The
OLD BOOK
Value Guide
Second Edition

25,000 Listings of Old Books with Current Values

By the Editors of Collector Books

COLLECTOR BOOKS
A Division of Schroeder Publishing Co., Inc.

The current values in this book should be used only as a guide. They are not intended to set prices, which vary from one section of the country to another. Auction prices as well as dealer prices vary greatly and are affected by condition as well as demand. Neither the author nor the Publisher assumes responsibility for any losses that might be incurred as a result of consulting this guide.

Additional copies of this book may be ordered from:

Collector Books
P.O. Box 3009
Paducah, KY 42002-3009

@$19.95 Add $2.00 for postage and handling.

Copyright: Schroeder Publishing Co., Inc. 1990

Introduction

This book was compiled to help the owner of old books evaluate his holdings and find a buyer for them. Most of us have a box, trunk, stack, or bookcase of old books. Chances are they are not rare books, but they may have value. Two questions that we are asked most frequently are 'Can you tell me the value of my old books?' and 'Where can I sell them?' *The Old Book Value Guide* will help answer both of these questions. Not only does this book place retail values on over 25,000 old books, it also lists scores of buyers along with the type of material each is interested in purchasing. Note that we list retail values (values that an interested party would be willing to pay to obtain possession of the book.) These prices are taken from recent dealers' selling lists.

If you were to sell your books to a dealer, you would expect to receive no more than 50% of the values listed in this book unless the dealer had a specific buyer in mind for some of your material. In many cases, a dealer will pay less than 50% of retail for a book to stock.

Do not ask a dealer to evaluate your old books unless you intend to sell your books to him. Most Antiquarian book dealers in the larger cities will appraise your books and ephemera for a fee that ranges from a low of $10.00 per hour to $50.00 per hour. If you were to have an extensive library of rare books, the $50.00-an-hour figure would be money well spent (assuming, of course, the appraiser to be qualified and honest.)

The Old Book Value Guide places values on the more common holdings that many seem to accumulate. You will notice that the majority of the books listed are in the $5.00 to $20.00 range. Many such guides list only the rare, almost non-existent books that the average person will never see. The format is very simple: the listings are alphabetized first by the name of the author, editor, or illustrator; if more than one book is listed for a particular author, each title is listed alphabetically under his or her name. Also dust jackets or wrappers are noted when present; and sizes when given are approximate.

In the back of the book, we have listed buyers of books and book-related material. When you correspond with these dealers, be sure to enclose a self-addressed, stamped envelope if you want a reply. Please do not send lists of books for an appraisal. If you wish to sell your books, quote the price that you want or negotiate price only on the items the buyer is interested in purchasing. When you list your books, do so by author, full title, publisher and place, date, and edition. Indicate condition, noting any defects on cover or contents.

When shipping your books, first wrap each book in paper such as brown kraft or a similar type of material. Never use newspaper for the inner wrap, since newsprint tends to rub off. (It may, however be used as a cushioning material within the outer carton.) Place your books in a sturdy corrugated box, and use a good shipping tape to seal it. Tape impregnated with nylon string is preferable, as it will not tear.

Books shipped by parcel post may be sent at a special fourth class book rate, which is much lower than regular parcel post zone rates.

The Editors of Collector Books

Listings of Standard Abbreviations

Am	American	OUP	Oxford University Press
bdg	binding	SftCvr	soft cover
BOMC	Book of Month Club	sgn	signature, signed
c	circa	TB	textbook
dj	dust jacket	Trans	translated
ed.	edition	U.	University
EX	excellent	VG	very good
fld	folded	wraps	wrappers
G	good	xl	ex-library
GPO	Government Printing Office	12mo.	about 7" tall
HrdCvr	hard cover	16mo	6 to 7" tall
Ills.	illustrated	24mo	5 to 6" tall
imp	impression	32mo	4 to 5" tall
inscr	inscribed	48mo	less than 4" tall
Lib.	library	64mo	about 3" tall
Ltd	limited	sm 8vo	7½ to 8" tall
M	mint	8vo	8 to 9" tall
MOMA	Museum of Modern Art	sm 4to.	about 10" tall
p	page	4to.	between 11 to 13" tall
pb	paperback	folio.	13" or larger
plt	plate	elephant folio	23" or larger
Pr	press	atlas folio	25"
Pub	publisher	double elephant folio	larger than 25"

A

A'BECKETT. *Comic History of England.* c 1850s. London. 1 vol ed. VG $35.00

AARONSOHN. *With Turks in Palestine.* 1916 Boston. Ills. cloth. VG $30.00

ABBE, Ernest. *Gesammelte Abhandlungen.* 1904 Verlag. Ills 1st ed. 486 p. G $35.00

ABBEY, Edward. *Beyond the Wall.* 1984 NY. Holt. 1st ed. dj. M $20.00

ABBEY, Edward. *Black Sun.* 1971 Simon Schuster. 1st ed. dj. EX $40.00

ABBEY, Edward. *Cactus Country.* 1973 Time Life. Ills. 184 p. EX $8.00

ABBEY, Edward. *Desert Solitaire.* 1968 NY. 1st ed. dj. VG $47.50

ABBEY, Edward. *Monkey Wrench Gang.* 1985 Salt Lake. Dream Garden. Deluxe Ltd ed. M $65.00

ABBEY, Edward. *Sunset Canyon.* 1972 London. Talmy. 1st ed. dj. $20.00

ABBOT, Willis J. *Blue Jackets of '61: History of War of Secession.* 1887 square 8vo. 318 p. fair. $40.00

ABBOTT, Berenice. *Greenwich Village: Today & Yesterday.* 1949 NY. Harper. 1st ed. 8vo. dj. VG $65.00

ABBOTT, Berenice. *Guide to Better Photography.* 1941 NY. Crown. Ills. 4to. dj. VG $75.00

ABBOTT, Berenice. *Last Rivet.* 1940 Columbia U Pr. Ills 1st ed. dj. EX $75.00

ABBOTT, Berenice. *New Guide to Better Photography.* 1953 NY. 1st ed. $12.00

ABBOTT, George. *Tryout.* 1979 NY. 1st ed. dj. M $11.00

ABBOTT, J.S.C. *Confidential Correspondence of Napoleon & Josephine.* 1856 NY. 1st ed. rebound. VG $25.00

ABBOTT, J.S.C. *History of Civil War in America.* 1863-1836. Springfield. 1st ed. 2 vols. $60.00

ABBOTT, J.S.C. *History of King Philip: Sovereign Chief of Wampandags.* 1857 NY. 1st ed. $65.00

ABBOTT, J.S.C. *Life of David Crockett.* 1874 NY. Ills. $7.50

ABBOTT, J.S.C. *Life of General Ulysses S. Grant.* 1868 Russell. Ills 1st ed. 12mo. 309 p. VG $25.00

ABBOTT, J.S.C. *Lives of the Presidents of the USA.* 1867 Boston. Ills. 8vo. 480 p. G $24.00

ABBOTT, Jacob. *Florence Stories.* 1865 NY. 1st ed. VG $10.00

ABBOTT, Jacob. *Hennebury.* no date. Chicago. 8vo. wine cloth. G $15.00

ABBOTT, Jacob. *History of King Richard the 3rd of England.* 1858 NY. Harper. Ills 1st ed. VG $35.00

ABBOTT, Jacob. *Rollo in Holland.* no date. Chicago. Conkey. 8vo. cloth. $20.00

ABBOTT, Jacob. *Rollo in London.* 1855 Boston. Reynolds. Ills. cloth. G $30.00

ABBOTT, Jacob. *Rollo on the Rhine.* c 1855. Boston. gilt cloth. VG $25.00

ABBOTT, Jacob. *Rollo's Museum.* no date. Phillips Sampson. Revised ed. $25.00

ABBOTT, John. *Child at Home.* 1834 Boston. 8vo. 155 p. VG $30.00

ABBOTT, Lyman. *Life & Literature of Ancient Hebrews.* 1901 Boston. G $7.00

ABBOTT, R.T. *American Seashells.* 1954 Van Nostrand. Ills. 541 p. dj. VG $35.00

ABBOTT, R.T. *Kingdom of the Seashell.* 1972 Crown. 1st ed. photos. 256 p. dj. EX $26.00

ABBOTT & SMITH. *We Pointed Them North.* 1955 Norman. New ed. dj. VG $35.00

ABBOTT. *American Watchmaker & Jeweler.* 1910 Chicago. 378 p. $30.00

ABDILL, G.B. *This Was Railroading.* 1958 Seattle. Ills. folio. dj. VG $12.00

ABEL, A.H. *Tabeau's Narrative of Loisel's Expedition to the Upper MS.* 1968 OK U Pr. 1st ed. 2nd print. dj. EX $35.00

ABEL, Joseph. *Apartment Houses.* 1947 NY. Reinhold. G $20.00

ABERCROMBIE, John. *Gardener's Pocket Dictionary.* 1786 London. Lockyer Davis. 1st ed. 12mo. $55.00

ABERCROMBIE, John. *Inquiries Concerning Intellectual Powers.* 1835 Harper. 12mo. 376 p. VG $20.00

ABERCROMBIE, John. *Kitchen & Fruit Gardener.* 1847 Phil. Lea Blanchard. 12mo. cloth. $50.00

ABERCROMBIE, Lascelles. *Tower in Italy: Romantic Play in 1 Act.* 1976 Toronto. Basilike. 1/175. 8vo. wraps. $25.00

ABERCROMBIE & WATSON. *Plan for Plymouth.* 1943 Plymouth. 2nd ed. photos. maps. cloth. G $15.00

ABERNATHY, J.R. *Catch 'Em Alive Jack.* 1936 NY. Ills 1st ed. 222 p. VG $20.00

ABERNATHY, T.P. *Burr Conspiracy.* 1954 NY. Oxford. 1st ed. dj. VG $15.00

ABERT, J.W. *Report of an Expedition Led by J.W. Abert.* 1846 WA. Ills. 75 p. wraps. $375.00

ABERT, J.W. *Through the Country of Comanche Indians in 1845.* 1970 San Francisco. Howell Books. 1/5,000. VG $45.00

ABRAHAM, Dorothy. *Lone Cove: Journal of Life on Coast of Vancouver Island.* 1945 Victoria. sgn. 103 p. wraps. VG $15.00

ABRAHAM, Gerald. *Slavonic & Romantic Music: Essays & Studies.* 1968 NY. 1st Am ed. dj. VG $20.00

ABRAHAM, James Johnston. *Lettsom: His Life, Time, Friends, & Decendants.* 1933 London. Heinemann. Ills 1st ed. 498 p. $45.00

ABRAMS, M.H. *Mirror & Lamp: Romantic Theory & Critical Tradition.* 1953 NY. dj. VG $7.50

ABRAMS, Peter. *Night of Their Own.* 1965 NY. 1st ed. dj. EX $15.00

ABRAMSON, Albert. *Electronic Motion Pictures: History of Television Camera.* 1955 Berkeley. CA U Pr. Ills. 212 p. xl. $20.00

ABU BAKR IBN TUFAIL. *History of Havy Ibn Yaqzan.* no date. NY. Stokes. Trans Ockley. 179 p. G $7.50

ABZUG, R.H. *Inside the Vicious Heart.* 1984 Oxford U Pr. dj. EX $20.00

ACHAD, Frater. *31 Hymns to the Star Goddess.* 1978 40 p. VG $22.00

ACHESON, Sam. *35,000 Days in TX: History of Dallas News & Its Forbearers.* 1938 Macmillan. 1st ed. VG $20.00

ACKLEY, Edith. *Dolls To Make for Fun & Profit.* 1938 NY. dj. VG $22.00

ACKROYD, Peter. *Hawksmore.* 1985 Harper. 1st Am ed. dj. EX $17.00

ACOMB, E. *Revolutionary Journal of Baron Ludwig von Closen 1780-1783.* 1958 Chapel Hill. 1st ed. dj. EX $20.00

ADAIR, J. *History of the American Indians.* 1973 reprint of 1930. dj. EX $30.00

ADAIR, J. *Navaho & Pueblo Silversmiths.* 1954 OK U Pr. Ills. 220 p. dj. VG $15.00

ADAMIC, Louis. *My Native Land.* 1943 NY. 1st ed. dj. VG $30.00

ADAMIC, Louis. *Robinson Jeffers: Portrait.* 1985 Covelo, CA. Yolla Bolly Pr. 1/260. 8vo. M $125.00

ADAMS, Adrienne. *Great Valentine's Day Balloon Race.* 1980 NY. Scribner. Ills 1st ed. 4to. cloth. dj. $12.50

ADAMS, Alice. *Families & Survivors.* 1974 NY. Knopf. 1st ed. dj. M $30.00

ADAMS, Alice. *Superior Women.* 1984 Knopf. Advance copy. wraps. EX $45.00

ADAMS, Andy. *Anthony Reed, Cowman: Autobiography.* 1907 Houghton Mifflin. 1st ed. xl. $18.50

ADAMS, Andy. *Anthony Reed, Cowman: Autobiography.* 1907 Houghton Mifflin. 1st ed. EX $75.00

ADAMS, Andy. *Corporal Segundo.* 1968 Encino. Ltd ed. 1/750. editor sgn. EX $40.00

ADAMS, Andy. *Log of a Cowboy.* 1903 Houghton Mifflin. 1st ed. EX $75.00

ADAMS, Andy. *Log of a Cowboy.* 1903 Houghton Mifflin. 2nd print. $50.00

ADAMS, Andy. *Outlet.* 1905 Houghton Mifflin. 1st ed. EX $85.00

ADAMS, Andy. *TX Matchmaker.* 1904 Houghton Mifflin. 1st ed. VG $35.00

ADAMS, Andy. *Wells Brothers: Young Cattle Kings.* 1911 Boy Scout ed. photos Erwin E Smith. dj. $40.00

ADAMS, Ansel. *Born Free & Equal.* 1944 US Camera. 1st ed. wraps. VG $225.00

ADAMS, Ansel. *My Camera in National Parks.* 1950 Houghton. 1st ed. sgn. spiral bdg. VG $225.00

ADAMS, Ansel. *Photographs of the Southwest.* 1976 NY Graphic Soc. 1st ed. inscr. dj. EX $75.00

ADAMS, Ansel. *This Is the American Earth.* 1960 Sierra Club. 1st ed. sgn. dj. EX $75.00

ADAMS, Ansel. *Yosemite & Range of Light.* 1979 NY Graphic Soc. 1st ed. 4to. cloth. dj. EX $120.00

ADAMS, Ansel. *Yosemite & Sierra, NV.* 1948 Houghton. 1st ed. cloth. VG $50.00

ADAMS, Ansel. *Yosemite Tales & Trails.* 1934 Crocker. 1st ed. sgn. cloth. G $125.00

ADAMS, C.S. *Hunting Crows Year Round.* 1953 NY. Macmillan. Ills. 101 p. dj. EX $7.50

ADAMS, Celeste Marie. *Art & the West.* 1986 NY. Ills. 4to. 131 p. dj. $25.00

ADAMS, Charles Francis. *Studies: Military & Diplomatic 1775 & 1865.* 1911 NY. Macmillan. 1st ed. 8vo. 424 p. xl. VG $25.00

ADAMS, Charles M. *Randall Jarrell: A Bibliography.* 1958 Chapel Hill. 1st ed. wraps. EX $37.50

ADAMS, Charles. *Charles Adams' Mother Goose.* 1967 Windmill Books. dj. VG $25.00

ADAMS, Charles. *Home Bodies.* 1954 Simon Schuster. 1st ed. dj. VG $25.00

ADAMS, Charlotte. *S.A.S. World-Wide Cookbook.* 1960 Random House. 1st ed. dj. EX $12.00

ADAMS, Douglas. *Hitchhiker's Guide to the Galaxy.* 1980 Harmony. 1st Am ed. dj. VG $15.00

ADAMS, Douglas. *Life, the Universe, & Everything.* 1982 Harmony. 1st Am ed. dj. EX $20.00

ADAMS, Douglas. *Restaurant at the End of the Universe.* 1980 Harmony. 1st Am ed. dj. EX $25.00

ADAMS, E.H. *Digging the Top Off.* 1887 16mo. EX $100.00

ADAMS, E.P. *Report of Radiation & the Quantum Theory.* 1924 London. 2nd ed. sgn. 86 p. wraps. VG $90.00

ADAMS, Franklin P. *In Other Words.* 1912 Garden City. Doubleday. 8vo. cloth. scarce. $20.00

ADAMS, H. *Mont-Saint-Michel & Chartres.* 1913 Boston. G $15.00

ADAMS, H.G. *Hummingbirds.* 1861 Ills. cloth. G $125.00

ADAMS, Harold. *Barbed Wire Noose.* 1987 1st Am ed. inscr. dj. $22.00

ADAMS, Harold. *When Rich Men Die.* 1987 1st Am ed. inscr. dj. $22.00

ADAMS, Henry. *History of USA. Vol. II.* 1890 NY. Scribner. inscr. ¾-morocco. slipcase. $575.00

ADAMS, Henry. *Letters to a Niece.* 1920 Boston. 1st ed. EX $25.00

ADAMS, Henry. *Letters to a Niece.* 1920 Boston. 1st ed. G $12.00

ADAMS, Henry. *Writings of Albert Gallatin.* 1968 NY. Antiquarian Pr. 3 vol set. $80.00

ADAMS, Herbert. *Golf House Murders.* 1933 NY. Black. 8vo. 316 p. ads. $30.00

ADAMS, John D. *Metal Work & Etching with Additional Designs.* 1911 Chicago. Popular Mechanics. Ills. 88 p. $30.00

ADAMS, John Q. *Oration on Life & Character of Gilbert Motier de Lafayette.* 1835 WA. 1st ed. wraps. xl. VG $50.00

ADAMS, John Q. *Oration on Life & Character of Gilbert Motier de Lafayette.* 1835 WA. Duff Green. 96 p. blue wraps. $17.50

ADAMS, L. *Mink Raising.* 1935 Columbus. 1st ed. 12mo. 222 p. $15.00

ADAMS, L.D. *Striped Bass Fishing in CA & OR.* 1958 Pacific Books. Ills. 228 p. maps. G $10.00

ADAMS, Marion S. *Alvin M. Owsley of TX.* 1971 Waco, TX. 8vo. sgn. cloth. dj. VG $20.00

ADAMS, Mary. *Count Your Numbers & Keep on Counting.* 1948 Chicago. Aries Pr. 201 p. dj. EX $22.00

ADAMS, Ramon. *Come an' Get It: Story of Old Cowboy Cook.* 1952 Norman. 1st ed. dj. G $25.00

ADAMS, Ramon. *Cowman Says It Salty.* 1971 Tucson. dj. VG $10.00

ADAMS, Ramon. *More Burrs Under the Saddle: Books & Histories of the West.* 1976 Norman. 1st ed. dj. VG $22.00

ADAMS, Ramon. *Rampaging Herd: Bibliography of Books on Cattle Industry.* 1982 Cleveland. reprint. VG $38.00

ADAMS, Ramon. *Rampaging Herd: Bibliography of Books on Cattle Industry.* Norman. 1st ed. dj. VG $100.00

ADAMS, Ramon. *Western Words: Dictionary of American West.* 1968 OK U Pr. New ed. dj. $37.50

ADAMS, Richard. *Girl in a Swing.* 1980 NY Knopf. 1st ed. dj. EX $9.50

ADAMS, Richard. *Iron Wolf & Other Stories.* 1980 Lane. 1st ed. dj. EX $15.00

ADAMS, Richard. *Nature Through the Seasons.* Simon Schuster. 1st Am ed. EX $15.00

ADAMS, Richard. *Plague Dogs.* 1978 NY. Knopf. 1st Am ed. dj. EX $9.50

ADAMS, Richard. *Shardik.* 1974 Simon Schuster. 1st Am ed. dj. EX $15.00

ADAMS, Richard. *Watership Down Film Picture Book.* 1978 NY. Macmillan. Ills 1st Am ed. EX $25.00

ADAMS, Richard. *Watership Down.* 1972 NY. Macmillan. 1st ed. dj. EX $17.50

ADAMS, S.H. *Grandfather Stories.* 1955 Random House. 1st ed. $7.00

ADAMS, Thomas. *Rural Development & Planning.* 1917 Ottawa. 281 p. cloth. G $10.00

ADAMS, W.H. Davenport. *Egypt: Past & Present.* 1894 London. Nelson. Ills. 384 p. VG $15.00

ADAMS, W.H. Davenport. *Lighthouses & Lightships.* 1871 London. Nelson. Ills. 322 p. $70.00

ADAMS, W.H. Davenport. *Witch, Warlock, & Magician.* 1971 MI. Gryphon Books. facsimile. EX $22.00

ADAMS, W.I. Lincoln. *Sunlight & Shadows: Book for Photographers.* 1897 NY. Ills HP Robinson/Stieglitz. EX $60.00

ADAMS & SEWALL. *Novanglus & Massachusettensis.* 1819 1st ed. rebound. VG $110.00

ADAMS & SINGER. *Drawing Animals.* 1979 NY. Ills. 160 p. $22.50

ADAMSON, Joy. *Born Free, a Lioness in 2 Worlds.* 1960 Pantheon. Ills. 220 p. dj. EX $5.00

ADAMSON, W.A. *Enterprising Angler.* 1945 Morrow. Ills 1st ed. 268 p. VG $14.00

ADDAMS, Jane. *Good Intentions.* 1st Am ed. dj. EX $10.00

ADDAMS, Jane. *My Friend Julia Lathrop.* 1935 NY. 1st ed. dj. VG $22.50

ADDAMS, Jane. *Spirit of Youth & City Streets.* 1912 NY. 9th print. VG $20.00

ADDAMS, Jane. *20 Years at Hull House.* 1910 NY. 1st ed. VG $75.00

ADDAMS, Jane. *20 Years at Hull House.* 1911 Macmillan. 1st ed. EX $100.00

ADDINGTON, Sarah. *Round the Year in Pudding Lane.* 1924 Little Brown. Ills Kay. 1st ed. 8vo. VG $20.00

ADDISON, J.D.W. *Arts & Crafts in Middle Ages.* 1914 Boston. Ills. 378 p. VG $27.50

ADDISON, Joseph. *Vision of Mirzah.* 1917 CA Book Club. Ltd ed. 1/300. EX $45.00

ADDISON, Joseph. *Works of Joseph Addison.* 1761 Birmingham. Baskerville Pr. 4 vol set. $225.00

ADE, George. *Bang Bang.* 1928 NY. Ills McCutheon. 1st ed. EX $15.00

ADE, George. *Fables in Slang.* 1972 Westvaco. Ills Sullivan. Ltd ed. boxed. $15.00

ADE, George. *More Fables.* 1900 Chicago. 1st ed. VG $17.00

ADE, George. *Old-Time Saloon: Not Wet, Not Dry, Just History.* 1931 NY. Ltd 1st ed. EX $95.00

ADE, George. *Old-Time Saloon: Not Wet, Not Dry, Just History.* 2nd ed. $17.50

ADE, George. *Slim Princess.* 1907 Bobbs Merrill. Ills 1st ed. fair. $20.00

ADE, John. *Artie: Story of Streets & Towns.* 1896 Stone. Ills McCutcheon. 1st ed. $60.00

ADE, John. *Fables in Slang.* 1899 Stone. 1st ed. $50.00

ADE, John. *Fables in Slang.* 1972 Westvaco. Ltd ed. boxed. $45.00

ADE, John. *Girl Proposition.* 1902 Russell. 1st ed. VG $35.00

ADE, John. *I Knew Him When: Hoosier Fable Dealing with Happy Days.* 1910 Chicago. Ltd ed. 1/1,000. $75.00

ADE, John. *In Princess New.* 1906 McClure Phillips. 1st ed. $30.00

ADE, John. *Knocking the Neighbors.* 1912 Ills Leverin. $35.00

ADE, John. *More Fables.* 1900 Stone. 1st ed. $40.00

ADE, John. *Single Blessedness & Other Observations.* 1922 2nd state. $60.00

ADE, John. *True Bills.* 1904 Harper. 1st ed. G $30.00

ADE, John. *40 More Fables.* 1901 Grosset Dunlap. G $7.00

ADELER, Max. *Elbow Room.* 1876 Phil. Stoddard. Ills AB Frost. VG $25.00

ADELMANN. *Marcello Malpighi & Evolution of Embryology.* 1966 4to. 5 vol set. glassine wraps. slipcase. EX $65.00

ADHEMAR, Jean. *Toulouse-Lautrec: His Complete Lithographs & Drypoints.* no date. NY. Abrams. Ills. folio. dj. $150.00

ADLER, Hermann. *Unsere Luftwaffe in Polen.* 1939 Berlin. wraps. G $18.00

ADLER, Jacob. *Claus Spreckels: Sugar King in HI.* 1966 Honolulu. HI U Pr. Ills J Feher. VG $15.00

ADLER, Mortimer. *Idea of Freedom.* 1958 NY. VG. $22.50

ADLINGTON, William. *Golden Ass of Lucius Apuleius.* 1924 London. Navarre Soc. Ills Hagreen. EX $45.00

ADLINGTON, William. *Golden Ass of Lucius Apuleius.* 1913 NY. Ltd ed. VG $35.00

ADRICH, Thomas B. *Course of True Love Never Did Run Smooth.* 1858 NY. 1st ed. 1st state. cloth. $20.00

AESOP. *Aesop for Children.* 1919 Rand McNally. Ills Milo Winter. olive cloth. $50.00

AESOP. *Aesop's Fables.* 1813 Chiswick Pr. Ills. 16mo. gilt leather. $85.00

AESOP. *Aesop's Fables.* 1908 NY. Stokes. Ills LF Perkins. 1st ed. EX $40.00

AESOP. *Aesop's Fables.* 1970 NY. Windmill. Ills Jacob Lawrence. 4to. dj. $15.00

AESOP. *Aesop's Fables: New Version From Original Sources.* 1861 Leavitt Allen. Ills Tenniel. 188 p. cloth. VG $40.00

AESOP. *Fables of Aesop.* 1981 Hodder. Ills Detmold. gilt leather. EX $60.00

AFLALO. *Sunshine & Sport in FL & West Indies.* no date. Phil. Ills. cloth. $25.00

AGAR, M. *Garden Design.* 1912 Philadelphia. 272 p. cloth. G $15.00

AGARD, Walter. *New Architectural Sculpture.* 1935 Oxford U Pr. fair. $20.00

AGASSIZ, Alexander. *Visit to the Bermudas in 1894.* 1895 Harvard U Pr. Ills. fld map. rebound. $22.00

AGASSIZ, Elizabeth C. *Louis Agassiz: His Life & Correspondence.* 1886 Boston. 2 vol set. VG $30.00

AGASSIZ, G.R. *Letters & Recollections of Alexander Agassiz.* 1913 Boston. Ills 1st ed. maps. VG $50.00

AGASSIZ, Louis. *Journey in Brazil.* 1975 Boston. Osgood. G $30.00

AGASSIZ, Louis. *Scientific Results of a Journey to Brazil.* 1868 London. 1st ed. 620 p. cloth. $150.00

AGASSIZ, Louis. *Scientific Results of a Journey to Brazil.* 1868 Boston. 1st ed. VG $150.00

AGASSIZ, Louis. *12 Lectures on Comparative Embryology.* H Flanders. reprint. 8vo. 108 p. wraps. $55.00

AGEE, James. *Collected Short Prose of James Agee.* 1968 Houghton Mifflin. 1st ed. dj. $20.00

AGEE, James. *Let Us Now Praise Famous Men.* 1960 Houghton. Ills Evans. dj. EX $25.00

AGEE, James. *Letters of James Agee to Father Flye.* 1962 Braziller. dj. VG $20.00

AGEE, James. *Morning Watch.* 1951 Riverside. dj. VG $50.00

AGEE, James. *On Film.* 1958 NY. McDowell Obolensky. 1st ed. VG $12.00

AGEE. *Knoxville: Summer 1915.* 1986 Caliban Pr. 1st ed. 1/125. EX. $60.00

AGGHAZY, Maria. *Alte Holzfiguren in Ungarn.* 1963 Budapest. Terra Verlag. Ills. dj. $60.00

AGNEL, H.R. *Book of Chess.* 1850 NY. Ills. 8vo. 509 p. VG $75.00

AGNEW, B. *Fort Gibson: Terminal on the Trail of Tears.* 1981 OK U Pr. Ills. 274 p. dj. EX $17.00

AGRICOLA. *De la Generatione de la Cose.* 1550 Venice. vellum. cloth ties. $500.00

AGRIPPA, Henry C. *Occult Philosophy or Magic.* 1973 NY. facsimile of 1897. dj. VG $45.00

AGRIPPA, Henry C. *Philosophy of Natural Magic.* 1974 NY. Universe Books. 307 p. dj. EX $35.00

AHEARN, Allen. *Book Collecting: Book of 1st Books.* 1986 Quill Brush. 4th ed. wraps. EX $13.00

AHLBERG & ALLAN. *Jolly Postman.* 1986 Little Brown. Ills 1st Am ed. M $25.00

AHLBORN, Richard E. *Man, Made Mobile: Early Saddles of Western North America.* 1980 Smithsonian. Ills. 4to. 157 p. wraps. $30.00

AHMAD, Shaikh Mahmud. *Economics of Islam: Comparative Study.* 1947 Lahore, India. VG $35.00

AHMED, Rollo. *Black Art.* 1936 London. 1st ed. 292 p. $60.00

AHREM. *Das Weib in der Antiken Kunst.* 1924 Jena. Ills. VG $20.00

AI. *Sin.* 1986 Houghton. Advance copy. wraps. EX $25.00

AICKMAN, R. *Painted Devils.* 1979 NY. Scribner. 1st Am ed. dj. EX $17.50

AIDA, K. *Japanese Brush Painting in Color.* 1973 Tokyo. Ills. 104 p. $25.00

AIKEN, Conrad. *Brownstone Ecologues.* 1942 Duell. 1st ed. dj. EX $50.00

AIKEN, Conrad. *Clerk's Journal.* 1971 NY. Eakins. Ltd ed. 1/300. sgn. dj. boxed. $75.00

AIKEN, Conrad. *Great Circle.* 1933 NY. Ltd 1st ed. sgn. blue cloth. G $98.00

AIKEN, Conrad. *Kid.* 1947 Lehmann. 1st English ed. dj. EX $40.00

AIKEN, Conrad. *Morning Song of Lord Zero.* 1963 Oxford U Pr. 1st ed. sgn. 8vo. dj. EX $85.00

AIKEN, Conrad. *Mr. Arcularis.* 1957 Harvard U Pr. 1st ed. dj. EX $35.00

AIKEN, Conrad. *Prelude.* 1929 Random House. Ills 1st ed. 1/475. wraps. EX $125.00

AIKEN, Conrad. *Seizure of Limericks.* 1964 NY. 1st ed. dj. EX $17.00

AIKEN, Conrad. *Seizure of Limericks.* 1965 Allen. 1st English ed. dj. EX $25.00

AIKEN, Conrad. *Selected Letters of Conrad Aiken.* 1978 Yale U Pr. 1st ed. dj. EX $20.00

AIKEN, Conrad. *Thee.* 1967 Braziller. Ills Baskin. 1st ed. dj. EX $30.00

AIKEN, Conrad. *Ushant.* 1952 NY. 1st ed. dj. VG $12.00

AIKEN, Joan. *Black Hearts in Battersea.* 1964 NY. Doubleday. Ills Jacques. 1st Am ed. dj. $10.50

AIKIN, Charles. *40 Years with the Damned; or, Life Inside the Earth.* 1895 Chicago. 1st ed. 422 p. VG $27.50

AIKIN, J. *Letters to a Young Lady on a Course of English Poetry.* 1806 NY. $25.00

AINGER, A.C. *Eton Songs.* 1892 London. Leadenhall. VG $85.00

AINSWORTH, Edward. *Cowboy in Art.* 1968 Bonanza. reprint. dj. EX $20.00

AINSWORTH, Edward. *Cowboy in Art.* 1969 NY. 2nd ed. 241 p. dj. VG $40.00

AINSWORTH, W.H. *Fairy Mythology.* 1828 London. Davison. 1st ed. 2 vol set. EX $350.00

AIRD, Catherine. *Harm's Way.* 1984 London. 1st ed. sgn. dj. EX $27.00

AK GEOGRAPHIC SOCIETY. *AK Mammals.* 1981 Ills. oblong 4to. 184 p. VG $12.00

AK GEOGRAPHIC SOCIETY. *AK Whales & Whaling.* 1978 Ills. oblong 4to. wraps. EX $12.00

AK GEOGRAPHIC SOCIETY. *Chilkat River Valley.* 1984 Ills. 111 p. pb. EX $12.00

AKELEY, Carl E. *In Brightest Africa.* 1925 Garden City. VG $24.00

AKELEY, Carl E. *In Brightest America.* 1923 Garden City. 267 p. G $10.00

AKELEY, D.J. *Jungle Portraits.* 1930 Macmillan. Ills 1st ed. 251 p. G $7.50

AKERS, Floyd. *Boy Fortune Hunters in Yucatan.* 1910 Reilly Britton. 1st ed. VG $175.00

AKSYONOV, Vassily. *Colleagues.* 1962 London. 1st ed. dj. VG $50.00

AKUTAGAWA. *Japanese Short Stories.* 1961 Ills. dj. VG $5.00

AL-AZZAWI, Abbas. *Palm Tree in History of Iraq.* 1962 Baghdad. 1st ed. Arabic text. wraps. EX $15.00

ALBAUGH, W.A. *Confederate Edged Weapons.* 1960 Harper. Ills. 4to. 198 p. dj. EX $30.00

ALBAUGH, W.A.; & SIMMONS, E.N. *Confederate Arms.* 1957 Bonanza. reprint. 4to. 278 p. dj. EX $45.00

ALBEE, Edward. *Everything in the Garden.* 1968 NY. 1st ed. dj. EX $15.00

ALBEE, Edward. *Everything in the Garden.* 1968 NY. 1st ed. dj. M $20.00

ALBEE, Edward. *Lady From Dubuque.* 1980 NY. 1st ed. dj. EX $20.00

ALBINUS, Bernard Siegfried. *Explicatio Tabularum Anatomicarum Bartholomaei Eustachii.* 1761 Verbeek. Leidae. $1000.00

ALCOCK, J. *Sonoran Desert Spring.* 1985 Chicago U Pr. Ills 1st ed. 194 p. dj. EX $18.00

ALCOCK, Nathaniel. *100 Years of IA Medicine.* 1950 IA City. 1st ed. $30.00

ALCOHOLICS ANONYMOUS. *Works of Alcoholics Anonymous.* 1939 NY. 1st ed. 1st print. red cloth. VG $2500.00

ALCOHOLICS ANONYMOUS. *Works of Alcoholics Anonymous.* July, 1951. 14th print. G $250.00

ALCOHOLICS ANONYMOUS. *Works of Alcoholics Anonymous.* 1943 NY. 4th print. green cloth. VG $550.00

ALCOTT, Louisa M. *Aunt Jo's Scrap Bag.* reprint of 1873. G $20.00

ALCOTT, Louisa M. *Hospital Sketches.* 1863 Boston. 1st ed. 2nd print. 102 p. cloth. G $135.00

ALCOTT, Louisa M. *Jo's Boys & How They Turned Out.* 1886 Boston. 1st ed. 2nd state. 365 p. fair. $22.50

ALCOTT, Louisa M. *Little Men.* 1871 Roberts. 1st ed. red cloth. G $40.00

ALCOTT, Louisa M. *Little Women.* 1950 NY. Ills Lonette. VG $10.00

ALCOTT, Louisa M. *Little Women.* Orchard House. Ills JW Smith. dj. EX $25.00

ALCOTT, Louisa M. *Old-Fashioned Girl.* 1928 Winston. Ills Burd. VG $12.00

ALCOTT, Louisa M. *Old-Fashioned Girl.* 1896 Boston. Ills Merrill. G $12.50

ALCOTT, Louisa M. *Old-Fashioned Girl.* 1870 Boston. 1st ed. VG $100.00

ALCOTT, Louisa M. *Plots & Counterplots.* 1976 NY. dj. M $11.00

ALCOTT, Louisa M. *Poppies & Wheat.* no date. Little Brown. G $15.00

ALCOTT, Louisa M. *Proverb Stories.* 1886 Boston. Loring. Ills Hoppin. 1st ed. $60.00

ALCOTT, Louisa M. *Rose in Bloom.* 1933 Winston. Ills Burd. VG $12.00

ALCOTT, Louisa M. *Rose in Bloom.* 1932 Saalfield. Ills George Lawson. VG $9.50

ALCOTT, Louisa M. *Spinning Wheel Stories.* 1884 Boston. 1st ed. 276 p. gilt green cloth. VG $60.00

ALCOTT, Louisa M. *Under the Lilacs.* 1878 Boston. Roberts. 16mo. gilt cloth. G $40.00

ALCOTT, Louisa M. *Under the Lilacs.* 1909 Boston. Little Brown. VG $12.50

ALCOTT, Louisa M. *8 Cousins.* 1890 Boston. Ills. 8vo. cloth. VG $20.00

ALCOTT, William A. *Letters to a Sister; or, Woman's Mission.* 1850 Buffalo. VG $50.00

ALCOTT, William A. *Young Man's Guide.* 1847 Boston. Ills. 16mo. 392 p. G $19.00

ALDCROFT, Derek H. *Bibliography of European Economic & Social History.* 1984 Manchester Pr. 243 p. gilt blue cloth. VG $27.50

ALDEN, John. *General Gage in America.* 1948 Baton Rouge. 1st Am ed. 313 p. dj. EX $35.00

ALDEN, R.M. *Why the Chimes Rang.* 1980 Ills. 8vo. EX $15.00

ALDEN, R.M. *Why the Chimes Rang.* 1924 Indianapolis. Ills Sturges. 8vo. dj. EX $17.50

ALDIN, Cecil. *Cathedrals & Abbey Churches of England.* 1950 London. Eyre Spottiswoode. fair. $20.00

ALDIN, Cecil. *Ratcatcher to Scarlet.* 1920 London. Ills 2nd ed. 4to. 123 p. VG $40.00

ALDIN, Cecil. *Romance of Road.* 1928 London. Ills. folio. dj. VG $200.00

ALDIN, Cecil. *Scarlet to M.F.H.* 1933 NY. Scribner. 1st ed. 4to. 151 p. $25.00

ALDIN, Cecil. *Time I Was Dead.* 1934 NY. 1st ed. 8vo. 389 p. red cloth. VG $125.00

ALDINGTON, Richard. *Death of a Hero.* 1929 London. Chatto Windus. 1st ed. inscr. $50.00

ALDINGTON, Richard. *Last Straws.* 1930 Paris. Ltd ed. 1/200. sgn. 61 p. VG $125.00

ALDINGTON, Richard. *Love of Myrrhine & Konallis & Other Prose Poems.* 1926 Chicago. 1st ed. 1/510. dj. EX $42.00

ALDINGTON, Richard. *Wreath for San Gemingnano.* 1945 NY. dj. M $12.00

ALDISS, Brian. *Barefoot in the Head: European Fantasia.* 1969 London. 1st ed. dj. VG $30.00

ALDISS, Brian. *Billion Year Spree.* 1973 London. 1st ed. dj. EX $30.00

ALDISS, Brian. *Frankenstein Unbound.* 1973 London. 1st ed. dj. EX $20.00

ALDISS, Brian. *Greybeard.* 1964 NY. 1st ed. dj. VG $65.00

ALDISS, Brian. *Helliconia Summer.* London. 1st ed. sgn. EX $36.00

ALDISS, Brian. *Rude Awakening.* London. 1st ed. sgn. EX $25.00

ALDRED, Cyril. *Jewels of the Pharoahs: Egyptian Jewelry of Dynastic Period.* 1971 NY. Praeger. Ills. 4to. 256 p. dj. $40.00

ALDRICH, Bess Streeter. *Drum Goes Dead.* 1941 NY. 1st ed. dj. VG $17.50

ALDRICH, Florence. *21st Century Cookbook.* 1978 Hollywood. dj. EX $15.00

ALDRICH, T.B. *Baby Bell.* 1878 Boston. Osgood. Ills. 12mo. gilt blue cloth. $10.00

ALDRICH, T.B. *Friar Jerome's Beautiful Book.* 1952 NY. Angelo. Ltd ed. 1/75. dj. VG $150.00

ALDRICH, T.B. *Friar Jerome's Beautiful Book.* 1896 Riverside. 1st ed. $235.00

ALDRICH, T.B. *Life of Thomas Bailey Aldrich.* 1908 Boston. Ills. ¾-red leather. VG $35.00

ALDRICH, T.B. *Old Town by the Sea.* c 1917. Boston. EX $20.00

ALDRICH, T.B. *Story of a Bad Boy.* 1927 Winston. Ills Prittie. EX $12.00

ALDRICH, T.B. *Story of a Bad Boy.* 1923 Houghton Mifflin. Ills Brent. $20.00

ALDRICH, T.B. *Story of a Bad Boy.* 1894 Houghton. Ills. 12mo. brown cloth. VG $20.00

ALDRIDGE, Alan. *Beatles Illustrated Lyrics.* 1969 NY. 1st Am ed. dj. VG $35.00

ALDRIDGE, Henry R. *Case for Town Planning.* 1915 London. G $30.00

ALDRIDGE, James. *Of Many Men.* 1946 Boston. 1st ed. inscr. G $10.00

ALDRIDGE, James. *Sea Eagle.* 1944 Boston. 1st ed. inscr. VG $15.00

ALDRIDGE, James. *With Their Honour.* 1942 Boston. 1st reprint ed. inscr. G $10.00

ALEICHEM, S. *Great Fair.* 1955 NY. Ills Chagall. 1st ed. dj. EX $25.00

ALEXANDER, Archibald. *Thoughts on Religious Experience.* 1844 Presbyterian Board. 3rd ed. G $15.00

ALEXANDER, Constance G. *Francesca Alexander: Hidden Servant.* 1927 Cambridge. 1/750. 4to. $65.00

ALEXANDER, Duke of Russia. *Religion of Love.* 1929 NY. 1st ed. EX $25.00

ALEXANDER, E.P. *Iron Horses.* 1941 NY. Ills. G $12.00

ALEXANDER, Edwin. *Civil War Railroads & Models.* 1977 Clarkston Potter. 1st ed. dj. $22.50

ALEXANDER, J. *Jews: Their Past, Present, & Future.* 1870 London. 218 p. EX $150.00

ALEXANDER, J.B. *History of Mecklenburg County.* 1902 Charlotte, NC. 1st ed. 431 p. VG $65.00

ALEXANDER, J.J.G. *Master of Mary of Burgundy: Book of Hours for Engelburt.* 1970 Oxford. 24mo. slipcase. M $35.00

ALEXANDER, Roy. *Cruise of the Raider Wolf.* 1939 Yale. 3rd print. EX $15.00

ALEXANDER, Shana. *Anyone's Daughter.* 1st Am ed. dj. EX $12.00

ALEXANDER, Shana. *Nutcracker.* Doubleday. 1st ed. dj. VG $10.00

ALEXANDER, William. *Picturesque Representation of Dress & Manners of Chinese.* 1814 London. Ills. folio. $250.00

ALFORD, Thomas Wildcat. *Civilization.* 1979 Norman. dj. VG $15.00

ALGER, Horatio. *Digging for Gold: Story of CA.* 1892 Phil. Ills 1st ed. cloth. G $42.00

ALGER, Horatio. *Frank's Campaign; or, The Farm & the Camp.* no date. Hurst. VG $12.00

ALGER, Horatio. *Luke Walton; or, Chicago Newsboy.* Burt. VG $8.00

ALGER, Horatio. *Only an Irish Boy.* no date. Chicago. Donohue. G $10.00

ALGER, Horatio. *Risen From the Ranks; or, Harry Walton's Success.* 1874 Boston. Loring. 1st ed. 1st issue. VG $150.00

ALGER, Horatio. *Rough & Ready.* 1869 Boston. 1st ed. $25.00

ALGER, Horatio. *Slow & Sure.* 1910 NY Book Co. VG $12.00

ALGER, Horatio. *Store Boy.* no date. Chicago. Donohue. VG $12.00

ALGER, Horatio. *Tattered Tom; or, Story of a Street Arab.* 1871 Boston. Loring. 1st ed. 1st issue. EX $250.00

ALGER, Horatio. *Tattered Tom; or, Story of a Street Arab.* 1871 Boston. Loring. 1st ed. gilt mauve cloth. VG $200.00

ALGER, Horatio. *Try & Trust; or, Story of a Bound Boy.* 1873 Boston. Loring. 1st ed. mauve cloth. $200.00

ALGER, Horatio. *Young Book Agent.* 1905 Stitt Pub. G $30.00

ALGOUD, Henri. *Le Mobilier Provencal.* no date. Paris. Massin. Ills. G $65.00

ALGREN, Nelson. *Chicago: City on the Make.* 1951 Doubleday. 1st ed. dj. $45.00

ALGREN, Nelson. *Last Carousel.* 1973 NY. 1st ed. dj. VG $22.00

ALGREN, Nelson. *Man with the Golden Arm.* 1952 Hamburg. 1st German ed. sgn/dtd. dj. EX $150.00

ALGREN, Nelson. *Never Come Morning.* 1950 Paris. 1st French ed. inscr. $150.00

ALGREN, Nelson. *Notes From a Sea Diary.* 1965 Putnam. 1st ed. dj. VG $20.00

ALGREN, Nelson. *Walk on the Wild Side.* 1956 NY. 1st print. dj. EX $40.00

ALI, Salim. *Indian Hill Birds.* 1949 Oxford U Pr. Ills 1st ed. dj. VG $22.50

ALINSKY, Saul. *John L. Lewis: Unauthorized Biography.* 1949 Putnam. 1st ed. dj. VG $17.50

ALLANSON-WINN. *Boxing with Note by Bat Mullins.* 1899 London. Ills. 12mo. 91 p. $35.00

ALLBEURY, Ted. *Alpha List.* 1979 London. 1st ed. dj. EX $18.00

ALLBUTT, Thomas C. *Science & Medieval Thought.* 1901 London. Cambridge. VG $25.00

ALLEGRO, John M. *Sacred Mushroom & the Cross.* 1970 349 p. dj. EX $28.00

ALLEN, A.A. *Stalking Birds with Color Camera.* 1951 Nat'l Geog Soc. Ills 1st ed. 328 p. EX $27.00

ALLEN, A.A. *Stalking Birds with Color Camera.* 1961 Nat'l Geog Soc. Ills 2nd print. 328 p. dj. EX $15.00

ALLEN, B. Spraque. *Tides in English Taste 1619-1800.* 1958 NY. Pageant. Ills. 8 vol set. slipcase. $65.00

ALLEN, Charles D. *American Book Plates.* 1905 NY. 12mo. VG $50.00

ALLEN, Douglas. *Frederic Remington & the Spanish American War.* 1971 Crown. Ills. 4to. 178 p. dj. EX $10.00

ALLEN, Durward. *Pheasants in North America.* 1956 Stackpole. 1st ed. dj. $35.00

ALLEN, Edward. *America's Story Told in Postage Stamps.* 1930 1st ed. VG $15.00

ALLEN, Ethan. *Narrative of Col. Ethan Allen's Captivity.* 1930 NY. Ltd ed. 1/540. 8vo. 134 p. VG $20.00

ALLEN, G. *Flowers & Their Pedigrees.* 1884 NY. 266 p. xl. G $10.00

ALLEN, G.W. *Privateers of Revolution.* 1927 Cambridge. Ills 1st ed. 356 p. VG $35.00

ALLEN, Gay Wilson. *Solitary Singer: Critical Biography of Walt Whitman.* 1955 NY. Macmillan. 1st ed. 8vo. cloth. dj. EX $95.00

ALLEN, George. *Life of Philidor.* 1863 Philadelphia. Ltd 1st ed. 8vo. tan morocco. $150.00

ALLEN, Glover. *Birds & Their Attributes.* 1948 Jones. Ills. 338 p. VG $13.00

ALLEN, Gracie. *How To Become President.* 1940 Duell Sloan. 1st ed. dj. VG $22.50

ALLEN, H. *Bedford Village.* 1944 Ills Wyeth. 1st ed. dj. VG $25.00

ALLEN, H. Warner. *Wines of France.* no date. NY. G $20.00

ALLEN, Hervey. *Action at Aquila.* 1938 NY. 1st ed. dj. VG $18.00

ALLEN, Hervey. *Action at Aquila.* 1938 NY. 1st ed. sgn. 369 p. dj. EX $30.00

ALLEN, Hervey. *Anthony Adverse.* 1934 NY. Ills Wyeth. 2 vol set. VG $65.00

ALLEN, Hervey. *Anthony Adverse.* 1937 pub/ sgn Wilson. gilt cloth. dj. VG $35.00

ALLEN, Ida Bailey. *When You Entertain: What To Do & How.* 1932 Atlanta. Coca Cola. 124 p. EX $95.00

ALLEN, James. *Bride of the Mistletoe.* 1909 NY. 1st ed. EX $10.00

ALLEN, James. *Flute & Violin & Other KY Tales & Romances.* 1923 NY. Macmillan. VG $10.00

ALLEN, James. *Flute & Violin & Other KY Tales & Romances.* 1899 NY. 208 p. VG $25.00

ALLEN, John L. *Passage Through the Garden.* 1975 IL U Pr. 412 p. dj. EX $30.00

ALLEN, Joseph L. *KY Cardinal & the Aftermath.* 1901 London. Ltd ed. 1/250. cloth. VG $60.00

ALLEN, M.D.L. *Siamene Home Treatments: Guide for Those Who Seek Health.* 1904 CA. 1st ed. 284 p. EX $65.00

ALLEN, Maury. *Now Wait a Minute Casy!* 1965 Doubleday. 1st ed. dj. G $17.50

ALLEN, Percy. *Talks with Elizabethans.* no date. London. Rider. 216 p. xl. G $22.00

ALLEN, R.P. *Birds of the Caribbean.* 1961 Viking. Ills 1st ed. 4to. dj. VG $23.00

ALLEN, R.S. *Danger Forward.* 1947 NY. 1st ed. dj. VG $27.50

ALLEN, R.S. *Lucky Forward: History of Patton's 3rd US Army.* 1947 NY. Ills 1st ed. sgn. 424 p. dj. $50.00

ALLEN, Steve. *Curses!* 1973 Los Angeles. Ills Marvin Rubin. 1st ed. dj. $8.50

ALLEN, Steve. *Meeting of Minds.* 1978 sgn. 181 p. dj. EX $15.00

ALLEN, Thomas. *Vanishing Wildlife of North America.* 1974 Nat'l Geog Soc. Ills. 207 p. dj. EX $18.00

ALLEN, Virginia. *Drawings of Jean Dubuffet.* 1968 MOMA. Ills. 4to. wraps. $10.00

ALLEN, Woody. *Side Effects.* 1980 Random House. 1st ed. dj. EX $15.00

ALLEN, Woody. *Side Effects.* 1981 London. 1st English ed. dj. EX $20.00

ALLEN, Woody. *Without Feathers.* 1975 NY. 1st ed. dj. VG $12.50

ALLEN & ALLEN. *N.C. Wyeth.* 1972 NY. Ills 1st ed. dj. EX $55.00

ALLEN & BRYANT. *Life of Napoleon Bonaparte.* 1896 Allen & Bryant. G $95.00

ALLEN & JONES. *Romanesque Lyric.* 1928 Chapel Hill. 1st ed. VG $25.00

ALLEN PRESS. *Allen Press Bibliography.* 1985 San Francisco. CA Book Club. New Revised ed. $110.00

ALLEN. *Panorama of London; or, Visitor's Companion.* 1830 London. Ills. 12mo. 318 p. worn. $10.00

ALLERS, C.W. *Das Deutsche Jagerbuch.* 1897 Stuttgart. Ills Engl. 1st ed. M $650.00

ALLINGHAM & PATERSON. *Homes of Tennyson.* 1905 London. Black. Ills. VG $30.00

ALLIS, F.A. *Battle of the Komandorskis.* 1946 Newport. SftCvr. VG $35.00

ALLISON, K.L. *35mm Photography with an Exakta.* 1952 Fountain Pr. 3rd imp. dj. $12.00

ALLISON, Philip. *African Stone Sculpture.* 1968 NY. 1st ed. VG $35.00

ALLYN, Rube. *Dictionary of Fishes.* 1963 Great Outdoors. Ills. 4to. 126 p. wraps. G $5.00

ALOMONSEN, Finn. *Birds of Greenland: Gronlands Fugle.* 1950-1951. Kobenhavn. Ills. 3 vol set. EX $275.00

ALPATOV, M.W. *Art Treasures of Russia.* no date. NY. Abrams. dj. VG $65.00

ALPERS, Anthony. *Katherine Mansfield: Biography.* 1953 NY. 1st Am ed. dj. EX $25.00

ALPINI, Prosperi. *Medicina Aegyptiorum Liber de Balsamo et Rhapontico.* 1745 Potvliet. Editio Nova. full leather. $125.00

ALTER, J.C. *Jim Bridger.* 1951 OK U Pr. Ltd ed. 1/1,000. sgn. $50.00

ALTER, J.C. *Jim Bridger.* 1979 OK U Pr. Ills. 358 p. dj. EX $18.00

ALTER, J.C. *UT: Storied Domain.* 1932 Chicago. 1st ed. 3 vol set. VG $175.00

ALTGELD, John P. *Our Penal Machinery & Victims.* 1890 Chicago. $25.00

ALTSHELER, Joseph. *Soldier of Manhattan.* 1897 Manhattan. VG $35.00

ALTSHELER, Joseph. *TX Star.* 1912 NY. 1st ed. VG $25.00

ALVAREZ, A. *Hers.* 1974 Random House. 1st ed. dj. VG $10.00

ALVAREZ, A. *Savage God.* 1972 NY. 1st ed. dj. VG $20.00

ALVAREZ, Walter. *Incurable Physician: Autobiography.* 1963 Prentice Hall. VG $8.00

ALVAREZ, Walter. *Nervous Indigestion.* 1931 NY. 2nd imp. VG $35.00

ALVORD, C.W. *MS Valley in British Politics.* 1917 Cleveland. Clark. Ills. 2 vol set. VG $125.00

ALVORD, C.W. *1st Explorations of Trans-Allegheny Region by Virginians.* 1912 Cleveland. 1st ed. EX $275.00

ALYWARD, W.J. *Ships & How To Draw Them.* 1957 NY. Pitman. EX $16.00

AMADO, Jorge. *Home Is the Sailor.* 1964 Knopf. 1st Am ed. dj. EX $30.00

AMADO, Jorge. *Swallow & the Tom Cat.* 1982 Delacorte. Ills 1st Am ed. dj. EX. $15.00

AMAYA, Mario. *Tiffany Glass.* 1967 NY. Walker. Collector Blue Book Series. $10.00

AMBASZ, Emilio. *Italy: New Domestic Landscape.* 1972 MOMA. Ills. 431 p. wraps. $38.50

AMBLER, Eric. *Intercom Conspiracy.* 1969 Atheneum. 1st Am ed. dj. EX $20.00

AMBLER, Eric. *Light of Day.* 1963 Knopf. 1st ed. 2nd print. dj. VG $6.50

AMBLER, Eric. *Nightcomers.* 1956 London. Heinemann. 1st ed. dj. VG $50.00

AMBLER, Eric. *Schirmer Inheritance.* 1953 NY. 1st ed. dj. VG $15.00

AMBLER, Eric. *Seige of the Villa Lipp.* 1977 NY. 1st ed. dj. EX $10.00

AMEREL. *Winter Holidays: Story for Children.* 1850 NY. Appleton. Ills. 16mo. 117 p. juvenile. $15.00

AMERICAN ARTIST GROUP. *Arnold Blanch Monograph.* 1946 NY. Ills. 16mo. $20.00

AMERICAN ARTIST GROUP. *Charles Burchfield Monograph.* 1945 NY. Ills. 16mo. 62 p. $20.00

AMERICAN ARTIST GROUP. *Gladys Rockmore Davis Monograph.* 1945 Ills. 16mo. 64 p. $20.00

AMERICAN ARTIST GROUP. *Stuart Davis Monograph.* 1945 NY. 1st ed. VG $25.00

AMERICAN ARTIST GROUP. *Thomas H. Benton Monograph.* 1945 NY. Ills. 16mo. 64 p. $20.00

AMERICAN GUIDE SERIES. *CO.* 1943 Hastings House. Ills 2nd print. maps. VG $19.00

AMERICAN GUIDE SERIES. *DE.* 1938 Viking. Ills 1st ed. dj. EX $28.00

AMERICAN GUIDE SERIES. *Death Valley.* 1939 Houghton Mifflin. 1st ed. dj. $22.00

AMERICAN GUIDE SERIES. *IL.* 1974 Hastings. dj. EX $15.00

AMERICAN GUIDE SERIES. *ME.* 1937 Houghton Mifflin. Ills. G $24.00

AMERICAN GUIDE SERIES. *New Orleans City.* 1938 Houghton Mifflin. dj. EX $17.00

AMERICAN GUIDE SERIES. *NH.* 1938 Houghton Mifflin. dj. VG $22.00

AMERICAN GUIDE SERIES. *RI.* 1937 Houghton Mifflin. Ills. G $25.00

AMERICAN GUIDE SERIES. *VA.* 1941 Oxford U Pr. Ills 2nd print. 710 p. VG $18.00

AMERICAN GUIDE SERIES. *VT.* 1966 Houghton Mifflin. 2nd ed. dj. $18.00

AMERICAN GUIDE SERIES. *WY.* 1948 Oxford U Pr. Ills. 490 p. fld map. VG $18.00

AMERICAN GUIDE SERIES. *WY.* 1941 NY. Oxford U Pr. dj. VG $25.00

AMERICAN HERITAGE. *American Heritage Book of Indians.* 1961 Am Heritage. 1st ed. boxed. EX $15.00

AMERICAN HERITAGE. *American Heritage Book of Natural Wonders.* 1963 Ills. 4to. 384 p. maps. VG $10.00

AMERICAN MEDICAL ASSN. *Code of Medical Ethics.* 1877 NY. Wood. 3rd ed. EX $12.00

AMERICAN RED CROSS. *1st Aid Textbook.* 1940 Blakiston. 1st ed. wraps. EX $7.50

AMERICAN TEMPERATE SOCIETY. *Permanent Temperance Documents.* 1835 Boston. 1st ed. 500 p. scarce. EX $50.00

AMERY, L.S. *Days of Fresh Air.* 1940 London. Hutchinsons U Book Club. VG $12.50

AMES, Daniel T. *Ames' Compendium of Practical & Ornamental Penmanship.* 1877 NY. folio. 48 p. G $150.00

AMICHAI, Yehuda. *Not of This Time, Not of This Place.* 1968 Harper. 1st ed. dj. VG $25.00

AMIRAN, R. *Ancient Pottery of Holy Land.* 1920 4to. cloth. dj. $60.00

AMIRANASHVILI, Shalva. *Georgian Metalwork From Antiquity to the 18th Century.* 1971 London/NY. Ills Neubert. 175 p. dj. $35.00

AMIS, Kingsley. *Everyday Drinking.* 1983 London. 1st ed. dj. EX $20.00

AMIS, Kingsley. *Green Man.* 1969 London. 1st English ed. dj. EX $20.00

AMIS, Kingsley. *I Like It Here.* 1958 Harcourt Brace. 1st Am ed. dj. EX $25.00

AMIS, Kingsley. *I Want It Now.* 1968 London. 1st ed. dj. EX $14.00

AMIS, Kingsley. *I Want It Now.* 1969 Harcourt Brace. 1st ed. dj. VG $8.50

AMIS, Kingsley. *Jake's Thing.* 1979 NY. 1st ed. dj. M $10.00

AMIS, Kingsley. *New Maps of Hell.* 1960 NY. 1st ed. dj. VG $25.00

AMIS, Kingsley. *1 Fat Englishman.* 1964 Harcourt. 1st Am ed. dj. $30.00

AMIS, Kingsley. *1 Fat Englishman.* 1963 London. 1st English ed. dj. EX $20.00

AMIS, Martin. *Money.* 1985 NY. Viking. 1st Am ed. M $15.00

AMIS, Martin. *Moronic Inferno & Other Visits to America.* 1986 London. Uncorrected proof. EX $40.00

AMIS, Martin. *Other People: Mystery Story.* 1981 NY. Viking. Advance copy. EX $15.00

AMIS, Martin. *Rachel Papers.* 1974 NY. Knopf. 1st ed. author's 1st book. dj. $25.00

AMMEN, D. *Old Navy & the New Navy.* 1891 Philadelphia. xl. $10.00

AMMONS, A.R. *Selected Longer Poems.* 1980 NY. 1st ed. dj. EX $15.00

AMORY, Cleveland. *Celebrity Register.* 1963 Harper Row. Ills 1st ed. 4to. 677 p. $35.00

AMORY, Cleveland. *Trouble with Nowadays.* 1979 NY. inscr. dj. EX $15.00

AMORY, Cleveland. *Who Killed Society?* 1960 Harper. NY. dj. G $12.50

AMORY, Martha Babcock. *Domestic & Artistic Life of John Singleton Copley, R.A.* 1882 Houghton Mifflin. 1st ed. VG $45.00

AMORY, Thomas C. *Materials for a History of the John Sullivan Family.* no date. Cambridge. Wilson. 8vo. cloth. $50.00

AMOS, Oz. *Elsewhere, Perhaps.* 1973 Harcourt. 1st Am ed. dj. EX $15.00

AMOS, W.H. *Wildlife of the Islands.* 1980 Abrams. Ills. 231 p. dj. EX $22.00

AMSLEY, H. Murray. *Symobolism of the East & West.* 1900 London. Redway. Ills. 212 p. VG $45.00

AMUNDSEN, L.; & ELLSWORTH, R. *Our Polar Flight.* 1925 NY. 1st ed. dj. VG $40.00

ANACREON. *Works of Anacreon.* 1735 London. Trans John Addison. 1st ed. VG $75.00

ANAND, Mulk Raj. *7 Summers: Story of Indian Childhood.* 1951 London. Hutchinson. 1st ed. VG $25.00

ANDERS, L. *18th MO.* 1968 Bobbs Merrill. Ills. 404 p. maps. dj. EX $40.00

ANDERS, W. *Hitler's Defeat in Russia.* 1953 1st ed. dj. EX $27.50

ANDERSCH, Alfred. *Flight to Afar.* 1958 NY. Coward McCann. 1st ed. dj. VG $35.00

ANDERSEN, Hans Christian. *Andersen's Fairy Tales.* 1926 Winston. Ills F Richardson. 8vo. 276 p. $25.00

ANDERSEN, Hans Christian. *Andersen's Fairy Tales.* 1942 Heritage. Ills Kredel. 8vo. 318 p. EX $28.00

ANDERSEN, Hans Christian. *Fairy Tales.* 1981 Viking. Ills Kay Nielsen. 1st ed. dj. $15.00

ANDERSEN, Hans Christian. *Fairy Tales.* 1914 NY. Ills DS Walker. 1st ed. VG $22.50

ANDERSEN, Hans Christian. *Fairy Tales.* 1912 London. Black. Ills Duncan Carse. 1st ed. VG $60.00

ANDERSEN, Hans Christian. *Fairy Tales.* 1976 London. Ills M Foreman. 1st ed. VG $12.50

ANDERSEN, Hans Christian. *Fir Tree.* 1970 NY. Ills N Burkert. 1st ed. dj. VG $7.50

ANDERSEN, Hans Christian. *Garden of Paradise & the Mermaid.* no date. Munchen. Dietrich. VG $35.00

ANDERSEN, Hans Christian. *Improvisatore.* 1898 Boston. 29 mounted photos of Italy. EX $120.00

ANDERSEN, Hans Christian. *Little Ellie.* c 1865. NY. Miller. 16mo. $25.00

ANDERSEN, Hans Christian. *Nove Quadri.* 1927 Chelsea. Ltd ed. 1/100. Italian text. $25.00

ANDERSEN, Hans Christian. *Sand Hills of Jutland.* 1860 NY. 1st Am ed. VG $30.00

ANDERSEN, Hans Christian. *Stories From Hans Christian Andersen.* no date. NY. Doran. Ills Dulac. 8vo. EX $125.00

ANDERSEN, Hans Christian. *Stories From Hans Christian Andersen.* 1911 NY. Ills Edmund Dulac. disbound. $45.00

ANDERSEN, Hans Christian. *25 Fairy Tales.* 1912 NY. Platt Peck. Ills. 4to. EX $25.00

ANDERSEN & WHISTLER. *Fairy Tales & Legends.* 1935 Cobden Sanderson. 1st ed. sgn. $70.00

ANDERSEN. *Olympic Winter Games 1952.* Oslo. ½-leather. $25.00

ANDERSON, A. *Our Garden Heritage.* 1961 NY. 622 p. dj. VG $8.00

ANDERSON, A.J. *ABC of Artistic Photography.* 1913 London. Ills. VG $145.00

ANDERSON, Alan. *Blue Reef.* 1979 Knopf. Ills 1st ed. 259 p. dj. EX $14.00

ANDERSON, Anne. *Anne Anderson's Fairy Tales & Pictures.* 1935 Whitman. Nouveau Ills. folio. 20 p. $35.00

ANDERSON, C.G. *James Joyce & His World.* 1968 NY. Scribner. Ills. 144 p. dj. EX $18.00

ANDERSON, C.G. *James Joyce & His World.* 1967 NY. Viking. dj. VG $25.00

ANDERSON, F. *Illustrated Treasury of Orchids.* 1979 NY. 156 p. dj. VG $10.00

ANDERSON, F. *In Search of the Holy Grail.* 1955 London. Ills. 288 p. xl. G $22.00

ANDERSON, H.B. *Facts Against Compulsory Vaccination.* 1929 NY. Citizens Medical Bureau. VG $35.00

ANDERSON, Isabel. *Great Sea Horse.* 1909 Little Brown. Ills J Ellot. inscr. VG $65.00

ANDERSON, J.L. *Night of the Silent Drums.* 1975 Scribner. 1st ed. 406 p. dj. EX $25.00

ANDERSON, John. *Motion Picture in America: History in the Making.* 1938 NY. Ills 1st ed. EX $35.00

ANDERSON, Kenneth. *Black Panther of Sivanipalli.* 1960 Rand McNally. Ills. 247 p. dj. VG $8.50

ANDERSON, Kenneth. *Maneaters & Jungle Killers.* 1957 Nelson. Ills 1st ed. 199 p. dj. VG $16.50

ANDERSON, Kenneth. *This Is the Jungle.* 1964 Allen Unwin. 1st ed. dj. $25.00

ANDERSON, Kenneth. *9 Maneaters & 1 Rogue.* 1955 Dutton. Ills 1st ed. 251 p. VG $15.00

ANDERSON, L.H. *Ancient Magic, Magnetism, & Psychic Forces.* 1895 Chicago. sgn. fair. $45.00

ANDERSON, M. *Guatemalan Textiles Today.* 1978 NY. Watson Guptil. $17.50

ANDERSON, Maxwell. *Wingless Victory: Play in 3 Acts.* 1936 WA, DC. 1st ed. 133 p. dj. $20.00

ANDERSON, Newton H. *Aircraft Layout & Detail Design.* 1946 McGraw Hill. 2nd ed. 436 p. VG $15.00

ANDERSON, Paul. *Avatar.* 1978 NY. 1st ed. sgn. dj. EX $30.00

ANDERSON, Paul. *Corridors of Time.* 1965 Doubleday. 1st ed. dj. EX $60.00

ANDERSON, Paul. *Time & Stars.* 1964 Doubleday. 1st ed. dj. EX $80.00

ANDERSON, Paul. *Trouble Twisters.* 1966 Doubleday. 1st ed. dj. VG $35.00

ANDERSON, R.B. *America Not Discovered by Columbus: Historical Sketch.* 1874 Chicago. 8vo. 104 p. xl. EX $25.00

ANDERSON, R.C. *Rigging of Ships in Days of Spritsail Topmast 1600-1702.* 1927 VG $60.00

ANDERSON, Robert. *Getting Up & Going Home.* 1978 NY. 1st ed. sgn. dj. M $15.00

ANDERSON, Romola & R.C. *Sailing Ship.* 1963 NY. Bonanza. dj. EX $18.00

ANDERSON, Rufus. *HI Islands: Progress & Condition Under Missionary Labors.* 1864 Gould Lincoln. Ills 2nd ed. 8vo. VG $70.00

ANDERSON, Sherwood. *Hometown.* 1940 NY. Alliance Books. 1st ed. 4to. $40.00

ANDERSON, Sherwood. *New Testament.* 1927 NY. Boni Liveright. 1/265. sgn. $90.00

ANDERSON, Sherwood. *Storyteller's Story.* 1924 NY. 2nd ed. sgn. VG $25.00

ANDERSON, Sherwood. *Winesburg, OH.* 1978 Ltd Ed Club. Ills/sgn Stahl. slipcase. EX $65.00

ANDERSON & COLLIER. *Riding & Driving.* 1905 NY. Ills. $15.00

ANDERSON & HANNAH. *Doubleday Cookbook.* 1975 NY. dj. EX $15.00

ANDERSON & NORTH. *Gospel Music Encyclopedia.* 1979 Sterling. VG $17.50

ANDRADE, C. *Structure of the Atom.* 1924 London. Bell. 2nd ed. 314 p. VG $12.00

ANDRAINI, Gotz. *Baumeister.* 1971 DuMont Schauberg. Ills. folio. $100.00

ANDRAL, G. *Diseases of the Chest.* 1843 Phil. 408 p. $25.00

ANDRAL, G. *Diseases of the Encephlon.* 1843 Phil. G $75.00

ANDRE, Eugene. *Naturalist in Guianas.* 1904 Scribner. 1st Am ed. 310 p. cloth. VG $75.00

ANDREAS, A.T. *History of Cook County.* 1884 ½-leather. $250.00

ANDREE. *Andree Diaries.* 1931 London. 1st English ed. $35.00

ANDRES, Fred. *Ice Palaces.* 1983 Abbeville. oblong 4to. $7.50

ANDREWARTHA, H.G. *Introduction to the Study of Animal Populations.* 1966 London. Ills. 281 p. EX $18.00

ANDREWS, Allen. *Proud Fortress.* 1959 NY. Ills 1st ed. 220 p. dj. VG $9.50

ANDREWS, Avery De Lano. *My Friend & Classmate, John J. Pershing.* 1939 Harrisburg. 1st ed. 291 p. G $25.00

ANDREWS, Eliza F. *Wartime Journal of a GA Girl.* 1908 NY. Appleton. Ills 1st ed. 8vo. cloth. $25.00

ANDREWS, John. *Price Guide to Victorian, Edwardian, & 1920s Furniture.* 1981 Suffolk. Baron. Ills. dj. $40.00

ANDREWS, Loring. *Isles of Eden.* 1932 NY. Long Smith. 1st ed. 8vo. dj. $16.00

ANDREWS, M.P. *Founding of MD.* 1933 Baltimore. 1st ed. VG $65.00

ANDREWS, M.P. *Women of the South in Wartime.* 1920 Remington. Ills. 466 p. EX $30.00

ANDREWS, Michael. *Flight of the Condor: Wildlife Exploration in the Andes.* 1982 Little Brown. Ills 1st Am ed. dj. EX $18.00

ANDREWS, R.C. *Ends of the Earth.* 1929 Garden City. Ills. 293 p. VG $10.00

ANDREWS, R.C. *Explorer Comes Home.* 1947 Doubleday. 276 p. EX $6.00

ANDREWS, R.C. *Meet Your Ancestors: Biography of Primitive Man.* 1945 Viking. Ills. 259 p. $5.00

ANDREWS, R.C. *Nature's Ways: How Nature Takes Care of Its Own.* 1951 Crown. Ills. 206 p. $14.00

ANDREWS, R.C. *On the Trail of Ancient Man.* 1926 Putnam. Ills. 375 p. fld map. VG $20.00

ANDREWS, R.C. *Under Luck Star.* no date. Viking. 1st ed. dj. VG $8.00

ANDREWS, Ruth. *How To Know American Folk Art.* 1977 NY. Dutton. Ills. 8vo. 223 p. wraps. $15.00

ANDREWS, Sidney. *South Since the War: GA & the Carolinas.* 1866 Boston. 1st ed. 8vo. 400 p. dj. VG $75.00

ANDREWS, W. *Architecture, Ambition, & Americans.* 1955 NY. Ills. EX $8.00

ANDREWS, William. *At the Sign of Barber's Pole: Studies in Hirsute History.* 1904 Cottingham. Ills 1st ed. 12mo. 121 p. $45.00

ANDREYEV, Leonid. *Judas Iscariot, Christians, & Phantoms.* 1947 London. Ills. 189 p. G $20.00

ANDRUS. *I Was the Nuremberg Jailor.* 1969 Coward McCann. 1st ed. dj. VG $20.00

ANET, Claude. *End of a World.* 1927 Knopf. Ills. $5.00

ANGAS, W.M. *Rivalry on the Atlantic.* 1939 NY. Ills 1st ed. 4to. dj. VG $25.00

ANGEL, Joan. *Angel of the Navy: Story of a Wave.* 1943 NY. 2nd ed. inscr. 200 p. G $20.00

ANGELL, Roger. *Late Innings: Baseball Companion.* 1982 NY. 1st ed. inscr. dj. M $35.00

ANGELL, Roger. *Stone Arbor.* 1960 Boston. Little Brown. 1st ed. dj. VG $25.00

ANGELL, Roger. *5 Seasons.* 1977 NY. 1st ed. sgn. dj. M $25.00

ANGELO, Valenti. *Come Over & Stay Till Domesday.* 1937 NY. Ltd ed. 1/100. sgn. EX $100.00

ANGELO, Valenti. *Marble Fountain.* 1951 NY. 1st ed. dj. EX $10.00

ANGELO, Valenti. *Nino.* 1938 NY. Viking. Ills 1st ed. 4to. 244 p. dj. $15.00

ANGELO, Valenti. *Song of Roland.* 1938 NY. Ills. 4to. dj. VG $75.00

ANGELOU, Maya. *Gather Together in My Name.* 1974 Random House. 1st ed. dj. EX $25.00

ANGELOU, Maya. *I Know Why the Caged Bird Sings.* 1969 NY. 1st ed. dj. M $35.00

ANGELOU, Maya. *I Know Why the Caged Bird Sings.* 1969 Random House. 1st ed. dj. VG $20.00

ANGELOU, Maya. *Just Give Me a Cool Drink of Water.* 1971 1st ed. VG $30.00

ANGELOU, Maya. *Shaker, Why Don't You Sing.* 1983 Random House. 1st ed. dj. EX $15.00

ANGER, Kenneth. *Hollywood Babylon.* 1975 San Francisco. dj. VG $25.00

ANGIER, Bradford & Vena. *At Home in the Woods.* 1951 Sheridan House. Ills. 255 p. dj. VG $13.00

ANGIER, Bradford. *How To Go Live in the Woods on 10 Dollars a Week.* 1959 Harrisburg. dj. VG $8.00

ANGIER, Bradford. *Living Off the Country.* 1959 Harrisburg. 3rd print. dj. VG $8.00

ANGIER, Bradford. *We Like It Wild.* 1963 Stackpole. 213 p. dj. VG $10.00

ANGIER, Bradford. *We Like It Wild.* 1961 Harrisburg. VG $7.00

ANGIER & WHELEN. *On Your Own in the Wilderness.* 1964 Harrisburg. dj. EX $8.00

ANGLE, B. *My Sporting Memories.* 1925 London. 1st ed. VG $30.00

ANGLE, P.M. *Pictorial History of the Civil War Years.* 1967 Doubleday. Ills. 242 p. maps. dj. VG $13.00

ANGLE, P.M.; & MIERS, E.S. *Ballad of the North & South.* 1959 Kingsport, TN. Ltd ed. 1/1,250. boxed. VG $30.00

ANGLICUS, Merlinus. *Astrologer of 19th Century.* 1825 London. Knight. Ills. 8vo. full calf. scarce. $585.00

ANGLUND, Joan. *Brave Cowboy.* 1959 NY. juvenile. dj. VG $15.00

ANGLUND, Joan. *Childhood Is a Time of Innocence.* 1964 Harcourt Brace. Ills 1st ed. 16mo. dj. EX $15.00

ANGLUND, Joan. *Christmas Is a Time of Giving.* 1961 Harcourt World. Ills 1st ed. 4to. 32 p. dj. VG $10.00

ANGLUND, Joan. *Cowboy & His Friend.* 1961 NY. 1st ed. juvenile. VG $20.00

ANGLUND, Joan. *Cowboy's Secret Life.* 1963 NY. Lib ed. juvenile. EX $15.00

ANGLUND, Joan. *Cup of Sun: Book of Poems.* 1967 NY. gift inscr. juvenile. VG $15.00

ANGLUND, Joan. *Friend Is Someone Who Likes You.* 1958 NY. juvenile. dj. EX $15.00

ANGLUND, Joan. *Good-Bye, Yesterday.* 1974 NY. 1st ed. juvenile. dj. VG $15.00

ANGLUND, Joan. *Joan Walsh Anglund Sampler.* no date. NY. Harcourt. Ills. boxed. EX $25.00

ANGLUND, Joan. *Look Out the Window.* 1959 NY. juvenile. VG $15.00

ANGLUND, Joan. *Love Is a Special Way of Feeling.* 1960 NY. juvenile. dj. VG $15.00

ANGLUND, Joan. *Nibble Nibble Mousekin: Tale of Hansel & Gretel.* 1962 NY. Ills 1st ed. 4to. VG $17.50

ANGLUND, Joan. *Nibble Nibble Mousekin: Tale of Hansel & Gretel.* 1962 NY. 1st ed. juvenile. dj. M $25.00

ANGLUND, Joan. *Pocketful of Proverbs.* 1964 NY. juvenile. dj. slipcase. EX $15.00

ANGLUND, Joan. *Slice of Snow: Book of Poems.* 1970 NY. 1st ed. juvenile. dj. EX $20.00

ANGLUND, Joan. *Spring Is a New Beginning.* 1963 NY. 1st ed. juvenile. dj. G $20.00

ANGLUND, Joan. *What Color Is Love?* 1966 NY. juvenile. dj. VG $15.00

ANNABEL, Russell. *Hunting & Fishing in AK.* 1948 Knopf. Ills 1st ed. 341 p. dj. EX $40.00

ANNESLEY, Patrick. *Hardy's Book of Fishing.* 1971 Dutton. Ills 1st Am ed. 304 p. dj. VG $20.00

ANNIS, John H. *Mystic Key or Bible Astrology.* 1927 Los Angeles. 1st ed. 184 p. VG $35.00

ANNIXTER, Paul. *Wilderness Ways.* 1930 Penn. Ills Bull. 313 p. VG $17.50

ANOBILE, Richard. *Flask of Fields.* 1972 NY. 1st ed. 8vo. dj. EX $12.50

ANON. *Adventures of Alphonso After Destruction of Lisbon.* 1787 Phil. Dobson. 32mo. 109 p. rare. VG $5000.00

ANON. *Chronology of 25 Years: Roxburghe Club of San Francisco.* 1953 Grabhorn. Ltd ed. 1/200. VG $120.00

ANON. *Das Lager Bergen-Belsen.* 1968 Hannover. Ills 2nd ed. German text. $12.50

ANON. *Fable for Critics.* 1848 NY. Putnam. $30.00

ANON. *Guide to Jenolan Caves, New South Wales.* 1922 Sydney. Ills. map. 90 p. VG $25.00

ANON. *Happy School Days: My Record. A Memory Book.* 1918 Reilly Britton. unused. EX $17.50

ANON. *Heraldry of Crests.* 1829 ¾-leather. rebound. $125.00

ANON. *Lawn Tennis at Home & Abroad.* 1903 London. Ills 1st ed. 328 p. $35.00

ANON. *Laws of Etiquette by a Gentleman.* 1836 Phil. 12mo. 172 p. cloth. VG $25.00

ANON. *Memoirs of General Reinhard Gehlen.* 1972 NY. Ills. dj. G $20.00

ANON. *Mother Goose's Rhymes, Jingles, & Fairy Tales.* 1896 Altemus. cloth. VG $85.00

ANON. *Neely's Panorama of Our New Posessions.* c 1898. Ills. 12mo. 128 p. cloth. G $27.00

ANON. *Parlor Magician; or, 100 Tricks for Drawing Room.* 1863 NY. 12mo. 126 p. $75.00

ANON. *Pocumtuc Housewife.* 1897 Deerfield. 1st reprint ed. wraps. VG $50.00

ANON. *Puppet State of Manchukuo.* 1935 Shanghai. China United Pr. 4to. 278 p. $20.00

ANON. *Recollections of a Society Clairvoyant.* 1911 London. 2nd ed. VG $20.00

ANON. *Regeneration: Gate of Heaven.* 1897 Boston. Barta Pr. 163 p. VG $35.00

ANON. *Rejected Stone: Insurrection vs. Resurrection in America.* 1862 Boston. 12mo. 131 p. brown cloth. VG $40.00

ANON. *Reply to John Stuart Mill on Subjection of Women.* 1870 Phil. 1st ed. VG $45.00

ANON. *Sachsenhausen.* 1982 East Berlin. Ills 2nd ed. German text. G $12.50

ANON. *Secret History of the Most Renowned Queen Elizabeth.* 1708 London. 1st ed. EX $300.00

ANON. *Shys at Shakespeare.* 1869 Phil. private print. Ills. cloth. EX $50.00

ANON. *Spiritual Resistance Art From Concentration Camps 1940-1945.* 1981 NY. Ills Ltd ed. 1/1,000. VG $40.00

ANON. *Story of Our Wonderful Victories.* 1899 Phil. Ills. 715 p. EX $80.00

ANON. *Tiny Book on Chafing Dish.* 1905 Providence. miniature. leather. VG $150.00

ANON. *Visits From the World of Spirits.* 1791 London. 302 p. VG $225.00

ANON. *Wax Flowers & How To Make Them.* 1864 Boston. Ills. 8vo. 116 p. VG $60.00

ANON. *We Have Not Forgotten.* 1961 Warszawa. Polonia Pub. Ills. scarce. G $40.00

ANON. *Who Killed Hitler?* 1947 NY. 2nd ed. dj. G $25.00

ANON. *Winning of NV for Woman Suffrage.* 1916 Carson City. $35.00

ANON. *Year of Wreck: True Story by a Victim.* 1880 NY. 1st ed. 472 p. EX $65.00

ANSON, George. *Voyage Around the World in the Years 1740-1744.* 1970 Dublin. 9th ed. leather. G $25.00

ANTHOLOGY. *Anchor Review, Number 2.* 1957 Doubleday. 1st ed, wraps. VG $10.00

ANTHOLOGY. *Artists As Professors.* 1976 Urbana. 1st ed. dj. EX $20.00

ANTHOLOGY. *Best American Short Stories 1969.* 1969 Houghton. 1st ed. dj. EX $25.00

ANTHOLOGY. *Best American Short Stories 1977.* 1977 Houghton. 1st ed. dj. EX $20.00

ANTHOLOGY. *Best American Short Stories 1978.* 1978 Houghton. 1st ed. dj. EX. $20.00

ANTHOLOGY. *Best American Short Stories 1979.* 1979 Houghton. 1st ed. dj. EX. $20.00

ANTHOLOGY. *Best British Short Stories of 1926.* 1926 NY. Review copy. dj. EX $25.00

ANTHOLOGY. *Bookfellow Anthology 1931.* 1931 Chicago. Bookfellow. 1st ed. 1/600. EX $65.00

ANTHOLOGY. *British Hills & Mountains.* 1950 London. VG $15.00

ANTHOLOGY. *Buying Time.* 1985 Graywolf. 1st ed. dj. EX $20.00

ANTHOLOGY. *Irish Jests & Anecdotes.* c 1890s. Edinburgh. 252 p. VG $20.00

ANTHOLOGY. *Little Folks' Black & White Painting Book.* c 1880. Galpin. 80 p. $35.00

ANTHOLOGY. *Murder Mystique Crime Writers on Their Art.* 1982 NY. 1st ed. sgns contributors. dj. $75.00

ANTHOLOGY. *New Stories From the South: Year's Best 1986.* 1986 Algonquin. Uncorrected proof. EX $25.00

ANTHOLOGY. *New Work by 5 Poets.* 1959 Rome. Am Academy. inscr Garrett. $100.00

ANTHOLOGY. *New World Writing.* 1952 Nalor. 1st ed. wraps. VG $10.00

ANTHOLOGY. *Of Art & Artists.* 1981 MS U Pr. 1st ed. dj. EX $25.00

ANTHOLOGY. *Out of the West by 5 Authors.* 1979 Ltd ed. 1/350. dj. EX $35.00

ANTHOLOGY. *Poems From the VA Quarterly Review 1925-1967.* 1969 VA U Pr. 1st ed. inscr Eberhart. 8vo. $30.00

ANTHOLOGY. *Prize Stories of 1970.* 1970 Doubleday. 1st ed. dj. VG $20.00

ANTHOLOGY. *Salmagundi Reader.* 1983 IN U Pr. 1st ed. dj. EX $20.00

ANTHOLOGY. *Yale Book of American Verse.* 1912 Yale U Pr. Ltd 1st ed. 1/1,250. $35.00

ANTHONY, Edward. *Don Marquis: Biography.* 1962 Garden City. Ills 1st ed. 670 p. dj. VG $9.50

ANTHONY, J. Garner. *HI Under Army Rule.* 1955 Stanford U Pr. 1st ed. $10.00

ANTHONY, Piers. *Bearing an Hourglass.* 1983 Del Rey. 1st ed. $150.00

ANTHONY, Piers. *Blue Adept*. 1981 Del Rey. 1st ed. $100.00

ANTHONY, Piers. *Out of Phaze*. Putnam. 1st ed. EX $15.00

ANTHONY, Piers. *Split Inifinity*. 1980 Del Rey. 1st ed. $100.00

ANTHONY, Piers. *Wielding a Red Sword*. 1986 Del Rey. 1st ed. $150.00

ANTHONY, Piers. *With a Tangled Skein*. 1985 Del Rey. 1st ed. $150.00

ANTOMINUS, Brother. *Rose of Solitude: Love Poem Sequence*. 1967 Doubleday. 1st ed. 8vo. dj. EX $22.00

ANTON, Ferdinand. *Art of the Maya*. 1970 NY. Putnam. Ills. 344 p. dj. $65.00

ANTON, Ferdinand. *Pre-Columbian Art & Later Indian Tribal Arts*. 1967 NY. Abrams. Ills. 4to. 264 p. $20.00

ANTUNANO, J. *Practical Education of Bird Dog*. 1959 Am Field Pub. 8th print. photo. VG $15.00

APENSZLAK, Jacob. *Black Book of Polish Jewry*. no date. 343 p. dj. VG $25.00

APPEL, B. *Raw Edge*. 1958 NY. 1st ed. dj. EX $12.50

APPEL, Paul P. *Homage to Sherwood Anderson*. 1970 Mamaroneck. 1st ed. 2nd print. inscr. dj. $20.00

APPERLEY, C.J. *Chase*. 1931 NY. Ills EP Buyck. EX $15.00

APPERLEY, C.J. *Life of a Sportsman*. 1903 NY. Appleton. 12mo. 396 p. red cloth. $35.00

APPERSON, G.L. *Social History of Smoking*. 1916 NY. 8vo. 255 p. red cloth. VG $30.00

APPLE, Max. *Oranging of America*. 1976 Viking. 1st ed. dj. EX $40.00

APPLEMAN, Roy. *War in the Pacific*. 1966 WA. reprint of 1948. fld maps. VG $35.00

APPLETON, Victor. *Moving Picture Boys; or, Perils of Great City Depicted*. 1913 Grosset Dunlap. dj. EX $12.00

APPLETON, Victor. *Tom Swift & Airship*. 1910 Grosset Dunlap. VG $10.00

APPLETON, Victor. *Tom Swift & Big Tunnel*. 1916 Grosset Dunlap. VG $10.00

APPLETON, Victor. *Tom Swift & His Motor Boat*. 1910 Grosset Dunlap. Ills. 12mo. 212 p. tan cloth. $15.00

APPLETON, Victor. *Tom Swift & His Wizard Camera*. 1912 Grosset Dunlap. VG $10.00

APPLETON, William W. *Charles Macklin: Actor's Life*. 1960 Cambridge, MA. 1st ed. dj. EX $20.00

APPOLLINAIRE, Guillaume. *Cubist Painters: Aesthetic Meditation 1913*. 1944 Wittenborn. Ills. 4to. wraps. $65.00

APTECKER, George. *Beyond Despair*. 1980 Morristown, NJ. 1st ed. dj. EX $45.00

AQUINAS, St. Thomas. *Summa Philosophica*. 1780 Rome. Part 2 of 2. xl. G $55.00

ARAGON, Louis. *Henri Matisse*. 1971 Harcourt Brace. 1st Am ed. 2 vol set. djs. EX $200.00

ARBUCKLE, John C. *Marching with Sherman: Civil War Experience of Foot Soldier*. 1930 Columbus, OH. 188 p. VG $40.00

ARCHER, Jeffrey. *Matter of Honor*. 1986 London. 1st ed. sgn. dj. EX $35.00

ARCHER, Jeffrey. *Matter of Honor*. 1986 Simon Schuster. 1st ed. sgn. dj. EX $15.00

ARCHER, Jeffrey. *Prodigal Daughter*. 1982 Simon Schuster. 1st ed. xl. G $12.00

ARCHER, Jeffrey. *Quiver Full of Arrows*. 1982 Simon Schuster. 1st ed. EX $15.00

ARCHER, Jeffrey. *Shall We Tell the President?* 1977 Advance copy. wraps. $15.00

ARDIZZONE, Edward. *Arcadian Ballads*. 1978 London. Heinemann. 1st ed. 4to. 48 p. $17.50

ARDIZZONE, Edward. *Dick Whittington*. 1970 NY. Walck. Ills. 8vo. 44 p. dj. VG $22.50

ARDIZZONE, Edward. *Long Ago When I Was Young*. 1966 London. Whiting Wheaton. 1st ed. dj. $40.00

ARDIZZONE, Edward. *Otterbury Incident*. 1969 NY. World. Ills. 8vo. 176 p. dj. G $15.00

ARDIZZONE, Edward. *Ship's Cook Ginger*. 1977 Bodley Head. 1st ed. EX $20.00

ARDOIN, John. *Art, Life, & Fitzgerald: The Great Years*. 1974 NY. 1st ed. dj. EX $75.00

ARDOIN, John. *Stages of Menotti*. 1985 NY. Ills Gerald Fitzgerald. dj. VG $25.00

ARENSBERG, Ann. *Sister Wolf*. 1980 Knopf. 1st ed. dj. EX $25.00

AREY, H.W. *Girard College & Its Founder*. 1853 Philadelphia. Sherman. 85 p. VG $15.00

ARIHHA, A. *Nicholas Poussin: Rape of the Sabines*. 1983 Houston. Ills. 68 p. pb. $10.00

ARISTOPHANES. *Lysistrata*. 1962 Heritage. Ills Picasso. boxed. EX $20.00

ARLEN, Michael. *Exiles*. 1970 NY. 1st ed. dj. EX $12.00

ARLEN, Michael. *May Fair*. 1925 NY. Ltd ed. 1/500. sgn. dj. EX $30.00

ARLOTT & DALEY. *Pageantry of Sports From Age of Chivalry to Age of Victoria*. 1968 NY. Ills. folio. 16 plts. dj. VG $40.00

ARMER, Laura Adams. *Southwest*. 1935 Longman Green. Ills 1st ed. dj. VG $26.50

ARMER, Laura Adams. *Waterless Mountain*. 1931 NY/Toronto. Longman Green. 1st ed. dj. VG $60.00

ARMES, George A. *Ups & Downs of an Army Officer*. 1900 WA. 1st ed. G $16.00

ARMITAGE, Flora. *Desert & Stars*. 1955 NY. 1st ed. dj. EX $16.00

ARMITAGE, John. *History of Brazil From Arrival of Braganza Family to 1831*. 1836 London. Smith Elder. 1st ed. G $125.00

ARMITAGE, Merle. *So-Called Abstract Art*. 1939 NY. Ward Ritchie. wraps. G $20.00

ARMITAGE, Tom. *History of the Baptists*. 1889 NY. Ills. 4to. 990 p. $45.00

ARMOR, W. *Lives of Governors of PA From 1609-1872*. no date. 8vo. 528 p. full leather. G $35.00

ARMOUR, R.C. *North American Fairy Tales*. 1905 Lippincott. Ills 1st ed. 192 p. VG $27.50

ARMOUR, Richard. *Drug Store Days*. 1959 NY. 1st ed. dj. VG $6.00

ARMOUR, Tommy. *How To Play Your Best Golf All the Time*. 1953 Simon Schuster. dj. G $6.00

ARMS, Dorothy. *Churches of France*. 1929 NY. Macmillan. G $20.00

ARMSTRON, Tom. *Whitney Museum of American Art: Bicentennial Exhibition*. 1976 NY. Ills. 4to. 336 p. wraps. $35.00

ARMSTRONG, Arnold. *Parched Earth*. 1934 Macmillan. 1st ed. inscr. VG $10.00

ARMSTRONG, D.A. *Bullets & Bureaucrats: Machine Gun & the US Army 1861-1916*. 1982 Westport, CT. Ills 1st ed. 239. cloth. M $20.00

ARMSTRONG, D.M. *Life & Lore of the Bird*. 1979 Crown. Ills. 4to. 271 p. dj. EX $10.00

ARMSTRONG, Margaret. *5 Generations: Life & Letters of American Family 1750-1900*. 1930 NY. Ills 1st ed. 425 p. VG $45.00

ARMSTRONG, R.H. *Guide to the Birds of AK*. 1983 AK Northwest. Revised ed. 332 p. wraps. EX $16.00

ARMSTRONG, Sir Walter. *Sir Joshua Reynolds*. 1900 London. Ills Ltd ed. 1/1,110. xl. $125.00

ARMSTRONG, William Jackson. *Heroes of Defeat.* 1905 Cincinnati. Ills 1st ed. 599 p. $22.50

ARNBERGER, L. *Flowers of Southwest Mountains.* 1952 Pueblo. 112 p. wraps. $5.00

ARNHEIM, Rudolph. *Art & Visual Perception: Psychology of the Creative Eye.* 1974 CA U Pr. 2nd ed. dj. EX $10.00

ARNO, Peter. *Peter Arno's Sizzling Platter.* 1949 Simon Schuster. 1st ed. dj. EX $12.50

ARNO, Peter. *Whoops Dearie!* 1927 NY. 1st ed. sgn. VG $25.00

ARNOLD, Eve. *Marilyn Monroe: An Appreciation.* 1987 NY. Viking. dj. VG $20.00

ARNOLD, Isaac N. *History of Abraham Lincoln & the Overthrow of Slavery.* 1866 Chicago. Clarke. 1st ed. 4to. 736 p. VG $45.00

ARNOLD, L.B. *Manual for Butter & Cheese Makers.* 1879 Rochester. Ills. 12mo. 354 p. $25.00

ARNOLD, L.R. *High on the Wild with Hemingway.* 1968 Caldwell, ID. Ills 1st ed. 4to. dj. EX $50.00

ARNOLD, Matthew. *Culture & Anarchy & Friendship's Garland.* 1901 NY. VG $20.00

ARNOLD, Matthew. *Empedocles on Etna.* 1900 Portland. Mosher. Ltd ed. 1/450. VG $75.00

ARNOLD, Matthew. *Essays in Criticism.* 1888 London. 1st ed. VG $40.00

ARNOLD, Oren. *Wildlife in the Southwest.* 1936 Upshaw. Ills. 274 p. G $12.00

ARNOLD, R. *Automatic & Repeating Shotguns.* 1960 NY. 1st Am ed. dj. VG $15.00

ARNOLD, R. *Automatic & Repeating Shotguns.* 1965 Barnes. Ills. 173 p. dj. EX $10.00

ARNOLD, Sir Edwin. *Light of Asia.* 1932 McKay. Ills Pogany. 4to. 182 p. VG $30.00

ARNOLD, Sir Edwin. *Light of Asia.* 1976 Ltd Ed Club. Ills Houghtelling. EX $50.00

ARNOLD, Sir Edwin. *Seas & Lands.* 1891 NY. Longman Green. 1st ed. 530 p. $20.00

ARNOLD, W.H. *Record of Books & Letters.* 1901 NY. Marion Pr. 1/145. 4to. cloth. VG $45.00

ARNOLD, W.H. *Ventures in Book Collecting.* 1923 NY. 1st ed. 8vo. VG $20.00

ARNOLD & HALE. *Hot Irons: Heraldry of the Range.* 1940 NY. 1st ed. sgn. 8vo. EX $60.00

ARNOT, Hugo. *Collection & Abridgement of Celebrated Criminal Trials.* 1785 Edinburgh. 4to. 400 p. VG $125.00

ARNOW. *Dollmaker.* 1954 NY. 1st ed. dj. G $15.00

ARRIOLA, Gus. *Gordo.* 1950 NY. 1st ed. 8vo. black cloth. VG $25.00

ARROWSMITH, Joseph. *Reformation: A Comedy.* 1673 London. 1st ed. cloth. VG $295.00

ARTHUR, T.S. *Advice to Young Ladies on Their Duties & Conduct in Life.* 1851 Boston. Ills. 16mo. 204 p. cloth. $20.00

ARTHUR, T.S. *Tired of Housekeeping.* 1843 NY. 1st ed. 12mo. cloth. VG $60.00

ARTHUR, T.S. *10 Nights in a Bar Room.* no date. NY. Ills. 12mo. 175 p. G $12.00

ARTHURS, Stanley. *American Historical Scene.* 1935 Phil. Ills 1st ed. 4to. 151 p. EX $40.00

ARTMAN, William; & HALL, L.V. *Beauties & Achievements of the Blind.* 1854 Dansville, NY. 387 p. EX $20.00

ARTMAN, William; & HALL, L.V. *Beauties & Achievements of the Blind.* 1858 NY. G $15.00

ARTZIBASHEV, Michael. *Sanine.* 1932 NY. Ills. dj. EX $12.00

ARTZYBASHEFF, Boris. *Fairy Shoemaker & Other Poems.* 1928 Macmillan. Ills 1st ed. 8vo. EX $95.00

ARUNDALE, George S. *Nirvana.* 1926 Chicago. 193 p. VG $16.00

ARUNDELL, Dennis. *Henry Purcell.* 1927 Oxford U Pr. EX $15.00

ARWAS, Victor. *Art Deco.* 1980 Abrams. Ills 1st ed. 316 p. dj. EX $55.00

ASBURY, H. *Great Illusion: Informal History of Prohibition.* 1950 Garden City. 1st ed. $28.50

ASH, C. *Whaler's Eye.* 1962 Macmillan. Ills. 245 p. VG $6.00

ASHBERY, John. *Selected Poems.* 1985 Viking. 1st ed. dj. EX $20.00

ASHBURN, T.Q. *History of 324th Field Artillery, US Army.* 1919 NY. Ills. 141 p. dj. VG $32.50

ASHDOWN, Mrs. Charles H. *British Costume During 19 Centuries.* 1910 Ills. plts. $85.00

ASHE, Thomas. *Quest for Arthur's Britain.* 1969 London. 2nd print. dj. EX $35.00

ASHE, Thomas. *Travels in America Performed in 1806.* 1808 Newburyport. 1st Am ed. 366 p. VG $140.00

ASHFORD, Bailey K. *Soldier in Science.* 1934 NY. Grosset Dunlap. reprint. G $8.00

ASHLEY, Clifford W. *Ashley Book of Knots.* 1944 1st ed. 4to. dj. VG $45.00

ASHLEY, Paul P. *Say It Safely.* 1966 Seattle. 8vo. 170 p. dj. M $20.00

ASHTON, Wendell J. *Voice in the West: Biography of a Pioneer Newspaper.* 1950 NY. Ills 1st ed. dj. VG $20.00

ASHURST. *Surgery: Its Principles & Practice.* 1914 Phil. Ills. 1,136 p. VG $20.00

ASIMOV, Isaac. *Currents of Space.* 1952 Doubleday. 1st ed. dj. EX $85.00

ASIMOV, Isaac. *Fantastic Voyage II.* 1987 Ltd ed. 1/450. sgn. VG $100.00

ASIMOV, Isaac. *Foundation & Empire.* 1952 NY. 1st ed. 1st issue. dj. VG $125.00

ASIMOV, Isaac. *Foundation.* London. 1st ed. dj. VG $40.00

ASIMOV, Isaac. *Foundation's Edge.* 1981 NY. 1st ed. dj. VG $18.00

ASIMOV, Isaac. *I, Robot.* London. 1st ed. dj. EX $60.00

ASIMOV, Isaac. *Pebble in the Sky.* 1950 NY. Doubleday. 1st ed. 12mo. tan cloth. EX $100.00

ASIMOV, Isaac. *Robots & Empire.* 1985 Phantasia. Ltd 1st ed. 1/650. boxed. EX $75.00

ASIMOV, Isaac. *Robots & Empire.* 1985 Garden City. 1st ed. dj. EX $17.00

ASIMOV, Isaac. *Robots of Dawn.* 1983 Phantasia. Ltd ed. 1/750. boxed. EX $75.00

ASIMOV, Isaac. *Robots of Dawn.* 1983 Garden City. 1st trade ed. dj. EX $16.00

ASIMOV, Isaac. *2nd Foundation.* 1953 NY. 1st ed. dj. VG $100.00

ASIMOV & JEPPSON. *Laughing Space: Anthology of Science Fiction Humor.* 1982 1st print. dj. VG $15.00

ASKINS, Charles. *African Hunt.* 1958 Stackpole. Ills. 189 p. VG $18.50

ASKINS, Charles. *American Shotgun.* 1910 Outing. Ills 1st ed. 321 p. VG $45.00

ASKINS, Charles. *Asian Jungle, African Bush.* 1959 Harrisburg. Stackpole. 1st ed. dj. EX $45.00

ASKINS, Charles. *Asian Jungle, African Bush.* 1959 Harrisburg. Stackpole. 1st ed. dj. VG $35.00

ASKINS, Charles. *Modern Shotguns & Loads.* 1929 Marshalton. Ills 1st ed. VG $20.00

ASKINS, Charles. *Wing & Trap Shooting.* 1948 Macmillan. Ills 1st ed. 205 p. dj. EX $12.50

ASLIN, Elizabeth. *19th Century English Furniture.* 1962 London. Ills. 93 p. dj. $60.00

ASQUITH, Cynthia. *Shudders.* 1929 NY. 1st Am ed. dj. EX $25.00

ASTAIRE, Fred. *Fred Astaire Dance Book.* 1955 NY. Arrowhead. Ills 1st ed. VG $27.50

ASTON, F.W. *Isotopes.* 1923 NY. Ills 1st ed. 8vo. 152 p. EX $70.00

ASTON, F.W. *Mass Spectra & Isotopes.* 1942 London. Arnold. 2nd ed. 276 p. xl. VG $12.00

ASTON, Sir George. *Letters to Young Fly-Fishers.* 1926 Allan. Ills 1st ed. 153 p. $10.00

ASTON, Sir George. *Mostly About Trout.* 1921 Allen Unwin. 1st ed. 223 p. VG $10.00

ASTON. *Curious Creatures in Zoology.* 1890 London. Ltd ed. 1/210. $95.00

ASTOR, Brooke. *Last Blossom on the Plum Tree.* 1986 NY. 1st ed. M $10.00

ASTOR, G. *Last Nazi: Life & Times of Dr. Joseph Mengle.* 1985 NY. Ills. dj. G $12.50

ASTURIAS, M. *Hombres de Maiz.* 1982 Alianza. Spanish text. pb. EX $7.50

ATGET, Eugene. *Photographie de Paris.* 1930 NY. Weyhe. 1st Am ed. silk boards. EX $375.00

ATGET, Eugene. *Vision of Paris.* 1963 Macmillan. 1st ed. folio. gilt cloth. VG $90.00

ATGET, Eugene. *Vision of Paris.* 1963 Macmillan. 1st ed. 4to. cloth. EX $100.00

ATGET, Eugene. *Works of Eugene Atget.* 1982 MOMA. 4 vol set. djs. M $75.00

ATHANASIUS, Kircher. *China Monumentis.* 1667 Amsterdam. Ills. Latin text. folio. $400.00

ATHEARN, R.G. *Forts of the Upper MO.* 1967 Prentice Hall. Ills. 339 p. maps. dj. VG $32.00

ATHERTON, G. *Golden Gate Country.* 1945 NY. 2nd print. Am Folkways Series. $6.50

ATHERTON, G. *My San Francisco.* 1946 Bobbs Merrill. Ills. 334 p. dj. G $6.00

ATHERTON, Gertrude. *Life in the War Zone.* 1916 NY. sgn. $25.00

ATHERTON, John. *Fly & the Fish.* 1971 Freshet. Ills. 195 p. slipcase. EX $13.50

ATHILL, Diana. *Instead of a Letter.* 1969 London. Chatto Windus. 1st ed. dj. $60.00

ATKINS, Elizabeth H. *Pot of Gold.* 1930 NY. Stokes. Ills St Clair la Dow. 1st ed. $30.00

ATKINS, F.H. *Joseph Atkins: Story of a Family.* 1891 153 p. VG $40.00

ATKINSON, D.T. *Magic, Myth, & Medicine.* 1956 NY. 320 p. dj. EX $22.00

ATKINSON, J.A. *British Dueling Pistol.* 1978 Arms Armour. Ills. 108 p. dj. EX $15.00

ATKINSON, R. *Complete Book of Ground Covers.* 1970 NY. 210 p. dj. $8.00

ATSHELER. *Sun of Quebec.* 1920 Appleton. Ills 1st ed. dj. VG $28.00

ATTENBOROUGH, David. *Life on Earth: Natural History.* 1979 Little Brown. Ills 1st Am ed. 319 p. dj. EX $10.00

ATTENBOROUGH, David. *Living Planet.* 1984 Little Brown. Ills. 320 p. dj. EX $16.00

ATTIE, David. *Saloon Society.* 1960 NY. 1st ed. dj. VG $12.00

ATWATER, R. *Secret History of Procopius.* 1927 Chicago. Covici. 1/760. sgn. VG $45.00

ATWOOD, Margaret. *Bluebeard's Egg & Other Stories.* 1986 Houghton. 1st Am Ed. dj. EX $17.00

ATWOOD, Margaret. *Bodily Harm.* 1982 Simon Schuster. 1st ed. sgn. dj. EX $25.00

ATWOOD, Margaret. *Journals of Susanna Moodie.* 1970 Toronto. 1st ed. sgn. wraps. EX $25.00

ATWOOD, Margaret. *Lady Oracle.* 1976 McClelland. 1st ed. dj. EX $25.00

ATWOOD, W.W. *Rocky Mountains.* 1945 Vangaurd. Ills. 324 p. dj. VG $16.00

ATWOOD. *Regional Vocabulary of TX.* 1962 Austin. TX Pr. dj. EX $15.00

AUB & HAPGOOD. *Pioneer in Modern Medicine: David Edsall of Harvard.* 1970 Harvard. dj. M $12.50

AUBERT, Marcel. *L'Art Monumental Roman en France.* 1955 Paris. 1st ed. folio. dj. VG $45.00

AUBRY, G.J. *Joseph Conrad: Life & Letters.* 1927 London. 2 vol set. djs. VG $45.00

AUCHINCLOSS, Louis. *Dark Lady.* 1977 Boston. 1st ed. dj. M $17.00

AUCHINCLOSS, Louis. *World of Profit.* 1968 Houghton Mifflin. 1st ed. dj. $20.00

AUCHINCLOSS, Louis. *Writer's Capital.* 1978 MN U Pr. 1st ed. sgn. dj. M $16.00

AUDEN, W.H. *Age on Anxiety.* 1947 Random House. 1st ed. 8vo. dj. EX $45.00

AUDEN, W.H. *Collected Poetry of W.H. Auden.* 1945 Random House. 1st ed. 1st issue. dj. EX $100.00

AUDEN, W.H. *Epistle to a Godson.* 1972 London. dj. EX $14.00

AUDEN, W.H. *Poems.* 1930 London. 1st ed. wraps. VG $300.00

AUDEN, W.H. *Shield of Achilles.* 1955 London. 1st ed. dj. EX $28.00

AUDEN, W.H. *Spain.* 1937 London. 1st ed. wraps. VG $65.00

AUDEN, W.H. *Thank You, Fog.* 1974 NY. dj. EX $16.00

AUDSLEY, G.A. *Ornamental Arts of Japan. Vol. II.* 1884 NY. rebound. $450.00

AUDSLEY, G.A.; & BOWES, J.L. *Ceramic Art of Japan.* 1875 Liverpool. 1st ed. 2 vol set. EX $600.00

AUDUBON, John James. *Birds of America Edited by Donald Culross Peattie.* 1940 Boston. 1st ed. VG $40.00

AUDUBON, John James. *Birds of America.* 1937 NY. Macmillan. slipcase. EX $150.00

AUDUBON, John James. *Birds of America.* 1953 NY. 4to. dj. VG $45.00

AUDUBON, John James. *Delineations of American Scenery & Character.* 1926 NY. 1st ed. 349 p. dj. VG $30.00

AUDUBON, John James. *Original Watercolor Paintings for Birds of America.* 1966 NY. 1st ed. folio. 2 vol set. EX $100.00

AUDUBON, John James. *Quadrupeds of North America Edited by Bachman.* 1948 NY. 155 plts. 3 vol set. $1900.00

AUDUBON, John James. *Quadrupeds of North America.* 1856 NY. tall 8vo. 3 vol set. full leather. VG $2500.00

AUEL, Jean. *Mammoth Hunters.* no date. Crown. Ltd 1st ed. sgn. $40.00

AUEL, Jean. *Mammouth Hunters.* 1985 NY. 1st ed. sgn. dj. EX $20.00

AUEL, Jean. *Valley of Horses.* no date. Crown. 1st ed. dj. VG $20.00

AUEL, Jean. *Valley of Horses.* 1982 NY. 1st ed. dj. EX $30.00

AUMONIER & BELCHER. *Odd Fish.* 1923 London. Cheswick. 8vo. cloth. VG $20.00

AUSLANDER, Joseph. *Sunrise Trumpets.* 1924 NY. 1st ed. 1st issue. sgn. VG $85.00

AUSTEN, Jane. *Everyman & Other Plays.* 1925 London. Chapman Hall. Ills. 8vo. EX $50.00

AUSTEN, Jane. *Persuasion.* 1977 Ltd Ed Club. Ills/sgn Bounpastore. EX $50.00

AUSTEN, Jane. *Pride & Prejudice.* 1940 Boston. boxed. $22.50

AUSTEN, Jane. *Pride & Prejudice.* 1940 Heritage. Ltd Ed Club. dj. slipcase. EX $25.00

AUSTEN, Jane. *Sense & Sensibility.* 1926 London. full leather. VG $20.00

AUSTEN, Jane. *3 Evening Prayers.* 1940 Colt. Ltd ed. 1/300. $30.00

AUSTIN, Alfred. *Fortunatus the Pessimist.* 1893 London. 1st ed. inscr. cloth. EX $30.00

AUSTIN, Alma H. *Romance of Candy.* 1938 Harper. Ills. VG $12.00

AUSTIN, G. *Practical Magic with Popular Patter.* 1919 London. 1st ed. VG $20.00

AUSTIN, John. *Shakespeare's Hamlet, Prince of Denmark.* no date. Selwyn Blout. Ills. 4to. $110.00

AUSTIN, Mary. *Isidro.* 1905 Boston. VG $30.00

AUSTIN, Mary. *Land of Little Rain.* 1903 Boston. 1st ed. G $25.00

AUSTIN, O.L. *Birds of the World.* 1961 Golden Pr. Ills. 4to. 319 p. dj. EX $24.00

AUTHOR, R.W. *Contact! Careers of US Naval Aviators.* 1967 1st ed. EX $45.00

AUTON, C. *Recollections of Auton House.* 1881 Boston. Houghton Mifflin. 99 p. G $9.00

AUTRY, Gene. *Back in the Saddle Again.* 1978 Doubleday. dj. VG $20.00

AVAULT, J.W. *Fresh-Water Crayfish.* 1975 LA U Pr. Ills. 676 p. VG $27.00

AVEBURY, Lord. *Notes on Life History of British Flowering Plants.* 1905 London. 450 p. EX $25.00

AVEDON, Richard. *Photographs of Avedon 1947-1977.* 1978 Farrar. 1st ed. sgn. glassine wraps. $200.00

AVEDON, Richard. *Portraits.* 1976 NY. Farrar. 1st ed. 4to. inscr. dj. VG $75.00

AVEDON & CAPOTE. *Observations.* 1959 Simon Schuster. 1st ed. dj. VG $85.00

AVEDON & CAPOTE. *Observations.* 1959 Simon Schuster. 1st ed. dj. EX $110.00

AVERELL, William Woods. *10 Years in the Saddle.* 1978 San Rafael, CA. 1st ed. dj. VG $20.00

AVERILL, Naomi. *Whistling-Two-Teeth & the 49 Buffalos.* 1939 Grosset Dunlap. Ills 1st ed. VG $25.00

AVERILL & STANLEY. *Daniel Boone.* 1931 Paris. Domino. Ills Rojankovsky. M $110.00

AXELROD, H.R. *African Cichlids of Lake Malawi & Tanganyika.* 1974 Ills. 256 p. EX $15.00

AXELSON. *Commy.* 1919 Reilly Lee. Ills 1st ed. 320 p. $27.50

AYER, Jean. *Donald Duck & His Friends.* 1939 Heath. Ills Disney Studios. G $30.00

AYERS, James. *Gold & Sunshine Reminiscences of Early CA.* 1922 Boston. 1st ed. VG $35.00

AYMAR, B. *Personality of the Bird.* 1945 Bonanza. Ills. 270 p. dj. EX $5.00

AYMAR, G.C. *Bird Flight.* 1936 Dodd Mead. Ills 2nd ed. 234 p. VG $17.00

AYNSLEY, H. Murray. *Symbolism of the East & West.* 1971 Gale Research. reprint of 1900. 212 p. VG $20.00

AYRES, James. *British Folk Art.* 1977 Woodstock. Overlook. Ills. 144 p. dj. $30.00

AZEMA, M.A. *Conquest of Fitzroy.* 1957 London. 1st ed. dj. VG $45.00

AZIZ, P. *Doctors of Death. Vol. I.* 1976 Geneva. Ferni. Ills. VG $25.00

AZOY, A.C.M. *They Were Not Afraid To Die.* 1939 Harris. dj. VG $18.00

AZUELA, A. *La Casa de las Mil Virgenes.* 1984 Plaza y Janes. Spanish text. pb. EX $7.50

BABCOCK, Havilah. *Best of Babcock.* 1974 Holt Rinehart. 1st ed. 262 p. dj. EX $25.00

BABCOCK, Havilah. *Education of a Pretty Boy.* 1960 NY. 1st ed. dj. EX $75.00

BABCOCK, Havilah. *I Don't Want To Shoot an Elephant.* 1958 NY. Holt. 1st ed. dj. EX $60.00

BABCOCK, Havilah. *Jaybirds Go to Hell on Friday.* 1965 NY. 1st ed. dj. VG $75.00

BABCOCK, Havilah. *My Health Is Better in November.* 1948 SC U Pr. 284 p. VG $18.50

BABCOCK, Havilah. *Tails of Quails & Such.* 1951 NY. facsimile. EX $35.00

BABCOCK, Louis L. *Tarpon.* 1921 private print. Corrected 2nd ed. 107 p. VG $200.00

BABCOCK, P.H. *Falling Leaves: Tales From a Gun Room.* 1937 Derrydale. Ltd ed. 1/950. EX $125.00

BABCOCK, Wayne. *Textbook of Surgery.* 1929 Phil. Saunders. Ills. 1,041 p. G $60.00

BABCOCK & WILCOX. *Steam: Its Generation & Use.* 1889 NY. Ills. G $20.00

BABCOCK & WILCOX. *Steam: Its Generation & Use.* 1920 NY. 8vo. cloth. VG $17.00

BABEL, Isaac. *Benya Krik the Gangster.* 1948 Schocken. 1st Am ed. dj. VG $20.00

BABINGTON-SMITH, Constance. *Testing Time: Story of British Test Pilots & Their Aircraft.* 1961 NY. Harper. Ills 1st ed. 225 p. dj. VG $15.00

BABITZ, Eve. *Eve's Hollywood.* 1974 Delacorte. 1st ed. dj. EX $30.00

BABITZ, Eve. *Slow Days, Fast Company.* 1977 Knopf. 1st ed. dj. EX $20.00

BABSON, Roger W. *Cheer Up! Better Times Ahead.* 1932 NY. 1st ed. printed glassine wraps. $35.00

BABSON, Stanley. *Bone Fishing.* 1972 NY. 1st ed. dj. VG $20.00

BACH, J. *America's Germany.* 1946 Random House. G $10.00

BACH, Richard. *Stranger to the Ground.* 1963 Harper. 1st ed. dj. VG $15.00

BACHMAN, Richard. *Thinner.* 1984 NY. 1st ed. 3rd print. dj. VG $25.00

BACHRACH, Max. *Fur: Practical Treatise.* 1946 Prentice Hall. Ills. 672 p. G $14.00

BACK, Sir George. *Narrative of the Arctic Land Expedition.* 1836 Phil. Ills 1st Am ed. 8vo. VG $350.00

BACKMANN, A. *Encyclopedia of the Violin.* 1926 NY. Ills 1st ed. 8vo. VG $45.00

BACKUS, Isaac. *Church History of New England From 1620 to 1804.* 1853 Phil. VG $95.00

BACON, A.C. *History of the Violoncello As a Solo Instrument.* 1969 NY. 1st ed. VG $18.00

BACON, Axel W. *Hypnotism.* 1960 Chicago. 12mo. 265 p. dj. VG $7.50

BACON, Edward R. *Catalogue of Chinese Art Objects.* 1919 NY. private print. 2 vol set. $225.00

BACON, Francis. *Advancement of Learning.* 1902 Collier. 431 p. VG $10.00

BACON, Francis. *Opera Omni.* 1730 London. folio. 4 vol set. $125.00

BACON, Francis. *Proficience & Advancement of Learning: Divine & Human.* 1633 London. Oxford. 3rd ed. 335 p. G $650.00

BACON, H. *Parisan Art.* 1883 Boston. Ills. 239 p. VG $25.00

BACON, Peggy. *Cat Calls.* 1935 Stated 1st ed. VG $12.00

BACON, R. *Yankee Magazine of Forgotten Arts.* 1978 NY. 219 p. dj. VG $10.00

BACON, T. *Orientalist.* London. Arnold. Ills Finden. 8vo. cloth. VG $50.00

BADCOCK, D. *My Kind of Country.* 1976 Christchurch. Ills. 8vo. dj. EX $25.00

BADE, W.F. *Life & Letters of John Muir.* 1924 Boston. 2 vol set. cloth. xl. G $25.00

BADEN-POWELL. *Memories of India: Recollections of Soldiering & Sport.* no date. Phil. Ills. dj. VG $30.00

BADER. *American Picture Books: Noah's Ark to the Beast Within.* 1976 NY. dj. EX $45.00

BAEDEKER, Karl. *Austria & Hungary.* 1905 EX $52.00

BAEDEKER, Karl. *Austria with Budapest, Prague, Karlsbad, & Marienbad.* 1929 Leipzig. Last Revised ed. 519 p. dj. EX $65.00

BAEDEKER, Karl. *Canada with Newfoundland & AK.* 1907 Leipzig. 13 maps. 12 plans. 332 p. EX $60.00

BAEDEKER, Karl. *Eastern Alps.* 1911 Ills. maps. VG $12.00

BAEDEKER, Karl. *Egypt: Handbook of Travellers.* 1902 Leipzig. 5th ed. 408 p. G $30.00

BAEDEKER, Karl. *Gettysburg: What To See.* 1873 Boston. Ills. wraps. G $30.00

BAEDEKER, Karl. *Mediterranean Including Canary Islands, Morocco, & Algeria.* 1911 Leipzig. 38 maps. 49 plans. 608 p. VG $95.00

BAEDEKER, Karl. *Norway, Sweden, & Denmark.* 1903 Leipzig. 37 maps. 22 plans. 486 p. EX $40.00

BAEDEKER, Karl. *Palestine & Syria.* 1898 EX $127.00

BAEDEKER, Karl. *Rhine From Rotterdam to Constance.* 1900 Leipzig. 45 maps. 25 plans. 448 p. VG $25.00

BAEDEKER, Karl. *Switzerland, Italy, Savoy, & Tryol.* 1897 Ills. maps. VG $12.00

BAEDEKER, Karl. *Switzerland, Italy, Savoy, & Tyrol.* 1909 72 maps. 19 plans. VG $10.00

BAEDEKER, Karl. *Switzerland, Italy, Savoy, & Tyrol.* 1911 Leipzig. 75 maps. 20 plans. 594 p. EX $30.00

BAEDEKER, Karl. *US with Excursion into Mexico.* 1899 Leipzig. 19 maps. 24 plans. 580 p. VG $80.00

BAGNOLD, Enid. *National Velvet.* 1935 Morrow. 1st ed. dj. VG $50.00

BAIGELL, Matthew. *Dictionary of American Art.* 1979 NY. 4to. 390 p. cloth. dj. $25.00

BAIGELL, Matthew. *Thomas Hart Benton.* no date. NY. Abrams. Ills. oblong folio. $90.00

BAIGELL, Matthew. *Thomas Hart Benton.* 1973 Abrams. Deluxe Ltd ed. sgn Benton. M $450.00

BAIKIE. *Through the Telescope.* 1906 London. VG $25.00

BAILEY, Adrian. *Lakelane Rock: Classic Climbs with Chris Bonington.* 1985 London. 1st ed. dj. VG $18.00

BAILEY, Alice Cooper. *Skating Gander.* 1927 NY. Wise Parslow. Ills MH Myers. $15.00

BAILEY, Arthur Scott. *Tale of Billy Woodchuck.* 1916 Grosset Dunlap. Ills Smith. G $6.00

BAILEY, Arthur Scott. *Tale of Grunty Pig.* 1921 NY. Ills HL Smith. VG $8.50

BAILEY, Bernadine. *Guatemala.* 1942 Whitman. Ills Kurt Wiese. 1st ed. 24mo. $12.50

BAILEY, Bernadine. *Pictured Geography. Boliva in Story & Picture.* 1942 Whitman. Ills Wiese. 4to. 28 p. dj. VG $10.00

BAILEY, Bernadine. *Pictured Geography. Ecuador in Story & Picture.* 1942 Whitman. Ills Wiese. 4to. 28 p. dj. VG $10.00

BAILEY, Bernadine. *Pictured Geography. Honduras in Story & Picture.* 1942 Whitman. Ills Wiese. 1st ed. 4to. 28 p. $10.00

BAILEY, Bernadine. *Pictured Geography. Peru in Story & Picture.* 1942 Whitman. Ills Wiese. 4to. 28 p. dj. VG $10.00

BAILEY, Carolyn. *Stories From an Indian Cave.* 1924 Whitman. Ills. VG $12.00

BAILEY, H. *Lost Language of Symbolism.* 1952 Norgate. 2 vol set. VG $45.00

BAILEY, Isaac. *American Naval Biography.* 1815 Providence. Mann. 258 p. scarce. $250.00

BAILEY, J.O. *Pilgrims Through Space & Time.* 1947 NY. 1st ed. dj. EX $35.00

BAILEY, John. *Grandfather Was a Trout.* 1961 Prentice Hall. 151 p. dj. EX $7.50

BAILEY, L.H. *Botany for Secondary Schools.* 1920 Macmillan. 465 p. G $8.00

BAILEY, L.H. *Concise Dictionary Gardening.* 1930 NY. Ills 1st ed. 652 p. VG $47.50

BAILEY, L.H. *Encyclopedia of American Horticulture.* 1906 NY. 4th ed. 6 vol set. slipcase. $160.00

BAILEY, L.H. *Encyclopedia of Horticulture.* 1935 NY. 4to. 3 vol set. VG $55.00

BAILEY, L.H. *Garden of Gourds.* 1937 NY. 1st ed. dj. $17.00

BAILEY, L.H. *Gardener's Handbook.* 1941 NY. 292 p. dj. VG $18.00

BAILEY, L.H. *Manuel of Gardening.* 1910 Macmillan. 539 p. VG $18.00

BAILEY, L.H. *Sketch of Evolution of Our Native Fruits.* 1911 Macmillan. 3rd ed. VG $20.00

BAILEY, Paul. *City in the Sun.* 1971 Los Angeles. Ills. 222 p. dj. VG $25.00

BAILEY, Pearl. *Raw Pearl.* 1968 NY. Harcourt Brace. photos. inscr. $30.00

BAILEY & CUSHING. *Classification of Tumors of Glioma Group.* 1926 1st ed. VG $245.00

BAILLIE, Matthew. *Morbid Anatomy of the Human Body.* 1833 London. Longman. rebound. $65.00

BAILYN, Bernard. *New England Merchants in 17th Century.* 1955 Harvard. G $18.00

BAIN, G.F. *Clyde Barrow & Bonnie Parker: Barrow Gang.* 1968 private print. 33 p. EX $12.00

BAIN, John. *Cigarettes in Fact & Fancy.* 1906 Boston. G $20.00

BAIN, Robert. *Clans & Tartans of Scotland.* 1948 London. 8vo. VG $14.00

BAIN & HARRIS. *Mickey Mouse: 50 Happy Years.* 1977 NY. dj. VG $20.00

BAINBRIDGE, Beryl. *Injury Time.* 1977 Braziller. 1st Am ed. dj. EX $15.00

BAINBRIDGE, Beryl. *Quiet Life.* 1977 Braziller. 1st Am ed. dj. EX $15.00

BAINBRIDGE, Beryl. *Sweet William.* 1976 Braziller. 1st Am ed. dj. EX $16.00

BAINBRIDGE, Beryl. *Weekend with Claude.* 1982 Braziller. 1st Am ed. dj. EX $10.00

BAINBRIDGE, Beryl. *Winter Garden.* 1981 Braziller. 1st Am ed. dj. EX $12.00

BAINBRIDGE, Beryl. *Young Adolf.* 1979 NY. 1st ed. dj. M $10.00

BAINBRIDGE, Beryl. *Young Adolph.* 1979 Braziller. 1st Am ed. dj. EX $12.00

BAINBRIDGE, H. *Peter Carl Faberge.* 1949 London. 1st ed. dj. EX $75.00

BAIRD, J. *15 Years in the Hawken Lode.* 1976 Gun Room Pr. Ills. 4to. 120 p. dj. EX $15.00

BAIRD, Robert. *American Cotton Spinners', Managers' & Carders' Guide.* 1852 Phil. Hart. 12mo. 252 p. $25.00

BAIRD, Robert. *Impressions & Experiences of West Indies & North America.* 1850 Phil. Lea Blanchard. 1st Am ed. VG $75.00

BAIRD, Viola. *Wild Violets of North America.* 1942 CA U Pr. Ltd ed. 1/1,000. sgn. dj. $30.00

BAIRD. *Brief History of Upshur County.* 1945 Gilmer Mirror. dj. EX $17.50

BAKELESS, John. *Daniel Boone: Master of the Wilderness.* 1939 480 p. VG $10.00

BAKER, A.T. *Mahatma Letters to A.P. Sinnett.* 1923 London. 492 p. VG $35.00

BAKER, Carlos. *Year & a Day.* 1963 Nashville. 1st ed. inscr. dj. EX $17.00

BAKER, Charles. *Bibliography of British Book Illustrators.* 1978 Birmingham. Ltd ed. 1/1,000. 4to. dj. M $50.00

BAKER, Charles. *Gentleman's Companion: Exotic Cookery Book.* 1939 Derrydale. Ltd ed. 1/1,250. boxed. VG $185.00

BAKER, Clyde. *Modern Gunsmithing.* 1933 Plantersville. 2nd ed. VG $25.00

BAKER, Clyde. *Modern Gunsmithing.* 1928 Small Arms. Ills 1st ed. 530 p. VG $32.50

BAKER, Dorothy. *Cassandra at the Wedding.* 1962 Boston. 1st ed. dj. VG $10.00

BAKER, Eugene C. *Speeches, Responses, & Essays: Critical & Historical.* 1954 1st ed. 307 p. VG $35.00

BAKER, G.P. *12 Centuries of Rome.* 1934 Dodd Mead. $10.00

BAKER, George. *Collected Poems 1930-1955.* 1957 NY. 1st ed. dj. EX $25.00

BAKER, J.A. *Peregrine.* 1968 Harper Row. 1st Am ed. 8vo. dj. EX $10.00

BAKER, Mrs. Sale. *Lily's Visit to Grandmama.* 1879 London. Ills George Routledge. VG $9.50

BAKER, Pearl. *Wild Bunch at Robbers Roost.* 1971 Abelard Schuman. dj. EX $25.00

BAKER, Russell. *American in WA.* 1961 NY. 1st ed. dj. VG $10.00

BAKER, Samuel W. *Great Basin of the Nile & Other Explorations.* 1874 London. Ills New ed. 499 p. G $30.00

BAKER, Virgil. *American Painting History & Interpretation.* 1950 NY. Ills 1st ed. 8vo. 717 p. VG $20.00

BAKER, W. *Maritime History of Bath, ME.* 1973 Bath. Ills 1st ed. 2 vol set. $40.00

BAKER, William. *Lares & Penates; or, Cilicia & Its Governors.* 1853 London. Ingram Cook. 8vo. 394 p. VG $50.00

BAKER & KUNZ. *Collector's Book of Railroadiana: Complete Guide.* 1976 240 p. dj. EX $15.00

BAKER. *Man in the Trap.* 1967 NY. 1st ed. dj. VG $17.50

BAKER. *Southern Nature Stories: Book 2.* 1939 TB. VG $10.00

BAKST, Leon. *Designs of Leon Bakst for Sleeping Princes.* 1923 London. Ltd ed. 1/1,000. folio. $650.00

BALAKIAN, Nona. *Critical Encounters: Literary Views & Reviews 1953-1977.* 1978 Indianapolis. dj. VG $7.00

BALCH, Thomas Willing. *AK Frontier.* 1903 Phil. 4to. 28 maps. $40.00

BALDET, Marcel. *Lead Soldiers & Figurines.* 1961 NY. Crown. Ills. 129 p. dj. $50.00

BALDRIDGE, C.S. *White Africans & Black.* 1929 NY. Norton. Ills. VG $20.00

BALDWIN, Faith. *Skyscraper.* 1931 NY. 1st ed. VG $25.00

BALDWIN, James. *Amen Corner.* 1961 NY. 1st ed. dj. VG $35.00

BALDWIN, James. *Blues for Mr. Charlie.* 1965 London. 1st ed. dj. M $20.00

BALDWIN, James. *Devil Finds Work.* 1976 Dial. 1st ed. dj. M $20.00

BALDWIN, James. *Devil Finds Work.* 1976 NY. 1st ed. dj. VG $15.00

BALDWIN, James. *Evidence of Things Not Seen.* 1985 NY. Holt. 1st ed. dj. M $10.00

BALDWIN, James. *Giovanni's Room.* 1956 NY. Dial. 1st ed. dj. VG $50.00

BALDWIN, James. *If Beale Street Could Talk.* 1974 NY. 1st ed. dj. EX $12.00

BALDWIN, James. *Just Above My Head.* 1979 Ltd ed. 1/500. sgn. $65.00

BALDWIN, James. *Nothing Personal.* 1964 NY. Dell. Ills Avedon. 1st ed. pb. EX $35.00

BALDWIN, James. *School Reading by Grades.* 1897 Am Book Co. VG $8.00

BALDWIN, James. *Story of Roland.* 1930 NY/London. Scribner. Ills Hurd. 1st ed. M $40.00

BALDWIN, James. *Story of Roland.* 1930 Scribner. Ills Peter Hurd. VG $15.00

BALDWIN, James. *Story of Siegfried.* 1931 NY. Scribner. Ills Peter Hurd. $28.00

BALDWIN, James. *Story of Siegfried.* 1882 NY. Ills Pyle. 1st ed. VG $25.00

BALDWIN, James. *Tell Me How Long the Train's Been Gone.* 1968 NY. 1st ed. dj. EX $12.00

BALDWIN, Leland D. *Keelboat Age on Western Waters.* 1941 Pittsburgh. 1st ed. VG $50.00

BALDWIN, Leland D. *Whiskey Rebels.* 1939 Pittsburgh. dj. EX $20.00

BALDWIN, Ralph B. *Deadly Fuze: Secret Weapon of World War II.* 1980 San Rafael. Presidio Pr. 1st ed. 332 p. VG $12.00

BALDWIN, William Charles. *African Hunting From Natal to Zambesi.* 1863 NY. Harper. 1st ed. 397 p. EX $145.00

BALDWIN, William Charles. *African Hunting From Natal to Zambesi.* 1863 NY. Harper. 1st ed. 8vo. G $85.00

BALFOUR, Graham. *Life of Robert Louis Stevenson.* 1901 London. Methuen. 2nd ed. 2 vol set. $35.00

BALFOUR, Walter. *Reply to Professor Stuart's Exegetical Essays.* 1831 Boston. 1st ed. scarce. VG $75.00

BALL, Charles. *Slavery in the US: Narrative of Life & Adventures of Ball.* 1836 Lewiston. 1st ed. 400 p. fair. $30.00

BALL, Don. *America's Colorful Railroads.* 1980 210 p. $19.00

BALL, John. *Autobiography of John Ball.* 1925 Grand Rapids. 1st ed. EX $65.00

BALL, John. *Phase 3 Alert.* 1977 2nd ed. dj. EX $8.00

BALL, Martha Jane. *Timothy Crunchit, the Calico Bunny.* 1930 Laidlaw Bros. Ills Gay Woodring. 4to. $22.00

BALL, Sir Robert S. *Story of the Heavens.* 1891 London. Ills. VG $150.00

BALL, W.W. *State That Forgot: SC Surrender to Democracy.* 1932 Indianapolis. 1st ed. VG $20.00

BALLAGH, James Curtis. *Letters of Richard Henry Lee.* 1911 Macmillan. $22.00

BALLANTINE, Bill. *Wild Tigers & Tame Fleas.* 1958 Rinehart. Ills. 344 p. G $5.00

BALLANTYNE, R.M. *Gorilla Hunters.* 1893 London. Nels. New ed. 8vo. VG $15.00

BALLANTYNE, R.M. *Hudson Bay.* 1886 London. 4th ed. 12mo. cloth. VG $25.00

BALLANTYNE, Sheila. *Inscriptions.* 1985 Nomad Pr. Ills 1st ed. 1/100. wraps. EX $90.00

BALLARD, E.G. *Captain Streeter: Pioneer.* 1914 Chicago. 1st ed. $25.00

BALLARD, J.G. *High Rise.* London. 1st ed. sgn. EX $85.00

BALLARD, J.G. *Love & Napalm: Export USA.* 1972 NY. Grove. 1st ed. dj. VG $45.00

BALLARD, J.G. *Unlimited Dream Company.* 1979 NY. Holt. 1st ed. dj. VG $10.00

BALLARD, Joseph. *England in 1815, Seen by a Young Boston Merchant.* 1913 Boston. Ltd ed. 1/525. EX $25.00

BALLERT, M.; & BREIHAN, C. *Billy the Kid: Date with Destiny.* 1970 Superior. Ills. 141 p. VG $20.00

BALLIETT, Mrs. Dow. *Philosophy of Numbers.* 1917 Atlantic City. 155 p. VG $50.00

BALLIETT, Whitney. *Ecstasy at the Onion.* 1971 Bobbs Merrill. 1st ed. dj. VG $20.00

BALLIETT, Whitney. *NY Notes.* 1976 Boston. Houghton Mifflin. 1st ed. dj. $15.00

BALLOU, M.M. *Due North.* 1887 Ticknor. VG $20.00

BALLOU, M.M. *History of Cuba.* 1854 Boston. Ills. 230 p. G $37.50

BALLOU, M.M. *New Eldorado.* 1891 Boston. 355 p. G $25.00

BALLOU, M.M. *Story of Malta.* 1893 Boston. 1st ed. presentation. VG $35.00

BALLU, Nicole. *Le Porcelaine Francaise.* no date. Paris. Lib Centrale des Beaux Arts. $60.00

BALNEAVES, Elizabeth. *Mountains of the Murgha Zerin.* 1972 London. 1st ed. dj. VG $18.00

BAMFIELD, K. *Story of Christmas.* 1952 London. Ills Tarrant. VG $12.50

BANCROFT, Caroline. *Silver Queen: Fabulous Story of Baby Doe Labor.* 1952 Denver. 3rd print. wraps. VG $20.00

BANCROFT, George. *History of the USA From the Discovery of the Continent.* 1892 NY. 6 vol set. $40.00

BANCROFT, George. *History of the USA From the Discovery of the Continent.* 1853-1854. Boston. 6 vol set. VG $75.00

BANCROFT, George. *Memorial Address on the Life & Character of Abraham Lincoln.* 1902 GPO. 4to. VG $20.00

BANCROFT, George. *Memorial Address on the Life & Character of Abraham Lincoln.* 1866 WA. inscr. ¾-leather. $85.00

BANCROFT, H.H. *History of AK 1730-1885.* 1960 Antiquarian Pr. reprint of 1886. 775 p. dj. EX $95.00

BANCROFT, H.H. *History of AZ & NM.* 1889 San Francisco. Ills. fld map. $45.00

BANCROFT, H.H. *History of UT 1540-1887.* 1890 San Francisco. 808 p. EX $65.00

BANCROFT, H.H. *Native Races of Pacific States.* 1882 San Francisco. VG $125.00

BANCROFT, Laura. *Mr. Woodchuck.* 1906 Reilly Britton. 1st ed. 16mo. scarce. $85.00

BANDEL, Eugene. *Frontier Life in the Army.* 1974 Phil. VG $20.00

BANDELIER, A.F. *Delight Makers.* 1957 Dodd Mead. Ills. 490 p. VG $15.00

BANDELIER, A.F. *Delight Makers.* 1890 NY. scarce. VG $100.00

BANDELIER, A.F. *Delight Makers.* 1918 NY. Dodd Mead. 3rd ed. $50.00

BANDINELLI, Ranuccio B. *Roman Art A.D. 200-400.* 1971 NY. Braziller. Ills. 4to. 473 p. dj. $60.00

BANDINI, Ralph. *Men, Fish, & Tackle: Story of J.A. Coxe.* 1936 private print. 1st #d ed. sliver bdg. VG $300.00

BANGS, John K. *Idiot.* 1895 NY. Harper. Ills Richards. 12mo. cloth. G $10.00

BANGS, John K. *Mr. Munchausen.* 1901 Boston. Noyes. Ills Peter Newell. VG $15.00

BANISTER, J. *English Silver.* 1966 NY. Ills. 251 p. $16.50

BANKO, W.E. *Trumpeter Swan.* 1980 NEU Pr. Ills. 214 p. wraps. EX $7.00

BANKS, C.E. *Artistic Guide to Chicago & World's Columbian Expo.* 1893 Peale. Ills. 419 p. G $10.00

BANKS, C.E. *Beautiful Homes & Social Customs of America.* 1902 Chicago. folio. EX $35.00

BANKS, C.E. *Winthrop Fleet of 1630.* 1930 Boston. Ltd 1st ed. 1/500. sgn. dj. EX $60.00

BANKS, Iain. *Bridge.* London. 1st ed. sgn. EX $55.00

BANKS, Iain. *Consider Phlebas.* 1987 London. 1st ed. sgn. dj. M $35.00

BANKS, Iain. *Consider Phlebas.* London. proof. EX $250.00

BANKS, Iain. *Consider Phlebas.* London. Ltd 1st ed. 1/176. sgn. EX $150.00

BANKS, Iain. *Espedair Street.* London. 1st ed. sgn. EX $40.00

BANKS, Iain. *Tales From Forbidden Planet.* London. Ltd 1st ed. 1/250. sgn. EX $120.00

BANKS, Iain. *Walking on Glass.* London. 1st ed. sgn. EX $55.00

BANKS, Louis Albert. *Immortal Songs of Camp & Field.* 1899 Cleveland. Ills. 298 p. VG $35.00

BANN, Stephen. *Tradition of Constructivism.* 1974 NY. Viking. Ills. 8vo. 384 p. dj. $25.00

BANNERMAN. *Histoire du Petit Negre Sambo.* 1921 NY. VG $50.00

BANNERMAN. *Little Black Sambo Storybook.* 1935 Platt Munk. Ills. EX $20.00

BANNERMAN. *Story of Little White Squibba.* 1966 London. 12mo. dj. M $30.00

BANNING, Margaret Culkin. *Lifeboat Number 2.* NY. 1st ed. sgn. dj. G $12.50

BANNING, Margaret Culkin. *Mesabi.* 1969 NY. 1st ed. sgn. dj. VG $12.50

BANNING, Margaret Culkin. *Women for Defense.* 1942 NY. 1st ed. dj. VG $12.50

BANNING, W. *6 Horses.* 1928 Century. Ills 2nd print. 410 p. VG $20.00

BANNISTER, Don. *Burning Leaves.* 1982 Routledge. 1st ed. dj. EX $15.00

BANSEMER, Roger. *Art of Hot Air Ballooning.* 4to. sgn. 165 p. dj. EX $15.00

BARADA, B. *Underwater Hunting: Its Techniques & Adventures.* 1969 Doubleday. Ills 1st ed. 237 p. dj. EX $14.00

BARAKA, Amiri. *Autobiography of Leroi Jones.* 1984 NY. 1st ed. dj. VG $15.00

BARBASETTI. *Art of the Foli.* 1932 NY. Ills 1st ed. 276 p. dj. G $32.50

BARBEAU, Marius. *Pathfinders in the North Pacific.* 1958 Caxton. 1st ed. dj. EX $15.00

BARBER, Edwin A. *Emily Johnson de Forest Collection of Mexican Majolica.* 1911 MOMA. Ills Ltd ed. 1/1,000. $30.00

BARBER, H. *Aerobatics.* 1928 NY. Ills. 4th print. VG $65.00

BARBER, Joel. *Wildfowl Decoys.* 1937 Garden City. Windward House. dj. VG $40.00

BARBER, Joel. *Wildfowl Decoys.* 1934 NY. Windward House. gilt red coth. $110.00

BARBER, Lynn. *Heyday of Natural History 1820-1870.* 1980 Doubleday. Ills 1st Am ed. 320 p. dj. EX $15.00

BARBER, Noel. *From the Land of Lost Content.* 1970 1st Am ed. 235 p. EX $25.00

BARBER, R. *Arthurian Legends: Illustrated Anthology.* 1979 1st Am ed. EX $15.00

BARBER, R. *Reign of Chivalry.* 1980 1st Am ed. dj. EX $20.00

BARBET, Pierre. *Doctor at Calvary: Passion of Our Lord Described by Surgeon.* 1953 NY. Kennedy. xl. VG $30.00

BARBOUR, Alan. *Pictorial History of Motion Picture Serial.* 1977 A&W Pub. Ills. cloth. dj. M $15.00

BARBOUR, Ralph Henry. *Cupid in Love.* 1912 Boston. Ills 1st ed. EX $12.00

BARBOUR, Ralph Henry. *Holly: Romance of a Southern Girl.* 1907 Phil. 1st ed. EX $14.00

BARCLAY, John. *Argenis.* 1671 Amsterdam. Latin text. full leather. VG $25.00

BARCLAY, W. *Land of Magellan.* no date. NY. Ills. maps. VG $18.00

BARCSAY, Jeno. *Drapery & the Human Form.* 1958 Budapest. Corvina. dj. $25.00

BARDACH, John. *Downstream: Natural History of a River.* 1964 Harper Row. Ills 1st ed. 278 p. dj. EX $10.00

BARDENS, Dennis. *Mysterious Worlds.* 1970 NY. 256 p. dj. EX $11.00

BARDESCHI. *Italian Villas Today.* 1967 Transatlantic. 1st ed. dj. M $16.00

BARHAM, R.H. *Ingoldsby Legends.* 1907 London. Ills. 4to. cloth. G $115.00

BARICH, Bill. *Laughing in the Hills.* 1980 NY. Viking. 1st ed. dj. EX $20.00

BARING, Maurice. *Postscript with Some Letters & Verse.* 1948 London. 1st ed. dj. EX $12.00

BARKER, Bill; & LEWIN, Jackie. *Denver!* 1972 Garden City. 1st ed. VG $12.50

BARKER, Clive. *Books of Blood. Vols. I-VI.* 1985-1986. Weidenfeld Nicolson. set. EX $300.00

BARKER, Clive. *Books of Blood. Vols. I-VI.* London. 1st trade ed. sgn. djs. set. M $330.00

BARKER, Clive. *Books of Blood. Vols. I-VI.* CA. Ltd 1st ed. 1/250. sgn. djs. $110.00

BARKER, Clive. *Books of Blood. Vols. I-VI.* London. 1st ed. sgn. djs. set. EX $275.00

BARKER, Clive. *Books of Blood. Vols. I-VI.* CA. Ltd ed. 1/26. sgn. djs. EX $250.00

BARKER, Clive. *Books of Blood. Vols. I-VI.* 1984-1985. Sphere. 1st ed. wraps. set. EX $75.00

BARKER, Clive. *Damnation Game.* 1987 NY. Putnam. 1st Am ed. dj. M $15.00

BARKER, Clive. *Damnation Game.* London. 1st ed. sgn. pb. VG $25.00

BARKER, Clive. *Damnation Game.* 1987 Ace. Advance copy. wraps. $50.00

BARKER, Clive. *Damnation Game.* 1985 London. 1st ed. dj. M $50.00

BARKER, Clive. *In the Flesh.* 1986 NY. 1st Am ed. dj. EX $30.00

BARKER, Clive. *In the Flesh.* NY. proof. EX $85.00

BARKER, Clive. *Inhuman Condition.* 1986 NY. 1st ed. dj. EX $30.00

BARKER, Clive. *Weaveworld.* no date. 1st Canadian ed. dj. M $65.00

BARKER, Clive. *Weaveworld.* 1987 Poseidon Pr. Uncorrected proof. VG $75.00

BARKER, Clive. *Weaveworld.* 1987 London. 1st trade ed. sgn. dj. M $40.00

BARKER, E.S. *Beatty's Cabin: Adventures in the Pecos High Country.* 1953 NM U Pr. Ills. 220 p. dj. VG $20.00

BARKER, F.C. *Lake & Forest As I Have Known Them.* 1903 Lee Shepherd. Ills. 230 p. G $5.00

BARKER, George. *Eros in Dogma.* 1944 London. dj. VG $35.00

BARKER, Will. *Familiar Reptiles & Amphibians of America.* 1964 Harper Row. Ills 1st ed. 220 p. VG $10.00

BARKLEY. *History of Travis County & Austin 1839-1890.* 1963 Waco. Texian Pr. dj. EX $17.00

BARLETT, Norman. *Pearl Seekers.* 1954 NY. dj. G $12.00

BARLOW, George. *Poetical Works of George Barlow.* 1890 London. Glaisher. 10 vol set. xl. VG $135.00

BARLOW, Joel. *Columbiad: Poem.* 1807 Phil. 1/384. 4to. 11 plts. G $80.00

BARLOW, T.D. *Woodcuts of Albrecht Durer.* 1948 London. King Penguin. 1st ed. 110 p. $15.00

BARNARD, George. *Switzerland: Drawn From Nature & on Stone.* 1843 London. Ills. folio. ½-morocco. VG $1200.00

BARNARD, Harry. *Eagle Forgotten: Life of John Peter Altgeld.* Ills 1st ed. $30.00

BARNARD. *Metric System of Weights & Measures.* 1872 Revised ed. sgn. 194 p. $40.00

BARNES, Albert C. *Art in Painting.* 1925 Phil. Ills. 530 p. index. G $15.00

BARNES, Djuna. *Creatures in an Alphabet.* 1982 NY. 1st ed. dj. M $10.00

BARNES, George W. *How To Make Bamboo Fly Rods.* 1977 Winchester. Ills. 110 p. dj. EX $10.00

BARNES, Julian. *Flaubert's Parrot.* 1985 Knopf. 1st Am ed. dj. EX $25.00

BARNES, M.F. *Historic Vistas.* 1930 NY. Payson. Ltd ed. 1/500. 121 p. $10.00

BARNES, Mary S. *Long-Distance Calling.* 1945 NY. 114 p. EX $15.00

BARNES, R.M. *History of Regiments & Uniforms of British Army.* 1957 London. Seeley. Ills 4th ed. dj. EX $35.00

BARNETT, L.D. *Brahma Knowledge.* 1907 London. Murray. 113 p. VG $22.00

BARNEY, M. Wright. *Valley of Gode Almighty Jones.* 1965 Appleton. 1st ed. dj. VG $30.00

BARNHART, John. *Valley of Democracy.* 1953 Bloomington. 1st ed. 338 p. dj. EX $35.00

BARNHART, Percy S. *Marine Fishes of Southern CA.* 1936 CA U Pr. 1st ed. 209 p. scarce. VG $30.00

BARNUM, P.T. *Humbugs of the World.* 1866 NY. 424 p. G $27.50

BARNUM, P.T. *Humbugs of the World.* 1866 NY. 424 p. VG $50.00

BARNUM, P.T. *Life of P.T. Barnum Written by Himself.* no date. Newark, OH. Ills. 520 p. VG $25.00

BARNUM, P.T. *Struggles & Triumphs; or, 40 Years Recollections.* 1880 Buffalo, NY. Ills. 12mo. 327 p. G $25.00

BARNUM, P.T. *Struggles & Triumphs; or, 40 Years Recollections.* 1869 Hartford. Large ed. G $25.00

BARNUM, P.T. *Struggles & Triumphs; or, 40 Years Recollections.* 1872 Buffalo. G $20.00

BARNUM, P.T. *30 Years Hustling.* 1890 Rutland. Ills 1st ed. 488 p. VG $37.50

BARNWELL, F.S. *Aeroplane Design & Simple Explanation of Inherent Stability.* 1917 NY. VG $30.00

BARO, Gene. *Claues Oldenburg: Drawings & Prints.* 1969 NY/London. Chelsea House. folio. 274 p. $175.00

BARR, Alfred H. *Cubism & Abstract Art.* 1964 MOMA. Ills 1st ed. 4to. 249 p. $12.50

BARR, Alfred H. *Henri Matisse: His Art & His Public.* 1951 MOMA. Ills. 4to. 591 p. dj. $35.00

BARR, Alfred H. *Masters of Modern Art.* 1954 MOMA. Ills. 4to. 239 p. $40.00

BARR, Alfred H. *MOMA 1st Loan Exhibition: Cezanne & Gauguin.* 1929 MOMA. Ltd 1st ed. 1/3,000. 152 p. $30.00

BARR, Alfred H. *Painting & Sculpture in MOMA.* 1948 Simon Schuster. Ills Ltd ed. 4to. 327 p. $15.00

BARR, Alfred H. *Recent Painting USA: The Figure.* 1962 MOMA. Ills. 4to. 40 p. wraps. $10.00

BARR, Alfred H. *What Is Modern Art?* 1943 MOMA. Ills Revised ed. 4to. 50 p. $6.00

BARR, Alfred H. *75th Anniversary Exhibition of Pablo Picasso.* 1957 MOMA. Ills. 4to. 115 p. wraps. $10.00

BARR, Gladys H. *Master of Geneva.* 1961 Holt Rinehart Winston. 1st ed. $5.00

BARR, Louise Farrow. *Presses of Northern CA.* 1934 Berkeley. 1st ed. 8vo. VG $85.00

BARR, Margaret S. *Medardo Rosso.* 1963 NY. Ills. 4to. 92 p. cloth. dj. $20.00

BARR, Robert. *Triumphs of Eugene Valmont.* 1906 NY. 1st Am ed. VG $70.00

BARR. *TX Politics 1876-1906.* 1971 Austin. TX U Pr. dj. EX $10.00

BARRAULT, Jean-Louis. *Theatre of Jean-Louis Barrault.* 1959 London. Trans Chiari. 1st ed. dj. EX $20.00

BARRERE, A.; & LELAND, C.G. *Dictionary of Slang, Jargon, & Cant.* 1889 Ballantyne. Ltd ed. 2 vol set. rebound. EX $250.00

BARRET, Richard Carter. *Bennington Pottery & Porcelain.* 1958 Bonanza. Ills. 4to. 352 p. cloth. xl. $30.00

BARRET, Richard Carter. *Blown & Pressed American Glass.* 1966 Bennington. 1st ed. spiral bdg. VG $7.00

BARRETT, E. *Drama of Exile & Other Poems.* 1845 NY. 1st Am ed. 2 vol set. G $400.00

BARRETT, Francis. *Magus or Celestial Intelligencer.* 1801 London. 1st ed. rebound. $695.00

BARRETT, J.H. *Life of Abraham Lincoln.* 1860 Cincinnati. 1st ed. VG $35.00

BARRETT, Paul. *Concordance to Darwin's Origin of Species.* 1981 Cornell. 1st ed. EX $30.00

BARRETT, Peter. *Great True Hunts.* 1967 Prentice Hall. Ills. 4to. 278 p. dj. VG $14.50

BARRETT, Peter. *In Search of Trout.* 1973 Prentice Hall. Ills 1st ed. 223 p. dj. EX $12.50

BARRETT, Peter. *Treasury of African Hunting.* no date. Winchester. Ills. 4to. dj. EX $18.50

BARRETT, Peter. *Treasury of African Hunting.* 1979 NY. dj. EX $28.00

BARRETT, Timothy. *Japanese Papermaking: Tradition, Tools, & Techniques.* 1983 Weatherhill. Ills. 317 p. dj. $32.50

BARRETT & JACKSON. *Nazi Conspiracy & Aggression.* 1946 WA. 9 vol set. G $75.00

BARRIE, Douglas M. *Australian Blood Horse.* 1956 Sydney. 1st ed. 503 p. EX $95.00

BARRIE, J.M. *Auld Light Idylls.* c 1900. NY. Caldwell. VG $20.00

BARRIE, J.M. *Courage.* 1922 London. 1st ed. EX $28.00

BARRIE, J.M. *Entrancing Life.* 1930 London. 1st ed. dj. EX $16.00

BARRIE, J.M. *Letters of James M. Barrie.* 1947 NY. 1st ed. dj. G $25.00

BARRIE, J.M. *Little White Bird.* 1902 NY. EX $36.00

BARRIE, J.M. *Little White Bird.* 1915 NY. Scribner. Ills Rackham. VG $10.00

BARRIE, J.M. *Peter Pan & Wendy.* 1911 Scribner. Ills 1st Am ed. 267 p. VG $40.00

BARRIE, J.M. *Peter Pan in Kensington Gardens.* 1906 Hodder Stoughton. Ills 1st ed. $295.00

BARRIE, J.M. *Peter Pan in Kensington Gardens.* 1916 NY. Ills Rackham. VG $75.00

BARRIE, J.M. *Peter Pan.* 1987 Parsippany. Ills Hildebrandt. 179 p. M $17.00

BARRIE, J.M. *Quality Street.* no date. Hodder Stoughton. Ills. 4to. $75.00

BARRIE, J.M. *Tommy & Grizel.* 1900 NY. Scribner. Ills Partridge. 1st ed. dj. EX $17.00

BARRIE, J.M. *Tommy & Grizel.* 1900 NY. Scribner. Ills Partridge. 1st ed. VG $15.00

BARRINGTON, Jonah. *Historic Ancedotes & Secret Memoirs of a Legislative Union.* 1809 London. folio. ½-morroco. rare. EX $400.00

BARRINGTON, Lewis. *Historic Restorations of Daughters of American Revolution.* 1941 NY. Ills. 210 p. dj. VG $17.50

BARRINGTON, Mrs. R. *Life, Letters, & Work of Frederic Leighton.* 1906 NY. 8vo. 154 plts. cloth. VG $40.00

BARRON, Greg. *Groundrush.* 1982 Random House. 1st ed. dj. VG $10.00

BARROW, John. *Account of Travels into Interior of Southern Africa.* 1802 NY. 1st Am ed. 386 p. calf. $150.00

BARROW, John. *Voyages of Discovery & Research.* 1846 London. Murray. Ills 1st ed. presentation. $400.00

BARROWS, Marjorie. *Muggins Mouse.* 1932 Whitman. Ills Keith Ward. EX $25.00

BARROWS, Marjorie. *100 Best Poems for Boys & Girls.* 1930 Whitman. Ills. G $12.50

BARROWS, W. *OR: Struggle for Possession.* 1885 Houghton Mifflin. 363 p. G $10.00

BARRUS, Clara. *Our Friend John Burroughs.* 1914 Cambridge. Riverside Pr. G $30.00

BARRY, G. *Man the Artist.* 1964 London. Ills. 367 p. $32.50

BARRY, P. *Fruit Garden: Treatise.* 1857 NY. G $15.00

BARRY, Wendell. *Place on Earth.* 1967 NY. 1st ed. sgn. EX $35.00

BARRYMORE, Ethel. *Memories: Autobiography by Ethel Barrymore.* 1956 London. 1st ed. dj. EX $25.00

BARSALI, Isa B. *Medieval Goldsmith's Work.* 1969 London. Hamlyn. Ills. 157 p. dj. $12.50

BARSIS, Max. *They're All Yours, Uncle Sam.* 1943 NY. Ills 1st ed. VG $17.50

BARSNESS, Larry. *Gold Camp: Alder Gulch & VA City, MT.* 1962 NY. 1st ed. 312 p. dj. VG $22.50

BARTH, John. *Chimera.* 1972 Random House. 1st ed. dj. EX $25.00

BARTH, John. *Don't Count on It.* 1984 Northridge. Ltd 1st ed. 1/150. sgn. EX $35.00

BARTH, John. *End of the Road.* 1958 NY. 1st ed. dj. EX $25.00

BARTH, John. *Giles Goat Boy.* 1966 Garden City. 1st ed. presentation. dj. EX $30.00

BARTH, John. *Letters of John Barth.* 1979 NY. 1st ed. dj. M $15.00

BARTH, John. *Letters of John Barth.* 1979 Putnam. Ltd 1st ed. sgn. slipcase. EX $60.00

BARTH, John. *Lost in the Fun House.* 1968 Doubleday. 1st ed. dj. VG $15.00

BARTH, John. *Sabbatical.* 1982 NY. 1st ed. sgn. dj. EX $35.00

BARTH, John. *Todd Andrews to the Author.* 1979 Ltd ed. 1/300. sgn. dj. EX $30.00

BARTH, M.; & ROGER, Henry. *Manual of Auscultation & Percussion.* 1849 Phil. Lindsay Blakeston. 2nd ed. $45.00

BARTH, M.; & ROGER, Henry. *Manual of Auscultation & Percussion.* 1866 Phil. Lindsay Blakeston. 164 p. $18.00

BARTHE, Grenville. *Engineer's Miscellany: Chronicle of Early Engineering.* 1938 Phil. Patterson White. 4to. 136 p. $45.00

BARTHELME, Abbe. *Travels of Anacharis the Younger in Greece.* 1794 London. 2nd ed. 7 vol set. $135.00

BARTHELME, Donald. *Amateurs.* 1977 London. dj. EX $14.00

BARTHELME, Donald. *City Life.* 1970 NY. 1st ed. dj. EX $12.50

BARTHELME, Donald. *Come Back, Dr. Caligari.* 1964 Little Brown. 1st ed. dj. EX $95.00

BARTHELME, Donald. *Dead Father.* 1977 London. dj. EX $12.00

BARTHELME, Donald. *Dead Father.* 1975 Farrar. 1st ed. inscr. dj. EX $35.00

BARTHELME, Donald. *Emerald.* 1980 Los Angeles. Ltd ed. 1/330. sgn. M $75.00

BARTHELME, Donald. *Guilty Pleasures.* 1974 NY. 1st ed. dj. EX $15.00

BARTHELME, Donald. *Paradise.* 1986 Putnam. 1st ed. dj. EX $17.00

BARTHELME, Donald. *Presents.* 1980 Pressworks. Ills 1st ed. 1/350. sgn. EX $65.00

BARTHELME, Donald. *Sadness.* 1972 Farrar. 1st ed. dj. EX $25.00

BARTHELME, Donald. *Unspeakable Practices, Unnatural Acts.* 1968 Farrar. 1st ed. dj. EX $40.00

BARTHELME, Donald. *60 Stories.* 1981 Putnam. 1st ed. dj. EX $16.00

BARTHELME, Frederick. *Moon Deluxe.* 1983 Simon Schuster. 1st ed. dj. EX $16.00

BARTHELME, Frederick. *Tracer.* 1985 Simon. 1st ed. dj. EX $14.00

BARTHELME, Frederick. *2nd Marriage.* 1984 Simon Schuster. 1st ed. dj. EX $16.00

BARTHES, Roland. *Erte.* 1972 Parma. Franco Maria Ricci. 1st ed. $150.00

BARTHOLOW, Robert. *Practical Treatise on Materia Medica & Therapeutics.* 1884 Appleton. 5th ed. VG $20.00

BARTLETT, Arthur C. *Pilgrim & Pluck: Dogs of the Mayflower.* 1936 Wilde. G $15.00

BARTLETT, D. *Flight of the Snow Geese.* 1975 Stein Day. Ills 1st ed. 189 p. dj. VG $10.00

BARTLETT, D. & J. *Flight of the Snow Geese.* 1975 Stein Day. Ills 1st ed. 189 p. dj. EX $9.00

BARTLETT, D.W. *Life & Public Services of Abraham Lincoln.* 1860 NY. 357 p. $20.00

BARTLETT, D.W. *Life & Public Services of Abraham Lincoln.* 1860 Cincinnati. cloth. scarce. $90.00

BARTLETT, D.W. *Life of General Franklin Pierce.* 1852 Auburn. 1st ed. EX $45.00

BARTLETT, Ella H. *Victor Herbert Songs for Children.* 1943 Whittlesey House. Ills Fry. VG $12.00

BARTLETT, John Russell. *Personal Narrative of Explorations & Incidents in TX.* 1854 Broadway. Appleton. 1st ed. 2 vol set. $325.00

BARTLETT, Richard D. *Great Surveys of the West.* 1962 Norman. 1st ed. presentation. dj. EX $35.00

BARTLETT, W.H. *Finden's Views of Ports, Harbors, & Watering Places.* 1837 London. Ills. 4to. leather. VG $180.00

BARTLETT, W.H. *History of the US of North America.* 1856 NY. 1st book ed. 3 vol set. VG $145.00

BARTLETT, W.H. *Nile Boat.* 1850 London. Ills Arthur Hall. ¾-leather. $17.50

BARTON, George A. *Archaelogy & the Bible.* 1917 Sunday School Union. 2nd ed. G $15.00

BARTON, Lucy. *Historic Costume for the Stage.* 1935 Boston. Ills Sarvis. 1st ed. 60 p. VG $25.00

BARTON, Margaret. *Garrick.* 1949 NY. 1st print. 312 p. dj. EX $20.00

BARTON, Phyllis. *Cecil C. Bell.* 1976 KS City. McGrew. Ills. 4to. 159 p. dj. $35.00

BARTON, Ralph. *God's Country.* 1929 Knopf. VG $14.50

BARTON, William E. *Life of Abraham Lincoln.* 1925 Indianapolis. sgn. 2 vol set. $65.00

BARTON, William E. *Lincoln & His Books.* 1920 Chicago. 108 p. VG $7.50

BARYSHNIKOV & FRACCI. *Meadea: Making of a Dance.* 1976 Holt. 1st ed. oblong 4to. wraps. VG $15.00

BARZUN, Jacques. *Use & Abuse of Art.* 1974 Princeton. dj. EX $25.00

BASHLINE & SAULTS. *America's Great Outdoors.* 1976 VG $18.00

BASILE, Gia. *Stories From the Pentamerone.* 1911 London. Ills Warwick. 4to. G $95.00

BASKET, Sir James. *History of Island of St. Domingo.* 1824 NY. Mahlon Day. 1st Am ed. 266 p. G $125.00

BASKIN, Esther & L. *Creatures of Darkness.* 1962 Ills L Baskin. 1st ed. 2nd print. dj. VG $35.00

BASKIN, Esther & L. *Poppy & Other Deadly Plants.* 1967 1st ed. dj. VG $35.00

BASKIN, Leonard. *Ars Anatomica: Medical Fantasia.* 1972 Medicina Rara. Ltd ed. folio. sgn. slipcase. $125.00

BASKIN, Leonard. *Caprices & Grotesques.* 1965 Northampton. Gehenna Pr. 1/500. slipcase. $150.00

BASKIN, Leonard. *Demons, Imps, & Friends.* 1976 Northampton. Gehenna Pr. 1/450. EX $150.00

BASKIN, Leonard. *Figures of Dead Men.* 1968 Boston. 1st ed. 8vo. sgn. cloth. M $375.00

BASKIN, Leonard. *Hosie's Alphabet.* 1972 NY. dj. VG $20.00

BASLER, Adolphe. *Henri Rousseau.* 1927 NY. Weyhe. Ltd ed. 1/1,000. 4to. wraps. $85.00

BASS, Althea. *Cherokee Messenger.* 1968 OK U Pr. Ills. 348 p. dj. EX $5.00

BASSANI, Giorgio. *Garden of the Finzi-Continis.* 1965 NY. 1st ed. VG $15.00

BASSO, Hamilton. *Light Infantry Ball.* 1959 London. 1st ed. dj. EX $17.00

BATCHELLER, G. *Golden Hours with Mother Goose.* c 1911. Phil. Sunshine Printery. Ills. 4to. $15.00

BATE, Philip. *Flute.* 1969 NY. VG $12.00

BATEMAN, Ruth Conrad. *50 Great Buffet Parties.* 1974 NY. dj. EX $10.00

BATES, Arlo. *Wheel of Fire.* 1885 NY. 1st ed. VG $15.00

BATES, Charles Frances; & ROE. *Custer Engages the Hostiles.* no date. Fort Collins. dj. VG $50.00

BATES, D. *Lincoln in the Telegraph Office.* 1907 NY. 1st ed. VG $32.50

BATES, Ely. *Rural Philosophy.* 1807 Hopkins. 1st Am ed. fair. $25.00

BATES, H.E. *Hessian Prisoner.* 1930 London. Cheswick. 1/550. sgn. EX $55.00

BATES, H.E. *Love for Lydia.* 1952 Michael Joseph. 1st ed. dj. VG $22.50

BATES, H.E. *Spring Song & View of Fact: 2 Stories.* 1927 San Francisco. Lantern Pr. Ltd 1st ed. wraps. $125.00

BATES, H.E. *7 Tales & Alexander.* 1929 London. Scholartis. 1st ed. 1/1,000. $50.00

BATES, H.W. *Naturalist on the River Amazon.* 1915 London. Murray. 8vo. cloth. VG $20.00

BATES, H.W. *Naturalist on the River Amazon.* 1892 London. Murray. 395 p. fld map. VG $40.00

BATES, Joe. *Atlantic Salmon Flies & Fishing.* 1970 Stackpole. Ills 1st ed. 362 p. dj. EX $15.00

BATES, Joe. *How To Find Fish & Make Them Strike.* 1979 Outdoor Life. Ills. 216 p. dj. EX $10.00

BATES, Joe. *Spinning for American Game Fish.* 1948 Little Brown. Ills. 247 p. VG $7.50

BATES, Joe. *Spinning for American Game Fish.* 1952 Boston. 6th print. dj. VG $20.00

BATES, Joe. *Spinning for Salt-Water Game Fish.* 1957 Little Brown. Ills 1st ed. 274 p. dj. EX $10.00

BATES, Joe. *Streamer Fly Tying & Fishing.* 1966 Stackpole. Ills 1st ed. 368 p. dj. EX $17.50

BATES, Marston. *Where Winter Never Comes.* 1952 Scribner. Ills 1st ed. 310 p. dj. VG $10.00

BATES, Miss L. *Stories of the Flowers.* 1872 Am Tract Soc. VG $25.00

BATES, Mrs. D.B. *Incidents on Land & Water; or, 4 Years in the Pacific.* 1857 Boston. Ills 1st ed. cloth. $30.00

BATES, N. *East of the Andes & West of Nowhere.* 1947 Scribner. dj. VG $15.00

BATES, Ralph. *Olive Field.* 1936 NY. Dutton. 3rd print. sgn. EX $15.00

BATESON, F.W. *Cambridge Bibliography of English Literature.* 1941 Macmillan. 4 vol set. VG $85.00

BATHE, Basil W. *7 Centuries of Sea Travel From Crusaders to Cruises.* 1973 NY. Tudor. Ills. $40.00

BATSFORD, H. *Greater English Church of the Middle Ages.* 1943 London. Ills. 136 p. $15.00

BATSFORD, H. *Homes & Gardens of England.* 1932 London. Ills 1st ed. G $35.00

BATSON, W.T. *Wild Flowers in SC.* 1964 SC U Pr. Ills. 146 p. EX $10.00

BATTE. *History of Milam County, TX.* 1956 San Antonio. Naylor. dj. G $25.00

BATTELLE, L.G. *Story of OH Accountancy.* 1954 Dayton. Ills 1st ed. sgn. 281 p. dj. G $22.50

BATTLE, Kemp. *Memories of Old-Time Tar Heel.* 1945 Chapel Hill. dj. VG $15.00

BATTY, J.H. *How To Hunt & Trap Buffalo, Elk, Moose, Deer, & Antelope.* 1878 NY. Ills W Cary. 1st ed. 223 p. EX $95.00

BATTY, Lt. Col. *Hanoverian & Saxon Scenery.* 1829 Lodnon. Jennings. 4to. G $20.00

BAUDELAIRE, Charles. *Les Fleurs du Mal.* 1947 no place. Eds de la Maison Francaise. $100.00

BAUER, C.M. *Yellowstone Geysers.* 1947 Haynes. Ills Revised ed. VG $15.00

BAUER, Erwin A. *Bass Fisherman's Bible.* 1961 Doubleday. Ills 1st ed. 191 p. wraps. VG $12.50

BAUER, Erwin A. *Deer in Their World.* 1983 Outdoor Life. Ills. 4to. 242 p. dj. EX $25.00

BAUER, Erwin A. *Fisherman's Digest.* 1973 Follett. Ills 9th ed. 320 p. wraps. VG $12.50

BAUER, Erwin A. *Treasury of Big Game Animals.* 1972 Outdoor Life. Ills. 4to. 398 p. dj. EX $12.50

BAUER, Harold. *His Book.* 1948 NY. 1st ed. G $10.00

BAUER, Helen. *CA Gold Days.* 1959 NY. Ills 1st ed. dj. VG $15.00

BAUER, Johann. *Kafka & Prague: Biography.* 1973 NY. Ills 1st Am ed. 4to. dj. EX $25.00

BAUGH, Hansell. *Frances Newman's Letters.* 1929 NY. 1st Am ed. dj. VG $65.00

BAUM, L. Frank. *American Fairy Tales.* 1901 Chicago. 1st ed. G $550.00

BAUM, L. Frank. *Black Beauty & Little Lame Prince.* Reilly Lee. 12mo. 58 p. olive cloth. VG $30.00

BAUM, L. Frank. *Captain Salt in Oz.* 1936 Reilly Lee. Ills Neill. 1st ed. VG $145.00

BAUM, L. Frank. *Dorothy & the Wizard of Oz.* c 1908. Reilly Lee. green-gray cloth. $215.00

BAUM, L. Frank. *Dorothy & the Wizard of Oz.* c 1928. Reilly Lee. 16 plts. G $175.00

BAUM, L. Frank. *Dorothy & Toto & Cowardly Lion & Hungry Tiger.* 1939 Rand McNally. Little Wizard Series. 60 p. G $20.00

BAUM, L. Frank. *Emerald City of Oz.* 1910 Reilly Britton. Ills Neill. 1st ed. 1st issue. $600.00

BAUM, L. Frank. *Emerald City of Oz.* c 1940. Reilly Lee. Ills Neill. 295 p. $35.00

BAUM, L. Frank. *Emerald City of Oz.* 1939 Rand McNally. Jr ed. 60 p. VG $20.00

BAUM, L. Frank. *Enchanted Isle of Yew.* 1903 Donohue. 3rd ed. VG $125.00

BAUM, L. Frank. *Father Goose: His Book.* 1900 Chicago. Hill. Ills Denslow. VG $125.00

BAUM, L. Frank. *Giant Horse of Oz.* 1928 Reilly Lee. Ills Neill. orange cloth. dj. $55.00

BAUM, L. Frank. *Giant Horse of Oz.* 1928 Reilly Lee. Ills Thompson. red cloth. VG $100.00

BAUM, L. Frank. *Glinda of Oz.* 1920 Reilly Lee. 1st ed. G $110.00

BAUM, L. Frank. *Glinda of Oz.* 1920 Reilly Lee. 1st ed. VG $125.00

BAUM, L. Frank. *Grandpa in Oz.* 1924 Reilly Lee. Ills Neill. 1st issue. VG $175.00

BAUM, L. Frank. *Grandpa in Oz.* 1924 Reilly Lee. Ills Thompson. dj. EX $95.00

BAUM, L. Frank. *Handy Mandy in Oz.* 1937 Reilly Lee. Ills Neill. VG $165.00

BAUM, L. Frank. *Hidden Vally of Oz.* 1951 Reilly Lee. 1st ed. dj. EX $100.00

BAUM, L. Frank. *Hungry Tiger of Oz.* 1926 Reilly Lee. Ills Neill. 1st ed. VG $185.00

BAUM, L. Frank. *Jack Pumpkinhead & Sawhorse.* 1939 Rand McNally. Little Wizard Series. 60 p. VG $20.00

BAUM, L. Frank. *John Dough & the Cherub.* 1906 Reilly Britton. Ills Neill. 1st ed. 2nd state. $75.00

BAUM, L. Frank. *Land of Oz.* 1939 Reilly Lee. Ills Neill. Popular ed. VG $15.00

BAUM, L. Frank. *Life & Adventures of Santa Claus.* 1902 Bowen Merrill. Ills Clark. 1st ed. red cloth. $200.00

BAUM, L. Frank. *Little Dorothy & Toto of Oz.* 1939 Rand McNally. G $30.00

BAUM, L. Frank. *Lost King of Oz.* 1925 Reilly Lee. Ills Thompson. VG $75.00

BAUM, L. Frank. *Lost King of Oz.* 1925 Reilly Lee. Ills Neill. 1st issue. G $175.00

BAUM, L. Frank. *Lost Princess of Oz.* 1917 Reilly Britton. Ills Neill. 1st issue. G $295.00

BAUM, L. Frank. *Lost Princess of Oz.* 1939 Rand McNally. Jr ed. 60 p. VG $20.00

BAUM, L. Frank. *Lucky Bucky Oz.* 1942 Reilly Lee. Ills Neill. 1st ed. EX $100.00

BAUM, L. Frank. *Magic of Oz.* 1919 Reilly Lee. 1st ed. 1st issue. G $115.00

BAUM, L. Frank. *Magical Mimics in Oz.* Reilly Lee. Ills Kramer. 1st ed. VG $115.00

BAUM, L. Frank. *Magical Mimics in Oz.* 1946 Reilly Lee. Ills Snow. 1st ed. VG $90.00

BAUM, L. Frank. *Magical Mimics in Oz.* 1946 Reilly Lee. Ills Snow. 1st ed. EX $120.00

BAUM, L. Frank. *Magical Monarch of Mo.* c 1900-1903. Indianapolis. Ills Verbeck. VG $110.00

BAUM, L. Frank. *Marvelous Land of Oz.* 1904 Reilly Britton. Ills Neill. 1st ed. 3rd issue. $215.00

BAUM, L. Frank. *Master Key.* 1901 Indianapolis. Ills Cory. 1st ed. G $125.00

BAUM, L. Frank. *Navy Alphabet.* 1900 Chicago. 1st ed. 4to. VG $450.00

BAUM, L. Frank. *New Wizard of Oz.* 1903 Bobbs Merrill. 2nd ed. 2nd state. VG $140.00

BAUM, L. Frank. *New Wizard of Oz. MGM Movie Version.* 1939 Bobbs Merrill. movie photos. EX $32.00

BAUM, L. Frank. *New Wizard of Oz. MGM Movie Version.* 1939 Bobbs Merrill. Ills Denslow. green cloth. G $20.00

BAUM, L. Frank. *Ojo in Oz.* 1933 Reilly Lee. Ills Neill. 1st issue. VG $145.00

BAUM, L. Frank. *Oz.* 1907 Reilly Britton. 1st issue. 40 pls. VG $450.00

BAUM, L. Frank. *Ozma of Oz.* c 1935. Reilly Lee. Ills Neill. 270 p. $40.00

BAUM, L. Frank. *Ozoplaning with the Wizard of Oz.* 1939 Reilly Lee. Ills Neill. 1st ed. VG $145.00

BAUM, L. Frank. *Patchwork Girl of Oz.* 1913 Reilly Britton. 1st ed. 2nd state. VG $175.00

BAUM, L. Frank. *Patchwork Girl of Oz.* 1939 Rand McNally. Jr ed. 60 p. VG $20.00

BAUM, L. Frank. *Pirates in Oz.* 1931 Reilly Lee. Ills Thompson. 1st ed. VG $135.00

BAUM, L. Frank. *Purple Prince of Oz.* 1932 Reilly Lee. Ills Neill. 1st ed. VG $135.00

BAUM, L. Frank. *Purple Prince of Oz.* 1932 Reilly Lee. Ills Thompson. EX $55.00

BAUM, L. Frank. *Rinkitink in Oz.* 1916 Reilly Britton. 1st ed. 1st issue. G $125.00

BAUM, L. Frank. *Rinkitink in Oz.* 1916 Reilly Lee. Ills Neill. yellow cloth. $55.00

BAUM, L. Frank. *Road to Oz.* 1909 Reilly Britton. 1st ed. 1st issue. VG $125.00

BAUM, L. Frank. *Road to Oz. Little Golden Book.* 1951 Simon Schuster. Ills McNaught. 1st ed. G $7.50

BAUM, L. Frank. *Royal Book of Oz.* 1921 Reilly Lee. Ills Neill. 1st issue. G $185.00

BAUM, L. Frank. *Scalawagons of Oz.* Reilly Lee. Ills Neill. 1st ed. VG $145.00

BAUM, L. Frank. *Scarecrow & Tin Woodman.* 1939 Rand McNally. Little Wizard Series. 60 p. VG $20.00

BAUM, L. Frank. *Scarecrow of Oz.* 1915 Reilly Britton. 1st ed. EX $250.00

BAUM, L. Frank. *Sea Fairies.* 1911 Reilly Britton. Ills Neill. 1st ed. 1st issue. $400.00

BAUM, L. Frank. *Sea Fairies.* c 1927. Reilly Lee. Ills 3rd ed. $100.00

BAUM, L. Frank. *Shaggy Man of Oz.* 1949 Reilly Lee. Ills Kramer. dj. EX $95.00

BAUM, L. Frank. *Silver Princess of Oz.* 1938 Reilly Lee. Ills Neill. VG $90.00

BAUM, L. Frank. *Sky Island.* 1912 Reilly Britton. Ills Neill. early issue. G $165.00

BAUM, L. Frank. *Tin Woodman of Oz.* 1918 Reilly Lee. Ills Neill. 1st issue. VG $225.00

BAUM, L. Frank. *Tin Woodman of Oz.* c 1940. Reilly Lee. Popular ed. EX $40.00

BAUM, L. Frank. *Tin Woodman of Oz.* c 1940. Reilly Lee. Ills Neill. VG $15.00

BAUM, L. Frank. *To Please a Child.* 1961 Chicago. M $30.00

BAUM, L. Frank. *Wishing Horse of Oz.* 1935 Reilly Lee. Ills Thompson. dj. VG $38.00

BAUM, L. Frank. *Wishing Horse of Oz.* 1935 Reilly Lee. Ills Neill. 1st issue. VG $145.00

BAUM, L. Frank. *Wizard of Oz.* 1958 Italy. Ills Maraja. 120 p. VG $50.00

BAUM, L. Frank. *Wizard of Oz.* 1903 Indianapolis. Ills Denslow. Ltd ed. 208 p. G $25.00

BAUM, L. Frank. *Wonder City of Oz.* 1940 Reilly Lee. Ills Neill. blue cloth. EX $60.00

BAUM, L. Frank. *Wonderful Wizard of Oz.* 1986 CA U Pr. Ills 1st ed. dj. EX $40.00

BAUM, L. Frank. *Wonderful Wizard of Oz.* 1900 Chicago. Hill Green Hanff. inscr. EX $900.00

BAUM, L. Frank. *Yellow Hen & Other Stories.* 1916 Reilly Britton. Snuggle Tales Series. $70.00

BAUM, L. Frank. *Yellow Knight of Oz.* 1930 Reilly Lee. 1st ed. dj. EX $160.00

BAUM, Vivki. *Theme for Ballet.* 1958 Doubleday. 1st ed. dj. VG $8.50

BAUR, John I.H. *Nature in Abstraction.* 1958 NY. Whitney. Ills. 8vo. 72 p. wraps. $25.00

BAUR-HEINHOLD, Margarete. *Baroque Theatre: Cultural History of 17th & 18th C.* 1967 NY. Ills 1st ed. 4to. 292 p. EX $35.00

BAUSCH, Edward. *Manipulation of the Microscope.* 1901 Rochester. Bausch Lomb. 4th ed. 202 p. $10.00

BAX, Ernest Belfort. *Reminiscences & Reflections of a Mid & Late Victorian.* 1920 NY. VG $30.00

BAXTER, John E. *Locker Room Ballads.* 1923 NY. Ills JM Flagg. 1st ed. 76p. $75.00

BAXTER, K.S. *Godchild of Washington: Picture of the Past.* 1897 NY. Ills 1st ed. 651 p. $95.00

BAXTER, K.S. *In Beautiful Japan.* 1904 NY. Ills. G $20.00

BAYER, H.G. *Belgians: 1st Settlers in NY & the Middle States.* 1925 no place. 1st ed. wraps. VG $15.00

BAYLEY, Barrington. *Seed of Evil.* 1979 London. 1st ed. dj. EX $16.00

BAYNE, S.G. *On an Irish Jaunting Car Through Donegal & Connemara.* 1902 NY. Ills. VG $15.00

BAZALGETTE, Leon. *Henry Thoreau: Bachelor of Nature.* 1924 NY. Trans Van Wyck Brooks. 357 p. $25.00

BAZIN, Germain. *Nat Neujean.* 1986 Bruxelles. Vokaer. Ills. 4to. dj. $45.00

BEACH, Rex. *Big Brother & Other Stories.* 1923 Harper. 1st ed. $8.00

BEACH, Rex. *Oh, Shoot!* 1921 Harper. Ills 1st ed. 280 p. VG $12.00

BEACH, Sylvia. *Shakespeare & Co.* 1959 NY. Harcourt. 1st ed. dj. EX $22.00

BEADLE, George & Murial. *Language of Life: Introduction to the Science of Genetics.* 1966 Doubleday. Ills. 242 p. dj. VG $10.00

BEADLE, J.H. *Life in UT; or, Mysteries & Crimes of Mormonism.* 1904 Ills Pub. 648 p. $35.00

BEADLE, J.H. *Life in UT; or, Mysteries & Crimes of Mormonism.* 1870 Phil. Ills 1st ed. VG $60.00

BEADLE, J.H. *Western Wilds & the Men Who Redeem Them.* 1878 Bancroft. rebound. scarce. VG $100.00

BEADLE, Maurice. *Fortnightly of Chicago: City & Its Women 1873-1973.* 1973 dj. VG $45.00

BEAGLE, P.S. *Fine & Private Place.* 1960 Viking. 1st ed. dj. VG. $45.00

BEAGLE, P.S. *I See My Outfit.* 1965 NY. Viking. 1st ed. with letter. $75.00

BEAGLE, P.S. *Lila the Werewolf.* 1974 Capra. 1st ed. wraps. EX $30.00

BEAL, Graham W.J. *5 Themes of Jim Dine.* 1983 Minneapolis. Ills. 4to. 156 p. cloth. dj. $35.00

BEAL, R. *Songs of the Sea.* 1891 NY. $18.00

BEAL. *Proletarian Journey.* 1937 NY. 1st ed. 352 p. xl. VG $10.00

BEALE, Lionel S. *Our Morality & the Moral Question.* 1887 London/Phil. EX $15.00

BEALER, A. *Tools That Built America.* 1976 Bonanza. Ills. EX $16.00

BEALS, Carleton. *Crime of Cuba.* 1933 Lippincott. Ills 1st ed. 8vo. VG $65.00

BEAMISH, Richard. *Psychometry of the Hand.* 1865 London. Ills. 104 p. VG $75.00

BEAN, Florence O. *Bookbinding for Beginners.* 1919 Worcester. Ills. G $15.00

BEAN, L.L. *Hunting, Fishing, & Camping.* 1942 private print. Ills. 104 p. maps. VG $7.50

BEAN, L.L. *Hunting, Fishing, & Camping.* 1950 Freeport, ME. Ills. photos. VG $12.00

BEANESLY, M. *Lolland Bible & Other Medieval Biblical Versions.* 1920 Cambridge. 1st English ed. 483 p. VG $20.00

BEARD, Augustus F. *Story of John Fredreic Oberlin.* 1909 Boston. Pilgrim Pr. VG $20.00

BEARD, C.A. *President Roosevelt & the Coming of the War 1941.* 1948 Yale U Pr. 3rd ed. VG $10.00

BEARD, Dan. *American Boys' Book of Birds & Brownies.* 1923 Lippincott. VG $15.00

BEARD, Patten. *Billy Cory: Adventurer.* 1936 Whitman. Ills E Mussey. 1st ed. cloth. $20.00

BEARDSLEY, A. *Le Morte d'Arthur.* Dover. reprint of 1894. pb. M $8.00

BEARDSLEY, Aubrey. *Aubrey Beardsley Drawings.* 1967 NY. United Book Guild. pb. wraps. $15.00

BEARDSLEY, Aubrey. *Selected Drawings.* 1967 Grove Pr. 1st ed. 4to. dj. EX $30.00

BEARDSLEY, Aubrey. *Story of Venus & Tannhausser.* 1907 London. 1/250. VG $100.00

BEARDSLEY, Aubrey. *Under the Hill.* 1959 NY. Grove. 1st print. dj. EX $25.00

BEARDSLEY & BEEHBOHM. *Savoy, #2.* 1896 London. sgn. VG $50.00

BEARSE, Ray. *Sporting Arms of the World.* 1976 Outdoor Life. Ills. 461 p. dj. EX $17.50

BEATON, Cecil. *Ballet.* 1951 NY. Ills Ltd 1st ed. sgn. EX $235.00

BEATON, Cecil. *Fair Lady.* 1964 Holt Rinehart. 128 p. dj. VG $15.00

BEATON, Cecil. *Glass of Fashion.* 1954 Doubleday. 1st ed. dj. VG $50.00

BEATON, Cecil. *Japanese.* 1959 NY. 1st ed. dj. EX $30.00

BEATON, Cecil. *Memoirs of the '40s.* 1972 310 p. dj. EX $15.00

BEATON, Cecil. *Photobiography.* 1951 NY. Ills 1st ed. 8vo. dj. EX $65.00

BEATON, Cecil. *Time Exposure.* 1946 London. Batsford. dj. EX $35.00

BEATON, Cecil. *Wandering Years 1922-1939.* 1961 Little Brown. Ills. VG $15.00

BEATON, Cecil; & TYNAN, K. *Persona Grata.* 1954 NY. Grove. 1st Am ed. dj. VG $50.00

BEATON, Cecil; & TYNAN, K. *Persona Grata.* 1954 NY. Grove. 1st Am ed. dj. EX $65.00

BEATON, K. *Enterprise in Oil: Shell Oil in US.* 1957 NY. 1st ed. 8vo. cloth. dj. VG $13.00

BEATTIE, Ann. *Burning House.* 1982 NY. 1st ed. dj. EX $10.00

BEATTIE, Ann. *Jacklighting.* 1981 Metacom. 1st ed. 1/250. sgn. wraps. EX $35.00

BEATTIE, Ann. *Love Always.* 1985 Random House. 1st ed. dj. EX $17.00

BEATTIE, Ann. *Secrets & Surprises.* 1978 NY. 1st ed. inscr. dj. EX $10.00

BEATTIE, Ann. *Where You'll Find Me.* 1986 Linden Pr. 1st ed. dj. EX $15.00

BEATTIE, May H. *Carpets of Central Persia.* 1976 Birmingham. Ills. 104 p. $18.50

BEATTY, K.J. *Human Leopards: Account of Trials of Human Leopards.* 1915 London. Ills. Intro WB Griffith. G $28.00

BEATTY, W. *Death of Lord Nelson.* 1807 London. Ills. VG $65.00

BEAUCLERK, Helen. *Green Lacquer Pavilion.* 1926 NY. Ills 1st ed. dj. EX $25.00

BEAUFORT. *Badminton Library.* 1894 London. Ills. VG $20.00

BEAUJON, Paul. *Graphic Arts.* 1936 Garden City. 4to. 318 p. VG $25.00

BEAUMONT, John. *Historical, Physiological & Theological Treatise on Spirits.* 1705 London. 400 p. VG $225.00

BEAWES, Wyndham. *Beawes's Lex Mercatoria.* 1792 London. Mortimer. 5th ed. folio. VG $155.00

BEAZLEY, John D. *Development of Attic Black Figure.* 1951 Berkeley/London. 176 p. dj. $50.00

BEAZLEY, John D. *Etruscan Vase Painting.* 1976 Hacker. Ills. VG $35.00

BEBEE, William. *Pheasant Jungles.* 1904 NY. Ills. VG $35.00

BECHDOLT, F.D. *Tales of the Old Timers.* 1924 Century. $15.00

BECK, Fred. *89 Years in a Sand Trap.* 1965 Hill Wang. Ills Coker. 1st ed. dj. VG $6.50

BECK, Henry C. *397th Bomb Group: Pictorial History.* 1966 Cleveland. Ills 1st ed. cloth. scarce. EX $35.00

BECK, L. Adams. *Opener of the Gate: Stories of the Occult.* 1930 Cosmopolitan. 1st ed. VG $35.00

BECK, L. Adams. *Story of Oriental Philosophy.* 1928 Farrar Rinehart. VG $12.50

BECK, L. Adams. *Story of Oriental Philosophy.* 1943 New Home Lib. dj. VG $6.00

BECKER, A.C. *Lure Fishing.* 1970 Barnes. Ills 1st ed. 189 p. dj. EX $8.50

BECKER, A.C. *Waterfowl in the Marshes.* 1969 Barnes. Ills. 155 p. dj. EX $12.50

BECKER, Bob. *Memo: Go Fishing.* 1931 Bobbs Merrill. Ills 1st ed. 349 p. dj. VG $15.00

BECKER, Charlotte. *Arabian Nights Fairy Tales.* 1928 Sears. Ills. 4to. 242 p. $40.00

BECKER, Peter. *Dingane, King of the Zulu 1828-1840.* 1965 Crowell. Ills 1st Am ed. 283 p. dj. VG $17.00

BECKETT, S.B. *Guide Book of Atlantic & St. Lawrence Railroads.* 1853 Portland. 1st ed. fld map. 180 p. EX $45.00

BECKETT, Samuel. *Attendant Godot.* 1952 Paris. wraps. G $375.00

BECKETT, Samuel. *Echo's Bones & Other Precipitates.* 1935 Paris. Europa. 1st ed. 1/250. 4to. wraps. EX $275.00

BECKETT, Samuel. *Ends & Odds.* 1976 NY. 1st ed. wraps. M $11.00

BECKETT, Samuel. *No's Knife: Collecter Shorter Prose 1945-1966.* 1967 Calder Boyars. Ltd 1st ed. sgn. slipcase. M $250.00

BECKETT, Samuel. *Proust: 3 Dialogues.* 1965 London. Calder. 1/100. 8vo. sgn. slipcase. M $250.00

BECKETT, Samuel. *Waiting for Godot.* 1954 Grove. dj. G $250.00

BECKFORD, Peter. *Thoughts on Hunting.* 1926 Knopf. Ills. 283 p. G $7.50

BECKFORD, William. *Descriptive Account of the Island of Jamaica.* 1790 London. Egerton. 1st ed. 405 p. $350.00

BECKFORD, William. *Vathek.* 1929 Bloomsbury. Ills MV Dorn. Ltd ed. 1/1,550. $50.00

BECKWITH, George C. *Peace Manual.* 1847 Boston. Am Peace Soc. G $20.00

BECKWITH, Martha. *Hawaiian Romance of Laieikawai.* 1918 Washington. Ills. 4to. 384 p. $25.00

BEDDALL, Barbara. *Wallace & Bates in the Tropics.* 1969 Macmillan. Ills. 241 p. dj. EX $16.00

BEDDARD, F.E. *Earthworms & Their Allies.* 1912 Cambridge U Pr. Ills. 150 p. VG $10.00

BEDDARD, F.E. *Textbook of Zoogeography.* 1895 Cambridge U Pr. 246 p. maps. VG $16.00

BEDDINGTON, Jack. *Young Artists of Promise.* 1957 London. 1st ed. dj. VG $25.00

BEDFORD, John. *Old English Lustreware.* 1968 NY. Walker. Ills. 66 p. dj. $8.50

BEDFORD, Sybille. *Trial of Dr. Adams.* 1959 Simon Schuster. 1st ed. dj. $30.00

BEDICHEK, Roy. *Karankaway Country.* 1950 Doubleday. Ills 1st ed. dj. xl. G $12.50

BEDICHEK, Roy. *Karankaway Country.* 1950 Doubleday. Ills 1st ed. dj. VG $20.00

BEEBE, Lucius. *Highliners.* 1960 NY. reprint. dj. VG $20.00

BEEBE, Lucius. *Mansions on Rails.* 1959 Berkeley. Ills Gold Coast ed. 1/1,950. $100.00

BEEBE, Lucius. *Saga of Wells Fargo.* Bonanza. reprint. 320 p. dj. VG $18.00

BEEBE, Lucius. *Saga of Wells Fargo.* 1949 NY. 1st ed. EX $35.00

BEEBE, Mary Blair & C.W. *Our Search for a Wilderness.* 1910 NY. Holt. 1st ed. photos. 408 p. VG $75.00

BEEBE, William. *Beneath Tropic Seas.* 1937 Halcyon House. Ills. 234 p. G $6.00

BEEBE, William. *Galapagos: World's End.* 1927 Putnam. Ills. 443 p. VG $20.00

BEEBE, William. *Zaca Venture.* 1938 NY. 1st ed. dj. G $25.00

BEEBE, William; & TEE-VAN, J. *Field Book of Shore Fishes of Bermuda.* 1933 London/NY. Ills. maps. 338 p. cloth. EX $55.00

BEEBE & CLEGG. *American West.* 1955 NY. Dutton. 1st ed. dj. G $25.00

BEECHER, G.A. *Bishop of the Great Plains.* 1950 Ills. $7.50

BEECHER, Henry Ward. *Norwood; or, Village Life in New England.* 1868 NY. Scribner. $35.00

BEEDOME, Thomas. *Select Poems: Divine & Humane.* 1928 Bloomsbury. Nonesuch. Ltd ed. 1/1,250. EX $50.00

BEELER, Joe. *Cowboys & Indians: Characters in Oil & Bronze.* 1967 OK U Pr. 1st ed. dj. EX $20.00

BEER, Thomas. *Hanna.* 1929 NY. 325 p. $7.50

BEER, Thomas. *Road to Heaven.* 1928 NY. Ltd 1st ed. sgn. blue cloth. $48.00

BEERBOHM, Max. *Around Theatres.* 1930 NY. 1st ed. 8 vol set. G $35.00

BEERBOHM, Max. *Christmas Garland.* 1908 NY. 1st ed. VG $20.00

BEERBOHM, Max. *Christmas Garland.* 1912 London. 1st ed. inscr. VG $95.00

BEERBOHM, Max. *Dreadful Dragon of Hay Hill.* 1928 London. 1st ed. dj. VG $22.50

BEERBOHM, Max. *Heroes & Heroines of Bitter Sweet.* 1931 London. Ltd ed. 1/900. 8vo. inscr. VG $200.00

BEERBOHM, Max. *Letters to Reggie Turner.* 1964 London. 1st ed. dj. EX $35.00

BEERBOHM, Max. *Mainly on the Air.* 1948 NY. 1st ed. dj. EX $17.00

BEERBOHM, Max. *Survey.* 1921 London. Heinemann. 4to. red cloth. $50.00

BEERBOHM, Max. *7 Men.* 1919 London. Heinemann. 1st ed. $35.00

BEETON, Mrs. S. *Book of Household Management. Part 9.* 1869 London. Ills. wraps. VG $15.00

BEETON, Mrs. S. *Mrs. Beeton's English Women Shilling Cookery Book.* c 1880. London. fair. $25.00

BEGAY, K. *Navajos & World War II.* 1977 Tsaile. Ltd 1st ed. 1/1,000. 153 p. VG $12.00

BEHAN, Brendan. *Brendan Behan's Island: Irish Sketchbook.* 1962 Geis. Ills Hogarth. 2nd print. dj. $7.00

BEHAN, Brendan. *Brendan Behan's NY.* 1964 NY. Ills Hogarth. 1st ed. dj. $25.00

BEHAN, Brendan. *Confessions of an Irish Rebel.* 1965 NY. 1st ed. dj. VG $20.00

BEHAN, Brendan. *Richard's Cork Leg.* 1974 Grove Pr. 1st Am ed. dj. EX $15.00

BEHAN, Brendan. *Scarperer.* 1964 Doubleday. 1st Am ed. dj. EX $25.00

BEHAN, Richard J. *Pain: Its Origin, Conduction, Perception, & Significance.* 1920 NY. Appleton. VG $40.00

BEHAN. *Hold Your Hour & Have Another.* 1963 Little Brown. 1st ed. dj. EX $15.00

BEHLER, J.L.; & KING, F.W. *Field Guide to North American Reptiles & Amphibians.* 1979 Knopf. Ills. 719 p. maps. EX $12.00

BEHN, Mrs. Aphra. *Plays, Histories, & Novels of the Ingenious Mrs. Behn.* 1871 London. Pearson. 8vo. 6 vol set. EX $250.00

BEHRMAN, S.N. *Lord Pengo.* 1963 NY. 1st ed. dj. M $14.00

BEHRMAN, S.N. *Suspended Drawing Room.* 1965 Stein Day. 1st ed. dj. VG $8.00

BEIGBEDER, Oliver. *Ivory.* 1965 NY. Putnam. Ills. 128 p. dj. $25.00

BEL GEDDES, Norman. *Magic Motorways.* 1940 NY. 1st print. dj. $40.00

BELASCO & BYRNE. *Fairy Tales Told by 7 Travellers at Red Lion Inn.* 1906 NY. Ills Bleekman. VG $25.00

BELBENOIT, Rene. *Dry Guillotine: 15 Years Among the Living Dead.* 1938 NY. 1st ed. dj. VG $20.00

BELDEN, Jack. *China Shakes the World.* 1944 NY. Harper. 1st ed. inscr. G $20.00

BELDEN, Jack. *China Shakes the World.* 1949 NY. dj. VG $10.00

BELDING. *Belding Brothers' Self-Instructor in Silk Knitting.* 1884 no place. 2nd ed. 12mo. 84 p. $20.00

BELDON, Jack. *Retreat with Stilwell.* 1943 NY. 8vo. 368 p. dj. VG $50.00

BELFIELD, W.T. *Disease of Urinary & Male Sexual Organs.* 1884 Wood. $12.50

BELKNAP, G.N. *OR Imprints 1845-1870.* 1968 Eugene. Ills 1st ed. 8vo. 305 p. dj. $35.00

BELKNAP, Henry. *Artists & Craftsmen of Essex City, MA.* 1927 Salem. 125 p. VG $50.00

BELL, Andrew. *History of Canada From Time of Its Discovery to Union Year.* 1866 Montreal. 2 vol set. VG $100.00

BELL, Archie. *Spell of China.* 1920 Boston. Page. Ills. 8vo. 404 p. VG $30.00

BELL, Bob. *Hunting the Long-Tailed Bird.* 1975 Freshet Pr. Ills. 212 p. dj. EX $14.00

BELL, Charles G. *Half-Gods.* 1968 Houghton. 1st ed. dj. EX $20.00

BELL, Clair. *Peasant Life in Old German Epics.* 1931 Columbia U Pr. dj. VG $16.00

BELL, Harold. *Ma Cinderella.* 1932 NY. 1st ed. VG $90.00

BELL, Isaac. *Foxiana.* 1929 London. 1st ed. 16 plts. EX $40.00

BELL, James Munro. *Furniture Designs of Chippendale, Hepplewhite, & Sheraton.* 1910 London. Gibbings. Ills. $125.00

BELL, Lillian. *Love Affairs of an Old Maid.* c 1893. NY. inscr. VG $50.00

BELL, Louise Price. *Kitchen Fun.* 1932 Cleveland. Ills JW Smith. 1st ed. scarce. $85.00

BELL, Madison Smartt. *WA Square Ensemble.* 1983 NY. Viking. Advance proof. scarce. $150.00

BELL, Madison Smartt. *WA Square Ensemble.* 1983 NY. Viking. 1st ed. dj. EX $45.00

BELL, Madison Smartt. *Waiting for the End of the World.* 1985 Ticknor Fields. 1st ed. dj. EX $17.00

BELL, Madison Smartt. *Waiting for the End of the World.* 1985 NY. Ticknor Fields. Advance proof. $50.00

BELL, Madison Smartt. *Waiting for the End of the World.* 1985 NY. Ticknor Fields. Review copy. $25.00

BELL, Millicent. *Marquand.* 1979 Little Brown. 1st ed. dj. VG $10.00

BELL, Quentin. *Victorian Artists.* 1967 Harvard U Pr. Ills. 8vo. dj. EX $22.50

BELL, Thomas. *Anatomy, Physiology, & Diseases of the Teeth.* 1837 Phil. 3rd Am ed. 11 plts. G $80.00

BELL, Thomas. *From This Day Forward.* 1946 Grosset Dunlap. 1st ed. dj. $15.00

BELL, W.D.M. *Karamojo Safari.* 1949 Harcourt Brace. 1st ed. 298 p. VG $30.00

BELL, W.D.M. *Wanderings of an Elephant Hunter.* 1976 K&S Arms. Ills. 187 p. dj. EX $16.50

BELL, W.S. *Anti-Prohibition.* 1886 Chicago. Stern. Enlarged 2nd ed. 43 p. wraps. $12.50

BELL, Walter. *Great Plague in London in 1665.* 1924 London. plts. VG $28.00

BELL, Whitfield. *John Morgan: Continental Doctor.* 1965 PA U Pr. 1st ed. dj. EX $12.50

BELL TELEPHONE LABORATORIES. *Radar Systems & Components.* 1949 NY. Van Nostrand. 1st ed. 1,042 p. $18.00

BELL. *Reminiscences of a Ranger.* 1881 Los Angeles. 1st ed. $125.00

BELL. *Straight Cut.* 1986 Ticknor. 1st ed. dj. EX $16.00

BELLAIRS, John. *Mummy, Will, & Crypt.* 1983 NY. Dutton. 1st ed. dj. EX $12.00

BELLAMY, Edward. *Duke of Stockbridge.* 1900 NY. 1st ed. EX $25.00

BELLAMY, Edward. *Looking Backward.* 1945 World. Ltd 1st ed. 1/950. slipcase. $40.00

BELLAMY, Edward. *Looking Backward.* 1941 Hollywood. Ills/sgn Cavanna. 1/1,500. EX $40.00

BELLARD, Alfred. *Gone for a Soldier.* no date. Ills 1st ed. dj. VG $35.00

BELLEW, Frank. *Art of Amusing.* 1867 Carleton. 8vo. green cloth. VG $50.00

BELLI, Melvin. *Blood Money.* 1956 NY. 1st ed. dj. EX $25.00

BELLIVEAU, Jim & Mary. *Riches Under Your Roof.* 1983 Holt. Advance copy. wraps. EX $7.00

BELLOC, Hilaire. *Bad Child's Book of Beasts.* 1930 NY. Knopf. Ills 1st Am ed. $15.00

BELLOC, Hilaire. *Cranmer, Archbishop of Canterbury.* 1939 4th print. 333 p. dj. VG $10.00

BELLOC, Hilaire. *Cruise of the Nona.* 1925 1st print. cloth. dj. $30.00

BELLOC, Hilaire. *General Sketch of the European War.* 1915 London. 377 p. maps. G $22.50

BELLOC, Hilaire. *Highway & Its Vehicles.* 1926 London. Studio. Ills 1st ed. 1/1,250. 4to. VG $100.00

BELLOC, Hilaire. *Shadowed.* 1929 NY. Ills GK Chesteron. 1st ed. $14.00

BELLOC, Hillaire. *Book of Bayeux Tapestry.* 1941 NY. Putnam. Ills 1st ed. 76 p. EX $85.00

BELLOC, Hillaire. *Wolsey.* 1920 Phil. 3rd print. VG $25.00

BELLOW, Saul. *Adventures of Augie March.* 1953 NY. Viking. 1st ed. 1st issue. dj. EX $90.00

BELLOW, Saul. *Adventures of Augie March.* 1965 Modern Library. 1st ed. dj. EX $10.00

BELLOW, Saul. *Adventures of Augie Marsh.* 1953 NY. Viking. 1st ed. 4th print. dj. VG $15.00

BELLOW, Saul. *Dean's December.* 1982 Ltd 1st ed. 1/500. sgn. VG $65.00

BELLOW, Saul. *Dean's December.* 1982 Harper. 1st trade ed. dj. EX $15.00

BELLOW, Saul. *Henderson the Rain King.* 1959 Weidenfield. 1st English ed. dj. EX $65.00

BELLOW, Saul. *Henderson the Rain King.* 1959 NY. Viking. 1st ed. 1st issue. dj. VG $85.00

BELLOW, Saul. *Herzog.* 1965 London. 1st ed. dj. VG $27.00

BELLOW, Saul. *Herzog.* 1964 Viking. 1st ed. dj. EX $30.00

BELLOW, Saul. *Him with His Foot in His Mouth.* 1984 Harper. 1st ed. dj. EX $16.00

BELLOW, Saul. *Humboldt's Gift.* 1975 Viking. 1st ed. dj. EX $25.00

BELLOW, Saul. *Mosby's Memoirs.* 1968 Viking. 1st ed. dj. EX $30.00

BELLOW, Saul. *Mr. Sammler's Planet.* 1970 1st ed. dj. EX $17.00

BELLOW, Saul. *Nobel Lecture.* 1979 NY. Targ. 1st ed. 1/350. sgn. $65.00

BELLOW, Saul. *Seize the Day.* 1956 Viking. 1st ed. 8vo. dj. VG $65.00

BELLOW, Saul. *To Jerusalem & Back.* 1976 Viking. 1st ed. dj. EX $20.00

BELLOW, Saul. *Victim.* 1947 NY. 1st ed. $125.00

BELO, Jane. *Essays on Traditional Balinese Culture.* 1970 Columbia U Pr. 1st ed. dj. EX $35.00

BELOW, Ida C. *Eugene Field in His Home.* 1898 NY. Ills 1st ed. $25.00

BEMELMANS, Ludwig. *Best of Times.* 1948 NY. 1st ed. 4to. dj. VG $30.00

BEMELMANS, Ludwig. *Blue Danube.* 1945 NY. Viking. Ills 1st ed. VG $45.00

BEMELMANS, Ludwig. *Eye of God.* 1949 NY. 1st ed. $30.00

BEMELMANS, Ludwig. *Father, Dear Father.* 1953 NY. Ltd ed. 1/150. sgn. EX $45.00

BEMELMANS, Ludwig. *High World.* 1954 NY. Ills. juvenile. dj. VG $30.00

BEMELMANS, Ludwig. *Hotel Splendide.* 1941 Viking. Ltd ed. 1/245. sgn. slipcase. $115.00

BEMELMANS, Ludwig. *La Bonne Table.* 1964 Simon Schuster. 1st ed. dj. EX $15.00

BEMELMANS, Ludwig. *Madeline & the Gypsies.* 1972 Viking. Ills 7th print. 4to. 56 p. dj. $15.00

BEMELMANS, Ludwig. *My Life in Art.* 1958 NY. Harper. Ills. 69 p. dj. VG $22.50

BEMELMANS, Ludwig. *Now I Lay Me Down To Sleep.* 1944 Viking. 1st ed. dj. VG $15.00

BEMELMANS, Ludwig. *Sunshine.* 1950 NY. dj. VG $15.00

BEMELMANS, Ludwig. *Woman of My Life.* 1957 NY. 1st ed. dj. EX $12.00

BEMENT, C. *American Poulterer's Companion.* 1871 NY. VG $18.00

BENCH, Johnny. *Catch You Later.* 1979 Harper. 1st ed. sgn. dj. VG $17.50

BENCHLEY, N. *Robert Benchley.* 1955 1st ed. dj. VG $20.00

BENCHLEY, Peter. *Deep.* 1976 Garden City. 1st ed. dj. M $15.00

BENCHLEY, Peter. *Girl of the Sea of Cortez.* 1982 Garden City. 1st ed. dj. EX $12.50

BENCHLEY, Peter. *Island.* 1979 Garden City. 1st ed. dj. M $15.00

BENCHLEY, Peter. *Jaws.* 1974 Garden City. 1st ed. dj. EX $15.00

BENCHLEY, Robert. *Benchley Beside Himself.* 1940 reprint. dj. VG $20.00

BENCHLEY, Robert. *Benchley or Else!* 1948 London. Ills Gluyas Williams. 1st ed. $55.00

BENCHLEY, Robert. *Early Worm.* 1927 NY. Holt. 1st ed. VG $25.00

BENCHLEY, Robert. *From Bad to Worse.* 1950 London. Ills G Williams. 1st ed. dj. $15.00

BENCHLEY, Robert. *Inside Benchley.* 1942 Harper. 1st ed. dj. VG $20.00

BENCHLEY, Robert. *My 10 Years in a Quandary.* 1951 London. Ills Gluyas Williams. 1st ed. $30.00

BENCHLEY, Robert. *No Poems; or, Around the World Backwards & Sideways.* 1932 Ills 1st ed. VG $27.50

BENDER, G.L. *Reference Handbook on Deserts of North America.* 1982 Westport. Ills 1st ed. 594 p. EX $35.00

BENDER. *Dynamic Psychopathology of Childhood.* 1954 Thomas. 1st ed. $20.00

BENE. *Feeding & Behavior of Hummingbirds.* c 1943. Boston. Ills. 78 p. dj. VG $40.00

BENEDETTA, M. *Street Markets of London.* 1936 London. Ills 1st ed. 8vo. EX $125.00

BENEDICT, Francis G. *Chemical Lecture Experiments.* 1901 NY. Macmillan. 1st ed. xl. $15.00

BENEDICT, Ruth. *Tales of the Cochiti Indians.* 1931 Smithsonian. wraps. G $17.00

BENEDICT, Ruth; & WELTFISH, G. *In Henry's Backyard.* 1948 NY. Ills. sgns. VG $10.00

BENESCH, O. *Egon Schiele As a Draughtsman.* no date. Vienna. 4to. 24 plts. VG $50.00

BENET, Laura. *Noah's Dove.* 1929 Garden City. 1st ed. slipcase. EX $18.00

BENET, S.V. *From Earth to Moon.* 1958 New Haven. private print. 12mo. M $12.00

BENET, S.V. *Heavens & Earth.* 1920 NY. 1st ed. VG $25.00

BENET, S.V. *John Brown's Body.* 1928 Garden City. 1st ed. dj. EX $38.00

BENET, S.V. *Tales Before Midnight.* 1939 NY. Rinehart. 1st ed. dj. EX $15.00

BENET, S.V. *Western Star.* 1943 Farrar. 1st ed. dj. EX $28.00

BENET, S.V. *Young Adventure.* 1918 NY. 1st ed. VG $20.00

BENET, William R. *Starry Harness.* 1933 NY. sgn. cloth. VG $15.00

BENFORD, G. *Jupiter Project.* 1975 Nelson. 1st ed. dj. EX $17.50

BENHAM, W. Gurney. *Putnam's Dictionary of Thoughts.* 1930 NY. 1,226 p. index. VG $20.00

BENHAM. *Playing Cards: History of Pack & Explanations of Secrets.* no date. London. 1st ed. 196 p. VG $35.00

BENHARD. *Das Ewige Antlitz.* 1926 Berlin. German text. photos. dj. VG $15.00

BENJAMIN, Asher. *Builder's Guide.* 1839 Boston. Perkins Marvin. 1st ed. 83 p. $350.00

BENJAMIN, Asher. *Practice of Architecture.* 1835 Boston. 2nd ed. 4to. 60 plts. VG $200.00

BENJAMIN, Susan. *English Enamel Boxes: 18th-20th Century.* 1978 NY. Viking. 1st ed. dj. EX $20.00

BENJAMIN & RAYNERD. *American Builder's Companion.* 1806 Boston. 1st ed. 4to. 44 plts. calf. $525.00

BENJAMIN & RAYNERD. *American Builder's Companion.* 1916 Boston. Ills 3rd ed. 4to. 61 plts. G $160.00

BENKARD, Ernst. *Das Selbstbildnis vom 15.* 1927 Berlin. 1st ed. German text. VG $60.00

BENNETT, Arnold. *Dream of Destiny & Venus Rising From the Sea.* 1932 London. 1st ed. dj. EX $20.00

BENNETT, Arnold. *Night Visitor & Other Stories.* 1913 Edinburgh. 1st ed. VG $15.00

BENNETT, Edna Mae. *Turquoise & the Indian.* 1970 Chicago. Revised ed. dj. VG $8.00

BENNETT, F.M. *Moniter & the Navy Under Steam.* 1900 Boston. VG $50.00

BENNETT, George. *Wanderings: New South Wales, Batavia, Pedir Coast, & China.* 1834 London. 2 vol set. $700.00

BENNETT, Ida. *Making of a Flower Garden.* 1919 NY. 248 p. VG $15.00

BENNETT, John Hughes. *Pathology & Treatment of Pulmonary Tuberculosis.* 1853 Edinburgh. Sutherland Knox. $40.00

BENNETT, John. *Doctor to the Dead.* 1946 Rinehart. 1st ed. dj. EX $30.00

BENNETT, Paul. *Books & Printing Treasury for Typophiles.* 1951 NY/Cleveland. Ills. 417 p. dj. VG $37.00

BENNETT, Paula Pogany. *Art of Hungarian Cooking.* 1954 NY. dj. EX $15.00

BENNETT, Richard. *Mr. Ole.* 1930 Doubleday. Jr Books. 1st ed. 4to. $20.00

BENNETT, Richard. *Puget Sound.* 1931 Seattle. Ills 1st ed. EX $30.00

BENNETT, Robert. *Wrath of John Steinbeck.* 1939 Albertson Pr. Ltd 1st ed. sgn. G $25.00

BENNETT, Wendell C. *Ancient Art of the Andes.* 1954 MOMA. Ills. 4to. 186 p. $40.00

BENNETT, Whitman. *Practical Guide to American Book Collecting.* 1931 1st ed. 8vo. VG $35.00

BENNETT, Whitman. *Practical Guide to American 19th Century Color Plate Books.* 1948 NY. Bennett Book Studios. 140 p. M $125.00

BENNEY, Mark. *Angels in Undress.* 1937 NY. Random House. 1st ed. dj. G $25.00

BENSON, E.F. *Dodo.* 1978 Crowell. 1st ed. dj. EX $15.00

BENSON, E.F. *Lucia in London.* 1928 1st ed. Lucia Mapp Series. VG $17.50

BENSON, E.F. *Miss Mapp.* 1924 1st ed. Lucia Mapp Series. VG $15.00

BENSON, E.F. *Old London.* 1937 NY. 1st ed. 4 vol set. djs. EX $50.00

BENSON, E.F. *Spook Stories.* c 1930s. Hutchinson. dj. EX $50.00

BENSON, E.F. *Trouble for Lucia.* 1939 1st ed. Lucia Mapp Series. VG $12.50

BENSON, E.F. *Visible & Invisible.* 1924 Doran. 2nd print. G $45.00

BENSON, Joseph. *Life of Rev. John W. de la Flechere.* 1848 NY. 12mo. original leather. $25.00

BENSON, Sally. *Meet Me in St. Louis.* 1942 Random House. 1st ed. dj. VG $18.00

BENSON, Sally. *Meet Me in St. Louis.* 1942 Random House. 1st ed. dj. EX $25.00

BENSON, Stella. *Christmas Formula & Other Stories.* 1932 London. Chiswick. 1st ed. 1/550. sgn. $36.00

BENSON, Stella. *Tobit Transplanted.* 1931 London. 1st ed. VG $10.00

BENT, A.C. *Life Histories of North American Diving Birds.* 1963 Dover. Ills. 239 p. wraps. EX $8.00

BENT, A.C. *Life Histories of North American Gallinaceous Birds.* 1963 Dover. Ills. 490 p. wraps. EX $12.00

BENT, A.C. *Life Histories of North American Gulls & Terns.* 1963 Dover. Ills. 337 p. wraps. EX $8.00

BENT, A.C. *Life Histories of North American Marsh Birds.* 1963 Dover. Ills. 392 p. wraps. EX $10.00

BENT, A.C. *Life Histories of North American Shore Birds.* 1962 Dover. Ills. 2 vol set. wraps. EX $18.00

BENT, A.C. *Life Histories of North American Woodpeckers.* 1964 Dover. Ills. 334 p. wraps. EX $8.00

BENT, Newell. *Jungle Giants.* 1936 Plimpton Pr. Ills 1st ed. 255 p. VG $65.00

BENT. *American Polo.* 1929 NY. Ills. cloth. VG $30.00

BENTLEY, J. *Great American Automobiles.* 1957 NY. Ills. 374 p. $20.00

BENTLEY, Phyllis. *Bronte Sisters.* 1959 London. Revised ed. $25.00

BENTLEY, W.A. *Snow Crystals.* 1931 1st ed. 4to. VG $85.00

BENTLEY & ALLEN. *Trent's Own Case.* 1936 London. 1st ed. VG $35.00

BENTON, Elbert J. *Movement for Peace Without a Victory During the Civil War.* 1918 Cleveland. Ills. 80 p. wraps. G $19.50

BENTON, J.H. *Samuel Slade Benton: His Ancestors & Descendants.* 1901 354 p. xl. G $55.00

BENTON, Thomas Hart. *Artist in America.* 1951 KS U Pr. Revised ed. 324 p. G $10.00

BENTON, Thomas Hart. *30 Years in US Senate.* 1854 NY. Appleton. 2 vol set. $90.00

BENTON, Thomas Hart. *30 Years View; or, History of Working American Government.* 1856 Appleton. 2 vol set. $40.00

BENY, R. *Persia Bridge of Turquoise.* 1975 Toronto. 1st ed. dj. VG $65.00

BERANEK, Leo L. *Music, Acoustics, & Architecture.* 1962 NY. Ills. G $35.00

BERENDSOHN, W. *Selma Lagerof: Her Life & Work.* 1931 London. 1st English ed. 1/130. inscr. $150.00

BERENSON. *Sketch for Self-Portrait.* 1949 Pantheon. Ills Kessel. 12mo. 184 p. G $7.50

BERG, L.S. *Natural Regions of the USSR.* 1950 Macmillan. Ills 1st ed. 436 p. dj. VG $22.00

BERG, L.S. *Warsaw Ghetto.* 1945 NY. cloth. $30.00

BERGEN, Candice. *Knock Wood.* 1984 NY. 1st ed. presentation. dj. M $25.00

BERGEN, Fanny D. *Current Superstitions.* 1896 London. Ltd ed. 1/450. 161 p. EX $60.00

BERGER, A.J. *Bird Study.* 1971 Dover. Ills. 389 p. wraps. G $4.00

BERGER, J.F. *Observations of Physical Structure of Devonshire & Cornwall.* 1811 London. 91 p. VG $55.00

BERGER, M. *Story of NY Times 1851-1951.* 1951 Simon Schuster. Ills 1st ed. inscr. 589 p. EX $35.00

BERGER, Oscar. *Famous Faces: Caricaturist's Scrapbook.* 1950 London. 1st ed. dj. VG $30.00

BERGER, Thomas. *Arthur Rex.* 1978 NY. dj. EX $20.00

BERGER, Thomas. *Killing Time.* 1967 NY. Advance copy. $30.00

BERGER, Thomas. *Killing Time.* 1967 Dial Pr. 1st ed. dj. VG $17.50

BERGER, Thomas. *Little Big Man.* 1964 NY. 1st ed. sgn. dj. EX $65.00

BERGER, Thomas. *Neighbors.* 1980 NY. 1st ed. dj. M $10.00

BERGER, Thomas. *Reinhart's Women.* 1981 NY. Delacorte. 1st ed. dj. EX $20.00

BERGER, Thomas. *Reinhart's Women.* 1981 NY. 1st ed. dj. M $11.00

BERGER, Thomas. *Who Is Teddy Villanova?* 1977 Delacorte. 1st ed. dj. EX $20.00

BERGH, L.J.V. *On the Trail of the Pygmies.* 1969 Negro U Pr. reprint of 1921. 264 p. EX $18.00

BERGHOLD, A. *Indians' Revenge; or, Days of Horror.* 1891 San Francisco. 1st English Trans. 240 p. $40.00

BERGMAN, Ingmar. *Serpent's Egg.* 1977 NY. 1st ed. dj. M $12.00

BERGMAN, Ray. *Fresh-Water Bass.* 1947 NY. Knopf. 6th print. VG $20.00

BERGMAN, Ray. *Just Fishing.* 1946 Knopf. Ills. 418 p. dj. VG $12.00

BERGMAN, Ray. *Trout.* 1952 Knopf. Revised ed. 482 p. EX $14.00

BERGMAN, Ray. *With Fly, Plug, & Bait.* 1949 Morrow. 640 p. VG $10.00

BERGONZI, Bernard. *Heroes' Twilight: Study of Literature of Great War.* 1966 NY. 1st Am ed. dj. G $20.00

BERGREEN, Lawrence. *James Agee by Lawrence Bergreen.* 1984 NY. 1st ed. dj. M $10.00

BERGSON, Henri. *Creative Evolution.* 1911 NY. EX $25.00

BERGSTROM, E. *Old Glass Paperweights.* 1948 NY. Crown. 2nd print. 142 p. dj. $20.00

BERGSTROM, E. *Old Glass Paperweights.* no date. Crown. 1st ed. dj. $40.00

BERGSTROM, E. *Old Glass Paperweights.* 1940 Lakeside Pr. Ills 1st ed. EX $50.00

BERKELEY, Daniel. *Updike & Merrymount Press.* 1940 NY. Ltd 1st ed. 1/1,000. sgn. dj. $45.00

BERKELEY, Grantley F. *Reminiscences of a Huntsman.* 1854 Ills Leech. 1st ed. EX $150.00

BERKMAN, A. *Prison Memoirs of an Anarchist.* 1912 NY. 1st ed. VG $25.00

BERKY, Andrew. *Practitioner in Physics: Biography of Abraham Wagner.* 1954 Schwenkfelder. VG $12.50

BERLIN, Ellin. *Best of Families.* 1970 Doubleday. 1st ed. dj. VG $8.00

BERLIN, Sven. *Alfred Wallis Primitive.* 1949 London. VG $30.00

BERLINGER, B. *Danger Down the Sights.* 1964 Vantage. Ills 1st ed. 202 p. dj. G $8.00

BERMAN, Eugene. *Graphic Work of Eugene Berman.* 1971 NY. Potter. Ills. 4to. dj. $50.00

BERMAN, Eugene. *Imaginary Promendes in Italy.* 1956 NY. Ltd ed. 1/850. sgn. slipcase. $65.00

BERNADAC, Claude. *Devil's Doctors: Medical Experiments on Humans.* 1978 Geneva. Ferni. Ills. EX $25.00

BERNADAC, Claude. *Experimental Medicine: Classics of Medicine.* 1980 full leather. EX $35.00

BERNARD, J. *Abyssal Crustacea.* 1962 Columbia U Pr. Ills. 4to. 223 p. dj. VG $25.00

BERNARD, J. *Fly Dressing.* 1932 London. 8vo. dj. VG $30.00

BERNARD, John. *Retrospections of America 1797-1811.* 1887 NY. 1st ed. $75.00

BERNARD, John. *Retrospections of the Stage.* 1830 Riviere. 2 vol set. VG $225.00

BERNARD, Raymond. *Hollow Earth.* 1964 Fieldcrest. New ed. pb. $15.00

BERNAYS, Anne. *NY Ride.* 1965 Trident. 1st ed. dj. EX $30.00

BERNAYS, Edward L. *Engineering of Consent.* 1956 Norman. OK U Pr. $10.00

BERNDT, G.; & SHULTZ, H. *Grundlagen und Gerate Technischer Langenmessungen.* 1921 Berlin. Springer. Ills. 216 p. xl. VG $15.00

BERNHARD, Ruth. *Eternal Body.* 1986 Carmel. Ltd Special ed. 1/375. EX $425.00

BERNHARDT, Sarah. *Memories of My Life.* 1907 NY. Ltd 1st ed. 1/250. sgn. EX $350.00

BERNHEIM. *Suggestive Theraputics, Nature, & Uses of Hypnotism.* 1895 NY. cloth. VG $45.00

BERNHEIMER, Charles. *Rainbow Bridge.* 1924 Garden City. 1st ed. VG $25.00

BERNSTEIN, Aline. *Masterpieces of Women's Costume in 18th & 19th Centuries.* 1959 Crown. $45.00

BERNSTEIN, Aline. *3 Blue Suits.* 1933 NY. Ltd ed. 1/600. sgn. 74 p. $115.00

BERNSTEIN, Burton. *Last Act.* 1963 World. Ills J Stevenson. 1st ed. VG $20.00

BERNSTEIN, Leonard. *Joy of Music.* 1959 Simon Schuster. 1st ed. dj. VG $15.00

BERNSTEIN, Leonard. *Leonard Bernstein's Young People's Concerts.* 1970 Revised ed. 1st print. dj. VG $12.00

BERNSTEIN. *Turbulent Years.* 1970 Houghton. 1st ed. dj. VG $30.00

BERRALL, Julia S. *Flowers & Table Settings.* 1951 NY. Corner Pub. VG $25.00

BERRIGAN, Daniel. *False Gods, Real Men.* 1969 NY. 1st ed. dj. EX $15.00

BERRIGAN, Daniel. *Love, Love at the End.* 1968 Macmillan. 1st ed. dj. EX $20.00

BERRIGAN, Daniel. *Prison Poems.* 1973 Unicorn. 1st ed. sgn. dj. EX $25.00

BERRIGAN, Daniel. *Time Without Number.* 1957 NY. dj. VG $30.00

BERRIGAN, Ted. *Clear the Range.* 1977 NY. sgn with poem. dj. M $17.00

BERRIGAN, Ted. *Train Ride.* 1971 Vehicle. 1st ed. presentation. wraps. $20.00

BERRIGAN. *America Is Hard To Find.* 1972 Doubleday. 1st ed. dj. EX $20.00

BERRONE. *James Joyce in Padua.* 1977 NY. 1st ed. 146 p. dj. VG $12.00

BERRY, Wendell. *Collected Poems.* 1985 San Francisco. North Point. 1st ed. dj. EX $17.50

BERRY, Wendell. *Farming: A Handbook.* 1970 NY. Harcourt. 1st ed. dj. VG $35.00

BERRY, Wendell. *Findings.* 1969 Iowa City. Prairie Pr. VG $35.00

BERRY, Wendell. *Nathan Coulter.* 1960 Boston. 1st print. dj. VG $45.00

BERRY, Wendell. *November 26, 1963.* 1964 Braziller. Ills 1st ed. slipcase. EX $25.00

BERRY, Wendell. *Salad.* 1980 Berkeley. North Point. 1st ed. 12 mo. $25.00

BERRY, Wendell. *Sayings & Doings.* 1975 Lexington. Gnome. $15.00

BERRY, Wendell. *Unsettling of America.* 1977 San Francisco. 1st ed. dj. VG $35.00

BERRYMAN, John. *Berryman's Sonnets.* 1967 NY. 1st ed. dj. EX $30.00

BERRYMAN, John. *Delusions.* 1972 NY. Farrar. 1st ed. dj. EX $25.00

BERRYMAN, John. *Dream Songs.* 1969 Farrar. 1st ed. dj. EX $15.00

BERRYMAN, John. *Henry's Fate & Other Poems.* 1977 NY. dj. EX $50.00

BERRYMAN, John. *His Toy, His Dream, His Rest.* 1968 NY. 1st ed. dj. EX $25.00

BERRYMAN, John. *Homage to Mistress Bradstreet.* 1956 Farrar. Ills Ben Shahn. 1st ed. dj. VG $50.00

BERRYMAN, John. *Love & Fame.* 1971 Faber. 1st English ed. dj. VG $20.00

BERRYMAN, John. *Poems.* 1942 New Directions. 1st ed. 1/1,500. wraps. EX $90.00

BERRYMAN, John. *Recovery.* 1973 NY. dj. M $14.00

BERRYMAN, O.L. *Pioneer Preacher.* 1948 Crowell. dj. VG $8.00

BERTELSMANN, H. & E. *Eye of the Beholder.* 1981 Hudson Hills. 1st ed. dj. EX $12.50

BERTHRONG, Donald J. *Southern Cheyennes.* 1963 Norman. 1st ed. dj. VG $40.00

BERTOLUCCI. *Last Tango in Paris.* 1972 NY. 1st ed. dj. VG $10.00

BERTON, Pierre. *Impossible Railway.* 1972 NY. 1st ed. dj. VG $15.00

BERTON, R. *Remembering Bix.* 1974 NY. Ills 1st ed. 428 p. dj. VG $17.50

BERTRAM, Anthony. *To the Mountains.* 1929 London. 1st ed. dj. VG $18.00

BESANT, Annie. *Birth & Evolution of the Soul.* 1895 London. 56 p. VG $25.00

BESANT, Annie. *Shri Rama Chandra, Ideal King.* 1905 Benares. 188 p. VG $22.00

BESANT, Sir W. *Survey of London.* 1901-1911. 4to. 10 vol set. $250.00

BESSIE. *Dwell in the Wilderness.* 1935 Covici Friede. 1st ed. dj. EX $125.00

BEST, Herbert. *25th Hour.* 1940 1st print. G $8.00

BESTERMAN, Theodore. *Annie Besant Calendar.* 1927 London. 1st ed. 200 p. VG $28.00

BESTIC, A.A. *Kicking Canvas.* 1957 London. Ills. G $12.50

BETJEMAN, John. *English Cities & Small Towns.* 1943 London. Collins. dj. VG $20.00

BETJEMAN, John. *Summoned By Bells.* 1960 London. dj. EX $24.00

BETJEMAN, John. *Victorian & Edwardian England.* 1969 London. 1st ed. photos. dj. EX $27.00

BETJEMAN, John. *Victorian & Edwardian London From Old Photographs.* 1969 Viking. dj. VG $15.00

BETTEN, H.L. *Upland Game Shooting.* 1940 Phil. Ills. 450 p. $30.00

BETTEN, H.L. *Upland Game Shooting.* 1944 NY. 4th print. dj. $25.00

BETTINI, Sergio. *Mosaici Antichi di San Marco a Venezia.* c 1944. Italina d'Arti Graphiche. G $25.00

BETTS, Doris. *Heading West.* 1981 Knopf. 1st ed. dj. VG $10.00

BETTS, Doris. *River to Pickle Beach.* 1972 NY. 1st ed. sgn. dj. EX $45.00

BEUCHNER, Frederick. *Lion Country.* 1971 Atheneum. 1st ed. dj. EX $20.00

BEUCHNER, Frederick. *Open Heart.* 1971 Atheneum. 1st ed. dj. EX $15.00

BEUCHNER, Frederick. *Treasure Hunt.* 1977 NY. 1st ed. dj. EX $10.00

BEVAN, E.R. *House of Seleucus.* 1902 London. Arnold. Ills 1st ed. 2 vol set. $50.00

BEVANS, John. *Brief View of Doctrines Professed by Society of Friends.* 1810 Phil. 1st ed. VG $90.00

BEVANS, Michael. *Book of Reptiles & Amphibians.* 1956 Doubleday. Ills. 87 p. dj. EX $12.00

BEVERIDGE, Albert J. *Abraham Lincoln 1809-1858.* 1928 Boston. 4th imp. gilt blue cloth. VG $40.00

BEVERIDGE, Albert J. *Life of John Marshall.* 1929 Boston. 2 vol set. $40.00

BEVERLY, R. *History of VA.* 1722 London. Ills 2nd ed. 8vo. VG $1200.00

BEYER, Ernestine Cobern. *Story of Lenghwise.* 1967 Chicago. Follet. Ills Madden. dj. EX $10.00

BEZUCHA, R.D. *Golden Anniversary Book of Scouting.* 1959 Golden Pr. Ills N Rockwell. 4to. dj. VG $30.00

BEZYMENSKI, L. *Death of Adolf Hitler.* 1968 Harcourt Brace. Ills. dj. EX $20.00

BHAVNANI, Enakshi. *Decorative Designs & Craftsmanship of India.* 1969 Bombay. Taraporevala. Ills. 109 p. dj. $65.00

BHIKSHU, Subhadra. *Buddhist Catechism.* 1890 London. Redway. 1st ed. 92 p. VG $45.00

BIANCHI, Martha; & HAMPSON, A. *Further Poems of Emily Dickinson.* 1929 Little Brown. 4th print. 208 p. VG $18.00

BIANCO, Margery Williams. *Candlestick.* 1929 NY. Doubleday. Ills Ludovic Rodo. 1st ed. VG $35.00

BIANCO, Margery Williams. *Poor Cecco.* 1925 NY. Ills Rackham. 4to. VG $100.00

BIANCO, Margery Williams. *Poor Cecco.* 1934 NY. Ills Rackham. G $20.00

BIANCO & O'DONNELL. *Alice & Jerry Basic Reading Program.* c 1957. Ills. VG $15.00

BIBLE. *Book of Common Prayer in Language of Ojibwa Indians.* 1911 NY. 12mo. cloth. $30.00

BIBLE. *Book of Common Prayer.* 1845 London. fore-edge of Westminster. $400.00

BIBLE. *Book of Common Prayer.* 1830 Cambridge. fore-edge of Cambridge. $450.00

BIBLE. *Book of Common Prayer.* 1917 Oxford. full leather. G $75.00

BIBLE. *Book of Ecclesiastes.* 1951 Prairie Pr. 1st ed. 1/375. sewn wraps. $60.00

BIBLE. *Book of Ecclesiastes.* 1968 Ltd Ed Club. full calf. slipcase. EX $80.00

BIBLE. *Gospel of St. John in English & Japanese.* 1873 NY. Am Bible Soc. 8vo. cloth. VG $85.00

BIBLE. *Gospel of St. Mark in English & Mandarin.* 1882 Shanghai. Am Presbyterian Mission Pr. VG $65.00

BIBLE. *Holy Bible.* 1637 Robert Baker. leather. rebound. EX $450.00

BIBLE. *Holy Bible.* Cassell Petter. Ills Dore. 2 vol set. leather. $190.00

BIBLE. *Holy Bible.* Oct 27, 1802. Phil. plts. maps. $80.00

BIBLE. *Le Nouveau Testament, La Forme des Prieres.* 1696 Geneva. rebound. xl. EX $200.00

BIBLE. *New Testament in Language of Choctaw Indians.* 1881 NY. Am Bible Soc. 8vo. G $100.00

BIBLE. *New Testament in Language of Ojibway Indians.* 1875 NY. Am Bible Soc. 8vo. calf. G $100.00

BIBLE. *Picture Bible of Late Middle Ages.* 1960 Stuttgard. facsmile of Freiburg Morgan. $45.00

BIBLE. *Sermon on the Mount.* 1977 Ltd Ed Club. 4to. 87 p. slipcase. EX $47.50

BIBLE. *Whole Book of Psalms with Hymns.* 1793 NY. Gaine. 8vo. leather. G $85.00

BIBLE. *23rd Psalm.* 1965 Worcester, MA. Ills T Tudor. leather. dj. M $50.00

BICHAT, Xavier. *General Anatomy Applied to Physiology & Medicine.* 1822-1823. Boston. 4 vol set. $300.00

BICKEL, Karl. *Mangrove Coast.* 1942 Coward McCann. 2nd ed. dj. VG $25.00

BICKINGHAM, N. *Shootinest Gentleman.* 1941 NY. 1st ed. VG $60.00

BIDDLE, Nicholas. *Address Before Philadelphia Society Promoting Agriculture.* 1822 Phil. 8vo. 39 p. wraps. $35.00

BIDDLECOMBE, G. *Art of Rigging.* 1925 Marine Research Soc. VG $120.00

BIDWELL, John. *Echoes of the Past.* 1914 Chicago. Ills. wraps. $90.00

BIDWELL, John. *Life in CA Before the Gold Discovery.* 1966 private print. Ills Ltd ed. 1/1,950. VG $35.00

BIEBER, M. *Sculpture of Hellenistic Age.* 1961 NY. Ills. folio. cloth. dj. VG $100.00

BIEBER, Ralph. *Marching with the Army of the West.* 1974 Phil. VG $20.00

BIEBER, Ralph. *Southern Trails to CA.* 1849 Glendale. 1st ed. EX $75.00

BIERCE, Ambrose. *Can Such Things Be?* 1926 Boni. 3rd print. 12mo. 427 p. VG $17.50

BIERCE, Ambrose. *Devil's Dictionary.* 1941 Tower Books. 1st print. dj. VG $12.00

BIERCE, Ambrose. *Shadow on Dial & Other Essays.* 1909 San Francisco. 1st ed. VG $40.00

BIERCE, Ambrose. *Write It Right.* 1909 NY. 73 p. dj. VG $22.50

BIERCE, Ambrose. *21 Letters.* 1922 Cleveland. Ltd 1st ed. 1/950. VG $25.00

BIERMANN, George. *Lovis Corinth.* 1913 Leipzig. 1st ed. VG $45.00

BIGELOW, Henry J. *Lithoplaxy or Rapid Lithotrity with Evacuation.* 1878 Boston. inscr. cloth. VG $125.00

BIGELOW, Jacob. *American Medical Botany. Part II.* 1818 Boston. Ills. $375.00

BIGELOW, John. *Autobiography of Benjamin Franklin.* 1868 PA. VG $35.00

BIGELOW, John. *Memoir of Life & Public Services of John Charles Fremont.* 1856 NY. Ills. VG $40.00

BIGELOW, O. *Mulberry Trout.* 1969 1st ed. dj. xl. EX $10.00

BIGELOW, Poultney. *Borderline of Czar & Baiser.* 1895 NY. Harper. Ills Remington. 8vo. $10.00

BIGGERS, Earl Derr. *Chinese Parrot.* 1926 Bobbs Merrill. 1st ed. green linen. EX $60.00

BIGGERS, Earl Derr. *7 Keys to Baldpate.* 1913 Indianapolis. 1st ed. $40.00

BIGLAND, Eileen. *Lake of the Royal Crocodiles.* 1939 Macmillan. Ills. 299 p. maps. dj. VG $16.00

BIGLER, M. *Navajo Indians.* 1934 OH. Ills. 8vo. 36 p. wraps. VG $12.00

BILBO, Jack. *Autobiography of Jack Bilbo.* 1948 London. Modern Art Gallery. 4to. dj. $70.00

BILBO, Jack. *Autobiography of Jack Bilbo.* 1948 London. private print. folio. plts. VG $40.00

BILGUER. *Handbuch der Schachspiels.* 1874 Leipzig. $24.00

BILL, A.H. *Beleagured City: Richmond 1861-1865.* 1946 Knopf. Ills 1st ed. 313 p. VG $16.00

BILLCLIFFE, Roger. *Mackintosh Textile Designs.* 1982 NY. Taplinger. Ills. 80 p. dj. $25.00

BILLINGHURST, P. *100 Fables of La Fontaine.* no date. Lane. 2nd ed. VG $60.00

BILLINGS, H. *Man Under Water.* 1955 NY. 2nd print. dj. G $5.00

BILLINGS, John. *Hardtack & Coffee.* 1982 Time Life. reprint of 1887. leather. M $40.00

BILLINGS, John. *Hardtack & Coffee.* 1960 Chicago. Lakeside. EX $25.00

BILLINGTON & CAMARILLO. *American Southwest: Image & Reality.* 1979 UCLA. 8vo. 129 p. wraps. VG $8.00

BINGHAM, C. *American Preceptor.* 1803 Boston. 17th ed. $20.00

BINGHAM, C. *Columbian Orator.* 1815 Troy. G $15.00

BINGHAM, Hiram. *Across South America.* 1911 Boston/NY. Houghton. 1st ed. 405 p. EX $60.00

BINGHAM, Hiram. *Inca Land.* 1922 Houghton. 1st ed. VG $45.00

BINGHAM, Hiram. *Residence of 21 Years in Sandwich Islands.* no date. (1848) Hartford. G $55.00

BINNS, Archie. *Peter Skene Ogden, Fur Trader.* 1967 Bifords Mort. Ills 1st ed. maps. dj. EX $10.00

BINYON, Laurence. *Attila.* 1907 London. 1st ed. EX $15.00

BINYON, Laurence. *Burning of Leaves.* 1944 London. wraps. scarce. G $40.00

BINYON, Laurence. *Engraved Designs of William Blake.* 1967 NY. DaCapo. reprint of 1926. dj. $65.00

BINYON, Laurence. *Engraved Designs of William Blake.* 1926 London. Benn. Ltd Deluxe ed. 1/100. G $120.00

BINYON, Laurence. *Engraved Designs of William Blake.* 1967 NY. Da Capo. 82 plts. $40.00

BINYON, Laurence. *Japanische Bunst.* 1912 Berlin. German text. VG $35.00

BINYON, Laurence. *North Star & Other Poems.* 1941 London. 1st ed. dj. EX $15.00

BINYON, Laurence. *Spirit of Man in Asian Art.* 1935 Cambridge. 1st ed. dj. VG $40.00

BIRBECK, Morris. *Notes on Journey in America to Territory of IL.* 1818 Cublin. fld map. $300.00

BIRCH, A.G. *Moon Terror.* 1927 Indianapolis. Popular Fiction. 1st ed. dj. $125.00

BIRCH, Samuel. *History of Ancient Pottery.* 1958 London. Murray. Ills. 2 vol set. VG $95.00

BIRD, E.A. *Fishing Off Puerto Rico.* 1960 Barnes. Ills 1st ed. 111 p. VG $5.00

BIRD, I.L. *Lady's Life in the Rocky Mountains.* 1960 OK U Pr. Review ed. 249 p. dj. EX $30.00

BIRD, I.L. *Lady's Life in the Rocky Mountains.* 1962 OK U Pr. Ills. 249 p. EX $15.00

BIRD, M.B. *Black Man; or, Haitian Independence.* 1869 NY. private print. 1st ed. 461 p. $75.00

BIRD, Sir W.D. *Direction of War.* 1925 Cambridge. 2nd ed. VG $20.00

BIRDSALL, S. *Log of the Liberators.* 1973 NY. dj. VG $22.50

BIRDWELL, C. *Amazons.* 1980 NY. 1st ed. dj. EX $10.00

BIRDWOOD, Lt. Col. Lord. *Worcestershire Regiment 1922-1950.* 1952 Aldorshot. 1st ed. dj. VG $20.00

BIRENBAUM, H. *Hope Is the Last To Die.* 1971 NY. SftCvr. G $15.00

BIRGE, J.C. *Awakening of Desert.* 1912 Boston. 2nd ed. 420 p. VG $15.00

BIRKHOLDT, George D. *Aesthetic Measure.* 1933 Harvard U Pr. Ills. 4to. 226 p. VG $65.00

BIRMINGHAM, George. *Lighter Side of Irish Life.* no date. Stokes. Ills Henry W Kerr. $10.00

BIRMINGHAM, Stephen. *Grandees.* 1971 Harper Row. 1st ed. dj. VG $10.00

BIRMINGHAM, Stephen. *Life at the Dakota.* 1979 NY. Ills. VG $7.00

BIRMINGHAM, Stephen. *Right People.* 1968 NY. Ills. VG $5.00

BIRRELL, Augustine. *Obiter Dicta.* 1891 NY. 2 vol set. VG $8.00

BIRREN, Faber. *American Colorist.* 1948 Sandusky. Prang. 2nd ed. sgn. wraps. $12.00

BIRREN, Faber. *Color Psychology & Color Theraphy.* 1965 NY U Books. 3rd print. 302 p. dj. EX $26.00

BIRREN, Faber. *Color: Survey in Words & Pictures.* 1963 New Hyde Park. Ills 1st ed. 4to. slipcase. EX $25.00

BIRREN, Faber. *History of Color in Painting.* 1965 NY. Reinhold. Ills. 4to. 32 plts. dj. EX $65.00

BIRREN, Faber. *Your Color & Yourself.* 1952 Sandusky. Prang. 1st ed. 8vo. inscr. VG $18.00

BISCHOF, Werner. *World of Werner Bischof.* 1959 Dutton. $30.00

BISHOP, Elizabeth. *Geography III.* 1976 NY. 1st ed. dj. $35.00

BISHOP, Elizabeth. *Selected Poems.* 1967 London. Chatto Windus. 1/1,200. dj. $75.00

BISHOP, J.B. *Our Political Drama.* 1904 1st ed. 236 p. VG $30.00

BISHOP, John Peale. *Collected Poems.* 1948 Scribner. 1st ed. dj. EX $20.00

BISHOP, R. *Painting of the Royal Collection.* 1937 London. Harrap. 1st ed. dj. VG $26.00

BISHOP, Richard. *Bishop's Birds: Etchings of Waterfowl & Upland Game Birds.* 1936 Phil. Ltd ed. 1/1,050. boxed. EX $295.00

BISHOP, Robert. *Folk Painters of America.* 1979 NY. 1st ed. 4to. dj. EX $45.00

BISHOP, Robert. *Gallery of Amish Quilts.* 1976 NY. Dutton. Ills. 4to. 96 p. wraps. $30.00

BISHOP, Robert. *How To Know American Antique Furniture.* 1973 Dutton. Ills. 8vo. 224 p. wraps. $15.00

BISHOP, T.J. *History of De Witt Clinton Council No. 22.* 1887 NY. Burdick Taylor. 51 p. $10.00

BISHOP, W.H. *Old Mexico & Her Lost Provinces.* 1883 Ills 1st ed. 8vo. 509 p. VG $35.00

BISHOP, Zealia. *Curse of Yig.* 1953 Arkham House. 1st ed. dj. VG $65.00

BISLAND, Elizabeth. *3 Wise Men of the East.* 1930 NC U Pr. 1st ed. EX $15.00

BISSELL, Richard. *My Life on MS; or, Why I Am Not Mark Twain.* 1973 Little Brown. 1st ed. dj. VG $11.00

BISSETT, Clark. *Abraham Lincoln: Universal Man.* 1923 Grabhorn. Ltd ed. 1/125. sgn. EX $45.00

BITTING, A.W. & K.G. *Canning & How To Use Canned Foods.* 1916 WA. Ills. G $65.00

BITTNER, Herbert. *Kaethe Kollwitz Drawings.* 1959 NY. Yoseloff. Ills. 4to. cloth. dj. $30.00

BJERRE, Jens. *Kalahari.* 1960 Hill Wang. Ills. 227 p. VG $8.00

BJORNDAL, K.A. *Biology & Conservation of Sea Turtles.* 1982 Smithsonian. Ills. 584 p. wraps. $30.00

BLACK, Alexander. *Photography Indoors & Out.* 1894 Boston. 2nd ed. scarce. VG $45.00

BLACK, Campbell. *Asterisk's Destiny.* 1978 Knopf. 1st ed. dj. VG $10.00

BLACK, George F. *Gypsy Bibliography.* 1909 Gypsy Lore Soc. 8vo. 139 p. wraps. $18.00

BLACK, J.M. *Families & Descendants in America of Golsan, Golson, Etc.* 1959 Salt Lake City. 815 p. EX $35.00

BLACK, John. *Cultivation of Peach & Pear on DE Peninsula.* 1886 Wilmington, DE. 1st ed. 8vo. 397 p. $35.00

BLACK, Robert. *Art of Jacob Epstein.* 1942 Cleveland. Ills 1st ed. 1/425. calf. $75.00

BLACK. *Black's Guide to Ireland.* 1906 London. Ills. 372 p. gilt cloth. VG $35.00

BLACKBURN, Robert. *New Horizon Book of Flying.* 1963 London. dj. VG $15.00

BLACKBURNE. *Games at Chess.* 1899 London. 8vo. 331 p. VG $60.00

BLACKER, Irwin. *Hakluyt's Voyages.* 1965 NY. Viking. 1st ed. 522 p. dj. EX $20.00

BLACKHOUSE, Sarah. *Memoir of James Blackhouse.* 1870 London. 1st ed. full leather. EX $50.00

BLACKMAN, R.V.B. *World's Warships.* 1961 NY. Ills 2nd ed. 8vo. cloth. dj. $16.00

BLACKMANTLE, Bernard. *English Spy.* 1907 London. Ills Cruikshank. 2 vol set. EX $80.00

BLACKMORE. *Lorna Doone.* 1893 Boston. 2 vol set. boxed. EX $52.00

BLACKSTONE, William. *Commentaries on Laws of England in 4 Books.* 1884 Chicago. 3rd ed. 4 vols in 2. leather. $125.00

BLACKWELDER, B. *Great Westerner: Story of Kit Carson.* 1962 Caxton. Ills. dj. EX $25.00

BLACKWELL, Sarah Ellen. *Forma Sara.* 1774 Boston. G $40.00

BLACKWELL, Sarah Ellen. *Military Genius: Life of Anna Ella Carroll of MD.* 1891 WA. 1st ed. 3 plts. cloth. $70.00

BLACKWOOD, Algernon. *Incredible Adventures.* 1914 London. Macmillan. 1st ed. VG $60.00

BLACKWOOD, Algernon. *Jimbo: Phantasy.* 1909 London. Macmillan. 1st ed. VG $60.00

BLACKWOOD, Algernon. *Lost Valley: Evelight Nash Fowside House.* 1910 London. 1st ed. 2nd imp. VG $35.00

BLACKWOOD, Algernon. *Strange Stories.* 1929 London. Heinemann. 1st ed. VG $60.00

BLACKWOOD, Algernon. *Tongues of Fire.* 1924 London. 1st ed. VG $35.00

BLADES, William. *Biography & Typography of Wm. Caxton, England's 1st Printer.* 1882 NY. Ills 2nd ed. VG $20.00

BLADES, William. *Pentateuch of Printing.* 1891 Chicago. McClurg. Ills. leather. G $12.00

BLAINE, James G. *20 Years of Congress: Lincoln to Garfield. Vols. I & II.* 1886 Norwich, CT. 2 vol set. G $50.00

BLAIR, Claude. *European & American Arms 1100-1850.* 1962 Crown. Ills 1st ed. 4to. dj. EX $30.00

BLAIR, Hugh. *Abridgment of Lectures on Rhetoric.* 1818 Haverhill. $15.00

BLAIR, Hugh. *Lectures on Rhetoric.* 1874 Phil. Aitken. 1st Am ed. $120.00

BLAIR, Robert. *Grave.* c 1890s. London. Routledge. Ills. $150.00

BLAIR, W. *Raft Pilot's Log: History of Rafting Industry on Upper MS.* 1929 Cleveland. Ills 1st ed. 328 p. VG $45.00

BLAIR, W.F. *Evolution of the Genus Bufo.* 1972 TX U Pr. Ills. 4to. dj. EX $35.00

BLAISDELL, H.F. *Tricks That Take Fish.* 1960 Holt. Ills. 299 p. dj. VG $10.00

BLAKE, E.R. *Birds of Mexico: Guide for Field Identification.* 1963 Chicago U Pr. Ills 644 p. dj. VG $25.00

BLAKE, J. *First Book Astronomy.* 1831 Boston. Ills. $35.00

BLAKE, Nicholas. *Beast Must Die.* 1938 NY. 1st Am ed. VG $75.00

BLAKE, William. *Pencil Drawings by William Blake.* 1927 London. 1/1,550. 4to. ½-linen. VG $125.00

BLAKE, William. *Selections From Writings of William Blake.* 1893 London. Intro Houseman. VG $35.00

BLAKE, William. *Songs of Innocence.* 1928 Yellow Springs. VG $20.00

BLAKE, William. *Tombstone & Its Mines.* 1902 Ills. inscr. scarce. VG $125.00

BLAKE, William. *XVII Designs to Thorton's Virgil.* 1909 Portland, ME. Ltd ed. 1/450. G $80.00

BLAKE & REVEIRS-HOPKINS. *Old English Furniture for the Small Collector.* 1930 NY/London. Ills. photos. VG $12.50

BLAKEBOROUGH, J. *Analysis of the Turf.* 1927 London. Ills. 8vo. 321 p. $25.00

BLAKESLEE & JARVIS. *Trees in Winter.* 1916 NY. Ills. G $20.00

BLAKEY, Robert. *Historical Sketches of Angling Literature.* 1856 London. 16mo. ½ leather. $150.00

BLANC, Charles. *Masterpieces of Italian Art. Vol. II.* no date. Phil. leather. $100.00

BLANCH, Lesley. *Journey into the Mind's Eye.* 1969 Atheneum. 1st Am ed. lavender cloth. dj. $15.00

BLANCHAN, Nellie. *Birds That Hunt & Are Hunted.* 1898 NY. 48 plts. VG $30.00

BLANCHAN. *Birds That Hunt & Are Hunted.* 1920 NY. Ills. xl. VG $12.00

BLANCHARD, Fessenden S. *Block Island to Nantucket.* 1961 Nostrand, NJ. Stated 1st ed. 8vo. 253 p. dj. $20.00

BLANCHARD, Mary Miles. *Basketry Book: 12 Lessons in Reed Weaving.* 1915 Scribner. Ills. sgn. 111 p. G $17.00

BLANCHARD, R. *How To Restore & Decorate Chairs.* 1952 NY. Ills. 128 p. $12.50

BLANCK, Jacob. *Bibliography of American Literature.* 1968-1983. New Haven/London. 7 vol set. $400.00

BLANCK, Jacob. *Peter Parley to Penrod.* 1938 NY. Bowker. Ltd ed. 1/500. xl. VG $100.00

BLANCO, A.D.F. *Journey of the Flame.* 1933 Houghton Mifflin. Ills. dj. EX $14.00

BLAND, E. *Flat Racing Since 1900.* 1950 London. Ills 1st ed. dj. VG $30.00

BLAND, Humphrey. *Treatise on Military Discipline.* 1759 London. 8vo. leather. $250.00

BLAND, J.O. *Recent Events & Present Policies in China.* 1912 Phil. 1st Am ed. 482 p. fld maps. G $20.00

BLAND, Jane Cooper. *Art of the Young Child, 3 to 5 Years.* 1957 MOMA. Ills. 4to. 47 p. xl. $5.00

BLAND, Oliver. *Adventures of a Modern Occultist.* 1920 NY. 221 p. G $25.00

BLANDFORD, Linda. *L.S.O.: Scenes From Orchestra Life.* 1984 London. dj. EX $12.00

BLANDING, Don. *Leaves From Grass House.* 1923 Honolulu. 1st ed. EX $52.00

BLANDING, Don. *Pictures of Paradise.* 1937 NY. 2nd ed. boxed. VG $27.50

BLANDING, Don. *Rest of the Road.* 1946 NY. Ills 13th print. VG $15.00

BLANKENBURG, Lucretia. *Blankenburgs of Philadelphia.* 1929 Phil. 1st ed. inscr. VG $30.00

BLASINGAME, Ike. *Dakota Cowboy: My Life in the Old Days.* 1958 Putnam. Ills. 317 p. dj. VG $28.00

BLASSO, H. *Cinnamon Seed.* 1934 NY. 1st ed. dj. VG $25.00

BLATTY, W.P. *Exorcist.* 1971 NY. dj. EX $19.00

BLATTY, W.P. *John Goldfarb, Please Come Home.* 1963 NY. 1st ed. dj. VG $17.50

BLAVATSKY, H.P. *Isis Unveiled: Master Key to Mysteries of Ancient Science.* 1919 Point Loma, CA. Aryan Theosophical Pr. 2 vols. $60.00

BLAVATSKY, H.P. *Isis Unveiled: Master Key to Mysteries of Ancient Science.* 1910 Point Loma, CA. 2 vol set. VG $125.00

BLAVATSKY, H.P. *Secret Doctrine.* 1917 Point Loma, CA. Aryan Theosophical Pr. $95.00

BLAXLAND, G. *Middlesex Regiment.* 1977 London. Ills. 144 p. dj. EX $15.00

BLAYLOCK, James P. *Elfin Ship.* 1982 Del Rey. 1st ed. $100.00

BLAYLOCK, James P. *Elfin Ship.* 1982 Ballantine. 1st ed. wraps. EX $25.00

BLAYLOCK, James P. *Paper Dragons.* 1986 Axolotl Pr. 1st ed. $100.00

BLAYLOCK, James P. *2 Views of a Cave Painting.* 1987 Axolotl Pr. Intro D Koontz. 1/500. sgns. $25.00

BLEANEY, B.I. *Electricity & Magnetism.* 1957 Oxford. 1st ed. dj. EX $30.00

BLEDSOE. *Essay on Liberty & Slavery.* 1856 NY. G $25.00

BLEECK, Oliver. *Highbinders.* 1974 NY. Morrow. 1st ed. dj. VG $20.00

BLEECK, Oliver. *Protocol for a Kidnapping.* 1971 NY. Morrow. 1st ed. dj. VG $25.00

BLEECKER, Ann Eliza. *History of Maria Kittle in Letter to Miss Ten Eyck.* 1802 Hartford. 2nd ed. 12mo. $250.00

BLEECKER, Ann Eliza. *Posthumous Works in Prose & Verse.* 1793 NY. 12mo. 375 p. leather. VG $125.00

BLEGVAD, Erik. *Moon-Watch Summer.* 1972 NY. Harcourt Brace Jovanovich. dj. $6.50

BLEGVAD, Lenore. *This Little Pig a Wig & Other Rhymes About Pigs.* 1978 Ills. 8vo. dj. EX $10.00

BLEVINS, Richard. *Clarel's Motel: Travel & Poetry in the USA.* no date. Santa Barbara. 1st ed. EX $10.00

BLEY, Wulf. *Das Buch der Spanienflieger.* 1939 Leipzig. $20.00

BLISH, Helen H. *Pictographic History of Oglala Sioux.* 1967 NE U Pr. G $35.00

BLISH, James. *Earthman Come Home.* 1955 Putnam. 1st ed. dj. EX $45.00

BLISH, James. *Spock Must Die!* 1975 Bantam. 14th print. pb. $5.00

BLISH, James. *Star Trek 8.* 1972 Bantam. 5th print. pb. VG $4.00

BLISHEN. *Oxford Book of Poetry for Children.* 1963 Watts. Ills Wildsmith. 1st print. dj. $20.00

BLISS, Carey S. *Autos Across America.* 1972 Los Angeles. Plantin Pr. Ltd 1st ed. EX $65.00

BLISS, D.P. *History of Wood Engraving.* 1964 London. Ills. 263 p. $25.00

BLOCH, Dr. J.S. *Gegen die Anti-Semiten. Eine Streitschrift.* 1882 Wien. Verlag. 39 p. wraps. xl. G $95.00

BLOCH, Robert. *Blood Runs Cold.* 1961 NY. 1st ed. dj. VG $22.00

BLOCH, Robert. *Bogey Men.* 1967 Pyramid. 1st ed. wraps. EX $10.00

BLOCH, Robert. *Dragons & Nightmares.* 1968 Mirage. Ltd 1st ed. 1/1,000. dj. EX $35.00

BLOCH, Robert. *Living Demons.* 1967 Belmont. 1st ed. wraps. EX $10.00

BLOCH, Robert. *Night of the Ripper.* 1984 Doubleday. 1st ed. EX $20.00

BLOCH, Robert. *Opener of the Way.* 1945 Arkham House. 1st ed. dj. EX $95.00

BLOCH, Robert. *Unholy Trinity.* 1986 Scream Pr. 1st ed. 1/250. sgn. slipcase. $85.00

BLOCK, Lawrence. *Ariel.* 1980 Ltd 1st Am ed. 1/500. sgn. dj. $25.00

BLOCK, Lawrence. *Burglar Who Studied Spinoza.* 1980 1st Am ed. inscr. dj. $20.00

BLOCK, Lawrence. *When the Sacred Gin Mill Closes.* 1986 1st Am ed. sgn. dj. $22.00

BLOCK, Maurice. *Francois Boucher & the Beauvais Tapestries.* 1933 Boston. Houghton Mifflin. Ills. 40 p. $32.50

BLOFELD, John. *Tantric Mysticism of Tibet.* 1970 NY. 257 p. VG $24.00

BLOHM, C.C. *Guide to Home Decorating.* 1953 NY. Ills. 151 p. $7.50

BLOM, Eric. *Mozart.* 1956 reprint. Master Musicians Series. dj. $8.00

BLOOMFIELD, Robert. *Poems.* 1809 London. full leather. G $20.00

BLOOMSDAY. *Interpretation of James Joyce's Ulysses.* c 1972. NY. Field Levitt. dj. $37.50

BLOSSFELDT, Karl. *Unformen der Kunst.* 1925 Berlin. Wasmuth. 1st ed. gilt cloth. $85.00

BLOSSUM, Frederick A. *Told at the Explorers' Club.* 1931 NY. Ills 1st ed. 425 p. G $25.00

BLOUGH, Glenn O. *Not Only for Ducks: Story of Rain.* 1954 Ills Bendick. 2nd ed. 4to. dj. $15.00

BLOW, Ben. *CA Highways.* 1920 San Francisco. Ills. maps. dj. G $36.00

BLUCHER, K. *Know Your Germans.* 1951 London. dj. G $12.50

BLUESTONE, George. *Novels Into Film.* 1957 John Hopkins. 1st ed. dj. VG $10.00

BLUM, H.F. *Time's Arrow & Evolution.* 1951 Princeton U Pr. 222 p. dj. EX $10.00

BLUME, Judy. *Iggie's House.* 1974 NY. Bradbury. 2nd print. 8vo. 117 p. dj. G $10.50

BLUME, Judy. *Wifey.* 1978 Putnam. Uncorrected proof. EX $20.00

BLUMENSON, Martin. *Breakout & Pursuit.* 1961 WA. Ills 1st ed. 748 p. maps. VG $27.50

BLUMENTHAL, Walter. *Heaven & Hades.* 1965 Worcester. 1/200. VG $15.00

BLUNDEN, Edmund. *Masks of Time.* 1925 London. Ltd ed. 1/390. VG $35.00

BLUNDEN, Edmund. *Near & Far.* 1930 NY. Ltd ed. 1/105. sgn. VG $15.00

BLUNT, Flight Lt. V.E.R. *Use of Air Power.* 1943 Harrisburg. Military Service Pub. 1st ed. $20.00

BLUNT, Reginald. *Gerald Blunt of Chelsea (England).* 1911 323 p. ancestral charts. xl. VG $25.00

BLUNT, Wilfrid. *Art of Botanical Illustration.* 1955 London. 3rd ed. 47 plts. dj. EX $40.00

BLY, Carol. *Letters From the Country.* 1981 Harper. 1st ed. dj. M $12.00

BLYTHE, W.J. *Effective Conjuring.* 1934 London. 3rd ed. 8vo. 224 p. dj. $20.00

BLYTHE, W.J. *Paper Magic.* 1920 London. 1st ed. VG $16.00

BOAS, F. *Handbook of American Indian Languages.* 1911 & 1922. 2 vol set. $100.00

BOAS, S. Louise. *Elizabeth Browning.* 1930 Longman Green. 1st ed. dj. VG $10.00

BOAS, Z. & L. *Cotton Mather, Keeper of the Puritan Conscience.* 1928 NY. Ills 1st ed. 271 p. VG $20.00

BOAZ & BADSWORTH. *How To Play Bridge.* 1900 London. 7th print. VG $20.00

BOBBE, Dorothie. *Mr. & Mrs. John Quincy Adams: Adventure in Patriotism.* 1930 Minton Balch. $12.50

BOBKER, Lee R. *Unicorn Group.* 1979 Morrow. 1st ed. dj. EX $12.00

BOCCACCIO, Giovanni. *Life of Dante.* 1904 Boston. Riverside. Ltd ed. 1/265. VG $65.00

BOCCACCIO, Giovanni. *Questions of Love.* c 1931. NY. 3 Sirens Pr. Ills Ltd ed. VG $45.00

BODDE, Derk. *Peking Diary: Year of Revolution.* 1950 NY. dj. VG $10.00

BODDINGTON, Harry. *University of Spiritualism.* 1967 481 p. VG $22.00

BODE, Winston. *Life of Great Texan: J. Frank Dobie.* 1965 Austin. 3rd print. dj. EX $25.00

BODENHEIM, Maxwell. *Introducing Irony.* 1922 NY. 1st ed. scarce. VG $35.00

BODENHEIM, Maxwell. *Minna & Myself.* 1918 NY. 1st issue. G $60.00

BODSWORTH, Fred. *Last of the Curlews.* 1955 NY. Ills TM Short. dj. xl. G $10.00

BOECK & SABARTES. *Picasso.* c 1955. Abrams. 1st ed. dj. EX $50.00

BOEHME, Jacob. *Way of Christ.* 1947 NY. 253 p. VG $35.00

BOEHME, Jacob. *Way of Christ.* 1775 Bristol. G $235.00

BOEHME, Jacob. *6 Theosophical Points & Other Writings.* 1920 NY. 220 p. VG $45.00

BOELDEKE, Alfred. *With Graciela to Headhunters.* 1958 McKay. Ills. 166 p. black linen. VG $9.00

BOGARDUS, A.H. *Field, Cover, & Trap Shooting.* 1874 Ford. Ills 1st ed. 343 p. VG $42.50

BOGEN, Nancy. *William Blake: Book of Thel.* 1971 Providence. Brown. 1st ed. dj. EX $25.00

BOGGS, Kate Doggett. *Prints & Plants of Old Gardens.* 1932 Richmond. Garrett Massie. 101 p. xl. G $35.00

BOGUET, Henry. *Examine of Witches.* 1929 Ltd ed. 1/1,275. 328 p. $70.00

BOHM, David. *Causality & Chance in Modern Physics.* 1957 Princeton. Van Nostrand. 1st ed. 170 p. $15.00

BOHMAN, Nils. *Jim, Jock, & Jumbo.* 1946 NY. Dutton. Ills E Norelius. 1st ed. VG $35.00

BOHR, Aage. *Peter Robertson: Early Years of Neils Bohr Institute.* 1979 Kobenhavn. Forlag. Ills. sgn. 173 p. EX $50.00

BOHR, Niels. *Atomic Physics & Human Knowledge.* 1958 NY. Wiley. 1st ed. 101 p. dj. VG $33.00

BOHR, Niels. *Drie Aufsatze uber Spektren und Atombau.* 1924 Braunschweig. Ills. 150 p. wraps. VG $35.00

BOHR, Niels. *Effect of Electric & Magnetic Fields on Spectral Lines.* 1922 London. VG $30.00

BOHR, Niels. *Niels Bohr Centenary Volume.* 1985 Cambridge. Harvard U Pr. 1st ed. 403 p. $27.00

BOHR, Niels. *Niels Bohr: The Man, His Science, & the World They Changed.* 1966 NY. Knopf. Ills 1st ed. 436 p. dj. VG $15.00

BOHU, Slava. *Story of Dukhobors.* 1940 Farrar. 1st ed. 437 p. dj. VG $35.00

BOIES, Henry M. *Science of Penology.* 1901 NY/London. Putnam. inscr. ¾-leather. VG $125.00

BOILEAU, D. *Introduction to the Study of Political Economy.* 1811 London. 1st ed. G $35.00

BOKER, George Henry. *Legend of the Hounds.* 1929 NY. Ills Ross. 1/800. slipcase. VG $25.00

BOKER, George Henry. *Legend of the Hounds.* 1929 NY. Ltd ed. 1/800. G $15.00

BOKSER, Benjamin Zion. *From the World of Cabbalah.* 1954 210 p. VG $25.00

BOLAND, K.T. *Dwight Moody: Man & Mission.* 1900 Memorial ed. Ills. VG $10.00

BOLIN, Major C. *Narrative of Life & Adventures of Major C. Bolin.* 1966 private print. Intro RH Dillion. 1/1,300. VG $40.00

BOLITHO, Hector. *Biographer's Notebook.* 1950 London. 1st ed. dj. VG $12.00

BOLITHO, Hector. *Without the City Wall: Adventures in London Street Names.* 1952 London. Murray. dj. VG $15.00

BOLITHO, William. *Camera Obscura.* 1930 NY. Intro Noel Coward. 1st ed. $15.00

BOLL, Heinrich. *Children & Civilians Too.* 1970 McGraw Hill. Advance copy. dj. EX $20.00

BOLL, Heinrich. *Irish Journal.* 1967 McGraw Hill. 1st Am ed. dj. EX $25.00

BOLL, Heinrich. *Lost Honor of Katharina Blum.* 1975 McGraw Hill. 1st Am ed. dj. EX $15.00

BOLL, Heinrich. *Never Said a Word.* 1978 McGraw Hill. 1st Am ed. dj. EX $15.00

BOLL, Heinrich. *Safety Net.* 1982 Knopf. 1st Am ed. dj. EX $15.00

BOLL, Heinrich. *Soldier's Legacy.* 1985 Knopf. 1st Am ed. dj. EX $12.00

BOLL, Heinrich. *Tomorrow & Yesterday.* 1957 Criterion. 1st Am ed. dj. EX $30.00

BOLL, Heinrich. *What's To Become of the Boy?* 1984 Knopf. 1st Am ed. dj. EX $12.00

BOLLAERT, William. *Antiquarian, Ethnological, & Researches in New Granada.* 1860 London. Trubner. 1st ed. 279 p. $125.00

BOLOGNA, Giafranco. *Birds of the World.* 1978 Simon Schuster. Ills. 511 p. wraps. EX $12.00

BOLOGNA, Giafranco. *World of Birds.* 1975 Abbeville. Ills. 256 p. EX $8.00

BOLTON, Arthur T. *Gardens of Italy.* 1919 London. Offices of Country Life. VG $250.00

BOLTON, E.S. *Wax Portraits & Silhouettes.* 1915 Boston. Ills. VG $55.00

BOLTON, Herbert Eugene. *Outpost of Empire: Founding San Francisco.* 1931 NY. Ills. 11 maps. VG $40.00

BOLTON, Herbert Eugene. *Rim of Christendom: Biography of Eusebio Francisco Kino.* 1936 NY. 1st ed. VG $35.00

BOLTON, Robert. *History of Several Towns, Manors, & Patents of Westchester.* 1881 NY. Roper. Ills. maps. 2 vol set. VG $100.00

BOLTON, Robert. *History of the County of Westchester.* 1848 NY. 1st ed. 2 vol set. VG $250.00

BOLTWEED, Lucius M. *Genealogy of Family of Thomas Noble of Westfield, MA.* 1878 Hartford. Ills 1st ed. black cloth. VG $50.00

BOMBAL, Maria Luisa. *New Islands.* 1982 Farrar. 1st Am ed. dj. EX $15.00

BONAPARTE, Louis. *Histoire du Parlement Anglais.* 1820 Paris. VG $20.00

BONAPARTE, M. *Origins of Psychoanalysis: Letters to W. Fliess 1887-1902.* Basic Books. 1st Am ed. 486 p. VG $14.00

BOND, B. *Drusilla & Her Dolls.* 1921 Ills. sgn. 57 p. VG $12.50

BOND, F. *Kodachrome & Ektachrome From All Angles.* 1947 San Francisco. Camera Craft. 3rd ed. 4to. dj. $15.00

BOND, Harold L. *Encyclopedia of Antiques.* 1945 NY. Tudor. Ills. 389 p. $30.00

BOND, James. *America's Number 1 Trophy.* 1950 Portland. sgn. wraps. VG $30.00

BOND, James. *From Out of the Yukon.* 1948 Portland. 1st ed. EX $40.00

BOND, James. *From Out of the Yukon.* 1948 Binfords Mort. Ills. 220 p. maps. dj. VG $27.50

BOND, James. *From Out of the Yukon.* 1948 Portland. Ills. inscr. dj. VG $35.00

BOND, James. *Rifleman in AK.* 1953 private print. Ills 1st ed. inscr. wraps. $22.50

BOND, Nelson. *Exiles of Time.* 1949 Prime Pr. 1st ed. EX $30.00

BOND, P.S. *Engineer in War.* 1916 NY. 1st ed. VG $15.00

BONE, Gavin. *Beowulf: In Modern Verse & Essay.* 1945 Oxford. Blackwell. Ills Bone. VG $12.50

BONE, J. Allen. *Letters to Strongheart.* 1942 241 p. VG $9.00

BONES, J. *TX West of the Pecos.* 1981 TX A&M U Pr. 1st ed. photos. 136 p. dj. EX $25.00

BONI, Ada. *Italian Regional Cooking.* 1969 NY. dj. EX $20.00

BONI, Margaret B. *Fireside Book of Favorite American Songs.* 1952 Simon Schuster. Ills Battaglia. 1st ed. EX $15.00

BONONSIENSI, Montio. *Methodus Medendi.* 1540 Augsburg. tooled full leather. $2250.00

BONTEKOE, Willem Ysbrantsz. *Memorable Description of East Indian Voyage 1618-1625.* 1929 NY. G $10.00

BONWICK, James. *Egyptian Belief & Modern Thought.* 1878 London. 454 p. VG $12.50

BOON, K.G. *Complete Etchings of Rembrandt.* no date. NY. Abrams. Ills. folio. dj. $65.00

BOORER, Michael. *Wildcats.* 1970 Grosset Dunlap. Ills. 159 p. dj. VG $10.00

BOORSTIN, Daniel. *Discoverers.* 1983 Random House. 1st ed. dj. EX $12.50

BOOTH. *In Darkest England.* 1890 NY. 8vo. 316 p. G $40.00

BOOTH. *Witches of Early America.* 1975 238 p. index. VG $7.50

BOOTHROYD, G. *Guns Through the Ages.* 1961 Bonanza. Ills. 190 p. dj. EX $12.50

BOOTHROYD, G. *Handgun.* 1970 Bonanza. Ills. 4to. 564 p. dj. EX $25.00

BORADMAN, Peter. *Shining Mountain.* 1979 London. Travel Book Club. dj. VG $18.00

BORBA DE MORAES, R. *Bibliographia Brasiliana.* 1958 Amsterdam/Rio. 2 vol set. EX $95.00

BORCHARD, Edwin M. *Convicting the Innocent.* 1932 Yale U Pr. fair. $10.00

BORD, J. & C. *Alien Animals: World-Wide Investigation.* 1981 Stackpole. dj. EX $15.00

BORDEN, Lucille Papin. *White Hawthorne.* 1935 NY. 1st ed. inscr. dj. EX $16.00

BORDEN, Spencer. *Arab Horse.* 1906 NY. Ills 1st ed. cloth. VG $50.00

BORDEN, W.C. *Use of Roentgen Ray by US Army in War with Spain.* 1898 WA. presentation. $175.00

BOREL, Emile. *Space & Time.* 1926 London. 1st ed. blue cloth. EX $95.00

BORENIUS, T. *40 London Statues & Public Monuments.* 1926 London. Ills 1st ed. 8vo. $65.00

BORGES & BIOY-CASARES. *Chronicles of Bustos-Donecq.* 1976 NY. 1st Am ed. dj. EX $36.00

BORIE, Lysbeth B. *Poems for Peter Set to Music by Ada Richter.* 1940 Presser Co. Ills Shaffer. 4to. 41 p. VG $20.00

BORLAND, Hal. *Country Editor's Boy.* 1970 Lippincott. 1st ed. 313 p. dj. EX $20.00

BORLAND, Hal. *Hill Country Harvest.* 1967 Lippincott. 2nd print. inscr. dj. VG $15.00

BORLAND, Hal. *Homeland.* no date. Family Bookshelf. 2nd ed. dj. $15.00

BORLAND, Hal. *Sundial of the Seasons.* 1964 Lippincott. 350 p. dj. VG $8.00

BORLAND, Hal. *Wapiti Pete.* 1938 NY. 1st ed. dj. G $27.50

BORMANN, Henry H. *Bridges.* 1934 Macmillan. Ills. 4to. 79 p. cloth. $20.00

BORN, Max. *La Constitution de la Matiere.* 1922 Paris. 81 p. wraps. VG $35.00

BORN, Max. *My Life & My Views.* 1968 NY. Scribner. 1st Am ed. 216 p. dj. VG $12.00

BORN, Max. *Physics in My Generation.* 1956 London. Pergamon. 1st ed. 232 p. xl. $20.00

BORNSTEIN, M. *Instruction in Use of Dumb Bells & Indian Clubs.* 1879 NY. Ills. 16mo. 128 p. $30.00

BORROW, George. *Lavengro.* 1936 London. Ltd Ed Club. 2 vol set. EX $100.00

BORUP, G. *Tenderfoot with Peary.* 1911 Stokes. Ills. 317 p. VG $20.00

BOSE, Sir Jagadis C. *Plant Autographs & Their Revelations.* 1927 NY. Ills 1st ed. $25.00

BOSE & HALDAR. *Tantras.* 1981 Calcutta. 3rd ed. $11.50

BOSSE, Malcolm. *Fire in Heaven.* 1985 Simon. 1st ed. sgn. dj. EX $30.00

BOSSERT, Helmuth T. *Das Ornamentwerk.* 1937 Berlin. folio. 120 plts. VG $65.00

BOSSERT, Helmuth T. *Encyclopedia of Color Decorations.* 1928 London. Ills. xl. VG $75.00

BOSSERT, Helmuth T. *Folk Art of Europe.* 1953 NY. Praeger. Ills. dj. $125.00

BOSSERT, Helmuth T. *Peasant Art of Europe & Asia.* 1959 Praeger. Ills. 4to. cloth. dj. VG $35.00

BOSTOCK, Frank C. *Training of Wild Animals.* 1903 NY. Ills. 256 p. red cloth. VG $45.00

BOSWELL, George C. *Litchfield Book of Days.* 1900 CT. Shumway. VG $20.00

BOSWELL, Harriet A. *Master Guide to Psychism.* 1969 Parker Pub. dj. EX $6.00

BOSWELL, James. *Boswell in Holland.* 1952 NY. 1st ed. sgn. dj. EX $18.00

BOSWELL, James. *Life of Samuel Johnson.* 1901 Dent. Ills Railton. 466 p. EX $100.00

BOSWELL, James. *London Journal.* 1950 NY. 1st ed. dj. EX $16.00

BOSWELL, P. *Modern American Painting.* 1940 NY. folio. dj. EX $28.00

BOSWORTH, A.R. *New Country.* 1962 Harper. Ills 1st ed. 334 p. dj. VG $7.00

BOSWORTH, Sheila. *Almost Innocent.* 1984 Simon Schuster. 1st ed. dj. EX $16.00

BOSWORTH, W.; & GENTHE, A. *Gardens of Kijkuit.* 1919 no place. private print. 1st ed. 4to. $195.00

BOSWORTH, Welles. *Altoviti Aphrodite.* 1920 private print. xl. G $35.00

BOSWORTH & TOLLER. *Anglo-Saxon Dictionary Supplement.* 1955 cloth. dj. xl. $60.00

BOTKIN. *Sidewalks of America.* 1954 Indianapolis. 1st ed. 8vo. 506 p. dj. VG $16.00

BOTTA, Charles. *History of the War of Independence of USA.* 1842 New Haven. 8vo. 2 vol set. EX $125.00

BOTTA, Charles. *History of the War of Independence of USA.* 1840 New Haven. Ills 4th ed. 2 vol set. G $75.00

BOTTOMLEY, Gordon. *Grauch & Britain's Daughter: 2 Plays.* 1922 London. VG $8.00

BOTTOMLEY, Julia. *Complete Course in Millinery.* 1919 NY. VG $20.00

BOTTONE, S.R. *Electric Bells & All About Them.* 1901 London. Whittaker. Revised 6th ed. VG $20.00

BOUBNOFF, S. *Institut d'Hygiene de l'Univrseite Imperiale de Moscou.* 1897 Kouchnereff. Ills. French text. wraps. VG $20.00

BOUCHARD, Georges. *Other Days, Other Ways: Silhouettes of Past French Canada.* 1928 Montreal/NY. 8vo. VG $22.00

BOUCHER, Francois. *20,000 Years of Fashion.* 1966 NY. Abrams. 1st ed. dj. VG $60.00

BOUCHER, John N. *William Kelly: True History of Bessemer Process.* 1924 private print. EX $17.50

BOUCHER, Louis. *La Salpetriere: Son Histoire de 1656-1790.* 1883 Paris. Siecle. wraps. G $20.00

BOUCHET, L. *Interieurs au Salon des Artistes Decorateurs.* 1929 Paris. Ills Pouchoir. VG $90.00

BOUGHAN, R.B. *Shotgun Ballistics for Hunters.* 1965 Barnes. Ills. 157 p. dj. EX $12.50

BOUGHTON, George H. *Sketching Rambles in Holland.* 1885 NY. Harper. Ills author/EA Abbey. 1st ed. $50.00

BOULENGER, E.G. *British Angler's Natural History.* 1946 Collins. 48 p. dj. VG $5.00

BOULESTIN, X.M. *Finer Cooking.* 1937 London. 1st ed. VG $20.00

BOULLE, Pierre. *Bridge Over the River Kwai.* 1954 Vanguard. 1st Am ed. dj. EX $40.00

BOULLE, Pierre. *Garden on the Moon.* 1965 Vanguard. 1st Am ed. dj. EX $20.00

BOULLE, Pierre. *Good Leviathan.* 1978 Vanguard. 1st Am ed. dj. EX $15.00

BOULLE, Pierre. *Photographer.* 1967 Vanguard. 1st Am ed. dj. EX $15.00

BOULLE, Pierre. *Planet of the Apes.* 1963 NY. 1st ed. dj. EX $25.00

BOULTON, Laura. *Music Hunter.* 1969 Garden City. Ills 1st ed. VG $18.00

BOUQUET, A.C. *European Brasses.* 1967 NY. Praeger. folio. $37.50

BOURDON, David; & TOMKINS, C. *Christo: Running Fence, Sonoma & Marin Counties, CA.* 1978 NY. Abrams. Ills. oblong folio. slipcase. $150.00

BOURJAILY, Vance. *Now Playing at Canterbury.* 1976 NY. 1st ed. dj. M $12.00

BOURJAILY, Vance. *Now Playing at Canterbury.* 1976 Dial. Review ed. sgn. wraps. EX $150.00

BOURKE, J.G. *Apache Campaign in Sierra Madre.* 1958 NY. Scribner. 128 p. dj. VG $10.00

BOURKE, J.G. *With General Crook in Indian Wars.* 1968 private print. Ills Ltd ed. ½,100. VG $35.00

BOURKE. *Snake Dance of the Moquis of AR.* 1884 NY. 1st ed. scarce. $495.00

BOURKE-WHITE, Margaret. *Dear Fatherland Rest Quietly.* 1946 Simon Schuster. 1st ed. dj. VG $35.00

BOURKE-WHITE, Margaret. *Eyes on Russia.* 1931 NY. 1st ed. dj. VG $60.00

BOURKE-WHITE, Margaret. *Halfway to Freedom.* 1949 NY. 1st ed. inscr. EX $55.00

BOURKE-WHITE, Margaret. *Portrait of Myself.* 1963 NY. 383 p. VG $9.00

BOURKE-WHITE, Margaret. *Shooting the Russian War.* 1942 NY. 1st ed. dj. G $65.00

BOURKE-WHITE, Margaret. *They Called It Purple Heart Valley.* 1944 NY. 1st ed. dj. VG $25.00

BOURKE-WHITE & CALDWELL. *Say Is This the USA?* 1941 NY. 1st ed. VG $25.00

BOURKE-WHITE & CALDWELL. *You Have Seen Their Faces.* 1937 NY. Modern Age Books. 1st ed. dj. $40.00

BOURKE-WHITE & KELLY. *1 Thing Leads to Another.* 1936 Boston/NY. Ills 1st ed. cloth. EX $35.00

BOURLIERE, Francois. *Natural History of Mammals.* 1964 Knopf. Ills. 387 p. dj. EX $10.00

BOURNE, B.F. *Captive in Patagonia.* 1853 Boston. 1st ed. $60.00

BOURNE, Edward G. *Narrative of Career of Hernando de Soto in Conquest of FL.* 1904 NY. 2 vol set. EX $35.00

BOURNON, Fernand. *Blois Chambord et les Chateaux du Blesois.* 1930 Paris. Librarie Renouard. fair. $24.00

BOUTELL, Henry S. *1st Editions of Today & How To Tell Them.* 1939 Berkeley. 3rd ed. 8vo. dj. VG $25.00

BOUTON, Josephine. *Poems for the Children's Hour.* 1962 NY. 363 p. VG $10.00

BOUVIER, Jacqueline. *Some Special Summer.* 1974 Delacorte. 1st ed. dj. EX $12.50

BOVA, Ben. *Star-Crossed.* 1975 Chilton. 1st ed. dj. EX $25.00

BOVEY, Martin. *Whistling Wings.* 1947 Doubleday. Ills 1st ed. 4to. 162 p. VG $20.00

BOVILL, F.W. *Niger Explored.* 1968 Oxford U Pr. Ills 1st ed. 263 p. dj. VG $28.00

BOVIN, M. *Jewelry Making for Schools, Tradesmen, & Craftsmen.* 1952 NY. Ills. 128 p. $15.00

BOVINI, Giusepe. *Ravenna Mosaics.* 1956 Greenwich. Ills. cloth. dj. $65.00

BOWDEN, B.V. *Faster Than Thought.* 1963 London. Pitman. later print. dj. VG $20.00

BOWDITCH, Henry I. *Memoir of Amos Twitchell, M.D.* 1851 Boston. Wilson. 212 p. VG $55.00

BOWEN, Catherine D. *Family Portrait.* 1970 Boston. 1st ed. sgn. dj. VG $10.00

BOWEN, Catherine D. *Temper of a Man.* 1963 245 p. EX $9.00

BOWEN, E. *High Sierra.* 1972 Time Life. photos. map. 184 p. EX $8.00

BOWEN, Elizabeth. *Eva Trout.* 1968 NY. 1st ed. dj. EX $17.00

BOWEN, Elizabeth. *House in Paris.* 1935 NY. later print. inscr. dj. VG $15.00

BOWEN, Elizabeth. *House in Paris.* 1936 NY. 1st Am ed. dj. EX $30.00

BOWEN, Elizabeth. *To the North.* 1952 London. 1st ed. VG $35.00

BOWEN, F.C. *American Sails the Seas.* 1938 NY. Ills 1st ed. 4to. 411 p. $12.50

BOWEN, John. *After the Rain.* 1967 NY. 1st ed. dj. EX $12.00

BOWEN, John. *Scale Model Warships.* 1978 NY. Mayflower Books. 1st Am ed. EX $21.00

BOWEN, W.S.; & NEAL, H.E. *US Secret Service.* 1960 Phil. Ills 1st ed. dj. VG $20.00

BOWEN. *Ivy Gripped the Steps.* 1946 Knopf. 1st ed. dj. EX $50.00

BOWER, B.M. *Heritage of Sioux.* 1916 Boston. 1st ed. 313 p. $35.00

BOWER, T. *Klaus Barbie: Butcher of Lyons.* 1984 Grosset Dunlap. Ills. dj. $12.50

BOWERS, Claude. *Beveridge & the Progressive Era.* 1932 Literary Guild. 1st ed. presentation. dj. VG $35.00

BOWERS, Claude. *Tragic Era After Lincoln.* 1929 Blue Ribbon. G $12.50

BOWERS, Clement G. *Rhododendrons & Azaleas.* 1960 NY. 525 p. dj. EX $25.50

BOWERS, Clement G. *Rhododendrons & Azaleas.* 1936 NY. 1st ed. 1st print. EX $65.00

BOWERS, Clement G. *Rhododendrons & Azaleas.* 1968 Macmillan. 2nd ed. VG $22.50

BOWERS, F. *Japan.* no date. NY. Ills. dj. VG $40.00

BOWIE, R. *When Jesus Was Born.* 1928 NY. Ills Falls. Ltd ed. 1/500. sgns. boxed. EX $25.00

BOWLES, Jane. *Collected Works of Jane Bowles.* 1966 NY. Farrar. 1st Am ed. dj. VG $60.00

BOWLES, Paul. *Let It Come Down.* 1952 Random House. 1st ed. dj. EX $50.00

BOWLES, Paul. *Spider's House.* 1955 1st ed. VG $25.00

BOWLES, Samuel. *Across the Continent: Summer's Journey to Pacific States.* 1865 Springfield. 1st print. fld map. scarce. VG $45.00

BOWLES, Samuel. *Across the Continent: Summer's Journey to Rocky Mountains.* 1866 Springfield. 2nd ed. fld map. leather. VG $55.00

BOWLES, Samuel. *Across the Continent: Summer's Journey to Rocky Mountains.* 1865 Springfield. 1st ed. fld map. EX $75.00

BOWLES, Samuel. *Our New West.* 1869 NY. Deluxe ed. ¾-leather. G $70.00

BOWLES, Samuel. *Our New West.* 1869 NY. Ills. 8vo. 524 p. brown cloth. $40.00

BOWLES, Samuel. *Summer Vacation in Parks & Mountains of CO.* 1869 Springfield. 12mo. 166 p. $85.00

BOWMAN, H.W. *Famous Guns From Famous Collectors.* 1957 Arco. Ills. 143 p. dj. VG $10.00

BOWMAN, Heath. *Death Is Incidental: Story of Revolution.* 1937 NY/Chicago. Ills Stirling Dickinson. dj. $16.50

BOWMAN, S. *Sherman & His Campaigns.* 1865 NY. $20.00

BOWNE, B.P. *Philosophy of Herbert Spencer.* 1874 NY. cloth. EX $45.00

BOY SCOUTS OF AMERICA. *Official Handbook for Boys.* 1911 NY. 12mo. 400 p. cloth. VG $110.00

BOYCE, W.D. *Illustrated South America.* 1912 Rand McNally. Ills. 638 p. map. EX $15.00

BOYCE, W.D. *US & Dependencies.* 1914 Rand McNally. Ills. 638 p. VG $20.00

BOYD, B.M. *Redneck Way of Knowledge.* 1982 NY. 1st ed. dj. EX $10.00

BOYD, E. *Saints & Saint Makers of NM.* 1946 Santa Fe. Laboratory of Anthropology. VG $30.00

BOYD, Ernest. *H.L. Mencken.* 1925 McBride. 2nd print. $25.00

BOYD, James. *Marching On.* 1927 NY. 1st ed. EX $10.00

BOYD, James. *Military & Civil Life of Ulysses S. Grant.* 1885 Ills. 12mo. 734 p. G $26.00

BOYD, James. *Roll River.* 1935 NY. 1st ed. dj. EX $16.00

BOYD, James. *Ulrich Fuetrer's Parzival: Materials & Sources.* 1936 Oxford. Blackwell. 1st ed. VG $30.00

BOYD, Jason. *Recent Indian Wars Under Leadership of Sitting Bull.* 1891 no place. 1st ed. 320 p. $25.00

BOYD, Julian P. *Bibliographical Record.* 1950 Princeton. Ltd ed. presentation. EX $35.00

BOYD, L. *Irvines & Their Kin.* 1908 Chicago. EX $50.00

BOYD, L.A. *Fiord Region of East Greenland.* 1935 Am Geog Soc. Ills. 369 p. slipcase. EX $45.00

BOYD, William. *Good Man in Africa.* 1982 NY. Morrow. Review copy. dj. VG $25.00

BOYER, Rick. *Billingsgate Shoal.* 1982 1st Am ed. sgn. dj. $35.00

BOYER, Rick. *Daisy Ducks.* 1986 1st Am ed. dj. $30.00

BOYER, Rick. *Penny Ferry.* 1984 1st Am ed. dj. $25.00

BOYINGTON, Gregory. *Tonya.* 1960 NY. 1st ed. VG $20.00

BOYLE, C. *Gibraltar Directory & Guide Book.* 1894 Gibralter. Ills 1st ed. red cloth. EX $125.00

BOYLE, E.V. *Story Without an End.* 1874 London. Ills. 4to. gilt cloth. VG $100.00

BOYLE, E.V. *Story Without an End.* 1868 London. Ills. 4to. blue cloth. VG $225.00

BOYLE, Kay. *Long Walk at the San Francisco State.* 1970 Grove. 1st ed. dj. EX $20.00

BOYLE, Kay. *Sea Gull on the Step.* 1955 London. 1st ed. sgn. dj. EX $50.00

BOYLE, Kay. *Short Stories.* 1929 Black Sun. Ltd 1st ed. 1/150. slipcase. $425.00

BOYLE, Kay. *Underground Woman.* 1975 Garden City. 1st ed. dj. M $12.00

BOYLE, Kay. *Words That Must Somehow Be Said.* 1985 London. 1st ed. dj. M $15.00

BOYLE, T.C. *Budding Prospects.* 1984 London. dj. M $14.00

BOYLE, T.C. *Descent of Man.* 1980 London. Gollancz. 1st ed. dj. VG $15.00

BOYLE, T.C. *Water Music.* 1981 Little Brown. 1st ed. dj. EX $20.00

BOYNTON, Capt. Edward C. *History of West Point.* 1863 NY. 1st ed. fld maps. EX $100.00

BOYNTON, W.W. *Early History of Lorain County.* 1876 Elyria. 1st ed. 35 p. wraps. VG $150.00

BOZMAN, John Leeds. *Sketch of History of MD.* 1811 Baltimore. 1st ed. $75.00

BRACE, C.L. *Dangerous Classes of NY.* 1880 NY. VG $20.00

BRACKENRIDGE, H. *Modern Chivalry; or, Adventures of Farrago & O'Regan.* 1846 Ills Darley. 2nd ed. 2 vols in 1. leather. $65.00

BRACKENRIDGE, H. *Views of LA.* 1817 Baltimore. 8vo. $125.00

BRACKENRIDGE, H. *Voyage to Buenos Ayres 1817-1818.* 1820 London. cloth. VG $145.00

BRACKENRIDGE, H. *Voyage to South America 1817-1818.* 1819 Baltimore. 1st ed. 2 vol set. calf. $150.00

BRACKETT, James. *Oration at Dartmouth College on 4th of July, 1805.* 1805 Hanover. 1st ed. wraps. EX $20.00

BRADBURY, Fred. *Carpet Manufacture.* 1904 Halifax. Ills 1st ed. 8vo. 301 p. $100.00

BRADBURY, John. *Fugitives: A Critical Account.* 1958 NC U Pr. 1st ed. dj. EX $20.00

BRADBURY, Ray. *Dark Carnival.* 1948 Hamilton. 1st English ed. dj. VG $225.00

BRADBURY, Ray. *Dark Carnival.* 1947 Arkham House. 1st ed. dj. G $400.00

BRADBURY, Ray. *Death Is a Lonely Business.* 1984 Franklin Mint. 1st ed. sgn. shrinkwrap. EX $50.00

BRADBURY, Ray. *Fahrenheit 451.* 1953 Ballantine. 1st ed. pb. wraps. EX $34.00

BRADBURY, Ray. *Fahrenheit 451.* 1982 Ltd Ed Club. sgn Bradbury/Mugnaini. dj. EX $125.00

BRADBURY, Ray. *Fahrenheit 451.* 1953 Ballantine. 1st ed. Curry D bdg. dj. EX $110.00

BRADBURY, Ray. *Golden Apples of the Sun.* 1953 Doubleday. 1st ed. dj. EX $85.00

BRADBURY, Ray. *Illustrated Man.* 1951 Doubleday. 1st ed. dj. EX $100.00

BRADBURY, Ray. *Love Affair & 2 Poems.* 1982 Lord John Pr. 1st ed. 1/300. sgn. dj. EX $45.00

BRADBURY, Ray. *Love Affair & 2 Poems.* 1982 Lord John Pr. Ills 1st ed. 1/100. sgn. EX $85.00

BRADBURY, Ray. *Machineries of Joy.* 1964 Simon Schuster. 1st ed. dj. EX $100.00

BRADBURY, Ray. *Martian Chronicles.* 1950 NY. dj. G $75.00

BRADBURY, Ray. *Medicine for Melancholy.* 1959 Doubleday. 1st ed. dj. EX $115.00

BRADBURY, Ray. *October Country.* 1955 Ballantine. 1st ed. dj. EX $95.00

BRADBURY, Ray. *S Is for Space.* 1966 Doubleday. 1st ed. dj. VG $60.00

BRADBURY, Ray. *S Is for Space.* 1966 Doubleday. 1st ed. inscr. dj. EX $95.00

BRADBURY, Ray. *Twice 22.* 1966 Doubleday. 1st ed. incr. dj. EX $200.00

BRADFORD, Charles. *Angler's Secret.* 1904 Putnam. Ills 1st ed. 206 p. VG $25.00

BRADFORD, N. *Battles & Leaders of the Civil War.* 1956 Appleton Century. Ills. 626 p. $15.00

BRADFORD, R. *Old Man & His Chillun.* 1928 Harper. VG $15.00

BRADFORD, Richard. *So Far From Heaven.* 1973 Lippincott. Advance proof. EX $20.00

BRADFORD, Roark. *Green Roller.* 1949 NY. Harper. 1st ed. dj. 8vo. EX $15.00

BRADFORD, Roark. *How Come Christmas: Modern Morality.* 1930 NY. Harper. 1st ed. 1/1,400. 8vo. EX $30.00

BRADFORD, Roark. *Let the Band Play Dixie & Other Stories.* 1934 NY. Harper. 1st ed. inscr. 8vo. EX $100.00

BRADFORD, Roark. *Ol' King David an' the Philistine Boys.* 1930 NY. Harper. 1st ed. inscr. 8vo. dj. EX $150.00

BRADFORD, Roark. *3-Headed Angel.* 1937 NY. Harper. 1st ed. inscr. dj. 8vo. EX $125.00

BRADLEY, A.G. *In the March & Borderland of Wales.* 1906 Boston. Ills 1st ed. 430 p. VG $35.00

BRADLEY, C. *Foxhound of 20th Century.* 1914 London. Ills 1st ed. VG $40.00

BRADLEY, C. *Good Sport with Famous Packs 1885-1910.* no date. (1910) London. Ills. 4to. cloth. VG $35.00

BRADLEY, David. *Chaneysville Incident.* 1981 Harper. 1st ed. dj. EX $25.00

BRADLEY, David. *South Street.* 1975 Grossman. 1st ed. dj. EX $85.00

BRADLEY, E.L. & M.M. *Allendale Annals.* 1926 Lake Villa, IL. G $25.00

BRADLEY, M.H. *On the Gorilla Trail.* 1922 Appleton. Ills 1st ed. 270 p. VG $30.00

BRADLEY, M.H. *Trailing the Tiger.* 1929 Appleton. Ills. 246 p. VG $30.00

BRADLEY, M.H. *Trailing the Tiger.* 1929 Appleton. Ills. 246 p. G $12.00

BRADLEY, Marion Z. *Jewel of Arwen.* no date. Baltimore. T-K Graphics. VG $10.00

BRADLEY, Marion Z. *Planet Savers.* Ace. 1st ed. wraps. VG $7.50

BRADLEY, R.T. *Outlaws of the Border.* 1882 St. Louis. Marsh. $40.00

BRADLEY, Van Allen. *Book Collector's Handbook of Values.* 1975 NY. 3rd ed. VG $75.00

BRADLEY, Van Allen. *Book Collector's Handbook of Values.* 1982 NY. Revised 4th ed. sgn. dj. EX $55.00

BRADLEY, Van Allen. *More Gold in Your Attic.* 1962 Ills 2nd print. 415 p. gilt navy cloth. dj. VG $17.50

BRADLEY, W. *Book of Ruth & Book of Esther.* 1897 NY. Russell. 1st ed. EX $175.00

BRADLEY, Willard King. *Inside Secrets of Photoplay Writing.* 1926 NY. 1st ed. dj. EX $27.50

BRADLEY, William. *Singing Carr & Other Song Ballads of Cumberlands.* 1918 NY. Knopf. 1st ed. VG $125.00

BRADNER, Enos. *Northwest Angling.* 1950 Barnes. Ills. 239 p. G $7.50

BRADSHAW, Gillian. *Beacon at Alexandria.* 1986 Houghton. Review ed. wraps. M $8.00

BRADY, Cyrus Townsend. *Border Fights & Fighters.* 1906 NY. Ills. 382 p. cloth. VG $22.50

BRADY, Cyrus Townsend. *Colonial Fights & Fighters.* 1907 NY. Ills. 341 p. maps. cloth. G $17.50

BRADY, Cyrus Townsend. *Northwestern Fighters & Fights.* 1913 NY. VG $20.00

BRADY, Cyrus Townsend. *Recollections of a Missionary in the Great West.* 1900 NY. Ltd ed. 12mo. 200 p. cloth. $45.00

BRADY, John. *Clavis Calendria; or, Compendious Analysis of Calendar.* 1812 London. Ills 2nd ed. 2 vol set. EX $100.00

BRAGDON, Claude. *Arch Lectures.* 1942 NY. 239 p. VG $16.00

BRAGDON, Claude. *Beautiful Necessity: 7 Essays on Theosophy & Architecture.* 1927 NY. Ills 2nd ed. 111 p. VG $35.00

BRAGDON, Claude. *Episodes From an Unwritten History.* 1910 NY. Manas Pr. 2nd English ed. 109 p. VG $25.00

BRAGDON, Claude. *Yoga for You.* 1949 NY. 3rd print. 180 p. VG $30.00

BRAGDON, Claude. *4-Dimensional Vistas.* 1916 NY. Knopf. 1st ed. VG $45.00

BRAGG, David W. *Flight Before Flying.* 1974 NY. Frederick Fell. 1st ed. dj. EX $15.00

BRAGG, W.H. *Relativity & the Electron Theory.* 1915 London. Longman. 1st ed. sgn. 96 p. $65.00

BRAGG, W.H. *Sir William Bragg: Old Trades & New Knowledge.* 1926 London. Bell. 1st ed. inscr/sgn. 226 p. VG $90.00

BRAGG. *Old Savannah Ironwork.* 1957 Savannah. 41 p. wraps. $12.00

BRAID, James. *Golf Guide & How To Play Golf.* c 1910. London. Ills. 12mo. 148 p. wraps. $40.00

BRAINERD, David. *Abridgement of Journal Among the Indians.* 1748 London. 1st English ed. 12mo. calf. VG $200.00

BRAITHWAITE. *Bewitched Parsonage: Story of Brontes.* 1950 NY. 238 p. dj. $17.00

BRAIVE, Michael. *Photography: Social History.* no date. NY. McGraw Hill. 1st Am ed. dj. EX $125.00

BRAKEFIELD, Tom. *Hunting Big Game Trophies: North American Guide.* 1976 Outdoor Life. Ills. 446 p. dj. EX $10.00

BRAMAH, Ernest. *English Farming & Why I Turned It Up.* 1894 London. 1st ed. 8vo. 181 p. EX $150.00

BRAMAH, Ernest. *Kai Lung's Golden Hours.* 1923 Doran. 1st ed. VG $45.00

BRAMAH, Ernest. *Kin Weng & the Miraculous Tusk.* 1941 Birmingham. School of Print. 1st ed. 1/50. $150.00

BRAMMER, William. *Gay Place.* 1961 Boston. Houghton Mifflin. 1st ed. dj. $45.00

BRAMWELL, J. *Hypnotism.* 1956 NY. VG $8.00

BRANAGAN. *Excellency of the Female Character Vindicated.* 1828 Harrisburg. 3rd ed. $225.00

BRANCH. *Hunting of Buffalo.* 1929 NY/London. Ills. dj. EX $40.00

BRAND, John. *Observations on Popular Antiquities of Great Britain.* 1850 London. 12mo. 3 vol set. $50.00

BRAND, Max. *Dionysus in Hades.* 1931 Shakespeare Head. G $75.00

BRAND, Max. *Thunderer.* 1933 Derrydale. Ills Brown. VG $65.00

BRANDBORG, Stewart. *Life History & Management of the Mountain Goat in ID.* 1955 Boise. 1st ed. wraps. EX $10.00

BRANDES, R. *Fontier Military Posts of AZ.* 1960 Globe. 94 p. wraps. VG $10.00

BRANDON, William. *American Heritage Book of Indians.* 1961 no place. Ills. 424 p. dj. VG $15.00

BRANDRETH. *John Gielgud.* 1984 Boston. dj. VG $7.50

BRANDT, Bill. *Literary Britain.* 1951 London. Cassell. 1st ed. green cloth. $70.00

BRANDT, H. *AK Bird Trails.* 1943 Cleveland. 1st ed. VG $100.00

BRANDT, H. *AZ & Its Bird Life.* 1951 Cleveland. Ills. 723 p. VG $45.00

BRANGWYN, Frank. *Girl & the Faun.* 1917 Phil. Lippincott. 4to. 78 p. VG $60.00

BRANN, W.C. *Brann the Iconoclast.* 1911 Waco. 2 vol set. $60.00

BRANNON, George. *Vectis Scenery: Original & Select Views.* 1823 London. Ills 2nd ed. oblong 4to. $100.00

BRATHURST, Bill. *For Julia: Poems.* 1967 Cranium Pr. sgn. $150.00

BRATT, John. *Trails of Yesterday.* 1921 Lincoln. 1st ed. VG $50.00

BRATTON, S.T. *Geography of St. Francis Basin.* 1926 MO U Pr. Ills. maps. pb. EX $10.00

BRAUN, E. *Baker's Book. Vol. I.* 1901 NY. Braun Bath Beach. G $25.00

BRAUN, E. *Grand Canyon of the Living CO.* 1970 Sierra Club. Ills. 144 p. dj. EX $10.00

BRAUN & BRANCHICK. *Thomas H. Benton: America Today Murals.* 1986 NY. Equitable Life Insurance Soc. $18.00

BRAUNE, Charles W. *Atlas of Topographical Anatomy.* 1877 Phil. Ills. 31 plts. VG $50.00

BRAUNFELS, Wolfgang. *Meisterwerke Europaischer Plastik.* 1958 Berlin. Ills. VG $25.00

BRAUTIGAN, Richard. *Dreaming of Babylon.* 1977 Delacorte. 1st ed. dj. EX $20.00

BRAUTIGAN, Richard. *Hawkline Monster.* 1974 Simon. 1st ed. dj. EX $20.00

BRAUTIGAN, Richard. *Sombrero Fallout.* 1976 NY. 1st ed. dj. M $15.00

BRAUTIGAN, Richard. *Tokyo-MT Express.* 1980 NY. Delacorte. 1st ed. dj. EX $15.00

BRAUTIGAN, Richard. *Tokyo-MT Express.* 1979 NY. Ltd 1st ed. 1/350. sgn. EX $50.00

BRAUTIGAN, Richard. *Tokyo-MT Express.* London. 1st ed. dj. EX $8.50

BRAWLEY, B. *Social History of the American Negro.* 1921 NY. 1st ed. VG $25.00

BRAZENDALE & ACETI. *Classic Cars.* 1983 NY. Exeter. Ills. inscr. dj. EX $20.00

BREAKENRIDGE, W. *Helldorado: Bringing Law to the Mesquite.* 1928 Boston. 1st ed. 256 p. VG $25.00

BREAKENRIDGE, W. *Helldorado: Bringing Law to the Mesquite.* 1928 Boston. 1st ed. 256 p. dj. EX $40.00

BREASTED, Jason H. *Oriental Forerunners of Byzantine Painting.* 1924 Chicago U Pr. 4to. black leather. $30.00

BREAZEALE, J.W.M. *Life As It Is; or, Matters & Things in General.* 1842 Knoxville. 256 p. full leather. rebound. $400.00

BRECKENRIDGE, Robert P. *Modern Camouflage.* 1942 NY. Ills 1st ed. $25.00

BREDES, Don. *Hard Feelings.* 1977 Atheneum. 1st ed. dj. EX $20.00

BREDES, Don. *Muldoon.* 1982 Holt. 2nd ed. sgn. dj. EX $30.00

BREDIUS. *Paintings of Rembrandt.* 1936 Vienna. Ills. 4to. VG $20.00

BREESKIN, Adelyn Dohme. *Catalogue Raisonne of Graphic Work of Mary Cassatt.* 1980 WA. Ills. 4to. 190 p. cloth. $45.00

BREIHAN, C.W. *Badmen of the Frontier Days.* 1957 McBride. 1st ed. 315 p. dj. VG $20.00

BREIHAN, C.W. *Complete Authentic Life of Jesse James.* 1953 Fell. Ills 1st ed. 287 p. VG $20.00

BREIHAN, C.W. *Killer Legions of Quantrill.* 1971 Superior. Ills 1st ed. 144 p. EX $20.00

BREIHAN, C.W. *Younger Brothers.* 1961 Naylor. 1st ed. sgn. dj. VG $25.00

BREMER, Fredrika. *Homes of the New World.* 1853 Harper. 1st Am ed. VG $25.00

BREMSER, Ray. *Born Again.* 1985 Santa Barbara. 1st ed. 1/250. 4to wraps. EX $10.00

BRENDAN, Behan. *Brendan Behan's Island.* 1962 Bernard Geis. Ills 1st ed. dj. VG $35.00

BRENNA, A. *Guide to Gustav Vigeland's Sculpture Park.* 1956 Oslo. Ills. pb. wraps. $15.00

BRENNAN, Joseph. *Nightmare Need.* 1964 Sauk City. 1st ed. dj. VG $100.00

BRENNER, Scott. *PA Dutch: Plain & Fancy.* 1957 Stackpole. 1st ed. dj. EX $12.50

BRENNI, Vito J. *Edith Wharton: A Bibliography.* 1966 WV U Lib. 1st ed. 8vo. beige cloth. M $10.00

BRENT, Stuart. *Mr. Toast & the Wooly Mammoth.* 1966 NY. Viking. dj. EX $8.00

BRESLIN, Jimmy. *Gang That Couldn't Shoot Straight.* c 1969. Viking. 1st ed. dj. EX $25.00

BRESLIN, Jimmy. *Gang That Couldn't Shoot Straight.* Taiwan. Pirated ed. dj. EX $10.00

BRESLIN, Jimmy. *How the Good Guys Won.* 1st Am ed. dj. EX $15.00

BRESLIN, Jimmy. *Table Money.* 1986 NY. 1st ed. sgn. dj. M $15.00

BRESS, Helene. *Macrame Book.* 1972 NY. Scribner. Ills. 274 p. dj. $25.00

BRESSON, Henri Cartier. *Decisive Moment.* 1952 NY. dj. $250.00

BRETT, Dorothy. *Lawrence & Brett.* 1974 Ltd New ed. 1/300. sgn. dj. EX $100.00

BRETT, Simon. *Cast in Order of Disappearance.* 1975 1st Am ed. dj. $20.00

BRETT, Simon. *Dead Giveaway.* 1986 Uncorrected proof. wraps. $30.00

BRETT, Simon. *Dead Romantic.* 1986 Uncorrected proof. dj. $30.00

BRETT, Simon. *Dead Side of the Mike.* 1980 1st Am ed. dj. $10.00

BRETT, V. *Phaidon Guide to Pewter.* 1983 NY. Ills. 256 p. $15.00

BRETT, William H. *Indian Tribes of Guiana: Their Condition & Habits.* 1868 London. Bell Daldy. 1st ed. fld map. $125.00

BREWER, D.C. *Conquest of New England by the Immigrant.* 1926 NY. 1st ed. xl. $15.00

BREWER, E. Cobham. *Character Sketches of Romance, Fiction, & Drama.* 1902 Selmar Hess. 4to. VG $80.00

BREWER, J. *Wings in the Meadow.* 1967 Houghton Mifflin. Ills. dj. VG $8.00

BREWER, L. *Love of Books.* 1923 Torch Pr. Ltd ed. 1/300. VG $25.00

BREWER, Luther A. *Marginalia.* 1926 Cedar Rapids. private print. $45.00

BREWER, Reginald. *Delightful Diversion.* 1935 NY. 1st ed. 8vo. VG $20.00

BREWER, Stella. *Chimps of Mount Asserik.* 1978 Knopf. Ills 1st Am ed. 302 p. dj. VG $12.00

BREWER, T. *Wilson's American Ornithology.* 1853 NY. 746 p. cloth. $125.00

BREWER, William. *Up & Down CA.* 1930 Yale. presentation. scarce. EX $110.00

BREWERTON, G.D. *In Buffalo Country.* 1970 private print. Intro D Lavender. 1/1,400. VG $35.00

BREWERTON, G.D. *Incidents of Travel in NM.* 1969 private print. Intro F Egan. 1/1,400. VG $35.00

BREWERTON, G.D. *Overland with Kit Carson.* 1930 NY. Ills 1st ed. 301 p. map. EX $50.00

BREWERTON, G.D. *Ride with Kit Carson Across American Desert & Mountains.* 1969 private print. Intro G Stewart. 1/1,400. VG $35.00

BREWINGTON, M.V. *Ship Carvers of North America.* 1972 Dover. Ills. 173 p. pb. VG $7.00

BREWINGTON, M.V. & Dorothy. *Marine Paintings & Drawings in Peabody Museum.* 1968 Salem, MA. Ills. 4to. dj. VG $100.00

BREWSTER, William. *Concord River.* 1937 Harvard. 1st ed. dj. VG $37.50

BREWSTER, William. *October Farm.* 1936 Cambridge. 1st ed. dj. VG $25.00

BREYER, S. *Guide to Soviet Navy.* 1970 Naval Inst. 8vo. 354 p. dj. VG $15.00

BRIAN, Dennis. *Enchanted Voyager: Life of J.B. Rhine, Parapsychologist.* 1982 367 p. dj. EX $16.00

BRICE, M.M. *Stonewall Brigade Band.* 1967 Verona, VA. gilt red cloth. EX $15.00

BRICKELL, John. *Natural History of NC.* 1743 Dublin. 2 fld plts. fld map. $800.00

BRICKNER, Richard. *Intellectual Functions of Frontal Lobes.* 1936 Macmillan. inscr. dj. EX $15.00

BRIDGE, Ann. *Singing Waters.* 1946 1st ed. VG $10.00

BRIDGE, Ann. *4-Part Setting.* 1939 Boston. 1st ed. dj. EX $10.00

BRIDGE, James H. *Inside History of Carnegie Steel Company.* 1903 NY. Ills. 8vo. ¾-leather. dj. VG $35.00

BRIDGER, A.E. *Man & His Maladies.* 1889 Harper. VG $10.00

BRIDGES, E.L. *Uttermost Part of the Earth.* 1949 Dutton. Ills. 558 p. maps. dj. EX $25.00

BRIDGES, T.C. *Wardens of the Wild.* 1937 Harrap. Ills. 271 p. VG $7.50

BRIDGMAN, F.A. *Winters in Algeria.* 1890 NY. Ills 1st ed. gilt cloth. VG $45.00

BRIDGMAN, G.B. *Constructive Anatomy.* 1920 NY/London. 2nd ed. 8vo. cloth. VG $17.50

BRIDGMAN, G.B. *7 Laws of Folds.* 1942 NY. Pelham. 1st ed. VG $25.00

BRIDGMAN, P.W. *Nature of Some of Our Physical Concepts.* 1952 NY. Philosophical Lib. 1st ed. VG $15.00

BRIDGMAN, P.W. *Physics of High Pressure.* 1952 London. Bell. 3rd ed. xl. VG $20.00

BRIDGMAN, P.W. *Reflections of a Physicist.* 1950 NY. Philosophical Lib. 1st ed. xl. $10.00

BRIDGMAN, P.W. *Way Things Are.* 1969 Cambridge. Harvard U Pr. 3rd print. dj. $10.00

BRIEGER, Gert. *Medical America in 19th Century: Readings From Literature.* 1972 John Hopkins. dj. M $22.50

BRIEGER, L. *Das Aquarell: Seine Geschickte und Seine Meister.* no date. Berlin. 8vo. cloth. VG $15.00

BRIGGS, Asa. *Power of Steam: Illustrated History of World's Steam Age.* 1982 Chicago U Pr. Ills 1st ed. 208 p. wraps. EX $12.00

BRIGGS, Barbara. *Our Friendly Trees.* no date. London. Butterworth Pr. G $25.00

BRIGGS, Barbara. *Some Other Friendly Trees.* no date. London. Butterworth Pr. G $25.00

BRIGGS, Ellis O. *Shots Heard Around World: Ambassador's Hunting Adventures.* 1957 NY. Viking. Ills Freund. dj. VG $6.00

BRIGGS, Loutrel W. *Charleston Gardens.* 1951 SC U Pr. Ills. 4to. 174 p. dj. $35.00

BRIGGS, R. *Father Christmas Goes on Holiday.* 1975 NY. 1st ed. juvenile. dj. EX $10.00

BRIGGS, W. *Without Noise of Arms.* 1976 Northland. Ills 1st ed. 4to. dj. EX $40.00

BRIGHAM, B. *Heaved From the Earth.* 1971 Knopf. 1st ed. inscr. dj. EX $15.00

BRIGHAM, Clarence. *History & Biography of American Newspapers 1690-1820.* 1947 Worcester. 1st ed. 2 vol set. EX $120.00

BRIGHT, Marion Converse. *Early GA Portraits 1715-1870.* 1975 Athens. 1st ed. dj. VG $40.00

BRILL, Frances. *Farm Gardening & Seed Growing.* 1872 Orange Judd. G $25.00

BRILLAT-SAVARIN. *Handbook of Dining; or, Corpulency & Leanness.* 1865 NY. Appleton. 1st Am ed. EX $100.00

BRILLAT-SAVARIN. *Physiology of Taste.* 1926 NY. Boni. 1st ed. dj. EX $75.00

BRIMER, Martin. *3 Essays in History, Religion, & Art of Ancient Egypt.* 1847 Cambridge. 86 p. ¾-leather. G $50.00

BRIN, David. *Postman.* 1985 NY. Bantam. Advance copy. sgn. M $50.00

BRIN, David. *Uplift War.* Phantasia. Ltd 1st ed. sgn. slipcase. M $120.00

BRIN, David. *Uplift War.* 1987 Bloomfield. 1st trade ed. dj. M $22.00

BRINDZE, Ruth. *All About Undersea Exploration.* 1960 Random House. dj. G $18.00

BRINGHAM, Charles S. *Paul Revere's Engravings.* 1969 NY. Atheneum. Revised ed. 4to. dj. $50.00

BRINGHAM, Clarence S. *Journals & Journeymen.* 1950 Phil. 8vo. 114 p. dj. M $18.00

BRININSTOOL, E.A. *Fighting Indian Warriors.* 1953 Stackpole. 1st ed. dj. VG $35.00

BRINK, Andre. *Looking on Darkness.* 1975 Morrow. 1st ed. dj. VG $30.00

BRINK, Andre. *Wall of Plague.* 1984 Summit. 1st Am ed. dj. EX $18.00

BRINK, Carol Ryrie. *All Over Town.* 1929 Macmillan. Ills D Bayley. 1st ed. dj. EX $25.00

BRINK, Carol Ryrie. *Winter Cottage.* 1968 Macmillan. Ills Rocker. 1st ed. 178 p. VG $30.00

BRINLEY, Gordon. *Away in the Canadian Rockies & British Columbia.* 1938 NY. Putnam. Ills 1st ed. red cloth. VG $55.00

BRINNIN, John Malcolm. *Sway of the Grand Saloon: Social History of North Atlantic.* 1971 NY. Ills 1st ed. 599 p. dj. EX $16.00

BRISTER, William. *Needlepoint Catalog.* 1983 Van Nostrand. 2nd ed. cream linen. dj. EX $22.00

BRISTOL, F.M. *Life of Chaplain McCabe.* 1908 Revell. Ills. 416 p. VG $20.00

BRISTOW, Archibald. *Old-Time Tales of Warren County.* 1932 no place. Ills Subscriber ed. 1/250. VG $45.00

BRITTEN, Emma Hardinge. *Art: Magic or Mundane?* 1876 NY. cloth. $30.00

BRITTEN, Evelyn Barrett. *Chronicles of Saratoga.* c 1959. Saratoga Springs. sgn. EX $50.00

BRITTON, Nan. *President's Daughter.* 1927 NY. Elizabeth Ann Guild. 1st ed. $25.00

BRITTON & ROSE. *Cactaceae.* 1963 Dover. 2 vol set. $30.00

BROBECK, Florence. *Best of All Cookbook.* 1950 NY. dj. EX $9.00

BROCK, David. *To Hunt the Fox.* no date. Philadelphia. Ills 1st ed. dj. $20.00

BROCK, Emma. *Beppo.* 1936 Whitman. Ills 1st ed. orange cloth. VG $8.00

BROCK, H.I. *Colonial Churches in VA.* 1930 Dale Pr. Ills Ltd ed. sgn. 95 p. EX $35.00

BROCK, S.E. *Jungle Cowboy.* 1972 Taplinger. Ills. 190 p. dj. EX $15.00

BROCK. *History of Fireworks.* 1949 London. Harrap. 1st ed. dj. VG $35.00

BROCKETT, L.P. *Woman's Work in the Civil War.* 1868 St. Louis/Boston. Ills. $40.00

BROCKMAN, C.F. *Trees of North America.* 1968 Golden Pr. Ills. 280 p. maps. G $6.00

BROCKWAY, T.J. *Essentials of Medical Physics.* 1892 Phil. Saunders. G $16.00

BROCKWELL, Maurice W. *Erasmus, Humanist & Painter: Study of Triptych.* 1918 no place. private print. 1/100. $50.00

BRODATZ & WATSON. *Human Form in Action & Repose: Photographic Handbook.* 1966 NY. 4to. dj. EX $25.00

BRODER, P.J. *Hopi Painting.* 1978 NY. Ills. 4to. sgn. 319 p. dj. EX $50.00

BRODERICK, M. *Concise Dictionary of Egyptian Archaeology.* 1924 London. Methuen. 3rd ed. 16mo. 193 p. $25.00

BRODERICK, M. *Handbook for Travellers in Lower & Upper Egypt.* 1896 London. Murray. 9th ed. maps. VG $25.00

BRODHEAD, L.W. *DE Water Gap.* 1870 Phil. Ills. G $28.00

BRODIE, F. *Devil Drives: Life of Sir Richard Burton.* 1967 Norton. Ills 1st Am ed. 390 p. dj. EX $35.00

BRODIE, F. *No Man Knows My History: Joseph Smith Biography.* 1945 Knopf. Ills 1st ed. 476 p. dj. VG $40.00

BRODIE, F. *Thomas Jefferson: Intimate History.* 1974 Norton. Ills. 594 p. dj. EX $12.00

BRODIE, John. *Open Field.* 1974 Boston. 2nd ed. EX $12.50

BRODIE, S. Dan. *66 Years on CA Gridiron.* 1949 Oakland. Ills 1st ed. 477 p. VG $25.00

BRODTKORB, R. *Flying Free.* 1965 Rand McNally. Ills. 141 p. dj. VG $10.00

BRODY, J.J. *Mimbres Painted Pottery.* 1977 Albuquerque. Ills. biblio. cloth. dj. $40.00

BROM, J.L. *Pitiless Jungle.* 1955 McKay. Ills. 309 p. dj. VG $12.00

BROMBERG, Norbert. *Hitler's Psychopathology.* 1983 International U Pr. dj. EX $15.00

BROMELL, H. *Slightest Distance.* 1974 Boston. 1st ed. dj. EX $10.00

BROMFIELD, Louis. *Animals & Other People.* 1955 Harper. Ills. 272 p. $5.00

BROMFIELD, Louis. *Rains Came.* 1937 NY. sgn. EX $17.50

BROMFIELD, Louis. *Strange Case of Miss Annie Spragg.* 1928 NY. 2nd print. sgn. dj. EX $15.00

BROMFIELD, Louis. *Wild Is the River.* 1941 NY. 1st ed. dj. EX $12.00

BRONAUGH, W.C. *Youngers' Fight for Freedom.* 1906 Columbia. 1st ed. 398 p. VG $40.00

BRONGERSMA, L.D. *To Mountains of Stars.* 1963 Doubleday. 1st ed. 318 p. dj. VG $8.50

BRONIEWSKI, W. *Le Combat la Mort Lee Souvenir 1929-1945.* Varsovie. Ills. French text. G $40.00

BRONSON, B.H. *Traditional Tunes of Child Ballads.* 1966 Princeton. dj. VG $45.00

BRONSON, Edgar B. *Cowboy Life on the Western Plains.* 1910 NY. Ills 1st ed. dj. VG $22.00

BRONSON, Henry. *Medical History & Biography.* 1877 New Haven. Hist Soc. 147 p. VG $15.00

BRONSON, W.S. *Horns & Antlers.* 1942 Harcourt Brace. Ills 1st ed. 143 p. VG $10.00

BRONTE, Charlotte. *Two Tales: Secret & Lily Hart.* 1978 London. Ills 1st ed. 1/300. slipcase. $65.00

BRONTE, Charlotte. *12 Adventurers & Other Stories.* 1925 London. EX $20.00

BRONTE, Emily. *Poems.* 1947 London. Curwen. 1st ed. dj. VG $30.00

BRONTE, Emily. *Wuthering Heights & Jane Eyre.* 1943 Random House. Ills Eichenberg. 2 vols. $15.00

BRONTE, Emily. *Wuthering Heights.* 1946 NY. Ills Eichenberg. dj. VG $25.00

BRONTE, Emily. *Wuthering Heights.* 1931 Random House. Ills 1st trade ed. 4to. 325 p. $17.50

BRONTE, P. *Detroit Murders.* 1948 NY. 1st ed. dj. VG $16.00

BROOKE, Iris. *Dress & Undress: Restoration & 18th Century.* 1958 London. Ills 1st ed. 161 p. dj. EX $25.00

BROOKE, Iris. *English Children's Costume Since 1775.* 1930 Black. 8vo. 87 p. VG $45.00

BROOKE, Iris; & LAVER, James. *English Costume From the 14th Through 19th Centuries.* 1937 NY. Macmillan. 4to. 426 p. VG $35.00

BROOKE, Iris; & LAVER, James. *English Costume of the 19th Century.* 1929 Black. Ills. 8vo. 88 p. VG $32.00

BROOKE, Jocelyn. *Crisis in Bulgaria.* 1956 London. Chatto Windus. 1st ed. dj. VG $25.00

BROOKE, Rupert. *1914 & Other Poems.* 1915 London. 1st ed. 12mo. cloth. scarce. $75.00

BROOKES, John. *Room Outside.* 1970 Viking. 2nd print. 192 p. dj. EX $15.00

BROOKES, R. *New Universal Gazetter of the Known World.* 1847 Boston. Ills. 8vo. 816 p. G $38.00

BROOKESMITH, Peter. *Unexplained.* 1984 London. 5 vol set. M $60.00

BROOKHAUSER, Frank. *Our Philadelphia.* 1957 NY. 1st ed. inscr. dj. VG $20.00

BROOKNER, Anita. *Family & Friends.* 1985 Cape. 1st ed. dj. EX $30.00

BROOKNER, Anita. *Family & Friends.* 1985 Cape. Advance copy. wraps. EX $75.00

BROOKNER, Anita. *Family & Friends.* 1985 London Ltd. 1st ed. 1/250. sgn. EX $90.00

BROOKNER, Anita. *Genius of the Future.* 1971 Phaidon. Ills. dj. VG $10.00

BROOKNER, Anita. *Jacques-Louis David: A Personal Interpretation.* 1974 Oxford U Pr. 1st ed. wraps. scarce. EX $75.00

BROOKS, A.H. *Blazing AK Trails.* 1953 AK U Pr. Ills. 528 p. maps. dj. EX $45.00

BROOKS, A.H. *Mineral Resources of AK.* 1905-1909. WA. GPO. Ills. 5 vol set. EX $75.00

BROOKS, Amy. *Dorothy Dainty at Foam Ridge.* 1918 Boston. 1st ed. VG $10.00

BROOKS, Charles S. *Chimney Pot Papers.* 1919 New Haven. Ills F Endell. 8vo. VG $12.00

BROOKS, Cleanth. *Well-Wrought Urn.* 1947 Reynal Hitchcock. 1st ed. dj. $45.00

BROOKS, G. *Street in Bronzeville.* 1945 NY. 1st ed. dj. EX $175.00

BROOKS, Gwendolyn. *Annie Allen.* 1949 Harper. 1st ed. sgn. VG $50.00

BROOKS, J. *Mt. Meadows Massacre.* 1950 dj. EX $48.00

BROOKS, Jennie. *Under Oxford Trees.* 1911 Cincinnati. EX $22.50

BROOKS, Joe. *Complete Book of Fly Fishing.* 1965 NY. 3rd print. VG $8.50

BROOKS, Joe. *Complete Book of Fly Fishing.* 1958 Outdoor Life. Ills. 352 p. VG $15.00

BROOKS, Joe. *Complete Book of Fly Fishing.* 1972 Outdoor Life. Ills. 405 p. EX $12.50

BROOKS, Joe. *Trout Fishing.* 1972 NY. 1st ed. dj. VG $15.00

BROOKS, Joe. *World of Fishing.* 1964 Van Nostrand. Ills 1st ed. 375 p. EX $15.00

BROOKS, Noah. *1st Across the Continent: Story of Lewis & Clark Expedition.* 1901 NY. map. VG $55.00

BROOKS, R. *Producer.* 1951 NY. 1st ed. dj. EX $15.00

BROOKS, R.; & OLMO, H. *Register of Fruit & Nut Varieties.* c 1920-1950. CA U Pr. green cloth. xl. VG $12.00

BROOKS, S. *Creole.* 1847 London. 1st ed. wraps. dj. EX $18.00

BROOKS, Van Wyck. *Flowering of New England.* 1941 Boston. Merrymount. Ills/sgn Holden. $55.00

BROOKS, Van Wyck. *Flowering of New England.* 1936 NY. 7th print. VG $8.00

BROOKS, Van Wyck. *John Sloan: Painter's Life.* 1955 Dutton. 1st ed. $22.50

BROOKS, Van Wyck. *Sketches in Criticism.* 1932 1st ed. sgn. 306 p. dj. VG $30.00

BROOKS, Van Wyck. *Writer in America.* 1953 NY. 1st ed. dj. EX $12.00

BROOMFIELD, S.S. *Kachalola; or, The Mighty Hunter.* 1931 NY. 1st ed. 310 p. EX $35.00

BROPHY, Brigid. *Black Ship to Hell.* 1962 NY. 1st Am ed. 492 p. dj. EX $17.00

BROPHY, J. *Face of the Nude.* 1968 NY. Ills. 160 p. $32.50

BROSSARD, Chandler. *Raging Joys, Sublime Violations.* 1981 Cherry Valley. 1st ed. inscr. 8vo. wraps. $20.00

BROSSARD, Chandler. *Spanish Scene.* 1968 NY. dj. EX $22.00

BROUGH, Robert B. *Life of Sir John Falstaff.* 1858 London. Ills Cruikshank. rebound. VG $225.00

BROUGHAN, Henry. *Critical & Miscellaneous Writings.* 1841 Phil. 1st Am ed. 2 vol set. EX $60.00

BROUGHTON, George H. *Flower Paintings Through 4 Centuries: Descriptive Catalogue.* 1952 1/500. 4to. 8 plts. G $100.00

BROUGHTON, J. *Thud Ridge.* 1969 NY. 1st ed. dj. VG $22.50

BROUGHTON, T. Alan. *Family Gathering.* 1977 Dutton. 1st ed. dj. EX $20.00

BROUGHTON, T. Alan. *Winter Journey.* 1980 Dutton. 1st ed. sgn. dj. EX $30.00

BROUGHTON. *Hob's Daughter.* 1984 Morrow. 1st ed. sgn. dj. EX $30.00

BROUGHTON. *Horsemaster.* 1981 Dutton. 1st ed. sgn. dj. EX $30.00

BROUN, Heywood. *Our Army at the Front.* 1919 Ills 1st ed. 332 p. VG $25.00

BROUN, Heywood. *Pieces of Hate.* 1922 1st ed. 227 p. VG $20.00

BROUN, Heywood; & LEECH, M. *Anthony Comstock: Roundsman of the Lord.* 1927 NY. Ills 1st ed. blue cloth. VG $20.00

BROWER, C.D. *50 Years Below Zero.* 1948 Dodd Mead. Ills. 310 p. VG $10.00

BROWER, David. *Meaning of Wilderness to Science.* 1960 Sierra Club. Ills. 129 p. dj. VG $8.00

BROWN, A.F. *Lonesomest Doll.* 1928 Ills Rackham. VG $35.00

BROWN, Alec. *Voyage of the Chelyuskin.* 1935 Macmillan. Ills. 325 p. maps. VG $35.00

BROWN, Alexander. *Cabells & Their Kin.* 1895 Boston/NY. 1st ed. 641 p. VG $55.00

BROWN, Beatrice Bradshaw. *Doll's Day.* 1931 Little Brown. Ills BH Brown. 1st ed. VG $30.00

BROWN, Bob. *Complete Book of Cheese.* 1955 NY. 1st ed. dj. EX $10.00

BROWN, C.A. *Wild Flowers of LA & Adjoining States.* 1972 LA U Pr. Ills. 247 p. dj. EX $18.00

BROWN, Christy. *Down All the Days.* 1970 Stein Day. Advance copy. dj. EX $25.00

BROWN, Christy. *Shadow on Summer.* 1875 Stein Day. 1st Am ed. dj. EX $15.00

BROWN, Claude. *Manchild in Promised Land.* 1965 NY. Advance copy. wraps. VG $65.00

BROWN, Colin; & PITTMAN, J. *Songs of Scotland: Collection of 190 Songs.* no date. NY. G $20.00

BROWN, D. *Photographs of American Wilderness.* 1976 NY. Amphoto. Ills. 8vo. dj. EX $25.00

BROWN, D.C. *Yukon Trophy Trails.* 1971 Gray. 213 p. map. dj. EX $27.50

BROWN, D.E. *Grizzly in the Southwest.* 1985 OK U Pr. Ills 1st ed. 274 p. dj. EX $20.00

BROWN, Dee. *Bold Cavaliers.* 1959 Lippincott. Ills 1st ed. 353 p. dj. VG $32.50

BROWN, Dee. *Bury My Heart at Wounded Knee.* 1970 NY. dj. VG $25.00

BROWN, Dee. *Bury My Heart at Wounded Knee.* 1970 NY. later print. dj. VG $10.00

BROWN, Dee. *Fort Phil Kearny: An American Saga.* 1962 NY. Putnam. 1st ed. dj. EX $35.00

BROWN, F.A. *Selected Invertebrate Types.* 1950 Wiley. Ills. 597 p. VG $18.00

BROWN, Frank E. *Roman Architecture.* 1967 NY. Braziller. G $8.00

BROWN, Fredric. *And the Gods Laughed.* 1987 Bloomfield. Ltd ed. 1/475. sgn. dj. M $50.00

BROWN, Fredric. *Compliments of a Fiend.* 1950 NY. Dutton. 1st ed. dj. M $50.00

BROWN, Fredric. *Far Cry.* 1951 1st ed. dj. VG $62.00

BROWN, Fredric. *Paradox Lost.* 1973 Random House. 1st ed. dj. EX $25.00

BROWN, Fredric. *Rogue in Space.* 1957 Dutton. 1st ed. dj. EX $50.00

BROWN, Fredric. *Space on My Hands.* 1951 Shasta. 1st ed. dj. EX $85.00

BROWN, George William. *Statues of Province of Saskatchewan.* 1914 Regina. ¾-leather. $20.00

BROWN, Glenn. *History of the US Capitol.* 1900 WA. 2 vol set. $275.00

BROWN, Harriet Connor. *Grandmother Brown's 100 Years.* October, 1929. Little Brown. G $15.00

BROWN, Harry. *Walk in the Sun.* 1944 NY. 1st ed. dj. EX $15.00

BROWN, Hazel. *Grant Wood & Marvin Cone: Artists of an Era.* 1972 NY. 1st ed. dj. EX $12.50

BROWN, Henry Collins. *From Alley Pond to Rockefeller Center.* 1936 NY. Ills Pyle/Gibson. 1st ed. VG $15.00

BROWN, Henry Collins. *Manual of Old NY.* 1922 private print. Ills. VG $35.00

BROWN, Henry Collins. *Manual of Old NY.* 1927 NY. Ills. $40.00

BROWN, Horatio. *Dalmatia.* 1905 London. Ills Tyndale. 1st ed. VG $12.00

BROWN, J. Moray. *Shikar Sketches with Notes on Indian Field Sports.* 1887 London. Ills 1st ed. dj. VG $20.00

BROWN, J. Wood. *Inquiry into the Life & Legend of Michael Scott.* 1897 London. 281 p. VG $95.00

BROWN, J.P.S. *Jim Kane.* 1970 NY. Dial. dj. EX $30.00

BROWN, Joe David. *Addie Pray.* 1971 Simon Schuster. 1st ed. dj. EX $10.00

BROWN, John Mason. *Art of Playgoing.* 1936 NY. 1st ed. sgn. G $20.00

BROWN, John P. *Old Frontier: Story of Cherokee Indians.* 1938 sgn. VG $90.00

BROWN, Kenneth. *Medchester Club.* 1938 NY. Derrydale. Ills Broadhead. 1/950. 224 p. $95.00

BROWN, Leonard. *American Patriotism.* 1869 Des Moines. 1st ed. 574 p. VG $60.00

BROWN, M.H.; & FELTON, W.R. *Frontier Years.* 1955 Bramhall. Ills. 4to. 272 p. dj. EX $9.00

BROWN, Marcia. *Backbone of the King.* 1966 NY. Ills 1st ed. VG $8.00

BROWN, Marcia. *Blue Jackal.* 1977 NY. Ills 1st ed. VG $15.00

BROWN, Marcia. *Dick Whittington & His CA.* 1950 NY. dj. VG $17.50

BROWN, Marcia. *Flying Carpet.* 1956 NY. Scribner. 1st ed. dj. VG $20.00

BROWN, Margaret W. *Fox Eyes.* 1977 NY. Pantheon. Ills Williams. 36 p. dj. EX $8.50

BROWN, Margaret W. *Streamlined Pig.* Ills K Wiese. 1st ed. 4to. orange cloth. VG $22.00

BROWN, Marion. *San Francisco: Old & New.* 1939 Grabhorn. $95.00

BROWN, Marion. *Southern Cookbook.* 1951 NC U Pr. 2nd print. 388 p. dj. VG $22.50

BROWN, Mark. *Before Barbed Wire.* 1956 NY. 1st ed. dj. VG $25.00

BROWN, Paul. *Daffy Taffy.* 1955 NY. Scribner. Ills 1st ed. 4to. EX $20.00

BROWN, Paul. *Draw Horses.* 1949 NY. dj. G $10.00

BROWN, Paul. *Horses of Destiny.* 1949 NY. Scribner. Ills. 8vo. 186 p. dj. VG $22.50

BROWN, Paul. *Plow Penny Mystery.* 1942 NY. Doubleday Doran. 1st ed. dj. $17.50

BROWN, Paul. *Silver Heels.* 1951 NY. Scribner. 1st ed. 8vo. 126 p. dj. VG $30.00

BROWN, Paul. *Something for Christmas.* 1958 NY. 1st ed. dj. EX $15.00

BROWN, Rita Mae. *Hand That Cradles the Rock.* Diana Pr. 1st ed. scarce. EX $32.00

BROWN, Rita Mae. *In Her Day.* 1976 Plainfield. Daughters Inc. 1st ed. wraps. $15.00

BROWN, Rita Mae. *Sudden Death.* 1983 Bantam. Advance copy. dj. M $20.00

BROWN, Robert. *Researches into Primitive Constellations of Greeks.* 1899 London. 2 vol set. VG $45.00

BROWN, Rosellen. *Autobiography of My Mother.* 1976 Doubleday. 1st ed. dj. EX $30.00

BROWN, Rosellen. *Civil Wars.* 1984 NY. 1st ed. dj. EX $35.00

BROWN, Rosellen. *Cora Fry.* 1977 Norton. sgn. dj. EX $25.00

BROWN, Rosellen. *Street Games.* 1974 Garden City. 1st ed. dj. EX $25.00

BROWN, Rosellen. *Tender Mercies.* 1978 NY. 1st ed. dj. EX $12.00

BROWN, Rosemary. *Immortals by My Side.* 1975 Chicago. 1st ed. dj. M $12.00

BROWN, Rosemary. *Unfinished Symphonies.* 1971 NY. Morrow. 192 p. dj. $5.00

BROWN, S. *Book of 40 Puddings.* 1882 NY. 1st ed. VG $25.00

BROWN, T. Graham. *Brenva.* 1944 London. 1st ed. VG $25.00

BROWN, T.M. *Margaret Bourke-White: Photojournalist.* 1972 Ithaca, NY. Cornell U Pr. 1st ed. dj. VG $50.00

BROWN, T.W. *Sharks: Silent Savages.* 1973 Little Brown. Ills. 134 p. dj. VG $12.00

BROWN, W.H. *On the South African Frontier.* 1899 NY. Ills 1st ed. VG $47.50

BROWN, Walter. *Fables.* 1884 London. Ills Bewick. 4to. VG $20.00

BROWN, William Robinson. *Horse & the Desert.* 1947 NY. Ills. folio. 217 p. VG $275.00

BROWN, William. *Carpenter's Assistant.* 1853 Boston. Ills. 4to. 77 plts. EX $400.00

BROWN & COCHRAN. *History of Dallas County, TX From 1837 to 1887.* 1966 Dallas. Aldredge Book Store. EX $35.00

BROWN & JAMES. *What's in a Name.* 1980 Akron. Ills 1st ed. spiral bdg. VG $6.50

BROWN & PECKHAM. *Henry Dearborn: Revolutionary War Journals 1775-1783.* 1939 Caxton. Ltd ed. 1/360. VG $75.00

BROWNE, D.G. *American Bird Fancier.* 1880 Orange Judd. Ills. 116 p. wraps. VG $30.00

BROWNE, D.G. *American Bird Fancier: Cage & House Birds.* 1860 NY. Saxton Baker. Ills. 120 p. EX $50.00

BROWNE, E.C. *Coming of the Great Queen.* 1888 London. Ills 1st ed. 451 p. VG $37.50

BROWNE, Frances. *Granny's Wonderful Chair & Tales of Fairy Times.* 1916 Dutton. Ills K Pyle. 1st ed. 211 p. VG $70.00

BROWNE, Francis. *Everyday Life of Abraham Lincoln.* 1886 NY. Ills. 747 p. G $20.00

BROWNE, Howard. *Paper Gun.* 1985 Macmillan. dj. EX $35.00

BROWNE, J.R. *Dangerous Journey.* 1972 private print. Intro F Egan. 1/600. VG $35.00

BROWNE, J.R. *Dangerous Journey.* 1950 Palo Alto. 1st ed. dj. EX $25.00

BROWNE, J.R. *Debates in the Convention of CA.* 1850 WA. 1st ed. VG $295.00

BROWNE, J.R. *Explorations in Lower CA.* 1952 Silouettes. reprint. 52 p. pb. VG $10.00

BROWNE, J.R. *Muleback to the Convention.* 1950 San Francisco. Ltd ed. 1/400. VG $50.00

BROWNE, J.R. *Peep at Washoe; or, Sketch of Adventure in VA City.* 1968 private print. Intro O Lewis. 1/1,400. VG $35.00

BROWNE, James. *History of Highlands & Highland Clans.* 1840 Glasgow. Fullarton. 8vo. 4 vol set. VG $42.50

BROWNE, James. *History of Scotland: Its Highlands, Regiments, & Clans.* 1909 Edinburgh. Caledonia ed. 1/1,000. VG $95.00

BROWNE, Junius Henri. *4 Years in Secessia: Adventures Within & Beyond Union Lines.* 1865 Hartford. 8vo. 450 p. VG $35.00

BROWNE, L.F. *J. Ross Browne: His Letters, Journals, & Writings.* 1969 NM U Pr. dj. EX $20.00

BROWNE, Maurice. *Recollections of Rupert Brooke.* 1927 Greene. Ills Ltd 1st ed. 1/510. VG $75.00

BROWNE, Thomas. *Religio Medici.* 1891 London. Green Hill. 24mo. leather. $18.00

BROWNE, Thomas. *Religio Medici.* 1955 London. Cambridge. dj. M $10.00

BROWNELL, Charles De Wolf. *Indian Races of North & South America.* 1853 Boston. Wentworth. 8vo. 640 p. VG $225.00

BROWNELL, F. *Teacher's Guide to Holbrook's School Apparatus.* 1856 1st ed. G $18.00

BROWNELL, L.W. *Natural History with a Camera.* 1942 Boston. dj. VG $20.00

BROWNING, Elizabeth & Robert. *2 Poems.* 1954 London. Chapman Hall. 1st ed. 8vo. EX $225.00

BROWNING, Elizabeth B. *Aurora Leigh.* 1857 NY. 1st Am ed. $20.00

BROWNING, Elizabeth B. *Aurora Leigh.* 1857 London. 3rd ed. 8vo. 403 p. EX $25.00

BROWNING, Elizabeth B. *Cada Guidi Windows.* 1851 London. 1st ed. calf over buckram. VG $55.00

BROWNING, Elizabeth B. *Sonnets From Portuguese.* 1925 San Francisco. 1st ed. sgn Nash. boxed. VG $150.00

BROWNING, Elizabeth B. *Sonnets From Portuguese.* c 1920s. Unwin. Ills Nestore Leoni. 4to. VG $75.00

BROWNING, Robert. *Aristophanes' Apology.* 1876 London. Smith Elder. 1st Am ed. G $40.00

BROWNING, Robert. *Asolando.* 1890 London. Smith. 1st ed. VG $25.00

BROWNING, Robert. *Dramatic Idyls, 2nd Series.* 1880 London. EX $33.00

BROWNING, Robert. *Dramatis Personae.* 1864 Boston. EX $45.00

BROWNING, Robert. *Fifine at the Fair.* 1872 London. Smith. 1st ed. VG $25.00

BROWNING, Robert. *In a Balcony.* 1902 Chicago. Ltd ed. 1/415. VG $100.00

BROWNING, Robert. *Inn Album.* 1875 London. EX $33.00

BROWNING, Robert. *Pied Piper of Hamelin.* 1910 Chicago. Ills Hope Dunlap. 1st print. $27.50

BROWNING, Robert. *Pippa Passes.* 1900 Dodd Mead. Ills Margaret Armstrong. VG $37.50

BROWNING, Robert. *Poetical & Dramatic Works of Robert Browning.* 1887 Boston. 5 of 6 vols. VG $50.00

BROWNING, Robert. *Rabbi Ben Ezra.* 1909 Mosher. Ltd ed. 1/925. EX $25.00

BROWNLOW, Kevin. *Parades Gone By.* 1968 NY. 1st ed. dj. VG $20.00

BROWNLOW, William. *Sketches of Rise & Decline of Secession.* 1862 Phil. 1st ed. EX $40.00

BRUCCOLI, M. *F. Scott Fitzgerald Collector's Handlist.* 1964 Columbus. 1st ed. wraps. $10.00

BRUCE, Florence G. *Lillie of 6-Shooter Junction.* 1946 Naylor. Ltd 1st ed. sgn. dj. EX $25.00

BRUCE, G. *Drummer's & Fifer's Guide.* 1880 NY. Ills. G $17.00

BRUCE, J.C. *Cougar Killer.* 1953 Comet Pr. Ills. inscr/sgn. 172 p. VG $18.50

BRUCE, Mrs. C.G. Kashmir. *Peeps at Many Lands.* 1915 Black. Ills. 12mo. 95 p. G $7.00

BRUCE, Philip A. *Social Life of VA in 17th Century.* 1907 Richmond. Ltd 1st ed. 1/1,000. VG $35.00

BRUCE, R.V. *Lincoln & the Tools of War.* 1956 Bobbs Merrill. Ills 1st ed. 368 p. VG $30.00

BRUCE, S.D. *Horse Breeder's Guide & Handbook.* 1883 Turf Field Farm. 1st ed. 8vo. $65.00

BRUETTE, William. *American Duck, Goose, & Brant Shooting.* 1929 NY. Ills 1st ed. cloth. VG $50.00

BRUETTE, William. *American Duck, Goose, & Brant Shooting.* 1934 Scribner. Ills. 415 p. EX $38.50

BRUETTE, William. *American Duck, Goose, & Brant Shooting.* 1943 Scribner. dj. VG $20.00

BRUMBAUGH, T.B. *Architecture of Middle TN.* 1974 Nashville. 1st ed. dj. EX $20.00

BRUNDAGE, B.C. *Empire of Inca.* 1963 Norman. Ills 1st ed. maps. 396 p. dj. $30.00

BRUNDAGE, Frances. *East of the Sun & West of the Moon.* 1924 Saalfield. Mayflower Series. 248 p. VG $25.00

BRUNHAMMER, Yvonne. *Anglais (Regency).* no date. Paris. Massin. Ills. $42.50

BRUNNER, Bernard. *Face of Night.* 1967 Frederick Fell. 1st ed. dj. xl. $5.00

BRUNNER, D.B. *Indians of Berks County, PA.* 1897 Reading, PA. Revised 2nd ed. 8vo. 255 p. $30.00

BRUNNER, John. *From This Day Forward.* 1972 Doubleday. 1st ed. dj. xl. $5.00

BRUNNER, John. *Plague on Both Your Causes.* 1969 Hodder Stoughton. 1st ed. dj. $7.50

BRUNNER, John. *Sheep Look Up.* 1972 Harper Row. 1st ed. dj. xl. G $6.00

BRUNNER, John. *Stone That Never Came Down.* 1976 New English Library. VG $7.00

BRUNS, Henry P. *Angling Books of the Americas.* 1975 Anglers Pr. 1st ed. 543 p. EX $65.00

BRUNTON, Paul. *Hermit in the Himalayas.* 1939 NY. Ills 2nd ed. 322 p. VG $25.00

BRUNTON, Paul. *Hidden Teachings Beyond Yoga.* 1969 NY. 431 p. dj. EX $22.00

BRUNTON, Paul. *Search in Secret Egypt.* 1936 NY. 287 p. G $17.50

BRUSH, D.H. *Growing Up in Southern IL 1820-1861.* 1944 Donnelley. Ills. 265 p. VG $15.00

BRUSSEL, James A. *Casebook of a Crime Psychiatrist.* 1968 no place. 1st ed. dj. $15.00

BRUST. *I Guarded Kings.* 1936 NY. Hellwin. Ills. 8vo. cloth. VG $12.00

BRUUN, Bertel. *Birds of Europe.* 1971 Golden Pr. Ills. 4to. 321 p. dj. EX $25.00

BRYAN, C.D.B. *National Air & Space Museum.* 1979 NY. Ills 1st ed. folio. dj. VG $35.00

BRYAN, Christopher. *Night of the Wolf.* 1983 Harper Row. 1st ed. dj. VG $15.00

BRYAN, Holme. *Master Drawings in Line.* 1948 Studio. dj. VG $12.00

BRYAN, William A. *Natural History of HI.* 1915 Honolulu. Ills. 4to. 596 p. VG $50.00

BRYAN, William S. *History of Pioneer Families of MO.* 1935 Columbia. Lucas. reprint. 8vo. 569 p. VG $45.00

BRYANT, Sara Cone. *Epaminondas & His Auntie.* 1938 Houghton Mifflin. Ills. 8vo. $20.00

BRYANT, Wilbur. *Blood of Abel.* 1887 Hastings. 1st ed. xl. scarce. VG $165.00

BRYANT, William Cullen. *Fountain & Other Poems.* 1842 NY. presentation. VG $250.00

BRYANT, William Cullen. *Letters of a Traveller.* 1859 NY. 2nd series. brown cloth. G $25.00

BRYANT, William Cullen. *Little People of the Snow.* 1873 Appleton. Ills Fredericks. EX $22.00

BRYANT, William Cullen. *Picturesque America.* 1872 NY. 4to. 2 vol set. full leather. $225.00

BRYANT, William Cullen. *Picturesque America*. 1872 & 1874. Appleton. 4to. 2 vol set. EX $375.00

BRYANT, William Cullen. *Popular History of the US to End of Civil War*. 1885-1886. NY. Ills. 4 vol set. G $150.00

BRYANT, William D. *19th Century Handbook on Manufacture of Liquors*. 1899 Chicago. 12mo. 307 p. $25.00

BRYANT & STRATON. *Counting House Bookkeeping*. 1863 NY/Chicago. Ills. 8vo. 375 p. $35.00

BRYANT. *History of the MN Valley*. 1882 1,016 p. G $125.00

BRYCE, James. *American Commonwealth*. 1889 London. 2nd print. 2 vol set. EX $75.00

BRYDEN, H.A. *Wildlife in South Africa*. 1936 Harrap. 282 p. VG $14.00

BRYERS, Duane. *Bunkhouse Boys From Lazy Daisy Ranch*. 1974 Northland. 1st ed. dj. VG $30.00

BRYSON, B. *20 Miracles of St. Nicholas*. 1950 1st ed. dj. VG $10.00

BUCHAN, John. *Castle Gay*. 1930 Hodder Stoughton. 1st ed. VG $30.00

BUCHAN, John. *Runagates Club*. 1928 Hodder Stoughton. 4th ed. VG $12.00

BUCHAN, Tom. *Dolphins at Cochin*. 1969 Hill. 1st Am ed. dj. EX $12.00

BUCHANAN, Angus. *Out of the World, North of Nigeria*. 1922 Dutton. Ills. 258 p. G $24.00

BUCHANAN, Lamont. *Pictorial History of the Confederacy*. 1959 Crown. Ills. 4to. 288 p. dj. VG $10.00

BUCHANAN-BROWN, J. *Phiz! Illustrator of Dickens' World*. 1978 NY. Ills 1st ed. dj. EX $20.00

BUCHENHOLZ, Bruce. *Doctor in the Zoo*. 1975 David Charles. Ills 1st English ed. dj. EX $14.00

BUCHHEIM, L.G. *Picasso: Pictorial Biography*. 1959 NY. Ills. 146 p. $28.00

BUCHNER, Alexandre. *Les Instruments de Musique Populaires*. 1969 Paris. Grund. Ills. 294 p. dj. $45.00

BUCK, Albert H. *Reference Handbook of Medical Sciences*. c 1885. NY. Williams Wood. 8 vol set. VG $300.00

BUCK, C.D. *Dictionary of Selected Synonyms in Indo-European Languages*. 1965 Chicago. 2nd imp. 1,515 p. EX $50.00

BUCK, Charles Nevelle. *Call of the Cumberlands*. no date. Grosset Dunlap. Photoplay ed. $7.00

BUCK, Daniel. *Indian Outbreaks*. 1965 Minneapolis. dj. VG $10.00

BUCK, Daniel. *Indian Outbreaks*. 1904 Mankato, MN. Ills 1st ed. G $47.50

BUCK, Frank. *Animals Are Like That*. 1939 McBride. Ills. sgn. 240 p. VG $28.00

BUCK, Frank. *Bring 'Em Back Alive*. 1930 Simon Schuster. 1st ed. sgn. EX $25.00

BUCK, Frank. *Fang & Claw*. 1935 NY. 1st ed. dj. VG $27.50

BUCK, J.H. *Old Plate*. 1888 NY. Gorham. Ills 1st ed. 268 p. VG $50.00

BUCK, Pearl S. *All Men Are Brothers*. Ltd Ed Club. 1/1,500. 2 vol set. EX $75.00

BUCK, Pearl S. *All Under Heaven*. 1973 NY. Ltd 1st ed. 1/1,000. sgn. dj. $15.00

BUCK, Pearl S. *Big Fight*. 1964 1st ed. dj. EX $12.50

BUCK, Pearl S. *Dragon Seed*. 1942 NY. 4th imp. inscr. VG $35.00

BUCK, Pearl S. *Good Earth*. no date. Grosset Dunlap. dj. EX $7.00

BUCK, Pearl S. *Kinfolk*. 1949 NY. 1st ed. dj. EX $75.00

BUCKBEE, Edna. *Saga of the Old Tuolumne*. 1935 NY. Pioneer Pr. 1st ed. VG $45.00

BUCKINGHAM, Nash. *Blood Lines: Tales of Shooting & Fishing*. 1947 Putnam. Ills. 192 p. dj. EX $35.00

BUCKINGHAM, Nash. *Shootinest Gentleman & Other Tales*. 1943 Putnam. 222 p. dj. VG $35.00

BUCKINGHAM, Nash. *Tattered Coat*. 1944 Putnam. Ills Fuller. 210 p. VG $37.50

BUCKLE, Richard. *Adventures of a Ballet Critic*. 1953 London. Ills 1st ed. dj. EX $20.00

BUCKLE, Richard. *Jacob Epstein: Sculptor*. 1963 Cleveland. World. $40.00

BUCKLEY, William F. *Marco Polo If You Can*. 1982 Doubleday. 1st ed. dj. EX $15.00

BUCKTON, Catherine M. *Health in the House: 25 Lectures*. 1893 London. 12mo. 207 p. $20.00

BUCKWALD, Art. *Getting High in Government Circles*. 1976 Putnam. 1st ed. cloth. dj. EX $7.00

BUDGE, E.A. Wallis. *Book of Dead: Papyrus of Ani*. 1913 London. Medici. 2 vol set. VG $200.00

BUDGE, E.A. Wallis. *Chronography of Bar Hebraeus*. 1932 Oxford. 4to. 2 vol set. scarce. EX $255.00

BUDGE, E.A. Wallis. *Dwellers of the Nile*. 1891 London. 3rd ed. 206 p. G $20.00

BUDGE, E.A. Wallis. *Egyptian Heaven & Hell: Book of Am-Tuat*. 1925 London. reprint. 3 vols in 1. 232 p. G $25.00

BUDGE, E.A. Wallis. *Egyptian Magic*. 1958 Evanston. Universtiy Books. 234 p. dj. G $15.00

BUDGE, E.A. Wallis. *Literature of the Ancient Egyptians*. 1914 London. 272 p. G $12.00

BUDGE, E.A. Wallis. *Mummy*. 1893 Cambridge. 1st ed. VG $60.00

BUDGE, E.A. Wallis. *Nile: Notes for Travellers in Egypt*. 1890 London. 6th ed. maps. 443 p. G $55.00

BUDGE, E.A. Wallis. *1st Steps in Egyptian*. 1923 London. 2nd imp. VG $30.00

BUECHNER, Frederick. *Long Day's Dying*. 1950 NY. 1st ed. dj. M $58.00

BUECHNER, Frederick. *Love Feast*. 1974 Atheneum. 1st ed. dj. EX $15.00

BUECHNER, Frederick. *Sacred Journey*. 1982 Harper. 1st ed. dj. EX $15.00

BUECHNER, Frederick. *Treasure Hunt*. 1977 Chatto Windus. 1st English ed. dj. EX $15.00

BUECHNER, Thomas S. *Norman Rockwell: Artist & Illustrator*. 1970 NY. Abrams. 1st ed. plts. dj. EX $85.00

BUEL, J.W. *Authorized Pictorial Lives of J.G. Blaine & John A. Logan*. 1884 Ills 1st ed. 502 p. VG $20.00

BUEL, J.W. *Border Outlaws*. 1883 St. Louis. Historical Co. rebound. rare. $125.00

BUEL, J.W. *Younger Brothers; Jessie & Frank James*. 1881 2 vols in 1. rebound. EX $63.00

BUELL, T. *Quiet Warrior*. 1974 Boston. 1st ed. dj. VG $30.00

BUERSCHAPER, Peter. *Arctic Journey*. 1977 Pagurian. cloth. VG $10.00

BUFF, Mary & Conrad. *Kobi: Boy of Switzerland*. 1944 NY. 2nd ed. VG $10.00

BUHLER, Kathryn. *Mount Vernon Silver*. 1957 Mount Vernon. Ills. 8vo. 75 p. wraps. $10.00

BUKOWSKI, Charles. *Barfly*. 1975 Black Sparrow. 1st ed. wraps. M $20.00

BUKOWSKI, Charles. *Factotum*. 1975 Black Sparrow. 1st ed. wraps. EX $15.00

BULAU, Alwin E. *Footprints of Assurance*. 1953 Macmillan. 1st print. dj. VG $20.00

BULEY, R.C. *Old Northwest*. 1940 Bloomington. 2 vol set. G $42.50

BULEY, R.C. *Old Northwest.* 1964 Bloomington. 4th print. 2 vol set. boxed. $45.00

BULFINCH, Thomas. *Age of Fable.* 1857 Boston. presentation. full calf. EX $300.00

BULFINCH, Thomas. *Age of Fable.* 1942 Heritage. VG $8.00

BULFINCH, Thomas. *Age of Fable.* 1942 Heritage. Ills Hayter. 369 p. VG $7.50

BULFORD, M.B. *Genealogy of Bulford Family in America.* 1903 San Francisco. 409 p. VG $100.00

BULL, John. *Birds of the NY Area.* 1964 Harper Row. Ills. 540 p. dj. VG $8.00

BULL, Sara C. *Ole Bull: Memoir with Ole Bull's Violin Notes.* 1986 London. Ills. ¾-leather. VG $55.00

BULLIET, C.J. *Apples & Madonnas: Emotional Experiences in Modern Art.* 1928 Chicago. Covici. 2nd print. 248 p. VG $10.00

BULLIVANT, Cecil. *Home Fun.* 1910 NY. Ills. 8vo. 549 p. $25.00

BULLOCK. *Hitler: Study in Tyranny.* 1964 Harper. Torchbooks. Revised ed. wraps. $6.00

BULLOUGH, W.S. *Evolution of Differentiation.* 1967 Academic Pr. 206 p. dj. EX $18.00

BULTMANN, Bernard. *Oskar Kokoschka.* no date. NY. Abrams. Ills. folio. 132 p. $75.00

BULWER-LYTTON, Edward George. *Pelham; or, Adventures of a Gentleman.* 1828 NY. Harper. 1st Am ed. 8vo. 2 vol set. VG $100.00

BULYGIN & KERENSKY. *Murder of the Romanovs.* 1935 London. VG $50.00

BUMGARDNER, G.B. *American Broadsides.* 1971 Imprint Soc. 1/1,950. folio. boxed. EX $55.00

BUMP, Gardiner. *Ruffed Grouse: Life History, Propagation, & Management.* 1947 Albany. Ills 1st ed. 4to. 915 p. VG $85.00

BUMPUS, John S. *History of English Cathedral Music 1549-1889.* no date. NY. Potts. Ills. fair. $18.00

BUNKER, M.N. *You Wrote It Yourself.* 1939 Ohio. 1st ed. 240 p. VG $22.00

BUNT, Cyril G.E. *Russian Arts From Scyths to Soviets.* 1946 London. Studio. 1st ed. 8vo. 272 p. VG $20.00

BUNYAN, John. *Pilgrim's Progress.* 1972 Charlotte, NC. Ills Frederick/Rhead. VG $25.00

BUNYAN, John. *Pilgrim's Progress.* 1880 London. Ills Barnard. Ltd Deluxe ed. $125.00

BUOLLE. *Marvelous Palace.* 1977 Vanguard. 1st Am ed. dj. EX $15.00

BURBA, George. *Our Bird Friends.* 1908 Outing. Ills. dj. VG $25.00

BURBRIDGE, Claude. *Scruffy: Adventures of Mongrel in Movie Land.* 1937 Hurst Blackett. Ills. G $10.00

BURCH, J.P. *Charles W. Quantrell: True History of His Guerilla Warfare.* 1923 Vega. 1st ed. EX $35.00

BURCHETT, George. *Memoirs of Tattooist.* 1958 NY. 1st Am ed. dj. EX $15.00

BURD, Clara. *Girls' Stories From Dickens.* 1929 Winston. Ills. G $14.00

BURDEN, W. Douglas. *Look To the Wilderness.* 1960 Little Brown. 1st ed. dj. VG $12.50

BURDEN, W. Douglas. *Look To the Wilderness.* 1960 Boston. 1st ed. dj. EX $15.00

BURDETT, Charles. *Life of Kit Carson: Great Western Hunter & Guide.* 1879 Cincinnati. 8vo. cloth. VG $25.00

BURDETT, Charles. *Life of Kit Carson: Great Western Hunter & Guide.* 1886 Phil. Potter. 12mo. $30.00

BURDICK, Arthur J. *Mystic Mid-Region: Deserts of the Southwest.* 1904 NY. 8vo. 237 p. cloth. $125.00

BURGE, C.G. *Encyclopedia of Aviation.* c 1933. London. 4to. 642 p. blue cloth. $65.00

BURGERS, F. *Antique Jewelry & Trinkets.* 1919 London. Ills. 399 p. G $50.00

BURGESS, Anthony. *But Do Blondes Prefer Gentlemen?* 1986 McGraw Hill. 1st Am ed. dj. EX $25.00

BURGESS, Anthony. *Clockwork Testament.* 1975 NY. 1st ed. dj. M $12.00

BURGESS, Anthony. *Coaching Days of England 1750-1850.* 1966 London. Elek. Ills. oblong folio. dj. $95.00

BURGESS, Anthony. *Earthly Powers.* 1980 NY. 1st ed. presentation. dj. M $35.00

BURGESS, Anthony. *End of the World News.* 1982 London. 1st ed. sgn. dj. EX $85.00

BURGESS, Anthony. *Enderby Outside.* 1968 London. 1st ed. dj. EX $45.00

BURGESS, Anthony. *Kingdom of the Wicked.* 1985 NY. 1st ed. sgn. dj. M $18.00

BURGESS, Anthony. *Long Day Wanes.* 1964 NY. 1st ed. dj. EX $15.00

BURGESS, Anthony. *Moses.* 1976 NY. 1st ed. dj. M $12.00

BURGESS, Anthony. *Napoleon Symphony.* 1974 NY. 2nd print. dj. VG $15.00

BURGESS, Anthony. *On Going to Bed.* 1982 London. Ills 1st ed. dj. EX $25.00

BURGESS, Anthony. *Piano Players.* 1986 London. 1st ed. $25.00

BURGESS, Anthony. *Right to an Answer.* 1960 London. 1st ed. dj. VG $85.00

BURGESS, Anthony. *Shorter Finnegan's Wage.* 1967 NY. Viking. dj. VG $25.00

BURGESS, Anthony. *99 Novels.* London. 1st English ed. dj. EX $30.00

BURGESS, Dale. *Just Us Hoosiers.* 1966 Unified College Pr. 1st ed. VG $11.00

BURGESS, Gelett. *Burgess Unabridged.* 1914 NY. Ills 1st ed. $15.00

BURGESS, Gelett. *Goop Song Book.* 1941 Cincinnati. Willis Music Co. 1st ed. EX $30.00

BURGESS, Gelett. *Maxims of Methuselah.* 1907 NY. dj. VG $17.00

BURGESS, Gelett. *More Goops & How Not To Be Them.* 1903 NY. Stokes. Ills. 4to. brown cloth. VG $30.00

BURGESS, L. *Garden Art.* 1981 NY. 192 p. dj. VG $10.00

BURGESS, M. *Royal New Zealand Navy.* 1981 Dunedin. Ills. 128 p. wraps. EX $10.00

BURGESS, Thornton W. *Adventurers of Bobby Coon.* 1920 Little Brown. Ills H Cady. gray cloth. VG $10.00

BURGESS, Thornton W. *Adventures of Old Man Coyote.* 1919 Little Brown. Ills H Cady. gray cloth. VG $10.00

BURGESS, Thornton W. *Adventures of Paddy Beaver.* 1920 Little Brown. Ills H Cady. 16mo. gray cloth. $10.00

BURGESS, Thornton W. *Adventures of Paddy Beaver.* 1917 Little Brown. Ills Cady. 1st ed. 16mo. G $10.00

BURGESS, Thornton W. *Adventures of Peter Cottontail.* 1943 Little Brown. Ills. 8vo. VG $10.00

BURGESS, Thornton W. *Adventures of Prickly Porky.* 1920 Little Brown. Ills H Cady. gray cloth. dj. $20.00

BURGESS, Thornton W. *Adventures of Reddy Fox.* 1914 Little Brown. 1st ed. $25.00

BURGESS, Thornton W. *Adventures of Reddy Fox.* 1944 Little Brown. Ills Cady. 8vo. 94 p. VG $16.00

BURGESS, Thornton W. *Adventures of Sammy Jay.* 1915 Little Brown. 1st ed. VG $10.00

BURGESS, Thornton W. *Adventures of Unc' Billy Possum.* 1919 Little Brown. Ills H Cady. 16mo. gray cloth. $10.00

BURGESS, Thornton W. *Animal World of Thornton Burgess.* 1961 Platt Munk. Ills H Cady. 1st ed. VG $8.50

BURGESS, Thornton W. *At Paddy the Beaver's Pond.* 1950 NY. Bonanza. Ills Harrison Cady. 146 p. dj. $10.50

BURGESS, Thornton W. *Bird Book for Children.* 1922 Little Brown. VG $30.00

BURGESS, Thornton W. *Crooked Little Path.* 1949 Little Brown. Ills Cady. 8vo. red cloth. VG $15.00

BURGESS, Thornton W. *Crooked Little Path.* 1946 Bonanza. reprint. 184 p. dj. VG $10.00

BURGESS, Thornton W. *Longlegs the Heron.* 1927 Little Brown. Ills Cady. 8vo. 207 p. VG $25.00

BURGESS, Thorton W. *Birds You Should Know.* 1933 Little Brown. Ills 1st ed. 256 p. EX $15.00

BURK, Bruce. *Waterfowl Studies.* 1976 Winchester. Ills. 4to. 254 p. dj. EX $17.50

BURK, Dale A. *New Interpretations.* 1960 Western Life. 1st ed. sgn. wraps. EX $20.00

BURK, John N. *Life & Works of Beethoven.* 1943 483 p. VG $12.00

BURKE, Billie. *With a Feather on My Nose.* 1959 NY. 5th print. inscr. VG $30.00

BURKE, Billie. *With a Feather on My Nose.* 1948 Appleton Century. inscr. G $14.00

BURKE, Edmund. *Works of Edmund Burke.* 1866 Boston. Ltd ed. 1/1,000. 2 vol set. VG $450.00

BURKE, J. *Buffalo Bill: Noblest Whiteskin.* 1973 Putnam. Ills. 320 p. dj. VG $15.00

BURKE, John. *Genealogical & Heraldric History of the Commoners.* 1836 London. 4 vols in 2. new cloth. VG $60.00

BURKE, Kenneth. *Poems 1915-1954.* 1955 Los Altos. dj. VG $25.00

BURKE, Thomas. *Song Book of Quong Lee of Limehouse.* 1920 London. Curwen. 1st ed. wraps. VG $30.00

BURKE, Thomas. *Streets of London Through the Centuries.* 1943 London. Batsford. VG $15.00

BURKHALTER. *Gideon Lincecum.* 1965 Austin. TX Pr. inscr. EX $10.00

BURLAND, Brian. *Fall From Aloft.* 1969 Random House. 1st ed. presentation. dj. $100.00

BURLAND, Brian. *Sailor & the Fox.* 1973 NY. Hill Wang. 1st ed. presentation. dj. $20.00

BURLAND, Brian. *Surprise.* 1974 NY. Harper Row. 1st Am ed. presentation. $20.00

BURLAND, Brian. *Undertow.* 1971 Barry Jenkins. 1st ed. presentation. dj. $60.00

BURLAND, Cottie. *Eskimo Art.* 1973 London. Hamlyn. Ills. 4to. 96 p. $20.00

BURLEIGH, T.D. *Birds of ID.* 1972 Caxton. Ills. 467 p. dj. EX $27.50

BURLEIGH, T.D. *GA Birds.* 1958 OK U Pr. Ills 1st ed. 746 p. dj. EX $70.00

BURLEND. *True Picture of Emigration.* 1848 London. Ills. wraps. $425.00

BURLINGAME, H.J. *Leaves From Conjurers' Scrapbooks.* 1891 Chicago. 1st ed. VG $30.00

BURNET, Jacob. *Notes on Early Settlement of Northwest Territory.* 1847 VG $80.00

BURNET, John. *Platonism.* 1928 CA U Pr. 1st ed. 130 p. VG $26.00

BURNETT, C.B. *Captain John Ericsson, Father of the Monitor.* 1960 Vanguard. 255 p. dj. VG $10.00

BURNETT, Charles. *Ear: Its Anatomy, Physiology, & Diseases.* 1884 2nd ed. leather. VG $125.00

BURNETT, Frances Hodgson. *Giovanni & the Other.* 1892 NY. 1st ed. EX $50.00

BURNETT, Frances Hodgson. *Head of the House of Coombe.* 1922 Stokes. G $8.50

BURNETT, Frances Hodgson. *In the Closed Room.* 1904 McClure. Ills JW Smith. 1st ed. 8vo. EX $50.00

BURNETT, Frances Hodgson. *Little Princess.* 1929 NY. Ills Betts. VG $25.00

BURNETT, Frances Hodgson. *Little Princess.* 1963 Lippincott. Ills T Tudor. 4to. 240 p. dj. $18.00

BURNETT, Frances Hodgson. *Racketty-Packetty House.* 1975 Lippincott. 1st ed. 4to. 60 p. red cloth. $17.50

BURNETT, Frances Hodgson. *Sara Crewe.* 1888 NY. Ills 1st ed. $8.00

BURNETT, Frances Hodgson. *Secret Garden.* 1962 Lippincott. Ills T Tudor. 4to. VG $20.00

BURNETT, Frances Hodgson. *Secret Garden.* 1911 Stokes. 1st ed. VG $45.00

BURNETT, J.H. *Fundamentals of Mycology.* 1968 St. Martin. Ills 1st ed. 546 p. dj. EX $30.00

BURNETT, W.R. *Asphalt Jungle.* 1949 NY. 1st ed. dj. EX $50.00

BURNETT, W.R. *Goodhues.* 1934 NY/London. Ills SJ Lankes. VG $12.00

BURNETT, W.R. *Little Caesar.* 1929 NY. 1st ed. EX $85.00

BURNETT, W.R. *Little Ceasar.* 1929 NY. 1st ed. G $40.00

BURNETT, Whit. *This Is My Best.* 1944 Halcyon House. 1,180 p. G $7.50

BURNEY, C. *Dungeon Democracy.* 1946 Duell Sloan. dj. xl. $25.00

BURNFORD, S. *1 Woman's Arctic.* 1973 Little Brown. 234 p. dj. EX $10.00

BURNS, Eugene. *Fresh-Water & Salt-Water Spinning.* 1952 Barnes. Ills 1st ed. 96 p. VG $5.00

BURNS, James Mac Gregor. *Roosevelt: Soldier of Freedom.* 1970 NY. Harcourt Brace Jovanovich. VG $18.00

BURNS, R. *Josephine C. Fox: Traveller, Opera Goer, & Art Collector.* 1973 TX Western Pr. 1st ed. 143 p. dj. $10.00

BURNS, Rex. *Avenging Angel.* 1983 1st Am ed. inscr. dj. $30.00

BURNS, Rex. *Farnsworth Score.* 1977 1st Am ed. dj. $20.00

BURNS, Robert. *Complete Works of Robert Burns.* c 1880. Dumont. 1/1,000. 8vo. 6 vols in 12. $400.00

BURNS, Robert. *Cotter's Saturday Night.* 1905 London. Chatto Windus. Ills Boyd. VG $25.00

BURNS, Robert. *Merry Muses of Caledonia.* no date. private print. 8vo. dj. $20.00

BURNS, Robert. *Poetical Works of Robert Burns.* 1823 Phil. $40.00

BURNS, Robert. *Some Early Editions of Works of Robert Burns.* 1946 Dartmouth. 22 p. wraps. EX $15.00

BURNS, W.N. *Saga of Billy the Kid.* 1926 Grosset Dunlap. reprint. 322 p. VG $10.00

BURNS, W.N. *Tombstone: Iliad of the Southwest.* 1929 Garden City. reprint. 388 p. VG $19.00

BURNS & CRITCHLEY. *H.M.S. Bulwark 1948-1984.* 1986 Liskeard. Ills. 128 p. dj. EX $22.50

BURR, Clincon S. *America's Race Heritage.* 1922 NY. 1st print. G $60.00

BURR & HINTON. *Life of Philip Sheridan.* 1888 Providence. 1st ed. G $22.00

BURRAGE, Charles D. *Favorite Drives Around Gardner.* 1896 Gardner, MA. Ills. VG $20.00

BURRAGE, H.S. *Baptist Hymn Writers & Their Hymns.* 1888 Portland, ME. 4to. 682 p. cloth. VG $35.00

BURRAND, G. *Identification of Firearms & Forensic Ballistics.* 1962 NY. Barnes. 1st Am ed. 217 p. VG $12.50

BURRELL, A. *That's Philadelphia with 2 Ls.* private print. VG $10.00

BURRISS, Eli Edward. *Taboo Magic Spirits.* 1931 NY. 1st ed. 250 p. dj. EX $30.00

BURROUGHS, Edgar Rice. *At the Earth's Core.* 1922 Grosset. reprint. dj. VG $25.00

BURROUGHS, Edgar Rice. *Back to the Stone Age.* 1937 Tarzana. 1st ed. dj. VG $250.00

BURROUGHS, Edgar Rice. *Bandit of Hell's Bend.* 1925 Chicago. 1st ed. VG $100.00

BURROUGHS, Edgar Rice. *Beasts of Tarzan.* 1916 NY. Burt. G $22.50

BURROUGHS, Edgar Rice. *Beasts of Tarzan.* 1916 NY. Burt. dj. VG $27.00

BURROUGHS, Edgar Rice. *Beasts of Tarzan.* 1916 McClurg. 1st ed. VG $40.00

BURROUGHS, Edgar Rice. *Carson of Venus.* 1939 Tarzana. 1st ed. dj. VG $150.00

BURROUGHS, Edgar Rice. *Chessman of Mars.* 1922 McClurg. 1st ed. G $50.00

BURROUGHS, Edgar Rice. *Escape on Venus.* 1946 Tarzana. Ills 1st ed. 347 p. dj. $47.50

BURROUGHS, Edgar Rice. *Fighting Man of Mars.* 1964 Ballantine. 1st print. G $10.00

BURROUGHS, Edgar Rice. *I Am a Barbarian.* 1967 Tarzana. 1st ed. dj. EX $60.00

BURROUGHS, Edgar Rice. *Jewels of Opar.* 1963 Chicago. 1st ed. green cloth. VG $85.00

BURROUGHS, Edgar Rice. *Jungle Girl.* 1933 London. 1st ed. dj. EX $100.00

BURROUGHS, Edgar Rice. *Jungle Tales of Tarzan.* 1919 McClurg. 1st ed. dj. EX $100.00

BURROUGHS, Edgar Rice. *Jungle Tales of Tarzan.* 1919 London. 1st ed. VG $80.00

BURROUGHS, Edgar Rice. *Jungle Tales of Tarzan.* 1919 McClurg. 1st ed. fair. $15.00

BURROUGHS, Edgar Rice. *Jungle Tales of Tarzan.* 1919 Chicago. Ills 1st ed. green cloth. G $35.00

BURROUGHS, Edgar Rice. *Land of Terror.* 1944 Tarzana. 1st ed. blue cloth. VG $70.00

BURROUGHS, Edgar Rice. *Land That Time Forgot.* 1946 NY. Doubleday. dj. M $15.00

BURROUGHS, Edgar Rice. *Lost on Venus.* 1935 Tarzana. 1st ed. G $30.00

BURROUGHS, Edgar Rice. *Mad King.* 1926 Chicago. 1st ed. VG $65.00

BURROUGHS, Edgar Rice. *Mastermind of Mars.* 1928 McClurg. 1st ed. VG $85.00

BURROUGHS, Edgar Rice. *Monster Men.* 1929 McClurg. 1st ed. G $45.00

BURROUGHS, Edgar Rice. *Oakdale Affair & the Rider.* 1937 Burroughs. 1st ed. G $62.50

BURROUGHS, Edgar Rice. *Outlaw of Torn.* 1927 London. 1st ed. dj. VG $75.00

BURROUGHS, Edgar Rice. *Outlaw of Torn.* 1927 McClurg. 1st ed. scarce. VG $125.00

BURROUGHS, Edgar Rice. *Pellicidar.* 1923 McClurg. 1st ed. VG $70.00

BURROUGHS, Edgar Rice. *Pirates of Venus.* 1934 Tarzana. Ills St John. 1st ed. xl. G $35.00

BURROUGHS, Edgar Rice. *Pirates of Venus.* 1934 Tarzana. Ills J Allen St John. 1st ed. $70.00

BURROUGHS, Edgar Rice. *Princess of Mars.* 1917 McClurg. 1st ed. EX $300.00

BURROUGHS, Edgar Rice. *Return of Tarzan.* 1915 NY. Burt. dj. G $40.00

BURROUGHS, Edgar Rice. *Return of Tarzan.* 1915 Chicago. 1st ed. VG $150.00

BURROUGHS, Edgar Rice. *Savage of Pellucidar.* 1963 Canaveral Pr. 1st ed. dj. EX $100.00

BURROUGHS, Edgar Rice. *Son of Tarzan.* 1941 Grosset Dunlap. dj. VG $25.00

BURROUGHS, Edgar Rice. *Son of Tarzan.* 1917 NY. Grosset Dunlap. dj. G $35.00

BURROUGHS, Edgar Rice. *Son of Tarzan.* 1917 Chicago. McClurg. 1st ed. G $40.00

BURROUGHS, Edgar Rice. *Swords of Mars.* 1936 Burroughs. 1st ed. dj. EX $250.00

BURROUGHS, Edgar Rice. *Tarzan & Forbidden City.* 1938 Burroughs. 1st ed. dj. EX $175.00

BURROUGHS, Edgar Rice. *Tarzan & Golden Lion.* 1923 Grosset Dunlap. dj. EX $30.00

BURROUGHS, Edgar Rice. *Tarzan & Jewels of Opar.* 1918 Chicago. McClurg. 1st ed. G $50.00

BURROUGHS, Edgar Rice. *Tarzan & Jewels of Opar.* 1918 NY. Burt. dj. fair. $22.00

BURROUGHS, Edgar Rice. *Tarzan & Jewels of Opar.* 1918 Grosset Dunlap. dj. VG $30.00

BURROUGHS, Edgar Rice. *Tarzan & Leopard Men.* 1935 Burroughs. 1st ed. dj. EX $350.00

BURROUGHS, Edgar Rice. *Tarzan & Madman.* 1964 Canaveral Pr. 1st ed. dj. EX $100.00

BURROUGHS, Edgar Rice. *Tarzan & the Ant Men.* 1925 London. 1st English ed. EX $35.00

BURROUGHS, Edgar Rice. *Tarzan & the Foreign Legion.* 1947 Tarzana. 1st ed. dj. EX $55.00

BURROUGHS, Edgar Rice. *Tarzan at Earth's Core.* 1930 Grosset Dunlap. dj. EX $35.00

BURROUGHS, Edgar Rice. *Tarzan Book No. 1.* 1929 Grosset Dunlap. Ills Harold Foster. G $98.00

BURROUGHS, Edgar Rice. *Tarzan of the Apes.* 1914 Toronto. 1st Canadian ed. VG $300.00

BURROUGHS, Edgar Rice. *Tarzan of the Apes.* 1914 McClurg. 1st ed. EX $850.00

BURROUGHS, Edgar Rice. *Tarzan the Terrible.* c 1940. Grosset Dunlap. dj. VG $25.00

BURROUGHS, Edgar Rice. *Tarzan the Untamed.* 1920 McClurg. 1st ed. EX $75.00

BURROUGHS, Edgar Rice. *Tarzan Triumphant.* 1932 Burroughs. 1st ed. dj. EX $200.00

BURROUGHS, Edgar Rice. *Tarzan Twins.* 1927 Joliet. 1st ed. dj. G $350.00

BURROUGHS, Edgar Rice. *Tarzan's Quest.* 1936 Tarzana. 1st ed. dj. VG $110.00

BURROUGHS, Edgar Rice. *Tarzen Bein Den Affen.* c 1920. Stuttgart. Ills. dj. $100.00

BURROUGHS, Edgar Rice. *Thuvia, Maid of Mars.* 1969 Ballantine. 3rd print. VG $10.00

BURROUGHS, Edgar Rice. *Warlord of Mars.* 1919 McClurg. 1st ed. VG $50.00

BURROUGHS, Edgar Rice. *Wizard of Venus & Pirate Blood.* 1970 NY. 1st ed. VG $15.00

BURROUGHS, John. *Bird & Bough.* 1806 Houghton Mifflin. VG $30.00

BURROUGHS, John. *Riverby.* 1895 Houghton Mifflin. 1st ed. G $10.00

BURROUGHS, John. *Squirrels & Other Furbearers.* 1900 Boston. Houghton Mifflin. Ills. 8vo. $15.00

BURROUGHS, John. *Writings of John Burroughs.* 1904-1922. Houghton Mifflin. 23 vol set. $235.00

BURROUGHS, Paul. *Southern Antiques.* c 1957. NY. dj. VG $25.00

BURROUGHS, William. *Adding Machine.* 1986 Seaver. 1st Am ed. dj. EX $17.00

BURROUGHS, William. *Adding Machine.* 1985 Holt. Uncorrected proof. wraps. VG $50.00

BURROUGHS, William. *Dead Star.* 1969 San Francisco. 1st ed. EX $15.00

BURROUGHS, William. *Dr. Benway.* 1979 Santa Barbara. Ltd ed. 1/150. dj. M $75.00

BURROUGHS, William. *Exterminator.* 1973 Viking. 1st ed. dj. VG $20.00

BURROUGHS, William. *Exterminator.* 1973 NY. 1st ed. dj. EX $65.00

BURROUGHS, William. *Naked Lunch.* 1959 NY. 1st ed. 1st print. dj. EX $75.00

BURROUGHS, William. *Naked Lunch.* 25th Anniversery ed. 1/500. M $75.00

BURROUGHS, William. *Place of Dead Roads.* 1983 NY. 1st ed. dj. EX $10.00

BURROUGHS, William. *Queer.* 1985 London. 1st ed. dj. M $30.00

BURROUGHS, William. *Soft Machine.* 1961 Paris. Olympia. 1st ed. wraps. dj. VG $75.00

BURROUGHS, William. *Speed.* 1970 NY. 1st ed. wraps. rare. EX $45.00

BURROUGHS, William. *Speed.* 1981 NY. 1st HrdCvr ed. dj. EX $25.00

BURROUGHS, William. *Ticket That Exploded.* 1967 Grove. 1st ed. dj. EX $20.00

BURROUGHS, William. *Ticket That Exploded.* 1963 Paris. Olympia. 2nd ed. wraps. dj. VG $35.00

BURROUGHS, William. *Wild Boys.* 1971 NY. 1st ed. dj. EX $12.00

BURROWAY, Janet. *Dancer From Dance.* 1965 London. Faber. 1st ed. dj. VG $50.00

BURROWS, E.H. *Capt. Owen of the African Survey 1774-1857.* 1979 Balkema. 1st ed. dj. EX $15.00

BURROWS, George. *Gentleman Charles: History of Fox Hunting.* 1951 Vinton. 1st ed. dj. EX $15.00

BURROWS, Guy. *Curse of Central Africa.* 1903 London. $95.00

BURROWS, Millar. *Dead Sea Scrolls.* 1956 NY. VG $12.00

BURRUS. *Kino's Plan for Development of Pimeria Alta, AZ & Upper CA.* 1961 Tucson. Ltd 1st ed. 1/500. EX $75.00

BURT, Calvin C. *Egyptian Masonic History of Original & Unabridged Ancients.* 1879 Utica, NY. G $30.00

BURT, O.W. *American Murder Ballads & Their Stories.* 1958 Oxford U Pr. Ills. 272 p. dj. VG $5.00

BURT, Struthers. *Powder River.* 1938 NY. 1st ed. G $12.00

BURTON, C.L. *Sense of Urgency: Memoirs of a Canadian Merchant.* 1952 Toronto. 1st ed. dj. VG $15.00

BURTON, E. Milby. *Charleston Furniture 1700-1825.* 1955 Charleston. 1st ed. EX $20.00

BURTON, E. Milby. *Thomas Elfe: Charleston Cabinetmaker.* 1970 Charleston Museum. 2nd print. $20.00

BURTON, Eric. *Long-Case Clock.* 1968 NY. Praeger. Ills. 146 p. dj. xl. VG $12.00

BURTON, Isabel. *Life of Sir Richard Burton.* 1893 NY. Appleton. G $40.00

BURTON, J.A. *Birds of the Tropics.* 1973 Bounty. Ills. 4to. 128 p. dj. EX $12.00

BURTON, J.A. *Small Amimals.* no date. Crescent. Ills 1st ed. dj. EX $8.00

BURTON, John Hill. *Book Hunter.* 1863 London. 2nd ed. VG $25.00

BURTON, Maurice & Robert. *Encyclopedia of Insects & Arachnids.* 1984 Finsbury. Ills. 4to. 252 p. dj. EX $24.00

BURTON, Maurice. *Animal Legends.* 1957 Coward McCann. Ills 1st Am ed. 318 p. dj. VG $5.00

BURTON, Maurice. *Encyclopedia of Animal Life.* 1986 Bonanza. Revised ed. 4to. 640 p. dj. EX $40.00

BURTON, Maurice. *Just Like an Animal.* 1978 Scribner. Ills. 215 p. dj. EX $10.00

BURTON, Maurice. *Systematic Dictionary of Mammals of the World.* 1962 Crowell. Ills. 307 p. dj. EX $12.00

BURTON, Miles. *Death Takes a Detour.* 1958 Collins. 1st ed. xl. VG $10.00

BURTON, Miles. *Hardway Diamonds Mystery.* 1930 Mystery League. 1st ed. VG $18.00

BURTON, Miles. *Secret of High Eldersham.* 1931 Mystery League. 1st ed. VG $18.00

BURTON, R.F. *Arabian Nights.* 1886 London. 6 vol set. VG $495.00

BURTON, R.F. *Book of 1,000 Nights & a Night.* private print. Ltd ed. 1/1,000. 17 vol set. $125.00

BURTON, R.F. *Kasidah of Haji Abdu El Yezdi.* 1931 McKay. Ills Pogany. 129 p. folio. EX $75.00

BURTON, R.F. *Lake Regions of Central Africa.* 1860 Harper. Ills 1st Am ed. map. G $100.00

BURTON, R.F. *Letters From Battle Bields of Paraguay.* 1870 London. Tinsley. 1st ed. VG $165.00

BURTON, R.F. *Personal Narrative of Pilgrimage to Medinah & Meccah.* 1856 Putnam. 1st ed. xl. G $75.00

BURTON, R.F. *1st Footsteps in East Africa.* no date. Dent. 16mo. 363 p. VG $6.50

BURTON, R.F. *1st Footsteps in East Africa.* 1896 London. Memorial ed. VG $70.00

BURTON, Robert. *Anatomy of Melancholy.* 1925 London. Ills Kauffer. 1/750. 2 vols. $250.00

BURTON, William. *Josiah Wedgwood & His Pottery.* 1922 NY. Ills. 1/1,500. $50.00

BURTT, Frank. *Cross-Channel & Coastal Paddle Steamers.* 1937 London. Richard Tilling. $41.00

BUSBY, Roger. *Main Line Kill.* 1968 Walker. 1st ed. dj. EX $7.00

BUSCH, Frederick. *Hawkes: Guide to His Fictions.* 1973 Syracuse. 1st ed. dj. EX $25.00

BUSCH, Frederick. *Invisible Mending.* 1984 Godine. Advance copy. wraps. EX $30.00

BUSCH, Frederick. *Sometimes I Live in the Country.* 1986 Godine. 1st ed. dj. EX $16.00

BUSCH, Frederick. *Too Late American Boyhood Blues.* 1984 Boston. 1st ed. sgn. dj. EX $18.00

BUSCH, Niven. *Duel in the Sun.* 1947 Allen. dj. VG $10.00

BUSCH, Niven. *Gentleman From CA.* 1965 Simon. 1st ed. dj. EX $10.00

BUSH, Christopher. *Case of the Counterfeit Colonel.* 1953 Macmillan. dj. VG $15.00

BUSH, Christopher. *Case of the Curious Client.* 1948 Macmillan. 1st ed. VG $15.00

BUSH, Christopher. *Case of the Extra Grave.* 1961 Macmillan. 1st ed. dj. xl. $5.00

BUSH, Christopher. *Dead Man Twice.* 1930 Crime Club. 1st ed. VG $20.00

BUSH, Christopher. *Perfect Murder Case.* no date. Grosset Dunlap. xl. $6.00

BUSH, Martin H. *Ben Shahn: Passion of Sacco & Vazetti.* 1968 Syracuse U Pr. Ills. 4to. 87 p. dj. $45.00

BUSH & WAUGH. *Character Analysis: How To Read People at Sight.* 1925 Chicago. 624 p. VG $35.00

BUSH-BROWN, Albert. *Louis Sullivan.* 1960 NY. Braziller. G $25.00

BUSHNELL, D.I. *Choctaw of LA.* 1909 GPO. $35.00

BUSHNELL, D.I. *Villages of the Algonquin, Siouan, & Caddoan Tribes.* 1922 WA. 211 p. VG $20.00

BUSHNELL, David J. *Choctaw of Bayou Lacomb St. Tammony Parish, LA.* 1909 Smithsonian. 8vo. VG $25.00

BUSHNELL, George Herbert. *Sir Richard Grenville: Turbulent Life of Hero.* 1936 London. 341 p. VG $27.00

BUSSETM, H.G.P. *Ship Ahoy!* no date. Liverpool. VG $25.00

BUTLER, Alfred. *Ancient Coptic Churches of Egypt.* 1884 Oxford. Ills. 2 vol set. scarce. VG $235.00

BUTLER, B.H. *Old Bethesda at Head of Rockfish.* 1933 NY. wraps. EX $8.00

BUTLER, Benjamin F. *Butler's Book.* 1892 Ills 1st ed. 8vo. 1,154 p. G $25.00

BUTLER, D.F. *US Firearms: 1st Century 1776-1876.* 1971 Winchester. Ills. 4to. dj. EX $17.50

BUTLER, George P. *School English.* 1919 Am Book Co. $2.00

BUTLER, H.E. *Goal of Life; or, Science & Revelation.* 1926 CA. Eso Pub. 2nd ed. 363 p. EX $22.00

BUTLER, Jack. *Hawk Bumbo.* 1982 August House. 1st ed. pb. wraps. EX $20.00

BUTLER, Jack. *Kid Who Wanted To Be a Spaceman.* 1984 August House. 1st ed. sgn. dj. EX $30.00

BUTLER, Jack. *West of Hollywood.* 1980 August House. 1st ed. sgn. dj. EX $30.00

BUTLER, Joseph T. *Candle Holders in America 1650-1900.* 1967 NY. Bonanza. dj. $32.50

BUTLER, Joseph T. *Candle Holders in America 1650-1900.* 1967 NY. Crown. Ills. 178 p. dj. $35.00

BUTLER, Margaret Manor. *Lakewood Story.* 1949 NY. Ills 1st ed. sgn. 271 p. VG $15.00

BUTLER, Octavia E. *Wild Seed.* 1980 Doubleday. 1st ed. dj. EX $30.00

BUTLER, Robert Olen. *On Distant Ground.* 1985 Knopf. 1st ed. dj. EX $15.00

BUTLER, Robert Olen. *Wabash.* 1987 Knopf. 1st ed. dj. EX $16.00

BUTLER, Samuel. *Atlas of Ancient Geography.* 1838 Phil. 21 plts. $115.00

BUTLER, Samuel. *Erewhon.* 1931 NY. Chesire. Ills Tomlinson. 1/1,200. VG $35.00

BUTLER, Samuel. *Erewhon; or, Over the Range.* 1917 Dutton. VG $20.00

BUTLER, Samuel. *Hudibras.* 1806 NY. Troy. 1st Am ed. 296 p. leather. EX $60.00

BUTLER, Samuel. *Way of All Flesh.* 1936 NY. Ltd ed. 1/1,500. 8vo. 2 vol set. VG $75.00

BUTLER, William. *Personal Reminiscences of India.* 1872 NY. Ills. map. gilt cloth. VG $25.00

BUTRES, Julia. *Rhythm of the Redman.* 1930 NY. Ills 1st ed. 8vo. dj. VG $30.00

BUTT, Archie. *Intimate Letters of Archie Butt: Military Aide.* 1930 NY. 1st ed. 2 vol set. EX $25.00

BUTT, G. Baseden. *Madame Blavatsky.* 1925 Phil. 268 p. fair. $35.00

BUTTERFIELD, C.W. *Historical Account of Expedition Against Sandusky.* 1873 Cincinnati. VG $125.00

BUTTERFIELD, Consul. *History of Seneca County, OH.* 1848 Sandusky. VG $90.00

BUTTERFIELD, Roger. *American Past: History of US From Concord to Hiroshima.* 1947 Simon Schuster. $30.00

BUTTERWORTH, Hezekiah. *Log Schoolhouse on Columbia.* 1890 NY. 1st ed. EX $30.00

BUTTERWORTH, Hezekiah. *Log Schoolhouse on Columbia.* 1901 Appleton. Ills 3rd ed. $12.50

BUTTERWORTH, John. *New Concordance & Dictionary to Holy Scriptures.* 1811 Phil. 4to. calf. $60.00

BUTTERWORTH, Michael. *Virgin on the Rocks.* 1985 Crime Club. 1st ed. dj. VG $13.00

BUXTORFI, Johannis. *Synagoga Judaica.* 1641 Basil. 8vo. 498 p. vellum. G $225.00

BUZZACOTT. *Complete Hunters, Trappers, & Campers' Library.* 1913 Milwaukee. VG $45.00

BYLES, Marie B. *Paths to Inner Calm.* 1965 208 p. dj. VG $18.00

BYLINSKY, Gene. *Life in Darwin's Universe.* 1981 Doubleday. 1st ed. dj. EX $10.00

BYNE, Mildred Stapley. *Sculptured Capital in Spain.* 1926 NY. Ills. VG $55.00

BYNNER, W. *New World.* 1915 NY. 1st ed. VG $12.00

BYNUM & JONES. *Biscailuz: Sheriff of New West.* 1950 NY. Intro ES Gardner. Ills. dj. $5.00

BYRD, C.K. *Bibliography of IL Imprints 1814-1858.* 1966 Chicago. dj. VG $40.00

BYRD, Richard E. *Discovery.* 1935 Putnam. 1st ed. 8vo. gilt blue cloth. $17.50

BYRD, Richard E. *Into the Home of the Blizzard.* 1928 private print. 1st ed. 1/1,000. 4to. EX $100.00

BYRD, Richard E. *Little America.* 1930 NY. 1st ed. sgn. VG $65.00

BYRD, Richard E. *Little America.* 1930 Putnam. Ltd ed. 1/1,000. sgn. $125.00

BYRD, Richard E. *Little America.* 1930 NY. 2nd ed. EX $20.00

BYRD, Richard E. *Little America.* 1930 NY. 1st ed. presentation. dj. EX $75.00

BYRD. *Skyward.* 1928 Putnam. 359 p. gilt blue cloth. $15.00

BYRNE, B.J. *Frontier Army Surgeon.* 1962 NY. Exposition. Revised 2nd ed. dj. EX $15.00

BYRNE, Donn. *Changling & Other Stories.* 1923 NY. VG $6.00

BYRNE, Donn. *Crusade.* 1928 Sampson Low. xl. $5.50

BYRNE, Donn. *Hangman's House.* no date. Grosset Dunlap. Photoplay ed. $14.00

BYRNE, Donn. *Stories Without Women.* 1931 NY. 1st ed. VG $10.00

BYRNES, Gene. *Regular Fellers.* 1929 NY. 8vo. VG $35.00

BYRNES, Thomas. *Professional Criminals of America.* 1969 Chelsea. reprint of 1886. dj. VG $65.00

BYRON, D. *Firearms Price Guide.* 1977 Crown. Ills. 340 p. wraps. EX $14.00

BYRON, John. *Narrative of John Byron.* 1768 London. Baker. 2nd ed. 257 p. ½-calf. $150.00

BYRON, Lord George. *Giaour.* 1857 Athens. 1st ed. Greek text. VG $185.00

BYRON, Lord George. *Island; or, Christian & His Comrades.* 1823 Phil. 1st Am ed. EX $120.00

BYRON. *Self-Portrait: Letters & Diaries 1798-1824.* 1967 NY. 2 vol set. $30.00

BYTWERK, R.L. *Julius Streicher.* 1983 Stein Day. Ills. dj. VG $15.00

C

CABELL, James Branch. *Ballads From the Hidden Way.* 1928 NY. Crosy Gaige. Ltd ed. 1/831. VG $40.00

CABELL, James Branch. *Beyond Life.* 1919 NY. 1st ed. EX $35.00

CABELL, James Branch. *Figures of Earth.* Ills Pape. 1st ed. 3rd print. VG $45.00

CABELL, James Branch. *Hamlet Had an Uncle.* 1940 NY. 1st ed. dj. EX $25.00

CABELL, James Branch. *Jewel Merchants: Comedy in 1 Act.* 1921 NY. Ltd ed. 1/1,000. VG $35.00

CABELL, James Branch. *Jurgen: Comedy of Justice.* 1921 Ills FC Pape. Ltd ed. 1/3,000. EX $145.00

CABELL, James Branch. *Jurgen: Comedy of Justice.* 1976 Ltd Ed Club. Ills/sgn Burnett. slipcase. EX $50.00

CABELL, James Branch. *Silver Stallion.* 1928 NY. McBride. Ills Pape. 1st ed. 8vo. 359 p. $35.00

CABELL, James Branch. *Smirt.* 1937 NY. 1st ed. dj. EX $30.00

CABELL, James Branch. *Smirt.* 1934 NY. McBride. Ltd 1st ed. 1/153. sgn. EX $100.00

CABELL, James Branch. *Some of Us: Essay in Epitaphs.* 1930 NY. Ltd ed. 1/1,295. sgn. slipcase. VG $35.00

CABELL, James Branch. *Taboo.* 1921 NY. Ltd 1st ed. 1/900. VG $20.00

CABELL, James Branch. *Way of Ecben.* Ills Pape. 1st ed. VG $50.00

CABELL, James Branch. *White Robe, Saint's Summery.* 1928 NY. McBride. Ills Locher. 1st ed. 4to. VG $85.00

CABELL, James Branch. *1st Gentleman of America.* 1942 Farrar Rinehart. 1st ed. dj. $10.00

CABELL, James Branch. *1st Gentlemen of America.* 1942 NY. 1st ed. dj. EX $30.00

CABLE, G.W. *Bonaventure.* 1898 NY. inscr. VG $35.00

CABLE, G.W. *Old Creole Days.* 1943 Heritage. Ills Cosgrave. EX $17.50

CABLE, G.W. *Old Creole Days.* 1879 NY. 1st ed. VG $50.00

CABOT, W.B. *Labrador.* c 1920. Ills. 354 p. G $25.00

CABRERA INFANTE, G. *Tres Tristes Tigres.* 1983 Seix Barral. Spanish text. pb. EX $7.50

CADBY, Carine. *Brownies in Switzerland.* 1924 Macaulay. Ills. 4to. VG $12.00

CADWALLADER, Sylvanus. *3 Years with Grant.* 1955 Knopf. 1st ed. 353 p. maps. dj. VG $15.00

CADY, D.L. *Rhymes of VT Rural Life.* 1923 Rutland. 5th ed. G $8.00

CADY, Jack. *McDowell's Ghost.* 1982 Arbor House. 1st ed. dj. EX $17.50

CAEN, Herbert. *Bagdad by the Bay.* 1950 Garden City. 1st ed. dj. EX $14.00

CAFFIN, C. *Photography As a Fine Art.* 1901 NY. Ills 1st ed. 4to. VG $65.00

CAGE, John. *Silence.* 1961 Wesleyan U Pr. 2nd print. VG $18.00

CAGE, John. *X: Writings 1979-1982.* 1983 Wesleyan U Pr. 1st ed. dj. EX $35.00

CAHALANE, V.H. *Alive in the Wind.* 1970 Prentice Hall. Ills. 244 p. dj. VG $10.00

CAHILL, Holger. *American Folk Art: Art of Common Man in America 1750-1900.* 1932 MOMA/Norton. Ills. 4to. $40.00

CAHILL, Holger. *American Painting & Sculpture 1862-1942.* 1932 NY. MOMA. Ills Ltd ed. 1/2,000. wraps. $40.00

CAHILL, Holger. *Art in America: Complete Survey.* 1935 NY. Reynal Hitchcock. 4to. $30.00

CAHILL, J. *Chinese Painting.* 1960 Skira. Treasures of Asia Series. dj. $55.00

CAHN, Joseph M. *Tennie Weenies' Book: Life & Art of William Donahey.* 1986 La Jolla, CA. Green Tiger. 1st ed. 127 p. M $30.00

CAHOONE, Sarah S. *Visit to Grand-Papa; or, Week at Newport.* 1840 NY. Taylor Dodd. 213 p. fair. $35.00

CAIN, Charles W. *Aircraft in Profile.* 1971 Garden City. Ills. 284 p. dj. xl. G $35.00

CAIN, James M. *Baby in the Icebox.* 1981 NY. 1st ed. dj. M $16.00

CAIN, James M. *Butterfly.* 1947 Knopf. 1st ed. dj. xl. $10.00

CAIN, James M. *For Men Only: Collection of Short Stories.* 1944 Cleveland. Ltd ed. 1/500. VG $40.00

CAIN, James M. *Galatea.* 1953 NY. 1st ed. VG $25.00

CAIN, James M. *Love's Lovely Counterfeit.* 1945 Tower. VG $10.00

CAIN, James M. *Magician's Wife.* 1965 NY. 1st ed. presentation. dj. EX $175.00

CAIN, James M. *Mildred Pierce.* 1945 World. Photoplay ed. $12.00

CAIN, James M. *Moth.* 1948 Knopf. 2nd ed. VG $20.00

CAIN, James M. *Moth.* 1948 NY. 1st ed. dj. VG $25.00

CAIN, James M. *Rainbow's End.* 1975 Mason Charter. 1st ed. dj. xl. $7.00

CAIN, James M. *Serenade.* 1943 Tower. VG $15.00

CAIN, James M. *Serenade.* 1937 NY. 1st ed. EX $20.00

CAIN, James M. *3 of Hearts.* 1949 Robert Hale. VG $25.00

CAINE, Hall. *Christian.* 1896-97. Ills Appleton. G $8.50

CAINE, L.S. *Salt-Water Tackle Digest.* 1947 Paul Richmond. Ills. 128 p. wraps. VG $17.50

CAIRD, Edward. *Critical Philosophy of Immanuel Kant.* 1889 Glasgow. presentation. 2 vol set. VG $45.00

CAIRD, Janet. *Murder Reflected.* 1965 Geoffrey Bles. 1st ed. dj. xl. $7.50

CAIRN, David. *Responses: Musical Essays & Reviews.* 1973 NY. 1st Am ed. dj. EX $10.00

CALDECOTT, M. *Son of the Sun.* 1986 London. 1st ed. dj. M $25.00

CALDECOTT, Randolph. *Frog He Would Go A-Wooing.* no date. Warne. Ills. oblong 8vo. M $10.00

CALDECOTT, Randolph. *Hey Diddle Diddle & Baby Bunting.* no date. Warne. Ills. oblong 8vo. M $10.00

CALDER, Alexander. *Autobiography.* 1966 NY. Pantheon/Random House. 285 p. $75.00

CALDWELL, Dorothy. *Murder on the House.* 1976 Musson. 1st ed. dj. xl. $5.00

CALDWELL, Erskine. *Close To Home.* 1962 London. 1st ed. dj. VG $25.00

CALDWELL, Erskine. *GA Boy.* 1943 Duell Sloan. 1st ed. dj. VG $20.00

CALDWELL, Erskine. *God's Little Acre.* 1948 Falcon. dj. VG $12.50

CALDWELL, Erskine. *Gretta.* 1955 Boston. 1st ed. dj. EX $22.00

CALDWELL, Erskine. *Journeyman.* 1935 NY. Ltd ed. 1/1,475. slipcase. VG $30.00

CALDWELL, Erskine. *Say Is This the USA?* 1941 NY. Ills 1st ed. 4o. VG $40.00

CALDWELL, H.M. *Jingle of a Jap.* c 1910. Boston. Ills CB Thurston. 8vo. EX $25.00

CALDWELL, J.A. *Caldwell's Atlas of Wayne County & City of Wooster, OH.* 1974 Evansville. reprint of 1873. VG $55.00

CALDWELL, R.G. *Red Hannah: DE Whipping Post.* 1947 Phil. Ills 1st ed. 144 p. dj. VG $20.00

CALDWELL, Steven. *Aliens in Space.* 1979 Crescent. dj. EX $7.50

CALDWELL, Steven. *Star Quest.* 1979 Crescent. dj. EX $7.50

CALDWELL, Steven. *Worlds at War.* 1980 Crescent. VG $5.00

CALDWELL, Taylor. *Captains & Kings.* 1972 Doubleday. 1st ed. dj. EX $25.00

CALDWELL, Taylor. *Ceremony of the Innocent.* 1976 Doubleday. 1st ed. dj. EX $10.00

CALDWELL, Taylor. *Dialogues with the Devil.* 1967 Doubleday. 1st ed. $7.00

CALDWELL, Taylor. *Late Clara Beame.* 1963 Crime Club. 1st ed. dj. VG $12.50

CALDWELL, Taylor. *Testimony of 2 Men.* 1968 Doubleday. 1st ed. dj. VG $15.00

CALDWELL, Taylor. *This Side of Innocence.* 1946 NY. 1st ed. VG $5.00

CALHOUN, John C. *Life of John C. Calhoun.* 1843 NY. 554 p. $25.00

CALISHER, Hortense. *Bobby-Soxer.* 1986 Doubleday. 1st ed. dj. EX $18.00

CALISHER, Hortense. *Extreme Magic.* 1964 Little Brown. 1st ed. dj. VG $20.00

CALISHER, Hortense. *Journey From Ellipsia.* 1965 Little Brown. 1st ed. dj. EX $20.00

CALISHER, Hortense. *Keeping Women.* 1977 Arbor House. 1st ed. dj. EX $10.00

CALISHER, Hortense. *Mysteries of Motion.* 1983 Doubleday. Review copy. dj. EX $25.00

CALISHER, Hortense. *Queenie.* 1971 Arbor House. 1st ed. dj. EX $20.00

CALISHER, Hortense. *Railway Police.* 1966 Boston. 1st ed. dj. EX $12.00

CALISHER, Hortense. *Standard Dreaming.* 1972 Arbor House. 1st ed. dj. VG $15.00

CALISHER, Hortense. *Textures of Life.* 1963 Little Brown. 1st ed. dj. EX $25.00

CALKINS, Frank. *Rocky Mountain Warden.* 1971 Knopf. 1st ed. 265 p. dj. VG $16.00

CALLAHAN, North. *Carl Sandburg: Lincoln of Our Literature.* 1970 NY U Pr. 2nd print. $25.00

CALLAHAN, North. *George Washington: Soldier & Man.* 1972 Morrow. Ills. 296 p. dj. EX $10.00

CALLOWAY, Cab. *Of Minnie the Moocher & Me.* 1976 NY. Ills 1st ed. 281 p. dj. VG $17.50

CALMET, Augustin. *Dictionnaire Historique de la Bible.* 1730 Paris. folio. plts. 4 vol set. G $875.00

CALSON, J.R. *Under Cover.* 1943 NY. 8th print. dj. G $10.00

CALTHROP, Dion Clayton. *English Costume.* 1926 London. Black. Ills. 463 p. xl. G $25.00

CALTHROP, Dion Clayton. *English Costume.* 1907 London. Black. Ills. 8vo. 463 p. VG $165.00

CALTHROP & BLACK. *Charm of Gardens.* 1911 London. 1st ed. 32 plts. $22.50

CALVERT, J. *Surface at the Pole.* 1960 1st ed. dj. VG $30.00

CALVIN, John. *Institution of Christian Religion.* 1587 London. 4th ed. rebound. VG $75.00

CALVINO, Italo. *Invisible Cities.* 1974 Harcourt Brace. 1st ed. dj. xl. $7.50

CALVINO, Italo. *Mr. Palomar.* 1985 Harcourt. 1st Am ed. dj. VG $15.00

CALZA, A. *Fausta Vittoria Mengarini.* 1928 Rome. Ills. ¾-red leather. VG $15.00

CAMBELL, Alice. *Veiled Murder.* 1949 Random House. 1st ed. $10.00

CAMBPELL, Alexander. *Millennial Harbinger. Vol. II.* 1831 Bethany, VA. 574 p. leather. G $60.00

CAMDEN, Brittannia. *Choreographical Description.* 1806 London. Ills. 4 vol set. $200.00

CAMDEN, John. *Hundredth Acre.* 1905 Turner. 1st ed. VG $20.00

CAMERON, Berl. *Cosmic Echelon.* 1952 Curtis. dj. VG $8.50

CAMERON, Don. *Dig Another Grave.* 1946 Mystery House. VG $9.00

CAMERON, Don. *White for a Shroud.* no date. Boardman. dj. VG $15.00

CAMERON, Ian. *White Ship.* 1975 NY. 1st ed. dj. EX $15.00

CAMERON, James R. *Motion Picture Projection.* 1928 NY. 4th ed. fair. $18.00

CAMERON, Julia. *Victorian Album.* 1975 NY. Da Capo. $27.50

CAMERON, Julia. *Victorian Photographs of Famous Men & Fair Women.* 1926 Hogarth Pr. 1/450. folio. EX $750.00

CAMERON, Margaret. *Experience in Psychic Phenomena.* 1918 NY. 314 p. G $23.00

CAMERON, Roderick. *Shadows From India.* 1958 London. Heinemann. VG $20.00

CAMERON & HOFFMAN. *Theatrical Response.* 1969 NY. 1st print. dj. M $15.00

CAMFIELD, William A. *Francis Picabia.* 1970 NY. 1st ed. stiff wraps. EX $25.00

CAMM, Dom Bede. *Pilgrim Paths in Latin Lands.* 1923 London. MacDonald Evans. 1st ed. VG $40.00

CAMMELL, Charles R. *Aleister Crowley.* 1951 London. 1st ed. 230 p. EX $45.00

CAMP, Raymond R. *Decoys & Eastern Seaboard Wildfowling.* 1952 NY. Ills G Don Ray. M $85.00

CAMP, Raymond R. *Fireside Book of Fishing.* 1959 Simon Schuster. 1st ed. 500 p. dj. EX $25.00

CAMP, Raymond R. *Hunting Trails.* 1961 NY. dj. VG $14.00

CAMP, Samuel G. *Fishing with Floating Flies.* 1916 NY. VG $30.00

CAMP, W.E. *World in Your Garden.* 1959 Nat'l Geog Soc. 2nd ed. dj. EX $7.50

CAMP, Walter. *Substitute: Football Story.* 1909 NY. Appleton. 8vo. 336 p. EX $35.00

CAMP. *Philo White's Narrative of Cruise in the Pacific.* Denver. Rosenstock. 1/1,000. EX $40.00

CAMPAN, Jeanne Louise H. *Memoirs of Private Life of Marie Antoinette.* 1917 NY. Brentano. 2 vol set. $40.00

CAMPANA, Michele. *European Carpets.* 1966 London. Ills. 158 p. dj. $12.50

CAMPANELLA, Roy. *It's Good To Be Alive.* 1959 2nd print. 306 p. dj. VG $9.00

CAMPBELL, Bruce. *Dictionary of Birds in Color.* 1983 Exeter. Ills. 4to. 352 p. dj. EX $25.00

CAMPBELL, Bruce. *Mystery of the Iron Box.* 1952 Grosset Dunlap. VG $6.00

CAMPBELL, Bruce. *Secret of Skeleton Island.* 1949 Grosset Dunlap. VG $6.00

CAMPBELL, George F. *Soldier of the Sky.* 1918 Chicago. Ills. 232 p. cloth. EX $35.00

CAMPBELL, Gerald. *Of True Experience.* 1947 NY. 1st ed. G $20.00

CAMPBELL, Guy. *Golf for Beginners.* 1923 London. 12mo. 124 p. $20.00

CAMPBELL, H.J. *Beyond the Visible.* 1952 Hamilton. dj. VG $25.00

CAMPBELL, H.J. *Case for Mrs. Surrat.* 1943 Putnam. 272 p. EX $15.00

CAMPBELL, J. *Flight of Wild Gander.* 1969 Viking. 1st ed. dj. EX $7.00

CAMPBELL, J.D. *American Military Insigna 1800-1851.* 1963 Smithsonian. Ills. 4to. 124 p. $25.00

CAMPBELL, J.D.S. *Trip to Tropics & Home Through America.* 1867 London. Hurst Blackett. 1st ed. G $75.00

CAMPBELL, John W. *Analog 3.* 1966 Dobson. dj. VG $12.00

CAMPBELL, John W. *Astounding Science Fiction Anthology.* 1951 Simon Schuster. 1st ed. dj. VG $75.00

CAMPBELL, John W. *Black Star Passes.* 1953 Fantasy Pr. Ltd 1st ed. 1/500. sgn. dj. EX $150.00

CAMPBELL, John W. *Black Star Passes.* 1953 Fantasy Pr. 1st ed. $35.00

CAMPBELL, John W. *Cloak of Aesir.* 1952 Shasta. 1st ed. dj. VG $35.00

CAMPBELL, John W. *Incredible Planet.* 1949 Fantasy Pr. Ltd 1st ed. 1/500. sgn. dj. EX $150.00

CAMPBELL, John W. *Mightiest Machine.* 1947 Hadley. 1st ed. dj. EX $75.00

CAMPBELL, John W. *Moon Is Hell!* 1951 Fantasy Pr. 1st ed. dj. G $35.00

CAMPBELL, John W. *Who Goes There?* no date. Shasta. 2nd ed. dj. VG $35.00

CAMPBELL, John W. *Who Goes There?* 1948 Chicago. 1st ed. dj. sgn. VG $65.00

CAMPBELL, John. *Travels in South Africa.* 1816 Andover. 1st Am ed. 8vo. map. $140.00

CAMPBELL, Julie. *Trixie Belden & Mystery Off Glen Road.* 1956 Whitman. VG $10.00

CAMPBELL, Keith. *Darling Don't.* 1950 MacDonald. dj. VG $7.00

CAMPBELL, Patrick. *Life in Thin Slices.* 1951 MacDonald. dj. VG $7.00

CAMPBELL, Ramsey. *Cold Print.* 1985 Scream Pr. Ills Potter. Ltd 1st ed. sgns. $100.00

CAMPBELL, Ramsey. *Demons by Daylight.* 1973 Arkham House. 1st ed. dj. EX $22.50

CAMPBELL, Ramsey. *Doll Who Ate His Mother.* 1977 Millinton. 1st English ed. sgn. dj. EX $75.00

CAMPBELL, Ramsey. *Height of the Scream.* 1976 Arkham House. 1st ed. dj. EX $15.00

CAMPBELL, Ramsey. *Inhabitant of Lake & Less Welcome Tenants.* 1964 Sauk City. 1st ed. sgn. dj. EX $125.00

CAMPBELL, Ramsey. *Medusa.* 1987 Footsteps Pr. Ltd 1st ed. 1/300. sgn. wraps. $30.00

CAMPBELL, Ramsey. *Parasite.* 1980 NY. 1st ed. dj. EX $10.00

CAMPBELL, Ramsey. *Scared Stiff.* 1987 Los Angeles. Ills Potter. Ltd ed. sgns. dj. $75.00

CAMPBELL, Ramsey. *Scared Stiff.* 1987 Scream Pr. Ills JK Potter. 1st ed. sgn. $75.00

CAMPBELL, Ramsey. *Scared Stiff.* 1987 Los Angeles. 1st trade ed. dj. M $25.00

CAMPBELL, Ramsey. *To Wake the Dead.* London. 1st ed. sgn. EX $50.00

CAMPBELL, Roy. *Light on a Dark Horse: Autobiography.* 1952 Chicago. 1st Am ed. dj. VG $18.00

CAMPBELL, Sheldon. *Lifeboats to Ararat.* 1978 Times. Ills. 240 p. VG $8.00

CAMPBELL, Thomas. *Gertrude of WY: PA Tale.* 1809 London. Longman Hurst. 4to. 134 p. $450.00

CAMPBELL, Thomas. *Poetical Works of Thomas Campbell.* 1840 London. Ills Harvey. fore-edge of men. $800.00

CAMPBELL, Tom W. *2 Fighters & 2 Fines.* 1941 Little Rock. 1st ed. 557 p. VG $15.00

CAMPBELL & ROBINSON. *Skeleton Key to Finnegan's Wake.* 1944 NY. 365 p. dj. VG $18.00

CAMPBELL & TWINING. *Survey of Northern Boundary of US.* 1878 Ills. 624 p. xl. VG $125.00

CAMPBELL. *Invaders From Infinite.* 1961 Gnome Pr. 1st ed. dj. VG $12.50

CAMUS, Albert. *Caligula & Cross Purpose.* 1947 London. 1st ed. dj. EX $25.00

CAMUS, Albert. *Exile & the Kingdom.* 1958 Knopf. 1st ed. dj. EX $15.00

CAMUS, Albert. *Happy Death.* 1972 Knopf. 1st Am ed. dj. VG $17.50

CAMUS, Albert. *Notebooks: 1935-1942.* 1963 Knopf. 1st Am ed. dj. EX $30.00

CANADY, John. *Lives of the Painters.* 1969 NY. 1st ed. 4 vol set. boxed. $40.00

CANBY, C. *History of Weaponry.* 1963 Hawthorne. Ills 1st ed. 105 p. VG $12.50

CANBY, C. *Lincoln & the Civil War.* 1960 Braziller. 416 p. dj. VG $10.00

CANBY, Henry S. *Thoreau.* 1939 Boston. Special ed. 1/265. sgn. EX $40.00

CANDACE, Flynt. *Sins of Omission.* 1984 NY. 1st ed. sgn. dj. EX $30.00

CANDEE, Helen Churchill. *Jacobean Furniture & English Styles in Oak & Walnut.* 1916 NY. Stokes. G $18.00

CANDEE, Helen Churchill. *Tapestry Book.* 1912 NY. Stokes. Ills 1st ed. 275 p. cloth. VG $50.00

CANDEE, Helen Churchill. *Weaves & Draperies: Classic & Modern.* 1930 NY. Stokes. xl. G $30.00

CANDEE, Helen Churchill. *Weaves & Draperies: Classic & Modern.* 1930 NY. Stokes. Ills 1st ed. 300 p. dj. VG $37.50

CANDY, Edward. *Words for Murder Perhaps.* 1971 Gollancz. 1st ed. dj. xl. $5.00

CANE, M. *Eloquent April.* 1971 NY. 1st ed. sgn. dj. EX $15.00

CANETTI, Elias. *Auto-Da-Fe.* NY. Stein Day. 1st Am ed. dj. EX $9.00

CANFIELD, Chauncey L. *City of 6.* 1970 Chicago. 365 p. $55.00

CANFIELD, Chauncey. *Diary of a Forty-Niner.* 1947 Stanford. Intro Oscar Lewis. dj. EX $15.00

CANFIELD, D. *Seasoned Timber.* 1939 NY. Harcourt. 1st ed. slipcase. EX $15.00

CANFIELD, D. *Seasoned Timber.* 1939 Harcourt Brace. boxed. VG $8.00

CANFIELD, D. *Understood Betsy.* 1917 NY. 1st ed. green cloth. juvenile. VG $20.00

CANHAM, Erwin D. *Commitment to Freedom: Story of Christian Science Monitor.* 1958 Boston. Houghton Mifflin. G $15.00

CANIFF, Milton. *April Kane & the Dragon Lady.* no date. Whitman. $9.00

CANIFF, Milton. *Male Call.* 1945 NY. 65 p. VG $17.50

CANNING, John. *So Strange Stories of Supernatural.* no date. Bell. 1st ed. dj. EX $10.00

CANNING, John. *50 Great Ghost Stories.* no date. Bell. 1st ed. dj. VG $10.00

CANNING, John. *50 Great Horror Stories.* 1969 Taplinger. dj. VG $15.00

CANNING, John. *50 True Tales of Terror.* no date. Bell. 4th ed. EX $10.00

CANNING, Victor. *Dragon Tree.* 1958 Sloane. 1st ed. dj. VG $10.00

CANNING, Victor. *Finger of Saturn.* 1974 Morrow. 1st ed. dj. EX $14.00

CANNING, Victor. *Man From the Turkish Slave.* 1954 Hodder Stoughton. dj. VG $16.50

CANNING, Victor. *Mr. Finchley Goes to Paris.* 1938 Carrick Evans. 1st ed. dj. VG $27.50

CANNING, Victor. *Painted Tent.* 1974 Heinemann. 1st ed. dj. xl. $5.00

CANNING, Victor. *Panthers' Moon.* 1948 Mill. 2nd ed. dj. VG $15.00

CANNING, Victor. *Python Project.* 1968 Morrow. 1st ed. dj. EX $14.00

CANNON, Carl J. *American Book Collectors.* 1941 NY. 1st ed. 8vo. VG $45.00

CANNON, Frank; & O'HIGGINS, H. *Under the Prophet in UT.* 1911 Boston. Clark. 402 p. $15.00

CANNON, H.G. *Evolution of Living Things.* 1958 Manchester U Pr. 180 p. dj. EX $10.00

CANNON, M. *Lola Montes: Tragic Story of a Liberated Woman.* 1973 Melbourne. Ltd 1st ed. 1/1,000. dj. VG $17.00

CANNON, Richard. *Historical Records of the 10th or Lincolnshire Regiment.* 1847 London. 3 plts. $110.00

CANNON, Walter. *Bodily Changes in Pain, Hunger, Fear, & Rage.* 1929 NY. 2nd ed. 1st print. 404 p. EX $60.00

CANNON, Walter. *Way of Investigator: Scientist's Experiences in Research.* 1945 Norton. 1st ed. dj. VG $15.00

CANTIN, Eugene. *Yukon Summer.* 1974 Chronicle. Ills. 198 p. dj. VG $9.00

CANTOR, Eddie. *Caught Short.* 1929 NY. Ills 1st ed. dj. VG $15.00

CANTWELL, R. *Alexander Wilson.* 1961 Phil. 4to. dj. VG $45.00

CAPA, Robert. *Images of War.* 1964 Grossman. 1st ed. dj. VG $30.00

CAPA, Robert. *Slightly Out of Focus.* 1947 Holt. 1st ed. VG $30.00

CAPEK, Karel. *Krakatit.* 1925 London. 1st English ed. $100.00

CAPEK, Karel. *War with the Newts.* 1937 Putnam. 1st ed. dj. EX $35.00

CAPELL, Frank A. *Strange Death of Marilyn Monroe.* c 1964 wraps. VG $45.00

CAPELL, James. *Something About Eve.* Ills Pape. Ltd 1st ed. 1/831. sgn. VG $125.00

CAPEN, Oliver Bronson. *Country Homes of Famous Americans.* 1905 NY. Ills. folio. 176 p. VG $100.00

CAPERS, G.M. *Occupied City: New Orleans Under Federals 1862-1865.* 1965 KY U Pr. dj. VG $15.00

CAPOTE, Truman. *Breakfast at Tiffany's.* 1958 NY. 1st ed. 8vo. yellow cloth. dj. $45.00

CAPOTE, Truman. *De Sang-Froid.* 1966 Paris. Ltd ed. 1/51. dj. EX $165.00

CAPOTE, Truman. *In Cold Blood.* 1965 NY. Advance copy. wraps. EX $75.00

CAPOTE, Truman. *In Cold Blood.* 1965 Random House. 1st ed. dj. M $25.00

CAPOTE, Truman. *Local Color.* 1950 NY. 1st ed. dj. EX $75.00

CAPOTE, Truman. *Muses Are Heard.* 1956 Random House. 1st ed. dj. EX $75.00

CAPOTE, Truman. *Music for Cameleons.* 1980 NY. 1st ed. dj. M $12.00

CAPOTE, Truman. *Other Voices, Other Rooms.* 1948 Random House. 1st ed. dj. G $40.00

CAPOTE, Truman. *Other Voices, Other Rooms.* 1948 London. 1st ed. dj. VG $55.00

CAPOTE, Truman. *Other Voices, Other Rooms.* 1948 Random House. 1st print. dj. EX $65.00

CAPOTE, Truman. *Thanksgiving Visitor.* 1969 London. 1st ed. dj. EX $36.00

CAPOTE, Truman. *Tree of Night.* 1949 NY. 1st ed. dj. EX $55.00

CAPOTE & AVEDON. *Observations.* 1959 Simon Schuster. 1st ed. slipcase. $95.00

CAPP, Al. *Hardhat's Bedtime Story.* 1971 NY. 1st ed. sgn. dj. $27.50

CAPPS, B. *Great Chiefs.* 1981 Time Life. Ills Revised ed. 240 p. EX $15.00

CAPPS, B. *Indians.* no date. Time Life. Ills Revised ed. $15.00

CAPRA, Frank. *Name Above the Title.* 1971 Macmillan. 1st ed. dj. VG $16.00

CAPSTICK, Peter. *Death in Long Grass.* 1977 St. Martin. photos. VG $15.00

CAPSTICK, Peter. *Death in Long Grass.* 1977 NY. 1st ed. inscr. dj. EX $20.00

CAPSTICK, Peter. *Death in the Silent Places.* 1981 NY. 1st ed. sgn. dj. EX $15.00

CAPSTICK, Peter. *Maneaters.* 1981 Peterson. Ills. 178 p. dj. EX $15.00

CAPUTO, Philip. *Del Corso's Gallery.* 1983 Holt. 1st ed. dj. EX $20.00

CAPUTO, Philip. *Del Corso's Gallery.* 1983 Harper Row. dj. VG $12.00

CAPUTO, Philip. *Horn of Africa.* 1980 NY. Ltd 1st ed. 1/200. boxed. M $55.00

CAPUTO, Philip. *Horn of Africa.* 1980 NY. Ltd ed. 1/250. sgn. boxed. M $35.00

CARAS, R.A. *Custer Wolf: Biography of an American Renegade.* 1966 Little Brown. Ills 1st ed. 175 p. dj. EX $10.00

CARAS, R.A. *Panther!* 1969 Little Brown. Ills 1st ed. 185 p. dj. EX $9.00

CARAS, Roger. *Dangerous to Man.* 1964 Chilton. Ills 1st ed. 433 p. dj. VG $15.00

CARAS, Roger. *Monarch of Deadman Bay: Life & Death of a Kodiak Bear.* 1969 Little Brown. Ills 1st ed. 185 p. EX $14.00

CARAS, Roger. *North American Mammals.* 1967 Galahad. Ills. 578 p. maps. dj. EX $18.00

CARAS, Roger. *Venomous Animals.* 1974 Prentice Hall. Ills 1st ed. 4to. dj. VG $18.00

CARD, O.S. *Capitol.* 1979 Baronet. 1st ed. wraps. EX $40.00

CARD, O.S. *Cardography.* 1987 Eugene. Ltd ed. 1/750. sgn. dj. M $35.00

CARD, O.S. *Hot Sleep.* 1979 Baronet. 1st ed. wraps. M $20.00

CARDEW, Margaret. *French Alphabet.* no date. London. Faber. Ltd ed. 4to. $40.00

CARDIN, Sir John. *Travels in Persia.* 1927 London. Argonaut Pr. Ltd ed. 1/975. VG $60.00

CARDOZO. *Lucky Eyes & a High Heart: Life of Maud Gonne.* 1978 IN. 1st ed. dj. EX $10.00

CARDWELL, Paul. *America's Camping Book.* 1969 Scribner. Ills. 591 p. dj. VG $10.00

CARELL. *Scorched Earth.* 1970 Boston. 1st Am ed. dj. VG $55.00

CAREW. *Glorious Glouster: History of Gloucestershire Regiments.* 1970 London. Ills 1st ed. maps. dj. VG $15.00

CAREY, A.M. *American Firearms Makers.* 1953 Crowell. Ills. 146 p. dj. VG $20.00

CAREY, Peter. *Fat Man in History & Other Stories.* 1908 Random House. 1st ed. dj. VG $15.00

CAREY, T. *History of Pirates.* 1827 no place. 2nd ed. 16mo. calf. $50.00

CARGILL, S.T. *Philosophy of Analogy & Symbolism.* c 1940s. London. Rider. 264 p. dj. VG $26.00

CARHART, A.H. *Fishing Is Fun.* 1950 Macmillan. 1st print. 122 p. dj. EX $7.50

CARHART, A.H. *Hunting North American Deer.* 1946 NY. 1st ed. dj. VG $20.00

CARL, Katharine A. *With the Empress Dowager of China.* 1926 Tientsin. Ills. 306 p. yellow silk. VG $120.00

CARL & CLEMENS. *Fresh-Water Fishes of British Columbia.* 1948 Ills. wraps. VG $20.00

CARLETON, George. *Our Artist in Cuba.* 1865 NY. Ills 1st ed. cloth. $60.00

CARLETON, George. *Traits & Stories of the Irish Peasantry.* c 1850. London. Ills. 2 vol set. VG $105.00

CARLETON, George. *Traits & Stories of the Irish Peasantry.* c 1870. London. Tegg. New ed. 703 p. G $35.00

CARLETON, J. *Moonflower Vine.* 1962 Simon Schuster. 1st ed. dj. EX $8.00

CARLETON, Will. *City Ballads.* 1885 NY. Ills. 180 p. G $18.00

CARLETON, Will. *Drifted In.* 1908 NY. 1st ed. VG $40.00

CARLIER, Auguste. *Marriage in the US.* 1867 Boston. 12mo. 179 p. $35.00

CARLISLE, Harry. *On the Drumhead: Selection From Writing of Mike Quinn.* 1948 San Francisco. Pacific Pub. Memorial Vol. VG $35.00

CARLQUIST, Sherwin. *HI: Natural History.* 1980 Honolulu. Ills. 468 p. wraps. EX $12.00

CARLQUIST, Sherwin. *Island Life.* 1965 NY. Nat Hist Pr. 1st ed. dj. VG $27.50

CARLSON, Eric. *Recognition of Edgar Allan Poe.* 1966 MI U Pr. 1st ed. dj. VG $15.00

CARLSON, John F. *Elementary Principles of Landscape Painting.* 1928 Bridgman Pub. Special ed. VG $15.00

CARLSON, Marvin. *Goethe & the Weimar Theatre.* 1978 Cornell U Pr. Ills 1st ed. dj. EX $8.00

CARLSON, Raymond. *Gallery of Western Paintings.* 1951 NY. Ills 1st ed. 4to. VG $35.00

CARLSON, W.S. *Lifelines Through Arctic.* 1962 NY. 1st ed. dj. VG $8.00

CARLSON & RODRIGUEZ. *Town Is Born: Pictorial Review of Winslow, AZ.* 1981 private print. 1st ed. sgn Carlson. 4to. EX $35.00

CARLSON. *Mirror for CA.* 1941 Indianapolis. 1st ed. G $10.00

CARLYLE, Alexander. *Love Letters of Thomas Carlyle & Jane Welsh.* 1909 London. Ills 1st ed. 2 vol set. $55.00

CARLYLE, Thomas. *On Heroes, Hero Worship, & the Heroic in History.* 1840 London. Routledge. 334 p. G $35.00

CARLYLE, Thomas. *On Heroes, Hero Worship, & the Heroic in History.* no date. NY. Crowell. VG $30.00

CARMAN, Harry. *Jesse Buel: Agricultural Reformer.* 1947 NY. 609 p. dj. G $18.00

CARMEAN, E.A. *Decade of American Abstraction: Modernist Art 1960-1970.* 1974 Houston. Museum Fine Art. 4to. 140 p. $17.50

CARMEN, J. Neale. *From Camelot to Joyous Guard.* 1974 KS U Pr. 1st ed. M $17.50

CARMER. *Songs of the Rivers of America.* 1942 NY. 1st ed. dj. VG $75.00

CARMICHAEL, Mrs. A.C. *Domestic Manners & Social Condition of West Indies.* 1833 London. Whitaker. 1st ed. 2 vol set. $125.00

CARNEGIE, Andrew. *Carnegie Anthology.* 1915 private print. Ills. dj. EX $35.00

CARNEGIE, Andrew. *Empire of Business.* 1902 Doubleday Page. G $20.00

CARNEGIE, Andrew. *Triumphant Democracy.* 1891 NY. inscr. VG $80.00

CARNEGIE, Dale. *How To Win Friends.* 1937 NY. sgn. EX $15.00

CARNEGIE, Dale. *Lincoln the Unknown.* 1932 NY. 1st ed. dj. VG $25.00

CAROZZI, A.V. *Microscopic Sedimentary Petrography.* 1960 Wiley. Ills. 485 p. EX $10.00

CARPENTER, Don. *Hard Rain Falling.* 1969 NY. 1st ed. dj. EX $10.00

CARPENTER, Don. *Murder of the Frogs.* 1969 NY. 1st ed. dj. EX $10.00

CARPENTER, F.B. *Inner Life of Abraham Lincoln.* 1872 NY. 12mo. 359 p. black cloth. G $24.00

CARPENTER, F.G. *AK: Our Northern Wonderland.* 1925 Doubleday Page. Ills. 319 p. maps. VG $7.50

CARPENTER. *Carpenter's New Geographical Reader: Europe.* 1924 Ills. maps. photos. TB. VG $10.00

CARR, Archie. *Everglades.* 1973 Time Life. Ills. 184 p. EX $10.00

CARR, Archie. *Reptiles.* 1963 Life. Ills. 4to. 192 p. EX $14.00

CARR, Archie. *So Excellent a Fish: Natural History of Sea Turtles.* 1967 NY. 1st ed. VG $25.00

CARR, John Dickson. *Capt. Cut-Throat.* 1955 London. 1st English ed. dj. EX $18.00

CARR, John Dickson. *Dead Man's Knock.* 1958 NY. 1st ed. dj. EX $22.50

CARR, John Dickson. *Dead Man's Knock.* 1958 London. 1st ed. EX $17.50

CARR, John Dickson. *Deadly Hall.* 1971 NY. 1st ed. dj. EX $15.00

CARR, John Dickson. *Demoniacs.* 1962 London. 1st ed. dj. EX $17.50

CARR, John Dickson. *Demoniacs.* 1962 NY. 1st ed. dj. EX $22.50

CARR, John Dickson. *Sleeping Sphinx.* 1947 NY. 1st ed. dj. $25.00

CARR, John Dickson. *Sleeping Sphinx.* 1947 London. 1st ed. dj. VG $22.00

CARR, Sir John. *Tour Through Holland.* 1807 Phil. 1st Am ed. 301 p. $30.00

CARR, Terry. *Cirque.* 1977 Indianapolis. 1st ed. dj. M $20.00

CARRE, Leon. *Au Jardin des Gemmes.* 1925 Paris. 10 plts. wraps. G $37.50

CARRICK, Alice van Leer. *Mother Goose for Antique Collectors.* 1927 Payson Clarke. Ills D Taylor. 1st print. VG $20.00

CARRICK, Alice van Leer. *Next-to-Nothing House.* 1922 Boston. Ills. 252 p. VG $22.00

CARRIGHAR, Sally. *Icebound Summer.* 1953 Knopf. Ills. 262 p. dj. VG $10.00

CARRIGHAR, Sally. *Moonlight at Midday.* 1959 Knopf. Ills. 392 p. VG $10.00

CARRIGHAR, Sally. *Wild Heritage.* 1965 Houghton Mifflin. 1st ed. dj. $6.00

CARRIGHAR, Sally. *Wild Voice of the North.* 1959 Doubleday. Ills. 191 p. dj. EX $14.00

CARRINGTON, M.I. *Absaraka, Home of the Crows.* 1950 Donnelley. Ills. reprint. fld map. EX $27.00

CARROLL, Alice. *Complete Guide to Modern Knitting & Crocheting.* 1942 NY. Ills. 8vo. 310 p. VG $15.00

CARROLL, James. *Fault Lines.* 1980 Little Brown. 1st ed. dj. EX $12.00

CARROLL, John A. *Reflections of Western Historians.* 1969 Tucson. VG $20.00

CARROLL, John M. *Benteen-Goldin Letters on Custer & His Last Battle.* 1974 Liveright. Ltd ed. sgn. slipcase. EX $65.00

CARROLL, John M. *Custer & the Battle of the Little Big Horn.* 1976 Garry Owen Pr. 1st ed. dj. EX $55.00

CARROLL, John M. *Custer in TX.* 1975 Lewis. Ills. 288 p. VG $25.00

CARROLL, John M.; & PRICE, B. *Roll Call on the Little Big Horn.* 1974 Old Army Pr. EX $50.00

CARROLL, Lewis. *Adventures Underground.* 1964 U Microfilms. facsimile. boxed. VG $22.00

CARROLL, Lewis. *Alice in Wonderland.* 1901 NY. Ills Peter Newell. VG $45.00

CARROLL, Lewis. *Alice in Wonderland. Pop-Up Classic.* 1968 Random House. Graphics Internat'l. 1st ed. $25.00

CARROLL, Lewis. *Alice's Adventures in Wonderland, Through the Looking Glass.* 1898 Lathrop. Ills Tenniel. 1st ed. 4to. EX $137.50

CARROLL, Lewis. *Alice's Adventures in Wonderland, Through the Looking Glass.* 1977 NY. St. Martin. Ills Tenniel. 1st ed. dj. EX $67.00

CARROLL, Lewis. *Alice's Adventures in Wonderland, Through the Looking Glass.* 1941 Heritage. Ills Tenniel. 8vo. 172 p. dj. $22.00

CARROLL, Lewis. *Alice's Adventures in Wonderland, Through the Looking Glass.* no date. Grosset Dunlap. Ills Tenniel. $7.50

CARROLL, Lewis. *Alice's Adventures in Wonderland, Through the Looking Glass.* c 1930. Siren. Ills Complete 1 vol ed. VG $20.00

CARROLL, Lewis. *Alice's Adventures in Wonderland, Through the Looking Glass.* 1872 London. Ills Tenniel. 2 vol set. 8vo. $225.00

CARROLL, Lewis. *Alice's Adventures in Wonderland, Through the Looking Glass.* 1929 London. Ills Tenniel. 2 vols. boxed. $100.00

CARROLL, Lewis. *Alice's Adventures in Wonderland, Through the Looking Glass.* 1898 Lathrop. Ills Tenniel. 1st ed. VG $125.00

CARROLL, Lewis. *Alice's Adventures in Wonderland.* 1871 Boston. Ills 3rd ed. 12mo. cloth. VG $50.00

CARROLL, Lewis. *Alice's Adventures in Wonderland.* no date. Garden City. Ills Jackson. VG $30.00

CARROLL, Lewis. *Alice's Adventures in Wonderland.* 1982 CA U Pr. Ills 1st ed. dj. EX $30.00

CARROLL, Lewis. *Alice's Adventures in Wonderland.* 1982 Hodder. Ills Hudson. gilt leather. EX $60.00

CARROLL, Lewis. *Alice's Adventures in Wonderland.* 1902 NY. Harper. Ills Peter Newell. EX $75.00

CARROLL, Lewis. *Alice's Adventures in Wonderland.* 1902 NY. Harper. Ills Peter Newell. VG $30.00

CARROLL, Lewis. *Annotated Alice.* 1940 Bramhall House. Ills Tenniel. dj. VG $15.00

CARROLL, Lewis. *Hunting Snark.* 1903 NY. Harper. Ills Peter Newell. VG $30.00

CARROLL, Lewis. *Lylvie & Bruno Concluded.* 1893 London. 1st ed. 1st issue. 423 p. dj. $38.00

CARROLL, Lewis. *Rhyme? Reason?* 1884 NY. Macmillan. Ills AB Frost. 1st Am ed. EX $75.00

CARROLL, Lewis. *Rhyme? Reason?* NY. Macmillan. Ills Frost/Holiday. 1st ed. VG $65.00

CARROLL, Lewis. *Through the Looking Glass.* 1935 NJ. Ills Tenniel. 1/1,500. 8vo. VG $300.00

CARROLL, Lewis. *Through the Looking Glass.* 1872 London. Ills Dodgson. 1st ed. rebound. $1000.00

CARROLL, Lewis. *Through the Looking Glass.* Ltd Ed Club. 1/1,500. sgn A Hargreaves. EX $500.00

CARROLL, Lewis. *Through the Looking Glass.* 1946 NY. Ills Tenniel. Special ed. VG $20.00

CARROLL, Lewis. *Through the Looking Glass.* 1935 NY. 8vo. gilt blue morocco. EX $225.00

CARRUTH, Hayden. *Crow & Heart.* 1959 NY. Macmillan. 1st ed. wraps. $45.00

CARRYL, Charles E. *Admiral's Caravan.* 1920 Houghton Mifflin. Ills Birch. $10.00

CARRYL, G.W. *Fables for the Frivolous.* 1904 NY. Ills Newell. VG $16.00

CARSON, R. *Gallery of Western Paintings.* 1951 NY. Crown. Ills Remington/Russell/others. $35.00

CARSON, Rachel. *Sea Around Us.* 1980 NY. Ltd Ed Club. 1/2,000. sgn. EX $50.00

CARSON, Rachel. *Sea Around Us.* 1951 NY. Oxford U Pr. 230 p. VG $12.00

CARSON, Rachel. *Silent Spring.* 1962 Boston. 1st ed. dj. EX $15.00

CARTER, A. *Nights at the Circus.* 1985 Scribner. 1st Am ed. dj. EX $15.00

CARTER, A.C. *Kingdom of Siam.* 1904 Putnam. Ills 1st ed. 280 p. VG $10.00

CARTER, Edward C. *Latrobe's Views of America 1795-1820.* 1985 Yale. 1st ed. 161 p. dj. EX $35.00

CARTER, Forrest. *Education of Little Tree.* 1980 Delacorte. 4th ed. dj. EX $15.00

CARTER, G.G. *Looming Lights: Story of the British Lightships.* 1947 Readers Union. London. G $8.50

CARTER, Hodding. *Doomed Road of Empire.* 1963 NY. 1st ed. dj. VG $17.50

CARTER, Hodding. *Lower MS.* 1942 NY. 1st ed. dj. VG $30.00

CARTER, Huntly. *New Spirit in Drama & Art.* 1912 London. 1st ed. VG $45.00

CARTER, Jimmy & Rosalynn. *Everything To Gain: Making the Most of Rest of Your Life.* 1987 1st trade ed. sgns. M $75.00

CARTER, Jimmy. *Keeping Faith.* 1983 Bantam. 1st trade ed. sgn. pb. EX $25.00

CARTER, Jimmy. *Outdoor Journal.* 1988 NY. 1st ed. sgn. dj. M $45.00

CARTER, John. *ABC for Book Collectors.* 1970 NY. Revised 4th ed. dj. VG $15.00

CARTER, John. *Taste & Technique in Book Collecting.* 1949 Cambridge U Pr. Revised 2nd imp. dj. VG $20.00

CARTER, John; & PERCY, H. *Printing & the Mind of Man.* 1967 London. Ills. folio. dj. $100.00

CARTER, John; & POLLARD, G. *Firm of Charles Ottley.* 1948 London. 1st ed. 8vo. wraps. scarce. VG $45.00

CARTER, Morris. *Isabella Stewart Gardner & Fenway Court.* 1925 Boston. 1st ed. cloth. VG $22.00

CARTER, Richard. *Breakthrough: Saga of Jonas Salk.* 1966 Trident. dj. VG $7.50

CARTER, Russell G. *101st Field Artillery AEF 1917-1919.* 1940 Boston. 1st ed. VG $30.00

CARTER, Samuel. *Boat Builders of Bristol.* 1970 Doubleday. 1st ed. dj. VG $17.50

CARTER, Samuel. *Cyrus Field: Man of 2 Worlds.* 1968 NY. Putnam. Ills 1st ed. 380 p. dj. VG $15.00

CARTER, Samuel. *Siege of Atlanta 1864.* 1973 St. Martin. dj. EX $25.00

CARTER, T.D. *Mammals of the Pacific World.* 1945 Macmillan. Ills 1st ed. 227 p. dj. VG $16.00

CARTER, W.H. *Horses of the World.* 1923 Nat'l Geog Soc. VG $25.00

CARTER & MACE. *Tomb of Tut-Ank-Amen.* 1923 2nd print. VG $37.50

CARTIER, J.O. *Getting the Most Out of Modern Waterfowling.* 1974 St. Martin. Ills. 396 p. dj. EX $12.50

CARTIER-BRESSON, Henri. *Decisive Moment.* 1952 NY. 1st Am ed. VG $145.00

CARTIER-BRESSON, Henri. *Face of Asia.* 1972 NY. 1st ed. 4to. dj. EX $55.00

CARTIER-BRESSON, Henri. *Flagrant Delits.* 1967 Paris. Delpire Editeur. 1st ed. 4to. $185.00

CARTIER-BRESSON, Henri. *France.* 1971 Viking. 1st Am ed. dj. VG $45.00

CARTIER-BRESSON, Henri. *From 1 China to the Other.* 1956 NY. 1st ed. 4to. 144 p. xl. fair. $35.00

CARTIER-BRESSON, Henri. *People of Moscow.* 1955 NY. Ills 1st ed. dj. EX $65.00

CARTIER-BRESSON, Henri. *World of Henri Cartier-Bresson.* 1968 Viking. 4to. wraps. VG $55.00

CARTLAND, Barbara. *Imperial Splendor.* 1979 NY. 1st ed. dj. M $10.00

CARTWRIGHT, D.W. *Natural History of Western Wild Animals.* 1875 Toledo. 2nd ed. EX $48.00

CARUSO, Dorothy. *Wings of Song.* no date. (1828) London. Ills. 256 p. G $22.50

CARUSO, John Anthony. *Great Lakes Frontier.* 1961 Bobbs Merrill. 1st ed. dj. EX $15.00

CARVALHO, D. *40 Centuries of Ink.* 1971 NY. EX $20.00

CARVALHO, S.N. *Incidents of Travel & Adventure in the Far West.* 1859 NY. Derby & Jackson. 12mo. $20.00

CARVER, Jeffrey. *Infinity Link.* 1984 NY. 1st ed. dj. M $17.00

CARVER, Raymond. *At Night the Salmon Move.* 1976 Capra. Ltd ed. 1/1,000. blue wraps. M $35.00

CARVER, Raymond. *At Night the Salmon Move.* 1983 Santa Barbara. Capra. 1st Separate ed. 1/25. $75.00

CARVER, Raymond. *At Night the Salmon Move.* 1976 Santa Barbara. Capra. 1/100. sgn. dj. VG $75.00

CARVER, Raymond. *Cathedral.* 1983 NY. Knopf. Uncorrected proof. $125.00

CARVER, Raymond. *Cathedral.* 1983 Knopf. 1st ed. dj. VG $25.00

CARVER, Raymond. *Early for the Dance.* 1986 Ltd 1st ed. 1/100. sgn. VG $55.00

CARVER, Raymond. *Fires.* 1983 Santa Barbara. Capra. 1st ed. pb. VG $35.00

CARVER, Raymond. *Fires.* 1985 London. Collins. 1st ed. dj. M $35.00

CARVER, Raymond. *Intimacy.* 1987 Concord. Ewert. Ltd ed. 1/75. sgn. M $125.00

CARVER, Raymond. *My Father's Life.* 1986 Derrydale. Ltd 1st ed. 1/40. sgn. wraps. $125.00

CARVER, Raymond. *Pheasant.* 1982 Worcester. Metacom. Ltd ed. 1/150. wraps. $50.00

CARVER, Raymond. *This Water.* 1985 Ewert. 1st ed. 1/100. sgn. blue wraps. M $60.00

CARVER, Raymond. *This Water.* 1985 Ewert. 1st ed. 1/36. sgn. M $125.00

CARVER, Raymond. *Those Days.* 1987 Elmwood. Raven Eds. 1st ed. 1/100. M $100.00

CARVER, Raymond. *Vitamins.* 1981 1st Separate ed. 1/25. sgn. $135.00

CARVER, Raymond. *What We Talk About When We Talk About Love.* 1981 NY. Knopf. 1st ed. dj. M $45.00

CARVER, Raymond. *What We Talk About When We Talk About Love.* 1981 NY. Knopf. Uncorrected proof. $150.00

CARVER, Raymond. *Will You Please Be Quiet, Please?* 1976 NY. McGraw Hill. 1st ed. EX $100.00

CARVER, Raymond. *Winter Insomnia.* 1970 Santa Cruz. Kayak. Ltd 1st ed. sgn. wraps. $125.00

CARVER, William. *Practical Horse Farrier.* 1820 Phil. 12mo. 251 p. G $50.00

CARY, A.T. *Arranging Flowers Throughout the Year.* 1933 NY. Ills. 230 p. $12.50

CARY, Elizabeth L. *Tennyson: His Homes, His Friends, & His Work.* 1898 Putnam. Ills Cameron. 2nd imp. 1/400. $85.00

CARY, J. *Actual Survey of Country 15 Miles Around London.* 1786 London. 8vo. 51 maps. calf. rebacked. $600.00

CARY, Joyce. *Horse's Mouth.* 1944 London. 1st ed. dj. VG $55.00

CARY, Joyce. *Horse's Mouth.* 1957 London. Curwen. 1/1,500. slipcase. $125.00

CARY, Joyce. *Memoir of the Bobotes.* 1960 TX U Pr. Ills 1st ed. dj. EX $45.00

CARY, Mrs. V. *Letters on Female Character.* 1828 Richmond, VA. Works. 199 p. xl. $35.00

CASE, A.D. *Dr. Case's New Recipe Book.* 1882 NY. 12mo. cloth. VG $50.00

CASE, F. *Wild Flowers of the Northeastern States.* 1978 NY. 34 p. dj. VG $20.00

CASE, Frank. *Tales of the Wayward Inn.* 1938 Phil. Ills. VG $25.00

CASE, Robert & Victoria. *Last Mountains.* 1945 Garden City. dj. VG $10.00

CASE, V. *We Called It Culture: Story of Chautauqua.* 1948 Garden City. 1st ed. 272 p. VG $10.00

CASENTINO, Andrew J. *Capital Image: Painters in WA 1800-1915.* 1983 Nat'l Museum Am Art. 280 p. $25.00

CASEY, Powell A. *Try Us: Story of WA Artillery in WWII.* 1971 Baton Rouge. 1st ed. dj. EX $65.00

CASEY, Robert J. *Black Hills & Their Incredible Characters.* 1949 Bobbs Merrill. dj. G $35.00

CASEY, Robert J. *Easter Island: Home of the Scornful Gods.* 1931 Bobbs Merrill. Ills 1st ed. 337 p. maps. EX $45.00

CASEY, Robert J. *Mr. Clutch: Story of George William Borg.* 1948 Bobbs Merrill. 1st ed. sgn Borg. VG $10.00

CASEY, Robert J. *TX Border & Some Border Liners.* 1950 Bobbs Merrill. Ills 1st ed. dj. VG $17.50

CASH, J.H. *Working the Homestake.* 1973 IA U Pr. Ills 1st ed. 141 p. dj. EX $30.00

CASPER, Leonard. *New Writings From the Philippines: Critique & Anthology.* 1966 NY. dj. EX $6.50

CASS, A.R.H. *Catching the Wily Sea Trout.* no date. Jenkins. Ills 1st ed. dj. VG $10.00

CASS, William. *In the Heart of the Heart of the Country.* 1968 Harper. 1st ed. dj. VG $75.00

CASSEDY, David; & SHROTT, G. *Works of William S. Mount in Museums of Stony Brook.* 1983 Stony Brook. Ills. 4to. 96 p. wraps. $13.50

CASSIDY, Claudia. *Europe on the Aisle.* 1954 Random House. 1st ed. dj. VG $10.00

CASSIDY, Claudia. *Lyric Opera of Chicago.* 1979 Chicago. Ills. 4to. dj. VG $45.00

CASSILL, R.V. *After Goliath.* 1985 Ticknor Fields. 1st ed. presentation. dj. $35.00

CASSILL, R.V. *Goss Women.* 1974 Doubleday. 1st ed. dj. EX $20.00

CASSILL, R.V. *In an Iron Time: Statements & Reiterations.* 1969 Purdue. 1st ed. presentation. dj. $40.00

CASSILL, R.V. *La vie Passionnee of Rodney Buckthorne.* 1968 Bernard Gies. 1st ed. dj. EX $25.00

CASSILL, R.V. *Labors of Love.* 1982 Arbor House. 1st ed. presentation. dj. EX $20.00

CASSILL, R.V. *President.* 1964 Simon Schuster. 1st ed. presentation. dj. EX $40.00

CASSON, Herbert. *History of the Telephone.* 1911 Chicago. Ills. 315 p. VG $8.50

CASSON, Herbert. *Romance of the Reaper.* 1908 NY. photos. VG $25.00

CASSON, Stanley. *Murder by Burial.* 1938 NY. 1st ed. dj. VG $12.50

CASTAGNETTA, G. *Good Tidings.* 1941 NY. Ills Van Loon. 16mo. dj. $15.00

CASTANEDA, Carlos. *Eagle's Gift.* 1981 Simon Schuster. 1st ed. dj. $20.00

COATS, Peter. *Roses.* 1973 Octopus. Ills. 95 p. dj. EX $5.00

COATSWORTH, Elizabeth. *Away Goes Sally.* 1934 NY. Macmillan. Ills Sewell. 1st ed. 122 p. VG $15.00

COATSWORTH, Elizabeth. *Cat Who Went to Heaven.* 1930 Ills Lynd Ward. 1st ed. 4to. 57 p. red cloth. $20.00

COATSWORTH, Elizabeth. *Enchanted.* 1951 NY. 1st ed. dj. EX $25.00

COATSWORTH, Elizabeth. *George & Red.* 1969 NY. Macmillan. Ills Giovanopoulos. 1st print. $10.00

COATSWORTH, Elizabeth. *House of the Swan.* 1948 NY. Macmillan. Ills K Voute. 1st print. dj. $10.00

COATSWORTH, Elizabeth. *Pure Magic.* 1973 NY. Macmillan. Ills Fetz. 1st ed. 69 p. dj. $10.00

COATSWORTH, Elizabeth. *Summer Green.* 1948 NY. Macmillan. Ills Nora Unwin. 1st print. G $15.00

COATSWORTH, Elizabeth. *Sun's Diary.* 1929 NY. Macmillan. Ills McIntosh. 1st ed. VG $20.00

COBB, Bertha & Ernest. *Dan's Boy.* 1926 Arlo Pub. Ills. juvenile. VG $12.50

COBB, Humphrey. *Paths of Glory.* 1935 NY. 1st ed. dj. EX $35.00

COBB, Irvin S. *Exit Laughing.* 1941 Indianapolis. sgn. VG $30.00

COBB, Irvin S. *Roughing It Deluxe.* 1914 Doran. Ills John McCutcheon. $10.00

COBB, William T. *Strenuous Life: Oyster Bay Roosevelts in Business.* 1946 NY. 1st ed. 100 p. cloth. scarce. $20.00

COBBOLD, R.P. *Innermost Asia: Travel & Sport in Pamirs.* 1900 London. Ills 1st ed. 354 p. G $70.00

COBDEN-SANDERSON, T.J. *Arts & Crafts Movement.* 1905 Chiswick Pr. Ills. full leather. $450.00

COBLENTZ, Stanton A. *Next To the Sun.* 1960 NY. 1st ed. dj. EX $35.00

COBLENTZ, Stanton A. *Senator Goose.* 1940 Wings Pr. dj. G $20.00

COBLENTZ, Stanton A. *Under the Triple Suns.* 1955 Fantasy. VG $7.50

COBLENTZ, Stanton A. *Villains & Vigilantes.* 1936 NY. dj. VG $35.00

COBURN, Alvin Langdon. *Alvin Langdon Coburn: Photographer.* 1966 NY/WA. Praeger. 1st ed. 4to. cloth. dj. EX $55.00

COBURN, F.D. *Book of Alfalfa.* 1912 NY. Ex-Chemists' Club. G $15.00

COBURN, Walt. *Walt Coburn: Autobiography.* 1973 Flagstaff. 1st ed. 255 p. dj. VG $25.00

COCCHIA, Admiral Aldo. *Hunters & the Hunted: Adventures of Italian Naval Forces.* 1958 Annapolis. 1st ed. dj. EX $30.00

COCHRAN, Hamilton. *Blockade Runners of the Confederacy.* 1958 Indianapolis. 1st ed. dj. VG $20.00

COCHRAN, Hamilton. *Noted American Duels & Hostile Encounters.* 1963 Chilton. Ills 1st ed. 319 p. dj. EX $18.00

COCHRAN, Jacqueline. *Stars at Noon.* 1954 Boston. 1st ed. dj. VG $15.00

COCHRAN & GOIN. *New Field Book of Reptiles & Amphibians.* 1970 Putnam. Ills. 359 p. dj. EX $14.00

COCHRANE, Charles Stuart. *Journal of Residence & Travels in Columbia.* 1825 London. Coburn. 1st ed. fld map. 2 vol set. VG $450.00

COCHRANE. *Dr. Johnson's Printer.* 1964 London. Ills 1st ed. dj. EX $28.00

COCKER, M.P. *Observer's Directory of Royal Navy Submarines 1901-1982.* 1982 London. Ills. 128 p. dj. EX $24.00

COCKERELL, Douglas. *Some Notes on Bookbinding.* 1929 Oxford U Pr. 1st ed. VG $40.00

COCKERELL, T.D. *Zoology of CO.* 1927 CO U Pr. Ills 1st ed. 262 p. VG $20.00

COCKRUM, E.L. *Mammals of the Southwest.* 1982 AZ U Pr. Ills. 176 p. maps. wraps. $6.00

COCKRUM. *Pioneer History of IN.* 1907 Oakland City. VG $20.00

COCTEAU, Jean. *Dessins.* 1924 Paris. 2nd ed. wraps. VG $50.00

COCTEAU, Jean. *Le Coq et L'Arlequin.* 1918 Paris. Ltd ed. 1/55. wraps. $295.00

CODMAN, Charles A. *Drive.* 1957 Boston. 1st ed. dj. VG $20.00

CODMAN, Charles A. *Drive.* 1957 Boston. Ills 1st ed. 335 p. dj. EX $35.00

CODMAN, John. *Arnold's Expediton to Quebec.* 1901 NY. Ills 1st ed. 340 p. G $40.00

CODMAN, John. *Brook Farm: Historic & Personal Memoirs.* 1894 Arena Pub. 12mo. 335 p. VG $20.00

CODY, William F. *Adventures of Buffalo Bill.* 1904 NY. VG $25.00

COE, W.R. *Nemerteans of the West & Northwest Coast of America.* 1905 Harvard U Pr. Ills. 318 p. EX $25.00

COFFEY, Frank. *Pride of Portland.* 1979 Everest. 1st ed. dj. EX $14.00

COFFEY, Frank. *40 Years on the Pacific.* 1920 NY. inscr. EX $35.00

COFFIN, Charles C. *Boys of '61.* 1896 Dana Estes. New Revised ed. VG $12.50

COFFIN, Charles C. *Boys of '76. History of Battles of the Revolution.* 1924 Harper. Ills Sturtevant. VG $10.00

COFFIN, Charles C. *Boys of '76. History of Battles of the Revolution.* 1876 NY. Harper. Ills. 4to. 398 p. VG $40.00

COFFIN, Charles C. *Old Times in the Colonies.* 1904 Harper. Ills. 460 p. VG $10.00

COFFIN, Charles C. *Our New Way Around the World.* 1869 Boston. Ills 1st ed. 12mo. 524 p. VG $30.00

COFFIN, Lewis. *Brick Architecture of Colonial Period in MD & VA.* 1919 NY. Arch Book Pub. G $60.00

COFFIN, Lewis. *Small French Buildings.* 1926 NY. Scribner. Ills. 4to. VG $45.00

COFFIN, Robert P. Tristram. *Collected Poems.* 1948 NY. inscr. dj. VG $25.00

COFFIN, Robert P. Tristram. *Kennebec.* 1937 1st ed. sgn. Rivers Series. dj. VG $45.00

COFFIN, Robert P. Tristram. *Kennebec.* 1937 6th print. G $15.00

COFFIN, Robert P. Tristram. *1 Horse Farm.* 1949 NY. 1st ed. dj. VG $15.00

COFFIN & COHEN. *Folklore in America.* 1966 NY. 1st ed. dj. VG $15.00

COGGINS, Jack. *Arms & Equipment of the Civil War.* 1962 Doubleday. Ills 1st ed. 4to. dj. VG $14.00

COGGINS, Jack. *Arms & Equipment of the Civil War.* 1983 Fairfax. Ills. 4to. 160 p. G $20.00

COGHLAN, Francis. *New Guide to Belgium.* 1837 London. Baily. 12mo. 2 fld maps. 378 p. $125.00

COGHLAN, Mrs. *Memoirs of Mrs. Coghlan.* 1795 NY. 8vo. ½-leather. G $45.00

COGSWELL, H.L. *Water Birds of CA.* 1977 CA U Pr. Ills. 399 p. dj. EX $14.00

COGSWELL, J.G. *History of the Revolutions in Europe.* 1852 Hartford. Ills. 8vo. 784 p. G $19.00

COHEN, Arthur A. *Admirable Woman.* 1983 Godine. 1st ed. dj. EX $15.00

COHEN, David. *Ramapo Mountain People.* 1974 New Brunswick. dj. EX $20.00

COHEN, I. Bernard. *Some Early Tools of American Science.* 1950 Cambridge. Harvard U Pr. 1st ed. 201 p. $25.00

COHEN, J.H. *They Builded Better Than They Knew.* c 1946. NY VG $25.00

COHEN, Leonard. *Favorite Game.* 1963 NY. 1st ed. dj. VG $25.00

COHEN, M. *Lewis Carroll, Photographer of Children: 4 Nude Studies.* 1979 Phil. 8vo. dj. EX $20.00

COHN, David. *God Shakes Creation.* 1935 Harper. Ills 1st ed. dj. VG $25.00

COIT, Dorothy. *Ivory Throne of Persia.* 1929 NY. Stokes. Ills 1st ed. 8vo. EX $25.00

COIT, J. *Citrus Fruits.* 1915 Macmillan. 520 p. G $5.00

COKE, Lady Mary. *Letters & Journals of Lady Mary Coke.* 1970 Bath, England. Ltd ed. 1/500. 4vo. dj. VG $85.00

COKE, Mr. & Mrs. Larry. *Calico.* 1941 Yermo, CA. 1st & only ed. wraps. EX $50.00

COKE, Van Deren. *Andrew Dashburg.* 1979 NM U Pr. Ills. 150 p. dj. $25.00

COKER, R.E. *Streams, Lakes, & Ponds.* 1954 NC U Pr. Ills. 327 p. dj. VG $18.00

COLBERT, E.H. *Age of Reptiles.* 1965 Norton. Ills 1st ed. 228 p. dj. VG $14.00

COLBERT, E.H. *Dinosaurs: Illustrated History.* 1983 Dembner. Ills. 4to. 224 p. dj. EX $20.00

COLBERT, E.H. *Great Dinosaurs Hunters & Their Discoveries.* 1984 Dover. Ills. 283 p. maps. wraps. EX $12.00

COLBERT, E.H. *Men & Dinosaurs.* 1968 Dutton. Ills 1st ed. 283 p. EX $14.00

COLBY. *1st Army in Europe.* 1969 GPO. Ltd ed. 1/1,500. wraps. VG $25.00

COLCORD, Joanna C. *Songs of American Sailormen.* 1938 NY. Revised ed. dj. VG $18.00

COLCORD, L. *Sailing Days on the Penebscot.* 1932 Salem, MA. 1st ed. photos. 465 p. VG $150.00

COLDEN, C. *History of the 5 Indian Nations of Canada.* 1902 1st ed. 8vo. 2 vol set. G $45.00

COLDERIDGE, Henry N. *6 Months in West Indies in 1825.* 1826 London. Murray. 1st ed. 332 p. fair. $125.00

COLE, F. Cooper. *Kincaid Prehistoric IL Metropolis.* 1951 Chicago. Ills 1st ed. 385 p. dj. VG $27.50

COLE, George R. Fitz-Roy. *Peruvians at Home.* 1884 London. Kegan Paul. 1st ed. 277 p. $75.00

COLE, L. *Fishing All Waters: Lake, Stream, & Ocean.* 1973 Galahad. Ills. 1960 p. dj. EX $7.50

COLE, N.R. *Arts in the Classroom.* 1940 NY. Ills. 137 p. dj. VG $10.00

COLE, Timothy. *Old Italian Masters.* 1892 NY. Century. VG $23.00

COLE, William. *Beastly Boys & Ghastly Girls.* 1964 World. Ills Ungerer. 1st ed. dj. VG $20.00

COLE, William. *Most of A.J. Liebling.* 1963 NY. 1st ed. dj. EX $20.00

COLEMAN, M.M. *From Mustanger to Lawyer 1890-1910.* 1952 San Antonio. Carleton. Ltd ed. 1/500. sgn. $25.00

COLEMAN, S.N. *Bells: History, Legends, Making, & Uses.* 1928 Chicago. Ills 1st ed. 462 p. VG $35.00

COLEMAN, Terry. *Southern Cross.* 1979 Viking. 1st ed. dj. VG $12.50

COLEMAN. *Collector Encyclopedia of Dolls.* 1971 Crown. dj. M $65.00

COLEMAN. *Eagle Wing.* 1956 NY. Greenwich. 1st ed. dj. EX $7.50

COLERIDGE, Samuel T. *Notes & Lectures on Shakespeare: Old Poets & Dramatists.* 1849 London. Pickering. 1st ed. 2 vol set. $75.00

COLERIDGE, Samuel T. *Poetical Works of Samuel T. Coleridge.* 1840 London. Pickering. 3 vol set. VG $75.00

COLERIDGE, Samuel T. *Rime of the Ancient Mariner.* 1945 Heritage. Ills Wilson. EX $10.00

COLERIDGE, Samuel T. *Rime of the Ancient Mariner.* 1875 London. Dore Gallery. 1st ed. folio. $125.00

COLES, Manning. *Brief Candles.* 1954 Doubleday. 1st ed. dj. EX $25.00

COLES, Manning. *Night Train to Paris.* 1952 London. 1st ed. red cloth. VG $7.50

COLES, Robert. *Children of Crisis: Study of Courage & Fear.* 1967 Boston. Little Brown. 1st ed. 8vo. $25.00

COLLENDER, H.W. *Modern Billiards: Complete Textbook of the Game.* no date. (1884) Ills New ed. 335 p. red cloth. $75.00

COLLENS, J.H. *Guide to Trinidad: Handbook for Tourists & Visitors.* 1888 London. Stock. Revised 2nd ed. 287 p. VG $35.00

COLLETT, Robert. *Centennial History of Sigma Chi Fraternity.* 1955 Evanston. Ills. 525 p. VG $20.00

COLLETTE. *Break of Day.* 1983 Ltd Ed Club. 1/2,000. sgn Gilot. dj. EX $95.00

COLLETTE. *Cheri & the Last of Cheri.* 1951 Farrar. dj. VG. $15.00

COLLETTI, Jack J. *Art of Wood Carving.* 1977 Prentice Hall. dj. VG $6.00

COLLIER, Eric. *3 Against the Wilderness.* 1960 Dutton. Ills. 349 p. dj. EX $10.00

COLLIER, John. *Fancies & Good Nights.* 1951 NY. 1st ed. dj. EX $60.00

COLLIER, John. *His Monkey Wife.* 1930 London. EX $100.00

COLLIER, John. *Patterns & Ceremonies of Indians of the Southwest.* 1949 NY. Ltd ed. 1/1,475. 192 p. dj. VG $180.00

COLLIER, Robert. *Book of Life.* 1925 NY. 7 vol set. G $25.00

COLLIER, W.R. *Dave Cook of the Rockies.* 1936 NY. Ills 1st ed. 224 p. dj. VG $30.00

COLLIN, Rodney. *Theory of Celestial Influence.* 1954 London. 1st ed. 393 p. EX $38.00

COLLINS, A.F. *Greatest Eye in the World.* 1942 NY. 1st ed. 266 p. dj. VG $20.00

COLLINS, A.F. *Handicraft for Boys.* 1918 NY. Stokes. 1st ed. dj. EX $10.00

COLLINS, A.F. *Manual of Wireless Telegraphy & Telephony (sic).* 1913 NY. 3rd ed. 300 p. VG $10.00

COLLINS, Alan C. *Story of the American in Pictures.* 1935 Garden City. reprint of 1953. dj. VG $8.00

COLLINS, C. Cody. *Love of a Glove.* 1947 NY. Fairchild. Revised ed. 8vo. 139 p. dj. $15.00

COLLINS, Clella Reeves. *Army Woman's Handbook.* 1942 NY. Revised ed. 239 p. G $8.50

COLLINS, Dale. *Sea Tracks of the Speejacks.* 1926 NY. Doubleday Page. G $26.00

COLLINS, George R. *Antonio Gaudi.* 1960 NY. Braziller. G $25.00

COLLINS, H.H. *Complete Field Guide to American Wildlife.* 1959 Harper. Ills. 683 p. VG $5.00

COLLINS, J. *Doctor Looks at Love & Life.* 1926 NY. New Home Lib. G $20.00

COLLINS, J.S. *My Experience in the West.* 1970 Donnelley. Ills. 245 p. EX $30.00

COLLINS, J.T. *Amphibians & Reptiles in KS.* 1982 KA U Pr. Revised ed. 256 p. EX $18.00

COLLINS, John O. *Panama Guide.* 1912 Mt. Hope. Ills. 8vo. fld map. 326 p. $25.00

COLLINS, Mabel. *When the Sun Moves Northward.* 1948 Il 148 p. EX $16.00

COLLINS, Max. *Baby Blue Ripoff.* 1983 1st Am ed. dj. $45.00

COLLINS, Max. *Kill Your Darlings.* 1984 1st Am ed. inscr. dj. $40.00

COLLINS, Vere H. *Talks with Thomas at May Gate 1920-1922.* 1928 NY. 1st ed. VG $35.00

COLLINS, Wilkie. *Armadale: Novel.* 1866 NY. $30.00

COLLINS, Wilkie. *Dead Alive.* 1874 Boston. 1st Am ed. 2nd bdg. VG $20.00

COLLINS, Wilkie. *Frozen Deep.* 1875 Boston. 1st Am ed. VG $95.00

COLLINS, Wilkie. *My Miscellanies.* 1963 London. 1st ed. 2 vol set. VG $85.00

COLLINS, Wilkie. *Tales of Suspense.* 1954 London. Folio Soc. VG $15.00

COLLINS, Wilkie. *Woman in White.* 1964 boxed. VG $35.00

COLLINS, Wilkie. *Woman in White.* 1860 NY. Harper. Ills. 260 p. cloth. EX $125.00

COLLINS. *Glamorous Sinners.* 1932 NY. Long Smith. Ills 1st ed. 269 p. dj. VG $17.50

COLLIS, Maurice. *Last & 1st in Burma.* 1956 NY. dj. VG $12.00

COLLISON, W.H. *In Wake of War Canoe.* c 1900. NY. Ills. 352 p. map. index. G $27.50

COLLODI, Carlo. *Pinocchio.* 1920 Lippincott. Ills Kirk. Deluxe ed. 8vo. VG $50.00

COLLODI, Carlo. *Pinocchio.* 1927 Boston. Houghton Mifflin. Ills. VG $35.00

COLLODI, Carlo. *Pinocchio.* no date. Florence. Italian text. 4to. $10.00

COLLODI, Carlo. *Pinocchio.* no date. Donohue. Ills. 264 p. 8vo. EX $10.00

COLLODI, Carlo. *Pinocchio.* 1940 Platt Munk. Ills Sarg. 1st ed. 122 p. dj. $25.00

COLLODI, Carlo. *Pinocchio.* no date. Winston. Ills Richardson. VG $15.00

COLLODI, Carlo. *Pinocchio.* 1946 Random House. Ills Lenski. 4to. dj. VG $15.00

COLLODI, Carlo. *Pinocchio.* 1929 Italy. Macmillan. Ills Mussino. VG $17.50

COLLODI, Carlo. *Pinocchio.* 1937 NY. Ills/ sgn Floethe. slipcase. VG $28.00

COLLODI, Carlo. *Pinocchio.* 1932 Garden City. Ills Petershams. VG $18.00

COLLODI, Carlo. *Pinocchio.* 1920 Phil. Ills Kirk. Gift ed. 4to. VG $35.00

COLMAN, George. *Broad Grins.* January 1804. Worcester. $35.00

COLOMBO, Alice. *Better Class.* 1980 NY. 1st ed. sgn. wraps. EX $12.00

COLQUHOUN, Patrick. *Treatise on Police of London.* 1798 Phil. 1st Am ed. VG $120.00

COLTON, Calvin. *Life & Times of Henry Clay.* 1846 NY. 1st ed. 8vo. 2 vol set. full leather. $100.00

COLTON, George. *Tecumseh; or, The West 30 Years Since.* 1842 NY. Wiley Putnam. 1st ed. $300.00

COLTON, Walter. *Deck & Port.* 1850 NY. Ills Sarony. VG $150.00

COLTON, Walter. *3 Years in CA.* 1949 Stanford. dj. VG $30.00

COLUM, M. *Our Friend James Joyce.* 1958 NY. 239 p. dj. VG $20.00

COLUM, Padraic. *Creatures.* 1927 NY. Ills Artzybasheff. 1st ed. VG $20.00

COLUM, Padraic. *Frenzied Prince: Being Heroic Stories of Ancient Ireland.* 1943 McKay. Ills Pogany. 1st issue. VG $30.00

COLUM, Padriac. *Children of Odin.* 1920 Macmillan. Ills Pogany. 1st ed. 282 p. $20.00

COLVILLE, W.J. *Spiritual Therapeutics.* 1888 Chicago. 1st ed. 332 p. VG $35.00

COLVIN, D.L. *Prohibition in the US: History of Prohibition Party.* 1926 NY. 1st ed. $35.00

COLVIN, H.M. *History of the King's Works.* 1963 London. 3 vol set. xl. VG $125.00

COLWIN, Laurie. *Family Happiness.* 1982 Knopf. 1st ed. dj. EX $15.00

COLWIN, Laurie. *Passion & Affect.* 1974 Viking. 1st ed. VG $25.00

COLWIN, Laurie. *Shine On Bright & Dangerous Object.* 1975 Chatto Windus. 1st English ed. dj. EX $25.00

COMBE, Andrew. *Physiology of Digestion.* 1840 Boston. 4th ed. 12mo. VG $15.00

COMBE, George. *System of Phrenology.* 1897 NY. Fowler & Wells. 516 p. EX $35.00

COMBE, J. *Hieronimus Bosch.* 1946 Paris. Pierre Tisne. 4to. 142 plts. $45.00

COMINI, Allessandra. *Schiele in Prison.* 1973 Greenwich. Graphic. $15.00

COMINO, Mary. *Gimson & the Barnsleys.* 1982 Van Nostrand. Ills. 224 p. $12.50

COMMAGER, H.S. *West: Illustrated History.* 1976 Promontory. Ills. 288 p. VG $10.00

COMMERY, E.W. *Artificial Light & Its Application in the Home.* 1932 McGraw Hill. Ills. tall 8vo. 153 p. dj. $35.00

COMOEDIAE, P. *Terentii Afri.* 1558 original vellum. VG $450.00

COMPTON-BURNETT, Ivy. *Mighty & Their Fall.* 1962 NY. 1st ed. dj. EX $10.00

COMRIE, John D. *Selected Works of Thomas Sydeham, M.D.* 1922 London. Bale. 4 plts. VG $20.00

COMSTOCK, Helen. *American Furniture: 17th, 18th, & 19th Century Styles.* 1952 NY. Viking. Ills. 326 p. dj. $50.00

COMSTOCK, Helen. *American Furniture: 17th, 18th, & 19th Century Styles.* 1962 NY. Viking. Ills. dj. EX $32.50

COMSTOCK, Helen. *100 Most Beautiful Rooms in America.* 1969 NY. Studio. 3rd print. EX $27.50

COMSTOCK, Henry Smith. *Hasty Recollections of Busy Life.* 1896 Peoria. Transcript Co. $30.00

COMSTOCK, J.H. *Introduction to Entomology.* 1933 Comstock. Ills. 1,044 p. VG $20.00

COMSTOCK, J.L. *Conversations on Chemistry.* 1833 Hartford. Ills. 356 p. full leather. $25.00

COMSTOCK, Jane. *I Go to the Blackboard (Ke hele Nei Au I Ka Papaeleele).* 1929 Honolulu. Ills. 32 p. Hawaiian verse. VG $15.00

COMTE, L.C. *Le Magicien de Societe.* 1825 Paris. 2nd ed. wraps. VG $115.00

CONARD, H.S.; & REDFEARN, P.L. *How To Know the Mosses & Liverworts.* 1979 Brown. Ills 1st ed. 302 p. EX $22.00

CONDE, J.W. *Jumping Kangaroo & the Apple Butter Cat.* 1900 McClure. 1st ed. 4to. VG $25.00

CONDON, Eddie. *We Called It Music.* 1947 NY. 1st print. G $18.00

CONDON, Richard. *Infinity of Mirrors.* 1964 NY. Advance copy. $25.00

CONDON, Richard. *Mile High.* 1969 Dial. 1st ed. dj. EX $15.00

CONDON, Richard. *Prizzi's Honor.* 1982 NY. Ltd ed. 1/100. sgn. dj. M $15.00

CONE, Mary. *2 Years in CA.* 1876 Chicago. 1st ed. 8vo. rust cloth. EX $85.00

CONGER, George. *Synoptic Naturalism.* 1960 MN U Lib Pr. 1st ed. 805 p. EX $20.00

CONGREVE, William. *Love for Love.* 1977 London. 1st ed. wraps. EX $17.00

CONISE, Titus. *Natural Wealth of CA.* 1868 San Francisco. 4to. VG $40.00

CONKLING, Margaret C. *Memoirs of the Mother & Wife of Washington.* 1851 Auburn. 12mo. 248 p. red cloth. xl. VG $17.00

CONNELL, E. *Diary of a Rapist.* 1966 NY. 1st ed. dj. EX $15.00

CONNELL, E. *Points for a Compass Rose.* 1973 NY. 1st ed. dj. EX $10.00

CONNELL, E.S. *Mr. Bridge.* 1969 Knopf. 1st ed. dj. EX $30.00

CONNELL, E.S. *Son of the Morning Star.* 1984 San Francisco. 1st ed. dj. EX $60.00

CONNELL, E.S. *Son of the Morning Star.* 1984 North Point. Uncorrected proof. EX $75.00

CONNELLEY, W.E. *Founding of Harman's Station & Wiley Captivity.* 1910 NY. 1st ed. scarce. VG $125.00

CONNELLEY, W.E. *Quantrill & Border Wars.* 1910 Torch Pr. Ills. 539 p. maps. scarce. $125.00

CONNELLEY, W.E. *Quantrill & Border Wars.* 1956 NY. Pageant. Ills. 542 p. dj. VG $25.00

CONNELLY, Marc. *Green Pastures.* 1929 NY. 1st ed. sgn. G $50.00

CONNER, Daniel Ellis. *Confederate in CO Gold Field.* 1970 Norman. 1st ed. dj. VG $17.50

CONNER, Dennis. *No Excuse To Lose.* 1978 Norton. 1st ed. 192 p. dj. VG $25.00

CONNETT, Eugene. *American Big Game Fishing.* 1935 Derrydale. Ltd ed. 1/850. EX $350.00

CONNETT, Eugene. *Any Luck? Trout Fishing.* 1939 Garden City. Ills. 231 p. dj. VG $9.00

CONNETT, Eugene. *Duck Decoys: How To Make, Paint, & Rig Them.* 1953 Ills Edgar Burke. dj. $30.00

CONNETT, Eugene. *Duck Shooting Along the Atlantic Tidewater.* 1956 2nd print. dj. VG $45.00

CONNETT, Eugene. *Duck Shooting Along the Atlantic Tidewater.* 1947 Bonanza. Ills. 4to. 308 p. dj. VG $25.00

CONNETT, Eugene. *Duck Shooting Along the Atlantic Tidewater.* 1947 NY. Ills Burke/Hunt. 1st ed. dj. $65.00

CONNETT, Eugene. *Duck Shooting Along the Atlantic Tidewater.* 1947 NY. 1st trade ed. VG $60.00

ONNETT, Eugene. *Upland Game Bird Shooting in America.* 1930 NY. Ills 1st ed. 1/850. 4to. $150.00

CONNETT, Eugene. *Wildfowling in the MS Flyway.* 1949 NY. 1st ed. dj. VG $150.00

CONNETT, Eugene. *Wing Shooting & Angling.* 1920 1st ed. $45.00

CONNINGHAM, F. *Currier & Ives Prints: Illustrated Check List.* 1983 NY. Crown. EX $16.00

CONNOLLY, Cyril. *Evening Colonnade.* 1975 Harcourt Brace. 1st Am ed. dj. VG $10.00

CONNOLLY, J.B. *Book of the Gloucester Fishermen.* 1927 John Day. 1st ed. 301 p. VG $10.00

CONNOLLY, Joseph. *P.G. Wodehouse.* 1979 London. Ills 1st ed. dj. EX $35.00

CONNOLLY & O'HARRA. *Mineral Wealth of the Black Hills.* 1929 Rapid City. Ills. 418 p. wraps. EX $25.00

CONNOR, Seymour V. *Broadcloth & Britches.* 1977 College Station. 1st ed. dj. $30.00

CONRAD, B. *Gates of Fear.* 1957 NY. Ills. 4to. 337 p. $12.50

CONRAD, Earl. *Jim Crow America.* 1947 NY. 1st print. G $12.50

CONRAD, Jessie. *Joseph Conrad As I Knew Him.* 1926 London. 1st ed. VG $45.00

CONRAD, Joseph. *Arrow of Gold.* 1919 Garden City. 2nd issue. EX $11.00

CONRAD, Joseph. *Congo Diary.* 1978 NY. 1st ed. dj. M $12.00

CONRAD, Joseph. *Conrad to a Friend.* 1928 London. 1st ed. VG $35.00

CONRAD, Joseph. *Conrad's Manifesto: Preface to Career.* 1966 Phil. Gehenna. Ltd ed. 1/1,100. boxed. VG $10.00

CONRAD, Joseph. *Last Essays.* 1926 London. 1st ed. dj. EX $45.00

CONRAD, Joseph. *Last 12 Years of Joseph Conrad.* 1928 London. 1st ed. VG $35.00

CONRAD, Joseph. *Laughing Anne & 1 More Day.* 1924 London. VG $25.00

CONRAD, Joseph. *Laughing Anne: Play.* 1923 London. 1/200. 8vo. sgn. vellum. EX $300.00

CONRAD, Joseph. *Lord Jim.* 1900 Edinburgh. gray-green cloth. slipcase. G $225.00

CONRAD, Joseph. *Lord Jim.* 1900 NY. 1st Am ed. EX $95.00

CONRAD, Joseph. *Nostromo.* 1961 NY. Ltd Ed Club. slipcase. EX $100.00

CONRAD, Joseph. *Notes on My Books.* 1921 NY/Toronto. 1/250. 8vo. sgn. dj. EX $225.00

CONRAD, Joseph. *Outcast of the Island.* 1975 Ltd Ed Club. 4to. 212 p. slipcase. EX $50.00

CONRAD, Joseph. *Personal Record.* 1912 Harper. 1st ed. $30.00

CONRAD, Joseph. *Rover.* 1923 Garden City. 1st Am ed. dj. EX $125.00

CONRAD, Joseph. *Secret Agent.* 1907 NY. Harper. 1st ed. VG $60.00

CONRAD, Joseph. *Shadowline.* 1917 Doubleday. 1st ed. VG $10.00

CONRAD, Joseph. *Suspense.* 1925 Garden City. 1st trade ed. dj. G $15.00

CONRAD, Joseph. *Tales of Hearsay.* 1925 NY. 1st Am ed. 120 p. dj. EX $45.00

CONRAD, Joseph. *Tales of Hearsay.* 1925 London. 1st English ed. VG $22.00

CONRAD, Joseph. *Tales of Hearsay.* 1925 London. Unwin. Ltd 1st ed. dj. $150.00

CONRAD, Joseph. *Tales of Unrest.* 1898 London. 1st English ed. VG $175.00

CONRAD, Joseph. *Within the Tides.* 1955 London. 1st ed. VG $75.00

CONRAD, Joseph. *Works of Joseph Conrad.* Luxury ed. reprint of 1921. 20 vol set. $2500.00

CONRAD, Joseph. *Works of Joseph Conrad.* 1980 NY. Ltd ed. 1/780. 20 vol set. M $2500.00

CONRAD, Joseph. *3 Plays.* 1934 London. dj. EX $20.00

CONRAD, Lawrence H. *Author's Mind.* 1925 Highland Falls. Editor Council. 1st ed. VG $25.00

CONRAD. *Uncle Dick Wooten.* 1890 Chicago. 1st ed. EX $150.00

CONRAN, T. *House Book.* 1983 NY. Ills. 448 p. $35.00

CONRAN, Terence. *Cookbook.* 1980 NY. 1st ed. dj. EX $25.00

CONROTTO, Eugene L. *Miwok Means People.* 1973 Fresno, CA. 8vo. 131 p. dj. VG $20.00

CONROY, Pat. *Great Santini.* 1976 Houghton. 1st ed. sgn. dj. EX $60.00

CONROY, Pat. *Lords of Discipline.* 1980 Boston. Houghton Mifflin. 1st ed. dj. $30.00

CONROY, Pat. *Prince of Tides.* 1986 Boston. Houghton Mifflin. 1st ed. dj. $12.00

CONSTANTINE, K.C. *Always a Body To Trade.* 1983 Uncorrected proof. wraps. $65.00

CONSTANTINE, K.C. *Man Who Liked To Look at Himself.* 1973 NY. Saturday Review. 1st ed. EX $35.00

CONSUMER GUIDE EDITORS. *Clay Cookery.* no date. Simon Schuster. 1st ed. dj. EX $10.00

CONTINI, Mila. *Fashion.* 1965 NY. dj. EX $15.00

CONWAY, A. *Reconstruction of GA.* 1966 MN U Pr. 248 p. EX $14.00

CONWAY, Moncure D. *My Pilgrimage to the Wise Men of the East.* 1906 Boston. Ills. 416 p. cloth. EX $45.00

CONWAY, W. *Climbing in Karakoram Himalayas.* 1894 NY. VG $250.00

CONWAY, W. *Writings of Albrecht Durer.* 1958 NY. Intro A Werner. VG $35.00

CONWAY, W. *1st Crossing of Spitzbergen.* 1897 London. Ills 1st ed. 371 p. VG $125.00

CONWELL, R.H. *Life, Travels, & Literary Career of Bayard Taylor.* 1879 Boston. Ills. 12mo. 358 p. cloth. xl. $17.00

CONWELL, R.H. *Life & Public Services of James A. Garfield.* 1880 Boston. Ills 1st ed. 12mo. 354 p. VG $21.00

COOK, Beatice. *Truth Is Stranger Than Fishin'.* 1955 Morrow. 303 p. G $5.00

COOK, Capt. James. *Journals of Voyage of Resolution & Discovery 1776-1780.* 1967 Cambridge U Pr. Hakluyt Soc. 2 vol set. $90.00

COOK, Capt. James. *3 Voyages of Capt. Cook Around the World.* c 1868. NY/London. 8vo. 2 vols. VG $150.00

COOK, J.H. *50 Years on the Old Frontier.* 1923 Yale U Pr. Ills 2nd print. $17.50

COOK, Roy Bird. *Family & Early Life of Stonewall Jackson.* 1967 Charleston, WV. 5th ed. wine cloth. dj. EX $25.00

COOK, Warren L. *Flood Tide of Empire: Spain & Pacific Northwest 1543-1819.* 1973 New Haven. Ills 1st ed. maps. dj. M $50.00

COOKE, Alistair. *Christmas Eve.* 1952 NY. Knopf. Ills Simont. 4to. 57 p. dj. G $15.00

COOKE, H.I. *Pictures Within Pictures in the National Gallery of Art.* 1970 Richmond. Ills. 64 p. $8.50

COOKE, J. *Dublin Book of Irish Verse 1828-1909.* no date. Dublin/London. 1st ed. EX $60.00

COOKE, John Esten. *Outlines From the Outpost.* 1961 Donnelley. 1st ed. 410 p. EX $35.00

COOLEY, A. *Encyclopedia of 6,000 Receipts.* 1846 NY. $18.00

COOLIDGE, Calvin. *Autography of Calvin Coolidge.* 1929 NY. 1st trade ed. inscr. G $120.00

COOLIDGE, Calvin. *Have Faith in MA.* 1919 Boston. inscr. EX $250.00

COOLIDGE, Calvin. *Price of Freedom.* 1924 NY/London. 1st ed. blue cloth. VG $10.00

COOLIDGE, Mary R. *Rain Makers of AZ & NM.* 1929 Boston. Ills. maps. G $20.00

COOLIDGE, W.A.B. *Alpine Studies.* 1912 London. Longman. Ills 1st ed. G $45.00

COON, C.S. *Hunting Peoples.* 1971 Little Brown. Ills 1st ed. 413 p. dj. EX $14.00

COON, C.S. *7 Caves: Explorations in the Middle East.* 1957 NY. Knopf. 1st ed. VG $15.00

COONEY, Barbara. *Chanticleer & the Fox.* 1958 Cowell. Ills 1st ed. dj. VG $30.00

COONEY, Barbara. *Little Juggler.* 1961 NY. 1st ed. dj. EX $17.50

COONEY, Ellen. *Quest for the Holy Grail.* 1981 Duir Pr. 1st ed. sgn. wraps. $20.00

COONEY, Ellen. *Silver Rose.* 1979 Duir Pr. 1st ed. sgn. wraps. EX $25.00

COOPER, C. *Scene.* 1960 NY. 1st ed. dj. EX $10.00

COOPER, C.; & LINDSAY, M. *Eli Whitney & the Whitney Armory.* 1980 Whitney Museum. Ills. 95 p. pb. EX $9.00

COOPER, Elizabeth. *My Lady of the Chinese Courtyard.* 1914 Stokes. 2nd print. $12.50

COOPER, Helen A. *John Turnbull: Hand & Spirit of a Painter.* 1986 New Haven. Ills. 4to. 300 p. dj. $47.00

COOPER, Helen A. *Winslow Homer Watercolors.* 1986 New Haven. Ills. 4to. 264 p. cloth. dj. $40.00

COOPER, J. Wesley. *Ante-Bellum Houses of Natchez.* 1970 Natchez. Ills. 208 p. dj. $50.00

COOPER, James Fenimore. *Bravo: Venetian Story.* 1831 Paris. Baudry Foreign Lib. VG $125.00

COOPER, James Fenimore. *History of the Navy.* 1847 Phil. 1st 1 vol ed. 8vo. 447 p. G $75.00

COOPER, James Fenimore. *History of the Navy.* 1839 Phil. 2 vol set. G $175.00

COOPER, James Fenimore. *Last of the Mohicans.* 1935 NY. Scribner. reprint. 4to. EX $20.00

COOPER, James Fenimore. *Last of the Mohicans.* 1956 NY. Scribner. Classic ed. Ills Wyeth. VG $10.00

COOPER, James Fenimore. *Last of the Mohicans.* 1939 NY. Scribner. Classic ed. Ills Wyeth. $35.00

COOPER, James Fenimore. *Leather Stocking Saga.* 1954 Pantheon. Ills. 833 p. $25.00

COOPER, James Fenimore. *Pathfinder.* 1840 Phil. 1st ed. 1st issue. 2 vol set. $225.00

COOPER, James Fenimore. *Works of James Fenimore Cooper.* no date. NY. Putman. Red Rover ed. 30 vols. $75.00

COOPER, James Fenimore. *Works of James Fenimore Cooper.* NY. Putnam. Ltd Leather Stocking ed. $300.00

COOPER, James Fenimore. *Works of James Fenimore Cooper.* Pathfinder ed. 1/1,000. 16 vol set. VG $90.00

COOPER, Jeff. *Complete Book of Modern Handgunning.* 1961 Prentice Hall. 1st ed. dj. VG $25.00

COOPER, John R. *Art of the Compleat Angler.* 1968 Duke U Pr. 1st ed. green cloth. M $10.00

COOPER, Lane. *Louis Agassiz As a Teacher.* 1951 Comstock. Ills. 90 p. wraps. $8.00

COOPER, Patricia. *Quilters, Women, & Domestic Art.* 1977 NY. Doubleday. Ills. 4to. 157 p. $15.00

COOPER, R.K. *Tenny Big.* 1953 Christopher. Ills Hobson. sgn. EX $10.00

COOPER, Rev. *History of North America.* 1815 Albany. 264 p. G $40.00

COOPER, Samuel. *1st Lines of the Practice of Surgery.* 1830 Phil. 3rd Am ed. 484 p. 2 vol set. $200.00

COOPER, W.D. *History of South America Containing Discoveries of Columbus.* 1789 London. 1st ed. 12mo. 168 p. calf. $125.00

COOPER, William H. *Incidents of Shipwreck; or, Loss of the San Francisco.* 1855 Phil. 1st ed. ½-calf. $60.00

COOPER, William. *Preventive Medicine.* 1905 Cleves. 1st ed. $15.00

COOVER, Robert. *Prick Songs & Descants.* 1969 NY. 1st ed. dj. VG $15.00

COOVER, Robert. *Prick Songs & Descants.* 1969 Dutton. Review copy. dj. EX $55.00

COOVER, Robert. *Prick Songs & Descants.* 1969 Dutton. 1st ed. sgn. dj. EX $25.00

COOVER, Robert. *Theological Position.* 1972 Dutton. Review copy. dj. EX $60.00

COPE, E.D. *Batrachia of North America.* 1963 Lundberg. reprint of 1889. 525 p. EX $45.00

COPLAND, Aaron. *Copland on Music.* 1960 Doubleday. 1st ed. dj. VG $15.00

COPLAND, Aaron; & PERLIS, V. *Copland: 1900 Through 1942.* 1984 NY. dj. EX $15.00

COPLESTON, Edward. *Advice to a Young Reviewer.* 1927 Oxford. dj. VG $45.00

COPLEY, Fred S. *Set of Alphabets.* 1870 NY. oblong 4to. 47 p. fair. $75.00

COPPARD, A.E. *Field of Mustard.* 1926 Cape. 1st ed. dj. EX $50.00

COPPARD, A.E. *Hips & Haws: Poems.* 1922 Golden Cockerell. 1/500. dj. $50.00

COPPARD, A.E. *Man From Kilsheelan.* 1930 London. Chiswick. 1/550. sgn. EX $50.00

COPPARD, A.E. *Nixey's Harlequin.* 1931 London. 1st ed. dj. EX $45.00

COPPARD, A.E. *Pink Furniture.* 1930 London. Cape. Ills Gurney. 1st ed. dj. EX $25.00

COPPARD, A.E. *Pink Furniture.* 1930 Cape. Ills Gurney. Ltd ed. sgn. EX $90.00

COPPARD, A.E. *Rummy: That Noble Game.* 1933 Boston. Golden Cockerell. 1st ed. dj. $40.00

COPPARD, A.E.; & ANGELO, V. *Cherry Ripe.* 1935 Hawthorn House. Ltd ed. 1/300. sgn. slipcase. $50.00

COPPEE, H. *General Thomas.* 1893 NY. Ills. Great Am Commanders Series. VG $25.00

COPPEE, H. *Grant & His Campaigns: Military Biography.* 1886 NY. Richardson. Ills. maps. 3/4 leather. VG $30.00

COPPEL, Alfred. *Dragon.* 1977 Harcourt. 1st ed. dj. EX $15.00

COPPENS, Rev. Charles S.J. *Brief History of Philosophy.* 1909 NY. 144 p. VG $25.00

COPPLESTONE, T. *Architecture: Great Art of Building.* 1971 London. Ills. 99 p. dj. M $15.00

CORBETT, Elizabeth. *She Was Carie Eaton.* 1938 NY. 1st ed. dj. M $14.00

CORBETT, James. *Jungle Lore.* 1953 Oxford U Pr. Ills. 172 p. dj. VG $17.50

CORBETT, James. *Maneaters of Kumaon.* 1946 Oxford U Pr. Ills 1st Am ed. 235 p. dj. VG $10.00

CORBETT, Jim. *Maneaters of India.* 1957 Oxford U Pr. dj. VG $10.00

CORDASCO, F. *American Medical Imprints 1820-1910.* 1985 Rowman. 2 vol set. EX $90.00

CORDELL, A. Richard. *20th Century Plays.* 1941 Ronald Pr. 3rd ed. $10.00

CORDELL, Eugene. *Medical Annals of MD 1799-1899.* 1903 Baltimore. 1st ed. 888 p. EX $50.00

CORE, Sue. *Panama's Jungle Book.* 1936 Clermont Pr. oblong 8vo. cloth. $16.00

COREY, Zane. *Adventures in Fishing.* 1952 Harper. dj. VG $35.00

CORLETT, William. *Medicine Man of American Indian: His Cultural Background.* 1935 Springfield. Ills 1st ed. 8vo. 369 p. VG $60.00

CORLISS, Philip G. *Hemerocallis.* 1951 San Francisco. Ltd 1st ed. 1/1,000. inscr. EX $22.00

CORMACK, A.J.R. *Famous Pistols & Handguns.* 1977 Barrie Jenkins. Ills. 160 p. dj. EX $22.50

CORMAN, Avery. *Kramer vs. Kramer.* 1977 NY. 1st ed. dj. M $15.00

CORMAN, Avery. *Old Neighborhood.* 1980 Linden. 1st ed. dj. EX $11.00

CORMAN, Cid. *Living, Dying.* 1970 New Directions. 1st ed. dj. EX $15.00

CORN, Alfred. *Tongues on Trees.* 1981 Parenthese. Ltd 1st ed. 1/150. inscr. EX $35.00

CORNELIUS, Brother. *Old Master of CA.* 1942 Putnam. 1st ed. $200.00

CORNELIUS, Charles O. *Furniture Masterpieces of Duncan Phyfe.* 1922 NY. Ills. 4to. 99 p. G $50.00

CORNELIUS, Mrs. *Young Housekeeper's Friend: Guide to Domestic Economy.* 1850 Boston. $60.00

CORNELL, Katherine. *Autobiography of Katherine Cornell.* 1939 Random House. presentation. sgn. dj. VG $37.50

CORNELL, Katherine. *I Wanted To Be an Actress.* 1939 NY. 1st ed. dj. VG $27.50

CORNER, William. *San Antonio de Bexar.* 1890 San Antonio. 1st ed. 8vo. map. plts. cloth. $80.00

CORNFORD, Frances. *Different Days.* 1928 London. 1st ed. VG $60.00

CORNING, Frederick Gleason. *Student Reverie: Album of Saxony Days.* 1920 NY. Ills. 4to. 98 p. rare. VG $40.00

CORNISH, B.W. *Some Family Letters of William M. Thackery.* 1911 Riverside. 1st ed. 1/550. $50.00

CORNISH, C.J. *Wild Animals in Captivity.* 1894 NY. VG $35.00

CORREA, Antonio B. *Alfaro.* 1981 Madrid. Universidad Complutense. 4to. $20.00

CORRI, E. *30 Years a Referee.* 1915 NY. VG $27.50

CORRIGAN, Douglas. *That's My Story.* 1938 Dutton. 1st ed. presentation. dj. VG $27.50

CORRIGAN, Douglas. *That's My Story.* 1938 NY. 1st ed. sgn. dj. EX $30.00

CORSON, M. William. *Armies of Ignorance: Rise of American Intelligence Empire.* 1977 Dial. 1st ed. dj. VG $10.00

CORTAZAR, Julio. *All Fires the Fire.* 1973 NY. 1st ed. dj. EX $8.00

CORTAZAR, Julio. *Certain Lucas.* 1984 Knopf. 1st Am ed. dj. EX $13.00

CORTAZAR, Julio. *Hopscotch.* 1967 London. Collins. 1st ed. dj. VG $25.00

CORTAZAR, Julio. *Hopscotch.* 1966 NY. Pantheon. 1st ed. dj. EX $45.00

CORTAZAR, Julio. *Manual for Manuel.* 1978 Pantheon. 1st Am ed. dj. EX $20.00

CORTAZAR, Julio. *Winners.* 1965 Pantheon. 1st Am ed. dj. EX $30.00

CORTAZAR, Julio. *62: A Model Kit.* 1972 NY. 1st ed. dj. EX $8.00

CORTI, Count. *Wizard of Monte Carlo.* 1935 NY. 1st ed. dj. VG $20.00

CORTI, Egon C. *Rise of the House of Rothschild.* 1928 NY. Ills 1st ed. 8vo. 427 p. VG $35.00

CORVO, Baron. *Letters to James Walsh.* 1972 London. Ltd 1st ed. dj. M $28.00

CORVO, Baron. *Rubaiyat.* 1925 Boston. Ills Hamzeh Carr. dj. VG $275.00

CORWIN, Hugh D. *Comanche & Kiowa Captives in OK & TX.* 1959 Lawton. private print. 1st ed. sgn. EX $75.00

CORY, David. *Puss Junior & Man in Moon.* 1922 Harper. G $15.00

COSENTINO, F.T. *Boehm's Birds: Porcelain Art.* 1960 NY. 1st ed. 4to. sgn. dj. VG $42.50

COSENTINO, F.T. *Porcelain Art of Edward Marshall Boehm.* 1961 NY. Ills. 206 p. $45.00

COSMAS & MURRAY. *US Marines in Vietnam.* 1986 GPO. Ills. 487 p. maps. dj. $34.00

COST, March. *Bitter Green of the Willow.* 1967 Phil. Ills Anderson. 1st ed. dj. EX $20.00

COSTAIN, Thomas. *Below the Salt.* 1957 Doubleday. 1st ed. dj. EX $10.00

COSTAIN, Thomas. *Black Rose.* 1945 Doubleday Doran. 1st ed. VG $20.00

COSTAIN, Thomas. *Darkness & the Dawn.* 1959 Doubleday. 1st ed. dj. EX $7.00

COSTAIN, Thomas. *White & Gold: French Regime in Canada.* 1954 Toronto. Doubleday Canada. 1st ed. dj. $20.00

COSTANTINO, Ruth T. *How To Know French Antiques.* 1961 NY. Potter. Ills. 240 p. dj. $40.00

COSTELLANO, Illion. *Maneaters; or, Cannibal Queen: Story of the South Pacific.* 1864 NY. Munro. 1st ed. 12mo. pink wraps. VG $165.00

COSTELLO, D.F. *Desert World.* 1972 Crowell. Ills. 264 p. dj. EX $12.00

COSTELLO, D.F. *Prairie World.* 1969 Crowell. Ills. 242 p. VG $12.00

COSTELLO, H.F. *Under the Rattlesnake Flag.* 1898 Boston. Ills J Steeple. VG $12.00

COSTON, H.E.T. *Swift Trout: Tale of Trout in 2 Rivers.* 1946 Collins. Ills. 160 p. G $7.00

COTE, Augustin. *Relations des Jesuites. Dans la Nouvelle-France.* 1858 Quebec. 8vo. 3 vol set. xl. VG $175.00

COTLER, Gordon. *Mission in Black.* 1967 Random House. 1st ed. dj. EX $10.00

COTLOW, Lewis. *In Search of the Primitive.* 1966 Little Brown. Ills. 454 p. dj. VG $10.00

COTLOW, Lewis. *Twilight of the Primitive.* 1971 Macmillan. Ills. 1st ed. 257 p. dj. VG $12.00

COTON, A.V. *New Ballet: Kurt Jooss & His Work.* 1946 London. Ills 1st ed. dj. VG $25.00

COTSAKIS, Roxane. *Wing & Thorn.* 1952 Atlanta. Tupper Love. 1st ed. sgn. $25.00

COTTERELL, H.H. *National Types of Old Pewter.* 1925 Boston. Ltd ed. 1/1,050. fair. $12.00

COTTON, J. *Narrative of Planting of MA Colony.* 1694 Boston. 19th C reprint. 1/2 calf. VG $30.00

COTTON, W.C. *Short Simple Letter From Conservative Beekeeper.* 1841 Boston. Ills 1st Am ed. 12mo. 24 p. $75.00

COTTRELL. *Recollection of Siberia in 1840 & 1841.* 1842 London. fld map. cloth. xl. VG $45.00

COUCH, William. *New Playwrights' Anthology.* 1969 LSU Pr. 8vo. 258 p. dj. EX $20.00

COUES, E. *Journal of Jacob Fowler.* 1898 NY. 1st ed. 1/950. VG $100.00

COUES, E. *Key to North American Birds.* 1887 Estes Lauriat. Revised ed. 985 p. VG $48.00

COUFFER, Jack. *Song of Wild Laughters.* 1963 Simon Schuster. Ills. 190 p. dj. EX $10.00

COULSON, Zoe. *Good Housekeeping Illustrated Cookbook.* 1980 NY. dj. EX $12.50

COULTER, E.M. *Civil War & Readjustment in KY.* 1926 Chapel Hill. 1st ed. VG $65.00

COULTER, John. *Adventures on Western Coast of South America.* 1847 London. Longman. 1st ed. 2 vol set. $200.00

COULTER, John. *Complete Story of Galveston Horror.* 1900 Ills. G $20.00

COULTER. *Short History of GA.* 1933 Chapel Hill. Ills. cloth. dj. VG $18.00

COUPIN, Henri. *Atlas de Botanique Microscopique.* 1908 Paris. Vigot Freres. 4to. 126 p. $20.00

COURLANDER, H. *Son of the Leopard.* 1974 NY. Ills 2nd ed. EX $7.00

COURT, Alfred. *My Life with the Big Cats.* 1955 Simon Schuster. Ills 1st ed. 178 p. VG $12.50

COURTHION, Pierre. *Georges Rouault.* no date. NY. Abrams. Ills. 490 p. dj. $100.00

COURTNEY, B.; & Burdsall, H.H. *Field Guide to Mushrooms & Their Relatives.* 1982 Van Nostrand. Ills 1st ed. 144 p. dj. EX $18.00

COUSINS, Frank. *Colonial Architecture.* 1912 Doubleday Page. fair. $65.00

COUSTEAU, Jacques-Yves. *Costeau's Underwater Treasury.* 1959 Harper. 1st ed. dj. VG $26.00

COUSTEAU, Jacques-Yves. *Living Sea.* 1963 Harper Row. EX $21.00

COUTURE, Thomas. *Conversation on Art Methods.* 1879 NY. 8vo. inscr. VG $45.00

COVARRUBIAS, Miguel. *In the Worst Possible Taste.* 1932 Scribner. 1st ed. dj. EX $25.00

COVARRUBIAS, Miguel. *Indian Art of Mexico & Central America.* 1957 NY. 1st ed. dj. VG $45.00

COVARRUBIAS, Miguel. *Island of Bali.* 1937 Knopf. 2nd ed. cloth. VG $40.00

COVARRUBIAS, Miguel. *Island of Bali.* 1937 NY. Ills. dj. EX $65.00

COVARRUBIAS, Miguel. *Mexico South: Isthmus of Tehuantepec.* 1946 NY. Knopf. 1st ed. 427 p. VG $30.00

COWAN, Robert Ernest. *Bibliography of History of CA & Pacific West 1510-1906.* 1952 Columbus. New ed. 4to. VG $65.00

COWAN, S.K. *Sergeant York & His People.* 1922 Grosset Dunlap. reprint. G $11.00

COWARD, Noel. *Blithe Spirit.* 1941 Garden City. dj. G $15.00

COWARD, Noel. *Future Indefinite.* 1954 London. 1st ed. presentation. dj. EX $25.00

COWARD, Noel. *Not Yet the Dodo & Other Verses.* 1967 London. 1st ed. dj. VG $18.00

COWARD, Noel. *Nude with Violin.* 1958 NY. 1st ed. dj. EX $17.50

COWARD, Noel. *Present Indicative.* 1937 Doubleday. Ills 1st ed. $15.00

COWARD, Noel. *Pretty Polly.* 1965 Garden City. 1st ed. dj. EX $10.00

COWARD, Noel. *Privilege of His Company.* 1975 NY. 1st ed. dj. M $15.00

COWBURN, Philip. *Warship in History.* 1964 NY. 1st print. dj. G $20.00

COWDEN, Jeanne. *Chameleons: Little Lions of the Reptile World.* 1977 McKay. Ills 1st ed. 58 p. dj. EX $10.00

COWDRY, E.V. *Problem of Aging: Biological & Medical Aspects.* 1939 Williams Wilkins. $12.50

COWELL, Adrian. *Heart of the Forest.* 1961 Knopf. Ills 1st ed. 238 p. dj. VG $10.00

COWEN, R.C. *Frontiers of the Sea: Story of Oceanographic Exploration.* 1960 Doubleday. Ills. 307 p. dj. VG $18.00

COWICK, K.L. *Story of KS City.* reprint of 1924. pb. EX $10.00

COWLES, Roger. *Distant Drums.* 1932 London. Methuen. 1st ed. inscr. G $12.00

COWLEY, Abraham. *Anacreon.* 1923 London. Ills Gooden. 1/725. 8vo. VG $100.00

COWLEY, Malcolm. *Blue Juniata: Poems.* 1929 NY. EX $100.00

COWLEY, Malcolm. *Exile's Return.* 1981 Ltd Ed Club. sgn Cowley/Abbott. dj. EX $95.00

COWLEY, Malcolm. *Flower & the Leaf.* 1985 Viking. 1st ed. dj. EX $25.00

COWLEY, Malcolm. *2nd Flowering: Works & Days of the Lost Generation.* 1973 NY. 1st ed. dj. EX $15.00

COWPER, R. *Unhappy Princess.* 1982 Cheap Street. 1st ed. 1/27. presentation. EX $300.00

COWPER, William. *Diverting History of John Gilpin.* c1888. London. Ills H Rosa. 8vo. $40.00

COWPER, William. *Poems.* 1845 Glasgow. fore-edge of men fishing. $310.00

COX, G.W. *Tales of the Gods & Heroes.* no date. London. Ills Fripp. dj. VG $25.00

COX, Herbert A. *Old London Illustrated; or, London in the 16th Century.* no date. London. Ills Brewer. 7th ed. $18.00

COX, James. *Journey Through My Years.* 1946 NY. Ills. inscr. cloth. dj. VG $75.00

COX, James. *My Native Land.* 1895 St. Louis. G $30.00

COX, M. *Notes on the History of the Irish Horse.* 1897 Dublin. Sealy Bryers Walker. 128 p. VG $95.00

COX, Nicholas. *Gentleman's Recreation.* 1928 Cresset Pr. Ltd ed. 1/650. 136 p. EX $18.50

COX, Palmer. *Brownies Around the World.* 1894 NY. De Vinne Pr. dj. $75.00

COX, Palmer. *Brownies' Kind Deed.* 1903 Chicago. WB Conkey. VG $25.00

COX, Peter. *Dwarf Rhododendrons.* 1973 London. 296 p. dj. VG $18.00

COX, Ross. *Adventures on Columbia River.* 1832 NY. 1st Am ed. $300.00

COX, Ruth Y. *Copperplate Textiles in the Williamsburg Collection.* 1964 Colonial Williamsburg. 8vo. $10.00

COX, S.C. *Orient Sunbeams; or, From Porte to Pyramids of Palestine.* 1890 NY. VG $20.00

COX, Warren. *Book of Pottery & Porcelain.* 1944 NY. Crown. Ills. 2 vol set. EX $35.00

COX, Warren. *Lighting & Lamp Design.* 1952 Crown. 1st ed. dj. VG $30.00

COXE, George Harmon. *Man Who Died Too Soon.* 1962 Knopf. 1st ed. dj. VG $15.00

COY, D.C. *Gold Days.* 1929 LA. EX $22.00

COY, Owen. *CA Country Boundaries.* 1923 Berkeley. 1st ed. scarce. EX $45.00

COYKENDALL, R. *Duck Decoys & How To Rig Them.* 1983 Winchester Pr. boxed. M $20.00

COYKENDALL, R. *Duck Decoys & How To Rig Them.* 1955 NY. 1st ed. dj. VG $30.00

COZZENS, J.G. *Confusion.* 1924 Boston. 1st print. VG $65.00

COZZENS, J.G. *Morning, Noon, & Night.* 1968 NY. 1st ed. dj. M $12.00

COZZENS, J.G. *S.S. San Pedro.* 1931 NY. dj. EX $22.00

COZZENS, S.S. *S.S. San Pedro.* 1931 NY. Stated 1st ed. cloth. G $10.00

CRABB, A.L. *Peace at Bowling Green.* 1955 Bobbs Merrill. Ltd 1st ed. sgn. dj. VG $20.00

CRABTREE, J.B. *Passing of Spain & Ascendency of America.* 1898 Springfield. Ills. 8vo. 460 p. leather. $16.00

CRADDOCK, Charles Egbert. *Down the Ravine.* 1885 Houghton Mifflin. 1st ed. G $15.00

CRADDOCK, Harry. *Savoy Cocktail Book.* 1930 NY. Smith. 8vo. VG $50.00

CRAFT, Robert. *Prejudices in Disguise.* 1974 NY. 1st ed. dj. VG $15.00

CRAFTS, W.A. *Life of Ulysses S. Grant.* 1868 Boston. Walker. $15.00

CRAFTY. *La Chasse a Courre. Notes et Croquis.* no date. Paris. Ills. oblong 4to. 48 p. VG $45.00

CRAIG, E.G. *Ellen Terry & Her Secret Self.* 1931 London. 1st ed. VG $45.00

CRAIG, John. *Danger Is My Business.* 1938 Simon Schuster. G $5.00

CRAIG, Lulu Alice. *Glimpses of Sunshine & Shade in the Far North.* 1900 Editor Pub Co. Ills 1st ed. inscr. EX $75.00

CRAIGHEAD, F.C. *Track of the Grizzly.* 1979 Sierra Club. Ills. 261 p. dj. VG $15.00

CRAIGHEAD, Frank & John. *Hawks in the Hand: Adventure in Photography & Falconry.* 1939 Boston. Ills. 57 plts. 290 p. VG $75.00

CRAIN, Hart. *Bridge.* 1981 Ltd Ed Club. sgn Benson. cloth. dj. EX $95.00

CRAINE & REINDORP. *Chronicles of Michoacan.* 1970 OK U Pr. 259 p. dj. EX $12.00

CRAM, Ralph Adams. *American Church Buildings of Today.* 1929 NY. Architect Book. Ills. 283 p. G $175.00

CRAM, Ralph Adams. *Impressions of Japanese Architecture & Allied Arts.* 1930 Boston. Revised ed. 1st issue. VG $15.00

CRAMER, Jesse Grant. *Letters of Ulysses S. Grant to His Father & Youngest Sister.* 1912 NY. Ills 1st ed. 192 p. VG $35.00

CRAMER. *Hudson River.* 1939 NY. 1st ed. sgn. dj. EX $45.00

CRAMLET, R.C. *Fundamentals of Leathercraft.* 1947 NY. Ills. 64 p. $5.00

CRAMOND, Michael. *Of Bears & Men.* 1986 OK U Pr. Ills 1st ed. 433 p. dj. EX $28.00

CRAMP, J.M. *Baptist History.* c 1870. Phil. 12mo. 498 p. gilt brown cloth. $20.00

CRANDALL, L.S. *Zoo Man's Notebook.* 1966 Chicago U Pr. Ills. 216 p. dj. EX $10.00

CRANE, H. *Bridge.* 1930 NY. 1st ed. 8vo. EX $110.00

CRANE, H. *Bridge.* 1984 NY. Ltd Ed Club. 1/2,000. EX $125.00

CRANE, H. *Robber Rocks.* 1968 Wesleyan U Pr. 1st ed. dj. M $17.00

CRANE, L. *China in Sign & Symbol.* 1926 Shanghai. Kelly. Ills. VG $175.00

CRANE, L. *Indians of Enchanted Desert.* 1925 Boston. G $20.00

CRANE, L. *Indians of Enchanted Desert.* 1927 3rd imp. G $12.00

CRANE, R. *Hero's Walk.* 1954 Ballantine. 1st ed. dj. EX $35.00

CRANE, Stephen. *Maggie: Girl of the Streets.* 1974 Ltd Ed Club. Ills/sgn S Abeles. slipcase. $65.00

CRANE, Stephen. *Maggie: Girl of the Streets.* 1896 Appleton. G $40.00

CRANE, Stephen. *O'Ruddy.* 1903 NY. Stokes. 1st ed. 8vo. cloth. VG $75.00

CRANE, Stephen. *Red Badge of Courage.* 1931 Grabhorn. Ltd ed. 1/980. VG $60.00

CRANE, Stephen. *Red Badge of Courage.* 1968 Westvaco. Ills Thompson. Ltd ed. boxed. $20.00

CRANE, Stephen. *Whilomville Stories.* 1900 London/NY. Harper. 1st ed. 8vo. VG $45.00

CRANE, Stephen. *Wounds in the Rain.* 1900 NY. 1st ed. G $40.00

CRANE, Walter. *Baby's Bouquet.* no date. London/NY. EX $45.00

CRANE, Walter. *Baby's Opera.* no date. Warne. VG $65.00

CRANE, Walter. *Baby's Own Aesop.* no date. London/NY. EX $45.00

CRANE, Walter. *Don Quixote.* 1917 NY. Lane. Ills. VG $65.00

CRANE, Walter. *Flora's Feast Masque of Flowers.* 1902 London. Ills. VG $55.00

CRANE, Walter. *Flora's Feast Masque of Flowers.* 1889 London. VG $135.00

CRANE, Walter. *Old Garden.* 1894 Houghton Mifflin. VG $85.00

CRANE, Walter. *Pothooks & Perseverance.* 1886 London. 1st ed. VG $195.00

CRANE, Walter. *Queen Summer: Journey of Lily & Rose.* London. EX $195.00

CRANE. *Newton Booth of CA.* 1894 NY. Ills. VG $25.00

CRANWELL & COVER. *Notes on Figures of Earth.* 1929 NY. Ltd ed. 1/865. VG $50.00

CRARY, Mary. *Daughter of the Stars.* 1939 London. Ills Dulac. 1st trade ed. G $15.00

CRARY, Mary. *Daughters of the Stars.* 1939 London. Hatchard. Ills Dulac. 190 p. $50.00

CRASCREDO. *Horse Sense & Sensibility.* 1927 Scribner. 2nd ed. 8vo. EX $28.00

CRAVEN, Margaret. *Home Front.* 1981 NY. Putnam. 1st ed. dj. EX $10.00

CRAVEN, Thomas. *Cartoon Cavalcade.* 1943 Simon Schuster. 1st ed. G $7.50

CRAVEN, Thomas. *Story of Painting From Cave Pictures to Modern Art.* 1943 Simon Schuster. white bdg. dj. VG $14.50

CRAVEN, Thomas. *Treasure of American Prints.* 1939 Simon Schuster. Ills. folio. spiral bdg. $15.00

CRAVEN, Thomas. *Treasury of Art Masterpieces: Renaissance to Present Day.* 1958 NY. reprint. dj. VG $15.00

CRAWFORD, Charles. *Christian: Poem in 6 Books.* 1802 Phil. 3rd ed. EX $80.00

CRAWFORD, I. *Kiowa: Story of a Blanket Indian Mission.* 1915 NY. Revell. $17.50

CRAWFORD, J.C. *Recollections of Travel in New Zealand & Australia.* 1880 London. Ills 1st ed. 468 p. G $50.00

CRAWFORD, J.H. *Wildlife of Scotland.* 1896 London. Ills John Williamson. VG $45.00

CRAWFORD, John Martin. *Kalevala: Epic Poem of Finland in English.* 1888 NY. Alden. 2 vols in 1. 744 p. VG $30.00

CRAWFORD, John. *Journal of an Embassy From Governor General of India.* 1834 London. 2nd ed. 2 vol set. $200.00

CRAWFORD, M.A. *Comparative Nutrition for Wild Animals.* 1968 Academic Pr. facsimile. 429 p. EX $18.00

CRAWFORD, M.D. *Heritage of Cotton.* c 1924. NY. Grosset Dunlap. VG $25.00

CRAWFORD, M.D. *Heritage of Cotton.* 1924 NY. Ills 1st ed. dj. EX $32.00

CRAWFORD, Mary C. *Romance of Old New England Rooftrees.* 1903 Boston. 8vo. 785 p. VG $35.00

CRAWFORD, Oswald. *By Path & Trail.* 1908 fair. $75.00

CRAWFORD, William P. *Mariner's Celestial Navigation.* 1972 444 p. dj. VG $15.00

CRAWFORD. *Cats in Prose & Verse.* 1947 Ills Diana Thorne. 1st ed. EX $20.00

CRAWFORD. *History of Irion County, TX.* 1966 Waco. TX Pr. dj. EX $20.00

CRAYON, Porte. *VA Illustrated.* 1857 NY. Harper. Ills. 8vo. blue cloth. VG $115.00

CREASEY, John. *Baron in France.* 1960 Walke. 1st ed. dj. VG $5.00

CREASY, Sir Edward. *Memoirs of Eminent Etonians.* 1876 London. fore-edge of dog with game. $475.00

CREELEY, Robert. *Charm.* 1969 Four Seasons. 1st ed. presentation. EX $150.00

CREELEY, Robert. *Echoes.* 1982 Toothpaste. Ltd ed. 1/200. sgn. cloth. M $55.00

CREELEY, Robert. *Hellow.* 1978 New Directions. 1st ed. dj. EX $15.00

CREELEY, Robert. *Later.* 1978 IA. Ltd ed. 1/100. sgn. wraps. VG $25.00

CREELEY, Robert. *Pieces.* 1968 Black Sparrow. Ills B Creeley. 1st ed. 1/150. $55.00

CREELEY, Robert. *St. Martins.* 1971 Los Angeles. Ltd ed. 1/250. sgn. dj. M $22.00

CREIGHTON, W.S. *Ants of North America.* 1950 Harvard U Pr. 585 p. EX $45.00

CREMER, Robert. *Lugosi: Man Behind the Cape.* 1976 Regency. Ills 1st ed. 307 p. dj. VG $35.00

CREMER, W.H. *Hanky-Panky: Book of Conjuring Tricks.* 1872 London. Ills 1st ed. 8vo. 250 p. G $50.00

CREMER, W.H. *Magician's Own Book.* 1872 London. 1st ed. 8vo. 325 p. $50.00

CREMONY, John C. *Life Among the Apaches.* 1868 San Francisco. presentation. VG $300.00

CRESSLER, A. *Vignettes of Writers & Artists.* 1946 Grabhorn. Ltd ed. 1/300. VG $40.00

CREWS, H. *Naked in Garden Hills.* 1969 1st ed. dj. EX $32.50

CREWS, Harry. *Enthusiast.* 1981 Palaemon. 1st ed. 1/50. sgn. EX $125.00

CREWS, Harry. *Feast of Snakes.* 1976 NY. 1st ed. dj. VG $35.00

CREWS, Harry. *Hawk Is Dying.* 1973 NY. 1st ed. dj. VG $20.00

CREWS, Harry. *2 By Crews.* 1984 Lord John. 1st ed. 1/200. sgn. M $50.00

CRICHTON, K.S. *Law & Order.* 1928 Santa Fe. Ltd ed. 1/350. sgn. dj. VG $27.00

CRICHTON, Michael. *Andromeda Strain.* 1969 Cape. 1st English ed. dj. EX $30.00

CRICHTON, Michael. *Andromeda Strain.* 1969 Knopf. 1st ed. dj. VG $20.00

CRICHTON, Michael. *Eaters of the Dead.* 1976 NY. Knopf. 1st ed. dj. VG $12.50

CRICHTON, Michael. *Eaters of the Dead.* 1976 NY. 1st ed. dj. M $17.00

CRICHTON, Michael. *Electronic Life.* 1983 NY. 1st ed. dj. M $15.00

CRICHTON, Michael. *Terminal Man.* 1972 Knopf. 1st ed. dj. VG $12.50

CRICHTON, Michael. *Terminal Man.* 1972 NY. 1st ed. sgn. M $16.00

CRIDLAND, R. *Practical Landscape Gardening.* 1926 NY. 276 p. VG $15.00

CRILE, Grace. *George Crile: Autobiography.* 1947 NY. Lippincott. 1st ed. 2 vol set. $25.00

CRILE, Grace. *Skyways to a Jungle Laboratory: African Adventure.* 1936 Norton. Ills 1st ed. 240 p. VG $8.50

CRISLER, Lois. *Captive Wild.* 1968 Harper. Ills 1st ed. 238 p. dj. VG $20.00

CRISP, N.J. *Brink.* 1982 Viking. Advance copy. wraps. EX $10.00

CRISPIN, Edmund. *Fen Country.* 1979 London. 1st ed. dj. VG $27.00

CRISSEY, Forest. *Alexander Legge 1886-1933.* 1936 private print. sgn. EX $45.00

CRITCHLEY & JAMES. *Maul & Pear Tree: 1811 Ratcliffe Highway Murders.* 1971 London. 1st ed. dj. EX $25.00

CRITTENDEN. *Yellowstone National Park.* 1924 St. Paul. Revised 3rd ed. map. G $10.00

CROCE. *Fred Astaire's & Ginger Rogers' Book.* 1972 Galahad. Ills 1st ed. dj. M $15.00

CROCKER, Betty. *Dinner for 2.* 1958 Simon Schuster. 1st ed. 1st print. VG $8.50

CROCKER, Betty. *Good & Easy Cookbook.* 1954 NY. 1st ed. G $8.50

CROFTS, Freeman W. *Antidote to Venom.* 1938 London. 1st ed. 8vo. cloth. VG $25.00

CROFTS, Freeman W. *Loss of the Jane Vosper.* 1936 London. 1st ed. VG $48.00

CROFTS, Freeman W. *Silence for the Murderer.* 1948 NY. Dodd. 1st ed. presentation. dj. $30.00

CROFUT, William. *Troubadour: Different Battlefield.* 1968 NY. Ills. dj. VG $10.00

CROGHAN, John. *Rambles in Mammoth Cave During the Year 1844.* 1845 Louisville. Ills 1st ed. 101 p. $50.00

CROMIE, Robert. *Dillinger: Short & Violent Life.* 1962 NY. 2nd ed. dj. VG $17.50

CROMIE, Robert. *Great Chicago Fire.* 1958 1st ed. sgn. dj. VG $25.00

CROMPTON, Sidney. *English Glass.* 1986 Hawthorne. 1st Am ed. 8vo. 255 p. dj. EX $15.00

CRON, Gretchan. *Roaring Veldt.* 1930 Putnam. Ills 1st ed. 286 p. VG $75.00

CRONE, G.R. *Explorers.* 1962 Crowell. 1st ed. 361 p. maps. dj. VG $12.00

CRONIN, A.J. *Green Years.* 1944 Little Brown. 1st Am ed. VG $10.00

CRONIN, A.J. *Keys of Kingdom.* 1942 London. Gollancz. 1st ed. dj. VG $25.00

CRONIN, A.J. *Northern Lights.* 1958 Little Brown. 1st Am ed. dj. EX $12.00

CRONIN, A.J. *Song of Sixpence.* 1964 Little Brown. 1st Am ed. dj. EX $15.00

CRONIN, A.J. *Spanish Garden.* 1950 Boston. 1st ed. dj. EX $17.00

CRONISE, Titus F. *Natural Wealth of CA.* 1868 San Francisco. Bancroft. 1st ed. 4to. 696 p. $30.00

CROSBIE, Robert. *Friendly Philosopher.* 1945 NY. 415 p. dj. EX $16.00

CROSBY, Bill. *Fatherhood.* 1986 Doubleday. 1st ed. dj. EX $14.00

CROSBY, Everett. *Vintage Years.* 1973 Harper. 227 p. dj. VG $10.00

CROSBY, Fanny. *Life Story of Fanny Crosby.* 1903 NY. Everywhere Pub. Ills 1st ed. $25.00

CROSBY, Katharine. *Blue Water Men & Other Cape Codders.* 1946 NY. 1st ed. G $20.00

CROSBY, Percy. *Dear Sooky: Letters From Skippy.* 1929 Knickerbocker. Ills 1st ed. juvenile. dj. G $35.00

CROSS, F.B.; & COLLINS, J.T. *Fishes in KS.* 1975 KS U Pr. Ills. 189 p. maps. wraps. EX $8.00

CROSS, G. *Little Heroes of Hartford.* 1947 NY. 1st ed. sgn. dj. VG $15.00

CROSS, J.L. *AZ: Its People & Resources.* 1960 U of AZ Pr. Ills. dj. VG $15.00

CROSSEN, F. *Western Yesterdays.* 1965 Boulder. Ills. 83 p. pb. G $5.00

CROSSMAN, E.C. *Military & Sporting Rifle Shooting.* 1932 Small Arms. Ills 1st ed. 499 p. EX $27.50

CROSSMAN, E.C. *Small Bore Rifle Shooting.* 1927 Small Arms. Ills. 337 p. VG $22.50

CROTHERS, S.M. *Children of Dickens.* 1942 NY. Scribner. Ills. JW Smith $35.00

CROTHERS, T.D. *Disease of Inebriety.* 1893 NY. 400 p. scarce. VG $35.00

CROUSE, N.M. *Search for the North Pole.* 1947 Smith. 376 p. VG $18.00

CROWE, C. *Fast Times at Ridgemont High.* 1981 NY. 1st ed. dj. EX $15.00

CROWE, John. *Book of Trout Lore.* 1947 Barnes. Ills 1st ed. 233 p. dj. EX $20.00

CROWE, P.K. *Sporting Journeys in Asia & Africa.* 1966 Barre. Ill Ltd ed. 1/2,500. dj. EX $10.00

CROWE, Sylvia. *Garden Design.* 1959 NY. Ills. dj. VG $10.00

CROWELL, M.R. *Great Blue: Odyssey of a Great Blue Heron.* 1980 Times. Ills. 143 p. dj. EX $10.00

CROWELL, P. *Cavalcade of American Horses.* 1951 NY. Ills. 4to. 311 p. VG $45.00

CROWEST, Frederick J. *Story of British Music From Earliest Times to Tudor Period.* 1896 NY. Scribner. VG $20.00

CROWLEY, Aleister. *Diary of a Drug Fiend.* 1923 NY. 1st ed. VG $35.00

CROWLEY, Aleister. *Diary of a Drug Fiend.* NY. University Books. dj. M $65.00

CROWLEY, Aleister. *Magic in Theory & Practice.* 1929 London. 1st ed. 436 p. VG $25.00

CROWLEY, Aleister. *Moon Child.* 1929 London. 1st ed. EX $45.00

CROWLEY, John. *Aegypt.* 1967 Bantam. Uncorrected proof. wraps. EX $60.00

CROWLEY, John. *Engine Summer.* 1979 Doubleday. 1st ed. dj. EX $30.00

CROWLEY, John. *Little Big.* London. 1st English ed. sgn. wraps. VG $25.00

CROWLEY. *777.* 1955 London. Neptune. Ltd 1st ed. 1/1,100. $50.00

CROWNFIELD, Gertrude. *Little Tailor of the Winding Way.* 1921 Macmillan. Ills Pogany. G $30.00

CROWNINSHIELD, Frank. *Unofficial Palace of NY: Tribute to Waldorf-Astoria.* 1939 Ltd ed. 1/5,000. 177 p. VG $35.00

CROWTHER, J.G. *Cavendish Laboratory 1874-1974.* 1974 London. 1st ed. 464 p. dj. VG $25.00

CROY, H. *Trial of Mrs. Abraham Lincoln.* 1962 NY. 1st ed. dj. VG $22.50

CROZIER, William. *How the Farm Pays.* 1884 Boston. 8vo. 191 p. red calf. $35.00

CROZIER, William. *How the Farm Pays.* 1902 NY. Henderson. 400 p. scarce. $10.00

CRUIKSHANK, George. *Comic Almanac.* 1871 London. Hotten. 1st & 2nd Series. 2 vol set. $210.00

CRUIKSHANK, George. *Humorous Illustrations.* no date. Ills 2nd ed. 400 plts. cloth. $45.00

CRUIKSHANK, George. *Table Book.* 1885 London. Ills New ed. ¾-red morocco. $300.00

CRUIKSHANK, George. *12 Sketches Illustrative of Sir Walter Scott's Demonology.* 1830 London. Robins. 1st ed. 1st issue. 4to. $140.00

CRUIKSHANK, Robert. *Devil's Visit.* 1830 London. Ills 1st ed. 12mo. 35 p. VG $75.00

CRUM, M. *Gullah.* 1940 Durham. Ills 1st ed. 351 p. VG $42.50

CRUME, Paul. *Texan at Bay.* 1961 McGraw Hill. 1st ed. sgn. 212 p. dj. EX $20.00

CRUMLEY, James. *Last Good Kiss.* 1978 Random House. Uncorrected proof. EX $250.00

CRUMLEY, James. *Last Good Kiss.* 1978 NY. 1st ed. sgn. dj. $55.00

CRUMLEY, James. *1 to Count Cadence.* 1969 Random House. 1st ed. dj. M $225.00

CRUMP, Irving. *Boy's Book of Airman.* 1927 Dodd Mead. Ills. $25.00

CRUMP, Irving. *Out of the Woods.* 1941 Dodd Mead. Ills Comstock. 269 p. dj. VG $10.00

CRUMP, W.B. *Leeds Woolen Industry 1780-1820.* 1931 Leeds. VG $15.00

CRUMRINE, Boyd. *Courts of Justice: Bench & Bar in WA County, PA.* 1902 Ills 1st ed. 4to. 352 p. cloth. VG $50.00

CUBBIN, Thomas. *Wreck of the Serica: Narrative of 1868.* 1950 London. Dropmore Pr. 8vo. dj. EX $45.00

CUDAHY, J. *African Horizons.* 1930 Duffield. Ills. 159 p. G $7.50

CULBERTSON, J.T. *Mathematics & Logic for Digital Devices.* 1958 NY. Nostrand. 8vo. 224 p. cloth. EX $75.00

CULLEN, Countee. *Copper Sun.* 1927 NY. Harper. Ills 6th print. sgn. $95.00

CULLEN, Countee. *Lost Zoo.* 1940 NY. Ills Sebree. 1st ed. dj. VG $150.00

CULLEN, William. *1st Lines of the Practice of Physics.* 1792 Phil. 2 vol set. $130.00

CULLUM, Albert. *Geranium on Windowsill Just Died, But Teacher, You Went On.* 1975 Quist. Ills 2nd ed. black cloth. VG $25.00

CULP, John H. *Whistle in the Wind.* 1978 NY. 1st ed. dj. EX $12.00

CULPEPPER. *Complete Herbal & English Physician.* 1981 reprint of 1826. dj. EX $25.00

CULVER, F.B. *Blooded Horses of Colonial Days.* 1922 Baltimore. 1st ed. wraps. VG $25.00

CULVER, Henry B. *Book of Old Ships.* 1935 NY. 4to. cloth. VG $15.00

CULVERWELL, Dr. R.J. *Porneio-Pathology: Treatise on Venereal & Other Diseases.* 1844 Redfield. Ills. 12mo. VG $35.00

CUMING, E.D. *Idlings in Arcadia.* 1935 Dutton. Ills 1st ed. 326 p. dj. VG $18.00

CUMMING, A. *Elements of Clock & Watchwork.* 1766 London. Ills. 4to. EX $2500.00

CUMMINGS, Charles S. *Everyday Ballistics.* 1950 Harrisburg. dj. VG $16.00

CUMMINGS, E.E. *Eimi.* 1933 NY. Ltd ed. 1/1,381. VG $155.00

CUMMINGS, E.E. *Poems 1923-1954.* 1954 Harcourt. Stated 1st ed. 8vo. 468 p. dj. $22.00

CUMMINGS, E.E. *Selected Poems 1923-1958.* 1960 London. 1st ed. dj. VG $27.00

CUMMINGS, E.E. *Tom.* 1935 NY. Arrow. Ills Shahn. rare. VG $30.00

CUMMINGS, E.E. *Tulips & Chimneys.* 1937 Mount Vernon. Ltd ed. 1/629. dj. EX $225.00

CUMMINGS, E.E. *45 Poems.* 1958 NY. Ltd ed. 1/300. slipcase. $60.00

CUMMINGS, E.E. *73 Poems.* 1963 NY. 1st ed. dj. EX $12.00

CUMMINGS, M.F. *Architectural Details.* 1873 NY. 1st ed. folio. plts. cloth. $250.00

CUMMINS, A.B. *Nottoway County, VA.* 1970 Richmond. 8vo. VG $20.00

CUMMINS, C. *My Days with the Diesel.* 1967 Ills 1st ed. 8vo. 190 p. dj. $10.00

CUMONT, Franz. *Mysteries of Mithra.* 1956 Dover. reprint of 1903. VG $9.00

CUNARD, Nancy. *Brave Poet, Indomitable Rebel 1896-1965.* 1972 Phil. Ills 1st ed. dj. VG $27.00

CUNEO, John. *Robert Rogers of the Rangers.* 1959 NY. Oxford U. 1st ed. dj. xl. G $24.00

CUNNINGHAM, Allan. *Lives of Most Eminent British Painters & Sculptors.* 1854 NY. Harper. Family Lib ed. 5 vol set. VG $75.00

CUNNINGHAM, C.C. *Let There Be Light.* 1964 Hartford. Wadsworth Atheneum. 4to. 54 p. $15.00

CUNNINGHAM, Eugene. *Triggernometry: Gallery of Gunfighters.* 1952 Caxton. Ills. 441 p. dj. VG $14.00

CUNNINGHAM, Graham. *Faith.* 1909 London. 1st ed. VG $25.00

CUNNINGHAM, J.T. *Treatise on the Common Sole.* 1890 Plymouth. 1st ed. 4to. 147 p. VG $150.00

CUNNINGHAM, J.V. *Judge Is Fury.* 1947 Swallow. 1st ed. dj. VG $35.00

CUNY, Hilaire. *Albert Einstein: The Man & His Theories.* 1965 NY. Eriksson. Ills 1st Am ed. 175 p. dj. VG $15.00

CUPPY, Will. *How To Become Extinct.* 1941 NY. Ills Steig. 1st ed. dj. VG $17.50

CUPPY, Will. *How To Become Extinct.* 1941 NY. Ills Steig. 1st ed. dj. EX $25.00

CURIE, Marie. *Pierre Curie.* 1926 NY. Macmillan. Trans Kellogg. VG $40.00

CURIE, Marie. *Radiologie et la Guerre.* 1921 Paris. 1st ed. 143 p. wraps. xl. G $75.00

CURIE, Marie. *Recherches sur les Substances Radioactives.* 1904 Paris. Gauthier Villars. 2nd ed. $300.00

CURIE, Marie. *Traite de Radioactivite.* 1910 Paris. 1st ed. 2 vol set. VG $280.00

CURLE, Richard. *Last 12 Years of Joseph Conrad.* 1928 London. 1st ed. 8vo. dj. VG $15.00

CURRAN, C.P. *Rotunda Hospital: Its Architects & Craftsmen.* 1945 Dublin. At Sgn of 3 Candles. G $27.00

CURRAN & CALKINS. *In Canada's Wonderful Northland.* 1917 NY. photos. dj. G $45.00

CURREY, J. Seymour. *Chicago: Its History & Its Builders.* 1912 rebound. $100.00

CURREY, Robert A. *Bahamian Lore.* 1928 Paris. Ills Ltd ed. 8vo. 125 p. G $20.00

CURRIE, Barton. *Tractor & Its Influence on Agricultural Implement Industry.* 1916 Phil. Curtis. 1st ed. presentation. EX $100.00

CURRIER, E.L. *Farm Accounting.* 1924 Macmillan. 287 p. VG $5.00

CURRIER, Richard S. *Genealogical History of Dickey Family.* 1935 Montpelier. Ills 1st ed. 8vo. 340 p. VG $45.00

CURRIER & TILTON. *Bibliography of Oliver Wendell Holmes.* 1953 NY. VG $125.00

CURRY, Larry. *8 American Masters of Watercolor.* 1968 NY/WA. Praeger. Ills. 8vo. cloth. dj. $25.00

CURTI, Merle. *1920s in Historical Perspective.* 1966 TX Western Pr. 1st ed. wraps. M $5.00

CURTIS, A.T. *Little Maid of MD.* 1923 Phil. dj. EX $10.00

CURTIS, A.T. *Little Maid of Narragansett Bay.* 1921 Phil. dj. EX $10.00

CURTIS, C.P. & R.C. *Hunting in Africa, East & West.* 1925 Houghton Mifflin. Ills. VG $23.50

CURTIS, David. *Experimental Cinema: 50 Year Evolution.* 1971 Universe Books. Ills. dj. VG $15.00

CURTIS, Edward S. *Portraits From North American Indian Life.* 1985 Castle. reprint. dj. EX $20.00

CURTIS, Edward S. *Portraits From North American Indian Life.* 1972 NY. Outerbridge. 1st ed. folio. EX $40.00

CURTIS, G.W. *Ars Recte Vivendi.* 1898 NY. 1st ed. EX $18.00

CURTIS, George T. *Life of Daniel Webster.* 1870 NY. $135.00

CURTIS, Kent. *Last Wanigan.* no date. Seymour. Ills. inscr. EX $23.50

CURTIS, L. *Apes & Angels: Irishman in Victorian Caricature.* 1971 Smithsonian. Ills. 126 p. dj. VG $20.00

CURTIS, M.M. *Story of Snuff & Snuff Boxes.* 1935 NY. Ills 1st ed. dj. VG $50.00

CURTIS, Natalie. *Songs & Legends of American Indians.* 1935 London/NY. Ills. 8vo. cloth. VG $55.00

CURTIS, Newton M. *Bride of Northern Wilds: Tale of 1743.* 1843 Troy. wraps. $50.00

CURTIS, P.A. *American Game Shooting.* 1927 Dutton. Ills. 279 p. dj. VG $10.00

CURTIS, P.A. *Guns & Gunning.* 1941 Outdoor Life. Ills. 384 p. VG $12.50

CURTIS, P.A. *Guns & Gunning.* 1934 Outdoor Life. Penn Pub. G $22.00

CURTIS, P.A. *Sporting Firearms of Today.* 1922 Dutton. Ills 1st ed. 264 p. VG $25.00

CURTIS, P.A. *Sportsmen All.* 1938 NY. Derrydale. Ltd ed. 1/950. EX $100.00

CURTIS, Tony. *Oriental Rugs.* 1980 NY. Quick Fox. Ills. 125 p. $4.00

CURTISS, H.A. & F.H. *Letters From the Teacher.* 1913 CA. 2nd ed. 249 p. $30.00

CURTISS. *Von Stroheim.* 1971 Farrar. 1st ed. dj. M $15.00

CURWEN & HATT. *Plough & Pasture.* 1953 NY. 329 p. dj. VG $10.00

CURWOOD, James. *Alaskan.* no date. Cosmo. 1st ed. VG $10.00

CURWOOD, James. *Country Beyond.* no date. Cosmo. 1st ed. VG $10.00

CURWOOD, Oliver James. *Hunted Woman.* 1926 Doubleday Page. $10.00

CURZON, Louis H. *Blue Ribbon of Turf: Chronicle of Race for Derby.* 1890 London. 1st ed. 8vo. 364 p. $40.00

CURZON, Robert. *Visit to Monasteries in Levant.* 1851 Putnam/Murray. Ills. fld plan. cloth. EX $125.00

CUSHING, Caleb. *Territory of OR.* 1839 WA. 8vo. 61 p. unbound. $375.00

CUSHING, Harvey. *Life of Sir William Osler.* 1925 Oxford. 3rd imp. 2 vol set. $50.00

CUSHING, Harvey. *Life of Sir William Osler.* 1940 London. Oxford U Pr. VG $27.50

CUSHING, W. *Initials & Pseudonyms.* 1886 NY. Revised ed. VG $40.00

CUSHMAN, D. *Great North Trail.* 1966 McGraw Hill. 1st ed. 383 p. dj. EX $20.00

CUST, Mrs. Henry. *Gentlemen Errant.* 1909 London. Murray. Ills. 551 p. VG $25.00

CUSTER, Elizabeth. *Boots & Saddles; or, Life in Dakota with General Custer.* 1885 NY. 12mo. 312 p. cloth. $60.00

CUSTER, Elizabeth. *Boots & Saddles; or, Life in Dakota with General Custer.* 1885 map. portrait. G $40.00

CUSTER, Elizabeth. *Following the Guidon.* 1890 Harper. 1st ed. VG $32.50

CUSTER, Elizabeth. *Tenting on the Plains.* 1887 NY. Webster. VG $75.00

CUSTER, Elizabeth. *Tenting on the Plains.* 1893 London. VG $35.00

CUTTER, Calvin. *1st Book on Anatomy, Physiology, & Hygiene.* 1850 Boston. Ills. 12mo. 180 p. G $18.00

CUTTER, Donald. *Malaspina in CA.* 1960 San Francisco. Ltd ed. 1/1,000. wraps. $65.00

CUTTER, William. *Life of Major General Israel Putnam.* 1854 Boston. VG $15.00

CUTTS, John P. *La Musique de Scene de la Troupe de Shakespeare.* 1959 Paris. 4to. bilingual text. VG $25.00

CUYLER, Susanna. *High-Pile Rug Book.* 1974 Harper Row. Ills 1st ed. 140 p. dj. $15.00

CZAJA, Michael. *Gods of Myth & Stone: Phallicism in Japanese Folk Religion.* 1974 Weatherill. Ills 1st ed. dj. EX $30.00

CZECH-JOCHBERG, Erich. *Vom 30 Januar zum 21 Mars.* 1933 Leipzig. with 2 records. VG $100.00

CZWIKLITZER, Christopher. *Picasso's Posters.* 1970-1971. Random House. folio. 365 p. $185.00

D

D'ANCONA, David A. *CA-NV Travel Diary of 1876.* 1975 Santa Monica. Ltd ed. 1/350. dj. VG $30.00

D'AULAIRE, Ingri. *East of the Sun & West of the Moon.* 1938 Viking. Ills 1st ed. tan cloth. VG $10.00

D'AULAIRE, Ingri; & PARIN, E. *Abraham Lincoln.* 1940 NY. Doubleday. Ills authors. 4to. VG $15.00

D'ESPOUY. *100 Plates From Fragments of Antique Architecture.* 1923 Pencil Points. Ills. 4to. 207 p. VG $30.00

D'EVREUX, Pere Yves. *Voyage dans le Nord de Bresil Fair les Annees 1614.* 1864 Paris. Librairie A Franck. 456 p. VG $100.00

D'HARNONCOURT, Rene. *New American Painting Shown in 8 European Countries.* 1959 MOMA. Ills. 4to. 96 p. wraps. $25.00

D'INDY, Vincent. *Cesar Franck.* 1922 Bodley Head. Trans Rosa Newmarch. G $15.00

D'OENCH & FEINBERG. *Jim Dine Prints 1977-1985.* 1986 Middletown/NY. Ills. 4to. 182 p. cloth. dj. $30.00

D'OLIVET, Fabre. *Hermeneutic Interpretation of Origin of Social State of Man.* 1915 Putnam. G $40.00

D'ORLEANS, Prince Henry. *From Tonkin to India by Sources of Irawadi.* 1898 NY. Dodd Mead. Ills. 8vo. 467 p. $20.00

D'UCEL, Jeanne. *Barber Art: Introduction.* 1932 Norman. Ills 1st ed. dj. VG $30.00

DA SILVA, Owen. *Mission Music of CA.* 1941 Los Angeles. Patron Ltd ed. 1/1,000. VG $110.00

DABROWSKI, Magdalena. *Contrasts of Form: Geometric Abstract Art 1910-1980.* 1985 MOMA. Intro John Elderfield. 302 p. $45.00

DACUS, J. *Life of Frank & Jesse James.* 1881 St. Louis. leather. G $125.00

DADD, George H. *American Cattle Doctor.* 1883 NY. VG $35.00

DADD, George H. *Curing & Diseases of Oxen, Cattle, Sheep, & Swine.* 1883 Orange Judd. New ed. VG $19.50

DADD, George H. *Modern Horse Doctor.* 1866 NY. 12mo. 432 p. $20.00

DAHL, Roald. *Charlie & the Great Glass Elevator.* 1972 NY. Knopf. Ills Schindelman. 1st ed. dj. $20.00

DAHL, Roald. *Danny: Champion of the World.* 1975 NY. Knopf. Ills Bennett. 1st print. dj. $15.00

DAHL, Roald. *Dirty Beasts.* 1983 NY. Farrar. Ills Fawcett. 1st Am ed. dj. $10.00

DAHL, Roald. *Kiss Kiss.* 1960 NY. Knopf. 1st ed. dj. VG $20.00

DAHL, Roald. *My Uncle Oswald.* 1979 London. 1st ed. dj. EX $20.00

DAHL, Roald. *Switch Bitch.* 1974 Knopf. 1st ed. dj. VG $15.00

DAHL, Roald. *Twits.* 1981 Knopf. Ills Q Blake. 1st ed. dj. EX $15.00

DAHLBERG, Edward. *Carnal Myth.* 1968 NY. 1st ed. dj. M $20.00

DAHLBERG, Edward. *Olive of Minerva.* 1976 NY. 1st ed. dj. M $12.00

DAHLBERG, Edward. *Sorrows of Priapus.* 1957 New Directions. Ills Shahn. $15.00

DAICHES, David. *2 Worlds: Edinburgh Jewish Childhood.* 1956 Harcourt Brace. 1st ed. dj. VG $6.50

DAILEY, Janet. *Great Alone.* 1986 Simon Schuster. 1st ed. dj. M $12.00

DAIN, M. *Faulkner's Co.* 1964 NY. 1st ed. dj. EX $35.00

DAINGERFIELD, Henrietta G. *Our Mammy & Other Stories.* 1906 Lexington. Ills. 8vo. 143 p. sgn. EX $80.00

DAKIN, Edwin F. *Mrs. Eddy: Biography of a Virginal Mind.* 1929 NY. 553 p. VG $22.00

DAL, Bjorn. *Butterflies of Northern Europe.* 1982 Croom Helm. Ills. 128 p. maps. dj. EX $12.00

DALBIEZ, Roland. *Psychoanalytical Method & the Doctrine of Freud.* 1948 Longman. 2nd print. 2 vol set. EX $22.50

DALE, Daphne. *Echoes From Story Land for Young People.* 1890 Elliott Beezley. 25 plts. G $57.50

DALE, Edward. *Frontier Ways.* 1959 TX U Pr. 1st ed. dj. EX $15.00

DALE, Edward. *Range Cattle Industry.* 1930 Norman. 1st ed. EX $150.00

DALE, Harrison. *Ashley-Smith Explorations 1822-1829.* 1941 Glendale. Clark. Revised ed. EX $75.00

DALES, R.P. *Pelagic Polychaetes of the Pacific Ocean.* 1957 CA U Pr. wraps. EX $12.00

DALEY, Robert. *Prince of the City.* 1978 Boston. 1st ed. dj. M $10.00

DALEY, Robert. *Swords of Spain.* 1966 NY. Ills 1st ed. 239 p. VG $10.00

DALEY, Robert. *Target Blue.* 1973 NY. 1st ed. dj. M $15.00

DALGLIESH, Alice. *Christmas Book of Stories, Old & New.* 1946 NY. Scribner. Ills Woodward. 323 p. dj. VG $25.00

DALGLIESH, Alice. *Courage of Sarah Noble.* 1954 NY. Scribner. Ills Weisgard. cocoa linen. EX $18.00

DALI, Salvador. *Diners de Gala.* 1973 Paris. French text. dj. EX $150.00

DALI, Salvador. *Secret Life of Salvador Dali.* 1942 NY. 4th ed. dj. VG $45.00

DALI, Salvador. *Study of My Life & Work.* 1957 NY. glassine dj. VG $95.00

DALI, Salvador. *Vins de Gala.* 1977 Paris. French text. dj. EX $150.00

DALL, Caroline. *Margaret & Her Family.* 1895 1st ed. G $25.00

DALLAS, Robert Charles. *History of Maroons From Origin to Establishment of Tribe.* 1803 London. Strahan. 1st ed. 2 vol set. $75.00

DALLAS, Sandra. *No More Than 5 in a Bed.* 1967 Norman. 1st ed. cloth. dj. VG $17.50

DALLIMORE, W. *Holly, Yew, & Box.* 1978 London. Ltd ed. 1/250. 284 p. $20.00

DALLIN, David J. *Soviet Russia's Foreign Policy 1939-1942.* 1947 Yale U Pr. 5th print. G $25.00

DALPHIN, Marcia. *50 Years in Rye 1904-1954.* 1955 NY. Rye. VG $20.00

DALRYMPLE, B.W. *Complete Book of Deer Hunting.* 1974 Winchester. Ills. 247 p. dj. EX $7.50

DALRYMPLE, B.W. *Complete Guide to Hunting Across North America.* 1970 Outdoor Life. 848 p. maps. dj. VG $7.50

DALRYMPLE, B.W. *Doves & Dove Shooting.* 1949 1st ed. VG $20.00

DALRYMPLE, B.W. *How To Rig & Fish Natural Baits.* 1976 Outdoor Life. Ills. 165 p. dj. EX $6.50

DALRYMPLE, B.W. *Ice Fishing for Everybody.* 1948 Lantern. Ills 1st ed. 257 p. G $5.00

DALRYMPLE, B.W. *Light Tackle Fishing.* 1947 Whittlesey. Ills. 398 p. G $10.00

DALRYMPLE, B.W. *Modern Book of Black Bass.* 1972 Winchester. Ills. 206 p. dj. EX $10.00

DALRYMPLE, B.W. *North American Game Animals.* 1978 Crown. Ills. 4to. 480 p. EX $15.00

DALTON, David. *Rolling Stones.* 1972 NY. Ills. dj. VG $22.00

DALTON, Henry G. *History of British Guiana.* 1855 London. Longman. 1st ed. 2 vol set. $175.00

DALTON, John C. *Treatise on Human Physiology.* 1861 Phil. Ills. 8vo. 690 p. brown cloth. $28.00

DALTON, John C. *Treatise on Human Physiology.* 1867 Phil. Ills. leather. $22.50

DALTON, Moray. *Night of Fear.* 1931 Stated 1st ed. dj. VG $10.00

DALY, J. *Ireland in the Days of Dean Swift.* 1887 London. 278 p. gilt cloth. VG $47.50

DALY, Joseph Francis. *Life of Augustin Daly.* 1917 NY. Ills 1st ed. 672 p. xl. VG $15.00

DALY. *Song in His Heart: Life & Times of James Bland.* 1951 Phil. 1st ed. dj. VG $30.00

DALZELL, Ralph. *Architectural Drawing & Detailing.* 1946 Chicago. Am Technol Soc. G $20.00

DALZIEL, Hugh. *National Nursey Rhymes & Nursery Songs.* 1870 Phil. Ills. G $25.00

DAMPIER, William. *Voyages & Discoveries.* 1931 Argonaut Pr. Ltd ed. 1/975. 4to. 311 p. EX $90.00

DANA, Charles A. *Art of Newspaper Making.* 1985 NY. Appleton. 1st ed. maroon buckram. dj. EX $135.00

DANA, Charles L. *Peaks of Medical History.* 1928 NY. Hoeber. Ills Revised 2nd ed. rebound. $16.00

DANA, Edmund. *Geographical Sketches on Western Country: Emigrant Guide.* 1819 Cincinnati. 1st ed. 12mo. rare. G $350.00

DANA, James D. *Geological Story.* c 1875. Ills. 12mo. 236 p. cloth. G $10.00

DANA, James D. *Manual of Mineralogy & Lithology.* 1884 NY. 3rd ed. fair. $50.00

DANA, Julian. *Man Who Built San Francisco.* 1936 Macmillan. Ills Rideout. 1st ed. 388 p. $15.00

DANA, R.H. *2 Years Before the Mast.* no date. London. Ward Lock. Ills. VG $12.50

DANE, G. Ezra. *Ghost Town.* 1941 NY. 1st ed. VG $25.00

DANE, G. Ezra. *Ghost Town.* 1948 Tudor. 311 p. G $7.00

DANESE, Reanto. *American Images.* 1979 McGraw Hill. 1st print. 4to. dj. EX $45.00

DANFORD, Capt. Robert. *Notes on Training: Field Artillery Details.* 1918 Yale. 7th print. VG $15.00

DANIEL, Dan. *Real Babe Ruth.* 1948 NY. Ills 1st ed. 164 p. VG $50.00

DANIEL, Elizabeth. *Happy Hours: Photographs of Happy Children.* 1935 Chicago. Ills. 62 p. VG $20.00

DANIEL, J.F. *Elasmobranch Fishes.* 1922 CA U Pr. Ills 1st ed. 334 p. VG $45.00

DANIEL, L.J.; & GUNTER, R.W. *Confederate Cannon Foundries.* 1977 Pioneer. Ills. 4to. 112 p. dj. EX $25.00

DANIEL, P.; & SMOCK, R. *Talent for Detail: Photographs of Miss Francis B. Johnston.* 1974 NY. 1st ed. 4to. wraps. VG $20.00

DANIELS, Jonathan. *Devil's Backbone: Story of Natchez Trace.* 1962 NY. 1st ed. Am Trails Series. dj. $20.00

DANIELS, Les. *Black Castle.* 1978 Scribner. 1st ed. dj. EX $20.00

DANIELS, Mary. *Morris.* 1974 Ills 1st ed. dj. G $7.50

DANNET, Sylvia. *Nobel Women of the North.* 1959 NY. Ills Yoseloff. VG $20.00

DANRIDGE, Dorothy. *Everything & Nothing.* 1970 Abelard Schuman. 1st ed. $15.00

DANTE. *Divine Comedy.* 1928 Nonesuch. Ills after Botticelli. Ltd ed. $225.00

DANTE. *Divine Comedy.* 1932 Ltd Ed Club. sgn Mardersteig. dj. VG $80.00

DANTE. *Purgatory & Paradise.* 1886 Chicago/NY. Ills Dore. xl. G $35.00

DARAUL, Arkon. *History of the Secret Societies.* 1961 NY. 256 p. dj. EX $33.00

DARDIS, Tom. *Some Time in the Sun.* 1976 NY. 1st ed. dj. M $12.00

DARK, Sidney. *London.* 1937 NY. Ills Pennell. xl. G $18.00

DARK, Sidney. *Paris.* 1936 NY. Macmillan. Ills Henry Rushbury. 139 p. VG $20.00

DARLEY, F.O.C. *Aladdin; or, The Wonderful Lamp.* 1846 Phil. Lindsay Blakiston. 118 p. VG $25.00

DARLEY, F.O.C. *Legend of Sleepy Hollow.* 1849 Am Art Union. folio. $60.00

DARLEY, F.O.C. *Rip Van Winkle.* 1848 Am Art Union. folio. wraps. $45.00

DARLEY, F.O.C. *War Pictures.* 1865 NY. Ills. green leather. G $25.00

DARO, August. *Inside Swing: Key to Better Golf.* 1972 NY. 1st ed. inscr. $75.00

DARRAH, Delmar D. *History & Evolution of Freemasonry.* 1954 Chicago. Ills. 422 p. dj. EX $18.00

DARROW, Clarence. *Prohibition Mania.* 1927 NY. Ills 1st ed. 254 p. VG $40.00

DARROW, Clarence. *Scott's Militia Tactics.* 1821 Hartford. Revised 2nd ed. full calf. VG $125.00

DARROW, Clarence. *Story of My Life.* 1960 495 p. dj. VG $10.00

DARTON, William. *Little Truths Better Than Great Fables. Vol. II.* 1800 Phil. 16mo. wraps. EX $80.00

DARWIN, Charles. *Descent of Man.* 1904 NY. Ills 2nd ed. 2 vol set. $30.00

DARWIN, Charles. *Different Forms of Flowers on Plants of Same Species.* 1899 NY. Ills. 351 p. $15.00

DARWIN, Charles. *Different Forms of Flowers on Plants of Same Species.* 1893 Appleton. Ills. 352 p. VG $18.00

DARWIN, Charles. *Expression des Emotions.* 1874 Paris. Reinwald. 1st ed. 8vo. cloth. $125.00

DARWIN, Charles. *Expression of Emotions in Man & Animals.* 1904 NY. Ills. 372 p. $20.00

DARWIN, Charles. *Expression of Emotions in Man & Animals.* 1873 NY. 1st Am ed. 8vo. xl. EX $75.00

DARWIN, Charles. *Expression of Emotions in Man & Animals.* 1872 London. Murray. 1st ed. 2nd issue. VG $280.00

DARWIN, Charles. *Expression of Emotions in Man & Animals.* 1873 Appleton. 1st Am ed. VG $150.00

DARWIN, Charles. *Journal of Researches in Geology & Natural History.* 1839 London. blue cloth. ½-leather box. $1800.00

DARWIN, Charles. *Naturalist's Voyage Around the World.* 1889 NY. Appleton. Revised 2nd ed. 12mo. 519 p. $35.00

DARWIN, Charles. *On the Origin of Species.* 1860 NY. 1st Am ed. 3rd print. VG $205.00

DARWIN, Charles. *On the Origin of Species.* 1963 NY. reprint of 6th ed. boxed. EX $15.00

DARWIN, Charles. *On the Origin of Species.* 1929 London. Thinker Lib. 1st ed. dj. VG $18.00

DARWIN, Charles. *Structure & Distribution of Coral Reefs.* 1984 AZ U Pr. 214 p. maps. wraps. EX $10.00

DARWIN, Charles. *Variation of Animals & Plants Under Domestication.* 1868 London. Murray. 1st ed. 2 vol set. VG $250.00

DARWIN, Charles. *Vegetable Mould & Earthworms.* 1881 London. G $32.00

DARWIN, E. *Beauties in the Botanic Garden.* 1805 London. VG $25.00

DARWIN, George Howard. *Tides & Kindred Phenomena in Solar System.* 1898 London. Murray. Ills 1st ed. 342 p. $25.00

DAS, Bhagavan. *Science of Peace.* 1904 London. 1st ed. 347 p. G $35.00

DASH, Samuel. *Chief Counsel.* 1976 NY. dj. M $12.00

DAUDET, Alphonse. *Fromont & Risler.* 1898 Boston. 1st ed. EX $17.00

DAUDET, Alphonse. *Kings in Exile.* 1900 Boston. blue cloth. VG $35.00

DAUGHERTY, James. *Daniel Boone.* 1940 NY. Viking. 2nd ed. 4to. 95 p. EX $15.00

DAUGHERTY, James. *Daniel Boone.* 1939 NY. Viking. Ills 1st ed. 94 p. cloth. VG $15.00

DAUGHERTY, James. *Of Courage Undaunted: Across Continent with Lewis & Clark.* 1951 NY. Viking. 1st ed. 4to. 168 p. dj. VG $16.00

DAUGHERTY, James. *Poor Richard.* 1941 NY. Viking. Ills 1st ed. VG $12.50

DAUGHERTY, James. *Sound of Trumpets.* 1971 NY. Viking. Ills 1st ed. 4to. 127 p. dj. $15.00

DAUGHERTY, James. *Their Weight in Wildcats: Tales of Frontier.* 1936 Boston. Houghton Mifflin. 1st ed. dj. $17.50

DAUGHERTY, James. *West of Boston.* 1956 NY. Viking. Ills 1st ed. 4to. 95 p. dj. $15.00

DAUGHERTY, James. *Wild, Wild West.* 1948 McKay. Ills. 4to 34 p. dj. $20.00

DAUTERMAN, C.C. *Sevres.* 1969 NY. Ills. 84 p. $10.00

DAUVILLIER, A. *Photochemical Origin of Life.* 1965 Academic Pr. Ills. 193 p. dj. VG $14.00

DAUZET, Marceline. *1 Happy Day: Picture Storybook.* 1939 Saalfield. Ills JL Scott. 4to. 18 p. dj. $20.00

DAVAMATA, Sister. *Days in an Indian Monastery.* 1927 326 p. EX $25.00

DAVENPORT, Basil. *Tales To Be Told in the Dark.* 1953 Dodd Mead. 1st ed. dj. EX $25.00

DAVENPORT, E. *Principles of Breeding.* 1907 NY. 727 p. VG $10.00

DAVENPORT, E.A. *History of 8th IL Cavalry.* 1888 Chicago. 1st ed. 450 p. EX $125.00

DAVENPORT, Guy. *Eudora Welty: G. Davenport Celebrates Writer & Photographer.* 1978 Aperture. 1st ed. EX $25.00

DAVENPORT, Homer. *My Quest of the Arab Horse.* 1909 NY. Dodge. Ills. 8vo. 276 p. VG $250.00

DAVENPORT, John. *Aphrodisiacs & Anti-Aphrodisiacs.* 1869 London. 154 p. EX $95.00

DAVENPORT, Millia. *Book of Costume.* 1948 NY. 1st ed. slipcase. VG $40.00

DAVEY, K.G. *Reproduction in the Insects.* 1965 Oliver Boyd. Ills 1st ed. 96 p. dj. EX $20.00

DAVEY, Peter. *Architecture of the Arts & Crafts Movement.* 1980 NY. Rizzoli. Ills. 4to. 224 p. dj. $30.00

DAVEY, W. *Arms, Angels, Epitaphs, & Bones.* 1935 Rydal Pr. $15.00

DAVID, Hans; & MENDEL, Arthur. *Bach Reader.* 1945 NY. 1st ed. dj. VG $22.00

DAVID, Maurice. *Who Was Columbus?* 1933 Research Pub. G $27.50

DAVID-NEEL, Alexander. *Magic & Mystery in Tibet.* 1932 NY. Kendall. VG $30.00

DAVID-NEEL, Alexander. *My Journey to Lhasa.* 1927 London. 1st ed. VG $20.00

DAVIDOFF, Z. *Connoisseurs Book of Cigars.* 1984 NY. Ills. 101 p. EX $15.00

DAVIDS, Arlette. *Flowers, Rock Plants.* 1939 Paris. 40 plts. dj. G $35.00

DAVIDS, R.C. *Lords of the Arctic.* 1982 Macmillan. Ills 1st ed. 140 p. dj. EX $18.00

DAVIDSON, Doherty. *Strange Crimes at Sea.* 1954 NY. dj. VG $12.00

DAVIDSON, Donald. *Poems 1922-1961.* 1966 MN U Pr. 1st ed. dj. EX $30.00

DAVIDSON, Donald. *Southern Writers in Modern World.* 1958 GA U Pr. 1st ed. dj. EX $30.00

DAVIDSON, H. *Edward Borein: Cowboy Artist.* 1974 Doubleday. Ills 1st ed. dj. VG $27.50

DAVIDSON, Homer K. *Black Jack Davidson.* 1974 Glendale. 1st ed. dj. VG $35.00

DAVIDSON, Jean. *Alexander Calder at the Zoo.* 1974 NY. Smithsonian. Ills. $5.00

DAVIDSON, Jo. *Between Sittings: Informal Autobiography.* 1951 NY. Dial. Ills 1st ed. dj. G $20.00

DAVIDSON, L.S. *South of Joplin: Story of a Tri-State's Diggin's.* 1939 NY. 1st ed. photos. dj. VG $15.00

AVIDSON, Marshall B. *Artists' America.* 1973 Am Heritage. 1st ed. dj. EX $18.00

DAVIDSON, Marshall B. *Life in America.* 1951 NY. MOMA. Ills. 2 vol set. $20.00

DAVIDSON, N.J. *Modern Exploration & Travel.* 1932 Lippincott. Ills. 318 p. maps. VG $16.00

DAVIDSON, Orlando. *Story of 96th Infantry Division in WWII.* 1947 Washington. 1st ed. VG $80.00

DAVIE, John Constanse. *Letters From Paraguay.* 1805 London. Robinson. 1st ed. 293 p. $150.00

DAVIE, Oliver. *Methods in the Art of Taxidermy.* 1900 McKay. Ills. 4to. 359 p. VG $33.00

DAVIE, Oliver. *Nests & Eggs of North American Birds.* 1889 Columbus. 4th ed. VG $25.00

DAVIE, Oliver. *Recollections of a Naturalist.* 1898 Columbus. Ltd ed. 1/200. VG $25.00

DAVIES, Charles Maurice. *Mystic London; or, Phases of Occult Life in the Metropolis.* 1875 London. 406 p. VG $45.00

DAVIES, Godfrey. *Bibliography of British History: Stuart Period 1603-1714.* 1928 Oxford. 1st ed. tall 8vo. VG $25.00

DAVIES, H.W. *Catalog of Early French Books in Library of Fairfax. Vol. I.* 1961 Holland Pr. dj. VG $80.00

DAVIES, Hunter. *Beatle Book.* 1964 Lancer, NY. Ills. pb. EX $12.50

DAVIES, Hunter. *Beatles.* 1969 Dell. Ills 1st print. VG $12.50

DAVIES, Nigel. *Voyages to the New World.* 1979 Morrow. Ills 1st Am ed. 287 p. dj. EX $16.00

DAVIES, Nina S. *Classics of the Doll World.* 1959 New Orleans. dj. EX $16.00

DAVIES, R. *6 Centuries of Painting.* no date. NY. Dodge. 40 plts. VG $22.50

DAVIES, Rhys. *Stars, World, & Women.* 1930 London. Chiswick. 1/550. sgn. EX $50.00

DAVIES, Robertson. *Papers of Samuel Marchbanks.* 1986 Viking. 1st Am ed. dj. EX $23.00

DAVIES, Robertson. *Rebel Angels.* 1982 Viking. 1st Am ed. dj. EX $14.00

DAVIES, Robertson. *Tempest-Tost.* 1951 Toronto. 1st ed. dj. VG $125.00

DAVIES, T. Maria. *Tinderbox.* 1913 Century. Ills Jackson. 1st ed. dj. $10.00

DAVIES, Valentine. *Miracle on 34th St.* 1984 NY. Harcourt Brace. dj. $15.00

DAVIES, Valentine. *Miracle on 34th Street.* 1947 NY. 1st ed. dj. EX $18.00

DAVIES, W.H. *Autobiography of a Super-Tramp.* 1908 London. 1st ed. VG $45.00

DAVIES, W.H. *Fries Rebellion 1798-1799.* 1899 Doylestown, PA. Ills 1st ed. 143 p. VG $75.00

DAVILA, Enrico Caterino. *Histoire des Guerres Civiles de France.* 1657 Paris. Rocolet. 3rd ed. 2 vol set. $135.00

DAVIS, Andrew Jackson. *Harbinger of Health.* 1909 19th ed. 428 p. EX $26.00

DAVIS, Andrew Jackson. *Temple Concerning Disease of the Brain & Nerves.* 1909 NY. 487 p. cloth. EX $35.00

DAVIS, B. *George Washington & the American Revolution.* 1975 Random House. 1st ed. 497 p. maps. dj. VG $20.00

DAVIS, B. *They Called Him Stonewall.* 1954 NY. 2nd ed. presentation. dj. G $25.00

DAVIS, Benjamin. *Southern Garden.* 1971 Phil. 252 p. dj. VG $9.00

DAVIS, Britton. *Truth About Geronimo.* 1951 Donnelley. Ills. 380 p. VG $20.00

DAVIS, Burke. *Get Yamamoto.* 1969 Random House. 1st ed. dj. VG $17.50

DAVIS, Burke. *To Appomattox, 9 April Days in 1865.* 1959 Rinehart. 433 p. maps. dj. VG $18.00

DAVIS, C.C. *Marine & Fresh-Water Plankton.* 1955 MI U Pr. Ills. 562 p. VG $30.00

DAVIS, C.C. *Pelagic Copepoda of the Northeastern Pacific Ocean.* 1949 WA U Pr. Ills. 117 p. wraps. EX $10.00

DAVIS, Charles. *Egyptian Book of the Dead.* 1895 NY/London. Putnam. Ills. 4to. 186 p. VG $125.00

DAVIS, Charles. *Report on Interoceanic Canals & Railroads.* 1867 WA. 1st ed. sgn. 14 maps. VG $175.00

DAVIS, Charles. *Report on Interoceanic Canals & Railroads.* 1886 WA. 13 fld maps. $60.00

DAVIS, Frank. *Country Life Book of Glass.* 1968 Middlesex. Country Life Books. 96 p. dj. $25.00

DAVIS, Frank. *Victorian Patrons of the Arts.* 1963 Country Life. 1st ed. dj. EX $15.00

DAVIS, G.E. *Practical Microscopy.* 1889 London. Ills. 436 p. blue cloth. G $65.00

DAVIS, H. Richard. *Scarlet Car.* 1907 Scribner. Ills Fred Steele. $10.00

DAVIS, Hubert J. *Great Dismal Swamp.* 1962 Richmond. Ills. dj. VG $12.00

DAVIS, J. *1st Settlers of VA.* 1806 NY. 2nd ed. 8vo. VG $500.00

DAVIS, J.C. *CA Salt-Water Fishing.* 1949 Barnes. Ills. 271 p. dj. VG $9.00

DAVIS, J.C. *Salt-Water Fishing on the Pacific Coast.* 1964 Barnes. Ills. 262 p. dj. VG $10.00

DAVIS, J.D. *Candi Token Wayusica (Sioux).* 1903 Santee. EX $17.50

DAVIS, J.F. *General Description of Empire of China.* 1836 NY. Ills. 16mo. 382 p. G $25.00

DAVIS, J.M. *Breaking of the Deadlock.* 1904 Springfield. Ills. 441 p. cloth. VG $25.00

DAVIS, Jefferson. *Rise & Fall of Confederate Government.* 1912 Appleton. 2 vol set. VG $10.00

DAVIS, Julia. *Shenadoah River.* 1945 NY. 1st ed. VG $15.00

DAVIS, Nicholas A. *Campaign From TX to MD with Battle of Fredericksburg.* 1961 Austin. facsimile of 1863. boxed. EX $40.00

DAVIS, R. *Reynolds.* 1913 London. Black. 4to. plts. VG $22.50

DAVIS, R.H. *About Paris.* 1895 Ills CD Gibson. 1st ed. 219 p. blue cloth. EX $20.00

DAVIS, R.H. *Bar Sinister.* 1903 NY. 1st ed. VG $20.00

DAVIS, R.H. *Congo & Coasts of Africa.* 1907 NY. 1st ed. dj. EX $20.00

DAVIS, R.H. *In the Fog.* 1901 NY. Russell. Ills Pierce/Steele. 8vo. $10.00

DAVIS, R.H. *Princess Aline.* 1895 NY. Ills. 163 p. $8.00

DAVIS, R.H. *West From a Car Window.* 1892 NY. Ills Remington. VG $65.00

DAVIS, Reed E. *From Aviation Section Signal Corps to USAF.* 1984 NY. Vantage. Ills 1st ed. 220 p. dj. EX $10.00

DAVIS, Sammy. *Hollywood in a Suitcase.* 1980 NY. 1st ed. dj. VG $17.50

DAVIS, T. *Vision Quest.* 1979 NY. 1st ed. dj. EX $15.00

DAVIS, W. *Dojo: Magic & Exorcism in Modern Japan.* 1980 Stanford U Pr. Ills. 332 p. dj. EX $18.00

DAVIS, W. Jefferson. *Air Conquest.* 1930 Los Angeles. Intro Lindbergh. 1st ed. $22.00

DAVIS, W.T. *Plymouth Memories of an Octogenarian.* 1906 Plymouth. VG $45.00

DAVIS, William Stearns. *Roots of War: Non-Technical History of Europe 1870-1914.* 1918 NY. G $17.00

DAVIS, William W. *Civil War & Reconstruction in FL.* 1913 NY. 8vo. 769 p. scarce. G $50.00

DAVIS, Winfield J. *History of Political Conventions in CA.* 1893 Sacramento. VG $70.00

DAVISON, V.E. *Bobwhites on the Rise.* 1949 Scribner. Ills 1st ed. 150 p. dj. EX $22.50

DAVY, Humphry. *Elements of Agricultural Chemisty: Course of 6 Lectures.* 1813 London. 1st ed. 323 p. $200.00

DAVY, Sir H. *Salmonia Days Fly Fishing.* 1851 VG $70.00

DAWES, Charles. *Journal As Ambassador to Great Britain.* 1939 NY. Ills 1st ed. inscr. VG $30.00

DAWES, Charles. *Journal of McKinley Years.* 1950 sgn. 458 p. VG $20.00

DAWSON, Aileen. *Masterpieces of Wedgwood in the British Museum.* 1984 Bloomington. Ills. cloth. $27.50

DAWSON, Aileen. *Porcelain of the 19th Century.* 1983 NY. Rizzoli. Ills. $85.00
j.

DAWSON, F. *Mandalay Dream.* 1971 NY. 1st ed. dj. EX $6.00

DAWSON, F. *Sun Rises into the Sky.* 1974 Los Angeles. Ltd ed. 1/250. sgn. wraps. EX $15.00

DAWSON, G.F *Life & Service of General Logan.* 1887 Chicago. 1st ed. 4to. cloth. xl. VG $20.00

DAWSON, Henry B. *Battles of US by Sea & Land.* 1858 NY. Johnson Fry. Ills Cappel. $75.00

DAWSON, Kenneth. *Casts From a Salmon Reel.* no date. Jenkins. Ills 1st ed. dj. VG $10.00

DAWSON, Kenneth. *Modern Salmon & Sea Trout Fishing.* 1938 VG $20.00

DAWSON, Kenneth. *Salmon & Trout in Moorland Streams.* 1947 Jenkins. Ills. 155 p. dj. VG $12.00

DAWSON, Percy. *Biography of Francois Magendie.* 1908 NY. Ltd 1st ed. 1/250. 8vo. 66 p. $50.00

DAWSON, Sarah Morgan. *Confederate Girl's Diary.* 1913 Boston. Houghton Mifflin. 1st ed. sgn. $25.00

DAWSON, William L. *Birds of OH.* 1903 Columbus. 2 vol set. ½-leather. VG $65.00

DAY, A. Grove. *Jack London in the South Seas.* 1971 NY. 4 Winds Pr. 1st ed. dj. EX $15.00

DAY, Avanelle. *Spice Cookbook.* 1964 NY. Book Club ed. dj. EX $10.00

DAY, Clarence. *Life with Father.* 1935 NY. 1st ed. dj. EX $20.00

DAY, Clarence. *Life with Mother.* 1937 NY. 1st ed. dj. EX $20.00

DAY, Cyrus L. *Songs of Thomas D'Urfey.* 1933 Harvard U Pr. EX $15.00

DAY, D. *Hunting & Exploring Adventures of Theodore Roosevelt.* 1955 Simon Schuster. 1st ed. dj. EX $15.00

DAY, David. *Doomsday Book of Animals.* 1983 Viking. Ills. 4to. 288 p. wraps. VG $10.00

DAY, David. *Tolkien Bestiary.* Crescent Books. 1st ed. dj. M $15.00

DAY, Donald. *Autobiography of Will Rogers.* 1949 Houghton Mifflin. sgn. 410 p. $8.00

DAY, Francis. *Point Lace & Diamonds.* 1891 Stokes. 1st ed. square 4to. VG $45.00

DAY, Kenneth. *Book Typography 1815-1965 in Europe & the US.* 1965 Chicago. 1st ed. dj. EX $20.00

DAY, L.B. *Folk Tales of Bengal.* 1912 London. Macmillan. 1st ed. red cloth. $85.00

DAY, Lewis C. *Magnetic Mountain.* 1933 London. Hogarth. Ltd ed. 1/100. $250.00

DAY, Lucella. *Tragedy of the Klondike.* 1906 NY. scarce. G $75.00

DAY, Mrs. Frank. *Princess of Manoa & Other Romantic Tales of HI.* 1906 San Francisco. Elder. Ills Hitchcock. G $20.00

DAY & DUNLAP. *Map Collection of TX State Archives 1527-1900.* 1962 Austin. TX State Lib. SftCvr. EX $7.00

DAY. *Jacob De Cordova: Land Merchant of TX.* 1962 Waco. Texian Pr. EX $10.00

DAYAN, Moshe. *Story of My Life.* 1976 Morrow. 1st ed. dj. VG $12.00

DE ALARCON, P.A. *3-Cornered Hat.* 1959 boxed. EX $30.00

DE ANDREA, William L. *Azrael.* 1987 NY. 1st Am ed. inscr. dj. $20.00

DE ANDREA, William L. *Lunatic Fringe.* 1980 NY. 1st Am ed. inscr. dj. $30.00

DE ANGELI, Arthur Craig. *Door in the Wall:* 1968 NY. Doubleday. Ills 1st ed. 153 p. dj. EX $15.00

DE ANGELI, Marguerite. *Book of Nursery & Mother Goose Rhymes.* 1954 NY. Doubleday. Ills. 4to. 192 p. dj. VG $35.00

DE ANGELI, Marguerite. *Bright April.* 1946 NY. Doubleday. Ills 1st ed. green cloth. VG $8.00

DE ANGELI, Marguerite. *Butter at the Old Price.* 1971 Doubleday. 5th ed. red cloth. dj. EX $10.00

DE ANGELI, Marguerite. *Covered Bridge.* 1936 NY. Macmillan. Ills 1st ed. square 8vo. VG $25.00

DE ANGELI, Marguerite. *Door in the Wall.* 1949 Kingswood. 1st English ed. 8vo. VG $15.00

DE ANGELI, Marguerite. *Door in the Wall.* 1949 NY. Ills 1st ed. dj. G $12.00

DE ANGELI, Marguerite. *Fiddle Strings.* 1974 Doubleday. Ills 1st ed. VG $20.00

DE ANGELI, Marguerite. *Lion in Box.* 1975 NY. 1st ed. dj. VG $8.00

DE ANGELI, Marguerite. *Little Book of Prayers & Graces.* 1952 NY. Doubleday. Ills. 4to. 28 p. dj. VG $15.00

DE ANGELI, Marguerite. *Skippack School.* 1939 NY. Doubleday. Jr Books. reprint. dj. G $15.00

DE ANGELI, Marguerite. *Whistle for the Crossing.* 1977 Ills 1st ed. dj. M $17.50

DE ARMOND, R.M. *Lady Franklin Visits Sitka, AK 1870.* 1981 AK Hist Soc. Ills. 134 p. M $25.00

DE BALZAC, Honore. *Droll Stories.* 1927 Boni Liveright. Ills R Barton. 1/2,050. 8vo. $85.00

DE BALZAC, Honore. *Droll Stories.* 1874 Bibliophilist. Ills Dore. G $17.00

DE BALZAC, Honore. *Les Contes Drolatiques.* no date. Paris. Ills Dore. 11th ed. leather. $55.00

DE BALZAC, Honre *Droll Stories.* London. Ills Dore. 1st English ed. $125.00

DE BARTHE, Joe. *Life & Adventures of Frank Grouard.* 1958 OK U Pr. Ills 1st ed. 268 p. dj. EX $25.00

DE BECOURT, R. *Grave of Human Philosophies: Ancient & Modern.* 1827 London. fld chart. VG $75.00

DE BLES, Arthur. *How To Distinguish the Saints in Art.* 1925 NY. Art Culture Pub. Ills. 4to. VG $30.00

DE BOGORY, Eugene. *Roaring Dusk.* 1928 Kenilworth. Ills 1st ed. 277 p. dj. VG $17.50

DE BOSSCHERE, Jean. *Folk Tales of Flanders.* Ills 1st Am ed. 4to. gilt green cloth. VG $150.00

DE BOUVIENNE, Louise Antoine. *Memoirs of Napoleon Bonaparte.* 1890 NY. Scribner. 4 vol set. $37.50

DE BROGLIE, Louis. *Matter & Light: New Physics.* 1946 Dover Pub. G $10.00

DE BROGLIE, Louis. *Theorie Generale des Particles a Spin.* 1954 Paris. 2nd ed. wraps. VG $40.00

DE BROKE, Willoughby. *Spirit of Our Ancestors.* no date. NY. Ills Armour. 1st Am ed. G $36.00

DE BROKE, Willoughby. *Sport of Our Ancestors.* no date. NY. Dutton. Ills Armour. $65.00

DE BRUNHOFF, Jean. *Histoire de Babar le Petit Elephant.* 1931 Paris. Ills 1st ed. folio. $375.00

DE BRUNHOFF, Jean. *Travels of Barbar.* 1934 NY. 1st Am ed. VG $65.00

DE BURY, Richard. *Philobiblon: Treatise on the Love of Books.* 1899 NY. Meyers. Ltd ed. 1/500. 8vo. wraps. EX $10.00

DE BUSSIGNY, H.L. *Handbook for Horsewomen.* 1884 NY. 16mo. 75 p. $45.00

DE CALABRELLA, Baroness. *Evenings at Haddon Hall.* 1846 London. Ills Cattermole. $75.00

DE CAMOENS, Luis. *Lusiad; or, Discovery of India: Epic Poem.* 1778 Oxford. 2nd ed. 4to. 496 p. calf. VG $165.00

DE CAMP, L. Sprague. *Footprints on Sand: Literary Sampler.* Ills Burnett. Ltd 1st ed. 1/1,500. sgn. dj. $95.00

DE CAMP, L. Sprague. *Great Fetish.* 1978 Garden City. 1st ed. sgn. dj. EX $20.00

DE CAMP, L. Sprague. *Great Monkey Trial.* 1968 NY. 1st ed. dj. EX $35.00

DE CAMP, L. Sprague. *Hand of Zei.* 1963 NY. 1st ed. dj. EX $63.00

DE CAMP, L. Sprague. *Heroes & Hobgoblins.* 1981 Grant. Ltd ed. 1/1,250. sgn. dj. M $30.00

DE CAMP, L. Sprague. *Lovecraft.* 1975 Doubleday. 1st ed. dj. EX $22.50

DE CAMP, L. Sprague. *Tritonian Ring.* 1968 Paperback Lib. 1st ed. VG $11.00

DE CAMP, L. Sprague. *Undesired Princess.* 1951 Fantasy. 1st ed. VG $15.00

DE CAMP, L. Sprague. *Warlocks & Warriors.* 1970 NY. 1st ed. dj. EX $20.00

DE CAMP, L. Sprague. *Wheels of If.* 1948 Chicago. 1st ed. sgn. dj. EX $125.00

DE CARDONNEL, Adam. *Picturesque Antiquities of Scotland.* 1788 London. Ills. 4to. 1/4 leather. VG $200.00

DE CARLE, D. *With the Watchmaker at the Bench.* 1945 NY. Ills. 243 p. $10.00

DE CASSERES, Benjamin. *Superman in America.* 1929 WA U Pr. inscr. 8vo. 30 p. dj. VG $35.00

DE CASSERES, Benjamin. *When Huck Finn Went Highbrow.* 1934 NY. Madigan. 1/125. boxed. VG $100.00

DE CASTRO, Josue. *Of Men & Crabs.* 1970 NY. 1st ed. dj. VG $25.00

DE CAULAINCORT. *Duke of Vicenza with Napoleon in Russia.* 1935 NY. Ills. fld map. VG $12.00

DE CHARDIN, Pierre Teilhard. *Phenomenon of Man.* 1959 London. Advance copy. 8vo. slipcase. $350.00

DE CLERCK, Jean. *Textbook of Brewing.* 1957 London. Chapman Hall. 1st ed. 2 vols. $50.00

DE COCK, L. *Ansel Adams.* 1972 NY Graphic Soc. 4to. dj. VG $30.00

DE COSTA, B.F. *Natural & Moral History of the Indies.* 1880 London. reprint of 1880. 551 p. dj. EX $95.00

DE COSTA, B.F. *Sailing Directions of Henry Hudson.* 1869 Albany. 8vo. ¾-leather. VG $30.00

DE COSTER, Charles. *Flemish Legends.* 1920 London. Ills Delstanche. VG $20.00

DE COSTER, Charles. *Glorious Adventures of Tyl Ulenspiegl.* 1934 Harlem. folio. $50.00

DE FAYET, M. *Louis XIII & Louis XIV.* no date. Paris. Ills. dj. $45.00

DE FELICE, Roger. *French Furniture Under Louis XVI & the Empire.* 1920 London. Heinemann. Ills. 142 p. $25.00

DE FELITTA, Frank. *Oktoberfest.* 1973 Doubleday. 1st ed. dj. EX $25.00

DE FILIPPI. *Karakora & Western Himalaya.* no date/place. Ills. maps. VG $150.00

DE FOE, Daniel. *Die Winderbare Lebensbeschreibung und Erstaunliche.* 1809 Phil. Zentler. 12mo. plts. fair. $60.00

DE FOE, Daniel. *Journal of Plague Year.* 1968 CT. Ills D Gnoli. Ltd ed. 1/1,500. $95.00

DE FOE, Daniel. *Life & Most Surprising Adventures of Robinson Crusoe.* 1819 NY. 4 plts. $60.00

DE FOE, Daniel. *Moll Flanders.* 1920 NY/London. Dodd Mead/Bodley Head. 1st ed. $40.00

DE FOE, Daniel. *Robinson Crusoe.* 1912 Houghton Mifflin. Ills Smith. $45.00

DE FOE, Daniel. *Robinson Crusoe.* 1930 Heritage. Ills E Wilson. slipcase. VG $10.00

DE FOE, Daniel. *Robinson Crusoe.* 1946 Grosset Dunlap. Ills Lynd Ward. dj. EX $10.00

DE FOE, Daniel. *Robinson Crusoe.* Belforde Clarke. reprint. VG $7.50

DE FOE, Daniel. *Roxana: Fortunate Mistress.* 1976 Ltd Ed Club. Ills/sgn Kroeber. slipcase. EX $50.00

DE FONTENOY, Marquise. *Eve's Glossary.* 1897 Stone. Ills Hazenplug. 4to. 285 p. VG $55.00

DE GIVRY, Grillot. *Pictorial Anthology of Witchcraft, Magic, & Alchemy.* 1958 NY. Universe Books. 1st Am ed. $28.00

DE GOURMONT, Remy. *Book of Masks.* 1921 Boston. EX $25.00

DE GOUY, L.P. *Derrydale Cookbook of Fish & Game.* 1937 Derrydale. Ltd ed. 1/1,250. VG $135.00

DE GRUNWALD, Constantin. *Napoleon's Nemesis: Life of Baron Stein.* 1936 Scribner. $10.00

DE GUILLEBON. *Porcelain of Paris 1770-1850.* 1972 NY. Ills. 4to. dj. VG $45.00

DE HARTOG, Jan. *Captain.* 1966 1st ed. VG $30.00

DE HARTOG, Jan. *Sailing Ship.* 1964 NY. Odyssey Pr. Ills Spier. G $11.00

DE JOINVILLE, Prince. *Army of the Potomac.* 1862 NY. Ills. VG $35.00

DE KAY, James E. *Natural History of NY Fauna: Part II, Birds.* 1844 Albany. 141 plts. $275.00

DE KOVEN, Mrs. Reginald. *Musician & His Wife.* 1926 NY. Harper. photos. VG $12.00

DE LA FERTE, Philip Joubert. *Rocket.* 1957 NY. Philosophical Lib. 190 p. dj. $10.00

DE LA FONTAINE, Jean. *Tales & Novels of Jean de la Fontaine.* 1929 Nijmegen. Ills C Tice. Ltd ed. 2 vols. $400.00

DE LA MANO. *De la Mano's Magic Book.* c 1880s. NY. 12mo. 28 p. EX $25.00

DE LA MARE, Walter. *Alone.* 1927 London. Ills Ralph Keene. proof. $45.00

DE LA MARE, Walter. *Before Dawn.* 1924 London. Ltd 1st ed. 1/100. wraps. $50.00

DE LA MARE, Walter. *Broomsticks & Other Tales.* 1925 NY. Knopf. Ills Bold. 1st ed. 8vo. VG $30.00

DE LA MARE, Walter. *Broomsticks.* 1952 London. Constable. 1st ed. VG $18.00

DE LA MARE, Walter. *Come Hither.* 1923 London. Ltd ed. 1/350. sgn. 2 vol set. $50.00

DE LA MARE, Walter. *Crossings: Fairy Play with Music.* 1923 Ills Lathrop. 1st ed. VG $30.00

DE LA MARE, Walter. *Fleeting.* 1933 London. 1st ed. dj. EX $17.00

DE LA MARE, Walter. *Flora.* no date. Phil. 4to. dj. VG $50.00

DE LA MARE, Walter. *Memory & Other Poems.* 1938 Constable. 1st ed. dj. EX $15.00

DE LA MARE, Walter. *Number 6 Joy Street.* 1927 NY. Ills. 8vo. plts. $35.00

DE LA MARE, Walter. *O Lovely England.* 1956 NY. 1st ed. dj. EX $15.00

DE LA MARE, Walter. *Peacock Pie.* 1924 NY. Ills C Lovat Fraser. 4to. $30.00

DE LA MARE, Walter. *Peacock Pie.* 1961 Ills Cooney. 1st ed. juvenile. dj. M $22.50

DE LA MARE, Walter. *Peacock Pie.* 1925 NY. Ills WH Robinson. cloth. VG $25.00

DE LA MARE, Walter. *Stories From the Bible.* 1929 NY. 1st Am ed. 343 p. dj. VG $15.00

DE LA MARE, Walter. *Stuff & Nonesense.* 1927 Constable. dj. EX $20.00

DE LA RAME, Louisa. *Bimbi (Ouida).* 1902 Lippincott. Ills. VG $12.00

DE LA ROCHE, Mazo. *Return to Jalna.* 1946 Toronto. 1st Canadian ed. dj. VG $20.00

DE LAMARTINE, A. *History of French Revolution of 1848.* 1849 Boston. 1st Am ed. 2 vols in 1. G $15.00

DE LANEY, Paul. *Toll of the Sands.* 1919 Denver. Smith Brooks. 1st ed. 333 p. $75.00

DE LAURENCE, L.W. *India's Hood Unveiled.* 1910 Chicago. DeLaurence. 204 p. VG $33.00

DE LAWRENCE, George. *Impromptu Magic with Patter.* 1922 Chicago. Ills. 12mo. 79 p. $20.00

DE LEEUW, Hendrik. *Conquest of the Air: History & Future of Aviation.* 1960 NY. Vantage. Ills 1st ed. 300 p. dj. VG $10.00

DE LEON, T.C. *Joseph Wheeler: Man, Statesman, & Soldier.* 1960 Continental. Ills. reprint. 142 p. EX $18.00

DE LILLO, Don. *End Zone.* 1976 Boston. Houghton Mifflin. 1st ed. EX $50.00

DE LILLO, Don. *Names.* 1982 Knopf. 1st ed. dj. EX $15.00

DE LINCY, M.L. *Recherches sur Jean Grolier sur sa Vie et Sa Bibliotheque.* 1866 Paris. fld plts. full leather. VG $45.00

DE LINT, Charles. *Ascian Rose.* 1986 Seattle. Intro Blaylock. 1/300. sgns. M $45.00

DE LIZARDI, J. *Itching Parrot.* 1942 NY. 1st ed. dj. VG $14.00

DE LONG, George W. *Voyage of the Jeannette.* 1883 Boston. 1st ed. maps. plts. 2 vol set. $120.00

DE MADARIAGA, Salvador. *Genius of Spain & Other Essays on Spanish Literature.* 1930 London. 2nd ed. VG $15.00

DE MAUPASSANT, Guy. *Works of Guy de Maupassant.* 1911 Classic. 4 vol set. leather. EX $25.00

DE MAURIER, G. *Peter Ibbetson.* 1891 NY. 1st ed. EX $28.00

DE MAURIER, G. *Trilby.* 1894 NY. 1st Am ed. VG $25.00

DE MENEVAL, Barou C. *Memoirs Illustrating History of Napoleon I.* 1894 NY. 3 vol set. xl. VG $35.00

DE MENIL, Alexander Nicolas. *Literature of LA Territory.* 1944 St. Louis. dj. VG $35.00

DE MILLE, A. *Where the Wings Grow.* 1978 Doubleday. Ills 1st ed. dj. VG $7.50

DE MILLE, James. *Doge Club; or, Italy in MDCCCLIX.* 1869 NY. Ills 1st ed. $35.00

DE MONTAIGNE, Michel. *De Montaigne's Essays.* 1932 London. Nonesuch. 1/900. 8vo. morocco. $95.00

DE MONTFAUCON, Bernard. *Antiquity Explained & Represented in Sculptures.* 1721-1722. London. folio. 5 vol set. VG $300.00

DE MONVEL. *Everybody's St. Francis.* 1912 NY. Ills 1st ed. G $15.00

DE MONVEL. *Joan of Arc.* 1918 McKay. Ills 1st Am ed. oblong 4to. VG $40.00

DE MORGAN, William. *Old Madhouse.* 1919 NY. 1st ed. EX $10.00

DE MUSSET, Alfred. *La Nuit Venitienne, Fantasio; Les Caprices de Marianne.* 1913 Paris. Ills Brunelleschi. wraps. VG $125.00

DE PAOLA, Tomie. *Fight the Night.* 1968 Lippincott. Ills 1st ed. sgn. dj. EX $25.00

DE PAOLA, Tomie. *Strega Nona.* 1975 Prentice Hall. Ills. sgn. 32 p. dj. VG $20.00

DE PAUW, Linda G.; & HUNT, C. *Remember the Ladies: Women in America 1750-1815.* 1976 NY. Viking. Ills. 168 p. dj. $30.00

DE PEYSTER, John W. *Personal & Military History of Philip Kearny.* 1869 NY. 1st ed. rebound. VG $50.00

DE PRATZ, Clair. *French Home Cooking.* 1929 NY. 8vo. 295 p. $20.00

DE PROFT, Melanie. *New World Encyclopedia of Cooking.* 1972 NY. Ills 1st ed. 768 p. dj. EX $25.00

DE QUEIROZ, Ela. *Sweet Miracle.* 1906 Mosher. 1st ed. dj. EX $10.00

DE QUILLE, Dan. *Big Bonanza.* 1947 Knopf. 1st Borzoi Book. dj. VG $16.50

DE QUINCEY. *CA & the Gold Mania.* 1945 Colt Pr. 1/500. EX $45.00

DE REAMUR, M. *Art de Faire E'Clorre, et d'E'Lever en Tout Saison.* 1749 Paris. Ills. 12mo. 2 vol set. VG $300.00

DE RICCI, S. *Book Collector's Guide.* 1970 NY. EX $17.50

DE SAINT-EXUPERY, Antoine. *Little Prince.* 1943 Reynal Hitchcock. dj. EX $15.00

DE SAINT-EXUPERY, Antoine. *Little Prince.* 1943 Harcourt Brace. Ills 1st Am ed. dj. VG $45.00

DE SAUVENIERE, A. *Le Levrier.* 1881 Paris. Ills. 8vo. full leather. VG $35.00

DE SAVITSCH, Eugene. *In Search of Complications.* 1940 NY. 1st ed. xl. VG $10.00

DE SCHAUENSEE, R.M. *Birds of China.* 1984 Smithsonian. Ills. 602 p. wraps. EX $35.00

DE SCUDERI, Madeleine. *La Promenade de Versailles.* 1920 Paris. Ills Robert Mahias. wraps. G $75.00

DE SEGUR, Countess. *Old French Fairy Tales.* 1920 Phil. Penn. Ills Sterett. 8vo. VG $15.00

DE SELINCOURT, E. *Journals of Dorothy Worsworth.* 1970 Archon. 2 vol set. $32.50

DE SERVIEZ. *Roman Empresses: Their Lives & Secret Intrigues.* 1932 Dingwall. VG $25.00

DE SORIA, R. *3 Tales.* 1923 Chatto Windus. Ills. tall 8vo. G $15.00

DE TAKATS, Geza. *Local Anesthesia.* 1928 Phil. Saunders. Ills 1st ed. G $35.00

DE TALLEYRAND, Prince. *Memoirs of the Prince de Talleyrand.* 1891-1892. NY. Putnam. Ills. 8vo. 5 vol set. $500.00

DE TROBRIAND, Phillippe. *Military Life in Dakota.* 1951 St. Paul. Trans Lucille M Kane. dj. EX $45.00

DE VECCHI, Pierluigi. *Complete Paintings of Piero Della Francesca.* 1967 NY. 1st Am ed. dj. $25.00

DE VECCHI, Pierluigi. *Complete Paintings of Raphael.* 1966 NY. 1st Am ed. dj. $25.00

DE VERE GREEN, Bertha. *Fans Over the Ages: Collector Guide.* 1975 NY. Barnes. Ills. 4to. 174 p. dj. $25.00

DE VOE, Shirley S. *English Papier-Mache of Georgian & Victorian Periods.* 1971 Wesleyan U Pr. Ills. 4to. 211 p. dj. $30.00

DE VOTO, Bernard. *Across the Wide MO.* 1947 Boston. Houghton Mifflin. 1st ed. dj. $37.50

DE VOTO, Bernard. *Course of Empire.* 1952 Houghton Mifflin. dj. EX $14.00

DE VOTO, Bernard. *House of Sun Goes Down.* 1928 Chicago. 1st ed. VG $17.50

DE VOTO, Bernard. *More Food for Thought.* 1929 NY. 1st ed. dj. VG $20.00

DE VRIES, Peter. *Comfort Me with Apples.* 1956 Little Brown. 1st ed. dj. EX $50.00

DE VRIES, Peter. *Consenting Adults.* 1980 Little Brown. 1st ed. dj. EX $15.00

DE VRIES, Peter. *Glory of the Hummingbird.* 1974 Little Brown. 1st ed. dj. EX $20.00

DE VRIES, Peter. *I Hear America Singing.* 1976 Little Brown. 1st ed. dj. EX $15.00

DE VRIES, Peter. *Madder Music.* 1977 Little Brown. 1st ed. dj. EX $15.00

DE VRIES, Peter. *Prick of Noon.* 1985 Little Brown. 1st ed. dj. EX $15.00

DE VRIES, Peter. *Sauce for the Goose.* 1981 Little Brown. 1st ed. dj. EX $15.00

DE WITT, C.H. *Story of the PA Dutch.* no date. Harper. Ills. 4to. $35.00

DE WOLFE, Elsie. *House in Good Taste.* 1913 NY. 1st ed. dj. VG $27.50

DE WOLFE, Fiske. *Flowers by the Wayside.* c 1908. Boston. Ills. dj. EX $8.50

DE YRAOLA, Gonzalo Diaz. *La Vuelta al Mundo de la Expedicion de la Vacuna.* 1945 Seville. dj. wraps. xl. G $12.50

DEACON, Mary R. *Clover Club of Philadelphia 1882-1897.* 1897 Phil. presentation. 364 p. $38.00

DEAN, Amos. *History of Civilization.* 1868 Albany. Munsell. 1st ed. 7 vol set. VG $110.00

DEAN, Harry. *Pedro Gorino: Adventures of Negro Sea Captain.* 1929 Boston. 1st ed. dj. EX $35.00

DEAN, John. *Microscopic Anatomy of Lumbar Enlargement of Spinal Cord.* 1861 Cambridge. Ills. wraps. $150.00

DEAN, R. *Dahlia: Its History & Cultivation.* 1903 London. Ills. $8.00

DEARBORN, Frederick M. *American Homepathy in the World War*. 1923 Chicago. Am Inst Homeopathy. 447 p. xl. $9.50

DEAS, Alston. *Early Ironwork of Charleston*. 1941 Columbia, SC. Ills RJ Bryan. 4to. 112 p. dj. $65.00

DEATHERAGE, C.P. *Steamboating on the MO River in the '60s*. 1924 private print. Ills. 39 p. pb. VG $14.00

DEBAR, J. *Prohibition: Temperance, Good Morals, & Government*. no date. 8vo. 311 p. VG $20.00

DEBECKER. *Sexual Life in Japan*. no date. NY. 3rd ed. VG $17.50

DEBIT, Ralph M. *After-Death States*. 1924 178 p. VG $23.00

DEBO, Angie. *History of the Indians of the US*. 1972 OK U Pr. Ills. 450 p. maps. dj. EX $18.00

DEBO, Angie. *Prairie City*. 1944 Knopf. Ills 1st ed. 245 p. VG $15.00

DEBO, Angie. *Rise & Fall of the Choctaw Republic*. 1961 OK U Pr. Ills. 314 p. maps. dj. EX $22.00

DEBS, Eugene V. *Walls & Bars*. 1927 Chicago. red cloth. VG $35.00

DEBUSSY, Claude. *Children's Corner*. 1908 Paris. Durand Fils. 4to. wraps. $100.00

DECARGUES, Pierre. *Picasso*. 1974 NY. Felicie. Ills. folio. dj. $85.00

DECARPENTRY, Colonel. *Piaffer & Passage*. 1961 Princeton. Ills Ltd ed. 1/1,000. 76 p. EX $45.00

DECK, John. *1 Morning, for Pleasure*. 1968 NY. 1st ed. dj. EX $20.00

DECREMPS, Henri. *Testament de Jerome Sharp*. 1789 Paris. 3rd ed. VG $200.00

DEFORMERO, Carlo. *Carranza & Mexico*. 1915 Kennerley. 1st ed. inscr. G $15.00

DEGENHARDT, Richard K. *Belleek: Complete Collector's Guide & Reference*. 1978 NY. Portfolio. Ills. 4to. 221 p. $40.00

DEHN, Virginia. *Drawings of Adolf Dehn*. 1971 Columbia. MO Pr. Ills. 4to. cloth. $30.00

DEIGHTON, Len. *Battle of Britain*. 1980 NY. 1st ed. dj. M $20.00

DEIGHTON, Len. *Catch a Falling Spy*. 1976 NY. 1st ed. dj. M $12.00

DEIGHTON, Len. *Close-Up*. 1972 Atheneum. 1st Am ed. dj. EX $20.00

DEIGHTON, Len. *Declarations of War*. 1971 Cape. 1st ed. dj. EX $35.00

DEIGHTON, Len. *Funeral in Berlin*. 1964 London. 1st ed. dj. EX $25.00

DEIGHTON, Len. *Good-Bye Mickey Mouse*. 1982 Knopf. 1st ed. 4to. 337 p. dj. EX $17.50

DEIGHTON, Len. *London Match*. 1985 Hutchinson. Uncorrected proof. EX $50.00

DEIGHTON, Len. *Mexico Set*. 1985 Knopf. 1st ed. dj. EX $12.50

DEIGHTON, Len. *Only When I Laugh*. 1987 Ltd ed. 1/250. sgn. slipcase. VG $50.00

DEIGHTON, Len. *Spy Story*. 1974 Harcourt. 1st Am ed. dj. EX $20.00

DEIGHTON, Len. *Twinkle, Twinkle, Little Spy*. 1976 Cape. 1st ed. dj. EX $25.00

DEIGHTON & SCHWARTZMAN. *Airship Wreck*. 1978 London. Cape. 1st ed. dj. EX $27.50

DEKNATEL, Frederick B. *Edward Munch*. 1950 Chanticleer Pr. Ills. 4to. 120 p. cloth. dj. $30.00

DEL CASTILLO, Bernal Diaz. *True History of Conquest of Mexico*. 1966 Readex Microprint. $20.00

DELACROIX, Eugene. *Charlet*. 1862 Paris. Imprimerie de J Claye. wraps. $850.00

DELACROIX, Eugene. *Journals of NY*. 1937 Covice Friede. Ills 1st Am ed. 4to. VG $30.00

DELAFIELD, R. *Report on Art of War in Europe in 1854-1856*. 1861 WA. Ills 1st ed. 4to. maps. VG $195.00

DELAMOTTE, F. *Amateur Artist*. 1906 Chicago. fair. $10.00

DELAND, Margaret. *Dr. Lavendar's People*. 1903 NY. Ills 1st ed. VG $75.00

DELAND, Margaret. *Wisdom of Fools*. 1897 Boston. 1st ed. inscr/sgn. VG $85.00

DELANO, Alonzo. *Across the Plains & Among the Diggings*. 1936 NY. Wilson Erickson. Ills. wraps. $45.00

DELANO, Alonzo. *Alonzo Delano's CA Correspondence*. 1952 Castle Pr. Ltd ed. 1/310. EX $75.00

DELARUE, J. *Les Tatouages du Milieu*. 1950 Paris. Ills 1st ed. VG $125.00

DELAVAN, J. *Notes on CA & Places*. 1956 Biobooks. Ills Ltd ed. 1/700. $35.00

DELBANCO, N. *Group Portrait*. 1982 NY. 1st ed. inscr. dj. EX $15.00

DELBANCO, N. *In the Middle Distance*. 1971 NY. 1st ed. dj. EX $10.00

DELDERFIELD, R.F. *Avenue*. 1964 Simon Schuster. 1st ed. dj. VG $20.00

DELDERFIELD, R.F. *Horseman Riding By*. 1966 Simon Schuster. 1st ed. dj. VG $18.00

DELDERFIELD, R.F. *Mr. Sermon*. 1962 Simon Schuster. 1st ed. dj. VG $15.00

DELDERFIELD, R.F. *Nobody Shouted Author*. 1951 London. 1st ed. dj. VG $25.00

DELDERFIELD, R.F. *To Serve Them All My Days*. 1972 London. 1st ed. dj. VG $18.00

DELL, J. *Layout for Advertising*. 1928 Chicago. 175 p. $10.00

DELL'ACQUA, G.A. *Tiziano*. 1956 Milano. Martello. 4to. plts. dj. VG $35.00

DELLENBAUGH, Frederick. *Canyon Voyage*. 1908 Putnam. Ills. EX $27.50

DELLENBAUGH, Frederick. *Canyon Voyage*. 1926 New Haven. Ills. presentation. VG $20.00

DELLENBAUGH, Frederick. *Romance of CO River*. 1909 NY. VG $35.00

DELMONT, Joseph. *Catching Wild Beasts Alive*. 1931 Stokes. Ills. 285 p. VG $12.50

DEMACHY, Alain. *Interior Architecture & Decoration*. 1974 NY. Morrow. Ills. 163 p. dj. $47.50

DEMARET, Jimmy. *My Partner, Ben Hogan*. 1954 McGraw Hill. 1st ed. dj. VG $17.50

DEMARGNE, Pierre. *Birth of Greek Art*. 1964 NY. Golden. Ills. 4to. 447 p. dj. $60.00

DEMARINIS, Rick. *Lovely Monster*. 1975 Simon. 1st ed. dj. EX $15.00

DEMENT, J. *Uranium & Atomic Power*. 1945 Brooklyn. 1st ed. dj. $25.00

DEMEYER, J. *Benjamin Franklin Calls on the President*. 1939 NY. 1st ed. 90 p. cloth. dj. $6.00

DEMPSEY, Jack. *Dempsey*. 1977 1st ed. dj. EX $12.50

DEMUS, Otto. *Byzantine Mosaic Decoration*. 1955 Boston. Ills. 97 p. cloth. $27.50

DEMUTH, Averil. *Trudi & Hansel: Story of the Austrian Tyrol*. 1938 Winston. Ills Lavrin. 1st ed. VG $20.00

DENDY, Walter Cooper. *Philosophy of Mystery*. 1841 London. 443 p. G $45.00

DENDY, Walter Cooper. *Philosophy of Mystery*. 1845 NY. 442 p. VG $48.00

DENISON, C. *Rocky Mountain Health Resorts*. 1880 Boston. 1st ed. 192 p. G $27.50

DENISON, G.T. *History of Cavalry.* 1913 London. 2nd ed. VG $25.00

DENKER, Eric. *Drawing Near: Whistler Etchings From Zelman Collection.* 1984 Los Angeles. Ills. 4to. 192 p. wraps. $25.00

DENMARK, E.R. *Architecture of Old South.* 1926 Atlanta. Ills 1st ed. 80 p. cloth. $27.50

DENNIS, A.W. *What To See in Salem.* 1915 MA. Ills. 18 p. wraps. $5.00

DENNIS, Felix. *Man-Eating Sharks.* 1976 Castle. Ills. 4to. 96 p. dj. EX $10.00

DENNIS, Patrick. *Around the World with Auntie Mame.* London. 1st English ed. dj. VG $35.00

DENNIS, W.H. *100 Years of Metallurgy.* 1964 Chicago. Aldine. 1st ed. 8vo. 342 p. $10.00

DENNIS, William J. *History & Incidents of Railway Postal Service.* 1916 Des Moines. VG $50.00

DENNY, J.H. *Chindit Indiscretion.* 1956 London. 1st ed. VG $10.00

DENSLOW, W.W. *Toyland ABC.* Donohue. 8vo. 8 p. printed on linen. $25.00

DENSMORE, F. *Chippewa Music.* 1910 & 1913. WA. 2 vol set. VG $40.00

DENSMORE, F. *Mandan & Hidatsa Music.* 1923 WA. 192 p. VG $20.00

DENSMORE, F. *Northern Ute Music.* 1922 WA. 213 p. VG $20.00

DENSON, Alan. *Printed Writings by George W. Russell.* 1961 Northwestern U. 1st ed. EX $20.00

DENT, Edward J. *Foundations of English Opera: Study of Musical Drama.* 1928 Cambridge. VG $20.00

DENWOOD, Philip. *Tibetan Carpet.* 1974 Warminster. Artis Phillips. Ills. 101 p. $55.00

DEPEW, C.M. *Life & Later Speeches.* 1894 NY. Ills 1st ed. 510 p. cloth. $7.50

DEPEW, C.M. *100 Years of American Commerce.* 1895 Haynes. 2 vol set. xl. G $18.50

DEPKE, J. *Tom Fawick Story.* 1972 Cleveland. sgn Fawick. VG $10.00

DEPPARD, C.W. *American Clocks & Clock Makers.* 1947 Garden City. Ills 1st ed. 312 p. dj. VG $25.00

DEPPARD, C.W. *American Pioneer Arts & Artists.* 1942 Springfield. Ills. 172 p. dj. $55.00

DEPPING, Warwick. *Roper's Row.* 1929 London. 1st ed. 1/500. dj. EX $30.00

DEPUY, H.W. *Ethan Allen & Green Mountain Heroes of 1776.* 1853 Buffalo. 1st ed. 428 p. $15.00

DERBY, George H. *Phoenixiana.* 1937 San Francisco. Grabhorn. Ills Ltd ed. 1/600. $85.00

DERECSKEY, Susan. *Hungarian Cookbook.* 1972 NY. dj. EX $10.00

DERIEUX, S.A. *Animal Personalities.* 1925 Garden City. Ills. 298 p. $10.00

DERLETH, August. *Chronicles of Solar Pons.* 1973 Sauk City. 1st ed. dj. EX $15.00

DERLETH, August. *Concord Rebel.* 1962 Chilton. 1st ed. 213 p. dj. EX $24.00

DERLETH, August. *Edge of Night.* 1945 Prairie City. 1st ed. dj. VG $30.00

DERLETH, August. *Evening in Spring.* 1945 Sauk City. 1st ed. sgn. VG $85.00

DERLETH, August. *Mr. Fairlie's Final Journey.* 1968 Mycroft Moran. Ltd 1st ed. 1/3,500. dj. EX $35.00

DERLETH, August. *Other Side of the Moon.* 1956 London. dj. VG $15.00

DERLETH, August. *Praed Street Dossier.* 1968 Sauk City. 1st ed. dj. EX $50.00

DERLETH, August. *Sherlock Holmes.* 1945 Sauk City. 1st ed. sgn. dj. VG $125.00

DERLETH, August. *Village Year: Sac Prairie Journal.* 1941 NY. Coward. Ills Utpatel. 1st ed. VG $15.00

DERLETH, August. *Who Knocks?* 1946 NY. Ills 1st ed. dj. EX $25.00

DERLETH, August. *Wind Over WI.* 1938 NY. Advance copy. SftCvr. wraps. G $95.00

DERLETH, August. *30 Years of Arkham House 1939-1969.* 1970 Sauk City. 1st ed. dj. EX $60.00

DERRY. *World of Robert Bateman.* 1985 Toronto. Viking. 1st ed. sgn. dj. EX $78.00

DERRYDALE PRESS. *Derrydale Cookbook of Fish & Game.* 1937 NY. Ltd ed. 1/1,250. 2 vol set. VG $130.00

DES CHENEZ, Baroness. *Lady Green Satin & Her Maid.* 1937 Macmillan. Ills Bromhall. green cloth. VG $15.00

DES PRES, T. *Survivor.* 1976 Oxford U Pr. 6th print. dj. VG $12.50

DESAI, Anita. *Clear Light of the Day.* 1980 NY. 1st ed. dj. EX $10.00

DESAI, Anita. *Games at Twilight.* 1978 Harper. 1st Am ed. dj. EX $15.00

DESCARGUES, Pierre. *Francois Fielder.* 1967 Paris. Derriere Le Miroir. folio. $40.00

DESCARGUES, Pierre. *Hartung.* 1977 NY. Rizzoli. $42.50

DESMOND, H.W. *Stately Homes in America.* 1903 NY. Ills 1st ed. 532 p. cloth. $27.50

DESMONDE, Kay. *All Color Book of Dolls.* 1974 Octopus Books. Ills 1st ed. dj. EX $20.00

DETCHARD. *In the Shadow of the Lost Pines.* 1955 Bastrop. Bastrop Advertiser. SftCvr. EX $7.50

DETMOLD, E.J. *Arabian Nights.* no date. (1924) 1st trade ed. 4to. VG $225.00

DETMOLD, E.J. *Book of Baby Birds.* 1919 London. Ills. 4to. G $125.00

DETMOLD, E.J. *Fabre's Book of Insects.* 1937 NY. Tudor. 7th ed. VG $20.00

DETMOLD, E.J. *Fabre's Book of Insects.* 1935 Later print. 4to. 12 plts. $55.00

DEVA, B.C. *Musical Instruments of India.* 1977 India. Nat'l Book Trust. 1/4 leather. $20.00

DEVERDUN, Alfred L. *True Mexico: Mexico-Tenochtitlan.* 1938 private print. 8vo. sgn. cloth. xl. G $10.00

DEVINNE, Theodore Low. *Modern Methods of Book Compostion.* 1921 NY. G $10.00

DEVINNE, Theodore Low. *Practice of Typography: Correct Composition.* 1901 NY. Century. 1st ed. presentation. VG $45.00

DEVINNE, Theodore Low. *Practice of Typography: Correct Composition.* 1916 NY. Oswald. VG $20.00

DEVINNE, Theodore Low. *Practice of Typography: Plain Printing Types.* 1900 NY. Century. 1st ed. presentation. sgn. G $45.00

DEVLIN, Albert. *Eudora Welty's Chronicles.* 1983 MS U Pr. 1st ed. dj. EX $20.00

DEW, Robb Forman. *Time of Her Life.* 1984 Morrow. Advance copy. dj. EX $20.00

DEWALD, E.T. *Illustrations of the Utrecht Psalter.* no date. Princeton U Pr. 144 plts. $125.00

DEWAR, George A.B. *Book of the Dry Fly.* 1897 London. 4 plts. $75.00

DEWEES, William P. *Compendious System of Midwifery.* 1833 Phil. Ills 6th ed. full leather. G $50.00

DEWEES, William P. *Compendious System of Midwifery.* 1847 Phil. full leather. G $40.00

DEWES. *Molly Maguires.* 1877 Phil. 1st ed. fair. $10.00

DUNCAN, David Douglas. *Good-Bye Picasso.* 1974 NY. 1st ed. dj. EX $65.00

DUNCAN, David Douglas. *I Protest.* 1968 NY. 1st ed. wraps. EX $35.00

DUNCAN, David Douglas. *Picassos' Picassos.* 1961 Harper. dj. VG $67.50

DUNCAN, David Douglas. *This Is War!* 1951 NY. Ills 1st ed. dj. G $65.00

DUNCAN, David Douglas. *War Without Heroes.* NY. Harper Row. 1st ed. dj. VG $70.00

DUNCAN, David Douglas. *Yankee Nomad: Photographic Odyssey.* 1966 NY. 1st ed. VG $25.00

DUNCAN, David Douglas. *Yankee Nomad: Photographic Odyssey.* 1967 NY. Ills 2nd imp. 4to. dj. EX $25.00

DUNCAN, Donald. *New Legions.* 1967 NY. 1st ed. dj. M $15.00

DUNCAN, Else S. *Collector's 1st Handbook on Antique Chinese Ceramics.* 1942 no place. Ills. wraps. $15.00

DUNCAN, George. *Present Day Golf.* 1921 NY. $30.00

DUNCAN, Isadora. *Art of the Dance.* 1928 NY. Ills Genthe/Steichen. 1st ed. $175.00

DUNCAN, R.F. *Cruising Guide to New England Coast.* 1952 NY. Ills. maps. 276 p. dj. $15.00

DUNCAN, W. *Webs in Wind: Habits of Web-Weaving Spiders.* 1949 NY. Ills. EX $30.00

DUNCAN-WINTER, Rev. Henry. *Sacred Philosphy of the Seasons.* 1846 Carter. Ills. VG $25.00

DUNGLISON, Robley. *Dictionary of Medical Science.* 1858 Phil. G $55.00

DUNGMORE, A.R. *Romance of Newfoundland Caribou.* 1913 Philadelphia/London. Ills. VG $75.00

DUNGMORE, A.R. *Vast Sudan.* 1924 NY. Stokes. Ills 1st Am ed. VG $45.00

DUNHAM, Barrows. *Men Against Myth.* 1947 Boston. inscr. G $15.00

DUNHILL, Alfred. *Pipe Book.* 1924 NY. 1st Am ed. 8vo. EX $85.00

DUNLAP, Henry A. *Atoms at Your Service: Primer for Layman on Nuclear Physics.* 1957 NY. 1st ed. dj. VG $25.00

DUNLAP, Hope. *Little Lame Prince.* 1909 Rand McNally. 1st ed. 4to. 121 p. linen. $35.00

DUNLAP, Hope. *Muffin Shop.* 1908 Rand McNally. 1st ed. folio. VG $45.00

DUNLAP, Jack. *American, British, & Continental Pepperbox Firearms.* 1964 Los Altos. 1st ed. dj. EX $50.00

DUNLAP, Susan. *As a Favor.* 1984 1st Am ed. inscr. dj. $15.00

DUNLAP, Susan. *Bohemian Connection.* 1985 1st Am ed. inscr. dj. $15.00

DUNN, E.D. *Double-Crossing America by Motor: Routes & Ranches of West.* 1933 NY. Ills. $8.00

DUNN, Laurence. *World's Tankers.* 1956 London. Ills 1st ed. dj. $35.00

DUNN, Nell. *Poor Cow.* 1967 Garden City. 1st ed. dj. EX $14.00

DUNNACK, H.E. *ME Book: Augusta.* 1920 Ills 1st ed. sgn. 321 p. cloth. $25.00

DUNNACK, H.E. *ME Forts: Augusta.* 1924 Ills 1st ed. maps. 248 p. $30.00

DUNNE, Finley Peter. *Dissertations by Mr. Dooley.* 1906 NY. 1st ed. G $20.00

DUNNE, John Gregory. *Quintana & Friends.* 1978 Dutton. 1st ed. dj. EX $15.00

DUNNETT, Dorothy. *Ringed Castle.* 1972 Putnam. 1st Am ed. G $22.50

DUNNING, C. *Rock to Riches.* 1959 Phoenix. Ills 1st ed. 406 p. dj. VG $22.50

DUNSANY, Lord. *Book of Wonder.* c 1930. Boston. Ills. $22.50

DUNSANY, Lord. *Plays of Gods & Men.* 1917 John Luce. 1st ed. dj. EX $30.00

DUNSANY, Lord. *Sword of Welleran.* 1908 London. Ills. $45.00

DUNSANY, Lord. *7 Modern Comedies.* 1929 NY. 1st ed. dj. VG $20.00

DUNSHEE, K.H. *As You Pass By.* 1952 NY. Ills 1st ed. maps. 261 p. $17.50

DUNTHORN, Gordon. *Flower & Fruit Prints of 18th & Early 19th Century.* 1970 NY. Da Capo. $150.00

DUPIN, Jacques. *Miro.* no date. Abrams. Ills. 4to. dj. EX $75.00

DUPLESSIS, Georges. *Histoire de la Gravure en France.* 1861 Paris. 1st ed. 8vo. 408 p. wraps. EX $35.00

DUPREY, Kenneth. *Old Houses on Nantucket.* 1959 NY. Architectural Book. Ills. 4to. $45.00

DUPUY, R.E.; & BREGSTEN, C.L. *Soldier's Album.* 1946 Houghton Mifflin. Ills. VG $8.00

DURAND, J. *Able Seaman of 1812.* 1926 Yale. 139 p. VG $12.50

DURAND, Sir Edward. *Rifle, Rod, & Spear in the East.* 1911 London. 1st ed. VG $45.00

DURANT, Ghislani. *Horseback Riding From a Medical Point of View.* 1879 NY. $75.00

DURANT, John & Alice. *Pictorial History of American Presidents.* 1955 NY. Ills 1st ed. dj. $12.50

DURANT, John & Alice. *Pictorial History of American Ships.* 1953 NY. 1st ed. VG $10.00

DURANT, John & Alice. *Pictorial History of the American Circus.* 1957 NY. Barnes. Ills. 4to. 336 p. dj. $20.00

DURANTY, Louis Emile Edmond. *Theatre des Marionettes.* 1880 Paris. Ills. 387 p. fair. $95.00

DURDEN, Kent. *Fine & Peaceful Kingdom.* 1975 Simon Schuster. Ills 1st ed. 159 p. dj. EX $8.00

DURER, Albrecht. *Durer Society. Series I-IX.* 1898-1907. Ills. 10 vol set. VG $750.00

DURER, Albrecht. *Little Passion.* 1971 Verona. Ills Ltd ed. 1/140. 8vo. $325.00

DURGNAT, Raymond. *Mirror for England.* 1971 Praeger. 1st ed. dj. VG $10.00

DURHAM, David. *Pearl-Headed Pin.* 1925 London. 1st ed. G $45.00

DURHAM, Marilyn. *Man Who Loved Cat Dancing.* 1972 NY. 2nd print. dj. EX $10.00

DURHAM, P. *Down These Mean Streets.* 1963 NC U Pr. 1st ed. dj. EX $20.00

DURKEE, Silas. *Treatise on Gonorrhoea or Syphilis.* 1859 Boston. Ills Bufford. VG $150.00

DURRELL, Gerald. *Beasts in My Belfrey.* 1973 London. 1st ed. dj. EX $18.00

DURRELL, Gerald. *Donkey Rustlers.* 1968 London. 1st ed. dj. EX $15.00

DURRELL, Gerald. *Golden Bats & Pink Pigeons.* 1977 Simon Schuster. Ills. 190 p. xl. dj. VG $10.00

DURRELL, Gerald. *Picnic & Suchlike Pandemonium.* 1979 London. 1st ed. dj. EX $22.00

DURRELL, Gerald. *Whispering Land.* 1962 Viking. Ills 1st ed. 235 p. dj. VG $10.00

DURRELL, Gerald. *Zoo in My Luggage.* 1960 London. 1st ed. dj. EX $18.00

DURRELL, Gerald. *Zoo in My Luggage.* 1962 Viking. Ills. 198 p. VG $10.00

DURRELL, Gerald. *2 in the Bush.* 1966 Viking. Ills. 256 p. dj. VG $10.00

DURRELL, Lawrence. *Black Book.* 1960 NY. Dutton. 1st Am ed. dj. EX $50.00

DURRELL, Lawrence. *Collected Poems 1931-1974.* 1980 Viking. 1st Am ed. dj. EX $23.00

DURRELL, Lawrence. *Constance; or, Solitary Practices.* 1982 Viking. 1st Am ed. dj. EX $16.00

DURRELL, Lawrence. *Ikons.* 1966 London. 1st ed. dj. M $18.00

DURRELL, Lawrence. *Mountolive.* 1959 NY. dj. EX $12.00

DURRELL, Lawrence. *Nunquam.* 1970 Faber. 1st ed. dj. EX $30.00

DURRELL, Lawrence. *Nunquam.* 1970 Dutton. 1st Am ed. dj. EX $20.00

DURRELL, Lawrence. *Quinx.* 1985 NY. 1st ed. sgn. dj. M $28.00

DURRELL, Lawrence. *Sauve Qui Peut.* 1966 Faber. Ills N Bentley. 1st ed. dj. EX $22.00

DURRELL, Lawrence. *Vega & Other Poems.* 1973 Faber. 1st ed. dj. EX $30.00

DURRIE, D.S. *History of Madison, Capital of WI.* 1874 Madison. Ills Jones. 420 p. $65.00

DUSANY. *Plays of Near & Far.* 1923 Putnam. 1st ed. dj. EX $16.00

DUSSEL, Raymond. *Bourgogne Romane.* 1968 Paris. Zodiaque. VG $20.00

DUTCHER, George. *Disinthralled: Story of My Life.* 1872 Hartford. 1st ed. scarce. EX $50.00

DUTTON, C. *Samaritans of Moloafowkai.* 1932 NY. Ills 1st ed. dj. VG $25.00

DUTTON, J.P. *Exploring America's Gardens.* 1959 London. Ills. 259 p. cloth. dj. $6.50

DUTTON, R. *English Garden.* 1950 London. 2nd print. 122 p. dj. VG $15.00

DUVOISIN, Roger. *Mother Goose.* 1943 Heritage. Ills 1st ed. 4to. dj. $18.00

DUVOISIN, Roger. *1,000 Christmas Beards.* 1955 NY. dj. VG $7.50

DUYCKINCK, E.A. *Encyclopedia of American Literature.* 1856 NY. 1st ed. 2 vol set. $25.00

DUYCKINCK, E.A. *National Gallery of Eminent Americans. Vol. I.* 1862 NY. Ills 1st ed. leather. $45.00

DUYCKINCK, Evert & George. *Encyclopedia of American Literature.* 1875 PA. Ills. 2 vol set. VG $75.00

DWIGGINS, Don. *Hollywood Pilot.* 1967 Doubleday. 1st ed. 249 p. dj. VG $20.00

DWIGGINS, Don. *They Flew the Bendix Race.* 1965 Lippincott. 1st ed. 198 p. dj. VG $25.00

DWIGGINS. *Strange Case of Dr. Jekyll & Mr. Hyde.* 1929 NY. Ills Ltd ed. 1/1,200. sgn. EX $75.00

DWIGHT, Edwin W. *Memoir of Henry Obookiah, Native of the Sandwich Islands.* no date. (1819) NY. scarce. VG $125.00

DWIGHT, Marianne. *Letters From Brook Farm 1844-1847.* 1928 NY. Vassar. 1st ed. 8vo. VG $25.00

DWIGHT, S.E. *Memoirs of Rev. David Brainerd, Missionary to Indians of NY.* 1822 New Haven. 506 p. full leather. VG $90.00

DWIGHT, S.E. *Memoirs of Rev. David Brainerd, Missionary to Indians of NY.* 1822 New Haven. 8vo. leather. G $60.00

DWIGHT, Thomas. *Variations of the Bones of the Hands & Feet.* 1907 Phil. Ills. $175.00

DWIGHT, Timothy. *Memories of Yale Life & Men 1845-1899.* 1903 NY. VG $45.00

DWIGHT, Timothy. *Travels in New England & NY.* 1822 New Haven. 1st ed. 3 fld maps. 4 vol set. $150.00

DWORACZK. *1st Polish Colonies of America in TX.* 1936 San Antonio. Naylor. inscr. pb. G $30.00

DYE, E.E. *Conquest: True Story of Lewis & Clark.* 1903 McClurg. 3rd ed. $7.50

DYE, E.E. *Soul of America: OR Iliad.* 1934 Pioneer Pr. $7.50

DYER, Anthony. *Classic African Animals.* 1973 Winchester. Ills. 4to. 154 p. dj. EX $18.50

DYER, W.A. *Country Cousins.* 1927 Garden City. Ills CL Bull. 1st ed. VG $20.00

DYER, W.A. *Lure of Antique.* 1910 NY. Ills 1st ed. 488 p. cloth. $15.00

DYKE, A.L. *Automobile Encyclopedia.* 1912 Ills 2nd ed. charts. dictionary. G $40.00

DYKE, Walter. *Son of Old Man Hat.* 1938 1st ed. dj. VG $50.00

DYKEMAN, W. *French Broad.* 1955 NY. 1st ed. dj. VG $50.00

DYKES, Jeff. *Collecting Range Life Literature.* 1982 Brazos Corral of Westerners. $20.00

DYKES, Jeff. *My Dobie Collection.* 1971 College Station. 1st ed. M $25.00

DYKES, Jeff. *50 Great Western Illustrators.* 1975 Northland. Ills 1st ed. 4to. dj. EX $35.00

DYKES, Jeff. *50 Great Western Illustrators.* no date. Northland Pr. Ltd ed. 1/200. M $125.00

DYLAN, Bob. *Tarantula.* 1971 Macmillan. Ltd ed. dj. $15.00

DYLAN, Bob. *Writings & Drawings.* 1977 NY. Knopf. VG $18.00

EADE, Charles. *Dawn of Liberation: War Speeches of Winston S. Churchill.* 1945 London. 1st ed. VG $20.00

EAGAN, Maurice Francis. *Confessions of a Book Lover.* 1922 NY. xl. G $20.00

EAKINS, Thomas. *Life & Works of Thomas Eakins.* 1974 NY. Grossman. Ills. 4to. 367 p. cloth. dj. $85.00

EAKINS, Thomas. *21 Photographs.* 1979 Olympia Galleries. 1st ed. EX $285.00

EAMES, Emma. *Fragrance in Violets.* 1973 NY. Vantage. 1st ed. dj. EX $10.00

EAMES, H. *Winner Lose All: Doctor Cook & the Theft of the North Pole.* 1973 Little Brown. Ills. 346 p. dj. EX $15.00

EAMES, H.E. *Rifle in War.* 1909 Leavenworth. US Cavalry Assn. Ills. 331 p. $10.00

EARHART, Amelia. *Fun of It.* 1932 NY. 1st ed. with record. VG $45.00

EARHART, Amelia. *Last Flight.* 1937 NY. Ills. 229 p. $20.00

EARHART, Amelia. *20 Hours 40 Minutes.* 1928 Putnam. 1st ed. sgn. VG $275.00

EARL, Lawrence. *Crocodile Fever.* 1954 Knopf. Ills 1st ed. 293 p. dj. VG $14.00

EARL, Lawrence. *Crocodile Fever.* 1954 London. Collins. 255 p. VG $17.50

EARLE, A.M. *Home Life in Colonial Days.* 1898 NY. Ills 1st ed. 451 p. cloth. $25.00

EARLE, A.M. *Home Life in Colonial Days.* 1899 NY. Ills. 451 p. cloth. $15.00

EARLE, A.M. *Stage Coach & Tavern Days.* 1900 NY. Ills 1st ed. 435 p. cloth. $25.00

EARLE, A.M. *Sun Dials & Roses of Yesterday.* 1922 NY. Ills. 446 p. cloth. $10.00

EARLE, S.A. *Chesapeake Bay Country.* 1924 Baltimore. Ills 2nd ed. VG $100.00

EARLE, S.A. *Exploring Deep Frontier.* 1980 WA. Ills 1st ed. 284 p. dj. $15.00

EARLE. *History of Clay County & Northwest TX.* 1963 Austin. Brick Row Book Shop. 64 p. EX $10.00

EARLY, E. *Adirondack Tales.* 1939 Boston. Ills 1st ed. 239 p. $10.00

EARLY, E. *And This Is Boston.* 1930 Boston. Ills 1st ed. 243 p. cloth. $10.00

EARLY, E. *And This Is Cape Cod.* 1936 Boston. Ills 1st ed. maps. 211 p. dj. $10.00

EARLY, E. *And This Is WA.* 1934 Boston. Ills 1st ed. maps. 269 p. dj. $10.00

EARLY, E. *Behold the White Mountains.* 1935 Boston. Ills 1st ed. 209 p. dj. $10.00

EARLY, E. *Cape Cod Summer.* 1949 Boston. 300 p. cloth. dj. $6.50

EARLY, E. *Island Patchwork.* 1941 Boston. Ills 1st ed. 290 p. cloth. $10.00

EARLY, E. *New England Sampler.* 1940 Boston. Ills. sgn. 372 p. cloth. $12.50

EARLY, E. *NY Holiday.* 1950 NY. 1st ed. 366 p. cloth. $7.50

EARNEST, A. *Art of the Decoy.* 1965 Bramall House. Ills. 4to. dj. EX $20.00

EAST, Ben. *Bears.* 1978 Crown. Ills. 269 p. dj. EX $14.00

EAST, Ben. *Ben East Hunting Book.* 1974 Outdoor Life. Ills. 360 p. dj. EX $10.00

EAST, Ben. *Narrow Escapes & Wilderness Adventures.* 1960 Outdoor Life. Ills. 321 p. VG $8.50

EAST, Henry R. *How To Train Dogs for the Home, Stage, & Moving Pictures.* 1937 NY. 175 p. VG $25.00

EAST, O.G. *Wright Brothers' National Memorial in NC.* 1963 WA. Ills. 63 p. wraps. $2.50

EAST. *History & Progress of Jefferson County, TX.* 1961 Dallas. Royal Pub. dj. EX $15.00

EASTLAKE, C. *Hints on Household Tasks.* 1872 Boston. Ills 1st Am ed. $35.00

EASTLAKE, Charles Lock. *Goethe's Theory of Colors Translated From German.* 1840 London. Murray. Ills. 423 p. cloth. VG $95.00

EASTLAKE, William. *Child's Garden of Verses for the Revolution.* 1970 Grove. 1st ed. dj. EX $20.00

EASTLAKE, William. *Long Naked Descent into Boston.* 1977 Viking. 1st ed. dj. EX $15.00

EASTMAN, C.A. *Soul of the Indian.* 1911 Boston/NY. 1st ed. VG $20.00

EASTMAN, E. *7 & 9 Years Among the Commanches & Apaches.* 1873 Jersey City. 1st ed. VG $30.00

EASTMAN, George. *Chronicles of an African Trip.* 1927 private print. Ills Johnson. 85 p. VG $35.00

EASTMAN, M.E. *East of the White Hills.* 1900 North Conway. Blanchard Book Pr. 139 p. $25.00

EASTMAN, Mary H. *American Aboriginal Portfolio.* 1853 Phil. Ills Seth Eastman. folio. $450.00

EASTMAN, Max. *Lot's Wife.* 1942 NY. Review ed. dj. EX $35.00

EASTMAN, Max. *Love & Revolution.* 1964 Random House. Ills 1st ed. 665 p. dj. VG $25.00

EASTMAN, Max. *Venture.* 1927 NY. Boni. 1st ed. inscr. VG $25.00

EASTMAN, S.E. *In Old South Hadley.* 1912 Chicago. Ills 1st ed. 221 p. cloth. $20.00

EASTMAN KODAK. *Eastman Kodak Camera Guide.* 1959 NY. Ills 1st ed. 219 p. wraps. $5.00

EASTON, C. *Straight Ahead: Story of Stan Kenton.* 1973 NY. 1st ed. 252 p. dj. VG $17.50

EASTWOOD, B. *Complete Manual for the Cultivation of the Cranberry.* 1860 NY. Ills. 12mo. 120 p. $35.00

EATON, Allen H. *Beauty for the Sighted & the Blind.* 1959 NY. St. Martin. Intro Helen Keller. 8vo. dj. $15.00

EATON, Allen H. *Handcrafts of New England.* 1949 NY. 1st ed. dj. VG $9.50

EATON, Allen H. *Handicrafts of the Northeast.* 1949 NY. Ills 1st ed. dj. VG $35.00

EATON, Allen H. *Handicrafts of the Southern Highlands.* 1948 NY. reprint. dj. $50.00

EATON, Anne Thaxter. *Animal's Christmas.* 1944 Ills V Angelo. 1st ed. 12mo. 124 p. dj. VG $12.00

EATON, Frank. *Pistol Pete: Veteran of Old West.* 1952 Little Brown. Ills 1st ed. 278 p. VG $10.00

EATON, J. *Gardening Under Glass.* 1973 NY. 360 p. dj. VG $6.00

EATON, Seymour. *Adventures of Travelling Bears.* 1915 NY. Barse Hopkins. 4to. 63 p. VG $50.00

EATON, Seymour. *Prince Domino & Muffles.* 1910 Stern. Ills Twelvetrees. 1st ed. 4to. $75.00

EATON, W.P. *Cape Cod.* 1931 MA. Ills 1st ed. 48 p. wraps. $7.50

EATON, W.P. *Green Trails & Upland Pasture.* 1925 Boston. Revised ed. 303 p. $6.50

EATON, W.P. *In Berkshire Fields.* 1926 Boston. Ills 1st ed. cloth. $15.00

EATON, W.P. *New England Vista.* 1930 Boston. Ills 1st ed. 121 p. cloth. $6.50

EATON, W.P. *On Yankee Hilltops.* 1933 Boston. Ills 1st ed. 128 p. cloth. $6.50

EATON, W.P. *Plymouth: 1620.* 1928 NY. Ills 1st ed. 47 p. wraps. $7.50

EATON, W.P. *Wild Gardens of New England.* 1936 Boston. Ills 1st ed. 114 p. dj. $8.50

EATON, William D. *Woodrow Wilson: His Life & Work.* 1919 1st ed. cloth. EX $45.00

EBAN, Abba. *Civilization & the Jews.* 1984 Heritage. 1st ed. dj. VG $15.00

EBERHART, Mignon. *Alpine Condo Cross Fire.* 1984 Random House. EX $12.00

EBERHART, Mignon. *Dark Garden.* 1933 NY. 1st ed. dj. EX $50.00

EBERHART, Mignon. *El Rancho Rio.* 1970 NY. 1st ed. dj. EX $5.00

EBERHART, Mignon. *2 Little Rich Girls.* 1972 London. 1st ed. inscr. dj. EX $25.00

EBERHART, Richard. *Quarry.* 1964 NY. 1st ed. dj. wraps. EX $15.00

EBERHART, Richard. *Ways of Light.* 1980 Oxford U Pr. 1st ed. sgn. dj. EX $25.00

EBERHART, Richard. *13 Dartmouth Poems.* 1958 Stinehour. 1st ed. 1/150. wraps. EX $20.00

EBERHART, Richard. *31 Sonnets.* 1967 Eakins. 1st ed. dj. EX $25.00

EBERLEIN, H.D. *Architecture of Colonial America.* 1925 Boston. Ills. 274 p. cloth. $12.50

EBERLEIN, H.D. *Diary of Independence Hall.* 1948 Phil. Ills 1st ed. 363 p. dj. $15.00

EBERLEIN, H.D. *Interiors, Fireplaces, & Furniture of Italian Renaissance.* 1927 NY. Ills. 82 p. dj. $20.00

EBERLEIN, H.D. *Manor Houses & Homes of Long Island & Staten Island.* 1928 Phil. Ltd 1st ed. 303 p. cloth. $50.00

EBERLEIN, H.D. *Practical Book of American Antiques.* 1948 Halcyon. reprint. 390 p. dj. VG $18.00

EBERLEIN, H.D. *Practical Book of Chinaware.* 1925 NY. Ills 1st ed. 299 p. cloth. $25.00

EBERLEIN, H.D. *Practical Book of Chinaware.* 1942 Garden City. Halcyon House. VG $18.00

EBERLEIN, H.D. *Practical Book of Chinaware.* 1938 Halcyon House. Ills. 325 p. cloth. $35.00

EBERLEIN, H.D. *Practical Book of Garden Structure & Design.* 1937 Philadelphia. Ills 1st ed. 135 p. cloth. $17.50

EBERLEIN, H.D. *Practical Book of Interior Decoration.* 1937 Phil. Ills. 477 p. VG $25.00

EBERLEIN & CORTLANDT. *American Georgian Architecture.* 1952 London. Pleiades. Ills Lear. 4to. dj. $25.00

EBERLEIN & CORTLANDT. *Historic Houses of the Hudson Valley.* no date. NY. Bonanza. Ills. 208 p. 4to. $25.00

EBERLEIN & RAMSDELL. *Small Manor Houses & Farmsteads in France.* 1926 Lippincott. Ills 1st ed. 4to. dj. EX $95.00

EBERS, George Moritz. *Egypt: Descriptive, Historical, & Picturesque.* 1881-1882. London. Cassel. 2 vol set. VG $175.00

EBERS, George Moritz. *Varda: Romance of Ancient Egypt. Vol. I.* 1884 NY. 332 p. EX $35.00

EBERSTADT, Edward. *William Robertson Coe Collection of Western Americana.* 1948 New Haven. private print. 1/100. rare. EX $250.00

EBERSTADT. *Annotated Eberstadt Catalogs of America.* 1965 NY. 1st ed. 4 vol set. EX $100.00

EBERT, Katherine. *Collecting American Pewter.* 1973 NY. Weathervane. Ills. 163 p. $20.00

EBEYER, Paul P. *Revelation Concerning Napoleon's Escape to St. Helena.* 1947 New Orleans. Ills. sgn. 398 p. EX $60.00

ECHARD, Laurence. *General Ecclesiastical History From Nativity of Savior.* 1719 London. Tonson. folio. 472 p. full leather. EX $150.00

ECKENRODE, H.J. *Randolfs: Story of a VA Family.* 1946 Bobbs Merrill. Ills. 8vo. cloth. VG $55.00

ECKENRODE, H.J. *Rutherford B. Hayes: Statesman of Reunion.* 1930 NY Ills 1st ed. 344 p. cloth. $27.50

ECKENRODE & CONRAD. *J. Longstrett: Lee's War Horse.* 1936 Chapel Hill. 1st ed. scarce. EX $75.00

ECKER, G.D. *Portrait of Old Georgetown.* 1933 Richmond. Ills 1st ed. 255 p. $27.50

ECKERT, A. *Hab Theory.* 1976 Boston. 1st ed. dj. VG $20.00

ECKERT, A.W. *Wild Season.* 1967 Little Brown. Ills 1st ed. 244 p. dj. VG $10.00

ECKERT, W.J. *Punched Card Methods in Scientific Computation.* 1940 NY. Columbia U. Ills. 4to. 136 p. xl. VG $45.00

ECKHARDT, G. *PA Clocks & Clockmakers.* 1955 4to. dj. M $8.00

EDDINGS, David. *Guardians of the West.* 1987 Ballantine. Uncorrected proof. wraps. EX $30.00

EDDINGS, David. *Guardians of the West.* 1987 Ballantine. dj. EX $12.00

EDDINGTON, A.S. *Fundamental Theory.* 1946 Cambridge. 1st ed. 4to. 292 p. scarce. VG $100.00

EDDINGTON, A.S. *Internal Constitution of the Stars.* 1926 Cambridge. 1st ed. 4to. 407 p. VG $95.00

EDDINGTON, A.S. *Mathematical Theory of Relativity.* 1923 Cambridge. 1st ed. 4to. 247 p. VG $90.00

EDDINGTON, A.S. *Nature of the Physical World.* 1927 NY. Macmillan. 361 p. dj. VG $20.00

EDDINGTON, A.S. *Nature of the Physical World.* 1933 NY. 361 p. dj. EX $25.00

EDDINGTON, A.S. *New Pathways in Science.* 1934 NY. Macmillan. Ills. 333 p. dj. VG $30.00

EDDINGTON, A.S. *Philosophy of Physical Science.* 1938 Cambridge. 1st ed. 230 p. VG $35.00

EDDINGTON, A.S. *Philosophy of Physical Science.* 1938 NY. Macmillan. reprint. 230 p. dj. VG $20.00

EDDINGTON, A.S. *Science & the Unseen World.* 1929 NY. Swarthmore. 91 p. dj. VG $22.00

EDDINGTON, A.S. *Space, Time, & Gravitation.* 1921 Cambridge. $65.00

EDDINGTON, A.S. *Stars & Atoms.* 1927 New Haven. Ills 2nd print. 127 p. dj. VG $20.00

EDDISON, E.R. *Mezentian Gate.* 1958 Curwen. 1st ed. dj. EX $150.00

EDDISON, E.R. *Mistress of Mistresses.* 1935 Faber. 1st ed. dj. scarce. EX $300.00

EDDISON, E.R. *Worn Ourobors.* 1926 Boni. 1st Am ed. G $25.00

EDDY, M.B. *Science & Health with Key to Scriptures.* 1888 Boston. G $60.00

EDDY, Mary Baker. *Poems.* 1910 Boston. 1st ed. 8vo. EX $35.00

EDDY, Mary O. *Ballads & Songs From OH.* 1939 JJ Augustin. dj. VG $15.00

EDDY, R.S.D. *Eddy Family in America.* 1930 Boston. 1,372 p. VG $45.00

EDEL, Leon. *Henry James: Les Annees Dramatiques.* 1931 Jouve & Cie. Ltd ed. 1/300. wraps. $375.00

EDEN, Anthony. *Reckoning.* 1965 Boston. Ills 1st print. cloth. dj. VG $60.00

EDEN, Timothy. *Tribulations of a Baronet: Memoir of Sir William Eden.* 1933 London. dj. VG $27.50

EDERSHEIM, Rev. Dr. *Sketches of Jewish Social Life in Days of Christ.* 1914 NY. Hodder Stoughton. red cloth. $60.00

EDGAR, F. *Mondrian.* 1968 NY. Ills. 256 p. $20.00

EDGAR, Matilda. *10 Years of Upper Canada in Peace & War 1805-1815.* 1890 Toronto. Briggs. Ills. 8vo. fld maps. $120.00

EDGELL, G.H. *American Architecture of Today.* 1928 NY. Scribner. fair. $35.00

EDGELL, G.H. *History of Sienese Painting.* 1932 NY. Ills. VG $100.00

EDGEWORTH, Maria. *Popular Tales.* 1890 Stokes. 2 vol set. EX $25.00

EDLIN, Herbert L. *Atlas of Plant Life.* 1973 Day. Ills. 4to. 128 p. dj. EX $8.00

EDLIN, Herbert L. *What Wood Is That?* 1969 NY. Studio/Viking. Ills. 160 p. $30.00

EDMINSTER, F.C. *Ruffed Grouse: Its Life Story, Ecology, & Management.* 1947 Macmillan. 1st ed. 385 p. VG $42.50

EDMONDS, I.G. *Kings of Black Magic.* 1981 197 p. dj. M $18.00

EDMONDS, S. Emma. *Nurse & Spy in the Union Army.* 1865 Hartford, CT. Ills. 12mo. 384 p. cloth. $30.00

EDMONDS, Walter. *Mostly Canallers.* 1934 Boston. 1st ed. dj. VG $40.00

EDMONDS, Walter. *They Fought with What They Had.* 1951 Boston. 1st ed. dj. EX $50.00

EDMONDS, William H. *Truth About AR.* 1895 St. Louis. Woodward Tieran. 16 p. wraps. $20.00

EDMUNDS, P.W. *Legends of NC Coast.* 1941 Richmond. Ills 1st ed. 35 p. cloth. $10.00

EDMUNDS, Simeon. *Miracles of the Mind: Introduction to Parapsychology.* 1965 IL. Thomas. 204 p. dj. EX $25.00

EDSON, James S. *Black Knights of West Point.* 1954 1st ed. 263 p. VG $15.00

EDWARDS, A. *Cape Cod: New & Old.* 1922 Boston. VG $7.50

EDWARDS, A. *Cape Cod: New & Old.* 1918 Boston. Ills 1st ed. map. 239 p. $10.00

EDWARDS, A. *Peoples of Old.* 1929 London. Benn. Ills 1st ed. 8vo. VG $20.00

EDWARDS, A. Cecil. *Persian Caravan.* 1928 London. 1st ed. inscr/sgn. $30.00

EDWARDS, Allen. *Jewel in the Lotus.* 1959 293 p. EX $22.00

EDWARDS, Amelia. *1,000 Miles Up the Nile.* 1888 Caldwell. Ills 2nd ed. VG $15.00

EDWARDS, Bryan. *Historical Survey of French Colony in Island of St. Domingo.* 1797 London. Stockdale. 1st ed. 247 p. $150.00

EDWARDS, Bryan. *Historical Survey of Island of Saint Domingo.* 1801 London. Stockdale. 4to. $150.00

EDWARDS, Bryan. *History, Civil & Commercial, of British Colonies.* 1801 London. Stockdale. 3rd ed. 3 vol set. $200.00

EDWARDS, Charles. *History & Poetry of Finger Rings.* 1889 Pollard Moss. 1st ed. Echo Series. wraps. VG $30.00

EDWARDS, E.I. *Enduring Desert.* 1969 LA. Ward Ritchie. slipcase. VG $85.00

EDWARDS, G.T. *Music & Musicians of ME 1604-1928.* 1928 Portland. Ills. sgn. 542 p. VG $20.00

EDWARDS, G.W. *Brittany & the Bretons.* 1910 Boston. Moffat Yard. Ills. 4to. VG $30.00

EDWARDS, G.W. *Vanished Halls & Cathedrals of France.* 1917 Phil. Ills 1st ed. 322 p. cloth. $25.00

EDWARDS, Harry Stillwell. *Sons & Fathers.* 1937 Atlanta. Brown. Ltd 1st ed. 1/1,000. dj. VG $25.00

EDWARDS, Jonathan. *Careful & Strict Engraving.* 1754 Boston. Kneeland. 1st ed. calf. G $395.00

EDWARDS, Julia. *Mandy.* 1971 NY. Harper Row. Ills JG Brown. 1st ed. dj. G $15.00

EDWARDS, Lionel. *Jerry Todd & the Talking Frog.* 1925 Grosset Dunlap. dj. EX $10.00

EDWARDS, Lionel. *Reminiscences of a Sporting Artist.* 1947 London. 1st print. VG $25.00

EDWARDS, Paul. *English Garden Ornament.* 1965 NY. Barnes. Ills. 4to. 110 p. dj. $25.00

EDWARDS, Ralph. *English Chairs.* 1965 London. Ills 2nd ed. $35.00

EDWARDS, Ralph; & RAMSEY, L.G. *Early Georgian Period 1714-1760.* no date. NY. Reynal. Ills. 4to. dj. $30.00

EDWARDS, William B. *Story of Colt's Revolvers.* 1953 Stackpole. Ltd ed. sgn. leather. EX $125.00

EDWARDS, William C. *Historic Quincy, MA.* 1945 Quincy. private print. Ills. 111 p. VG $15.00

EDWARDS, William H. *Voyage Up the River Amazon Including Residence at Para.* 1847 NY. Appleton. 1st ed. 256 p. EX $100.00

EDWORDS, Clarence. *Bohemian San Francisco: Its Restuarants & Their Recipes.* 1919 San Francisco. Elder. 8vo. 138 p. $50.00

EELLS, Rev. M. *10 Years of Missionary Work Among the Indians at Skokomish.* 1886 Boston. Ills. G $18.00

EFFINGER, George A. *Planet of the Apes #3: Journey into Terror.* 1975 Award. 1st ed. VG $8.00

EFFINGER, George A. *Wolves of Memory.* 1981 NY. 1st ed. inscr. dj. EX $25.00

EGGLESTON, Edward. *Hoosier School Boy.* 1883 NY. 1st ed. 1st state. VG $75.00

EGGLESTON, George C. *American War Ballads & Lyrics 1725-1865.* c 1889. NY. Ills. 16mo. 2 vols. G $20.00

EGGLESTON. *Christ in Art.* no date. NY. Ills Bida. leather. xl. VG $45.00

EGLE, William H. *Andrew Gregg Curtin: His Life & Services.* 1895 Avil Print Co. G $30.00

EHRENBURG, Ilya. *Storm.* 1948 Moscow. English text. VG $15.00

EHRENSTEIN, A. *Tubutsch.* 1946 Abrams. Ills Kokoschka. 1/1,000. dj. $25.00

EHRLICH, A. *Celebrated Violinists: Past & Present.* 1897 London. VG $35.00

EHRLICH, Gretel. *Geode Rock Baby.* 1970 Santa Barbara. 1st ed. inscr. wraps. M $17.00

EHRMANN, Eric. *Hummel Guide & Reference.* 1976 NY. 1st ed. EX $40.00

EICHENBERG, F. *Nantucket Woodcuts.* 1967 Barre, MA. Ills 1st ed. 60 p. $12.50

EICHENBERG. *Pigs & Eagles.* 1978 Thistle Hills. 1/500. 4to. sgn. slipcase. EX $95.00

EIFERT, V.S. *Land of the Snowshoe Hare.* 1961 Dodd Mead. Ills. 271 p. dj. EX $10.00

EIGNER, Larry. *Things Stirring Together or Far Away.* 1974 Black Sparrow. Ltd ed. 1/26. sgn. cloth. EX $35.00

EILAND, Murray L. *Oriental Rugs: Comprehensive Guide.* 1976 Boston. Ills. 214 p. dj. $95.00

EINSTEIN, Albert. *Albert Einstein: Philosopher-Scientist.* 1949 Evanston. Ltd 1st ed. 1/760. sgn/dtd. EX $850.00

EINSTEIN, Albert. *Atomic War or Peace.* 1947 Princeton. 1st separate ed. wraps. $175.00

EINSTEIN, Albert. *Debate on the Theory of Relativity.* 1927 Chicago. Intro WL Bryan. 1st ed. 154 p. $25.00

EINSTEIN, Albert. *Die Grundlage der Allgemeinen Relativitaetstheorie.* 1916 Leipzig. 1st separate print. wraps. VG $250.00

EINSTEIN, Albert. *Meaning of Relativity.* 1950 Princeton U Pr. 150 p. VG $5.00

EINSTEIN, Albert. *Out of My Later Years.* 1950 NY. 1st Am ed. EX $25.00

EINSTEIN, Albert. *Quantentheorie des Einatomigen Idealen Gases.* 1925 Berlin. 1st ed. 4to. orange wraps. $150.00

EINZIG, Paul. *Montague Norman: Study in Financial Statesmanship.* 1932 London. 1st ed. 8vo. cloth. dj. VG $13.00

EISELEY, Loren. *Darwin & the Mysterious Mr. X.* 1979 London. 1st ed. dj. M $10.00

EISEN, G.A. *Portraits of WA.* 1932 NY. Hamilton. sgn. 3 vol set. slipcase. EX $375.00

EISENBERG & TAYLOR. *Ultimate Fishing Book.* 1981 Boston. 1st ed. dj. EX $40.00

EISENHOWER, D.D. *Crusade in Europe.* 1948 NY. Ills 1st ed. map. 478 p. dj. $10.00

EISENHOWER, D.D. *Crusade in Europe.* 1948 Garden City. Ltd ed. 1/426. dj. VG $50.00

EISENHOWER, D.D. *In Review: Pictorial Autobiography.* 1969 NY. Ills 1st ed. 237 p. dj. $15.00

EISENHOWER, D.D. *Peace with Justice.* 1961 NY. Ills 273 p. dj. $6.00

EISENHOWER, D.D. *White House Years: Mandate for Change & Waging Peace.* 1956 & 1961. 2 vol set. $25.00

EISENHOWER, D.D. *White House Years: Mandate for Change.* 1963 NY. Ills 1st ed. maps. 658 p. $12.50

EISENSCHIML, Otto. *Otto Eisenschiml: Historian Without an Armchair.* 1963 Bobbs Merrill. 224 p. sgn. dj. VG $11.00

EISENSCHIML, Otto. *Why the Civil War?* 1958 Bobbs Merrill. 1st ed. 208 p. dj. VG $10.00

EISENSCHIML, Otto. *Why Was Lincoln Murdered?* 1937 Boston. Ills 1st ed. 503 p. G $15.00

EISENSCHIML & NEWMAN. *American Iliad: Epic Story.* 1947 Bobbs Merrill. Ltd ed. 1/555. sgns. boxed. EX $65.00

EISENSTAEDT. *Witness to Our Time.* 1966 NY. Viking. Ills 1st ed. 4to. dj. VG $35.00

EISLEY, Robert. *Man into Wolf.* no date. London. Spring Books. dj. EX $25.00

EISNER, T.; & WILSON, E.O. *Animal Behavior.* 1975 Freeman. Ills. 4to. 339 p. wraps. VG $12.00

ELAM, A. *History of Shakers.* c 1960. NH. 11 p. wraps. $2.00

ELBIQUET. *Supplementary Magic with Illustrations.* 1917 London. Ills 1st ed. 8vo. 200 p. $35.00

ELDER, Paul. *Old Spanish Missions of CA.* 1913 Elder. EX $25.00

ELDER, William. *Biography of Elisha Kent Kane.* 1859 Phil. Ills. 416 p. G $20.00

ELDERFIELD, John. *Fauvism: Wild Beasts & Affinities.* 1976 MOMA. Ills. oblong 8vo. 168 p. wraps. $9.00

ELDERFIELD, John. *Modern Drawing: 100 Works on Paper From MOMA.* 1983 MOMA. Ills. 4to. 216 p. cloth. dj. $37.50

ELDERFIELD, John. *Morris Louis Monograph.* 1986 MOMA. Ills. 4to. 176 p. cloth. dj. $40.00

ELDRIDGE, Charlotte. *Godey Lady Doll.* 1953 NY. Hastings House. 1st ed. dj. EX $15.00

ELDRIDGE, Ethel J. *Yen-Foh.* 1935 Whitman. Ills 1st ed. inscr. 4to. $35.00

ELDRIDGE, Ethel J. *You Can Write Chinese.* 1946 Viking. Ills 2nd print. 4to. cloth. $22.00

ELDRIDGE, Fred. *Wrath in Burma: Uncensored Story of Gen. Stilwell.* 1946 Garden City. Ills 1st ed. 320 p. G $17.50

ELEY, V. *Monk at the Potter's Wheel.* no date. Condon. Ills 1st ed. dj. VG $25.00

ELGAR, Franck. *Picasso.* 1974 NY. 1st ed. dj. VG $25.00

ELGIN, Robert. *Tiger Is My Brother.* 1980 Morrow. Ills 1st ed. 220 p. dj. EX $12.00

ELGOOD, George E. *Italian Gardens.* 1907 London. Ills. 4to. 157 p. VG $85.00

ELIOT, Alexander. *300 Years of American Painting.* 1957 NY. Time. Intro John Walker. 4to. cloth. $35.00

ELIOT, George. *Adam Bede.* 1896 Estes Lauriat. Ltd ed. 1/250. 2 vol set. G $80.00

ELIOT, George. *Complete Works of George Eliot.* Estes Lauriat. Lib ed. 14 vol set. leather. G $27.50

ELIOT, George. *Complete Works of George Eliot.* 1883 Estes Lauriat. 12 vol set. G $40.00

ELIOT, George. *Silas Marner.* 1953 Ills/sgn Lyntom Lamb. VG $55.00

ELIOT, George. *Silas Marner.* 1953 London. boxed. $35.00

ELIOT, George. *2 Lovers.* 1909 Moffat. Ills Christy. G $20.00

ELIOT, T.S. *Cocktail Party.* 1950 London. 1st ed. 2nd state. dj. M $26.00

ELIOT, T.S. *Confidential Clerk.* 1954 London. 1st ed. 1st issue. dj. M $38.00

ELIOT, T.S. *Cultivation of Christmas Trees.* 1956 Farrar. Ills 1st Am ed. EX $15.00

ELIOT, T.S. *Elder Statesman.* 1959 NY. Farrar. 1st ed. dj. EX $25.00

ELIOT, T.S. *Elder Statesman.* 1959 London. dj. M $45.00

ELIOT, T.S. *From Poe to Valery.* 1948 NY. private print. 1st ed. $40.00

ELIOT, T.S. *Journey of Magi.* no date. London. 1st trade ed. wraps. $22.50

ELIOT, T.S. *Notes Toward the Definition of Culture.* no date. London. 1st ed. dj. VG $30.00

ELIOT, T.S. *To Criticize the Critic.* 1955 Faber. 1st ed. dj. EX $18.00

ELIOT, T.S. *Undergraduate Poems.* 1948 Cambridge. 1st ed. wraps. G $35.00

ELIOT, T.S. *3 Voices of Poetry.* 1953 London. 1st ed. wraps. EX $18.00

ELISOFON, E.; & FAGG, W. *Sculpture of Africa.* 1958 Praeger. Ills. folio. cloth. dj. VG $150.00

ELISOFON, Eliot. *Java Diary.* 1969 Macmillan. Ills 1st ed. 298 p. dj. EX $15.00

ELIZABETH, Charlotte. *Chapters on Flowers.* 1844 Ills 6th ed. cloth. $25.00

ELIZABETH, Charlotte. *Judea Capta.* 1848 NY. 12mo. VG $15.00

ELKIN, Robert. *Old Concert Rooms of London.* 1955 London. Ills 1st ed. dj. VG $15.00

ELKIN, Stanley. *Bad Man.* 1967 Random House. 1st ed. dj. EX $30.00

ELKIN, Stanley. *Criers & Kibitzers, Kibitzers & Criers.* 1965 NY. 1st ed. dj. EX $45.00

ELKIN, Stanley. *Dick Gibson Show.* 1971 NY. 1st ed. dj. EX $25.00

ELKIN, Stanley. *Eligible Men.* 1974 London. 1st ed. dj. EX $15.00

ELKIN, Stanley. *Franchiser.* 1976 NY. Review copy. dj. EX $25.00

ELKIN, Stanley. *George Mills.* 1982 Dutton. 1st ed. dj. EX $16.00

ELKIN, Stanley. *Greatest Hits.* 1980 NY. 1st ed. dj. EX $10.00

ELKIN, Stanley. *Living End.* 1979 Dutton. 1st ed. dj. EX $20.00

ELKIN, Stanley. *Living End.* 1980 London. 1st ed. dj. EX $12.00

ELKIN, Stanley. *Living End.* 1979 NY. 1st ed. sgn. dj. EX $25.00

ELKIN, Stanley. *Magic Kingdom.* 1985 NY. 1st ed. sgn. dj. M $25.00

ELKIN, Stanley. *Stanley Elkin's Greatest Hits.* 1980 Dutton. 1st ed. dj. EX $15.00

ELKIN, Stanley. *1st George Mills.* 1980 Dallas. 1st ed. sgn. dj. EX $30.00

ELKIN, Stanley. *6 Year Old Man.* 1987 Flint. proof. wraps. EX $20.00

ELLER, John. *Charlie & the Ice Man.* 1981 St. Martin. Advance copy. dj. EX $15.00

ELLER, John. *Rage of Heaven.* 1982 St. Martin. 1st ed. dj. EX $15.00

ELLICOTT, Andrew. *Journal of Andrew Ellicott.* 1803 Phil. 6 fld maps. ½-morocco. G $850.00

ELLIN, Stanley. *Winter After This Summer.* 1960 Random House. 1st ed. dj. EX $35.00

ELLIOT, Bob. *Making of an Angler.* 1975 Winchester. Ills. 209 p. EX $8.00

ELLIOT, C. *Practical Farm Drainage.* 1906 NY. 92 p. VG $6.00

ELLIOT, C.W. *Winfield Scott: Soldier & Man.* 1937 Macmillan. Ills 1st ed. 817 p. maps. VG $7.50

ELLIOT, Charles Wyllys. *Pottery & Porcelain: Early Times to Philadelphia Exhibition.* 1878 NY. Appleton. xl. fair. $30.00

ELLIOT, Charles. *Fading Trails: Endangered American Wildlife.* 1947 Ills. 279 p. VG $11.00

ELLIOT, Charles. *Gone Huntin'.* 1954 Stackpole. Ills. 270 p. dj. EX $12.50

ELLIOT, H. Chandler. *Reprieve From Paradise.* 1955 Gnome. 1st ed. dj. VG $25.00

ELLIOT, M.H. *My Cousin: F. Marion Crawford.* 1934 Macmillan. Ills. sgn. VG $15.00

ELLIOTT, H. *Our Arctic Province: AK & Seal Islands.* 1887 NY. Ills. 473 p. G $50.00

ELLIS, Charles. *History of Roxbury Town.* 1847 Boston. rebound. VG $20.00

ELLIS, Daniel. *Thrilling Adventures of Daniel Ellis.* 1867 NY. Ills. 430 p. M $75.00

ELLIS, Edward. *Life & Deeds of Admiral Dewey.* 1899 Scull. Ills. 244 p. VG $12.00

ELLIS, Elmer. *Henry Moore Tuller: Defender of the West.* 1941 1st ed. dj. VG $20.00

ELLIS, G.H. *Portsmouth Book.* c 1900. Boston. Ills 1st ed. 52 p. wraps. $20.00

ELLIS, H. Havelock. *Studies in Psychology of Sex: Evolution of Modesty.* 1901 Phil. Davis. scarce. $50.00

ELLIS, H. Havelock. *Studies in Psychology of Sex: Modesty, Sexual Periodicity.* 1901 Phil. Davis. Ills. scarce. VG $35.00

ELLIS, Keith. *American Civil War.* 1971 Putnam. Ills. 128 p. dj. EX $5.00

ELLIS, O.O. *Plattsburg Manual: Handbook for Military Training.* 1918 NY. VG $12.50

ELLIS, Richard N. *General Pope & Indian Policy.* 1970 Albuquerque. 1st ed. dj. VG $18.00

ELLIS, William Donohue. *Cuyahoga.* 1966 NY. Ills 1st ed. dj. VG $17.50

ELLIS, William. *3 Visits to Madagascar During Years 1853, 1854, & 1856.* 1859 NY. Ills. 514 p. $30.00

ELLISON, Harlan. *Again, Dangerous Visions.* 1972 Doubleday. 1st ed. sgn. dj. EX $100.00

ELLISON, Harlan. *Approaching Oblivion.* 1974 NY. 1st ed. dj. EX $55.00

ELLISON, Harlan. *Essential Ellison.* 1987 Omaha. 1/1,200. sgn. dj. slipcase. M $60.00

ELLISON, Harlan. *Gentleman Junkie.* 1975 Pyramid. 1st ed. wraps. EX $15.00

ELLISON, Harlan. *Man with 9 Lives & Touch of Infinity.* 1960 Ace Doubles. EX $25.00

ELLISON, Harlan. *Medea: Harlan's World.* 1985 Bantam. Uncorrected proof. wraps. EX $75.00

ELLISON, Harlan. *Partners in Wonder.* 1971 NY. 1st ed. sgn. dj. M $50.00

ELLISON, Ralph. *Invisible Man.* 1952 Signet. 1st ed. wraps. VG $5.00

ELLISON, Virginia H. *Pooh Party Book.* 1971 NY. Dutton. Ills Shepard. 1st ed. dj. EX $15.00

ELLISON, William Henry. *Life & Adventures of George Nidever 1802-1883.* 1937 Berkeley. dj. EX $35.00

ELLISTON, Thomas. *Organs & Tuning.* 1898 London. 3rd ed. 8vo. 399 p. cloth. VG $30.00

ELLMAN, R.; & GILBERT, S. *Letters of James Joyce.* 1966 NY. Viking. dj. M $65.00

ELLROY, James. *Blood on the Moon.* 1984 1st Am ed. inscr. dj. $20.00

ELLROY, James. *Silent Terror.* 1987 Ltd 1st Am ed. 1/350. sgn. dj. $30.00

ELLROY, James. *Suicide Hill.* 1986 1st Am ed. sgn. dj. $20.00

ELLSWORTH, L.R. *Hilibut Schooner.* 1953 NY. sgn. 242 p. maps. EX $10.00

ELLSWORTH, William W. *Golden Age of Authors.* 1919 Boston. presentation. 8vo. 304 p. VG $35.00

ELLUL, Jacques. *Propaganda.* 1965 NY. Knopf. 1st Am ed. VG $12.00

ELLWOOD, G.M. *Model und Raumkunst in England 1680-1800.* 1919 Stuttgart. Verlag. fair. $25.00

ELM, Capt. I. *Avigation by Dead Reckoning.* 1929 Phil. fld map. 120 p. VG $18.00

ELM, H. *Zen Schock Knack-Nusse.* 1877 Leipzig. Ills. German text. juvenile. $15.00

ELMAN, R. *Badmen of the West.* 1974 Castle. Ills. 4to. 256 p. dj. EX $23.00

ELMAN, R.; & PEPER, G. *Hunting America's Game Animals & Birds.* 1975 Winchester. Ills. 368 p. dj. EX $12.50

ELMAN, Robert. *All About Deer Hunting in America.* 1976 Winchester. Ills. 255 p. dj. EX $7.50

ELMAN, Robert. *Atlantic Flyway.* 1972 Winchester. Ills. 4to. 203 p. dj. EX $25.00

ELMER, R.P. *Archery.* 1926 Penn. Ills 1st ed. scarce. VG $25.00

ELON, Amos. *Timetable.* 1980 Doubleday. 1st Am ed. dj. EX $15.00

ELSEN, Albert E. *Purposes of Art.* 1967 NY. 2nd ed. dj. VG $25.00

ELSEN, Albert E. *Rodin.* 1963 MOMA. Ills. 4to. 228 p. dj. $30.00

ELSON, Arthur. *Critical History of Opera.* 1901 Page. 1st ed. $20.00

ELSON, Arthur. *Woman's Work in Music.* 1904 Page. G $18.00

ELSTOB, P. *Bastogne: Road Block.* 1972 NY. 4th ed. $7.50

ELUARD, Paul. *Pablo Picasso.* no date. Phil. Ills. dj. $30.00

ELWOOD, Louie. *Queen Calafia's Land.* 1940 Grabhorn. leather. VG $35.00

ELWOOD, Roger. *Continuum 1.* 1975 London. Allen. dj. VG $7.50

ELWOOD, Roger. *Continuum 3.* 1974 Berkley. dj. VG $7.50

ELY, F. *Lost Dutchman Mine.* 1964 NY. 5th print. dj. EX $7.50

ELYTIS, Odysseus. *Maria Nephele.* 1981 Houghton. 1st Am ed. dj. EX $10.00

EMANUEL, Walter. *Dog Day.* 1902 Dutton. Ills Cecil Aldin. 24mo. $28.00

EMBREE, Edwin R. *Indians of the Americas.* 1939 Houghton Mifflin. 1st ed. VG $30.00

EMBURY, Aymar. *Building the Dutch Colonial House.* 1929 NY. Ills. G $18.00

EMBURY, Aymar. *Early American Churches.* 1914 NY. Ills 1st ed. 184 p. cloth. $25.00

EMBURY, Aymar. *100 Country Houses.* 1909 NY. Ills 1st ed. 261 p. $35.00

EMDEN. *Powers of Europe in the 19th & 20th Centuries.* 1930 NY. 428 p. xl. VG $10.00

EMERSON, Caroline D. *Merry-Go-Round of Modern Tales.* 1927 NY. Dutton. Ills Lenski. 1st ed. VG $25.00

EMERSON, Edwin. *Aspirations.* 1907 Tokyo. 1st ed. presentation. wraps. G $25.00

EMERSON, J. *Evangelical Primer.* 1815 Boston. Ills 6th ed. G $20.00

EMERSON, P.H. *Naturalistic Photography for Students of Art.* 1899 Scovill Adams. Revised 3rd ed. 8vo. xl. VG $55.00

EMERSON, Ralph Waldo. *Letter of Emerson to Solomon Corner of Baltimore in 1842.* 1934 Boston. Ills 1st ed. dj. VG $15.00

EMERSON, Ralph Waldo. *Love & Friendship.* c 1902. NY. Crowell. dj. VG $45.00

EMERSON, Ralph Waldo. *Society & Solitude.* 1879 Boston. 1st ed. VG $35.00

EMERSON, Ralph Waldo. *Trandcendentalism.* 1886 NY. 12mo. ½-leather. VG $60.00

EMERSON, Ralph Waldo. *Works of Ralph Waldo Emerson.* 1903 Boston. Concord ed. 12 vol set. $200.00

EMERSON, W. *When North Winds Blow.* 1922 Lewiston. Ills. G $10.00

EMERSON, W. *When North Winds Blow.* 1922 Lewiston. Ills 1st ed. 229 p. VG $15.00

EMERSON, Walter. *Latchstring: ME Woods & Waters.* 1916 Cambridge. Riverside Pr. Ills. dj. VG $25.00

EMERSON, Walter. *Latchstring: ME Woods & Waters.* 1916 Boston. Ills 1st ed. 229 p. $15.00

EMERSON, William. *History of the Town of Douglas.* 1879 Boston. Ills 1st ed. $40.00

EMERSON, William. *Lancaster on the Nashua.* 1904 MA. Ills 1st ed. 96 p. $20.00

EMERSON, William. *Picturesque Lake Winnipesaukee.* 1905 Calter Bay. Ills 1st ed. 64 p. wraps. $12.50

EMERSON, Willis G. *Smoky God.* 1908 Chicago. 1st ed. $45.00

EMERY, Frederic B. *Violin Concerto.* 1928 Chicago. 8vo. VG $20.00

EMERY, I.C. *WA Monument.* 1920 VA. Ills 1st ed. maps. wraps. $6.00

EMERY, Sara A. *My Generation.* 1893 Neburyport. G $17.50

EMERY, W.B. *Nubian Treasures: Discoveries at Ballana & Qustul.* 1948 London. Ills. VG $20.00

EMMERLING, Mary E. *American Country.* 1980 Potter/Crown. Ills. 292 p. dj. $30.00

EMMERTON, C.O. *Chronicles of 3 Old Houses.* 1935 Boston. Ills 1st ed. 58 p. $12.50

EMMETT, Chris. *Shanghai Pierce: A Fair Likeness.* 1953 OK U Pr. Ills. 338 p. maps. G $10.00

EMMETT, Rowland. *Early Morning Milk Train.* 1977 Battleboro, VT. Ills. 4to. sgn. dj. M $25.00

EMMONS, Earl H. *Reward of Virtue.* 1938 NY. Ltd 1st ed. 1/100. EX $15.00

EMMONS, F. *Pacific Liners 1927-1972.* 1973 Newton Abbot. Ills. 135 p. dj. G $20.00

EMMONS, Sam F. *Downtown District of Leadville, CO.* 1907 GPO. Ills 1st ed. 83 p. wraps. VG $25.00

EMMONS, Sam F. *Ore Deposits.* 1913 NY. Ills 1st ed. 954 p. EX $65.00

EMPSON, William. *Some Versions of Pastoral.* no date. New Directions. 1st ed. dj. EX $30.00

EMRICH, Duncan. *Comstock Bonanza: Rare Western Americana of Twain.* 1950 NY. dj. VG $10.00

EMRICH, Duncan. *It's an Old Wild West Custom.* 1949 NY. 1st ed. dj. VG $25.00

ENDE, Michael. *Neverending Story.* 1983 Doubleday. Ills 1st stated ed. dj. EX $15.00

ENDICOTT, Wendell. *Adventures in AK & Along the Trail.* 1928 NY. Ills 1st ed. green cloth. VG $20.00

ENDICOTT, Wendell. *Adventures with Rod & Harpoon Along FL Keys.* 1925 NY. Stokes. 1st ed. EX $35.00

ENDORE, Guy. *Babouk.* 1934 Vanguard, NY. inscr. G $17.50

ENESEE. *History of Dungeon Rock.* 1856 Boston. 1st ed. wraps. G $20.00

ENFIELD, William. *History of Philosophy.* 1819 London. 2 vol set. VG $85.00

ENGEL, Carl. *Music of Most Ancient Nations.* 1909 London. Reeves. 379 p. VG $50.00

ENGELBRECHT, H.C. *Merchants of Death.* 1934 NY. 1st ed. VG $25.00

ENGELS, Vincent. *Adirondack Fishing in the 1930s.* 1978 Syracuse U Pr. Ills 1st ed. 155 p. dj. EX $10.00

ENGLE, Paul. *Break the Heart's Anger.* 1936 NY. 1st ed. sgn. dj. VG $35.00

ENGLE, Paul. *Golden Child.* 1926 NY. Ills LE Fisher. 1st ed. dj. EX $10.00

ENGLE, Paul. *West of Midnight.* 1941 NY. 1st ed. dj. EX $35.00

ENGLEHARDT, Zephyrin. *San Gabriel Mission & Beginnings of Los Angeles.* 1927 Ills 1st ed. 370 p. cloth. VG $75.00

ENGLEMAN, Paul. *Catch a Fallen Angel.* 1986 Uncorrected proof. wraps. $25.00

ENGLISH, H. *Mining Almanac for 1849.* 1849 London. rebound. VG $30.00

ENNEMOSER, Joseph. *History of Magic.* 1854 London. 1st ed. 2 vol set. rebound. VG $195.00

ENTWISLE, E.A. *Book of Wallpaper: Its History & Appreciation.* 1954 London. Barker. Ills. 151 p. $37.50

EPARVIER, Jean. *Paris Sous la Botte des Nazis.* 1944 Paris. Ills. 4to. dj. VG $22.50

EPHRON, Nora. *Heartburn.* 1983 Knopf. 1st ed. dj. EX $12.00

EPICURUS. *Extant Remains of Epicurus.* 1947 Ltd Ed Club. 1/1,500. $80.00

EPSTEIN, Edward. *Rise & Fall of Diamonds.* 1982 Simon Schuster. 1st ed. EX $12.00

EPSTEIN. *Autobiography.* 1955 NY. Dutton. 1st ed. dj. EX $75.00

EPSTEIN. *Lady Epstein's Drawings.* 1962 Cleveland. World. 1st ed. dj. EX $37.50

ERDRICH, Louise. *Beet Queen.* 1986 NY. Holt. Advance copy. VG $15.00

ERDRICH, Louise. *Beet Queen.* 1986 Holt. 1st ed. dj. EX $20.00

ERICKSON, C. *Invisible Immigrants.* 1972 Miami U Pr. 1st ed. dj. $15.00

ERICKSON, J. *Road to Stalingrad.* 1975 NY. 1st ed. dj. M $35.00

ERICSON, Jack T. *Folk Art in America: Painting & Sculpture.* 1979 NY. Mayflower. Ills. 175 p. $8.00

ERITH, John. *Erith on Portraiture.* 1948 Fountain Pr. 160 p. dj. $20.00

ERLANGER, Philippe. *Age of Courts & Kings.* 1967 Harper Row. 1st Am ed. VG $12.00

ERNEST, Griset. *Aesop's Fables.* 1882 Boston. Ills. gilt edges. VG $17.50

ERNST, Abbe. *Eine Lebensbeschreibung.* 1918 Leipzig. Ills. 512 p. wraps. VG $40.00

ERNST & CARRINGTON. *Houdini & Conan Doyle.* 1933 London. 1st ed. VG $85.00

ERRINGTON, P.L. *Muskrats & Marsh Management.* 1978 NE U Pr. Ills. 183 p. wraps. EX $6.00

ERSKINE, Albert R. *History of Studebaker Corp.* 1924 4to. 229 p. cloth. VG $25.00

ERSKINE, Gladys Shaw. *Broncho Charlie: Saga of the Saddle.* 1934 NY. photos. G $40.00

ERSKINE, John. *NY.* 1945 Chicago. 1st ed. 101 p. dj. $22.50

ERSKINE, John. *Penelope's Man.* 1928 Indianapolis. 1st ed. dj. EX $14.00

ERSKINE, John. *Private Life of Helen of Troy.* 1925 Indianapolis. 1st ed. sgn. dj. boxed. M $26.00

ERSKINE, John. *Private Life of Helen of Troy.* 1925 Indianapolis. VG $5.00

ERSKINE, John. *This Kind of Poetry & Other Essays.* 1920 1st ed. VG $30.00

ERTELL, Viviane B. *Colorful World of Buttons.* 1973 Princeton. Pyne. Ills. 4to. cloth. dj. $25.00

ERWIN. *Southwest of John Horton Slaughter.* 1965 1st ed. dj. EX $90.00

ERWOOD, William J. *Spiritualism & the Catholic Church.* 1917 187 p. VG $22.00

ESCOFFIER, A. *Guide to Modern Cookery.* 1907 NY. 1st Am ed. VG $100.00

ESDAILE, James. *Mesmerism in India & Its Practical Application in Medicine.* 1902 Chicago. 165 p. VG $65.00

ESHLEMAN, Clayton. *Gull Wall.* 1975 Ltd ed. 1/200. sgn. VG $35.00

ESHLEMAN, H. Frank. *Swiss & German Pioneers.* 1917 Lancaster. 386 p. M $65.00

ESKELUND, K. *While God Slept.* 1961 London. 1st ed. dj. VG $10.00

ESKEW, G.L. *Cradle of Ships.* 1958 Putnam. Ills 1st ed. 279 p. dj. VG $22.50

ESKEW, G.L. *Pageant of Packets: Book of American Steamboating.* 1929 NY. 1st ed. dj. EX $35.00

ESLER, L.A. *Presidents of Our US.* 1936 Chicago. Ills. 63 p. $3.00

ESPINOSA, Carmen. *Shawls, Crinolines, Filigree.* 1970 TX Western Pr. 1st ed. 61 p. dj. $12.00

ESPY, James. *Philosophy of Storms.* 1841 Boston. Ills 1st ed. 552 p. EX $150.00

ESQUEMELING, John. *Buccaneers of America Now Faithfully Rendered into English.* 1893 London. Swan Sonnenschein. Ills. 8vo. $100.00

ESSARY, Fred. *Ships.* 1916 John Murphy. Ltd ed. 1/1,000. 199 p. $15.00

ESSARY, J.F. *Selected Addresses of C. Bascom Slemp.* 1938 WA. inscr Slemp. VG $20.00

ESSER, Hermann. *Draughtsman's Alphabets.* 1877 NY/Chicago. 6th ed. oblong 4to. 31 p. VG $95.00

ESTES, Eleanor. *Moffat Museum.* 1983 Harcourt Brace. Ills 1st ed. 262 p. dj. EX $17.50

ESTES, Eleanor. *Rufus M.* 1959 Harcourt Brace. Ills Slobodkin. 320 p. dj. VG $8.50

ESTEY, P.C. *Woodchuck Hunter.* 1936 Small Arms. Ills. 135 p. dj. EX $30.00

ESTLEMAN, Loren D. *Every Brilliant Eye.* 1986 Advance copy. wraps. $15.00

ESTLEMAN, Loren D. *Roses Are Dead.* 1985 Uncorrected proof. wraps. $40.00

ESTVAN, B. *War Pictures From the South.* 1863 NY. green cloth. VG $55.00

ETCHISON, Dennis. *Dark Country.* 1983 Scream Pr. Ills Potter. 1st ed. sgns. dj. $135.00

ETCHISON, Dennis. *Dark Country.* 1982 Scream Pr. Ills Potter. 1/100. sgns. dj. $450.00

ETCHISON, Dennis. *Halloween II.* 1981 Zebra. 1st ed. wraps. EX $8.00

ETCHISON, Dennis. *Red Dreams.* 1985 Scream Pr. Ills Potter. 1st ed. sgns. dj. $100.00

ETIENNE, Drioton. *Egyptian Art.* 1951 Golden Griffin. 2nd print. dj. VG $16.00

ETTINGHAUSEN, R. *Le Peinture Arabe.* 1962 Skira. Ills. French text. dj. EX $22.50

EULER, L. *Lettres de M. Euler a une Princesse d'Allemagne.* 1787-1789. Paris. Nouvelle ed. 3 vol set. $125.00

EUNSON, D. *Day They Gave Babies Away.* 1947 NY. Ills F Kredel. 1st ed. dj. EX $8.50

EUNSON, D. *Up the Rim.* 1970 NY. dj. VG $7.50

EUSTACE, Rev. John C.A. *Classical Tour Through Italy.* 1815 London. 3rd ed. 2 vol set. VG $145.00

EUSTIS, Celestine. *Cooking in Old Creole Days.* 1903 NY. Ills 1st ed. VG $65.00

EVANOFF, V. *Fishing Rigs for Fresh-Water & Salt-Water.* 1977 Harper Row. Ills 1st ed. dj. EX $7.50

EVANOFF, V. *Fresh-Water Fisherman's Bible.* 1964 Doubleday. Ills. 180 p. wraps. $10.00

EVANOFF, V. *Hunting Secrets of the Experts.* 1964 Doubleday. Ills 1st ed. 251 p. VG $7.00

EVANOFF, V. *Make Your Own Fishing Lures.* 1975 Barnes. 158 p. dj. EX $8.50

EVANS, Allen. *Reindeer Trek.* no date. (1930) Coward. 1st ed. EX $15.00

EVANS, Bessie. *American Indian Dance Steps.* 1931 Barnes. 1st ed. 104 p. VG $37.50

EVANS, Charles. *Friends in 17th Century.* 1876 Phil. 668 p. VG $60.00

EVANS, E.L. *Documented History of Long Family.* 1956 Atlanta. 1st ed. 316 p. EX $35.00

EVANS, Edwin. *Technics of the Organ.* no date. London. Reeves. VG $20.00

EVANS, Eva Knox. *Emma Belle & Her Kinfolks.* 1940 NY. Putnam. Ills Flavia Gag. 1st ed. dj. $15.00

EVANS, Fredrick William. *Autobiography of a Shaker & Revelation of the Apocalypse.* June 1869. Mt. Lebanon. 1st ed. cloth. $60.00

EVANS, G. *Sir Geraint Evans: Knight at the Opera.* 1984 London. Ills 1st ed. dj. VG $25.00

EVANS, G.G. *Visitor's Companion at Our Nation's Capital.* 1892 Phil. Ills 1st ed. 192 p. wraps. $15.00

EVANS, G.W. *Slash Ranch Hounds.* 1951 NM U Pr. Ills. 244 p. dj. VG $38.00

EVANS, George Bird. *Best of Nash Buckingham.* 1973 Winchester. 320 p. dj. EX $20.00

EVANS, George Bird. *Bird Troubles with Bird Dogs.* 1985 Old Hemlock. Ltd ed. sgn. dj. slipcase. EX $85.00

EVANS, George Bird. *Upland Shooting Life.* 1971 Knopf. Ills. 301 p. dj. EX $12.50

EVANS, H.E. *Life on a Little Known Planet.* 1968 Dutton. Ills. 318 p. dj. EX $6.00

EVANS, J. *Art in Medieval France.* 1948 London. Oxford U Pr. 280 plts. EX $125.00

EVANS, Joe M. *About All I Know I Learned From a Cow.* 1964 Ills 5th ed. 71 p. wraps. EX $15.00

EVANS, Joe M. *Corral Full of Stories.* 1939 McMath. 4th ed. inscr. wraps. $50.00

EVANS, John. *Halo in Blood.* 1946 Bobbs Merrill. 1st Paul Pine Mystery. scarce. $75.00

EVANS, Mary. *Costume Throughout the Ages.* 1950 Phil. dj. VG $10.00

EVANS, Max. *One-Eyed Sky.* 1974 Los Angeles. Ills 1st ed. dj. M $14.00

EVANS, Oliver. *Young Millwright & Miller's Guide.* 1836 Phil. Carey Lea Blanchard. 392 p. $75.00

EVANS, Oliver. *Young Millwright & Miller's Guide.* 1794 Phil. Ills 1st ed. 8 vol set. $1300.00

EVANS, R. *Lyndon B. Johnson: Exercise of Power.* 1966 NY. 1st ed. 574 p. dj. $15.00

EVANS, W.F. *Border Skylines: 50 Years Tallying Out on Round-Up Ground.* 1940 Cecil Baugh. sgn. dj. scarce. $125.00

EVANS, W.F. *Mental Medicine: Theory & Practical.* 1872 Boston. Carter Pettee. 4th ed. $18.00

EVANS, Walker. *American Photographs.* 1938 NY. MOMA. Ills 1st ed. dj. EX $135.00

EVANS, Walker. *Message From the Interior.* 1966 NY. Ills. folio. EX $185.00

EVANS-WENTZ, W.Y. *Tibetan Book of the Great Liberation.* 1954 London. Oxford U Pr. EX $35.00

EVE, A.S.; & CREASY, C.H. *Life & Work of John Tyndall.* 1945 London. Macmillan. 1st ed. 404 p. xl. $25.00

EVELYN, John. *Acetaria: Discourse on Sallets.* 1937 Brooklyn. reprint of 1699. 1/1,000. $50.00

EVERETT, Dick. *Vanguards of the Frontier.* 1941 NY. Ills 1st ed. dj. VG $20.00

EVERETT, E. *Life of George Washington.* 1860 NY. 1st ed. 272 p. cloth. $15.00

EVERETT, Michael. *Birds of Paradise.* 1978 Putnam. Ills. 144 p. dj. EX $80.00

EVERETT-GREEN, Evelyn. *Princess's Token.* no date. London/NY. Ills Dixon. 48 p. $10.00

EVERITT, C. *Birds of the Edward Marshall Boehm Aviaries.* 1973 Boehm. Ills. 4to. 297 p. VG $10.00

EVERITT, Charles P. *Adventures of Treasure Hunter.* 1951 Boston. 1st ed. 265 p. gilt cloth. $15.00

EVERS, A. *Catskills.* 1972 NY. 1st ed. plts. maps. dj. VG $16.00

EVERS, John C. *Artists of the Old West.* 1965 NY. Ills 1st ed. dj. EX $35.00

EVERSON, William. *Black Hills.* 1973 Didymus Pr. Ills Hopkins. 1st ed. 1/285. $115.00

EVERSON, William. *Robin Jeffers.* 1968 Oyez. 1st ed. $30.00

EVERSON, William. *Tendril in the Mesh.* 1973 Cayucos Pr. 1st ed. 1/250. sgn. EX $110.00

EVERTS, L.H. *Compilation Atlas Map of Stark County.* 1975 Phil. Ills 1st ed. 121 p. cloth. EX $175.00

EVES, C. Washington. *West Indies Published Under Auspices Royal Colony Institute.* 1889 London. Sampson Low. Ills 1st ed. VG $75.00

EWAN, Joseph & Nesta. *Biographical Dictionary of Rocky Mountain Naturalists.* 1981 Hauge. 253 p. EX $60.00

EWAN, Joseph & Nesta. *John Banister & His Natural History of VA 1678-1692.* 1970 IL U Pr. Ills. 485 p. dj. EX $15.00

EWAN, Joseph. *Rocky Mountain Naturalists.* 1950 Denver. 1st ed. 358 p. dj. VG $25.00

EWART, Gavin. *9 New Poems.* 1986 Bitts Pr. 1st ed. 1/300. sgn. wraps. EX $10.00

EWBANK, Thomas. *Descriptive & Historical Account of Hydraulic Machines.* 1842 NY. Appleton. Ills. 582 p. VG $120.00

EWBANK, Thomas. *Life in Brazil; or, Journal of Visit to Land of Cocoa.* 1856 NY. Harper. Ills 1st ed. 8vo. 469 p. EX $100.00

EWELL, R. *Dining Out in America's Cities.* 1954 Boston. 1st ed. 214 p. wraps. $5.00

EWEN, David. *Book of European Light Opera.* 1962 NY. Holt. 1st ed. dj. VG $15.00

EWERS, J.C. *Artists of the Old West.* 1973 NY. Enlarged ed. VG $40.00

EWERS, J.C. *Artists of the Old West.* 1965 Doubleday. Ills. 4to. 240 p. dj. EX $25.00

EWING, Douglas. *Pleasing the Spirits: Catalogue Collection Am. Indian Art.* 1982 NY. Ghylen. Ills. 4to. 401 p. M $25.00

EWING, Elizabeth. *Fur in Dress.* 1981 London. Batsford. Ills. 4to. 168 p. $25.00

EWING, J.H. *Grandmother's Spring.* c 1885. London. Ills. VG $25.00

EWING, J.H. *Jackanapes & the Peace Egg.* 1928 Winston. Ills Fitz. 1st ed. VG $25.00

EWING, J.H. *Jackanapes.* 1903 Phil. Altemus. Ills R Caldecott. VG $20.00

EWING, J.H. *Lob Lie-by-the-Fire, Brownies, & Other Tales.* 1891 Boston. Roberts. Ills Cruikshank. G $15.00

EXLEY, Frederick. *Fan's Notes.* 1968 Harper. Advance copy. wraps. scarce. $150.00

EXMAN, Eugene. *House of Harper: 150 Years of Publishing.* 1967 NY. Ills 1st ed. 326 p. dj. G $20.00

EYO, Ekpo. *2,000 Years of Nigerian Art.* 1977 Nigeria. Dept Antiquities. Ills Held. $60.00

EYRE, Alice. *Famous Fremonts & Their America.* 1948 Fine Arts Pr. 1st ed. inscr/sgn. EX $50.00

EYTON, T.C. *History of Rarer British Birds.* 1836 London. Longman. Ills. brown cloth. VG $275.00

EZELL, E.C. *Small Arms of the World.* 1977 Stackpole. Revised ed. 4to. dj. EX $25.00

EZICKSON, A.J. *Roosevelt Album.* 1945 NY. Ills 1st ed. 96 p. wraps. $10.00

FABBRO, Mario. *How To Build Modern Furniture. Vol. I.* 1951 NY. Dodge. Ills. 170 p. $42.50

FABBRO, Mario. *Modern Furniture: Its Design & Construction.* 1949 NY. Reinhold. Ills. 158 p. dj. $47.50

FABIAN, Dietrich. *Modern Swimming Pools of World.* 1958 Florence. Nat'l Pool Equipment Co. dj. $25.00

FABLES, Robert H. *Romance of a Bookshop 1904-1938.* 1938 Revised ed. 8vo. VG $28.00

FABRE, J. *Picasso en Cataluna.* 1966 Barcelona. trilingual text. dj. EX $35.00

FABRE, J.H. *Bramble Bees & Others.* 1915 NY. 1st English ed. VG $20.00

FABRE, J.H. *Hunting Wasps.* 1919 Dodd Mead. 427 p. G $8.00

FABRE, J.H. *Life of the Grasshopper.* 1919 Dodd Mead. 453 p. G $8.00

FABRE, J.H. *Life of the Spider.* 1912 NY. Intro Maurice Maetterlinck. $45.00

FADALA, Sam. *Black Powder Hunting.* 1978 Stackpole. Ills. 256 p. dj. EX $10.50

FADIMAN. *Joys of Wine.* 1975 NY. Abrams. dj. EX $50.00

FAGAN, J.O. *Old South; or, Romance of Early New England History.* 1925 Boston. Ills. 125 p. wraps. $6.00

FAGES, R. *Historical, Political, & Natural Description of CA.* 1937 Berkeley. 12mo. dj. EX $65.00

FAHEY, J. *Inland Empire.* 1965 WA U Pr. Ills. 270 p. maps. dj. EX $20.00

FAHNESTOCK, William Baker. *Statuvolism; or, Artificial Somnambulism.* 1871 328 p. G $60.00

FAIRBAIRN, A. *Call Him George.* 1969 NY. Ills 1st ed. 304 p. dj. VG $20.00

FAIRBANK, Alfred. *Book of Scripts.* 1949 King Penguin. Ills. 12mo. 64 p. $7.50

FAIRBANK, Calvin. *Rev. Calvin Fairbank During Slavery Time.* 1890 Chicago. inscr. VG $55.00

FAIRBANKS, Douglas. *Laugh & Live.* 1917 NY. Britton. 2nd print. VG $15.00

FAIRBANKS, Douglas. *Making Life Worthwhile.* 1918 NY. Ills. 157 p. EX $25.00

FAIRBRIDGE, D. *Historic Houses of South Africa.* 1922 London. Ills 1st ed. 4to. gilt cloth. $150.00

FAIRBRIDGE, Rhodes W. *Encyclopedia of Oceanography.* 1966 NY. Reinhold. 1st ed. dj. EX $36.00

FAIRCHILD, David & Marian. *Book of Monsters.* 1914 Nat'l Geog Soc. 1st ed. red cloth. VG $60.00

FAIRCHILD, David. *Book of Monsters.* 1914 Nat'l Geog Soc. 1st ed. 266 p. VG $95.00

FAIRCHILD, David. *Garden Islands of Great East.* 1943 Scribner. 1st ed. EX $15.00

FAIRCHILD, David. *World Grows Round My Door.* 1947 Scribner. 1st ed. VG $12.50

FAIRCHILD, David. *World Was My Garden.* 1939 NY. Scribner. VG $16.50

FAIRFIELD, Jane. *Life of Sumner Lincoln Fairfield.* 1846 NY. fair. $20.00

FAIRMONT, Ethel. *Rhymes for Kindly Children.* 1937 Ills Gruelle. Revised ed. 1st print. dj. VG $30.00

FAIRMONT, Ethel. *Rhymes for Kindly Children.* 1916 Volland. Ills Gruelle. 16th ed. 8vo. $36.00

FAIRRIE, Geoffrey. *Sugar.* 1925 Fairrie & Co. Ltd 1st ed. VG $15.00

FAISON, S. Lane. *New England Eye: Master American Paintings From New England.* 1983 Williamston. presentation. 4to. $10.00

FALCONER, Sheila. *Lorgaireacht an Tsoidhigh Naomtha.* 1953 Dublin. scarce. VG $40.00

FALCONER, William. *Mushrooms: How To Grow Them.* 1906 NY. Ills. 12mo. 169 p. VG $15.00

FALCONER, William. *Shipwreck.* 1868 London. Ills Birket Foster. EX $25.00

FALCONER, William. *Universal Dictionary of the Marine.* 1769 London. Cadell. Ills 1st ed. 4to. $325.00

FALK, Bernard. *Thomas Rowlandson: His Life & Art.* 1952 NY. 1st Am ed. 4to. 236 p. VG $70.00

FALK, E.A. *Togo & Rise of Japanese Sea Power.* 1936 London. 1st ed. 508 p. EX $35.00

FALL, B. *Hell in Small Place.* 1966 Lippincott. 1st ed. dj. VG $25.00

FALLACI, Oriana. *Letter to a Child Never Born.* 1976 Simon Schuster. 1st Am ed. dj. EX $20.00

FALLACI, Oriana. *Man.* 1980 NY. 1st ed. presentation. dj. M $35.00

FALLON, Capt. David M.C. *Big Fight.* c 1918. NY. 1st ed. sgn. VG $15.00

FALLS, Dewitt Clinton. *History of 7th Regiment 1889-1922.* 1948 NY. Ills. 302 p. VG $25.00

FALLS. *Battle of Caporetto.* 1966 Lippincott. 1st ed. dj. M $25.00

FANKHAUSER, W. *Financial History of CA.* 1913 Berkeley. 408 p. wraps. VG $55.00

FANT, J. *Faulkner at West Point.* 1964 NY. 1st ed. dj. EX $30.00

FANTA, J. Julius. *Winning America's Cup.* 1969 NY. Sea Lore. 1st ed. dj. VG $21.00

FAR, Isabella. *De Chirico.* 1968 NY. Abrams. Ills. 4to. cloth. slipcase. $65.00

FARADAY, Cornelia Bateman. *European & American Carpets & Rugs.* 1929 Grand Rapids. Ills 1st ed. 4to. 382 p. VG $125.00

FARADAY, Michael. *Experimental Researches in Chemistry & Physics.* 1859 London. Taylor/Francis. 1st ed. xl. $425.00

FARAGO, L. *Aftermath: Martin Bormann & the 4th Reich.* 1974 NY. Ills. dj. G $17.50

FARAGO, L. *Patton Ordeal & Triumph.* 1963 Obolensky. 1st ed. dj. VG $25.00

FARBER, E. *Great Chemists.* 1961 NY. $17.50

FARBER, E. *Nobel Prize Winners in Chemistry 1901-1950.* 1953 NY. Schuman. 1st ed. G $10.00

FARBER, N. *How Does It Feel To Be Old?* 1979 NY. Dutton. 1st ed. dj. VG $15.00

FARGEON, Jefferson. *Complete Smuggler.* 1937 Indianapolis. dj. G $12.00

FARINA, Richard. *Long Time Coming & Long Time Gone.* 1969 NY. 1st ed. dj. VG $30.00

FARIS, J.T. *Old Gardens in & About Philadelphia.* 1932 Indianapolis. Ills 1st ed. 301 p. $20.00

FARIS, J.T. *On Trail of Pioneers.* 1920 NY. VG $25.00

FARIS, J.T. *Roaming Eastern Mountains.* 1932 NY. Ills 1st ed. maps. 319 p. $6.00

FARIS, J.T. *Romance of the Boundaries.* 1926 Harper. 1st ed. VG $15.00

FARIS, J.T. *Seeing PA.* 1919 Phil. Lippincott. Ills 2nd ed. G $20.00

FARIS, J.T. *Seeing the Eastern States.* 1922 Lippincott. dj. VG $15.00

FARIS, Lillie. *Old Testament Stories Retold for Children.* 1938 Platt Munk. Ills WF White. 4to. EX $12.00

FARIS & ELMER. *Arab Archery.* 1945 Princeton. Ills. dj. VG $45.00

FARISH, Thomas Edwin. *Gold Hunters of CA.* 1904 Chicago. Ills. VG $50.00

FARISH. *History of AR.* 1915 Phoenix. 1st ed. 2 vol set. EX $75.00

FARLEY, Edward J. *Fighter Planes P-1 to F-107.* c 1961. Aero. 3rd ed. dj. VG $17.50

FARLEY, F.A. *Unitarianism Defined.* 1870 Boston. Am Unit Assn. G $25.00

FARLEY, J.A. *Jim Farley's Story.* 1948 NY. Ills 1st ed. 377 p. cloth. $12.50

FARLEY, Walter. *Black Stallion's Filly.* 1952 NY. Ills 1st print. dj. EX $7.50

FARMER, Fannie. *Boston Cooking School Cookbook.* 1950 Boston. dj. EX $20.00

FARMER, Fannie. *Chafing Dish Possibilites.* 1899 Boston. cloth. $50.00

FARMER, Fannie. *New Book of Cookery.* 1912 Boston. Ills 1st ed. G $20.00

FARMER, G. *MA: Anatomy of Quality.* 1967 MA. Ills 1st ed. 127 p. boxed. $10.00

FARMER, P.J. *Green Odyssey.* 1957 NY. Ballantine. 1st ed. wraps. VG $25.00

FARMER, P.J. *Image of the Beast.* 1968 Essex House. 1st ed. dj. EX $75.00

FARMER, P.J. *Magic Labyrinth.* 1980 Berkeley. 1st ed. dj. EX $15.00

FARMER, P.J. *Maker of the Universe.* 1975 Garland. 1st HrdCvr ed. dj. EX $75.00

FARMER, P.J. *Night of Light.* 1975 Garland. 1st HrdCvr ed. dj. EX $80.00

FARMER, P.J. *Unreasoning Mask.* 1981 Putnam. 1st ed. dj. EX $15.00

FARMER. *Realm of Rusk County.* 1951 Henderson. Henderson Times. dj. VG $30.00

FARNHAM, T.J. *Life, Adventures, & Travels of CA.* 1849 NY. 8vo. 468 p. gilt cloth. VG $70.00

FARNOL, Jeffery. *Money Moon.* 1911 Dodd Mead. Ills Keller. 1st ed. 386 p. $35.00

FARNUM, Alex. *Visits of Northmen to RI.* 1877 Providence. 1st ed. 1/250. wraps. EX $60.00

FARQUHAR, Francis P. *Big Trees & High Sierra.* 1948 Berkeley. 1st ed. dj. rare. EX $175.00

FARR, F. *Margaret Mitchell of Atlanta.* 1965 NY. 1st ed. dj. EX $15.00

FARR, Finis. *Chicago.* 1973 dj. EX $20.00

FARRAR, E.F. *Old VA House Along the James.* 1957 Hastings House. Ills. 4to. 231 p. dj. EX $15.00

FARRAR, E.F. *Old VA Houses: Mobjack Bay Country.* c 1960s. NY. Bonanza. Ills. 169 p. dj. $10.00

FARRAR, E.F. *Old VA Houses: Mobjack Bay Country.* 1955 NY. Bonanza. 1st ed. dj. $20.00

FARRELL, Andrew. *John Cameron's Odyssey.* 1928 Macmillan. $25.00

FARRELL, James T. *Misunderstanding.* 1949 NY. 1st ed. 1/300. rare. VG $75.00

FARRELL, James T. *Reflections at 50.* 1954 NY. 1st ed. dj. VG $20.00

FARRELL, James T. *Reflections at 50.* 1956 London. 1st ed. dj. VG $35.00

FARRELL, James T. *Young Lonigan: Boyhood in Chicago Streets.* 1932 NY. Vanguard. 1st ed. EX $125.00

FARRINGTON, Chisie. *Women Can Fish.* 1951 Coward McCann. Ills. 238 p. VG $10.00

FARRINGTON, S.K. *Atlantic Game Fishing.* 1939 Garden City. Deluxe ed. 4to. 298 p. dj. VG $30.00

FARRINGTON, S.K. *Book of Fishes.* 1946 Balkiston. Ills 1st ed. 88 p. dj. VG $15.00

FARRINGTON, S.K. *Ducks Came Back: Story of Ducks Unlimited.* 1945 Coward McCann. Ills. 4to. 138 p. EX $20.00

FARRINGTON, S.K. *Fishing the Atlantic.* 1949 NY. 1st ed. presentation. dj. EX $45.00

FARRINGTON, S.K. *Fishing the Atlantic.* 1949 Coward McCann. Ills. 312 p. dj. VG $10.00

FARRINGTON, S.K. *Fishing the Pacific.* 1953 Coward McCann. Ills. inscr/sgn. 297 p. EX $12.50

FARRINGTON, S.K. *Fishing with Hemingway & Glassell.* 1971 McKay. Ills. 118 p. dj. EX $8.00

FARRINTON, Margaret Vere. *Tales of King Arthur.* 1888 NY. Ills Fredericks. 1st ed. VG $22.00

FARRIS, John. *Son of Endless Night.* 1985 NY. 1st ed. dj. EX $20.00

FARRIS, John. *Uninvited.* 1982 Delacorte. 1st ed. dj. EX $13.00

FARRIS, John. *Wildwood.* 1986 NY. 1st ed. dj. M $20.00

FARROW, Edward S. *Farrow's Military Encyclopedia.* 1885 NY. Ills 1st ed. 3 vol set. $350.00

FARROW, M.H. *Troublesome Time in TX.* 1960 Naylor. Ills 2nd ed. 106 p. dj. VG $25.00

FARSON, Negley. *Going Fishing.* no date. Harcourt Brace. 1st Am ed. dj. $12.50

FASSETT, N.C. *Manual of Aquatic Plants.* 1975 WI U Pr. Ills. 405 p. VG $14.00

FAST, Howard. *Departure & Other Stories.* 1949 Little Brown. 1st ed. VG $10.00

FAST, Howard. *My Glorious Brother.* 1948 Boston. 1st ed. inscr. VG $15.00

FAST, Howard. *Spartacus.* 1951 NY. 1st ed. sgn. dj. EX $20.00

FAST, Howard. *Story of Lola Gregg.* 1956 Blue Heron Pr. 1st ed. dj. VG $15.00

FATIO, Louise. *3 Happy Lions.* 1959 NY. Whitlesey House. Ills 1st ed. $15.00

FAULK, John Henry. *Fear on Trial.* 1964 NY. 1st ed. sgn. dj. G $30.00

FAULK, O.B. *Geronimo Campaign.* 1969 Oxford U Pr. Ills. 245 p. maps. EX $15.00

FAULK, O.B. *Short History of AZ.* 1970 OK U Pr. Ills Review of 1st ed. dj. EX $15.00

FAULKNER, Georgene. *Little Peachling & Other Tales of Old Japan.* 1928 Wise Parslow. Ills Richardson. green cloth. $20.00

FAULKNER, J. *Men Working.* 1941 NY. 1st ed. sgn. dj. EX $25.00

FAULKNER, John. *My Brother Bill.* 1963 Trident Pr. 1st ed. dj. EX $20.00

FAULKNER, Ray. *Art Today.* 1969 NY. 5th ed. 1st issue. 542 p. dj. $25.00

FAULKNER, William. *Absalom, Absalom!* 1936 Random House. 1st ed. VG $15.00

FAULKNER, William. *Big Woods.* 1955 NY. 1st ed. dj. VG $60.00

FAULKNER, William. *Dr. Matino & Other Stories.* 1934 NY. Ltd 1st ed. 1/360. sgn. EX $500.00

FAULKNER, William. *Early Prose & Poetry.* 1963 London. 1st ed. dj. EX $30.00

FAULKNER, William. *Fable.* 1954 Random House. 1st trade ed. crimson cloth. $45.00

FAULKNER, William. *Fable.* 1954 NY. 1st ed. dj. VG $55.00

FAULKNER, William. *Fable.* 1954 NY. 2nd ed. dj. VG $12.00

FAULKNER, William. *Flags in the Dust.* 1973 NY. 1st ed. dj. EX $25.00

FAULKNER, William. *Intruder in the Dust.* 1949 Signet. 1st print. wraps. VG $50.00

FAULKNER, William. *Intruder in the Dust.* 1948 NY. 1st ed. dj. VG $55.00

FAULKNER, William. *Knight's Gambit.* 1949 NY. 1st ed. dj. scarce. VG $65.00

FAULKNER, William. *Mansion.* 1959 Random House. 1st ed. 8vo. gilt cloth. dj. $75.00

FAULKNER, William. *Mansion.* 1959 NY. 1st ed. 8vo. blue cloth. dj. $70.00

FAULKNER, William. *Mayday.* 1978 U Notre Dame. 1st ed. dj. EX $15.00

FAULKNER, William. *Moustiques.* 1948 Paris. 1st French ed. wraps. EX $30.00

FAULKNER, William. *MS Poems.* 1979 Oxford, MS. Review ed. 1/125. VG $140.00

FAULKNER, William. *MS Poems.* 1979 Yoknapatawpha. 1st ed. 1/500. slipcase. EX $100.00

FAULKNER, William. *New Orleans Sketches.* 1958 Rutgers. Intro C Collins. 1st ed. dj. $50.00

FAULKNER, William. *New Orleans Sketches.* 1959 London. 1st English ed. dj. VG $25.00

FAULKNER, William. *Pylon.* 1935 NY. Ltd ed. 1/310. sgn. VG $600.00

FAULKNER, William. *Pylon.* 1935 NY. Smith Haas. 1st trade ed. 1st print. VG $75.00

FAULKNER, William. *Pylon.* 1935 Harrison Smith. 1st ed. dj. VG $250.00

FAULKNER, William. *Pylon.* 1935 NY. 1st ed. 1st print. 8vo. dj. EX $200.00

FAULKNER, William. *Reivers.* 1962 NY. 1st ed. dj. VG $35.00

FAULKNER, William. *Reivers.* 1962 NY. Ltd 1st ed. 1/500. 8vo. wraps. $275.00

FAULKNER, William. *Reivers.* 1962 Random House. 1st ed. dj. EX $50.00

FAULKNER, William. *Reivers.* 1962 Chatto Windus. 1st English ed. dj. EX $45.00

FAULKNER, William. *Requiem for a Nun.* 1951 Random House. 1st ed. 1st issue. 8vo. dj. EX $40.00

FAULKNER, William. *Requiem for a Nun: A Play.* 1959 NY. Ills 1st ed. 8vo. dj. EX $20.00

FAULKNER, William. *Selected Letters of William Faulkner.* 1977 NY. 1st ed. dj. M $22.00

FAULKNER, William. *Town.* 1957 Random House. 1st ed. 2nd issue. dj. VG $55.00

FAULKNER, William. *Town.* 1957 Random House. 1st ed. 1st issue. dj. VG $65.00

FAULKNER, William. *Town.* 1957 NY. Ltd ed. 1/450. sgn. EX $525.00

FAULKNER, William. *Vision in Spring.* 1984 TX U Pr. 1st ed. dj. M $20.00

FAULKNER, William. *Wild Palms.* 1939 Random House. 1st ed. G $20.00

FAULKNER & COWLEY. *Faulkner-Cowley File.* 1966 London. 1st ed. dj. EX $15.00

FAUST, A.B. *German Element in the US.* 1927 NY. Revised ed. 2 vols in 1. $32.50

FAUST, E.C. *Life History Studies of MT Trematodes.* 1917 IL U Pr. Ills. 120 p. G $8.00

FAVOUR, A.H. *Old Bill Williams, Mountain Man.* 1962 OK U Pr. Ills 1st ed. maps. dj. EX $10.00

FAVOUR, A.H. *Old Bill Williams, Mountain Man.* 1936 Chapel Hill. Ills 1st ed. 229 p. maps. G $57.50

FAWCETT, Clara Hallard. *On Making, Mending, & Dressing Dolls.* 1949 NY. dj. EX $12.00

FAWCETT, P.H. *Lost Trails, Lost Cities.* 1953 Funk Wagnall. Ills. 332 p. dj. G $14.00

FAY, Bernard. *George Washington: Republican Aristocrat.* 1931 Boston/NY. 1st ed. presentation. G $25.00

FAY, Bernard. *George Washington: Republican Aristocrat.* 1931 Boston. Ills 1st ed. maps. 274 p. $15.00

FAY, Theodore S. *Views in the City of NY & Its Environs.* 1831 NY. 1st ed. map. 13 plts. rare. $1000.00

FEACHEM, R. *Guide to Prehistoric Scotland.* 1977 Toronto. 223 p. VG $10.00

FEARING, Clarence. *Contemporary Kindred of Abraham Lincoln.* 1929 Weymouth, MA. EX $45.00

FEARING, Kenneth. *Dead Reckoning.* 1938 NY. 1st ed. dj. EX $30.00

FEARN. *Diary of a Refugee.* 1910 NY. Ills. G $50.00

FECHHEIMER, Hedwig. *Die Plastik der Agypter.* 1922 Berlin. VG $15.00

FEDDERSEN, Martin. *Japanese Decorative Art: Handbook for Collectors.* 1962 NY. Yoseloff. Ills 1st Am ed. 296 p. dj. $40.00

FEDER, Norman. *American Indian Art.* 1965 NY. 445 p. dj. VG $50.00

FEDER & JOESTEN. *Luciano Story.* 1954 NY. 1st ed. sgns. dj. scarce. $35.00

FEDUCCIA, Alan. *Catesby's Birds of Colonial America.* 1985 NC U Pr. Ills. 4to. 176 p. dj. EX $35.00

FEEDLEY, George. *Mr. Cat.* 1961 Ills VJ Dowling. dj. VG $10.00

FEEK, A.J. *Every Man His Own Trainer.* 1889 Syracuse, NY. 8vo. 302 p. $45.00

FEHRENBACH, T.R. *This Kind of Peace.* 1966 NY. 1st ed. dj. VG $20.00

FEHRENBACH, T.R. *This Kind of War.* 1963 NY. 1st ed. dj. EX $37.50

FEIBLEMAN, J.K. *Aesthetics.* 1968 NY. 463 p. $25.00

FEIBLEMAN, P.S. *Bayous.* no date. Time Life. Ills. 184 p. EX $8.00

FEIFFER, Jules. *Ackroyd.* 1977 Simon Schuster. 1st ed. dj. EX $15.00

FEIFFER, Jules. *Harry: The Rat with Women.* 1963 McGraw Hill. 1st ed. dj. EX $20.00

FEIFFER, Jules. *Tantrum.* 1979 Knopf. proof. wraps. EX $40.00

FEIFFER, Jules. *Tantrum.* 1979 Knopf. 1st ed. dj. VG $15.00

FEIKEMA, Feike. *Golden Bowl.* 1944 St. Paul. 1st ed. sgn. EX $20.00

FEININGER, A. *Trees.* 1968 NY. Ills. 116 p. dj. VG $15.00

FEININGER, T.L. *Lyonel Feininger Monograph.* 1985 Geneva. Ills. 76 p. wraps. $20.00

FEIS, H. *Between War & Peace.* 1960 Princeton. 1st ed. dj. VG $10.00

FEJES, C. *People of the Noatak.* 1967 NY. dj. $17.50

FELCHER, Cecelia. *Complete Book of Rug Making: Folk Methods & Ethnic Designs.* 1975 NY. Hawthorne. Ills. 208 p. dj. $17.50

FELD & PICASSO. *Picasso: His Recent Drawings 1966-1968.* 1969 NY. Abrams. Ills. 4to. dj. $75.00

FELDMAN, H. *Prohibition: Its Economic & Industrial Aspects.* 1927 NY. 1st ed. $28.00

FELL, Herbert Grandville. *Book of Job.* 1896 London/NY. Ills. 4to. tan cloth. $110.00

FELLOWES, Edmund H. *Orlando Gibbons: Short Account of His Life & Work.* 1925 Oxford. Clarendon Pr. VG $15.00

FELLOWES, Edmund H. *William Byrd: Short Account of His Life & Work.* 1928 Oxford. Clarendon Pr. VG $15.00

FELLOWES, W.D. *Visit to La Trappe.* 1818 Ills 2nd ed. VG $125.00

FELLOWS, P.F.M. *1st Over Everest.* 1934 NY. dj. VG $25.00

FELT, E.P. *Manual of Tree & Shrub Insects.* 1926 Macmillan. 382 p. blue cloth. VG $20.00

FENN, George Manville. *Young Robin Hood.* 1898 London/NY. Ills Venner. 8vo. 72 p. VG $15.00

FENNELLY, Catherine. *Garb of Country New Englanders 1790-1840.* 1966 Ills. 8vo. 48 p. wraps. $10.00

FENNELLY, Catherine. *Life in Old New England Country Village.* 1969 NY. Ills 1st ed. 203 p. dj. $17.50

FENOLLOSA, Ernest F. *Epochs of Chinese & Japanese Art.* 1921 London. New Revised ed. 2 vol set. VG $120.00

FENOLLOSA, Mary. *Blossoms From a Japanese Garden.* 1913 NY. Stokes. Ills 1st ed. gray cloth. EX $50.00

FENTON, Carroll. *Our Amazing Earth.* 1943 Garden City. 346 p. maps. VG $8.00

FENTON, Richard. *Tour in Quest of Genealogy.* 1811 London. Ills. new cloth. VG $35.00

FENTON, Robert W. *Big Swingers: Biography of Edgar Rice Burroughs & Tarzan.* 1967 Prentice Hall. Ills. dj. EX $25.00

FERBER, Edna. *Cheerful by Request.* 1918 Doubleday. G $15.00

FERBER, Edna. *Cimarron.* 1930 NY. 1st ed. VG $6.00

FERBER, Edna. *Come & Get It.* 1935 Doubleday. Stated 1st ed. VG $10.00

FERBER, Edna. *Giant.* 1952 Doubleday. 1st ed. VG $20.00

FERBER, Edna. *Gigalo.* 1922 Doubleday. 1st ed. G $10.00

FERBER, Edna. *Ice Palace.* 1958 NY. 1st ed. dj. EX $12.00

FERBER, Edna. *Peculiar Treasure.* 1939 Doubleday. 1st ed. sgn. 398 p. $25.00

FERBER, Edna. *Peculiar Treasure.* 1940 NY. 398 p. $9.50

FERBER, Edna. *Show Boat.* 1926 NY. Doubleday. Ltd 1st ed. 1/201. sgn. EX $150.00

FERBER, Edna. *Show Boat.* 1926 Doubleday Page. Ltd ed. 1/1,000. presentation. $30.00

FERBER, Linda S. *New Path: Ruskin & American Pre-Raphaelities.* 1985 NY. Brooklyn Mus. 4to. 288 p. $30.00

FERGER, F. *Les Progres de l'Aviation.* 1905 Paris. 2nd ed. 53 p. wraps. G $25.00

FERGUSON, Robert. *Arctic Harpooner.* 1938 PA U Pr. 1st ed. dj. VG $35.00

FERGUSSON, E. *Dancing Gods: Indian Ceremonies of NM & AZ.* 1957 reprint of 1931. dj. VG $12.00

FERGUSSON, E. *Our Southwest.* 1941 2nd ed. dj. VG $10.00

FERGUSSON, Harvey. *Life of Riley.* 1937 NY. 1st ed. EX $17.00

FERGUSSON, James. *History of Modern Styles of Architecture.* 1891 London. Revised 3rd ed. 2 vol set. $40.00

FERGUSSON, Sir William. *System of Practical Surgery.* 1943 Phil. Ills 1st Am ed. 629 p. VG $65.00

FERLINGHETTI, Lawrence. *After the Cries of Birds.* 1967 San Francisco. 1st ed. wraps. EX $10.00

FERLINGHETTI, Lawrence. *Back Roads to Far Places.* 1971 New Directions. 1st ed. wraps. EX $15.00

FERLINGHETTI, Lawrence. *Mexican Night.* 1970 New Directions. 1st ed. wraps. EX $15.00

FERLINGHETTI, Lawrence. *Populist Manifesto.* 1981 San Francisco. 1st ed. wraps. EX $7.50

FERLINGHETTI, Lawrence. *Secret Meaning of Things.* 1968 New Directions. 1st ed. wraps. EX $20.00

FERLINGHETTI, Lawrence. *Starting From San Francisco.* 1961 New Directions. 1st ed. with record. VG $20.00

FERLINGHETTI, Lawrence. *Tyranus Nix.* 1969 NY. 1st ed. wraps. G $12.50

FERN, O'SULLIVAN, & HUGHES. *Complete Prints of Leonard Baskin: Catalogue Raisonne.* 1984 Boston. Ills. 4to. 304 p. cloth. dj. $60.00

FERNE, John. *Blazon of Gentrie.* 1586 London. Windet. Ills 1st ed. 12mo. $335.00

FERNOW, B. *NY in the Revolution. Vol. XV.* 1887 Albany. 4to. G $50.00

FERREE, Barr. *American Estates & Gardens.* 1906 NY. Munn. 306 p. green cloth. VG $100.00

FERRELL, Anderson. *Where She Was.* 1985 NY. 1st ed. dj. EX $15.00

FERRELL, Anderson. *Where She Was.* 1985 NY. Uncorrected proof. EX $30.00

FERRIS, C.D.; & BROWN, F.M. *Butterflies of Rocky Mountain States.* 1981 OK U Pr. Ills 1st ed. 442 p. dj. EX $40.00

FERRIS, H. *Girl Scout Short Stories.* 1926 Doubleday Page. Official GSA Pub. 1st ed. VG $16.00

FERRIS, Jacob. *States & Territories of the Great West.* 1856 NY. Ills. 12mo. 352 p. G $30.00

FERRO, R.; & GRUMLEY, M. *Atlantis: Autobiography of a Search.* 1970 NY. dj. VG $14.00

FETHERSTONHAUGH, R.C. *Royal Canadian Mounted Police.* 1940 Garden City. Ills. 294 p. maps. VG $8.50

FETSCHRIFT, Joseph Needham. *Explorations in History of Science & Technology in China.* 1982 Shanghai. Ills. cloth. $52.00

FETTER, R. *Mountain Men of WY.* 1982 Johnson. Ills. 60 p. pb. EX $7.00

FEUCHTERSLEBEN, Ernst. *Health & Suggestion.* 1910 NY. Trans Lewisohn. 1st ed. G $15.00

FEYRER, Ernest C. *Call of the Soul.* 1926 198 p. dj. VG $18.00

FICKE, Arthur D. *Mountain Against Mountain.* 1929 NY. 1st ed. inscr. VG $15.00

FIEDLER, Arkady. *Squadron 303.* 1943 NY. Ills 1st ed. photos. 182 p. G $65.00

FIEDLER, H.G. *Oxford Book of German Verse.* 1911 Oxford U Pr. inscr. German text. G $5.00

FIELD, Eugene. *Christmas Tales & Verse.* 1912 NY. Scribner. Ills Storer. 8vo. EX $30.00

FIELD, Eugene. *Echoes From Sabine Farm.* 1893 Chicago. Ltd ed. 1/500. $75.00

FIELD, Eugene. *House.* 1896 NY. Scribner. 1st ed. VG $65.00

FIELD, Eugene. *Little Book of Tribune Verse.* 1901 Denver. 1st ed. 1/750. VG $25.00

FIELD, Eugene. *Little Book of Western Verse.* 1890 NY. $25.00

FIELD, Eugene. *Love Affairs of a Bibliomaniac.* 1896 NY. 1st ed. 8vo. VG $35.00

FIELD, Eugene. *Love Affairs of a Bibliomaniac.* 1903 NY. 253 p. cloth. $10.00

FIELD, Eugene. *Poems of Childhood.* 1904 NY. Ills Parrish. 1st ed. 199 p. G $75.00

FIELD, Eugene. *Sugar Plum Tree & Other Verses.* 1930 Saalfield. Ills FB Peat. 1st ed. VG $38.00

FIELD, Eugene. *Tribune Primer.* 1900 Boston. Ills JC Frohn. VG $30.00

FIELD, Henry M. *History of Atlantic Telegraph.* 1866 NY. Scribner. Ills 1st ed. 364 p. VG $50.00

FIELD, Henry M. *Story of the Atlantic Telegraph.* 1893 NY. Scribner. Ills. 415 p. xl. $40.00

FIELD, Louise A. *Peter Rabbit & His Pa.* c 1916. Saalfield. Ills Albert. VG $15.00

FIELD, M.C. *Prairie & Mountain Sketches.* 1957 OK U Pr. Ills 1st ed. 236 p. dj. EX $45.00

FIELD, Rachel. *All Through the Night.* 1940 NY. Ills 1st ed. 24mo. dj. G $15.00

FIELD, Rachel. *American Folk & Fairy Tales.* 1929 NY. Scribner. Ills Margaret Freeman. 302 p. $40.00

FIELD, Rachel. *Calico Bush.* 1931 NY. Ills Lewis. presentation. G $65.00

FIELD, Rachel. *Pointed People.* 1930 NY. New ed. 12mo. inscr. VG $60.00

FIELD, Robert D. *Art of Walt Disney.* 1942 NY. 4to. cloth. VG $100.00

FIELD, S. *Personal Reminiscences of Early Days in CA.* 1893 no place. 2nd ed. VG $100.00

FIELDER, Mildred. *Sioux Indian Leaders.* 1975 Superior. Ills 1st ed. 4to. dj. EX $16.00

FIELDING, Henry. *Adventures of Joseph Andrews.* 1931 Boston. Bibliophile Soc. 2 vol set. VG $30.00

FIELDING, Henry. *Adventures of Joseph Andrews.* 1749 London. 2 vol set. full leather. VG $155.00

FIELDING, Henry. *Adventures of Joseph Andrews.* 1832 London. Ills Cruikshank. full leather. $60.00

FIELDING, Henry. *Fielding's Novels.* 1926 London. Shakespeare Head Pr. 1/520. VG $225.00

FIELDING, Henry. *History of Tom Jones.* 1749 London. 4 vol set. rebound. $150.00

FIELDING, Henry. *Miscellanies & Poems Edited by James P. Browne, M.D.* 1872 London. 1st ed. leather. G $40.00

FIELDING, Henry. *Tom Jones.* 1931 Ltd Ed Club. Ills Alex King. 1/1,500. sgn. $20.00

FIELDING, Henry. *Works of Henry Fielding.* 1771 London. 12 vol set. full leather. $225.00

FIELDING, Sarah. *Governess; or, Little Female Academy.* 1968 facsmile of 1749. dj. EX $20.00

FIELDING, T.H. *Art of Engraving, Etching, & Lithography.* 1844 London. ½-sheepskin. $125.00

FILIPPINI, Alexander. *International Cookbook.* 1906 NY. 4to. 1,059 p. red cloth. G $40.00

FILISOLA. *Evacuation of TX.* 1965 Waco. Texian Pr. dj. EX $15.00

FILLEY, William. *Life & Adventures of William Filley.* 1867 Chicago. Ills 2nd ed. rare. $200.00

FILLMORE, Myrtle. *Wee Wisdom's Way.* 1928 KS City. Ills Heitland. 6th ed. 8vo. VG $10.00

FILSTRUP, Chris & Janie. *Beadazzled: Story of Beads.* 1982 London/NY. Warne. Ills. 145 p. dj. $15.00

FINCH, Christopher. *Norman Rockwell's America.* 1975 Abrams. Ills Rockwell. 1st ed. 312 p. $65.00

FINDEN, E. *Landscape Illustrations of the Bible.* 1836 London. 4to. 2 vol set. ½-leather. $85.00

FINDLAY, Hugh. *Garden Making & Keeping.* 1928 NY. 252 p. VG $12.00

FINEY, Martha. *Elsie Dinsmore.* 1896 Burt. juvenile. $10.00

FINGER, C.J. *Give a Man a Horse.* 1938 Winston. Ills Henry Pitz. $12.50

FINGER, C.J. *Ozark Fantasia.* 1927 Golden Horseman. Ills. sgn. VG $10.00

FINK, Leo G. *Old Jesuit Trail in Penn's Forest.* 1933 NY. Paulist Pr. 8vo. 270 p. xl. VG $10.00

FINK, W.H. *Surgery of the Oblique Muscles of the Eye.* 1951 St. Louis. Ills 1st ed. 350 p. VG $55.00

FINKELSTEIN, Sidney. *Jazz: People's Music.* 1948 NY. Citadel. dj. VG $12.50

FINLEY, R.E. *Old Patchwork Quilts.* 1929 2nd imp. G $35.00

FINLEY, Rev. James. *Pioneer Life in the West.* 1854 2nd ed. VG $35.00

FINNEY, Charles G. *Circus of Dr. Lao.* 1982 NY. Ltd Ed Club. 1/2,000. sgn. $300.00

FINNEY, Charles G. *Circus of Dr. Lao.* 1935 Viking. 1st ed. dj. EX $75.00

FINNEY, Charles G. *Unholy City.* 1937 Vanguard. 1st ed. dj. EX $40.00

FINNIE, R. *Canol.* 1945 San Francisco. folio. $125.00

FINTA, Alex; & EATON, J. *Herd Boy of Hungary.* 1932 NY. Harper. Ills 1st ed. dj. VG $30.00

FINTON, Walter. *Alaskan Bear Adventures.* 1937 NY. Ryerson. 1st ed. presentation. sgn. VG $80.00

FIRBANK, Ronald. *Prancing Niger.* 1924 NY. Brentano. dj. EX $32.50

FIRBANK, Ronald. *Sorrow Sunlight.* 1925 London. 1st ed. 1/1,000. VG $45.00

FIRESIDE, Frank. *Lights & Shadows on the Wall: Political Celebrities.* c 1860. London. Ills. 4to. wraps. VG $45.00

FIRESTONE, Harvey. *Man on the Move: Story of Transportation.* 1967 Putnam. dj. VG $10.00

FIRMAN, Sidney G. *Winston Readers. 3rd Reader.* 1918 Phil. Winston. Ills Frederick Richardson. G $8.00

FIRSOFF, V.A. *On Foot in the Cairngorms.* 1965 Edinburgh. 1st ed. dj. VG $15.00

FIRSOFF, V.A. *Tatra Mountains.* no date. London. 1st ed. dj. VG $20.00

FISCHER, Erling Gunnar. *Peter Och Kajan Pa Lagresa.* 1946 Stockholm. Ills. 4to. Swedish text. VG $30.00

FISCHER, G. *Beethoven: Character Study.* 1905 NY. VG $25.00

FISCHER, J. *Discoveries of Norsemen in America.* 1970 NY. $15.00

FISCHER, Karl. *Die Wehrmacht.* 1941 Berlin. G $35.00

FISCHER, Martin. *Gracian's Manual.* 1939 Thomas. 4th ed. slipcase. dj. EX $12.00

FISH, Helen D. *Animals of American History.* 1939 Stokes. Ills Bransom. 1st ed. 4to. $20.00

FISH, R. *Assassination Bureau Limited.* 1963 NY. McGraw Hill. 1st ed. dj. EX $15.00

FISHBAUGH, Charles P. *From Paddle Wheels to Propellers: Howard Shipyard.* 1970 IN. VG $20.00

FISHBEIN, Morris. *Autobiography of Morris Fishbein.* 1969 Garden City. Doubleday. Ills 1st ed. 505 p. $10.00

FISHBEIN, Morris. *Fads & Quackery in Healing.* 1932 Blue Ribbon. VG $8.00

FISHBEIN, Morris. *Medical Follies.* 1925 Boni Liveright. VG $9.00

FISHBOUGH, William. *Macrocosm & Microcosm; or, Universe Without & Within.* 1852 176 p. G $65.00

FISHCHER, L.H. *Lincoln's Gadfly: Adam Gurowski.* 1964 OK U Pr. Ills 1st ed. 301 p. dj. EX $8.00

FISHER, Anne B. *Salinas River.* 1945 NY. Ltd 1st ed. sgn. dj. VG $45.00

FISHER, Bud. *Mutt & Jeff Cartoons.* 1910 Boston. $45.00

FISHER, D.C. *VT Tradition.* 1953 Boston. 485 p. dj. $7.50

FISHER, Douglas A. *Steel Serves the Nation 1901-1951.* 1951 NY. US Steel. Ills. 4to. 227 p. VG $20.00

FISHER, Harrison. *Bachelor Belles.* 1908 NY. Ills 1st ed. G $145.00

FISHER, Harrison. *Bachelor Belles.* 1908 Grosset Dunlap. 18 plts. VG $165.00

FISHER, Harrison. *Harrison Fisher Book.* 1908 NY. Scribner. Ills. G $150.00

FISHER, Irving. *Prohibition Still at Its Worst.* 1928 NY. 1st ed. $37.50

FROTHINGHAM, Richard. *Centennial: Battle of Bunker Hill.* 1875 Boston. Ills. 136 p. wraps. $75.00

FROTHINGHAM, Richard. *History of Seige of Boston & Battles of Lexington & Concord.* 1849 Boston. Ills 1st ed. maps. 359 p. $35.00

FROTHINGHAM, T.G. *George Washington: Commander in Chief.* 1930 Boston. Ills 1st ed. 389 p. dj. $17.50

FROUDE, J.A. *English Seamen in 16th Century.* 1901 London. G $18.00

FRY, Christopher. *Curtmantle.* 1961 NY. dj. M $11.00

FRY, Christopher. *Dark Is Light Enough.* 1954 NY. dj. EX $12.00

FRY, Christopher. *Dark Is Light Enough.* 1954 London. 1st ed. dj. VG $18.00

FRY, Christopher. *Root & Sky.* 1975 Boston. Ltd 1st ed. 1/220. boxed. EX $150.00

FRY, Christopher. *Transformation.* no date. (1926) NY. Ills. 4to. green cloth. VG $25.00

FRY, Christopher. *Venus Observed.* 1950 London. 1st ed. dj. VG $35.00

FRY, P.M. *Jefferson Hotel of Richmond, VA.* 1909 NY. Ills 1st ed. 16 p. wraps. $7.50

FRY, W.; & WHITE, J.R. *Big Trees.* 1945 Stanford U Pr. Ills. 126 p. VG $10.00

FRY. *Word to Women.* 1840 Phil. 1st Am ed. cloth. VG $125.00

FUCHIDA & OKUMIYA. *Midway: Battle That Doomed Japan.* 1955 Annapolis, MD. Ills 1st ed. 266 p. cloth. $35.00

FUCHS, Eduard. *Das Erotische Element in der Karikatur.* 1904 Berlin. Ills 1st ed. 4to. 264 p. $150.00

FUCHS, Eduard. *Geschichte der Erotischen Kunst.* 1912 Munich. VG $35.00

FUCHS, Eduard; & KRAEMER, H. *Die Karikatur der Europaischen volker vom Altertum.* 1901 Berlin. Ills. 494 p. ½-leather. VG $55.00

FUCHS, Madeleine. *Sols & Carrelages Rustiques.* 1969 Paris. Massin. Ills. dj. $35.00

FUENTES, Carlos. *Distant Relations.* 1982 Farrar. 1st Am ed. dj. EX $15.00

FUENTES, Carlos. *Hydra Head.* 1978 NY. 1st ed. dj. M $12.00

FUENTES, Carlos. *La Muerte de Artemio Cruz.* 1983 Spanish text. pb. EX $7.50

FUENTES, Carlos. *Old Gringo.* 1985 NY. 1st Am ed. 199 p. dj. EX $8.50

FUENTES, Carlos. *Where the Air Is Clear.* 1960 NY. 1st ed. dj. EX $45.00

FUENTES, N. *Hemingway in Cuba.* 1984 Stuart. 1st ed. dj. EX $20.00

FUERMANN, George. *Reluctant Empire: Mind of TX.* 1957 Doubleday. 1st ed. dj. EX $20.00

FUERTES, L.A. *Book of Dogs.* 1919 WA. Ills 1st ed. 96 p. $7.50

FUESS, C.M. *Calvin Coolidge: Man From VT.* 1940 Boston. Ills 1st ed. 500 p. $25.00

FUGARD, Sheila. *Revolutionary Woman.* 1983 Braziller. 1st Am ed. dj. EX $15.00

FULBRIGHT, T. *Cow-Country Counselor.* 1968 NY. 1st ed. 196 p. dj. VG $10.00

FULD, M. *Flower Lore.* 1916 NY. 101 p. wraps. $12.00

FULDHEIM, Dorothy. *1,000 Friends.* 1974 NY. sgn. 183 p. dj. VG $8.00

FULFORD, Harry. *Potted Golf.* 1910 Glasgow. Ills 1st ed. 12mo. 148 p. VG $45.00

FULLAONDO, Juan D. *Le Pari de Chillida.* 1968 Paris. Derriere Le Miroir. wraps. $40.00

FULLER, Buckminster. *Dymaxion World of Buckminster Fuller.* 1973 NY. Anchor Books. G $10.00

FULLER, Buckminster. *Lord's Prayer.* 1975 Doubleday Page. 1st ed. 1st separate print. $135.00

FULLER, Buckminster. *9 Chains to the Moon.* 1938 Advance copy. dj. VG $50.00

FULLER, Buckminster. *9 Chains to the Moon.* 1938 Phil. 1st trade ed. $40.00

FULLER, J.C.F. *Armament & History.* 1946 London. 1st ed. VG $15.00

FULLER, J.F.C. *Armament & History.* 1945 NY. 1st Am ed. 207 p. VG $12.50

FULLER, J.F.C. *Decisive Battles: Their Influence on History & Civilization.* 1940 1st ed. 1,060 p. EX $45.00

FULLER, J.F.C. *Military History of Western World.* no date. NY. Minerva. 3 vol set. VG $45.00

FULLER, Jack. *Convergence.* 1982 Doubleday. 1st ed. dj. EX $20.00

FULLER, John G. *Day of St. Anthony's Fire.* 1968 NY. Macmillan. 1st ed. 310 p. dj. VG $10.00

FULLER, M.L. *Geology of Long Island.* 1914 WA. GPO. Ills. 4to. 231 p. $45.00

FULLER, M.W. *Story of Deerfield 1630-1930.* 1930 Brattleboro. Ills 1st ed. map. 48 p. cloth. $7.50

FULLER, Margaret. *Recollections of Richard F. Fuller.* 1926 Boston. private print. 102 p. $20.00

FULLER, Oliver. *History of Warwick, RI.* 1875 Providence. 1st ed. EX $45.00

FULLER, Richard E. *Chinese Snuff Bottles in the Seattle Art Museum.* 1970 Ills. spiral bdg. $8.50

FULLER, Roy. *That Distance Afternoon.* 1959 Macmillan. 1st Am ed. dj. EX $20.00

FULLER, T. *Harvard Has a Homicide.* 1936 NY. Triangle. dj. VG $10.00

FULLER, W.O. *Old Town by the Sea.* 1912 Portsmouth. Ills. 16 p. $6.00

FULLER. *Book of Friendly Giants.* 1914 Ills P Smith. 1st ed. VG $22.50

FULOP-MILLER, Rene. *Triumph Over Pain.* 1938 Literary Guild. dj. G $8.50

FULTON, E.G. *Vegetarian Cookbook: Substitutes for Flesh Foods.* 1914 Mountain View. 2nd ed. 12mo. 271 p. $25.00

FULTON, J.F.; & THOMPSON, E.H. *Benjamin Silliman: Pathfinder in American Science.* 1947 NY. Ills 1st ed. 294 p. VG $60.00

FULTON, John F. *Physiology of the Nervous System.* 1938 London. 675 p. $150.00

FULTON, John. *Harvey Cushing: Biography.* 1946 Charles Thomas. 1st ed. VG $16.50

FULTON, M.G. *Diary & Letters of Josiah Gregg.* 1941-1944. Norman, OK. 1st ed. 2 vol set. $50.00

FUMET, Stanislas. *Braque.* 1948 Paris/NY. Braun & Cie/Tudor. 4to. dj. $20.00

FUNDABURK & FOREMAN. *Sun Circles & Human Hands: Southeastern Indian Art & Hist.* 1968 3rd print. dj. EX $5.00

FUNKHOUSER, William D. *Wildlife in KY.* 1925 Frankfort. Ltd 1st ed. 1/1,000. EX $95.00

FURLONG, C.W. *Let 'Er Buck: Story of the Passing of the Old West.* 1921 NY. Putnam. Ills. 242 p. VG $15.00

FURMAN, Laura. *Shadow Line.* 1982 NY. Viking. 1st ed. dj. VG $15.00

FURMAN, Laura. *Tuxedo Park.* 1986 Summit. Advance copy. dj. EX $25.00

FURMAN, Laura. *Watch Time Fly.* 1985 NY. Viking. 1st ed. dj. VG $15.00

FURST, Herbert. *Decorative Art of Frank Brangwyn.* 1924 London. Lane/Bodley Head. Ills. 231 p. $85.00

FUTRELL, Robert F. *US Air Force in Korea 1950-1953.* 1961 NY. Ills 1st ed. 774 p. dj. VG $38.00

FUTSIAKA, K. *Police Jiu-Jitsu.* 1937 NY. Ills. VG $9.00

FYLEMAN, Rose. *Gay Go Up.* 1930 Doubleday. Ills Merwin. 1st ed. VG $20.00

FYNMORE, J. *Central Adirondacks: Picture Story.* 1955 Prospect, NY. Ills 1st ed. 100 p. dj. $10.00

G

GABRIELSON, I.N. *Wildlife Refuges.* 1943 Macmillan. Ills 1st ed. 257 p. maps. G $15.00

GADDIS, Thomas. *Birdman of Alcatraz.* 1955 NY. 1st ed. dj. VG $15.00

GAG, Wanda. *Millions of Cats.* 1928 NY. Ills. narrow oblong 8vo. VG $45.00

GAG, Wanda. *Tales From Grimm.* 1936 Coward McCann. 237 p. VG $8.00

GAGE, Mrs. Frances. *Elsie Magoon; or, Old Still-House in the Hollow.* 1867 Lippincott. 1st ed. G $12.00

GAGEY, E. *History of San Francisco Stage.* 1950 NY. Ills 1st ed. 264 p. dj. VG $22.50

GAGLIARDO, Ruth. *Let's Read Aloud.* 1962 Lippincott. Ills Angelo. 1st ed. 8vo. dj. $15.00

GAIDZAKIAN, Ohan. *Illustrated Armenia & the Armenians.* 1898 Boston. 1st ed. 8vo. VG $40.00

GAINES, F.P. *Background of Great Decision.* 1934 Lexington, VA. Ills 1st ed. wraps. $7.50

GALASSI, Peter. *Before Photography: Painting & Invention of Photography.* 1981 MOMA. Ills. 8vo. 152 p. wraps. $7.00

GALBREATH, Charles B. *History of OH.* 1925 Chicago. Ills. 4to. 4 vol set. VG $65.00

GALE, D.C. *Proctor: Story of Marble Town.* 1922 Brattleboro. Ills 1st ed. 259 p. $15.00

GALLAND, A. *1st & Last.* 1954 NY. 1st ed. dj. VG $37.50

GALLICO, Ludmila. *Story of Lichtenstein.* 1960 Vaduz. presentation. sgn. dj. EX $9.50

GALLICO, Paul. *Abandoned.* 1950 NY. 1st ed. dj. VG $17.50

GALLICO, Paul. *Abandoned.* 1953 Knopf. 4th ed. inscr. dj. VG $35.00

GALLICO, Paul. *Abandoned.* 1950 Knopf. 2nd ed. sgn. dj. VG $25.00

GALLICO, Paul. *Boy Who Invented Bubble Gum.* 1974 NY. 1st ed. dj. M $12.00

GALLICO, Paul. *Farewell to Sport.* 1945 Pocket. VG $7.50

GALLICO, Paul. *Golf Is a Friendly Game.* 1942 NY. 1st ed. dj. VG $45.00

GALLICO, Paul. *Hand of Mary Constable.* 1964 Garden City. 1st ed. dj. VG $35.00

GALLICO, Paul. *Hurricane Story.* 1959 London. 1st ed. dj. EX $15.00

GALLICO, Paul. *Jennie.* 1953 Michael Joseph. 12th print. dj. EX $15.00

GALLICO, Paul. *Ludmila.* 1960 Liechtenstein. G $12.50

GALLICO, Paul. *Ludmila.* 1960 Vaduz. juvenile. dj. VG $7.00

GALLICO, Paul. *Manxmouse.* 1968 NY dj. EX $12.00

GALLICO, Paul. *Matilda.* 1970 Coward McCann. 1st ed. dj. VG $12.50

GALLICO, Paul. *Mrs. 'Arris Goes to Paris.* 1958 NY. 1st ed. dj. M $14.00

GALLICO, Paul. *Mrs. 'Arris Goes to Parliament.* 1965 Doubleday. Ills Fiammenghi. 1st Am ed. EX $12.50

GALLICO, Paul. *Poseidon Adventure.* 1969 NY. 1st ed. dj. EX $12.00

GALLICO, Paul. *Thief Is an Ugly Word.* 1951 Dell. EX $25.00

GALLICO, Paul. *Zoo Gang.* 1971 Coward McCann. 1st Am ed. dj. VG $12.00

GALONIO, Antonio. *Tortures & Torments of Christian Martyrs.* no date. Paris. Fortune Pr. Ltd ed. 242 p. EX $45.00

GALSWORTHY, John & Ada. *Carmen: Opera in 4 Acts.* 1932 London. Ltd ed. 1/650. sgns. dj. VG $40.00

GALSWORTHY, John. *Flowering Wilderness.* 1932 London. Ltd ed. 1/400. sgn. VG $50.00

GALSWORTHY, John. *Flowering Wilderness.* 1932 NY. Scribner. 1st ed. EX $7.00

GALSWORTHY, John. *Fraternity.* 1909 NY. 1st ed. 3rd print. dj. VG $25.00

GALSWORTHY, John. *Jocelyn.* 1977 NY. 1st ed. dj. M $14.00

GALSWORTHY, John. *Maid in Waiting.* 1931 NY. 1st ed. dj. EX $17.00

GALSWORTHY, John. *Soames & the Flag.* 1930 Scribner. 1st ed. 1/680. sgn. EX $75.00

GALSWORTHY, John. *Swan Song.* 1928 London. Ltd 1st ed. sgn. $30.00

GALSWORTHY, John. *Swan Song.* 1928 NY. Scribner. 1st ed. dj. EX $20.00

GALSWORTHY, John. *White Monkey.* 1924 London. Ltd ed. 1/265. sgn. VG $22.00

GALSWORTHY, John. *Works of John Galsworthy.* 1922 NY. Scribner. Manaton ed. 1/780. 30 vol set. $300.00

GALSWORTHY, John. *1 More River.* 1933 NY. Scribner. 1st ed. EX $8.00

GALSWORTHY, John. *2 Forsyte Interludes.* 1928 NY. 1st Am ed. VG $10.00

GALT, John. *Bachelor's Wife.* 1824 Edinburgh/ London. 1st ed. VG $95.00

GALT, John. *Works of John Galt.* 1895 Blackwood. 1st ed. 8 vol set. scarce. EX $100.00

GALTON, Francis. *Fingerprints.* 1892 London. Macmillan. 1st ed. 8vo. 216 p. $400.00

GALTON, Francis. *Hereditary Genius: Inquiry into Laws & Consequences.* 1871 NY. Appleton. 2nd Am ed. 390 p. $70.00

GALTON, Francis. *Natural Inheritance.* 1889 London. Macmillan. 1st ed. 259 p. G $45.00

GALVIN, John. *Record of Travels in AZ & CA 1775-1776.* 1965 San Francisco. Ltd ed. 1/1,250. EX $50.00

GAMBLE, F.W. *Flatworms & Mesozoa.* 1896 Macmillan. Ills. 560 p. $8.00

GAMBLE, T. *Savannah: City of Opportunity.* 1904 GA. Ills 1st ed. 60 p. wraps. $20.00

GAMBRILL & MACKENZIE. *Sporting Stables & Kennels.* 1935 NY. Appleton. Ltd ed. 1/950. red cloth. G $150.00

GAMMELL, W. *Address on Opening of New RI Historical Headquarters.* 1844 28 p. wraps. $6.50

GAMMOND, Peter. *Musical Instruments in Color.* NY. Macmillan. Ills R Bird. 1st Am ed. dj. EX $12.00

GAMONEDA, E. *Monumentos Arquitectonicos de Espana.* 1905 Madrid. Ills. 456 p. G $55.00

GANDHI, Mahatma. *All Men Are Brothers: Life & Thoughts of Mahatma Gandhi.* 1958 196 p. VG $15.00

GANDHI, Mahatma. *Sermon on the Sea.* 1924 Chicago. 1st ed. EX $10.00

GANN, Ernest K. *Aviator.* 1981 Arbor House. 1st ed. dj. VG $10.00

GANN, Ernest K. *Blaze of Noon.* 1946 NY. 310 p. VG $5.00

GANN, Ernest K. *Flying Circus.* 1974 Macmillan. 1st ed. dj. VG $45.00

GANN, Ernest K. *Twilight for the Gods.* 1956 NY. 1st ed. dj. VG $17.50

GANN, T.W.F. *Maya Indians.* 1918 GPO. Ills. G $50.00

GANN, W.D. *Tunnel Through the Air.* 1927 NY. 1st ed. VG $20.00

GANO, H. *Souvenir: Past, Present, & Future Presidents.* 1904 Louisville. Ills 1st ed. 32 p. wraps. $5.00

GANS-RUEDIN, Erwin. *Connoisseur's Guide to Oriental Carpets.* 1971 Rutland/Tokyo. Tuttle. 431 p. dj. $125.00

GANS-RUEDIN, Erwin. *Indian Carpets.* 1984 NY. Rizzoli. Ills. oblong 4to. dj. $60.00

GANSON, Dai Vernon. *Inner Secrets of Card Magic.* 1959 Devon. 8vo. 76 p. dj. $15.00

GANTZ, C.O. *Naturalist in Southern FL.* 1972 Miami U Pr. Ills. inscr. dj. VG $18.00

GARAGIOLA, Joe. *Baseball Is a Funny Game.* 1960 Lippincott. dj. VG $12.00

GARAVAGLIA, Niny. *Complete Paintings of Mantegna.* 1967 NY. 1st ed. VG $25.00

GARBER, J.P. *Valley, DE & Its Place in American History.* 1934 Phil. Ills 1st ed. 40 p. $25.00

GARBERI, Mercedes P. *Frescoes From Venetian Villas.* 1971 NY. Phaidon. Ills. 4to. 514 p. dj. $125.00

GARD, W. *Chisholm Trail.* 1954 OK U Pr. Ills 1st ed. dj. EX $30.00

GARD, W. *Chisholm Trail.* 1954 OK U Pr. Ills 2nd print. 296 p. dj. VG $23.00

GARD, W. *Great Buffalo Hunt.* 1960 Knopf. Ills. 324 p. VG $10.00

GARDINER, Allen F. *Visit to Indians on Frontiers of Chili.* 1841 London. Seeley. 1st ed. 194 p. cloth. $125.00

GARDINER, C.H. *Prescott & His Publishers.* 1959 Southern IL U Pr. 1st ed. dj. $15.00

GARDINER, Dorothy. *West of the River.* 1941 NY. Ills 1st ed. dj. VG $20.00

GARDINER, G. *Greenhouse Gardening.* 1968 NY. 214 p. dj. G $8.00

GARDINER & WALKER. *Raymond Chandler Speaking.* 1962 Boston. 1st Am ed. dj. EX $50.00

GARDNER, Albert Ten Eyck. *History of Watercolor Painting in America.* 1966 Reinhold. Ills 1st ed. dj. EX $50.00

GARDNER, Albert Ten Eyck. *Winslow Homer, American Artist: His World & His Work.* 1961 NY. Bramhall House. 4to. dj. $30.00

GARDNER, Arthur. *English Medieval Sculpture.* 1973 Hacker. 4to. $25.00

GARDNER, Augustus K. *Causes & Curative Treatment of Sterility.* 1856 NY. Ills T Sinclair. cloth. $75.00

GARDNER, Charles. *William Blake: The Man.* 1919 London. Ills 1st ed. VG $15.00

GARDNER, D.P. *Farmer's Dictionary.* 1846 NY. 1st ed. sgn Levi Lincoln. $50.00

GARDNER, E.S. *Case of the Silent Partner.* 1940 NY. Morrow. 1st ed. dj. VG $40.00

GARDNER, E.S. *Hunting the Desert Whale.* 1963 London. Ills 1st ed. dj. VG $15.00

GARDNER, E.S. *Neighborhood Frontiers.* 1954 Morrow. Ills. 272 p. dj. EX $18.00

GARDNER, F. *Life & Death of San in VA.* 1856 Richmond. Morris. 308 p. scarce. $65.00

GARDNER, G. *Shining Moments of John F. Kennedy.* 1964 Ills 1st ed. 96 p. $5.00

GARDNER, John. *Art of Living.* 1981 NY. 1st ed. dj. M $12.00

GARDNER, John. *Art of Living.* 1981 London. 1st ed. dj. VG $15.00

GARDNER, John. *For Services Rendered.* 1982 London. 1st ed. dj. EX $12.50

GARDNER, John. *For Special Services.* 1982 Coward McCann. Review copy. dj. EX $35.00

GARDNER, John. *For Special Services.* 1982 Coward McCann. 1st Am ed. dj. VG $12.50

GARDNER, John. *Freddy's Book.* 1980 Knopf. 1st ed. dj. EX $22.50

GARDNER, John. *Freddy's Book.* 1981 Secker Warburg. 1st English ed. dj. EX $15.00

GARDNER, John. *Icebreaker.* 1983 Putnam. 1st Am ed. dj. VG $12.50

GARDNER, John. *Icebreaker.* 1983 London. 1st ed. dj. EX $12.00

GARDNER, John. *In Suicide Mountains.* 1977 Knopf. 1st ed. dj. VG $45.00

GARDNER, John. *King of the Hummingbirds.* 1977 Knopf. 1st ed. dj. EX $45.00

GARDNER, John. *King's Indian.* 1975 London. 1st ed. dj. M $20.00

GARDNER, John. *King's Indian.* 1974 NY. 1st Am ed. sgn. dj. EX $55.00

GARDNER, John. *Life & Times of Chaucer.* 1977 Knopf. 1st ed. dj. EX $30.00

GARDNER, John. *Mickelsson's Ghosts.* 1982 NY. 1st ed. 590 p. dj. EX $20.00

GARDNER, John. *Mickelsson's Ghosts.* 1982 Knopf. proof. wraps. $45.00

GARDNER, John. *Nickel Mountain.* 1973 NY. 1st ed. dj. VG $12.00

GARDNER, John. *Nickel Mountain.* 1973 NY. Knopf. 1st ed. dj. EX $15.00

GARDNER, John. *Nobody Lives Forever.* 1986 Putnam. 1st Am ed. dj. EX $15.00

GARDNER, John. *October Light.* 1976 NY. 1st ed. sgn. dj. EX $75.00

GARDNER, John. *October Light.* 1976 NY. 1st ed. dj. EX $55.00

GARDNER, John. *October Light.* 1976 NY. proof. sgn. wraps. M $160.00

GARDNER, John. *On Moral Fiction.* 1977 NY. 1st ed. dj. EX $12.50

GARDNER, John. *Poems.* 1978 NY. Ltd ed. 1/300. sgn. EX $40.00

GARDNER, John. *Role of Honor.* 1984 Putnam. 1st Am ed. dj. VG $12.50

GARDNER, John. *Stillness & Shadows.* 1986 Knopf. 1st ed. dj. EX $19.00

GARDNER, John. *Sunlight Dialogues.* 1972 Knopf. 1st ed. dj. VG $55.00

GARDNER, John. *Sunlight Dialogues.* 1973 Cape. 1st English ed. dj. EX $45.00

GARDNER, John. *Sunlight Dialogues.* 1977 Knopf. VG $10.00

GARDNER, John. *Wreckage of Agathon.* 1970 NY. 1st ed. dj. VG $65.00

GARDNER, Leonard. *Fat City.* 1969 NY. 1st ed. dj. EX $25.00

GARDNER, M. *Journey to Earth's Interior.* 1920 Aurora, IL. VG $40.00

GARDNER, William James. *History of Jamaica From Its Discovery to 1872.* 1909 NY. Appleton. fld map. 510 p. cloth. $50.00

GAREISSEN, M.F. *Little Sketches & Glimpses of Our National Capital.* 1907 Baltimore. Ills 1st ed. 74 p. $20.00

GARFIELD, Brian. *Death Sentence.* 1975 1st Am ed. dj. EX $25.00

GARFIELD, James A. *Wild Life of the Army: Civil War Letters.* 1964 MI State U Pr. Ills. blue cloth. dj. VG $15.00

GARFIELD, V.E.; & FORREST, L. *Wolf & the Raven: Totem Poles of Southeastern AK.* 1971 WA U Pr. 6th imp. 150 p. wraps. VG $15.00

GARGIA MARQUEZ, G. *Cien Anos de Soledad.* 1985 Oveja Negra. Spanish text. pb. EX $7.50

GARIS, Howard. *Curly Tops at Cherry Farm.* 1918 Cupples Leon. Ills J Greene. VG $8.50

GARIS, Howard. *Uncle Wiggily & His Friends.* c 1955. NY. Platt Munk. Ills. VG $25.00

GARIS, Howard. *Uncle Wiggily & His Friends.* 1939 Platt Munk. Ills G Carlson. 8vo. 93 p. dj. $10.50

GARIS, Howard. *Uncle Wiggily & the Black Cricket.* 1943 Ills Stover. 4to. wraps. EX $8.00

GARIS, Howard. *Uncle Wiggily & the Littletails.* 1942 NY. Platt Munk. Ills. G $16.00

GARIS, Howard. *Uncle Wiggily & the Milkman.* 1943 Ills M&W Stover. wraps. EX $8.00

GARIS, Roger. *My Father Was Uncle Wiggily.* 1966 McGraw Hill. 1st ed. 8vo. 217 p. dj. EX $20.00

GARLAND, Hamlin. *Afternoon Neighbors.* 1934 NY. 1st ed. dj. VG $10.00

GARLAND, Hamlin. *Back Trailers From the Middle Border.* 1928 NY. 1st ed. sgn. VG $25.00

GARLAND, Hamlin. *Book of the American Indian.* 1923 Harper. Ills Remington. 1st ed. 274 p. $150.00

GARLAND, Hamlin. *Book of the American Indian.* 1923 Harper. Ills Remington. 1st ed. G $60.00

GARLAND, Hamlin. *Boy's Life on the Prairie.* 1899 NY. Ills 1st ed. VG $37.50

GARLAND, Hamlin. *My Friendly Contemporaries.* 1932 Macmillan. Ills Constance Garland. dj. G $30.00

GARLAND, Hamlin. *Roadside Meetings.* 1931 Macmillan. Ills Garland. dj. G $30.00

GARLAND, Hamlin. *Son of the Middle Border.* 1917 NY. 1st ed. 467 p. $10.00

GARLAND, Hamlin. *Under the Wheel: Modern Play in 6 Scenes.* 1890 Boston. Barta Pr. 8vo. wraps. VG $150.00

GARLAND, Hamlin. *Wayside Courtships.* 1897 NY. Ills Deming. 1st ed. VG $40.00

GARLAND, Hamlin. *40 Years of Psychic Reasearch.* 1936 NY. 1st ed. VG $35.00

GARLAND, Joseph. *Story of Medicine.* 1949 Houghton Mifflin. VG $10.00

GARNER, Alan. *Alan Garner's Book of British Fairy Tales.* 1984 1st Am ed. dj. EX $12.00

GARNER, Elvira. *Ezekiel.* 1937 NY. Ills 1st ed. dj. EX $50.00

GARNER, Philippe. *Emille Galle.* 1984 St. Martin. Ills. 4to. 167 p. dj. $30.00

GARNER, Philippe. *World of Edwardiana.* 1974 London/NY. Hamlyn. Ills. dj. $35.00

GARNER, R.L. *Apes & Monkeys: Their Life & Language.* 1900 Ginn. Ills 1st ed. 297 p. cloth. EX $23.00

GARNER & STRATTON. *Domestic Architecture of England During the Tudor Period.* 1911 London. 1st ed. 2 vol set. VG $150.00

GARNETT, A. Campbell. *Instinct & Personality.* 1928 London. sgn. dj. G $45.00

GARNETT, Christopher Browne. *Taste.* 1968 NY. 1st ed. dj. EX $14.00

GARNETT, David. *Familiar Faces.* 1963 Harcourt. 1st Am ed. dj. VG $10.00

GARNETT, David. *Lady into Fox & Man in the Zoo.* 1946 Penguin. VG $10.00

GARNETT, David. *Lady into Fox.* 1945 Armed Services. VG $20.00

GARNETT, David. *Letters of T.E. Lawrence.* 1927 NY. 1st ed. dj. VG $40.00

GARNETT, Louis Ayres. *Merrymakers.* 1918 Rand McNally. Ills McCraken. 1st ed. cloth. $40.00

GARNETT, Porter. *Green Knight.* 1909 San Francisco. Bohemian Club. presentation. $40.00

GARNETT, Richard; & GOSSE, E. *English Literature: Illustrated Record.* 1903 NY/London. only ed. 4 vol set. VG $55.00

GARNIER, Edouard. *Soft Porcelain of Serves.* 1892 London. Ills. folio. ½-morocco. $600.00

GARON, Marco. *Black Sport.* 1951 Warren. VG $15.00

GARON, Marco. *Fire Tribes.* no date. Warren. VG $25.00

GARRARD. *Running Away with Nebby.* 1944 McKay. Ills Pogany. 1st ed. G $10.00

GARREAN-DOMBASLE, Man'Ha. *Aztlan: Songes Mexicans.* 1952 Paris. Ills Tamayo. Ltd ed. 1/125. EX $700.00

GARRETT, A. *History of Wood Engraving.* 1986 London. Ills. 404 p. $35.00

GARRETT, E.H. *Pilgrim Shore of MA Coast.* 1902 Boston. Ills 1st ed. 234 p. $12.50

GARRETT, E.H. *Romance & Reality of Puritan Coast.* 1897 Boston. Ills 1st ed. 221 p. $15.00

GARRETT, Eileen J. *Many Voices.* 1968 NY. 252 p. dj. EX $11.00

GARRETT, George. *King of the Mountain.* 1957 NY. Scribner. 1st ed. sgn. dj. VG $25.00

GARRETT, P.F. *Authentic Life of Billy the Kid.* 1946 Atomic Books. 128 p. wraps. VG $5.00

GARRETT, P.F. *Authentic Life of Billy the Kid.* 1980 Time Life. reprint of 1882. leather. EX $20.00

GARRETT, Randall. *Pagan Passions.* 1959 Galaxy Beacon. VG $30.00

GARRETT, Randall. *Takeoff!* 1980 Donning. EX $6.00

GARRICK, David. *Pineapples of Finest Flavor.* 1930 Cambridge. Harvard U Pr. Ltd ed. 1/400. $35.00

GARRISON, Fielding Hudson. *William MacMichael: The Gold-Headed Cane.* 1827 London. Murray. Ills Brooke. 1st ed. calf. $450.00

GARRISON, Omar V. *Lost Gems of Secret Knowledge.* 1973 252 p. dj. EX $22.00

GARRISON, W.L. *Writings & Speeches.* 1852 Boston. inscr. cloth. $60.00

GARRY, Margaret. *Legendary Tales.* 1858 London. 1st & only ed. ¾-calf. EX $110.00

GARSIDE, J.T. *Old English Furniture. Division I: Oak Period 1500-1630.* 1924 NY/London. Ills. photos. VG $60.00

GARSON, Helen. *Truman Capote.* 1980 Ungar. 1st ed. pb. wraps. EX $10.00

GARTNER, J. *All About Pickup Campers, Van Conversions, & Motor Homes.* 1969 CA. Ills 1st ed. 224 p. wraps. $5.00

GARWOOD, D. *Artist in IA.* 1944 NY. 1st ed. dj. VG $20.00

GARY, Romain. *European Education.* 1960 NY. 1st ed. dj. M $12.00

GARY, Romain. *Promise at Dawn.* 1961 NY. 1st ed. dj. EX $18.00

GASCOIGNE, Bamber. *World Theatre: Illustrated History by Bamber Gascoigne.* 1968 Boston. 1st ed. dj. EX $20.00

GASH, Jonathan. *Gondola Scam: Lovejoy Narrative.* 1984 London. 1st ed. sgn. dj. EX $27.00

GASH, Jonathan. *Sleepers of Erin.* 1983 London. 1st ed. dj. EX $22.00

GASKELL, G.A. *How To Write for the Press.* 1884 NY. Penman Gazette. 1st ed. 152 p. $18.00

GASPER, Howland. *Complete Sportsman.* 1893 NY. Forest & Stream. 1st ed. 8vo. $35.00

GASQUE, Jim. *Bass Fishing: Techniques, Tactics, & Tales.* 1945 Knopf. Ills 1st ed. 204 p. dj. EX $14.00

GASS, William. *Habitations of the Word.* 1985 Simon Schuster. 1st ed. dj. EX $20.00

GASS, William. *In the Heart of the Country.* 1968 NY. Harper. Advance copy. M $45.00

GASS, William. *Omensetter's Luck.* 1966 NY. 1st ed. dj. EX $65.00

GASS, William. *Willie Master's Lonesome Wife.* 1971 NY. Knopf. M $25.00

GASS, William. *1st Winter of My Married Life.* Lord John. Ltd 1st ed. 1/275. sgn. EX $75.00

GASSER, H. *Casein Painting: Methods & Demonstrations.* 1950 NY. Watson Guptill. 1st ed. 4to. $22.50

GASSON, Roy. *Illustrated Lewis Carroll.* 1978 London. Jupiter. 1st print. dj. EX $10.00

GAST, R. *Hibiscus Around the World.* 1980 FL. 140 p. VG $6.00

GATES, Charles. *5 Fur Traders of the Northwest.* 1965 St. Paul. MN Historical Soc. dj. EX $20.00

GATES, Doris. *Blue Willow.* 1981 NY. Viking. Ills P Lantz. reprint. dj. EX $15.00

GATES, Josephine. *Little Girl Blue.* 1910 Houghton Mifflin. 1st ed. VG $10.00

GATES, Josephine. *Story of Live Dolls.* 1901 Indianapolis. Ills V Keeps. VG $27.50

GATES, Susa Young. *Life Story of Bringham Young.* 1931 NY. 2nd print. 388 p. VG $40.00

GATES, Susa Young. *Life Story of Bringham Young.* 1930 London. VG $15.00

GATTI, Attilio. *Killers All!* 1943 McBride. Ills 1st ed. 245 p. dj. VG $11.50

GATTI, Attilio. *King of the Gorillas.* 1932 Garden City. Ills 1st ed. 254 p. VG $10.00

GATTI, Attilio. *South of the Sahara.* 1945 McBride. Ills 1st ed. 266 p. VG $15.00

GATTY, Mrs. Alfred. *Parables From Nature.* 1881 London. 2 vols. fore-edge paintings. EX $750.00

GAUDREAU, Leo. *Anvils, Horseshoes, & Cannons: History of Strongmen.* 1975 East Kingston. private print. 1st ed. 4to. EX $35.00

GAUGUIN, Emil. *Intimate Journals.* 1936 Crown. Trans Van Wyck Brooks. VG $12.50

GAULT, W.P. *OH at Vicksburg.* 1906 Columbus. Ills 1st ed. 374 p. G $45.00

GAUNT, W. *Etchings of Frank Bragwyn.* 1924 London. Ltd ed. 1/125. 4to. VG $375.00

GAUSE, G.F. *Search for New Antibiotics.* 1960 Yale. G $7.50

GAUTHIER, Joseph. *Le Mobilier des Vielles Provinces de France.* no date. Paris. Massin. Ills. 221 p. $65.00

GAUTHIER, S. *Bretons.* no date. Paris. Massin. Ills. dj. $45.00

GAUTIER, E.F. *Sahara, the Great Desert.* 1935 Columbia U Pr. Revised ed. 264 p. fld map. EX $18.00

GAUTINGER, George. *How To Ski.* 1936 NY. Ills. 12mo. 79 p. $25.00

GAVIN, Angus. *Wildlife of the North Slope: 5 Year Study 1969-1973.* 1974 photos Steven C Wilson. 67 p. $10.00

GAVIN, Anthony. *Great Red Dragon; or, Master Key to Popery.* 1854 Boston. 1st ed. 408 p. G $27.00

GAY, John. *Beggar's Opera.* 1937 Heritage. 4to. with music. slipcase. EX $15.00

GAY, John. *Fables.* 1792 1 vol ed. tree calf. VG $125.00

GAY, S.H. *James Madison.* 1898 Boston. 324 p. cloth. $8.00

GAYE, Selina. *World's Lumber Room.* 1885 Cassell. G $15.00

GEARY, Edward R. *Depredations & Massacre by the Snake River Indians.* 1861 WA. 1st ed. 8vo. 16 p. wraps. $200.00

GEDALGE, Andre. *Traite de la Fugue.* c 1900. Paris. 4to. 379 p. G $45.00

GEDALOF, Robin. *Paper Stays Put.* 1980 Hurtig, CA. cloth. VG $10.00

GEDDES, D.P. *Franklin Delano Roosevelt: A Memorial.* 1945 NY. Ills. 218 p. dj. $6.00

GEE, Ernest. *Meynellian Science.* 1926 Derrydale. Ltd ed. 1/28. EX $1450.00

GEE, Harry. *Saxophone Soloists & Their Music.* 1986 IN U Pr. EX $12.00

GEER. *Beyond the Lines; or, Yankee Prisoner Loose in Dixie.* 1863 Phil. VG $30.00

GEFFROY, Gustave. *Les Gobelins.* no date. Paris. Ills. 162 p. maroon cloth. $125.00

GEHMAN, Dr. Jesse Mercer. *Smoke Over America.* 1943 Roycroft. inscr. $25.00

GEIGER, Maynard. *Life & Times of Father Serra.* 1959 WA. 1st ed. sgn. 2 vol set. EX $120.00

GEIJER, Agnes. *History of Textile Art.* 1979 London. Wilson. Ills. 317 p. dj. $37.50

GEIST, Valerius. *Mountain Sheep: Study in Behavior & Evolution.* 1974 Chicago U Pr. Ills. 383 p. dj. EX $18.50

GELDARD, James. *Handbook of Cotton Manufacture.* 1867 NY. Ills 1st ed. 8vo. 298 p. $50.00

GELLENS, R.J. *Freer Chinese Bronzes.* 1969 Smithsonian. Oriental Studies #7. dj. EX $30.00

GELLER, Stephen. *She Let Him Continue.* 1966 NY. 1st ed. dj. VG $40.00

GEMMILL, C.; & JONES, M. *Pharmacology at University of VA School of Medicine.* 1966 inscr Gemmill. M $12.50

GENAILLE, Robert. *La Peinture dans les Anciens Pays-Bas de Van Eyck a Bruegel.* 1954 Bruxelles. 1st ed. dj. VG $50.00

GENAUER, Emily. *Modern Interiors: Today & Tomorrow.* 1939 NY. Ills. photos. VG $40.00

GENET, Jean. *Balcony.* 1958 London. 1st English ed. dj. VG $50.00

GENET, Jean. *Balcony.* 1958 NY. Grove. 1st Am ed. 1/26. sgn. EX $650.00

GENET, Jean. *Funeral Rites.* 1969 Grove. 1st Am ed. dj. EX $20.00

GENET, Jean. *Miracle of the Rose.* 1966 Grove. 1st Am ed. dj. VG $20.00

GENET, Jean. *Thief's Journal.* 1964 Grove. dj. EX $10.00

GENIN, Thomas H. *Selections From Writings of Late Thomas H. Genin.* 1869 NY. sgn. $25.00

GENT, Peter. *TX Celebrity Turkey Trot.* 1978 Morrow. 1st ed. dj. VG $8.00

GENT, R.G. *Brief & True Report for Traveler Concerning Williamsburg.* 1936 Richmond. 1st ed. 192 p. leather. $12.50

GENT, W.H. *Road to OR.* 1934 NY. Ills. 274 p. $10.00

GENTHE, A.; & IRWIN, W. *Pictures of Old China Town.* 1908 NY. Moffat. 1st ed. cloth. xl. VG $85.00

GENTHE, A.; & IRWIN, W. *Pictures of Old Chinatown.* 1908 NY. G $40.00

GENTHE, Arnold. *As I Remember.* 1936 NY. Ills Genthe. Ltd ed. 1/250. VG $140.00

GENTHE, Arnold. *As I Remember.* 1936 NY. 1st ed. VG $60.00

GENTHE, Arnold. *As I Remember.* 1946 NY. 2nd print. VG $40.00

GENTHE, Arnold. *Impressions of Old New Orleans.* 1926 NY. Doran. 1st ed. 4to. cloth. EX $75.00

GEORGE, Margaret. *Autobiography of Henry VIII.* 1986 St. Martin. Review copy. wraps. EX $10.00

GEORGE, N.J.T. *Gentlemen & Ladies' Pocket Dictionary.* 1831 Concord. 16mo. $60.00

GEORGE, Uwe. *In the Deserts of This Earth.* 1977 Harcourt Brace. Ills. 307 p. VG $14.00

GERBER, Will. *Judishus.* 1945 Hebberd. Ills GD Mack. 1st ed. 8vo. EX $15.00

GERBING, G.C. *Camellias.* 1943 Fernandina, FL. plts. VG $22.00

GERDTS, William H. *Washington Allston, Man of Genius 1779-1843.* 1979 Boston. Museum Fine Arts. 255 p. dj. $35.00

GERE, Charlotte. *Victorian Jewelry Design.* 1973 Chicago. Regnery. Ills. 285. $40.00

GERGER, Thomas. *Reinhart's Women.* 1981 Delacorte. 1st ed. dj. EX $15.00

GERHART, E.C. *America's Advocate: Robert Jackson.* 1958 Indianapolis. dj. G $20.00

GERHART, Genevra. *Russian's World, Life, & Language.* 1974 NY. 257 p. $8.00

GERLING, Curt. *Smugtown, USA.* 1957 2nd ed. sgn. 201 p. dj. VG $15.00

GERNSBACK, Hugo. *Ralph 124C 41+: Romance of the Year 2660.* 1925 Boston. Stratford. 1st ed. blue cloth. $125.00

GERNSHEIM, H. *Alvin Langdon Coburn, Photographer: Autobiography.* 1966 London. 1st ed. dj. EX $50.00

GERNSHEIM, H. *Concise History of Photography.* 1965 Grosset Dunlap. 1st Am ed. wraps. VG $35.00

GERNSHEIM, H. *Concise History of Photography.* 1965 London. Thames Hudson. dj. EX $35.00

GERNSHEIM, H. *History of Photography.* 1955 London. 1st ed. 4to. VG $175.00

GERNSHEIM, H. *Julia Margaret Cameron: Her Life & Photographic Work.* 1948 London/NY. 1st ed. 8vo. EX $70.00

GERNSHEIM, H. *Lewis Carroll, Photographer: Autobiography.* 1949 NY. VG $50.00

GERNSHEIM, H. *Recording Eye.* 1960 Putnam. 1st ed. dj. EX $35.00

GERNSHEIN, H.; & DAGUERRE, L. *World's 1st Photographer.* 1956 NY/Cleveland. 1st ed. 8vo. dj. VG $50.00

GEROME, Jean-Leon. *Collection of the Works of Jean-Leon Gerome.* 1881 NY. Hall. 100 photos in 10 linen folios. $225.00

GERRISH, Theodore. *Life in the World's Wonderland.* 1887 ME. Ills. 421 p. G $25.00

GERROLD, David. *Man Who Folded Himself.* 1973 Random House. 1st ed. dj. EX $10.00

GERSHMAN, Herbert. *Surrealist Revolution in France.* 1966 MI U Pr. dj. EX $15.00

GERSHON, Freddie. *Sweetie Baby Cookie Honey.* 1986 Arbor House. Review ed. wraps. M $8.00

GERSON, Horst. *Rembrandt Paintings.* 1968 Reynal/Morrow. Ills. folio. 527 p. dj. $85.00

GERSON, Noel B. *Kit Carson.* 1964 Garden City. 1st ed. dj. VG $12.00

GERSTACKER, Frederick. *Gerstacker's Travels.* 1854 London. Nelson. 290 p. cloth. $100.00

GERSTACKER, Frederick. *Scenes of Life in CA.* 1942 San Francisco. Ltd ed. 1/500. VG $100.00

GERSTACKER, Frederick. *Wild Sports of the Far West.* 1860 Boston. Ills Weir. 2nd Am ed. VG $90.00

GERSTACKER, Frederick. *Wild Sports of the Far West.* 1968 Duke U Pr. 409 p. dj. EX $50.00

GESELL, Arnold. *Child From 5 to 10.* 1946 Harper. 1st ed. 475 p. $20.00

GESSLER, Clifford. *Tropic Landfall: Port of Honolulu.* 1942 Doubleday Doran. Ill 1st ed. G $15.00

GESTON, M.S. *Siege of Wonder.* 1976 Doubleday. 1st ed. dj. EX $17.50

GETLEIN, Frank. *Chaim Gross.* 1974 NY. Abrams. folio. presentation. dj. EX $200.00

GETLEIN, Frank. *Jack Levine.* no date. c 1966. NY. Abrams. sgn. EX $110.00

GETLEIN, Frank. *Lure of the Great West.* 1973 Country Beautiful. 1st ed. dj. $18.00

GHEERBRANT, Alain. *Journey to the Far Amazon.* 1954 Simon Schuster. Ills. 353 p. dj. VG $12.00

GHIRSHMAN, Roman. *Art of Ancient Iran.* 1964 NY. Golden. Ills. 4to. 461 p. dj. $60.00

GIACOMOTTI, Jeanne. *French Faience.* 1963 NY. Universe. Ills. 4to. 270 p. dj. $60.00

GIBB, D.E.W. *Lloyds of London.* 1957 London. 1st ed. 8vo. cloth. dj. VG $11.00

GIBBINGS, Robert. *Sweet Thames Run Softly.* 1940 London. 3rd print. EX $12.00

GIBBINGS, Robert. *Wood Engravings of Robert Gibbings.* 1959 London. Dent. Ills. dj. VG $125.00

GIBBON, Edward. *History of Decline & Fall of Roman Empire.* 1838 London. Cadell Strand. 8 vol set. G $25.00

GIBBON, Monk. *Branch of Hawthorne Tree.* 1927 Grayhound Pr. Ills P Le Doux. 1/460. 83 p. $12.00

GIBBON, Monk. *Tales of Hoffmann: Study of the Film.* 1951 England. Saturn Pr. Ills. VG $12.00

GIBBONEY, S.G. *Historic Monticello Home of Thomas Jefferson.* c 1920s. NY. Ills. 42 p. wraps. $10.00

GIBBS, James. *Pacific Graveyard.* 1964 Binfords Mort. Ills. 296 p. dj. EX $15.00

GIBBS, Jerry. *Bass Myths Exploded: Newest Ways to Catch Largemouth.* 1978 McKay. Ills. 200 p. dj. EX $10.00

GIBBS, Josiah. *Manual of Hebrew & English Lexicon.* 1828 Andover. leather. VG $65.00

GIBBS, Rebecca W. *Gardens Through the Ages.* 1937 private print. 2nd ed. sgn. 103 p. VG $15.00

GIBBS, W.M. *Species & How To Know Them.* 1909 Buffalo. Ills 1st ed. 8vo. EX $45.00

GIBBS. *Buckeye Horology: Chicago Clocks & Clockmakers.* 1971 Columbia, PA. 4to. EX $22.50

GIBBS-SMITH, Charles H. *Fashionable Lady in the 19th Century.* 1960 London. Ills. plts. wraps. $10.00

GIBSON, Arrell. *Chickasaws.* 1971 Norman. 1st ed. dj. G. $30.00

GIBSON, Charles Dana. *Gibson Book.* 1907 NY. 2 vol set. VG $130.00

GIBSON, Charles Dana. *London As Seen by Charles Dana Gibson.* 1897 NY. 1st ed. folio. VG $90.00

GIBSON, Charles Dana. *Our Neighbors.* 1905 NY. Scribner. 1st ed. folio. EX $110.00

GIBSON, Charles Dana. *Pictures of People.* 1896 Russell. 1st ed. folio. VG $175.00

GIBSON, Charles Dana. *Stuff & Nonsense.* 1888 NY. 1st Gibson book. VG $20.00

GIBSON, F. *6 French Artists of the 19th Century.* 1925 London. 78 p. $20.00

GIBSON, George Rutlege. *Journal of a Soldier Under Kearney & Doniphan.* 1974 Philadelphia. VG $20.00

GIBSON, Katharine. *Nathaniel's Witch.* 1941 Longman. Ills Vera Bock. 1st ed. VG $20.00

GIBSON, L.H. *Beautiful Houses: Study in House Building.* 1895 NY. Ills 1st ed. 346 p. cloth. $25.00

GIBSON, Litzka R. & Walter B. *Mystic & Occult Arts: Guide to Their Use in Daily Living.* 1969 Parker Pub. dj. VG $10.00

GIBSON, W.H. *Pastoral Days of Memories of New England Year.* 1882 NY. Ills. 153 p. cloth. $35.00

GIBSON, William. *Burning Chrome.* 1986 Arbor House. Uncorrected proof. wraps. EX $60.00

GIBSON, William. *Count Zero*. 1986 NY. Review copy. dj. M $20.00

GIBSON, William. *Neuromancer*. 1986 Phantasia. 1st Am HrdCvr ed. 1/375. sgn. $110.00

GIBSON, William. *Neuromancer*. 1984 Ace. 1st ed. wraps. EX $35.00

GIBSON, William. *Neuromancer*. 1984 Gollancz. 1st English HrdCvr ed. sgn. EX $110.00

GIBSON. *Amateur Telescopists' Handbook*. 1894 NY. $32.00

GIBSON. *Goldsmith of Florence*. 1929 NY. 1st ed. VG $15.00

GIDDENS, Paul H. *Standard Oil Company: Oil Pioneer of the Middle West*. 1955 NY. Ills 1st ed. EX $65.00

GIDDINGS, R.W. *Yaqui Myths & Legends*. 1959 Tucson. 180 p. dj. VG $15.00

GIDE, Andre. *Oscar Wilde: A Study*. 1905 Oxford. Ltd 1st ed. 1/500. $75.00

GIDE, Andre. *Secret Drama of My Life*. 1951 Paris. 1st ed in English. wraps. EX $25.00

GIEDION S. *Time & Architecture*. 1965 Harvard. 4th ed. dj. EX $20.00

GIELGUD, John. *Early Stages*. 1939 London. Macmillan. 1st ed. inscr. EX $175.00

GIFFORD, D. *Notes for Joyce: Annotation of Ulysses*. 1974 NY. Ills 1st ed. 544 p. dj. EX $48.00

GIFFORD, T. *Anglers & Muscleheads*. 1960 Dutton. Ills 1st ed. 186 p. dj. G $10.00

GIFFORD, Thomas. *Man From Lisbon*. 1977 McGraw Hill. 1st ed. dj. M $20.00

GIFFORD & LEE. *Jack's Books*. 1978 St. Martins. Ills 1st ed. 337 p. dj. VG $22.50

GILBERT, B. *Trailblazers*. 1973 Time Life. Ills. 236 p. leather. EX $15.00

GILBERT, F. *American Literature*. 1882 Chicago. Ills 1st ed. 110 p. cloth. $5.00

GILBERT, G. *Nuremberg Diary*. 1947 NY. G $35.00

GILBERT, G.K. *Geology of Henry Mountains*. 1877 WA. xl. VG $50.00

GILBERT, Henry. *King Arthur*. 1929 Saalfield. Ills Frances Brundage. G $20.00

GILBERT, Henry. *Robin Hood*. 1929 Saalfield. Ills Frances Brundage. G $20.00

GILBERT, James. *Flier's World*. 1976 NY. Ridge Pr. EX $10.00

GILBERT, James. *Historical Rhymes for Boys & Girls*. 1885 $15.00

GILBERT, Julie. *Ferber*. 1978 Doubleday. 1st ed. dj. VG $10.00

GILBERT, Michael. *Black Seraphim*. 1983 London. 1st ed. sgn. dj. EX $27.00

GILBERT, Michael. *Dust & Heat*. 1967 London. 1st ed. dj. VG $25.00

GILBERT, W.S. *Bab Ballads*. 1869 Camden. Ills 1st ed. 2 vol set. VG $150.00

GILBERT, W.S. *Mikado*. 1928 London. Ills Flint/Brock. 9vo. 96 p. $50.00

GILBERT, W.S. *Pinafore Picture Book*. 1908 Macmillan. Ills AB Woodward. 1st ed. VG $45.00

GILBERT, W.S. *50 Bab Ballads*. 1877 London. Ills 1st ed. VG $30.00

GILBERT, William. *On the Lodestone & Magnetic Bodies*. 1893 NY. Wiley. 1st ed. VG $135.00

GILBRETH, Frank B. *Motion Study*. 1911 NY. Van Nostrand. 1st ed. VG $300.00

GILBY, Walter. *George Morland: His Life & Works*. 1907 London. Black. 1st ed. sgn. VG $95.00

GILCHRIST, Ellen. *Annunciation*. 1983 Little Brown. proof. wraps. VG $85.00

GILCHRIST, Ellen. *Annunciation*. 1983 Little Brown. 1st ed. EX $40.00

GILCHRIST, Ellen. *Drunk with Love*. 1986 London. 1st ed. VG $40.00

GILCHRIST, Ellen. *Drunk with Love*. 1986 Little Brown. Advance copy. wraps. EX $90.00

GILCHRIST, Ellen. *In Land of Dreamy Dreams*. 1981 Fayetteville. 1st ed. sgn. wraps. $20.00

GILCHRIST, Ellen. *In Land of Dreamy Dreams*. 1982 London. Faber. 1st ed. dj. M $30.00

GILCHRIST, Ellen. *Victory Over Japan*. 1985 Ferber. 1st English ed. dj. EX $45.00

GILCHRIST, Ellen. *Victory Over Japan*. 1985 Little Brown. 1st ed. sgn. VG $35.00

GILDER, R. *Statue of Liberty Enlightening the World*. 1943 NY. Ills 1st ed. 40 p. cloth. $7.50

GILDER, Richard W. *Inscriptions for Pan-American Exposition at Buffalo 1901*. 1901 NY. Gilliss Pr. 1st ed. $30.00

GILES, J.H. *Kinta Years*. 1973 Houghton Mifflin. 1st ed. dj. $5.00

GILKERSON, William. *Scrimshander*. 1975 Troubador Pr. 1st ed. pb. VG $15.00

GILL, Brendan. *Here at the New Yorker*. 1975 NY. 2nd print. dj. EX $5.00

GILL, Brendan. *Many Masks: Life of Frank Lloyd Wright*. 1987 NY. 1st ed. sgn. dj. M $18.00

GILL, E.M. *Practical Dry-Fly Fishing*. 1912 Scribner. Ills 1st Am ed. 216 p. VG $47.50

GILL, Eric. *Art & Love*. 1927 Bristol. Golden Cockerell. 1/260. VG $130.00

GILL, Eric. *Song of Songs*. 1925 Golden Cockerell. 1/750. $300.00

GILL, Richard. *White Water & Black Magic*. 1940 Holt. Ills. 369 p. VG $14.00

GILLELAN, G.H. *Complete Book of the Bow & Arrow*. 1971 Stackpole. Ills. 320 p. dj. VG $7.50

GILLESPIE, Janet. *Peacock Manure & Marigolds*. 1964 NY. Viking. 1st ed. dj. EX $20.00

GILLESPIE, W.M. *Roads & Railroads*. 1848 NY. 2nd ed. $125.00

GILLET, L. *La Peinture XVIIe et XVIIIe Siecles*. 1913 Paris. Ills. French text. VG $30.00

GILLETT, J.P. *6 Years with TX Rangers*. 1925 New Haven. Ills 1st ed. 259 p. index. VG $27.50

GILLIARD, E.T. *Living Birds of the World*. 1958 Doubleday. Ills. 400 p. VG $12.00

GILLIATT, Mary. *English Style in Interior Decoration*. 1967 NY. Viking. Ills. 144 p. dj. $75.00

GILLIES, John. *Memoirs of the Life of Rev. George Whitefield*. 1912 VG $33.00

GILLIS, W.R. *Gold Rush Days with Mark Twain*. 1930 Boni. Ills. $30.00

GILLMORE, Q.A. *Practicle Treatise on Roads, Streets, & Pavements*. 1876 NY. Ills. 8vo. 158 p. cloth. VG $40.00

GILMAN, B. *Roosevelt: Happy Warrior*. 1921 Boston. Ills 1st ed. 360 p. cloth. $10.00

GILMAN, Charles. *Reports of Cases Argued & Determined in Supreme Court IL*. 1848 Quincy. leather. G $40.00

GILMAN, Lawrence. *Music & the Cultivated Man*. 1929 NY. Rudge. Ltd ed. 8vo. blue cloth. EX $12.00

GILMORE, J.C. *Art for Conservation: Federal Duck Stamps*. 1971 Barre. Ills. 4to. 94 p. dj. EX $25.00

GILMORE, James R. *Rear Guard of Revolution*. 1897 NY. VG $65.00

GILOT, Francoise; & LAKE, O. *Life with Picasso*. 1964 1st ed. 373 p. VG $9.00

GILOU, Albert. *Les Merveilles de la France.* 1961 Paris. Librarie Hachette. VG $40.00

GILPIN, Laura. *Temples in Yucatan: Camera Chronicle.* 1948 NY. 1st ed. dj. VG $50.00

GILPIN, William. *Observations on Mountains & Lakes of Cumberland.* 1792 London. Ills 3rd ed. 4to. 2 vol set. $350.00

GILPIN, William. *Observations on River Wye & Several Parts of South Wales.* 1789 London. 2nd ed. 4to. 152 p. scarce. VG $200.00

GILPIN, William. *Observations on Western Parts of England.* 1798 London. Ills 1st ed. 4to. 359 p. calf. $250.00

GILPIN, William. *Remarks on Forest Scenery & Other Woodland Views.* 1794 3 vol in 2. 3/4 leather. rebound. EX $250.00

GILPIN, William. *Remarks on Forest Scenery.* 1791 London. Ills 1st ed. 4to. 2 vol set. $250.00

GINCKEL, John E. *Boyville: History of 15 Years Work Among Newsboys.* 1905 Toledo, OH. 8vo. 219 p. VG $10.00

GINGER, Ray. *Bending Cross: Biography of Eugene Victor Debs.* 1949 New Brunswick. Rutgers. 1st ed. sgn. dj. VG $22.50

GINGER, Ray. *6 Days or Forever? TN vs John Thomas Scopes.* c 1958. Boston. dj. VG $25.00

GINGRICH, Arnold. *Joys of Trout.* 1973 NY. Crown. Ills. 275 p. dj. EX $10.00

GINGRICH, Arnold. *Well-Tempered Angler.* 1965 Knopf. Ills 1st ed. 331 p. dj. EX $17.50

GINGRICH, Arnold. *1,000 Mornings of Music: Journal of Obsession with Violin.* 1970 NY. Crown. dj. VG $20.00

GINSBERG, Allen. *Allen Verbatim.* 1974 McGraw Hill. 1st ed. sgn. dj. EX $35.00

GINSBERG, Allen. *Fall of America.* 1972 City Lights. 1st ed. sgn. EX $40.00

GINSBERG, Allen. *Planet News.* 1968 City Lights. 1st ed. EX $35.00

GINZBURG, Ralph. *Eros.* 1962 1st ed. 4 vol set. EX $85.00

GINZBURG, Ralph. *Unhurried View of Erotica.* 1958 Helmsman. boxed. VG $15.00

GIOVANNETTI. *Nothing But Max.* 1959 Macmillan. 1st Am ed. VG $12.50

GIPSON, F. *Fabulous Empire: Colonel Zack Miller's Story.* 1946 Houghton Mifflin. dj. G $8.50

GIPSON, L.H. *British Isles & American Colonies: Southern Plantations.* 1960 NY. Ills Revised ed. 280 p. $3.00

GIRAULT, Francois. *Tale of Gargantua & King Arthur.* 1932 Harvard U Pr. 1st ed. dj. VG $22.00

GIRL SCOUTS OF AMERICA. *Girl Scout Handbook.* 1917 1st ed. blue linen. VG $125.00

GISH, Lillian. *Movies, Mr. Griffith, & Me.* 1969 1st ed. 2nd print. inscr/sgn. $25.00

GISSING, George. *Brownie.* 1931 Columbia U Pr. Ltd ed. dj. G $45.00

GISSING, George. *Life's Morning.* 1919 reprint. G $15.00

GISSING, George. *Town Traveller.* 1956 4th ed. dj. VG $16.00

GISSING, George. *Town Traveller.* 1898 1st Am ed. EX $60.00

GISSING, George. *Veranilda.* 1904 London. 1st ed. VG $75.00

GIST, B.D. *High Sierra Adventure.* 1950 private print. 108 p. G $8.00

GITTINGER, Mattiebelle. *Textiles & Tradition in Indonesia.* 1979 NY/Singapore. Oxford. Ills. 243 p. $30.00

GLACKENS, I. *Glackens & the Ashcan Group.* 1957 Crown. 1st ed. dj. EX $20.00

GLADDEN, Washington. *From the Hub to the Hudson.* 1869 Boston. Ills. 16mo. 149 p. cloth. G $29.00

GLADDING, Effie. *Across the Continent by the Lincoln Highway.* 1915 NY. Ills 1st ed. fld map. cloth. G $20.00

GLADSTONE, W.E. *Studies on Homer & the Homeric Age.* 1858 Oxford. 1st ed. 8vo. 3 vol set. VG $450.00

GLASGOW, Ellen. *Deliverance.* 1904 NY. Ills Schoonover. 1st ed. 8vo. $12.00

GLASGOW, Ellen. *In This Our Life.* 1941 NY. dj. EX $22.00

GLASGOW, Ellen. *They Stooped to Folly.* 1929 Garden City. dj. EX $10.00

GLASGOW, Ellen. *They Stooped to Folly.* 1st ed after Special ed. VG $5.00

GLASGOW, Ellen. *Vein of Iron.* 1935 NY. 1st ed. VG $6.00

GLASGOW, Ellen. *Vein of Iron.* 1935 NY. 1st ed. dj. scarce. EX $15.00

GLASS, F.R. *Pictorial History of Fort Dearborn Massacre 1812.* 1933 Chicago. Ills. 8vo. wraps. $30.00

GLASS, Mary Lou. *Recipes for 2.* 1947 NY. 387 p. EX $5.00

GLASSCOCK, C.B. *War of the Copper Kings.* 1934 NY. photos. G $40.00

GLASSER, Otto. *Handbuch der Physick.* 1927 Berlin. Springer. Ills. sgn. 413 p. $25.00

GLAZIER, R. *Manual of Historic Ornament.* 1948 NY. Ills. 184 p. M $18.00

GLAZIER, R. *Manual of Historic Ornament.* 1926 London. Ills. 184 p. VG $35.00

GLAZIER, W. *Headwaters of the MS.* 1894 VG $30.00

GLAZIER, W. *Ocean to Ocean on Horseback.* 1900 Phil. Edgewood. Ills. VG $25.00

GLAZIER, W. *3 Years in the Federal Cavalry.* 1873 Ills. VG $17.50

GLAZIER, Willard. *Peculiarities of American Cities.* 1886 Phil. Ills. 12mo. 570 p. cloth. G $20.00

GLEASON, Herbert. *Through the Year Within Thoreau.* 1917 Boston. Ills 1st ed. EX $125.00

GLEESON, Alice. *Colonial RI.* 1926 Pawtucket. Ills. 260 p. $12.00

GLENN, T.A. *Some Colonial Mansions & Those Who Lived in Them.* 1900 Phil. Ills. 483 p. cloth. $12.50

GLENNON, J.F. *Where Time Bears Witness to Sound Building.* 1935 Mobile, AL. Ills 1st ed. 124 p. $17.50

GLICK, Wendell. *Recognition of Thoreau.* 1969 Ann Arbor. dj. xl. VG $37.00

GLINES, Lt. Col. C.V. *Polar Aviation.* c 1964. NY. dj. VG $25.00

GLOAG, John. *British Furniture Makers.* c 1950. NY. Hastings. G $10.00

GLOAG, John. *Georgian Grace: Social History of Design From 1660-1830.* 1967 London. Spring. Ills. 426 p. dj. $65.00

GLYN, Elinor. *Elizabeth Visits America.* 1909 NY. 1st ed. dj. EX $20.00

GOBLE, Warwick. *Green Willow & Other Japanese Fairy Tales.* 1910 London. Macmillan. Ills. VG $275.00

GOCHER, W.H. *Trotalong, Pacealong, Racealong.* 1928 Hartford. 3 vol set. VG $85.00

GODARD, Keith; & WILLAMS, E. *Little Night Book.* 1983 Works. 1st ed. accordion format. juvenile. $14.00

GODDARD, P.E. *Indians of the Northwest Coast.* 1945 Mus Nat Hist. Ills. 175 p. fld map. VG $18.00

GODDARD, P.E. *Indians of the Southwest.* 1931 Mus Nat Hist. Ills. 205 p. VG $18.00

GODDARD, Robert H. *Liquid Fuel Rocket Research.* 1941 Prentice Hall. Ills. 222 p. wraps. $8.00

GODDARD, Robert H. *Papers of Robert H. Goddard.* 1970 NY. Ills. 1,707 p. 3 vol set. $95.00

GODDEN, Geoffrey. *Coalport & Coalbrookdale Porcelains.* 1970 NY. Praeger. dj. VG $27.00

GODDEN, Goeffrey. *British Porcelain.* 1974 Potter Crown. Ills. 451 p. cloth. dj. $35.00

GODDEN, Rumer. *China Court.* 1961 Viking. 1st Am ed. dj. EX $25.00

GODDEN, Rumer. *Dark Horse.* 1982 Viking. 1st Am ed. dj. EX $12.00

GODDEN, Rumer. *Dragon of Og.* 1981 London. Ills P Baynes. 1st ed. dj. M $15.00

GODDEN, Rumer. *Episode of Sparrows.* 1955 Viking. 1st ed. dj. VG $10.00

GODDEN, Rumer. *Fugue in Time.* 1945 London. 1st ed. dj. $25.00

GODDEN, Rumer. *Gone.* 1968 Viking. 1st Am ed. dj. EX $20.00

GODDEN, Rumer. *Greenage Summer.* 1958 Viking. 1st ed. dj. VG $20.00

GODDEN, Rumer. *Little Plum.* 1963 Viking. Ills Jean Primorose. 1st ed. $25.00

GODDEN, Rumer. *Operation Sippacik.* 1969 Viking. Ills Bryan. 1st Am ed. dj. EX $20.00

GODDEN, Rumer. *Peacock Spring.* 1976 Viking. 1st ed. dj. VG $10.00

GODDEN, Rumer. *River.* 1946 Boston. 1st ed. dj. EX $10.00

GODDEN, Rumer. *River.* 1946 London. dj. VG $18.00

GODFREY & DUFRESNE. *Great Outdoors.* 1947 St. Paul. 1st ed. $20.00

GODFREY & DUFRESNE. *Lure of the Open.* 1954 Ltd ed. Intro D Darling. VG $25.00

GODLEE, Sir Rickman John. *Lord Lister.* 1917 London. Macmillan. Ills 1st ed. VG $35.00

GODOLPHIN, Mary. *Sandford & Merton in Words of 1 Syllable.* no date. NY. Ills. juvenile. $15.00

GODSELL, Philip. *Red Hunters of Snows.* 1938 Toronto. 1st ed. VG $55.00

GODWIN, Frank. *King Arthur & His Knights.* 1927 Phil. Winston. VG $20.00

GODWIN, Gail. *Dream Children.* 1976 Knopf. 1st ed. dj. EX $35.00

GODWIN, Gail. *Finishing School.* 1985 Viking. 1st ed. sgn. dj. M $20.00

GODWIN, Gail. *Mother & 2 Daughters.* Uncorrected proof. sgn. wraps. $60.00

GODWIN, James. *Dream Chintz & Other Tales.* 1851 London. fore-edge of Thames River. $310.00

GODWIN, Tom. *Survivors.* 1958 NY. 1st ed. dj. VG $25.00

GODWIN, William. *Memoirs of Mary Wollstonecraft.* 1927 London/NY. Ltd 1st ed. 1/700. VG $15.00

GOELL. *Tramping Through Palestine: American Student in Israel.* 1926 NY. Ills. cloth. VG $20.00

GOERL, Stephen. *Paper Making in America: Pictorial Account.* 1945 NY. Bulkly. Ills Robert Greco. $30.00

GOERNER, Fred. *Search for Amelia Earhart.* 1966 Garden City. 1st ed. dj. VG $17.50

GOETHE. *Faust.* 1930 NY. Ltd ed. 1/501. Trans/sgn L Ward. VG $65.00

GOETZMAN, W.H. *Army Explorations in the American West.* 1979 NEU Pr. Ills. 489 p. maps. EX $32.00

GOGOL, Nikolai. *Overcoat: Government Inspector.* 1976 Ltd Ed Club. Ills/sgn S Field. slipcase. EX $50.00

GOHL, Heinrich. *AK: Vast Land on the Edge of the Arctic.* 1970 Kimmerly Frey Bern. slipcase. $22.00

GOLD, Herbert. *Birth of a Hero.* 1951 NY. 1st ed. sgn. dj. EX $35.00

GOLD, Herbert. *Family.* 1981 NY. dj. M $21.00

GOLD, Herbert. *Man Who Was Not With It.* 1956 Boston. 1st ed. dj. $15.00

GOLD, Herbert. *Mr. White Eyes.* 1984 NY. 1st ed. dj. EX $14.00

GOLD, Herbert. *Mr. White Eyes.* 1984 Arbor House. Review copy. dj. EX $20.00

GOLD, Herbert. *Optimist.* 1959 Little Brown. 1st ed. dj. EX $20.00

GOLD, Herbert. *Slave Trade.* 1979 NY. 1st ed. dj. M $15.00

GOLD, Ivan. *Nickel Miseries.* 1963 NY. 1st ed. inscr. dj. EX $35.00

GOLD. *Fiction of the '50s.* 1959 Doubleday. 1st ed. dj. VG $10.00

GOLDBARTH, Albert. *Ink Blood Semen.* 1980 Bits. 1st ed. sgn. wraps. EX $10.00

GOLDBERG, Howard. *Angler's Book of Fly Tying & Fishing.* 1973 Scribner. Ills. 4to. 107 p. dj. EX $12.00

GOLDBERG, Isaac. *Man Menchen: Biographical & Critical Survey.* 1925 NY. Ills. VG $25.00

GOLDBERG, M. *Namesake.* 1982 Yale U Pr. Ills. dj. G $10.00

GOLDBERG, Michael. *Carlyle & Dickens.* 1972 GA U Pr. 1st ed. dj. EX $25.00

GOLDBERGER, E. *Unipolar Lead Electrocardiography.* 1947 Phil. Ills 1st ed. VG $45.00

GOLDEN, H. *Little Girl Is Dead.* 1965 Cleveland. 1st ed. dj. xl. VG $12.50

GOLDEN, H. *Mr. Kennedy & the Negros.* 1964 Cleveland. Ills 1st ed. 264 p. dj. $10.00

GOLDEN, Harry. *Carl Sandburg.* 1961 World. 1st ed. dj. $35.00

GOLDFINGER, Myron. *Villages in the Sun.* 1969 NY. Praeger. VG $20.00

GOLDING, Louis. *Doomington Wanderer.* 1934 London. Gollancz. dj. VG $17.50

GOLDING, Louis. *Glory of Elsie Silver.* Hutchinson. 1st ed. inscr. dj. VG $25.00

GOLDING, Louis. *Pursuer.* no date. (1948) Capetown. 12mo. VG $20.00

GOLDING, William. *Close Quarters.* 1987 NY. 1st ed. dj. EX $15.00

GOLDING, William. *Darkness Visible.* 1979 Farrar. 1st Am ed. dj. EX $20.00

GOLDING, William. *Free Fall.* 1959 London. 1st ed. dj. VG $80.00

GOLDING, William. *Hot Gates.* 1966 NY. dj. EX $30.00

GOLDING, William. *Marathon Man.* 1974 Delacorte. 1st ed. dj. VG $25.00

GOLDING, William. *Moving Target.* 1982 London. 1st ed. dj. EX $25.00

GOLDING, William. *Moving Target.* 1982 Farrar. 1st Am ed. dj. EX $20.00

GOLDING, William. *Nobel Lecture.* 1984 6th Chamber Pr. 1st ed. 1/500. wraps. EX $25.00

GOLDING, William. *Paper Men.* 1984 NY. 1st ed. dj. EX $16.00

GOLDING, William. *Pyramid.* 1980 Pyramid. 1st ed. dj. VG $50.00

GOLDING, William. *Pyramid.* 1967 Harcourt. 1st Am ed. dj. EX $25.00

GOLDING, William. *Rites of Passage.* 1980 NY. 1st ed. dj. $20.00

GOLDING, William. *Scorpion God.* 1971 Harcourt. 1st Am ed. dj. EX $25.00

GOLDING, William. *Scorpion God.* 1971 London. 1st ed. dj. EX $25.00

GOLDING, William. *Spire.* 1964 Harcourt. 1st Am ed. dj. EX $30.00

GOLDMAN, Albert. *Elvis.* 1981 600 p. dj. VG $18.00

GOLDMAN, Emma. *Living My Life.* 1931 NY. 1st ed. VG $18.50

GOLDMAN, William. *Boys & Girls Together.* 1964 NY. 1st ed. dj. EX $20.00

GOLDMAN, William. *Control.* 1982 Delacorte. 1st ed. dj. VG $12.00

GOLDMAN, William. *Marathon Man.* 1975 Macmillan. 1st English ed. dj. VG $25.00

GOLDMAN, William. *Season.* 1969 Harcourt. 1st ed. dj. EX $35.00

GOLDMAN, William. *Temple of Gold.* 1957 NY. Knopf. 1st ed. dj. $40.00

GOLDMAN, William. *Thing of It Is.* 1967 NY. 1st ed. dj. EX $32.50

GOLDMAN. *Death in Locker Room.* 1984 South Bend. 1st ed. dj. VG $22.50

GOLDSCHEIDER. *Kokoschka in Full Color.* 1967 Phaidon. Ills 3rd print. 4to. dj. EX $30.00

GOLDSCHMITT, Bruno. *Die Shriften Salomos.* 1922 Munich. Ills Ltd ed. 1/250. sgn. $175.00

GOLDSMITH, Joel S. *Mystical.* 1971 Harper Row. dj. VG $10.00

GOLDSMITH, Oliver. *Beauties of Goldsmith; or, Moral & Sentimental Treasury.* 1797 Phil. 1st Am ed. 12mo. $175.00

GOLDSMITH, Oliver. *Citizen of the World.* 1792 London. 2 vol set. full leather. VG $80.00

GOLDSMITH, Oliver. *Elegy on the Glory of Her Sex: Mrs. Mary Blaize.* Caldecott. Color Picture Book. $15.00

GOLDSMITH, Oliver. *Goldsmith's Poetical Works.* c 1860. London. fore-edge of harvest scene. $350.00

GOLDSMITH, Oliver. *History of Earth & Animated Nature.* 1774 London. 1st ed. 8vo. 8 vol set. $30.00

GOLDSMITH, Oliver. *Mad Dog.* Caldecott. Color Picture Book. $25.00

GOLDSMITH, Oliver. *Roman History From Foundation of City of Rome.* 1769 London. 19th C reprint. 1st ed. calf. $125.00

GOLDSMITH, Oliver. *She Stoops To Conquer.* no date. NY. Ills H Thomson. 4to. 198 p. EX $75.00

GOLDSMITH, Oliver. *Vicar of Wakefield.* 1798 Hereford. Ills T Bewick. G $95.00

GOLDSMITH-CARTER, George. *Sailors, Sailors.* 1966 London. Paul Hamlyn. dj. G $21.00

GOLDSTEIN, B. & Estette T. *Toy Soldiers.* 1982 Cincinnati. miniature. leather. M $25.00

GOLDSTEIN, Milton. *Magnificent West: Yosemite.* 1972 Doubleday. Ills. dj. EX $25.00

GOLDSTON, Will. *Tricks & Illusions.* c 1914. London. 12mo. 249 p. $25.00

GOLDSTON, Will. *Young Conjuror.* no date. London. Ills. 8vo. $20.00

GOLDSTONE & SWEETSER. *Bibliography of Arthur Machen.* 1965 TX U Pr. Ltd 1st ed. 1/500. dj. VG $75.00

GOLDWATER, Barry. *AZ.* 1978 Rand McNally. photos D Muench. folio. dj. EX $25.00

GOLDWATER, Barry. *Speeches of Henry Fountain Ashurst of AZ.* no date. Goldwater. sgn. VG $35.00

GOLDWATER, Marge. *Jennifer Bartlett.* 1985 Minneapolis. Ills. square 4to. 174 p. dj. $35.00

GOLDWATER, P. *Paul Gaugiun.* 1957 NY. Abrams. M $30.00

GOLDWATER, Robert. *John & Dominque de Menil Collection.* 1962 NY. Museum of Primitive Art. $30.00

GOLDWATER, Robert. *Senufo Sculpture From West Africa.* 1964 NY. Museum of Primitive Art. 4to. $40.00

GOLDWATER, Robert. *What Is Modern Sculpture?* 1969 MOMA. Ills. 4to. 146 p. wraps. $10.00

GOLLANCZ, Victor. *My Dear Timothy.* 1953 NY. 1st ed. dj. EX $14.00

GOLLWITZER, G. *Drawing From Nature.* 1970 NY. Ills. 96 p. $7.50

GOLOMB, J. *Master Man Hunters.* 1926 NY. G $20.00

GOLOWNIN, Capt. *Memoirs of Captivity in Japan During Years 1811-1813.* 1824 London. 2nd ed. 3 vol set. VG $200.00

GOLUB, P. *Bolsheviks & Armed Forces in 3 Revolutions.* 1979 Moscow. 304 p. cloth. dj. EX $12.50

GONNARD, P. *Exile of St. Helena.* 1909 Phil. VG $30.00

GONOVIOUS, J. *Flora Virginica.* 1946 Harvard U Pr. 183 p. wraps. VG $15.00

GOOCH, Bob. *Weedy World of the Pickerels.* 1970 Barnes. Ills 1st ed. 184 p. dj. VG $10.00

GOOCH, D.W. *Fort Pillow Massacre.* 1864 WA. GPO. 1st ed. 128 p. $75.00

GOOD HOUSEKEEPING. *Good Housekeeping Cookbook.* 1933 NY. 1st ed. dj. VG $25.00

GOOD HOUSEKEEPING. *Good Housekeeping Needlework Manual.* 1905 Springfield. Ills. 8vo. 296 p. $25.00

GOODALL, D.W. *Evolution of Desert Biota.* 1976 TX U Pr. Ills. 250 p. EX $22.00

GOODALL, John S. *Edwardian Christmas.* 1978 NY. Atheneum. Ills. 4to. dj. VG $15.00

GOODMAN, David. *Western Panorama 1849-1875.* 1966 Glendale. EX $25.00

GOODMAN, Jack. *Fireside Book of Dog Stories.* 1943 Simon Schuster. 591 p. dj. VG $8.00

GOODMAN, L.; & GILMAN, A. *Pharmacological Basis of Therapeutics.* 1941 NY. 1st ed. VG $125.00

GOODMAN, P. *Art & Social Nature.* 1941 NY. dj. $15.00

GOODMAN, P. *Hawkweed.* 1967 NY. 1st ed. dj. EX $10.00

GOODMAN, P. *Illustrated Essays on Jewish Bookplates.* 1971 KATV Pub. EX $15.00

GOODMAN, Ryah T. *Toward the Sun.* 1952 Boston. inscr. dj. VG $10.00

GOODRICH, A.L. *Birds of KS.* 1946 Topeka. 1st ed. 340 p. wraps. VG $15.00

GOODRICH, C.A. *Lives of Signers to Declaration of Independence.* 1829 NY. Reed. Ills. full calf. $15.00

GOODRICH, Lloyd. *Artist in America.* 1967 NY. 1st ed. dj. VG $12.50

GOODRICH, Lloyd. *Edward Hopper.* no date. Abrams. oblong 4to. 306 p. dj. $110.00

GOODRICH, Lloyd. *Graphic Art of Winslow Homer.* 1968 Smithsonian. Ills. square 4to. cloth. dj. $35.00

GOODRICH, Lloyd. *Raphael Soyer.* no date. NY. Abrams. Ills. 349 p. dj. $225.00

GOODRICH, Lloyd. *Reginald Marsh.* no date. NY. Abrams. folio. 307 p. dj. $250.00

GOODRICH, Lloyd. *Winslow Homer Monograph.* 1959 Braziller. Ills. 4to. 127 p. cloth. $20.00

GOODRICH, S.G. *Animal Kingdom.* 1880 Ann Arbor. Ills. 2 vol set. $50.00

GOODRICH, S.G. *Garden.* 1834 Boston. Carter Hendee. mauve cloth. EX $200.00

GOODRICH, S.G. *Goodrich's Universal Geography.* 1833 Boston. Carter Hendee. 2nd ed. G $100.00

GOODRICH, S.G. *Manners, Customs, & Antiquities of Indians of the Americas.* 1844 Ills 1st ed. 336 p. VG $30.00

GOODRICH. *Rolls of Soldiers in Revolutionary War 1775 to 1783.* 1904 Routledge. VG $150.00

GOODRUM, C.A. *Treasures of the Library of Congress.* 1980 NY. 1st ed. dj. EX $25.00

GOODSELL, Daniel A. *Nature & Character at Granite Bay.* 1901 NY. VG $10.00

GOODSPEED, Bernice I. *Paricutin.* 1945 Mexico City. 1st ed. large pb. wraps. VG $45.00

GOODSPEED, C.E. *Treasury of Fishing Stories.* 1946 Barnes. Ills. 4to. 600 p. VG $15.00

GOODSPEED, C.E. *Yankee Bookseller.* 1937 Boston. Ills 1st ed. 305 p. $20.00

GOODSPEED, T.H. *Plant Hunters in the Andes.* 1941 NY. 429 p. VG $30.00

GOODSPEED, T.H. *Plant Hunters in the Andes.* 1941 NY. Ills 1st ed. dj. EX $50.00

GOODSTONE, Tony. *Pulps: 50 Years of American Pop Culture.* 1970 238 p. dj. VG $15.00

GOODWIN, Cardinal. *John Charles Fremont: Explanation of His Career.* 1930 Stanford. EX $25.00

GOODWIN, Derek. *Pigeons & Doves & the World.* 1983 Cornell U Pr. Revised 3rd ed. 363 p. dj. EX $35.00

GOODWIN, Jan. *Caught in Cross Fire: American Woman's Secret & Journey.* 1987 NY. Dutton. 1st ed. $20.00

GOODWIN, M.W. *Historic NY.* 1897 NY. Ills 1st ed. 2 vol set. $50.00

GOODWIN, P.A. *Biography of Andrew Jackson.* 1854 Hartford. 12mo. 456 p. brown cloth. G $32.00

GOODWIN, P.A. *Biography of Andrew Jackson.* 1832 Hartford. 1st ed. 422 p. full calf. VG $45.00

GOODWIN, R.A. *Brief & True Report Concerning Williamsburg, VA.* 1941 Richmond. Ills Revised ed. 123 p. $27.50

GOODWIN, R.N. *Sower's Seed: Tribute to Adlai Stevenson.* 1965 NY. Ills 1st ed. 15 p. boxed. $7.50

GOODWIN, W.A.R. *Bruton Parish Church Restored & Its Historic Environment.* 1907 Petersburg, VA. Ills 1st ed. 198 p. cloth. $20.00

GOODWYN, Frank. *Lone Star Land.* 1955 Knopf. 1st ed. dj. VG $17.00

GOOLD, N. *Wadsworth-Longfellow House.* 1960 Portland. Ills. 44 p. wraps. $3.00

GOOLD, W. *Portland in Past with Historic Notes of Old Falmouth.* 1886 Portland, ME. Ills 1st ed. 527 p. $35.00

GOOLRICK, J.T. *Fredericksburg & Cavalier Country.* 1935 Richmond. Ills 1st ed. maps. 92 p. dj. $20.00

GORAN, M. *Story of Fritz Haber.* 1967 Norman. OK U Pr. 1st ed. dj. VG $10.00

GORDIMER, Nadine. *Burger's Daughter.* 1979 Cape. 1st English ed. dj. VG $25.00

GORDIMER, Nadine. *Burger's Daughter.* 1979 Cape. Advance copy. wraps. EX $50.00

GORDIMER, Nadine. *Burger's Daughter.* 1979 Viking. Review copy. dj. EX $40.00

GORDIMER, Nadine. *Burger's Daughter.* 1979 Viking. 1st Am ed. dj. EX $25.00

GORDIMER, Nadine. *July's People.* 1981 Cape. 1st ed. dj. EX $30.00

GORDIMER, Nadine. *Late Bourgeois World.* 1966 Viking. 1st Am ed. dj. VG $35.00

GORDIMER, Nadine. *Livingston's Companions.* 1971 Viking. 1st Am ed. dj. EX $35.00

GORDIMER, Nadine. *Livingston's Companions.* 1972 London. Cape. 1st ed. dj. VG $25.00

GORDIMER, Nadine. *Not for Publication.* 1965 London. 1st ed. VG $50.00

GORDIMER, Nadine. *Not for Publication.* 1965 Viking. 1st Am ed. VG $30.00

GORDIMER, Nadine. *Selected Stories.* 1976 NY. Viking. 1st ed. dj. VG $20.00

GORDIMER, Nadine. *Soldier's Embrace.* 1980 Cape. Advance copy. wraps. EX $45.00

GORDIMER, Nadine. *Soldier's Embrace.* 1980 NY. 1st ed. dj. M $12.00

GORDIMER, Nadine. *Something Out There.* 1984 Cape. 1st English ed. dj. EX $30.00

GORDIMER, Nadine. *World of Strangers.* 1958 Simon Schuster. 1st Am ed. dj. VG $35.00

GORDIMER, Nadine. *6 Feet of Country.* 1956 Simon Schuster. 1st ed. dj. VG $45.00

GORDON, A.C. *In Picturesque Shenandoah Valley.* 1930 Richmond. Ills 1st ed. maps. $15.00

GORDON, B.L. *Secret Lives of Fishes.* 1977 Grosset Dunlap. Ills 1st ed. 305 p. dj. EX $10.00

GORDON, Caroline. *Aleck Maury Sportsman.* 1934 NY. Scribner. 1st ed. dj. EX $250.00

GORDON, Caroline. *Collected Stories.* 1981 Farrar Straus. 1st ed. dj. EX $20.00

GORDON, Caroline. *Collected Stories.* 1981 NY. Review copy. dj. EX $30.00

GORDON, Caroline. *Green Centuries.* 1941 NY. Scribner. 1st ed. dj. scarce. EX $85.00

GORDON, Caroline. *How To Read a Novel.* 1957 NY. Viking. 1st ed. dj. EX $60.00

GORDON, Caroline. *Old Red & Other Stories.* 1963 NY. 1st ed. presentation. VG $45.00

GORDON, Caroline. *Strange Children.* 1951 NY. Scribner. 1st ed. dj. EX $65.00

GORDON, Caroline. *Women on the Porch.* 1944 NY. Scribner. 1st ed. dj. EX $60.00

GORDON, Clifton R. *12th US Infantry.* 1919 NY. Ills. 425 p. xl. G $35.00

GORDON, Craig E. *Book of Portraits.* 1899 Chicago. Stone. Ills 1st ed. folio. EX $250.00

GORDON, Elizabeth. *Billy Bunny's Fortune.* 1919 Volland. 22nd ed. 12mo. $18.00

GORDON, Elizabeth. *Bird Children.* 1912 Volland. Ills MT Ross. 14th ed. 8vo. VG $50.00

GORDON, Elizabeth. *Buddy Jim.* 1935 Wise Parslow. Ills John Rae. 8vo. 109 p. $18.00

GORDON, Elizabeth. *King Gumdrop.* 1916 Whitman. Ills H Frazee. 112 p. boxed. $40.00

GORDON, Elizabeth. *More Really-So Stories.* no date. Wise Parslow. Ills Rae. VG $15.00

GORDON, Elizabeth. *Really-So Stories.* 1924 Wise Parslow. Ills John Rae. 8vo. VG $15.00

GORDON, Elizabeth. *Really-So Stories.* 1924 Volland. Ills. $18.00

GORDON, Elizabeth. *Really-So Stories.* 1937 Wise Parslow. Ills John Rae. 8vo. 96 p. VG $18.00

GORDON, G.S. *English Literature & the Classics.* 1969 NY. EX $7.50

GORDON, H. *Old English Furniture.* 1949 NY. Ills 1st ed. 154 p. cloth. $5.00

GORDON, J. *On Wandering Wheels.* 1929 London. Ills 1st ed. 336 p. cloth. $15.00

GORDON, J. *Reminiscences of the Civil War.* 1903 NY. 1st ed. G $50.00

GORDON, Lesley. *Pageant of Dolls.* 1949 NY. dj. EX $22.00

GORDON, Mary. *Company of Women.* 1980 NY. Knopf. 1st ed. dj. VG $20.00

GORDON, Mary. *Men & Angels.* 1985 Random House. 1st ed. dj. VG $17.50

GORDON, S.W. *How To Fish From Top to Bottom.* 1957 Stackpole. 384 p. VG $12.50

GORDON, Theodore. *American Trout Fishing.* 1972 Knopf. Ills. 247 p. dj. EX $10.00

GORDON, W.J. *Our Country's Fishes.* c 1920s. London. Ills. 8vo. VG $20.00

GORDON, W.J. *Under the Avalanche.* 1889 NY. cloth. VG $18.00

GORDON, William Hugh. *Lettering for Commercial Purposes.* 1918 Cincinnati. 4th ed. oblong 4to. 173 p. VG $45.00

GORES, Joe. *Come Morning.* 1986 NY. 1st Am ed. inscr. dj. $25.00

GORES, Joe. *Come Morning.* 1986 NY. Advance copy. wraps. $35.00

GORES, Joe. *Dead Skip.* 1973 London. 1st English ed. sgn. dj. EX $30.00

GORES, Joe. *Hammett.* 1975 NY. Putnam. 1st ed. VG $20.00

GORES, Joe. *Interface.* 1974 NY. 1st Am ed. dj. EX $25.00

GOREY, Edward. *Broken Spoke.* 1976 Dodd Mead. 1st ed. sgn. dj. VG $20.00

GOREY, Edward. *Doubtful Guest.* 1978 NY. Dodd Mead. 1st ed. sgn. dj. $30.00

GOREY, Edward. *Dwindling Party.* 1982 Random House. 1st ed. EX $15.00

GOREY, Edward. *Fletche & Zenobia Save the Circus.* 1971 Dodd Mead. Ills V Chess. 1st ed. dj. VG $30.00

GOREY, Edward. *Improvable Landscape.* 1986 Albondocani. Ltd ed. 1/300. sgn. wraps. EX $35.00

GOREY, Edward. *Les Echanges Malandreux.* 1985 Worcester. Ltd 1st ed. 1/500. sgn. wraps. $25.00

GOREY, Edward. *Les Urnes Utiles.* 1980 Cambridge, MA. Ltd 1st ed. 1/400. sgn. wraps. $25.00

GOREY, Edward. *Object Lesson.* 1958 NY. Doubleday. 1st ed. dj. VG $160.00

GOREY, Edward. *Unstrung Harp; or, Mr. Earbrass Writes a Novel.* 1953 NY. Ills. 1st ed. $150.00

GOREY, Edward. *Utter Zoo.* 1967 Meredith. EX $12.50

GORHAM, A. *Indian Mason's Marks of Moghul Dynasty.* c 1900. London. 62 p. G $125.00

GORKY, Maxim. *Selected Short Stories.* 1974 Moscow. 3rd ed. VG $10.00

GORKY, Maxim. *26 & 1, & Other Stories From the Vagabond Series.* 1902 NY. Intro Strannik. 1st Am ed. $50.00

GORLING, A. *Art Treasures of Germany.* c 1880. Boston. Ills. 4to. ½-leather. VG $75.00

GORLING, L. *491.* 1966 NY. 1st ed. dj. EX $7.00

GORMAN, H. *James Joyce.* 1939 NY. Farrar Rinehart. VG $25.00

GORMAN, John A. *Western Horse: Its Types & Training.* 1944 Danville, IL. Interstate. Ills. 8vo. VG $45.00

GORMAN. *Lithographs.* 1974 Flagstaff. Ltd ed. 1/100. M $1000.00

GORSE. *Golden Moorland Mousie.* 1930 NY. Scribner. Ills Lionel Edwards. EX $20.00

GOSLING, N. *Nadar.* 1976 NY. Ills. dj. VG $24.00

GOSNELL, H.A. *Rebel Raider.* 1948 Chapel Hill. Ills 1st ed. 218 p. dj. VG $20.00

GOTTESMAN, Rita Susswein. *Arts & Crafts in NY 1777-1799.* 1954 NY Hist Soc. $35.00

GOTTLIEB, Abraham. *Story of Fur Business.* 1927 Harper. 1st ed. VG $16.50

GOTTSCHALK, Lillian. *American Toy Cars & Trucks 1894-1942.* 1986 NY. Abbeville. Ills. oblong folio. 328 p. $60.00

GOTTSCHALK, Louis. *Lafayette in America.* 1975 Bicentennial 1st ed. 458 p. $40.00

GOTTSCHALK, Louis. *Lafayette in America.* 1975 Arveyres. Ltd ed. sgn. 3 vols in 1. EX $25.00

GOTTSCHANG, J.L. *Guide to the Mammals of OH.* 1981 OH U Pr. Ills. 4to. 176 p. dj. EX $30.00

GOUDGE, Elizabeth. *God So Loved the World.* 1951 London. 1st ed. sgn. dj. EX $25.00

GOUDGE, Elizabeth. *Little White House.* 1946 London U Pr. 1st ed. G $25.00

GOUDGE, Elizabeth. *Rosemary Tree.* 1956 Coward McCann. 1st ed. dj. VG $15.00

GOUGE. *Fiscal History of TX.* 1968 NY. Kelly Pub. fair. $17.00

GOULD, A.A. *Report on Invertebrata of MA.* 1870 Boston. 2nd ed. green cloth. $35.00

GOULD, E.W. *50 Years on the MS.* 1951 Columbus. Ills. 750 p. dj. VG $45.00

GOULD, F.C. *Froissart's Modern Chronicles.* 1903 London. Ills 1st ed. 8vo. cloth. dj. $25.00

GOULD, George E. *American Yearbook of Medicine & Surgery.* 1900 2 vol set. VG $20.00

GOULD, J. *Good Fight: Story of F.D.R.'s Conquest of Polio.* 1960 NY. 1st ed. 308 p. cloth. dj. $8.50

GOULD, J. *New England Town Meeting.* 1940 Brattleboro. Ills 1st ed. 61 p. dj. $12.50

GOULD, John. *Fastest Hound Dog in the State of ME.* 1953 NY. 1st ed. dj. VG $20.00

GOULD, John. *John Gould's Birds.* 1981 Chartwell. Ills. 239 p. dj. EX $35.00

GOULD, Lois. *Not Responisble for Personal Articles.* 1978 Random House. 1st ed. dj. EX $15.00

GOULD, Lois. *Sea Change.* 1976 Simon Schuster. 1st ed. dj. EX $15.00

GOULD, Lois. *Such Good Friends.* 1970 Random House. 1st ed. dj. EX $35.00

GOULD, M.E. *Antique Tin & Toleware: Its History & Romance.* 1967 Tuttle. Ills. 2nd print. 152 p. dj. $20.00

GOULD, M.E. *Early American House.* 1965 Rutland. reprint. 144 p. dj. $12.50

GOULD, Robert Freke. *History of Free Masonry.* no date. London. 4to. 6 vol set. EX $175.00

GOULDEN, W.O. *German-English Medical Dictionary.* 1955 Little Brown. 1st ed. VG $12.50

GOULDEN. *Best Years 1945-1950.* 1976 Athenium. 1st ed. dj. VG $12.50

GOUNOD, Charles F. *Memoirs of an Artist.* 1895 Chicago. 1st ed. 8vo. cloth. VG $15.00

GOVERNMENT PRINTING OFFICE. *Principles Underlying Radio Communication.* 1922 WA. GPO. Revised 2nd ed. 619 p. G $18.00

GOVINDA, Lama Anagarika. *Way of the White Clouds: Buddhist Pilgrim in Tibet.* 1966 London. 1st ed. 305 p. VG $22.00

GOWANS, A. *Architecture in NJ.* 1964 Ills 1st ed. maps. 152 p. dj. $10.00

GOWEN, Emmett. *Joys of Fishing.* 1961 Rand McNally. Ills 1st ed. 191 p. dj. VG $7.00

GOWING, Lawrence. *Tuner: Imagination & Reality.* 1966 Doubleday. Ills. 4to. 64 p. $12.50

GOYEN, William. *Arcadio.* 1938 NY. 1st ed. wraps. EX $20.00

GOYEN, William. *Collected Stories of William Goyen.* 1975 Doubleday. 1st ed. dj. VG $20.00

GOYEN, William. *Come, the Restorer.* 1974 Garden City. 1st ed. dj. EX $10.00

GOYEN, William. *Fair Sister.* 1963 Doubleday. 1st ed. sgn. dj. VG $20.00

GOYEN, William. *Ghost & Flesh.* 1952 NY. 1st ed. dj. VG $12.00

GOYEN, William. *House of Breath.* 1950 Random House. 1st ed. dj. EX $40.00

GRABAR, Andre. *Golden Age of Justinian.* 1967 NY. Odyssey. Ills. 4to. 440 p. dj. $60.00

GRABAR, Oleg. *Formation of Islamic Art.* 1973 New Haven. Yale U Pr. $20.00

GRABHORN, Robert. *19th Century Type Displayed.* 1959 San Francisco. 1st ed. sgn. VG $75.00

GRACE, Harvey. *Organ Works of Bach.* no date. London. VG $18.00

GRACQ, Julien. *Castle of Argol.* no date. Direction 22. dj. VG $10.00

GRADY, James. *Hard Bargains.* 1985 Uncorrected proof. wraps. $25.00

GRADY, James. *6 Days of the Condor.* 1974 1st Am ed. dj. $30.00

GRAFTON, Sue. *A Is for Alibi.* 1982 NY. 1st ed. dj. M $45.00

GRAFTON, Sue. *B Is for Burglar.* 1985 London. 1st English ed. sgn. dj. $35.00

GRAFTON, Sue. *B Is for Burglar.* 1985 NY. 1st Am ed. inscr. dj. $35.00

GRAFTON, Sue. *C Is for Corpse.* 1986 NY. 1st Am ed. inscr. dj. $30.00

GRAHAM, Ada & Frank. *Falcon Flight.* 1978 Delacorte. Ills 1st ed. 112 p. dj. EX $10.00

GRAHAM, Billy. *Peace with God.* 1953 sgn. 222 p. dj. VG $15.00

GRAHAM, E. *ME Charm String.* 1946 NY. 1st ed. 231 p. $7.50

GRAHAM, E. *My Window Looks Down East.* 1951 NY. 1st ed. 218 p. dj. $7.50

GRAHAM, F. *Since Silent Spring.* 1970 Houghton Mifflin. 332 p. dj. $6.00

GRAHAM, Frank. *Gulls: Social History.* 1975 Random House. Ills 1st ed. 179 p. dj. EX $10.00

GRAHAM, G.W. *Mecklenburg Declaration of Independence, May 20, 1775.* 1905 NY/WA. Neale. 1st ed. EX $150.00

GRAHAM, Harvey. *Eternal Eve.* 1950 London. 1st ed. dj. EX $35.00

GRAHAM, Harvey. *Surgeons All.* 1939 London. Rich Cowan. 2nd print. $28.00

GRAHAM, Jesse M. *Smoke Over America.* 1943 Roycroft. presentation. 572 p. VG $35.00

GRAHAM, Lynda. *Pinky Marie: Her Adventures with 7 Bluebird.* 1939 Saalfield. Ills. 4to. 24 p. dj. EX $28.00

GRAHAM, Mary N. *Book of Christmas Carols.* 1938 Grosset Dunlap. Ills Pelagie Doane. 4to. VG $12.00

GRAHAM, Philip. *Showboats.* 1951 Austin. Ills 1st ed. sgn. dj. VG $35.00

GRAHAM, R.B.C. *Horses of the Conquest.* 1949 OK U Pr. Ills. 145 p. dj. EX $35.00

GRAHAM, R.B.C. *Horses of the Conquest.* 1949 OK U Pr. Ills. 4to. 145 p. VG $18.00

GRAHAM, S. *You Will Find It in MD.* 1945 Baltimore. Ills 1st ed. 91 p. $10.00

GRAHAM, Virginia. *Consider the Years.* 1946 London. 1st ed. dj. EX $25.00

GRAHAM, W.A. *Custer Myth.* NY. Bonanza. Ills. 8vo. dj. VG $40.00

GRAHAM, W.A. *Custer Myth.* 1953 Harrisburg. Stackpole. VG $25.00

GRAHAM, Winston. *Marnie.* 1961 London. 1st ed. dj. EX $25.00

GRAHAM. *Story of Surgery.* 1939 Doubleday. Ills. 425 p. G $7.00

GRAHAM-MULHALL, Sara. *Opium: Demon Flower.* 1926 NY. presentation. G $50.00

GRAHAME, Kenneth. *Dream Days.* 1899 NY/London. Bodley Head. 1st ed. 8vo. VG $75.00

GRAHAME, Kenneth. *Dream Days.* 1899 1st ed. slipcase. boxed. G $90.00

GRAHAME, Kenneth. *Dream Days.* 1902 Lane. Ills Parrish. 233 p. VG $45.00

GRAHAME, Kenneth. *Golden Age.* 1915 London. Ills Moony. 1st ed. $40.00

GRAHAME, Kenneth. *Golden Age.* 1900 Lane. Ills Parrish. 252 p. VG $50.00

GRAHAME, Kenneth. *Golden Age.* 1900 NY/London. Bodley Head. Ills Parrish. EX $110.00

GRAHAME, Kenneth. *Golden Age.* 1915 NY/London. Bodley Head. Ills Parrish. VG $70.00

GRAHAME, Kenneth. *Golden Age.* 1895 Stone Kimball. EX $75.00

GRAHAME, Kenneth. *Headswoman.* 1898 London. wraps. EX $85.00

GRAHAME, Kenneth. *Pagan Papers.* 1894 Chicago/London. Ltd ed. 1/450. scarce. EX $75.00

GRAHAME, Kenneth. *Wind in the Willows.* 1908 Scribner. 1st Am ed. 8vo. VG $100.00

GRAHAME, Kenneth. *Wind in the Willows.* 1959 NY. Ills Rackham. VG $16.00

GRAHAME, Kenneth. *Wind in the Willows.* 1940 Heritage House. Ills Rackham. 1st ed. VG $40.00

GRAHAME, Kenneth. *1st Whisper of Wind in the Willows.* 1945 Lippincott. Ills Grahame. 1st Am ed. VG $45.00

GRAHAME, Kenneth. *1st Whisper of Wind in the Willows.* 1923 Lippincott. Ills 2nd imp. dj. VG $17.50

GRAMATKY. *Little Toot on the MS.* 1973 inscr. dj. M $18.00

GRAND, Gordon. *Col. Weatherford & His Friends.* 1933 Derrydale. Ltd ed. 1/1,450. EX $50.00

GRAND, Gordon. *Col. Weatherford's Young Entry.* 1935 Derrydale. Ltd ed. 1/1,350. $50.00

GRAND, Gordon. *Old Man & Other Col. Weatherford Stories.* 1934 Derrydale. Ltd ed. 1/1,150. EX $50.00

GRAND, Gordon. *Redmond C. Stewart: Fox Hunter & Gentleman of MD.* 1938 NY. 1st ed. boxed. EX $40.00

GRANGE, Red. *Zuppke of IL.* 1937 Chicago. 1st ed. dj. VG $25.00

GRANGER, Bill. *AZ Place Names.* 1974 AZ U Pr. $20.00

GRANGER, Bill. *Hemingway's Notebook.* 1986 Crown. 1st ed. dj. EX $14.00

GRANT, Anne. *Memoirs of American Lady with Sketches of Manners.* 1808 London. 1st ed. 2 vol set. leather. G $75.00

GRANT, Charles. *Dark Cry of the Moon.* 1985 Grant. Ills Krupowicz. 1/300. sgn. $100.00

GRANT, David. *Beauties of Modern British Poetry.* 1865 London. fore-edge of whaling scene. $650.00

GRANT, Gordon. *Greasy Luck: Whaling Sketchbook.* 1932 NY. Ills 1st ed. 4to. VG $50.00

GRANT, Gordon. *Life & Adventures of John Nicol.* 1936 NY. Rinehart. Ills Grant. Intro Laing. $20.00

GRANT, Hamil. *Last Days of Archduke Rudolph.* 1916 NY. Ills. 286 p. EX $35.00

GRANT, J.A. *Through Evangeline's Country.* 1894 Boston. Knight. Ills. 100 p. VG $10.00

GRANT, J.J. *More Single-Shot Rifles.* 1959 Morrow. Ills. 322 p. dj. VG $20.00

GRANT, J.J. *More Single-Shot Rifles.* 1976 Gun Room Pr. Ills. 322 p. dj. EX $22.50

GRANT, Joan. *Winged Pharoah.* 1938 Harper. 1st ed. VG $17.50

GRANT, John B. *Our Common Birds & How To Know Them.* 1891 NY. Ills. 12mo. 224 p. tan cloth. $17.00

GRANT, John Cameron. *Ethiopian.* 1935 Black Hawk Pr. VG $17.50

GRANT, Joseph W. *My 1st Campaign.* 1863 Boston. 152 p. scarce. $125.00

GRANT, Madison. *Caribou.* 1902 NY. Ills. sgn. VG $15.00

GRANT, U.S. *American Civil War Book & Grant Album.* 1894 NY. oblong 4to. cloth. G $50.00

GRANT, U.S. *Personal Memoirs.* 1885-1886. 1st ed. 2 vol set. leather. G $35.00

GRANTZ, G.J. *Home Book of Taxidermy & Tanning.* 1977 Stackpole. Ills. 160 p. dj. VG $10.00

GRASS, Gunter. *From Diary of Snail.* 1973 Harcourt. 1st Am ed. dj. EX $15.00

GRASS, Gunter. *Local Anaesthesia.* 1969 Harcourt. 1st Am ed. dj. EX $20.00

GRASS, Gunter. *New Poems.* 1968 Harcourt. 1st Am ed. dj. EX $20.00

GRASS, Gunther. *Dog Years.* 1965 NY. dj. EX $20.00

GRATTAN, Thomas Colley. *Civilized America.* 1859 Bradbury Evans. 2 vol set. $30.00

GRAU, Shirley Ann. *Black Prince.* 1955 Knopf. 1st ed. dj. VG $45.00

GRAU, Shirley Ann. *Black Prince.* 1955 NY. Knopf. 1st ed. sgn. dj. EX $100.00

GRAU, Shirley Ann. *Condor Passes.* 1971 Knopf. 1st ed. dj. EX $15.00

GRAU, Shirley Ann. *Condor Passes.* 1971 NY. Knopf. Advance copy. dj. EX $60.00

GRAU, Shirley Ann. *Evidence of Love.* 1977 Knopf. 1st ed. dj. EX $15.00

GRAU, Shirley Ann. *Evidence of Love.* 1977 Hamilton. 1st English ed. dj. EX $15.00

GRAU, Shirley Ann. *Hard Blue Sky.* 1958 NY. Knopf. 1st ed. dj. scarce. EX $75.00

GRAU, Shirley Ann. *Hard Blue Sky.* 1958 NY. Knopf. 1st ed. dj. VG $55.00

GRAU, Shirley Ann. *House on Coliseum Street.* 1961 Knopf. 1st ed. dj. EX $20.00

GRAU, Shirley Ann. *Keepers of the House.* 1964 NY. Knopf. 1st ed. dj. EX $15.00

GRAU, Shirley Ann. *Wind Shifting West.* 1973 Knopf. 1st ed. dj. EX $15.00

GRAVES, Charles. *Leather Armchairs: Guide to the Great Clubs of London.* 1964 NY. 1st Am ed. dj. VG $25.00

GRAVES, E.L. *Foreshore of Old VA.* c 1920. Norfolk. Ills 1st ed. 56 p. $12.50

GRAVES, John. *Good-Bye to a River.* 1960 NY. 1st ed. dj. VG $25.00

GRAVES, John. *Good-Bye to a River.* 1960 Knopf. 1st ed. dj. EX $45.00

GRAVES, Morris. *Retrospective Exhibition of Works.* 1956 CA U Pr. Ills. 4to. 78 p. wraps. $20.00

GRAVES, Robert. *Ancient Castle.* 1981 NY. 1st ed. dj. M $20.00

GRAVES, Robert. *Antigua Stamp.* 1937 NY. 1st Am ed. $40.00

GRAVES, Robert. *Count Belisarius.* 1938 London. 1st English ed. dj. VG $70.00

GRAVES, Robert. *Good-Bye to All That.* 1929 London. Cape. 3rd ed. $7.50

GRAVES, Robert. *I, Claudius.* 1934 London. 1st English ed. dj. $150.00

GRAVES, Robert. *I, Claudius.* 1934 NY. 1st ed. dj. EX $75.00

GRAVES, Robert. *Love Respelt Again.* 1969 NY. Ltd ed. 8vo. sgn. cloth. dj. $45.00

GRAVES, Robert. *On English Poetry.* 1922 London. 1st ed. dj. EX $125.00

GRAVES, Robert. *Poems 1938-1945.* 1946 London. 1st ed. dj. VG $35.00

GRAVES, Robert. *Song of Songs.* no date. (1973) Ills Hans Erni. 1st Am ed. dj. $15.00

GRAVES, Robert. *10 Poems More.* 1930 Hours Pr. Ltd 1st ed. 1/200. sgn. $150.00

GRAVES, Robert. *2 Wise Children.* 1966 NY. 1st ed. dj. M $17.00

GRAVES & HART. *T.E. Lawrence to His Biographers.* 1939 NY. Ltd 1st ed. 1/500. 2 vol set. $35.00

GRAY, Alan. *Marconi Rigging & Sailmaking.* c 1937. NY. 3rd ed. VG $15.00

GRAY, Asa. *Gray's New Manual of Botany.* 1908 Revised ed. VG $7.00

GRAY, Asa. *Gray's School & Field Botany.* 1887 NY. Review copy. $45.00

GRAY, Asa. *How Plants Grow, with a Popular Flora.* 1869 Ivison/Phinney/Blakeman. Ills. $55.00

GRAY, Asa. *Introduction to Structural & Systematic Botany Physiology.* 1864 NY. Revised 5th ed. 555 p. $20.00

GRAY, Butler. *Poetical Works of Thomas Gray.* 1867 Phil. gilt leather. VG $75.00

GRAY, Cecil & Margery. *Bed.* 1946 London. Nicholson Watson. Ills Ayrton. $15.00

GRAY, Cleve. *Hans Richter by Hans Richter.* 1971 NY. Holt Rinehart Winston. 191 p. $40.00

GRAY, David. *Gallops 2.* 1903 NY. 1st ed. VG $14.00

GRAY, David. *Mr. Carteret.* 1910 NY. Ills 1st ed. red cloth. VG $14.00

GRAY, G.A. *Descendants of George Holmes of Roxbury.* 1908 Boston. VG $25.00

GRAY, George W. *Frontiers of Flight.* 1948 NY. Knopf. 1st ed. 362 p. xl. $10.00

GRAY, Henry. *Anatomy: Descriptive & Surgical.* 1878 leather. G $12.50

GRAY, Henry. *Anatony: Descriptive & Surgical.* 1901 Ills. leather. rebound. G $20.00

GRAY, Jerry & Vivian. *Space Flight Report.* 1962 NY. Basic Books. Ills 1st ed. dj. $10.00

GRAY, M. Etheldreda. *Treasure Book of Children's Verse.* c 1910. Hodder Stoughton. 4to. VG $135.00

GRAY, O.W. *Atlas of the US.* 1874 Phil. folio. G $350.00

GRAY, R.L. *Wonderful Shenandoah Valley.* 1932 Stauton, VA. Ills 1st ed. 307 p. $12.50

GRAY, Thomas. *Elegy Written in a Country Churchyard.* 1931 Ills F Adams. small folio. tan cloth. EX $65.00

GRAY, Thomas. *Elegy Written in a Country Churchyard.* 1938 London. Ills AM Parker. 4to. dj. VG $60.00

GRAYDON, N.S. *Tales of Edisto.* 1960 Atlanta. Ills. 166 p. dj. $12.50

GREACEN, Robert. *Art of Noel Coward.* 1953 Hand Flower Pr. dj. EX $25.00

GREAVES, R.P. *Brewster's Millions.* 1903 Chicago. Lakeside Pr. 1st ed. VG $35.00

GREELEY, Horace. *American Conflict.* 1865 & 1866. 2 vol set. rebound. VG $50.00

GREELEY, Horace. *Great Industries of the US.* 1972 Hartford. Ills. 1,304 p. G $35.00

GREELEY, Horace. *Life & Public Services of Henry Clay.* 1852 Auburn, NY. 1st ed. VG $45.00

GREELEY, Horace. *Women of the Age.* 1868 Hartford. 1st ed. G $25.00

GREEN, Abel; & LAURIE, Joe. *Show Biz: From Vaude to Video.* 1951 Holt. 8vo. 613 p. cloth. dj. VG $15.00

GREEN, Anna K. *Filigree Ball.* 1903 Indianapolis. Ills 1st ed. VG $25.00

GREEN, Anna K. *Leavenworth Case: Lawyer's Story.* 1879 NY. 1st ed. later print. cloth. EX $75.00

GREEN, Anna K. *Mystery of the Hasty Arrow.* 1917 Dodd Mead. Ills Ballinger. 432 p. G $12.00

GREEN, Ben A. *Biography of the TN Walking Horse.* 1960 Nashville. 1st ed. VG $25.00

GREEN, Benny. *P.G. Wodehouse: Literary Biography.* 1981 London. 1st ed. dj. EX $40.00

GREEN, D. *Handbook of Pottery Glazes.* 1978 NY. 280 p. $27.50

GREEN, Donald E. *Panhandle Pioneer.* 1979 Norman. dj. VG $8.50

GREEN, Doron. *History of Old Homes on Radcliffe Street.* 1938 Bristol. Ills 1st ed. VG $40.00

GREEN, Edith Pinero. *Perfect Fools.* 1982 NY. 1st ed. dj. EX $8.50

GREEN, Elizabeth Shippen. *Songs of Bryn Mawr College.* 1903 Philadelphia. oblong 4to. cloth. VG $75.00

GREEN, G. Garrow. *In Irish Constabulary.* no date. Dublin. Hodges Figgis. 259 p. $30.00

GREEN, Gerald. *Blockbuster.* 1972 Doubleday. 1st ed. dj. EX $15.00

GREEN, Henry. *Back.* 1950 NY. 1st Am ed. VG $30.00

GREEN, Henry. *Back.* 1946 London. Hogarth. dj. EX $75.00

GREEN, Henry. *Loving.* 1949 NY. 1st Am ed. VG $20.00

GREEN, Henry. *Nothing.* 1950 NY. 1st Am ed. VG $30.00

GREEN, Henry. *Nothing.* 1950 London. 1st ed. dj. EX $50.00

GREEN, Horace. *General Grant's Last Stand.* 1936 NY. 1st ed. dj. VG $16.00

GREEN, J. *Edmund Thornton Jenkins: Life & Times of Black Composer.* 1982 Westport, CT. Ills. VG $20.00

GREEN, J.R. *Short History of English People.* c 1892. Harper. Ills. EX $60.00

GREEN, John D. *Birds (girls) of Britain.* 1967 NY. 1st ed. folio. dj. EX $25.00

GREEN, Margaret. *Big Book of Animal Fables.* 1965 NY. Watts. Ills Grabianski. 1st Am ed. EX $15.00

GREEN, Margaret. *Big Book of Animal Stories.* 1961 NY. Watts. Ills Grabianski. 1st Am ed. VG $12.50

GREEN, Martin. *Tolstoy & Gandhi: Men of Peace.* 1983 NY. Basic Books. 1st ed. dj. EX $20.00

GREEN, R. *Asiatic Primulas.* 1976 Surrey. 163 p. dj. VG $12.00

GREEN, S. *Amateur Fruit Growing.* 1918 Webb. 138 p. VG $5.00

GREEN, William. *Famous Fighters of the 2nd World War.* 1967 Garden City. Ills 2nd series. 132 p. dj. VG $12.50

GREEN & DAVIE. *Old Cottages & Farmhouses in Surrey.* 1908 London. Batsford. Ills 1st ed. VG $65.00

GREENAWAY, Kate. *A Apple Pie.* no date. London/NY. Warne. 4to. VG $60.00

GREENAWAY, Kate. *April Baby's Book of Tunes.* 1900 NY. Macmillan. 1st ed. $35.00

GREENAWAY, Kate. *Birthday Book for Children.* no date. London. Routledge. 1st ed. VG $125.00

GREENAWAY, Kate. *Day in a Child's Life.* c 1900. Warne. VG $125.00

GREENAWAY, Kate. *Kate Greenaway Pictures.* 1921 Warne. 1st ed. dj. EX $375.00

GREENAWAY, Kate. *Kate Greenaway's Almanac for 1887.* 1887 London. $95.00

GREENAWAY, Kate. *Kate Greenaway's Almanac for 1928.* 1928 London. Ills. VG $50.00

GREENAWAY, Kate. *Language of Flowers.* no date. London/NY. 80 p. VG $35.00

GREENAWAY, Kate. *Life & Works of Bracken Books.* 1968 London. reprint of 1905. 8vo. M $30.00

GREENAWAY, Kate. *Little Ann.* 1882 Routledge. 1st ed. EX $225.00

GREENAWAY, Kate. *Marigold Garden.* no date. London. Warne. fair. $15.00

GREENAWAY, Kate. *Mother Goose.* no date. Routledge. 1st ed. VG $110.00

GREENAWAY, Kate. *Mother Goose.* NY/London. Warne. VG $65.00

GREENAWAY, Kate. *Mother Goose.* NY/London. Warne. fair. $17.50

GREENAWAY, Kate. *Pictures From Originals.* 1921 London. 4to. cloth. dj. EX $315.00

GREENAWAY, Kate. *Under the Window.* no date. Routledge. 1st Am ed. VG $135.00

GREENAWAY, Kate. *Under the Window.* no date. Routledge. 1st Am ed. G $85.00

GREENBERG, Cara. *Mid-Century Furniture of the 1950s.* 1984 NY. 1st ed. dj. EX $25.00

GREENBERG. *Coming Attractions.* 1957 Gnome. 1st ed. G $5.00

GREENBURG & O'MALLEY. *How To Avoid Love & Marriage.* 1983 Freundlich. 1st ed. dj. EX $15.00

GREENE, Asa. *Yankee Among the Nullifiers: Autobiography.* 1833 NY. 1st ed. 152 p. rebound. G $65.00

GREENE, F.W. *Report on Russian Army: Its Campaigns in Turkey.* 1879 Appleton. VG $50.00

GREENE, G.W. *Short History of RI.* 1877 Providence. 1st ed. map. 287 p. $15.00

GREENE, Graham. *African Sketchbook.* 1961 London. 1st ed. VG $40.00

GREENE, Graham. *Burnt-Out Case.* 1961 Viking. 1st Am ed. dj. EX $30.00

GREENE, Graham. *Comedians.* 1966 NY. 1st ed. dj. M $26.00

GREENE, Graham. *Comedians.* 1966 London. 1st ed. dj. EX $45.00

GREENE, Graham. *Complaisant Lover.* 1961 NY. 1st Am ed. dj. VG $15.00

GREENE, Graham. *Dr. Fischer of Geneva; or, Bomb Party.* 1980 Simon Schuster. 1st Am ed. dj. EX $15.00

GREENE, Graham. *End of the Affair.* 1951 London. 1st ed. dj. VG $35.00

GREENE, Graham. *End of the Affair.* 1951 Viking. 1st Am ed. dj. EX $45.00

GREENE, Graham. *Getting To Know the General.* 1984 London. 1st ed. dj. M $14.00

GREENE, Graham. *Heart of the Matter.* 1948 NY. 1st Am ed. dj. VG $40.00

GREENE, Graham. *Heart of the Matter.* 1948 NY. 1st trade ed. dj. EX $20.00

GREENE, Graham. *Honorary Consul.* 1973 London. 1st ed. dj. EX $35.00

GREENE, Graham. *Honorary Consul.* 1973 Simon Schuster. 1st ed. dj. EX $15.00

GREENE, Graham. *Human Factor.* 1978 Simon Schuster. 1st Am ed. dj. EX $15.00

GREENE, Graham. *Monsignor Quixote.* 1982 London. 1st ed. VG $40.00

GREENE, Graham. *Monsignor Quixote.* 1982 Simon Schuster. 1st Am ed. dj. EX $15.00

GREENE, Graham. *Our Man in Havana.* 1958 NY. 1st Am ed. dj. VG $25.00

GREENE, Graham. *Our Man in Havana.* 1958 London. Heinemann. 1st ed. dj. EX $60.00

GREENE, Graham. *Quiet American.* 1956 NY. 1st ed. EX $30.00

GREENE, Graham. *Sort of Life.* 1971 NY. dj. M $14.00

GREENE, Graham. *Travels with My Aunt.* 1969 Bodley Head. 1st ed. dj. EX $35.00

GREENE, Graham. *3rd Man.* 1950 NY. 1st ed. cloth. dj. G $50.00

GREENE, Hugh. *Cosmopolitan Crimes.* 1971 NY. 1st Am ed. dj. EX $50.00

GREENE, L.G. *Long Live the Delta Queen.* 1973 NY. 1st ed. dj. VG $15.00

GREENE, R. *Calvary in China.* 1953 xl. VG $8.00

GREENE, Robert. *Pandosto: Triumph of Time.* 1902 Elston Pr. Ltd ed. 1/160. VG $60.00

GREENE, S. *Amateur Fruit Growing.* 1918 Webb. 138 p. VG $5.00

GREENE, S.E. *Illustrated History of Baltimore, MD.* 1980 Ills 1st ed. maps. 315 p. dj. $12.50

GREENE, V. *English Dolls' Houses of 18th & 19th Centuries.* 1955 London. Batsford. Ills. 4to. dj. VG $40.00

GREENE. *Living Room.* 1953 Heinemann. 1st ed. G $15.00

GREENE. *May We Borrow Your Husband?* 1966 Viking. 1st ed. dj. EX $20.00

GREENE. *Quiet American.* 1956 Viking. dj. EX $45.00

GREENEWALT, C.H. *Hummingbirds.* 1960 NY. dj. EX $90.00

GREENEWALT, C.H. *Hummingbirds.* 1960 NY. 1st trade ed. dj. VG $150.00

GREENEWALT, C.H. *Hummingbirds.* 1960 Garden City. Ills. dj. EX $225.00

GREENFELD. *Waters of November.* 1969 Chicago. Ills 1st ed. 4to. 160 p. dj. $20.00

GREENHOW, R. *History of OR, CA, & Other Territories of Northwest.* 1844 Boston. ½-leather. xl. G $65.00

GREENLAW, Barry A. *New England Furniture at Williamsburg.* 1975 Colonial Williamsburg. 4to. $50.00

GREENLEAF, Stephen. *Death Bed.* 1980 1st Am ed. dj. $30.00

GREENLEAF, Stephen. *Ditto List.* 1985 1st Am ed. inscr. dj. $35.00

GREENLEAF, Stephen. *Grave Error.* 1979 1st Am ed. dj. $40.00

GREENSLET, Ferris. *Lowells & Their 7 Worlds.* 1946 Boston. 1st ed. dj. VG $25.00

GREENWALT, E.A. *Point Loma Community.* 1955 Berkeley. G $10.00

GREENWAY, Dale. *Kenya Trees & Shrubs.* 1961 Nairobi. Ills 1st ed. maps. 654 p. VG $50.00

GREENWAY, John. *Down Among the Wild Men.* 1972 Little Brown. Ills 1st ed. 361 p. dj. EX $15.00

GREENWOOD, Annie Pike. *We Sagebrush Folks.* 1934 Appleton. 1st ed. 483 p. dj. $25.00

GREENWOOD, George. *Golfing Really Explained.* c 1920. London. 16mo. 88 p. dj. $25.00

GREENWOOD, Grace. *New Life in New Lands.* c 1872. Brooklyn. sgn. 413 p. G $35.00

GREENWOOD, Grace. *Stories From Famous Ballads.* 1860 Ticknor Fields. G $15.00

GREER, Germaine. *Female Eunuch.* 1971 NY. 1st Am ed. dj. VG $10.00

GREER, Germaine. *Obstacle Race: Fortunes of Women Painters & Their Works.* 1979 NY. 1st ed. dj. EX $25.00

GREER, R. *Introduction to Arts & Crafts.* 1975 NY. Ills. 122 p. $15.00

GREER, T.H. *What Roosevelt Thought.* 1958 Lansing. 1st ed. 213 p. $8.50

GREGG, E.C. *How To Tie Flies.* 1940 Barnes. Ills. 83 p. VG $8.00

GREGG, F.M. *Founding of a Nation.* 1915 Cleveland. Ills 1st ed. 683 p. maps. $27.50

GREGG, K.L. *History of Fort Osage.* 1940 MO Hist Soc. pb. EX $12.00

GREGOR, Arthur S. *Amulets, Talismans, & Fetishes.* 1975 NY. Scribner. Ills. 120 p. VG $24.00

GREGORIETTI, Guido. *Jewelry Through the Ages.* 1969 NY. American Heritage. Ills. 4to. $40.00

GREGORY, Franklin. *White Wolf.* 1941 Random House. 1st ed. VG $30.00

GREGORY, H.F. *Helicopter.* 1976 NY. sgn. dj. VG $45.00

GREGORY, Horace. *Another Look: Poem.* 1976 NY. 1st ed. dj. EX $12.50

GREGORY, Lady. *Image & Other Plays.* 1922 London. 1st ed. dj. $65.00

GREGORY, Lady. *Image.* 1910 Dublin. sgn. 12mo. $125.00

GREGORY, Lady. *Irish Folk History Plays: Tragedies.* 1912 NY. Putnam. VG $10.00

GREGORY, Lady. *On the Racecourse.* 1926 London. 1st ed. wraps. $55.00

GREGORY, Lady. *7 Short Plays.* 1909 Dublin. 1st ed. EX $18.00

GREGORY, W. *Animal Magnetism or Mesmerism & Its Phenomena.* 1884 London. 3rd ed. 252 p. xl. VG $45.00

GREGORY, W. *Letters on Animal Magnetism.* 1851 London. cloth. $85.00

GREGSON, H. *Collection of Book Plate Designs.* 1907 Boston. xl. VG $20.00

GREHAN, Ida. *Waterford: Irish Art.* 1981 NY. Rowe/Portfolio. Ills. 4to. dj. $50.00

GREIFF, C.M. *Great Houses From Pages of Magazine Antiques.* c 1970s. NY. Ills. 166 p. dj. $7.50

GREINER, James. *Wager with the Wind: The Don Sheldon Story.* 1974 Rand McNally. Ills. blue cloth. dj. EX $35.00

GRENIER, Jean. *Francois Fiedler.* 1961 Paris. Derriere Le Miroir. folio. $100.00

GRESHAM, Grits. *Complete Book of Bass Fishing.* 1966 Outdoor Life. Ills. 246 p. dj. VG $6.50

GRESHAM, Grits. *Complete Wildfowler.* 1973 Winchester. Ills. 294 p. VG $7.50

GREULICH, W. *Radiographic Atlas of Skeletal Development of Hand & Wrist.* 1950 Stanford. xl. VG $10.00

GREVEN, Philip J. *4 Generations: Population, Land, & Family in Andover, MA.* 1970 Ithaca. 1st ed. dj. VG $22.50

GREY, Beryl. *Red Curtain Up.* 1958 NY. Ills. dj. VG $25.00

GREY, Lt. Gen. C. *Early Years of His Royal Highness the Prince Consort.* 1867 NY. VG $50.00

GREY, Romer. *Cruise of Fisherman.* 1929 Harper. Ills 1st ed. 268 p. dj. VG $40.00

GREY, Zane. *Adventures in Fishing.* 1952 NY. Harper. 1st ed. dj. VG $85.00

GREY, Zane. *AZ Ames.* 1932 NY. Harper. 1st ed. VG $25.00

GREY, Zane. *Black Mesa.* 1955 NY. Harper. 1st ed. dj. VG $80.00

GREY, Zane. *Blue Feather.* 1961 NY. Harper. 1st ed. dj. xl. VG $70.00

GREY, Zane. *Call of the Canyon.* 1930 London. Hodder Stoughton. 1st ed. dj. $175.00

GREY, Zane. *Captivities of the Desert.* 1952 NY. Harper. 1st ed. dj. VG $100.00

GREY, Zane. *Deer Stalker.* 1949 NY. Harper. 1st ed. dj. VG $85.00

GREY, Zane. *Desert Gold.* 1926 Nelson. 1st ed. dj. EX $250.00

GREY, Zane. *Desert of Wheat.* London. Hodder Stoughton. 1st ed. dj. $250.00

GREY, Zane. *Fishing Virgin Waters.* 1925 NY. 1st ed. cloth. VG $35.00

GREY, Zane. *Forlorn River.* 1927 NY. Harper. 1st ed. VG $25.00

GREY, Zane. *Fugitive Trail.* 1957 NY. Harper. 1st ed. dj. VG $100.00

GREY, Zane. *Heritage of the Desert.* London. Nelson. 1st ed. dj. EX $250.00

GREY, Zane. *Horse Heaven Hill.* 1959 NY. Harper. 1st ed. dj. G $60.00

GREY, Zane. *Last of the Plainsmen.* London. Hodder Stoughton. 1st ed. dj. $200.00

GREY, Zane. *Last of the Plainsmen.* 1909 Outing Pub. rare. G $100.00

GREY, Zane. *Lone Star Ranger.* 1926 London. Nelson. 1st ed. dj. EX $250.00

GREY, Zane. *Man of the Forest.* no date. Hodder Stoughton. 1st ed. dj. $250.00

GREY, Zane. *Maverick Queen.* 1950 NY. Harper. 1st ed. dj. VG $80.00

GREY, Zane. *Mysterious Rider.* 1921 NY/London. Harper. green cloth. VG $14.00

GREY, Zane. *NV, Romance of the West.* 1929 NY. Harper. 1st ed. 12mo. tan cloth. VG $15.00

GREY, Zane. *Rainbow Trail.* 1926 London. Nelson. 1st ed. dj. EX $225.00

GREY, Zane. *Ranger & Other Stories.* 1979 Franklin Lib. Ltd ed. EX $60.00

GREY, Zane. *Reef Girl.* 1977 NY. Harper. 1st ed. dj. EX $50.00

GREY, Zane. *Roaring U.P. Trail.* 1918 London. Hodder Stoughton. 1st ed. dj. $200.00

GREY, Zane. *Robber's Roost.* 1932 London. Hodder Stoughton. 1st ed. dj. $300.00

GREY, Zane. *Roping Lions in the Grand Canyon.* London. Hodder Stoughton. 1st ed. dj. $175.00

GREY, Zane. *Rouge River Feud.* 1930 NY. Harper. 1st ed. dj. VG $65.00

GREY, Zane. *Round-Up (Omnibus).* 1943 Grosset Dunlap. dj. VG $90.00

GREY, Zane. *Stairs of Sand.* 1943 NY. Harper. 1st ed. dj. VG $60.00

GREY, Zane. *Stranger From the Tonto.* 1957 London. 1st ed. dj. VG $50.00

GREY, Zane. *Sunset Pass.* 1931 NY. Harper. 1931 A-F ed. VG $20.00

GREY, Zane. *Tales of Fishes.* no date. Hodder Stoughton. 1st ed. dj. $275.00

GREY, Zane. *Tales of Fishes.* 1919 NY. Harper. dj. xl. VG $80.00

GREY, Zane. *Tales of Fresh-Water Fishing.* 1928 Grosset Dunlap. 4to. dj. EX $52.00

GREY, Zane. *Tales of Lonely Trails.* 1922 Harper. Ills 1st ed. 394 p. VG $32.50

GREY, Zane. *Tales of Southern Rivers.* 1924 Grosset Dunlap. Ills. 249 p. VG $30.00

GREY, Zane. *Tales of Swordfish & Tuna.* 1927 NY. Harper. Ills 1st ed. 4to. 203 p. G $30.00

GREY, Zane. *Tales of the Angler's Eldorado New Zealand.* 1926 Grosset Dunlap. Ills. 4to. VG $35.00

GREY, Zane. *Tappan's Burro.* 1923 NY. Harper. Ills 1st ed. VG $125.00

GREY, Zane. *Thunder Mountain.* 1935 NY. Grosset Dunlap. sgn. dj. G $45.00

GREY, Zane. *Thundering Herd.* 1925 Leipzig. Tauchnitz. 1st ed. dj. EX $375.00

GREY, Zane. *Under the Tonto Rim.* no date. Hodder Stoughton. 1st ed. dj. $225.00

GREY, Zane. *Valley of Wild Horses.* NY. Harper. 1st ed. dj. VG $85.00

GREY, Zane. *Wanderer of the Wasteland.* 1923 Harper. 1st ed. 3 plts. VG $15.00

GREY, Zane. *West of the Pecos.* 1937 Collier. VG $20.00

GREY, Zane. *Zane Grey's Book of Camps & Trails.* 1931 NY. Harper. xl. G $225.00

GRIESENGER, Theodore. *Jesuits: Compete History of Open & Secret Proceedings.* 1885 London. 8vo. green cloth. EX $145.00

GRIEVE, R. *New England Coast.* 1890 Providence. Ills. 216 p. wraps. $15.00

GRIFFEN, Jeff. *Hunting Dogs of America.* 1964 Doubleday. Ills. 311 p. dj. VG $12.00

GRIFFIN, E.F. *Westchester Co. & Its People.* 1946 NY. 3 vol set. EX $45.00

GRIFFIN, F. *Old Salem in Pictures.* 1966 Charlotte, NC. Ills 1st ed. sgn. maps. dj. $12.50

GRIFFIN, J. *Chemical Handicraft: Classified & Descriptive Catalog.* 1877 London. Ills. VG $175.00

GRIFFIN, John H. *Nuni.* 1956 Boston/Dallas. 1st ed. dj. VG $32.00

GRIFFIN. *Commodore J. Barry.* c 1900. Phil. private print. 1/600. xl. VG $8.00

GRIFFIS, Eliot. *Story of Wallons at Home, in Lands of Exile, & America.* 1923 Boston. VG $30.00

GRIFFIS. *9 Lives of Deaf Smith.* 1958 Dallas. dj. EX $20.00

GRIFFITH, Fuller. *Lithographs of Childe Hassam.* 1980 reprint of 1962. $35.00

GRIFFITHS, D. *2 Years' Residence in New Settlements of OH, North America.* 1835 London. EX $1000.00

GRIFFITHS, M. *Hidden Menace: History of Mine Warfare at Sea.* 1981 Greenwich. Ills. dj. EX $12.50

GRIFFS, W.E. *Millard Fillmore.* 1915 Ithaca. 1st ed. sgn. 144 p. $25.00

GRIGGS, Nathan. *Lyrics of the Lariat.* 1893 Fleming Revell. cloth. EX $25.00

GRIGGS, R.F. *Valley of 10,000 Smokes.* 1922 Nat'l Geog Soc. Ills. 341 p. maps. EX $75.00

GRIGGS. *Indian Art in Marlborough House.* c 1900. Griggs. Ills. folio. black leather. $225.00

GRIMES, Absalom. *Confederate Mail Runner.* 1926 New Haven. xl. VG $25.00

GRIMM, Brothers. *Grimm's Fairy Tales.* 1946 NY. Scribner. Ills Abbott. 8vo. EX $25.00

GRIMM, Brothers. *Grimm's Fairy Tales.* 1922 Bavaria. Winston. Cozy Hour Series. VG $10.00

GRIMM, Brothers. *Grimm's Fairy Tales: 20 Stories.* 1973 Viking. Ills Rackham/others. VG $20.00

GRIMM, Brothers. *Household Tales.* 1973 London. Methuen. Ills Peake. dj. VG $15.00

GRIMM, Brothers. *King Grisly Beard.* 1973 NY. Ills Sendak. 1st ed. EX $15.00

GRIMSCHITZ, Bruno. *Austrian Painting From Biedermeier to Modern Times.* 1963 Wein. Wolfrum. Ills. 4to. $75.00

GRIMSHAW, Beatrice. *Fiji & Its Possibilities.* 1907 NY. Ills 1st ed. 315 p. VG $35.00

GRINNELL, G.B. *American Game Bird Shooting.* 1910 NY. 1st ed. 2 plts. VG $75.00

GRINNELL, G.B. *American Game Bird Shooting.* 1910 NY. Forest Stream. Ills. 558 p. $45.00

GRINNELL, G.B. *Beyond the Old Frontier.* 1976 Williamstown. dj. VG $20.00

GRINNELL, G.B. *Cheyenne Indians.* 1923 New Haven. 1st ed. 2 vol set. EX $225.00

GRINNELL, G.B. *Fighting Cheyennes.* 1915 NY. 1st ed. VG $125.00

GRINNELL, G.B. *Fighting Cheyennes.* 1956 OK U Pr. Ills Review copy. 452 p. dj. $42.50

GRINNELL, G.B. *When Buffalo Ran.* 1969 OK U Pr. Ills 2nd ed. 114 p. dj. VG $10.00

GRINNELL, G.B. *When Buffalo Ran.* 1920 Yale. 1st ed. dj. EX $75.00

GRINNELL, Joseph. *Gold Hunting in AK.* 1901 Elgin, IL. Ills. square 8vo. $95.00

GRINNELL, Joseph. *Gold Hunting in AK.* 1983 AK Northwest. Ills. 4to. 78 p. maps. pb. EX $8.00

GRINNELL & MILNE. *Silent Victory, September 1940.* 1958 London. Ills. dj. G $18.00

GRISERI, Andreina. *La Palazzina di Stupinigi.* 1982 Novara. Ills. 76 p. $20.00

GRISMER, J.P. *Way Down East: New England Life.* 1900 NY. Ills 1st ed. 190 p. $7.50

GRISMER, Karl H. *History of Kent: Historical & Biographical.* 1932 Kent, OH. Ills 1st ed. photos. 296 p. EX $75.00

GRISWOLD, F.G. *Clipper Ships & Yachts.* 1927 Ills. $22.50

GRISWOLD, F.G. *Fish Facts & Fancies.* 1926 NY. Ills Ltd ed. 1/1,000. VG $75.00

GRISWOLD, F.G. *Some Fish & Some Fishing.* 1921 NY. Ills 1st ed. VG $20.00

GRISWOLD, Rufus Wilmot. *Female Poets of America.* 1849 Phil. 1st ed. presentation. leather. $200.00

GROBER. *Picturesque Palestine, Arabia, & Syria.* 1925 NY/Berlin. Ills. 4to. cloth. VG $45.00

GROHMAN, W.B. *Sport in the Alps.* 1896 NY. Ills 1st ed. 356 p. G $47.50

GROHMANN, Will. *Drawings of Paul Klee.* 1960 NY. Abrams. Ills. square 4to. 176 p. $75.00

GROHMANN, Will. *Drawings of Paul Klee.* 1955 NY. Abrams. Ills. 4to. 441 p. dj. $125.00

GROHMANN, Will. *Drawings of Paul Klee.* 1945 NY. Valentin. Ills 2nd print. 4to. $95.00

GROHMANN, Will. *Kandinsky.* 1958 NY. Abrams. dj. VG $100.00

GROHMANN, Will. *Willi Baumeister.* 1952 Stuttgart. German/English text. 4to. $125.00

GROMAIRE, Francois. *Gromaire.* 1949 Paris. Braun & Cie. Ills. 4to. $35.00

GRONAU, George. *Correggio des Meisters Gemalde.* 1907 Stuttgart. 1st ed. VG $65.00

GRONEFELD, G. *Understanding Animals.* 1965 Viking. Ills. 319 p. VG $10.00

GRONEMAN, C.H. *Applied Leathercraft.* 1942 IL. Ills. 210 p. $12.50

GROPIUS, Walter. *New Architecture & the Bauhaus.* 1936 1st Am ed. VG $40.00

GROPMAN, D. *Say It Ain't So Joe.* 1979 Boston. 1st ed. dj. VG $15.00

GROSE, F. *Classical Dictionary of Vulgar Tongue.* 1785 Hooper. 1st ed. 8vo. G $200.00

GROSE, Francis. *Antiquities of Scotland.* 1789-1791. London. 1st ed. 2 vol set. VG $250.00

GROSE, Francis. *Antiquities of England & Wales.* 1773-1787. London. folio. 6 vol set. VG $600.00

GROSE, Francis. *Antiquities of Ireland.* 1791-1795. London. 2 vol set. scarce. $450.00

GROSS, Chaim. *Fantasy Drawings.* 1956 Beechhurst Pr. 1st ed. dj. EX $25.00

GROSS, L. *Last Jews in Berlin.* 1982 NY. dj. G $17.50

GROSS, M. *Hiawatha.* 1926 NY. Ills 1st ed. dj. VG $15.00

GROSS, Polly. *Western Motel.* 1985 Atheneum. Advance copy. dj. EX $20.00

GROSSINGER, R. *Solar Journal.* 1970 Los Angeles. Ltd 1st ed. sgn. mylar wraps. $15.00

GROSZ, George. *Ecce Homo.* 1965 NY. Brussell. Ills. boxed. $50.00

GROSZ, George. *Little Yes & Big No.* 1946 NY. 1st ed. dj. $50.00

GROSZ, George. *30 Drawings & Watercolors.* 1944 NY. Herrmann. Ills 1st ed. spiral bdg. VG $45.00

GROTH-MARNAT, Gary. *Handbook of Psychological Assessment.* 1984 Van Nostrand. dj. EX $15.00

GROTIUS, Hugo. *Le Droit de la Guierre de la Paix.* 1724 Amsterdam. Pierre de Coup. 2 vols in 1. $130.00

GROUEFF, S. *Manhattan Project.* 1967 Boston. 1st ed. dj. EX $28.50

GROUSSET, Rene. *La Chine et Son Art.* 1951 Paris. Libraire Plon. wraps. G $18.00

GROUT, A.J. *Mosses with a Hand Lens.* 1924 private print. Ills. 339 p. VG $20.00

GROVE, A.R. *Lure & Lore of Trout Fishing.* 1971 Freshet. Ills. 336 p. slipcase. EX $10.00

GROVER, Eulaile O. *Mother Goose Rhymes.* 1925 Volland. Ills F Richardson. Favor ed. $40.00

GROVER, Eulalie O. *Mother Goose Rhymes.* 1915 Chicago. Donohue. Volland ed. slipcase. $75.00

GROVER, Eulalie O. *Overall Boys.* 1905 Rand McNally. VG $25.00

GROVER, Ray & Lee. *Art Glass Nouveau.* 1972 Tuttle. slipcase. M $125.00

GROVER, Ray & Lee. *Art Glass Nouveau.* 1975 Rutland. Tuttle. 424 plts. dj. EX $25.00

GROVER, Ray & Lee. *English Cameo Glass.* 1980 NY. Crown. Ills. 4to. 498 p. dj. $40.00

GROVES, Lt. Col. P. *History of the 2nd Dragoons: The Royal Scots Grays.* 1893 Edinburgh. Ills Harry Payne. 4to. $100.00

GROVES, Lt. Col. P. *History of the 42nd Royal Highlanders: The Black Watch.* 1893 Edinburgh. Ills Harry Payne. 4to. $100.00

GROVES & THORPE. *Chemical Technology, Vol. I.* 1889 Phil. Ills. 4to. 802 p. VG $55.00

GRUBAR. *William Ranney: Painter of the Early West.* 1962 Corcoran Gallery of Art. EX $30.00

GRUBB, Davis. *Night of the Hunter.* 1953 NY. dj. VG $8.00

GRUELLE, Johnny. *Beloved Belinda.* Voland. 2nd ed. boxed. $75.00

GRUELLE, Johnny. *Friendly Fairies.* Volland. 19th print. $25.00

GRUELLE, Johnny. *Little Sunny Stories.* 1919 Sunny Book. Ills 29th ed. VG $18.00

GRUELLE, Johnny. *Little Sunny Stories.* c1919. 11th ed. 40 p. G $15.00

GRUELLE, Johnny. *Little Sunny Stories.* Volland. 24th print. $22.00

GRUELLE, Johnny. *Magical Land of Noom.* 1922 Chicago/NY. Donahue. Ills. VG $32.50

GRUELLE, Johnny. *My Very Own Fairy Stories.* Volland. 39th print. $35.00

GRUELLE, Johnny. *Original Raggedy Ann Stories.* no date. Chicago. dj. EX $35.00

GRUELLE, Johnny. *Orphan Annie Storybook.* 1921 Bobbs Merrill. Ills. cloth. VG $35.00

GRUELLE, Johnny. *Raggedy Andy Stories.* Volland. 59th print. $22.00

GRUELLE, Johnny. *Raggedy Andy Stories.* 1920 NY. Volland. VG $40.00

GRUELLE, Johnny. *Raggedy Ann & Andy & Camel with the Wrinkled Knees.* 1951 Gruelle Co. Ills. green cloth. G $7.50

GRUELLE, Johnny. *Raggedy Ann & Andy & Camel with the Wrinkled Knees.* Volland. 26th print. boxed. $30.00

GRUELLE, Johnny. *Raggedy Ann & Betsy Bonnet String.* 1943 Gruelle Co. 1st ed. dj. EX $20.00

GRUELLE, Johnny. *Raggedy Ann in the Deep Woods.* 1930 Chicago. Donohue. Ills. 8vo. VG $20.00

GRUELLE, Johnny. *Raggedy Ann Stories.* 1918 Donohue Volland. G $20.00

GRUELLE, Johnny. *Raggedy Ann's Magical Wishes.* 1928 Donahue. Ills. VG $18.00

GRUELLE, Johnny. *Raggedy Ann's Wishing Pebble.* 1925 Chicago/NY. 1st ed. dj. VG $30.00

GRUELLE, Johnny. *Rhymes for Kindly Children.* 1937 Wise Parslow. Ills. 8vo. VG $18.00

GRUEN, John. *Menotti.* 1978 NY. Macmillan. 1st print. VG $18.00

GRUENIG, P. *Dobermann Pinscher.* 1939 NY. Orange Judd. VG $22.00

GRUENING, Ernest. *Battle for AK Statehood.* 1967 AK U Pr. Centennial ed. cloth. dj. EX $10.00

GRUMBACH, Doris. *Company She Kept.* 1967 Macmillan. Ills 2nd imp. dj. VG $7.50

GRUMBACH, Doris. *Ladies.* 1984 Dutton. 1st ed. dj. EX $15.00

GRUMBACH, Doris. *Missing Person.* 1981 Putnam. 1st ed. dj. EX $12.00

GRUMBACH, Doris. *Spoil of the Flowers.* 1962 Doubleday. 1st ed. dj. VG $65.00

GRUNDY, F. *Handbook for Social Medicine.* 1947 Luton/London. Leagrave Pr. 4th ed. VG $20.00

GUARESCHI, Giovanni. *Don Camillo's Dilemma.* 1954 NY. 1st ed. dj. EX $17.00

GUARMANI, C. *Northern Najd.* 1928 London. cloth. VG $50.00

GUDIOL, Jose. *El Greco 1541-1614.* 1973 NY. Viking. plts. $45.00

GUEDALLA, Philip. *Bonnet & Shawl: An Album.* 1927 Crosby Gaige. Ltd ed. 1/571. sgn. EX $35.00

GUERMAN, M. *Art of the October Revolution.* 1979 Abrams. Ills. 4to. dj. VG $25.00

GUEROT, Alfred. *French Cooking for Everyone.* 1963 Paris. Golden Pr. dj. VG $10.00

GUEST, Edgar. *Heap Livin'.* 1906 Reilly Lee. sgn. VG $10.00

GUEST, Judith. *Ordinary People.* 1976 Viking. 1st ed. dj. EX $20.00

GUEST, Judith. *2nd Heaven.* 1982 Viking. Advance copy. dj. EX $15.00

GUGGENHEIM, Peggy. *Out of This Century: Confessions of an Art Addict.* 1979 NY. Review copy. sgn. dj. $45.00

GUGGISBERG, C.A.W. *Wild Cats of the World.* 1975 Taplinger. Ills. 328 p. dj. EX $12.50

GUIART, Jean. *Arts of South Pacific.* 1963 Golden. Ills 1st ed. 461 p. dj. VG $50.00

GUILD, Curtis. *Over the Ocean; or, Sights & Scenes in Foreign Lands.* 1880 Boston. 12mo. 558 p. G $16.00

GUILD, J. *Old Times in TN.* 1878 Nashville. 1st ed. G $50.00

GUILD, L.V.A. *Geography of American Antiques.* 1927 NY. Doubleday. G $30.00

GUILFORD, Carol. *Easiest Cookbook.* no date. NY. 1st ed. dj. EX $10.00

GUILFOYLE, J.H. *On Trail of Forgotten Man.* 1933 Boston. Ills 1st ed. 190 p. $7.50

GUILLAUME, Paul; & MUNRO, T. *Primitive Negro Sculpture.* 1946 NY. Ills. 4to. VG $75.00

GUINNESS, Alec. *Blessings in Disguise.* 1986 Knopf. 1st Am ed. dj. VG $10.00

GUITERMAN, A. *Death & General Putnam.* 1935 NY. 1st ed. dj. VG $17.00

GUITERMAN, Arthur. *Laughing Muse.* 1915 NY. 1st ed. sgn. VG $25.00

GULLAND, W.G. *Chinese Porcelain.* 1911 London. 3rd ed. 4to. 2 vol set. VG $145.00

GULLEGO, Julia. *Zurbaran 1598-1664.* 1977 NY. Rizzoli. $42.50

GUMMERE, J. *Treatise on Surveying.* 1845 Phil. Ills. 266 p. $15.00

GUMUCHIAN. *Les Livres de l'Enfance.* 1985 Holland Pr. 2 vol set. djs. VG $85.00

GUN, N.E. *Day of the Americans.* 1966 NY Ills. dj. G $27.50

GUNES, C.V. *Grand Old Lady.* 1959 Cleveland. Pennington Pr. 1st ed. dj. VG $15.00

GUNN, James. *Breaking Point.* 1972 NY. Walker. 1st ed. dj. EX $15.00

GUNN, John C. *Gunn's Family Physician.* 1889 Cincinnati. Ills. 1,230 p. black leather. $20.00

GUNN, John C. *Gunn's Newest Family Physician or Home Book of Health.* 1878 Ills. Moore. 1,230 p. G $195.00

GUNN, John C. *New Domestic Physician.* 1864 Cincinnati. Ills. plts. 1,128 p. VG $50.00

GUNN, Thomas. *To the Air.* 1974 MA. Godine. 1st ed. sgn. EX $18.00

GUNNARSSON, Gunnar. *Good Shepherd.* 1940 Indianapolis. Ills Simkovitch. 1st ed. dj. $7.00

GUNNING, I.C. *Prehistoric People of Eastern OK & Their Culture.* 1974 OK Hist Soc. Ills. 56 p. pb. EX $14.00

GUNNISON, Almon. *Rambles Overland: Trip Across the Continent.* 1884 Boston. VG $25.00

GUNNISON, J.W. *Mormons or Latter Day Saints.* 1853 Phil. VG $40.00

GUNSAULUS, Frank W. *Monk & Knight: Historical Study in Fiction.* 1891 McClurg. 1st ed. 2 vol set. EX $20.00

GUNST, F. *Martyrs of Spanish Inquisition.* 1870 San Francisco. 1st Am ed. VG $75.00

GUNTER, A.C. *Mr. Potter of TX.* 1888 NY. 1st ed. 1/60,000. $40.00

GUNTHER, J. *Behind the Curtain.* 1949 NY. 351 p. $5.00

GUNTHER, J. *Days To Remember: America 1945-1955.* 1956 NY. Ills 1st ed. 237 p. dj. $12.50

GUNTHER, J. *Inside Africa.* 1955 NY. 1st ed. map. 892 p. dj. $7.50

GUNTHER, J. *Inside Europe.* 1937 London. Ills. 527 p. dj. $6.00

GUNTHER, J. *Inside USA.* 1947 NY. 1st ed. maps. 920 p. cloth. $10.00

GUNTHER, J. *Roosevelt in Retrospect.* 1950 NY. 1st ed. 379 p. cloth. $10.00

GUNTHER, R.T. *Earth Movements in Bay of Naples.* 1903 London. Ills. VG $20.00

GUPTILL, Arthur L. *Norman Rockwell: Illustrator.* 1946 NY. 1st ed. presentation. sgn Rockwell. EX $120.00

GURLEY, W. & L.E. *Manual of Principal Instruments Used in American Surveying.* 1873 Troy. 10 plts. cloth. EX $60.00

GURN, J. *Charles Carroll of Carrollton 1737-1832.* 1932 NY. Ills 1st ed. 297 p. $17.50

GURNEY, C.S. *Portsmouth: Historic & Picturesque.* 1902 NH. Ills 1st ed. maps. 228 p. $27.50

GURNEY, C.W. *Northwestern Pomology.* 1894 Concord, NE. 12mo. 293 p. $35.00

GUSTAFSON, A. *Burrowing Birds.* 1981 Lothrop Lee. Ills 1st ed. 64 p. dj. EX $6.00

GUSTAFSON, A. *Soils & Soil Management.* 1947 NY. McGraw. 424 p. brown cloth. VG $10.00

GUSTAVSON, Leland. *Enjoy Your Golf.* 1954 Harcourt Brace. Ills 1st ed. dj. VG $10.00

GUSTON, Philip. *New Paintings.* 1974 Boston. Ills. oblong 8vo. 20 p. wraps. $5.00

GUTHE. *Pueblo Pottery Making: Study at San Ildefonso.* 1925 Yale U Pr. 1st ed. VG $65.00

GUTHRIE, A.B. *Big Sky.* 1947 Sloane. 1st ed. dj. G $25.00

GUTHRIE, A.B. *Big Sky.* 1947 Houghton Mifflin. 1st ed. sgn. $70.00

GUTHRIE, A.B. *Last Valley.* 1975 Houghton Mifflin. 1st ed. dj. $15.00

GUTHRIE, W. *Seeds of Man.* 1976 NY. 1st ed. dj. EX $20.00

GUTHRIE, William. *New Geographical, Historical, & Commercial Grammer.* 1795 London. 8vo. 26 fld maps. VG $100.00

GUTTFIELD, F. *Fishing Tackle & Baits.* 1973 Crescent. Ills. 64 p. G $6.50

GUY, Rosa. *Bird at My Window.* 1966 Lippincott. 1st ed. dj. EX $40.00

GUY, Rosa. *Measure of Time.* 1983 Holt. Advance copy. wraps. EX $35.00

GUYOT, Guillaume Germain. *Histoire de France.* 1788-1796. Paris. Ills. 5 vol set. $100.00

GWYNN, S. *Captain Scott.* 1930 Harper. Ills 1st ed. 240 p. VG $5.00

H

HAAGENSEN, C.D. *100 Years of Medicine.* 1943 NY. Sheridan House. 1st ed. VG $18.00

HAAK, Bob. *Golden Age: Dutch Painters of the 17th Century.* 1984 NY. Abrams. Ills. 536 p. dj. $75.00

HAAK, Bob. *Rembrandt: His Life, His Work, & His Time.* no date. NY. Abrams. Ills. 348 p. dj. $100.00

HAARD, K. & R. *Foraging for Edible Wild Mushrooms.* 1978 Cloudburst. Ills. 156 p. wraps. EX $6.00

HAAS, Arthur. *Vektoranalysis.* 1922 Berlin. Ills 1st ed. 149 p. EX $45.00

HAAS, Emmy. *Pride's Progress: Story of a Family of Lions.* 1967 Harper Row. Ills. 116 p. dj. EX $10.00

HAAS, Gerda. *These I Do Remember.* 1982 Freeport, ME. 1st ed. dj. VG $15.00

HAAS, Joseph; & LOVITZ, Gene. *Carl Sandburg: Pictorial Biography.* 1978 Putnam. 1st ed. dj. $35.00

HABENSTEIN, Robert W. *History of American Funeral Directory.* 1955 Milwaukee, WI. Bulfin Printers. 1st ed. G $10.00

HABER, F. *Thermodynamics of Technical Gas Reactions.* 1908 NY. Longman. 356 p. xl. $40.00

HABERLY, L. *Medieval English Paving Tiles.* 1937 Shakespeare Head. 1/425. EX $125.00

HABERLY, L. *Pursuit of Horizon: Life of George Catlin.* 1948 NY. Ills 1st ed. 239 p. dj. VG $27.50

HABERLY, L. *Sacrifice of Spring: Masque of Queens.* 1927 Long Crendon. 7 Acres Pr. 1/124. 4to. 20 p. $350.00

HABERLY, L. *4th of July; or, OR Orator.* 1942 St. Louis. private print. 1/350. 8vo. VG $50.00

HACHETTE, M. *Traite Elementaire des Machines.* 1819 Paris. 2nd ed. 4to. 374 p. EX $170.00

HACKETT. *Narrative of Expedition To Join the South American Patriots.* 1818 London. rebound. $145.00

HACKLE, Sparse Grey. *Fishless Days, Angling Nights.* 1971 Crown. Ills. 223 p. dj. EX $5.00

HADDOCK, J.A. *Picturesque St. Lawrence River.* 1895 NY. Ills 1st ed. 416 p. VG $95.00

HADER, Berta & Elmer. *Billy Butter.* 1936 Macmillan. Ills 1st ed. oblong 8vo. dj. $30.00

HADER, Berta & Elmer. *Cricket.* 1938 Macmillan. Ills 1st ed. 8vo. red cloth. $25.00

HADER, Berta & Elmer. *Little Antelope.* 1962 NY. Macmillan. Ills 1st print. 41 p. dj. G $30.00

HADER, Berta & Elmer. *Skyrocket.* 1946 Macmillan. 1st ed. 8vo. dj. $25.00

HADFIELD, M. *Gardens.* 1962 NY. 128 p. slipcase. G $6.00

HADFIELD, Robert A. *Work of Metallurgical Chemist.* 1921 Sheffield. Ills. 97 p. VG $40.00

HADFIELD, William. *Brazil, River Plate, & Falkland Islands.* 1854 London. Longman. 1st ed. fld map. $150.00

HADLOCK, Adah. *My Life in the Southwest.* 1969 TX Western Pr. 1st ed. 113 p. dj. M $12.00

HAECKEL, E. *Evolution of Man: Human Embryology & Ontogeny.* 1906 NY. Ills 5th ed. 8vo. 364 p. VG $28.00

HAESAERTS, Paul. *James Ensor.* 1959 NY. Abrams. Ills. 4to. 386 p. dj. $100.00

HAFEN, L.R. *Fremont's 4th Expedition.* 1966 Glendale. 1st ed. dj. EX $50.00

HAFEN, L.R. *Mountain Men & Fur Traders of the Far West.* 1982 NE U Pr. Ills. 401 p. pb. EX $10.00

HAFEN, L.R. *Overland Routes to the Gold Fields.* 1859 Glendale. Clark. 1st ed. EX $62.00

HAFEN, L.R. & Ann W. *Reports From CO.* 1961 Glendale. 1st ed. dj. VG $27.50

HAFEN & GHENT. *Broken Hand.* 1931 Denver. 1st ed. sgn. $200.00

HAFEN & YOUNG. *Ft. Laramie 1834-1890.* 1938 CA. AH Clark. inscr. VG $300.00

HAFTMANN, Werner. *Paul Klee Watercolors, Drawings, & Writings.* 1969 NY. Abrams. Ills. 4to. cloth. dj. $50.00

HAGEDORN, Hermann. *Americanism of Theodore Roosevelt.* 1923 Houghton Mifflin. 1st ed. EX $10.00

HAGEDORN, Hermann. *Roosevelt Family of Sagamore Hill.* 1954 NY. Ills 1st ed. 424 p. dj. $10.00

HAGEDORN, Hermann. *Roosevelt in the Bad Lands.* 1912 NY. 8vo. 491 p. cloth. $85.00

HAGEDORN, Hermann. *Roosevelt in the Bad Lands.* 1921 Cambridge. Riverside Pr. photos. fair. $35.00

HAGEDORN, Hermann. *Rough Riders.* 1927 NY. Harper. 1st ed. scarce. G $20.00

HAGEN, Uta. *Love of Cooking.* 1976 NY. 1st ed. dj. EX $10.00

HAGERBAUMER, David. *Selected American Game Birds.* 1972 Caxton. Ills. oblong 4to. sgn. EX $40.00

HAGERTY, H.J. *Jasmine Trail.* 1936 Boston. 1st ed. dj. EX $8.50

HAGGARD, H. *Winter Pilgrimage.* 1902 London. 2nd imp. VG $22.00

HAGGARD, H. Rider. *Allen Quatermain.* 1922 London. Longman. reprint. EX $7.00

HAGGARD, H. Rider. *Brethren.* 1904 NY. Ills. gilt blue cloth. VG $12.00

HAGGARD, H. Rider. *King Solomon's Mine.* London. reprint of 1885. G $6.00

HAGGARD, H. Rider. *Moon of Israel.* 1918 London. Murray. reprint. wraps. VG $7.00

HAGGARD, H. Rider. *Private Diaries 1914-1925.* 1980 NY. 1st ed. dj. M $14.00

HAGGARD, H. Rider. *She & Allan.* 1921 NY. 1st ed. dj. VG $35.00

HAGGARD, H. Rider. *She.* 1927 London. Longman. reprint. EX $6.00

HAGGARD, H. Rider. *When the World Shook.* 1919 NY. Longman Green. 1st Am ed. VG $27.50

HAGGARD, H. Rider. *Witch's Head.* no date. NY/London. Street Smith. VG $8.50

HAGGARD, Howard W. *Doctor in History.* 1935 New Haven. Yale U Pr. 2nd print. dj. $15.00

HAGGARD, Howard W. *Mystery, Magic, & Medicine.* 1929 Harper. dj. G $10.00

HAGGIN, B.H. *Music in the Nation.* 1949 NY. 1st print. VG $8.50

HAGIE, C.E. *American Rifle for Hunting & Target Shooting.* 1946 NY. 4th ed. dj. VG $10.00

HAGIE, C.E. *How To Hunt North American Big Game.* 1946 Macmillan. Ills 1st ed. 195 p. VG $7.50

HAGUE, Eleanor. *Latin American Music: Past & Present.* 1934 Santa Ana. Ills. VG $25.00

HAGUE, Michael. *World of Unicorns Pop-Up Book.* 1986 NY. Holt. Ills 1st ed. M $12.50

HAHNEMANN, Samuel. *Organon of Homeopathic Medicine.* 1843 NY. 2nd Am ed. $80.00

HAIG-BROWN, R.L. *Fisherman's Spring.* 1951 Morrow. Ills. 222 p. dj. VG $20.00

HAIG-BROWN, R.L. *Fisherman's Summer.* 1959 Morrow. Ills 1st ed. 253 p. dj. VG $20.00

HAIG-BROWN, R.L. *Fisherman's Winter*. 1954 Morrow. Ills. 288 p. dj. VG $20.00

HAIG-BROWN, R.L. *Measure of the Year*. 1950 NY. 1st ed. dj. VG $40.00

HAIG-BROWN, R.L. *Return to the River*. 1954 NY. dj. VG $25.00

HAIG-BROWN, R.L. *Return to the River*. 1941 Morrow. Ills Charles De Foe. dj. G $40.00

HAIG-BROWN, R.L. *River Never Sleeps*. 1981 NY. SftCvr. EX $10.00

HAIG-BROWN, R.L. *Western Angler*. 1981 NY. SftCvr. EX $10.00

HAIGHT, WHEELER, & CHARLOT. *Portraits of Latin America Seen by Her Print Makers*. 1946 NY. Hastings. English/Spanish text. dj. EX $40.00

HAILEY, Arthur. *Airport*. 1968 Doubleday. 1st ed. dj. EX $15.00

HAILEY, Arthur. *Final Diagnosis*. 1959 Doubleday. 1st ed. dj. VG $15.00

HAINES, D.P. *Life on KY Stock Farm*. 1947 NY. Hobson. Ills. 174 p. VG $10.00

HAINES, H.A. *History of English Literature*. 1877 London. 4vo. $40.00

HAINING, Peter. *Complete Birdman: Illustrated History of Man-Powered Flight*. 1977 NY. St. Martin. Ills 1st ed. 160 p. dj. EX $15.00

HAIRSTON, T. Beatrice. *Brief History of Danville, VA 1728-1954*. 1955 Richmond. dj. VG $30.00

HAJEK, L. *Chinese Art*. c 1960s. London. Spring Books. 4to. dj. $30.00

HAJOS, A. *Souvenir of Athens, GA*. 1900 NY. Ills 1st ed. 68 p. $22.50

HAKANSON-COLBY, Joy. *Art & City*. 1956 Detroit. Wayne State U Pr. VG $15.00

HALAAS, David Fridtjof. *Boom Town Newspapers*. 1981 Albuquerque. 1st ed. dj. VG $12.00

HALASZ, Nicholas. *Biography of Alfred Nobel*. 1959 NY. Orion. 1st ed. 281 p. VG $10.00

HALDANE, R.A. *Hidden World*. 1976 NY. 1st ed. dj. EX $15.00

HALE, D.E. *Great Dane*. 1938 Judy Pub. Ills 2nd ed. 8vo. 110 p. dj. $20.00

HALE, E.E. *Franklin in France*. 1888 Boston. 2 vol set. VG $42.50

HALE, E.E. *Franklin in France*. 1887 Boston. Roberts. Ills. 4to. VG $90.00

HALE, E.E. *Historic Boston & Its Neighborhood*. 1898 NY. Ills 1st ed. 181 p. xl. $6.50

HALE, E.E. *Ingram Papers*. 1869 Boston. 1st ed. G $30.00

HALE, E.E. *KS & NE: History & Direction to Emigrants*. 1854 Boston. 1st ed. fld map. VG $75.00

HALE, E.E. *Life & Letters of Edward Hale*. 1957 Boston. 1st ed. 2 vol set. VG $65.00

HALE, E.E. *Man Without a Country & Other Patriotic Stories*. 1926 Winston. Ills. G $25.00

HALE, E.E. *Man Without a Country*. 1891 Boston. Silmon Smith. inscr. G $100.00

HALE, E.E. *Man Without a Country*. c 1908. Chicago. Ills. 45 p. $7.50

HALE, E.E. *Man Without a Country*. 1902 NY. Ltd ed. 1/80. sgn. VG $145.00

HALE, E.E. *New England History in Ballads*. 1904 Little Brown. Ills. 4to. 82 p. $35.00

HALE, E.E. *Stories of Invention*. 1887 London. Ills 1st ed. 301 p. $5.00

HALE, E.E. *Story of MA*. 1891 Boston. Ills 1st ed. 354 p. $8.50

HALE, George E. *Depths of the Universe*. 1925 NY. EX $65.00

HALE, George E. *Robert Fulton, Engineer & Artist: His Life & Works*. 1913 London. Lane. Ills. sgn. 333 p. $35.00

HALE, K. *Orlande Becomes a Doctor*. 1949 London. Country Life Ltd. 2nd ed. VG $40.00

HALE, L.C. *American's London*. 1920 NY. Ills 1st ed. 349 p. cloth. $10.00

HALE, L.C. *We Discover New England*. 1915 NY. Ills 1st ed. map. 314 p. $15.00

HALE, L.C. *We Discover Old Dominion*. 1916 NY. Ills 1st ed. 374 p. xl. $10.00

HALE, M.F. *How To Know the Lichens*. 1979 Brown. Ills. 246 p. EX $18.00

HALE, P. *Woods & Timbers of NC*. 1883 Raleigh. 1st ed. G $25.00

HALE, R.W. *Story of Bar Harbor*. 1949 NY. Ills 1st ed. map. 342 p. dj. $15.00

HALE, Robert B. *American Sculpture 1951*. 1951 NY. MOMA. G $30.00

HALE, Sarah. *Countries of Europe*. no date. NY. McLoughlin. 24mo. wraps. G $10.00

HALES, J.G. *Survey of Boston & Its Vicinity*. 1821 Boston. 1st ed. xl. $35.00

HALEY, J. Evetts. *Jeff Milton: Good Man with a Gun*. 1948 Norman. 1st ed. dj. G $20.00

HALEY, J. Evetts. *Robbing Banks Was My Business*. 1973 Canyon TX. sgn. dj. VG $35.00

HALEY, J.W. *Providence Illustrated Guide*. 1931 RI. Ills 1st ed. maps. 143 p. $8.50

HALFORD, Fred M. *Dry-Fly Man's Handbook*. 1913 London. 1st ed. 44 plts. $80.00

HALFPENNY, William. *Practical Architecture*. 1736 London. Bowles. 12mo. calf. G $125.00

HALIBURTON, Thomas C. *Historical & Statistical Account of Nova Scotia*. 1829 Halifax. 2 vol set. ¾-leather. xl. EX $150.00

HALL, Anna Gertrude. *Nansen*. 1940 NY. Viking. Ills 1st ed. presentation. EX $40.00

HALL, Ansell F. *Handbook of Yosemite National Park*. 1921 NY. Ills. G $20.00

HALL, B. *3 Acres & Liberty*. 1908 Grosset Dunlap. 441 p. VG $10.00

HALL, Basil. *Travels in North America in Years 1827 & 1828*. 1829 Edinburgh. presentation. 3 vol set. EX $180.00

HALL, Basil. *40 Etchings From Sketches Made with the Camera Lucida*. 1829 London. Ills. 4to. $180.00

HALL, Bill. *Year in Forest*. 1973 McGraw Hill. Ills Rojankovsky. 1st ed. dj. $17.50

HALL, E.C. *Book of Hand-Woven Coverlets*. 1925 Boston. VG $75.00

HALL, E.H. *Philipse Manor Hall at Yonkers*. 1912 NY. Ills 1st ed. 255 p. cloth. $15.00

HALL, Gordon Langley. *Vinnie Ream: Story of the Girl Who Sculptured Lincoln*. 1963 NY. 1st ed. dj. VG $50.00

HALL, H.J. *Benjamin Thomas: 1st Native Born American Poet*. 1924 Boston. Houghton Mifflin. 1/400. G $50.00

HALL, H.M. *Woodcock Ways*. 1946 Oxford U Pr. Ills. 84 p. dj. VG $20.00

HALL, James Norman. *Fairy Lands of South Seas*. 1921 Star. reprint. dj. EX $15.00

HALL, James Norman. *Far Lands*. 1950 Little Brown. 298 p. VG $8.00

HALL, James Norman. *High Adventure: Air Fighting in France*. 1918 Boston. 1st ed. $30.00

HALL, James Norman. *My Island Home*. 1952 Boston. 1st ed. dj. VG $25.00

HALL, John. *Staffordshire Portrait Figures*. 1972 NY. World. Collector Guide. dj. $9.50

HALL, Kay. *Irrepressible Churchill*. 1966 NY. Ills 1st ed. dj. VG $16.00

HALL, L. *Life Along an Ozark River*. 1958 Chicago U Pr. Ills. inscr. dj. VG $12.00

HALL, M.E. *Roger Williams*. 1917 Boston. Ills 1st ed. 212 p. dj. $7.50

HALL, Madeline. *Miss Browne: Story of a Superior Mouse.* 1978 NY. Hart. Ills. 4to. 24 p. dj. VG $10.00

HALL, Manly P. *Facing the Future.* 1935 1935 2nd ed. VG $22.00

HALL, Manly P. *Lecture in Ancient Philosophy.* 1929 Los Angeles. 1st ed. sgn. VG $35.00

HALL, Manly P. *Mystical Christ.* 1956 Los Angeles. 3rd ed. dj. VG $15.00

HALL, Monica. *Life & Legend of Wyatt Earp.* 1958 Simon Schuster. Ills Mel Crawford. 1st print. $7.50

HALL, Norman S. *Balloon Buster: Frank Luke of AZ.* 1928 NY. 1st ed. $45.00

HALL, P.F. *Immigration.* 1922 NY. 1st ed. $23.50

HALL, R.N. *Prehistoric Rhodesia.* 1909 Phil. Jacobs. 1st ed. photos. maps. plans. $40.00

HALL, Radclyffe. *Well of Loneliness.* 1928 NY. Ltd ed. 1/500. VG $50.00

HALL, Robert A. *Comic Style of P.G. Wodehouse.* 1974 Archon Books. 1st ed. dj. VG $35.00

HALL, S.C. *Book of Thames From Its Rise to Its Fall.* 1867 London. Ills. gilt leather. VG $175.00

HALL, Sharlot. *Sharlot Hall on the AZ Strip.* 1975 Flagstaff. 1st ed. 97 p. dj. VG $15.00

HALL, T.F. *Has the North Pole Been Discovered?* 1917 Boston. 1st ed. presentation. 539 p. $42.50

HALL, Thomas B. *Purity & Destiny of Modern Spiritualism.* 1899 Boston. $27.00

HALL, W.W. *Health at Home; or, Hall's Family Doctor.* 1883 Boston. Ills. 8vo. 891 p. leather. VG $30.00

HALLE, Edward. *Union of 2 Noble Families of Lancaster & York.* 1970 London. Scolar Pr. facsimile of 1550. $100.00

HALLE, Johann. *Fortgesetzte Magie. Oder, Die Zauberkrafte der Natur. Vol 6.* 1794 Berlin. Ills. 8vo. 578 p. $150.00

HALLE, L. *Storm Petrel & the Owl of Athena.* 1970 Princeton U Pr. Ills. 268 p. maps. dj. EX $10.00

HALLECK, H. Wager. *Elements of Military Art & Science.* 1861 NY. Ills 2nd ed. green cloth. G $35.00

HALLECK, Henry. *International Law & Laws of War.* 1861 San Francisco. full calf. G $125.00

HALLENBECK. *Spanish Missons of the Old Southwest.* 1926 Garden City. 1st ed. dj. EX $65.00

HALLER, William. *Tracts on Liberty in Puritan Revolution 1638-1647.* 1933 NY. Columbia U Pr. 3 vol set. $60.00

HALLETT, J.P. *Animal Kitabu.* 1967 Random House. Ills 1st ed. 292 p. VG $12.00

HALLETT, J.P. *Congo, Kitabu.* 1966 Random House. Ills. 436 p. maps. dj. VG $10.00

HALLEY, Edmund. *Genius in Eclipse.* 1970 London. Macdonald. 1st English ed. dj. $22.00

HALLEY, William. *Centennial Year Book of Alameda County, CA.* 1876 Oakland. wraps. VG $100.00

HALLGREN, M.A. *Gay Reformer: F.D.R.* 1935 NY. 1st ed. 316 p. cloth. $10.00

HALLIBURTON, Richard. *Richard Halliburton's Book of Marvels.* 1941 Bobbs Merrill. dj. VG $10.00

HALLIBURTON, Richard. *Richard Halliburton's Complete Book of Marvels.* 1941 NY. Ills. 634 p. M $16.50

HALLIBURTON, Richard. *7 League Boots.* 1935 Indianapolis. 1st ed. dj. $17.50

HALLIDAY, Brett. *Blond Cried Murder.* 1956 NY. 1st ed. presentation. dj. EX $35.00

HALLION, Richard P. *Legacy of Flight: Guggenheim Contribution to Flight.* 1977 Seattle. WA U Pr. Ills 1st ed. 292 p. $12.00

HALLOCK, Charles. *Fishing Tourist: Angler's Guide & Reference Book.* 1873 Harper. 239 p. rebound. scarce. VG $37.50

HALPER, Vicki. *Clay Revisions: Plate, Cup, & Vase.* 1987 Seattle. Art Museum. 64 p. wraps. $12.50

HALSEY, F.W. *Authors of Our Day in Their Homes.* 1902 NY. Ills 1st ed. 290 p. cloth. $7.50

HALSEY, M.D. *Tenderfoot in Southern CA.* 1912 Ltd ed. $10.00

HALSEY, R.T. *Homes of Our Ancestors.* 1925 NY. Ills 1st ed. 288 p. cloth. $25.00

HALSEY, R.T. *Metropolitan Museum of Art: American Wing.* 1928 NY. Ills 4th ed. 8vo. wraps. $5.00

HALSEY, R.T.; & TOWER, E. *Homes of Our Ancestors.* 1934 NY. Ills. dj. VG $26.00

HALSEY & BRYAN. *Admiral Halsey's Story.* 1947 NY. Ills 1st ed. 310 p. dj. EX $50.00

HALSMAN. *Frenchman: Photographic Interview with Fernandel.* 1949 Simon Schuster. Ills. VG $34.00

HALSTEAD, B.W. *Dangerous Marine Animals.* 1959 Cornell. Ills. 146 p. dj. VG $10.00

HALSTEAD, Isabella. *Visit with Wolf Kahn.* 1983 Barrytown, NY. Station Hill Pr. 8vo. dj. $15.00

HALSTEAD, Murat. *Gaveston: Horrors of a Stricken City.* 1900 Am Pub. Ills. $20.00

HALSTEAD, Murat. *Life & Achievements of Admiral Dewey.* c 1899. Ills. 8vo. 452 p. cloth. G $18.00

HAMBIDGE, Jay. *Dynamic Symmetry: Greek Vase.* 1920 Yale U Pr. 4to. 161 p. photos. G $25.00

HAMBLETON, Jack. *Fisherman's Paradise.* 1946 Longman Green. Ills. 172 p. G $12.00

HAMERTON, P.G. *Etching & Etchers.* 1868 London. 1st ed. ½-leather. EX $97.50

HAMERTON, P.G. *Etching & Etchers.* 1878 Boston. Roberts. Revised Enlarged ed. $42.00

HAMERTON, P.G. *Graphic Arts.* 1882 London. Ills 1st ed. 378 p. fair. $37.50

HAMERTON, P.G. *Landscape.* 1885 London. Ills. xl. VG $175.00

HAMERTON, P.G. *Man in Art.* 1892 London. Ills 1st ed. 344 p. xl. G $125.00

HAMILTON, A. *Hamilton's Itinerarium: Being Narrative of a Journey.* 1907 St. Louis. Ills 1st ed. maps. 487 p. $35.00

HAMILTON, Bernard. *1 World at a Time.* no date. c 1910. London. 320 p. xl. G $16.00

HAMILTON, Count A. *Memoirs of Count Grammont.* London. Revised 2nd ed. 3 vol set. G $22.50

HAMILTON, Count A. *Memoirs of Count Grammont.* 1809 London. 3 vol set. full leather. $175.00

HAMILTON, H. *Zachary Taylor: Soldier in the White House.* 1951 Bobbs Merrill. Ills 1st ed. 496 p. EX $24.00

HAMILTON, Ian. *Gallipoli Diary.* 1920 Doran. Ills. 2 vol set. wraps. VG $35.00

HAMILTON, Ian. *Staff Officers' Scrapbook During Russo-Japanese War.* 1906 London. Ills 4th print. blue cloth. VG $25.00

HAMILTON, J.P. *Travels Through Interior Province of Columbia.* 1827 London. Murray. 1st ed. 8 vol set. rebound. $250.00

HAMILTON, J.T. *20 Years of Pioneer Missions to Nyasaland.* 1912 Bethlehem, PA. Ills. 192 p. VG $15.00

HAMILTON, L. *Canada.* 1926 Berlin. folio. photos. VG $45.00

HAMILTON, T.M. *Colonial Frontier Guns.* 1980 Fur Pr. Ills. 4to. 176 p. pb. $20.00

HAMILTON, W.T. *My 60 Years on the Plains.* 1960 OK U Pr. Ills Russell. 12 mo. $10.00

HAMLIN, A.D.F. *History of Ornament: Ancient & Medieval.* 1916 NY. Ills. 406 p. $20.00

HAMLIN, A.D.F. *Textbook of History of Architecture.* 1900 NY. Longman Green. G $18.00

HAMLIN, H. *9 Mile Bridge, ME.* 1947 NY. Ills. map. 233 p. dj. $5.00

HAMLIN, T. *Greek Revival Architecture in America.* 1945 NY. Ills. 337 p. $25.00

HAMMER, Armand. *Quest of Romanoff Treasure.* 1936 Paisley Pr. 3rd ed. VG $30.00

HAMMER, K.M. *Springfield Carbine on the Western Frontier.* 1970 Old Army Pr. Ills. 18 p. pb. EX $5.00

HAMMERTON, J.A. *George Meredith: In Anecdote & Critisism.* 1909 NY. Kennerley. EX $15.00

HAMMERTON, J.A. *Wonders of the Past: Romance of Antiquity & Its Splendors.* 1923 NY. Putnam. Ills. 4 vol set. EX $145.00

HAMMETT, A.B. *History of Gold.* 1966 Braswell. Ills. sgn. dj. EX $30.00

HAMMETT, Dashiell. *Adventures of Sam Spade.* 1945 Tower. 1st ed. dj. VG $25.00

HAMMETT, Dashiell. *Man Named Thin.* 1962 NY. Ferman. 1st ed. wraps. EX $50.00

HAMMETT, Dashiell. *Worlds of Robert A. Heinlein.* 1966 NY. Ace. 1st ed. wraps. VG $15.00

HAMMETT, R.W. *Romanesque Architecture of Western Europe.* 1927 NY. Arch Book. 1st ed. tall 4to. dj. EX $85.00

HAMMOND, Geoffrey F. *Showdown at Newport: Race for the America's Cup.* 1974 216 p. VG $14.00

HAMMOND, George P. *Coronado's 7 Cities.* 1940 Albuquerque. Ills. 82 p. wraps. EX $95.00

HAMMOND, J.M. *Colonial Mansions of ME & DE.* 1914 Phil. Ills 1st ed. 294 p. G $17.50

HAMMOND, J.M. *Quaint & Historic Forts of North America.* 1915 Lippincott. 1st ed. G $40.00

HAMMOND, John Hays. *Autobiography.* 1937 NY. 1st ed. 2 vol set. VG $15.00

HAMMOND, L.D. *News From New Cythera: Report of Bougainville's Voyage.* 1970 MN U Pr. Ltd ed. 1/750. glassine dj. EX $12.50

HAMMOND, N.H. *New Adventures in Needlepoint Design.* 1973 NY. Ills. 128 p. dj. M $12.50

HAMMOND, Nicholas. *20th Century Wildlife Artists.* 1986 Overlook. Ills. 224 p. dj. EX $60.00

HAMMOND, R. *Anti-Bellum Mansions of AL.* c 1960s. NY. Bonanza. Ills. maps. dj. $7.50

HAMMOND, S.T. *Practical Dog Training.* 1885 NY. VG $35.00

HANCHETT, W. *Charles G. Halpine in Civil War America.* 1970 NY. Syracuse. 208 p. dj. cloth. VG $12.50

HANCOCK, Campbell. *Amateur Pottery & Glass Painting.* c 1880. London. Ills 4th ed. 8vo. 212 p. VG $35.00

HANCOCK, H. Irving. *Motor Boat Club & the Wireless.* 1909 Phil. 1st ed. dj. EX $25.00

HANCOCK, W. *Emigrant's 5 Years in the Free States of America.* 1860 London. Ills. 12mo. 321 p. blue cloth. $45.00

HANCOCK & VAN DER POEL. *Selections From Smuts Papers.* 1966 Cambridge. 4 vol set. xl. VG $40.00

HAND, W. *Who's Hoover?* July, 1928. Dodd Mead. 2nd print. dj. VG $11.00

HAND, William M. *House Surgeon & Physician.* 1818 Hartford. 1st ed. $120.00

HANDFORD, Thomas W. *Our Babies.* 1885 Belford Clarke. Ills. 96 p. cloth. VG $15.00

HANDKE, Peter. *Across.* 1986 Farrar. 1st Am ed. dj. EX $15.00

HANDKE, Peter. *Moment of True Feelings.* 1977 Farrar. 1st Am ed. dj. EX $15.00

HANDKE, Peter. *Short Letter, Long Farewell.* 1974 Farrar. 1st Am ed. dj. EX $15.00

HANES, Col. Bailey. *Bill Doolin: Outlaw.* 1968 OK U Pr. 1st ed. dj. EX $20.00

HANGER, George. *Life, Adventures, & Opinions of Col. George Hanger.* 1801 London. Beuiett. 12mo. 2 vol set. G $250.00

HANKS, C.S. *Camp Kits & Camp Life.* 1906 Scribner. Ills 1st ed. 259 p. VG $17.50

HANKS, David A. *Decorative Designs of Frank Lloyd Wright.* 1978 Renwick Gallery. wraps. xl. $10.00

HANLE, Paul A. *Bringing Aerodynamics to America.* 1982 Cambridge. MIT Pr. Ills 1st ed. 184 p. EX $15.00

HANLEY, James. *Last Voyage.* 1931 London. Chiswick. Ltd ed. 1/550. sgn. $125.00

HANLEY, Mike. *Owyhee Trails.* 1973 Caxton. Ills 1st ed. maps. dj. EX $17.50

HANNA, E. *Wit & Wisdom of Adlai Stevenson.* 1965 NY. Ills 1st ed. 95 p. dj. $5.00

HANNA, K.A. *FL Golden Sands.* 1950 Indianapolis. Ills 1st ed. 380 p. dj. $15.00

HANNA, K.A. *FL: Land of Change.* 1945 Chapel Hill. Enlarged ed. 399 p. dj. $15.00

HANNAH, Barry. *Black Butterfly.* 1982 Palaemon. Ltd ed. 1/150 sgn. dj. $45.00

HANNAH, Barry. *Captain Maximus.* 1985 Knopf. Advance copy. yellow wraps. EX $120.00

HANNAH, Barry. *Captain Maximus.* 1985 Knopf. 1st ed. sgn. dj. M $35.00

HANNAH, Barry. *Captain Maximus.* 1985 Knopf. 1st ed. sgn. dj. EX $25.00

HANNAH, Barry. *Geronimo Rex.* 1972 NY. Viking. Book Club ed. sgn. dj. $60.00

HANNAH, Barry. *Nightwatchman.* 1973 Viking. 1st ed. dj. EX $50.00

HANNAH, Barry. *Tennis Handsome.* 1983 NY. 1st ed. dj. EX $15.00

HANNAH, Barry. *2 Stories.* 1982 Nouveau Pr. Ills 1st ed. 1/200. sgn. M $55.00

HANNAH, Barry. *2 Stories.* 1982 Nouveau Pr. Ltd ed. 1/226. sgn. EX $50.00

HANNAH. *Darkness Visible.* 1954 London. 1st ed. 222 p. dj. VG $22.50

HANNAVY, J. *Roger Fenton of Crimble Hall.* 1976 Boston. 1st ed. 4to. EX $45.00

HANNON, Jessie Gould. *Boston-Newton Company Venture.* 1969 Lincoln. 1st ed. dj. VG $20.00

HANRAHAN, E.J. *Bent's Bibliography of White Mountains.* 1971 NH. wraps. EX $15.00

HANRATTY, Peter. *Book of Modred.* no date. Ace. 1st ed. pb. M $4.00

HANS, Fred M. *Great Sioux Nation.* 1907 Donahue. Ills 1st ed. 575 p. VG $110.00

HANSCOM, Adelaide. *Rook.* 1905 NY. Ills. square 4to. VG $75.00

HANSEN, Gottfried. *Nauticus: Jahrbuch fur Deutschland Seeinterssen.* 1944 Berlin. $35.00

HANSEN, Harry. *Chicago River.* 1942 NY. 1st ed. sgn. dj. EX $35.00

HANSEN, Harry. *Midwest Portraits.* 1923 Harcourt Brace. $45.00

HANSEN, Henry H. *Costume Cavalcade.* 1956 London. Ills 1st ed. 160 p. dj. EX $25.00

HANSEN, J.J. *European Folk Art.* 1973 NY. McGraw. Ills. $40.00

HANSEN, Joseph. *Job's Year.* 1983 Holt. Advance copy. dj. EX $20.00

HANSEN, Joseph. *Smile in His Lifetime.* 1981 Holt. 1st ed. dj. EX $15.00

HANSEN, Joseph. *Troublemaker.* 1975 London. Harrap. 1st ed. dj. VG $25.00

HANSFORD, S. Howard. *Chinese Jade Carving.* 1950 London. Ills 2nd imp. 4to. 156 p. $40.00

HANSFORD, S. Howard. *Jade: Essence of Hills & Streams.* 1969 NY. Am Elsevier. 4to. 220 p. $60.00

HANSON, C.E. *Northwest Gun.* 1976 NE Hist Soc. Ills. 4to. 85 p. pb. EX $12.00

HANSON, C.E. *Plains Rifle.* 1960 Stackpole. Ills. 4to. sgn. dj. EX $37.50

HANSON, H.C.; & KOSSACK, C.W. *Mourning Dove in IL.* 1963 IL U Pr. Ills. 133 p. maps. dj. EX $15.00

HANSON, Norwood Russell. *Concept of the Positron: Philosophical Analysis.* 1963 Cambridge. 1st ed. 236 p. dj. VG $15.00

HANSSON, Laura M. *We Women & Our Authors.* 1899 London. Bodley Head. VG $30.00

HAPGOOD, I. *Steel Flea.* 1916 Merrymount. Trans NS Lyeskoff. EX $25.00

HAPPEL, R.V. *Berkshire: 200 Years in Pictures.* 1961 Pittsfield. Ills 1st ed. 105 p. wraps. $7.50

HARA, O. Hashnu. *Mental Alchemy; or, Wonders of Thought Force.* 1909 Chicago. Occult Pub. 122 p. VG $22.00

HARAND, Irene. *His Struggle.* 1937 Chicago. Artcraft Pr. 1st ed. dj. EX $75.00

HARBAUGH, H. *Harbaugh's Harfe. Gedichte in Pennsylvanisch-Deutscher.* 1902 Phil. Ills Revised ed. 121 p. $12.50

HARBORD, Maj. Gen. J.C. *Leaves From a War Diary.* 1926 NY. 4to. 407 p. blue cloth. xl. VG $15.00

HARBOUR, Henry. *Where Flies the Flag.* c 1904. Ills Rackham. 2nd ed. scarce. $35.00

HARBY, Clifton. *Bible in Art.* 1936 Covici Friede. Ills. 4to. 392 p. $18.00

HARD, W. *Matter of 50 Houses.* 1952 Middlebury, VT. 90 p. dj. $7.50

HARD, W. *Memory of VT.* 1967 NY. 1st ed. 242 p. dj. $12.50

HARD, W. *VT Valley.* 1958 Middlebury, VT. 1st ed. 187 p. dj. $7.50

HARDACRE, Val. *Woodland Nuggets of Gold: Story of American Ginseng.* 1974 Northville. Revised 2nd ed. dj. VG $15.00

HARDEMAN, Nicholas Perkins. *Wilderness Calling.* 1977 Knoxville. 1st ed. dj. VG $12.50

HARDIN, John Wesley. *Life of John Wesley Hardin.* 1896 Seguin, TX. 1st ed. 1st issue. wraps. EX $200.00

HARDIN, N.L. *Friendship.* 1911 Taylor. Ltd ed. 1/400. inscr. $35.00

HARDING, A.R. *Fur Buyer's Guide.* 1915 Harding. Ills. 16mo. 366 p. VG $12.50

HARDING, A.R. *Mink Trapping.* 1906 Harding. Ills. 16mo. 171 p. G $7.50

HARDING, A.R. *Wolf & Coyote Trapping.* 1909 Harding. Ills. 252 p. G $10.00

HARDING, M. Ester. *Psychic Energy: Its Source & Transformation.* 1963 Princeton U Pr. Bollingen Series X. 2nd ed. M $26.00

HARDING, S.B. *IN University 1820-1904.* 1904 Bloomington. IN U Pr. Ills. 8vo. 348 p. $17.50

HARDING, Walter. *Days of Henry David Thoreau.* 1965 NY. 1st ed. 468 p. dj. EX $42.00

HARDING, Walter. *Thoreau Handbook.* 1959 NY. 1st ed. 229 p. EX $20.00

HARDINGE, Emma. *Modern American Spiritualism.* 1970 NY U Books. 565 p. dj. M $24.00

HARDINGE, Lord. *On Hill & Plains.* 1933 Murray. Ills 1st ed. 110 p. G $11.50

HARDWICH, T.F. *Manual of Photographic Chemistry.* 1859 London. Churchill. 8vo. cloth. scarce. $135.00

HARDWICK, Elizabeth. *Barteby in Manhattan.* 1983 NY. 1st ed. dj. M $14.00

HARDWICK, Elizabeth. *Seduction & Betrayal.* 1974 Random House. 1st ed. dj. EX $15.00

HARDWICKE, R. *Petroleum & Natural Gas Bibliography.* 1937 TX U Pr. 1st ed. presentation. EX $45.00

HARDY, A. *Wild Bill Hickock: King of the Gunfighters.* 1943 Haldeman Julius. 23 p. pb. EX $10.00

HARDY, A.C. *Merchant Navy at War.* 1941 London. Ills. 72 p. cloth. G $20.00

HARDY, T. *Indiscretion in Life of an Heiress.* 1935 Baltimore. dj. G $50.00

HARDY, Thomas. *Dynasts.* 1927 London. Ltd ed. 1/525. 4to. 3 vol set. $150.00

HARDY, Thomas. *Famous Tragedy of Queen of Cornwall.* 1930 London. gilt blue cloth. VG $12.50

HARDY, Thomas. *Far From the Madding Crowd.* 1958 Ltd Ed Club. 1/1,500. boxed. EX $60.00

HARDY, Thomas. *Jude the Obscure.* 1896 London. Ills. map. $22.50

HARDY, Thomas. *Jude the Obscure.* 1969 NY. Ills/sgn AM Parker. slipcase. $85.00

HARDY, Thomas. *Late Lyrics & Earlier.* 1922 London. 1st English ed. green cloth. G $35.00

HARDY, Thomas. *Life & Art.* 1925 Greenburg. 1st ed. VG $75.00

HARDY, Thomas. *Life's Little Ironies.* 1894 NY. 1st Am ed. green cloth. G $35.00

HARDY, Thomas. *Return of the Native.* 1972 NY. Harper. 485 p. VG $5.00

HARDY, Thomas. *Selected Poems.* 1921 Boston/London. Ltd ed. $70.00

HARDY, Thomas. *Thomas Hardy in ME.* 1942 Portland. Ltd ed. 1/425. VG $30.00

HARDY, Thomas. *Well-Beloved.* 1897 NY. 1st ed. VG $26.00

HARDY, Thomas. *Wessex Tales.* 1888 London. 1st ed. 2 vol set. VG $97.50

HARDY & SHAFFER. *Wicker Man.* 1978 Crown. 1st ed. dj. EX $30.00

HARDY. *Best Stories: Child's Own Way Series.* 1934 TB. VG $12.00

HARE, Augustus J.C. *Walks in London.* 1880 London. Routledge. 2 vols in 1. $22.00

HARE, Augustus J.C. *Walks in London.* 1878 London. Daldy Isbister. 2 vol set. $35.00

HARGRETT. *Bibliography of Constitutions & Laws of American Indians.* 1947 Harvard U Pr. 1st ed. dj. EX $45.00

HARING. *Our Catskill Mountains.* 1931 Putnam. 1st ed. 350 p. dj. VG $17.50

HARK, A. *Blue Hills & Shoofly Pie.* 1952 Phil. Ills 1st ed. 284 p. $8.50

HARKEY, Dee. *Mean As Hell.* 1948 1st ed. 1st state. dj. VG $12.50

HARKEY, Dee. *Mean As Hell.* 1948 1st ed. 2nd state. dj. VG $7.50

HARKNESS, Ruth. *Lady & the Panda: An Adventure.* 1938 NY. Ills. 288 p. red cloth. dj. EX $55.00

HARLAN, George. *Illustrated Horse Owner's Guide.* 1876 Toledo, OH. Ills. 12mo. chart. $35.00

HARLAND, M. *Cookery for Beginners.* 1884 Boston. VG $30.00

HARLECH, Pamela. *Feast Without Fuss.* 1977 NY. 1st ed. dj. EX $10.00

HARLING, Robert. *Modern Furniture & Decorating.* 1971 Galahad. folio. dj. VG $12.00

HARLOW, Alvin. *Old Bowery Days.* 1931 Ills 1st ed. 565 p. EX $35.00

HARLOW, Alvin. *Old Post Bags.* 1928 NY. Appleton. 1st ed. dj. G $75.00

HARLOW, Alvin. *Old Waybills: Romance of the Express Companies.* 1934 NY. Appleton. 1st ed. presentation. EX $65.00

HARLOW, Alvin. *Old Wires & New Waves.* 1936 NY. Ills 1st ed. 548 p. EX $45.00

HARLOW, Alvin. *Paper Chase: Amenities of Stamp Collecting.* 1940 NY. 1st ed. dj. VG $35.00

HARLOW, Alvin. *Steelways of New England.* 1946 NY. Ills 1st ed. 461 p. dj. VG $27.50

HARLOW, Enid. *Crashing.* 1980 NY. 1st ed. dj. M $10.00

HARLOW, V.F. *Delinquent & Forfeited Lands: Acts of VA & WV Legislatures.* 1877 Lewisburg, WV. Harlow Argabrite. 175 p. VG $15.00

HARMAN, J.P. *Virgin Magic Islands.* 1961 NY. Ills 1st ed. sgn. 269 p. dj. $7.50

HARMS, L. *Butterflies of GA.* 1972 OK U Pr. Ills 1st ed. 326 p. dj. VG $28.00

HARMSEN, Dorothy. *Harmsen's Western Americana.* 1971 Flagstaff. Northland. 4to. cloth. dj. $20.00

HARNACK, Dr. A. *History of Dogma.* 1895-1898. Boston. 3rd German ed. 4 vols. $35.00

HARNEY, Gen. William. *Council with Sioux Indians at Fort Pierre.* 1856 WA. GPO. 1st ed. VG $65.00

HARPER, F. *Travels of William Bartram.* 1967 Yale U Pr. 2nd print. dj. EX $25.00

HARPER, Francis. *Barren Ground Caribou of Keewatin.* 1955 KS U Pr. Ills. 163 p. wraps. EX $6.50

HARPER, Francis. *Birds of the Ungava Peninsula.* 1958 KS U Pr. Ills. 171 p. maps. wraps. $10.00

HARPER, George Mills. *Neoplatonism of William Blake.* c 1961. Chapel Hill. 1st ed. dj. G $30.00

HARPER, H.H. *Byron's Malach Hamoves.* 1918 Boston. 1st ed. sgn. wraps. $75.00

HARPER, H.H. *Byron's Malach Hamoves.* 1919 private print. inscr. $65.00

HARPER, H.H. *Genius of Henry Fielding.* 1919 Boston. 208 p. VG $25.00

HARPER, H.H. *Letters From Outsider to Insider.* 1932 Cedar Rapids. private print. G $35.00

HARPER, H.H. *Tides of Fate.* 1918 Boston. Ills Bicknell. 1st ed. 323 p. $25.00

HARPER, I. *Life & Works of Susan B. Anthony. Vol. II.* 1898 Indianapolis. 1st ed. xl. G $25.00

HARPER, Robert S. *Lincoln & the Press.* 1951 McGraw Hill. 418 p. dj. G $10.00

HARRER, H. *I Come From Stone Age.* 1965 NY. 1st Am ed. dj. VG $8.00

HARRER, Heinrich. *White Spider (Mountain Climbing) Eiger's North Face.* 1960 NY. Dutton. Ills 1st ed. 240 p. dj. VG $40.00

HARRER, Heinrich. *White Spider (Mountain Climbing) Eiger's North Face.* 1962 London. Ills 4th ed. 240 p. dj. VG $22.50

HARRER, Heinrich. *7 Years in Tibet.* 1954 Dutton. Ills 1st ed. 314 p. dj. VG $14.00

HARRILL, L. *Reminiscences 1861-1865.* 1910 Statesville. 1st ed. EX $175.00

HARRING, H.K. *Synopsis of the Rotatoria.* 1913 USNM. 226 p. VG $12.00

HARRINGTON, M.R. *Dickson Among the Lenape Indians.* 1938 Chicago. Winston. Ills 1st ed. 8vo. EX $20.00

HARRIS, Burton. *John Colter: His Years in the Rockies.* 1952 Scribner. 180 p. maps. G $5.00

HARRIS, F. *Bernard Shaw.* 1931 NY. 1st ed. VG $10.00

HARRIS, Frank. *Bomb.* 1969 NY. 1st Am ed. VG $25.00

HARRIS, Frank. *Elder Conklin & Other Stories.* 1895 London. 2nd ed. sgn. G $95.00

HARRIS, Frank. *Latest Contemporary Portraits.* 1927 NY. 1st ed. dj. EX $10.00

HARRIS, Frank. *My Life: Vol. II.* 1925 private print. 1/1,000. VG $50.00

HARRIS, Frank. *My Live & Loves.* 1945 Obelisk Pr. 1st ed. 1st issue. 4 vol set. $75.00

HARRIS, Frank. *My Secret Life.* 1966 Grove. 11 vols in 2. slipcase. $20.00

HARRIS, Frank. *Oscar Wilde: His Life & Confessions.* 1918 NY. private print. 2nd ed. 2 vols. $85.00

HARRIS, Frank. *Shakespeare & His Tragic Life Story.* 1923 NY. VG $25.00

HARRIS, J.R. *Angler's Entomology.* 1973 Barnes. Ills. 268 p. maps. dj. EX $10.00

HARRIS, Joel Chandler. *Nights with Uncle Remus.* 1926 London. cloth. VG $55.00

HARRIS, Joel Chandler. *On the Plantation.* 1892 NY. Appleton. 1st ed. 233 p. $35.00

HARRIS, Joel Chandler. *Plantation Pageant.* 1899 Ills EB Smith. 1st ed. G $50.00

HARRIS, Joel Chandler. *Tar Baby & Other Tales of Uncle Remus.* 1904 Appleton. Ills Frost/Kemble. 1st ed. $75.00

HARRIS, Joel Chandler. *Uncle Remus: His Songs & Sayings.* 1921 Appleton Century. Ills Frost. $30.00

HARRIS, Joel Chandler. *Uncle Remus: His Songs & Sayings.* 1927 London. cloth. VG $55.00

HARRIS, Joel Chandler. *Uncle Remus: His Songs & Sayings.* 1881 Appleton. 1st ed. VG $140.00

HARRIS, Joel Chandler. *Uncle Remus: His Songs & Sayings.* 1880 NY. 1st ed. 1st issue. VG $500.00

HARRIS, Joel Chandler. *Wally Wanderoon.* 1903 NY. 1st ed. 8vo. tan cloth. VG $65.00

HARRIS, John S. *Barbed Wire.* 1974 Bringham Young U Pr. 1st ed. $10.00

HARRIS, Kenn. *Renata Tebaldi.* 1974 NY. Ills 1st ed. dj. VG $20.00

HARRIS, Lewine. *Good-Bye to All That.* 1970 McGraw Hill. presentation. dj. EX $35.00

HARRIS, Lois. *World of Jo Davidson.* 1958 Covenant Books. Ills. 180 p. $5.00

HARRIS, Lucien. *Butterflies of GA.* 1972 OK U Pr. Ills 1st ed. 326 p. dj. EX $15.00

HARRIS, Mark. *Southpaw.* 1953 Bobbs Merrill. 1st ed. dj. VG $25.00

HARRIS, Richard. *Honor Bound.* 1982 St. Martin. Advance copy. wraps. EX $20.00

HARRIS, Sara. *Talks with Spirit Friends.* 1931 London. Watkins. 229 p. xl. VG $18.00

HARRIS, Seale. *Woman Surgeon: Life Story of J. Marion Sims.* 1950 NY. Macmillan. 1st ed. dj. VG $12.00

HARRIS, Thomas. *Black Sunday.* 1975 NY. dj. EX $11.00

HARRIS, Thomas. *Great Republic: Poem of the Sun.* 1867 NY. 261 p. fair. $19.00

HARRIS, Thomas. *Red Dragon.* 1981 NY. Putnam. 1st ed. dj. M $35.00

HARRIS, Thomas. *Red Dragon.* 1980 Putnam. Uncorrected proof. wraps. G $45.00

HARRIS, W. *Age of the Rainmakers.* 1971 London. Review copy. dj. EX $18.00

HARRIS, W. *Ascent to Omai.* 1970 London. 1st ed. dj. VG $18.00

HARRIS, W. *Highlands of Aethiopia.* 1844 London. 1st ed. VG $140.00

HARRIS, W. *Journey Through Yemen.* 1893 Edinburgh/London. VG $58.00

HARRIS, W. Cornwallis. *Highlands of Ethiopia.* c 1850s. NY. Winchester. 8vo. 392 p. VG $40.00

HARRIS, Walter. *Salmon Fishing in IA.* 1967 Barnes. Ills. 143 p. dj. EX $10.00

HARRIS, Wilson. *Secret Ladder.* 1963 London. Faber. 1st ed. dj. VG $35.00

HARRIS & KIRI. *Music & a Maori Girl.* 1966 Sydney. 1st ed. dj. EX $40.00

HARRIS. *Selling Hitler.* 1986 NY. 1st Am ed. dj. EX $10.00

HARRISON, C. *Gold Mine in the Front Yard.* 1905 Webb. 279 p. VG $10.00

HARRISON, George H. *Roger T. Peterson's Dozen Birding Hot Spots.* 1976 Simon Schuster. Ills. 288 p. dj. VG $17.00

HARRISON, H.H. *Wood Warblers World.* 1984 Simon Schuster. Ills 1st ed. 335 p. dj. EX $25.00

HARRISON, Harry. *Great Balls of Fire.* London. 1st ed. sgn. EX $45.00

HARRISON, Harry. *Winter in Eden.* 1986 Bantam. Ills 1st ed. dj. EX $20.00

HARRISON, Jim. *Farmer.* 1976 NY. Viking. Advance copy. $25.00

HARRISON, Jim. *Farmer.* 1976 Viking. 1st ed. sgn. dj. EX $55.00

HARRISON, Jim. *Legends of the Fall.* 1979 NY. Delacorte. 1st 1 vol ed. dj. VG $15.00

HARRISON, Jim. *Legends of the Fall.* 1980 Collins. 1st English ed. dj. EX $30.00

HARRISON, Jim. *Locations.* 1968 Norton. 1st ed. sgn. dj. EX $110.00

HARRISON, Jim. *Selected & New Poems 1961 to 1981.* 1982 NY. Ltd 1st ed. 1/250. sgn. EX $55.00

HARRISON, Jim. *Selected & New Poems.* 1982 NY. Delacorte. Advance copy. dj. EX $15.00

HARRISON, Jim. *Sundog.* 1984 Dutton. 1st ed. sgn. dj. EX $35.00

HARRISON, Jim. *Warlock.* 1981 Delacorte. Ltd 1st ed. sgn. slipcase. M $125.00

HARRISON, Jim. *Warlock.* 1981 Delacorte. 1st trade ed. dj. EX $25.00

HARRISON, Jim. *Wolf.* 1971 Simon Schuster. 1st ed. dj. EX $40.00

HARRISON, Michael. *History of Hat.* 1960 London. Ills 1st ed. 188 p. dj. EX $20.00

HARROLD, John. *Capture, Imprisonment, Escape, & Rescue of Union Soldier.* 1870 Phil. black cloth. G $75.00

HARRYHAUSEN, Ray. *Film Fantasy Scrapbook.* 1972 Barnes. Ills. cloth. dj. G $18.00

HARSHBERGER, M. *Madrigal & Minstrelsy.* 1927 Boni. Art Deco plts. VG $75.00

HART, A.B. *How Our Grandfathers Lived.* 1902 NY. Ills 1st ed. 371 p. $12.50

HART, A.B. *Varick Court of Inquiry to Investigate Col. Varick.* 1907 Boston. Bibliophile. 1/470. EX $125.00

HART, Bret. *Heritage of Dedlow Marsh & Other Tales.* 1889 Boston/NY. 1st ed. G $25.00

HART, F.R. *Admirals of Caribbean.* 1922 Riverside. VG $15.00

HART, H.M. *Old Forts of the Southwest.* 1964 Bonanza. reprint. 192 p. dj. EX $15.00

HART, H.M. *Old Forts of the West.* 1965 Superior. Ills 1st ed. 4to. dj. EX $22.00

HART, H.M. *Pioneer Forts of the West.* 1967 Superior. Ills 1st ed. 4to. dj. EX $22.00

HART, J. *Female Prose Writers of America.* 1870 Phil. VG $12.00

HART, James D. *Rare Book Stores in San Francisco 50 Years Ago.* 1984 Ltd 1st ed. wraps. VG $25.00

HART, Joseph C. *Miriam Coffin; or, The Whale Fisherman.* 1834 Allen Ticknor. 2 vol set. fair. $125.00

HART, M. *Winged Victory.* 1943 Random House. 1st ed. 8vo. 201 p. VG $55.00

HART, Willaim S. *My Life East & West.* 1929 Houghton Mifflin. 1st ed. $22.50

HART, William S. *Bill Hart's Pinto Pony Told Under a White Oak Tree.* 1922 Boston. Ills JM Flagg. VG $35.00

HART, William S. *Pinto Ben.* 1919 NY. EX $24.00

HART-DAVIS & RUPERT. *Catalogue of Caricatures of Max Beerbohm.* 1972 Harvard U Pr. Ills. 4to. cloth. dj. $40.00

HARTE, Bret. *Bell Ringer of Angels.* 1894 London. 1st ed. inscr. rebound. VG $200.00

HARTE, Bret. *East & West Poems.* 1871 Boston. 1st ed. G $20.00

HARTE, Bret. *Heathen Chinee.* 1871 Boston. Ills Eytinge. 12mo. wraps. $90.00

HARTE, Bret. *Heathen Chinee.* 1936 San Francisco. Nash. Ills Little. slipcase. $80.00

HARTE, Bret. *Her Letter, His Answer, & Her Last Letter.* 1905 Boston. Ills Arthur Keller. $25.00

HARTE, Bret. *In a Hollow of the Hills.* 1895 Boston. 1st ed. VG $35.00

HARTE, Bret. *In the Carquiez Woods.* 1883 London. 1st ed. VG $30.00

HARTE, Bret. *Poems.* 1871 Boston. Osgood. 1st ed. VG $20.00

HARTE, Bret. *Poems.* 1871 Boston. 1st issue. slipcase. boxed. $150.00

HARTE, Bret. *Queen of the Pirate Isle.* 1887 NY/Boston. Ills Greenaway. 1st Am ed. EX $125.00

HARTE, Bret. *Queen of the Pirate Isle.* 1900 London/NY. Ills Greenaway. VG $30.00

HARTE, Bret. *Story of a Mine.* 1878 Boston. Osgood. 1st ed. 16mo. 172 p. VG $15.00

HARTE, Bret. *Under the Red Woods.* 1901 Boston. 1st ed. 12mo. red cloth. VG $50.00

HARTE, Bret. *3 Partners.* 1897 Boston. 1st ed. EX $22.00

HARTE, G. & K.B. *Island in Sun.* 1937 Little Brown. Ills Merman. 1st ed. EX $10.00

HARTER, T.H. *Boonastiel.* 1893 Middleburgh. 1st ed. 240 p. VG $65.00

HARTING, P. *Das Microscope.* 1859 Braunschweig. Vieweg. Ills. 965 p. wraps. VG $90.00

HARTLAND, Michael. *Down Among the Dead.* 1983 Macmillan. Advance copy. wraps. EX $10.00

HARTLEY, E.N. *Ironworks on the Saugus.* 1971 Norman. OK U Pr. Ills 2nd print. VG $5.00

HARTLEY, Marsden. *Adventures in the Arts.* 1921 NY. 1st ed. dj. VG $35.00

HARTLEY, Marsden. *Collected Poems 1904-1943.* 1987 Black Sparrow. Deluxe 1st ed. 1/150. sgn. $30.00

HARTLEY, Marsden. *Lyonel Feininger.* 1944 MOMA. 89 plts. 96 p. dj. VG $15.00

HARTMAN, William. *Nudist Society.* 1970 NY. Ills 1st ed. dj. EX $25.00

HARTMANN, Franz. *Life of Jehoshua: Prophet of Nazareth.* 1909 198 p. VG $65.00

HARTMANN, Franz. *Life of Paracelsus.* 1887 London. Redway. 1st ed. VG $45.00

HARTMANN, Franz. *Occult Science of Medicine.* 1893 1st ed. 100 p. VG $75.00

HARTMANN & KESTER. *Plant Propagation.* 1975 NJ. 662 p. dj. VG $20.00

HARTREE, Douglas R. *Calculating Instruments & Machines Urbana.* 1953 Urbana. IL U Pr. 2nd print. 138 p. VG $25.00

HARTSHORNE, A. *Antique Drinking Glasses: History of Drinking Vessels.* 1968 NY. EX $55.00

HARTSHORNE, Anna C. *Japan & Her People.* 1902 Phil. Ills 1st ed. 2 vol set. EX $100.00

HARTSHORNE, Henry. *Essentials of Principles & Practices of Medicine.* 1869 2nd ed. leather. rebound. VG $30.00

HARTT, Frederick. *History of Italian Renaissance Art.* 1974 NY. 1st ed. 636 p. dj. VG $85.00

HARTWIG, G. *Polar & Tropical Worlds.* 1874 Nichols. Ills. 811 p. VG $11.50

HARTWIG, G. *Polar World.* 1869 NY. Ills 1st ed. 486 p. VG $55.00

HARVEY, Captain C.M. *New US Navy.* 1898 St. Louis. Ills. 8vo. oblong. $12.00

HARVEY, D.C. *French Regime in Prince Edward Island.* 1926 New Haven. 1st ed. fld map. 265 p. $20.00

HARVEY, George. *Henry Clay Frick: The Man.* 1936 NY. dj. VG $10.00

HARVEY, J. *Study in Environment.* 1949 London. Ills. 116 p. $38.50

HARVEY, John. *Victorian Novelists & Their Illustrators.* 1971 NY U Pr. 1st ed. dj. EX $35.00

HARVEY, Virginia. *Color & Design in Macrame.* 1967 Van Nostrand. 1st ed. 4to. red linen. dj. EX $17.00

HARVEY, William. *Anatomical Exercises of Dr. William Harvey.* no date. London. Nonesuch. 1/1,450. VG $120.00

HARVEY, William. *Arm of Mrs. Eagan.* 1952 NY. 1st ed. dj. EX $25.00

HARVEY, William. *Beast with 5 Fingers.* 1947 Dutton. 1st ed. dj. EX $25.00

HARVEY, William. *Lectures on the Whole of Anatomy.* 1961 Berkeley. CA U Pr. 1st ed. dj. EX $15.00

HARWELL, R.B. *Confederate Reader.* 1957 Longman Green. Ills. 389 p. EX $16.00

HARWELL. *British Atomic Energy Research Establishment 1946-1951.* 1952 NY. 1st Am ed. VG $12.50

HARWOOD, Earl of. *Flat Racing.* 1940 Edinburgh. Ills. dj. VG $35.00

HARWOOD, M. *In Shadow of Presidents.* 1966 Phil. 1st ed. 223 p. dj. $8.50

HASBROUCK, Jacob L. *History of McLean Co.* 1924 Topeka. Hist Pub. 2 vol set. EX $45.00

HASBROUCK, K.E. *Street of Huguenots.* 1958 Rutland. Ills. 41 p. cloth. $10.00

HASELTON, S.E. *Cacti for the Amateur.* 1941 Abbey Garden. Ills. 134 p. VG $10.00

HASENFUS, N.J. *More Vacation Days in ME.* 1949 Roxbury. Ills 1st ed. sgn. 245 p. dj. $20.00

HASKEL, A. *Australia.* 1941 London. 1st ed. maps. 48 p. $7.50

HASKELL, Barbara. *Ralston Crawford Monograph.* 1985 NY. Whitney Mus. 160 p. wraps. $20.00

HASKIN, Frederic J. *Panama Canal.* 1913 Doubleday Page. Ills. 386 p. G $10.00

HASKINS, Charles Homer. *Studies in History of Medieval Science.* 1960 NY. Unger. $15.00

HASKINS, Frederic J. *Panama Canal.* 1913 NY. 1st ed. cloth. G $125.00

HASKINS, R. *New England & the West.* 1843 Buffalo. 1st ed. wraps. EX $25.00

HASLETT, William. *Advices & Meditations of the Late Haslett.* 1825 Phil. Neal. G $25.00

HASLOPE, P.L. *Practical Sea Fishing Handbook.* 1905 Gill. 272 p. rebound. VG $7.50

HASLUCK, F.W. *Athos & Its Monasteries.* 1924 London. Ills. 8vo. $60.00

HASLUCK, F.W. *Cycle Buildings & Repairing.* 1904 Phil. Ills. EX $75.00

HASLUND, H. *Men & Gods in Mongolia.* 1935 NY. 358 p. index. VG $20.00

HASS, Hans. *Men & Sharks.* 1954 Doubleday. Ills 1st Am ed. 318 p. dj. VG $10.00

HASSARD, H. *Medical Malpractice: Risks, Protection, & Prevention.* 1966 Oradell. 1st ed. VG $15.00

HASSAUREK, F. *4 Years Among Spanish-Americans.* 1868 NY. Hurd Houghton. 1st ed. cloth. $75.00

HASSEL, Sven. *Legion of the Damned.* 1957 NY. 1st ed. dj. EX $15.00

HASSLER, Jon. *Love Hunter.* 1981 Morrow. Advance copy. wraps. EX $15.00

HASSLER, Jon. *Simon's Night.* 1979 Atheneum. 1st ed. dj. EX $15.00

HASSRICK, Royal B. *George Catlin Book of American Indians.* 1981 Castle. reprint. dj. EX $20.00

HASTINGS, T. *Psalmista; or, Choir Melodies.* 1956 NY. Ivison Phinney. 8vo. 352 p. G $20.00

HASTINGS. *English Sporting Guns & Accessories.* 1969 London. Ills. cloth. dj. VG $15.00

HASTINGS. *Ranchman's Recollections.* 1921 Breeder's Gazette. VG $100.00

HATCH, A. *Franklin D. Roosevelt: Informal Biography.* 1947 NY. Ills 1st ed. 381 p. dj. $8.50

HATCH, Benton. *Check List of Publications of Mosher Press.* 1966 Gehenna. 1/500. boxed. EX $225.00

HATCH, F.H. *Petrology of Sedimentary Rocks.* 1965 Ills. VG $15.00

HATCHER, Harlan. *Giant From the Wilderness.* 1955 Cleveland. Ills. 338 p. VG $9.50

HATCHER, Harlan. *Great Lakes.* 1945 Oxford U Pr. Ills. 384 p. maps. $9.00

HATCHER, Harlan. *Lake Erie.* 1945 Indianapolis. Ills 1st ed. sgn. 416 p. VG $12.50

HATCHER, Julian S. *Firearms, Investigation, Identification, & Evidence.* 1957 Harrisburg. Ills Revised ed. 387 p. dj. VG $22.50

HATHAWAY, B. *League of the Iroquois.* 1881 Chicago. lacks frontis. $50.00

HATHAWAY, Kenneth A. *Modern Radio Essentials.* 1935 Chicago. 1st ed. dj. G $25.00

HATTIE, B.M. *Early Settlers of Lee County, VA.* 1977 Greensboro. Ills. 2 vol set. $95.00

HAUASHI, T. *New Steinbeck Bibliography: 1971-1981.* 1983 Scarecrow Pr. 1st ed. 8vo. EX $18.50

HAUFF, Wilhelm. *Monkey's Uncle.* 1969 NY. Farrar. Ills 1st Am ed. EX $8.00

HAUG, Hans. *Alsaciens.* no date. Paris. Massin. Ills. dj. $50.00

HAUN, Mildred. *Hawks Done Gone.* 1940 Indianapolis. 1st ed. dj. VG $30.00

HAUPT, Herman. *General Theory of Bridge Construction.* 1853 NY. Ills. 16 plts. black cloth. VG $150.00

HAUSENSTEIN, Wilhelm. *Das Bild Atlanten zur Kunst.* 1922 Muchen. 1st ed. VG $40.00

HAUSER, Thomas. *Ashworth & Palmer.* 1981 Morrow. Advance copy. wraps. EX $15.00

HAVARD, V. *Military Hygiene.* 1917 NY. 8vo. maroon cloth. G $15.00

HAVEL, E.A. *Handbook to Agra, Etc.* 1924 2nd ed. 8vo. cloth. VG $24.00

HAVEN & BELDEN. *History of the Colt Revolver.* 1940 NY. 1st ed. sgns. dj. slipcase. VG $75.00

HAVERSTOCK, Mary. *American Bestiary.* 1979 Abrams. Ills. 4to. 248 p. dj. EX $20.00

HAVIGHURST, Walter. *OH: Bicentennial History.* 1976 NY. Ills. 211 p. VG $12.50

HAVIGHURST, Walter. *Voices on River.* 1964 Macmillan. Ills 1st ed. 310 p. dj. VG $15.00

HAVILAND, Virginia. *Favorite Fairy Tales Told in Italy.* 1965 Little Brown. Ills Ness. 1st ed. dj. EX $17.50

HAVILAND, Virginia. *Favorite Fairy Tales Told in Poland.* 1963 Little Brown. Ills Hoffman. 1st ed. 90 p. VG $17.50

HAVILAND, Virginia. *Favorite Fairy Tales Told in Scotland.* 1963 Little Brown. Ills Adrienne Adams. 1st ed. $15.00

HAVILAND, Virginia. *Favorite Fairy Tales Told in Spain.* 1963 Little Brown. Ills Barbara Cooney. 1st ed. $15.00

HAVILAND & CAUGHLAN. *Yankee Doodle's Literary Sampler of Prose.* 1947 NY. Ills 1st ed. 4to. dj. EX $17.50

HAWES, C. *King of the Thundering Herd: Biography of an American Bison.* 1911 Phil. Ills. $6.50

HAWES, C.B. *Gloucester: Land & Sea.* 1923 Boston. Ills 1st ed. 220 p. cloth. $20.00

HAWES, Charles. *Whaling.* 1924 NY. Ills 1st ed. 358 p. $25.00

HAWES, H.B. *Fish & Game: Now or Never.* 1935 NY. 1st ed. dj. VG $40.00

HAWES, H.B. *My Friend the Black Bass.* 1930 Stokes. 288 p. EX $12.50

HAWK, Dave. *100 Years on Bass.* 1970 Naylor. Ills. 134 p. dj. EX $17.50

HAWKER, P. *Instructions to Young Sportsmen in All That Relates to Guns.* 1922 Phil. reprint. VG $25.00

HAWKES, C. *Patches: WY Cow Pony.* Springfield. Ills Griswold Tyng. G $20.00

HAWKES, Clarence. *Shaggy Coat.* 1906 Phil. Jacobs. Ills Copeland. 1st ed. VG $10.00

HAWKES, John. *Beetleleg.* 1951 New Directions. 1st ed. orange bdg. EX $25.00

HAWKES, John. *Blood Oranges.* 1971 New Directions. 1st ed. dj. EX $25.00

HAWKES, John. *Death, Sleep, & the Traveller.* 1974 NY. 1st ed. sgn. dj. M $35.00

HAWKES, John. *Death, Sleep, & the Traveller.* 1974 New Directions. 1st ed. dj. EX $30.00

HAWKES, John. *Innocent Party.* 1966 New Directions. 1st ed. dj. EX $55.00

HAWKES, John. *Lime Twig.* 1961 New Directions. 1st ed. dj. EX $65.00

HAWKES, John. *Passion Artist.* 1979 Harper. 1st ed. dj. EX $15.00

HAWKES, John. *Travesty.* 1976 Chatto Windus. 1st English ed. dj. EX $25.00

HAWKES, John. *Virginie.* 1982 Harper. 1st trade ed. dj. EX $14.00

HAWKINS, Arthur. *Steak Book.* 1966 NY. Doubleday. dj. VG $10.00

HAWKINS, B.L. *15 Poems.* 1974 Berkeley. 1st ed. 1/426. wraps. EX $10.00

HAWKINS, R.E. *Jim Corbett's India.* 1978 Oxford U Pr. 250 p. dj. EX $15.00

HAWKINS, Wallace. *Case of John C. Watrous: US Judge for TX.* 1950 SMU Pr. 1st ed. 1/1,200. dj. EX $25.00

HAWKS, Francis L. *Adventures of Daniel Boone: KY Rifleman.* 1851 NY. 24mo. cloth. $35.00

HAWKS, Francis L. *Monuments of Egypt with Notes on a Voyage.* 1950 NY. gilt cloth. VG $25.00

HAWKS, Frank. *Speed.* 1931 NY. Brewer Warren Putnam. 314 p. $10.00

HAWLEY, Harriet Smith. *Goose Girl of Nuremberg.* 1936 Suttonhouse. Ills Willy Pogany. 4to. EX $20.00

HAWTHORN, A. *Kwakiutl Art.* 1979 Seattle. Ills. 292 p. $38.00

HAWTHORNE, Daniel. *Ships of the 7 Seas.* 1925 NY. Doubleday Page. 1st ed. G $86.00

HAWTHORNE, H. *Lure of the Garden.* 1911 NY. Ills 1st ed. 259 p. cloth. $17.50

HAWTHORNE, H. *Old Seaport Towns of New England.* 1916 NY. Ills 1st ed. 312 p. cloth. $12.50

HAWTHORNE, H. *Rambles in Old College Towns.* 1917 NY. Ills 1st ed. 364 p. cloth. $7.50

HAWTHORNE, Nathaniel. *House of 7 Gables.* 1851 Boston. Ticknor Reed Fields. VG $200.00

HAWTHORNE, Nathaniel. *In Colonial Days.* 1913 Boston. Ills. 104 p. cloth. $7.50

HAWTHORNE, Nathaniel. *In Colonial Days.* 1911 Page. Ills FT Merrill. 3rd imp. VG $17.50

HAWTHORNE, Nathaniel. *Life of Franklin Pierce.* 1852 Boston. 1st ed. 144 p. $75.00

HAWTHORNE, Nathaniel. *Marble Faun.* 1860 Boston. 1st ed. 1st issue. 2 vol set. $175.00

HAWTHORNE, Nathaniel. *Marble Faun.* 1860 Leipzig. 2 vols in 1. dj. VG $250.00

HAWTHORNE, Nathaniel. *Marble Faun.* 1899 Boston. 2 vol set. $48.00

HAWTHORNE, Nathaniel. *Maypole of Merrymount.* 1947 Merrymount Pr. 12mo. gray wraps. $10.00

HAWTHORNE, Nathaniel. *Mr. Higginbotham's Catastrophe.* 1931 Boston. Berkeley Printers. Ltd ed. VG $30.00

HAWTHORNE, Nathaniel. *Our Old Home.* 1883 Boston. 1st ed. 1st issue. $85.00

HAWTHORNE, Nathaniel. *Scarlet Letter.* 1941 NY. Ills HV Poor. 4to. sheepskin. $75.00

HAWTHORNE, Nathaniel. *Scarlet Letter.* no date. NY. Ills Thompson. VG $30.00

HAWTHORNE, Nathaniel. *Scarlet Letter.* 1850 Boston. 2nd ed. EX $300.00

HAWTHORNE, Nathaniel. *Snow Image & Other Twice Told Tales.* 1952 Ticknor Reed. 1st ed. 8vo. brown cloth. VG $55.00

HAWTHORNE, Nathaniel. *Snow Image.* 1852 Boston. 1st ed. $80.00

HAWTHORNE, Nathaniel. *Tanglewood Tales.* 1913 Rand McNally. Windermere Series. 1st ed. VG $15.00

HAWTHORNE, Nathaniel. *Tanglewood Tales.* 1921 Phil. Penn. Ills Sterrett. 1st ed. $125.00

HAWTHORNE, Nathaniel. *Tanglewood Tales.* no date. NY. Crowell. Ills George Soper. VG $25.00

HAWTHORNE, Nathaniel. *Transformation, Monte Beni.* 1860 Leipzig. Tauchnitz. photos. 2 vols. VG $150.00

HAWTHORNE, Nathaniel. *Wonder Book & Tanglewood Tales.* 1938 Dodd Mead. Ills Parrish. 15th ed. VG $22.50

HAWTHORNE, Nathaniel. *Wonder Book for Boys & Girls.* c 1940s. Saalfield. Ills FB Peat. dj. $8.00

HAWTHORNE, Nathaniel. *Wonder Book for Girls & Boys.* 1893 Boston. Ills Crane. VG $50.00

HAWTHORNE, Nathaniel. *Wonder Book.* 1913 Rand McNally. Ills Milo Winter. 4to. VG $20.00

HAWTHORNE, Nathaniel. *Wonder Book.* 1899 Boston. Houghton Mifflin. Ills Church. $50.00

HAWTHORNE, Nathaniel. *Works of Nathaniel Hawthorne.* 1890 Boston. 13 vol set. G $100.00

HAWTHORNE, Nathaniel. *Works of Nathaniel Hawthorne.* 1882 Boston. Little Classic ed. 25 vol set. $100.00

HAY, J. *Great Beach: Cape Cod.* 1963 NY. Ills 1st ed. 131 p. dj. $10.00

HAY, J. *Nature's Year: Seasons of Cape Cod.* 1961 NY. Ills 1st ed. 199 p. dj. $12.50

HAY, John. *Castilian Days.* 1871 Boston. 1st ed. 414 p. $50.00

HAY, John. *Castilian Days.* 1903 Boston/NY. Ills Pennell. 1st ed. VG $17.50

HAY, John. *Little Breeches.* 1871 NY. Ills Engel. 1st ed. 2nd print. wraps. $30.00

HAYASHI, T. *Study Guide to Steinbeck: Handbook to His Major Works.* 1974 Netuchen. 1st ed. 8vo. cloth. EX $18.50

HAYCRAFT, H. *Murder for Pleasure: Life & Times of Detective Story.* 1941 NY. sgn. VG $25.00

HAYDEN. *Great West.* 1880 Bloomington. Ills. map. fair. $25.00

HAYDON, A.L. *Riders of the Plains: Northwest Mounties 1873-1910.* 1910 Chicago. Ills. EX $35.00

HAYES, A.A. *New CO & Santa Fe Trail.* 1881 London. 1st English ed. EX $60.00

HAYES, A.A. *New CO & Santa Fe Trail.* 1880 NY. Ills 1st ed. 200 p. G $35.00

HAYES, H.W. *Attractive Bits Along Shore.* 1890 Portland. Ills. maps. 104 p. cloth. $25.00

HAYES, I.I. *Land of Desolation: Greenland.* 1872 NY. Ills. xl. G $10.00

HAYES, I.I. *Open Polar Sea.* 1867 NY. Ills 1st ed. maps. 454 p. G $95.00

HAYES, J.G. *Sheriff Thompson's Day.* 1968 Tucson. 1st ed. 190 p. dj. VG $15.00

HAYES, L.S. *CT River Valley.* 1929 Rutland. 1st ed. rebound. $20.00

HAYES, L.S. *High Water at Bellows Falls.* 1927 VT. Ills 1st ed. 40 p. wraps. $8.50

HAYES, Tom. *Hunting the White-Tail Deer.* 1960 NY. dj. VG $10.00

HAYES & LOOS. *Twice Over Lightly.* 1972 NY. 1st ed. sgns. dj. VG $20.00

HAYLEY, William. *Triumphs of Temper.* 1796 London. Ills 9th ed. VG $30.00

HAYLEY, William. *Triumphs of Temper: Poem in 6 Cantos.* 1804 Kennebuck, ME. 2nd Am ed. $60.00

HAYMAKER, Webb. *Founders of Neurology.* 1953 Thomas. 1st ed. inscr/sgn. dj. EX $105.00

HAYMAN, Ronald. *Brecht: Biography.* 1983 Oxford U Pr. 1st ed. dj. M $7.00

HAYMAN & ANDERSON. *In the Wake of the Wake.* 1978 WI U Pr. 1st print. 210 p. VG $12.00

HAYNE, C. *Vanguard of the Caravans: Life Story of John Mason Peck.* 1931 Judson. Ills 1st ed. 157 p. VG $6.50

HAYNES, G.W. *American Paint Horse.* 1976 OK U Pr. Ills 1st ed. 351 p. dj. EX $22.00

HAYS, Donald. *Dixie Association.* 1984 Simon Schuster. 1st ed. inscr. dj. VG $45.00

HAYS, Will H. *See & Hear: Brief History of Motion Pictures & Sound.* 1929 no place. presentation. G $35.00

HAYTER, William Stanley. *Death of Hektor.* 1979 Circle Pr. Ltd ed. 1/300. sgn. slipcase. $600.00

HAYWARD, C.H. *Period Furniture Designs.* 1975 London. Ills. $15.00

HAYWARD, C.H. *Staining & Polishing.* 1975 London. Ills. 214 p. $16.50

HAYWARD, Charles B. *Practical Aeronautics with Introduction by Orville Wright.* 1917 Chicago. Am Technical Soc. 769 p. VG $45.00

HAYWARD, John. *Gazetteer of the US of America.* 1853 Hartford, CT. 8vo. 861 p. $35.00

HAYWARD, John. *N.E. Gazetter.* 1839 Concord. 9th ed. VG $50.00

HAYWOOD, Charles. *Bibliography of North American Folklore & Folk Song.* 1961 NY. Dover. Revised 2nd ed. 2 vol set. xl. $25.00

HAZARD, A.G. *Mr. Hazard's Discourse.* 1848 Providence. 1st ed. 45 p. wraps. $7.50

HAZARD, Samuel. *Santo Domingo: Past & Present.* 1873 NY. Harper. 1st ed. 511 p. cloth. VG $100.00

HAZELTINE. *Hazeltine's Pocket Almanac for 1894.* 1894 Warren, PA. wraps. EX $50.00

HAZELTON, G.C. *National Capital.* 1911 NY. Ills. 261 p. cloth. $12.50

HAZELTON, G.C.; & BENRIMO. *Yellow Jacket: Chinese Play Done in Chinese Manner.* 1913 Bobbs Merrill. Ills Genthe. 8vo. cloth. EX $30.00

HAZLETON, Joseph. *Scouts, Spies, & Heroes of Great Civil War.* 1893 Providence. Ills. G $25.00

HAZLITT, William. *Conversations of James Northcote.* 1830 London. 1st ed. ¾-morocco. rebound. $100.00

HAZLITT, William. *Lectures on the English Comic Writers.* 1819 Phil. 1st Am ed. 343 p. scarce. $60.00

HEACOX, C.E. *Compleat Brown Trout.* 1974 Winchester. Ills. 182 p. dj. EX $12.50

HEAD, F.B. *Journeys Across the Pampas & Among the Andes.* 1967 IL U Pr. dj. EX $18.00

HEAD, Henry. *Studies in Neurology.* 1920 London. 2 vol set. VG $250.00

HEADLAND, Fred. *On Actions of Medicines in the System.* 1874 Lindsay Blakiston. G $15.00

HEADLEY, J.T. *Great Rebellion: History of Civil War in US.* 1864 & 1866. Hartford. Ills. 8vo. 2 vols. G $43.00

HEADLEY, J.T. *Great Rebellion: History of Civil War in US.* 1863 Hartford. Ills. 2 vol set. full leather. $75.00

HEADLEY, J.T. *Illustrated Life of George Washington.* 1860 NY. Ills. 528 p. cloth. $20.00

HEADLEY, J.T. *Life of Kossuth.* 1852 Auburn, NY. 8vo. 461 p. VG $20.00

HEADLEY, J.T. *Life of U.S. Grant.* 1868 NY. Ills. $35.00

HEADLEY, J.T. *Naval Commanders 1861-65.* 1867 NY. $30.00

HEADLEY, J.W. *Confederate Operations in Canada & NY.* 1984 Time Life. facsimile of 1906. 480 p. M $30.00

HEADLEY, P.C. *Life of General Layayette.* 1851 Auburn. 1st ed. 12 mo. 377 p. G $20.00

HEADLEY, P.C. *Life of Louis Kossuth.* 1852 Auburn. 12mo. 461 p. cloth. VG $16.00

HEADON, Deidre; & HELLER, J. *Knight.* 1982 1st Am ed. M $20.00

HEADSTROM, Richard. *Beetles of America.* 1977 Barnes. Ills. 488 p. EX $13.00

HEADSTROM, Richard. *Your Reptile Pet.* 1978 McKay. Ills. 120 p. dj. EX $10.00

HEALD, Edward Thornton. *William McKinley Story.* 1964 no place. Stark Co Hist Soc. 1st ed. $17.50

HEALY, Jeremiah. *Blunt Darts.* 1984 NY. 1st ed. dj. M $45.00

HEALY, Mary. *Lakeville; or, Substance & Shadow.* 1873 NY. Ills 1st ed. cloth. $60.00

HEANEY, Seamus. *Haw Lantern.* 1987 London. 1st ed. VG $45.00

HEANEY, Seamus. *Makings of Music: Poetry of Wordsworth & Yeats.* 1978 Liverpool. 1st ed. wraps. $20.00

HEANEY, Seamus. *Selected Poems 1965-1975.* 1980 London. 1st ed. dj. EX $65.00

HEANEY, Seamus. *Songs of the Soul That Delights in Knowing God by Faith.* 1983 no place. 1st ed. 1/50. wraps. $185.00

HEANEY, Seamus. *Sweeney Astray.* 1983 Ltd ed. 1/350. sgn. VG $75.00

HEAP, David Potter. *Report on International Exhibition of Electricity in Paris.* 1884 WA. GPO. Ills 1st ed. 287 p. VG $70.00

HEARN, Lafcadio. *Exotics & Retrospectives.* 1898 Boston. Ills 1st ed. 299 p. VG $40.00

HEARN, Lafcadio. *Gleanings in Buddha's Fields.* 1897 Boston. xl. $30.00

HEARN, Lafcadio. *In Ghostly Japan.* 1899 Boston. 1st ed. cloth. VG $50.00

HEARN, Lafcadio. *Interpretations of Literature.* 1926 NY. 2 vol set. VG $20.00

HEARN, Lafcadio. *Japan.* 1904 NY/London. 1st ed. EX $95.00

HEARN, Lafcadio. *Kokoro.* 1896 Boston. Houghton Mifflin. Ills. 12mo. $12.50

HEARN, Lafcadio. *Life & Literature.* 1925 Tokyo. Hokuseido. VG $10.00

HEARN, Lafcadio. *Shadowings.* Boston. Ills 1st ed. VG $65.00

HEARN, Lafcadio. *Stories & Sketches.* 1925 Tokoyo. Hokuseido. VG $10.00

HEARN, Lafcadio. *2 Years in the French West Indies.* 1890 NY. Ills Green. floral cloth. VG $50.00

HEARON, S. *Small Town.* 1985 NY. Review ed. dj. EX $10.00

HEATH, Irene P. *Heard by a Mouse.* 1931 London. Warne. Ills. dj. EX $10.00

HEAVEY, W.F. *Story of Army Amphibian Engineers.* 1946 WA. 1st ed. VG $35.00

HEBARD, G.R. *Bozeman Trail.* 1960 Clark. Ills. 2 fld maps. EX $85.00

HEBARD, G.R. *Bozeman Trial.* 1922 Cleveland. 1st ed. 2 vol set. VG $200.00

HECHT, Anthony. *Love for 4 Voices.* 1983 Penmaen Pr. Ills M McCurdy. 1/50. sgns. EX $60.00

HECHT, Ben. *Champion From Far Away.* 1931 NY. VG $20.00

HECHT, Ben. *Fantazius Mallare.* 1922 Chicago. Ills Wallace Smith. 1/2,025. $45.00

HECHT, Ben. *Perfidy.* 1962 NY. VG $35.00

HECHT, Ben. *Sensualists.* 1959 NY. 1st ed. dj. VG $20.00

HECHT, Ben. *To Quito & Back.* 1937 Covici Friede. dj. VG $20.00

HECHT, Ben; & FOWLER, Gene. *Great Magoo.* 1933 Van Rees Pr. Ills 1st ed. 208 p. G $30.00

HECK, J.G. *Complete Encyclopedia of Illustration.* 1979 Crown. dj. EX $25.00

HECK, J.G. *Iconographic Encyclopedia of Science, Literature, & Art.* 1851 NY. Garrigue. Ills. 8vo. 4 vol set. VG $300.00

HECKER. *Recollections & Experiences in Spanish American War.* 1913 Detroit. private print. presentation. $25.00

HECKETHORN, Charles W. *Secret Societies of All Ages & Countries.* 1897 London. Redway. 2 vol set. EX $135.00

HECKMAN, Hazel. *Island Year.* 1972 WA U Pr. Ills. 255 p. VG $6.00

HECTLINGER, A. *American Quilts, Quilting, & Patchwork.* 1974 NY. Ills 1st ed. 349 p. dj. $10.00

HEDGE, L. *Elements of Logick.* 1818 Boston. 12mo. 202 p. leather. VG $14.00

HEDGES, E.S. *Tin in Social & Economic History.* 1964 St. Martin. 1st ed. dj. EX $12.50

HEDGES, F.A.M. *Battles with Giant Fish.* 1924 Small Maynard. Ills 1st ed. 300 p. VG $15.00

HEDIN, Sven. *Riddles of the Gobi Desert.* 1933 Dutton. Ills 1st Am ed. 382 p. G $24.00

HEDIN & SPRINGER. *Creative Needlework.* 1969 NY. Ills. 128 p. $10.00

HEDREN, Paul *First Scalp for Custer: Skirmish at Warbonnet Creek, NE.* 1980 Arthur Clark. Ltd ed. 1/350. M $65.00

HEDRICK, U.P. *Plums of NY.* 1911 Albany. 4to. VG $85.00

HEER, Frederich. *Medieval World: Europe 1100-1350.* 1961 Cleveland. 1st ed. 365 p. dj. VG $25.00

HEERWAGEN, Paul K. *Indian Scout & Western Painter: Capt. Charles L. Von Berg.* 1969 Little Rock. Pioneer Pr. dj. EX $25.00

HEGAN, Alice Caldwell. *Mrs. Wiggs of the Cabbage Patch.* 1903 NY. Ills. cloth. VG $7.00

HEGAN, Alice Caldwell. *Mrs. Wiggs of the Cabbage Patch.* 1901 NY. Century. 1st ed. 12mo. EX $50.00

HEGNER, Robert. *Parade of the Animal Kingdom.* 1951 Macmillan. Ills. 675 p. G $10.00

HEILBRON, J.L. *Dilemmas of an Upright Man.* 1986 Berkeley. 1st ed. 238 p. dj. EX $15.00

HEILNER, V.C. *Adventures in Angling.* 1922 OH. Ills 1st ed. VG $45.00

HEILNER, V.C. *Salt-Water Fishing.* 1940 PA. Ills. 452 p. G $8.50

HEILNER, V.C. *Salt-Water Fishing.* 1943 Intro Zane Grey. VG $25.00

HEILNER, V.C. *Salt-Water Fishing.* 1937 PA. Ills 2nd print. VG $25.00

HEILPERN, G.J. *Wedgewood: 18th-Century English Potter.* 1967 Carbondale. 4to. 66 p. VG $7.50

HEIN, G. *Printing Fabrics by Hand.* 1972 NY. Ills. 79 p. $10.00

HEINE, Heinrich. *Poems & Ballads.* 1881 NY. Trans Lazarus. 1st ed. VG $25.00

HEINEN, Dr. Henry. *Gesundheits Schatzkammer.* 1840 Phil. 2nd print. 118 p. leather. VG $25.00

HEINEY, D. *Recent American Literature.* 1961 NY. 573 p. wraps. $3.00

HEINIGER, E.A. *Great Book of Jewels.* 1974 Graphic Soc. Ills. 316 p. dj. EX $50.00

HEINIGER, E.A. *Great Book of Jewels.* 1974 Graphic Soc. 316 p. dj. VG $40.00

HEINL, Col. R.D. *Soldiers of the Sea: USMC 1775-1962.* 1965 Annapolis. Ills. maps. dj. VG $25.00

HEINLEIN, Robert. *Assignment in Eternity.* 1953 Fantasy Pr. 1st ed. 1st bdg. sgn. dj. VG $175.00

HEINLEIN, Robert. *Between Planets.* 1951 NY. Ills 1st ed. 222 p. dj. VG $75.00

HEINLEIN, Robert. *Beyond This Horizon.* 1948 Fantasy Pr. 1st ed. 1/500. inscr. dj. VG $180.00

HEINLEIN, Robert. *Cat Who Walks Through Walls.* 1985 NY. 1st ed. 1st issue. dj. EX $25.00

HEINLEIN, Robert. *Cat Who Walks Through Walls.* 1985 Putnam. Uncorrected proof. wraps. VG $75.00

HEINLEIN, Robert. *Citizen of Galaxy.* 1957 Scribner. 1st ed. dj. EX $150.00

HEINLEIN, Robert. *Die Augestofener der Erde.* 1963 Munchen. 1st German ed. wraps. G $30.00

HEINLEIN, Robert. *Door Into Summer.* 1957 Garden City. Doubleday. 1st ed. dj. EX $195.00

HEINLEIN, Robert. *Double Star.* 1956 Doubleday. 1st ed. scarce. EX $895.00

HEINLEIN, Robert. *Expanded Universe: Worlds of Robert A. Heinlein.* 1980 Grosset Dunlap. 1st ed. EX $100.00

HEINLEIN, Robert. *Farmer in the Sky.* 1950 Scribner. 1st ed. EX $270.00

HEINLEIN, Robert. *Farnham's Freehold.* 1964 Putnam. 1st ed. dj. scarce. EX $395.00

HEINLEIN, Robert. *Friday.* 1982 Harper Row. Uncorrected proof. EX $95.00

HEINLEIN, Robert. *Glory Road.* 1963 Putnam. 1st ed. dj. EX $450.00

HEINLEIN, Robert. *Green Hills of Earth.* 1951 Chicago. Shasta. 1st ed. dj. EX $210.00

HEINLEIN, Robert. *Have Space Suit, Will Travel.* 1958 Scribner. 1st ed. dj. EX $295.00

HEINLEIN, Robert. *Man Who Sold the Moon.* 1950 Shasta. 1st ed. dj. EX $110.00

HEINLEIN, Robert. *Menace From Earth.* 1959 Hicksville. Gnome. 1st ed. EX $260.00

HEINLEIN, Robert. *Methuselah's Children.* 1963 Munchen. 1st ed. German text. wraps. G $15.00

HEINLEIN, Robert. *Methuselah's Children.* 1958 Hicksville. Gnome. 1st ed. dj. VG $145.00

HEINLEIN, Robert. *Moon Is a Harsh Mistress.* 1966 Putnam. 1st ed. EX $875.00

HEINLEIN, Robert. *Orphans of the Sky.* 1963 London. Gollancz. 1st ed. scarce. EX $725.00

HEINLEIN, Robert. *Orphans of the Sky.* 1964 NY. Putnam. 1st Am ed. dj. VG $225.00

HEINLEIN, Robert. *Past Through Tomorrow.* 1967 Putnam. 1st ed. dj. EX $295.00

HEINLEIN, Robert. *Podkayne of Mars.* 1963 Putnam. 1st ed. dj. VG $215.00

HEINLEIN, Robert. *Puppet Masters.* 1951 Doubleday. 1st ed. EX $60.00

HEINLEIN, Robert. *Red Planet.* 1949 Scribner. 1st ed. EX $325.00

HEINLEIN, Robert. *Revolt in 2100.* 1957 Gengensha. 1st Japanese ed. inscr. wraps. $225.00

HEINLEIN, Robert. *Robert Heinlein Omnibus.* 1958 London. Sidgwick Jackson. 1st ed. dj. $145.00

HEINLEIN, Robert. *Rocket Ship Galileo.* 1947 NY. 1st ed. dj. EX $200.00

HEINLEIN, Robert. *Rolling Stones.* 1952 NY. 1st ed. dj. EX $195.00

HEINLEIN, Robert. *Space Cadet.* 1948 Scribner. 1st ed. dj. VG $310.00

HEINLEIN, Robert. *Space Family Stone.* 1969 London. Gollancz. 1st ed. scarce. EX $135.00

HEINLEIN, Robert. *Star Beast.* 1954 Scribner. 1st ed. dj. VG $165.00

HEINLEIN, Robert. *Starman Jones.* 1953 NY. 1st ed. dj. EX $195.00

HEINLEIN, Robert. *Starship Troopers.* 1959 Putnam. 1st ed. dj. EX $625.00

HEINLEIN, Robert. *Stranger in a Strange Land.* 1961 Putnam. 1st ed. dj. EX $795.00

HEINLEIN, Robert. *Time Enough for Love.* 1973 Putnam. 1st ed. sgn. dj. EX $395.00

HEINLEIN, Robert. *Time for Stars.* 1956 Scribner. 1st ed. dj. EX $225.00

HEINLEIN, Robert. *Tomorrow the Stars.* 1952 Garden City. Doubleday. 1st ed. dj. EX $245.00

HEINLEIN, Robert. *Tunnel in the Sky.* 1955 Scribner. 1st ed. EX $175.00

HEINLEIN, Robert. *Universe.* 1951 Dell. 1st ed. wraps. VG $35.00

HEINLEIN, Robert. *Unpleasant Profession of Jonathan Hoag.* 1959 Hicksville. Gnome Pr. 1st ed. sgn. dj. EX $295.00

HEINLEIN, Robert. *Waldo & Magic, Inc.* 1950 Doubleday. 1st ed. dj. EX $90.00

HEINLEIN, Robert. *6th Column.* 1949 Gnome. 1st ed. EX $175.00

HEINOLD, G. *Burglar in the Treetops.* 1952 NY. Ills 1st ed. 242 p. dj. $12.50

HEINRICH, Boll. *Acquainted with the Night.* 1954 Holt. 1st Am ed. dj. VG $40.00

HEINS, Henry Hardy. *Golden Anniversary Bibliography of Edgar Rice Burroughs.* 1964 dj. EX $275.00

HEINSCHEIMER, Hans W. *Best Regards to Aida.* 1968 NY. Ills 1st ed. dj. VG $15.00

HEINTZELMAN, A.W. *Watercolor Drawings of Thomas Rowlandson.* 1947 Boston Pub Lib. Ills 1st ed. dj. G $20.00

HEINTZELMAN, D.S. *Manual for Bird Watching in the Americas.* 1979 Universe. Ills. 254 p. maps. dj. EX $10.00

HEINTZELMAN, D.S. *North American Ducks, Geese, & Swans.* 1978 Winchester. Ills. 236 p. maps. dj. EX $20.00

HEIPOUN, A. *Explorations on West Coast of FL.* 1887 Phil. Ills 1st ed. 153 p. VG $95.00

HEISE, Kenan; & EDGERTON, M. *Chicago: Center for Enterprise.* 1980 Ills. 2 vol set. boxed. EX $35.00

HEISENBERG, Werner. *Cosmic Radiation.* 1946 NY. Dover. 1st Am ed. 192 p. VG $22.00

HEISENBERG, Werner. *Physical Principles of the Quantum Theory.* no date. NY. Dover. reprint. wraps. VG $8.00

HEISENBERG, Werner. *Physicist's Conception of Nature.* 1958 NY. Harcourt Brace. 1st Am ed. xl. $15.00

HEISENBERG, Werner. *Physics & Beyond: Encounter & Conversations.* 1971 NY. Harper Row. 1st Am ed. 247 p. dj. VG $15.00

HEITZMANN & ZUCKERKANDL. *Anatomischer Atlas.* 1902 & 1905. Wein Leipzig. 2 vol set. $85.00

HELCK, Peter. *Checkered Flag: History of Road Racing in America.* 1961 NY. Scribner. $40.00

HELD, John. *Held's Angels.* 1952 NY. VG $25.00

HELD, John. *Saga of Frankie & Johnny.* 1972 facsimile of 1930. dj. EX $20.00

HELD, Robert. *Age of Firearms: Pictorial History.* 1957 Harper. Ills. 4to. 192 p. dj. VG $12.50

HELDENBRAND, Sheila. *Prose Poems.* 1976 Tideline Pr. Ltd ed. 1/65. EX $40.00

HELLAMN, Renee. *Celebrity Cooking.* 1967 London. dj. EX $10.00

HELLER, B. *Candle Making: Step-By-Step Guide.* 1972 NY. Ills. 118 p. $8.50

HELLER, J. *Print Making Today.* 1966 NY. Ills. 266 p. $20.00

HELLER, Joseph. *God Knows.* 1984 NY. 1st ed. sgn. dj. M $28.00

HELLER, Joseph. *God Knows.* 1984 Knopf. 1st trade ed. sgn. dj. EX $17.00

HELLER, Joseph. *Good As Gold.* 1979 NY. 1st ed. sgn. dj. M $25.00

HELLER, Joseph. *Something Happened.* 1974 Knopf. 1st ed. dj. EX $20.00

HELLER, Joseph. *Something Happened.* 1974 Knopf. Ltd 1st ed. sgn. slipcase. EX $150.00

HELLER, Joseph. *We Bombed in New Haven: A Play.* 1968 NY. Knopf. 1st ed. 8vo. maroon cloth. dj. $275.00

HELLER, S. *Artist's Christmas Cards.* 1979 1st ed. dj. EX $20.00

HELLER. *Catch 22.* 1966 1st Modern Lib ed. dj. EX $10.00

HELLMAN, A.A. *Amnesia & Analgesia in Parturition.* 1915 NY. 1st ed. presentation. 8vo. VG $45.00

HELLMAN, Lillian. *Maybe.* 1980 Little Brown. 1st ed. dj. EX $15.00

HELLMAN, Lillian. *Searching Wind.* 1944 NY. 1st ed. dj. VG $30.00

HELLMAN, Lillian. *Three.* 1979 Boston. Ltd ed. 1/500. sgn. slipcase. $90.00

HELLMAN, Lillian. *Unfinished Woman.* 1969 Little Brown. 1st ed. dj. EX $7.50

HELLMANN, G.S. *Memoirs of Comte de Mercy Argenteau.* 1917 NY. Ltd 1st ed. 1/500. 2 vol set. $25.00

HELLUM & GOTTSHALL. *You Can Whittle & Carve.* 1942 Ills. dj. $10.00

HELM, Clementine. *Cecily (Elf Goldihair).* 1924 Lippincott. Ills Kay. 1st ed. blue cloth. $45.00

HELM, MacKinley. *John Marin.* 1948 Boston. Inst Contemporary Art. 1st ed. $185.00

HELM, Thomas. *Dangerous Sea Creatures.* 1976 Funk Wagnall. Ills. 278 p. dj. VG $10.00

HELM, Thomas. *Hurricanes: Weather at Its Worst.* 1967 NY. Ills 1st ed. 213 p. dj. $5.00

HELM, Thomas. *Shark: Unpredictable Killer of the Sea.* 1965 Dodd Mead. Ills. 260 p. VG $13.00

HELMERICKS, Constance. *Hunting in North America.* 1959 Harrisburg. 2nd ed. dj. VG $18.00

HELMERICKS, Harmon. *Last of the Bush Pilots.* 1969 Knopf. 1st ed. dj. VG $20.00

HELMS, Anthony Zachariah. *Travels From Buenos Ayres by Potosi to Lima.* 1807 London. Phillips. Abridged ed of 1st. $100.00

HELPRIN, Mark. *Ellis Island & Other Stories.* 1981 London. Hamish. 1st ed. dj. VG $25.00

HELPRIN, Mark. *Winter's Tale.* 1983 Harcourt. 1st ed. dj. EX $15.00

HELPS, Racey. *Footprints in the Snow.* no date. Canada. Collins. 4to. 22 p. VG $25.00

HEMANS, F. *Forest Sanctuary.* 1827 Boston. ½-leather. VG $35.00

HEMENWAY, H.D. *How To Make a School Garden.* 1909 Doubleday. 110 p. VG $15.00

HEMINGWAY, Ernest. *Across the River & into the Trees.* 1950 London. 1st English ed. dj. EX $120.00

HEMINGWAY, Ernest. *Across the River & into the Trees.* 1950 NY. Scribner. 1st ed. 8vo. cloth. dj. VG $40.00

HEMINGWAY, Ernest. *Big Two-Hearted River.* 1925 Paris. 1st ed. wraps. EX $75.00

HEMINGWAY, Ernest. *Collected Poems.* no date. Paris. 2nd issue. wraps. VG $35.00

HEMINGWAY, Ernest. *Collected Poems.* 1960 no place. Pirated ed. wraps. EX $25.00

HEMINGWAY, Ernest. *Farewell to Arms.* 1929 NY. 1st ed. 2nd print. VG $40.00

HEMINGWAY, Ernest. *Farewell to Arms.* 1929 NY. 1st ed. G $35.00

HEMINGWAY, Ernest. *Fifth Column.* 1969 NY. dj. M $22.00

HEMINGWAY, Ernest. *For Whom the Bell Tolls.* 1965 Bucharest. 1st Rumanian ed. VG $35.00

HEMINGWAY, Ernest. *For Whom the Bell Tolls.* 1940 Scribner. 1st ed. 2nd issue. dj. VG $100.00

HEMINGWAY, Ernest. *For Whom the Bell Tolls.* 1940 NY. 1st ed. 1st state. dj. G $125.00

HEMINGWAY, Ernest. *Garden of Eden.* 1987 NY. Collier. 1st ed. 8vo. wraps. EX $10.00

HEMINGWAY, Ernest. *Hemingway Manuscripts.* 1969 Ltd ed. 1/300. VG $40.00

HEMINGWAY, Ernest. *In Our Time.* 1930 NY. Scribner. Intro Edmund Wilson. G $75.00

HEMINGWAY, Ernest. *Islands in the Stream.* 1970 NY. 1st ed. dj. M $35.00

HEMINGWAY, Ernest. *Men Without Women.* 1927 NY. 1st ed. 1st state. VG $70.00

HEMINGWAY, Ernest. *Moveable Feast.* 1964 NY. 1st ed. dj. EX $35.00

HEMINGWAY, Ernest. *Moveable Feast.* 1964 Scribner. 1st English ed. dj. EX $40.00

HEMINGWAY, Ernest. *Nick Adams Stories.* 1972 Scribner. 1st ed. dj. VG $20.00

HEMINGWAY, Ernest. *Old Man & the Sea.* Scribner. 1st ed A. dj. VG $30.00

HEMINGWAY, Ernest. *Old Man & the Sea.* 1952 NY. 1st ed. dj. VG $75.00

HEMINGWAY, Ernest. *Old Man & the Sea.* 1953 Reprint Soc. VG $27.50

HEMINGWAY, Ernest. *To Have & Have Not.* 1937 NY. 1st ed. 1st state. M $75.00

HEMINGWAY, Ernest. *To Have & Have Not.* 1937 NY. 1st ed. 2nd state. EX $22.00

HEMINGWAY, Ernest. *Torrents of Spring.* 1930 NY. Scribner. not 1st ed. dj. VG $75.00

HEMINGWAY, Ernest. *Treasure for Free World.* 1946 NY. 1st ed. dj. EX $35.00

HEMINGWAY, Ernest. *Treasury for Free World.* 1946 NY. 1st ed. dj. VG $25.00

HEMINGWAY, Ernest. *Winner Take Nothing.* 1933 Scribner. 1st ed. dj. G $30.00

HEMINGWAY, Jack. *Misadventures of Fly Fisherman: My Life with & Without Papa.* 1986 Dallas. Ills 1st ed. 8vo. dj. EX $15.00

HEMINGWAY, Mary. *How It Was.* 1976 NY. 1st ed. dj. $15.00

HEMPHILL, Paul. *Nashville Sound: Bright Lights & Country Music.* 1970 NY. Simon Schuster. EX $10.00

HEMSTREET, C. *Story of Manhattan.* 1901 NY. 1st ed. VG $20.00

HENDEL, Max. *Mysteries of the Great Operas.* 1921 Oceanside, CA. 1st ed. scarce. $9.00

HENDERSON, Archibald. *Mark Twain.* 1912 NY. Stokes. Ills L Coburn. 230 p. EX $350.00

HENDERSON, D. *From the Volga to the Yukon.* 1944 NY. dj. $15.00

HENDERSON, D. *Hidden Coasts: Biography of Admiral Charles Wilkes.* 1953 NY. 1st ed. dj. EX $15.00

HENDERSON, Dion. *Season of Birds.* 1976 Tamarack. Ills 1st ed. 87 p. dj. EX $10.00

HENDERSON, Helen. *Loiterer in New England.* 1919 NY. Ills 1st ed. 445 p. $10.00

HENDERSON, Helen. *Loiterer in NY.* 1917 NY. Ills 1st ed. 454 p. xl. $10.00

HENDERSON, Mrs. L.R.S. *Magic Aeroplane.* 1911 Reilly Britton. Ills. 4to. VG $40.00

HENDERSON, Peter. *Practical Floriculture.* 1869 NY. 12mo. 249 p. $15.00

HENDERSON, Philip. *William Morris: His Life, Work, & Friends.* 1967 NY. McGraw Hill. Ills. 388 p. dj. $45.00

HENDERSON, R. *On Desert Trails Today & Yesterday.* 1961 Westlore Pr. Ills. dj. EX $20.00

HENDERSON, W.J. *Art of the Singer.* 1906 NY. Scribner. 1st ed. xl. VG $8.00

HENDERSON. *Henderson's Garden Guide & Record.* 1942 Revised ed. wraps. EX $5.00

HENDRICK, Burton. *Lees of VA.* 1935 Boston. 1st ed. dj. EX $22.00

HENDRICKS, Gordon. *Albert Bierstadt.* 1972 Forth Worth. Ills. 8vo. 48 p. wraps. $12.50

HENDRICKS, Gordon. *Bad Men of the West.* 1970 Naylor. Ills. 254 p. dj. VG $25.00

HENDRICKS, Gordon. *Life & Works of Winslow Homer.* 1979 NY. Abrams. Ills. oblong 4to. 346 p. dj. $100.00

HENDRICKS, Gordon. *Photographs of Thomas Eakins.* 1972 NY. 1st ed. dj. VG $110.00

HENDRIX, John. *If I Can Do It Horseback: Cow Country Sketchbook.* 1964 UT Pr. 1st ed. dj. EX $25.00

HENDRON, J.W. *Frijoles: Hidden Valley in New World.* 1946 Santa Fe. Rydal. sgn. dj. EX $30.00

HENDY, Philip. *Catalog of Exhibited Paintings & Drawings.* 1931 Boston. Merrymount. Ills. 8vo. VG $40.00

HENIE, Sonja. *Wings on My Feet*. 1940 Prentice Hall. Ills 1st ed. 177 p. dj. VG $25.00

HENIE, Sonja. *Wings on My Feet*. 1940 NY. Ills 1st print. presentation. $150.00

HENIUS, Frank. *Stories From the Americas*. 1944 no place. Scribner. Ills 1st ed. EX $25.00

HENKIN, Harmon. *Complete Fisherman's Catalog*. 1977 Lippincott. Ills 1st ed. 4to. dj. EX $12.50

HENKIN, Harmon. *Fly Tackle: Guide to the Tools of the Trade*. 1976 Lippincott. Ills 1st ed. 240 p. dj. EX $12.50

HENLE, Faye. *Au Clare de Luce: Portrait of a Luminous Lady*. 1943 NY. 1st ed. dj. VG $12.50

HENRI, Robert. *Art Spirit*. 1939 NY. Lippincott. Ills 9th print. 292 p. dj. $15.00

HENRICI, Max. *Das Buch der Deutschen in Amerika*. 1909 Phil. Ills. 4to. German text. 974 p. VG $37.50

HENRY, Arthur. *Nicholas Blood Candidate*. 1890 NY. 1st ed. VG $40.00

HENRY, D. Scott. *Iron & Steel in Wheeling*. 1929 Toledo. Ltd ed. $25.00

HENRY, G.M. *Guide to the Birds of Ceylon*. 1955 London. Ills 1st ed. 432 p. xl. $70.00

HENRY, J.D. *Red Fox: Catlike Canine*. 1986 Smithsonian. Ills. 176 p. EX $22.00

HENRY, Marguerite. *Brighty of the Grand Canyon*. 1960 Rand McNally. Ills Wesley Dennis. $12.00

HENRY, Marguerite. *Canada in Story & Picture*. 1943 Whitman. Ills Wiese. Revised ed. 28 p. $8.00

HENRY, Marguerite. *Misty of Chincoteague*. 1948 NY. dj. VG $20.00

HENRY, May; & HALFORD, Kate. *Dainty Dinners & Dishes for Jewish Families*. 1907 London. Ills 2nd ed. 12mo. 190 p. $75.00

HENRY, O. *Cabbages & Kings*. 1904 NY. 1st ed. 1st issue. G $75.00

HENRY, O. *Stories of O. Henry*. 1965 Ltd Ed Club. Ills Groth. dj. slipcase. EX $150.00

HENRY, R.S. *Story of the Mexican War*. 1950 Bobbs Merrill. Ills 1st ed. 424 p. dj. VG $25.00

HENRY, R.S. *1st with Most Forrest*. 1944 Indianapolis. Ltd 1st ed. sgn. dj. VG $67.50

HENRY, Stuart. *Conquering Our Great American Plains*. 1930 Dutton. Ills 1st ed. 395 p. G $40.00

HENRY, Will. *Alias Butch Cassidy*. 1967 Random House. 1st print. 209 p. dj. VG $5.00

HENRY, Will. *Who Rides with Wyatt*. 1955 Random House. Review of 1st ed. 241 p. EX $18.00

HENSHALL, J.A. *Bass, Pike, Perch, & Other Game Fishes of America*. 1923 Stewart Kidd. Ills. 410 p. EX $14.00

HENSHALL, J.A. *Book of the Black Bass*. 1881 Clarke. facsimile. 463 p. EX $17.50

HENSHALL, J.A. *Favorite Fish & Fishing*. 1908 NY. 1st ed. VG $30.00

HENSLEE, Helen. *Pretty Redwing*. 1983 Holt. Advance copy. dj. EX $15.00

HENSLOW, Rev. Prof. G. *Religion of the Spirit World Written by Spirits Themselves*. 1920 London. Kegan Paul. 223 p. EX $30.00

HENSON, Matthew. *Black Explorer at the North Pole*. 1969 NY. dj. $17.50

HENSON, Matthew. *Negro Explorer at North Pole*. 1912 NY. 200 p. xl. VG $70.00

HENSON, Truman. *Sporting Rifles & Scope Sights*. 1950 NY. VG $16.00

HENTOFF, Nat. *1st Freedom*. 1981 Dell. 1st ed. sgn. wraps. EX $10.00

HENTY, G.A. *By Conduct & Courage*. 1904 NY. VG $15.00

HENTY, G.A. *Knight of the White Cross*. 1895 NY. VG $15.00

HENTY, G.A. *March on London*. 1897 NY. 1st ed. EX $20.00

HENTY, G.A. *Point of a Bayonet*. 1901 NY. 1st ed. EX $28.00

HENTY, G.A. *St. Bartholomew's Eve*. 1894 Ills. gilt cloth. EX $18.00

HENTY, G.A. *St. George & England*. no date. London. Blackie. VG $20.00

HENTY, G.A. *When London Burned*. 1894 NY. Scribner. Ills 1st Am ed. VG $20.00

HENTY, G.A. *With the British Legion*. 1903 London. 1st ed. VG $25.00

HEPBURN, A. *Complete Guide to NY City*. 1957 London. Ills. maps. 165 p. dj. $6.00

HEPBURN, A. *Complete Guide to NY City*. 1972 NY. Ills 1st ed. 114 p. wraps. $5.00

HEPBURN, A. Barton. *History of Currency in the USA*. 1915 NY. 8vo. VG $16.00

HERBERT, A.P. *Water Gypsies*. 1930 NY. VG $6.00

HERBERT, E. *Michael Reasor & Anna Herbert Descendants*. 1968 Burbank. 700 p. EX $45.00

HERBERT, F. *Santaroga Barrier*. 1970 Rapp Whiting. 1st ed. dj. EX $30.00

HERBERT, Frank. *Chapterhouse: Dune*. 1985 Putnam. 1st ed. dj. EX $20.00

HERBERT, Frank. *Chapterhouse: Dune*. 1985 Putnam. Ltd ed. 1/750. sgn. slipcase. EX $75.00

HERBERT, Frank. *Dosadi Experiment*. 1977 Berkeley. dj. VG $20.00

HERBERT, Frank. *Dragon in the Sea*. 1956 Doubleday. 1st ed. dj. $125.00

HERBERT, Frank. *Dune Messiah*. 1969 Putnam. 1st ed. dj. VG $90.00

HERBERT, Frank. *Dune*. 1970 Chilton. 1st ed. 3rd print. dj. VG $50.00

HERBERT, Frank. *Dune*. 1965 Chilton. 1st ed. blue cloth. VG $75.00

HERBERT, Frank. *God Emperor of Dune*. 1981 NY. Putnam. 7th imp. dj. EX $10.00

HERBERT, Frank. *God Emperor of Dune*. 1981 NY. Putnam. Ltd 1st ed. sgn. slipcase. VG $85.00

HERBERT, Frank. *God Emperor of Dune*. 1981 NY. Putnam. 1st trade ed. dj. EX $25.00

HERBERT, Frank. *Heretics of Dune*. 1984 NY. Putnam. Ltd 1st ed. sgn. slipcase. VG $75.00

HERBERT, Frank. *Lazarus Effect*. 1983 Putnam. 1st ed. dj. VG $15.00

HERBERT, Frank. *Man of 2 Worlds*. 1986 proof. VG $50.00

HERBERT, Frank. *White Plague*. 1982 Putnam. 1st ed. dj. EX $25.00

HERBERT, George B. *Popular History of the Civil War*. 1885 NY. Ills. 12mo. 552 p. cloth. xl. $20.00

HERBERT, George. *Temple*. 1927 London. Nonesuch. Ltd ed. 1/1,500. VG $50.00

HERBERT, Henry William. *Frank Forester's Fish & Fishing of US & British Provinces*. 1859 NY. Dinks. New Revised ed. 512 p. $25.00

HERBERT, James. *Moon*. no date. Crown. Review ed. wraps. M $8.00

HERBERT, James. *Sepulchre*. London. 1st ed. sgn. EX $35.00

HERBERT. *Why the Solid South?* 1890 Baltimore. 1st ed. VG $25.00

HERBST, Josephine. *Nothing Is Sacred*. 1928 NY. 1st ed. VG $42.50

HERFORD, Oliver. *Laughing Willow*. 1918 NY. 1st ed. sgn. VG $35.00

HERFORD, Oliver. *Rubaiyat of a Persian Kitten.* 1904 NY. Scribner. Ills 1st ed. square 12mo. dj. $45.00

HERGESHEIMER, J. *Party Dress.* 1930 NY. Ltd ed. 1/60. sgn. EX $30.00

HERGESHEIMER, J. *Presbyterian Child.* 1923 NY. Knopf. Ltd ed. 1/950. sgn. boxed. VG $30.00

HERGESHEIMER, J. *3 Black Pennys.* 1917 NY. ¾-morocco. EX $35.00

HERLIHY, James Leo. *Midnight Cowboy.* 1965 NY. 1st ed. dj. EX $35.00

HERLIHY, James Leo. *Season of the Witch.* 1971 Simon Schuster. 1st ed. dj. EX $25.00

HERMAN, Zvi. *Peoples, Seas, & Ships.* 1967 NY. Putnam. 1st Am ed. G $36.00

HERMES, Walter G. *Truce Tent & Fighting Front: US Army in Korean War.* 1966 WA. 1st print. EX $35.00

HERNANDEZ, Francisco J. *El Jugete Popular en Mixico.* 1950 Mexico. Mexicana. Ills. 158 p. $50.00

HERNANDEZ, J. *Martin Fierro: Gaucho Epic.* 1948 NY. Hispanic Institute. 1st ed. VG $14.00

HERNDON & GIBBON. *Exploration of Valley of Amazon.* 1853 & 1854. WA. presentation. 2 vol set. G $300.00

HERNE, Brian. *Uganda Safaris.* 1979 Clinton. Amwell Pr. Ltd ed. sgn. M $420.00

HEROLD, C.J. *Wisdom of Woodrow Wilson.* 1919 NY. 1st ed. 196 p. cloth. $5.00

HERON, G. Scott. *Nigger Factory.* 1972 NY. 1st ed. dj. VG $27.50

HERRICK, C.J. *Neurological Foundations of Animal Behavior.* 1924 Holt. Ills. 334 p. VG $17.00

HERRICK, F. *American Eagle.* 1934 NY. Ills 1st ed. 267 p. dj. VG $35.00

HERRICK. *American Lobster: Habits & Development.* 1895 54 pls. wraps. $40.00

HERRIMAN, G. *Krazy Kat.* 1946 NY. Intro Cummings. 1st ed. VG $42.50

HERRIOT, James. *It Shouldn't Happen to a Vet.* 1972 London. 1st ed. dj. VG $15.00

HERRITT, Sarah. *Keepsake, Dedicated to My Friends.* 1876 Cincinnati. 158 p. G $30.00

HERRLIGKOFFER, Karl M. *Nanga Parbat.* 1954 London. 1st ed. VG $18.00

HERRLINGER, Robert. *History of Medical Illustration.* 1970 NY. Ed Medicina Rara. 1st ed. 4to. $50.00

HERRMANN, Paul. *Conquest by Man.* 1954 Harper. Ills. 455 p. maps. VG $13.00

HERSCHBERGER, Ruth. *Way of Happening.* 1948 Pelligrini. 1st ed. dj. VG $20.00

HERSCHEL, John. *Treatise on Astronomy.* 1834 London. Longman. New ed. 422 p. xl. $37.00

HERSCHEL, John. *Treatise on Astronomy.* 1834 Phil. Ills 1st Am ed. VG $65.00

HERSEY, John. *Bell for Adano.* 1944 Knopf. 1st ed. dj. VG $25.00

HERSEY, John. *Letter to the Alumni.* 1970 NY. 1st ed. dj. M $10.00

HERSEY, John. *My Petition for More Space.* 1974 Knopf. 1st ed. dj. EX $15.00

HERSEY, John. *Wall.* 1950 NY. 1st ed. dj. EX $15.00

HERSEY, John. *Walnut Door.* 1977 NY. dj. M $12.00

HERSHELL, J.F.W. *Treatise on Astronomy.* 1842 London. New ed. 16mo. calf. VG $25.00

HERT, Carl. *Tracking the Big Cat.* 1955 Caxton. Ills. 330 p. dj. EX $28.50

HERTER, G.L. *Bull Cook & Authentic Historical Recipes & Practices.* 1963 MN. Ills. 324 p. VG $10.00

HERTER, G.L. *Bull Cook & Authentic Historical Recipes & Practices.* 1960 Waseca. Ills 1st ed. VG $12.00

HERTER, G.L. *Professional Fly Tying & Tackle Making Manual.* 1949 Herters. Ills. 416 p. wraps. VG $10.00

HERTER, G.L. *Professional Fly Tying Manual.* 1950 Herters. Ills. 96 p. wraps. VG $5.00

HERTZ, Louis H. *Toy Collector.* 1969 NY. Funk Wagnall. 8vo. 304 p. $40.00

HERTZ, R. *Congregational Woope (Sioux).* 1926 Santee. 24mo. 24 p. wraps. VG $12.50

HERTZLER, Arthur. *Diseases of Thyroid Gland.* 1922 Mosby. VG $10.00

HERVEY, John. *Lady Suffolk.* 1936 NY. Ltd ed. 1/500. 8vo. VG $110.00

HERVEY, John. *Racing in America 1665-1865.* 1944 NY. Ltd ed. 1/800. EX $350.00

HERVEY, John. *Racing in America 1922-1936.* 1937 NY. private print. Ills. EX $300.00

HERZFELD. *Archaeological History of Iran.* 1935 London. Ills. cloth. VG $35.00

HERZOG, Arthur. *Make Us Happy.* 1978 NY. 1st ed. dj. VG $15.00

HESKSCHER, Morrison H. *Furniture in Metropolitan Museum of Art: Late Colonial.* 1985 NY. Ills. 4to. 384 p. cloth. dj. $45.00

HESLER, L.R. *Mushrooms of the Great Smokies.* 1963 TN U Pr. Ills. 289 p. EX $14.00

HESS, Stephen; & KAPLAN, M. *Ungentlemanly Art: History of American Political Cartoons.* 1968 NY. Macmillan. 1st print. dj. VG $20.00

HESS, Thomas B. *Barnett Newman.* 1971 MOMA. Ills. 4to. 160 p. wraps. $20.00

HESS, Thomas B. *Willem De Kooning.* 1968 MOMA. Ills. 4to. 170 p. cloth. $20.00

HESS. *Taste of America.* 1977 1st ed. 384 p. dj. VG $5.00

HESSE, Hermann. *Klingsor's Last Summer.* 1970 Farrar. 1st Am ed. dj. EX $20.00

HESSE, Hermann. *Peter Camenzind.* 1969 Farrar. 1st Am ed. dj. EX $25.00

HESSE, Hermann. *Steppenwolf.* 1977 Ltd Ed Club. Ills/sgn Kazin. slipcase. EX $65.00

HETTES, Karel. *Venezianisches Glass.* 1960 Prague. Artia. Ills Forman. dj. $42.50

HEUVELMANS, B. *On Track of Unknown Animals.* 1959 NY. 1st ed. 558 p. dj. VG $22.50

HEVESY, George. *Radioactive Indicators.* 1948 NY. Intersciences. 1st ed. 556 p. $30.00

HEWES, A. *Boy of the Last Crusade.* 1923 Boston. Ills. EX $27.50

HEWETT, Edgar L. *Ancient Life in American Southwest.* Indianapolis. Ltd ed. 1/1,930. G $25.00

HEWETT, Edgar L. *Ancient Life in Mexico & Central America.* 1936 Indianapolis. Ills 1st ed. 364 p. dj. EX $45.00

HEWETT, Edgar L. *Chaco Canyon & Its Monuments.* 1936 NM U Pr. 1st ed. 234 p. dj. EX $60.00

HEWITT, Charles. *Tribute to Memory of Edward Jenner.* 1896 Chicago. 1st ed. wraps. EX $25.00

HEWITT, E.R. *Hewitt's Handbook of Fly Fishing.* 1933 Marchbanks. Ills. 116 p. scarce. EX $40.00

HEWITT, E.R. *Secrets of the Salmon.* 1925 NY. Ills. EX $20.00

HEWITT, E.R. *Trout & Salmon Fisherman for 75 Years.* 1950 Scribner. Ills. 338 p. dj. EX $20.00

HEWITT. *Cornell History.* 1905 4 vol set. EX $125.00

HEWLETT, Maurice. *Extemporary Essays.* 1922 London. EX $15.00

HEWLETT, Maurice. *Works of Maurice Hewlett.* 1898 NY. Macmillan. Ltd ed. 1/500. EX $150.00

HEXAMER, F.M. *Asparagus: Its Culture for Home & Use for Market.* 1918 NY. Ills. G $10.00

HEY, W. *Ausgewahlte Fabeln Fur Kinder.* no date. Reutlingen. Ills. 4to. dj. EX $50.00

HEYDENREICH, Ludwig H. *Leonardo the Inventor.* 1980 Ills. 192 p. dj. EX $9.00

HEYEN, William. *Trains.* 1981 Metacom. Ltd ed. 1/150. sgn. wraps. EX $45.00

HEYERDAHL, Thor. *Aku-Aku: Secrets of Easter Island.* 1958 Rand McNally. Ills. 384 p. VG $7.00

HEYERDAHL, Thor. *Kon-Tiki Expedition.* 1965 Rand McNally. Ills 1st English ed. dj. VG $13.00

HEYERDAHL, Thor. *Kon-Tiki: Across the Pacific by Raft.* 1950 Rand McNally. Ills. 304 p. G $5.00

HEYLEN, Peter. *Aerius Redivivus: History of Presbyterians.* 1670 Oxford. folio. VG $150.00

HEYLEN, Peter. *Cosmographie in Source Bookes Contayning Chorographie.* 1657 London. Seile. Ills. folio. 1,113 p. rebound. $400.00

HEYWARD, Du Bose; & ALLEN, H. *Carolina Chansons.* 1922 NY. 1st ed. EX $20.00

HEYWARD, M. *Illustrated Guide to Savannah, GA.* 1917 Ills 1st ed. wraps. $10.00

HEYWOOD, D. Herbert. *Personal Development Through Mind Power Building.* 1923 San Francisco. 120 p. rope bdg. G $15.00

HEYWOOD, Rosalind. *Beyond the Reach of Sense.* 1961 NY. Dutton. Book Club ed. dj. VG $3.00

HIATT. *Picture Posters.* 1896 London. Ills 2nd ed. cloth. VG $100.00

HIBBARD, C.P. *Souvenir of Crawford Notch, NH.* 1892 NY. Ills 1st ed. 24 p. wraps. $12.50

HIBBARD, F.G. *Palestine: Its Geography & Bible History.* 1851 NY. Ills. 354 p. gilt black cloth. $150.00

HIBBARD, G.A. *Lenox, MA.* 1896 NY. Ills. 54 p. cloth. $8.50

HIBBARD, Howard. *Caravaggio.* 1983 NY. Harper Row. Ills. 4to. 416 p. dj. $45.00

HIBBEN, Frank C. *Hunting American Bears.* 1950 Phil. 1st ed. $37.50

HIBBEN, Frank C. *Hunting in Africa.* 1962 NY. 1st Am ed. dj. EX $40.00

HIBBEN, Frank C. *Hunting in Africa.* 1962 Hill Wang. dj. EX $45.00

HIBBEN, Frank C. *Treasure in the Dust: Exploring Ancient North America.* 1951 Phil. 1st ed. dj. VG $15.00

HIBBERD, Shirley. *Rustic Adorments for Homes of Taste.* 1870 London. Revised Enlarged ed. 402 p. G $125.00

HIBBERT, C. *Disraeli & His World.* 1978 NY. Ills. 128 p. $15.00

HIBLER, C. *Down in AR.* 1902 Abbey Pr. $10.00

HICHENS, R. *Egypt & Its Monuments.* 1908 Century. Ills Jules Guerin. VG $25.00

HICKEL, Walter J. *Who Owns America?* 1971 Prentice Hall. dj. EX $10.00

HICKENS, R. *Green Carnation.* 1874 NY. 1st Am ed. inscr. VG $45.00

HICKMAN, Janet. *Zoar Blue.* 1978 NY. 1st ed. inscr. juvenile. dj. $10.00

HICKS, Granville. *Great Tradition: Interpretation of American Literature.* 1935 NY. Revised ed. inscr. $35.00

HICKS, J.E. *Adventures of a Tramp Printer 1880-1890.* 1890 KS City. 8vo. 285 p. dj. M $20.00

HICKS, J.E. *US Military Firearms 1776-1956.* 1962 Hicks & Son. Ills. 4to. 127 p. dj. EX $17.50

HIDY, V.S. *Pleasures of Fly Fishing.* 1972 Winchester. Ills. 4to. 127 p. VG $12.50

HIGGINBOTHAM, Jay. *Fast Train Russia.* 1983 Dodd Mead. 1st ed. dj. EX $12.50

HIGGINS, A. *New Castle, DE 1651-1939.* 1939 Boston. Ills Ltd 1st ed. sgn. 765 p. $100.00

HIGGINS, Colin. *Harold & Maude.* 1971 NY. 1st ed. dj. EX $25.00

HIGGINS, G.V. *Friends of Eddie Coyle.* 1972 NY. 1st ed. dj. M $17.00

HIGGINS, G.V. *Kennedy for the Defense.* 1980 NY. 1st ed. dj. M $10.00

HIGGINS, G.V. *Kennedy for the Defense.* 1980 NY. Uncorrected proof. dj. $20.00

HIGGINS, Jack. *Day of Judgment.* 1978 London. 1st ed. dj. EX $35.00

HIGGINS, Jack. *Eagle Has Landed.* 1975 NY. 1st ed. EX $18.00

HIGGINS, Jack. *East of Desolation.* 1968 London. 1st English ed. dj. VG $45.00

HIGGINS, Jack. *Solo.* 1986 London. 1st ed. dj. EX $30.00

HIGGINS, V. *Crassulas in Cultivation.* 1964 London. 78 p. dj. VG $12.00

HIGGINSON, A. Henry. *British & American Sporting Authors: Writings & Biographies.* 1949 Berryville, VA. Blue Ridge. Ills 1st ed. 4to. $35.00

HIGGINSON, A. Henry. *Try Back.* 1931 NY. Huntington Pr. 1/401. EX $55.00

HIGGINSON, Ella. *AK, the Greatest Country.* 1919 Macmillan. Ills. 583 p. fld map. VG $18.00

HIGGINSON, Ella. *AK, the Greatest Country.* 1908 NY. Ills 1st ed. VG $35.00

HIGGINSON, Thomas W. *Tales of Enchanted Islands of Atlantic.* c 1890s. NY. Ills 1st ed. cloth. $30.00

HIGGINSON & CHAMBERLAIN. *Hunting in US & Canada: History of Hunt Clubs.* 1928 Garden City. Ltd ed. 1/450. sgn. boxed. $150.00

HIGHAM. *Ziegfeld.* 1972 Chicago. dj. VG $7.50

HIGHSMITH, Patricia. *People Who Knock at the Door.* 1985 Uncorrected proof. dj. $40.00

HIGHTOWER, John. *Pheasant Hunting.* 1946 Knopf. Ills 1st ed. 227 p. dj. VG $15.00

HILBERRY, Conrad. *Man in the Attic.* 1980 Bits Pr. 1st ed. sgn. wraps. EX $10.00

HILDEBRAND, S.F. *Descriptive Catalog of the Shore Fishes of Muda.* 1946 USNM. Ills. 530 p. wraps. VG $45.00

HILDEBRANDT, Greg. *Christmas Treasury.* 1984 Unicorn Pub. Ills 1st ed. oblong 4to. EX $17.50

HILDERANDT, Dr. Hans. *Alexander Archipenko.* 1923 Berlin. Ukrainshe Slowo. tall 4to. $50.00

HILDRETH, Richard. *Archie Moore: White Slave.* 1856 Brown. Ills Baker-Smith. 408 p. fair. $45.00

HILDRETH, Richard. *Archie Moore: White Slave.* 1971 NY. Kelley. reprint of 1856. EX $20.00

HILER, Hilaire. *From Nudity to Raiment: Introduction to Study of Costume.* 1929 NY. Wyehe. 4to. 303 p. VG $110.00

HILER, Hilaire. *From Nudity to Raiment: Introduction to Study of Costume.* 1929 London. Ills 1st ed. 4to. 303 p. VG $45.00

HILL, A.F. *Secrets of the Sanctum.* 1875 Phil. 8vo. 312 p. VG $20.00

HILL, Carol. *Jeremiah 8:20.* 1970 Random House. 1st ed. dj. EX $30.00

HILL, Elizabeth. *My Childhood's Home & Other Poems.* 1889 Shelbyville. 1st ed. G $30.00

HILL, F.T. *Lincoln the Lawyer.* 1906 NY. Ills 1st ed. 332 p. VG $30.00

HILL, G.J. *Story of the War in La Vendee & Little Chouannerie.* c 1850s. NY/Montreal. Sadlier. 324 p. $10.00

HILL, Grace Livingston. *War Romance in the Salvation Army.* 1919 Phil. 1st ed. dj. VG $27.50

HILL, H.C. *Roosevelt & the Caribbean.* 1927 Chicago. 1st ed. map. 213 p. $7.50

HILL, Howard. *Hunting the Hard Way.* 1953 Chicago. Wilcox Follett. 1st ed. dj. EX $125.00

HILL, Howard. *Hunting the Hard Way.* 1956 Wilcox Follett. reprint. dj. EX $25.00

HILL, J.E.; & SMITH, J.D. *Bats: Natural History.* 1984 TX U Pr. Ills. 243 p. maps. dj. EX $30.00

HILL, M. *Permanent Way: Story of Kenya & Uganda Railway.* 1949 Nairobi. 1st ed. 582 p. cloth. EX $35.00

HILL, N.E. *Fisherman's Notes to His Son.* no date. Jenkins. Ills 1st ed. VG $8.00

HILL, N.E. *Fisherman's Recollections.* no date. Jenkins. Ills 1st ed. G $5.00

HILL, N.P. *Birds of Cape Cod, MA.* 1965 Morrow. Ills. 364 p. xl. VG $8.00

HILL, Pati. *Pit & the Century Plant.* 1955 Harper. 1st ed. dj. VG $10.00

HILL, R.N. *Contrary Country: VT.* 1950 NY. Ills 1st ed. 292 p. dj. $6.50

HILL, R.N. *Story of Shelburne Museum.* 1950 VT. Ills 1st ed. sgn. 56 p. $8.50

HILL, R.N. *Story of Ticonderoga.* 1957 VT. Ills 1st ed. 107 p. wraps. $7.50

HILL, Thomas E. *Hill's Manual of Social & Business Forms.* 1884 Chicago. Ills. 4to. cloth. VG $38.00

HILL, W. *Onionhead.* 1957 NY. 1st ed. dj. EX $17.00

HILL, W. Henry. *Stradivari: His Life & Work.* 1909 London. 2nd ed. VG $85.00

HILLARD, G.S. *Life & Campaigns of G.B. McClellan.* 1864 Lippincott. $25.00

HILLARY, Edmund. *High Adventure.* 1955 London. 1st ed. dj. VG $12.50

HILLARY, Edmund. *High Adventure.* 1955 NY. 1st ed. dj. EX $25.00

HILLARY & DOIG. *High in the Thin Cold Air.* 1962 Garden City. 1st ed. dj. VG $15.00

HILLBERG, R. *Documents of Destruction: Germany & Jewry 1933-1945.* 1971 Chicago. Quadrangle. $25.00

HILLEN, William. *Blackwater River.* 1972 Norton. 1st Am ed. 169 p. dj. EX $11.00

HILLERMAN, Tony. *Dark Wind.* 1982 Harper. 1st Am ed. inscr. dj. $20.00

HILLERMAN, Tony. *Ghostway.* 1984 1st Am ed. sgn. dj. $25.00

HILLERMAN, Tony. *Skinwalkers.* 1986 NY Advance copy. sgn. dj. $35.00

HILLHOUSE, A.M. *Pierre Gibert, French Huguenot: Background & Decendants.* 1977 Danville. 1st ed. dj. VG $45.00

HILLIAR, William J. *Modern Magicians' Handbook.* 1902 Chicago. 1st ed. 8vo. 440 p. $40.00

HILLS, Chester. *Builder's Guide: Practical Treatise on Grecian Architecture.* 1846 Hartford. Ills. folio. calf. EX $400.00

HILLS, J.W. *History of Fly Fishing for Trout.* 1971 Freshet. 244 p. slipcase. EX $12.50

HILLS, J.W.; & DUNBAR, I. *Golden River: Sport & Travel in Paraguay.* 1922 Allan. Ills. 187 p. map. G $7.00

HILLS, Patricia. *Eastman Johnson.* 1972 NY. 1st ed. dj. VG $35.00

HILLYER, Robert. *Death of Captain Nemo.* 1949 NY. 1st ed. dj. M $11.00

HILLYER, V.M. *Child's Geography of the World.* 1929 NY. 3rd print. VG $25.00

HILOWITZ, B. *Great Historic Places of Europe.* 1974 NY. Ills 1st ed. maps. 383 p. dj. $12.50

HILTON, James. *To You Mr. Chips.* 1938 Great Britain. Hodder Stoughton. 1st ed. dj. $50.00

HILTON, James; & BROCK, H.M. *Good-Bye Mr. Chips.* 1935 Boston. Birthday ed. 1/600. sgns. EX $125.00

HILTON. *Rest & Pain.* 1950 Lippincott. 8vo. slipcase. EX $25.00

HIMES, Chester. *All Shot Up.* 1960 NY. Avon. 1st ed. pb. EX $10.00

HIMES, Chester. *Heat's On.* 1966 Putnam. 1st ed. dj. VG $35.00

HIMES, Chester. *Lonely Crusade.* 1947 NY. 1st ed. dj. VG $60.00

HIMMELWRIGHT, A.L.A. *Pistol & Revolver Shooting.* 1928 NY. Macmillan. New Revised ed. 482 p. VG $15.00

HINCHCLIFF, Thomas Woodbine. *South American Sketches.* 1863 London. Longman. 1st ed. VG $125.00

HINDLEY, Charles. *True History of Tom & Jerry.* 1888 London. Reeves Turner. Ills. 8vo. sgn. $85.00

HINDLEY, Geoffrey. *Book of Houses.* 1973 London. Triune Copplestone Pub. VG $10.00

HINE, Robert V. *Community on the American Frontier.* 1980 Norman. 1st ed. dj. VG $12.50

HINES, C.G. *NY & Albany Post Road.* 1905 NY. 1st ed. VG $25.00

HINES, C.G. *Old Dutch Burying Ground of Sleepy Hollow.* 1953 Boston. private print. VG $35.00

HINES, G. *OR: Its History, Condition, & Prospects.* c 1881. NY. 12mo. 437 p. blue cloth. VG $18.00

HINES, N.E. *Medical History of Contraception.* 1936 Baltimore. 1st ed. 519 p. VG $75.00

HINGSTON, R.W.G. *Naturalist in Guiana Forest.* 1932 NY. 1st Am ed. 384 p. G $40.00

HINKLEY, F. Lewis. *Directory of Antique Furniture.* 1953 NY. Bonanza. Ills. 4to. dj. $25.00

HINTON, John H. *History & Topography of USA. Vol. I.* 1853 Boston. 3rd ed. ½-leather. G $45.00

HINTON, S.E. *Outsiders.* 1967 Viking. 1st ed. dj. EX $100.00

HIORNS, Arthur H. *Metallographie.* 1903 Paris. Beranger. Ills. 205 p. VG $15.00

HIRSCH, Richard. *World of Benjamin West.* 1962 Allentown Art Mus. 4to. wraps. $30.00

HIRSCH & DOHERTY. *1st 100 Years of Mount Sinai Hospital of NY 1852-1952.* 1952 Random House. 1st ed. $12.50

HIRSCHFELD, Al. *American Theater As Seen by Braziller.* 1961 Braziller. 1st ed. dj. VG $25.00

HIRSCHFELD, Al. *Sexual History of WWI.* Panurge Pr. Ills separate supplement. VG $25.00

HIRSHORN, Joseph H. *Modern Sculpture From J.H. Hirshorn Collection.* 1962 NY. Guggenheim Museum. 1st ed. dj. $30.00

HIRST, F.W. *Early Life & Letters of John Morley.* 1927 London. Macmillan. 2 vol set. $37.50

HIRTH, Fred. *Scraps From a Collector's Notebook.* 1905 NY/Leipzig. Ills 1st ed. 8vo. 135 p. VG $85.00

HIRTH, George. *Picture Book of the Graphic Arts 1500-1800.* 1972 NY. VG $75.00

HISS, A. Emil. *Standard Manual of Soda & Other Beverages.* 1897 Chicago. 1st ed. 8vo. $150.00

HISS, Alger. *Court of Public Opinion.* 1957 NY. 1st ed. dj. G $85.00

HITCHCOCK, A.S. *Manual of the Grasses of the US.* 1950 USDA. Revised ed. 1,051 p. VG $35.00

HITCHCOCK, C.H. *Mount WA in Winter.* 1871 Boston. Ills 1st ed. 357 p. cloth. $45.00

HITCHCOCK, Edward. *Plates Illustrating Geology & Scenery of MA.* 1834 Boston. 2nd ed. 4to. plts. rare. $600.00

HITCHCOCK, Edward. *Sketch of Scenery of MA.* 1842 Northampton. Separate 1st ed. 4to. 14 plts. $700.00

HITCHCOCK, Enos. *Farmer's Friend.* 1793 Boston. 1st ed. calf. $280.00

HITCHCOCK, Ethan Allen. *50 Years in Camp & Field.* 1909 NY. 1st ed. VG $40.00

HITCHCOCK, Henry Russell. *American Architectural Books.* 1946 MN U Pr. Revised 3rd ed. EX $25.00

HITCHCOCK, Henry Russell. *Antoni Gaudi.* 1957 MOMA. Ills. 4to. 47 p. wraps. $12.50

HITCHCOCK, Henry Russell. *Built in USA: Post-War Architecture.* 1952 NY. Ills 1st ed. 128 p. dj. $25.00

HITCHCOCK, Henry Russell. *Latin American Architecture.* 1955 NY. MOMA. VG $25.00

HITCHCOCK, Henry Russell. *Nature of Materials: Buildings of Frank Lloyd Wright.* 1942 4th print. oblong 4to. 413 plts. VG $37.50

HITCHING, Francis. *Neck of Giraffe: Where Darwin Went Wrong.* 1982 279 p. dj. VG $20.00

HITCHINS, Capt. H.L. *From Lodestone to Gyro-Compass.* 1955 London. Hutchinson. 2nd ed. 219 p. dj. $15.00

HITLER, Adolf. *My Political Testament: My Private Testament & Addendum.* no date/place. EX $22.00

HITT, Thomas. *Treatise of Fruit Trees.* 1758 Dublin. Ills 3rd ed. 8vo. 176 p. VG $225.00

HIX, John. *Strange As It Seems.* 1931 NY. Ills. $30.00

HJORTSBERG, William. *Falling Angel.* 1978 Harcourt Brace. 1st ed. dj. EX $25.00

HJORTSBERG, William. *Gray Matters.* 1971 Simon Schuster. 1st ed. dj. EX $35.00

HOADLY, Charles. *Public Records of CT From October 1776 to February 1778.* 1894 Hartford. 653 p. VG $40.00

HOAGLAND, H. *Pacemakers in Relation to Aspects of Behavior.* 1935 Macmillan. 138 p. dj. EX $10.00

HOAR, J.S. *Small Town Motion Pictures & Sketches of Franklin City.* 1969 ME. Ills Ltd ed. 1/800. sgn. dj. $17.50

HOARE, Clement. *Practical Treatise on Cultivation of Grape Vine.* 1837 Boston. 1st Am ed. $90.00

HOBAN, Russell. *Lion of Boaz-Jachin.* 1973 NY. 1st ed. dj. EX $12.00

HOBAN, Russell. *Pilgermann.* 1983 Summit. 1st Am ed. dj. EX $16.00

HOBAN & BAYLEY. *La Corona & Tin Frog.* 1979 London. 1st ed. EX $8.00

HOBART, Alice Tisdale. *Yang & Yin.* 1936 Indianapolis. 1st ed. dj. EX $15.00

HOBBES, John Oliver. *Margaret Maison: Her Life & Work.* 1976 London. 1890s Soc. 8vo. wraps. EX $10.00

HOBBS, Robert. *American Art in 18th Century Furniture.* 1986 IA U of Art. Ills. 24 p. $10.00

HOBBS, William H. *Fortress Islands of Pacific.* 1946 Ann Arbor. Edwards. Ills 2nd ed. dj. VG $15.00

HOBHOUSE, L.T. *L.T. Hobhouse: His Life & Work.* 1931 London. 1st ed. inscr. dj. VG $10.00

HOBSON, Anthony. *Great Libraries.* 1970 NY. 4to. 320 p. dj. EX $25.00

HOBSON, R.L. *Art of the Chinese Potter.* 1923 London. Ltd ed. 1/1,500. $175.00

HOBSON, R.L. *Guide to Islamic Pottery of the Near East.* 1932 London. British Mus. Ills. 104 p. $30.00

HOBSON, R.L. *Wares of the Ming Dynasty.* 1923 London. Benn. Ills Ltd ed. 1/500. 240 p. $225.00

HOBSON, R.P. *Grass Beyond the Mountains.* 1951 Lippincott. 256 p. dj. VG $15.00

HOCHBAUM, H.A. *Canvasback on a Prairie Marsh.* 1981 NE U Pr. Ills. 207 p. maps. EX $20.00

HOCHBAUM, H.A. *Travels & Traditions of Waterfowl.* 1960 Branford. Ills. 301 p. dj. EX $12.00

HOCHHUTH, Rolf. *Deputh.* 1964 NY. 1st ed. dj. EX $15.00

HOCKING, W.E. *Self: Its Body & Freedom.* 1928 New Haven. VG $10.00

HOCKING, W.E. *Thoughts on Death & Life.* 1937 NY. 1st ed. presentation. VG $12.00

HODGDON, M.J. *Historic Nashua.* 1902 NH. Ills 1st ed. maps. wraps. $10.00

HODGE, Frederick Webb. *Handbook of American Indians North of Mexico.* 1907-1910. WA. GPO. 2 vol set. $85.00

HODGE, Frederick Webb. *Handbook of American Indians North of Mexico.* 1912 Smithsonian. 4th print. 2 vol set. scarce. $125.00

HODGE, Gene. *Kachinas Are Coming.* 1967 AZ. 4to. dj. VG $30.00

HODGE. *AR As It Is; or, Coming Country.* 1877 NY. 1st ed. VG $225.00

HODGE. *History of Fannin County, TX.* 1966 Hereford, TX. Pioneer Pub. EX $17.00

HODGESON, William B. *Notes on Northern Africa, Sahara, & Soudan.* 1844 NY. Ills 1st ed. wraps. VG $85.00

HODGINS, Eric. *Mr. Blandings Builds His Dream House.* 1946 NY. Ills. 237 p. G $7.50

HODGINS, Eric. *Sky High, Story of Aviation.* 1929 Boston. Little Brown. 1st ed. 337 p. $10.00

HODGKIN, J. *Rariora.* 1902 London. 1st ed. 3 vol set. VG $200.00

HODGKIN, R. *History of Anglo-Saxons.* 1952 Oxford U Pr. 3rd ed. 2 vol set. djs. $37.50

HODGSON, Fred T. *Builders' Reliable Estimator & Contractors' Guide.* 1912 Chicago. Sears. G $30.00

HODGSON, W.E. *Trout Fishing.* 1904 Black. 2nd print. VG $12.00

HODGSON, William H. *Carnacki the Ghost Finder.* 1947 Mycroft Moran. 1st ed. 1/3,000. dj. EX $35.00

HODGSON, William H. *Deep Waters.* 1967 Arkham House. Ltd 1st ed. dj. EX $75.00

HODGSON, William H. *Poems of the Sea.* 1977 London. Ferret. Ills Ltd ed. EX $70.00

HODGSON, William Noel. *Verse & Prose in Peace.* 1916 London. 1st ed. $45.00

HODNETT, Edward. *English Woodcuts 1480-1535.* 1973 Ills. cloth. EX $150.00

HOEHLING, A.A. *Great Epidemic.* 1961 Boston. Little Brown. 1st ed. dj. VG $12.00

HOEHLING, A.A. *Last Train From Atlanta.* 1958 NY. Yosoloff. Ills 1st ed. dj. VG $17.50

HOEHLING, A.A. *Lexington Goes Down.* 1971 Prentice Hall. Ills. 208 p. $7.00

HOEK, Henry. *Parsenn.* 1933 London. 1st English ed. VG $25.00

HOFER, E. *Arctic Riviera.* 1957 Berne. Ills. VG $22.00

HOFER, Philip. *Othello: 15 Etchings by Theodore Chasseriau.* 1969 Walker/Harvard College Lib. $45.00

HOFF, C.C. *Ostracods of IL.* 1942 IL U Pr. Ills. 196 p. wraps. $12.00

HOFF, Sid. *Hunting Anyone?* 1963 Bobbs Merrill. Ills 1st ed. 183 p. dj. VG $6.00

HOFF, Sid. *Upstream, Downstream, & Out of My Mind.* 1961 Bobbs Merrill. Ills 1st ed. 191 p. dj. EX $7.50

HOFF, W. *Wilhelm Lehmbruck.* 1969 London. Revised ed. 4to. 103 plts. xl. $20.00

HOFFA, Jimmy. *Trials of Jimmy Hoffa: Autobiography of James R. Hoffa.* 1970 Chicago. 1st ed. sgn. dj. scarce. EX $160.00

HOFFER. *Working & Thinking on the Waterfront.* 1969 Harper. 1st ed. dj. VG $8.00

HOFFMAN, Abbie. *Steal This Book.* 1971 NY. 1st ed. pb. VG $25.00

HOFFMAN, Abbie. *Woodstock Nation.* 1969 NY. 3rd print. trade pb. VG $15.00

HOFFMAN, Alice. *Angel Landing.* 1982 Severn House. 1st English ed. dj. EX $15.00

HOFFMAN, Alice. *Drowning Season.* 1979 Dutton. Advance copy. dj. EX $25.00

HOFFMAN, Alice. *Property of Alice.* 1977 Farrar. 1st ed. dj. EX $30.00

HOFFMAN, Calvin. *Man Who Was Shakespeare.* 1955 London. 1st ed. dj. VG $12.50

HOFFMAN, Frederic J. *Freudianism & the Literary Mind.* 1945 Baton Rouge. 1st ed. 346 p. VG $20.00

HOFFMAN, Frederick. *Achievement of Randall Jarrell.* 1970 Scott Foresman. 1st ed. wraps. EX $12.50

HOFFMAN, Malvina. *Heads & Tales.* 1936 NY. 1st ed. 416 p. VG $25.00

HOFFMAN, Malvina. *Yesterday Is Tomorrow.* 1965 Crown. Ills 1st ed. 378 p. dj. VG $17.50

HOFFMAN, Professor. *Drawing Room Conjuring.* 1887 London/NY. 1st ed. VG $100.00

HOFFMAN, Professor. *Modern Magic.* c1940s. Phil. 563 p. dj. VG $27.50

HOFFMAN, Professor. *Modern Magic.* 1877 London. 2nd ed. 8vo. 511 p. G $75.00

HOFFMAN, Ralph. *Birds of the Pacific Coast.* 1955 Boston. Houghton Mifflin. dj. VG $15.00

HOFFMAN & GRIMM. *Beyond Reach: Search for Titanic.* 1982 NY. Beaufort Books. 1st ed. dj. EX $30.00

HOFFMAN. *Der Stewelpeter, Pestalozzi.* no date. Germany. 4to. VG $20.00

HOFFMAN. *Nutcracker.* 1983 Crown. Ills Sendak. 2nd print. dj. EX $18.00

HOFMANN, Werner. *George Braque: His Graphic Work.* 1962 London. Thames & Hudson. 119 p. dj. $60.00

HOFSTADER, R. *American Higher Education: Documentary History.* 1961 1st ed. 8vo. 1,016 p. 2 vol set. djs. G $25.00

HOGARTH, Paul. *Artists on Horseback.* 1972 NY. 1st ed. 4to. 288 p. dj. EX $15.00

HOGBEN, Carol. *British Art & Design 1900-1960.* 1984 London. Victoria & Albert Mus. 2nd ed. $15.00

HOGBEN, L. *From Cave Painting to the Comic Strip.* 1949 London. Ills. dj. VG $20.00

HOGG, I.V. *German Pistols & Revolvers 1871-1945.* 1971 Stackpole. Ills. 160 p. dj. EX $15.00

HOGG, I.V. *Textbook of Automatic Pistols.* 1975 London/Harrisburg. Revised ed. $22.50

HOGG, Jabez. *Microscope: Its History, Construction, & Application.* 1898 London. Ills 15th ed. 704 p. VG $86.00

HOGG, Jabez. *Microscope: Its History, Construction, & Application.* 1861 Ills 5th ed. 621 p. red cloth. VG $85.00

HOGG & BATCHELOR. *Armies of the American Revolution.* 1975 Mayer. Ills. VG $18.00

HOGGSON, N. *Squires' Homemade Wine.* 1924 NY. reprint of 1765. 1/1,524. VG $20.00

HOGNER, D.C. *Conversation in America.* 1958 Lippincott. Ills 1st ed. 240 p. dj. G $5.00

HOGNER, D.C. *Sea Mammals.* 1979 Crowell. Ill 1st ed. 80 p. dj. EX $8.00

HOGROGIAN, Nonny. *Renowned History of Little Red Riding Hood.* 1967 Crowell. Ills 2nd print. 16mo. VG $12.00

HOHN, R.; & PETERMAN, J. *Curiosities of the Plant Kingdom.* 1980 Universe. Ills. 4to. 212 p. dj. EX $12.00

HOHNE, Heinz. *Order of Death's Head.* 1969 London. 1st ed. dj. scarce. M $38.50

HOHNE, Heinz. *Order of Death's Head.* 1970 Coward McCann. 1st ed. dj. EX $30.00

HOIG, Stan. *Sand Creek Massacre.* 1961 OK U Pr. 1st ed. dj. EX $35.00

HOKE, John. *1st Book of Photography.* 1854 Franklin Watts. Ills Hamilton. 8vo. 69 p. $12.00

HOLBEIN, Hans. *Family of Sir John Moore.* 1977 NY. Ills. 8 acquatints. M $175.00

HOLBROOK, Arthur T. *From the Log of a Trout Fisherman.* 1949 Norwood. private print. 1st ed. VG $200.00

HOLBROOK, Hal. *Mark Twain Tonight.* 1959 Ives Washburn. 1st ed. dj. VG $25.00

HOLBROOK, Stewart H. *Down on the Farm.* 1964 NY. Life. 188 p. dj. G $10.00

HOLBROOK, Stewart H. *Old Post Road.* 1962 NY. 1st ed. 3rd print. Am Trails Series. $35.00

HOLBROOK, Stewart H. *Wyatt Earp, US Marshall.* 1956 Random House. Ills. 180 p. dj. VG $15.00

HOLBROOK. *Hiawatha Primer.* 1898 Houghton Mifflin. Ills. EX $15.00

HOLCIK, J. *Fresh-Water Fishes.* 1972 Spring. Ills. 128 p. dj. EX $5.00

HOLDEN, C.H. *City of London: Record of Destruction & Survival.* 1951 London. Arch Pr. Ills. fld maps. VG $25.00

HOLDEN, G.P. *Streamcraft Angling Manual.* 1920 Stewart Kidd. Ills. 263 p. VG $12.50

HOLDEN. *Country Diary of an Edwardian Lady.* 1977 NY. facsimile. dj. EX $8.00

HOLDER, Charles F. *Along the FL Reef.* 1899 NY. Appleton. Ills. 8vo. EX $15.00

HOLDER, Charles F. *Ivory King.* 1886 Scribner. Ills. 12mo. 330 p. 23 plts. G $125.00

HOLDREDGE, Helen. *Mammy Pleasant's Partner.* 1954 NY. 1st ed. dj. VG $15.00

HOLDREDGE, Helen. *Woman in Black: Life of Fabulous Lola Montez.* 1955 NY. 1st ed. dj. VG $10.00

HOLDSTOCK, Robert. *Mythago Wood.* 1984 London. 1st ed. sgn. EX $85.00

HOLECEK, J. *Ein Jagerparadies.* 1962 Hamburg. Ills. 4to. 240 p. dj. EX $65.00

HOLIDAY. *USA in Color.* 1956 Phil. Ills 1st ed. maps. 190 p. $10.00

HOLLAND, A.J. *Ships of British Oak.* 1971 Newton Abbot. Ills. dj. EX $18.00

HOLLAND, Bob, Dan, & Ray. *Good Shot: Book of Rod, Gun, & Camera.* 1946 Knopf. 1st ed. inscr. G $25.00

HOLLAND, Cecelia. *City of God.* 1979 NY. 1st ed. dj. M $12.00

HOLLAND, Cecelia. *Earl.* 1971 NY. 1st ed. dj. EX $11.00

HOLLAND, Cecelia. *Floating Worlds.* 1975 Knopf. 1st ed. dj. M $12.00

HOLLAND, Cecelia. *Great Maria.* 1974 Knopf. 1st ed. dj. EX $10.00

HOLLAND, Cecelia. *Home Ground.* 1981 NY. 1st ed. dj. M $10.00

HOLLAND, J.G. *Life of Abraham Lincoln.* 1866 Springfield. Ills. 8vo. 544 p. VG $20.00

HOLLAND, J.G. *Marble Prophecy.* 1872 NY. scarce. EX $33.00

HOLLAND, M. *English Provincial Silver.* 1971 NY. Ills. 240 p. $18.00

HOLLAND, R.P. *Nip & Tuck.* 1939 Penn. Ills Fuller. 182 p. EX $13.50

HOLLAND, R.P. *Shotgunning in the Lowlands.* 1946 Barnes. Ills Ltd ed. 1/2,500. VG $28.50

HOLLAND, R.P. *Shotgunning in the Uplands.* 1945 NY. Barnes. Ills 2nd ed. 4to. cloth. VG $45.00

HOLLAND, Rupert S. *Freedom's Flag: Story of Francis Scott Key.* 1943 Phil. 1st ed. 356 p. cloth. $7.50

HOLLAND, Rupert S. *Yankee Ships in Pirate Waters.* 1931 Garden City. Ills Schoonover. blue cloth. $20.00

HOLLAND, V. *Oscar Wild: Pictorial Biography.* 1960 NY. Viking. dj. VG $45.00

HOLLAND, W.J. *Moth Book.* 1916 Doubleday Page. Ills. 479 p. VG $14.00

HOLLAND, W.J. *To the River Plate & Back.* 1913 Putnam. 1st ed. dj. VG $37.50

HOLLANDER, Eugene. *Die Karikatur und Satire in der Medizin.* 1905 Stuttgart. Enke. EX $150.00

HOLLANDER, John. *Town & Country Matters: Erotica & Satirica.* 1972 Boston. Godine. Ltd ed. 1/3,850. dj. $20.00

HOLLANDS, David. *Eagles, Hawks, & Falcons of Australia.* 1984 Nelson. Ills 1st ed. 4to. dj. EX $23.00

HOLLAWAY, D. *Lewis & Clark & the Crossing of North America.* 1974 Saturday Review. Ills. dj. EX $20.00

HOLLERAN, Andrew. *Dancer From the Dance.* 1978 NY. Morrow. 1st ed. dj. EX $15.00

HOLLEY, Marietta. *My Opinions & Betsy Bobbet's.* 1875 Hartford, CT. Ills. 12mo. 432 p. cloth. G $23.00

HOLLEY, Marietta. *Sweet Cicely.* 1885 NY. 1st ed. VG $15.00

HOLLEY, Mary A. *TX Diary 1835-1838.* 1965 Austin. TX Pr. dj. EX $7.00

HOLLEY, Mary A. *TX Observations.* 1981 Austin. Ltd ed. 1/325. M $250.00

HOLLIDAY, Carl. *Woman's Life in Colonial Days.* 1968 Corner House. 319 p. index. dj. VG $10.00

HOLLING, Clancy. *Choo-Me-Shoo.* 1928 Volland. Ills L Holling. 3rd print. $15.00

HOLLING, Clancy. *Claws of the Thunderbird.* 1928 Volland. Ills 1st ed. 8vo. cloth. dj. $25.00

HOLLING, H.C. *Book of Cowboys.* 1939 Platt Munk. Ills. sgn. $22.50

HOLLING, H.C. *Book of Cowboys.* 1936 Platt Munk. Ills. VG $15.00

HOLLING, H.C. *Book of Indians.* 1935 NY. Platt Munk. VG $25.00

HOLLING. *Tree in the Trail.* 1943 Boston. Ills. 4to. dj. EX $17.50

HOLLINGWORTH, Clare. *Mao & the Men Against Him.* 1985 London. Cape. M $12.00

HOLLISTER, O.J. *Mines of CO.* 1974 Promontory. 450 p. dj. EX $5.00

HOLLISTER & CHAMBERLAIN. *Beauport at Gloucester.* 1951 Hastings House. Ills. 8vo. cloth. dj. $20.00

HOLLON, W.E. *Southwest: Old & New.* 1961 Knopf. Review of 1st ed. dj. EX $24.00

HOLLON, W.E. *Southwest: Old & New.* 1961 Knopf. Ills 1st ed. 487 p. maps. VG $18.00

HOLLOWAY, C.M. *History of Niagara Steam Fire Engine Co. No. 1.* 1900 New London. Ills. wraps. VG $125.00

HOLLOWAY, E.S. *American Furniture & Decoration: Colonial & Federal.* 1928 Phil/London. Ills. VG $30.00

HOLLOWAY, Laura C. *Hearthstone; or, Life at Home Household Manual.* 1889 Chicago/NY. Ills. 8vo. 582 p. $45.00

HOLLOWAY, Laura C. *Ladies of the White House.* 1885 Phil. Ills. 768. cloth. fair. $10.00

HOLLOWAY, Laura C. *Ladies of the White House.* 1881 Phil. Ills. ½-leather. G $20.00

HOLLOWAY, Laura C. *Ladies of the White House.* 1870 NY. Ills. 685 p. EX $45.00

HOLLOWAY, M. *Bibliography of 19th Century British Topographical Books.* 1977 Holland Pr. dj. VG $30.00

HOLLOWAY, W.L. *Wildlife on the Plains & Horrors of Indian Warfare.* 1969 Arno Pr. Ills. dj. VG $15.00

HOLLOWAY, W.R. *Indianapolis: Historical & Statistical Sketch of the City.* 1870 1st ed. 8vo. 390 p. maps. ads. VG $235.00

HOLM, T. *Vegetation of the Alpine Region of the Rocky Mountains.* 1923 4to. 45 p. wraps. $25.00

HOLMAN, Albert M. *Pioneering in the Northwest: Niobrare-VA City Wagon Road.* 1924 Sioux City. EX $15.00

HOLMAN, Felice. *At the Top of My Voice & Other Poems.* 1970 NY. Norton. Ills Gorey. 1st print. dj. EX $20.00

HOLMAN, J.C. *Views on Homosassa River.* 1885 Boston. Ills. sgn. 24 p. cloth. $20.00

HOLMAN & PERSONS. *Buckskin & Homespun.* 1979 Austin. Ltd ed. 1/450. M $200.00

HOLME, C. Geoffrey. *Children's Toys of Yesterday.* 1932 London. Studio. Ills. 4to. 128 p. G $30.00

HOLME, C. Geoffrey. *Color Photography & Recent Developments of Art & Camera.* 1908 London. Ills 1st ed. VG $125.00

HOLMES, Anne Middleton. *Algernon Sydney Sullivan.* 1929 NY. Southern Soc. EX $25.00

HOLMES, D.H. *Under a Fool's Cap.* 1914 Mosher. Ltd ed. 1/900. slipcase. EX $10.00

HOLMES, F.L. *George Washington Travelled This Way.* 1935 Boston. Ills 1st ed. 281 p. cloth. $12.50

HOLMES, J.C. *Get Home Free.* 1964 NY. 1st ed. dj. EX $30.00

HOLMES, Kenneth L. *Ewing Young.* 1967 Portland. 1st ed. dj. VG $12.50

HOLMES, Oliver Wendell. *Addresses at the Inauguration of Jared Sparks.* 1849 Cambridge. wraps. $30.00

HOLMES, Oliver Wendell. *Astraea: Balance of Illusions.* 1850 Boston. $90.00

HOLMES, Oliver Wendell. *Autocrat of the Breakfast Table.* 1858 Boston. 1st ed. 2nd print. $30.00

HOLMES, Oliver Wendell. *Breakfast Table Series.* no date. London. 3 vol set. VG $47.50

HOLMES, Oliver Wendell. *Common Law.* 1881 Boston. 1st ed. VG $350.00

HOLMES, Oliver Wendell. *Currents & Counter Currents in Medical Science.* 1861 Boston. 1st ed. cloth. $100.00

HOLMES, Oliver Wendell. *Elsie Venner: Romance of Destiny.* 1861 Boston. Ticknor Fields. 3rd print. $60.00

HOLMES, Oliver Wendell. *Our 100 Days in Europe.* 1887 Boston/NY. Houghton Mifflin. 1st ed. VG $25.00

HOLMES, Oliver Wendell. *Over Their Teacups.* 1891 Boston. 1st ed. later issue. $30.00

HOLMES, Oliver Wendell. *Poet at Breakfast Table.* 1872 Boston. 1st ed. 1st state. EX $85.00

HOLMES, Oliver Wendell. *Professor at Breakfast Table.* 1885 2 vols. green calf/gilt edges. EX $150.00

HOLMES, Oliver Wendell. *Psychiatric Novels of Oliver Wendell Holmes.* 1944 Columbia. 2nd print. $17.00

HOLMES, Oliver Wendell. *Traveller From Altruria.* 1894 Harper. red cloth. G $95.00

HOLMES, Oliver Wendell. *Urania: Rhymed Lesson.* 1846 Boston. G $125.00

HOLMES, R.R. *Queen Victoria Monograph.* 1897 London/Paris. Goupie. 1/350. slipcase. EX $495.00

HOLMES, W.D. *Safari: R.S.V.P.* 1960 Coward McCann. Ills. 179 p. VG $13.50

HOLMS, A. Champbell. *Facts of Psychic Science & Philosophy.* 1969 NY U Books. 512 p. dj. EX $22.00

HOLROYDE, Peggy. *Music of India.* 1972 NY. Ills. dj. VG $16.00

HOLT, Arden. *Fancy Dresses; or, What To Wear at Fancy Balls.* 1887 London. Aebenham & Freebody. G $95.00

HOLT, J.R. *Historic Frederick, MD.* 1949 Ills 1st ed. 53 p. wraps. $7.50

HOLT, L.E. *Care & Feeding of Children.* 1907 Appleton. VG $14.00

HOLT, Rosabelle. *Rugs: Oriental & Occidental, Antique & Modern.* 1901 Chicago. McClurg. Ills. 4to. 165 p. VG $175.00

HOLT. *Schleicher County: The Eldorado Success.* 1930 Eldorado. VG $20.00

HOLTON, Isaac F. *New Granada: 20 Months in Andes.* 1967 IL U Pr. 223 p. dj. EX $22.00

HOLTON, Isaac F. *New Granada: 20 Months in Andes.* 1857 NY. Harper. 1st ed. maps. 605 p. cloth. $125.00

HOLTZCLAW, William. *Black Man's Burden.* 1915 Neale. Intro BT Washington. Ills. G $15.00

HOLWAY, M.G. *Art of the Old World in Spain & Mission Days of Alta, CA.* 1922 San Francisco. Ltd ed. 1/1,000. EX $30.00

HOLYOKE, Samuel. *Columbian Repository of Sacred Harmony.* 1802 Exeter, NH. 1st ed. 4to. $280.00

HOLZER, Erika. *Double Crossing.* 1983 Putnam. Advance copy. dj. EX $18.00

HOLZER, Hans. *New Pagans: Inside Report on the Mystery Cults of Today.* 1972 203 p. dj. EX $16.00

HOLZER, Hans. *Psychic Photography: Threshold of a New Science.* 1969 NY. 117 p. dj. EX $18.00

HOLZWORTH, J.M. *Wild Grizzlies of AK.* 1930 NY. Ills. G $30.00

HOMANS, I.S. *Sketches of Boston: Past & Present.* 1851 Boston. 1st ed. fld map. VG $85.00

HOMANS, James E. *Self-Propelled Vehicles: Practical Treatise on Theory.* 1907 NY. Audel. Ills Revised 6th ed. 598 p. VG $25.00

HOMANS, James E. *Self-Propelled Vehicles: Practical Treatise on Theory.* 1912 NY. Ills. 8vo. 667 p. cloth. VG $35.00

HOME, D.D. *Incidents in My Life.* 1972 288 p. dj. EX $15.00

HOME, Gordon. *Inns of Court.* 1909 London. Ills 1st ed. VG $45.00

HOME, Gordon. *Yorkshire Coast & Moorland Scenes.* 1907 London. Ills. VG $35.00

HOME, Madame Dunglas. *Dunglas D. Home: His Life & Mission.* 1921 London. Intro AC Doyle. 1st ed. 230 p. $45.00

HOMER, Sidney. *My Wife & I.* 1939 Macmillan. 1st ed. dj. VG $15.00

HOMER. *Iliad Translated by A. Pope.* 1771 London. 5 vol set. G $35.00

HOMER. *Odyssey.* 1861 Edinburgh. Blackwood. 2 vol set. VG $22.00

HONE, Nathaniel J. *Mannor & Court Baron.* 1909 London. Manorial Society. VG $25.00

HONNESS, Elizabeth. *Flight of Fancy.* 1941 Oxford. Ills Pelagie Doane. dj. VG $12.50

HONOUR, Hugh. *Goldsmiths & Silversmiths.* 1971 NY. Putnam. Ills. 4to. 320 p. dj. $50.00

HONRI, Peter. *Working Halls: Honris in 100 Years of British Music Hall.* 1973 England. Ills. 4to. dj. with record. VG $20.00

HOOD, Graham. *History of American Silver 1650-1900.* 1971 NY. Praeger. Ills. turquoise linen. dj. EX $25.00

HOOD, Grant. *Modern Methods in Horology.* 1944 Peoria. Bradley Polytechnic. Ills. $25.00

HOOD, I.W. *Betsy Gaskins, Wife of Jobe Gaskins.* 1897 Wabash Pub. Ills CB Falls. $27.00

HOOD, J.B. *Advance & Retreat.* 1880 New Orleans. 1st ed. 358 p. G $135.00

HOOD, T. *Epping Hunt.* 1930 Derrydale. VG $30.00

HOOD, T. *Faithless Sally Brown.* 1928 Larchmont. earlier Peter Pauper imp. $20.00

HOOD, Thomas. *Poetical Works.* 1888 London. full leather. VG $20.00

HOOD, Thomas. *Serious Poems.* 1879 London. VG $20.00

HOOD, Thomas. *Up the Rhine.* 1840 London. 1st ed. ½-leather. EX $250.00

HOOK, Andrew. *Scotland & America: Study of Cultural Relations.* 1975 Glasgow. Ills 1st ed. 8vo. dj. VG $25.00

HOOKE, Nathaniel. *Account of Conduct of Dowager Duchess of Marlborough.* 1742 London. calf. scarce. VG $675.00

HOOPER, Elizabeth. *American Historical Dolls.* 1941 Baltimore. sgn. VG $16.00

HOOPER, Has. *Country House.* 1911 NY. Ills. 330 p. VG $35.00

HOOPER, Lucy. *Poetical Works.* 1848 NY. 1st ed. 404 p. $15.00

HOOPER, M. *New England River Life Along the CT.* 1939 Brattleboro. Ills 1st ed. maps. 120 p. $12.50

HOOPES, Donelson F. *Watercolors of Thomas Eakins.* 1971 Watson Guptil. Ills. square 4to. 87 p. dj. $40.00

HOOPES, Donelson F. *William Zorach Paintings, Watercolors, & Drawings 1911-1922.* 1969 Brooklyn. Ills. 8vo. 71 p. wraps. $15.00

HOOVER, Helen. *Gift of the Deer.* 1968 Knopf. Ills. 210 p. dj. VG $5.00

HOOVER, Herbert. *Challenge to Liberty.* 1934 London/NY. 1st ed. cloth. VG $15.00

HOOVER, Herbert. *Challenge to Liberty.* 1934 NY. 1st ed. dj. EX $17.00

HOOVER, Herbert. *Fishing for Fun & To Wash Your Soul.* 1963 Random House. Ills 1st ed. dj. EX $9.00

HOOVER, Herbert. *Fishing for Fun & To Wash Your Soul.* 1963 NY. Ills Ltd ed. 1/200. cloth. VG $80.00

HOOVER, Herbert. *Hoover After Dinner.* 1933 NY. inscr. cloth. $50.00

HOOVER, Herbert. *Ordeal of Woodrow Wilson.* 1958 NY. Ills 1st ed. 303 p. dj. $7.50

HOOVER, Herbert. *Remedy for Disappearing Game Fishes.* 1930 NY. Huntington. Ltd ed. 1/990. slipcase. EX $100.00

HOOVER, Herbert. *This Crisis in American Life.* 1948 Phil. wraps. VG $50.00

HOOVER, J. Edgar. *Masters of Deceit.* 1958 4th ed. inscr. VG $40.00

HOPE, Anthony. *Dolly Dialogues.* 1926 Woolcott. leather. $65.00

HOPE, Bob. *They Got Me Covered.* 1941 Hollywood. 1st ed. wraps. EX $20.00

HOPE, J. *River for the Living: The Hudson.* 1975 Barre, MA. Ills 1st ed. 224 p. dj. $13.50

HOPE, Laurence. *Complete Love Lyrics.* 1940 NY. 12mo. blue leather. slipcase. $20.00

HOPKINS, C. *Story of Soil.* 1911 Boston. 350 p. G $10.00

HOPKINS, J. *Elvis: Biography.* 1971 NY. Ills 1st ed. 448 p. dj. VG $32.50

HOPKINS, Kenneth. *Collected Poems.* 1964 IL U Pr. 1st ed. slipcase. EX $15.00

HOPKINS, Kenneth. *She Died Because.* 1964 1st Am ed. dj. EX $15.00

HOPKINS, N.M. *Over the Threshold of War.* 1918 Phil. 8vo. blue cloth. VG $15.00

HOPKINS, Nevil. *20th Century Magic & Construction of Modern Apparatus.* 1898 NY/London. 1st ed. 8vo. 160 p. $50.00

HOPKINS, Sarah W. *Life Among the Piutes: Their Wrongs & Claims.* 1883 Boston. 1st ed. G $45.00

HOPPE, E.O. *Book of Fair Women.* no date. NY. Knopf. 1/500. 32 plts. EX $135.00

HOPPE, E.O. *London.* 1932 Boston. Hale Cushman. 1st ed. 8vo. VG $35.00

HOPPE, E.O. *Picturesque Great Britain.* 1926 Berlin. Wasmuth. 1st ed. 4to. cloth. $45.00

HOPPE, E.O. *5th Continent.* 1931 London. 1st ed. 4to. inscr. cloth. VG $70.00

HOPPER, Edward L. *Goodrich.* 1978 Abrams. dj. EX $150.00

HOPPIN, Benjamin. *Diary Kept While with Peary Arctic Expedition of 1896.* no date. no place. dj. scarce. $125.00

HORA, Bayard. *Encyclopedia of Trees of the World.* 1981 Oxford U Pr. Ills. 4to. 288 p. dj. EX $28.00

HORACE. *Odes & Epodes.* 1961 NY. Ltd ed. 1/1,500. 2 vol set. EX $90.00

HORAN, J.D. *Confederate Agent.* 1960 Crown. Ills. 326 p. maps. EX $15.00

HORAN, J.D. *Confederate Agent.* 1954 Crown. Ills. gray cloth. VG $15.00

HORAN, J.D. *Confederate Agent.* 1954 NY. Ills 1st ed. sgn. dj. M $35.00

HORAN, J.D. *Desperate Men.* Bonanza. reprint. 296 p. dj. EX $20.00

HORAN, J.D. *Desperate Men.* 1949 NY. 2nd print. dj. VG $35.00

HORAN, J.D. *Desperate Women.* 1952 Bonanza. reprint. 336 p. dj. EX $20.00

HORAN, J.D. *Life & Art of Charles Schreyvogel: Painter-Historian.* 1969 NY. 4to. plts. VG $50.00

HORAN, J.D. *Matthew Brady: Historian with a Camera.* 1955 Bonanza. reprint. 4to. 244 p. dj. EX $20.00

HORAN, J.D. *Pictorial History of Wild West.* 1954 NY. 1st ed. G $20.00

HORAN, Kenneth. *Remember the Day.* 1937 NY. 1st ed. boxed. scarce. EX $17.00

HORGAN, Paul. *Approaches to Writing.* 1973 NY. 1st ed. dj. EX $10.00

HORGAN, Paul. *Centuries of Santa Fe.* 1956 Dutton. Review ed. dj. EX $23.00

HORGAN, Paul. *Centuries of Santa Fe.* 1956 Dutton. 1st ed. 363 p. maps. VG $16.00

HORGAN, Paul. *Centuries of Santa Fe.* 1956 Dutton. 1st ed. dj. EX $30.00

HORGAN, Paul. *Encounters with Stravinsky.* 1972 NY. 1st ed. dj. EX $20.00

HORGAN, Paul. *Everything To Live For.* 1969 London. 1st ed. dj. VG $20.00

HORGAN, Paul. *Great River: Rio Grande in North American History.* 1954 Book of Month. slipcase. VG $20.00

HORGAN, Paul. *Great River: Rio Grande in North American History.* 1954 NY/Toronto. Rinehart. 2 vol set. boxed. VG $22.50

HORGAN, Paul. *Heroic Triad.* 1970 NY. 1st ed. inscr. dj. EX $22.00

HORGAN, Paul. *Lamy of Santa Fe.* 1975 NY. 3rd print. dj. VG $12.50

HORGAN, Paul. *Lamy of Santa Fe.* 1975 NY. Ills 1st ed. 523 p. EX $22.50

HORGAN, Paul. *Lamy of Sante Fe.* 1975 NY. 1st ed. sgn. dj. VG $35.00

HORGAN, Paul. *Lamy of Sante Fe.* 1975 Farrar Straus. Ills 1st print. dj. EX $25.00

HORGAN, Paul. *No Quarter Given.* 1935 NY. 1st ed. dj. VG $27.50

HORINE, Emmett Field. *Pioneer in KY 1785-1800.* 1948 NY. 257 p. cloth. $22.00

HORLER, Sydney. *Curse of Doone.* 1930 NY. 1st ed. dj. VG $12.00

HORN, Madeline Darrough. *Log Cabin Family.* 1939 NY/London. Scribner. 1st ed. dj. EX $30.00

HORN, S.F. *Army of TN.* 1953 OK U Pr. Ills. 503 p. maps. dj. EX $35.00

HORN, S.F. *Army of TN.* 1941 Indianapolis. 1st ed. dj. VG $45.00

HORN, S.F. *Hermitage Home of Old Hickory.* 1950 NY. Ills. 206 p. cloth. $10.00

HORNADAY, W.T. *Campfires in the Canadian Rockies.* 1907 Scribner. Ills. 353 p. maps. VG $23.50

HORNADAY, W.T. *Campfires in the Canadian Rockies.* 1906 NY. Ills 1st ed. 353 p. G $32.50

HORNADAY, W.T. *Campfires in the Canadian Rockies.* 1906 NY. 1st ed. VG $40.00

HORNADAY, W.T. *Campfires on Desert & Lava.* 1909 Scribner. Ills. 366 p. maps. EX $40.00

HORNADAY, W.T. *Campfires on Desert & Lava.* 1908 NY. 1st ed. G $60.00

HORNBEIN, Thomas F. *Everest: West Ridge.* 1965 San Francisco. Sierra Club. 1st ed. sgn. dj. $110.00

HORNBLOW. *History of the Theater in America.* 1919 Lippincott. 2 vol set. $75.00

HORNE, Richard Henry. *Memoirs of London Dolls.* 1967 NY. Macmillan. Ills Gillies/Smith. 1st print. $15.00

HORNELL, James. *Fishing in Many Waters.* 1950 Cambridge U Pr. Ills. 210 p. dj. EX $14.00

HORNER, Dave. *Clues to Millions in Sunken Gold & Silver.* 1971 259 p. EX $14.00

HORNER, J.W. *Silver Town.* 1950 Caldwell. Ills 1st ed. 322 p. dj. VG $32.50

HORNEY, Dr. Karen. *Neurotic Personality of Our Time.* 1937 Norton. dj. G $8.00

HORNUNG, C.P. *Trademarks.* 1930 NY. 1/750. 12mo. slipcase. $60.00

HORNUNG, C.P. *Treasury of American Design & Antiques.* no date. NY. 1st ed. 2 vol set. EX $50.00

HORNUNG, C.P. *Treasury of American Design & Antiques.* 1986 NY. Crown. 2 vols in 1. dj. EX $30.00

HORNUNG, C.P. *Treasury of American Design: Pictorial Survey of Folk Arts.* c 1972. 2 vol set. wraps. VG $35.00

HORNUNG, C.P. *Treasury of American Design: Pictorial Survey of Folk Arts.* 1976 NY. Abrams. Ills. 4to. 2 vol set. VG $70.00

HORNUNG, E.W. *Amateur Cracksman.* 1899 NY. 1st ed. $20.00

HORNUNG, E.W. *Thief in the Night.* 1905 London. 1st ed. $15.00

HORODISCH, Abraham. *Picasso As a Book Artist.* 1962 World. 1st ed. dj. VG $25.00

HOROWITZ, Frances. *High Tower.* 1970 London. 1st ed. 1/25. sgn. $25.00

HORSFORD, E.N. *Report on Vienna Bread.* 1875 WA. Ills. 8vo. 122 p. wraps. $30.00

HORSIA, Olga; & PETRESCU, P. *Artistic Handicrafts in Romania.* 1971 Ltd ed. 1/4,000. $52.50

HORSLEY, T. *Fishing for Trout & Salmon.* 1947 Witherby. Ills. 180 p. dj. G $7.00

HORTON, R.G. *Life & Public Service of James Buchanan.* 1856 NY/Cincinnati. 1st ed. 428 p. $30.00

HORWITZ, Elinor L. *Contemporary American Folk Artists.* 1975 Phil. Lippincott. Ills. 143 p. $7.50

HOSEMANN, Theodore. *Slovenly Kate.* c 1870. NY. Miller. 1st ed. rebound. $65.00

HOSHOR, J. *God in a Rolls Royce.* 1936 NY. 1st ed. dj. VG $22.50

HOSKING, Arthur N. *Artist's Yearbook.* 1906 Chicago. Art League Pub. inscr. fair. $25.00

HOSKING & NEWBERRY. *Art of Bird Photography.* 1948 London. Revised Enlarged ed. dj. VG $20.00

HOSMER, J.K. *History of Expedition of Lewis & Clark.* 1902 Chicago. 1st ed. 2 vol set. EX $70.00

HOSMER, James. *Life of Thomas Hutchinson.* 1896 Boston. 1st ed. 8vo. VG $45.00

HOSOKAWA, Bill. *Thunder in the Rockies.* 1976 NY. 1st ed. dj. VG $12.00

HOSPITALIER, E. *Modern Applications of Electricity.* 1882 NY. Appleton. Ills 1st ed. 463 p. $35.00

HOSTETTER, G.L.; & BEESLEY, T. *It's a Racket.* 1929 Chicago. Les Quinn Books. 1st ed. dj. $100.00

HOTCHKISS, G.B. *Outline of Advertising.* 1922 Macmillan. 1st print. VG $40.00

HOTCHNER, A.E. *Papa Hemingway.* 1966 Random House. 1st ed. dj. EX $14.00

HOTTENROTH, Frederick. *Le Costume Chez Peuples Anciens et Moderns.* no date. NY. Weyhe, 8vo. 213 p. VG $95.00

HOTTES, Alfred C. *My Garden Helper.* c 1940s. Merideth. EX $5.00

HOTTES, Alfred C. *1,001 Garden Questions Answered.* 1935 NY. De La Mare Co. $7.00

HOUART, Victor. *Miniature Silver Toys.* 1981 NY. Alpine. Ills. folio. 237 p. dj. $45.00

HOUDIN, Robert. *Les Secrets de la Prestidigitation et de la Magie.* 1868 Paris. 1st ed. 8vo. 442 p. $150.00

HOUDINI, H. *Houdini's Paper Magic.* 1922 NY. 1st ed. VG $70.00

HOUGH, Don. *Coctail Hour in Jackson Hole.* 1956 NY. 1st ed. 253 p. dj. VG $10.00

HOUGH, Emerson. *John Rawn.* 1912 Bobbs Merrill. Ills Leone Bracker. 1st ed. EX $12.00

HOUGH, Emerson. *MS Bubble.* 1902 Bowen Merrill. 1st ed. 1st bdg. VG $20.00

HOUGH, Franklin B. *History of Jefferson County, NY.* 1854 Albany. Ills 1st ed. 8vo. black cloth. $95.00

HOUGH, Henry Beetle. *Thoreau of Walden.* 1956 NY. 1st ed. 1st print. dj. VG $22.00

HOUGH, Olney. *Practical Exporting: Foreign Manufacturing & Merchandise.* 1919 NY. 1st ed. 8vo. cloth. dj. VG $10.00

HOUGH, Richard. *Blind Horn's Hate.* 1971 Norton. Ills 1st ed. 336 p. dj. EX $18.00

HOUGH, Richard. *Great Admirals.* 1977 NY. Morrow. VG $10.00

HOUGH, Richard. *Motor Car Lover's Companion.* 1965 Harper Row. Ills 1st ed. dj. VG $12.00

HOUGH, W. *Fire As an Agent in Human Culture.* 1926 Mus Nat Hist. Ills. 270 p. pb. EX $20.00

HOUGHTON, W. *British Fresh-Water Fishes.* 1981 London. 2nd ed. G $25.00

HOUGHTON, W.R. *Kings of Fortune: Noble Self-Made Men.* 1888 Chicago. Ills. 621 p. cloth. $10.00

HOUR, George F. *Autobiography of 70 Years.* 1903 NY. 2 vol set. VG $45.00

HOURTICQ, L. *La Peinture des Origines au XVIe Siecle.* 1926 Paris. Ills. French text. VG $32.50

HOUSE, B. *Roaring Ranger: Worlds Biggest Boom.* 1951 Naylor. Ills. 122 p. dj. VG $20.00

HOUSE, E.J. *Hunter's Campfires.* 1909 NY. Ills 1st ed. 402 p. VG $57.50

HOUSE, H.D. *Wild Flowers.* 1936 Macmillan. Ills. 4to. 362 p. VG $25.00

HOUSE & GARDEN. *House & Garden's Cookbook.* 1958 NY. Bonanza. EX $10.00

HOUSE & GARDEN. *House & Garden's Cookbook.* 1958 Simon Schuster. 1st print. 4to. 324 p. dj. VG $11.00

HOUSEMAN, Laurence. *Bethlehem: Nativity Play.* 1927 London. Macmillan. 8vo. 45 p. VG $35.00

HOUSEMAN, Laurence. *Stories From the Arabian Nights.* c 1930. Garden City. Ills Dulac. M $25.00

HOUSMAN, A.E. *Introductory Lecture.* 1937 NY. 1st ed. dj. EX $20.00

HOUSMAN, A.E. *More Poems.* 1936 London. 1st ed. 71 p. $50.00

HOUSMAN, A.E. *Shropshire Lad.* 1914 London. Ltd ed. 1/1,000. VG $195.00

HOUSTOUN, R.A. *Introduction to Mathematical Physics.* 1920 London. 200 p. red cloth. VG $30.00

HOUVET, Etienne. *Illustrated Monograph of Chartres Cathedral.* 1938 Chartres. Imprimerie Durand. Ills. VG $45.00

HOVEY, C. *Stonewall Jackson.* 1900 Boston. 1st ed. 12mo. EX $35.00

HOVEY, H.C. *Celebrated American Caverns: Mammoth, Wyandot, & Luray.* 1882 Cincinnati. Ills 1st ed. maps. 219 p. $50.00

HOVEY, H.C. *Mammouth Cave of KY.* 1912 Louisville. Revised ed. 8vo. VG $45.00

HOVORTA & KRONFELD. *Bergleichende Volksnedizin.* 1909 Stuttgart. Ills. 2 vol set. $100.00

HOWARD, Alexander. *Howard's Guide to Jerusalem & Vicinity.* 1895 octavo. 140 p. cloth. $75.00

HOWARD, B. *50 Years in MD Kitchen.* 1877 Baltimore. 3rd ed. VG $55.00

HOWARD, B.C. *Report of Decision of Supreme Court in Dred Scott Case.* 1857 WA. 1st ed. wraps. $175.00

HOWARD, H.W. *Salmon Fishing of Puget Sound.* 1947 Binfords Mort. Ills. 123 p. VG $6.00

HOWARD, Horton. *Improved System of Botanic Medicine.* 1836 Columbus, OH. 3rd ed. 33 plts. 3 vol set. $60.00

HOWARD, J.T. *Our American Music: 300 Years of It.* 1931 Ills 1st ed. sgn. 713 p. G $65.00

HOWARD, J.T. *Stephen Foster: America's Troubadour.* 1939 NY. Ills. 429 p. cloth. $13.00

HOWARD, John H. *In the Shadow of the Pines: Tale of Tidewater, VA.* c 1926. NY. VG $25.00

HOWARD, Joseph Kinsey. *Strange Empire.* 1952 Morrow. dj. G $25.00

HOWARD, Maureen. *Expensive Habits.* 1986 Summit. Advance copy. wraps. $30.00

HOWARD, O. *Famous Indian Chiefs I Have Known.* 1908 NY. Century. Ills G Varian. EX $65.00

HOWARD, O. *My Life & Experiences Among Our Hostile Indians.* 1907 Hartford. Ills 1st ed. 570 p. xl. VG $85.00

HOWARD, R.W. *Horse in America.* 1965 Follett. Ills. 298 p. VG $10.00

HOWARD, R.W. *This Is the South.* 1959 Chicago. Ills 1st ed. map. 288 p. dj. $15.00

HOWARD, Robert E. *Conan the Barbarian.* 1954 Gnome. 1st ed. dj. EX $75.00

HOWARD, Robert E. *Conan the Conqueror.* 1950 NY. 1st ed. dj. EX $65.00

HOWARD, Robert E. *Dark Man & Others.* 1963 Sauk City. 1st ed. dj. VG $100.00

HOWARD, Robert E. *Echoes From an Iron Harp.* 1972 W. Kingston. 1st ed. dj. EX $70.00

HOWARD, Robert E. *Hour of the Dragon.* 1977 NY. Ills. 296 p. dj. EX $25.00

HOWARD, Robert E. *King Conan.* 1953 Gnome. 1st ed. dj. EX $85.00

HOWARD, Robert E. *Lost Valley of Iskander.* 1974 W. Linn. 1st ed. dj. EX $15.00

HOWARD, Robert E. *Pride of Bear Creek.* 1966 1st Am ed. dj. $55.00

HOWARD, Robert E. *Return of Conan.* 1957 Gnome. 1st ed. dj. EX $75.00

HOWARD, Robert E. *Singers in the Shadows.* 1970 Ltd 1st Am ed. 1/500. dj. $80.00

HOWARD, Robert E. *Skull Face.* 1946 Sauk City. 1st ed. dj. EX $150.00

HOWARD, Robert E. *Sowers of Thunder.* 1973 W. Kingston. 1st ed. dj. M $35.00

HOWARD, Robert E. *Sword of Conan.* 1952 Gnome. 1st ed. dj. VG $40.00

HOWARD, Robert E. *Sword of Conan.* 1952 Gnome. 1st ed. dj. EX $60.00

HOWARD, Robert E. *Tales of Conan.* 1955 Gnome. 1st ed. dj. EX $60.00

HOWARD, Robert E. *Tigers of the Sea.* 1974 Grant. 1st ed. dj. EX $15.00

HOWARD, Robert E. *Valley of the Lost.* 1975 Phil. Ills Ltd ed. 1/777. wraps. $22.00

HOWARD, Robert E. *Worms of the Earth.* 1974 1st Am ed. dj. $25.00

HOWARD. *War Chief Joseph.* 1946 ID. Caldwell. 2nd ed. dj. VG $15.00

HOWARTH, David. *Waterloo: Day of Battle.* 1969 NY. Ills 1st Am ed. 239 p. dj. VG $9.50

HOWAT, John K. *Hudson River & Its Painters.* 1983 Am Legacy Pr. reprint. 4to. 208 p. dj. $40.00

HOWAT, John K. *Hudson River & Its Painters.* 1972 NY. Viking. Ills 1st ed. 4to. 208 p. dj. $75.00

HOWAT, John K. *Hudson River & Its Painters.* NY. Studio. Ills. map. dj. $22.50

HOWE, Helen. *Whole Heart.* 1944 London. 1st ed. dj. EX $12.00

HOWE, Henry. *Historical Collections of VA.* 1846 Charleston. Ills 2nd print. 544 p. $125.00

HOWE, Henry. *MA: There She Is, Behold Her.* 1960 NY. Ills 1st ed. maps. 268 p. dj. $10.00

HOWE, J.V. *Amateur Gun Craftsman.* 1943 Funk Wagnall. Ills. 301 p. VG $12.50

HOWE, M.A. *Boston: Place & People.* 1907 NY. Ills. maps. 388 p. cloth. $10.00

HOWE, Mark De Wolfe. *Holmes-Pollock Letters.* 1941 Cambridge. Harvard U Pr. 2 vol set. $30.00

HOWE, W.H. *Butterflies of North America.* 1975 Doubleday. Ills 1st ed. 633 p. dj. EX $65.00

HOWE, W.J. *Professional Gunsmithing.* 1946 Small Arms. Ills. 526 p. dj. EX $25.00

HOWELL, E.M. *Soviet Partisan Movement: 1941-1944.* 1956 GPO. 9 fld maps. VG $25.00

HOWELL, James. *Certain Letters of James Howell.* 1928 NY. Day. Rudge. Ltd ed. 1/1,000. VG $25.00

HOWELL, John W. *History of Incandescent Lamp.* 1927 Schenectady. Maqua. Ills 1st ed. 208 p. VG $25.00

HOWELLS, W.D. *Boy's Town.* 1890 NY. 1st ed. VG $50.00

HOWELLS, W.D. *Heroines of Fiction.* 1901 NY. 1st ed. 2 vol set. EX $26.00

HOWELLS, W.D. *Lady of the Aroostook.* 1879 Boston. ½-leather. G $110.00

HOWELLS, W.D. *Literary Friends & Acquaintances.* 1900 NY. 1st ed. EX $15.00

HOWELLS, W.D. *Mouse Trap & Other Farces.* 1889 NY. Ills 1st ed. 184 p. G $25.00

HOWELLS, W.D. *Mrs. Farrell.* 1921 Harper. 1st ed. dj. G $20.00

HOWELLS, W.D. *My Mark Twain: Reminiscences & Criticisms.* 1910 NY. 1st ed. 1st issue. VG $65.00

HOWELLS, W.D. *My Mark Twain: Reminiscences & Criticisms.* 1910 NY. Harper. 1st ed. sgn. EX $75.00

HOWELLS, W.D. *No Lost Love.* 1869 1st ed. VG $25.00

HOWELLS, W.D. *Pastels in Prose.* 1890 NY. 1st ed. EX $28.00

HOWELLS, W.D. *Rise of Silas Lapham.* 1885 Boston. Ticknow. 1st ed. 1st issue. VG $55.00

HOWELLS, W.D. *Seen & Unseen at Stratford-on-Avon.* 1914 NY. 1st ed. EX $17.00

HOWELLS, W.D. *Their Wedding Journey.* 1881 Boston. Houghton Mifflin. Ills Hoppin. $9.50

HOWELLS, W.D. *Undiscovered Country.* 1880 Houghton Mifflin. 1st ed. VG $20.00

HOWELLS, W.D. *Venetian Days.* 1893 Boston. Ills Hassam/others. VG $50.00

HOWELLS, W.D. *Venetian Life.* 1892 Houghton. Ills. 2 vol set. djs. M $50.00

HOWELLS, W.D. *Years of My Youth.* 1916 NY. 1st ed. EX $18.00

HOWER, Ralph. *History of an Advertising Agency.* 1939 Harvard. 1st ed. 8vo. cloth. VG $20.00

HOWES, C.B. *Recreational Vehicle Handbook.* 1974 Chicago. Ills 1st ed. 102 p. wraps. $5.00

HOWES, W. *US Iana.* 1962 NY. 2nd ed. 1st print. EX $60.00

HOWITT, M. *Birds & Flowers.* 1871 London. Ills 1st ed. 202 p. cloth. $12.50

HOWITT, Mary. *Our Cousins in OH From Diary of American Mother.* 1849 NY. 1st Am ed. VG $50.00

HOWITT, Mary. *Queens of Great Britain.* 1851 London. 1st ed. fore-edge portraits of queens. $675.00

HOWITT, William. *Ruined Abbeys & Castles of Great Britain & Ireland.* 1864 London. Bennett. 1st ed. 8vo. cloth. $135.00

HOWLAND, C.R. *Military History of the World War.* 1923 Ft. Leavenworth. 2 vol set. $145.00

HOWLAND, E. *Grant: Soldier & Statesman.* 1868 Hartford. Burr. Ills. ¾-leather. xl. $25.00

HOWLAND, E.A. *New England Economical Housekeeper.* 1847 Worcester. 2nd ed. VG $25.00

HOWORTH, Muriel. *Greatest Discovery Ever Made: Memoirs of Frederick Soddy.* 1935 London. New World. 1st ed. wraps. VG $25.00

HOYLE, Fred. *Nature of the Universe.* 1950 Harper. dj. VG $4.00

HOYLE, Rafael L. *Checan: Essay on Erotic Elements in Peruvian Art.* 1965 Geneva. Nagel. Ills. folio. dj. $85.00

HOYLE. *Hoyle's Games Improved.* 1814 Boston. 296 p. G $49.00

HOYT, E. *Brief Sketch of 1st Settlement of Deerfield, MA.* 1833 Greenfield. James Fogg. 48 p. sewn. rare. $200.00

HOYT, Harlowe. *Town Hall Tonight.* 1955 Prentice. dj. EX $25.00

HOYT, Murray. *Fish in My Life.* 1964 Crown. Ills. 210 p. dj. EX $5.00

HOYT, Norris D. *12 Meter Challenges for the America's Cup.* 1977 NY. Brandywine Pr. 1st ed. dj. VG $40.00

HSIEH, Tehyi. *Confucius Said It 1st.* 1939 Boston. 2nd ed. sgn. G $20.00

HSIEH, Tehyi. *Our Little Manchurian Cousin.* 1935 Boston. Ills. inscr. 106 p. dj. VG $40.00

HSU, Francis L.K. *Americans & Chinese.* 1953 NY. dj. G $12.00

HUANG, W.T. *Petrology.* 1962 NY. Ills. 4to. VG $15.00

HUANG SU MUEI. *Chinese Cuisine: Wei-Chuan Cooking Book.* 1979 Ills Revised ed. dj. EX $20.00

HUBBARD, Bernard S. *Mush You Malemutes.* 1932 America Pr. Ills 1st ed. maps. VG $15.00

HUBBARD, Charles D. *Old New England Village.* 1947 Portland. Ills. 107 p. black cloth. VG $25.00

HUBBARD, Elbert. *Friendship, Love, & Marriage.* 1923 Roycroft. 12mo. 95 p. VG $25.00

HUBBARD, Elbert. *Health & Wealth.* 1908 Roycroft. VG $50.00

HUBBARD, Elbert. *Liberators.* 1919 Roycroft. 1st ed. EX $20.00

HUBBARD, Elbert. *Little Journeys to Great Musicians.* 1905 East Aurora. Ltd ed. 1/940. sgn. suede. VG $32.50

HUBBARD, Elbert. *Little Journeys to Homes of English Authors: William Morris.* 1900 Roycroft. Ills/sgn Hubbard. 1/947. EX $70.00

HUBBARD, Elbert. *Little Journeys to the Homes of Great Scientists.* 1905 Roycroft. wraps. $10.00

HUBBARD, Elbert. *Little Journeys.* 1928 Aurora, NY. Roycroft. Memorial ed. EX $100.00

HUBBARD, Elbert. *Man of Sorrows: Little Journey to Home of Jesus of Nazareth.* 1905 Roycroft. Ltd ed. 1/200. sgn. VG $35.00

HUBBARD, Elbert. *Man of Sorrows: Little Journey to Home of Jesus of Nazareth.* 1904 Roycroft. 1st ed. suede. boxed. EX $45.00

HUBBARD, Elbert. *Notebook of Elbert Hubbard: Elbert Hubbard's Scrapbook.* 1923 & 1927. Wise, NY. 2 vol set. VG $22.00

HUBBARD, Elbert. *Rubaiyat.* 1899 Roycroft. Ltd ed. sgn. VG $225.00

HUBBARD, Elbert. *Rubaiyat.* 1900 Roycroft. Ills Griffin. Ltd ed. suede. $125.00

HUBBARD, Elbert. *Thomas Jefferson.* 1906 Roycroft. 1st ed. boxed. EX $40.00

HUBBARD, Elbert. *White Hyacinths.* 1907 Roycroft. Ills Dard Hunter. VG $65.00

HUBBARD, Frederick A. *Other Days in Greenwich.* 1913 NY. Ills 1st ed. 1/1,000. sgn. VG $50.00

HUBBARD, G.S. *Incidents & Events in Life of Gurdon Saltonstall Hubbard.* 1888 Chicago. Rand McNally. 189 p. scarce. $100.00

HUBBARD, Harlan. *Shantyboat.* 1953 NY. 1st ed. VG $30.00

HUBBARD, Kin. *Abe Martin: Hoss Sense & Nonsense.* 1926 Indianapolis. Ills. orange cloth. EX $18.00

HUBBARD, Kin. *Abe Martin's Broadcast.* 1930 Indianapolis. 1st ed. dj. VG $32.50

HUBBARD, L. Ron. *Dianetics.* 1950 NY. Hermitage. 1st ed. dj. VG $100.00

HUBBARD, L. Ron. *Dianetics.* 1950 NY. Hermitage. 4th print. dj. VG $45.00

HUBBARD, L. Ron. *Final Blackout.* 1948 Providence. 1st ed. dj. EX $65.00

HUBBARD, L. Ron. *Lives You Wished To Lead But Never Dared.* 1978 Theta. 1st ed. dj. EX $50.00

HUBBARD, L. Ron. *Mission Earth.* 1985 Bridge Pub. Uncorrected proof. wraps. $65.00

HUBBARD, L. Ron. *Slaves of Sleep.* 1948 Shasta. 1st ed. dj. EX $50.00

HUBBARD, L. Ron. *Typewriter in the Sky & Fear.* 1951 Gnome. 1st ed. dj. EX $45.00

HUBBARD, L. Ron. *7 Steps to Arbiter.* 1975 Major. wraps. VG $15.00

HUBBARD, W.P. *Notorious Grizzly Bears.* 1960 Sage. Ills. 205 p. dj. EX $14.50

HUBERMAN, Leo. *Labor Spy Racket.* 1937 NY. Modern Age. 8vo. dj. wraps. $45.00

HUCKE, Agnes. *Tale of 10 Little Toys.* NY. Gabriel. Ills. G $20.00

HUCKEL, J. *American Indians.* 1934 Albuquerque. 5th ed. VG $35.00

HUDDLE, Rev. W.D. *History of Descendants of John Hottel.* 1930 Strasburg, VA. Ills. 1,183 p. VG $50.00

HUDEN, J. *Indian Place Names of New England.* 1962 NY. wraps. $22.50

HUDSON, Derek. *Arthur Rackham: His Life & Work.* 1973 Scribner. folio. 181 p. $85.00

HUDSON, Derek. *Arthur Rackham: His Life & Work.* 1975 NY. Ills. 4to. cloth. $25.00

HUDSON, Derek. *Arthur Rackham: His Life & Work.* 1960 Scribner. Ills. small folio. dj. EX $100.00

HUDSON, G.H. *Amphibians & Reptiles of NE.* 1958 NE U Pr. Ills. 146 p. maps. wraps. EX $10.00

HUDSON, Thompson Jay. *Law of Mental Medicine.* 1903 Chicago. 2nd ed. 281 p. VG $22.00

HUDSON, Thompson Jay. *Scientific Demonstration of the Future Life.* 1899 Chicago. 4th ed. 326 p. EX $26.00

HUDSON, W.H. *Birds of La Plata.* 1952 London. Ills Magno. 12mo. dj. EX $25.00

HUDSON, W.H. *Birds of La Plata.* 1920 London/Toronto. Ltd 1st ed. 4to. 2 vol set. VG $175.00

HUDSON, W.H. *Book of a Naturalist.* 1919 NY. 1st Am ed. $45.00

HUDSON, W.H. *Far Away & Long Ago: History of My Life.* 1931 Dent. London. Revised ed. 337 p. VG $16.00

HUDSON, W.H. *Green Mansions & Purple Land.* c 1930s. NY. 3 Siren Pr. Ills Henderson. VG $25.00

HUDSON, W.H. *Little Boy Lost.* 1919 NY. Knopf. Ills McCormick. square 8vo. EX $15.00

HUEBNER & KRAMER. *Foreign Trade: Principles & Practice.* 1930 NY. 1st ed. 8vo. cloth. dj. VG $12.00

HUEFFER. *High Germany.* 1911 London. 1st ed. wraps. $150.00

HUESSER, Albert. *History of Silk Dyeing Industry in the US.* 1927 Paterson, NJ. Ills. 4to. 604 p. $75.00

HUFF, Gershom. *Electro-Physiology.* 1853 NY. Barnes. Ills 1st ed. 386 p. cloth. G $55.00

HUFF, Theodore. *Charlie Chaplin.* 1951 NY. Ills 1st ed. 354 p. VG $15.00

HUGHART, Barry. *Bridge of Birds.* 1984 World. 1st ed. sgn. EX $25.00

HUGHES, Edan M. *Artist in CA 1786-1940.* 1986 San Francisco. 1st ed. dj. EX $60.00

HUGHES, Graham. *International Survey of Modern Jewelry.* 1968 Crown. Revised ed. folio. 250 p. EX $45.00

HUGHES, John. *Letters of Abeland & Eloifa.* 1800 Vienna. 2nd ed. leather. G $75.00

HUGHES, Langston. *Black Misery.* 1969 Eriksson. 1st print. dj. $20.00

HUGHES, Langston. *Not Without Laughter.* 1930 NY. 1st ed. fair. $12.00

HUGHES, Langston. *Poetry of the Negro 1746-1949.* 1949 NY. Doubleday. Book Club ed. dj. VG $25.00

HUGHES, Langston. *Selected Poems of Gabriela Mistral.* 1957 Bloomington. 1st ed. dj. VG $20.00

HUGHES, Langston. *Simple Stakes a Claim.* 1957 1st ed. VG $60.00

HUGHES, Langston. *Tambourines to Glory.* 1958 NY. Hill Wang. pb. VG $22.50

HUGHES, Langston. *Tambourines to Glory.* 1958 NY. Day. 1st ed. dj. EX $50.00

HUGHES, R.D. *Principles & Practice of Fly & Bait Casting.* 1924 London. Black. Ills. 80 p. $10.00

HUGHES, R.S. *Beyond the Red Pony: Reader's Companion to Short Stories.* 1987 Scarcrow Pr. Ills 1st ed. 8vo. cloth. M $20.00

HUGHES, Richard. *Fox in Attic.* 1961 Chatto Windus. 1st ed. dj. EX $30.00

HUGHES, Sukey. *Washi: World of Japanese Paper.* 1978 Tokyo/NY. Kodanscha. 1st ed. 1/1,000. $325.00

HUGHES, Ted. *Gaudette.* 1977 Harper. dj. M $18.00

HUGHES, Ted. *Gaudette.* 1977 London. 1st ed. dj. EX $35.00

HUGHES, Ted. *Lupercal.* 1960 London. 1st ed. dj. scarce. EX $150.00

HUGHES, Ted. *Scapegoats & Rabies.* 1967 London. 1st ed. wraps. EX $22.00

HUGHES, Ted. *Season Songs.* 1975 NY. Ills Baskin. 1st ed. dj. VG $25.00

HUGHES, Ted. *What Is the Truth?* 1984 Harper. Ills 1st ed. dj. EX $18.00

HUGHES, Ted. *What Is the Truth?* 1984 London. Ills 1st ed. dj. EX $27.00

HUGHES, Therle & Bernard. *English Painted Enamels.* 1967 London. Spring. Ills. 156 p. $35.00

HUGHES, Therle. *Old English Furniture.* 1969 NY. Praeger. Ills. 202 p. dj. $30.00

HUGHES, Wendell L. *Reconstructive Surgery of the Eyelids.* 1954 St. Louis. Ills 2nd ed. 260 p. red cloth. $55.00

HUGHES, William. *Atlas of Classical Geography.* 1861 Phil. 8vo. maps. plts. ½-leather. $35.00

HUGHES & BASKIN. *Cave Birds.* 1978 London. 1st ed. dj. EX $32.00

HUGHES & BASKIN. *Cave Birds.* 1978 NY. Ills/sgn Baskin. 4to. dj. VG $27.50

HUGHESA, W.J. *Century of Traction Engines.* 1968 Newton Abbot. Ills. 262 p. dj. VG $15.00

HUGO, Richard. *Right Madness on Skye.* 1980 NY. Norton. 1st ed. dj. EX $15.00

HUGO, Richard. *Run of Jacks.* 1961 MN U Pr. 1st ed. dj. EX $125.00

HUGO, Richard. *What Thou Lovest Well Remains American.* 1975 NY. Norton. Uncorrected proof. $125.00

HUGO, Victor. *Battle of Waterloo.* 1977 Ltd Ed Club. Ills Detaille. 4to. slipcase. $65.00

HUGO, Victor. *Les Miserables.* 1938 NY. Ills Lynd Ward. 4 vol set. EX $85.00

HUGO, Victor. *Notre Dame de Paris.* 1955 NY. Ltd Ed Club. 1/4,300. boxed. M $50.00

HUGO, Victor. *Toilers of the Sea.* 1960 Verona. Ltd Ed Club. 1/1,500. boxed. M $100.00

HUGO, Victor. *Toilers of the Sea.* 1866 NY. Harper. VG $40.00

HUGO, Victor. *Works of Victor Hugo.* 1894 Phil. Ills Ltd ed. 41 vol set. $200.00

HUIE, William Bradford. *Hotel Mamie Stover.* 1963 Potter. 1st ed. dj. EX $20.00

HUIE, William Bradford. *Klansman.* 1967 Delacorte. 1st ed. dj. EX $15.00

HUISH, Marcus B. *American Pilgrim's Way in England.* 1907 London. Fine Arts Soc. Ills Chettel. $55.00

HULBERT, Archer B. *Forty-Niners Chronicle of the CA Trail.* 1949 Boston. dj. VG $25.00

HULBERT, Archer B. *Future of Road Making in America.* 1905 Cleveland. Ills. 211 p. VG $12.50

HULIT, L. *Salt-Water Angler.* 1924 NY. 1st ed. VG $35.00

HULL, E.M. *Sons of the Sheik.* 1927 NY. Burt. Ills. dj. VG $20.00

HULME, F. Edward. *Familiar Swiss Flowers.* 1908 Cassell. 100 plts. $65.00

HULME, Kathryn. *Look a Lion in the Eye: Safari Through Africa.* 1974 Little Brown. Ills 1st ed. 223 p. dj. EX $10.00

HULST, Cornelia S. *Pere Marquette & Last of Pattauitomic Chiefs.* 1912 Longman Green. Ills 1st ed. 113 p. VG $22.50

HULTEN, K.G. *Machine: As Seen at the End of the Mechanical Age.* 1968 Greenwich. Ills. 4to. 218 p. metal cover. $30.00

HULTZEN. *Old Fort Niagara.* 1938 no place. 1st ed. wraps. VG $20.00

HUMBERT, Claude. *Ornamental Design.* 1970 Fribourg. Office du Livre. bilingual. $40.00

HUME, David. *Essays: Moral, Political, & Literary.* 1898 London. sgn. 2 vol set. VG $40.00

HUME, David. *History of England.* 1816 Albany, NY. 8vo. 8 vol set. full calf. EX $300.00

HUME, E.E. *Ornithologists of the US Army Medical Corps.* 1942 Baltimore. 1st ed. inscr. 583 p. $165.00

HUME, E.H. *American Physicians's Life in China.* 1946 NY. Ills. dj. VG $20.00

HUME, Fergus. *Chronicles of Fairyland.* 1893 Lippincott. Ills Dunlop. 191 p. G $15.00

HUMMEL, B. *Hummel Book.* 1953 Ills 5th ed. Trans Eytel. 8vo. 62 p. VG $30.00

HUMPHREY, J.R. *Lost Towns & Roads of America.* 1967 Ills Revised ed. dj. VG $20.00

HUMPHREY, Maud. *Wild Flowers of America. Vol. I.* 1894 NY. Ills. 8vo. $150.00

HUMPHREY, W. *Farther Off From Heaven.* 1977 NY. 1st ed. dj. M $12.00

HUMPHREY, W. *Spawning Run.* 1970 Knopf. 1st ed. 80 p. dj. EX $10.00

HUMPHREYS, H.N. *British Butterflies & Their Transformations.* 1849 42 pls. cloth. VG $850.00

HUMPHREYS, J. *Bermuda Houses.* 1923 Boston. 1st ed. plts. 317 p. VG $175.00

HUNEKER, James. *Painted Veils.* 1928 NY. Ltd 1st ed. dj. EX $30.00

HUNEKER, James. *Painted Veils.* 1920 Boni Liveright. 1st ed. 1/120. sgn. EX $90.00

HUNGERFORD, E. *History of Rome, Watertown, & Ogdensburgh.* 1922 McBride. Ills 1st ed. 269 p. dj. VG $35.00

HUNGERFORD, E. *Story of the B&O Railroad 1827-1927.* 1928 NY. Putnam. 1st ed. 2 vol set. VG $65.00

HUNGERFORD, E. *Wells Fargo.* 1949 NY. 1st ed. 8vo. cloth. dj. VG $12.00

HUNNEWELL, James. *England's Chronicle in Stone.* 1886 London. Murray. xl. fair. $27.00

HUNNICUTT, Samuel J. *20 Years of Hunting & Fishing in Great Smoky Mountains.* no date. (1926) Knoxville. Ills. 216 p. G $12.50

HUNT, A. *Textile Design.* 1951 London. 96 p. VG $18.50

HUNT, Albert Bushell. *American Nation: From Original Sources.* 1904 NY. Harper. 28 vol set. VG $100.00

HUNT, Aurora. *Kirby Benedict.* 1961 Glendale. 1st ed. dj. VG $60.00

HUNT, Aurora. *Major General James Henry Carleton 1814-1873.* 1958 Arthur Clark. Frontier Military Series. EX $55.00

HUNT, Blanche Seale. *Little Brown Koko Has Fun.* 1945 Chicago. Am Colortype. dj. VG $22.50

HUNT, Blanche Seale. *Stories of Little Brown Koko.* 1953 Ills. 4to. VG $40.00

HUNT, Frazier. *Cap Mossman: Last of Great Cowmen.* 1951 NY. 1st ed. 277 p. dj. VG $30.00

HUNT, Frazier. *Untold Story of Douglas MacArthur.* 1954 NY. 1st ed. sgn. maps. 533 p. dj. G $12.50

HUNT, Gaillard. *Writings of James Madison.* 1910 NY. 9 vol set. $195.00

HUNT, John. *Ascent of Everest.* 1954 London. dj. VG $18.00

HUNT, John. *My Favorite Mountaineering Stories.* 1978 London. 1st ed. dj. EX $15.00

HUNT, John. *Our Everest Adventure.* 1954 Leicester. 1st ed. dj. VG $22.50

HUNT, L. *Men, Women, & Books.* 1847 NY. 2 vol set. G $90.00

HUNT, Leigh. *Jar of Honey From Mount Hybla.* 1848 London. 1st ed. VG $37.00

HUNT, Lewis W. *People Versus Tuberculosis.* 1966 Chicago. Tuberculosis Institute. VG $15.00

HUNT, Mrs. Alfred. *Our Grandmothers' Gowns.* no date. London. Field & Tuer. 8vo. EX $95.00

HUNT, Peter. *Peter Hunt's How To Do It Book.* 1952 NY. Ills. 294 p. $28.00

HUNT, Peter. *Peter Hunt's Workbook.* 1945 Ziff Davis Pub. Ills 4th print. photos. VG $25.00

HUNT, Rockwell Dennis. *Oxcart to Airplane.* 1929 Los Angeles. Ills 1st ed. 458 p. G $17.50

HUNT, Sir John. *Conquest of Everest.* 1954 Ills 1st ed. G $15.00

HUNT, T.F. *Exemplars of Tudor Architecture.* 1830 London. Longman. Ills. VG $250.00

HUNT, Thomas P. *Drunkard's Friend: Jesse Johnston & His Times.* 1945 Phil. Griffith & Simon. Ills. 12mo. $75.00

HUNT, W.S. *Frank Forester: Tragedy in Exile.* 1933 Newark. 1/200. EX $110.00

HUNT, William. *American Biographical Panorama.* 1849 Munsell. Ills. 8vo. 480 p. cloth. $20.00

HUNTER, Dard. *Papermaking Through 18 Centuries.* 1930 NY. Rudge. Ills 1st ed. 8vo. 358 p. $150.00

HUNTER, Dard. *Papermaking Through 18 Centuries.* 1971 NY. EX $35.00

HUNTER, Dard. *Papermaking: History & Technique of an Ancient Craft.* 1947 NY. Ills 2nd ed. 647 p. dj. EX $125.00

HUNTER, Edward. *Story of Mary Liu.* 1957 NY. 1st ed. inscr. dj. EX $12.00

HUNTER, Evan. *Buddwing.* 1964 Simon Schuster. 1st ed. dj. EX $20.00

HUNTER, Evan. *Come Winter.* 1973 Doubleday. 1st ed. sgn. dj. EX $30.00

HUNTER, Evan. *Easter Man.* 1972 Doubleday. 1st ed. sgn. dj. EX $30.00

HUNTER, Evan. *Matter of Conviction.* 1959 Simon Schuster. 1st ed. dj. EX $20.00

HUNTER, Evan. *Walk Proud.* 1979 Bantam. 1st ed. sgn. dj. EX $15.00

HUNTER, G.L. *Italian Furniture & Interiors.* 1920 NY. Helburn. Ills. 2 vol set. rebound. $325.00

HUNTER, G.L. *Tapestries: Their Origin, History, & Renaissance.* 1912 NY/London. Lane. Ills. cloth. VG $35.00

HUNTER, G.L. *Tapestries: Their Origin & History.* 1913 NY. Ills 1st ed. 1/550. 4to. sgn. $95.00

HUNTER, Hiram. *Little Folk's Book of Nature.* 1922 NY. Ills. 63 p. $5.00

HUNTER, J.A. *Hunter.* 1952 NY. BOMC. 1st ed. dj. VG $12.00

HUNTER, J.A. *Hunter's Tracks.* 1957 NY. BOMC. 1st ed. dj. EX $14.00

HUNTER, J.M. *Pioneer History of Bandera County.* 1970 Hunter House. reprint of 1922. 287 p. EX $30.00

HUNTER, J.M. *Story of Lottie Deno.* 1959 Bandera. 1st ed. 199 p. dj. VG $20.00

HUNTER, John D. *Captivity Among Indians of North America.* 1823 London. Enlarged ed. $110.00

HUNTER, Joseph. *New Illustrations of Life, Studies, Writings of Shakespeare.* 1845 London. 1st ed. 2 vol set. VG $95.00

HUNTER, M. *Canadian Wilds.* 1907 Harding. 277 p. EX $15.00

HUNTER, Sam. *American Art of the 20th Century.* 1972 Abrams. Ills. 4to. dj. EX $40.00

HUNTER, V.; & HAMMA, E. *Stagecoach Days.* 1963 Lane. Ills. 4to. 63 p. pb. EX $7.00

HUNTER & MANNIX. *African Bush Adventures.* 1954 London. dj. VG $45.00

HUNTINGTON, Archer M. *Notebook in Northern Spain.* 1898 NY. Ills. linen. VG $35.00

HUNTINGTON, H. *View of South America & Mexico Comprising Their History.* 1827 NY. 2 vols in 1. 239 p. $125.00

HUNTLEY, Florence. *Great Psychological Crime.* 1906 405 p. VG $24.00

HURD, Charles. *Compact History of the American Red Cross.* 1959 NY. Hawthorne. 1st ed. 308 p. dj. VG $10.00

HURD. *When the New Deal Was Young & Gay.* 1965 Hawthorne. 1st ed. dj. VG $12.00

HURLBERT. *McClellan & the Conduct of the War.* 1864 1st ed. maps. G $45.00

HURLBUT, C.S. *Minerals & Man.* 1970 Ills. 4to. dj. M $35.00

HURLBUT, Henry. *Chicago Antiquities.* 1881 Chicago. Fergus. EX $150.00

HURLEY, Vic. *Jungle Patrol.* 1938 NY. 1st ed. dj. VG $27.50

HURLEY, Vic. *Men in Sun Helmets.* 1936 Dutton. 1st ed. VG $17.50

HURLEY, Vic. *Swish of the Kris.* 1936 Dutton. 1st ed. VG $17.50

HURLIMANN, Martin. *English Cathedrals.* 1961 NY. Viking. VG $18.00

HUROK, S. *Hurok Presents: Memoir of the Dance World.* 1953 NY. Hermitage House. 1st ed. VG $22.00

HURSTON, Zora. *Mules & Men.* 1935 Phil. Ills 1st ed. dj. VG $100.00

HUSSEIN, M.A. *Origins of the Book.* 1972 NY. boxed. M $30.00

HUSSEY, Roland Dennis. *Caracas Company 1728-1784.* 1934 Cambridge. Harvard U Pr. 1st ed. EX $35.00

HUSSEY, Tait. *Sculptor of Youth.* 1930 Phil. Ills 1st ed. 4to. 108 p. VG $27.50

HUSTON. *Those S.O.B's at Tarryall & Other Tales of the Rockies.* 1974 Wichita Falls. dj. EX $25.00

HUTCHENS, J. *One Man's MT: Informal Portrait of a State.* 1964 Lippincott. 1st ed. dj. VG $15.00

HUTCHENS, John K. *American 1920s: Literary Panorama.* 1952 Phil. VG $7.50

HUTCHESON, M.B. *Spirit of the Garden.* 1923 Boston. xl. VG $25.00

HUTCHINGS, Jason M. *Scenes of Wonder & Curiosity in CA.* 1870 NY VG $40.00

HUTCHINS, James. *Boots & Saddles at the Little Big Horn.* 1976 Old Army Pr. Ills. 81 p. pb. EX $10.00

HUTCHINS, P. *James Joyce's Dublin.* 1950 London. Ills. 101 p. VG $32.00

HUTCHINSON, Bruce. *Fraser.* 1950 Rinehart. Ills. 368 p. dj. VG $13.00

HUTCHINSON, Frederick W. *Men Who Found America.* 1909 Grosset Dunlap. Ills Prittie. green cloth. VG $12.50

HUTCHINSON, Hazel. *Toward Daybreak.* 1950 NY. Ills Chagall. 1st ed. sgn. dj. $35.00

HUTCHINSON, Horace G. *Big Game Shooting. Vol. II.* 1905 London. Ills. VG $55.00

HUTCHINSON, Peter. *Diary & Letters of Thomas Hutchinson.* 1884 Boston. VG $25.00

HUTCHINSON, R.W. *Prehistoric Crete.* 1968 Penguin. Ills. 12mo. 373 p. dj. VG $15.00

HUTCHINSON, T. *American Soldier Under Greek Flag at Bezanie.* 1913 Nashville. Ills. VG $25.00

HUTCHINSON, Thomas. *Ballads & Other Rhymes of Country Bookworm.* 1888 London. 1st ed. 1/140. stiff wraps. VG $75.00

HUTCHINSON, Thomas. *Parana with Incidents of the Paraguayan War.* 1868 London. Ills. fld map. rebound. VG $30.00

HUTCHINSON, Thomas. *2 Years in Peru with Exploration of Its Antiquities.* 1873 London. Sampson Low. 1st ed. 334 p. $150.00

HUTCHINSON, W.H. *CA: 2 Centuries of Men, Land, & Growth.* 1969 Am West Pub. $15.00

HUTSON, Martha Young. *George Henry Durrie.* 1978 Santa Barbara. Ills 1st ed. 4to. 238 p. dj. $50.00

HUTTON, E. *Pageant of Venice.* 1922 London. Ills Frank Bragwyn. 147 p. VG $125.00

HUTTON, Laurence. *Literary Landmarks of Jerusalem.* 1895 NY. Ills. VG $25.00

HUTTON. *Trout & Salmon Fishing.* 1949 Ills 1st ed. dj. VG $32.00

HUXLEY, Aldous. *After Many a Summer.* 1939 London. 1st ed. presentation. dj. $125.00

HUXLEY, Aldous. *Along the Road.* 1925 NY. 1st Am trade ed. $12.00

HUXLEY, Aldous. *America & the Future.* 1970 NY. 1st ed. dj. M $17.00

HUXLEY, Aldous. *Antic Hay.* 1923 London. 1st ed. 1st issue. VG $20.00

HUXLEY, Aldous. *Brave New World Revisited.* 1958 NY. 1st ed. dj. VG $15.00

HUXLEY, Aldous. *Brave New World.* 1974 Avon. Ltd Ed Club. 1st ed. boxed. VG $40.00

HUXLEY, Aldous. *Brave New World.* 1932 NY. 1st Am ed. dj. xl. VG $20.00

HUXLEY, Aldous. *Complete Etchings of Goya.* 1943 NY. 1st ed. dj. VG $35.00

HUXLEY, Aldous. *Crome Yellow.* 1921 London. 1st ed. dj. $45.00

HUXLEY, Aldous. *Genius & the Goddess.* 1955 NY. 1st ed. dj. $22.00

HUXLEY, Aldous. *Leda.* 1929 Doubleday. Ltd ed. 1/361. 8vo. sgn. VG $95.00

HUXLEY, Aldous. *Little Mexican & Other Stories.* 1924 London. 1st ed. dj. VG $85.00

HUXLEY, Aldous. *Mortal Coils.* 1922 London. 1st ed. VG $40.00

HUXLEY, Aldous. *On the Margin.* 1923 NY. 1st Am ed. G $15.00

HUXLEY, Aldous. *Point Counter Point.* 1928 Doubleday. 432 p. $35.00

HUXLEY, Aldous. *Vulgarity in Literature.* 1930 London. Chatto Windus. 1st trade ed. $25.00

HUXLEY, Aldous. *World of Light.* 1931 London. dj. EX $55.00

HUXLEY, Elspeth. *Mottled Lizzard.* 1985 Chatto Windus. 311 p. dj. EX $12.00

HUXLEY, Elspeth. *Shining Eldorado: Journey Through Australia.* 1967 Morrow. Ills. 432 p. maps. dj. VG $15.00

HUXLEY, Francis. *Raven & Writing Desk.* 1976 NY. 1st Am ed. dj. EX $12.50

HUXLEY, Julian. *Biological Aspects of Cancer.* 1958 NY. Harcourt. 1st Am ed. 156 p. dj. xl. $10.00

HUXLEY, Julian. *Huxley's Diary of the Voyage of HMS Rattlesnake.* 1936 NY. Ills 1st ed. dj. VG $20.00

HUXLEY, Julian. *Religion Without Revelation.* 1927 London. 1st ed. presentation. $200.00

HUXLEY, Leonard. *Life & Letters of Thomas Henry Huxley.* 1901 Appleton. Ills. 2 vol set. 539 p. VG $25.00

HUXLEY, T.H. *More Criticisms on Darwin & Administrative Nihilism.* 1872 NY. 1st Am ed. 86 p. cloth. VG $35.00

HUXLEY, T.H. *On the Physical Basis of Life.* 1869 New Haven. 1st Am ed. G $25.00

HUXLEY, T.H. *Science & Christian Tradition.* 1898 NY. Appleton. VG $25.00

HUYETTE, H.C. *Coal Is King.* 1903 Chicago. $15.00

HUYGHE. *Art Treasures of Louvre.* 1951 NY. Ills. 4to. dj. VG $10.00

HVASS, E. & H. *Mushrooms & Toadstools.* 1973 Hippocrene. Ills 1st Am ed. 156 p. dj. EX $10.00

HYDE, C.W.; & STODDARD, W. *History of Great Northwest & Its Men of Progress.* 1901 full leather. G $100.00

HYDE, D.O. *Yamsi.* 1971 Dial. Ills 1st print. 318 p. dj. VG $9.00

HYDE, George E. *Spotted Tail's Folks: History of Brule Sioux.* 1961 OK U Pr. Ills 1st ed. 329 p. dj. VG $40.00

HYDE, H. Montgomery. *Trials of Oscar Wilde.* 1948 London. VG $15.00

HYDE, William Dewitt. *Practical Idealism.* 1908 NY. 335 p. index. EX $18.00

HYDE & BROWER. *Navajo Wild Lands.* 1967 San Francisco. Sierra Club. 1st ed. dj. EX $80.00

HYERDAHL. *Aku Aku.* 1958 London. 1st ed. VG $10.00

HYMAN, Trina Schart. *Popular Girls Club.* 1972 Simon Schuster. Ills 1st print. 8vo. 47 p. dj. $7.50

HYMAN, Trina Schart. *Stuck with Luck.* 1967 Little Brown. Ills 1st ed. 88 p. dj. VG $10.50

HYMAN, Trina Schart. *Wreath of Carols.* 1968 2nd print. dj. EX $15.00

HYND, Noel. *Revenge.* 1976 NY. Dial. 1st ed. dj. EX $30.00

I

IAMPORT. *Scrap Irony.* 1961 Boston. Ills Gorey. 1st ed. dj. M $22.50

IBSEN, Henrik. *Peer Gynt.* 1929 NY/Dublin. Ills MacKinstry. 1st ed. VG $50.00

IBSEN, Henrik. *Peer Gynt.* 1929 Doubleday. Ills MacKinstry. 1st ed. 4to. $40.00

IBSEN, Henrik. *Peter Gynt.* 1955 Oslo. boxed. EX $35.00

IBSEN, Henrik. *Vilanden (Wild Duck).* 1884 Kobenhaven. 2nd ed. gilt cloth. VG $30.00

IBSEN, Henrik. *When We Dead Awaken.* 1900 NY. 1st Am ed. G $20.00

IDYLL, C.P. *Exploring the Ocean World: History of Oceanography.* 1969 NY. Crowell. dj. EX $21.00

IGELOW, Jean. *Shepherd Lady & Other Poems.* 1876 Boston. 1st ed. cloth. VG $20.00

ILES, George. *Flame, Electricity, & the Camera.* 1900 NY. Doubleday McClure. 398 p. $45.00

ILLICK, J.S. *PA Trees.* 1919 Harrisburg. Ills. G $20.00

ILYINSKY & PERRY. *Good-Bye, Coney Island, Good-Bye.* 1972 Englewood. Ills. sgn Ilyinsky. G $10.00

IMLAY, G. *Topographical Description of North American Territory.* 1793 NY. Ills. leather. G $500.00

INFELD, Leo. *Albert Einstein: His Work & Its Influence on Our World.* 1950 NY. Scribner. 1st ed. 132 p. dj. EX $40.00

INGALESE, Isabella. *Mata the Magician.* 1901 2nd ed. 183 p. G $35.00

INGALLS, Fay. *Valley Road.* 1949 Cleveland. 1st ed. sgn. VG $20.00

INGALLS. *Tahl.* 1945 Knopf. 1st ed. dj. EX $35.00

INGE, William. *Good Luck, Miss Wyckoff.* 1970 Boston. 1st ed. dj. EX $12.00

INGE, William. *Outspoken Essays.* 1921 London. VG $6.50

INGERSOLL, Robert. *Ghosts.* 1878 WA. 1st ed. VG $20.00

INGERSOLL, Robert. *Vision of War 1899.* 1899 NY. 1st ed. wraps. VG $95.00

INGHAM, G.T. *Digging Gold Among the Rockies.* 1880 Phil. Hubbard. 1st ed. scarce. G $115.00

INGLE, Dean. *Platonic Tradition in English Religious Thought.* 1926 NY. 1st ed. dj. VG $25.00

INGLES, L.G. *Mammals of CA & Its Coastal Waters.* 1957 Stanford U Pr. Ills. 396 p. VG $18.00

INGLIS, O. *Dental Pathology & Theapeutics.* 1892 Philadelphia. VG $30.00

INGOLDSBY, Thomas. *Ingoldsby Legends; or, Myths & Marvels.* 1898 London. Dent Aldine. Ills Rackham. EX $250.00

INGOLDSBY, Thomas. *Ingoldsby Legends; or, Myths & Marvels.* 1913 London. Ills Rackham. fair. $50.00

INGRAHAM, J.H. *Prince of the House of David.* London. Routledge. Ills. VG $9.00

INGRAHAM, J.H. *Prince of the House of David.* no date. c 1910. Chicago. 520 p. $17.00

INGRAHAM, J.H. *Prince of the House of David.* 1859 NY. VG $35.00

INGRAM, R. *Mars in the House of Death.* 1939 NY. 1st ed. dj. EX $12.00

INGWERSEN, W. *Alpine Garden Plants.* 1981 Poole. 153 p. dj. VG $10.00

INMAN, Henry. *Old Santa Fe Trail.* 1898 Macmillan. tan bdg. G $35.00

INMAN, Henry. *Tales of the Trail.* 1898 Crane. Ills 1st ed. 279 p. VG $47.50

INMAN, Thomas. *Ancient Pagan & Modern Christian Symbolism.* 1874 2nd ed. 146 p. VG $85.00

INMAN & CODY. *Great Salt Lake Trail.* 1966 Haines. reprint. dj. EX $17.50

INMAN & CODY. *Great Salt Lake Trail.* 1914 Topeka. Ills. 529 p. maps. index. VG $50.00

INMAN & CODY. *Great Salt Lake Trail.* 1978 Williamstown. dj. VG $15.00

INMAN & CODY. *Great Salt Lake Trail.* 1898 NY. Ills 1st ed. map. VG $65.00

INNES, Hammond. *Atlantic Fury.* 1962 Knopf. 1st Am ed. dj. VG $7.00

INNES, Hammond. *Big Footprints.* 1977 Collins. 1st ed. dj. EX $17.00

INNES, Hammond. *Golden Soak.* 1973 Knopf. 1st Am ed. dj. EX $14.00

INNES, Hammond. *Lekvas Man.* 1971 Knopf. 1st Am ed. dj. VG $7.00

INNES, Hammond. *North Star.* 1975 Knopf. 1st Am ed. dj. VG $7.00

INNES, Hammond. *White South.* 1949 London. 1st ed. dj. VG $18.00

INNES, Hammond. *Wreck of Mary Deare.* 1956 Knopf. 1st Am ed. dj. VG $7.00

INNES, Michael. *Ampersand Papers.* 1978 London. 1st ed. dj. EX $22.00

INNES, Michael. *Sheiks & Adders.* 1982 Dodd Mead. 1st Am ed. dj. EX $12.00

INNES, W.T. *Exotic Aquarium Fishes.* 1966 Metaframe. Ills. 593 p. VG $12.00

INOUYE, T. *Modern Linguist.* 1896 Tokyo. 4to. 167 p. VG $15.00

IRBY, Kenneth. *Relation.* 1970 Black Sparrow. Ltd ed. 1/26. sgn. EX $35.00

IRELAN, W. *9th Annual Report of the State.* 1890 Sacramento. EX $60.00

IRELAND, B. *Warships of the World.* 1980 London. Ills. 160 p. dj. VG $15.00

IRELAND, John. *Hogarth Illustrated.* 1884 London. Ills. 8vo. cloth. VG $45.00

IRELAND, Leroy. *Work of George Innes.* 1965 TX U Pr. Ills. dj. $150.00

IRELAND, Mary E. *Siberian Exile.* 1894 Richmond, VA. Presbyterian. VG $20.00

IRISH, W. *Deadman Blues.* 1948 Phil. 1st ed. dj. VG $35.00

IRISH, W. *Eyes That Watch You.* 1952 NY. 1st ed. dj. EX $50.00

IRISH, W. *Waltz into Darkness.* 1947 Phil. 1st ed. dj. VG $30.00

IRVING, Clifford. *Tom Mix & Pancho Villa.* 1982 St. Martin. 1st ed. dj. EX $17.00

IRVING, Clifford. *38th Floor.* 1965 McGraw Hill. 1st ed. dj. EX $20.00

IRVING, David. *Mare's Nest.* 1964 Boston. 1st ed. dj. VG $22.50

IRVING, Helen. *Ladies' Wreath.* 1852 J.M. Fletcher. VG $35.00

IRVING, John. *Cider House Rules.* 1985 Franklin. Ltd 1st ed. sgn. full leather. $52.00

IRVING, John. *Hotel New Hampshire.* 1981 NY. dj. M $19.00

IRVING, John. *Water-Method Man.* 1972 Random House. 1st ed. dj. EX $100.00

IRVING, John. *World According to Garp.* 1978 Dutton. 1st ed. dj. EX $40.00

IRVING, John. *World According to Garp.* 1978 NY. 1st ed. later issue. sgn. dj. $45.00

IRVING, R.L.G. *Alps.* 1942 London. 1st ed. dj. VG $18.00

IRVING, R.L.G. *10 Great Mountains.* 1942 London. Travel Book Club. G $10.00

IRVING, Washington. *Adventures of Capt. Bonneville.* 1837 London. Bentley. 1st ed. 3 vol set. $250.00

IRVING, Washington. *Adventures of Capt. Bonnneville.* 1837 Paris. Baudry. 303 p. gilt green leather. G $75.00

IRVING, Washington. *Astoria; or, Anecdotes of Enterpise Beyond Rocky Mountains.* no date. Donohue Henneberry. xl. G $27.50

IRVING, Washington. *Irving's Roost* 1855 NY. 1st ed. G $100.00

IRVING, Washington. *Knickerbocker's History of NY.* 1900 NY. Ills Parrish. 1st print. VG $225.00

IRVING, Washington. *Legend of Catskill Mountains.* 1870 NY. Ills 1st ed. 8vo. G $110.00

IRVING, Washington. *Old Christmas & Bracebridge Hall.* 1886 NY. Combined 1st ed. VG $20.00

IRVING, Washington. *Old Christmas in Merrie England.* no date. Peter Pauper. Ills McKay. dj. $12.00

IRVING, Washington. *Rip Van Winkle.* 1939 Garden City. Ills Shinn. 4to. dj. VG $35.00

IRVING, Washington. *Rip Van Winkle. Sleepy Hollow.* 1914 Medici Soc. Ltd ed. 1/1,000. M $25.00

IRVING, Washington. *Tales of the Alhambra.* no date. Tuck McKay. Ills Dixon Brock. $30.00

IRVING, Washington. *Voyage d'Un Americaine a Londres.* 1822 Paris. 8vo. wraps. G $150.00

IRVING, Washington. *Wolferts Roost.* 1855 1st ed. VG $75.00

IRWIN, W. *Pictures of Pictures of Old Chinatown.* 1908 NY. 1st ed. xl. scarce. VG $85.00

ISELIN, John N. *Heinrich Iselin of Rosenfeld & His Descendants.* 1910 NY. 1/100. ½-leather. VG $125.00

ISENBART, H.H. *Imperial Horse: Saga of Lippazzeners.* 1968 Knopf. VG $27.50

ISHAM, Samuel. *History of American Painting.* 1910 NY. later print. 573 p. G $100.00

ISHERWOOD, Christopher. *Christopher & His Friends 1929-1939.* 1976 NY. Ltd 1st ed. 1/130. sgn. M $325.00

ISHERWOOD, Christopher. *Christopher & His Kind.* 1976 NY. 1st ed. dj. M $15.00

ISHERWOOD, Christopher. *Condor & Cows.* 1948 Random House. 1st print. dj. G $35.00

ISHERWOOD, Christopher. *Exhumations.* 1966 Simon Schuster. 1st Am ed. dj. EX $15.00

ISHERWOOD, Christopher. *Lions & Shadows.* 1947 New Directions. 1st Am ed. dj. VG $45.00

ISHERWOOD, Christopher. *Meeting by the River.* 1967 NY. 1st ed. dj. VG $10.00

ISHERWOOD, Christopher. *Prater Violet.* 1946 London. 1st ed. dj. VG $65.00

ISK-KISHOR, Sulamith. *Jews To Remember.* 1941 Hebrew Pub. Ills. 127 p. G $10.00

ISRAFEL. *Life & Times of Edgar Allan Poe.* 1927 NY. Doran. 2 vol set. $35.00

ITOH, Teiji. *Design & Tradition of the Japanese Storehouse.* 1973 Kyoto. Kodansha. $60.00

IVERSON, M.D. *American Chair 1630-1890.* 1957 NY. Ills. 241 p. $45.00

IVES, A.G.L. *British Hospitals.* 1948 London. Collins. 1st ed. 50 p. dj. VG $12.00

IVES, Joseph C. *Report on CO River of the West.* 1861 WA. 4to. 28 maps. plts. cloth. $215.00

IVINS, William M. *Prints & Books.* 1926 Cambridge. Harvard. Ills 1st ed. dj. EX $35.00

IZAX, Ikabod. *High Art & Sport in Brief Chapters.* 1875 Springfield. Ills Louis A Roberts. $15.00

IZZARD, Ralph. *Abominable Snowman Adventure.* 1955 London. 1st ed. dj. VG $20.00

IZZARD, Ralph. *Innocent on Everest.* 1955 London. G $10.00

J

JABOTINSKY, Vladimir. *Prelude to Delilah.* 1945 NY. VG $40.00

JACK, Ellen E. *Fate of Fairy.* 1910 Chicago. Donohue. 12mo. red cloth. VG $25.00

JACKH, Ernest. *Rising Crescent: Turkey of Yesterday, Today, & Tomorrow.* c 1944. NY. sgn. photos. map. VG $65.00

JACKMAN, E.R.; & LONG, R.A. *OR Desert.* 1964 Caxton. Ills. 407 p. dj. VG $20.00

JACKMAN, William. *Australian Captive.* 1853 Auburn. 1st ed. G $110.00

JACKSON, A.E. *Arabian Nights.* no date. Ward Lock. Ills. dj. VG $20.00

JACKSON, A.V. *Persia: Past & Present; Book of Travel & Research.* 1906 NY. Macmillan. 1st ed. 4to. 471 p. VG $40.00

JACKSON, Andrew. *Messages of Andrew Jackson.* 1837 Concord/NY. 1st ed. VG $35.00

JACKSON, Charles J. *English Goldsmiths & Their Marks.* 1921 London. Macmillan. 2nd ed. $90.00

JACKSON, Charles T. *Report on Geological & Agricultural Survey of RI.* 1840 Providence. 1st ed. maps. plts. half calf. $100.00

JACKSON, Charles. *Lost Weekend.* 1944 NY. inscr. dj. G $45.00

JACKSON, Charles. *Secondhand Life.* 1967 Macmillan. 1st ed. dj. EX $10.00

JACKSON, D.D.; & WOOD, P. *Sierra Madre.* 1975 Time Life. Ills. 184 p. EX $7.00

JACKSON, Donald. *Journals of Zebulon Montgomery Pike.* 1966 Norman. 1st ed. 2 vol set. EX $50.00

JACKSON, E.N. *History of Silhouettes.* 1911 London. Ills. VG $85.00

JACKSON, F. *Birds of Kenya Colony & Uganda.* 1938 London. 1st ed. 4to. 3 vol set. VG $1000.00

JACKSON, G. *British Whaling Trade.* 1978 Archon. 1st Am ed. dj. EX $15.00

JACKSON, George. *Soledad Brother: Prison Letters.* 1970 NY. 1st ed. dj. VG $17.50

JACKSON, H.H. *Glimpses of 3 Coasts.* 1888 Boston. $6.50

JACKSON, H.H. *Sonnets & Lyrics.* 1886 1st ed. EX $15.00

JACKSON, Harry. *Lost Wax Bronze Casting.* 1972 Ltd 1st ed. 1/100. $75.00

JACKSON, Helen Hunt. *Ah-Wah-Ne Days.* 1971 San Francisco. Ltd ed. 1/450. dj. VG $90.00

JACKSON, Holbrook. *Anatomy of Bibliomania.* 1930 London. Ltd ed. 1/1,048. 2 vol set. VG $240.00

JACKSON, Holbrook. *Anatomy of Bibliomania.* 1911 London. Heinemann. 2 vol set. EX $180.00

JACKSON, Holbrook. *Occasions.* 1923 NY. 1st ed. dj. fair. $20.00

JACKSON, Holliday. *Civilization of Indian Natives.* 1830 Phil. 1st ed. 120 p. $125.00

JACKSON, J.C. *Grant's Strategy & Other Addresses.* 1910 Westerville, OH. 8vo. VG $10.00

JACKSON, J.H. *Bad Company.* 1949 NY. 1st ed. sgn. dj. EX $25.00

JACKSON, James. *Letters to a Young Physician Entering Practice.* 1861 London. Tickner Fields. 5th ed. $12.00

JACKSON, Joseph Henry. *Encyclopedia of Philadelphia.* 1931-1933. Harrisburg. 4 vol set. VG $80.00

JACKSON, Joseph Henry. *Mexican Interlude.* 1935 Macmillan. 1st ed. inscr. VG $17.50

JACKSON, Laura. *Some Communications of Broad Reference.* 1983 Northridge. Lord John Pr. 1st ed. 1/125. $35.00

JACKSON, Leroy F. *Peter Patter Book.* 1918 Rand McNally. Ills Blanche Fisher Wright. EX $55.00

JACKSON, R. *Hawker Hunter.* 1982 London. Ills. dj. EX $11.00

JACKSON, Sheldon. *AK & Missions on North Pacific Coast.* 1880 NY. Ills 1st ed. 400 p. map. VG $50.00

JACKSON, Shirley. *Bird's Nest.* 1954 NY. 1st ed. dj. EX $35.00

JACKSON, Shirley. *Come Along with Me.* 1968 NY. 1st ed. dj. EX $20.00

JACKSON, Shirley. *Lottery: Adventures of James Harris.* 1949 NY. 1st ed. dj. EX $125.00

JACKSON, Shirley. *Road Through the Wall.* 1948 NY. 1st ed. VG $95.00

JACKSON, Shirley. *Sundial.* 1958 London. 1st ed. dj. VG $38.00

JACKSON, Shirley. *We Have Always Lived in the Castle.* 1962 Viking. 1st ed. dj. VG $35.00

JACKSON, Thomas W. *I'm From TX: You Can't Steer Me.* 1907 Chicago. 1st ed. $25.00

JACKSON, W.H. *Time Exposure.* 1940 NY. G $20.00

JACKSON, W.T. *Enterprising Scot: Investors in American West After 1873.* 1968 Edinburgh. Ills. dj. VG $22.00

JACKSON, W.T. *Wells Fargo Pony Expresses.* 1972 Ills. pb. EX $8.00

JACKSON, W.T. *Wells Fargo Staging Over the Sierras.* 1970 CA Hist Soc. Ills. pb. EX $9.00

JACOBI, Charles T. *Gesta Typographica.* 1897 London. Elkin Matthews. 12mo. 132 p. $275.00

JACOBI, Charles T. *Printers' Handbook.* 1905 London. 3rd ed. 12mo. 464 p. VG $30.00

JACOBI, Charles T. *Some Notes on Books & Printing.* 1892 London. Chiswick. 1st ed. $175.00

JACOBS, Carl. *Guide to American Pewter.* 1957 NY. McBride. Ills. 8vo. 216 p. dj. $40.00

JACOBS, D.H. *Fundamentals of Optical Engineering.* 1943 McGraw Hill. gilt blue cloth. EX $27.50

JACOBS, Helen Hull. *By Your Leave, Sir: Story of a Wave.* 1943 NY. 1st ed. inscr. 260 p. VG $22.50

JACOBS, James Ripley. *Beginning of US Army 1783-1812.* 1st ed. 397 p. G $30.00

JACOBS, Jay. *Color Encyclopedia of World Art.* 1975 NY. 1st ed. dj. VG $35.00

JACOBS, Michel. *Art of Color.* 1923 NY. Ills 1st ed. 4to. 90 p. fair. $50.00

JACOBS, W.W. *Lady of the Barge.* c 1920s. Thomas Nelson. VG $10.00

JACOBS, W.W. *Night Watches.* 1914 London. 1st ed. 1st issue. dj. EX $265.00

JACOBSEN, Charles W. *Oriental Rugs.* 1962 Tokyo/Rutland. Ills. 479 p. dj. $35.00

JACOBSON, P. *City of the Golden '50s.* 1941 CA U Pr. dj. EX $20.00

JACOBY, H. *New Techniques of Architectural Rendering.* 1981 NY. Ills. 157 p. $32.00

JACOLLIOT, Louis. *Bible in India.* no date/place. Dillingham. 324 p. $35.00

JACOLLIOT, Louis. *Occult Science in India & Among the Ancients.* 1971 Universe Books. dj. EX $24.00

JACOMB, C.E. *Violin Harmonics: What They Are & How To Play Them.* 1924 London. Strad Lib #25. VG $18.00

JACQUEMART, A. *History of Furniture.* 1878 NY/London. Ills. 8vo. cloth. VG $95.00

JACQUES, Robin. *Book of Ghosts & Goblins.* 1969 NY. 1st ed. dj. VG $8.50

JAEGER, B. *Life of North American Insects.* 1854 Providence. Sayles, Miller & Symons. Ills. $275.00

JAEGER, E.C. *Desert Wild Flowers.* 1964 Stanford U Pr. Revised ed. VG $10.00

JAEGER, E.C. *Desert Wildlife.* 1978 Stanford U Pr. Ills. 308 p. wraps. $5.00

JAEGER, E.C. *North American Deserts.* 1957 Stanford U Pr. Ills. 308 p. maps. dj. EX $17.00

JAEGER, E.C. *Our Desert Neighbors.* 1955 Stanford U Pr. Ills. 239 p. dj. EX $14.00

JAEGER, E.C. *Tracks & Trail Crafts.* 1948 Macmillan. Ills 1st ed. 381 p. VG $12.00

JAEGER, E.C. *Tracks & Trail Crafts.* 1967 Macmillan. Ills. 381 p. dj. EX $5.00

JAFFA. *Crisis of House Divided.* 1959 Doubleday. 1st ed. 451 p. dj. VG $22.50

JAFFE, H.L.C. *Mondrain.* NY. Abrams. Ills. 4to. cloth. dj. EX $65.00

JAFFE, Irma B. *John Trumbull: Patriot-Artist of the American Revolution.* 1975 Boston. Ills. 4to. cloth. dj. $60.00

JAFFRAY, Julia K. *Prison & the Prisoner: Symposium.* 1917 Boston. 1st ed. EX $37.50

JAHN, T.L. & F.F. *How To Know the Protozoa.* 1949 Brown. Ills. 234 p. VG $18.00

JALOVEC, Karel. *German & Austrian Violin Makers.* 1967 London. Ills 1st ed. 4to. dj. VG $195.00

JAMEISON, Tulitas Wulff. *Tulitas of Torreon: Reminiscences of Life in Mexico.* 1969 TX Western Pr. Ills 1st ed. dj. M $12.00

JAMES, Alice. *Alice James: Her Brothers, Her Journal.* 1935 Dodd Mead. 2nd print. VG $12.50

JAMES, Bill. *Great American Stat Book.* no date. 1st ed. wraps. M $10.00

JAMES, George Wharton. *AZ: The Wonderland.* 1920 Boston. Page. Ills 3rd ed. maps. 478 p. dj. $35.00

JAMES, George Wharton. *CA: Romantic & Beautiful.* 1914 NY. Ills 1st ed. 433 p. cloth. dj. $45.00

JAMES, George Wharton. *CA: Romantic & Beautiful.* 1914 Boston. Page. Ills 1st ed. 4to. 433 p. $40.00

JAMES, George Wharton. *Grand Canyon of AZ: How To See It.* 1910 Boston. Ills 1st ed. VG $10.00

JAMES, George Wharton. *Indian Basketry.* 1901 NY. Ills 1st ed. 238 p. index. VG $67.50

JAMES, George Wharton. *Out of Old Missions of CA.* 1927 Boston. Revised ed. xl. VG $17.50

JAMES, George Wharton. *What the White Race May Learn From the Indian.* 1908 Chicago U Pr. 1st ed. dj. VG $30.00

JAMES, Gilbert. *Rook.* no date. c 1895. Fenno. Ills. 12mo. VG $15.00

JAMES, Harlean. *Romance of the National Parks.* 1941 Macmillan. Ills. 240 p. VG $5.00

JAMES, Henry. *Abolitionism Unveiled.* 1856 Cincinnati. 252 p. cloth. $60.00

JAMES, Henry. *Ambassadors.* 1903 NY. 1st ed. dj. EX $200.00

JAMES, Henry. *Awkward Age.* 1899 NY/London. 1st ed. VG $45.00

JAMES, Henry. *Better Sort.* 1903 NY. 1st Am ed. $110.00

JAMES, Henry. *Better Sort.* 1903 London. $35.00

JAMES, Henry. *Charles W. Eliot: President of Harvard 1869-1909.* 1930 Boston. 1st ed. 2 vol set. EX $25.00

JAMES, Henry. *English Hours.* 1905 Cambridge. Ltd 1st Am ed. 1/400. VG $150.00

JAMES, Henry. *House of Fiction.* 1957 London. Hart Davis. dj. EX $15.00

JAMES, Henry. *In the Cage.* 1898 Chicago. 1st Am ed. VG $75.00

JAMES, Henry. *Little Tour in France.* 1900 Houghton Mifflin. EX $70.00

JAMES, Henry. *Novels & Tales of Henry James.* 1908-1909. NY. Scribner. 17 of 26 vols. EX $500.00

JAMES, Henry. *Outcry.* 1911 NY. Scribner. 1st ed. VG $45.00

JAMES, Henry. *Picture & Text.* 1893 NY. Harper. 1st ed. $70.00

JAMES, Henry. *Question of Our Speech.* 1905 Boston. 1st ed. $65.00

JAMES, Henry. *Sacred Fount.* 1901 NY. Scribner. 1st ed. 1st print. 319 p. $35.00

JAMES, Henry. *Sense of Past.* 1917 London. 1st ed. dj. VG $90.00

JAMES, Henry. *Siege of London.* 1883 London. 1st English ed. VG $85.00

JAMES, Henry. *Small Boy & Others.* 1913 NY. Scribner. 1st ed. VG $30.00

JAMES, Henry. *Terminations.* 1895 London. 1st English ed. VG $185.00

JAMES, Henry. *View & Reviews.* 1908 Boston. Ltd 1st ed. 1/160. VG $40.00

JAMES, Henry. *Watch & Ward.* 1923 London. 1st ed. VG $45.00

JAMES, Henry. *William Wetmore Story & His Friends.* 1903 Boston. 2 vol set. $50.00

JAMES, Henry. *Wings of Dove.* 1902 NY. 1st ed. 2 vol set. VG $20.00

JAMES, Henry. *Within the Rim.* 1919 London. Collins. 1st ed. dj. EX $175.00

JAMES, Henry. *Works of Henry James.* 1921-1923. London. 35 vol set. $275.00

JAMES, J.A. *Life of George Rogers Clark.* 1968 Greenwood. reprint of 1928. 934 p. EX $25.00

JAMES, Jesse S. *Early US Barbed Wire Patents.* 1966 Maywood, CA. Ills. 291 p. wraps. VG $25.00

JAMES, M.R. *5 Jars.* 1922 London. Ills 1st ed. scarce. EX $185.00

JAMES, Marquis. *Biography of a Bank.* 1954 NY. Harper. dj. VG $10.00

JAMES, Marquis. *Biography of Business.* 1942 Bobbs Merrill. Ills 1st ed. dj. VG $12.50

JAMES, Marquis. *Cherokee Strip: Tale of an OK Boyhood.* 1945 Viking. 294 p. dj. G $10.00

JAMES, Marquis. *Raven: Biography of Sam Houston.* 1929 Bobbs Merrill. Ills. 489 p. VG $15.00

JAMES, Marquis. *Singing Tower Carillon & Other Poems.* 1952 Winter Park. 1st ed. wraps. G $15.00

JAMES, P.D. *Black Tower.* 1975 NY. 1st ed. dj. EX $20.00

JAMES, P.D. *Innocent Blood.* 1980 NY. 1st ed. inscr. dj. EX $20.00

JAMES, P.D. *Innocent Blood.* 1980 NY. 1st ed. dj. VG $10.00

JAMES, P.D. *Skull Beneath the Skin.* 1982 NY. 2nd ed. dj. EX $5.00

JAMES, P.D. *Skull Beneath the Skin.* 1982 NY. 1st ed. sgn. dj. M $28.00

JAMES, Philip. *Children's Books of Yesterday.* 1933 London. Ills. cloth. VG $45.00

JAMES, Philip. *Early Keyboard Instruments.* 1930 NY. Stokes. Ills. 4to. cloth. dj. VG $350.00

JAMES, Philip. *English Book Illustration 1800-1900.* 1947 London. Ills 1st ed. VG $22.00

JAMES, Thomas. *3 Years Among Indians & Mexicans.* 1916 St. Louis. Ltd ed. 1/356. EX $135.00

JAMES, Will. *American Cowboy.* 1942 NY. 1st ed. VG $35.00

JAMES, Will. *Cow Country.* 1927 Grosset Dunlap. reprint. 242 p. EX $8.00

JAMES, Will. *Cowboys North & South.* 1924 NY. Scribner. Ills. 217 p. $20.00

JAMES, Will. *Cowboys North & South.* Grosset Dunlap. reprint. 217 p. dj. VG $9.00

JAMES, Will. *Drifting Cowboy.* 1925 NY. Scribner. Ills. 241 p. $20.00

JAMES, Will. *Horses I Have Known.* 1945 Forum. Ills. 280 p. VG $9.00

JAMES, Will. *Lone Cowboy, My Life Story.* 1930 Scribner. 1st ed. 1st print. dj. $40.00

JAMES, Will. *Smoky the Cow Horse.* Grosset Dunlap. reprint. dj. VG $10.00

JAMES, Will. *Smoky the Cow Horse.* Oct 1929. NY. Ills Classics ed. dj. VG $45.00

JAMES, Will. *Smoky the Cow Horse.* Scribner. reprint. VG $5.00

JAMES, Will. *Smoky the Cow Horse.* 1957 NY. Scribner. Ills. 8vo. rust cloth. dj. EX $15.00

JAMES, Will. *Sun Up: Tales of Cow Camps.* Grosset Dunlap. reprint. 312 p. $8.00

JAMES, Will. *Uncle Bill.* 1932 NY. 1st ed. G $17.50

JAMES, William. *Human Immortality: Supposed Objections to the Doctrine.* 1898 70 p. VG $22.00

JAMESON, A.B. *Winter Studies & Summer Rambles in Canada.* 1944 Nelson. Ills. 276 p. VG $10.00

JAMESON, Anna. *Shakespeare's Heroines.* 1898 London. Bell. 2nd ed. 8vo. 341 p. $45.00

JAMESON, Storm. *Before the Crossing.* 1947 NY. 1st ed. dj. VG $6.00

JAMESON & EASTLAKE. *History of Our Lord.* 1872 London. Longman. Ills 3rd ed. VG $30.00

JAMIESON & SEWALL. *Trends in Nursing History.* 1955 Saunders. 4th ed. VG $10.00

JAMIESON. *At the Edge of the Yellow Sky.* 1905 NY. sgn. 125 p. $35.00

JAMIESON. *Chinese Family & Commerical Law.* 1921 Shanghai. cloth. VG $35.00

JANES, E.C. *Fishing with Ray Bergman.* 1970 Knopf. 1st ed. 328 p. dj. EX $12.50

JANES, E.C. *Hunting Ducks & Geese.* 1954 Stackpole. Ills. 4to. 187 p. VG $20.00

JANES, E.C. *Ringneck! Pheasants & Pheasant Hunting.* 1975 Crown. Ills. 145 p. dj. EX $12.50

JANIS, Harriet & Sidney. *Picasso's Recent Years: 1939-1946.* 1946 NY. Doubleday. Ills. 4to. dj. EX $60.00

JANNEY, Russell. *So Long As Love Remembers.* 1953 NY. 1st ed. dj. EX $12.00

JANOVY, John. *Back in Keith County.* 1981 St. Martin. 1st ed. 179 p. dj. EX $10.00

JANOWITZ, Tama. *Slaves of NY.* 1986 Crown. 1st ed. dj. EX $25.00

JANUS, H. *Nature As Architect.* 1957 NY. 119 p $18.50

JANVIER, Thomas A. *In Old NY.* 1922 Harper. Ills. dj. VG $20.00

JANVIER. *Aztec Treasure House.* 1980 NY. Ills Remington. 1st ed. G $25.00

JAPP, A.H. *Our Common Cuckoo, Other Cuckoos, & Parasitical Birds.* 1899 London. Burleigh. Ills. 292 p. G $12.50

JAQUES, Florence. *Snowshoe Country.* 1945 MN U Pr. Ills. 4to. 110 p. dj. VG $15.00

JAQUET, E. *Technology & History of the Swiss Watch.* 1953 Switzerland. 278 p. VG $50.00

JARA, Joan. *Unfinished Song: Life of Victor Jara.* 1984 NY. Ills 1st Am ed. dj. VG $12.00

JARRATT, Vernon. *Eat Italian Once a Week.* 1967 NY. Bonanza. 1st ed. EX $10.00

JARRELL, Randall *Fly by Night.* 1976 NY. Farrar. Ills Sendak. 1st ed. 8vo. dj. $15.00

JARRELL, Randall. *About Popular Culture.* 1981 Paelaemon Pr. Ltd 1st ed. 1/125. wraps. EX $25.00

JARRELL, Randall. *Anchor Book of Stories.* 1958 NY. Doubleday. 1st ed. 12mo. wraps. EX $35.00

JARRELL, Randall. *Animal Family.* 1965 NY. Ills Sendak. G $15.00

JARRELL, Randall. *Animal Family.* 1965 NY. Pantheon. Ills Sendak. 1st ed. dj. EX $25.00

JARRELL, Randall. *Bat Poet.* 1977 Collier. Ills 1st ed. EX $10.00

JARRELL, Randall. *Complete Poems.* 1969 Farrar Straus. 1st ed. sgn. dj. scarce. EX $75.00

JARRELL, Randall. *Little Friend, Little Friend.* 1945 NY. 1st ed. dj. EX $85.00

JARRELL, Randall. *Lost World.* 1965 NY. Macmillan. 1st ed. sgn. dj. EX $30.00

JARRELL, Randall. *Lost World.* 1966 NY. Collier. 1st ed. sgn. pb. EX $12.50

JARRELL, Randall. *Lost World.* 1966 London. Eyre & Spottiswoode. 1st ed. $37.50

JARRELL, Randall. *Pictures From an Institution.* 1954 Knopf. 1st ed. dj. VG $60.00

JARRELL, Randall. *Poetry & the Age.* 1955 NY. 1st ed. dj. EX $20.00

JARRELL, Randall. *Selected Poems.* 1955 NY. Knopf. 1st ed. sgn. dj. EX $60.00

JARRELL, Randall. *Woman at the WA Zoo.* 1960 NY. Atheneum. 1st ed. 8vo. dj. EX $37.50

JARVIS, Edward. *Insanity & Idiocy in MA: Report of Commission on Lunacy.* Cambridge. reprint of 1855. dj. EX $10.00

JASEN, David. *Theatre of P.G. Wodehouse.* 1979 London. Ills 1st ed. dj. EX $30.00

JASTROW, Morris. *Song of Songs: Love Lyrics From Ancient Palestine.* 1922 Grabhorn. Ltd ed. 1/310. slipcase. VG $125.00

JAVOBS, T.C.H. *Appointment with the Hangman.* 1936 NY. 1st ed. dj. VG $20.00

JAYNE, Walter. *Healing Gods of Ancient Civilizations.* 1962 Universe Books. reprint of 1925. dj. VG $12.50

JAYNES, Julian. *Origin of Consciousness in Breakdown of Bicameral Mind.* 1976 Boston. 1st ed. dj. EX $25.00

JEAFFRESON, J. Cordy. *Book About Doctors.* 1860 London. 1st ed. 2 vol set. VG $45.00

JEAN, Marcel. *History of Surrealist Painting.* 1967 NY. Grove. Ills 2nd print. 4to. 383 p. $75.00

JEAN-AUBRY, G. *Joseph Conrad in the Congo.* 1926 Book Journal. Ltd ed. 1/470. sgn. EX $85.00

JEAN-AUBRY, G. *Joseph Conrad: Life & Letters.* 1927 Doubleday. 1st ed. 2 vol set. VG $35.00

JEAN-JAVAL, Lily. *Fortune's Caravan.* 1933 NY. Ills Salcedo. 1st ed. 8vo. dj. $18.00

JEFFERIES, R. *Saint Guido.* 1908 Mosher. 3rd ed. slipcase. EX $10.00

JEFFERS, Le Roy. *Call of the Mountains.* 1922 NY. 1st ed. VG $35.00

JEFFERS, Robinson & Una. *Where Shall I Take You: Love Letters of Una & Robinson.* 1987 Covelo. Yolla Bolly Pr. 1/225. 8vo. M $225.00

JEFFERS, Robinson. *Alpine Christ & Other Poems.* 1974 Cayucos Books. dj. EX $12.50

JEFFERS, Robinson. *Cowdor.* 1985 Covelo, CA. Yolla Bolly Pr. 1/225. M $250.00

JEFFERS, Robinson. *Descent to the Dead.* 1931 Random House. 1st ed. 1/500. sgn. VG $285.00

JEFFERS, Robinson. *Give Your Heart to the Hawks & Other Poems.* 1933 NY. Random. 1st trade ed. brown cloth. VG $20.00

JEFFERS, Robinson. *Meadea.* 1946 NY. 1st ed. 1st print. inscr. dj. $125.00

JEFFERS, Robinson. *Not Man Apart.* 1965 Sierra Club. Ills Ansel Adams/Weston. EX $100.00

JEFFERS, Robinson. *Roan Stallion Tamar & Other Poems.* 1935 NY. Modern Lib. Advance copy. $160.00

JEFFERS, Robinson. *Solstice & Other Poems.* 1935 Random. 1st trade ed. green cloth. $20.00

JEFFERS, Robinson. *Such Counsels You Gave to Me & Other Poems.* 1937 Random House. 1st trade ed. 12mo. dj. EX $37.50

JEFFERS. *Dear Judas.* 1929 NY. 1st trade ed. dj. EX $40.00

JEFFERSON, Joseph. *Autobiography of Joseph Jefferson.* 1890 Century. Ills 1st 1 vol ed. wraps. VG $55.00

JEFFERSON, Joseph. *Rip Van Winkle: Autobiography of Joseph Jefferson.* 1949 London. Reinhardt. Ills. dj. VG $25.00

JEFFERSON, Thomas. *Life & Morals of Jesus of Nazareth.* 1904 Washington. 1st ed. full leather. VG $50.00

JEFFERSON, Thomas. *Purchase & Exploration of LA in 1804.* 1904 NY. Houghton Mifflin. G $35.00

JEFFREY, E.C. *Anatomy of Woody Plants.* 1917 Chicago U Pr. Ills 1st ed. 478 p. G $18.00

JEFFRIES, John P. *Natural History of the Human Races.* 1869 NY. 1st ed. 380 p. G $40.00

JEFFS, Rae Brendan. *Behan: Man & Showman.* 1968 Cleveland. World. 1st ed. dj. EX $15.00

JEHL, J.R.; & SMITH, B.A. *Birds of the Churchill Region, Manitoba.* 1970 Manitoba Mus. Ills. 87 p. maps. wraps. $6.00

JEKYLL, Gertrude. *Gardens for Small Country Houses.* 1927 London. VG $65.00

JELLINEK, G. *Callas: Portrait of Prima Donna.* 1960 NY. Ills 1st ed. 354 p. dj. VG $17.50

JENKINS, C. Francis. *Vision by Radio: Radio Photographs & Radio Photograms.* 1925 WA. Jenkin's Lab. 1st ed. 140 p. $120.00

JENKINS, D. Vivin. *Past & Future of Mankind.* 1932 London. Rider. 1st ed. VG $25.00

JENKINS, Dan. *Dead Solid Perfect.* 1974 NY. 1st ed. dj. VG $17.50

JENKINS, Dan. *Dogged Victims of Inexorable Fate.* 1970 Boston/Toronto. 1st ed. dj. EX $25.00

JENKINS, Dan. *Semi-Tough.* 1972 Atheneum. 1st ed. dj. EX $20.00

JENKINS, Herbert. *Bindle Omnibus: Introduction to P.G. Wodehouse.* 1932 London. 1st ed. VG $30.00

JENKINS, J. *Decorative Furniture.* 1984 NY. Ills. 127 p. $15.00

JENKINS, J.G. *Evan Thomas Radcliffe: Cardiff Ship-Owning Company.* 1982 Cardiff. Ills. 92 p. wraps. EX $12.50

JENKINS, J.S. *Daring Deeds of American Generals.* c 1857. NY. 12mo. 407 p. red cloth. G $21.00

JENKINS, J.S. *Life of Gen. Andrew Jackson.* 1859 NY. Saxton. $10.00

JENKINS, J.S. *Voyage of US Exploring Squadron Commanded by Capt. Wilkes.* 1852 Auburn, NY. calf. VG $30.00

JENKINS, John H. *Basic TX Books: Annotated Bibliography.* 1983 Austin. Ills 1st ed. inscr. 648 p. dj. $50.00

JENKINS, Nancy. *Boat Beneath the Pyramid.* 1980 Holt Rinehart Winston. dj. EX $30.00

JENKINS, Paul B. *Book of Lake Geneva.* 1922 Chicago. dj. VG $20.00

JENKINS, Stephen. *Greatest Street in the World: Story of Broadway, Old & New.* 1911 NY. Ills 1st ed. gilt cloth. VG $95.00

JENKINSON, Isaac. *Aaron Burr: His Personal & Political Relations.* 1902 Richmond, IN. 1st ed. inscr. 389 p. VG $45.00

JENKINSON, Michael. *Beasts Beyond the Fire.* 1980 Dutton. Ills. 248 p. dj. VG $12.00

JENNEWEIN, J. Leonard. *Calamity Jane of West; or, Life & Adventures of Black Hawk.* 1849 Cincinnati. Conclin. G $75.00

JENNINGS, Hargrave. *Rosicrucians: Rites & Mysteries.* 1870 London. Ills. 339 p. rebound. VG $145.00

JENNINGS, John. *Tattered Ensign.* 1966 Crowell. Ills 1st print. dj. EX $8.00

JENNINGS, Mike. *Instinct Shooting.* 1959 Dodd Mead. Ills. 157 p. dj. VG $12.50

JENNINGS, N.A. *TX Ranger.* 1899 NY. 1st ed. 8vo. 321 p. G $95.00

JENNINGS, N.A. *TX Ranger.* 1960 Frontier. facsimile of 1899. 321 p. EX $20.00

JENNINGS, P.J. *Book of Trout Flies.* 1935 NY. Derrydale. Ltd ed. 1/850. slipcase. EX $350.00

JENNISON, George. *Animals for Show & Pleasure in Ancient Rome.* 1937 Manchester. Ills. 209 p. VG $20.00

JENSEN, A.C. *Cod.* 1972 Crowell. Ills 1st ed. 182 p. dj. EX $8.00

JENSEN, Amy L. *White House & Its 32 Families.* 1958 McGraw. 1st ed. dj. VG $12.00

JENSEN, Lt. O. *Carrier War.* 1945 NY. Ills 1st ed. 175 p. wraps. VG $27.50

JENYNS, R. Soame; & WATSON, W. *Chinese Art II.* 1980 NY. Rizzoli. Ills 2nd ed. 277 p. $30.00

JENYNS, Soame. *Later Chinese Porcelain.* 1971 London. Faber. Ills 4th ed. dj. EX $16.00

JEPSON, W.L. *Trees of CA.* 1909 San Francisco. Ills. G $20.00

JEROME, C. *History of the American Clock Business.* 1860 New Haven. 1st ed. wraps. G $30.00

JEROME, Jerome K. *2nd Thoughts of an Idle Fellow.* 1898 NY. Dodd Mead. 1st ed. EX $30.00

JEROME, Jerome K. *3 Men in a Boat.* 1890 NY. 1st Am ed. 8vo. cloth. VG $50.00

JEROME, Jerome K. *3 Men in a Boat.* 1975 Iswich. Ltd Ed Club. 4to. slipcase. $40.00

JEROME, K. *Stage Land: Curious Habits & Customs of Its Inhabitants.* 1890 NY. Ills 1st ed. 12mo. EX $55.00

JESERICH, Dr. Paul. *Die Mikrophotographie.* 1888 Berlin. Ills. 246 p. cloth. VG $75.00

JESSUP, M.K. *UFOs & the Bible.* 1956 Citadel. 1st ed. dj. VG $15.00

JESSUP, Philip C. *Elihu Root.* 1938 Dodd Mead. VG $30.00

JESSUP, Richard. *Quiet Voyage Home.* 1970 Boston. dj. EX $14.00

JESSUP, Richard. *Sailor.* 1969 Boston. 1st ed. dj. EX $16.00

JETTMAR, K. *Art of the Steppes.* 1967 NY. Ills. 272 p. $18.00

JEWETT, Charles. *Speeches, Poems, & Miscellaneous Writings.* 1849 Boston. 1st ed. $30.00

JEWETT, Sarah O. *Country Doctor.* 1884 Boston. 1st ed. cloth. VG $90.00

JEWETT, Sarah O. *Deephaven.* 1877 Boston. 1st ed. 1st issue. VG $90.00

JEWETT, Sarah O. *Tory Lover.* 1901 Boston/ NY. 1st ed. EX $45.00

JEWITT, Edwin. *Manual of Illuminated Missal Painting.* c 1865. London. 12mo. 6 plts. very scarce. VG $95.00

JILLSON, Willard Rouse. *Rare KY books 1776-1926.* 1939 Louisville. Ltd 1st ed. 1/350. 199 p. $100.00

JINARAJADASA, G. *Did Madame Blavatsky Forge the Mahatma Letters?* 1934 Madras. VG $20.00

JINARAJADASA, G. *1st Principles of Theosophy.* 1923 India. 3rd ed. 254 p. EX $33.00

JINGWEI, Zhang. *Alpine Plants of China.* 1982 Breach. Ills 1st ed. 134 p. dj. EX $18.00

JINKS, R.G. *History of Smith & Wesson.* 1977 Beinfield. Ills. 290 p. dj. EX $20.00

JOBE, Joseph. *Great Tapestries: Web of History From 12th Through 20th C.* 1965 Lausanne. Ills. 278 p. dj. slipcase. $125.00

JOERG. *Problems of Polar Research.* 1928 NY. Ills. 479 p. soiled. $35.00

JOHANNSEN, Albert. *House of Beadle & Adams: Its Dime & Nickel Novels.* 1950 Norman. Ills 1st ed. 2 vol set. VG $35.00

JOHL, Janet Pagter. *Fascinating Story of Dolls.* 1941 NY. 1st ed. sgn. dj. EX $45.00

JOHL, Janet Pagter. *Still More About Dolls.* 1950 NY. Linquist. Ills 1st ed. 300 p. dj. VG $32.00

JOHL, Janet Pagter. *Your Dolls & Mine.* 1952 NY. sgn. dj. VG $18.00

JOHNS, Bud. *Ombibulous Mr. Mencken.* 1968 San Francisco. 1st ed. VG $25.00

JOHNS, E. *Thomas Eakins: Heroism of Modern Life.* 1983 Princeton. 4to. dj. VG $25.00

JOHNS, E.B. *Camp Travis.* 1919 NY. 4to. VG $68.00

JOHNS, R. *Our Friend the Irish Setter.* 1933 NY. 1st ed. dj. VG $15.00

JOHNSGARD, P.A. *Bird Decoy: American Art Form.* 1976 NE U Pr. Ills. 190 p. dj. EX $20.00

JOHNSGARD, P.A. *Cranes of the World.* 1983 London. Helm. 1st English ed. dj. EX $55.00

JOHNSGARD, P.A. *Diving Birds of North America.* 1987 NE U Pr. Ills. 4to. 292 p. dj. EX $45.00

JOHNSGARD, P.A. *Ducks, Geese, & Swans of the World.* 1978 NE U Pr. Ills. 404 p. dj. EX $35.00

JOHNSGARD, P.A. *Grouse of the World.* 1983 NE U Pr. Ills. 413 p. maps. dj. EX $45.00

JOHNSGARD, P.A. *Guide to North American Waterfowl.* 1979 IN U Pr. Ills. 274 p. wraps. EX $12.00

JOHNSGARD, P.A. *Hummingbirds of North America.* 1984 Smithsonian. Ills. 304 p. dj. EX $35.00

JOHNSGARD, P.A. *Plovers, Sandpipers, & Snipes of the World.* 1981 NE U Pr. Ills. 493 p. maps. dj. EX $45.00

JOHNSGARD, P.A. *Waterfowl of North America.* 1975 IN U Pr. Ills 1st ed. 575 p. dj. EX $44.00

JOHNSGARD, P.A. *Waterfowl: Their Biology & Natural History.* 1968 NE U Pr. Ills. 138 p. dj. EX $15.00

JOHNSON, A. *Swedish Settlements on DE River 1638-1664.* 1970 NY. 2 vol set. $27.50

JOHNSON, Alfred. *Johnson Genealogy 1500-1914.* 1914 Boston. 219 p. VG $35.00

JOHNSON, Borough. *Technique of Pencil Drawing.* 1930 London. Pitman. 1st ed. plts. dj. VG $40.00

JOHNSON, Brita Elizabeth. *Maher-Shala-Hash-Baz; or, Rural Life in Old VA.* 1923 Claremont. Olson. 328 p. VG $15.00

JOHNSON, Charles. *Lives of Most Notorious Pirates.* Folio Soc. Ills. VG $12.50

JOHNSON, Clifford. *Pirated Junk.* 1934 NY. G $12.00

JOHNSON, Clifton. *Highways & Byways of Pacific Coast.* 1908 NY. Ills. 323 p. $10.00

JOHNSON, Clifton. *Highways & Byways of the MS Valley.* 1906 NY. VG $15.00

JOHNSON, Clifton. *Historic Hampshire in CT Valley.* 1932 Bradley. Ills. VG $12.50

JOHNSON, D.M. *Bloody Bozeman: Perilous Trail to MT Gold.* 1971 NY. Ills 1st ed. Am Trail Series. $15.00

JOHNSON, Denis. *Stars at Noon.* 1986 Knopf. 1st ed. dj. EX $16.00

JOHNSON, Diane. *American Art Nouveau.* 1979 NY. Abrams. Ills. 311 p. $45.00

JOHNSON, Diane. *Lying Low.* 1978 Knopf. 1st ed. dj. EX $15.00

JOHNSON, Dorothy. *Hanging Tree.* 1957 Ballantine. 1st ed. dj. scarce. $30.00

JOHNSON, E. *History of Libraries of the Western World.* 1970 Metuchen. 2nd ed. EX $25.00

JOHNSON, E.B. *Technique of Flower Painting.* 1931 London. Pitman. Ills. 4to. plts. VG $25.00

JOHNSON, Edgar. *Sir Walter Scott: Great Unknown.* 1970 Macmillan. 3 vol set. boxed. $40.00

JOHNSON, Elaine L. *Contemporary Painters & Sculptors As Printmakers.* 1966 MOMA. Ills. square 8vo. 48 p. wraps. $10.00

JOHNSON, Emory. *Principles of Railroad Transportation.* 1922 NY. Revised ed. dj. EX $25.00

JOHNSON, Franklyn A. *1 More Hill.* 1949 NY. 1st ed. maps. 181 p. dj. VG $45.00

JOHNSON, Gene. *Ship Model Building.* 1961 MD. Cornell Maritime Pr. dj. EX $16.00

JOHNSON, H. *Recipes for the Sutterly Chafing Dish.* 1894 Phil. wraps. VG $20.00

JOHNSON, Harold. *Who's Who in Major Leagues.* 1936 Chicago. 1st ed. VG $47.50

JOHNSON, Harold. *Who's Who in the American League.* 1935 Chicago. Ills 1st ed. red cloth. VG $40.00

JOHNSON, I.D. *Therapeutic Key: Practical Guide for Homeopathic Treatment.* 1875 Boericke. VG $10.00

JOHNSON, Irving. *Round the Horn in a Square Rigger.* 1932 Bradley. Ills. 219 p. G $4.00

JOHNSON, J. *Parachute.* c 1890. Routledge. Ills CE Brock. G $40.00

JOHNSON, J. Stewart. *Modern American Poster From Graphic Design Collection MOMA.* 1984 MOMA. Ills. bilingual text. 144 p. wraps. $17.00

JOHNSON, Josephine. *Inland Island.* 1969 NY. dj. EX $9.00

JOHNSON, Josephine. *Now in November.* 1935 NY. VG $5.00

JOHNSON, L.R. *How To Landscape Your Grounds.* 1950 NY. Ills. 221 p. $15.00

JOHNSON, Lady Bird. *White House Library.* 1967 WA. Ltd ed. 1/300. sgn. ½-morocco. M $100.00

JOHNSON, M. &. H. *Black Bruce.* 1938 Harcourt Brace. 1st ed. VG $12.50

JOHNSON, M.M. *Rifles & Machine Guns.* 1944 Morrow. Ills 1st ed. 390 p. VG $25.00

JOHNSON, Malcolm. *Great Locofoco Juggernaut.* 1971 Imprint Soc. 1/1,950. EX $15.00

JOHNSON, Martin. *Camera Trails in Africa.* 1924 Grosset Dunlap. Ills. 342 p. VG $14.00

JOHNSON, Martin. *Camera Trails in Africa.* 1924 Century. Ills. 342 p. G $8.00

JOHNSON, Martin. *Lion: African Adventures with the King of Beasts.* 1929 Putnam. Ills. EX $20.00

JOHNSON, Martin. *Lion: African Adventures with the King of Beasts.* 1934 Blue Ribbon. Ills. 281 p. VG $12.50

JOHNSON, Martin. *Safari: Saga of African Adventure.* 1928 Grosset Dunlap. Ills. 294 p. G $10.00

JOHNSON, Martin. *Safari: Saga of the African Blue.* 1928 Putnam. Ills. G $12.50

JOHNSON, Merle. *Howard Pyle's Book of Pirates.* 1949 NY. Ills Pyle/others. dj. G $15.00

JOHNSON, Osa. *Bride in the Solomons.* 1944 Houghton Mifflin. Ills. 251 p. $6.50

JOHNSON, Osa. *I Married Adventure.* no date. (1940) Lippincott. 4to. 371 p. $10.00

JOHNSON, Osa. *4 Years in Paradise.* 1941 London. 1st ed. sgn. VG $37.50

JOHNSON, Osa. *4 Years in Paradise.* 1941 Lippincott. Ills 1st ed. 345 p. dj. G $8.50

JOHNSON, Owen. *Wasted Generation.* 1921 Boston. 343 p. $5.00

JOHNSON, P.H. *Good Listener.* 1975 NY. 1st ed. dj. M $11.00

JOHNSON, Pamela Hansford. *Corkstreet Next to the Hatters.* 1965 Scribner. 1st ed. dj. VG $35.00

JOHNSON, Pamela Hansford. *Survival of the Fittest.* 1968 Scribner. 1st ed. dj. VG $30.00

JOHNSON, Peter H. *America's Finest Shotgun.* 1963 Harrisburg. Stackpole. 2nd ed. VG $25.00

JOHNSON, Peter. *Collecting Antique Furniture.* 1976 NY. Galahad. Ills. 128 p. dj. $22.50

JOHNSON, R.U.; & BUEL, C.C. *Battles & Leaders of the Civil War.* 1956 Yoseloff. Ills. 4 vol set. maps. dj. EX $45.00

JOHNSON, Raynor C. *Imprisoned Splendour.* 1953 NY. 1st ed. 424 p. dj. EX $16.00

JOHNSON, Ronald. *Book of the Green Man.* 1967 NY. 1st ed. dj. EX $20.00

JOHNSON, Rossitar. *Campfire & Battlefield.* 1894 NY. Ills. 4to. 648 p. VG $15.00

JOHNSON, Samuel. *Journey to Western Island of Scotland.* 1810 Baltimore. 1st Am ed. $175.00

JOHNSON, Samuel. *Rambler.* 1824 Phil. 4 vols in 2. leather. VG $125.00

JOHNSON, Samuel. *Rambler.* 1779 London. 9th ed. 12mo. 4 vol set. G $60.00

JOHNSON, T.R. *Amphibians of MO.* 1977 KS U Pr. Ills. 142 p. maps. wraps. EX $8.00

JOHNSON, Una E. *American Prints & Printmakers.* 1980 Garden City. Doubleday. 4to. cloth. dj. $40.00

JOHNSON, V.E. *Chemistry & Chemical Magic.* 1912 London. 12mo. 150 p. $15.00

JOHNSON, W.F. *Life of Sitting Bull & History of Indian War 1890-1891.* 1891 Phil. Ills. EX $45.00

JOHNSON, W.F. *Life of William Tecumseh Sherman: Late Retired General.* 1891 Ills 1st ed. maps. G $20.00

JOHNSON, W.W. *Baja, CA.* 1972 Time Life. Ills. 184 p. EX $8.00

JOHNSON, W.W. *Forty-Niners.* 1974 Time Life. Ills 1st ed. 240 p. EX $15.00

JOHNSON, William. *Christopehr Phlem: Father of Swedish Technology.* 1963 Trinity College. 1st ed. EX $15.00

JOHNSON & HAVEN. *Automatic Arms.* 1941 NY. 1st ed. presentation. EX $100.00

JOHNSON & HAVEN. *Automatic Weapons of World.* 1945 NY. 1st ed. dj. VG $35.00

JOHNSON & SNOOK. *Seashore Animals of the Pacific Coast.* 1935 NY. 1st ed. 2nd print. dj. M $50.00

JOHNSTON, Abraham J. *Surgeon's Log: Impressions of the Far East.* 1926 London. Ills. 8vo. 286 p. dj. VG $18.00

JOHNSTON, Annie Fellows. *In League with Israel: Tale of Chattanooga Conference.* 1897 Nashville. $25.00

JOHNSTON, Annie Fellows. *Miss Santa Claus of the Pullman.* 1913 Boston. Page. Ills Reginald Birch. 172 p. VG $25.00

JOHNSTON, Charles H.L. *Famous Scouts.* 1910 Boston. 1st ed. 8vo. cloth. VG $75.00

JOHNSTON, Edward. *Writing, Illuminating, & Lettering.* 1908 London. Revised 2nd ed. 12mo. 510 p. $45.00

JOHNSTON, F.B. *Hampton Album.* 1966 NY. 1st ed. 8vo. wraps. EX $20.00

JOHNSTON, J. *Grenfell of Labrador.* no date. London. Ills. xl. VG $10.00

JOHNSTON, Johanna. *Eagle in Fact & Fiction.* 1966 Quist. Ills 1st ed. 160 p. dj. EX $8.00

JOHNSTON, Joseph E. *Narrative of Military Operations Directed During War.* 1874 NY. Ills 1st ed. rebound. G $45.00

JOHNSTON, Margaret A. *In Acadia.* 1893 New Orleans. Hansell. photos. cloth. G $15.00

JOHNSTON, Mary. *Cease Firing.* 1912 Boston. Ills Wyeth. 1st ed. EX $20.00

JOHNSTON, Paul. *Biblio-Typographica.* 1930 NY. Covicci. Ltd ed. 1/1,050. 8vo. $50.00

JOHNSTON, Reginald F. *Twilight in the Forbidden City.* 1934 NY. Appleton. Ills. EX $50.00

JOHNSTONE, Ann Graham. *My Pop-Up Book of Nursery Rhymes.* 1983 London. Dean International Pub. VG $7.50

JOLINE, Adrian Hoffman. *Edgehill Essays.* 1911 Boston. Gorham. 1st ed. VG $15.00

JOLLEY, Elizabeth. *Foxy Baby.* 1985 Viking. Advance copy. dj. EX $20.00

JOLLEY, Elizabeth. *Milk & Honey.* 1984 Persea. 1st Am ed. dj. EX $15.00

JOLY, W.P. *Sir Oliver Lodge, Psychical Researcher & Scientist.* 1974 Rutherford. Ills 1st ed. 256 p. dj. VG $12.00

JONE, Adrienne. *Wild Voyageur: Story of a Canada Goose.* 1966 Little Brown. Ills 1st ed. 174 p. VG $6.00

JONES, Anson. *Republic of TX: Its History & Annexation 1836-1946.* Rio Grande. reprint of 1859. $30.00

JONES, Bobby. *Golf Is My Game.* 1960 Doubleday. 1st ed. dj. VG $20.00

JONES, David. *In Parenthesis.* 1961 NY. 1st ed. 1st issue. dj. VG $30.00

JONES, David. *Western Horse Advice & Training.* 1966 OK U Pr. dj. VG $10.00

JONES, Dewitt. *John Muir's America.* 1976 Crown. Ills 1st ed. 159 p. dj. EX $16.00

JONES, E. *Life & Work of Freud.* 1953-1957. Basic Books. 1st ed. 3 vols. $50.00

JONES, E. Alfred. *Gold & Silver of Windsor Castle.* 1911 Arden Pr. Ltd ed. 1/285. 4to. 103 plts. $650.00

JONES, Elizabeth Orton. *Small Rain.* 1943 Viking. 1st ed. dj. VG $45.00

JONES, G. *Autumn of the U-Boats.* 1984 London. Ills. dj. EX $25.00

JONES, Gayl. *Defeat of the Wolf Packs.* 1986 London. Ills. maps. dj. EX $26.50

JONES, Gayl. *White Rat: Short Stories.* 1977 Random House. 1st ed. VG $20.00

JONES, George W. *Georgics of Vergil.* 1931 London. Ills Carrick. 1/500. VG $35.00

JONES, Gertrude Manly. *Old Mammy's Lullaby Songs.* 1901 Phil. Ills. folio. EX $50.00

JONES, H.L. *Masterpieces of CA Decorative Style.* 1980 Santa Barbara. 8vo. cloth. dj. EX $17.50

JONES, Howard. *Key for the Identification of Nests & Eggs of Common Birds.* 1927 Circleville. 44 p. wraps. VG $35.00

JONES, J.B. *Wild Western Scenes.* 1891 Phil. Ills. 12mo. $7.50

JONES, J.W. *Christ in the Camp.* 1888 Richmond. 2nd print. VG $55.00

JONES, J.W. *Salmon.* 1959 Harper. Ills. 192 p. dj. VG $6.50

JONES, James. *From Here to Eternity.* 1951 NY. 1st ed. dj. fair. $65.00

JONES, James. *Ice Cream Headache.* 1968 NY. 1st ed. dj. EX $22.00

JONES, James. *Pistol.* 1958 Scribner. 1st ed. dj. VG $40.00

JONES, James. *Touch of Danger.* 1973 Garden City. dj. M $19.00

JONES, James. *Viet Journal.* 1974 NY. 1st ed. dj. EX $20.00

JONES, James. *Whistle.* 1978 NY. dj. M $12.00

JONES, K. *Plantation South.* 1957 1st ed. 8vo. 412 p. dj. G $35.00

JONES, K.M. *Heroines of Dixie.* 1955 Indianapolis. 1st ed. dj. EX $27.50

JONES, Laurence. *Piney Woods & Its Story.* 1922 Revell. Ills. $18.00

JONES, Le Roi. *Dutchman & the Slave.* 1964 Morrow Quill. 1st ed. wraps. EX $15.00

JONES, Le Roi. *Home: Social Essays.* 1966 Morrow. 1st ed. dj. EX $25.00

JONES, Le Roi. *Preface to a 20 Volume Suicide Note.* 1961 NY. Totem/Corinth. 1st ed. VG $20.00

JONES, Le Roi. *Raise: Essays Since 1965.* 1971 Random House. 1st ed. dj. EX $20.00

JONES, N. *Seattle.* 1972 Doubleday. Ills. 371 p. VG $5.00

JONES, S.C. *Reminiscences of 22nd IA Volunteer Infantry.* 1907 IA City. 1st ed. rare. VG $150.00

JONES, S.R. *Posters & Their Designers.* 1924 Studio. disbound. $10.00

JONES, Sydney. *Art & Publicity: Fine Printing & Design.* 1925 London. Ills. 4to. VG $17.00

JONES, T. *Star To Steer Her By.* 1985 London. xl. dj. VG $8.50

JONES, Ted. *Challenge '77: Newport & the America's Cup.* 1978 1st ed. 266 p. dj. VG $14.00

JONES, Thelma. *Piety Hill.* 1977 Turtinen. Ills. sgn. 136 p. dj. EX $8.00

JONES, Thomas H. *Experience of T.H. Jones: Slave for 43 Years.* 1862 Boston. Ills. inscr. salmon wraps. VG $350.00

JONES, Tom. *Henry Tate 1819-1899.* 1960 Tate Lyle Ltd. 8vo. cloth. VG $15.00

JONES, Virgil Carrington. *Hatfields & McCoys.* 1948 Chapel Hill. dj. VG $15.00

JONES, Virgil Carrington. *Ranger Mosby.* 1944 Chapel Hill. Ills 4th print. 347 p. dj. VG $37.50

JONES, W.H.S. *Medical Writings of Anonymous Londinensis.* 1947 Cambridge. 1st ed. dj. EX $35.00

JONES, Weimar. *Affair with a Weekly.* 1960 Winston Salem. 8vo. 116 p. cloth. dj. M $12.50

JONES, William. *History of Christian Church.* 1837 Dover. 2 vols in 1. full leather. VG $20.00

JONES & BOUCHER. *Baluchi Rugs.* 1974 WA. Ills. spiral bdg. $22.50

JONES. *Ladies of Richmond.* 1962 Indianapolis. 1st ed. dj. VG $18.00

JONG, Erica. *Fear of Flying.* 1975 Holt Rinehart. dj. EX $15.00

JONG, Erica. *Fear of Flying.* 1973 Holt Rinehart. 1st ed. dj. EX $25.00

JONG, Erica. *Fruits & Vegetables.* 1971 NY. 1st ed. dj. EX $20.00

JONG, Erica. *Parachutes & Kisses.* 1984 London. 1st ed. dj. M $15.00

JONG, Erica. *Serenissima.* 1987 Houghton. Advance copy. wraps. $30.00

JONNSON, Crockett. *Barnaby.* 1943 NY. dj. VG $15.00

JORAY, Marcel; & VASARELY, V. *Plastic Arts of the 20th Century: Vasarely II.* 1970 Neuchatel. Griffon. Ills. square 4to. dj. $85.00

JORDAN, David Starr. *Scientific Aspects of Luther Burbank's Work.* 1909 San Francisco. Philopolis Pr. 1st ed. 115 p. $65.00

JORDAN, David; & EVERMANN, B. *American Food & Game Fishes.* 1902 NY. Ills 1st ed. 4to. VG $95.00

JORDAN, E.L. *Pictorial Travel Atlas of Scenic America.* 1973 Hammond. Bicentennial ed. 1/150. EX $200.00

JORDAN, J. *Give Me the Wind.* 1971 Prentice Hall. 235 p. dj. EX $15.00

JORDAN, J. *Things That I Do in the Dark.* 1977 Random House. dj. EX $25.00

JORDAN, Jim; & GOLDWATER, R. *Paintings of Arshile Gorky.* 1982 NY. Ills. 4to. 576 p. dj. $125.00

JORDAN, John A. *Elephants & Ivory.* 1956 Rinehart. Ills. 250 p. dj. EX $30.00

JORDAN, Neil. *Night in Tunisia.* 1976 Dublin. Irish Writer Co-Op. 1st ed. EX $45.00

JORDAN, Robert Furneaux. *Le Corbusier.* 1972 London. Dent. Ills. photos. dj. EX $8.00

JORDANOFF, A. *Illustrated Aviation Dictionary.* 1942 NY. G $12.00

JORDANOFF, A. *Through the Overcast.* 1938 NY. Ills. 8vo. sgn. VG $15.00

JORDANOFF, A. *Your Wings.* 1937 NY. Ills. 8vo. sgn. VG $15.00

JORGENSEN, P. *Salmon Flies: Their Character, Style, & Dressing.* 1978 Stackpole. Ills. 4to. 256 p. dj. EX $17.50

JOSEPH, Browell. *Telephone Directory As a Cultural Guide.* 1929 NY. Coventry. 1st ed. 4to. cloth. dj. VG $55.00

JOSEPHY, Alvin M. *Indian Heritage of America.* 1968 NY. Knopf. Ills 2nd print. VG $7.50

JOSEPHY, Alvin M. *Long & Short & Tall.* 1946 NY. Ills. 221 p. xl. $20.00

JOSEPHY, Alvin M. *Nez Perce Indians.* 1965 New Haven. 1st ed. dj. VG $45.00

JOSLIN, Sesyle. *Baby Elephant's Baby Book.* 1964 NY. Ills Weisgard. 1st ed. dj. $15.00

JOURDAIN, F. *Toulouse-Lautrec.* 1951 NY. Paris Book Center. 8vo. dj. VG $45.00

JOVAN & DE VILLOA. *Voyage to South America.* 1806 London. Ills. 2 vols in 1. G $420.00

JOY, Charles R. *Animal World of Albert Schweitzer.* 1950 Boston. dj. VG $20.00

JOY, Charles R. *Music in the Life of Albert Schweitzer.* 1951 NY. Harper. 1st ed. dj. VG $20.00

JOY, William. *Aviators.* 1966 London. dj. VG $20.00

JOYCE, James. *Anna Livia Plurabelle.* 1930 London. 1st ed. wraps. EX $60.00

JOYCE, James. *Cat & the Devil.* 1964 NY. Ills Erdoes. 1st ed. $17.50

JOYCE, James. *Collected Poems of James Joyce.* 1936 NY. Black Sun. Ltd 1st ed. 1/800. 12mo. VG $300.00

JOYCE, James. *Epiphanies.* 1956 Buffalo U Pr. Ltd ed. 1/550. 12mo. cloth. EX $65.00

JOYCE, James. *Exiles.* 1918 NY. Huebsch. 1st Am ed. 8vo. green cloth. $135.00

JOYCE, James. *Finnegan's Wake.* 1947 NY. EX $15.00

JOYCE, James. *Finnegan's Wake.* 1939 London. 1st ed. dj. EX $275.00

JOYCE, James. *Giacomo Joyce.* 1968 NY. Viking. 1st ed. 8vo. slipcase. EX $50.00

JOYCE, James. *My Impossible Health.* 1977 London. Revised 2nd ed. wraps. $15.00

JOYCE, James. *Portrait.* 1977 Garland Pub. facsmile. 4to. 2 vols set. EX $85.00

JOYCE, James. *Portrait.* no date. NY. Ltd Ed Club. Ills. EX $110.00

JOYCE, James. *Portrait.* 1921 Egoist Pr. 3rd English ed. $40.00

JOYCE, James. *Portrait.* 1965 Folio Soc. VG $15.00

JOYCE, James. *Portrait.* 1917 Huebsch. 2nd Am ed. VG $75.00

JOYCE, James. *Schauspiel in 3 Akten.* 1919 Zurich. 1st ed. 8vo. 154 p. scarce. EX $75.00

JOYCE, James. *Stephen Hero.* 1944 New Directions. 1st ed. 234 p. VG $18.00

JOYCE, James. *Ulysses.* 1934 Random House. 1st Am ed. dj. VG $100.00

JOYCE, James. *Ulysses.* 1927 Paris. 9th print. G $60.00

JOYCE, James. *Ulysses.* 1935 Ills/sgn Matisse. 1/1,500. EX $1200.00

JOYCE, James. *2 Tales of Shem & Shaun.* 1932 London. 1st ed. VG $36.00

JOYCE, James. *7 Poems Set to Music by E. Moeran.* 1930 Oxford. 20 p. G $12.00

JOYCE, Stanislaus. *My Brother's Keeper.* 1958 NY. Ltd 1st ed. 1/375. dj. $30.00

JUDD, N.M. *Men Met Along the Trail.* 1968 OK U Pr. Ills 1st ed. 162 p. dj. EX $12.00

JUDSON, Katharine B. *Myths & Legends of AK.* 1911 Chicago. Ills. 8vo. 149 p. dj. VG $65.00

JUDSON, Katherine B. *Early Days in Old OR.* 1936 Metropolitan. Ills. 275 p. maps. dj. EX $35.00

JUDSON, Katherine B. *Myths & Legends of the Great Plains.* 1913 McClurg. 1st ed. dj. VG $40.00

JUENGST, Charles A. *Inventor.* 1921 no place. Ills. leather. dj. VG $30.00

JUETTNER, Otto. *Daniel Drake & His Followers.* 1909 Cincinnati. EX $100.00

JUMEAU, M.E. *Jumeau Doll Story.* 1957 Nina Davies. sgn Davies. dj. VG $10.00

JUNG, Carl G. *Man & His Symbols.* 1964 Doubleday. dj. EX $15.00

JUNIUS. *Letters of Junius.* 1791 Phil. 1st Am ed. EX $200.00

JUSDSON, Clara. *Jerry & Jean Detectors.* 1923 Chicago. Ills Gregory. VG $12.50

JUSTER, Norton; & GNOLI, D. *Alberic the Wise.* 1965 Pantheon. Ills 1st ed. dj. VG $25.00

K

KABOTIE, Fred. *Designs From the Ancient Mimbrenos with Hopi Interpretation.* 1982 Northland. Ltd 2nd ed. 1/100. slipcase. $50.00

KAFKA, Franz. *Amerika.* no date. (1940) New Directions. 1st ed. dj. EX $85.00

KAFKA, Franz. *Basic Kafka.* 1979 NY. Pocket Books. wraps. EX $22.50

KAFKA, Franz. *Metamorphosis.* 1984 Ltd Ed Club. Ills/sgn Cuevas. dj. EX $250.00

KAFKA, Franz. *Trial.* 1937 Knopf. 1st ed. dj. VG $25.00

KAGAWA, Toyohiko. *Songs From the Slums.* 1935 Nashville. Cokesbury Pr. VG $35.00

KAGE, Joseph. *With Faith & Thanksgiving.* 1962 Montreal. 1st ed. EX $45.00

KAHLENBERG, Mary H. *Grass.* 1977 Los Angeles. Ills. $15.00

KAHLENBERG, Mary H. *Rites of Passage: Textiles of Indonesian Archipelago.* 1979 San Diego. Ills. 46 p. $10.00

KAHLER, E. *Man the Measure.* 1943 NY. 1st ed. presentation. 8vo. cloth. EX $16.00

KAHN, David. *Codebreakers.* 1967 NY. Ills 1st ed. 1,164 p. dj. VG $45.00

KAHN, E.J. *Voice.* 1947 Harper. Ills 1st ed. 125 p. dj. VG $17.50

KAHN, Roger. *Boys of Summer.* 1972 NY. Harper Row. inscr. dj. VG $30.00

KAHO, Noel. *Will Rogers Country.* 1941 OK U Pr. 1st ed. 48 p. map. VG $5.00

KAHO, Noel. *Will Rogers Country.* 1950 private print. 32 p. pb. EX $5.00

KAINSINGER, Jean & Robert. *Village of Walton Hills: Tracing Our Heritage.* 1986 Walton Hills. Ills. 160 p. wraps. M $10.00

KAKUZO, Okakura. *Book of Tea.* 1919 Edinburgh/London. Ills. 8vo. $30.00

KALES, Anthony. *Sleep Physiology & Pathology: Symposium.* 1969 Lippincott. EX $15.00

KALINSKY, G. *From Behind the Plate.* 1972 Prentice Hall. sgn. dj. EX $30.00

KALLIER, Jane. *Viennese Design & the Weiner Werkstatte.* 1986 NY. Braziller. Ills. 4to. 152 p. dj. $25.00

KALLIR, Otto. *Egon Schiele: Oeuvre Catalogue of Paintings.* 1966 NY. Crown. Ills. folio. 561 p. $275.00

KALLIR, Otto. *Grandma Moses.* 1975 NY. Abrams. New Concise ed. dj. VG $10.00

KALLIR, Otto. *Grandma Moses.* 1973 NY. Abrams. Ills. 357 p. dj. VG $50.00

KAMAL, A. *Sacred Journey.* 1961 NY. 1st ed. dj. EX $7.00

KAMINSKY, Max. *My Life in Jazz.* 1963 NY. Ills 1st ed. dj. VG $25.00

KANE, Elisha Kent. *Arctic Explorations.* 1856 Phil. Ills 1st ed. maps. 2 vol set. $125.00

KANE, Elisha Kent. *US Grinnell Expedition in Search of Sir John Franklin.* 1854 NY. Harper. Ills 1st ed. fld map. VG $90.00

KANE, H.T. *Gentlemen, Swords, & Pistols.* 1951 Bonanza. 306 p. dj. EX $5.00

KANE, H.T. *Lady of Arlington.* 1953 Doubleday. dj. VG $10.00

KANE, H.T. *Pathway to the Stars.* 1950 Doubleday. 1st stated ed. $10.00

KANE, H.T. *Spies for the Blue & Gray.* 1954 Hanover. 1st ed. sgn. EX $25.00

KANE, H.T. *Spies for the Blue & Gray.* 1954 Hanover. 311 p. dj. VG $10.00

KANE, Patricia E. *300 Years of American Seating Furniture.* 1976 Boston. Ills. oblong 4to. 319 p. dj. $50.00

KANE, Paul. *Wanderings of Artist Among Indians of North America.* 1925 Toronto. Ills. 329 p. cloth. VG $35.00

KANIN, Garson. *Born Yesterday.* 1946 Viking. 1st ed. inscr. dj. EX $25.00

KANIN, Garson. *Moviola.* 1979 1st ed. inscr. dj. EX $15.00

KANIUT, Larry. *AK Bear Tales.* 1985 AK Northwest. 318 p. wraps. EX $10.00

KANTOR, MacKinlay. *Daughter of Bugle Ann.* 1953 Random House. 1st ed. 122 p. dj. EX $12.00

KANTOR, MacKinlay. *Hamilton County.* 1970 NY. 1st ed. dj. VG $20.00

KANTOR, MacKinlay. *Romance of Rosy Ridge.* 1937 Coward McCann. Ills Crawford. 96 p. dj. VG $6.50

KANTOR, MacKinlay. *Voice of Bugle Ann.* 1935 Coward McCann. 128 p. dj. VG $8.00

KAPLAN, C. *Salt & Bitter & Good.* 1975 Paddington. Ills. dj. VG $12.50

KAPLAN, M.N. *Big Game Salt-Water Angler's Paradise.* 1937 NY. map. G $18.00

KAPPEL, Philip. *New England Gallery.* 1966 Boston. 1st ed. 4to. inscr. VG $45.00

KAPR, Albert. *Deutsche Schrift Kunst.* c 1950s. Dresden. folio. VG $100.00

KAPROW. *Assemblages, Environments, & Happenings.* 1966 Abrams. $225.00

KARASZ. *12 Days of Christmas.* 1949 NY. juvenile. dj. G $8.50

KARGON, Robert H. *Rise of Robert Millikan.* 1982 Ithaca. 1st ed. 203 p. dj. VG $20.00

KARLEN, T. *Encyclopedia of Basic Craft Techniques.* 1973 NY. Ills. 433 p. $30.00

KARLSTROM, Paul J. *Louis Michel Eilshemius.* 1978 NY. Abrams. Ills. oblong folio. 264 p. dj. $65.00

KARMALI, John. *Birds of Africa.* 1980 Viking. Ills 1st ed. 4to. dj. EX $25.00

KARNOSH, Louis. *Psychiatrist's Anthology.* 1935 Cleveland. 4th ed. VG $15.00

KAROLEVITZ & FEHN. *Flight of Eagles.* 1974 Sious Falls. Ills 1st ed. 281 p. dj. VG $32.50

KARPEL. *Arts in America: Bibliography.* 1979 Smithsonian. 4 vol set. EX $150.00

KARPELES, Gustav. *Jews & Judaism in the 19th Century.* 1905 Phil. 1st ed. 83 p. EX $55.00

KARPELES, Maud. *Cecil Sharp.* 1967 Chicago. Ills 1st ed. dj. VG $20.00

KARPINSKI, L.C. *Bibliography of Printed Maps of MI.* 1931 Lansing. 8vo. cloth. VG $250.00

KARPINSKI, L.C. *History of Arithmetic.* 1925 Rand McNally. 8vo. sgn. cloth. VG $15.00

KARR, Phyllis Ann. *King Arthur Companion.* 1983 Reston. 1st ed. dj. M $30.00

KARRAS, A.L. *North to Cree Lake.* 1970 Trident. Ills. 256 p. dj. EX $14.00

KARSH, Yousuf. *Karsh Portfolio.* 1967 Toronto. Nelson. folio. dj. $50.00

KARSNER, David. *Silver Dollar: Story of the Tabors.* 1949 Crown. Ills. 354 p. dj. EX $10.00

KARTINI, Raden Adjing. *Letters of a Japanese Princess.* 1920 NY. VG $15.00

KASPAR, K. *International Window Display.* 1966 NY. Ills. 151 p. $20.00

KASSLER, Elizabeth B. *Modern Gardens & Landscapes.* 1964 MOMA. Ills. 4to. 96 p. wraps. $12.50

KASTNER, Erich. *Emil & Detectives.* 1930 NY. Ills Trier. 8vo. 235 p. EX $15.00

KASTNER, Erich. *Till Eulenspiegel the Clown.* 1957 NY. Messner. Ills Trier. 1st Am ed. dj. EX $40.00

LANHAM, Url. *Insects.* 1964 Columbia U Pr. Ills. 292 p. dj. EX $10.00

LANIER, H.W.; & FROST, A.B. *American Sportsman's Artist.* 1933 NY. Derrydale. Ills Ltd ed. 1/950. cloth. $115.00

LANIER, Henry W. *Greenwich Village Today & Yesterday.* 1949 NY. 1st ed. 4to. cloth. dj. EX $75.00

LANIER, Sidney. *Boy's King Arthur.* 1943 Scribner. Ills Wyeth. gilt cloth. EX $35.00

LANIER, Sidney. *Boy's King Arthur.* 1933 NY. Scribner. VG $35.00

LANIER, Sidney. *Hymns of the Marshes.* 1907 Scribner. Ills Troth. 1st ed. $35.00

LANIER, Sterling. *Unforsaken Hero.* 1983 NY. 1st ed. dj. VG $10.00

LANKESTER, E. Ray *Extinct Animals.* 1905 Holt. Ills. VG $45.00

LANKESTER, Mrs. *Wild Flowers Worth Noticing.* 1861 Ills JE Sowerby. VG $45.00

LANMAN, Charles. *Tour to River Saguenay in Lower Canada.* 1848 Phil. 12mo. 231 p. G $22.00

LANNER, R. *Trees of the Great Basin.* 1984 Reno. Ills. 215 p. EX $10.00

LANNING, John. *St. Augustine Expedition of 1740.* 1954 Columbia. 1st ed. presentation. VG $35.00

LANTZ, L.K. *Old American Kitchenware 1925-1925.* 1970 NY. Ills. 290 p. $22.50

LANWORN, R.A. *Book of Reptiles.* 1972 Hamlyn. Ills. 4to. 127 p. dj. EX $8.00

LAPMAN, Ben Hur. *Here Comes Somebody.* 1935 Metropolitan. Ills Blaine. 1st ed. tall 8vo. $50.00

LAPSLEY, Brooks. *Writings of Abraham Lincoln.* 1905 NY. Putnam. 8 vol set. $175.00

LARDNER, Dionysius. *Origin, Progressive Improvement & State of Silk Manufacture.* 1832 Phil. Ills 1st Am ed. 12mo. 276 p. $45.00

LARDNER, Dionysius. *Rudimentary Treatise on Steam Engine.* 1848 London. Ills. red cloth. EX $55.00

LARDNER, Dionysius. *Treatise on Hydrostatics & Pneumatics.* 1832 Phil. Ills 1st Am ed. scarce. VG $95.00

LARDNER, John. *Strong Cigars & Lively Women.* 1951 NY. Ills Walt Kelly. dj. EX $30.00

LARDNER, Ring. *Bib Ballads.* 1915 Volland. 1st ed. $85.00

LARDNER, Ring. *Big Town.* 1921 1st ed. 244 p. VG $30.00

LARDNER, Ring. *Ecstacy of Owen Muir.* 1954 NY. 1st ed. dj. EX $20.00

LARDNER, Ring. *Ecstasy of Owen Muir.* 1954 London. 1st ed. dj. VG $15.00

LARDNER, Ring. *How To Write Short Stories.* 1924 NY. 1st ed. VG $25.00

LARDNER, Ring. *My 4 Weeks in France.* 1918 1st ed. 187 p. VG $30.00

LARDNER, Ring. *Own Your Own Home.* 1919 Ills 1st ed. 8vo. 123 p. G $45.00

LARDNER, Ring. *Portable Ring Lardner.* 1946 NY. Viking. Intro Seldes. 1st ed. dj. EX $30.00

LARDNER, Ring. *Round Up.* 1929 NY. 1st ed. cloth. EX $40.00

LARDNER, Ring. *Symptoms of Being 35.* 1921 Indianapolis. 1st ed. VG $20.00

LARDNER, Ring. *Treat 'Em Rough.* 1918 Indianapolis. Ills 1st ed. 2nd issue. G $20.00

LARDNER, Ring. *Treat 'Em Rough.* 1918 Bobbs Merrill. Ills Frank Crerie. 1st ed. VG $55.00

LARDNER, Ring. *What of It?* 1925 NY. 1st ed. VG $30.00

LARDNER, Ring. *1st & Last.* 1934 Scribner. 1st ed. EX $30.00

LARGE, Laura. *Little Stories of a Big Country.* 1935 Platt Munk. dj. VG $12.50

LARIAR, L. *Hunt & Be Damned.* 1956 Prentice Hall. 4to. 96 p. dj. G $6.00

LARKIN, David. *Rousseau.* 1975 NY. 1st ed. wraps. xl. VG $15.00

LARKIN, Lew. *MO Heritage.* 1968 private print. Ills. sgn. 172 p. pb. VG $9.00

LARKIN, Philip. *High Window.* 1974 NY. 1st ed. wraps. M $11.00

LARKIN, Stillman Carter. *Pioneer History of Meigs County.* 1908 Columbus. 1st ed. 208 p. G $85.00

LARNER, E.T. *Practical Television.* 1928 London. Benn. Ills 1st ed. 8vo. 180 p. VG $45.00

LARRABEE, Eric. *American Panorama.* 1957 1st ed. 376 p. dj. VG $25.00

LARSEN, Ernest. *Not a Through Street.* 1981 Random House. Review copy. dj. EX $12.00

LARSEN, Jack Lenor. *Fabrics for Interiors: Guide for Architects & Designers.* 1975 Van Nostrand Reinhold. dj. $25.00

LARSEN, Thor. *World of the Polar Bear.* 1978 Hamlyn. Ills. 4to. dj. EX $12.00

LARSON, Judy L. *Illustration 1890-1925: Romance, Adventure, Suspense.* 1986 Calgary. Ills. 4to. 159 p. wraps. $20.00

LARSON, Knut. *Rugs & Carpets of the Orient.* 1962 London/NY. Revised ed. 219 p. dj. $37.50

LARSON, Knut. *Rugs & Carpets of the Orient.* 1978 London. Warne. Ills Revised ed. 4to. 220 p. $25.00

LARSON, P. *Deserts of America.* 1970 Prentice Hall. Ills. 340 p. dj. EX $18.00

LARSON. *WY War Years 1941-1945.* 1954 WY U Pr. 1st ed. dj. VG $14.00

LARTEGUY, J. *Bronze Drums.* 1967 NY. 1st ed. dj. VG $10.00

LARTIGUE, J.H. *Diary of a Century.* 1970 NY. 1st Am ed. 4to. cloth. VG $85.00

LARTIGUE, J.H. *Les Femmes aux Cigarettes.* 1980 NY. Viking. 1st Am ed. 8vo. cloth. dj. EX $25.00

LARTIGUE, J.H. *Les Femmes.* 1974 NY. 1st Am ed. 4to. cloth. EX $45.00

LARTIGUE, J.H. *Les Photographies de J.H. Lartigue.* 1966 Ami Guichard Editeur. EX $200.00

LASCELLES, Gerald. *Art of Falconry.* 1971 Spearman. reprint of 1892. 163 p. dj. EX $10.00

LASDUN, Susan. *Victorians at Home.* 1981 Studio/Viking. Ills. 4to. 160 p. dj. $20.00

LASHLEY, K. *Brain Mechanisms & Intelligence.* 1929 Chicago. 1st ed. VG $50.00

LASKY, Muriel. *Proud Little Kitten.* 1944 NY. Universal. Ills Erika. slim 4to. VG $15.00

LASSAIGNE, Jacques. *Drawings & Watercolors for the Ballet.* 1969 Paris. Ills Chagall. dj. slipcase. EX $85.00

LASSAIGNE, Jacques. *Marc Chagall: Ceiling of the Paris Opera.* 1966 NY. Praeger. Ills. 4to. cloth. dj. $100.00

LASSIMONNE & FERGUSON. *Myra Hess by Her Friends.* 1967 NY. Vanguard. VG $8.00

LASSWELL, Mary. *Tio Pepe.* 1963 Boston. 1st ed. dj. M $16.00

LATHAM, Aaron. *Crazy Sundays: F. Scott Fitzgerald in Hollywood.* 1971 NY. Viking. 1st ed. 8vo. dj. EX $40.00

LATHAM, Jean Lee. *On Stage, Mr. Jefferson!* 1958 NY. Harper. Ills Shenton. 1st ed. dj. VG $12.50

LATHAM, Philip. *5 Against Venus.* 1952 Winston. 1st ed. juvenile. dj. EX $20.00

LATHAM, R.M. *Complete Book of the Wild Turkey.* 1977 Stackpole. New Revised ed. 228 p. dj. EX $8.50

LATHAM, Wilfrid. *States of River Plate.* 1868 London. Longman Green. 2nd ed. 381 p. $75.00

LATHROP, D. *History of 59th Regiment IL Volunteers.* 1865 Indianapolis. VG $120.00

LATHROP, Dorothy P. *Silverhorn: Hilda Conkling Book for Other Children.* 1924 Stokes. Ills. 8vo. 159 p. cloth. VG $50.00

LATHROP, Dorothy P. *Skittle-Skattle Monkey.* 1945 Macmillan. Ills 1st ed. 8vo. red cloth. $20.00

LATHROP, Elise. *Early American Inns & Taverns.* 1935 NY. Ills. VG $20.00

LATHROP, Elise. *Early American Inns & Taverns.* 1946 NY. Ills. dj. $15.00

LATHROP, William G. *Brass Industry in US.* 1926 Mt. Carmel, CT. Revised ed. 174 p. VG $12.50

LATHROP. *Migration into East TX 1835-1860.* 1949 Austin. TX State Hist Assn. VG $10.00

LATIMORE, S.R.; & HASKELL, G. *Arthur Rackham: A Bibliography.* 1936 Los Angeles. Ritchie. Ltd ed. 1/550. 8vo. $100.00

LATROBE, Ferdinand C. *Iron Men & Their Dogs.* 1941 Baltimore. Ills. VG $22.50

LATTIMORE, Owen. *Desert Road to Turkestan.* 1929 Little Brown. Ills 1st ed. 373 p. G $7.50

LATTIMORE, Owen. *Desert Road to Turkestan.* 1929 Boston. 1st ed. 8vo. 373 p. VG $15.00

LATTIMORE, Owen. *Inner Asian Frontiers of China.* 1940 Am Geog Soc. 585 p. maps. VG $35.00

LAUDAN, Stanley. *White Baton.* 1957 London. 1st ed. dj. VG $15.00

LAUDER, Harry. *Minstrel in France.* 1918 Hearst. Ills. 338 p. VG $6.50

LAUFE, Abe. *Broadway's Greatest Musicals.* 1977 Funk Wagnall. Ills Revised ed. VG $12.00

LAUFER, Berthold. *Jade: Study in Chinese Archaeology & Religion.* 1912 South Pasadena. Perkins. Ills 2nd ed. $70.00

LAUFER, Berthold. *Jade: Study in Chinese Archaeology & Religion.* 1912 Chicago. wraps. xl. $95.00

LAUGHLIN, C.J. *Ghosts Along the MS.* 1961 NY. 4to. cloth. dj. EX $35.00

LAUGHLIN, C.J. *Ghosts Along the MS.* 1948 NY. Ills 1st ed. 4to. dj. $50.00

LAUGHLIN, James. *New Directions in Prose & Poetry.* 1939 Norfolk. Ills. 390 p. VG $30.00

LAUMER, Keith. *Time Trap.* 1970 NY. Review copy. dj. VG $20.00

LAURENCE, Margaret. *Fire Dwellers.* 1969 NY. 1st ed. dj. EX $12.50

LAURENCE, Margaret. *Tomorrow-Tamer: Short Stories.* 1963 London. Macmillan. 1st ed. VG $75.00

LAURENCE, William L. *Dawn Over Zero: Story of the Atomic Bomb.* 1946 NY. 1st ed. inscr. VG $35.00

LAURENTS, Arthur. *Clearing in the Woods.* 1957 NY. 1st ed. dj. EX $12.00

LAURIE, Andre. *Schoolboys in Japan.* 1895 Boston. Ills. G $40.00

LAURIE, David. *Reminiscences of a Fiddle Dealer.* no date. London. VG $35.00

LAURIE, Joe. *Vaudeville From Honkytonks to the Palace.* 1953 NY. Holt. 1st ed. 525 p. dj. $20.00

LAUT, A.C. *Blazed Trail of Old Frontier.* 1926 NY. Ills Charles Russell. VG $50.00

LAUT, A.C. *Fur Trade of America.* 1921 Macmillan. Ills 1st ed. 314 p. VG $30.00

LAUTERBACH, R.E. *Danger From the East.* 1947 NY/London. G $12.00

LAVALLE, Major A.J.C. *Air Power & the 1972 Spring Invasion.* 1976 GPO. Ills. 113 p. maps. wraps. EX $10.00

LAVALLE, Major A.J.C. *Tale of 2 Bridges & the Battle for Skies Over North Vietnam.* 1984 GPO. Ills. 193 p. wraps. EX $10.00

LAVALLE, Major A.J.C. *Vietnamese Air Force 1951-1975.* 1977 GPO. Ills. 161 p. wraps. EX $10.00

LAVENDER, David. *Bent's Fort.* 1954 Garden City. 1st ed. dj. VG $20.00

LAVENDER, David. *CA: Land of New Beginnings.* 1972 Harper Row. 1st stated ed. dj. $10.00

LAVENDER, David. *Great Persuader: Biography of Collis P. Huntington.* 1970 Garden City. Doubleday. 1st ed. dj. G $20.00

LAVENDER, David. *Land of the Giants.* 1958 Doubleday. dj. VG $14.50

LAVENDER, David. *Westward Vision: OR Trail.* 1963 London. 1st ed. 3rd print. dj. VG $30.00

LAVENDER, David. *Westward Vision: OR Trail.* 1963 McGraw Hill. 1st ed. dj. G $20.00

LAVENDER, David. *Westward Vision: OR Trail.* 1963 NY. 1st ed. Am Trails Series. dj. VG $45.00

LAVENDER, David. *1 Man's West.* 1956 Garden City. New ed. dj. VG $12.50

LAVER, James. *Costume of the Western World.* 1951 NY. Ills 1st Am ed. 4to. 390 p. EX $25.00

LAVER, James. *Costume of the Western World.* 1963 London. Ills 1st ed. 4to. 136 p. dj. $25.00

LAVER, James. *Ladies' Mistakes.* 1933 London. Nonesuch. Ltd ed. VG $35.00

LAVER, James. *Ladies' Mistakes.* 1934 NY. Knopf. 1st ed. 8vo. dj. VG $15.00

LAVER, James. *Love's Progress; or, Education of Araminta.* 1929 Bloomsbury. Ltd ed. 1/1,525. 4to. VG $55.00

LAVER, James. *Stitch in Time; or, Prevents a Fall.* 1927 London. Ltd ed. 1/1,525. 4to. dj. VG $60.00

LAVIN, Mary. *At Sallygap & Other Stories.* 1947 Little Brown. 1st ed. inscr. dj. VG $75.00

LAVIN, Mary. *Memory & Other Stories.* 1973 Boston. 1st ed. dj. VG $12.50

LAW, William. *Extract From a Serious Call to a Devout & Holy Life.* 1757 Dublin. 264 p. rebound. VG $195.00

LAWING, Nellie N. *AK Nellie.* 1940 Chieftan Pr. Ills. 201 p. EX $40.00

LAWLER, James J. *Lawler's American Sanitary Plumbing.* 1896 NY. Revised ed. 313 p. G $27.50

LAWLESS, Ray M. *Folk Singers & Folk Songs in America.* 1960 NY. 1st ed. G $12.00

LAWRENCE, D.H. *Aaron's Rod.* 1922 London. Martin Secker. 1st English ed. $40.00

LAWRENCE, D.H. *Apropos of Lady Chatterley's Lover.* 1930 Mandrake Pr. 1st ed. dj. VG $65.00

LAWRENCE, D.H. *Frieda Lawrence Collection of D.H. Lawrence Manuscripts.* 1948 Albuquerque. 1st ed. 8vo. 333 p. EX $27.00

LAWRENCE, D.H. *Glad Ghosts.* 1926 London. Ltd ed. 1/500. 12mo. 77 p. wraps. EX $175.00

LAWRENCE, D.H. *Kangaroo.* 1923 London. 1st ed. dj. VG $140.00

LAWRENCE, D.H. *Lady Chatterley's Lover.* 1928 Florence. private print. Ltd 1st ed. dj. $250.00

LAWRENCE, D.H. *Lady Chatterley's Lover.* 1956 Stockholm. Continental ed. scarce. EX $45.00

LAWRENCE, D.H. *Mornings in Mexico.* 1927 NY. 1st ed. 1st print. dj. EX $65.00

LAWRENCE, D.H. *Mornings in Mexico.* 1927 London. 1st ed. 2nd imp. VG $20.00

LAWRENCE, D.H. *My Skirmish with Jolly Roger.* 1929 Random House. Ltd 1st ed. 1/600. EX $50.00

LAWRENCE, D.H. *New Poems.* 1918 London. 1st ed. 3/4 morocco. EX $30.00

LAWRENCE, D.H. *Paintings of D.H. Lawrence.* 1964 NY. Viking. 1st ed. dj. EX $25.00

LAWRENCE, D.H. *Phoenix: Posthumous Papers of D.H. Lawrence.* 1936 NY. Viking. 852 p. dj. VG $65.00

LAWRENCE, D.H. *Rainbow.* 1915 London. Methuen. blue-green cloth. VG $375.00

LAWRENCE, D.H. *Rawdon's Roof.* 1928 London. Mathews Marrot. 1st ed. 1/530. $400.00

LAWRENCE, D.H. *Sea & Sardina.* 1921 NY. Ills Juta. 1st ed. VG $35.00

LAWRENCE, D.H. *Ship of Death & Other Poems.* 1933 London. Ills B Hughes-Stanton. VG $25.00

LAWRENCE, D.H. *Sons & Lovers.* 1975 Ltd Ed Club. Ills/sgn S Robinson. slipcase. $60.00

LAWRENCE, D.H. *St. Mawr.* 1925 NY. Knopf. 1st Am ed. VG $15.00

LAWRENCE, D.H. *St. Mawr.* 1925 London. 1st ed. cloth. VG $15.00

LAWRENCE, D.H. *Widowing of Mrs. Holroyd.* 1914 NY. Kennerley. 1st ed. 8vo. red cloth. VG $125.00

LAWRENCE, David. *True Story of Woodrow Wilson.* 1924 Doran. VG $10.00

LAWRENCE, Frieda. *Not I But the Wind.* 1934 Santa Fe. Ltd ed. 1/1,000. sgn. dj. $175.00

LAWRENCE, H. *Bloody War 1939-1945.* 1979 Ontario. Ills. 193 p. maps. dj. EX $20.00

LAWRENCE, J. *Caves Beyond.* 1955 NY. Ills 1st ed. 283 p. dj. VG $25.00

LAWRENCE, John. *Clergyman's Recreation.* 1717 London. Ills. G $110.00

LAWRENCE, John. *Rogues, Vagabonds, & Sturdy Beggars.* 1973 Impression Soc. dj. slipcase. EX $40.00

LAWRENCE, Margery. *Number 7 Queer Street.* 1969 Sauk City. 1st ed. $25.00

LAWRENCE, Maude; & SHELDON, C. *Use of the Plant in Decoration.* 1912 NY. Ills Teacher ed. 4to. 78 p. VG $35.00

LAWRENCE, Robert. *Lohengrin.* 1938 NY. Ills Serebriafoff. dj. EX $12.00

LAWRENCE, T.E. *Crusader Castles.* 1936 Golden Cockerel. Ltd ed. 4to. $425.00

LAWRENCE, T.E. *Die Sieben Saulen der Weisheit.* 1936 Leipzig. 1st German ed. VG $55.00

LAWRENCE, T.E. *Letters of T.E. Lawrence.* 1939 NY. 1st ed. VG $25.00

LAWRENCE, T.E. *Minorities.* 1971 London. Rota Cape. 1st ed. 1/125. EX $250.00

LAWRENCE, T.E. *Odyssey.* 1932 NY. 2nd print. VG $25.00

LAWRENCE, T.E. *Revolt in the Desert.* 1927 Garden City. 1st Am ed. 12mo. 335 p. $20.00

LAWRENCE, T.E. *Revolt.* NY. reprint of 1927. VG $14.00

LAWRENCE, T.E. *Wilderness of Zin.* 1915 London. Ills. 2 fld maps. 4to. $275.00

LAWRENCE, T.E. *7 Pillars of Wisdom.* 1935 Garden City. Ills 1st ed. 672 p. dj. $15.00

LAWRENCE, T.E. *7 Pillars of Wisdom.* 1935 London. Ills. gilt red morocco. $90.00

LAWRENCE, T.E. *7 Pillars of Wisdom.* 1935 Ills 1st trade ed. 672 p. dj. $8.00

LAWRENCE, Vera B. *Music for Patriots, Politicians, & Presidents.* 1975 NY. Ills 1st ed. 480. dj. EX $35.00

LAWRENCE. *Condoliers.* 1940 Grosset Dunlap. Ills 1st ed. VG $10.00

LAWRIE, W.H. *English Trout Flies.* 1969 Barnes. Ills 1st Am ed. dj. EX $10.00

LAWSON, Marie A. *Sea Is Blue.* 1946 NY. Viking. Ills 1st ed. 8vo. dj. EX $15.00

LAWSON, Robert. *Country Colic.* 1944 Little Brown. 1st ed. VG $25.00

LAWSON, Robert. *I Discover Columbus.* 1941 Boston. 1st ed. dj. EX $35.00

LAWSON, Robert. *Pilgrim's Progress.* 1939 Stokes. 1st ed. dj. VG $27.50

LAWSON, Robert. *Rabbit Hill.* 1944 NY. Viking. Ills. tall 8vo. VG $10.00

LAWSON, Robert. *Tough Winter.* 1954 NY. Viking. Ills 1st ed. tall 8vo. VG $20.00

LAWSON, Robert. *Wee Men of Ballywooden.* 1939 Doran. Ills 1st ed. black cloth. VG $25.00

LAWSON, W.P. *Log of a Timber Cruiser.* 1926 Duffield. photos. $10.00

LAWSON, Will. *Between the Lights.* 1906 Wellington. 8vo. sgn. VG $20.00

LAWSON & KRAMER. *Conversations with Walker Percy.* 1985 MS U Pr. 1st ed. dj. EX $25.00

LAYARD. *Suppressed Plates.* 1907 London. Black. VG $30.00

LAYCOCK, George. *Autumn of the Eagle.* 1973 Scribner. Ills 1st ed. 239 p. dj. EX $14.00

LAYCOCK, George. *Wild Hunters: North American Preditors.* 1978 McKay. Ills 1st ed. 121 p. dj. EX $8.00

LAYMAN, R.D. *Cuxhaven Raid: World's 1st Carrier Air Strike.* 1985 Greenwich. Ills. dj. EX $22.50

LAYNG, C. *Cross Word Puzzles: 1st Book.* 1924 Chicago. 1st ed. dj. $45.00

LAYTHA, Edgar. *North Again for Gold.* 1939 Stokes. 1st ed. presentation. sgn. G $35.00

LAZAREV, V.N. *Novgorodian Icon Painting.* 1969 Moscow. Ills. Russian/English text. dj. VG $40.00

LAZAREV, Viktor. *Old Russian Murals & Mosaics.* 1966 London. Phaidon. Ills. 4to. dj. $60.00

LAZELL, J.A. *Alaskan Apostle: Life Story of Sheldon Jackson.* 1960 Harper. Ills. 218 p. dj. VG $18.00

LAZENBY, Elizabeth. *Ireland: Catspaw.* 1929 Charter. 12mo. dj. $5.00

LAZLO, Kate. *Forever After.* 1981 Dial. Advance copy. wraps. $10.00

LE BLANC, Georgette. *Children's Bluebird.* 1945 NY. Ills Paus. inscr. G $15.00

LE BLONDE, Mrs. Aubrey. *Adventures on the Roof of the World.* no date. London. G $12.50

LE CARRE, John. *Call for the Dead.* 1962 Walker. 1st Am ed. dj. EX $25.00

LE CARRE, John. *Call for the Dead.* 1961 reprint of 1st English ed. dj. $15.00

LE CARRE, John. *Clandestine Muse.* 1986 Portland. Ltd ed. 1/250 sgn. wraps. M $75.00

LE CARRE, John. *Honorable Schoolboy.* 1977 Knopf. 1st Am ed. dj. EX $20.00

LE CARRE, John. *Little Drummer Girl.* 1983 Knopf. 1st ed. dj. VG $12.00

LE CARRE, John. *Looking Glass War.* NY. Coward McCann. 320 p. $5.00

LE CARRE, John. *Looking Glass War.* 1965 London. Heinemann. 1st ed. cloth. dj. $25.00

LE CARRE, John. *Murder of Quality.* 1962 reprint of 1st English ed. $15.00

LE CARRE, John. *Naive & Sentimental Lover.* 1972 Knopf. 1st Am ed. dj. EX $20.00

LE CARRE, John. *Perfect Spy.* 1986 Advance copy. SftCvr. red wraps. EX $75.00

LE CARRE, John. *Perfect Spy.* 1986 NY. 1st Am ed. sgn. dj. EX $95.00

LE CARRE, John. *Perfect Spy.* 1986 Knopf. 1st ed. dj. EX $20.00

LE CARRE, John. *Perfect Spy.* 1986 London. Ltd ed. 1/250. sgn. wraps. M $150.00

LE CARRE, John. *Small Town in Germany.* 1968 Heinemann. 1st English ed. dj. EX $60.00

LE CARRE, John. *Small Town in Germany.* 1968 Coward McCann. 1st Am ed. dj. EX $30.00

LE CARRE, John. *Smiley's People.* 1979 London. 1st ed. dj. EX $35.00

LE CARRE, John. *Smiley's People.* 1980 Knopf. 1st Am ed. dj. EX $15.00

LE CARRE, John. *Spy Who Came in From the Cold.* 1964 Coward McCann. 1st Am ed. dj. EX $35.00

LE CARRE, John. *Tinker, Tailor, Soldier, Spy.* 1974 Knopf. 1st Am ed. dj. EX $20.00

LE CARRE, John. *Tinker, Tailor, Soldier, Spy.* 1974 London. Hodder Stoughton. 1st ed. dj. $30.00

LE CLEZIO, J.M.G. *War.* 1973 NY. 1st ed. dj. EX $12.00

LE CORBEILLER. *Snuff Boxes.* Viking. dj. EX $75.00

LE CORBUSIER & HEPPERESTALL. *Cistercian Abbey of Le Thornonnet in Provence.* 1957 NY. 1st Am ed. VG $35.00

LE CORBUSIER. *Looking at City Planning.* 1971 NY. Grossman. dj. EX $15.00

LE CORBUSIER. *When Cathedrals Were White.* 1947 NY. 1st Am ed. dj. VG $25.00

LE FROY, Anna Austen. *Jane Austen's Sandition.* 1983 Chicago. Ltd 1st ed. 1/500. dj. $40.00

LE GALLIENNE, Richard. *Old Country House.* 1905 Harper. 4to. VG $40.00

LE GALLIENNE, Richard. *Religion of a Literary Man.* 1893 London. 1st ed. presentation. G $75.00

LE GALLIENNE, Richard. *Romance of Perfume.* 1928 NY/Paris. Ills Barbier. VG $60.00

LE GRAND, Edy. *Macao et Cosmage.* 1919 Paris. square folio. G $80.00

LE GUIN, U.K. *Beginning Place.* 1980 NY. proof. sgn. VG $60.00

LE GUIN, U.K. *Beginning Place.* 1980 NY. 1st ed. dj. EX $25.00

LE GUIN, U.K. *City of Illusions, Planet of Exile, & Rocannon's World.* 1975 Garland Pr. 1st HrdCvr ed. 3 vols in 1. $450.00

LE GUIN, U.K. *Compass Rose.* 1982 NY. 1st ed. sgn. dj. EX $25.00

LE GUIN, U.K. *Dispossessed.* 1974 NY. 1st ed. dj. VG $20.00

LE GUIN, U.K. *Dreams Must Explain Themselves.* 1975 NY. Ltd ed. wraps. EX $20.00

LE GUIN, U.K. *Eye of the Heron.* 1978 NY. 1st ed. M $15.00

LE GUIN, U.K. *From Elfland to Poughkeepsie.* 1973 Portland. Ltd 1st ed. wraps. M $45.00

LE GUIN, U.K. *Hard Words & Other Poems.* 1981 NY. 1st ed. dj. EX $25.00

LE GUIN, U.K. *Language of the Night.* 1979 NY. 1st ed. M $25.00

LE GUIN, U.K. *Left Hand of Darkness.* 1979 NY. 1st ed. dj. EX $20.00

LE GUIN, U.K. *Malafrena.* 1979 NY. 1st ed. M $25.00

LE GUIN, U.K. *Orsinian Tales.* 1976 NY. 1st ed. dj. EX $25.00

LE GUIN, U.K. *Planet of Exile & Rocannon's World.* Ace Doubles. 1st ed. EX $25.00

LE GUIN, U.K. *Planet of Exile.* 1966 NY. Ace. 1st ed. 8vo. wraps. VG $35.00

LE GUIN, U.K. *Planet of Exile.* 1978 NY. 1st ed. dj. EX $20.00

LE GUIN, U.K. *Torrey Pines Reserve.* 1980 Lord John. Ltd ed. EX $35.00

LE GUIN, U.K. *Very Far Away From Anywhere Else.* 1976 NY. 1st ed. 2nd state. M $25.00

LE GUIN, U.K. *Water Is Wide.* 1976 Portland. Ills Ltd ed. 1/50. sgn. M $80.00

LE GUIN, U.K. *Wizard of Earthsea.* 1968 Berkeley. 1st ed. 2nd state. dj. EX $80.00

LE GUIN, U.K. *World for World Is Forest.* 1972 NY. 1st ed. dj. EX $65.00

LE JEUNE, General. *Reminiscences of a Marine.* 1930 Phil. 2nd print. dj. VG $32.50

LE MARCHAND, Elizabeth. *Death on Doomsday.* 1971 London. 1st ed. dj. VG $20.00

LE MAY, Curtis E. *Mission with Le May.* 1965 sgn. 581 p. dj. VG $20.00

LE MOINE, J.M. *Picturesque Quebec.* 1882 Montreal. Dawson. 8vo. gilt blue cloth. $52.00

LE MOINE, J.M. *Quebec: Past & Present 1608-1876.* 1876 Quebec. Augustic Cote. 1st ed. 8vo. VG $75.00

LE MOINE, J.M. *Seaside Series: Chronicles of the St. Laurence.* 1878 Montreal. Dawson. 8vo. gilt brown cloth. $65.00

LE PLONGEON, Augustus. *Queen Moo & Egyptian Sphinx.* 1900 private print. presentation. 277 p. G $135.00

LE PLONGEON, Augustus. *Sacred Mysteries Among Themayas & the Quiches.* 1886 NY. Ills 1st ed. 163 p. EX $95.00

LE ROUX & GARNIER. *Acrobats & Mountebanks.* 1890 London. Ills 1st ed. 8vo. 336 p. $125.00

LEA, Tom. *Hand of Catu.* 1964 Ills 2nd ed. sgn. cloth. VG $22.00

LEA, Tom. *King Ranch.* 1957 Boston. 1st ed. 1st state. boxed. VG $75.00

LEA, Tom. *Picture Gallery.* 1968 Little Brown. Ills 1st ed. slipcase. $85.00

LEA, Tom. *Wonderful Country.* 1952 Ills 2nd print. 8vo. cloth. VG $6.00

LEA, Zilla R. *Ornamented Chair: Its Development in America 1700-1890.* 1960 Tuttle. Ills 4to. 173 p. dj. $100.00

LEACH, Brownie. *KY Derby Jubilee 1875-1949.* 1949 Review copy. 4to. 192 p. dj. EX $75.00

LEACH, Charles R. *In Tornado's Wake.* 1956 Chicago. Ills 1st ed. 232 p. cloth. VG $45.00

LEACH, David G. *Rhododendrons of the World.* 1961 NY. Scribner. 1st ed. 544 p. EX $75.00

LEACH, Frank A. *Recollections of a Newspaperman.* 1917 San Francisco. 8vo. dj. VG $20.00

LEACH, H.G. *Pageant of Old Scandinavia.* 1946 Princeton U Pr. dj. EX $13.00

LEACH, Joseph. *Typical Texan: Biography of an American Myth.* 1952 SMU Pr. 1st ed. dj. EX $25.00

LEACOCK, S. *Arcadian Adventures with Idle Rich.* 1914 NY. fair. $12.00

LEACOCK, S. *Greatest Pages of Charles Dickens.* 1934 Doubleday. 1st ed. dj. VG $15.00

LEACOCK, S. *Nonsense Novels.* 1921 Ills Kettlewell. VG $75.00

LEADBEATER, C.W. *Inner Life.* 1911 263 p. G $16.00

LEADBEATER, C.W. *Some Glimpses of Occultism: Ancient & Modern.* 1919 CA. 3rd ed. 382 p. VG $26.00

LEAF, Horace. *What Mediumship Is.* 1948 168 p. dj. VG $18.00

LEAF, Munro *Story of Ferdinand the Bull.* 1936 NY. Ills Lawson. 14th print. VG $45.00

LEAF, Munro. *Aesop's Fables.* c 1941. NY. Heritage. Ills Lawson. G $12.00

LEAF, Munro. *El Cuento de Ferdinando.* 1962 NY. Viking. Ills Lawson. 1st ed. dj. EX $15.00

LEAF, Munro. *Ferdinandus Taurus.* 1962 McKay. Ills Lawson. 1st ed. dj. VG $14.00

LEAF, Munro. *Geography Can Be Fun.* 1951 Lippincott. Ills 1st ed. 4to. EX $15.00

LEAF, Munro. *Grammar Can Be Fun.* 1934 NY. Ills 2nd print. VG $12.00

LEAF, Munro. *Manners Can Be Fun.* 1936 Stokes. VG $15.00

LEAF, Munro. *Story of Ferdinand the Bull.* 1936 NY. Ills Lawson. 20th print. EX $47.50

LEAF, Munro. *Story of Ferdinand the Bull.* 1938 NY. Ills Robert Lawson. VG $17.50

LEAF, Munro. *Story of Ferdinand the Bull.* 1936 NY. Viking. Ills Lawson. 3rd print. $20.00

LEAF, Munro. *War-Time Handbook for Young Americans.* 1942 Stokes. 1st ed. VG $20.00

LEAKEY, L.S.B. *Animals of East Africa.* 1969 Nat'l Geog Soc. Ills. 199 p. maps. EX $14.00

LEANTE, C. *Capitan de Cimarrones.* 1982 Argos Vergara. Spanish text. pb. EX $7.50

LEAR, Edward. *Collected Nonsense Songs.* 1947 London. Ills 1st ed. dj. VG $18.00

LEAR, Edward. *Nonsense Books.* 1888 Little Brown. Ills 5th ed. red cloth. VG $20.00

LEAR, Edward. *Scroobious Pip.* 1968 Harper Row. Ills Burkert. folio. linen. VG $22.00

LEAR, Edward. *Story of the 4 Little Children Who Went Round the World.* 1967 Harlin Quist. Ills Mack. 1st HrdCvr ed. $15.00

LEARY, Timothy. *High Priest.* 1968 NY. 1st ed. dj. VG $25.00

LEARY, Timothy. *Psychedelic Experience: Manual on Tibetan Book of Dead.* 1964 NY. 1st ed. EX $90.00

LEASK, H. *Irish Castles & Castelated Houses.* 1951 Dunkalk. Ills. 170 p. dj. VG $18.00

LEASOR, James. *Who Killed Sir Harry Oakes?* 1983 Boston. Houghton Mifflin. 1st ed. dj. $10.00

LEAT, Harry. *Magic of the Depots.* 1923 London. 1st ed. 8vo. 79 p. wraps. $35.00

LEAVITT, David. *Family Dancing.* 1984 NY. Knopf. 1st ed. dj. M $30.00

LECKY, S.T.S. *Wrinkles in Practical Navigation.* 1904 London. Ills 14th ed. 812 p. VG $15.00

LECLER, Rene. *Sahara.* 1954 Hanover House. Ills 1st ed. 280 p. dj. VG $14.00

LECLERC, Leon. *Normads.* no date. Paris. Massin. Ills. dj. $40.00

LECORCHE, E.; & TALAMON, C. *Traite de l'Albuminure et du Mal de Bright.* 1888 Paris. 774 p. EX $25.00

LEDOUX-LEBARD, Denise. *2nd Empire.* no date. Paris. Massin. Ills. dj. $45.00

LEE, Albert. *Tommy Toddles.* 1896 Harper. Ills Newell. 1st ed. 192 p. VG $25.00

LEE, Bourke. *Death Valley.* 1930 NY. Ills 1st ed. 210 p. VG $32.50

LEE, Charles Carter. *Observations on Writings of Thomas Jefferson.* 1839 Phil. 2nd ed. 8vo. cloth. G $85.00

LEE, Edward M. *CA Gold: Quarters, Halves, Dollars.* 1932 Glendale. private print. rare. EX $120.00

LEE, Frederic P. *Azalea Book.* 1958 Princeton. 1st ed. EX $45.00

LEE, Frederic P. *Azalea Book.* 1958 Van Nostrand. VG $20.00

LEE, Gerald Stanley. *Inspired Millionaires.* 1908 Northampton. 12mo. inscr. VG $20.00

LEE, H. *Radio Joke Book.* 1935 Phil. Ills 1st ed. wraps. VG $25.00

LEE, Harper. *To Kill a Mockingbird.* 1960 London. Heinemann. 1st ed. dj. VG $45.00

LEE, John B. *Fighter Facts & Fallacies.* 1942 NY. Ills. cloth. dj. $50.00

LEE, Laurie. *As I Walked Out Midsummer Morning.* 1985 Norton. 1st Am ed. dj. EX $23.00

LEE, Laurie. *Cider with Rosie.* 1959 London. Ills J Ward. 1st ed. dj. VG $17.00

LEE, Laurie. *Edge of Day.* 1960 NY. Ills J Ward. 1st Am ed. VG $15.00

LEE, Mable Barbee. *Cripple Creek.* 1958 Garden City. dj. VG $15.00

LEE, Nathanael. *Dramatic Works of Nathanael Lee.* 1734 London. rebound. VG $45.00

LEE, Robert E. *Wartime Papers.* 1961 944 p. dj. VG $18.50

LEE, Ruth Webb. *Antique Fakes & Reproductions.* 1950 Lee Pub. Ills 7th ed. 8vo. 335 p. $20.00

LEE, Ruth Webb. *Early American Pressed Glass.* 1960 Lee Pub. Ills 34th ed. 8vo. 696 p. dj. $25.00

LEE, S.P. *Report & Charts of the Cruise of US Dolphin.* 1854 WA. G $50.00

LEE, Sherman E. *History of Far Eastern Art.* 1964 NY. 1st ed. dj. VG $45.00

LEE, Tina. *How To Make Dolls & Doll Houses.* 1948 Garden City. dj. EX $12.00

LEE, Vernon. *Snake Lady & Other Stories.* 1954 Grove Pr. 1st ed. dj. EX $35.00

LEECH, John. *Little Tour of Ireland.* 1896 London. Arnold. 3rd ed. 255 p. VG $95.00

LEECH, John. *Little Tour of Ireland.* 1859 London. Bradbury Evans. 1st ed. 200 p. $275.00

LEECH, John. *Pictures of Life & Character From Collection of Mr. Punch.* 1854-1869. London. 5 Series in 2 vols. $225.00

LEECH, John. *Young Troublesome; or, Master Jack's Holidays.* Ills. ¾-calf. rebound. EX $200.00

LEECH, Margaret. *In the Days of McKinley.* 1959 NY. Ills 1st ed. 686 p. dj. VG $12.50

LEECH, Margaret. *Reveille in WA 1860-1865.* 1941 Harper. Ills. 483 p. VG $15.00

LEEDALE, G.F. *Euglenoid Flagellates.* 1967 Prentice Hall. Ills 1st ed. 242 p. dj. VG $14.00

LEEDER, S.H. *Veiled Mysteries of Egypt.* 1913 Scribner. Ills. 411 p. purple cloth. VG $26.00

LEEDS, Lewis W. *Lectures on Ventilation.* 1868 NY. Wiley. Ills 1st ed. 60 p. xl. VG $35.00

LEEMING, J. *Modern Ship Stowage.* 1942 GPO. Ills. G $12.00

LEEPER, David Rohrer. *Argonauts of '49: Recollections of Plains & Diggings.* 1950 Columbus. reprint of 1894. 95 p. wraps. $35.00

LEEPER, Janet. *Edward Gordon Craig Designs for the Theatre.* 1948 Middlesex. Penguin. Ills. 8vo. scarce. $35.00

LEEPER, John P. *Jules Pascin's Caribbean.* 1964 TX U Pr. Ills. 4to. 116 p. dj. $50.00

LEES, A.D. *Physiology of Diapause in Arthropods.* 1955 Cambridge U Pr. Ills. 151 p. dj. EX $15.00

LEES, J. *Masting & Rigging of English Ships of War 1625-1860.* 1984 Greenwich. New Revised ed. dj. EX $38.00

LEFEVRE, Edwin. *Reminiscences of Stock Operator.* 1923 Larchmont. dj. fair. $25.00

LEFEVRE, Felicite. *Topsy Turvy.* 1928 Macrae Smith. Ills Thomas. plts/silhouettes. $16.00

LEFKOFF, Gerald. *Computer Applications in Music.* 1967 Morgantown, WV. Ills Review copy. VG $12.00

LEGGE, James. *Li Chi Book of Rites.* 1967 NY. University Books. 2 vol set. $75.00

LEGGETT, John. *Ross & Tom: 2 American Tragedies.* 1974 Simon Schuster. 1st ed. inscr. dj. xl. VG $25.00

LEGMAN, Gershon. *Fake Revolt.* 1967 Breaking Point. 1st ed. 8vo. wraps. $30.00

LEGMAN, Gershon. *Horn Book.* 1964 New Hyde Park. 1st ed. dj. EX $20.00

LEGMAN, Gershon. *Love & Death: Study in Censorship.* 1949 NY. Breaking Point. 1st ed. wraps. $45.00

LEGMAN, Gershon. *New Limerick. 2nd Series.* 1977 NY. Crown. Review copy. dj. EX $25.00

LEGRAND, E. *Macao et Cosmage.* 1919 Paris. Fab Pochior. VG $225.00

LEGRAND, E. *Voyages des Grands Navigateurs.* 1921 Paris. Fab Pochoir. VG $250.00

LEHMAN, Milton. *This High Man: Life of Robert Goddard.* 1963 Farrar Straus. Ills 1st ed. 8vo. 430 p. dj. $15.00

LEHMANN, Rosamund. *Echoing Grove.* 1953 London. 1st ed. dj. VG $22.00

LEHMANN, V.W. *Bobwhites in the Rio Grande Plain of TX.* 1984 TX A&M U Pr. Ills 1st ed. 4to. dj. EX $30.00

LEHMANN, V.W. *Forgotten Legions: Sheep in Rio Grande Plain of TX.* 1969 TX Western Pr. Ills 1st ed. 266 p. dj. M $12.00

LEHMANN-HAUPT, Christopher. *Me & Dimaggio.* 1986 Simon Schuster. 1st ed. sgn. dj. M $15.00

LEHMANN-HAUPT, Hellmut. *Art Under Dictatorship.* NY. Oxford U Pr. dj. G $13.00

LEHMANN-HAUPT, Hellmut. *70 Books About Bookmaking.* 1941 Columbia U Pr. 66 p. VG $10.00

LEHNER, Ernest. *Alphabets & Ornaments.* 1952 Cleveland/NY. 1st ed. folio. 256 p. dj. EX $55.00

LEIBER, Fritz. *Best of Fritz Leiber.* 1974 NY. Ballantine. 1st print. inscr. wraps. $20.00

LEIBER, Fritz. *Big Time.* 1961 NY. Ace. 1st Separate ed. sgn. wraps. $15.00

LEIBER, Fritz. *Conjure Wife.* 1970 NY. Award. sgn. wraps. $15.00

LEIBER, Fritz. *Gather, Darkness!* 1950 Berkeley. 1st Medallion ed. sgn. wraps. $15.00

LEIBER, Fritz. *Green Millennium.* 1953 NY. Ace. later print. sgn. wraps. $15.00

LEIBER, Fritz. *Green Millennium.* 1954 NY. 1st Lion ed. sgn. wraps. VG $15.00

LEIBER, Fritz. *Night Black Agents.* 1947 Sauk City. Arkham House. 1st ed. inscr. $70.00

LEIBER, Fritz. *Night Black Agents.* 1961 NY. Ballantine. Ills 1st ed. sgn. wraps. VG $15.00

LEIBER, Fritz. *Night of the Wolf.* 1966 NY. 1st ed. inscr. G $15.00

LEIBER, Fritz. *Our Lady of Darkness.* 1977 Berkeley. 1st ed. inscr. dj. EX $70.00

LEIBER, Fritz. *Specter Is Haunting TX.* 1971 NY. Bantam. 1st ed. inscr. wraps. $15.00

LEIBER, Fritz. *Specter Is Haunting TX.* 1969 Walker. 1st ed. dj. EX $60.00

LEIBER, Fritz. *Swords & Deviltry.* 1970 NY. Ace. 1st ed. 2nd print. inscr. $30.00

LEIBER, Fritz. *Swords Against Death.* 1970 NY. Ace. 1st ed. later print. wraps. VG $15.00

LEIBER, Fritz. *Swords Against Wizardry.* 1968 NY. Ace. 1st ed. sgn. wraps. VG $15.00

LEIBER, Fritz. *Swords in the Mist.* 1968 NY. Ace. later print. inscr. $35.00

LEIBER, Fritz. *Swords of Lankhmar.* 1968 NY. Ace. later print. inscr. $35.00

LEIBER, Fritz. *2 Sought Adventure.* Gnome Pr. 1st ed. sgn. dj. EX $175.00

LEIBIG. *Chemistry of Food.* 1848 Lowell. Bixby. 1st Am ed. VG $85.00

LEIDY, J. *Fresh-Water Rhizopods of North America.* 1879 Ills 324 p. $50.00

LEIGH, Samuel. *Leigh's New Pocket Road Book to England & Wales.* 1837 London. 6th ed. 12mo. gilt green morocco. $75.00

LEIGHTON, C.C. *Life at Puget Sound with Sketches of Travel.* 1884 Boston. 1st ed. 258 p. xl. G $25.00

LEIGHTON, Clare. *Sometime-Never.* 1939 NY. Ills 1st Am ed. cloth. dj. VG $15.00

LEIGHTON, Clare. *Sometime-Never.* 1939 NY. 1st ed. 4to. dj. slipcase. EX $60.00

LEIGHTON, Clare. *Tempestuous Petticoat.* 1947 NY. 1st ed. dj. VG $25.00

LEIGHTON, Clare. *Tempestuous Petticoat.* 1947 NY. 1st ed. dj. wraps. EX $60.00

LEIGHTON, Clare. *Where Land Meets Sea.* 1954 Rinehart. Ills. dj. VG $8.50

LEIGHTON, Clare. *Wood Engraving & Woodcuts.* 1932 London. Studio. 1st ed. 4to. sgn. VG $125.00

LEIGHTON, Clare. *Wuthering Heights.* 1931 NY. Ills Ltd ed. 1/450. sgn. EX $125.00

LEIGHTON, Clare. *4 Hedges: A Gardener's Chronicle.* 1935 NY. Macmillan. 1st ed. 4to. green cloth. dj. $30.00

LEIGHTON, Margaret. *Singing Cave.* c 1945. Boston. dj. VG $15.00

LEIMBACH, P.P. *All My Meadows.* 1977 Prentice Hall. Ills. 235 p. dj. EX $8.00

LEINSDORF, Erich. *Composer's Advocate: Radical Orthodoxy for Musicians.* 1981 Yale U Pr. 1st ed. EX $15.00

LEISENRING, J.E.; & HIDY, V.S. *Art of Tying the Wet Fly.* 1971 Crown. Ills. 160 p. VG $6.50

LEITAO, M. *Boats of the Libson River.* 1978 London. Ills. 154 p. wraps. EX $12.00

LEITCH, Gordon B. *Chinese Rugs.* 1935 NY. Tudor. New ed. 8vo. 183 p. $75.00

LEITCH, M. & M. *7 Years in Ceylon.* 1980 NY. Ills 1st ed. VG $45.00

LEIVE & BERGMAN. *History of Military Government Detachment F-13.* 1945 Offenbach. Ills 1st ed. maps. photos. VG $45.00

LEJARD, Andre. *Art of the French Book.* no date. London. Elek. Ills. 166 p. $50.00

LELAND, Charles G. *Etruscan Magic & Occult Remedies.* 1963 NY. University Books. dj. EX $26.00

LELAND, Charles G. *Kuloskap the Master & Other Algonkin Poems.* 1902 Funk Wagnall. Ills. 370 p. VG $32.50

LELAND, Charles G. *Leather Work: Practical Manual for Learners.* 1892 London. Ills 1st ed. state A. $60.00

LELAND, Christopher T. *Mean Time.* 1982 Random House. 1st ed. dj. EX $15.00

LEM, Stanislaw. *Return From the Stars.* 1980 NY. 1st ed. dj. M $10.00

LEMAITRE, Solange. *Ramakrishna & the Vitality of Hinduism.* 1969 NY. Trans Markmann. 244 p. M $16.00

LEMAY, J.A.L. *Men of Letters in Colonial MD.* 1972 Knoxville. 1st ed. dj. VG $20.00

LEMERY. *Cours de Chymie.* 1698 Dresden. Ills. German text. 1,100 p. $450.00

LEMMER, K. *Deutsche Schauspieler der Gegenwart.* 1955 West Berlin. 240 photos. $10.00

LEMMON & JOHNSON. *Wild Flowers of North America in Full Color.* 1961 Hanover House. VG $10.00

LEMMON & SHERMAN. *Flowers of World.* 1958 Hanover. 1st ed. dj. EX $5.00

LEMONNIER. *Birds & Beasts.* 1911 London. Ills EJ Detmold. 1st ed. VG $50.00

LEMOS, P.J. *Applied Art: Drawing, Painting, Design, & Handcraft.* 1920 Pacific Pr. Ills. 379 p. G $18.00

LEMPRIERE, William. *Practical Observations on Diseases of Army in Jamaica.* 1799 London. only ed. 8vo. 2 vol set. G $100.00

LENGYEL, Emil. *Hitler.* 1932 NY. inscr. G $30.00

LENIN, Nikolai. *Imperialism: State & Revolution.* 1926 NY. 1st Am ed. brown cloth. VG $30.00

LENIN, Nikolai. *Soviets at Work.* 1918 NY. Rand School. green wraps. $65.00

LENNIE, Campbell. *Landseer: Victorian Paragon.* 1976 London. dj. EX $12.50

LENNON, John. *Penguin John Lennon.* 1966 Penguin. 1st ed. wraps. VG $18.00

LENNON, John. *Skywriting by Word of Mouth.* 1986 NY. Ltd 1st ed. 1/500. sgn Yoko. boxed. M $85.00

LENNON, John. *Spaniard in the Works.* 1965 London. 1st ed. EX $85.00

LENNON, John. *Spaniard in the Works.* 1965 NY. 1st ed. VG $32.50

LENORMANT, Francois. *Chaldean Magic: Its Origin & Development.* no date. (1887) London. 1st ed. 414 p. VG $135.00

LENS, Andre. *Le Costuem de Plsieurs Peuples de L'Antiquite.* 1776 Aliege. Ills. 4to. VG $95.00

LENSKI, Lois. *Blueberry Corners.* 1940 NY. Stokes. 1st ed. 4to. dj. VG $10.00

LENSKI, Lois. *Book of Enchantment Tales.* 1928 Dodd Mead. 1st ed. 4to. 230 p. scarce. VG $45.00

LENSKI, Lois. *Fireside Poems.* 1930 Minton Balch. Ills 1st ed. 4to. cloth. $30.00

LENSKI, Lois. *Judy's Journey.* 1947 Lippincott. reprint. 8vo. 212 p. dj. $10.00

LENSKI, Lois. *San Francisco Boy.* 1955 Phil/NY. Ills 1st ed. dj. EX $26.00

LENSKI, Lois. *Shoo-Fly Girl.* 1963 Lippincott. Ills 1st ed. 176 p. cloth. $15.00

LENSKI, Lois. *Skipping Village.* 1927 Stokes. 1st print. 4to. VG $35.00

LENSKI, Lois. *Strawberry Girl.* 1945 Lippincott. Ills 1st ed. 193 p. VG $15.00

LENSSEN, H. *Art & Anatomy.* 1946 NY. 80 p. $16.50

LENTON, H.T. *American Submarines.* 1973 London. Ills. dj. EX $12.50

LENTON, H.T. *British Warships.* 1962 London. ABC Series. Ills 6th ed. G $5.00

LENTRIVCHIA, F. & M.L. *Robert Frost: A Bibliography 1913-1974.* 1976 Metuchen. 1st ed. 8vo. M $9.00

LENTZ, Perry. *Falling Hills.* 1967 NY. Scribner. 1st ed. dj. VG $15.00

LENTZ, T.L. *Cell Biology of Hydra.* 1966 North Holland. Ills. 199 p. dj. EX $12.00

LENYGON, Francis. *Decoration in England From 1660-1770.* 1920 London. Batsford. Ills. 296 p. $225.00

LENZ, E.C. *Rifleman's Progress.* 1946 Standard. Ills. 4to. 162 p. dj. EX $20.00

LEONARD, Elmore. *Bounty Hunters.* 1954 Ballantine. 1st ed. wraps. $45.00

LEONARD, Elmore. *City Primeval.* 1980 NY. Arbor. 1st ed. sgn. EX $25.00

LEONARD, Elmore. *City Primeval.* 1981 London. Allen. 1st ed. dj. EX $30.00

LEONARD, Elmore. *Dutch Treat.* Mysterious Pr. Ltd 1st ed. 1/350. sgn. dj. $50.00

LEONARD, Elmore. *Gold Coast.* 1982 London. 1st English ed. dj. EX $40.00

LEONARD, Elmore. *La Brava.* 1983 London. 1st English ed. dj. EX $25.00

LEONARD, Elmore. *Last Stand at Saber River.* 1959 NY. 1st ed. wraps. VG $37.50

LEONARD, Elmore. *Moonshine War.* 1970 NY. Dell. 1st ed. pb. EX $15.00

LEONARD, Elmore. *Moonshine War.* 1969 NY. 1st ed. dj. xl. VG $17.50

LEONARD, Elmore. *Split Images.* 1981 NY. Arbor. 1st ed. sgn. EX $25.00

LEONARD, Elmore. *Split Images.* 1981 London. 1st English ed. dj. EX $30.00

LEONARD, Elmore. *Swag.* 1965 NY. Delacorte. 1st ed. M $45.00

LEONARD, Elmore. *Switch.* 1979 London. 1st ed. dj. EX $40.00

LEONARD, Elmore. *40 Lashes Less 1.* 1972 NY. Bantam. 1st ed. pb. scarce. EX $30.00

LEONARD, Iris F. *Professional Candy Making.* 1926 NY. Ills. 131 p. sliver cloth. $20.00

LEONHART, O. *New Orleans Drawn & Quartered.* 1938 Richmond. Ltd ed. 1/1,000. 4to. VG $40.00

LEOPOLD, A.S. *Wildlife of Mexico: Game Birds & Animals.* 1972 CA U Pr. Ills. 568 p. maps. dj. EX $47.50

LEOPOLD, Aldo. *Game Management.* 1939 Scribner. Ills Brooks. 481 p. VG $12.00

LEOPOLD, Aldo. *Game Management.* 1933 Scribner. Ills. 481 p. dj. EX $18.00

LEOPOLD, Aldo. *Round River.* 1953 Oxford U Pr. Ills Schwartz. 173 p. EX $14.00

LEOPOLD, Aldo. *Sand County Almanac Illustrated.* 1977 Tamarack Pr. Ills Algire. 152 p. dj. EX $20.00

LEOPOLD, Aldo. *Sand County Almanac.* 1949 Oxford U Pr. Ills Schwartz. 226 p. VG $10.00

LEOPOLD, J.H. *Almanus Manuscript: Rome Circa 1475-1485.* 1971 London. Hutchinson. Ills. 306 p. dj. $55.00

LEPPER, John Heron. *Famous Secret Societies.* no date. London. 344 p. VG $45.00

LEREBOURS, N.P. *Galerie Microscopique.* 1843 Paris. Ills. 224 p. wraps. rare. $175.00

LERMAN, Rhoda. *Eleanor.* 1979 Holt. 1st ed. dj. EX $15.00

LERMAN, Rhoda. *Girl That He Marries.* 1976 Holt. 1st ed. dj. EX $15.00

LERMONTOV. *Sheaf From Lermontov.* 1923 NY. 1st ed. VG $20.00

LEROUX, Gaston. *Phantom of the Opera.* 1911 NY/Indy. Ills Castaigne. 1st ed. EX $75.00

LESCARBOURA, Austin C. *Behind the Motion Picture Screen.* 1919 NY. Ills 1st ed. EX $25.00

LESIS, Sinclair. *Cass Timberlane.* 1945 NY. dj. EX $18.00

LESLEY, J.P. *Geographical Hand Atlas of 67 Counties of PA.* 1885 Harrisburg. Ills. 4to. VG $40.00

LESLIE, Chane. *Skill of Swift: An Extempore Exhumation.* 1928 Indianapolis. VG $25.00

LESLIE, Frank. *Famous Leaders & Battle Scenes of the Civil War.* 1896 NY. folio. 544 p. half morocco. VG $125.00

LESLIE, Frank. *Frank Leslie Christmas Book.* 1895 Frank Leslie. G $20.00

LESLIE, Frank. *Illustrated History of the Civil War.* 1895 NY. private print. 512 p. folio. $100.00

LESLIE, Frank. *Soldier in Our Civil War: Pictorial History of Conflict.* 1890 NY. folio. 2 vol set. VG $175.00

LESLIE, R.F. *Wild Pets.* 1970 Crown. Ills. 240 p. dj. VG $6.00

LESSING, Doris. *Canopus in Argos.* 1979-1983. 1st ed. 5 vol set. djs. EX $50.00

LESSING, Doris. *Children of Violence: Ripple From Storm & Landlocked.* 1966 Simon Schuster. 1st Am ed. dj. EX $30.00

LESSING, Doris. *Diary of Good Neighbor.* 1983 Knopf. 1st Am ed. dj. EX $25.00

LESSING, Doris. *Documents Relating to Sentimental Agents.* 1983 Knopf. 1st Am ed. dj. EX $13.00

LESSING, Doris. *Four-Gated City.* 1969 Knopf. 1st Am ed. dj. EX $30.00

LESSING, Doris. *Good Terrorist.* 1985 NY. 1st ed. dj. M $14.00

LESSING, Doris. *Habit of Loving.* 1957 Crowell. 1st Am ed. dj. EX $35.00

LESSING, Doris. *Habit of Loving.* 1957 London. VG $16.00

LESSING, Doris. *Memoirs of a Survivor.* 1975 Knopf. 1st Am ed. dj. EX $15.00

LESSING, Doris. *Sirian Experiments.* 1981 Knopf. 1st Am ed. dj. EX $15.00

LESSING, Doris. *Summer Before the Dark.* 1973 NY. dj. EX $14.00

LESSING, Doris. *Summer Before the Dark.* 1973 London. Cape. 1st ed. dj. EX $45.00

LESTER, C. Edwards. *Life & Achievement of Sam Houston, Hero & Statesman.* 1883 Alden. 12mo. VG $20.00

LESTER, Katherine Morris. *Accessories of Dress.* 1940 Peoria, IL. Ills. 4to. 587 p. VG $45.00

LESTER, Lewis. *Touch of Rot.* 1952 NY. Woodford. dj. EX $20.00

LESY, Michael. *WI Death Trip.* 1973 NY. Ills 1st ed. dj. VG $27.50

LETHABY, W. *Architecture, Mysticism, & Myth.* 1975 NY. 280 p. $20.00

LETHBRIDGE, I. *Herdsmen & Hermits: Celtic Seafarers in Northern Seas.* 1950 London. dj. $15.00

LETHBRIDGE, T.C. *Boats & Boatmen.* 1952 London. Ills. dj. G $12.00

LEUZINGER, Elsy. *Art of Black Africa.* 1972 NY. 1st ed. dj. VG $40.00

LEVENTHAL, Albert R. *War.* c 1973. Chicago. 4to. 252 p. dj. EX $14.00

LEVER, Charles. *Jack Hinton.* 1843 Phil. 1st Am ed. VG $40.00

LEVER, Charles. *Roland Cashel.* 1850 NY. Ills Phiz. 1st ed. G $30.00

LEVER, Charles. *St. Patrick's Eve.* 1845 London. Ills Phiz. 1st ed. 203 p. VG $145.00

LEVERTOV, Denise. *Conversations in Moscow.* 1973 Havey St Pr. 1/1,000. wraps. $20.00

LEVERTOV, Denise. *Freeing of Dust.* 1975 New Directions. 1st ed. dj. EX $25.00

LEVERTOV, Denise. *Life in the Forest.* 1978 New Directions. Ltd ed. 1/150. sgn. slipcase. $50.00

LEVERTOV, Denise. *O Taste & See.* 1964 New Directions. 1st ed. dj. EX $30.00

LEVERTOV, Denise. *Poet in the World.* 1973 New Directions. 1st ed. dj. EX $20.00

LEVERTOV, Denise. *To Stay Alive.* 1971 New Directions. Advance copy. dj. EX $30.00

LEVERTOV, Denise. *With Eyes at the Back of Our Heads.* 1959 New Directions. sgn. dj. VG $45.00

LEVEY, Michael. *Life & Death of Mozart.* 1971 NY. Ills 1st ed. dj. VG $25.00

LEVI, Eliphas. *Mysteries of Magic: Digest of Writings of G. Legman.* 1886 London. 1st ed. rebound. VG $135.00

LEVI, Eliphas. *Transcendental Magic.* 1958 London. dj. EX $48.00

LEVI, Eliphas. *Transcendental Magic.* 1896 London. Redway. 1st ed. 406 p. VG $145.00

LEVI, Wendell Mitchell. *Pigeon.* 1969 Ills. 667 p. VG $20.00

LEVIN, Bob. *Best Ride to NY.* 1978 NY. 1st ed. dj. M $12.00

LEVIN, Ira. *Rosemary's Baby.* 1967 Random House. dj. EX $12.50

LEVIN, Ira. *Stepford Wives.* 1972 dj. EX $14.00

LEVIN, L. & S. *Practical Benchwork for Horologists.* c 1945. Levin. 4th ed. VG $20.00

LEVIN, M. *In Search.* 1950 NY. dj. G $15.00

LEVIN, M. *Obsession.* 1973 NY. 1st ed. dj. $10.00

LEVIN, N. *Holocaust: Destruction of European Jewry 1933-1945.* 1973 Schocken Books. Sftcvr. G $15.00

LEVIN, Phyllis Lee. *Wheels of Fashion.* 1965 Garden City. Ills. 244 p. dj. VG $7.50

LEVINE, David. *Arts of David Levine.* 1978 NY. Ills 1st ed. dj. VG $25.00

LEVINE, I. *Francis Bacon.* 1925 Boston. Small Maynard. 1st ed. dj. VG $12.00

LEVINE, S.A.; & HARVEY, W.P. *Clinical Auscultation of the Heart.* 1949 Phil. Ills 1st ed. VG $75.00

LEVINE. *Life & Times of Snow Lake 1878-1978.* 1978 Ltd 1st ed. 1/600. 4to. EX $45.00

LEVINSON, Leonard L. *Wall Street: Pictorial History.* 1961 NY. Ills 1st ed. 4to. dj. boxed. $65.00

LEVISON, J.J. *Home Book of Trees & Shrubs.* 1940 NY. Ills. inscr. G $20.00

LEVRON. *Images de Versailles.* no date. Paris. Les Heures Claire. 8vo. dj. VG $75.00

LEVY, G.R. *Gate of Horn.* c 1946. Book Collectors Society. VG $50.00

LEVY, Julien. *Surrealism.* 1936 NY. Black Sun. Ltd 1st ed. 1/500. 8vo. EX $150.00

LEVY, M.J. *Family Revolution in Modern China.* 1949 Harvard U Pr. dj. VG $12.00

LEVY, Melvin. *Last Pioneers.* 1934 NY. inscr. VG $15.00

LEVY, Mervyn. *Liberty Style: Classic Years 1898-1910.* 1986 NY. Rizzoli. Ills. 4to. 160 p. dj. $25.00

LEWER, H.W. *Book of Simples.* 1908 London. Chiswich Pr. 2nd imp. 226 p. $45.00

LEWIN, F. *Characters From Dickens.* 1912 London. 20 plts. VG $42.00

LEWINSOHN, R. *Animals, Men, & Myths.* 1954 Harper. Ills 1st ed. 422 p. dj. VG $8.00

LEWIS, A.H. *Worlds of Chippy Patterson.* 1960 NY. dj. VG $15.00

LEWIS, Albert B. *Block Prints From India for Textiles.* 1924 Chicago. Field Mus. Ills. 4to. scarce. $40.00

LEWIS, Albert B. *Decorative Art of New Guinea.* 1925 Chicago. Field Museum of Natural Hist. $45.00

LEWIS, Alfred Henry. *Black Lion Inn.* 1903 NY. Russell. Ills Remington. EX $18.00

LEWIS, Alfred Henry. *Wolfville.* 1897 NY. Stokes. 1st ed. sgn. EX $125.00

LEWIS, Benjamin. *Ridings Illustrated with Photos.* 1939 NY. 4to. 141 p. tan buckram. VG $45.00

LEWIS, Bernard. *Behind the Type: Life Story of Frederic W. Goudy.* 1941 Pittsburgh. Ills. VG $30.00

LEWIS, C. Day. *Gate.* 1962 London. dj. M $17.00

LEWIS, C.S. *Abolition of Man.* 1947 Macmillan. 1st ed. dj. EX $20.00

LEWIS, C.S. *Perelandra.* 1950 Avon. VG $25.00

LEWIS, C.S. *Perelandra.* 1944 Macmillan. 1st print. dj. VG $16.00

LEWIS, C.S. *Reflection on the Psalms.* 1958 London. 1st English ed. dj. VG $30.00

LEWIS, C.S. *Reflection on the Psalms.* 1958 NY. 1st ed. dj. EX $18.00

LEWIS, C.S. *Surprised by Joy.* 1955 London. dj. M $35.00

LEWIS, C.T. *George Baxter, Color Printer: His Life & Work.* 1908 London. 1st ed. G $75.00

LEWIS, D. *Gypsies; or, Why We Went Gypsying in the Sierras.* 1881 Boston. 1st ed. 27 plts. fair. $30.00

LEWIS, E. *Trader Horn.* 1927 Simon Schuster. 302 p. map. G $10.00

LEWIS, Frank. *Best Design Versus Best Seller.* 1965 Lewis. Ills. 4to. dj. $40.00

LEWIS, G.W. *Ape I Knew.* 1961 Caxton. Ills. 263 p. VG $14.00

LEWIS, Griffin. *Mystery of the Oriental Rug.* 1914 Phil. Ills 1st ed. 8vo. 103 p. VG $35.00

LEWIS, Griffin. *Practical Book of Oriental Rugs.* 1920 Phil. $110.00

LEWIS, Griselda. *Collector's History of English Pottery.* 1969 NY. Viking. Studio Book. Ills. 224 p. dj. $40.00

LEWIS, Isaac Newton. *Pleasant Hours in Sunny Lands in a Tour Around the World.* 1888 Boston. inscr. EX $18.00

LEWIS, Janet. *Good-Bye, Son & Other Stories.* 1946 Doubleday. 1st ed. dj. VG $20.00

LEWIS, John. *Redemption of Lower Schuylkill.* 1924 Phil. City Park Assn. xl. G $35.00

LEWIS, Lloyd. *Captain Sam Grant.* 1950 Little Brown. 1st ed. 512 p. dj. VG $17.00

LEWIS, Lloyd. *Sherman, Fighting Prophet.* 1932 Harcourt Brace. Ills. 690 p. maps. VG $17.00

LEWIS, Lloyd; & SMITH, H.J. *Chicago: History of Its Reputation.* 1929 EX $20.00

LEWIS, Oscar. *Family of Builders.* 1961 San Francisco. Grabhorn. 1st ed. VG $15.00

LEWIS, Oscar. *Sutter's Fort: Gateway to the Gold Field.* 1966 NY. Ills 1st ed. dj. VG $12.50

LEWIS, Richard. *Few Flowers for Shiner.* 1950 NY. 1st ed. dj. EX $11.00

LEWIS, S. *Keep Out of the Kitchen.* 1929 NY. scarce. $350.00

LEWIS, Sinclair. *Ann Vicker.* 1933 Doubleday Doran. 562 p. $27.50

LEWIS, Sinclair. *Arrowsmith.* 1925 Grosset Dunlap. 448 p. $27.50

LEWIS, Sinclair. *Bethel Merriday.* 1940 NY. 1st ed. dj. G $30.00

LEWIS, Sinclair. *Bethel Merriday.* 1940 Doubleday. 1st ed. dj. EX $50.00

LEWIS, Sinclair. *Dodsworth.* 1929 Harcourt Brace. 1st ed. $27.50

LEWIS, Sinclair. *Elmer Gantry.* 1927 NY. 1st ed. 1st issue. VG $75.00

LEWIS, Sinclair. *God Seeker.* 1949 Random House. 1st ed. dj. VG $17.50

LEWIS, Sinclair. *Kingsblood Royal.* 1947 Random House. 1st ed. dj. EX $12.00

LEWIS, Sinclair. *Work of Art.* 1934 Doubleday. 1st ed. dj. VG $80.00

LEWIS, Thomas; & KNEBERG, M. *Hiwassee Island.* 1946 Knoxville. Ills 1st ed. 188 p. wraps. VG $75.00

LEWIS, V.A. *History of WV.* 1889 Hubbard. Ills 1st ed. 744 p. VG $55.00

LEWIS, W.S. *3 Tours Through London in Years 1748, 1776, & 1797.* 1941 Yale U Pr. VG $15.00

LEWIS, Wilmarth. *Horace Walpole's Library.* 1958 Cambridge. 1st ed. 1/750. 8vo. 74 p. dj. $40.00

LEWIS, Wyndham. *Demon of Progress in the Arts.* 1954 London. 1st ed. dj. VG $20.00

LEWIS, Wyndham. *Tarr.* 1918 NY. Knopf. 1st ed. 8vo. VG $110.00

LEWIS & CLARK. *History of Expedition Under Command of Lewis & Clark.* 1814 Phil. Ills. 8vo. 2 vol set. $3000.00

LEWIS & CLARK. *Journeys of Lewis & Clark.* 1962 NY. Heritage. 2 vol set. boxed. VG $75.00

LEWIS & DIGNAM. *Marriage of Diamonds & Dolls.* 1947 NY. 1st ed. dj. EX $25.00

LEWIS & SMITH. *Graphic Reproductions & Photography of Works of Art.* 1969 London. Cowell. 1st ed. dj. EX $17.00

LEWIS & YARNELL. *Pathological Firesetting.* 1951 NY. $10.00

LEY, Willy. *Bombs & Bombing.* 1941 NY. Ills. 124 p. VG $8.50

LEY, Willy. *Watchers of the Skies: Informal History of Astronomy.* 1966 NY. Viking. Ills 4th print. 529 p. dj. xl. $7.00

LEYDET, Francois. *Coyote: Defiant Song Dog of the Southwest.* 1977 Chronicle. Ills. 221 p. dj. EX $15.00

LEYLAND, John. *Gardens: Old & New.* c 1900. London. Country Life. 3rd ed. 2 vols. $130.00

LEYMARIE, Jean. *Balthus.* 1979 NY. Skira/ Rizzoli. square folio. $150.00

LEYMARIE, Jean. *French Painting: 19th Century.* 1962 Skira. Ills. 4to. plts. VG $45.00

LEYMARIE, Jean. *Graphic Works of Impressionists.* 1971 NY. 1st ed. dj. VG $125.00

LEYMARIE, Jean. *Impressionist Drawing From Manet to Renoir.* 1969 Geneva. Ills. 103 p. $18.00

LEZAMA-LIMA, J. *Paradiso.* 1985 Era. Spanish text. pb. EX $7.50

LHOTE, Andre. *La Peinture.* 1922 Paris. Ltd ed. 1/85. inscr. wraps. $20.00

LIBERMAN, A. *Artist in His Studio.* 1960 NY. presentation. dj. EX $100.00

LIBERMAN, William S. *Designs for a Midsummer Night's Dream.* 1968 MOMA. Ills. 12mo. 32 p. wraps. $12.00

LIBRARY OF CONGRESS. *Paper-Making Art & Craft.* 1968 Ills. 96 p. $12.50

LICHTEN. *Folk Art of Rural PA.* 1946 Scribner. Ills. folio. 276 p. G $30.00

LIDDELL, Hart. *War in Outline.* 1936 London. fld maps. dj. VG $15.00

LIDDY, G. Gordon. *Will.* 1980 NY. 1st ed. dj. VG $15.00

LIDMAN, Hans. *People of the Forest.* 1963 NY. 1st ed. 4to. photos. dj. VG $20.00

LIEB, F.G. *St. Louis Cardinals.* 1947 NY. Ills 8th print. 8vo. VG $10.00

LIEBERMAN, Max. *Max Ernst.* 1961 MOMA. Ills. 4to. 63 p. wraps. $12.50

LIEBERMAN, Max. *Sein Leben und Seine Werke von Erich Hancke.* 1914 Berlin. Ills. 547 p. ¾-calf. VG $375.00

LIEBERMAN, William S. *Art of the '20s.* 1979 MOMA. Ills. oblong 4to. wraps. $9.00

LIEBERMAN, William S. *Manhattan Observed Selections of Drawings & Prints.* 1968 MOMA. Ills. oblong 8vo. 43 p. wraps. $20.00

LIEBERMAN, William S. *Sculptor's Studio: Etchings by Picasso.* 1952 MOMA. Ills. 4to. 31 p. wraps. $15.00

LIEBERMAN, William S. *Seurat to Matisse: Drawing in France.* 1974 MOMA. Ills. 8vo. 103 p. wraps. $10.00

LIEBLING, A.J. *Back Where I Came From.* 1938 NY. 1st ed. dj. VG $140.00

LIEBLING, A.J. *Honest Rainmaker.* 1953 Doubleday. 1st ed. dj. VG $30.00

LIEBLING, A.J. *Mollie & Other War Pieces.* 1964 Ballantine. 1st ed. wraps. VG $15.00

LIEF, A. *It Floats.* 1958 Troy, NY. Ills 1st ed. dj. VG $22.50

LIFAR, Serge. *Ma Vie: From Kiev to Kiev.* 1970 NY. World. 1st print. 332 p. dj. VG $15.00

LILIUOKALANI. *HI Story by HI Queen.* 1898 Boston. VG $75.00

LILLARD, R.G. *Desert Challenge: Interpretation of NV.* 1942 NY. Ills. dj. G $35.00

LILLIE, F.R. *Problems of Fertilization.* 1919 Chicago U Pr. 278 p. VG $6.00

LILLY, Eli. *Schliemann in Indianapolis.* 1961 IN Hist Soc. 8vo. dj. EX $15.00

LILLYS, William. *Persian Miniatures: Story of Rustam.* 1958 Rutland. 1st ed. dj. VG $25.00

LIMEBEER, Ena. *Market Town.* 1931 London. Cape. 1st ed. inscr. dj. VG $15.00

LINCOLN, F.S. *Charleston.* 1946 NY. Corinthian. VG $22.00

LINCOLN, Harry B. *Computer & Music.* 1979 Ithaca. VG $22.00

LINCOLN, Joseph C. *Back Numbers.* 1933 Coward McCann. 1st ed. VG $22.50

LINCOLN, Joseph C. *Big Mogul.* 1926 NY. Appleton Century. $12.00

LINCOLN, Joseph C. *Bradshaw of Harris.* 1943 NY. Appleton Century. $12.00

LINCOLN, Joseph C. *Cape Cod Ballads.* 1902 Brandt. 1st ed. $65.00

LINCOLN, Joseph C. *Old Home House.* 1907 NY. Barnes. Ills 1st ed. 291 p. $30.00

LINCOLN, Joseph; & BRETT, H. *Cape Cod Yesterdays.* 1935 Little Brown. Chatham ed. 1/1,075. sgns. VG $65.00

LINCOLN, Mrs. D. *Carving & Serving.* 1896 Boston. inscr. VG $40.00

LINCOLN, Mrs. D. *Mrs. Lincoln's Boston Cookbook.* 1894 Boston. dj. G $35.00

LINCOLN, Mrs.; & LEMCHE, Mrs. *365 Breakfast Dishes.* 1901 Phil. 12mo. dj. EX $25.00

LINCOLN, P.R. *Black Bass Fishing: Theory & Practice.* 1952 Stackpole. Ills 1st ed. 376 p. dj. VG $17.50

LINCOLN & FREEMAN. *Blair's Attic.* 1929 NY. 1st ed. 8vo. blue cloth. dj. $50.00

LINCOLN & FREEMAN. *Ownley Inn.* 1939 Coward McCann. 2nd ed. dj. VG $18.50

LIND, L.R. *Studies in Pre-Vasalian Anatomy.* 1975 Phil. Am Philosophical Soc. 1st ed. $20.00

LINDBERGH, Anne Morrow. *Bring Me a Unicorn: Diaries & Letters 1922-1928.* 1972 Harcourt Brace. 2nd print. dj. VG $12.00

LINDBERGH, Anne Morrow. *Gift From the Sea.* 1955 Ills Special ed. 8vo. 120 p. $25.00

LINDBERGH, Anne Morrow. *Listen! The Wind.* 1938 Harcourt Brace. 1st ed. VG $30.00

LINDBERGH, Charles A. *Of Flight & Life.* 1948 NY. Scribner. 1st ed. 12mo. inscr. EX $275.00

LINDBERGH, Charles A. *Spirit of St. Louis.* presentation. glassine wraps. G $135.00

LINDBERGH & SCHEINGOLD. *Regional Integration Theory & Research.* 1971 Harvard. 1st ed. dj. $15.00

LINDBLAD, Jan. *Journey to the Red Birds.* 1969 Hill Wang. Ills. 176 p. dj. VG $18.00

LINDER, Leslie. *Journal of Beatrix Potter From 1881 to 1897.* 1966 London/NY. Ills 2nd print. xl. VG $25.00

LINDERMAN, Frank Bird. *Recollections of Charley Russell.* 1963 OK U Pr. 1st ed. dj. EX $30.00

LINDGREN, A. *Christmas in a Noisy Village.* 1964 NY. Ills Wikland. dj. EX $15.00

LINDLEY, Harlow. *History of Ordinance of 1787 & Old Northwest Territory.* 1937 Marietta. Ills. 95 p. wraps. $12.50

LINDLEY, John. *Vegetable Kingdom.* 1853 London. Ills. 908 p. rebound. $25.00

LINDOP, A.E. *Singer Not the Song.* 1953 London. 1st ed. dj. M $15.00

LINDROTH, C.H. *Faunal Connections Between Europe & North America.* 1957 Wiley. Ills. 344 p. maps. EX $18.00

LINDSAY, David. *Voyage to Arcturus.* 1946 Gollancz. 1st reissue ed. dj. EX $25.00

LINDSAY, Jack. *Homer's Hymns to Aphrodite.* c 1930. Fanfrolico Pr. 1/500. 4to. VG $25.00

LINDSAY, Jack. *Inspiration.* 1928 London. Fanfrolico Pr. 1/725. VG $35.00

LINDSAY, John S. *Anatomy of English Wrought Iron.* 1965 NY. Taplinger. Ills. 4to. 60 p. $40.00

LINDSAY, Merrill. *Miniature Arms.* 1970 NY. Ills Pendleton. 1st ed. 8vo. $12.50

LINDSAY, Merrill. *Miniature Arms.* 1970 Winchester. Ills. oblong 8vo. VG $10.00

LINDSAY, Suzanne. *Mary Cassatt & Philadelphia.* 1985 Phil. Ills. 4to. 96 p. cloth. dj. $35.00

LINDSAY, Vachel. *Going to the Stars.* 1926 Appleton. 1st ed. VG $25.00

LINDSEY, David. *OH Western Reserve.* 1955 Cleveland. Ills. 111 p. wraps. G $10.00

LINE, L.; & RICCIUTI, E.R. *Audubon Society Book of Wild Cats.* 1985 Abrams. Ills. 4to. 256 p. dj. EX $45.00

LINE, L.; & RUSSELL, F. *Audubon Society Book of Wild Birds.* 1976 Abrams. Ills. 4to. 292 p. dj. EX $20.00

LINGUIST, G.E.E. *Red Man in the US.* 1923 Ills 1st ed. 8vo. 461 p. VG $55.00

LINK, M.C. *Sea Diver.* 1961 NY. 2nd print. dj. VG $6.00

LINK, S. *Combat Jiu-Jitsu.* 1943 Portland. Ills. VG $9.00

LINKLATER. *Juan in America.* 1931 London. 1st ed. dj. EX $20.00

LINNE, Sir Charles. *General System of Nature.* 1806 London. leather. $45.00

LINNEHAN & COGSWELL. *Driving Clubs of Greater Boston.* 1914 Boston. Ills. 4to. 291 p. $40.00

LINS DO REGO, Jose. *Plantation Boy.* 1966 NY. Knopf. 1st ed. dj. EX $15.00

LINZEY, A.V. & D.W. *Mammals of the Great Smoky Mountains.* 1971 TN U Pr. Ills 1st ed. 114 p. wraps. $5.00

LIONEL, Edwards. *My Hunting Sketchbook.* 1928 London. Ills Ltd ed. 1/250. 4to. $70.00

LIPCHITZ, Jacques. *Amedeo Modigliani.* 1954 NY. 1st Am ed. wraps. VG $75.00

LIPMAN, Jean. *American Primitive Painting.* 1942 NY/London. Oxford U Pr. folio. cloth. dj. $50.00

LIPMAN, Jean. *Primitive Painters in America 1750-1950.* 1950 NY. Dodd Mead. Ills. 4to. 182 p. cloth. $60.00

LIPMAN, Jean. *Rufus Porter: Yankee Pioneer.* 1968 NY. Ills 1st ed. 4to. dj. EX $60.00

LIPMAN. *Calder's Universe.* 1976 Whitney Mus. Ills. square 4to. 350 p. dj. $25.00

LIPPINCOTT, J.W. *Wilderness Champion.* 1944 NY. Ills Bransom. 1st ed. dj. VG $17.50

LIPPMANN, Walter. *Preface to Morals.* 1929 NY. 1st ed. inscr. $25.00

LIPTON, Lawrence. *Erotic Revolution.* 1965 Sherbourne Pr. 1st ed. presentation. EX $45.00

LIPTON, Lawrence. *Holy Barbarians.* 1959 NY. Messner. 1st ed. dj. EX $45.00

LIPTON, Lawrence. *Holy Barbarians.* 1959 NY. Messner. 1st ed. G $20.00

LISLE, Edward. *Observations in Husbandry.* 1757 London. 1st ed. 4to. 452 p. rebound. $300.00

LISTER, Raymond. *Decorated Porcelains of Simon Lissim.* 1955 Cambridge. Golden Head Pr. Ltd ed. 1/480. $40.00

LISTER, Raymond. *Decorative Wrought Iron-work in Great Britain.* 1970 Rutland. Tuttle. Ills. 267 p. dj. $35.00

LISTER, Raymond. *Samuel Palmer & His Etchings.* 1969 NY. 1st ed. dj. VG $35.00

LITCHFIELD, Frederick. *Pottery & Porcelain Guide for Collectors.* 1925 NY. Macmillan. Ills Revised 4th ed. 464 p. $45.00

LITTAUER, Vladimir S. *Be a Better Horseman.* 1941 NY. Ills Ltd ed. 1/1,500. 4to. VG $45.00

LITTLE, G. *Life on the Ocean; or, 20 Years at Sea.* 1845 Boston. Waite Peirce. 3rd ed. 395 p. $20.00

LITTLE, Mrs. Sophia. *Thrice Through the Furnace: A Tale.* 1852 Pawtucket. 1st ed. cloth. EX $60.00

LITTLE, Nina F. *American Decorative Wall Painting 1700-1850.* 1952 NY. Studio. 4to. 160 p. dj. $60.00

LITTLE, Nina F. *Floor Coverings in New England Before 1850.* 1967 Old Strubridge Village. 83 p. $12.50

LITTLE, Nina F. *Neat & Tidy.* 1980 NY. Dutton. Ills. 8vo. 223 p. wraps. $20.00

LITTLEFIELD, George Emery. *Early MA Press 1638-1711.* 1907 Boston. Ltd 1/175. VG $110.00

LITTLEFIELD, S. *Seaside Gardening.* 1986 NY. 96 p. dj. EX $12.00

LITTLEHALES, Lillian. *Pablo Cassals.* 1929 NY. Ills 1st ed. 1/150. sgn. VG $275.00

LITTLEJOHN, E.G. *TX History Stories.* 1901 Johnson. Ills. 255 p. G $6.00

LIVERMORE, Mary A. *My Story of the War.* 1890 Hartford. Ills. 8vo. 700 p. red cloth. G $40.00

LIVERMORE, Mary A. *Story of My Life; or, Sunshine & Shadow of 70 Years.* 1898 Hartford. Ills. inscr. EX $25.00

LIVINGSTON, A.D. *Advanced Bass Tackle & Boats.* 1975 Lippincott. Ills 1st ed. 240 p. EX $12.50

LIVINGSTON, A.D. *Fly Rodding for Bass.* 1976 Lippincott. Ills 1st ed. 203 p. VG $10.00

LIVINGSTON, Jane; & BEARDSLEY. *Black Folk Art in America 1930-1980.* 1982. Ills 2nd print. sgn. $30.00

LIVINGSTONE, David & Charles. *Narrative of Expedition to Zambesi & Its Tributaries.* 1866 NY. Ills 1st Am ed. map. cloth. $65.00

LIVIUS, T. *Romane Historie.* 1659 London. Trans P Holland. folio. G $175.00

LIVSEY, C. *Manson Women.* 1980 NY. 1st ed. dj. VG $17.50

LIZARS, Robina & Kathleen. *In Days of Canada Company.* 1896 Toronto. Briggs. Ills. 8vo. EX $25.00

LLEWELLEN, Richard. *Few Flowers for Shiner.* 1950 Macmillan. 1st Am ed. dj. VG $13.00

LLEWELLEN, Richard. *Mr. Hamish Hamilton.* 1956 Doubleday. 1st Am ed. dj. EX $13.00

LLEWELLEN, Richard. *Night of Bright Stars.* 1979 Garden City. 1st ed. dj. M $12.00

LLEWELLEN, Richard. *None But the Lonely Heart.* 1943 Macmillan. 1st Am ed. dj. VG $25.00

LLEWELLEN, Richard. *Sweet Morn of Judas' Day.* Doubleday. 1st Am ed. dj. EX $12.00

LLOSA, Mario Vargas. *Conversation in Cathedral.* 1975 Harper. Trans Rabassa. 1st Am ed. dj. $25.00

LLOSA, Mario Vargas. *Perpetual Orgy.* 1986 Farrar. 1st Am ed. dj. VG $18.00

LLOSA, Mario Vargas. *War of the End of the World.* 1984 Farrar. 1st ed. 1/250. sgn. slip-case. $90.00

LLOYD, J.U. *Etidorpha; or, The End of the Earth.* 1896 Cinncinati. Ills. 386 p. VG $48.00

LLOYD, J.U. *Right Side of the Car.* 1897 Boston. 59 p. green cloth. $45.00

LLOYD, N. *Golden Encyclopedia of Music.* 1968 Golden Pr. 1st ed. EX $10.00

LLOYD, Ward. *Investing in Georgian Glass.* 1969 London. $17.50

LLOYD, Wyndham. *100 Years of Medicine.* 1939 London. Duckworth. VG $12.50

LO, Kenneth. *Complete Encyclopedia of Chinese Cooking.* 1979 London. dj. EX $15.00

LOBB, A. *Indian Baskets of the Northwest Coast.* 1978 Portland. Ills. 4to. dj. EX $20.00

LOBENSTINE, W.C. *Extracts From Diary of W.C. Lobenstine.* 1966 Flagstaff. Ills/sgn Perceval. Ltd 1st ed. $60.00

LOBLEY, J.L. *Mt. Vesuvius.* 1889 London. Ills. 400 p. red cloth. VG $40.00

LOBSANG, Rampa. *Doctor From Lhasa.* 1959 1st Am ed. 239 p. VG $8.50

LOCK, L. Leland. *Ancient Quipu; or, Peruvian Knot Record.* 1923 Am Mus Nat Hist. 4to. plts. EX $75.00

LOCK & WHITFIELD. *Men of Mark.* 1883 London. Sampson Low. 1st ed. 4to. $125.00

LOCKER-LAMPSON, Frederick. *London Lyrics.* 1862 London. Pickering. 2nd ed. sgn. VG $125.00

LOCKHART, J.G. *Mary Celeste & Other Strange Tales of the Sea.* 1952 London. Mariners Library ed. G $12.00

LOCKRIDGE, Richard. *Mr. & Mrs. North.* 1936 NY. Stokes. 1st ed. dj. EX $85.00

LOCKRIDGE, Ross. *Raintree County.* 1948 Boston. dj. EX $75.00

LOCKWOOD, Douglas. *Australia's Pearl Harbor.* 1942 Sydney. Darwin. 1st ed. sgn. dj. EX $40.00

LOCKWOOD, F.C. *Apache Indians.* 1938 Macmillan. 1st ed. 1st print. VG $75.00

LOCKWOOD, F.C. *More AZ Characters.* 1943 Tucson. 1st ed. 79 p. wraps. VG $15.00

LOCKWOOD, F.C. *Pioneer Days in AZ.* 1932 NY. Ills 1st ed. 387 p. VG $37.50

LOCKWOOD, F.C. *Pioneer Days in AZ.* 1932 NY. 1st ed. sgn. slipcase. EX $75.00

LOCKWOOD, George. *New Harmony Communities.* 1902 Marion, IN. Ills 1st ed. VG $60.00

LOCKYER, J. Norman. *Elements of Astronomy.* 1880 NY. Appleton. Ills Revised ed. 312 p. G $12.00

LODDER, Christina. *Russian Constructivism.* 1983 Yale U Pr. Ills. 4to. 336 p. dj. $60.00

LODER, George T. *Wonderful Ride: Journal of Mr. G.T. Loder.* 1978 NY. Harper Row. Ills 1st ed. 146 p. dj. VG $8.00

LODGE, Henry Cabot. *Theodore Roosevelt.* 1919 Boston. Ltd ed. 1/1,500. cloth. dj. $50.00

LODGE, Henry Cabot. *Works of Alexander Hamilton.* no date. NY. Putnam. 9 vol set. $175.00

LODGE, Oliver J. *Lightning Conductors & Lightning Guards.* 1892 Whittaker. Ills 1st ed. 544 p. VG $38.00

LODGE, Oliver J. *Signalling Through Space Without Wires.* no date. London. Electrician. 3rd ed. $90.00

LOENING, Grover. *Air Road Will Widen.* 1969 NY. Ills. 41 p. dj. VG $65.00

LOENING, Grover. *Our Wings Grow Faster.* 1935 Garden City. Ills 1st ed. 4to. dj. VG $75.00

LOESELL, Clarence M. *History of Kiwanis in MI.* 1956 Charlotte, MI. photos. 218 p. VG $12.50

LOESSER, Arthur. *Humor in American Song.* 1942 NY. Howell Soskin. Ills Adler. VG $15.00

LOESSER, Arthur. *Men, Women, & Pianos: Social History.* 1954 Simon Schuster. 1st ed. dj. VG $25.00

LOEWENSTEIN, Prince Huburtus. *After Hitler's Fall.* 1934 London. Faber. inscr. VG $35.00

LOFTING, Hugh. *Dr. Dolittle & the Green Canary.* 1950 Lippincott. Ills 1st ed. 8vo. VG $20.00

LOFTING, Hugh. *Dr. Doolittle's Return.* 1933 NY. Stokes. Ills 1st ed. VG $40.00

LOFTING, Hugh. *Dr. Doolittle's Zoo.* 1925 NY. Stokes. Ills 1st ed. 8vo. 338 p. VG $30.00

LOFTING, Hugh. *Voyages of Dr. Dolittle.* 1922 NY. Stokes. Ills. 364 p. VG $25.00

LOFTUS. *Maltser: Art of Malting.* 1876 London. Ills Revised ed. $40.00

LOGAN, H.C. *Under-Hammer Guns.* 1960 Stackpole. Ills. 4to. 249 p. dj. EX $23.50

LOGAN, J. *Ulster in the X-Rays.* c 1920s. London. 188 p. G $20.00

LOGAN, John A. *Great Conspiracy.* 1886 NY. cloth. VG $50.00

LOGAN, Mrs. John A. *30 Years in WA.* 1901 Hartford. Ills. 752 p. gilt cloth. M $75.00

LOGAN, Mrs. John A. *30 Years in WA.* 1901 Hartford. Ills. VG $15.00

LOGAN, Olive. *Mimic World & Public Exhibitions.* 1871 New World. G $12.00

LOHRMAN, H.P. *History of Tuscarawas County, OH.* 1937 New Phil. Ills. 60 p. wraps. G $12.50

LOISY, Alfred. *My Duel with the Vatican.* 1924 NY. VG $15.00

LOMASK, Milton. *Aaron Burr: Years From Princeton to Vice President.* 1979 Farrar. $12.00

LOMAX, J.A. *Adventures of a Ballad Hunter.* 1947 NY. 1st ed. VG $20.00

LOMBARDO, Josef V. *Chaim Gross: Sculptor.* 1949 NY. Ills. 4to. 254 p. $85.00

LONDON, Jack. *Before Adam.* 1907 NY. 1st ed. EX $55.00

LONDON, Jack. *Before Adam.* 1907 NY. Macmillan. 1st ed. 1st issue. wraps. VG $30.00

LONDON, Jack. *Burning Daylight.* 1910 NY. Macmillan. 1st print. VG $135.00

LONDON, Jack. *Call of the Wild.* 1903 NY. 1st ed. 1st bdg. VG $110.00

LONDON, Jack. *Cruise of the Snark.* 1911 NY. 1st ed. blue cloth. VG $100.00

LONDON, Jack. *Game.* 1905 NY. 1st ed. 2nd state. EX $45.00

LONDON, Jack. *House of Pride & Other Tales of HI.* London. 1st English ed. EX $27.50

LONDON, Jack. *Iron Heel.* 1948 NY. 1st ed. blue cloth. dj. G $55.00

LONDON, Jack. *John Barleycorn.* 1913 NY. Century. 1st ed. dj. VG $50.00

LONDON, Jack. *Little Lady of the Big House.* 1916 NY. 1st ed. VG $70.00

LONDON, Jack. *Lost Face.* 1913 Regent Pr. G $12.50

LONDON, Jack. *Love of Life.* 1907 NY. Macmillan. 1st ed. gilt blue cloth. VG $85.00

LONDON, Jack. *Michael, Brother of Jerry.* 1917 NY. Macmillan. 1st ed. 1st issue. red cloth. $80.00

LONDON, Jack. *Moon Face.* 1906 NY. Macmillan. 1st ed. VG $145.00

LONDON, Jack. *Mutiny of the Elsinore.* 1914 NY. 1st ed. VG $55.00

LONDON, Jack. *Night Born.* 1913 NY. Century. 1st ed. 8vo. dj. VG $95.00

LONDON, Jack. *Road.* 1907 NY. 1st ed. VG $200.00

LONDON, Jack. *Scarlet Plague.* 1915 NY. 1st ed. G $200.00

LONDON, Jack. *Sea Wolf.* 1961 Ltd Ed Club. Ills F Martin. 1/1,500. dj. EX $65.00

LONDON, Jack. *Smoke Bellew.* 1912 NY. Ills 1st ed. 385 p. $50.00

LONDON, Jack. *Son of the Wolf.* 1900 Boston. 1st ed. gray cloth. G $175.00

LONDON, Jack. *Valley of the Moon.* 1913 NY. Macmillan. 1st ed. EX $175.00

LONDON, Jack. *When God Laughs & Other Stories.* 1911 NY. Ills 1st ed. 319 p. G $175.00

LONDON, Jack. *White Fang.* 1906 NY. Macmillan. 1st ed. 8vo. green cloth. EX $75.00

LONDON, John C. *Encyclopedia of Agriculture.* 1839 London. 4th ed. rebound. VG $150.00

LONDON & BOYERS. *Robert Lowell: Portrait of the Artist in His Time.* 1970 Lewis. 1st ed. dj. EX $30.00

LONG, A.L. *Memoirs of Robert E. Lee.* 1886 NY. rebound. VG $35.00

LONG, F.B. *Hounds of Tindalos.* 1946 Arkham House. 1st ed. G $75.00

LONG, F.B. *Rim of the Unknown.* 1972 Arkham House. 1st ed. 1/3,500. dj. EX $20.00

LONG, F.B. *3 Steps Space Forward.* 1963 NY. 1st ed. dj. EX $30.00

LONG, Huey. *Every Man a King.* 1933 New Orleans. 1st ed. dj. $22.50

LONG, Mason. *Life of Converted Gambler.* 1878 Chicago. Ills 1st ed. $40.00

LONG, W.J. *Fowls of the Air.* 1901 Boston. Atheneum. 1st ed. inscr. EX $65.00

LONG, W.J. *Wilderness Ways.* 1900 Ginn. Ills Copeland. 154 p. G $6.50

LONG & BLISS. *Clinical & Experimental Use of Sulfanilimide.* 1939 Macmillan. VG $30.00

LONGFELLOW, Henry Wadsworth. *Aftermath.* 1873 Boston. 1st ed. G $30.00

LONGFELLOW, Henry Wadsworth. *Courtship of Miles Standish & Other Poems.* 1858 Boston. 1st ed. 1st issue. VG $38.00

LONGFELLOW, Henry Wadsworth. *Courtship of Miles Standish & Other Poems.* 1903 Indianapolis. Bobbs Merrill. Ills Christy. $20.00

LONGFELLOW, Henry Wadsworth. *Courtship of Miles Standish & Other Poems.* 1858 Boston. 1st ed. 1st issue. rebound. $85.00

LONGFELLOW, Henry Wadsworth. *Courtship of Miles Standish & Other Poems.* 1859 2nd ed. 215 p. VG $40.00

LONGFELLOW, Henry Wadsworth. *Divine Tragedy.* 1871 Boston. 1st ed. VG $35.00

LONGFELLOW, Henry Wadsworth. *Evangeline.* 1905 Indianapolis. Ills Christy. Spanish text. VG $55.00

LONGFELLOW, Henry Wadsworth. *Evangeline.* 1905 Indianapolis. Ills Christy. 1st ed. EX $55.00

LONGFELLOW, Henry Wadsworth. *Hanging of the Crane.* 1947 Centennial ed. 1/1,000. dj. VG $65.00

LONGFELLOW, Henry Wadsworth. *In the Harbor.* 1882 Boston. 1st ed. EX $20.00

LONGFELLOW, Henry Wadsworth. *Masque of Pandora.* 1875 Boston. gilt green cloth. $75.00

LONGFELLOW, Henry Wadsworth. *New England Tragedies.* 1868 Boston. 1st ed. VG $25.00

LONGFELLOW, Henry Wadsworth. *Poems by Henry Wadsworth Longfellow.* 1845 Carey Hart. Ills D Huntington. G $15.00

LONGFELLOW, Henry Wadsworth. *Saggi de Novellieri Italiani d'Ogni Scrittori.* 1832 Boston. Presso Gray e Bowen. 1st ed. $150.00

LONGFELLOW, Henry Wadsworth. *Song of Hiawatha.* 1895 Boston. Ills Remington. VG $40.00

LONGFELLOW, Henry Wadsworth. *Song of Hiawatha.* 1888 Smith Andrews. Minnehaha ed. G $12.50

LONGFELLOW, Henry Wadsworth. *Tales of Wayside Inn.* 1863 Ticknor Fields. G $37.00

LONGFELLOW, Henry Wadsworth. *Tales of Wayside Inn.* 1863 Boston. 1st Am ed. VG $50.00

LONGFELLOW, Henry Wadsworth. *Tales of Wayside Inn.* 1864 London. 1st English ed. EX $40.00

LONGLEY, Mary T. *Nameless.* 1912 Chicago. Progressive Thinker Pub. VG $15.00

LONGSTAFF, R. *Submarine Command.* 1984 London. Ills. dj. EX $28.00

LONGSTREET, Stephen. *Century on Wheels: Story of Studebaker History 1852-1952.* 1952 NY. Holt. Ills 1st ed. 121 p. VG $15.00

LONGSTREET, Stephen. *Treasure of World's Great Prints.* 1961 NY. 1st print. dj. VG $25.00

LONGSTRETH, T. Morris. *Catskills.* 1918 NY. Century. Ills. 321 p. green cloth. G $18.50

LONGSTRETH, T. Morris. *Sky Through Branches.* 1930 NY. 1st ed. presentation. 12mo. $25.00

LONGUS. *Daphnis & Chloe.* 1972 Impression Soc. Ills Felix Hoffman. sgn. dj. $25.00

LONGWITH, Benjamin. *Observations on Dr. Arbuthnot's Dissertaions.* 1747 ¾-calf. $100.00

LONGYEAR, Edmund J. *Descendants of Jacob Longyear of Ulster County, NY.* 1942 private print. 622 p. EX $25.00

LOOMIS, Alfred F. *Ocean Racing: Great Blue Water Yacht Races 1866-1935.* 1936 NY. Morrow. 1st ed. G $36.00

LOOMIS, Andrew. *Successful Drawing.* 1951 NY. Viking. dj. VG $35.00

LOOMIS, B.F. *Pictorial History of Lassen Volcano.* no date/place. dj. EX $14.00

LOOS, Anita. *Gentlemen Prefer Blondes.* 1925 NY. Ills Ralph Barton. 9th print. $5.00

LOOS, Anita. *Kiss Hollywood Good-Bye.* 1974 London. dj. EX $19.00

LOPEZ, Barry. *Arctic Dreams.* 1986 Scribner. 464 p. maps. dj. EX $18.00

LOPEZ, Barry. *Desert Reservations.* 1980 Ltd 1st ed. 1/300. sgn. wraps. M $45.00

LOPEZ, Barry. *Giving Birth to Thunder, Sleeping with His Daughter.* 1977 KS City. Sheed. 1st ed. dj. VG $40.00

LOPEZ, Barry. *Of Wolves & Men.* 1978 Scribner. Ills. 309 p. dj. EX $16.00

LOPEZ, Barry. *River Notes.* 1979 Andrews McMeel. 1st ed. M $25.00

LOPEZ, Barry. *River Notes.* 1979 Andrews McMeel. Uncorrected proof. $45.00.

LOPEZ, Barry. *Winter Count.* 1981 NY. Scribner. 1st ed. dj. M $10.00

LOPEZ-REY, Jose. *Valazquez' Work & World.* 1968 Greenwich. Ills. 4to. 172 p. dj. $50.00

LOPEZ-REY, Jose. *Velazquez: Catalogue Raisonne.* 1963 London. Faber. $40.00

LORANT, Stephan. *New World.* 1946 NY. Ills J White/J LeMoyne. VG $35.00

LORANT, Stephan. *Sieg Heil! Illustrated History of Germany.* 1974 Norton. 1st ed. dj. VG $18.50

LORD, F.A. *Civil War Sutlers & Their Wares.* 1969 Yoseloff. Ills. 162 p. dj. VG $45.00

LORD, F.A. *They Fought for the Union.* 1960 Harrisburg. Ills 1st ed. 375 p. dj. VG $32.00

LORD, James. *Giacometti Portrait.* 1965 MOMA/Doubleday. Ills. 8vo. 68 p. wraps. $15.00

LORD, John. *Beacon Lights of History.* 1921 8 vol set. VG $95.00

LORENZ, K.Z. *King Solomon's Ring: New Light on Animal Ways.* 1952 Crowell. Ills. 202 p. dj. G $6.00

LORING, John. *Tiffany Taste.* 1986 NY. 4to. linen. dj. M $32.00

LOSSING, Benson J. *Biography of James A. Garfield.* 1882 NY. 1st ed. VG $20.00

LOSSING, Benson J. *Hudson: Wilderness to Sea.* 1866 Troy, NY. Ills 1st ed. VG $140.00

LOSSING, Benson J. *Pictorial Field Book of the Revolution.* 1860 NY. Harper. 2 vol set. G $45.00

LOSSING, Benson J. *Pictorial Field Book of the Revolution.* 1976 NY. 2 vol set. $47.50

LOSSING, Benson J. *Pictorial Field Book of the Revolution.* 1855 NY. 2nd ed. 2 vol set. $110.00

LOSSING, Benson J. *Pictorial Field Book of War of 1812.* 1868 NY. Ills 1st ed. 1,084 p. xl. G $55.00

LOSSING, Benson J. *Washington & Mount Vernon.* 1859 NY. Ills 1st ed. VG $50.00

LOTHROP, Elise. *Historic Houses of Early America.* 1927 NY. McBridge. Ills. $47.50

LOTHROP, S.K. *Robert Woods Bliss Collection: Pre-Columbian Art.* 1959 Phaidon. Ills. folio. cloth. VG $230.00

LOTI, Pierre. *Carmen Sylva.* 1912 NY. 1st ed. EX $15.00

LOTTO. *Fayette County: Her History & Her People.* 1902 Schulenberg. Sticker Steam Pr. wraps. G $90.00

LOUDON, J.C. *Encyclopedia of Agriculture.* 1826 London. Ills 1st ed. 2 vol set. $125.00

LOUDON, J.C. *Encyclopedia of Agriculture.* 1839 London. 4th ed. rebound. $150.00

LOUDON, J.C. *Encyclopedia of Cottage, Farm, & Villa Architecture.* 1842 London. Ills New ed. 8vo. 1,306 p. VG $125.00

LOUIS & YAZIJIAN. *Cola Wars.* 1980 NY. 1st ed. dj. M $27.50

LOUNSBERRY, Alice. *Sir William Phips: Treasure Fisherman & Governor of MA.* 1941 NY. Ills 1st ed. dj. VG $15.00

LOUYS, Pierre. *Ancient Manners.* no date. Paris. Ltd ed. 1/1,000. VG $60.00

LOUYS, Pierre. *Aphrodite.* 1925 no place. Ills Ltd ed. 1/1,500. dj. VG $40.00

LOUYS, Pierre. *Aphrodite.* 1932 Willis Parker. Ills Deluxe ed. VG $35.00

LOUYS, Pierre. *Aphrodite.* 1932 Falstaff Pr. Ltd ed. 1/500. EX $35.00

LOUYS, Pierre. *Song of Bilitis.* 1926 NY. Masius. Ills/sgn W Pogany. 1/2,000. VG $30.00

LOVAT-FRASER. *Book of Lovat.* 1923 London. McFall Dent. VG $95.00

LOVE, Albert G. *Tabulating Equipment & Army Medical Statistics.* 1958 WA. Office of Surgeon General. xl. $15.00

LOVE, Aseaide. *Enchanted Drum.* 1950 Chicago. Dierkes Pr. 8vo. wraps. VG $20.00

LOVE, Edwin M. *Rocking Island.* 1927 NY. 1st ed. 4to. 182 p. cloth. VG $30.00

LOVE, P.M. *Will Rogers Book.* 1972 Texian. Ills. 212 p. dj. EX $8.00

LOVE, P.M. *Will Rogers Book.* 1961 1st ed. dj. EX $30.00

LOVE, R. *Rise & Fall of Jesse James.* 1939 Blue Ribbon. reprint. 446 p. G $25.00

LOVECRAFT, H.P. *Best Supernatural Stories.* 1945 Cleveland. World. 2nd print. VG $50.00

LOVECRAFT, H.P. *Collected Poems.* 1963 Sauk City. Arkham House. 1st ed. 1/2,000. $55.00

LOVECRAFT, H.P. *Dagon & Other Macabre Tales.* 1965 Arkham House. 1st ed. 1/3,500. 8vo. dj. EX $55.00

LOVECRAFT, H.P. *Dark Brotherhood & Other Pieces.* 1966 Arkham House. 1st ed. dj. VG $35.00

LOVECRAFT, H.P. *Dunwich Horror.* 1963 Arkham House. 1st ed. dj. EX $100.00

LOVECRAFT, H.P. *Horror in the Museum & Other Revisions.* 1970 Arkham House. 1st ed. 1/4,000. 8vo. dj. EX $30.00

LOVECRAFT, H.P. *Marginalia.* 1944 Arkham House. 1st ed. dj. VG $175.00

LOVECRAFT, H.P. *Selected Letters 11.* 1968 Arkham House. 1st ed. dj. EX $45.00

LOVECRAFT, H.P. *Selected Letters.* 1965 Arkham House. 1st ed. dj. EX $50.00

LOVECRAFT, H.P. *Shuttered Room.* 1959 Arkham House. 1st ed. dj. VG $100.00

LOVECRAFT, H.P. *Supernatural Horror in Literature.* 1945 NY. 1st ed. dj. VG $50.00

LOVECRAFT, H.P. *Weird Shadow Over Innsmouth.* 1944 Bart House. pb. G $85.00

LOVECRAFT, H.P. *3 Tales of Horror.* 1967 Arkham House. 1st ed. dj. EX $100.00

LOVECRAFT & DERLETH. *Lurker at the Threshold.* 1945 Arkham House. 1st ed. sgn Derleth. dj. VG $125.00

LOVECRAFT & DERLETH. *Lurker at the Threshold.* 1945 Arkham House. 1st ed. dj. VG $75.00

LOVECRAFT & DERLETH. *Waters Out of Time & Others.* 1974 Arkham House. 1st ed. dj. EX $25.00

LOVEJOY, A. *Primitivism & Related Ideas.* 1935 John Hopkins. dj. VG $17.00

LOVEJOY, Esther Poel. *Certain Samaritans.* 1927 Macmillan. 302 p. $20.00

LOVELACE, Leland. *Lost Mines & Hidden Treasures.* 1956 Naylor. 252 p. EX $8.00

LOVELACE, Maud Hart. *Betsy-Tacy.* 1940 NY. Crowell. Ills Lenski. 1st ed. dj. $35.00

LOVELACE, Maud Hart. *Heaven to Betsy.* no date. NY. Crowell. Ills Neville. 268 p. $7.50

LOVELL, Ernest J. *Captain Medwin: Friend of Byron & Shelley.* 1962 Austin. dj. VG $12.50

LOVELL, Malcolm R. *2 Quaker Sisters.* 1937 NY. 1st ed. sgn. dj. VG $20.00

LOVELL, Margaretta M. *Venice: American View 1860-1920.* 1984 San Francisco. Ills. 4to. 137 p. wraps. $20.00

LOVELL, Sir Bernard. *Story of Jodrell Bank.* 1968 NY. Harper Row. Ills 1st Am ed. 265 p. dj. xl. $10.00

LOVEMAN, S. *21 Letters of Ambrose Bierce.* 1922 Kirk. Ltd ed. 1/1,000. rare. G $28.00

LOVEMAN, Samuel. *Hermaphrodite & Other Poems.* 1936 Caxton. 1st ed. VG $75.00

LOVERIDGE, A. *Tomorrow's Holiday.* 1947 Harper. 1st ed. 278 p. VG $18.00

LOVETT, James. *Old Boston Boys & Games They Played.* 1906 Boston. Ills 1st trade ed. 8vo. 241 p. $35.00

LOW. *Cruise of Neptune 1903-1904.* 1906 Ottowa. Ills. map. cloth. VG $80.00

LOWDERMILK, W.C. *Palestine: Land of Promise.* 1944 NY. Stated 1st ed. 263 p. dj. VG $17.50

LOWE, David. *Lost Chicago.* 1975 dj. EX $45.00

LOWE, David. *Will All Faults.* 1973 Tehran. Intro Graham Greene. 1st ed. $25.00

LOWE, Percival. *5 Years a Dragoon.* 1006 KS City. 1st ed. rebound. VG $35.00

LOWELL, Amy. *John Keats.* 1925 Boston. Later ed. 2 vol set. $30.00

LOWELL, Amy. *Legends.* 1921 Boston. 1st ed. EX $11.00

LOWELL, Amy. *What's O'Clock.* 1925 Boston. Houghton Mifflin. 1st ed. VG $25.00

LOWELL, F. *Jiu-Jitsu.* 1942 NY. Ills. VG $8.00

LOWELL, James Russell. *Among My Books.* 1870 Boston. 1st ed. $20.00

LOWELL, James Russell. *Among My Books.* 1887 Houghton Mifflin. Later ed. EX $40.00

LOWELL, James Russell. *Biglow Papers. 2nd Series.* 1867 Boston. 2nd state. EX $24.00

LOWELL, James Russell. *Heartsease & Rue.* 1888 NY/Boston. 1st ed. G $25.00

LOWELL, James Russell. *Impressions of Spain.* 1899 Boston. 1st ed. VG $25.00

LOWELL, James Russell. *Last Poems.* 1895 Boston. 1st ed. EX $20.00

LOWELL, James Russell. *Poems.* 1849 Boston. 2 vol set. ½-leather. $90.00

LOWELL, James Russell. *Poems. 2nd Series.* 1848 Cambridge. 1st ed. pub presentation. $50.00

LOWELL, James Russell. *Political Essays.* 1888 Boston. 1st ed. M $20.00

LOWELL, Joan. *Cradle of the Deep.* 1929 Simon Schuster. G $21.00

LOWELL, Robert. *Day by Day.* 1977 NY. dj. M $14.00

LOWELL, Robert. *Dolphin.* 1973 NY. 1st ed. dj. EX $18.00

LOWELL, Robert. *Dolphin.* 1973 London. 1st ed. dj. M $22.00

LOWELL, Robert. *For the Union Dead.* 1964 NY. dj. EX $25.00

LOWELL, Robert. *History.* 1973 NY. dj. M $19.00

LOWELL, Robert. *Life Studies.* 1959 NY. 1st ed. dj. VG $100.00

LOWELL, Robert. *Lord Weary's Castle.* 1946 NY. 1st ed. cloth. dj. VG $75.00

LOWELL, Robert. *Notebook.* 1970 NY. Revised Expanded ed. dj. M $15.00

LOWELL, Robert. *Old Glory.* 1965 Farrar. 1st ed. dj. EX $40.00

LOWELL, Robert. *Phaedra & Figaro.* 1961 Farrar. Ills F Parker. 1st ed. dj. EX $40.00

LOWELL, Robert. *Selected Poems.* 1976 NY. 1st ed. 243 p. $15.00

LOWELL, T.H. *1st World Flight.* 1925 Ills 1st ed. VG $24.00

LOWENTHAL, Leo. *Literature & Image of Man.* 1957 Boston. VG $7.00

LOWENTHAL, Marvin. *Memoirs of Glukel of Hamelin.* 1932 NY. Ills 1st ed. G $20.00

LOWERY, G.H. *LA Birds.* 1955 LA U Pr. 1st ed. dj. VG $40.00

LOWERY, G.H. *Mammals of LA & Its Adjacent Waters.* 1974 LA U Pr. Ills. 565 p. maps. VG $22.00

LOWES, John Livingston. *Road to Xanadu.* 1927 Boston. Ltd 1st ed. 1/300. 8vo. $100.00

LOWINSKY, Ruth. *Lovely Food: A Cookery Notebook with Table Decorations.* 1931 NY. Random/Nonesuch. 1st ed. 8vo. $25.00

LOWMAN. *Printing Arts in TX.* 1975 Ltd ed. 1/395. EX $150.00

LOWRIE, Walter. *Art in Early Church.* 1947 NY. 1st ed. dj. VG $45.00

LOWRY, Beverly. *Daddy's Girl.* 1981 Viking. 1st ed. dj. EX $20.00

LOWRY, Beverly. *Daddy's Girl.* 1981 Viking. Uncorrected proof. EX $35.00

LOWRY, Malcolm. *Hear Us O Lord From Heaven Thy Dwelling Place.* 1961 Lippincott. 1st ed. dj. EX $75.00

LOWRY, Malcolm. *Lunar Caustic.* 1963 Paris. 1st ed. yellow wraps. EX $70.00

LOWRY, Malcolm. *October Ferry to Gabriola.* 1970 World. 1st ed. dj. EX $20.00

LOWRY, Malcolm. *Selected Letters.* 1965 Phil. 1st ed. dj. scarce. EX $35.00

LOWRY, Robert. *Big Cage.* 1949 Garden City. 1st ed. dj. EX $15.00

LOWRY, Robert. *Casualty.* 1946 NY. 1st ed. dj. G $50.00

LOWRY, Robert. *Find Me in Fire.* 1948 NY. 1st ed. 8vo. dj. EX $20.00

LOWRY, Robert. *Happy New Year Kamerades!* 1954 Garden City. 1st ed. dj. EX $17.00

LOWRY, Robert. *What's Left of April.* 1956 Garden City. 1st ed. dj. EX $15.00

LOWRY, Robert. *Wolf That Fed Us.* 1949 NY. 1st ed. 8vo. dj. EX $20.00

LOWTHER, C.C. *Panhandle Parson.* 1942 Parthenon. Ills 253 p. dj. EX $18.00

LOWTHER, M.K. *Blenner Hasset Island in Romance & Tragedy.* 1936 Rutland. Tuttle. 1st ed. sgn. EX $32.50

LOWTHER, M.K. *Blenner Hasset Island in Romance & Tragedy.* 1936 Rutland. Tuttle. 1st ed. 200 p. VG $20.00

LOZANO, Pedro. *True & Particular Relation of Earthquake at Lima.* 1748 London. Osborne. 2nd ed. maps. 341 p. $300.00

LUARD, N. *Last Wilderness: Journey Across the Great Kalahari Desert.* 1981 Simon Schuster. Ills 1st ed. 222 p. dj. EX $14.00

LUBBOCK, B. *Down-Easters: American Deep-Water Sailing Ships 1869-1929.* 1980 Glasgow. Ills. dj. EX $38.00

LUBELL, Cecil. *Textile Collections of the World: France.* 1977 Van Nostrand. Ills. 4to. 240 p. dj. $40.00

LUCAS, A. *Ancient Egyptian Materials & Industries.* 1934 2nd ed. 447 p. VG $45.00

LUCAS, E.V. *At the Shrine of St. Charles.* 1934 NY. 1st ed. dj. scarce. EX $20.00

LUCAS, E.V. *Cat Book.* 1927 Harper. Ills Pat Sullivan. 1st Am ed. $50.00

LUCAS, E.V. *Selected Essays.* 1954 London. 1st ed. dj. EX $12.00

LUCAS, F. *Animals of the Past.* 1901 NY. Ills 1st ed. 258 p. VG $35.00

LUCAS, Jason. *Lucas on Bass Fishing.* 1962 Dodd Mead. Ills. sgn. 381 p. dj. EX $15.00

LUCAS, W.E. *Eagle Fleet.* 1955 Weidenfeld Nicolson. dj. G $21.00

LUCAS. *Netherlanders in America.* 1955 Ann Arbor. 1st ed. VG $50.00

LUCE, J.V. *Lost Atlantis: New Light on Old Legend.* 1970 McGraw Hill. 8vo. dj. EX $20.00

LUCIE-SMITH, Edward. *Henri Fantin-Latour.* 1977 NY. Rizzoli. Ills. 4to. 176 p. dj. $30.00

LUCKIESH, M. *Light & Work: Discussion of Quality & Quantity of Light.* 1924 NY. Ills. EX $95.00

LUDLUM, Robert. *Bourne Identity.* 1980 Marek. 1st ed. dj. VG $13.00

LUDLUM, Robert. *Bourne Supremacy.* 1986 Random House. 1st ed. dj. EX $20.00

LUDLUM, Robert. *Materese Circle.* 1979 Marek. 1st ed. dj. EX $15.00

LUDLUM, Robert. *Osterman Weekend.* 1972 World. 1st ed. glassine dj. VG $40.00

LUDLUM, Robert. *Parsifal Mosiac.* 1982 Random House. 1st ed. dj. EX $16.00

LUDLUM, Robert. *Scarlatti Inheritance.* 1971 NY/Cleveland. 1st ed. dj. EX $47.50

LUDLUM, S.D. *Great Shooting Stories.* 1947 Doubleday. 1st ed. 303 p. dj. VG $10.00

LUDWIG, C. *Maxfield Parrish.* 1975 3rd ed. dj. EX $30.00

LUDWIG, E. *Nile: Life Story of a River.* 1937 Viking. Ills. 619 p. fld map. VG $11.00

LUDWIG, R. *Goegenische und Geognostische Studien.* 1862 Darmstadt. Ills. 267 p. wraps. VG $50.00

LUERERS, Edward. *Carl Van Vechten & the '20s.* 1955 NM U Pr. 1st ed. $11.00

LUETKENS, Charlotte. *Women & New Society, New Democracy.* 1946 London. Ills. 128 p. $12.00

LUHAN, M.D. *Winter in Taos.* 1935 NY. 1st ed. VG $30.00

LUKEMAN, Tim. *Witchwood.* 1983 NY. Uncorrected proof. EX $25.00

LUKER, Julia. *Yoeman's Daughter.* 1953 NY. 1st ed. dj. VG $15.00

LULL, R.S. *Hadrosaurian Dinosaurs of North America.* 1942 Am Geol Soc. Ills. 242 p. wraps. VG $10.00

LUMIERE, C. *Beneath the 7 Seas.* 1956 London. 1st ed. dj. VG $8.00

LUMISDEN, Andrew. *Remarks on Antiquities of Rome.* 1797 London. 1st ed. 11 plts. 2 fld maps. calf. EX $400.00

LUMMIS, C.F. *Goldfish of Gran Chimu.* 1911 Chicago. 1st ed. VG $28.00

LUMMIS, C.F. *Land of Poco Tiempo.* 1921 NY. G $15.00

LUNDBERG, Ferdinand. *Rich & the Super Rich.* 1968 5th print. 812 p. dj. VG $14.50

LUNGWWITZ, A. *Guide to Blacksmithing, Horseshoeing, Wagon Building.* 1902 Chicago. Ills. 222 p. EX $95.00

LUNN, Arnold. *Switzerland in English Prose & Poetry.* 1947 London. 1st ed. dj. VG $18.00

LUNTZ, Charles E. *Challenge of Reincarnation.* 1954 154 p. dj. VG $16.00

LUPOFF, R. *Wristwatch of Philip K. Dick.* 1985 Canyon Pr. Ills Ltd ed. 1/50. dj. EX $100.00

LUPOFF. *Edgar Rice Burroughs.* 1965 NY. 1st ed. dj. VG $47.50

LUPOLD, Jean. *Orchidees.* 1955 Service D'Images Silva Zurich. $45.00

LURIA & DARNELL. *General Virology.* 1967 Wiley. VG $15.00

LURIE, Alison. *Imaginary Friends.* 1967 London. 1st English ed. dj. EX $45.00

LUSK, William. *Science & Art of Midwifery.* 1893 Appleton. 4th ed. leather. $15.00

LUSTGARTEN, Edgar. *Verdict in Dispute.* 1950 NY. Scribner. 1st ed. dj. EX $12.50

MAULDIN, Bill. *Mud, Mules, & Mountains.* 1944 no place. 1st ed. VG $25.00

MAULDIN, Bill. *Mud, Mules, & Mountains.* 1944 Italy. inscr. wraps. $25.00

MAULDIN, Bill. *This Damn Tree Leaks.* 1945 NY. 1st ed. original wraps. EX $20.00

MAULDIN, Bill. *This Damn Tree Leaks.* 1945 Italy. 117 p. wraps. VG $15.00

MAUNDER, S. *History of the World.* 1849 NY. Ills. 8vo. 2 vol set. xl. VG $15.00

MAURIAC, Francois. *Questions of Precedence.* 1958 London. 1st ed. dj. M $12.00

MAURIAC, Francois. *Therese.* 1947 NY. 1st ed. dj. EX $15.00

MAURICE, A.B. *Paris of the Novelists.* 1919 NY. 1st ed. 8vo. VG $15.00

MAUROIS, Andre. *Illustrated History of France.* 1960 NY. 1st Am ed. dj. VG $25.00

MAUROIS, Andre. *Life of Sir Alexander Fleming: Discoverer of Penicillin.* 1959 Dutton. 1st ed. dj. VG $17.50

MAUROIS, Andre. *Voyage to Island of Articoles.* 1929 NY. 1st ed. dj. EX $20.00

MAURY, M.F. *Physical Geography of the Sea.* 1855 NY. 5th ed. 287 p. $25.00

MAURY, M.F. *Physical Geography of the Sea.* 1856 Harper. 6th ed. 8vo. 348 p. VG $50.00

MAUS, C.P. *Christ & the Fine Arts.* 1959 NY. Ills. 813 p. VG $18.00

MAVOR, William. *Catechism of Botany.* 1820 NY. Wood. 12mo. wraps. EX $60.00

MAW, Henry Lister. *Journal of Passage From Pacific to Atlantic Crossing Peru.* 1829 London. Murray. 1st ed. fld map. 486 p. $350.00

MAXIM, Hudson. *Defenseless America.* 1915 NY. VG $15.00

MAXWELL, Arthur. *Uncle Arthur's Bedtime Stories.* 1964 Ills. 5 vol set. VG $45.00

MAXWELL, G. *People of the Reeds.* 1957 Harper. Ills. 224 p. maps. dj. VG $14.00

MAXWELL, G. *Raven Seek Thy Brother.* 1969 Dutton. Ills 1st ed. 210 p. dj. VG $8.00

MAXWELL, G. *Ring of Bright Water.* 1961 Dutton. Ills 1st ed. 211 p. dj. VG $8.00

MAXWELL, G. *Rocks Remain.* 1963 Dutton. Ills 1st ed. 209 p. dj. EX $10.00

MAXWELL, James Clerk. *Treatise on Electricity & Magnetism.* 1881 Oxford. Clarendon. 2nd ed. 2 vol set. $95.00

MAXWELL, William Hamilton. *History of the Irish Rebellion in 1798.* 1854 London. Bohn. Ills 4th ed. 8vo. $175.00

MAY, Phil. *Phil May's ABC.* 1897 Leadenhall Pr. Ills Ltd ed. 1/1,050. 4to. $150.00

MAY, Robin. *Story of the Wild West.* 1978 Hamlyn. Ills. 4to. 155 p. dj. EX $18.00

MAYER, A. *Old Spain.* 1921 NY. Brentano. 1st ed. VG $35.00

MAYER, A.M. *Sport with Gun & Rod in American Woods & Waters.* 1883 NY. fair. $30.00

MAYER, August L. *Matthias Grunewald.* 1919 Munchen. 1st ed. 87 p. cloth. VG $60.00

MAYER, C. *Traping Wild Animals in the Malay Jungle.* 1921 Garden City. 207 p. dj. EX $18.00

MAYER, Mercer. *2 More Moral Tales.* 1974 NY. 4 Winds Pr. Ills Mayer. 1st print. dj. EX $15.00

MAYER-OAKES, W.J. *Prehistory of Upper OH Valley.* 1955 Pittsburgh. Carnegie Mus. 8vo. 296 p. $25.00

MAYERSON, Charlotte Leon. *Shadow & Light: Life, Friends, & Opinions of Maurice Sterne.* 1965 NY. Harcourt Brace/World. 4to. dj. $45.00

MAYFIELD, J. *Hit.* 1957 NY. 1st ed. dj. EX $10.00

MAYHEW, E. *Martha's Vineyard: History with Maps & Pictures.* 1956 Edgartown. $20.00

MAYHEW, Edward. *Illustrated Horse Doctor.* 1877 Phil. 522 p. green cloth. VG $17.00

MAYNARD, C.J. *Naturalist Guide in Collecting & Preserving Objects.* 1877 Salem, MA. Ills Revised ed. G $35.00

MAYNARD, Dr. Felix. *Whalers.* 1937 Curl. Ills 1st ed. 414 p. dj. VG $25.00

MAYNARD, L.D. *Animal Nutrition.* 1979 McGraw Hill. Ills. 602 p. VG $12.00

MAYNARD, Mrs. Nellie Colburn. *Was Abraham Lincoln a Spiritualist?* 1891 Phil. VG $35.00

MAYR, Ernst. *Systematics & Origin of Species: Viewpoint of Zoologist.* 1942 NY. 1st ed. sgn. $110.00

MAYRANX, M. *Dr. Fragments d'Hubert sur les Abeilles.* 1839 Paris. 16mo. 317 p. $50.00

MAYS, David J. *Edmund Pendleton.* 1952 Harvard U Pr. 2 vol set. dj. $17.50

MAYUYANA, Junkichi. *Chinese Ceramics in the West.* 1960 Tokyo. Mayuyama. bilingual text. 4to. $85.00

MAZZULLA, F. & J. *Outlaw Album.* 1966 private print. Ills. 48 p. pb. EX $2.00

MC ADOO. *Crowded Years.* Ills Autograph ed. 1/650. $30.00

MC ALLISTER, Anna. *Ellen Ewing: Wife of Gen. Sherman.* 1936 NY. 1st ed. dj. EX $30.00

MC ALLISTER, J.T. *VA Militia in Revolutionary War.* 1913 Hot Springs. 1st ed. VG $45.00

MC ALPINE, D. & A. *Biological Atlas: Guide.* 1881 Edinburgh. Ills. VG $45.00

MC ARTHUR, Alexander. *Pianoforte Study.* 1897 Phil. Presser. 8vo. beige cloth. dj. $50.00

MC ARTHUR, Edwin. *Flagstad: Personal Memoir.* 1965 Knopf. 1st ed. dj. VG $10.00

MC BAIN, Ed. *Beauty & the Beast.* 1982 Holt. Uncorrected proof. EX $40.00

MC BAIN, Ed. *Blood Relatives.* 1975 Random House. 1st ed. sgn. dj. EX $30.00

MC BAIN, Ed. *Cinderella.* 1986 Holt. dj. EX $15.00

MC BAIN, Ed. *Guns.* 1976 Random House. 1st ed. sgn. dj. EX $30.00

MC BAIN, Ed. *Hail, Hail, the Gang's All Here!* 1971 Doubleday. 1st ed. sgn. dj. EX $30.00

MC BAIN, Ed. *Hail to the Chief.* 1973 Random House. 1st ed. sgn. dj. EX $30.00

MC BAIN, Ed. *Long Time No See.* 1977 Random House. 1st ed. sgn. dj. EX $30.00

MC BAIN, Ed. *Shotgun.* 1969 Doubleday. 1st ed. dj. EX $35.00

MC BAIN, Ed. *So Long As You Both Shall Live.* 1976 Random House. 1st ed. sgn. dj. EX $30.00

MC BAIN, Ed. *Where There's Smoke.* 1975 Random House. 1st ed. dj. EX $15.00

MC BEY, J. *Etchings & Drypoints.* 1925 London. Ltd ed. 1/500. 4to. $210.00

MC BRIDE, Bill. *Pocket Guide to Identification of 1st Editions.* 1985 McBride. Revised 3rd ed. 1st print. EX $6.00

MC BRIDE, Bill. *Points of Issue.* 1987 McBride. 2nd ed. 1st print. wraps. EX $6.00

MC BRIDE, John G. *Vanishing Bracero.* 1963 Naylor. 1st ed. dj. EX $25.00

MC BRIDE, Robert Medill. *Furnishing with Antiques.* 1939 NY. folio. VG $28.00

MC CAFFREY, Anne. *Cooking Out of This World.* 1973 Ballantine. 1st ed. wraps. VG $45.00

MC CAFFREY, Anne. *Dragon Drums.* 1979 Argo. 1st ed. dj. EX $20.00

MC CAFFREY, Anne. *Moreta: Dragon Lady of Pern.* 1983 London. 1st English ed. sgn. dj. EX $27.00

MC CAFFREY, Anne. *Moreta: Dragon Lady of Pern.* 1983 Ballantine. 1st ed. dj. EX $25.00

MC CALL, Dan. *Jack the Bear.* 1974 Doubleday. 1st ed. dj. EX $20.00

MC CALLUM. *Tiger Wore Spikes.* 1956 Barnes. 1st ed. dj. VG $17.50

MC CANN. *Ship Model Making.* 1926 1st ed. G $20.00

MC CARRY, Charles. *Miernik Dossier.* 1973 NY. Saturday Review. 1st ed. VG $35.00

MC CARTER, Margaret Hill. *Winning the Wilderness.* 1914 Chicago. Ills JN Marchand. 1st ed. VG $16.50

MC CARTHY, Cormac. *Orchard Keeper.* 1965 Random House. 1st ed. dj. VG $50.00

MC CARTHY, Eugene. *Familiar Fish: Their Habits & Capture.* 1900 Appleton. Ills 1st ed. 216 p. VG $17.50

MC CARTHY, Mary. *Cannibals & Missionaries.* 1979 NY. 1st ed. dj. M $10.00

MC CARTHY, Mary. *Cast a Cold Eye.* 1950 Harcourt. 1st ed. dj. EX $45.00

MC CARTHY, Mary. *Memories of Catholic Girlhood.* 1957 NY. 1st ed. dj. $15.00

MC CARTHY, Mary. *17th Degree.* 1974 Harcourt. 1st ed. dj. EX $25.00

MC CASKIE, H.B. *Poems of Francois Villon.* 1946 London. Ills Ardizzone. G $15.00

MC CAUSLAND, Elizabeth. *Charles W. Hawthorne.* 1947 Am Artist Group. dj. VG $18.00

MC CAUSLAND, Elizabeth. *George Inness: American Landscape Painter.* 1946 NY. 1st ed. VG $45.00

MC CAUSLAND, Elizabeth. *Marsden Hartley Monograph.* 1952 MN U Pr. Ills. 4to. 84 p. wraps. $25.00

MC CAUSLAND, H. *Snuff & Snuff Boxes.* 1951 London. Batchworth. Ills. 144 p. VG $15.00

MC CLELLAN, Elizabeth. *Historic Dress in America 1800-1870.* 1910 Phil. Ills Steel/Trout. 4to. 458 p. $50.00

MC CLELLAN, G.B. *Manual of Bayonet Exercise.* 1852 Phil. 1st ed. VG $40.00

MC CLELLAN, G.B. *McClellan's Own Story.* 1887 NY. Webster. 1st ed. 8vo. inscr. $275.00

MC CLELLAN, G.B. *McClellan's Report & Campaigns.* 1864 NY. fld map. embossed black cloth. $45.00

MC CLELLAND, Alice W. *Harmony Circle Cookbook.* c 1910-1920. Syracuse. 12mo. 145 p. $25.00

MC CLELLAND, Nancy. *Furnishing the Colonial & Federal House.* 1947 Lippincott. Ills New Revised Enlarged ed. $45.00

MC CLELLAND, Nancy. *Historic Wallpapers.* 1924 Phil/London. Ills 1st ed. 4to. cloth. VG $150.00

MC CLERAND. *With the Indian & Buffalo in MT 1870-1878.* 1969 Clark. Ltd 1st ed. 1/300. M $250.00

MC CLINTOCK, W. *Old North Trail.* 1910 London. 1st ed. VG $75.00

MC CLINTON, K.M. *American Glass.* 1950 Cleveland. World. Ills. 64 p. $15.00

MC CLINTON, K.M. *Art Deco Collector's Guide.* 1972 Potter. 1st ed. dj. M $45.00

MC CLINTON, K.M. *Collecting American 19th Century Silver.* 1968 NY. Bonanza. Ills. 280 p. dj. $28.50

MC CLINTON, K.M. *Complete Book of Small Antiques Collecting.* 1965 NY. Ills. 255 p. $12.50

MC CLUNG, John A. *Sketches of Western Adventure.* 1844 Dayton. Ells & Chaflin. Ills. 12mo. $35.00

MC CLUNG, John A. *Sketches of Western Adventure.* 1832 Maysville, KY. full leather. rare. VG $500.00

MC CLUNG, R. *Lost Wild Worlds.* 1976 Morrow. Ills 1st ed. 288 p. dj. VG $15.00

MC CLURE, A.K. *Lincoln & Men of War Times.* 1892 Phil. 1st ed. VG $45.00

MC CLURE, A.K. *Recollections of Half a Century.* 1902 Salem. Ills. cloth. VG $25.00

MC CLURE, James. *Steam Pig.* 1971 NY. Harper. 1st ed. dj. EX $25.00

MC CLURE, Michael. *Gorf.* 1976 New Directions. 1st ed. dj. EX $15.00

MC CLURE, Michael. *Josephine: Mouse Singer.* 1980 New Directions. 1st ed. 8vo. wraps. EX $75.00

MC CLURE, Michael. *Scratching the Beat Surface.* 1980 San Francisco. North Point. 1st ed. dj. EX $60.00

MC COLL, D.D. *Sketches of Old Marlboro.* 1916 Columbia. 8vo. 108 p. wraps. VG $30.00

MC CONKEY, Harriet B. *Dakota War Whoops.* 1970 Minneapolis. dj. VG $20.00

MC CONKEY, James. *To a Distant Island.* 1984 NY. Dutton. 1st ed. dj. M $10.00

MC CONNELL, Burt M. *Mexico at the Bar of Public Opinion.* 1939 NY. $20.00

MC CORMICK, A.D. *Artist in the Himalayas.* 1895 NY. Ills 1st ed. 306 p. fld map. $47.50

MC CORMICK, L.M. *Descriptive List of the Fishes of Lorain County, OH.* 1892 Oberlain U Pr. 33 p. wraps. scarce. VG $15.00

MC CORMICK, Robert R. *War Without Grant.* 1950 NY. Ills 1st ed. 245 p. dj. VG $37.50

MC COSH, Rev. James. *Intuitions of the Mind Inductively Investigated.* 1872 NY. 3rd ed. 451 p. VG $48.00

MC COURT, Edward. *Yukon & Northwest Territories.* 1969 St. Martin. Ills. 236 p. maps. dj. EX $10.00

MC COWAN, D. *Animals of the Canadian Rockies.* 1941 Macmillan. Ills. sgn. 302 p. VG $12.00

MC COWAN, D. *Animals of the Canadian Rockies.* 1936 NY. Ills. sgn. $20.00

MC COWAN, D. *Naturalist in the Rockies.* 1946 Macmillan. Ills. 294 p. VG $6.00

MC COY, Esther. *Richard Neutra.* 1960 NY. Braziller. G $18.00

MC COY, John Pleasant. *Swing the Big-Eyed Rabbit.* 1944 Dutton. 1st ed. dj. VG $20.00

MC COY, Joseph G. *Historical Sketches of the Cattle Trade of West & Southwest.* 1940 Clark. 1st ed. EX $100.00

MC COY & MELLNIK. *10 Escape From Tojo.* 1944 NY. Ills. 106 p. wraps. G $12.50

MC CRACKEN, Harold. *American Cowboy.* 1973 Garden City. Ltd ed. sgn. $200.00

MC CRACKEN, Harold. *Beast That Walks Like a Man: Story of the Grizzly Bear.* 1955 Hanover House. Ills 1st ed. 319 p. dj. VG $18.50

MC CRACKEN, Harold. *Charles M. Russell Book: Life & Work of Cowboy Artist.* 1957 NY. Ills 1st ed. 35 plts. 235 p. $75.00

MC CRACKEN, Harold. *Frank Tenney Johnson Book: Life & Work of Master Painter.* 1974 Doubleday. 1st ed. dj. EX $35.00

MC CRACKEN, Harold. *Frederic Remington Book.* 1966 Garden City. Ltd ed. sgn. boxed. $150.00

MC CRACKEN, Harold. *Frederic Remington: Artist of the Old West.* 1947 Phil. 1st ed. 3rd imp. 48 plts. $40.00

MC CRACKEN, Harold. *Frederic Remington's Own West.* Promontory Pr. Ills. 4to. dj. VG $15.00

MC CRACKEN, Harold. *Frederic Remington's Own West.* 1960 Dial. dj. VG $15.00

MC CRACKEN, Harold. *George Catlin & the Old Frontier.* 1959 NY. Ills 1st ed. 216 p. dj. EX $40.00

MC CRACKEN, Harold. *Nicolai Fechin.* 1961 NY. $80.00

MC CRACKEN, Harold. *Portrait of the Old West.* 1952 McGraw Hill. 1st ed. dj. VG $30.00

MC CRACKEN, Harold. *Roughnecks & Gentlemen: Memoirs of a Maverick.* 1968 Doubleday. 1st ed. dj. VG $25.00

MC CRACKEN, Harold. *Son of the Walrus King.* 1944 Phil/NY. Ills Lynn Bogue Hunt. dj. VG $20.00

MC CRAE, John. *In Flanders Field & Other Poems.* 1919 NY. 1st ed. dj. EX $18.00

MC CRAKEN, James. *Topsy Turvy Tales.* no date. (1920) Donohue. folio. VG $35.00

MC CRAKIN, Joseph Clifford. *Woman Who Lost Him: Tales of Army Frontier.* 1913 Pasadena. James. $25.00

MC CREADY, T.L. *Biggity Bantam.* 1954 NY. Ariel Books. Ills Tasha Tudor. $18.00

MC CREERY, John. *Press: Part I & Part II.* 1803 & 1827. 2 vols in 1. 4to. rebound. EX $350.00

MC CULLERS, Carson. *Ballad of the Sad Cafe.* 1951 Boston. Houghton Mifflin. 1st ed. dj. $35.00

MC CULLERS, Carson. *Clock Without Hands.* 1961 London. 1st English ed. dj. EX $18.00

MC CULLERS, Carson. *La Ballade du Cafe Triste et Autres Nouvelles Americaines.* 1946 Paris. wraps. EX $150.00

MC CULLERS, Carson. *Member of the Wedding.* 1946 Boston. 1st ed. VG $15.00

MC CULLERS, Carson. *Mortgaged Heart.* 1971 Boston. 1st ed. dj. EX $15.00

MC CULLERS, Carson. *Reflections in a Golden Eye.* 1941 Boston. 1st ed. dj. VG $45.00

MC CULLOUGH, Colleen. *Creed for the 3rd Millennium.* 1985 Harper. 1st ed. sgn. dj. EX $35.00

MC CULLOUGH, Colleen. *Indecent Obsession.* 1977 NY. 1st ed. dj. $30.00

MC CULLOUGH, Colleen. *Thorn Birds.* 1977 NY. 2nd print. dj. EX $10.00

MC CULLOUGH, David. *Building of the Brooklyn Bridge.* 1972 NY. 1st ed. presentation. dj. VG $50.00

MC CUTCHEON, George Barr. *Castle Craneycrow.* no date. Stone. 1st ed. $15.00

MC CUTCHEON, George Barr. *Graustark.* 1901 Chicago. Stone. 1st ed. 459 p. $30.00

MC CUTCHEON, George Barr. *Graustark.* 1901 Stone. 1st ed. later state. VG $25.00

MC CUTCHEON, George Barr. *Jane Cable.* Dodd Mead. Ills H Fisher. 1st ed. VG $20.00

MC CUTCHEON, George Barr. *Nedra.* 1905 Dodd Mead. 1st ed. G $10.00

MC CUTCHEON, George Barr. *Purple Parasol.* 1905 NY. Dodd Mead. Ills Harrison Fischer. dj. VG $20.00

MC CUTCHEON, George Barr. *Quill's Window.* 1931 Dodd Mead. 1st ed. $8.00

MC CUTCHEON, George Barr. *Sherrods.* 1903 Dodd Mead. 1st ed. $8.00

MC CUTCHEON, J.T. *Bird Center Cartoons.* 1904 Ills 1st ed. folio. VG $25.00

MC CUTCHEON, J.T. *Drawn From Memory.* 1950 Indianapolis. Ills 1st ed. cloth. VG $25.00

MC CUTCHEON, J.T. *To CA & Back.* 1900 Chicago. 176 p. map. $35.00

MC CUTCHEON, J.T. *To CA Over the Santa Fe Trail.* 1915 Chicago. Ills McCutcheon. $30.00

MC DERMAND, Charles. *Waters of the Golden Trout Country.* 1946 Putnam. Ills. 162 p. map. G $12.50

MC DERMAND, Charles. *Yosemite & Kings Canyon Trout.* 1947 Putnam. Ills. 178 p. dj. VG $18.50

MC DERMOTT, J. *Audubon in the West.* 1965 OK U Pr. Ills 1st ed. 131 p. dj. EX $10.00

MC DERMOTT, J. *Western Journals of Washington Irving.* 1966 OK U Pr. Ills. 201 p. dj. EX $25.00

MC DONALD, J. *Curiosities of Bird Life.* 1967 Castle. Ills. 152 p. dj. EX $5.00

MC DONALD, J. *Quill Gordon.* 1972 Knopf. Ills 1st ed. 195 p. dj. EX $15.00

MC DONALD, Lucile Saunders. *Sheker's Lucky Piece.* 1941 NY. Oxford. Ills Weda Yap. 1st ed. dj. EX $20.00

MC DONALD, W.N. *History of Laurel Brigade.* 1907 private print. 1st ed. G $250.00

MC DOWELL, B. *American Cowboy in Life & Legend.* no date. National Geographic Soc. dj. $15.00

MC ELLIGOTT, James N. *American Debater.* 1855 NY. 1st ed. G $25.00

MC ELROY, C.J. *African Safari of Amateur Hunter.* 1961 Vantage Pr. dj. VG $95.00

MC ELROY, C.J. *McElroy Hunts Africa.* 1976 AZ. Sincere Pr. dj. VG $30.00

MC ELROY, J.M. *Scotch-Irish McElroys in America.* 1901 Albany. VG $35.00

MC ELROY, John. *This Was Andersonville.* 1957 NY. 1st ed. 4to. sgn. dj. VG $30.00

MC ELROY, R. *Jefferson Davis.* 1937 1st ed. 2 vol set. EX $85.00

MC ELROY, T.P. *Habitat Guide to Birding.* 1974 Knopf. Ills. 257 p. dj. EX $10.00

MC ELROY, T.P. *Handbook of Attracting Birds.* 1951 Knopf. Ills. 163 p. dj. VG $8.00

MC ENERNY, Agnes. *Pithy Anecdotes of Sam Houston.* 1939 private print. 16 p. wraps. VG $12.00

MC EVOY, H.K.; & GRUZANSKI, C. *Knife Throwing As a Modern Sport.* 1965 IL. Ills 1st ed. dj. VG $20.00

MC EWAN, Ian. *In Between the Sheets.* 1979 Simon Schuster. Review copy. dj. EX $15.00

MC EWEN, Todd. *Fisher's Hornpipe.* 1983 Harper. 1st ed. dj. EX $15.00

MC FALL, Haldane. *Beautiful Children.* 1909 NY. Ills. 4to. gilt blue buckram. $85.00

MC FALL, W.F. *Taxidermy Step by Step.* 1975 Winchester. Ills. 230 p. dj. VG $10.00

MC FARLAND, Dorothy. *Flannery O'Connor.* 1984 Ungar. 1st ed. pb. wraps. EX $10.00

MC FARLAND, J.H. *Getting Acquainted with the Trees.* 1904 NY. Outlook Co. Ills. 241 p. VG $12.50

MC FARLAND, Jeanette. *1 Mad Scramble.* 1940 Cambridge, OH. private print. 116 p. VG $20.00

MC FARLAND, Marvin. *Papers of Wilbur & Orville Wright.* 1953 NY. Ills 1st ed. 2 vol set. dj. VG $50.00

MC FEE, William. *Conrad Argosy.* 1942 NY. Doubleday Doran. 1st ed. EX $26.00

MC FEE, William. *Harbor Master.* 1931 Garden City. Ltd ed. 1/377. sgn. VG $35.00

MC FEE, William. *In the 1st Watch.* 1946 NY. 1st ed. dj. VG $25.00

MC FEE, William. *Life of Martin Frobisher.* 1928 Harper. Ills 1st ed. 276 p. maps. VG $32.00

MC FEELY, W.S. *Grant Biography.* 1981 Norton. Ills 1st ed. 592 p. dj. EX $18.00

MC GAHERN, John. *Pornographer.* 1979 London. Faber. 1st ed. VG $10.00

MC GEHEE, R. *Fit for a King: Merle Armitage Book of Food.* 1939 Duell Sloan. Ills Weston. 1st ed. 8vo. EX $75.00

MC GEORGE, W. *Copy of Private Report of Rico-Aspen Mining Co.* 1892 Phil. 1st ed. wraps. G $25.00

MC GILL, W.M. *Caverns of VA.* 1933 VA U Pr. Ills. 187 p. EX $22.00

MC GINLEY, Patrick. *Goosefoot.* 1982 Dutton. 1st Am ed. dj. EX $14.00

MC GINLEY, Phyllis. *Merry Christmas! Happy New Year!* 1958 Ills I Karasz. dj. VG $7.50

MC GINLEY, Phyllis. *Times 3.* 1960 Viking. Intro WH Auden. 1st ed. dj. EX $20.00

MC GLASHAN, C.F. *History of the Donner Party.* 1907 Sacramento. Ills 8th ed. 261 p. $35.00

MC GOVERN, Ann. *Huckleberry Hound Builds a House.* 1959 Golden Pr. Ills Eisenbert/ White. 1st ed. $6.50

MC GOVERN, James. *Crossbow & Overcast.* 1964 NY. Morrow. Ills 1st ed. 279 p. dj. VG $10.00

MC GOVERN, W.M. *Early Empires of Central Asia.* 1939 Chapel Hill. 1st ed. 529 p. VG $15.00

MC GOVERN, W.M. *Jungle Paths & Inca Ruins.* 1927 Century. Ills. 526 p. maps. G $20.00

MC GOWN, Pearl K. *Dreams Beneath Design.* 1939 Boston. Humphries. Ills 8vo. 96 p. $20.00

MC GRATH, Thomas. *To Walk a Crooked Mile.* 1947 Swallow Pr. 1st ed. dj. VG $20.00

MC GRAW, E.J.; & WAGNER, L.M. *Merry Go Round in Oz.* 1963 Reilly Lee. Ills Dick Martin. 1st ed. dj. $250.00

MC GREGOR, C. *Bob Dylan Retrospective.* 1972 NY. Ills 1st ed. 407 p. dj. VG $15.00

MC GUANE, Thomas. *Bushwacked Piano.* 1971 NY. 1st ed. sgn. dj. EX $115.00

MC GUANE, Thomas. *MO Breaks.* 1976 Ballantine. 1st ed. wraps. EX $20.00

MC GUANE, Thomas. *Nobody's Angel.* 1982 Random House. Uncorrected proof. EX $75.00

MC GUANE, Thomas. *Nobody's Angel.* 1982 Random House. 1st ed. sgn. dj. EX $30.00

MC GUANE, Thomas. *Outside Chance.* 1980 Farrar. Advance copy. sgn. wraps. EX $120.00

MC GUANE, Thomas. *Outside Chance.* 1980 Farrar. 1st ed. sgn. dj. EX $35.00

MC GUANE, Thomas. *Panama.* 1978 Farrar Straus. 1st ed. 8vo. dj. EX $20.00

MC GUANE, Thomas. *Panama.* 1978 Farrar. Uncorrected proof. EX $85.00

MC GUANE, Thomas. *Something To Be Desired.* 1984 Random House. 1st ed. 8vo. dj. EX $20.00

MC GUANE, Thomas. *Something To Be Desired.* 1984 Random House. Review copy. sgn. dj. $45.00

MC GUANE, Thomas. *Sporting Club.* 1968 Simon Schuster. 1st ed. dj. EX $50.00

MC GUANE, Thomas. *To Skin a Cat.* 1986 NY. Dutton. Uncorrected proof. $35.00

MC GUANE, Thomas. *92 in the Shade.* 1973 NY. 1st ed. dj. EX $30.00

MC GUANE, Thomas. *92 in the Shade.* 1973 Farrar. 1st ed. sgn. dj. EX $60.00

MC GUFFEY, William H. *4th Eclectic Reader.* 1879 Cincinnati. VG $35.00

MC HARG, I.L. *Design with Nature.* 1969 NY. Ills. 198 p. pb. $15.00

MC HARGUE, Georgess. *Elidor & the Golden Ball.* 1973 Dodd Mead. Ills Schongut. 1st ed. dj. EX $10.00

MC HUGH, Tom. *Time of the Buffalo.* 1972 Knopf. Ills 1st ed. 339 p. dj. EX $24.00

MC ILVAINE, Charles. *1,000 American Fungi.* 1902 Indianapolis. Ills. 729 p. VG $45.00

MC ILVANNEY, William. *Papers of Tony Veitch.* 1983 Pantheon. 1st Am ed. dj. EX $13.00

MC INERNEY, Jay. *Bright Lights, Big City.* 1985 London. Cape. 1st ed. 1st HrdCvr issue. VG $25.00

MC INERNEY, Jay. *Ransom.* 1985 Vintage. Advance copy. wraps. EX $15.00

MC INERNEY, Jay. *Ransom.* 1985 Vintage. 1st ed. wraps. EX $10.00

MC INTOCH, Christopher. *Eliphas Levi & the French Occult Revival.* 1972 NY. 238 p. VG $35.00

MC INTYRE, Vonda. *Wrath of Khan.* London. 1st ed. EX $24.00

MC KAY, Claude. *Banjo.* 1929 NY. 1st ed. VG $42.50

MC KAY, Donald. *Some Famous Sailing Ships.* 1928 NY. 1st Am ed. VG $60.00

MC KAY, Winsor. *Little Nemo.* 1972 NY. Nostalgia. Ills 1st ed. 263 p. slipcase. $45.00

MC KEARIN, Helen & George S. *200 Years of American Blown Glass.* 1958 NY. Crown. Ills 9th print. 4to. dj. $30.00

MC KEARIN, Helen. *American Glass.* 1950 NY. Crown. VG $25.00

MC KEENE, H.A. *Growing Alfalfa in IL.* 1912 IL. Ills. 116 p. wraps. VG $8.00

MC KELVEY, S.D. *Lilac: Monograph.* 1928 Macmillan. Ills 1st ed. 4to. 581 p. EX $55.00

MC KELWAY, St. Clair. *Big Little Man From Brooklyn.* 1969 Boston. 1st ed. dj. M $12.00

MC KENDREE, Charles. *Neurological Examination.* 1928 Saunders. G $8.50

MC KENNA, Richard. *Sand Pebbles.* 1962 Harper Row. 1st ed. inscr. dj. EX $75.00

MC KENNEY, Ruth. *Industrial Valley.* 1939 NY. 1st ed. 379 p. dj. VG $25.00

MC KENNEY, Thomas L. *Sketch of Tour to Lakes & Character of Chippeway Indians.* 1972 Imprint Soc. Ltd ed. 8vo. slipcase. EX $85.00

MC KENNY, M. *Book of Wayside Frivits.* 1945 NY. Ills EF Johnston. 1st ed. 8vo. $20.00

MC KENNY, M. *Wildlife of the Pacific Northwest.* 1954 Binfords Mort. Ills. 299 p. dj. EX $8.00

MC KENZIE, Dan. *Infancy of Medicine.* 1927 London. Macmillan. 1st ed. VG $25.00

MC KEOWN, M.F. *Trail Let North: Mont Hawthorne's Story.* 1949 NY. 4th print. inscr. dj. VG $18.50

MC KILLOP, P.S. *Britain & America: Lost Israelites or 10 Tribes.* 1902 St. Albans, VT. Ills. VG $45.00

MC KITTERIC, David. *New Specimen Book of Curwen Pattern Papers.* 1987 Andoversford. Ltd ed. 1/335. boxed. EX $250.00

MC KNIGHT, Charles. *Our Western Border.* 1875 Phil. Ills. 756 p. half leather. $50.00

MC KNIGHT, T.L. *Camel in Australia.* 1969 Melbourne U Pr. Ills 1st ed. 154 p. dj. EX $14.00

MC KUEN, Rod. *Fields of Wonder.* 1971 NY. Ltd 1st ed. 1/750. slipcase. $15.00

MC LANATHAN, Richard. *American Tradition in Arts.* 1968 NY. 1st ed. wraps. VG $15.00

MC LANE, A.J. *McLane's Standard Fishing Encyclopedia.* 1965 Holt Rinehart. 5th print. dj. VG $20.00

MC LAREN, Francis. *Women of the War.* 1918 Doran. Ills. 160 p. dj. $20.00

MC LAUGHLIN, J. *Gettysburg: Long Encampment.* 1963 Bonanza. reprint. 244 p. dj. EX $20.00

MC LAUGHLIN, J. *My Friend the Indian.* 1974 Superior Pub. Ills D Buisson. Deluxe ed. EX $30.00

MC LEAN, E. Walsh. *Father Struck It Rich.* 1936 Boston. 1st ed. dj. VG $17.50

MC LEAN, J.H. *Peace Makers.* 1880 NY. Baker Godwin. 1st ed. 197 p. $100.00

MC LEOD, Fiona. *Hills of Ruel.* 192 London. Ills Lawrence. 1st ed. 4to. VG $37.50

MC LEOD, G. Winsor. *Station X.* 1975 Gregg. 1st HrdCvr ed. M $20.00

MC LUHAN, Herbert Marshall. *Mechanical Bride: Folklore of Industrial Man.* 1951 Vanguard. 1st ed. dj. EX $75.00

MC LUHAN, Marshall. *From Cliche to Archetype.* 1970 NY. 1st ed. dj. EX $15.00

MC MAHON, Thomas. *McKay's Bees.* 1979 Harper. 1st ed. dj. EX $20.00

MC MARTHY, Mary. *Group.* 1963 NY. 1st ed. dj. VG $10.00

MC MASTER, J.B. *Daniel Webster.* 1902 NY. 1st ed. 1/4 leather. G $10.00

MC MILLAN, D. *Transition: History of Literary Era 1927-1938.* 1976 NY. Ills. 303 p. dj. VG $12.00

MC MILLAN, G. *Old Breed: 1st Marine Division of WWII.* 1949 Washington. 1st ed. dj. VG $65.00

MC MILLAN, I. *Man & the CA Condor.* 1968 Dutton. Ills 1st ed. 191 p. VG $10.00

MC MILLEN, W. *Bugs or People.* 1965 NY. 228 p. dj. VG $6.00

MC MULLEN, J.P. *Cry of the Panther.* 1984 Pineapple Pr. 391 p. VG $20.00

MC MULLEN, Roy. *World of Marc Chagall.* 1968 NY. Doubleday. photos Izis. folio. cloth. dj. $65.00

MC MURTRIE, Douglas. *Alphabets.* 1941 NY. 5th print. dj. EX $15.00

MC MURTRIE, Douglas. *Invention of Printing: Bibliography.* 1970 NY. reprint of 1936. EX $25.00

MC MURTRIE, Douglas. *Printing Press Moves Westward.* 1934 St. Paul. Ills. 25 p. $15.00

MC MURTRIE, Douglas. *Wings for Words.* 1940 NY. 8vo. sgn. dj. VG $25.00

MC MURTRY, Larry. *All My Friends Are Going To Be Strangers.* 1972 NY. 1st ed. dj. EX $45.00

MC MURTRY, Larry. *Cadillac Jack.* 1982 Simon Schuster. 1st ed. dj. M $15.00

MC MURTRY, Larry. *Cadillac Jack.* 1982 Simon Schuster. 1st ed. dj. EX $8.00

MC MURTRY, Larry. *Cadillac Jack.* NY. Ltd ed. sgn. slipcase. EX $27.50

MC MURTRY, Larry. *Desert Rose.* 1983 NY. Ltd 1st ed. 1/250. boxed. M $125.00

MC MURTRY, Larry. *Desert Rose.* 1983 Simon Schuster. 1st ed. dj. EX $8.00

MC MURTRY, Larry. *Desert Rose.* 1985 Allen. 1st English ed. dj. EX $35.00

MC MURTRY, Larry. *In a Narrow Grave.* 1968 NY. 1st ed. 2nd state. dj. EX $55.00

MC MURTRY, Larry. *Lonesome Dove.* 1985 NY. 1st ed. dj. EX $25.00

MC MURTRY, Larry. *Moving On.* 1970 Simon Schuster. 1st ed. dj. EX $25.00

MC MURTRY, Larry. *Terms of Endearment.* 1977 London. 1st ed. sgn. VG $75.00

MC MURTRY, Larry. *Terms of Endearment.* 1975 Simon Schuster. 1st ed. VG $25.00

MC MURTRY, Larry. *Texasville.* 1987 NY. 1st ed. sgn. dj. M $75.00

MC NAB, Tom. *Flanagan's Run.* 1982 Morrow. Advance copy. wraps. EX $20.00

MC NAIR, J. *Livingstone's Travels.* no date. Macmillan. Ills. 429 p. VG $16.00

MC NAIR, James. *Rhus Dermatitis: Its Pathology & Chemotherapy.* 1923 Chicago U Pr. G $8.50

MC NAIRN, Alan. *Young Van Dyck.* 1980 Ottawa. 1st ed. VG $35.00

MC NALLY, M.C. *Kit Carsen's Will.* 1933 private print. facsimile. pb. $3.00

MC NALLY, Tom. *Fly Fishing.* 1978 Outdoor Life. Ills. 420 p. dj. EX $13.50

MC NEER, M. *Gold Rush.* 1944 NY. Ills Lynd Ward. juvenile. VG $15.00

MC NEER, M. *Martin Luther.* 1953 Abingdon. Ills Lynn Ward. juvenile. VG $25.00

MC NEER, M. *Wolf of Lambs' Lane.* 1967 Boston. Houghton Mifflin. 1st ed. dj. $20.00

MC NEILL, Bedford. *Mining & General Telegraphic Code.* 1903 London/NY. 807 p. gilt cloth. VG $50.00

MC NEILL, D. *Moving Through Here.* 1970 NY. 1st ed. dj. EX $10.00

MC NEILL, W.A. *Cabellian Harmonics.* 1928 NY. Georgian Pr. Ltd ed. 1/1,500. $25.00

MC NEIR, Forest W. *Forest McNeir of TX.* 1956 Naylor. 1st ed. dj. EX $40.00

MC NITT, Frank. *Indian Traders.* 1963 OK U Pr. Ills 2nd print. 393 p. dj. EX $17.00

MC NITT, V. *Bob's 30 Years: Story of Robert B. McNitt by His Father.* 1945 private print. Ltd ed. 1/300. boxed. EX $30.00

MC NULTY, F. *Great Whales.* 1974 Doubleday. Ills 1st ed. 100 p. dj. EX $8.00

MC NULTY, F. *Whooping Crane: Bird That Defies Extinction.* 1966 Dutton. Ills 1st ed. 190 p. dj. EX $10.00

MC NULTY, J. *My Son Johnny.* 1955 NY. Review ed. dj. EX $15.00

MC NULTY, John. *World of John McNulty.* 1957 Garden City. 1st ed. dj. VG $18.00

MC NULTY, Kneeland. *Collected Prints of Ben Shahn.* 1967 Phil. Ills. folio. 150 p. wraps. $35.00

MC PHEE, John. *Coming into the Country.* 1977 Farrar. 1st ed. green cloth. dj. EX $14.00

MC PHEE, John. *Crofter & Laird.* 1970 NY. 1st ed. dj. VG $20.00

MC PHEE, John. *Deltoid Pumpkin Seed.* 1973 Farrar. 1st stated ed. orange boards. $25.00

MC PHEE, John. *Giving Good Weight.* 1979 NY. Stated 1st ed. dj. G $8.00

MC PHEE, John. *Giving Good Weight.* 1979 NY. 1st ed. sgn. dj. EX $45.00

MC PHEE, John. *Levels of Game.* 1969 NY. 1st ed. dj. EX $35.00

MC PHEE, John. *Oranges.* 1967 NY. 1st ed. dj. EX $35.00

MC PHEE, John. *Pine Barrens.* 1981 NY. Ills Curtsinger. 1st ed. dj. $25.00

MC PHEE, John. *Roomful of Hovings.* 1979 NY. green cloth. dj. M $16.00

MC PHEE, John. *Sense of Where You Are.* 1966 no place. 1st ed. dj. EX $50.00

MC PHEE, John. *Sense of Where You Are: Profile of William Warren Bradley.* 1965 NY. Farrar. 1st ed. inscr/sgn. dj. EX $175.00

MC PHEE, John. *Wimbledon: Celebration.* 1972 NY. Ills Eisenstaedt. 1st ed. dj. $35.00

MC PHERSON, Alexander. *History of Faulkner County, AR.* 1927 Conway. private print. pb. EX $15.00

MC QUADE, James. *Cruise of Montauk to Bermuda, West Indies, & FL.* 1885 NY. Knox. G $35.00

MC QUADE, James. *Cruise of Montauk to Bermuda, West Indies, & FL.* 1885 NY. 1st ed. VG $45.00

MC REYNOLDS, E.C. *MO: History of the Crossroads State.* 1962 OK U Pr. Ills 1st ed. 483 p. maps. EX $20.00

MC REYNOLDS, E.C. *OK: History of the Sooner State.* 1956 OK U Pr. 2nd print. $10.00

MC SHANE, Charles. *Locomotive Up To Date.* 1906 Chicago. Ills. 711 p. $45.00

MC SHERRY. *History of MD.* 1904 Baltimore. 1/50. 437 p. VG $75.00

MC SHINE, K.L. *Information.* 1970 MOMA. Ills. 4to. 207 p. wraps. $10.00

MC SHINE, K.L. *Joseph Cornell.* 1980 MOMA. Ills. 4to. 296 p. wraps. $40.00

MC TAGGART, Lt. Col. M.F. *Mount & Man.* 1930 London. Ills L Edwards. 4to. 163 p. VG $40.00

MC VAUGH, Rogers. *Edward Palmer: Plant Explorer of the West.* 1956 OK U Pr. Ills 1st ed. 430 p. dj. EX $25.00

MC VICKER, M.L. *Writings of J. Frank Dobie.* 1968 Lawton. 1st ed. $35.00

MC WHORTER, L.V. *Yellow Wolf: His Own Story.* 1948 Caxton. Ills Revised 2nd ed. dj. VG $47.50

MC WILLIAMS, C. *Southern CA.* 1946 Duell. 1st print. Am Folkways Series. $12.50

MC WILLIAMS, Vera. *Lafcadio Hearn.* 1946 Boston. 1st ed. dj. $25.00

MEACHAM, L. *Lessons in Hypnotism.* 1898 Cincinnati. VG $8.00

MEAD, A.R. *Giant African Snail: Problem in Economic Malacology.* 1961 Chicago U Pr. Ills. 257 p. dj. VG $20.00

MEAD, Franklin. *Heroic Statues in Bronze of Abraham Lincoln.* 1932 Ft. Wayne. Ills Ltd ed. 1/300. 93 p. $30.00

MEAD, G.R.S. *Appolonius of Tyana.* 1901 London. 1st ed. 159 p. rebound. EX $75.00

MEAD, G.R.S. *Selected Works of Plotinus.* 1914 London. 1st ed. 343 p. VG $65.00

MEAD, Harold. *Bright Phoenix.* 1956 Ballantine. 1st ed. pb. EX $5.00

MEAD, Margaret. *Changing Culture of an Indian Tribe.* 1932 COU Pr. 1st ed. 313 p. index. G $35.00

MEAD, Margaret. *Male & Female.* 1971 Rio De Janiero. 1st Brasilian ed. inscr. $165.00

MEAD, Margaret. *Maoris & Their Arts.* 1928 NY. Am Museum. Ills 1st ed. wraps. rare. $250.00

MEAD, Margaret. *Moeurs et Sexualite en Oceanie.* 1963 Paris. 1st ed. sgn. wraps. VG $275.00

MEAD, Margaret. *New Lives for Old. Cultural Transformation: Manua 1928-1953.* 1956 NY. 1st ed. EX $30.00

MEAD, Margaret. *Social Organization of Manua.* 1930 Honolulu. 1st ed. sgn. 4to. scarce. EX $350.00

MEADE, Bishop. *Old Churches, Ministers, & Families of VA.* 1857 Lippincott. 2 vol set. $35.00

MEADE, R. *Patrick Henry.* 1957 Phil. 1st VA ed. presentation. EX $30.00

MEADOWCROFT, William H. *Boys' Life of Edison with Autobiographical Notes by Edison.* 1929 NY. Harper. Ills. 289 p. cloth. EX $55.00

MEADOWS, Lorena E. *Sagebrush Heritage: Story of Ben Edwards.* 1972 San Jose. dj. G $12.00

MEAGHER, S. *Accessory After Fact.* 1967 Indianapolis. 1st ed. dj. VG $30.00

MEANS, P.A. *Ancient Civilizations of Andes.* 1931 NY. Scribner. 1st ed. 8vo. inscr. EX $150.00

MEANS, P.A. *Spanish Main.* 1965 NY. VG $20.00

MEANY, Dee Morrison. *Iseult.* 1985 Ace. 1st ed. pb. M $4.00

MEANY, E.S. *History of the State of WA.* 1909 Macmillan. Ills 1st ed. 406 p. EX $25.00

MEARA, David. *Victorian Memorial Brasses.* 1983 London. Routledge. Ills. 173 p. $17.50

MEASE, James. *On the Causes, Cure, & Prevention of the Sick Headache.* 1832 Phil. 4th ed. EX $85.00

MEATYARD, R.E. *Photographs of R.E. Meatyard.* 1974 Millerton. Ills. 4to. wraps. EX $20.00

MECH, L.D. *Wolves of Isle Royale.* 1966 GPO. Ills. 210 p. wraps. EX $6.00

MECHANICUS, P. *Year of Fear.* 1964 NY. Hawthorne Books. EX $25.00

MECK, C.R. *Meeting & Fishing the Hatches.* 1977 Winchester. Ills. 194 p. dj. EX $12.50

MECKLENBURG, George. *Last of the Old West.* 1927 WA. Ills 1st ed. 149 p. dj. VG $22.50

MEEHAN, Jeanette Porter. *Lady of Limberlost: Life & Letters of Gene Stratton Porter.* 1928 Doubleday. 1st ed. dj. VG $250.00

MEEKER, Ezra. *Busy Life of 85 Years.* 1916 Seattle. private print. sgn. $85.00

MEEKER, Ezra. *Ox-Team Days on OR Trail.* 1922 NY. Pioneer Life Series. VG $45.00

MEGINESS. *Biography of Frances Slocum: Lost Sister of WY.* 1891 Ills. VG $170.00

MEGQUIER, Mary Jane. *Apron Full of Gold.* 1949 San Marino. 1st ed. dj. $27.50

MEHL, Robert Franklin. *Brief History of Science of Metals.* 1948 NY. 1st ed. 83 p. VG $10.00

MEHRING, Walter. *George Grosz Biography.* 1944 NY. Herrmann. Ills. 4to. $60.00

MEIER, M.S. *Chicanos: History of Mexican Americans.* 1972 NY. 1st ed. dj. $15.00

MEIER, W.H. *School & Home Gardens.* 1913 Boston. 319 p. xl. VG $10.00

MEIER-GRAEFE. *Spanish Journey.* no date. Harcourt Brace. plts. VG $20.00

MEIER-GRAEFE. *Vincent Van Gogh.* 1922 London. Medici Soc. 2 vol set. EX $95.00

MEIGS, A. *American Country House.* 1925 NY. 1st ed. folio. dj. VG $100.00

MEIGS, Cornelia. *Call of the Mountain.* 1940 Little Brown. Ills Daugherty. 1st ed. EX $20.00

MEIGS, Cornelia. *Trade Wind.* 1927 Little Brown. Ills Pitz. 8vo. black cloth. $15.00

MEIKLEJOHN, I.M.D. *Golden Primer Part I.* c 1880s. Blackwood. Ills Crane. 1st ed. $75.00

MEILACH, Dona Z. *Creating Art From Anything.* 1968 NY. Ills. 119 p. $15.00

MEILACH, Dona Z. *Creative Stitchery.* 1969 NY. Galahad. Ills. 118 p. dj. $20.00

MEILACH & TEN HOOR. *Collage & Found Art.* 1965 Reinhold. Ills 2nd print. 4to. 68 p. dj. $10.00

MEINERS. *History of the Female Sex.* 1808 London. 4 vol set. cloth. EX $300.00

MEINHOLD, William. *Sidonia the Sorceress.* 1893 London. Kelmscott Pr. 4to. $225.00

MEISS, Millard. *Great Age of Fresco.* 1970 NY. Braziller. Ills. folio. cloth. dj. $95.00

MEISS, Millard. *Visconti Hours.* 1972 NY. dj. slipcase. EX $40.00

MEISSNER, Hans P. Otto. *Magna Goebbels: 1st Lady of the 3rd Reich.* 1980 NY. 1st Am print. dj. VG $20.00

MEISTER, Helen. *Palestine 1933.* 1933 Chicago. private print. 8vo. VG $35.00

MELCHIOR, M. *Rabbi Remembers.* 1968 Lyle Stuart. 2nd ed. dj. VG $12.50

MELHAM, T. *John Muir's Wild America.* 1976 Nat'l Geog Soc. Ills. 199 p. maps. dj. EX $12.00

MELIGAKES, N.A. *Spirit of Gettysburg.* 1950 Bookmark. Ills. inscr. maps. EX $35.00

MELLEN, Grenville. *Book of the US.* 1841 NY. Ills. 8vo. 804 p. leather. G $49.00

MELLEN, Grenville. *Book of the US.* 1842 Hartford, CT. Ills. 8vo. 847 p. G $37.00

MELLEN, I.M. *Natural History of the Pig.* 1952 Exposition. Ills 1st ed. 157 p. G $8.00

MELLOR, J.E.M. *Notes on Falconry.* 1949 private print. Ills. 83 p. EX $20.00

MELTZER, David. *Around the Poem Box.* 1968 Black Sparrow. Ltd 1st ed. 1/26. sgn. wraps. $75.00

MELVILLE, Fred J. *Chats on Postage Stamps.* 1920 Unwin. 2nd imp. 361 p. VG $25.00

MELVILLE, George W. *In the Lena Delta.* 1885 Boston. Ills 1st ed. 8vo. 497 p. VG $45.00

MELVILLE, Herman. *Benito Cereno.* 1972 Barre. Ills Garrick Palmer. 1/1,950. $27.00

MELVILLE, Herman. *Benito Cereno.* 1926 London. Ills Kauffer. 1/1,650. $95.00

MELVILLE, Herman. *Mardi & Voyage Thither.* 1923 Boston. Botolph Soc. 1st imp. $13.00

MELVILLE, Herman. *Omoo.* 1924 Dodd Mead. Ills Schaeffer. 1st ed. VG $40.00

MELVILLE, Herman. *On the Slain Collegians.* 1971 NY. Ills Frasconi. 1/1,000. dj. EX $75.00

MELVILLE, Herman. *Redburn: His 1st Voyage.* 1848 NY. 1st ed. cloth. fair. $30.00

MELVILLE, Herman. *Tragedy of Mind.* 1944 Cambridge. 1st ed. dj. VG $25.00

MEMPES, Mortimer. *World Pictures.* no date. London. 100 plts. cloth. EX $50.00

MENABONI, A. & S. *Menaboni's Birds.* 1984 Potter. Revised ed. 4to. 176 p. dj. EX $23.00

MENCKEN, H.L. *American Language.* 1919 NY. Ltd ed. 1/1,500. $45.00

MENCKEN, H.L. *Bathtub Hoax.* 1958 NY. 1st ed. dj. VG $40.00

MENCKEN, H.L. *Choice of Days.* 1980 NY. Knopf. 1st ed. dj. VG $20.00

MENCKEN, H.L. *Heathen Days.* 1943 NY. 1st ed. sgn. dj. VG $90.00

MENCKEN, H.L. *James Branch Cabell.* 1927 NY. Ills 1st ed. wraps. $47.50

MENCKEN, H.L. *Letters of H.L. Mencken.* 1961 NY. 1st ed. dj. EX $45.00

MENCKEN, H.L. *Little Book in C Major.* 1916 NY. VG $75.00

MENCKEN, H.L. *Philosophy of Friedrich Nietzsche.* 1913 Boston. Luce. 3rd ed. 8vo. inscr. VG $60.00

MENCKEN, H.L. *Treatise on Right & Wrong.* 1934 NY. 1st ed. dj. EX $85.00

MENCKEN, H.L. *Treatise on the Gods.* 1958 NY. 1st ed. dj. VG $35.00

MENDALL, H.L. *Ring-Necked Duck in the Northeast.* 1958 ME U Pr. 317 p. maps. wraps. VG $22.50

MENDEL, G. *Experiments in Plant Hybridization.* 1967 Harvard U Pr. 41 p. wraps. G $10.00

MENEN, Aubrey. *Ramayana.* 1954 NY. dj. VG $10.00

MENJOU. *It Took 9 Tailors.* 1948 Whittlesey. 1st print. sgn. dj. VG $20.00

MENNELL & GARLEPP. *Bismarck Denkmal fur das Deutsche Volk.* 1985 Chicago. Werner. Ills. photos. wraps. $95.00

MENON & PANDALAI. *Coconut Palm: Monograph.* 1958 Ernakulam. Ills. 4to. dj. VG $37.50

MENPES, D. *Japan.* 1905 London. Ills Mortimer Menpes. 207 p. $30.00

MENPES, Mortimer & Dorothy. *Durbar.* 1903 London. Ills. 4to. sgn. cloth. EX $135.00

MENPES, Mortimer. *Gainsborough.* 1909 London. Black. Ills. folio. plts. VG $32.50

MENPES, Mortimer. *Rembrandt.* 1905 London. Black. Ills. VG $65.00

MENPES, Mortimer. *Whistler As I Knew Him.* 1904 London. Ltd ed. 1/500. $75.00

MENUHIN, Moshe. *Decadence of Judaism in Our Time.* 1969 Beirut. 4to. 579 p. VG $35.00

MENZIE, J.W. *New Methods: Wool Washing, Fleece Scouring, & Sheep Dipping.* 1882 Liverpool. 8vo. 32 p. wraps. $50.00

MERCER & HAY. *Gardens & Gardening.* 1954 London. 144 p. dj. VG $5.00

MERCER & HOLME. *Gardens & Gardening.* 1940 London. 116 p. dj. G $20.00

MERCHANT, Elizabeth. *King Arthur.* 1957 NY. Ills Frank Godwin. VG $4.50

MEREDITH, George. *Ordeal of Richard Feverel.* 1859 London. 1st ed. full leather. 3 vols. $225.00

MEREDITH, Roy. *Face of Robert E. Lee in Life & Legend.* 1947 Scribner. Ills 1st ed. 143 p. VG $20.00

MEREDITH, Roy. *Mr. Lincoln's Camera Man: Matthew B. Brady.* 1946 Scribner. Ills. 4to. 368 p. VG $30.00

MEREDITH, Roy. *Mr. Lincoln's General: U.S. Grant.* 1981 NY. Bonanza. Ills. VG $16.00

MEREJKOWSKI, D. *Romance of Leonardo da Vinci.* 1940 NY. 12mo. brown leather. slipcase. $25.00

MEREJKOWSKI, D. *Romance of Leonardo da Vinci.* 1928 NY. Ills. 574 p. EX $12.50

MERFIELD, Fred. *Gorilla Hunter.* 1956 NY. Ills. dj. VG $15.00

MERFIELD, Fred. *Gorillas Were My Neighbors.* 1956 Longman. Ills 1st ed. 249 p. G $10.00

MERIMEE, Prosper. *Carmen.* 1941 Ltd Ed Club. Aldus Printers. slipcase. EX $250.00

MERIMEE, Prosper. *Carmen.* 1931 NY. Trans Albert Sterner. 4to. G $22.00

MERK, Frederick. *Fur Trade & Empire: George Stimson's Journal 1824-1825.* 1968 Harvard. dj. VG $25.00

MERLE, Robert. *Day of the Dolphin.* 1969 NY. dj. EX $14.00

MERRIAM, H.G. *Way Out West: Recollections & Tales.* 1970 OK U Pr. 296 p. dj. EX $10.00

MERRIAM, Robert E. *Dark December: Full Account of Battle of Bulge.* 1947 Chicago. Ziff Davis. 1st ed. dj. EX $35.00

MERRICK, James Kirk. *Brian.* 1948 Rockport Pr. Ills. oblong 4to. cloth. VG $18.00

MERRICK. *In the World's Attic.* 1931 NY. Ills 1st ed. 259 p. VG $37.50

MERRILL, Elmer D. *Index Rafinesquianus.* 1949 Harvard U Pr. 4to. 296 p. black cloth. M $60.00

MERRILL, Henry A. *Alexander Gifford or Vi'let's Boy.* 1905 1st ed. 331 p. G $30.00

MERRILL, James. *Braving the Elements.* 1972 NY. Atheneum. 1st ed. 8vo. dj. EX $40.00

MERRILL, James. *Spurs to Glory: Story of the US Cavalry.* 1966 Rand McNally. Ills 1st ed. 302 p. dj. EX $12.50

MERRIMAN, A.T.A. *Type Comparison Book.* 1965 Indianapolis. Anniversary ed. VG $15.00

MERRITT, A. *Black Wheel.* 1947 NY. Ltd 1st ed. 1/1,000. dj. VG $45.00

MERRITT, A. *Face in Abyss.* 1931 Liveright. 1st ed. VG $50.00

MERRITT, A. *Moon Pool.* 1949 Putnam. 1st ed. VG $50.00

MERRITT, A. *Ship of Ishtar.* 1926 Putnam. 1st ed. VG $50.00

MERRITT, A. *7 Footprints to Satan.* 1928 Boni Liveright. 1st ed. VG $50.00

MERRYMAN, Richard. *Andrew Wyeth.* 1968 Boston. 1st ed. dj. EX $225.00

MERRYMAN, Richard. *Andrew Wyeth.* 1968 Boston. 2nd print. dj. EX $150.00

MERSHON, W.B. *Passenger Pigeon.* 1907 NY. Outing Pub. G $30.00

MERSHON, W.B. *Recollections of My 50 Years Hunting & Fishing.* 1923 Boston. cloth. $100.00

MERTENS. *Moderne Meubels en Interieurs.* c 1935. Antwerp. xl. G $14.00

MERTLE & MONSEN. *Photomechanics & Printing.* 1957 Chicago. Ills. folio. $50.00

MERTON, Thomas. *Christmas Sermons of B. Gueric of Ingny.* 1959 Abbey of Gethsemani. 62 p. VG $45.00

MERTON, Thomas. *Disputed Questions.* 1960 NY. 1st ed. dj. $15.00

MERTON, Thomas. *Living Bread.* 1956 NY. 1st ed. dj. EX $20.00

MERTON, Thomas. *Love & Living.* 1979 1st ed. VG $35.00

MERTON, Thomas. *Seeds of Destruction.* 1964 1st ed. VG $30.00

MERTON, Thomas. *Spiritual Direction & Meditation.* 1960 Collegeville. Liturgical Pr. 8vo. dj. $46.50

MERTON, Thomas. *Tears of the Blind Lions.* 1949 New Directions. 1st ed. 8vo. wraps. EX $20.00

MERTON, Thomas. *What Are These Wounds?* 1950 1st ed. dj. EX $75.00

MERTON, Thomas. *What Is Contemplation?* 1948 Holy Cross, IN. 1st ed. wraps. scarce. EX $117.50

MERWIN, W.S. *Green with Beasts.* 1956 London. 1st ed. dj. EX $65.00

MERWIN, W.S. *Lice.* 1969 London. 1st English ed. dj. EX $15.00

MESSEL, Oliver. *Stage Designs & Costumes.* 1933 London. Ills Ltd 1st ed. 1/1,000. 4to. $100.00

MESSER, Thomas M. *Emergent Decade: Latin American Painting in the '60s.* 1966 Cornell U Pr. Ills Cornell Capa. 187 p. dj. $75.00

MESSITER, C.A. *Sport & Adventures Among the North American Indians.* 1966 Abercrombie Fitch. Ills. EX $20.00

MESTA, Perle. *My Story by Perle Mesta.* 1960 NY. 1st ed. dj. EX $25.00

METCALFE, John. *Feasting Dead.* 1954 Sauk City. 1st ed. dj. VG $65.00

METEYARD, Eliza. *Wedgewood Handbook.* 1963 Trace. reprint. 8vo. 438 p. dj. $25.00

METKEN, Gunter. *Agam.* 1977 NY. Ills. oblong 4to. 78 p. dj. $20.00

METRAUX, Alfred. *Voodoo.* 1959 NY. Oxford U Pr. 1st ed. dj. EX $18.00

METZ, L.C. *John Selman: TX Gunfighter.* 1966 Hastings House. Ills. 254 p. dj. EX $10.00

METZ, L.C. *Shooters.* 1983 Mangan. Ills. 299 p. dj. EX $20.00

METZ, L.C. *Shooters.* 1976 El Paso, TX. Ills 2nd ed. sgn. dj. VG $20.00

MEURER, A. *Der Kraftfahrsport im Neuen Deutschland.* 1935 Berlin. Ills. German text. VG $40.00

MEYER, F. *Marc Chagall.* no date. NY. Abrams. dj. EX $75.00

MEYER, R.C.V. *Theodore Roosevelt: Patriot & Statesman.* 1901 private print. Ills. 485 p. VG $5.00

MEYER, S.E. *40 Watercolorists & How They Work.* 1976 NY. Ills. 176 p. $28.00

MEYER-ABICH, Asolf. *Alexander von Humboldt 1769-1969.* 1969 Bonn. Ills. 8vo. 169 p. wraps. $25.00

MEYNELL, Alice. *Mary, Mother of Jesus.* 1912 London. Medici Soc. Ills Bell. 1/250. $90.00

MEYNELL, Alice. *School of Poetry.* 1924 NY. cloth. dj. VG $25.00

MEYNELL, Francis. *My Lives.* 1971 NY. 1st ed. dj. M $24.00

MEYNELL, Francis. *My Lives.* 1971 NY. 1st Am ed. EX $16.00

MEYNELL, Francis. *Typography.* 1923 Pelican Pr. Ills 1st ed. EX $125.00

MEYNEN, Emil. *Bibliography on German Settlements in Colonial America.* 1937 Leipzig. 636 p. M $85.00

MEZEY, Robert. *Love Maker.* 1961 Cummington Pr. 1st ed. dj. EX $26.00

MEZZROW. *Really the Blues.* 1946 Random House. 1st ed. VG $22.50

MIALL, Agnes M. *Making Home Furnishings.* 1937 London. Pittman. xl. G $25.00

MIALL, L.C. *Natural History of Aquatic Insects.* 1922 Macmillan. Ills. 395 p. VG $14.00

MICHAUX, Henri. *Light Through Darkness.* 1963 NY. Orion. 1st ed. dj. VG $15.00

MICHEL, Emile. *Reubens.* 1899 NY/London. Ills. folio. 2 vol set. VG $150.00

MICHEL, Walter. *Wyndham Lewis: Paintings & Drawings.* 1971 Berkeley. $40.00

MICHELANGELO. *Drawings of Michelangelo.* 1965 NY. 1st ed. folio. ½-calf. slipcase. VG $350.00

MICHELL, Sir Lewis. *Life & Times of Cecil Thodes 1853-1902.* 1910 NY. Mitchell Kennerley, 2 vol set. $100.00

MICHELMAN, Joseph. *Violin Varnish.* 1946 Cincinnati. Michelman. VG $25.00

MICHELSON, T. *Contributions to Fox Ethnology.* 1927 BAE Bull. 168 p. VG $18.00

MICHENER, James A. *About Centennial.* 1974 NY. Ltd 1st ed. sgn. dj. M $27.00

MICHENER, James A. *Bridge at Andau.* 1957 NY. 1st ed. dj. VG $25.00

MICHENER, James A. *Centennial.* 1974 NY. 1st ed. dj. VG $20.00

MICHENER, James A. *Centennial.* 1974 Random House. dj. VG $14.50

MICHENER, James A. *Chesapeake.* 1978 NY. 1st ed. dj. VG $17.00

MICHENER, James A. *Covenant.* 1980 Random House. 1st ed. dj. EX $16.00

MICHENER, James A. *Drifters.* 1971 NY. 1st ed. dj. VG $20.00

MICHENER, James A. *Floating World.* 1954 Random House. Ills. 403 p. cloth. dj. $60.00

MICHENER, James A. *James A. Michener's USA.* 1981 Crown. 1st ed. dj. EX $25.00

MICHENER, James A. *Japanese Prints.* 1959 Rutland. 1st ed. dj. boxed. EX $95.00

MICHENER, James A. *Kent State.* 1971 Ramdom House. 1st ed. dj. EX $15.00

MICHENER, James A. *Michener Miscellany.* 1973 NY. 1st ed. dj. VG $20.00

MICHENER, James A. *Poland.* 1983 Random House. 1st ed. dj. EX $18.00

MICHENER, James A. *Quality of Life.* 1970 Girard Bank. Ltd ed. slipcase. EX $40.00

MICHENER, James A. *Rascals in Paradise.* 1957 NY. 1st ed. dj. VG $15.00

MICHENER, James A. *Rascals in Paradise.* 1957 London. 1st ed. dj. VG $25.00

MICHENER, James A. *Report of the Country Chairman.* 1961 NY. 1st ed. dj. EX $25.00

MICHENER, James A. *Sayonara.* 1954 NY. 1st ed. dj. VG $25.00

MICHENER, James A. *Source.* 1965 NY. 1st ed. dj. VG $20.00

MICHENER, James A. *Space.* 1982 Random House. 1st ed. dj. VG $30.00

MICHENER, James A. *Texas.* Random House. 1st ed. dj. VG $14.50

MICHENER, James A. *Texas.* no date. Special Deluxe ed. 1/400. EX $900.00

MICKEL, J.T. *How To Know the Ferns & Fern Allies.* 1979 Brown. Ills. 229 p. EX $18.00

MICKOLLS, L.C. *Scientific Investigation of Crime.* 1956 London. Ills 1st ed. dj. VG $20.00

MIDDLEDORF, Ulrich. *Sculpture of the Kress Collection.* 1976 NY. Phaidon. $32.50

MIDDLEMAS, Keith. *Antique Glass in Color.* 1971 NY. Doubleday. Ills. 4to. 120 p. dj. $25.00

MIDDLETON, George. *Hiss! Boom! Bah!* 1933 NY. 12mo. VG $12.00

MIERS, Earl. *Last Campaign: Grant Saves the Union.* 1972 Lippincott. 1st ed. 213 p. maps. VG $14.00

MIERS, Earl. *Web of Victory: Grant at Vicksburg.* 1955 Knopf. Ills 1st ed. 320 p. maps. VG $18.00

MIGDALSKI & FICHTER. *Fresh-Water & Salt-Water Fishes of the World.* 1976 NY. Ills Weaver. 1st ed. 4to. dj. $30.00

MIGEL, J.M. *Masters of the Dry Fly.* 1977 Lippincott. Ills 1st ed. 246 p. dj. EX $10.00

MIKES, Dr. G. *Epic of Lofoten.* no date. London. Ills. 79 p. wraps. G $10.00

MIKESH, R.C. *Zero Fighter.* 1981 London. Ills Watanabe. VG $25.00

MIKKELSON, Ejnar. *Lost in the Arctic.* 1913 NY. 1st ed. 395 p. dj. VG $135.00

MILBANK, Jeremiah. *1st Century of Flight in America.* 1943 Princeton. Ills 1st ed. 248 p. dj. VG $35.00

MILES, E.B. *Spirit of the Mountains.* 1975 Knoxville. TN U Pr. Ills. VG $12.00

MILES, Henry Downes. *Puglistica: History of British Boxing.* 1906 Edinburgh. 8vo. 3 vol set. VG $175.00

MILES, Nelson A. *Personal Recollections.* 1896 Chicago/NY. Ills 1st ed. 1st issue. VG $125.00

MILFORD, Nancy. *Zelda: Biography.* 1970 Harper. 1st ed. sgn. dj. EX $20.00

MILHAUSER, Steven. *Edwin Mullhouse.* 1979 London. Rutledge. 1st ed. dj. VG $30.00

MILHAUSER, Steven. *From Realm of Morpheus.* 1986 Morrow. 1st ed. dj. EX $18.00

MILHAUSER, Steven. *In the Penny Arcade.* 1985 Knopf. 1st ed. dj. EX $15.00

MILL, John Stuart. *Autobiography of John Stuart Mill 1806-1873.* 1873 London. 1st ed. xl. G $70.00

MILL, John Stuart. *Autobiography of John Stuart Mill 1806-1873.* 1873 NY. Holt. 1st Am ed. brown cloth. VG $70.00

MILL, John Stuart. *Subjection of Women.* 1870 NY. 1st Am ed. dj. EX $85.00

MILLAR, Kenneth. *Blue City.* 1947 NY. 1st ed. dj. EX $325.00

MILLAR, Kenneth. *3 Roads.* 1948 NY. 1st ed. dj. EX $250.00

MILLAR, Kenneth. *3 Roads.* 1950 London. 1st ed. dj. EX $95.00

MILLAR, Margaret. *Beast in View.* 1955 NY. 1st ed. dj. EX $17.50

MILLAR, Margaret. *Fiend.* 1964 NY. 1st ed. dj. EX $15.00

MILLARD, Christopher. *Bibliography of Oscar Wilde.* 1914 London. Ills 1st ed. VG $75.00

MILLAY, Edna St. Vincent. *Aria da Copo.* 1921 NY. Kennerly. 1st ed. dj. EX $35.00

MILLAY, Edna St. Vincent. *Buck in the Snow & Other Poems.* 1928 NY. Ltd ed. 1/515. 8vo. boxed. EX $160.00

MILLAY, Edna St. Vincent. *Buck in the Snow.* 1928 NY. 1st ed. dj. EX $12.00

MILLAY, Edna St. Vincent. *Collected Sonnets.* 1941 NY. Golden Hind. 1st ed. slipcase. $25.00

MILLAY, Edna St. Vincent. *Conversation at Midnight.* 1937 NY/London. Harper. 1st ed. 8vo. VG $55.00

MILLAY, Edna St. Vincent. *Few Figs & Thistles.* 1922 Harper. 12mo. gilt black cloth. VG $7.50

MILLAY, Edna St. Vincent. *Huntsman, What Quarry?* 1939 NY/London. Harper. 1st ed. 8vo. EX $25.00

MILLAY, Edna St. Vincent. *Lamp & Bell.* 1921 Harper. 12mo. black cloth. VG $7.50

MILLAY, Edna St. Vincent. *Make Bright the Arrows.* 1940 NY. 1st ed. dj. EX $28.00

MILLAY, Edna St. Vincent. *Poems Selected for Young People.* 1929 NY. Ills J Paget-Fredericks. VG $35.00

MILLAY, Edna St. Vincent. *Renaissance.* 1917 Mitchell Kennedy. 1st ed. VG $65.00

MILLAY, Edna St. Vincent. *There Are No Islands Anymore.* 1940 NY. EX $22.00

MILLAY, Edna St. Vincent. *Wine From These Grapes.* 1934 NY. 1st ed. dj. VG $15.00

MILLAY, Edna St. Vincent. *2nd April.* 1921 Harper. 112 p. VG $30.00

MILLER, A. *MS: Life & Legends of America's Greatest River.* 1975 Crescent. Ills. 4to. 127 p. maps. EX $12.00

MILLER, A.J. *Pioneer Doctor in the Ozarks White River Country.* 1949 Burton. Ills. 161 p. dj. VG $12.00

MILLER, A.J. *West of Alfred Jacob Miller.* 1968 OK U Pr. Revised ed. 1st print. dj. $35.00

MILLER, Arthur. *After the Fall.* 1964 NY. Viking. Ltd ed. 1/500. sgn. slipcase. $60.00

MILLER, Arthur. *After the Fall.* 1964 Viking. 1st ed. 1/995. sgn. slipcase. $110.00

MILLER, Arthur. *Salesman in Beijing.* 1984 NY. sgn. dj. M $24.00

MILLER, Arthur. *View From the Bridge.* 1955 Viking. 1st ed. dj. EX $45.00

MILLER, C. *Battle for Bundu.* 1974 NY. 1st ed. dj. EX $25.00

MILLER, D. *Measured Drawings of Colonial & Georgian Houses.* 1915 NY. Ills 1st ed. VG $85.00

MILLER, D. *Story of Walt Disney.* 1959 Dell. Ills 1st ed. pb. VG $6.00

MILLER, D. *You Can't Do Business with Hitler.* 1941 Little Brown. 3rd ed. G $10.00

MILLER, D.R. *Criminal Classes, Causes, & Cures.* 1903 Dayton. VG $30.00

MILLER, Dayton C. *Sparks, Lightning, & Cosmic Rays.* 1939 NY. Macmillan. Ills 192 p. dj. VG $12.00

MILLER, Dorothy C. *Americans 1963.* no date. MOMA. Ills. 112 p. wraps. $15.00

MILLER, Dorothy C. *Modern Masters From European & American Collections.* 1940 MOMA. Ills Ltd ed. spiral bdg. $10.00

MILLER, Dorothy C. *Sculpture of John B. Flannagan.* 1942 MOMA. Ills. 4to. 40 p. wraps. $30.00

MILLER, E.B. *Bataan Uncensored.* 1949 Long Prairie. 1st ed. sgn. EX $50.00

MILLER, E.G. *American Antique Furniture.* 1937 NY. 1st ed. 4to. 2 vol set. VG $50.00

MILLER, E.G. *American Antique Furniture.* 1937 Lord Baltimore Pr. 2 vol set. $85.00

MILLER, F.T. *Armies & the Leaders.* 1957 Castle. reprint. 10 vol set. VG $10.00

MILLER, F.T. *Photographic History of the Civil War.* 1957 Castle. 10 vol set. EX $52.50

MILLER, F.T. *World in the Air: Story of Flying in Pictures.* 1930 Putnam. Ills. 4to. 2 vol set. EX $55.00

MILLER, F.T. *2 Years of Grim War.* 1957 Castle. reprint. 2 vol set. VG $10.00

MILLER, Floyd. *Bill Tilghman, Marshall of the Last Frontier.* 1968 Doubleday. Ills 1st ed. 252 p. dj. EX $13.50

MILLER, G.S. *List of North American Recent Mammals.* 1924 USNM. 673 p. wraps. EX $18.00

MILLER, H. *In Conservation.* 1972 Quadrangle. dj. EX $7.00

MILLER, H. *Plexus.* 1953 Olympia Pr. 1st ed. VG $250.00

MILLER, H.M. *Comparative Studies of Furcocercous Cercariae.* 1926 IL U Pr. Ills. 112 p. wraps. $10.00

MILLER, Heather Ross. *Adams's 1st Wife.* 1983 Briarpatch. 1st ed. 12mo. $15.00

MILLER, Helen. *Realms of Arthur.* 1969 1st ed. dj. scarce. VG $15.00

MILLER, Helen. *Westering Women.* 1961 Doubleday. 1st ed. 8vo. brown cloth. EX $12.50

MILLER, Henry. *Black Spring.* 1963 Grove. VG $16.00

MILLER, Henry. *Book of Friends.* 1976 Santa Barbara. 1st ed. dj. M $11.00

MILLER, Henry. *Cosmological Eye.* 1939 NY. 1st ed. sgn. dj. EX $250.00

MILLER, Henry. *Gliding into the Everglades & Other Essays.* 1977 Santa Barbara. Ltd 1st ed. 1/250. sgn. M $35.00

MILLER, Henry. *Insomnia.* 1974 Garden City. 1st ed. dj. M $12.00

MILLER, Henry. *Joey: Book of Friends Vol. III.* 1979 Santa Barbara. Ltd ed. 1/250. sgn. dj. M $35.00

MILLER, Henry. *My Life & Times.* 1971 Playboy Pr. dj. EX $50.00

MILLER, Henry. *Obscenity & Law of Reflection.* 1945 Yonkers. Alicat Bookshop. 1/750. VG $65.00

MILLER, Henry. *Opus Pistorum.* 1983 NY. 1st ed. dj. M $25.00

MILLER, Henry. *Order & Chaos: Chez Hans Reichel.* 1966 Loujon Pr. Cork ed. 1/1,399. dj. boxed. M $50.00

MILLER, Henry. *Remember to Remember.* 1952 London. 1st English ed. dj. VG $35.00

MILLER, Henry. *Tropic of Cancer.* 1961 Grove. VG $16.00

MILLER, Henry. *Tropic of Capricorn.* 1964 London. 1st English ed. dj. VG $27.50

MILLER, Henry. *Tropic of Capricorn.* 1961 Grove. VG $16.00

MILLER, Henry. *Wisdom of the Heart.* 1941 Norfolk. 1st ed. dj. EX $100.00

MILLER, Henry. *World of Sex.* 1940 private print. Ltd ed. 1/250. dj. EX $100.00

MILLER, Joaquin. *Song of the Sierras.* 1871 Boston. 299 p. VG $25.00

MILLER, Joaquin. *Songs of the Sierras.* 1871 Boston. 1st ed. 299 p. EX $45.00

MILLER, Joaquin. *True Bear Stories.* 1900 Chicago. Ills 1st ed. VG $35.00

MILLER, Joaquin. *1st Families of Sierras.* 1876 Chicago. 1st Am ed. 258 p. rebound. VG $25.00

MILLER, John C. *Origins of the American Revolution.* 1943 Little Brown. 1st ed. 519 p. dj. VG $17.00

MILLER, John C. *Triumph of Freedom 1775-1783.* 1948 Little Brown. 1st ed. 718 p. dj. EX $10.00

MILLER, Joseph. *AZ Indians: People of the Sun.* 1941 NY. Ills 1st ed. photos. 57 p. VG $25.00

MILLER, Joseph. *AZ Story.* 1952 Hastings. Ills Ross Santee. dj. VG $22.50

MILLER, L. *Prize Articles.* 1954 Ballantine. 1st ed. dj. EX $75.00

MILLER, Leo E. *In the Wilds of South America.* 1919 NY. Ills 1st ed. map. EX $55.00

MILLER, Margaret. *Paul Klee.* 1946 MOMA. Ills. 4to. 64 p. cloth. dj. $25.00

MILLER, Margery. *Joe Louis: American.* 1945 NY. Ills 1st ed. presentation. dj. $85.00

MILLER, Mary Britton. *Menagerie.* 1928 NY. Macmillan. Ills Sewell. 1st ed. dj. EX $45.00

MILLER, Max. *Far Shore.* 1945 dj. VG $18.00

MILLER, Max. *Skinny on Your Own Side.* 1958 NY. 1st ed. dj. EX $9.00

MILLER, Max. *Town with Funny Nose.* 1948 NY. 1st ed. dj. EX $11.00

MILLER, Olive Beaupre. *Engines & Brass Bands.* 1933 NY. Ills 1st ed. dj. EX $15.00

MILLER, Olive Beaupre. *Little Pictures of Jampa.* 1925 Book House for Children. VG $20.00

MILLER, Olive Beaupre. *My Book House.* 1937 Chicago. 1st ed. 12 vol set. VG $45.00

MILLER, Olive Beaupre. *My Travelship.* *Little Pictures of Japan.* 1925 Chicago. Ills Sturges. 4to. VG $20.00

MILLER, Olive Beaupre. *My Travelship.* *Nursery Friends From France.* 1927 Chicago. Ills. VG $20.00

MILLER, Olive Beaupre. *My Travelship.* *Tales Told in Holland.* 1926 Chicago. Ills Petershams. VG $20.00

MILLER, Olive Beaupre. *My Travelship.* *Tales Told in Holland.* 1952 Chicago. Book House Series. Ills. G $12.50

MILLER, Paul. *Faces of the Living Dead.* 1943 London. Ills. 54 p. dj. VG $18.00

MILLER, Stewart. *FL Fishing.* 1931 Watt. Ills. 320 p. VG $10.00

MILLER, Sue. *Good Mother.* 1986 Harper. Advance copy. wraps. $30.00

MILLER, T.S. *Cotton Trade Guide & Student's Manual.* 1915 Flat, TX. 1st ed. 8vo. 431 p. $25.00

MILLER, Townsend. *Letter From TX.* 1939 Dallas. Ltd ed. 1/450. VG $200.00

MILLER, Walter M. *Canticle for Leibowitz.* 1960 Phil. 1st ed. 320 p. purple cloth. dj. VG $50.00

MILLER, Zane. *Boss Cox's Cincinnati.* 1968 NY. Oxford U Pr. 1st ed. dj. VG $15.00

MILLER & FOWLIE. *Letters of 1943-1972.* 1975 Grove Pr. 1st print. dj. EX $15.00

MILLER & MYERS. *Barnard College: 1st 50 Years.* 1939 Chicago U Pr. Ills. VG $10.00

MILLER. *Diary of James Knox Pold: Road to VA City.* 1960 OK U Pr. 1st ed. dj. VG $21.00

MILLER. *Why the West Was Wild.* 1963 KS Historial Soc. 1st ed. EX $100.00

MILLES, Thomas. *Catalogue of Honor.* 1610 London. Iaggard. 1st ed. folio. $395.00

MILLET, Rev. Joshua. *History of Baptists in ME.* 1845 Portland. 472 p. VG $100.00

MILLHAUSER, Steven. *Edwin Mullhouse.* 1972 NY. Knopf. 1st ed. M $25.00

MILLICAN, Charles Bowie. *Spenser & the Round Table.* 1932 Harvard. 1st ed. dj. EX $20.00

MILLIGAN, Spike. *Book of Bits.* 1965 London. Ills 1st ed. dj. EX $22.00

MILLIGAN & HOBBS. *Milligan's Ark.* 1971 London. 1st ed. dj. VG $7.50

MILLIKAN, Robert A. *Cosmic Rays.* 1939 Cambridge. 1st ed. sgn. 134 p. dj. VG $20.00

MILLING, C.J. *Buckshot & Hounds.* 1967 Barnes. Ills. 132 p. dj. EX $10.00

MILLIS, Walter. *Forrestal Diaries.* 1951 581 p. VG $9.50

MILLS, E.A. *Spell of the Rockies.* 1911 Houghton Mifflin. 1st ed. EX $18.00

MILLS, E.A. *Spell of the Rockies.* 1911 Cambridge. Riverside Pr. Ills. G $25.00

MILLS, E.A. *Trees That Twist.* Estes Park. photos. pb. $6.00

MILLS, John Brent. *Will: 62nd Bohemian Grove Play.* 1967 Grabhorn. EX $12.00

MILLS, Robert. *Statistics of SC.* 1826 Charlston. 1st ed. map. slipcase. boxed. $200.00

MILLS & DUNN. *Story of Old Dolls & How To Make New Ones.* 1940 NY. 1st ed. dj. VG $14.00

MILLSTEIN, Gilbert. *NY: True North.* 1964 Doubleday. 1st ed. dj. VG $20.00

MILMAN, H.H. *History of the Jews.* 1878 London. sgn BF Dos Passos. G $15.00

MILMINE, Georgine. *Life of Mary Baker Eddy & History of Christian Science.* 1909 1st ed. ghost writer Willa Cather. EX $145.00

MILNE, A.A. *Autobiography.* 1939 NY. Dutton. 1st ed. dj. VG $40.00

MILNE, A.A. *Gallery of Children.* 1925 McKay. Ills 1st Am ed. scarce. VG $60.00

MILNE, A.A. *Gallery of Children.* 1925 London. Ltd ed. 1/500. sgn. folio. VG $250.00

MILNE, A.A. *House at Pooh Corner.* 1928 London. VG $45.00

MILNE, A.A. *House at Pooh Corner.* 1st Am ed. VG $25.00

MILNE, A.A. *House at Pooh Corner.* London. 1st ed. 12mo. 178 p. dj. EX $275.00

MILNE, A.A. *House at Pooh Corner.* 1928 Dutton. Ills Shepard. 1st ed. VG $50.00

MILNE, A.A. *Now We Are 6.* 1927 London. Methuen. Ills 1st ed. dj. VG $135.00

MILNE, A.A. *Now We Are 6.* 1927 London. 1st ed. 8vo. red cloth. EX $175.00

MILNE, A.A. *Now We Are 6.* 1927 London. Methuen. 1st ed. octavo. VG $85.00

MILNE, A.A. *Prince Rabbit & the Princess Who Could Not Laugh.* 1966 NY. Dutton. Ills Shepard. 4to. 72 p. dj. $30.00

MILNE, A.A. *Secrets & Other Stories.* 1929 NY. G $65.00

MILNE, A.A. *Success: A Play.* 1923 London. 1st ed. dj. EX $20.00

MILNE, A.A. *When We Were Very Young.* 1939 Dutton. dj. VG $10.00

MILNE, A.A. *Willine Ille Pu.* 1960 NY. 1st ed. dj. EX $22.00

MILNE, A.A. *Winnie the Pooh.* 1946 Kenosha. Ills Page. 1st ed. square 4to. $20.00

MILNE, A.A. *Winnie the Pooh.* 1926 London. Ltd ed. sgn. dj. EX $400.00

MILNE, A.A. *Winnie the Pooh.* 1926 NY. Dutton. 1st Am ed. green cloth. G $35.00

MILNE, Hamish. *Bartok.* 1982 NY. Ills 1st ed. dj. VG $18.00

MILNE, L.J. & M. *Cougar Doesn't Live Here Anymore.* 1971 Prentice Hall. Ills. 258 p. dj. EX $15.00

MILNE, L.J. & M. *Nature of Life.* 1972 Crown. Ills. 360 p. VG $4.00

MILNE, L.J. & M. *Paths Across the Earth.* 1958 Harper. Ills. 216 p. dj. VG $4.00

MILNER & TULLY. *Essays on Fevers & Other Medical Subjects.* 1823 Middletown. 1st ed. calf. $60.00

MILORADOVICH, Milo. *Art of Fish Cookery.* 1949 NY. 1st ed. EX $10.00

MILOSZ, Czeslaw. *Captive Mind.* 1983 Ltd Ed Club. sgn Milosz/Kapusta. linen. EX $85.00

MILTON, John. *History of Britain.* 1695 London. Chiswell. rebound. G $125.00

MILTON, John. *Mask of Comus.* no date. NY. Heritage Pr. cloth. slipcase. $20.00

MILTON, John. *Mask of Comus.* 1937 Bloomsbury. Ltd ed. 1/950. folio. VG $85.00

MILTON, John. *Paradise Lost, Paradise Regained.* 1785 Birmingham. Baskerville. 2 vol set. $250.00

MILTON, John. *Paradise Lost, Paradise Regained.* 1936 San Francisco. Ills C Petrina. folio. VG $50.00

MILTON, John. *Paradise Regained.* 1924 London. Fleuron. Ills Lowinsky. 1/350. $30.00

MILTON, John. *Penseroso: L'Allegro.* 1954 Ltd Ed Club. Ills W Blake. 1/1,780. boxed. $40.00

MILTON, John. *Poetical Works of John Milton.* 1866 Boston. Ltd ed. 1/100. 3 vol set. $100.00

MILTON, John. *Poetical Works of John Milton.* 1794 London. Ills Westal. 3 vol set. G $75.00

MILTOUN, Francis. *In the Land of Mosques & Minarets.* 1908 Boston. Ills 1st ed. beige cloth. EX $35.00

MILTOUN, Francis. *Rambles on the Riviera.* 1906 Boston. VG $20.00

MIMS, Edwin. *Sidney Lanier.* 1905 Boston/ NY. 1st ed. G $25.00

MINAHAN, John. *Great Hotel Robbery.* 1982 Norton. Advance copy. wraps. EX $15.00

MINARIK, E.H. *Kiss for Baby Bear.* 1968 Harper. Ills Sendak. 1st print. dj. VG $16.00

MINDLER, Dr. *Anatomical Manikin of the Human Body. Vol. I & II.* c 1885. NY. Am Thermo-Ware. Student ed. $265.00

MINDLIN, Henrique. *Modern Architecture in Brazil.* 1956 NY. Reinhold. VG $28.00

MINER, Chas. *History of WY.* 1845 Phil. 1st ed. 8vo. black cloth. VG $75.00

MINGAZZINI, Paolino. *Greek Pottery Painting.* 1969 London. Hamlyn. Ills. 157 p. dj. $15.00

MINGOTTI, Antonio. *Gershwin: Eine Bildbiographie.* 1958 Munich. Ills. dj. VG $35.00

MINGUS, Charles. *Beneath the Underdog.* 1971 NY. 1st ed. dj. VG $25.00

MINNICH, H. *William Holmes McGuffey & His Readers.* 1936 NY. 2 vol set. slipcase. VG $25.00

MINNINGER, E. *Fantastic Trees.* 1967 Viking. Ills 1st ed. 304 p. dj. VG $14.00

MINTER, J.E. *Chagres: River of Westward Passage.* 1948 Rinehart. Ills 1st ed. 418 p. dj. VG $22.00

MINTON, S.A. & M.R. *Giant Reptiles.* 1973 Scribner. Ills. 345 p. wraps. EX $14.00

MINTON, S.A. & M.R. *Venomous Reptiles.* 1969 Scribner. Ills. 274 p. dj. VG $18.00

MIRACLE, Leonard. *Complete Book of Camping.* 1963 Outdoor Life. Ills. 594 p. dj. EX $5.00

MIRSKY, J.; & NEVINS, A. *World of Eli Whitney.* 1952 Macmillan. Ills 1st ed. 346 p. dj. EX $14.00

MIRSKY, Jeannette. *Elisha Kent Kane & the Seafaring Frontier.* 1954 Little Brown. 1st ed. 201 p. dj. EX $25.00

MISTRAL, Frederic. *Memoires et Recits.* 1906 Paris. EX $35.00

MITCHAM, S.W. *Triumphant Fox: Rommel & Rise of Africa Corps.* 1984 NY. 1st ed. dj. EX $18.00

MITCHEL, George. *Kernel Cob & Little Miss Sweet Clover.* 1918 Volland. Ills Tony Sarg. 1st ed. VG $20.00

MITCHELL, A. *Splendid Sisters.* 1966 London. Ills. dj. G $25.00

MITCHELL, Donald G. *American Lands & Letters: Leather Stocking to Poe's Raven.* 1899 NY. Scribner. Ills. 412 p. G $18.00

MITCHELL, E.V. *Adrift Among Books.* 1929 NY. 1st ed. morocco. dj. VG $20.00

MITCHELL, E.V. *Great Fishing Stories.* 1946 Doubleday. 1st ed. 285 p. dj. VG $11.50

MITCHELL, Gladys. *Here Lies Gloria Mundy.* 1982 NY. 1st Am ed. dj. VG $7.50

MITCHELL, Gladys. *Winking at Brim.* 1974 NY. 1st Am ed. dj. EX $8.50

MITCHELL, H. Frank. *Treasures of Irish Art 1500 B.C.-1500 A.D.* 1977 NY. 1st ed. dj. VG $35.00

MITCHELL, Horace. *Raising Game Birds.* 1936 Phil. Penn. Ills Shutts. 315 p. VG $17.50

MITCHELL, James R. *Antique Metalware: Brass, Bronze, Copper, Tin, Iron.* 1976 NY. Main St/Antiques Library. 4to. $30.00

MITCHELL, Joan. *My 5 Years in the Country.* 1972 Syracuse. Ills. 4to. disbound as issued. $20.00

MITCHELL, John. *Guide to Principals & Practice of Congregational Churches.* 1838 Northampton. $45.00

MITCHELL, Joseph. *My Ears Are Bent.* 1938 NY. dj. EX $50.00

MITCHELL, Margaret. *Gone with the Wind.* Heritage Club. 2 vols. slipcase. EX $25.00

MITCHELL, Margaret. *Gone with the Wind.* 1937 Hamburg. 1st German ed. VG $25.00

MITCHELL, Margaret. *Gone with the Wind.* 1936 Macmillan. 1st June print. dj. VG $37.50

MITCHELL, Margaret. *Gone with the Wind.* 1936 London. Macmillan. 1st ed. 1,037 p. G $75.00

MITCHELL, Margaret. *Gone with the Wind.* 1936 NY. Macmillan. 1st ed. 1st issue. EX $350.00

MITCHELL, Paige. *Wilderness of Monkeys.* 1965 Dutton. 1st ed. dj. EX $20.00

MITCHELL, R.T.; & ZIM, H.S. *Butterflies & Moths.* 1964 Golden Pr. Ills. 160 p. wraps. $4.00

MITCHELL, Ruth. *Old San Francisco.* 1933 NY. 1st ed. 4 vol set. slipcase. $50.00

MITCHELL, S. Weir. *Wager & Other Poems.* 1900 NY. 1st ed. inscr. green cloth. G $125.00

MITCHELL, S. Weir. *Wonderful Stories of Fuz-Buz the Fly.* 1867 Phil. G $45.00

MITCHELL, T.L. *3 Expeditions into the Interior of Eastern Australia.* 1838 London. 2 vol set. ¾-leather. $1850.00

MITCHELL, W.O. *Vanishing Point.* 1973 Toronto. 1st ed. dj. EX $20.00

MITCHELL, W.O. *Who Has Seen the Wind.* 1947 Toronto. 1st ed. dj. G $30.00

MITCHELL, William. *Winged Defense.* 1925 NY. Putnam. Ills 1st ed. scarce. VG $40.00

MITCHINSON, David. *Henry Moore: Unpublished Drawings.* 1976 Abrams. 8vo. plts. dj. EX $30.00

MITCHINSON, Naomi. *Swan's Road.* 1954 London. 1st ed. VG $8.50

MITFORD, A.B.F. *Attache at Peking.* 1900 London. Macmillan. 8vo. 386 p. VG $20.00

MITFORD, Jessica. *Fine Old Conflict.* 1977 London. 1st ed. dj. EX $25.00

MITFORD, Mary Russell. *Our Village.* 1910 Ills Thomson/Rawlings. EX $20.00

MITFORD, Nancy. *Noblesse Oblige.* 1956 London. Ills Lancaster. 1st ed. dj. VG $25.00

MITFORD, Nancy. *Water Beetle.* 1962 London. 1st ed. dj. VG $18.00

MIZWA, Stephen P. *Nicholas Copernicus.* 1945 NY. Kosciuszko Foundation. 28 p. $18.00

MOCK, Elisabeth. *If You Want To Build a House.* 1946 NY. MOMA. VG $20.00

MOE, Virginia. *Animal Inn.* 1946 Boston. Houghton Mifflin. 1st ed. dj. $15.00

MOENS, W. *English Travellers & Italian Brigands.* 1866 London. 2 vol set. 3/4 leather. VG $50.00

MOERLEIN, George. *Trip Around the World.* 1886 Cincinnati. Ills. 4to. gilt cloth. EX $95.00

MOFFAT, Alfred. *Little Songs of Long Ago.* 1912 Phil/London. Augener/McKay. Ills Le Mair. $20.00

MOFFATT, Adah Terrell. *Queen's Gift.* 1923 Boston. 1st ed. EX $30.00

MOFFETT, Kenworth. *Jules Olitski.* 1981 NY. Abrams. Ills. 4to. 240 p. dj. $65.00

MOHERMAN, T.S. *History of Church of Brethren in Northeastern OH.* 1914 Elgin, IL. Ills. 366 p. VG $22.50

MOHOLY, Lucia & Sibyl. *Experiment in Totality.* 1950 NY. Harper. 1st ed. inscr. EX $125.00

MOHOLY, Lucia & Sibyl. *Experiment in Totality.* 1950 NY. Harper. 1st ed. 8vo. cloth. EX $65.00

MOHOLY, Lucia. *100 Years of Photography.* 1939 England. Penguin. 1st ed. 8vo. wraps. $60.00

MOHOLY, Lucia; & FERGUSSON, B. *Portrait of Eton.* 1949 London. Muller. 1st ed. 8vo. cloth. dj. $70.00

MOHOLY, Sibyl. *Matrix of Man: Illustrated History of Urban Environment.* 1968 NY. Praeger. VG $35.00

MOHR, M.H. *Bibliography of Westmoreland Co., PA, 1773-1949.* 1949 Harrisburg. 8vo. 73 p. cloth. xl. VG $10.00

MOISENKO, Rena. *Realist Music: 25 Soviet Composers.* 1949 London. Meridian Books Ltd. VG $15.00

MOISSAN, Henri. *Traite de Chimie Minerale.* 1904-1906. Paris. 5 vol set. xl. VG $80.00

MOJTABAI, A.G. *Stopping Place.* 1979 Simon Schuster. 1st ed. dj. EX $20.00

MOLINA, Abbe Don J. Ignatius. *Geographical, Natural, & Civil History of Chili.* 1808 Middletown, CT. 1st Am/English eds. 2 vol set. $150.00

MOLLER, Borge J.C. *Dansk Jazz Discography.* 1945 Copenhagen. Danish text. wraps. VG $20.00

MOLONEY, M. *Irish Ethno-Botany & Evolution of Medicine in Ireland.* 1919 Dublin. 96 p. cloth. VG $45.00

MOLYNEAUX, Peter. *Romantic Story of TX.* 1936 Cordova. 463 p. VG $20.00

MOMA. *Art in Our Time.* 1939 NY. 1st ed. dj. VG $40.00

MOMA. *Flight of Butterflies.* 1979 Thames. facsimile. VG $25.00

MOMADAY, N. Scott. *House Made of Dawn.* 1968 NY. Harper. 1st ed. dj. VG $35.00

MOMSON, Samuel Eliot. *Rope Makers of Plymouth.* 1950 Boston. 1st ed. dj. VG $22.50

MONACHESI, Mrs. N.A. *Manual for China Painters.* 1907 Boston. Revised Enlarged ed. 12mo. VG $45.00

MONAGHAN, Frank. *French Travellers in US 1765-1932.* 1933 NY. 1st ed. 8vo. 114 p. scarce. VG $50.00

MONAGHAN, Frank. *French Travellers in US 1765-1932.* 1961 Antiquarian Pr. Ltd ed. 1/750. VG $15.00

MONAGHAN, Jay. *Australians & the Gold Rush: CA & Down Under.* 1966 CA U Pr. Ills. 317 p. dj. EX $30.00

MONAGHAN, Jay. *Book of the American West.* 1963 Messner. Ills 1st ed. 4to. 608 p. EX $25.00

MONAGHAN, Jay. *Civil War on the Western Border 1854-1865.* 1955 Little Brown. 1st ed. 454 p. EX $35.00

MONAGHAN, Jay. *Great Rascal: Exploits of Amazing Ned Buntline.* 1952 Boston. Ills. dj. VG $15.00

MONAGHAN, Jay. *Lincoln Bibliography.* 1945 Springfield. 2 vol set. VG $65.00

MONAGUE, C.E. *Right Off the Top.* 1927 London. Ltd 1st ed. 1/260. sgn. cloth. $30.00

MONBODDO, James Burnet. *Ancient Metaphysics; or, Science of Universals.* 1779-1799. Edinburgh. 6 vols in 3. rare. $400.00

MONCRIEFF, M.M. *Clairvoyant Theory of Perception.* 1951 London. dj. EX $26.00

MONEYPENNY & BUCKLE. *Life of Benjamin Disraeli.* 1968 NY. Russell. 4 vol set. $45.00

MONITT, Frank. *Indian Trader.* 1963 Norman, OK. Ills 2nd ed. dj. VG $20.00

MONKHOUSE, W.C. *Studies of Sir Edwin Landseer: With History of His Art.* no date. London. Virture. folio. VG $55.00

MONKHOUSE, W.C. *Works of Sir Edwin Landseer.* 1879-1880. London. Virtue. 3/4 leather. $200.00

MONROE, A.S. *Feelin' Fine: Bill Hanley's Book.* 1931 NY. Ills. $6.00

MONROE, Marilyn. *My Story.* 1974 NY. 1st ed. dj. EX $15.00

MONSARRAT, Nicholas. *Cruel Sea.* 1951 NY. Knopf. 1st ed. dj. $10.00

MONSARRAT, Nicholas. *East Corvette.* 1943 London. Ills 1st ed. wraps. $50.00

MONSARRAT, Nicholas. *H.M. Frigate.* 1946 London. 1st ed. wraps. $45.00

MONSARRAT, Nicholas. *Kapillan of Malta.* 1974 NY. 1st ed. dj. EX $12.50

MONSARRAT, Nicholas. *Leave Cancelled.* 1945 NY. 1st ed. dj. EX $11.00

MONTAGNE, Prosper. *Larousse Gastronomique.* 1966 Crown. 7th print. dj. G $25.00

MONTAGU, Ashley. *Touching: Human Significance of the Skin.* 1971 Columbia U Pr. dj. VG $12.00

MONTAGU, Basil. *Works of Francis Bacon, Lord Chancellor of England.* 1842 Phil. 3 vol set. rebound. VG $145.00

MONTAGU, Lady M.W. *Letters & Works.* 1866 London/Bohn. Ills 3rd ed. 2 vol set. xl. VG $18.00

MONTAGUE, Gilbert H. *Rise & Progress of Standard Oil Company.* July, 1903. Harper. G $12.50

MONTALL, R.J. *Mycobacterial Infections in Zoo Animals.* 1978 Smithsonian. Ills. 4to. 275 p. wraps. EX $10.00

MONTENGON, Don Pedro. *Eudoxia Hija de Belisario.* 1793 Madrid. 8vo. 390 p. leather. G $40.00

MONTGOMERIE, G.A. *Digital Calculating Machines.* 1956 Princeton. Van Nostrand. 1st ed. xl. G $10.00

MONTGOMERY, Frances Trego. *Billy Whiskers' Grandchildren.* 1909 Chicago. VG $18.00

MONTGOMERY, Frances Trego. *Billy Whiskers' Kids.* 1931 Akron. Ills Fry. Popular ed. 8vo. VG $12.50

MONTGOMERY, Frances Trego. *Chickens & Chicks.* 1908 NY. Ills. 61 p. fair. $12.50

MONTGOMERY, L.M. *Emily of New Moon.* 1923 NY. Stokes. 1st ed. dj. VG $25.00

MONTGOMERY, L.M. *Rainbow Valley.* 1919 NY. Burt. green cloth. dj. EX $15.00

MONTGOMERY, L.M. *Tangled Web.* 1931 Toronto. 1st Canadian ed. VG $30.00

MONZERT, L. *Independant Liquorist: Art of Manufacturing & Preparing.* 1866 NY. 1st ed. cloth. $60.00

MOODY, B. *Ocean Ships.* 1974 London. Ills 5th ed. VG $20.00

MOODY, D.W. *Life of a Rover.* 1926 Chicago. 116 p. $22.50

MOODY, Margaret J. *American Decorative Arts at Dartmouth.* 1981 Hanover. Ills. $8.50

MOODY, Ralph. *Horse of a Different Color.* 1968 NY. 1st ed. 8vo. 272 p. dj. $30.00

MOODY, Ralph. *Little Britches: Father & I Were Ranchers.* 1950 NY. Ills. dj. VG $7.00

MOODY, Ralph. *Stagecoach West.* 1967 Promontory. Ills. 341 p. maps. dj. EX $8.50

MOODY, W.R. *Life of D.L. Moody.* 1900 Revell. 1st ed. VG $12.50

MOODY, William V. *Poems.* 1901 Boston. Ltd 1st ed. 1/778. $50.00

MOON, Grace. *Chi-Wee: Adventures of Little Indian Girl.* 1951 NY. Ills. dj. VG $15.00

MOON, Grace. *Runaway Papoose.* 1928 1st ed. EX $16.00

MOONEY, Ted. *Easy Travel to Other Planets.* 1981 Farrar. 1st ed. dj. EX $25.00

MOORCOCK, Michael. *City in Autumn Stars.* London. 1st ed. sgn. EX $38.00

MOORCOCK, Michael. *End of All Songs.* 1976 NY. 1st ed. dj. EX $20.00

MOORCOCK, Michael. *English Assassin.* 1972 Harper Row. 1st Am ed. dj. EX $25.00

MOORCOCK, Michael. *Vanishing Tower.* 1970 Archival Pr. 1st HrdCvr Am ed. slipcase. EX $30.00

MOORE, A.C. *Nicholas: Manhattan Christmas Story.* 1924 NY. Ills JV Everen. 1st ed. VG $17.50

MOORE, Brian. *Catholics.* 1972 1st ed. VG $40.00

MOORE, Brian. *Feast of Lupercal.* 1957 Little Brown. 1st ed. dj. VG $35.00

MOORE, Brian. *Great Victorian Collection.* 1975 NY. 1st ed. dj. M $12.00

MOORE, C.B. *Book of Wild Pets.* 1954 Branford. Ills. 553 p. dj. xl. VG $8.00

MOORE, C.H. *WA: Past & Present.* 1929 Ills Suydham. 1st print. VG $22.00

MOORE, C.L. *Scarlet Dream.* 1981 Grant. Ltd ed. $45.00

MOORE, C.L. *Shambleau.* 1953 NY. Gnome. 1st ed. dj. EX $45.00

MOORE, Cecil A. *Restoration Literature: Poetry & Prose 1660-1700.* 1962 Appleton Century. 604 p. VG $18.00

MOORE, Charles A. *French Volunteer of War of Independence.* 1897 Paris. 1st ed. EX $125.00

MOORE, Clement C. *Night Before Christmas.* 1958 Whitman. Ills FS Winship. wraps. EX $12.00

MOORE, Clement C. *Night Before Christmas.* 1947 Lilja. Ills Winter. 4to. wraps. EX $12.00

MOORE, Clement C. *Night Before Christmas.* 1961 Random House. Ills Grandma Moses. dj. VG $12.50

MOORE, Clement C. *Night Before Christmas.* 1939 Whitman. Ills Johnson. linen wraps. VG $12.00

MOORE, Colleen. *Colleen's Dollhouse.* 1935 Garden City. Ills. 8vo. 32 p. wraps. VG $25.00

MOORE, Colleen. *Enchanted Castle.* 1935 Garden City. Ills Marie Lawson. 1st ed. dj. $60.00

MOORE, Colleen. *Silent Star.* 1968 NY. 1st ed. sgn. dj. VG $22.50

MOORE, Damrell. *Boston Almanac for 1854.* 1854 Boston. 24mo. fld map. 180 p. G $19.00

MOORE, Daniel G. *Log of a 20th Century Cowboy.* 1965 AZ U Pr. Ills. inscr. dj. VG $25.00

MOORE, Doris Langley. *Woman in Fashion.* 1949 London. Ills 1st ed. 184 p. dj. EX $30.00

MOORE, E.M. *Spoil of the North Wind.* 1901 Chicago. Ltd ed. 1/600. EX $120.00

MOORE, George. *Avowals.* 1919 NY. private print. rebound. G $125.00

MOORE, George. *Brook Kerith.* 1929 London. Ills Gooden. Ltd ed. sgns. $125.00

MOORE, George. *Esther Waters.* 1920 London. private print. Ltd ed. sgn. G $95.00

MOORE, George. *Heloise & Abelard.* 1921 London. Ltd ed. 8vo. sgn. 2 vol set. djs. VG $20.00

MOORE, George. *Heloise & Abelard.* 1921 NY. Ltd ed. 1/1,250. 2 vol set. $40.00

MOORE, George. *Modern Painting.* 1893 London. 1st ed. VG $95.00

MOORE, George. *Peronnik the Fool.* 1926 Rudge. Ltd ed. 1/785. VG $30.00

MOORE, George. *Pure Poetry.* no date. Nonesuch. Ltd ed. VG $40.00

MOORE, George. *Ulick & Soracha.* 1926 NY. Ltd ed. sgn. EX $33.00

MOORE, Harry T. *Intelligent Heart: Story of D.H. Lawrence.* 1954 NY. 1st ed. dj. VG $20.00

MOORE, Isabel. *Supercook's Cookbook.* 1978 London. 1st ed. EX $15.00

MOORE, J. Read. *Moore's Seminole Role & Land Guide.* c 1915. Wewoka, OK. EX $175.00

MOORE, John W. *History of NC.* 1880 Raleigh. 1st ed. scarce. VG $300.00

MOORE, John W. *Roster of NC Troops in War Between the States.* 1882 Raleigh. 8vo. 4 vol set. VG $400.00

MOORE, John. *View of Society & Manners in France, Switzerland, & Germany.* 1792 Boston. 1st Am ed. VG $125.00

MOORE, Joseph W. *Picturesque WA.* 1884 Provinance. Ills 1st ed. EX $50.00

MOORE, Marianne. *Marianne Moore Reader.* 1961 NY. Viking. inscr/sgn/poem. VG $250.00

MOORE, Marianne. *Predilections.* 1955 NY. 1st ed. dj. VG $35.00

MOORE, Marianne. *Selected Poems.* 1935 NY. Macmillan. 1st Am ed. 8vo. sgn. $175.00

MOORE, Marianne. *Tell Me, Tell Me.* 1966 NY. Viking. 1st ed. sgn. dj. EX $35.00

MOORE, Merrill. *Case Record From a Sanitarium.* 1951 NY. Ills E Gorey. 1st ed. dj. EX $75.00

MOORE, Merrill. *Clinical Sonnets.* 1950 Twayne. 3rd print. sgn. dj. $20.00

MOORE, Merrill. *Illegitimate Sonnets.* 1950 Twayne. 1st ed. dj. $12.50

MOORE, Merrill. *Sonnets From New Directions.* 1938 New Directions. #2 of Phamphlet Series. EX $45.00

MOORE, N. Hudson. *Collector's Manual.* 1905 NY. Tudor. 5th print. 329 p. cloth. $30.00

MOORE, N. Hudson. *Lace Book.* 1904 NY. xl. G $45.00

MOORE, N. Hudson. *Old Glass: European & American.* 1924 NY. Tudor. Ills. 394 p. cloth. $42.50

MOORE, N. Hudson. *Old Pewter, Brass, Copper, & Sheffield Plate.* 1905 Garden City. Ills. 229 p. dj. $25.00

MOORE, Nathan Grier. *Man & His Manor.* 1935 Chicago. private print. VG $25.00

MOORE, P.H. *Gun & Rod in Canada.* 1922 Houghton Mifflin. Ills 1st ed. $20.00

MOORE, R. *Universal Assistant & Complete Mechanic.* c 1879. NY. Ills. 12mo. 1,016 p. cloth. $36.00

MOORE, R.; & JENNINGS, H. *Treasure Hunter.* 1974 Prentice Hall. Ills 1st ed. 261 p. dj. EX $14.00

MOORE, T. Sturge. *Roderigo of Bivar.* 1925 NY. Rudge. Ltd ed. 1/500. VG $30.00

MOORE, T. Sturge. *Self-Portrait Taken From Letters & Journals of C. Ricketts.* 1939 London. Ills 1st ed. VG $40.00

MOORE, Thomas. *Letters & Journals of Lord Byron & Notices of His Life.* 1830 NY. Harper. 8vo. 2 vol set. scarce. VG $100.00

MOORE, Thomas. *Utopia.* 1944 Golden Cockerell. 1/500. 4to. $100.00

MOORE, W. *Roswell Incident.* 1980 NY. 1st ed. dj. VG $20.00

MOORE-BETTY, Maurice. *Maurice Moore-Betty Cookbook.* 1979 NY. 1st ed. EX $10.00

MOORE-LANDECKER, E. *Fundamentals of the Fungi.* 1982 Prentice Hall. Revised 2nd ed. 578 p. VG $34.00

MOOREHEAD, Alan. *Blue Nile.* 1962 Harper Row. Ills 1st ed. 308 p. dj. VG $7.00

MOOREHEAD, Alan. *Cooper's Creek.* 1963 Harper Row. Ills 1st ed. dj. EX $20.00

MOOREHEAD, Alan. *Darwin & the Beagle.* 1970 Harper Row. Ills. 280 p. maps. dj. EX $20.00

MOOREHEAD, Alan. *Darwin & the Beagle.* 1983 Crescent. Ills. 224 p. dj. EX $18.00

MOOREHEAD, Alan. *No Room in the Ark.* 1959 Harper Row. Ills. 227 p. VG $5.00

MOOREHEAD, Alan. *Russian Revolution.* 1958 Harper Row. 1st ed. dj. $17.00

MOOREHEAD, Alan. *White Nile.* 1971 Harper Row. Revised ed. 368 p. dj. VG $20.00

MOOREHEAD, Alan. *White Nile.* 1960 Harper Row. Ills. 385 p. maps. dj. VG $8.00

MOOREHEAD, Warren K. *Archaeology of the AR River Valley.* 1931 New Haven. 204 p. VG $65.00

MOOREHEAD, Warren K. *Etowah Papers.* 1932 New Haven. 1st ed. 178 p. VG $175.00

MOOREHEAD, Warren K. *Primitive Man in OH.* 1892 NY. Ills. 246 p. cloth. VG $65.00

MOORHOUSE, G. *Fearful Void.* 1974 Lippincott. Ills. 288 p. maps. dj. EX $8.00

MOORMAN, J.J. *Mineral Springs of North America.* 1873 Phil. Ills 1st ed. fld maps. VG $75.00

MOOSDORF, J. *Next Door.* 1964 Knopf. dj. VG $10.00

MOOTZ, H.E. *Pawnee Bill: Romance of OK.* 1928 Excelsior. Ills. 285 p. scarce. G $5.00

MORAND, Paul. *Le Voyage.* 1930 NY. Heron Pr. Ltd ed. 1/535. silhouettes. VG $50.00

MORATH & AUBIER. *Fiesta in Pamplona.* 1956 Paris/NY. 4to. dj. EX $45.00

MORATH & MILLER. *Chinese Encounters.* 1979 Farrar. 1st ed. dj. EX $25.00

MORATH & MILLER. *In Russia.* 1969 Studio/Viking. Ills. cloth. dj. VG $18.00

MORAVIA, Alberto. *Voyeus.* 1987 NY. 1st ed. sgn. dj. M $20.00

MORAVIA, Alberto. *1934.* 1983 Farrar. 1st Am ed. dj. EX $15.00

MORCOMBE, M. *Birds of Australia.* 1971 Scribner. Ills. 4to. 80 p. dj. VG $10.00

MORE, Hannah. *Sacred Drames.* 1787 Phil. 1st Am ed. 1/2 calf. $80.00

MORELL. *Thesaures Graecae Poeses.* 1767 Venice. Hogarth. leather. $90.00

MORELLA, J. *It Girl.* 1976 NY. Ills 1st ed. 284 p. dj. VG $17.50

MORETON, C. *Oscar. Old Carnations & Pinks.* 1955 Rainbird. Ills McEwen. VG $30.00

MORGAN, A.P. *How To Build a 20 Foot Biplane Glider.* 1909 NY. Spon Chamberlain. Ills. 60 p. $25.00

MORGAN, Ann Lee. *Arthur Dove: His Life & Work with a Catalogue Raisonne.* 1984 Newark. Ills. 4to. 380 p. wraps. $35.00

MORGAN, Barbara. *Martha Graham.* 1941 NY. Ills 1st ed. 4to. $95.00

MORGAN, Berry. *Mystic Adventures of Roxie Stoner.* 1974 Houghton. 1st ed. dj. EX $30.00

MORGAN, C.H. *Life of Michelangelo.* 1960 NY. Ills. 253 p. $15.00

MORGAN, Charles Lamb. *Martin Lewis Monograph.* 1931 Am Etchers Series XI. dj. $40.00

MORGAN, Frederick. *Refractions.* 1981 Omaha. Ltd ed. 1/290. EX $30.00

MORGAN, Gwenda. *Wood Engravings of Gwenda Morgan.* 1985 Ltd ed. 1/335. sgn. VG $60.00

MORGAN, Hal. *Prairie Fires & Paper Moons.* 1981 Boston. Godine. $17.50

MORGAN, J.M. *Recollections of Rebel Reefer.* 1917 Boston/NY. 1st trade ed. 491 p. VG $45.00

MORGAN, John Hill. *Sketch of Life of John Ramage: Miniature Painter.* 1930 NY. 1st ed. VG $35.00

MORGAN, Lewis H. *American Beaver & His Works.* 1868 Lippincott. Ills 1st ed. 330 p. $95.00

MORGAN, Lewis H. *Houses & House Life of the American Aborigines.* 1881 GPO. Ills. 4to. cloth. VG $100.00

MORGAN, Lewis H. *Houses & House Life of the American Aborigines.* 1881 GPO. Ills. 4to. cloth. G $50.00

MORGAN, M. *1 Man's Gold Rush.* 1977 WA U Pr. Ills. 213 p. pb. EX $17.00

MORGAN, Maurice. *Essay on Sir John Falstaff.* 1777 London. rebound. EX $200.00

MORGAN, Murray. *Last Wilderness.* 1956 Viking. Ills. 275 p. VG $12.00

MORGAN, Shirley. *Rain, Rain Don't Go Away.* 1972 NY. Dutton. Ills Ardizzone. 1st ed. VG $10.00

MORGAN, T.H. *Experimental Embryology.* 1927 Columbia U Pr. 1st ed. 766 p. VG $15.00

MORGAN & GRAHAM. *16 Dances in Photographs.* 1980 Dobbs Ferry. Revised 1st ed. inscr. dj. EX $40.00

MORGAN. *Trinity Protestant Episcopal Church. Gaveston, TX 1841-1953.* 1954 Houston. Anson Jones Pr. inscr. G $20.00

MORIBANA & HEIKWA. *Selected Arrangements of Moribana & Heikwa.* 1934 Japan. 200 plts. 2 vol set. $45.00

MORIER, James. *Adventures of Hajji Baba of Isphahan in England.* 1828 London. 2 vol set. full calf. EX $180.00

MORISON, S. *John Bell.* 1930 London. 1st Ed Club. 1/100. rare. EX $500.00

MORISON, Samuel Eliot. *Admiral of the Ocean Sea: Life of Christopher Columbus.* 1942 1st ed. 680 p. VG $15.00

MORISON, Samuel Eliot. *Development of Harvard University 1869-1929.* 1930 Cambridge. 1st ed. EX $40.00

MORISON, Samuel Eliot. *European Discovery of America.* 1974 Oxford U Pr. 1st ed. dj. VG $10.00

MORISON, Samuel Eliot. *European Discovery of America.* 1971 NY. Book Club ed. dj. VG $10.00

MORISON, Samuel Eliot. *History of US Naval Operations in WWII.* 1947 Little Brown. 1st ed. 15 vol set. djs. EX $325.00

MORISON, Samuel Eliot. *Maritime History of MA.* 1921 no place. xl. VG $22.50

MORISON, Samuel Eliot. *Old Bruin.* 1967 Boston. 1st ed. dj. EX $17.00

MORISON, Samuel Eliot. *Samuel de Champlain: Father of New France.* 1972 Boston. EX $30.00

MORISON, Stanley. *Art of the Printer: 250 Title Pages 1500-1900.* 1925 London. 1st ed. 4to. 244 p. dj. VG $100.00

MORISON, Stanley. *Typographic Design in Relation to Photographic Composition.* 1959 CA Book Club. 1st ed. 1/400. EX $60.00

MORKEL, Bill. *Hunting in Africa.* 1980 South Africa. dj. EX $16.00

MORLEY, A. *Strength of Materials.* 1911 London. 8vo. cloth. 495 p. VG $10.00

MORLEY, C. *Inward Ho!* 1923 Garden City. 1st ed. dj. VG $25.00

MORLEY, Christopher. *Arrow.* 1927 NY. 1st ed. sgn. dj. VG $25.00

MORLEY, Christopher. *Book of Days.* 1931 NY. Day. 2nd ed. sgn. blue cloth. VG $50.00

MORLEY, Christopher. *Goldfish Under the Ice.* 1929 London. Ltd ed. 1/530. sgn. dj. VG $30.00

MORLEY, Christopher. *Haunted Bookshop.* 1919 NY. 1st ed. 1st state. VG $80.00

MORLEY, Christopher. *Hostages to Fortune.* 1925 private print. 8vo. inscr. 121 p. VG $40.00

MORLEY, Christopher. *Old Loopy: Love Letter for Chicago.* 1935 Ills Gary Ederheimer. 1st ed. $35.00

MORLEY, Christopher. *Powder of Sympathy.* 1923 NY. Ills 1st ed. sgn. 304 p. G $25.00

MORLEY, Christopher. *Travels in Philadelphia.* 1920 Phil. Ills 1st ed. inscr. dj. $100.00

MORLEY, Christopher. *Where the Blue Begins.* 1922 Phil. Ills Rackham. 1st ed. sgn. VG $75.00

MORLEY, Christopher. *Where the Blue Begins.* 1922 NY. Ills 1st ed. 4to. sgn. VG $150.00

MORLEY, Christopher. *Where the Blue Begins.* 1922 Lippincott. Ills Rackham. dj. VG $30.00

MORLEY, F.V. *My 1 Contribution to Chess.* 1945 NY. VG $22.50

MORLEY, H.T. *Old & Curious Playing Cards.* 1931 London. Ills 1st ed. 4to. 235 p. dj. $185.00

MORLEY, H.T. *Old & Curious Playing Cards.* no date. London. Batsford. 4to. 235 p. $55.00

MORLEY, Henry. *Journal of a London Playgoer 1851-1866.* 1866 London. 1st ed. scarce. VG $65.00

MORLEY, M. *Few Familiar Flowers.* 1897 Boston. Ills. juvenile. VG $12.00

MORLEY, M. *Seed Babies.* 1896 Boston. 1st ed. juvenile. VG $12.00

MORLEY, S.G. *Ancient Maya.* 1947 Stanford U Pr. 2nd ed. 520 p. maps. dj. EX $40.00

MORLEY, S.G. *Maya Hieroglyphs.* 1915 GPO. Ills. G $50.00

MORNAND, P. *Visage du Christ.* 1939 Paris. Ills. folio. French text. VG $35.00

MORRELL, David. *Testament.* 1975 Evans. 1st ed. dj. EX $15.00

MORRICE, F.L.H. *Nightless North: Walk Across Lapland.* 1891 London. Kent. 1st ed. 8vo. cloth. EX $150.00

MORRIS, A.A. *Digging in the Southwest.* 1933 NY. Ills 1st ed. 301 p. dj. VG $17.50

MORRIS, Anne C. *Diary & Letters of Governor Morris.* 1888 NY. Ills 1st ed. 2 vol set. EX $65.00

MORRIS, C. *Morris' Story of the Great Earthquake of 1908.* c 1909. Ills. 8vo. 448 p. VG $10.00

MORRIS, C. *Volcano's Deadly Work From Fall of Pompeii to St. Pierre.* 1902 Phil. black cloth. G $12.00

MORRIS, Desmond. *Animal Days.* 1980 Morrow. Ills. 304 p. dj. EX $10.00

MORRIS, Desmond. *Naked Ape: Zoologist's Study of the Human Animal.* 1967 McGraw Hill. Ills 1st Am ed. 252 p. dj. VG $6.00

MORRIS, Donald. *Washing of the Spears.* 1965 Simon Schuster. Ills 1st ed. 655 p. dj. VG $32.50

MORRIS, Donald. *Washing of the Spears.* 1965 Simon Schuster. Book Club ed. dj. VG $20.00

MORRIS, Edmund. *Derrick & Drill.* 1965 NY. EX $80.00

MORRIS, F.O. *History of British Butterflies.* 1895 London. Nimmo. 8th ed. VG $175.00

MORRIS, F.O. *Natural History of British Moths.* 1872 London. Ills. 4to. 4 vol set. $150.00

MORRIS, George P. *Deserted Bride & Other Poems.* 1843 NY. Ills Chapman/Weir. 2nd ed. $60.00

MORRIS, Henry. *Omnibus.* 1967 Bird & Bull Pr. Ills. 8vo. $110.00

MORRIS, Joanna. *Encyclopedia of Cooking.* 1985 NY. Exeter Books. EX $20.00

MORRIS, L. *Epic of Hades.* 1876 Phil. G $10.00

MORRIS, Ron. *Wallenda.* 1976 Chatham. 1st ed. sgn Wallenda. EX $15.00

MORRIS, W. *About Fiction.* 1975 NY. 1st ed. dj. M $12.00

MORRIS, Whit. *Morris Family of Mecklenburg County, NC.* 1956 San Antonio. Clegg. 128 p. index. VG $15.00

MORRIS, William. *Art & Beauty of the Earth.* 1898 London. Longman. xl. $135.00

MORRIS, William. *Earthly Paradise.* 1868 Boston. 1st Am ed. G $45.00

MORRIS, William. *Story of Sigurd the Volsung.* 1877 London. 8vo. G $30.00

MORRIS, Willie. *Always Stand In Against the Curve.* 1983 Yoknapatawpha. 1st ed. sgn. dj. EX $35.00

MORRIS, Willie. *Courting of Marcus Dupree.* 1983 Doubleday. 1st ed. sgn. dj. EX $35.00

MORRIS, Willie. *Good Old Boy.* 1974 Deutsch. 1st English ed. dj. EX $30.00

MORRIS, Willie. *Good Old Boy.* 1980 Yoknapatawpha. Ltd 1st ed. 1/300. sgn. dj. EX $40.00

MORRIS, Willie. *James Jones: Friendship.* 1978 Doubleday. 1st ed. dj. EX $30.00

MORRIS, Willie. *Last of the Southern Girls.* 1973 Knopf. 1st ed. dj. EX $35.00

MORRIS, Willie. *North Toward Home.* 1967 Houghton. 1st ed. dj. EX $35.00

MORRIS, Willie. *Yazoo.* 1971 Harper. 1st ed. dj. EX $35.00

MORRIS, Wright. *Cat's Meow.* 1975 Los Angeles. Ltd 1st ed. 1/125. sgn. dj. M $100.00

MORRIS, Wright. *Cause for Wonder.* 1963 Atheneum. 1st ed. dj. EX $25.00

MORRIS, Wright. *Fire Sermon.* 1969 NY. 1st ed. dj. EX $10.00

MORRIS, Wright. *Fire Sermon.* 1971 Harper. 1st ed. dj. EX $20.00

MORRIS, Wright. *Here Is Einbaum.* 1973 Los Angeles. Ltd ed. 1/226. sgn. dj. M $45.00

MORRIS, Wright. *Home Place.* 1948 NY/ London. Scribner. 1st ed. 8vo. dj. EX $75.00

MORRIS, Wright. *Inhabitants.* 1946 NY. Scribner. 1st ed. 4to. cloth. $75.00

MORRIS, Wright. *Inhabitants.* 1946 NY. Scribner. Ills 1st ed. 4to. cloth. dj. $100.00

MORRIS, Wright. *Love Affair: Venetian Journal.* 1972 NY. Harper. Ills 1st ed. 4to. cloth. dj. $45.00

MORRIS, Wright. *Love Among the Cannibals.* 1957 NY. 1st ed. dj. EX $28.00

MORRIS, Wright. *Origins of Sadness.* 1984 AL U Pr. Ltd ed. 1/115. sgn. dj. M $75.00

MORRIS, Wright. *Plains Song.* 1980 Harper. 1st ed. dj. EX $15.00

MORRIS, Wright. *What a Way To Go.* 1962 Atheneum. 1st ed. dj. EX $30.00

MORRIS, Wright. *Works of Love.* 1951 Knopf. 1st ed. dj. EX $55.00

MORRIS & EAMES. *Our Wild Orchids.* 1929 Scribner. xl. VG $15.00

MORRIS. *Nelson Rockefeller: Biography.* 1960 NY. Ills. cloth. VG $25.00

MORRIS. *World in the Attic.* 1949 Scribner. 1st ed. dj. VG $25.00

MORRISON, H.R.; & LEE, C.E. *Americas Atlantic Isles.* 1981 Nat'l Geog Soc. Ills. 199 p. maps. dj. EX $12.00

MORRISON, John H. *History of American Steam Navigation.* 1958 NY. Stephen Daye Pr. $32.50

MORRISON, M. *Here's How in Fishing.* 1949 Doubleday. Ills. 128 p. G $4.00

MORRISON, Neil F. *Garden Gateway to Canada.* 1954 Toronto. Ills 1st ed. 344 p. VG $35.00

MORRISON, Philip. *Search for Extraterrestrial Intelligence.* 1977 WA. 1st ed. 276 p. wraps. G $7.00

MORRISON, Phyllis. *Spiders' Games: Book for Beginning Weavers.* 1979 Seattle. WA U Pr. Ills. 4to. 128 p. VG $25.00

MORRISON, Toni. *Beloved.* 1987 Knopf. 1st ed. sgn. dj. M $75.00

MORRISON, Toni. *Beloved.* 1987 Knopf. 1st ed. dj. $35.00

MORRISON, Toni. *Beloved.* 1987 Knopf. Uncorrected proof. EX $75.00

MORRISON, Toni. *Tar Baby.* 1981 Knopf. 1st ed. dj. EX $35.00

MORRISON, W. *Recovery of Jerusalem.* 1871 Appleton. 1st Am ed. maps. VG $45.00

MORRISON. *TX Book Prices.* 1973 Waco. EX $20.00

MORRITT, H.E. *Constant Fisherman.* 1957 London. Ills Shepard. 1st ed. cloth. $30.00

MORRITT, H.E. *Fishing Ways & Wiles.* 1929 London. 1st ed. plts. cloth. VG $30.00

MORROW, Elizabeth. *Painted Pig.* 1930 NY. Knopf. Ills D'Harnoncourt. 1st ed. VG $30.00

MORROW, Elizabeth. *Point of Judgement.* 1939 NY. Knopf. Ills S Suba. 4to. 43 p. dj. G $10.00

MORROW, J.E. *Fresh-Water Fishes of AK.* 1980 AK Northwest. Ills. 4to. 248 p. wraps. EX $24.00

MORSE, A. Reynolds. *Dali: Study of His Life & Work.* 1958 Greenwich, CT. Ills. folio. 96 p. $85.00

MORSE, A. Reynolds. *Salvador Dali 1910-1965.* 1965 Greenwich, CT. Ills. 4to. 150 p. dj. $40.00

MORSE, Arthur D. *While 6 Million Died.* 1968 NY. 2nd print. dj. VG $20.00

MORSE, Edward S. *Japanese Homes & Their Surroundings.* 1886 Salem. Peabody Academy of Science. VG $125.00

MORSE, H.G. *Robert Louis Stevenson As I Found Him.* 1902 no place. wraps. EX $10.00

MORSE, J.E. *New Rhubarb Culture.* 1903 NY. Judd. Ills. 12mo. 130 p. xl. $25.00

MORSE, Jedidiah. *American Gazetteer.* 1797 1st ed. maps. VG $85.00

MORSE, Jedidiah. *Annals of American Revolution.* 1824 Hartford. 1st ed. 6 plts. VG $85.00

MORSE, Jedidiah. *Geography Made Easy.* 1819 Utica. 20th ed. 16mo. full leather. $25.00

MORSE, John T. *American Statesmen.* 1898 Houghton. 32 vol set. EX $160.00

MORSE, S.F.B. *Foreign Conspiracy Against Liberties of the US.* 1835 NY. 1st ed. 208 p. fair. $27.50

MORSE, Sidney. *Household Discoveries: Encyclopedia of Recipes.* 1909 NY. Petersburg. 1st ed. EX $35.00

MORTENSEN, W. *Book on Problems of Posing.* 1948 San Francisco. 2nd ed. 8vo. cloth. dj. VG $20.00

MORTENSEN, William. *Monsters & Madonnas.* 1967 Jacques de Langre. dj. EX $50.00

MORTFORD, Henry. *Over Sea: England, France, & Scotland Seen by an American.* 1855 NY. 1st ed. G $35.00

MORTIMER, John. *Charade.* 1947 London. 1st ed. dj. EX $80.00

MORTIMER, Penelope. *Daddy's Gone a Hunting.* 1958 London. 1st ed. dj. VG $18.00

MORTIMER, Penelope. *Pumpkin Eaters.* 1962 London. 1st ed. dj. VG $22.00

MORTIMER, William W. *History of the Hundred of Wirral.* 1847 London. Ills. 4to. 36 p index. $100.00

MORTON, A.Q. *Literary Detection.* 1978 NY. 219 p. EX $20.00

MORTON, Edgar. *Great Pyramid: Its Scientific Features.* 1924 Glasgow. 217 p. wraps. VG $35.00

MORTON, Grace Margaret. *Arts of Costume & Personal Appearance.* 1943 NY. Ills 1st ed. 400 p. VG $7.50

MORTON, Henry. *Report of Translate of Inscription on the Rosetta Stone.* 1859 Phil. 2nd ed. 4to. 176 p. gilt red cloth. VG $250.00

MORTON, Richard L. *Colonial VA.* 1960 VA Hist Soc. 2 vol set. slipcase. VG $35.00

MORTON, Robert. *Southern Antiques & Folk Art.* 1976 Birmingham. Oxmoor House. $25.00

MORTON, Samuel G. *Crania Americana.* 1839 Phil. Ills 1st ed. folio. $250.00

MOSBY, John S. *Stuart's Cavalry in Gettysburg Campaign.* 1908 NY. 1st ed. xl. G $25.00

MOSCHCOWITZ, Eli. *Biology of Disease.* 1948 NY. 1st ed. VG $25.00

MOSCHINI, V. *Francesco Guardi.* 1956 Milan. Ills. 4to. dj. VG $25.00

MOSE, Brick. *CA Football History.* 1937 Berkeley. sgn. 257 p. $25.00

MOSER, Charles K. *Cotton Textile Industry of Far Eastern Countries.* 1930 Boston. Pepperell. Ills. 4to. 144 p. $35.00

MOSES, Henry. *Series of 29 Designs of Modern Costume.* 1823 London. Pall Mall. Ills. ½-leather. $225.00

MOSES, L.G.; & WILSON, R. *Indian Lives: Essays on 19th & 20th Century Indian Leaders.* 1985 NM U Pr. Ills. 227 p. dj. EX $20.00

MOSES, Montrose J. *British Plays From the Restoration to 1820.* 1929 Little Brown. 2 vol set. boxed. VG $40.00

MOSKOWITZ, Sam. *Strange Horizons: Spectrum of Science Fiction.* 1976 NY. 1st ed. dj. EX $30.00

MOSS, Howard. *Notes From the Castle.* 1979 Atheneum. Ltd ed. 1/750. dj. $25.00

MOSS, Howard. *Poet's Story.* 1973 NY. 1st ed. dj. EX $45.00

MOSS, Howard. *Swimmer in the Air: Poems.* 1957 NY. 1st ed. dj. EX $35.00

MOSS, Howard. *Whatever Is Moving.* 1981 Little Brown. 1st ed. dj. EX $16.00

MOSS, Howard. *Writing Against Time.* 1969 Morrow. Advance copy. dj. EX $20.00

MOTHERWELL, Robert. *Dada.* 1981 NY. Wittenborn Schultz. 460 p. $20.00

MOTHNER, Ira. *Man of Action: Life of Teddy Roosevelt.* 1966 Platt Munk. Ills. 90 p. dj. EX $5.00

MOTLEY, John Lathrop. *History of the United Netherlands.* 1888 2vol set. VG $25.00

MOTLEY, W. *Let Noon Be Fair.* 1966 NY. 1st ed. dj. EX $10.00

MOTTHEAU, Jacques. *Louis XVI.* no date. Paris. Massin. Ills. dj. $45.00

MOTTHEAU, Jacques. *Regence Louis XV.* no date. Paris. Massin. Ills. dj. $45.00

MOTTLEY, John. *History of Life of Peter I, Emperor of Russia.* 1740 Dublin. 1st ed. 12mo. $200.00

MOUNTFIELD, David. *History of Polar Exploration.* 1974 Dial. Ills. 4to. 208 p. dj. EX $12.50

MOUNTFORT, G. *Tigers.* 1973 Crescent. Ills. 96 p. dj. EX $6.50

MOURON, Henri. *A.M. Cassandre.* 1985 NY. Rizzoli. Ills. 4to. 315 p. dj. $50.00

MOWAT, F. *Never Cry Wolf.* 1963 Little Brown. 247 p. dj. EX $8.00

MOWAT, F. *People of the Deer.* 1952 Little Brown. Ills. 344 p. VG $11.00

MOWAT, F. *Polar Passion: Quest for the North Pole.* 1967 Little Brown. Ills 1st Am ed. 4to. dj. EX $15.00

MOWAT, F. *Snow Walker.* 1975 Toronto. 1st ed. dj. VG $20.00

MOWATT, Anna C. *Autobiography of an Actress; or, 8 Years on the Stage.* 1854 Boston. 12mo. gilt brown cloth. VG $35.00

MOWBRAY, George M. *Tri-Nitro-Glycerin: Applied in the Hoosac Tunnel.* 1872 North Adams. 1st ed. 8vo. plts. photos. $160.00

MOWERY, Jeannette H. *Dolls & People.* 1956 Portland. 1st ed. sgn. dj. EX $18.00

MOXON, Edward. *Moxon's Mechanic Exercises Applied to the Art of Printing.* 1896 NY. Typothetae. Ills. 1/450. 4to. 2 vol set. $200.00

MUCHA, J. *Alphonse Muncha: His Life & Art.* 1966 London. 1st ed. dj. EX $17.50

MUCHERY, George. *Astrological Tarot.* no date. London. Rider. 312 p. VG $15.00

MUDIE, Rosmary & Colin. *Story of Sailing Ship.* 1980 NY. Exeter. dj. EX $16.00

MUELLER, H.A. *Woodcuts & Wood Engravings: How I Make Them.* 1929 NY. Pynson. 1/3,000. VG $37.00

MUELLER, J. *Growing Your Own Mushrooms.* 1976 Garden Way. Ills. 174 p. wraps. EX $5.00

MUENSCHER, W.C. *Poisonous Plants of the US.* 1951 NY. Ills Revised 1st ed. dj. VG $20.00

MUENSCHER, W.C. *Poisonous Plants of the US.* 1960 Macmillan. Revised ed. 277 p. dj. VG $20.00

MUENSTERBERGER, Warner. *Sculpture of Primitive Man.* 1955 NY. Abrams. Ills. tall 4to. cloth. dj. $85.00

MUHLBACH, Louisa. *Works of Louisa Muhlbach.* 1883-1886. Ills. 18 vol set. EX $65.00

MUIR, John. *Cruise of Corwin.* 1917 Boston. 1st ed. 1/550. dj. VG $85.00

MUIR, John. *Mountains of CA.* 1901 NY. VG $40.00

MUIR, John. *My 1st Summer in the Sierra.* 1911 Boston. 2nd ed. dj. $40.00

MUIR, John. *My 1st Summer in the Sierra.* 1911 Boston/NY. Ills 1st ed. 8vo. gilt cloth. $65.00

MUIR, John. *Notes on My Journeys in CA's Northern Mountains.* 1974 private print. Ills Ltd ed. 1/700. VG $35.00

MUIR, John. *Our National Parks.* 1901 Riverside Pr. 1st ed. $75.00

MUIR, John. *Our National Parks.* 1901 Cambridge. 1st ed. xl. VG $50.00

MUIR, John. *Our National Parks.* 1909 Boston. Ills 2nd ed. 382 p. VG $85.00

MUIR, John. *Stickeen.* 1909 Boston. Houghton Mifflin. 6th imp. EX $40.00

MUIR, John. *Stickeen.* 1910 Boston. 8th imp. VG $40.00

MUIR, John. *Story of My Boyhood & Youth.* 1913 Boston. VG $45.00

MUIR, John. *Travels in AK.* 1916 Boston. 6th imp. $40.00

MUIR, John. *1,000 Mile Walk to the Gulf.* 1916 Boston. Ills 1st ed. VG $50.00

MUIR, John. *1,000 Mile Walk to the Gulf.* Boston. Ltd ed. 220 p. dj. VG $110.00

MUIR, John. *2 Essays on the Sights & Sounds of Sierra, NV.* 1973 private print. Ills Ltd ed. 1/1,000. VG $35.00

MUIR, Percy. *Victorian Illustrated Books.* 1971 NY. M $38.00

MUIR, Percy. *Victorian Illustrated Books.* 1971 London. Ills 1st ed. dj. VG $55.00

MUKERJI, Dhan G. *Gay-Neck.* 1927 NY. Dutton. Ltd Newberry Medal ed. dj. EX $100.00

MUKERJI, Dhan G. *Gay-Neck.* 1927 NY. Dutton. Ills Artzybasheff. 1/1,000. VG $65.00

MUKERJI, Dhan G. *Jungle Beasts & Men.* 1924 Dutton. Ills. 160 p. VG $6.50

MUKERJI, Dhan G. *Son of Mother India Answers.* 1962 NY. $20.00

MULDOON, G. *Leopards in the Night.* 1955 NY. 1st ed. dj. VG $30.00

MULFORD, Clarence. *Bar-20 Days.* 1911 Chicago. 1st ed. presentation. G $75.00

MULHANE, L.W. *Leprosy & the Charity of the Church.* 1898 Chicago. 8vo. 30 p. xl. VG $10.00

MULLAY, John. *Laying of the Cable; or, The Ocean Telegraph.* 1858 NY. Appleton. Ills. 329 p. VG $95.00

MULLEN, R.J. *Dominican Architecture in 16th Century Oaxaca.* 1975 AZ U Pr. Ills. 260 p. dj. EX $10.00

MULLER, Charles G. *How They Carried the Goods.* 1932 NY. Dodd Mead. Ills Tenggren. 1st ed. dj. EX $20.00

MULLER, F. *Eyewitness Auschwitz: Years in Gas Chambers.* 1981 Stein Day. Ills. SftCvr. G $12.50

MULOCK, Dinah T. *Adventures of a Brownie: The Little Prince.* 1948 Grosset Dunlap. Ills Lucille Corcos. boxed. EX $15.00

MULOCK, Dinah T. *Little Lame Prince.* 1930 Whitman. Ills Higgins. 2nd print. G $15.00

MUMEY, Nolie. *Alexander Taylor Rankin 1803-1885: His Diary & Letters.* 1966 Ltd ed. 1/400. $50.00

MUMEY, Nolie. *Art & Activities of John Dare Howland.* 1973 Boulder. Ills 1st ed. 237 p. slipcase. $50.00

MUMEY, Nolie. *Rocky Mountain Dick.* 1953 Ltd ed. 1/500. sgn. EX $55.00

MUMEY, Nolie. *Saga of Auntie Stone & Her Cabin.* 1964 Centenary ed. 1/500. sgn. EX $67.50

MUMFORD, J. *Doctor's Table Talk.* 1912 Boston/NY. Houghton Mifflin. 1st ed. VG $25.00

MUMFORD, John Kimberly. *Oriental Rugs.* 1909 NY. Scribner. Ills. 4to. 278 p. G $80.00

MUNDUS, F.; & WISNER, B. *Sport Fishing for Sharks.* 1976 Collier. Ills. 380 p. wraps. VG $12.00

MUNDY, Talbot. *Eye of Zeitoon.* 1920 Indianapolis. 1st ed. dj. VG $22.50

MUNDY, Talbot. *Old Ugly Face.* 1940 1st print. VG $150.00

MUNK, J.A. *AZ Sketches.* 1905 NY. G $30.00

MUNK, J.A. *Features of an AR Library.* 1926 Los Angeles. private print. 1st ed. sgn. EX $95.00

MUNK, J.A. *Southwest Sketches.* 1920 Putnam. Ills 1st ed. $35.00

MUNK, J.A. *Story of Munk Library of Arizoniana.* 1927 Los Angeles. private print. 1st ed. boxed. $85.00

MUNOZ, Frank J. *Microscope & Its Uses.* 1943 Brooklyn. Chemical Pub. 1st ed. 334 p. $6.00

MUNRO, D. *Treatment of Injuries to the Nervous System.* 1952 Phil. 1st ed. 284 p. EX $75.00

MUNRO, R.W.; & BROWN, L.C. *Practical Guide to Cocoa Nut Planting.* 1920 London. Ills 2nd ed. 12mo. 203 p. $25.00

MUNROE, David Hoadley. *Grand National 1839-1930.* 1930 NY. 1st ed. presentation. G $45.00

MUNSELL, A.H. *Color Notation.* 1926 Baltimore. Ills. 8vo. 105 p. VG $30.00

MUNSELL, A.H. *Color Notation.* 1916 Boston. Revised 4th ed. 12mo. 113 p. $55.00

MUNSEY, Cecil. *Illustrated Guide of Collecting Coca Cola.* 1972 NY. Hawthorne. 4to. M $35.00

MUNSEY, Cecil. *Illustrated Guide to Collecting Bottles.* 1970 NY. Hawthorne. Ills. 4to. 320 p. $20.00

MUNSEY, Cecil. *Walt Disney Collectibles.* 1974 NY. Ills. 395 p. dj. EX $50.00

MUNSON, Edward Lyman. *Soldier Foot & Military Shoe.* 1912 Ft. Leavenworth. 1st ed. G $15.00

MUNSON, G. *Waldo Frank: A Study.* 1923 NY. Ltd ed. 1/500. G $135.00

MUNSON. *Mister Charlie: Memoir of a TX Lawman 1902-1910.* 1975 Austin. Madrona Pr. 1st ed. dj. EX $25.00

MUNSTERBERG, Hugo. *Arts of Japan.* 1957 London. 1st ed. dj. EX $58.00

MUNSTERBERG, Hugo. *Japanese Print.* 1982 Weatherhill. Ills. 220 p. dj. M $35.00

MUNSTERS, George Chaworth. *At Home with the Patagonians.* 1871 London. Murray. 1st ed. 322 p. ¾-calf. $125.00

MURARO & GRABAR. *Treasures of Venice.* 1963 Skira. Ills. 4to. red linen bdg. dj. $60.00

MURATORIO, Ricardo. *Feast of Color: Corpus Christi Dance Costumes.* 1981 Smithsonian. Ills. 32 p. $12.50

MURBARGER. *Ghosts of Glory Trail.* 1956 Palm Desert. Ills 1st ed. 291 p. VG $32.50

MURDOCH, Harold. *19th of April 1775.* 1923 Houghton Mifflin. 1/525. $35.00

MURDOCH, Iris. *Accidental Man.* 1971 Viking. 1st Am ed. dj. EX $20.00

MURDOCH, Iris. *Black Prince.* 1973 Viking. 1st ed. dj. VG $12.50

MURDOCH, Iris. *Black Prince.* 1973 Viking. 1st Am ed. dj. EX $15.00

MURDOCH, Iris. *Henry & Cato.* 1977 Viking. 1st Am ed. dj. EX $15.00

MURDOCH, Iris. *Nice & Good.* 1968 Chatto Windus. 1st ed. dj. EX $25.00

MURDOCH, Iris. *Sacred & Profane Love Machine.* 1974 Viking. 1st Am ed. dj. EX $15.00

MURDOCH, Iris. *Under the Net.* 1954 Viking. 1st Am ed. dj. EX $45.00

MURDOCH, Iris. *Unicorn.* 1963 London. 1st ed. dj. EX $30.00

MURDOCH, Iris. *Unicorn.* 1963 Viking. 1st Am ed. dj. EX $20.00

MURDOCH, Iris. *Unofficial Rose.* 1962 Viking. 1st Am ed. dj. EX $20.00

MURDOCK, J.B. *Notes on Electricity & Magnetism.* 1884 NY. Ills. 140 p. red cloth. EX $30.00

MURDOCK, K.B. *Portraits of Increase Mather.* 1924 Cleveland. Ltd ed. 1/250. VG $75.00

MURDOCK, Myrtle. *Constantino Brumidi: Michaelangelo of the US Capitol.* 1950 WA. dj. VG $65.00

MURHACH, Ernst. *Painted Romanesque Ceiling of St. Martin in Zillis.* 1967 NY. Praeger. Ills. square 4to. dj. $40.00

MURIE, Adolph. *Naturalist in AK.* 1961 Devin Adair. Ills Murie. 302 p. dj. EX $15.00

MURIE, Adolph. *Wolves of Mt. McKinley.* 1971 GPO. Ills. 238 p. wraps. EX $8.50

MURIE, Alaus. *Journeys to the Far North.* 1973 Palo Alto. dj. EX $15.00

MURIE, M.E. *AK Bird Sketches of Olaus Murie.* 1979 AK Northwest. Ills. oblong 4to. wraps. EX $12.00

MURIE, M.E. *2 in the Far North.* 1983 AK Northwest. Ills New ed. 385 p. pb. EX $9.00

MURIE, M.E. *2 in the Far North.* 1962 Knopf. Ills Murie. 1st ed. 438 p. M $50.00

MURIE, M.E. *2 in the Far North.* 1963 Knopf. Ills. 438 p. dj. VG $14.00

MURIE, M.E. & O. *Wapiti Wilderness.* 1966 Knopf. Ills 1st ed. 302 p. dj. $28.00

MURPHEY, C.C. *Around the US by Bicycle.* 1906 Detroit. Ills 1st ed. 362 p. VG $37.50

MURPHY, Audie. *To Hell & Back.* 1949 NY. Holt. dj. VG $25.00

MURPHY, J.M. *Sporting Adventures in the Far West.* 1880 Harper. 469 p. VG $25.00

MURPHY, Robert Cushman. *Oceanic Birds of South America.* 1936 NY. Ills 1st ed. 2 vols in 1. $95.00

MURPHY, Robert Cushman. *Oceanic Birds of South America.* 1936 NY. 2 vol set. VG $50.00

MURPHY, Thomas D. *OR the Picturesque.* 1917 Boston. 40 plts. 16 maps. VG $35.00

MURPHY, Thomas D. *Sunset Highways.* 1915 Boston. Ills 1st ed. $40.00

MURPHY, Walter F. *Vicar of Christ.* 1979 NY. 1st ed. dj. M $15.00

MURPHY & AMADON. *Land Birds of America.* 1953 McGraw Hill. 1st ed. dj. VG $18.00

MURPHY & AMADON. *Land Birds of America.* 1953 McGraw Hill. 1st ed. 4to. sgns. EX $30.00

MURPHY & AMADON. *Land Birds of America.* 1953 McGraw Hill. Ills 1st ed. 340 p. G $10.00

MURRAY, Albert. *Good Morning Blues: Autobiography of Count Basie.* 1985 Random House. 1st ed. EX $18.00

MURRAY, Arthur. *Dance Secrets.* 1946 NY. Ills. dj. $15.00

MURRAY, Arthur. *How To Become a Good Dancer.* 1942 Simon Schuster. Revised 1st ed. 4to. dj. VG $15.00

MURRAY, D. *Birds of the Virgin Islands.* 1969 private print. Ills. 4to. 28 p. wraps. EX $5.00

MURRAY, Francis J. *Mathematical Machines. Vol. I. Digital Computers.* 1961 NY. Columbia U Pr. 300 p. xl. $10.00

MURRAY, G. *Legacy of Al Capone.* 1975 NY. 1st ed. dj. VG $17.50

MURRAY, H.J.R. *History of Chess.* 1913 Oxford. Ills. 900 p. $50.00

MURRAY, J. *Picturesque Tour of the River Thames.* 1862 London. Ills. VG $45.00

MURRAY, K.M. *Caught in Web of Words.* 1977 Yale. dj. VG $15.00

MURRAY, Keith A. *Modocs & Their War.* 1959 Norman. Ills 2nd ed. map. 346 p. dj. $20.00

MURRAY, Margaret Alice. *Witch Cult in Western Europe.* 1921 Oxford. VG $65.00

MURRAY, N. *Legacy of an Assassination.* 1964 NY. 1st ed. dj. VG $32.50

MURRAY, N. *Love of Elephants.* 1976 Octopus. Ills. 4to. dj. EX $10.00

MURRAY, Peter & Linda. *Dictionary of Art & Artists.* 1965 Praeger. 1st Am ed. dj. VG $35.00

MURRAY, Sheilagh. *Peacock & the Lions.* 1982 Stocksfield. Oriel. Ills. 8vo. 86 p. dj. $20.00

MURRAY, W. John. *Mental Medicine.* 1923 NY. dj. EX $25.00

MURRAY, W.H. *Adirondack Tales.* 1877 Boston. Ills 1st ed. G $35.00

MURRAY, W.H. *Adventures in the Wilderness.* 1869 Boston. Ills 1st ed. 236 p. fair. $27.50

MURRAY, W.H. *Holiday Tales: Christmas in the Adirondacks.* 1897 Springfield. inscr. VG $60.00

MURRAY. *Handbook for Travellers in Russia, Poland, & Finland.* 1888 London. 4th ed. fld map. VG $30.00

MURRAY. *Handbook to Algeria & Tunis.* 1890 London. Murray. Revised 4th ed. maps. plans. $40.00

MURRAY. *Lake Champlain & Its Shores.* 1896 Boston. G $25.00

MURRAY. *Muskoka & Haliburton 1615-1875.* 1963 Toronto. 445 p. VG $30.00

MURRAY. *System of Materia Medica & Pharmacy.* 1828 NY. leather. $30.00

MURREY, Thomas J. *Puddings & Dainty Desserts.* 1889 NY. 6th ed. EX $25.00

MURREY, Thomas J. *50 Salads.* 1885 NY. 7th ed. VG $20.00

MUSCATINE, Doris. *Cook's Tour of Rome.* 1964 NY. 1st ed. EX $10.00

MUSCHENHEIM, William. *Elements of Art of Architecture.* 1964 NY. Viking. VG $22.00

MUSIL, Alois. *Arabia Deserta.* 1927 NY. cloth. VG $90.00

MUSMANNO, M. *Eichmann Kommandos.* 1962 London. G $17.50

MUSMANNO, M. *10 Days To Die.* 1951 Doubleday. Ills. G $15.00

MUSSOLINI, Benito. *Cardinal's Mistress: A Novel.* 1928 NY. 1st Am & 1st Book ed. dj. EX $80.00

MUYBRIDGE, E. *Human Figure in Motion.* 1955 NY. Ills. 416 p. $18.00

MUYBRIDGE, E. *Muybridge's Complete Human & Animal Locomotion.* 1979 NY. 4to. cloth. dj. EX $20.00

MUZUMDAR, Haridas. *Gandhi the Apostle: His Trial & His Message.* 1923 Chicago. Universal. 1st ed. sgn. VG $20.00

MYERS, Frederick W.H. *Human Personality & Its Survival of Bodily Death.* 1936 London. 307 p. EX $35.00

MYERS, George Michael. *Alethea.* 1919 Boston. Gorham Pr. sgn. VG $25.00

MYERS, J.M. *Alamo.* 1948 Dutton. 1st ed. 240 p. maps. VG $20.00

MYERS, J.M. *Alamo.* 1948 NY. Special TX 1st ed. $25.00

MYERS, J.M. *Death of the Bravos.* 1962 Little Brown. 1st ed. 467 p. dj. $18.00

MYERS, J.M. *Doc Holiday.* 1955 Boston. 1st ed. $9.00

MYERS, J.M. *Last Chance: Tombstone's Early Years.* 1950 NY. 1st ed. dj. VG $35.00

MYERS, J.M. *Pirate, Pawnee, & Mountain Men: Saga of Hugh Glass.* 1963 Boston. 1st ed. dj. $10.00

MYERS, J.M. *San Francisco's Reign of Terror.* 1966 Doubleday. Ills 1st ed. 301 p. dj. EX $5.00

MYERS, L.H. *Pool of Vishnu.* 1940 NY. 1st ed. dj. M $15.00

MYERS, Louis G. *Some Notes on American Pewterers.* 1926 Garden City. Ltd ed. 1/1,000. $60.00

MYERS, M. John. *Deaths of the Bravos.* 1962 Boston. 1st ed. dj. VG $21.00

MYERS, Robert C.V. *Theodore Roosevelt: Patriot & Statesman.* c 1901. Ills. 8vo. 526 p. cloth. xl. G $14.00

MYERS, Sandra. *Cavalry Wife: Diary of Eveline M. Alexander 1866-1867.* 1977 TX A&M U Pr. Ills 1st ed. 175 p. VG $17.00

MYRER, Anton. *Evil Under the Sun.* 1951 Random House. 1st ed. dj. EX $35.00

MYRER, Anton. *Intruder.* 1965 Little Brown. 1st ed. dj. EX $30.00

NABOKOV, Vladimir. *Ada.* 1969 London. 1st ed. dj. EX $25.00

NABOKOV, Vladimir. *Ada.* 1969 McGraw Hill. 1st Am ed. dj. VG $30.00

NABOKOV, Vladimir. *Despair.* 1966 Putnam. 1st Am ed. dj. EX $50.00

NABOKOV, Vladimir. *Eye.* 1965 NY. Phaedra. 1st ed. 8vo. cloth. dj. EX $45.00

NABOKOV, Vladimir. *Glory.* 1971 McGraw Hill. 1st Am ed. dj. EX $30.00

NABOKOV, Vladimir. *Invitation to a Beheading.* 1959 NY. 1st ed. dj. VG $10.00

NABOKOV, Vladimir. *Lolita.* 1955 Paris. Olympia. 1st ed. 2 vol set. wraps. G $300.00

NABOKOV, Vladimir. *Lolita: A Screenplay.* no date. NY. Nabokov Verson. dj. EX $27.50

NABOKOV, Vladimir. *Look at the Harlequins!* 1974 McGraw Hill. 1st Am ed. dj. EX $25.00

NABOKOV, Vladimir. *Mary.* 1970 NY. 1st ed. Trans Michael Glenny. dj. VG $25.00

NABOKOV, Vladimir. *Nabokov's Dozen.* 1958 NY. 1st ed. dj. EX $50.00

NABOKOV, Vladimir. *Nikolai Gogol.* 1944 Hartford. 1st ed. dj. VG $17.00

NABOKOV, Vladimir. *Pale Fire.* 1962 NY. 1st ed. 1st imp. dj. EX $75.00

NABOKOV, Vladimir. *Transparent Things.* 1972 McGraw Hill. 1st Am ed. dj. EX $25.00

NABOKOV, Vladimir. *Waltz Invention.* 1966 Phaedra. 1st ed. dj. EX $95.00

NABOKOV, Vladimir. *9 Stories.* 1947 New Directions. 1st ed. VG $45.00

NACK, James. *Romance of Ring.* 1859 Delisser. VG $20.00

NACK, W. *Big Red of Meadow Stable.* 1975 NY. 1st ed. dj. VG $27.50

NADEAU, R. *Ghost Towns & Mining Camps of CA.* 1965 Ritchie Pr. 8vo. dj. VG $10.00

NAEF, Weston J. *Collection of Alfred Stieglitz.* 1978 NY. 4to. dj. M $50.00

NAEF, Weston J. *Era of Exploration: Rise of Landscape Photography.* 1975 NY Graphic Soc. 8vo. cloth. dj. EX $75.00

NAHMEE, Leon S. *Oriental Piano Selections.* 1925 NY. Syrian-Am Pr. Ills. folio. EX $95.00

NAINFA, John Abel. *Costume of Prelates of the Catholic Church.* 1926 Baltimore. Ills. 8vo. 293 p. $25.00

NAIPAUL, V.S. *Bend in the River.* 1979 NY. 1st ed. dj. EX $20.00

NAIPAUL, V.S. *Guerrillas.* 1975 London. 1st ed. dj. EX $45.00

NAIPAUL, V.S. *Miguel Street.* 1959 NY. 1st ed. dj. EX $15.00

NAIPAUL, V.S. *Return of Eva Peron.* 1980 NY. 1st ed. dj. EX $20.00

NAKAMURA, Ktsua. *Tokonoma.* 1958 Japan. Ills. 4to. 133 p. VG $50.00

NANSEN, Fridtjof. *Eskimo Life.* 1894 London. 2nd ed. scarce. EX $100.00

NANSEN, Fridtjof. *Farthest North.* 1897 Harper. 1st ed. 2 vol set. VG $85.00

NANSEN, Fridtjof. *In Nacht und Eis.* 1897 Leipzig. Ills. 8vo. 2 vol set. VG $70.00

NAPHEYS, G.H. *Modern Surgical Therapeutics.* 1879 Phil. 8vo. 605 p. brown cloth. G $30.00

NAPHEYS, G.H. *Prevention & Cure of Disease.* c 1871. Ills. 8vo. 1,151 p. leather. G $35.00

NAPP, Richard. *Argentine Republic Written for Central Argentine Commission.* 1876 Buenos Aires. 1st ed. 463 p. 3/4 leather. $75.00

NARAMORE, Earl. *Principles & Practice of Loading Ammunition.* 1954 Small Arms. Ills. 952 p. VG $47.50

NARAYAN, R.K. *Maneater of Malgudi.* 1961 NY. Viking. 1st ed. 8vo. inscr. dj. EX $22.50

NARAYAN, R.K. *Sweet Vendor.* 1967 London. 1st ed. dj. EX $15.00

NARKISS, Bezalel. *Hebrew Illuminated Manuscripts Encyclopedia Judaica.* 1969 Jerusalem. dj. VG $12.00

NARNBERG, Rolf. *Lindbergh, Hauptmann, & Amerika.* 1936 Leipzig. German text. inscr. VG $10.00

NASH, J.R.; & OFFEN, R. *Dillinger: Dead or Alive?* 1970 Regnery. Ills. 204 p. dj. EX $8.50

NASH, Ogden. *Animal Garden.* 1965 Ills Hilary Knight. dj. EX $15.00

NASH, Ogden. *Christmas That Almost Wasn't.* 1957 Little Brown. 1st ed. 8vo. 63 p. G $10.00

NASH, Ogden. *Hard Lines.* 1931 NY. 1st ed. 3rd print. VG $35.00

NASH, Ogden. *Marriage Lines.* 1964 Boston. 1st ed. dj. M $15.00

NASH, W. *2 Years in OR.* 1882 NY. Ills 2nd ed. VG $35.00

NASMYTH, James. *Autobiography of James Nasmyth.* 1883 NY. VG $95.00

NASON, Elias. *Sir Charles Henry Frankland: Baronet.* 1865 Albany. 1st ed. 8vo. blue cloth. EX $65.00

NATHAN, Archie. *Costumes by Nathan.* 1960 London. Ills 1st ed. 207 p. dj. EX $20.00

NATHAN, B. *Select Poems.* 1935 NY. 1st ed. dj. EX $12.00

NATHAN, Robert. *Married Look.* 1950 NY. 1st ed. dj. VG $12.50

NATIONAL GEOGRAPHIC SOCIETY. *AK: Highroads to Adventure.* 1976 Ills. 199 p. maps. dj. EX $10.00

NATIONAL GEOGRAPHIC SOCIETY. *America's Magnificent Mountains.* 1980 Ills. 207 p. dj. VG $10.00

NATIONAL GEOGRAPHIC SOCIETY. *America's Majestic Canyons.* 1979 Ills. 207 p. maps. dj. EX $10.00

NATIONAL GEOGRAPHIC SOCIETY. *America's Seashore Wonderlands.* 1985 Ills. 199 p. maps. dj. EX $10.00

NATIONAL GEOGRAPHIC SOCIETY. *America's Wild & Scenic Rivers.* 1983 Ills. 199 p. map. dj. EX $10.00

NATIONAL GEOGRAPHIC SOCIETY. *America's Wild Woodlands.* 1985 Ills. 199 p. dj. EX $10.00

NATIONAL GEOGRAPHIC SOCIETY. *American Mountain People.* 1973 Ills. 199 p. dj. EX $15.00

NATIONAL GEOGRAPHIC SOCIETY. *Canada's Wilderness Lands.* 1982 Ills. 199 p. maps. dj. EX $10.00

NATIONAL GEOGRAPHIC SOCIETY. *Discovering Man's Past in America.* 1973 Ills. 211 p. dj. EX $10.00

NATIONAL GEOGRAPHIC SOCIETY. *Exploring America's Back Country.* 1979 Ills. 215 p. maps. dj. EX $10.00

NATIONAL GEOGRAPHIC SOCIETY. *Great American Deserts.* 1972 Ills. 207 p. dj. EX $10.00

NATIONAL GEOGRAPHIC SOCIETY. *Mysteries of the Ancient World.* 1979 Ills. 223 p. maps. dj. EX $8.00

NATIONAL GEOGRAPHIC SOCIETY. *Nature's World of Wonders.* 1983 Ills. 199 p. maps. dj. EX $10.00

NATIONAL GEOGRAPHIC SOCIETY. *Secret Corners of the World.* 1982 Ills. 199 p. maps. dj. EX $10.00

NATIONAL GEOGRAPHIC SOCIETY. *Those Inventive Americans.* 1971 Ills. 231 p. dj. EX $8.00

NATIONAL GEOGRAPHIC SOCIETY. *Trails West.* 1983 WA. dj. VG $14.00

NATIONAL GEOGRAPHIC SOCIETY. *Wild Animals of North America.* 1967 Revised ed. 398 p. EX $11.00

NATIONAL GEOGRAPHIC SOCIETY. *Wild Animals of North America.* 1960 Ills 1st ed. 399 p. dj. EX $15.00

NATIONAL GEOGRAPHIC SOCIETY. *Wondrous World of Fishes.* 1965 Ills 1st ed. 367 p. EX $13.00

NATIONAL GEOGRAPHIC SOCIETY. *World of the American Indian.* 1974 Ills 1st ed. 399 p. EX $25.00

NATIONAL PARK SERVICE. *Yellowstone National Park.* 1929 Ills. 88 p. fld map. G $5.00

NAUD, Yves. *UFOs & Extra Terrestrials in History.* 1978 Geneva. Ferni. 4 vol set. EX $75.00

NAUHAUS, Eugene. *Art of the Exposition.* 1915 San Francisco. Ills. $35.00

NAULT, Andy. *Staying Alive in AK's Wild.* 1980 Loftion. Ills. 210 p. pb. EX $8.00

NAVILLE, Edouard. *Festival Hall of Osorkon II in Temple of Bubastis.* 1892 London. Ills. VG $40.00

NAYLOR, B. *Technique of Dress Design.* 1967 London. Ills. 154 p. dj. EX $22.50

NAYLOR, E.W. *Elizabethan Virginal Book.* 1905 London. Dent. VG $18.00

NAYLOR, Gillian. *Arts & Crafts Movement.* 1980 Cambridge. MIT Pr. Ills. 208 p. $20.00

NAYLOR, James Ball. *Sign of the Prophet.* 1901 Saalfield. 1st ed. 416 p. cloth. VG $22.50

NAYLOR, James Ball. *Under Mad Anthony's Banner.* 1903 Akron. Ills 1st ed. 394 p. G $17.50

NAYLOR, James Ball. *Vagrant Verse.* 1935 McConnelsville. 47 p. wraps. G $25.00

NEAL, Daniel. *History of Puritans or Protestant Non-Conformists.* 1754 London. Buckland. Corrected 2nd ed. $175.00

NEAL, H.V.; & RAND, H.W. *Chordate Anatomy.* 1939 Phil. Ills. 467 p. VG $22.50

NEAL, Julia. *Journal of Eldress Nancy.* 1963 Nashville. sgn. 256 p. $50.00

NEAL. *Pressed Glass Salt Dishes of Lacy Period 1825-1850.* 1962 Phil. private print. 1st ed. 468 p. $30.00

NEALE, Richard. *Medical Digest. Means of Ready Reference.* 1877 London. New Sydenham Soc. 1st ed. VG $35.00

NEARING, H. *Sinister Researches of C.P. Ransom.* 1954 Doubleday. 1st ed. dj. EX $35.00

NEARING, Scott; & HARDY, Jack. *Economic Organization of the Soviet Union.* 1927 NY. 1st ed. VG $25.00

NEEDHAM, Joseph. *Science & Civilization in China Vol. IV, Part 2.* 1965 Cambridge. wraps. EX $85.00

NEEL, Edith K. *Cats: How To Care for Them in Health & Treat Them When Ill.* 1902 Phil. Boericke Tafel. Ills. EX $30.00

NEELY, Ruth. *Women of OH.* no date. Clarke. 3 vol set. rare. VG $45.00

NEHRU, J. *Nuclear Explosions & Effects.* 1958 Delhi. VG $12.00

NEIDER, Charles. *Great West.* 1958 Bonanza. 457 p. dj. VG $14.00

NEIGHBOURS. *Indian Exodus: TX Indian Affairs 1835-1859.* 1973 no place. no publisher. Ills. dj. VG $28.50

NEIHARDT, John G. *Collected Poems.* 1926 Ltd ed. 1/250. sgn. 2 vol set. VG $45.00

NEIHARDT, John G. *River & I.* 1910 NY. 1st ed. 8vo. 325 p. $20.00

NEIHARDT, John G. *When the Tree Flowered.* 1951 Macmillan. 1st ed. dj. VG $20.00

NEIL, Miss E. *Everyday Cookbook & Encyclopedia of Practical Recipes.* c 1900. Chicago. 12mo. 316 p. $25.00

NEILL, C. Wilson. *Silver Stampede: Career of Death Valley's Hell Camp.* 1937 NY. 1st ed. VG $25.00

NEILL, John R. *Rab & His Friends.* 1908 Reilly Britton. 1st ed. VG $40.00

NEIMAN, Le Roy. *Art & Lifestyle.* no date. 1st ed. sgn. dj. EX $90.00

NELSON, Bruce. *Brothers.* 1975 NY. 1st ed. dj. EX $10.00

NELSON, Bruce. *Land of the Dakotahs.* 1947 MN U Pr. Ills. 354 p. dj. EX $22.00

NELSON, Donald. *Sam & Emma.* 1971 Parents Mag Pr. Ills Gorey. 1st ed. dj. EX $20.00

NELSON, Donald. *Sam & Emma.* 1971 Ills Gorey. 1st ed. VG $12.50

NELSON, Henry L. *Uniforms of the US Army.* 1959 NY. Ills Ogden. dj. VG $75.00

NELSON, Ozzie. *Ozzie.* 1973 NY. 1st ed. sgn. dj. VG $20.00

NELSON, Richard K. *Shadow of the Hunter.* 1980 TX U Pr. cloth. VG $10.00

NELSON & OGDEN. *Uniforms of the US Army.* 1959 NY. dj. VG $32.50

NEMEROV, Howard. *Commodity of Dreams & Other Stories.* 1959 NY. 1st ed. sgn. dj. EX $45.00

NEMEROV, Howard. *Federigo; or, Power of Love.* 1954 Boston. 1st ed. sgn. dj. M $65.00

NEMEROV, Howard. *Image & the Law.* 1947 NY. 1st ed. sgn. dj. EX $100.00

NEMEROV, Howard. *Journal of the Fictive Life.* 1965 NJ. 1st ed. dj. EX $10.00

NEMEROV, Howard. *Mirrors & Windows: Poems.* 1958 Chicago. 1st ed. dj. EX $50.00

NEMEROV, Howard. *Painter Dreaming in the Scholar's House.* 1968 NY. Phoenix Book Shop. 1/26. sgn. $125.00

NERNST, W. *New Heat Theorem. Its Foundations in Theory & Experiment.* 1926 London. Methuen. 1st English ed. xl. $40.00

NERO, R.W. *Redwings.* 1984 Smithsonian. Ills. 160 p. wraps. EX $12.00

NERUDA, Pablo. *Heights of Macchu Picchu.* 1966 London. 1st English ed. proof. wraps. $75.00

NERY, Bron de Santa-Anna. *Land of Amazons Translated From French.* 1901 London. Sands. Revised Enlarged 2nd ed. VG $50.00

NESBIT, E. *Bastable Children: Treasure Seekers, Would-Be-Goods.* 1928 Coward McCann. Ills 1st Am ed. 944 p. G $15.00

NESBIT, R.C. *Torpedo Airmen.* 1983 London. Ills. dj. EX $23.00

NESBIT & BRIGGS. *When a Feller Needs a Friend.* 1914 Chicago. Volland. Ills. inscr. VG $16.00

NESS, Elliot. *Untouchables.* 1957 NY. 1st ed. dj. VG $20.00

NESSEN, Ron. *It Sure Looks Different From the Inside.* 1978 Playboy. 1st ed. inscr. dj. VG $125.00

NETBOY, Anthony. *Atlantic Salmon: Vanishing Species?* 1968 Houghton Mifflin. Ills 1st ed. $20.00

NETBOY, Anthony. *Salmon: World's Most Harassed Fish.* 1980 Winchester. Ills. 304 p. dj. EX $14.00

NETHERCOT, Arthur H. *Last 4 Lives of Annie Besant.* 1963 Chicago. 483 p. dj. M. $22.00

NETSCHER, P.M. *Les Hollandais au Bresil.* 1853 La Haye. Belinfante Freres. 209 p. EX $75.00

NETTL, Bruno. *Music in Primitive Culture.* 1956 Cambridge. Harvard U Pr. 1st ed. dj. VG $15.00

NETTL, Paul. *Other Casanova: Contribution to 18th C Music & Manners.* 1950 NY. Ills. dj. VG $25.00

NETTLEFORD & LAYACONA. *Roots & Rhythms: Jamaica's National Dance Theatre.* 1969 London. 1st ed. sgn Layacona. dj. EX $20.00

NETTLETON, A. *Village Hymns for Social Worship.* 1828 NY. 12mo. full leather. G $22.50

NEUGEBOREN, Jay. *Listen Ruben Fontanez.* 1968 Houghton. 1st ed. dj. EX $35.00

NEUHAUS, Eugene. *Art of Exposition.* 1915 San Francisco. EX $25.00

NEUHAUS, Eugene. *Art of Treasure Island.* 1939 CA. VG $35.00

NEUMANN, Arthur. *Elephant Hunting in East Equatorial Africa.* 1966 Abercrombie Fitch. reprint. VG $50.00

NEUMANN, Erich. *Archetypal World of Henry Moore.* 1959 NY. Pantheon. Ills. 4to. 138 p. dj. $20.00

NEUMANN, G.C. *History of Weapons of the American Revolution.* 1967 Bonanza. Ills. 373 p. dj. EX $13.50

NEUMANN, R. *Hitler Aufsteig und Untergang des Dritten Reiches.* 1961 Munchen. Verlag. Ills. German text. $35.00

NEUMEYER, Peter F. *Why We Have Day & Night.* 1970 NY. Young Scott Books. 1st ed. dj. $20.00

NEVILL, Ralph. *Sport of Kings.* 1926 London. Ills 1st English ed. dj. VG $75.00

NEVILLE. *Jet Propulsion Progress.* 1948 NY. 1st ed. G $15.00

NEVILLE. *Red River Valley Then & Now.* 1948 Paris. North TX Pub. dj. M $50.00

NEVIN, D. *Expressmen.* 1974 Time Life. Ills. 240 p. leather. EX $15.00

NEVIN, D. *Soldier's.* 1973 Time Life. Ills 1st ed. leather. EX $20.00

NEVIN, D. *Texans.* 1982 Time Life. Revised ed. 240 p. leather. EX $15.00

NEVINS, Allan. *Diary of John Quincy Adams.* 1928 NY. inscr. cloth. VG $40.00

NEVINS, Allan. *Fremont: Pathfinder of the West.* 1955 NY. dj. EX $35.00

NEVINS, Allan. *Fremont: West's Greatest Adventurer.* 1928 NY/London. Harper. 1st ed. 2 vol set. VG $75.00

NEVINS, Allan. *John D. Rockefeller.* 1940 NY. 1st ed. 2 vol set. slipcase. $65.00

NEWARK, Peter. *Cowboys.* 1982 London. Ills. 4to. 159 p. dj. EX $12.00

NEWBERRY, Clare. *Mittens.* 1936 1st ed. 4to. dj. VG $20.00

NEWBY, P.H. *Kith.* 1977 London. 1st ed. dj. M $12.00

NEWCOMB, Harvey. *How To Be a Lady.* 1863 Boston. Gould Lincoln. 16mo. 224 p. VG $28.00

NEWCOMB, Harvey. *How To Be a Lady: Book for Girls.* 1848 Boston. 16mo. 224 p. brown cloth. G $19.00

NEWCOMB, M.A. *4 Years of Personal Reminiscenes of the War.* 1893 Chicago. 1st ed. 131 p. VG $25.00

NEWCOMB, R. *Old KY Arch.* 1940 NY. Ills 1st ed. 130 p. VG $60.00

NEWELL, A.D. *Gunstock Finishing & Care.* 1975 Stackpole. Ills. 473 p. dj. EX $15.00

NEWELL, C.M. *Kalani of Oahu.* 1881 Boston. private print. 12mo. $20.00

NEWELL, Gordon. *Ocean Liners of the 20th Century.* 1963 NY. Bonanza. VG $21.00

NEWELL, Peter. *Cobb's Anatomy.* 1912 NY. Doran. 1st ed. 12mo. VG $18.00

NEWELL, Peter. *Hole Book.* 1908 NY. Ills 1st ed. wraps. G $60.00

NEWELL, Peter. *Pictures & Rhymes.* 1899 NY. Harper. Intro John Bangs. 1st ed. 8vo. $80.00

NEWELL, Peter. *Rocket Book.* 1912 NY. Harper. 1st ed. 8vo. scarce. VG $150.00

NEWELL, Peter. *Slant Book.* 1910 NY. 1st ed. G $75.00

NEWELL, Peter. *Topsys & Turvys Number 2.* 1894 NY. 1st ed. G $85.00

NEWELL & VERBEEK. *Mother Goose for Grownups.* 1900 Harper. Ills 1st ed. 116 p. cloth. VG $50.00

NEWELL & VERBEEK. *Mother Goose for Grownups.* 1900 Harper. Ills 1st ed. G $25.00

NEWHALL, B. *History of Photography From 1839 to Present Day.* 1964 NY. MOMA. Revised Enlarged ed. 215 p. EX $25.00

NEWHALL, B. *History of Photography From 1839 to Present Day.* 1949 MOMA. 4to. cloth. $20.00

NEWHALL, B. *In Plain Sight.* 1983 Salt Lake City. Intro Ansel Adams. dj. EX $25.00

NEWHALL, B. *Photography 1839-1937.* no date. NY. 1st ed. VG $50.00

NEWHALL, M. *Photographs of M. Newhall.* 1946 NY. 1st ed. 8vo. VG $25.00

NEWHALL, Nancy. *Eloquent Light.* 1963 San Francisco. Ills A Adams. 1st ed. dj. EX $75.00

NEWHALL, Nancy. *P.H. Emerson: Fight for Photography & Fine Art.* 1975 NY. 1st ed. 4to. wraps. EX $25.00

NEWHALL, Nancy. *Paul Strand Photographs: 1915-1945.* 1945 NY. Ltd 1st ed. 1/6,000. wraps. VG $30.00

NEWHALL, Nancy. *Portfolio of 16 Photographs by Alvin Langdon Cogburn.* 1962 Eastman House. 1st ed. folio. EX $110.00

NEWHALL, Nancy. *This Is the American Earth.* 1960 San Francisco. Ills A Adams. 2nd print. dj. $50.00

NEWHALL, Nancy. *Time in New England: Photographs by Paul Strand.* 1950 NY. Ills 1st ed. 4to. dj. $65.00

NEWLANDS, John A.R. *Discovery of Periodic Law & Relations Among Atomic Weights.* 1884 London. Spon. 39 p. wraps. VG $90.00

NEWMAN, Arnold. *1 Mind's Eye.* 1974 NY Graphic Soc. Ills 1st ed. 8vo. inscr. EX $35.00

NEWMAN, Ernest. *Fact & Fiction About Wagner.* 1931 London. 1st ed. G $20.00

NEWMAN, Ernest. *Life of Richard Wagner, 1813 to 1848. Vol. I.* 1933 Knopf. 1st Am ed. $11.00

NEWMAN, Ernest. *Unconscious Beethoven.* 1927 Knopf. 1st ed. dj. VG $15.00

NEWMAN, Ernest. *Wagner As Man & Artist.* 1941 399 p. VG $9.00

NEWMAN, H.H. *Nature of the World & of Man.* 1933 Garden City. Ills. 562 p. dj. VG $4.00

NEWMAN, Harold. *Illustrated Dictionary of Glass.* 1977 London. Thames & Hudson. Ills. 351 p. $30.00

NEWMAN, J.R. *World of Mathematics.* 1956 NY. 1st ed. 4 vol set. slipcase. $35.00

NEWMAN, J.R. *World of Mathematics.* 1956 NY. 2nd print. 4 vol set. slipcase. VG $25.00

NEWMAN, William S. *Pianist's Problems.* 1956 NY. Harper. Revised ed. dj. VG $15.00

NEWNAN, William L. *Escape in Italy.* 1945 Rangers, MI. inscr. VG $20.00

NEWSOME, W. *Whitetailed Deer.* 1926 NY. 1st ed. VG $30.00

NEWTON, A. Edward. *A. Edward Newton on Books & Business.* 1930 Apellicon. Ltd ed. 1/325. 8vo. sgn. EX $45.00

NEWTON, A. Edward. *Amenities of Book Collecting & Kindred Affections.* 1922 4th imp. 373 p. VG $18.00

NEWTON, A. Edward. *Amenities of Book Collecting.* 1918 Atlantic Monthly. 1st ed. EX $40.00

NEWTON, A. Edward. *Amenities of Book Collecting.* 1920 3rd ed. G $15.00

NEWTON, A. Edward. *Derby Day & Other Adventures.* 1934 Boston. Ltd 1st ed. sgn. G $50.00

NEWTON, A. Edward. *End Papers: Literary Recreations.* 1933 Boston. Ltd ed. sgn. VG $45.00

NEWTON, A. Edward. *Magnificent Farce.* 1921 Boston. 2nd imp. G $12.00

NEWTON, A. Edward. *Newton on Blackstone.* 1937 Phil. Ills Ltd 1st ed. sgn. dj. EX $55.00

NEWTON, A. Edward. *This Book-Collecting Game.* 1928 Boston. 1st trade ed. VG $35.00

NEWTON, A. Edward. *This Book-Collecting Game.* 1928 Boston. Ltd ed. sgn. VG $45.00

NEWTON, Arthur Percival. *Colonizing Activities of English Puritans.* 1944 Yale U Pr. $22.50

NEWTON, Isaac. *Philosophiae Naturalis Principia Mathematica.* 1883 London. Tegg. 2nd Glasgow ed. 2 vol set. $190.00

NEWTON, John Marshall. *Memoirs of John Marshall Newton.* 1913 no place. VG $150.00

NEWTON, Ruth E. *Kittens & Puppies.* 1934 Racine. Whitman. Ills. 4to. VG $15.00

NEWTON. *Mr. Strahan's Dinner Party.* 1930 San Francisco. 1st ed. sgn. folio. VG $65.00

NIAUDET, Alfred. *Elementary Treatise on Electric Batteries.* 1880 NY. Trans Fishback. 1st ed. 266 p. $75.00

NICHERSON, R. *Sea Otters: Natural History & Guide.* 1984 Chronicle. Ills. 110 p. wraps. EX $10.00

NICHOLLS, Robert. *Life of Josiah Wedgwood.* 1930 Hanley. Webberley Ltd. sgn. $32.50

NICHOLS, Beverly. *Book of Old Ballads.* 1934 London. Ills Brock. 4to. tan cloth. EX $50.00

NICHOLS, Beverly. *Cats' ABC.* 1960 Ills Sayer. 1st Am ed. dj. VG $22.50

NICHOLS, Beverly. *Old Ballads.* 1934 London. Hutchinson. Ills Brock. 279 p. $65.00

NICHOLS, Bob. *Shotgunner.* 1949 Putnam. 373 p. VG $14.00

NICHOLS, C. *Arna Bontemps & Langston Hughes: Letters 1925-1967.* 1980 Dodd Mead. 529 p. dj. VG $12.00

NICHOLS, George. *Story of the Great March.* 1865 NY. Ills 1st ed. map. G $85.00

NICHOLS, J. *Biographical Anecdotes of William Hogarth.* 1781 London. 157 p. 3/4 leather. EX $45.00

NICHOLS, J.L. *Busy Man's Friend; or, Guide to Success by Facts & Figures.* 1896 Naperville. Ills. leather. VG $18.00

NICHOLS, John. *Serile Cuckoo.* 1965 NY. 1st ed. dj. VG $60.00

NICHOLS, John. *Wizard of Loneliness.* 1966 NY. 1st ed. dj. VG $40.00

NICHOLS, Perry Wampler. *Deep in the Hearts of Texans.* 1957 Naylor. 1st ed. dj. EX $20.00

NICHOLS, R. *Spanish & Portuguese Gardens.* 1924 NY. Ills 1st ed. $40.00

NICHOLS, Robert. *Budded Branch.* 1918 Westminster. Beaumont Pr. 1st ed. 8vo. VG $125.00

NICHOLS, Ruth. *Wings for Life.* 1957 NY. 1st ed. dj. VG $32.50

NICHOLSON, Benedict. *Joseph Wright of Derby: Painter of Light.* 1968 Mellon Foundation. 2 vol set. $100.00

NICHOLSON, John. *Farmer's Assistant.* 1820 Phil/Richmond. 8vo. 468 p. $25.00

NICHOLSON, T.R. *Passenger Cars 1905-1912. Cars of the World in Color.* 1971 NY. Macmillan. Ills 1st ed. 12mo. 162 p. dj. $7.00

NICHOLSON, William. *Introduction to Natural Philosophy.* 1788 Phil. Dobson. 3rd ed. full leather. $90.00

NICHOLSON & LEE. *Oxford Book of English Mystical Verse.* 1924 cloth. G. $25.00

NICKELLS, L.A. *1st Family: Diary of the Royal Year.* 1950 London. 1st ed. VG $7.00

NICKERSON, David. *English Furniture of the 18th Century.* 1963 NY. Putnam. Ills. 4to. 128 p. dj. $15.00

NICLAUSSE, Juliette. *Tapisseries et Tapis de la Ville de Paris.* 1948 Paris. Grund. folio. loose as issued. $50.00

NICOL, C.W. *From the Roof of Africa.* 1972 Knopf. Ills 1st ed. 362 p. EX $12.50

NICOLL, A. *Masks, Mimes, & Miracles: Studies in Popular Theatre.* 1963 NY. $25.00

NICOLLET, I.N. *Hydrographical Basin of Upper MS River.* 1843 WA. 1st ed. 1st issue. VG $1500.00

NICOLS. *Wizard of Loneliness.* 1966 Putman. 1st ed. VG $40.00

NICOLSON, Harold. *Tennyson: Aspects of His Life, Character, & Poetry.* 1925 Boston/NY. VG $9.00

NICOLSON, J.W. *Canterbury Tales in Modern English.* no date. Garden City. Ills Kent. dj. VG $15.00

NICOLSON, John. *AZ of Joseph Pratt Allyn.* 1974 Tucson. 1st ed. dj. VG $10.00

NIDA, William. *Tree Boys: Story of Man.* c 1929. Laidlaw. EX $15.00

NIEBAUM, Gustave. *Discoveries of Norsemen on Northeast Coast of America.* 1910 1st English ed. fld plt. 81 p. cloth. EX $28.00

NIELSEN, Kay. *East of the Sun, West of the Moon.* no date. NY. Doran. Ills 1st ed. dj. EX $300.00

NIELSEN, Kay. *East of the Sun, West of the Moon.* c 1930s. Doran. Ills. 204 p. gold linen. EX $195.00

NIELSEN, Kay. *East of the Sun, West of the Moon.* no date. Garden City. 1st ed. VG $25.00

NIEMAN, Leroy. *My 30 Years in Sports.* 1983 Abrams. sgn. dj. EX $40.00

NIETZCHE, Friedrich. *Thoughts Out of Season Part II. Vol. II.* 1910 London. Foulis. 1/2,000. EX $15.00

NIGHTINGALE, Florence. *Notes on Nursing: What It Is & What It Is Not.* 1946 Lippincott. reprint. xl. VG $10.00

NIJINSKY, Romola. *Last Years of Nijinsky.* 1952 Simon Schuster. Ills 1st print. dj. VG $20.00

NIJINSKY, Romola. *Nijinsky.* 1934 NY. 2nd print. dj. G $18.00

NIKELSBURGER, Jacob. *Koul Jacob in Defense of the Jewish Religion.* 1816 NY. 8vo. 79 p. scarce. VG $300.00

NILES, Blair. *James River.* 1939 NY. 1st ed. dj. G $25.00

NILES, John Jacob. *Ballad Book.* 1961 Boston. 1st print. sgn. EX $75.00

NIMROD. *Hunting Reminiscences.* 1843 London. 1st ed. fore-edge of hunt scene. $750.00

NIN, Anais. *D.H. Lawrence: Unprofessional Study.* 1964 Chicago. wraps. VG $20.00

NIN, Anais. *Four-Chambered Heart.* 1950 NY. Duell Sloan Pearce. 1st ed. $175.00

NIN, Anais. *Ladders to Fire.* 1946 Franklin Lib. 1st ed. dj. EX $45.00

NIN, Anais. *Spy in House of Love.* 1954 Franklin Lib. 1st ed. dj. EX $40.00

NIN, Anais. *Spy in House of Love.* 1954 NY. 1st ed. dj. EX $25.00

NISHIHARA, Kiyoyuki. *Japanese House: Patterns for Living.* 1968 Ills 1st print. dj. EX $30.00

NISHIMURA, T. *Ikenobo School of Japanese Floral Art.* 1951 Kyoto. Ills 1st ed. VG $35.00

NISSENSON, George N. *India Rubber: Its Manufacture & Use.* 1891 NY. private print. xl. G $8.00

NIVEDITA, Sister. *Master As I Saw Him.* 1948 India. 6th ed. 409 p. dj. EX $20.00

NIVEN, Larry. *Gift From Earth.* 1970 NY. Walker. 1st Am ed. dj. EX $30.00

NIVEN, Larry. *Ringworld Engineers.* 1980 Holt. 1st ed. dj. EX $25.00

NIVEN, Larry. *Ringworld Engineers.* 1979 Phantasia. Ltd ed. 1/500. sgn. boxed. EX $175.00

NIVEN, Larry. *Ringworld.* 1977 Holt. 1st ed. sgn. dj. EX $70.00

NIVEN, Larry. *World Out of Time.* 1976 Holt. 1st ed. sgn. dj. EX $25.00

NIVEN & PURNELLE. *Lucifer's Hammer.* 1977 Playboy. 1st ed. dj. EX $15.00

NIXON, Herman. *Possum Trot: Rural Community South.* 1941 Norman. Ltd ed. $35.00

NIXON, Pat I. *Century of Medicine in San Antonio.* 1936 San Antonio. private print. 1st ed. dj. EX $75.00

NIXON, Richard. *Memoirs of Richard Nixon.* 1978 NY. Ltd ed. sgn. slipcase. EX $100.00

NIXON, Richard. *1999: Victory Without War.* 1988 NY. Ltd 1st ed. 1/600. sgn. dj. boxed. M $125.00

NIXON, Richard. *6 Crises.* 1962 NY. 1st ed. sgn. dj. VG $35.00

NIXON, S. *Redwood Empire: Illustrated History of CA Redwood Country.* 1966 Dutton. dj. VG $20.00

NIZER, L. *What To Do with Germany.* 1941 Ziff Davis. G $15.00

NOAKES, A. *Sportsmen in Landscape.* 1954 Phil. 8vo. cloth. dj. VG $12.50

NOBLE, L.F. *Nitrate Deposits in Southwestern CA.* 1931 18 plts. fld map. $12.50

NOBLE, Louis. *After Icebergs with a Painter: Summer Voyage to Labrador.* 1861 NY. Appleton. Ills 1st ed. 8vo. cloth. EX $650.00

NOBLE & BRADLEY. *Mating Behavior of Lizards.* 1933 NY. Academy of Sciences. 8vo. G $16.00

NOBLE. *Beautiful Dolls.* 1972 Hawthorne. 4to. dj. EX $40.00

NOEL, J. *Footloose in Arcadia.* 1904 NY. 1st ed. VG $17.50

NOFF, Charles. *Sketches in Prison Camps.* 1865 NY. 3rd ed. 8vo. 204 p. G $75.00

NOFFSINGER, James Philip. *WWI Aviation Books in English.* 1987 Metuchen, NJ. Ills. 305 p. M $32.50

NOICE, H. *Back of Beyond.* 1939 Putnam. Ills. 247 p. VG $12.00

NOICE, H. *With Stefansson in the Arctic.* 1925 London. Ills 2nd ed. inscr. dj. VG $30.00

NOLAN, Sidney. *Legend of Ned Kelly: Australia's Outlaw Hero.* 1964 NY. EX $25.00

NOLAN, W.F. *Hammett: Life at the Edge.* no date. Congdon. 1st ed. dj. EX $8.00

NOLAN, W.F. *Ray Bradbury Companion.* 1975 Gale. 1st ed. slipcase. EX $95.00

NOLAN & JOHNSON. *Logan's Run.* 1968 Gollancz. 1st English ed. dj. EX $55.00

NOLAN & JOHNSON. *Logan's Run.* 1967 Dial. 1st ed. inscr. dj. EX $125.00

NOLAN. *Bark-Covered House.* 1937 Lakeside Pr. EX $12.50

NOLL, H.J. *Guide to Trout Flies & How To Use Them.* 1970 private print. Ills. 48 p. wraps. EX $10.00

NOLL, M. *Angling Success.* 1935 Macmillan. Ills. 291 p. dj. VG $10.00

NOLLET, M. L'Abbe. *Essai sur l'Ellectricite des Corps.* 1746 Paris. 1st ed. 12mo. 227 p. VG $275.00

NOMAD, Ali. *Cosmic Consciousness.* 1913 Chicago. Advance Thought Pub. 310 p. VG $22.00

NOMAD, Ali. *Sex: Unknown Quanity.* 1916 Chicago. 240 p. VG $22.00

NONTE, G.C. *Complete Book of the Air Gun.* 1970 Stackpole. Ills. 288 p. dj. VG $17.50

NONTE, G.C. *Modern Hand Loading.* 1974 Winchester. Ills. 410 p. EX $10.00

NONTE, G.C. *Pistol Smithing.* 1980 Stackpole. Ills. 560 p. dj. EX $17.50

NORDEN, Frederic Lewis. *Antiquities, Natural History, Ruins, Curiosities of Egypt.* 1792 London. Ills 1st ed. folio. rare. VG $750.00

NORDENSKIOLD, Erik. *History of Biology: A Survey.* 1938 NY. Tudor. $17.50

NORDHALL, Charles. *CA for Health, Pleasure, & Residence.* 1882 NY. Ills. maps. cloth. VG $30.00

NORDHOFF, Charles. *Men Against the Sea.* 1934 Boston. 1st ed. dj. VG $30.00

NORDHOFF, Charles. *Whaling & Fishing.* no date. Dodd Mead. Ills. 383 p. G $25.00

NORDHOFF & HALL. *High Barbaree.* 1945 Boston. 1st ed. dj. EX $10.00

NORDOHOFF & HALL. *Bounty Trilogy.* 1951 Little Brown. Ills Wyeth. dj. G $20.00

NORDYKE, L. *John Wesley: TX Gunman.* 1957 Morrow. 1st ed. 278 p. dj. VG $27.00

NORELLI, M.R. *American Wildlife Painting.* 1982 Galahad. Ills. 4to. 224 p. dj. EX $30.00

NORFLEET, J. Frank. *Norfleet.* 1927 Sugar Land, TX. Revised ed. dj. VG $25.00

NORMAN, Charles. *Magic Maker: E.E. Cummings.* 1958 NY. 1st print. VG $25.00

NORMAN, Charles. *Poets & People.* 1972 Bobbs Merrill. 1st ed. sgn. dj. VG $25.00

NORMAN, Charles. *Soldier Diary.* 1944 NY. 1st ed. dj. EX $10.00

NORMAN, Dorothy. *Dualities.* 1933 NY. private print. 1/400. 8vo. VG $75.00

NORMAN, J.R. *History of Fishes.* 1963 Hill Wang. Revised 2nd ed. 398 p. dj. VG $27.00

NORMAN, P.E. *Sculpture in Wood.* 1973 London. Ills. 112 p. pb. $8.00

NORRIS, F. *Pit.* 1903 NY. 1st ed. VG $20.00

NORRIS, Frank. *Story of San Francisco.* 1899 NY. Doubleday McClure. 1st ed. VG $300.00

NORRIS, Gloria. *Looking for Bobby.* 1985 Knopf. 1st ed. sgn. dj. EX $30.00

NORRIS, H.T. *Shinqiti Folk Literature & Song.* 1968 Oxford. 1st ed. dj. EX $10.00

NORRIS, Kathleen. *Foolish Virgin.* 1928 Garden City. 1st ed. dj. EX $25.00

NORRIS, P.W. *Calumet of Coteau & Other Poems.* 1883 Phil. Ills. 375 p. $35.00

NORTH, Oliver. *Rambles After Sport; or, Travels & Adventures in Americas.* 1874 London. 1st ed. cloth. VG $30.00

NORTH, S.N.D. & R.H. *Simeon North: 1st Official Pistol Maker of the US.* 1972 Gunroom Pr. reprint of 1913. 207 p. EX $10.00

NORTH, Sterling. *Night Outlasts the Whippoorwill.* 1936 NY. 1st ed. dj. EX $35.00

NORTH, Sterling. *Wolfing.* 1969 NY. 1st ed. dj. VG $10.00

NORTHEN, H. & R.T. *Ingenious Kingdom: Remarkable World of Plants.* 1970 Prentice Hall. Ills. 274 p. VG $5.00

NORTHEN, R.T. *Home Orchid Growing.* 1950 Van Nostrand. Ills. 286 p. G $6.00

NORTHROP & BANKS. *World's Fair Seen in 100 Days.* 1893 Phil. Ills. 736 p. VG $60.00

NORTON, Andre. *Forerunner: 2nd Venture.* 1987 NY. 1st ed. sgn. dj. M $25.00

NORTON, Andre. *Tales of Witch World.* 1987 NY. 1st ed. sgn. dj. M $25.00

NORTON, Andre. *Victory on Janus.* 1966 NY. 1st ed. dj. VG $25.00

NORTON, Charles. *Handbook of FL: Atlantic Coast.* 1890 NY. Ills 1st ed. red cloth. VG $100.00

NORTON, Charles. *Henry Wadsworth Longfellow.* 1907 Ltd ed. 121 p. VG $50.00

NORTON, Charles. *Rudyard Kipling: Biographical Sketch.* 1899 NY. Ltd ed. 1/100. VG $25.00

NORTON, E.F. *Fight for Everest.* 1924 NY/London. Ills 1st Am ed. maps. VG $90.00

NORTON, Elijah. *Careful & Candid Inquiry Respecting Subject of Baptism.* 1802 Stockbridge. 1st ed. wraps. G. $95.00

NORTON, Mary. *Borrowers Afield.* 1955 Harcourt Brace. Ills Krush. 1st ed. 215 p. VG $15.00

NORTON, Mary. *Borrowers.* 1953 Harcourt Brace. Ills Krush. reprint. 180 p. $10.50

NORTON, Roy. *Plunderer.* 1912 Burt. 1st ed. cloth. dj. EX $15.00

NORVELL, Joseph E. *Lost Guide.* 1910 Chicago. 12mo. 249 p. $75.00

NORWOOD, V. *Jungle Life in Guiana.* 1964 Hale. 1st ed. VG $15.00

NOTOVITCH, Nicolas. *Unknown Life of Jesus Christ.* 1916 Chicago. Indo-American Book. 4th ed. VG $26.00

NOTT, S.C. *Chinese Jade.* 1936 London. 4to. VG $70.00

NOTT, S.C. *Chinese Jades in the S.C. Nott Collection.* 1942 VG $300.00

NOURSE, J.E. *Narrative of the 2nd Arctic Expedition.* 1879 Ills. maps. G $65.00

NOUVEL, Odile. *Wallpapers of France 1800-1850.* 1981 NY. Rizzoi. Ills. 4to. 132 p. dj. $60.00

NOVA, Craig. *Geek.* 1975 Harper. Ills B Holland. 1st ed. dj. EX $20.00

NOVA, Craig. *Incandescence.* 1979 Harper. 1st ed. dj. EX $12.00

NOVAK, Emil. *Menstruation & Its Disorders.* 1921 NY. Ills 1st ed. VG $55.00

NOWELL, Elizabeth. *Thomas Wolfe: Biography.* 1960 456 p. VG $9.50

NOYES, Alfred. *Collected Poems.* 1947 Phil/NY. Collected 1 vol 1st ed. G $90.00

NOYES, Alfred. *In Land of the Chinook; or, Story of Blaine County, MT.* 1917 Helena. 1st ed. plts. cloth. EX $125.00

NOYES, Alfred. *2 Worlds for Memory.* 1953 London. Sheed & Ward. 1st ed. dj. EX $35.00

NOYES, John H. *Manual for Help of Those Who Seek Faith of Primitive Church.* 1847 Putney, VT. 1st ed. $175.00

NUMEY, N. *Study of Rare Books.* 1930 Denver. Ltd ed. 1/1,000. sgn. 572 p. $315.00

NUNIS, D.B. *Golden Frontier: Recollections of Herman Francis Reinhart.* 1962 Austin. Ills 1st ed. dj. VG $25.00

NUNN, Ancel. *Dreamscapes.* 1982 Ltd ed. 1/1,250. M $35.00

NUNN, George A. *Origin of the Strait of Anian Concept.* 1929 Phil. Ltd ed. 1/200. EX $40.00

NURA. *Buttermilk Tree.* 1934 NY. Nura. Ltd ed. 1/650. 4to. dj. VG $35.00

NURA. *Nura's Garden of Betty & Booth.* 1935 NY. Morrow. Ills Nura. 4to. dj. EX $35.00

NURA. *Silver Bridge.* 1937 NY. Ills Ltd ed. 1/650. 4to. VG $32.00

NUTCHUK. *Son of the Smoky Sea.* 1953 Messner. Ills. 245 p. dj. VG $10.00

NUTTALL, T. *Journal of Travels into AR Territory During the Year 1819.* 1980 OK U Pr. Ills. maps. dj. EX $25.00

NUTTALL, T. *Manual of Ornithology of the US & Canada.* 1832 Cambridge. xl. VG $50.00

NUTTING, Wallace. *American Windsors.* 1917 Old America. Ills 1st ed. VG $47.50

NUTTING, Wallace. *Clock Book.* 1924 Framingham, MA. Old Am Co. Ills. 4to. $45.00

NUTTING, Wallace. *Clock Book.* 1935 Garden City. 1st ed. dj. VG $42.50

NUTTING, Wallace. *CT Beautiful.* 1923 Old Am Co. Ills 1st ed. 304 p. EX $35.00

NUTTING, Wallace. *England Beautiful.* 1936 NY. Ills. 284 p. $12.50

NUTTING, Wallace. *Furniture of Pilgrim Period of American Origin 1620-1720.* 1924 Framingham, MA. Old Am Co. Revised ed. 4to. VG $50.00

NUTTING, Wallace. *Ireland Beautiful.* 1925 Old Am Co. Ills. 302 p. VG $20.00

NUTTING, Wallace. *MA Beautiful.* 1935 reprint. inscr. dj. VG $45.00

NUTTING, Wallace. *ME Beautiful.* 1935 Garden City. sgn. EX $22.50

NUTTING, Wallace. *PA Beautiful.* 1924 Farmingham. Ills 1st ed. 302 p. $15.00

NUTTING, Wallace. *VA Beautiful.* 1935 NY. Ills. dj. VG $25.00

NUTTING, Wallace. *VA Beautiful.* 1930 Old Am Co. Ills 1st ed. sgn. EX $55.00

NYANATILOKA. *Buddha's Path to Deliverance.* 1952 Colombo. 1st ed. 199 p. wraps. VG $22.00

NYCE, Vera. *Jolly Christmas at the Patterprints.* 1971 NY. Ills Helen Nyce. 27 p. cloth. $7.50

NYE, Elwood L. *Marching with Custer.* 1964 Arthur Clark. Ltd ed. 1/300. VG $125.00

NYE, N. *Not Grass Alone.* 1961 NY. 1st ed. 150 p. dj. VG $10.00

NYE, N. *Wolf That Rhode.* 1960 NY. 1st ed. 158 p. dj. VG $10.00

NYE, W.S. *Bad Medicine & Good.* 1962 Norman. Ills 1st ed. maps. dj. EX $18.00

NYE, W.S. *Carbine & Lance: Story of Old Fort Sill.* 1943 OK U Pr. 4th print. dj. VG $20.00

NYE, W.S. *Carbine & Lance: Story of Old Fort Sill.* 1951 OK U Pr. Ills. 345 p. G $5.00

NYGREN, Edward J. *Of Time & Place: Figurative Art From Corcoran Gallery.* 1981 WA. Ills. 4to. 208 p. wraps. $25.00

O

O'BRIAN, Patrick. *Mauritius Command.* 1977 London. 1st ed. dj. EX $40.00

O'BRIAN, Patrick. *Surgeon's Mate.* 1980 London. 1st ed. dj. VG $35.00

O'BRIAN, Patrick. *Treason's Harbor.* 1983 London. 1st ed. dj. EX $35.00

O'BRIAN, Robert. *This Is San Francisco.* 1948 McGraw Hill. Ills 1st ed. sgn. cloth. VG $15.00

O'BRIEN, Edna. *Country Girls Trilogy & Epilogue.* 1986 Farrar. 1st Am ed. dj. EX $20.00

O'BRIEN, H. *Round Towers of Ireland.* 1834 London. Whittaker. 1st ed. 8vo. rare. $195.00

O'BRIEN, Jack. *Silver Chief, Dog of the North.* 1933 Winston. Jr Guild. Ills Wiese. dj. VG $22.50

O'BRIEN, John. *Fun with Dick & Jane.* 1941 Chicago. VG $22.00

O'BRIEN, Kate. *Romance of English Literature.* 1944 NY. dj. EX $12.00

O'BRIEN, Tim. *Going After Cacciato.* 1978 NY. Delacorte. Advance copy. dj. M $65.00

O'BRIEN, Tim. *Going After Cacciato.* 1978 London. 1st ed. dj. EX $35.00

O'BRIEN, Tim. *Going After Cacciato.* 1978 NY. 1st ed. dj. EX $45.00

O'BRIEN, Tim. *Northern Lights.* 1975 Delacorte. 1st ed. dj. EX $50.00

O'BRIEN, Tim. *Nuclear Age: A Poem.* 1981 Portland. Ltd 1st ed. 1/125. dj. wraps. $40.00

O'BRIEN. *Timothy Murphy: Hero of the American Revolution.* 1941 1st ed. sgn. xl. VG $8.00

O'CALLAGHAN. *Documentary History of State of NY.* 1850 Albany. 3 vols of 4. VG $110.00

O'CASEY, Sean. *Bishop's Bonfire.* 1955 NY. Macmillan. 1st ed. 8vo. dj. EX $25.00

O'CASEY, Sean. *Feathers From the Green Crow.* 1962 MO U Pr. 1st ed. dj. M $12.00

O'CASEY, Sean. *Green Crow.* 1956 NY. 1st ed. dj. EX $20.00

O'CASEY, Sean. *Plough & the Stars.* 1926 London. 1st ed. dj. VG $45.00

O'CONNELL, R.F. *Fresh-Water Aquarium of St. Petersburg, FL.* 1971 Great Outdoors. dj. EX $10.00

O'CONNER, Francis V. *Jackson Pollock.* 1967 MOMA. Ills. 4to. 148 p. wraps. $15.00

O'CONNOR, Flannery. *Correspondence of O'Connor & the Brainard Cheneys.* 1986 Jackson, MS. proof. spiral bdg. wraps. EX $35.00

O'CONNOR, Flannery. *Everything That Rises Must Converge.* 1965 Farrar. 1st ed. dj. EX $100.00

O'CONNOR, Flannery. *Greyfriar: Siena Studies in Literature. Vol. VII.* 1964 Loudonville. wraps. $10.00

O'CONNOR, Flannery. *Habit of Being: Letters of Flannery O'Connor.* 1979 NY. Farrar. 1st ed. dj. VG $25.00

O'CONNOR, Flannery. *Memoir of Mary Ann.* 1961 NY. 1st ed. dj. VG $20.00

O'CONNOR, Flannery. *Memoir of Mary Ann.* 1961 Farrar Straus. 1st ed. dj. EX $75.00

O'CONNOR, Flannery. *Violent Bear It Away.* 1960 Farrar. 1st ed. dj. EX $190.00

O'CONNOR, Flannery. *Wiseblood.* 1962 NY. 1st ed. 2nd print. dj. EX $135.00

O'CONNOR, Frank. *Set of Variations.* 1969 NY. 1st ed. dj. VG $20.00

O'CONNOR, H. *Astors.* 1941 NY. Knopf. Ills 1st ed. 488 p. dj. VG $22.50

O'CONNOR, Jack. *Art of Hunting Big Game in North America.* 1967 Knopf. Ills. 404 p. dj. EX $20.00

O'CONNOR, Jack. *Big Game Animals of North America.* 1961 Outdoor Life. 4to. 264 p. maps. dj. VG $25.00

O'CONNOR, Jack. *Big Game Hunts.* 1963 NY. 1st & only ed. dj. $45.00

O'CONNOR, Jack. *Big Game Rifle.* 1952 NY. Knopf. 1st ed. scarce. EX $125.00

O'CONNOR, Jack. *Hunting in the Rockies.* 1947 NY. 1st ed. dj. VG $125.00

O'CONNOR, Jack. *Hunting Rifle.* 1970 NY. 1st ed. dj. VG $20.00

O'CONNOR, Jack. *Sheep & Sheep Hunting.* 1981 Tulsa. Memorial ed. dj. EX $15.00

O'CONNOR, Jack. *Sheep & Sheep Hunting.* 1974 Winchester. Ills. 308 p. dj. EX $10.50

O'CONNOR, Jack. *Shotgun Book.* 1965 NY. 1st ed. dj. VG $17.50

O'CONNOR, Jack. *Sportsman's Arms & Ammunition Manual.* 1952 Outdoor Life. Ills 1st ed. 252 p. VG $20.00

O'CONNOR, John. *Amadis de Gaule & Its Influence on Elizabethan Literature.* 1970 New Brunswick. dj. EX $10.00

O'CONNOR, Mrs. T.P. *I Myself.* 1914 NY. Ills. sgn. $15.00

O'CONNOR, R. *Sheridan the Inevitable.* 1953 Bobbs Merrill. Ills 1st ed. 400 p. maps. EX $45.00

O'CONNOR, Richard. *Bat Masterson.* 1957 NY. 1st ed. dj. VG $10.00

O'CONNOR, Richard. *Golden Summers.* 1974 Putnam. 1st ed. dj. VG $15.00

O'CONNOR, Richard. *Pat Garrett: Biography of Famous Marshall.* 1960 NY. 1st ed. dj. $17.50

O'CONNOR. *History of Turkey.* 1877 Chicago. 1st ed. 12mo. fld maps. VG $25.00

O'CROULEY, Pedro A. *Description of the Kingdom of New Spain.* 1972 Howells. Trans Sean Galvin. Ills. 4to. $40.00

O'DONNELL, E.P. *Great Big Doorstep: Delta Comedy.* 1979 Carbondale. Lost Am Fiction Series. $20.00

O'DONNELL, E.P. *Green Margins.* 1936 Boston. Houghton Mifflin. $15.00

O'DONNELL, Elliott. *Strange Cults & Secret Societies of Modern London.* 1935 NY. 1st ed. dj. scarce. $45.00

O'DONNELL, Elliott. *Strange Cults & Secret Societies of Modern London.* 1934 London. 1st ed. G $33.00

O'DONNELL, Elliott. *Werewolves.* 1912 London. Methuen. 1st ed. 12mo. 292 p. $55.00

O'DONNELL. *Ladder of Rickety Rungs.* 1943 Volland. Ills 1st ed. $15.00

O'DONOGHUE, D. *Poets of Ireland.* 1892-1893. London. VG $28.00

O'DONOGHUE & SPRINGER. *Adventures of Phoebe Zeit-Geist.* 1968 NY. Ills 1st ed. 4to. dj. EX $100.00

O'DRISCOLL, R. *Celtic Consciousness.* 1981 Toronto. McClelland. 1st ed. 1/500. EX $125.00

O'FAOLAIN, Sean. *Come Back to Erin.* 1940 NY. 1st ed. dj. VG $17.50

O'FAOLAIN, Sean. *Vanishing Hero.* 1956 Best. 1st ed. 204 p. dj. VG $18.00

O'FLAHERTY, Liam. *Civil War.* 1925 London. Archer. 1st ed. 1/100. sgn. VG $85.00

O'FLAHERTY, Liam. *Darkness: Tragedy in 3 Acts.* 1926 London. Archer. 1st ed. 1/100. sgn. wraps. EX $100.00

O'FLAHERTY, Liam. *Hollywood Cemetery.* 1935 London. Gollancz. dj. EX $150.00

O'FLAHERTY, Liam. *Informer.* 1925 London. VG $30.00

O'FLAHERTY, Liam. *Red Barbara & Other Stories.* 1928 Crosby Gaige. Ills Salkeld. Ltd ed. sgn. EX $90.00

O'GERAN, Graeme. *History of Detroit Street Railways.* 1931 Detroit. Conover Pr. $37.50

O'HAGEN, H. *Wilderness Men.* 1958 Doubleday. 1st ed. 263 p. dj. G $10.00

O'HAIR, Madalyn Murray. *Freedom Under Siege.* 1974 Los Angeles. 1st ed. sgn. dj. VG $27.50

O'HANLON & O'LEARY. *History of Queen's Country. Vol. I.* 1907 Dublin. cloth. VG $30.00

O'HARA, Frank. *Collected Peoms of Frank O'Hara.* 1971 NY. 2nd print. dj. VG $35.00

O'HARA, Frank. *In Memory of My Feelings.* 1967 NY. Ltd ed. 1/2,500. slipcase. EX $500.00

O'HARA, Frank. *Jackson Pollock.* 1959 NY. Braziller. Ills. 4to. 125 p. cloth. $30.00

O'HARA, Frank. *New Spanish Painting & Sculpture.* 1960 MOMA. Ills. 4to. 63 p. wraps. $12.50

O'HARA, J. *Sermons & Soda Water.* 1960 Random House. 3 vol set. slipcase. VG $30.00

O'HARA, John. *Appointment in Samarra.* 1934 NY. 1st ed. dj. VG $35.00

O'HARA, John. *Butterfield 8.* 1951 London. 1st ed. dj. EX $18.00

O'HARA, John. *Ewings.* 1972 NY. 1st ed. dj. EX $12.00

O'HARA, John. *Family Party.* 1956 Random House. 1st ed. dj. EX $30.00

O'HARA, John. *Farmer's Hotel.* 1951 Random House. 1st ed. dj. EX $15.00

O'HARA, John. *From the Terrace.* 1958 NY. 1st ed. dj. EX $18.00

O'HARA, John. *From the Terrace.* 1958 Ramdom House. 1st ed. 8vo. dj. VG $17.00

O'HARA, John. *Hat on the Bed.* 1963 Random House. Stated 1st ed. VG $12.50

O'HARA, John. *Hellbox.* 1947 Random House. 1st print. G $16.50

O'HARA, John. *Here's O'Hara.* 1946 NY. Duell Sloan Pearce. 1st ed. EX $40.00

O'HARA, John. *Lockwood Concern.* 1965 NY. 1st ed. 1/300. sgn. slipcase. $90.00

O'HARA, John. *Lockwood Concern.* 1965 NY. dj. EX $12.00

O'HARA, John. *Lovey Childs.* 1969 Random House. 1st ed. dj. EX $20.00

O'HARA, John. *Lovey Childs.* 1969 NY. Ltd 1st ed. 1/200. sgn. slipcase. EX $75.00

O'HARA, John. *Other Stories.* 1968 NY. 1st ed. dj. M $15.00

O'HARA, John. *Waiting for Winter.* 1966 Random House. 1st ed. dj. EX $20.00

O'HARA, John. *10 North Frederick.* 1955 Random House. 1st ed. dj. EX $35.00

O'KANE, Walter. *Intimate Desert.* 1969 AZ U Pr. Ills. 143 p. dj. EX $10.00

O'KEEFFE, Georgia. *Georgia O'Keeffe.* 1976 NY. 1st ed. folio. dj. VG $100.00

O'LAUGHLIN, John Callan. *Imperiled America.* 1916 Chicago. sgn. VG $17.50

O'MEARA, Walter. *Guns at the Forks.* 1965 Prentice Hall. Ills. 273 p. maps. VG $23.00

O'MEARA, Walter. *Savage Country.* 1960 Houghton Mifflin. Ills. dj. EX $35.00

O'NEILL, Charles. *Wild Train: Story of the Andrews Raiders.* 1956 dj. EX $20.00

O'NEILL, Eugene. *Ah, Wilderness.* 1972 Ltd Ed Club. Ills/sgn Sterneveis. slipcase. $60.00

O'NEILL, Eugene. *Ah, Wilderness.* 1933 NY. Ltd ed. 1/325. sgn. VG $175.00

O'NEILL, Eugene. *Ah, Wilderness.* 1933 Random House. 1st ed. dj. VG $40.00

O'NEILL, Eugene. *All God's Children: Wings & Welded.* 1924 NY. 1st ed. VG $20.00

O'NEILL, Eugene. *Complete Works of Eugene O'Neill.* 1924 NY. 1/1,200. sgn. 2 vol set. VG $250.00

O'NEILL, Eugene. *Desire Under the Elms.* 1925 NY. 1st ed. G $20.00

O'NEILL, Eugene. *Dynamo.* 1929 NY. Liveright. dj. VG $40.00

O'NEILL, Eugene. *Hairy Ape.* Ills A King. Ltd 1st ed. 1/750. sgn. boxed. $180.00

O'NEILL, Eugene. *History & Explanation for Boys & Girls.* 1916 London. Ills. G $20.00

O'NEILL, Eugene. *Iceman Cometh.* 1946 NY. 1st ed. dj. EX $60.00

O'NEILL, Eugene. *Lost Plays of Eugene O'Neill.* no date. NY. Citadel Pr. dj. EX $15.00

O'NEILL, Eugene. *Plays of Eugene O'Neill.* 1964 Random House. 3 vol set. VG $12.00

O'NEILL, Eugene. *Strange Interlude.* 1928 NY. Ltd 1st ed. 1/775. 8vo. wraps. boxed. $175.00

O'NEILL, Eugene. *Strange Interlude.* 1928 Boni. 6th print. VG $10.00

O'NEILL, Eugene. *Thirst & Other 1-Act Plays.* 1914 Boston. 1st ed. 12mo. EX $350.00

O'NEILL, Eugene. *Touch of the Poet.* 1957 New Haven. 2nd print. dj. M $11.00

O'NEILL, George & Rose. *Tomorrow's House; or, Tiny Angel.* 1932 Dutton. Ills 1st ed. VG $35.00

O'NEILL, R. *Dream of Eagles.* 1973 Boston. 1st ed. dj. VG $47.50

O'NEILL, Rose. *Loves of Edwy.* 1904 Ills 1st ed. 432 p. gilt cloth. EX $45.00

O'REILLY, B. *Life of John MacHale: Archbishop of Tuam.* 1890 NY/Cincinnati. 4to. 2 vol set. VG $45.00

O'REILLY, Bernard. *Green Mountains.* Smith Paterson. 1st ed. 13th imp. $7.50

O'SULLIVAN, Seamus. *Earth-Lover & Other Verses.* 1909 Dublin. New Nations Pr. 1st ed. VG $60.00

OAKESHOTT, Walter. *Mosaics of Rome.* 1967 Greenwich, CT. Ills. folio. cloth. dj. $150.00

OAKHURST, Walter. *Founded on the Seas.* 1942 Cambridge. 1st ed. 200 p. dj. VG $25.00

OATES, Joyce Carol. *All the Good People I've Left Behind.* 1979 Black Sparrow. Ltd 1st ed. 1/300. sgn. EX $35.00

OATES, Joyce Carol. *Angel of Light.* 1981 Dutton. 1st ed. dj. EX $16.00

OATES, Joyce Carol. *Angel of Light.* 1981 London. Cape. proof. wraps. $80.00

OATES, Joyce Carol. *Assassins.* 1975 NY. 1st ed. dj. EX $12.00

OATES, Joyce Carol. *Bellefleur.* 1981 NY. 1st ed. dj. EX $10.00

OATES, Joyce Carol. *Bloodsmoor Romance.* 1982 Dutton. 1st ed. dj. VG $17.50

OATES, Joyce Carol. *Crossing the Border.* 1976 Vanguard. 1st ed. dj. VG $15.00

OATES, Joyce Carol. *Cybele.* 1979 Black Sparrow. 1st ed. 1/300. sgn. EX $35.00

OATES, Joyce Carol. *Dreaming American & Other Poems.* 1973 Aloe. 1st ed. 1/150. sgn. wraps. EX $75.00

OATES, Joyce Carol. *Expensive People.* 1968 Vanguard. 1st ed. dj. EX $45.00

OATES, Joyce Carol. *Fabulous Beasts.* 1975 Baton Rouge. Ills 1st ed. dj. EX $15.00

OATES, Joyce Carol. *Goddess.* 1974 NY. dj. EX $24.00

OATES, Joyce Carol. *Miracle Play.* 1974 Black Sparrow. Ltd 1st ed. 1/300. sgn. EX $40.00

OATES, Joyce Carol. *Mysteries of Winterthurn.* Franklin Lib. 1st ed. EX $50.00

OATES, Joyce Carol. *Night Side.* 1977 NY. Sgn Ltd Eds. 1/100. dj. M $18.50

OATES, Joyce Carol. *Queen of the Night.* 1979 Northridge. Lord John Pr. 1/300. sgn. EX $35.00

OATES, Joyce Carol. *Sentimental Education.* 1980 NY. Dutton. 1st ed. dj. $25.00

OATES, Joyce Carol. *Unholy Loves.* 1979 Vanguard. 1st ed. dj. EX $15.00

OATES, Joyce Carol. *Wild Nights: A Story.* 1985 Athens, OH. Ltd ed. 1/300. sgn. dj. M $45.00

OATES, Joyce Carol. *Women Whose Lives Are Food, Men Whose Lives Are Money.* 1978 Baton Rouge. Ills 1st ed. dj. EX $10.00

OATES, Joyce Carol. *Wonderland.* 1971 NY. 1st ed. dj. EX $18.00

OATES, S.B. *To Purge This Land with Blood: Biography of John Brown.* 1970 Harper Row. Ills. 434 p. EX $20.00

OATES, S.B. *Visions of Glory: Texans on the Southwestern Frontier.* 1970 OK U Pr. 1st ed. dj. EX $20.00

OATES, W.C. *Wild Ducks: How To Rear & Shoot Them.* 1905 Longman Green. Ills 80 p. G $10.00

OBER, F.A. *Travels in Mexico & Life Among the Mexicans.* 1884 Estes Lauriat. Ills. 672 p. maps. VG $40.00

OBERFIRST, R. *Al Jolson.* 1980 San Diego. Ills 1st ed. dj. VG $14.00

OBERJOHANN, H. *My Best Friends Are Apes.* 1959 Dutton. Ills 1st Am ed. 191 p. dj. VG $6.00

OBERJOHANN, H. *Wild Elephant Chase: Adventure in the Lake Chad Region.* 1953 Dobson. Ills. 189 p. VG $11.00

OBERT, Karl. *This Is CA.* 1957 Menlo Park. Lane. Ills. 214 p. dj. $25.00

OCHOROWICZ, Dr. J. *Mental Suggestion.* 1891 NY. 361 p. VG $45.00

ODETS, Clifford. *Night Music: A Play.* 1940 NY. 1st ed. dj. EX $60.00

ODHAMS. *Duke of Edinburgh.* 1953 London. Intro Malcolm Thompson. VG $12.00

ODHAMS. *Royal Family in Wartime.* 1945 London. photos. VG $12.00

OEMLER, A. *Truck Farming in the South.* 1883 NY. 1st ed. 8vo. 270 p. $25.00

OESTERREICH, T. *Occultism & Modern Science.* 1923 181 p. EX $26.00

OESTERREICH, T. *Possession: Demonical & Other.* 1966 NY. 400 p. EX $30.00

OGDEN, N. *Versus.* 1949 1st ed. dj. EX $18.00

OGDEN, Ruth. *His Little Royal Highness.* no date. NY. Dutton. Ills Rainey. $20.00

OGDEN, Ruth. *Little Pierre & Big Peter.* Ills ML Kirk. 8vo. gilt green cloth. VG $18.00

OGG, F.A. *Old Northwest: Chronicle of the OH Valley & Beyond.* 1921 Yale U Pr. Ills. 220 p. fld map. VG $25.00

OGG, F.A. *Opening of the MS.* 1968 NY. facsimile. 670 p. VG $17.50

OGILVIE, M.A. *Wildfowl of Britain & Europe.* 1982 Oxford U Pr. Ills. 84 p. dj. EX $25.00

OGILVIE, M.A. *Winter Birds of the Arctic.* 1976 Praeger. Ills. 4to. maps. dj. EX $14.00

OGILVIE, W.H. *American Journey, a Diary, Sept. 1937 to Nov. 1937.* no date. London. Ash. Ills. inscr. VG $20.00

OGILVIE, Will. *Collected Sporting Verse of Will Ogilvie.* 1933 NY. Ills L Edwards. 4to. 396 p. VG $35.00

OGLESBY, Catherine. *French Provincial Decorative Art.* 1951 NY/London. Ills. 214 p. dj. $60.00

OHTA, T. *Golden Wind.* 1929 NY. Boni. Ills R Kent. 1st ed. wraps. VG $15.00

OJETTI, Ugo. *I Monumenti Italiani e la Guerra.* 1917 Milan. Alfieri Lacroix. fair. $22.00

OKIE, Howard P. *Old Silver & Old Sheffield Plate.* 1928 Doubleday. 420 p. dj. VG $40.00

OLCOTT, Henry Steel. *Old Diary Leaves.* 1895 NY. fair. $25.00

OLCOTT, Henry Steel. *Old Diary Leaves.* 1932 India. 5th Series. 531 p. VG $35.00

OLCOTT, Henry Steel. *People From the Other World.* 1875 CT. 492 p. VG $35.00

OLCOTT, Henry Steel. *Theosophy, Religion, & Occult Science.* 1885 London. Redway. 384 p. EX $60.00

OLDEN, Sarah Emilia. *People of Tipi Sapa.* 1918 Morehouse. Ills. photos. G $45.00

OLDER, Frederick. *My Own Story.* 1926 Macmillan. 1st ed. inscr. VG $12.00

OLDER, Mrs. Fremont. *Savages & Saints.* 1934 Dutton. 1st ed. inscr. G $10.00

OLENDORF, R.R. *Golden Eagle Country.* 1975 Knopf. Ills 1st ed. 4to. dj. EX $18.00

OLENDORF, William. *Addison Mizner: Architect to Affluent Fort Lauderdale.* 1983 FL. Gale Graphic. VG $12.00

OLFERS, Sibylle. *Etwas von den Wurzelkindern.* 1949 Germany. Ills. German text. VG $15.00

OLIPHANT, Mrs. *Reign of Queen Anne.* 1894 NY. Century. $75.00

OLIPHANT, Mrs. *Stories of the Seen & Unseen.* 1902 Blackwood. 1st ed. VG $35.00

OLIVER, R. *Why War Came in Korea.* 1950 NY. 1st ed. 260 p. dj. VG $12.50

OLLIVANT, Alfred. *Bob: Son of Battle.* 1901 NY. Doubleday McClure. Ills. G $10.00

OLMSTEAD, Frederick Law Jr. *Frederick Law Olmstead: Landscape Architect 1882-1903.* 1928 NY. Ills. $60.00

OLNEY, J. *Practical System of Modern Geography.* 1846 NY. Pratt Woodford. 300 p. EX $150.00

OLSEN, Jack. *Night of the Grizzlies.* 1969 Putnam. 254 p. dj. VG $10.00

OLSEN, O.A. *Elk Below.* 1945 private print. Ills. 104 p. dj. VG $14.00

OLSON, Charles. *Y & X: Poems by Charles Olson.* no date/place. Black Sun. Ills Cagli. wraps. $55.00

OLSON, Elder. *Cock of Heaven.* 1940 Macmillan. 1st ed. $15.00

OLSON, F. *Lonely Land.* 1961 Knopf. Ills. 273 p. dj. EX $14.00

OLSON, Fred. *Exiter Fishing.* 1978 Winchester. Ills. 270 p. dj. EX $12.50

OLSON, K.E. *Music & Musket: Bands & Bandsmen of the American Civil War.* 1981 Greenwood. Ills 1st ed. 299 p. dj. EX $25.00

OLSON, Sidney. *Young Henry Ford: Picture History of the 1st 40 Years.* 1963 Detroit. dj. VG $15.00

OLSON, Sigurd. *Open Horizons.* 1969 Knopf. Ills Kouba. 3rd print. 229 p. $15.00

OLSON, Sigurd. *Runes of the North.* 1964 Knopf. Ills. 255 p. dj. VG $8.00

OLSON, Sigurd. *Singing Wilderness.* 1956 NY. 1st ed. dj. VG $35.00

OLSON, Sigurd. *Wilderness Days.* 1973 Knopf. Ills 1st ed. 233 p. dj. EX $18.00

OLSON. *Olson's Book of the Rifle.* 1974 1st ed. dj. $14.00

OLSTED, F. *Journey Through TX.* 1969 NY. $17.50

OLTAR-JEVSKY, W. *Contemporary Babylon.* 1933 NY. Architecture Books. 4to. VG $200.00

OMAN & HAMILTON. *Wallpapers.* 1982 NY. Abrams. Ills. 4to. 486 p. dj. EX $60.00

ONDAATJE, Michael. *Collected Works of Billy the Kid.* 1974 NY. 1st Am ed. VG $15.00

ONDERDONK, Henry. *Revolutionary Incidents of Suffolk & Kings Counties.* 1849 NY. Leavitt. 1st ed. map. $75.00

ONIONS, Oliver. *Painted Face.* 1929 Heinemann. 1st ed. dj. VG $95.00

ONO, Yoko. *John Lennon Summer of 1980.* 1983 NY. 1st print. pb. EX $8.00

OPIE, Iona & Peter. *Nursery Companion.* 1980 Oxford U Pr. Ills. dj. VG $50.00

OPMEER & BEYERLINCK. *Opus Chronographicum Orbis Universi.* 1611 Antwerp. folio. 2 vols in 1. $135.00

OPPE, A.P. *Thomas Rowlandson: His Drawings & Watercolors.* 1923 London. Ills Ltd ed. 1/200. folio. $50.00

OPPEN, George. *Primitive.* 1978 Black Sparrow. Ills 1st ed. 1/226. dj. $25.00

OPPENHEIM. *American Jewish Yearbook 1918.* 1918 Phil. G $15.00

OPPENHEIMER, G. *Treatise on Medical Jurisprudence.* 1935 Baltimore. Williams Wood. VG $20.00

OPPENHEIMER, J. Robert. *Electron Theory: Description & Analogy.* 1955 Ames, IA. IA State College. wraps. $35.00

OPPIANUS. *Della Pesca, Della Caccia.* 1728 Florence. 16mo. xl. VG $30.00

OPTIC, Oliver. *Haste & Waste: Lake Champlain.* c 1894. Boston. Lee Shepherd. Ills. G $8.00

OPTIC, Oliver. *Popular Amusements for School & Home.* c 1875. Boston. 12mo. 159 p. $35.00

ORCUTT, Charles Dana. *Kingdom of Books.* 1927 Boston. 1st ed. dj. $25.00

ORCUTT, P. *White Road of Mystery.* 1918 NY. Am Ambulance Field Service. VG $15.00

ORCUTT, William Dana. *Book in Italy.* 1928 London. Harrap. Ills Ltd ed. 1/750. folio. VG $90.00

ORCUTT, William Dana. *Flower of Destiny.* 1905 Chicago. Ills Weber. 1st ed. $125.00

ORCUTT, William Dana. *Magic of the Book.* 1930 Boston. 1st trade ed. dj. VG $27.50

ORCUTT, William Dana. *Princess Kallisto & Other Tales of the Fairies.* 1902 Boston. Ills Amsden. 1st ed. EX $175.00

ORCZY, Baroness. *Scarlet Pimpernel.* 1905 NY. Ills 1st ed. VG $55.00

ORGAIN, Kate Alma. *Southern Authors in Poetry & Prose.* 1908 NY/WA. Neale. VG $35.00

ORLIAC, A. *Veronese.* 1940 London. Hyperion Pr. Ills. 4to. VG $20.00

ORLOVITZ, G. *Milkbottle H.* 1967 London. 1st ed. dj. EX $15.00

ORMAND, K. *Lord Leighton.* 1975 New Haven/London. 4to. dj. VG $45.00

ORMOND, Clyde. *Bear!* 1961 Harrisburg. dj. VG $12.00

ORMOND, Clyde. *Hunting Our Medium-Size Game.* 1958 Stackpole. Ills. 219 p. dj. VG $10.00

ORMOND, Clyde. *Outdoorsman's Handbook.* 1973 Outdoor Life. Ills. 336 p. dj. VG $8.00

ORMSBEE, T.H. *Early American Furniture Makers.* 1930 NY. Crowell. Ills. VG $37.50

ORMSBEE, T.H. *Windsor Chair.* 1962 NY. Hearthside. Ills. 223 p. dj. $37.50

ORMSBY. *Butterfield Overland Mail.* 1942 1st ed. EX $40.00

ORR, Clifford. *Dartmouth Murders.* 1929 NY. 1st ed. presentation. VG $35.00

ORR, R.T. *Animals in Migration.* 1970 Macmillan. Review copy. dj. EX $11.00

ORR, R.T. *Mammals of North America.* 1970 Doubleday. Ills. 250 p. dj. EX $12.50

ORTLOFF & RAYMORE. *Color & Design for Every Garden.* 1951 NY. 301 p. dj. $10.00

ORTON, James. *Andes & Amason; or, Across the Continent of South America.* 1870 NY. Harper. 1st ed. fld map. 356 p. VG $75.00

ORTON, Vrest. *Goudy: Master of Letters.* 1939 Chicago. Black Cat. Ltd ed. 1/500. EX $40.00

ORVIS & CHENEY. *Fishing with the Fly.* 1889 Houghton Mifflin. rebound. EX $25.00

ORWELL, George. *Animal Farm.* 1954 Ills Batchelor. 1st ed. dj. EX $20.00

ORWELL, George. *Animal Farm.* 1946 Harcourt. 1st Am ed. dj. EX $110.00

ORWELL, George. *Animal Farm.* 1985 Folio Soc. Ills Quentin Blake. boxed. M $20.00

ORWELL, George. *Animal Farm.* 1946 Harcourt. 1st ed. dj. VG $65.00

ORWELL, George. *Collected Essays.* no date. Harcourt. 4 vol set. dj. EX $70.00

ORWELL, George. *English People.* 1961 London. dj. EX $50.00

ORWELL, George. *Keep the Aspidistra Flying.* 1956 Harcourt. 1st Am ed. dj. EX $65.00

ORWELL, George. *Orwell Reader.* 1956 NY. 1st ed. dj. VG $20.00

ORWELL, George. *Such, Such Were the Joys.* 1953 NY. 1st ed. dj. $100.00

ORWELL, George. *1984.* 1949 Harcourt. 1st Am ed. dj. EX $55.00

ORWELL, George. *1984.* 1949 NY. Advance copy. wraps. scarce. $250.00

ORWELL, George. *1984.* 1949 NY. 1st Am ed. gray cloth. $35.00

ORWELL, George. *1984.* 1949 London. Seeker Warburg. 1st ed. VG $65.00

OSBORN, Albert S. *Questioned Documents.* 1929 Albany. Ills 1st ed. 1,028. cloth. $65.00

OSBORN, Albert S. *Questioned Documents.* 1910 Rochester. sgn. brown buckram. EX $100.00

OSBORN, Arthur W. *Meaning of Personal Existence.* 1967 Ills. 232 p. dj. EX $15.00

OSBORN, C.S. *Iron Hunter.* 1919 NY. Macmillan. Ills. 316 p. $12.50

OSBORN, Chase S. & Stella B. *Conquest of a Continent.* 1939 MI. 190 p. $12.00

OSBORNE, J. *Entertainer.* 1958 NY. 1st ed. dj. EX $10.00

OSBORNE, Lloyd. *3 Speeds Forward: Auto Love Story with 1 Reverse.* 1907 NY. Ills 1st ed. dj. $165.00

OSBOURNE, K. *Robert Louis Stevenson in CA.* 1911 McClurg. 1st ed. 8vo. photos. VG $25.00

OSGOOD. *Field Notes of Capt. William Clark.* 1964 New Haven. 1st ed. dj. EX $300.00

OSLER, William. *Aequanimitas & Other Addresses.* 1905 Phil. Blakiston. 1st ed. VG $150.00

OSLER, William. *Aequanimitas.* 1932 Phil. Ills 3rd ed. VG $65.00

OSLER, William. *AL Student & Other Biographical Essays.* 1908 Oxford U Pr. Ills. 334 p. rebound. $65.00

OSLER, William. *Counsels & Ideals.* 1905 Houghton Mifflin. G $15.00

OSLER, William. *Evolution of Modern Medicine.* 1922 Yale U Pr. 5th print. xl. G $20.00

OSLER, William. *Old Humanities & New Science.* 1920 Houghton Mifflin. 1st ed. VG $10.00

OSLER, William. *Principles & Practice of Medicine.* 1924 NY. Appleton. 9th ed. VG $22.50

OSLER, William. *Principles & Practice of Medicine.* 1902 NY. 4th ed. VG $50.00

OSLER, William. *Way of Life.* 1932 Baltimore. Remington Putnam. dj. VG $20.00

OSLER, William. *Way of Life.* 1926 Oxford U Pr. VG $10.00

OSSA, Helen. *They Saved Our Birds.* 1973 Hippocrene. Ills. 287 p. dj. EX $10.00

OSSENDOWSKI, Ferdinand. *Beasts, Men, & Gods.* 1923 Dutton. 22nd ed. 325 p. xl. VG $25.00

OSTRANDER. *Social Crisis.* 1898 NY. presentation. cloth. $25.00

OSTWALD, Wilhelm. *Historical Development of General Chemistry.* 1906 Columbia U Pr. reprint. 84 p. wraps. $20.00

OSTWALD, Wilhelm. *Manual of Physico-Chemical Measurements.* 1894 London. Macmillan. 255 p. xl. $35.00

OSWALD, Marianne. *1 Small Voice.* 1945 NY. Whittlesey House. 1st ed. VG $25.00

OTENBURGER, Leigh. *Climbers Guide to the Tetons Range.* 1956 Sierra Club. Ills 1st ed. 159 p. dj. EX $15.00

OTERO, Robert. *Forever Picasso: Intimate Look at His Last Years.* 1974 NY. Ills. folio. $25.00

OTT, E. *Plantation Cookery of Old LA.* 1938 New Orleans. 1st ed. VG $12.00

OTTINGEN. *Horse Breeding.* 1909 Simpson Lowe. 4to. red cloth. VG $95.00

OTTO, A.F.; & CHIPIEZ, C. *History of Art.* 1884 Chapman Hall. Trans W Armstrong. 12 vol set. $1200.00

OTTO, H.W. *Pauvres Saltim Bangues.* c 1890. Dusseldorf. rare. VG $200.00

OTWAY, Thomas. *Complete Works of Thomas Otway.* 1926 Bloomsbury. 1/1,250. 4to. 3 vol set. VG $95.00

OUIDA. *Nurnberg Stove.* c 1895. NY. Fenno. VG $12.50

OUTCAULT, R.F. *Buster Brown Abroad.* 1904 NY. Stokes. Ills 1st ed. blue buckram. VG $50.00

OUTDOOR LIFE. *Anthology of Hunting Adventures.* 1946 NY. dj. VG $50.00

OUTDOOR LIFE. *Great Outdoor Adventures.* 1961 NY. dj. VG $15.00

OUTDOOR LIFE. *Story of American Hunting & Firearms.* 1959 NY. Ills 1st ed. 4to. 172 p. dj. $15.00

OUTHWAITE, Leonard. *Atlantic: History of an Ocean.* 1957 NY. Coward McCann. dj. VG $8.00

OVENDEN, G. *Victorian Album: Julia Margaret Cameron & Her Circle.* 1975 NY. 1st Am ed. dj. EX $45.00

OVERBECK, Alice. *Sven the Wise & Sven the Kind & Other Stories of Lappland.* 1932 Harper. Ills Gergely. 1st ed. VG $15.00

OVERTON, G. *American Nights Entertainment.* 1923 NY. VG $15.00

OVERTON, G. *Cargoes for Crusoes.* 1924 NY. VG $15.00

OVERTON, G. *When Winter Comes to Main Street.* 1922 NY. dj. EX $15.00

OVERTON, R.C. *Burlington West: Colonization History of Burlington R.R.* 1941 Harvard. 8vo. $60.00

OVINGTON, Ray. *Tactics on Trout.* 1969 Knopf. Ills 1st ed. 327 p. VG $8.50

OWEN, Daniel E. *Old Times in Saco.* 1891 Saco, ME. Ills. maps. $75.00

OWEN, David Dale. *Report of Geological Survey of WI, IA, & MN.* 1852 Phil. 1st ed. 2nd issue. maps. plts. $75.00

OWEN, Guy. *Cape Fear Country & Other Poems.* 1958 Lake Como. 1st ed. sgn. wraps. VG $50.00

OWEN, M.A. *Voodoo Talks As Told by Negroes of the Southwest.* 1893 NY. 1st ed. 310 p. VG $75.00

OWEN, Rev. G. Vale. *Facts & the Future Life.* 1922 3rd ed. 191 p. VG $26.00

OWEN. *Story of Royal Copenhagen Christmas Plates.* 1961 Viking. Ills. spiral bdg. dj. EX $22.00

OWENS, H.J. *Dr. Faust.* 1953 Chicago. Caxton. Ills Kredel. 1/350. EX $40.00

OWINGS, Mark. *Robert A. Heinlein: Bibliography.* 1973 Baltimore. Croatan House. 1st ed. wraps. $40.00

OWINGS, N.A. *Spaces in Between: Architect's Journey.* 1973 Boston. 1st ed. sgn. dj. $10.00

OXX, William Gardener. *Oxx Family in America.* 1973 Northridge. Ltd ed. 1/150. 4to. 778 p. EX $200.00

OYAMA, Masutatsu. *Advanced Karate.* 1970 Japan Pub. 1st print. EX $12.50

OZ, Amos. *Hills of Evil Counsel.* 1978 Harcourt. 1st Am ed. dj. EX. $15.00

OZ, Amos. *Touch the Water, Touch the Wind.* 1973 Harcourt. 1st Am ed. dj. EX. $15.00

OZ, Amos. *Unto Death.* 1975 Harcourt. 1st ed. dj. EX. $13.00

OZICK, Cynthia. *Cannibal Galaxy.* 1983 NY. 1st ed. dj. EX $10.00

OZICK, Cynthia. *Levitation: 5 Fictions.* 1982 NY. Knopf. 1st ed. VG $15.00

OZICK, Cynthia. *Pagan Rabbi.* 1971 Knopf. 1st ed. dj. EX $45.00

PACH, Walter. *Art Museum in America.* 1948 NY. Ills 1st ed. inscr. VG $45.00

PACH, Walter. *Georges Seurat.* 1923 NY. Duffield. Ills. 4to. dj. $50.00

PACIONI, G. *Guide to Mushrooms.* 1981 Simon Schuster. Ills 1st Am ed. 511 p. dj. EX $18.00

PACKARD, Francis W. *Guy Patin & Medical Profession in Paris in 17th Century.* 1925 NY. Hoeber. Ills Ltd ed. 1/1,050. sgn. xl. $25.00

PACKARD, William. *Saturday Night at San Marcos.* 1985 NY. 1st ed. M $15.00

PACKARD, Winthrop. *FL Trails.* 1983 Pineapple. reprint of 1910. pb. EX $10.00

PACKARD, Winthrop. *FL Trails.* 1910 Maynard. Ills. VG $27.50

PACKER, Charles. *Paris Furniture by the Master Ebonists.* 1956 Newport. Ceramic Book. 1/1,000. 4to. $125.00

PADDOCK, Mrs. A.G. *Fate of Madame La Tour: Tale of Great Salt Lake.* 1881 Fords, Howard, Hurlbert. 12mo. $50.00

PADEN, Irene. *Wake of the Prairie Schooner.* 1943 Macmillan. EX $25.00

PADFIELD, Peter. *Titanic & the Californian.* 1966 NY. Day. 1st ed. photos. dj. VG $35.00

PADILLA, H. *En Mi Jardin Pastan Los Heroes.* 1981 Argos Vergara. Spanish text. pb. EX $7.50

PADOVER, S. *Psychologist in Germany.* 1946 Phoenix House. G $17.50

PADOVER, S. *Psychologist in Germany.* 1946 London. G $17.50

PAGANO, Jo. *Paesanos.* 1940 Boston. 2nd print. inscr. G $15.00

PAGE, Elizabeth. *Wagons West: Story of OR Trail.* 1930 NY. photos. G $30.00

PAGE, Elizabeth. *Wild Horses & Go: From WY to the Yukon.* 1932 NY. Ills. $8.50

PAGE, Harry S. *Between Flags: Recollections of Gentleman Rider.* Derrydale. Ills Ltd ed. 1/850. EX $110.00

PAGE, Marco. *Shadowy 3rd.* 1946 Dodd Mead. 1st ed. inscr. dj. VG $15.00

PAGE, Thomas J. *La Plata, Argentine Confederation, & Paraguay.* 1859 NY. Harper. Ills 1st ed. fld map. 632 p. $150.00

PAGE, Thomas Nelson. *In Old VA.* 1896 NY. Ills Frost/Pyle. 1st ed. $35.00

PAGE, Thomas Nelson. *In Ole VA.* 1892 Scribner. 16mo. 239 p. $10.00

PAGE, Thomas Nelson. *Old Gentleman of Black Stock.* 1900 NY. Ills Christy. VG $25.00

PAGE, Thomas Nelson. *Santa Claus's Partner.* 1899 NY. Ills W Glackens. 1st ed. VG $15.00

PAGE, Thomas Nelson. *Under the Crust.* 1907 NY. 1st ed. VG $20.00

PAGE, Thomas Nelson. *2 Little Confederates.* 1939 Scribner. Ills Thomason. dj. boxed. EX $20.00

PAGET, Guy. *Sporting Pictures of England.* 1946 London. dj. EX $11.00

PAINE, A.B. *Capt. Bill McDonald: TX Ranger.* 1986 State House Pr. facsimile of 1909. dj. M $20.00

PAINE, Albert W. *New Philosophy.* 1884 168 p. EX $35.00

PAINE, Gregory. *Southern Prose Writers.* 1969 Freeport, NY. 8vo. 392 p. VG $15.00

PAINE, Lauran. *Tom Horn: Man of the West.* 1963 Barre. 186 p. dj. EX $6.50

PAINE, Ralph. *Story of Martin Coe.* 1906 NY. Outing Pub. Ills H Giles. $45.00

PAINE, Thomas. *Common Sense.* 1792 London. wraps. disbound. VG $35.00

PAINE. *Conquest of the Great Northwest.* 1959 NY. Ills 1st ed. dj. VG $20.00

PAINE. *Gen. Custer's Story.* 1960 Fireside Pr. 144 p. $22.00

PAISLEY, F. *Al Capone: Biography of a Self-Made Man.* 1930 Ives Washburn. 1st ed. $60.00

PAL, Pratapaditya. *Art of Tibet.* 1969 NY. Asia Soc. pb. wraps. $25.00

PAL, Pratapaditya. *Elephants & Ivories in South Asia.* 1981 Los Angeles. Ills. 112 p. $12.50

PALAU-FABRE, Joseph. *Picasso: Early Years 1881-1907.* 1985 Barcelona. Poligrafa. Ills. folio. 361 p. $150.00

PALEY, Grace. *Enormous Changes at the Last Minute.* 1974 NY. 1st ed. dj. EX $15.00

PALEY, Morton D. *William Blake.* 1978 Oxford. Phaidon. Ills. 4to. 192 p. dj. $40.00

PALLISER, Mrs. Bury. *History of Lace.* 1875 London. 3rd ed. $85.00

PALLOTTINO, Massimo. *Etruscan Painting.* 1952 Luasanne. 1st ed. G $25.00

PALMER, Arnold; & FURLONG, B. *Go for Broke!* Simon Schuster. wraps. M $6.00

PALMER, Brooks. *Book of American Clocks.* 1950 NY. Ills 1st ed. 318 p. VG $35.00

PALMER, Brooks. *Book of American Clocks.* 1965 NY. 4to. sgn. dj. VG $25.00

PALMER, Brooks. *Treasury of American Clocks.* 1971 Macmillan. Ills. 371 p. dj. VG $15.00

PALMER, Fanny Purdy. *Sonnets of CA.* 1927 Purdy. Ltd 2nd ed. 1/50. 35 p. EX $12.50

PALMER, Fanny Purdy. *Sonnets.* 1909 San Francisco. Elder. Ltd ed. 1/250. inscr. $20.00

PALMER, Frederick. *Clark of the OH.* 1930 NY. 3rd print. 482 p. VG $18.00

PALMER, Howard. *Mountaineering & Exploration in the Selkirks.* 1914 NY. Ills. fld maps. 440 p. VG $200.00

PALMER, John. *Studies in Contemporary Theatre.* 1927 Boston. G $10.00

PALMER, Lilli. *Lobsters & Dance.* 1975 NY. sgn. dj. VG $25.00

PALMER, R.R. *12 Who Rules.* 1958 Princeton. dj. VG $10.00

PALMER, W.T. *English Lakes.* 1908 London. Ills AH Cooper. G $20.00

PALMER & CROWQUILL. *Wanderings of a Pen & Pencil.* 1846 London. 1st ed. VG $100.00

PALMER. *Riding High.* 1956 NY. 1st ed. 192 p. dj. VG $17.50

PAMP, Capt. Frederic E. *Normandy to the Elbe, XIX Corps.* 1945 Ills. 4to. 57 p. wraps. VG $32.50

PANETTI, Charles. *Pleasure of Rory Malone.* 1982 St. Martin. 1st ed. dj. EX $10.00

PANGBORN, Edgar. *Davy.* 1964 NY. St. Martin. 1st ed. dj. EX $75.00

PANGBORN, Edgar. *West of the Sun.* 1966 Dell. 1st ed. wraps. EX $5.00

PANGBURN, Edgar. *Good Neighbors & Other Strangers.* 1972 Macmillan. 1st ed. dj. EX $20.00

PANOFSKY, Erwin. *Early Netherlandish Painting: Its Origins & Character.* 1958 Harvard U Pr. 2nd print. 2 vol set. djs. EX $250.00

PANSY, Isabella Alden. *Man of the House.* 1883 Boston. Lathrop. Ills 1st ed. EX $20.00

PANSY, Isabella Alden. *Wise Alice.* no date. Boston. Lathrop. Ills. G $8.00

PAPACHRISTOU, Tician. *Marcel Breuer: New Buildings & Projects.* 1970 NY. Praeger. Ills. 4to. 240 p. dj. $85.00

PAPADAKI, Stamo. *Oscar Niemeyer.* 1960 NY. Braziller. G $18.00

PAPE, Frank C. *Lives of the 12 Caesers.* 1930 NY. Argus. Ills. gilt cloth. EX $45.00

PAPERT, Emma. *Illsutrated Guide to American Glass.* 1972 NY. Hawthorne. 4to. 299 p. dj. $20.00

PAPUS. *Tarot of the Bohemians.* 1910 London. Rider. rebound. VG $65.00

PARAMANANDA, Swami. *Upanishads.* 1919 2nd ed. 116 p. EX $15.00

PARAMORE, Edward E. *Ballad of Yukon Jake.* 1928 NY. Coward McCann. 1st ed. dj. G $50.00

PARDEE, R.G. *Complete Manual for Cultivation of the Strawberry.* 1865 NY. Orange Judd. 157 p. VG $15.00

PARDOE. *Beauties of Bosphorus.* 1839 London. Ills Bartlett. calf. xl. $100.00

PARETO, Vilfredo. *Mind & Society.* 1935 Harcourt. 1st ed. 4 vol set. xl. VG $45.00

PARETO, Vilfredo. *Trattato di Sociologia Generale.* 1923 Firenze. 2nd ed. 3 vol set. VG $75.00

PARGELLIS, Stanley. *Military Affairs in North America 1748-1765.* 1969 Archon. reprint. dj. EX $45.00

PARGELLIS, Stanley. *Military Affairs in North America 1748-1765.* 1969 Archon. reprint. dj. VG $35.00

PARIS, J.A. *Philosophy in Sort-Made Science.* 1847 Phil. 12mo. 432 p. $75.00

PARIS, William F. *Decorative Elements in Architecture.* 1917 NY. Ills. 4to. 152 p. $20.00

PARISH, Sir Woodbine. *Buenos Ayres & Provinces of Rio de la Plata.* 1852 London. Murray. Ills 2nd ed. maps. 434 p. VG $100.00

PARK, Benjamin. *Wrinkles & Recipes.* 1875 NY. Ills. 12mo. 252 p. $25.00

PARK, Mungo. *Travels in the Interior of Africa.* 1858 Black Edinburgh. Ills. VG $22.50

PARKER, DeWitt H. *Analysis of Art.* 1926 Yale U Pr. Ills. 190 p. $16.50

PARKER, Dorothy. *Death & Taxes.* 1931 NY. Viking. Ltd ed. 1/250. sgn. scarce. VG $250.00

PARKER, Dorothy. *Laments for the Living.* 1930 London. 1st ed. VG $25.00

PARKER, F. *Caryl Chessman: Red Light Bandit.* 1975 NY. 1st ed. dj. VG $15.00

PARKER, Frank. *Anatomy of the San Francisco Cable Car.* 1946 Stanford U Pr. Ills. 61 p. maps. dj. VG $15.00

PARKER, J. & P. *Ornamental Waterfowl & Exotic Garden Birds.* 1970 Barnes. Ills 1st Am ed. 184 p. dj. EX $12.00

PARKER, K.T. *Drawings of Hans Holbein: At Windsor Castle.* 1983 NY. 4to. cloth. dj. M $50.00

PARKER, Lester Shepard. *Nancy MacIntyre: Tale of the Prairies.* 1911 St Louis. 4th ed. $20.00

PARKER, R. *Pale Kings & Princes.* 1987 NY. Ltd ed. 1/225. sgn. slipcase. $60.00

PARKER, R.M. *Images of American Architecture.* 1982 NY. Ills. oblong. 143 p. $10.00

PARKER, Richard. *Historical Recollections of Robertson County, TX.* 1955 Salado. Anson Jones. 1/1,000. $30.00

PARKER, Richard. *School Compendium of Natural & Experimental Philosophy.* 1863 NY. Ills. 12mo. 470 p. cloth. G $21.00

PARKER, Robert B. *Catskill Eagle.* 1985 Delacorte. 1st ed. dj. EX $15.00

PARKER, Robert B. *Catskill Eagle.* 1985 Delacorte. 1st ed. sgn. dj. EX $30.00

PARKER, Robert B. *Ceremony.* 1982 Delacorte. 1st ed. dj. EX $20.00

PARKER, Robert B. *Godwulf Manuscript.* 1974 Boston. Houghton Mifflin. 1st ed. dj. $100.00

PARKER, Robert B. *Love & Glory.* 1983 NY. 1st ed. sgn. dj. M $35.00

PARKER, Robert B. *Mortal Stakes.* 1975 Boston. 1st ed. dj. EX $170.00

PARKER, Robert B. *Surrogate: Spenser Story.* 1982 Northridge. Ltd 1st ed. 1/300. sgn. dj. M $100.00

PARKER, Robert B. *Taming a Sea Horse.* 1986 proof. 1/500. sgn. wraps. M $65.00

PARKER, Robert B. *Taming a Sea Horse.* 1986 Delacorte. 1st ed. 4to. 250 p. dj. EX $20.00

PARKER, Robert B. *Valediction.* 1984 NY. 1st ed. sgn. dj. M $25.00

PARKER, Samuel. *Journal of an Exploring Tour Beyond the Rocky Mountians.* 1967 Minneapolis. dj. VG $15.00

PARKER, Wyman. *Henry Stevens of VT.* 1963 Amsterdam. VG $25.00

PARKER & BRYAN. *Old Quebec: Fortress of New France.* 1904 NY. Macmillan. Ills 2nd ed. G $25.00

PARKER & JENKINS. *Mushrooms: Separate Kingdom.* 1979 Oxmoor. Ills 1st ed. 101 p. dj. EX $12.00

PARKER & PAUDRAS. *To Bird with Love.* 1981 France. Ills. bilingual text. EX $160.00

PARKER. *Savage Place.* 1981 Delacorte. 1st ed. dj. EX $15.00

PARKES, J. *Story of Jerusalem.* 1949 London. maps. dj. G $8.00

PARKES, Samuel. *Chemical Essays.* 1815 London. Ills. 5 vol set. xl. G $58.00

PARKINS. *Young Man's Best Companion.* 1812 London. Ills. 12mo. 328 p. leather. $30.00

PARKINSON, C. Northcote. *Mrs. Parkinson's Law & Other Stories in Domestic Science.* 1968 London. Ills Osborn. 1st ed. dj. VG $25.00

PARKINSON, C. Northcote. *So Near So Far.* 1981 London. 1st ed. dj. EX $18.00

PARKINSON, E.S. *Wonderland.* 1894 Trenton. Ills. 12mo. $35.00

PARKMAN, Francis. *Count Frontenac & New France Under Louis XIV.* 1897 Little Brown. 463 p. fld map. VG $20.00

PARKMAN, Francis. *Half-Century of Conflict.* 1892 Little Brown. 1st ed. 2 vol set. maps. VG $65.00

PARKMAN, Francis. *Journals of Francis Parkman.* 1947 Harper. Ills 1st ed. 2 vol set. EX $50.00

PARKMAN, Francis. *Letters of Francis Parkman.* 1960 OK U Pr. Ills 1st ed. 2 vol set. EX $50.00

PARKMAN, Francis. *Montcalm & Wolfe.* 1898 Little Brown. 2 vol set. maps. VG $35.00

PARKMAN, Francis. *Old Regime in Canada.* 1898 Little Brown. Revised ed. 508 p. fld map. VG $20.00

PARKMAN, Francis. *OR Trail.* 1943 Heritage Pr. Ills. 297 p. VG $6.50

PARKMAN, Francis. *OR Trail.* 1945 Doubleday. Ills/sgn Benton. 1/1,000. VG $35.00

PARKMAN, Francis. *Pioneers of France in the New World.* 1897 Little Brown. Revised ed. maps. cloth. EX $20.00

PARKMAN, Francis. *Works of Francis Parkman.* 1899 Boston. Frontenac ed. 17 vol set. EX $250.00

PARKS, Gordon. *Camera Portraits: Techniques & Principles.* 1948 NY. Watts. 1st ed. 8vo. red cloth. dj. G $20.00

PARKS, Gordon. *Poet & His Camera.* 1968 NY. 8vo. dj. EX $25.00

PARLEY, Peter. *Voyages, Travels, & Adventures of Gilbert Go Ahead.* 1956 NY. 12mo. G $50.00

PARNELL, E.A. *Dyeing & Calico Printing.* 1849 London. 1st ed. 228 p. 22 cloth swatches. $150.00

PARNELL, E.A. *Practical Treatise on Dyeing & Calico Printing.* 1846 NY. 1st ed. 8vo. 10 plts. $160.00

PARNELL, Thomas. *Poems Selected by Lennox Robertson.* 1927 Caula Pr. Ltd ed. 1/200. $90.00

PARR, Hallam. *Further Training & Employment of Mounted Infantry.* 1888 London. $35.00

PARRIS, John. *Roaming the Mountains.* 1955 Asheville. 1st ed. dj. VG $30.00

PARRISH, Anne. *Floating Island.* 1930 NY/ London. Harper. Ills. square 8vo. VG $20.00

PARRISH, Maxfield. *Knave of Hearts.* 1925 spiral bdg. EX $475.00

PARRISH. *Phantom Bouquet: Treatise on Skeletonizing Leaves.* 1862 Phil. 1st ed. G $20.00

PARROT, Andre. *Arts of Assyria.* 1961 NY. Golden. Ills. 4to. 396 p. dj. $60.00

PARRY, Leonard A. *Some Famous Medical Trials.* 1928 NY. cloth. $25.00

PARRY, William Edward. *Journal of a Voyage for Discovery of Northwest Passage.* Greenwood Pr. reprint of 1918. VG $28.00

PARRY, William Edward. *Journal of 2nd Voyage for Discovery of Northwest Passage.* 1824 London. Murray. 1st ed. 4to. 571 p. leather. $350.00

PARRY, William Edward. *Journal of 2nd Voyage for Discovery of Northwest Passage.* 1824 NY. 1st Am ed. xl. VG $90.00

PARSONS, Arthur Jeffrey. *Catalog of Gardiner Greene Hubbard Collection of Engravings.* 1905 WA. 517 p. rebound. VG $125.00

PARSONS, E.C. *American Indian Life.* 1922 NY. Ills 1st ed. 4to. slipcase. EX $75.00

PARSONS, Edward C. *I Flew with the Lafayette Escadrille.* 1963 Indianapolis. dj. VG $45.00

PARSONS, Eugene. *Guidebook to CO.* 1911 Boston. Ills 1st ed. fld map. VG $12.50

PARSONS, Flora T. *Calisthenic Songs Illustrated.* 1969 NY/Chicago. Ills. 12mo. cloth. VG $30.00

PARSONS, Horatio A. *Book of Niagara Falls.* 1839 Buffalo. Revised 3rd ed. 12mo. 112 p. $75.00

PARSONS, J.E. *1st Winchester: Story of the 1866 Repeating Rifle.* 1969 Winchester. Ills. 207 p. dj. EX $15.00

PARSONS, J.E. *1st Winchester: Story of the 1866 Repeating Rifle.* 1955 NY. Ills 1st ed. dj. VG $20.00

PARSONS, P.A. *Complete Book of Fresh-Water Fishing.* 1963 Outdoor Life. Ills. 332 p. VG $6.50

PARSONS, R.H. *Steam Turbine & Other Inventions of Sir Charles Parsons.* 1948 London. Longman. reprint. wraps. VG $6.00

PARSONS, Robert P. *Mob 3: Naval Hospital in South Sea Jungle.* 1945 Indianapolis. Ills. 348 p. dj. VG $35.00

PARSONS, Samuel. *Parsons on the Rose.* 1891 NY. 12mo. 211 p. $25.00

PARSONS, Samuel. *Art of Landscape Architecture.* 1915 NY. Ills 1st ed. green cloth. VG $45.00

PARSONS, U. *Lecture on Reciprocal Influence Between Brain & Stomach.* 1841 Providence. 1st ed. wraps. VG $40.00

PARSONS, William Barkley. *Robert Fulton & the Submarine.* 1922 Columbia U Pr. dj. EX $20.00

PARTON, James. *Famous Americans of Recent Times.* 1879 Boston. 12mo. 473 p. green cloth. G $20.00

PARTON, James. *Life of Aaron Burr.* 1858 NY. Ills. plts. 696 p. G $35.00

PARTON, James. *Life of Andrew Jackson.* 1861 NY. 3 vol set. VG $125.00

PARTON, James. *Life of John Jacob Astor.* 1865 NY. 8vo. 122 p. blue cloth. VG $75.00

PARTRIDGE, E. *Dictionary of Underworld.* 1968 London. Enlarged ed. dj. $27.50

PARTRIDGE, E. *Sube Cane.* 1921 Phil. Penn. Ills. G $7.00

PARTRIDGE, M. *Farm Tools Through the Ages.* 1973 Boston. 240 p. dj. VG $18.00

PASKMAN & SPAETH. *Gentlemen, Be Seated: Parade of Old-Time Minstrels.* 1928 Doubleday. Ills 1st ed. VG $65.00

PASOLINI, Pier Paolo. *Ragazzi.* 1968 NY. Grove. 1st ed. VG $25.00

PASSMORE, Michael J. *Porcelain Allach.* 1972 Ills. 8vo. 107 p. dj. $25.00

PASTERNAK, Boris. *Adolescence of Zhenya Lovers.* 1961 Philosophical. 1st Am ed. dj. EX $15.00

PASTERNAK, Boris. *Blind Beauty.* 1969 NY. 1st ed. dj. EX $10.00

PASTERNAK, Boris. *Blind Beauty.* 1969 Collins. 1st English ed. dj. EX $15.00

PASTERNAK, Boris. *Essay in Autobiography.* 1959 Collins. 1st English ed. dj. EX $35.00

PASTERNAK, Boris. *My Sister.* 1976 NY. 1st ed. dj. M $15.00

PAT, J. *Ashes & Fire.* 1947 NY. dj. G $20.00

PATAI. *Encounters: Life of Jacques Lipchitz.* 1961 NY. 1st ed. 8vo. cloth. dj. VG $20.00

PATCHEN, Kenneth. *Before the Brave.* 1936 Random House. 1st ed. dj. EX $200.00

PATCHEN, Kenneth. *Poem-Scapes,* 1958 Highlands, NC. Williams. Ltd ed. 1/75. $275.00

PATCHEN, Kenneth. *See You in the Morning.* 1947 NY. 1st ed. dj. VG $45.00

PATCHEN, Kenneth. *Teeth of the Lion.* 1942 New Directions. 1st ed. dj. $50.00

PATCHEN, Kenneth. *They Keep Riding Down All the Time.* 1946 Padell. 1st ed. wraps. EX $20.00

PATEL, Harshad. *Vanishing Herds.* 1973 Stein Day. VG $35.00

PATER, Walter. *Gaston De Latour: An Unfinished Romance.* 1907 Portland. 1st ed. 1/925. full morocco. $95.00

PATER, Walter. *Marriage of Cupid & Psyche.* 1951 Heritage. Ills. 64 p. slipcase. VG $20.00

PATER, Walter. *Sebastian Van Storch.* 1927 London. Ills Alastair. Ltd ed. sgn. VG $110.00

PATERSON, A. *Birds of the Bahamas.* 1972 Durrell. Ills 1st ed. 180 p. dj. EX $15.00

PATERSON, David. *Science of Color Mixing for Dyers, Printers, & Chemists.* 1900 London. 1st ed. 8vo. 128 p. 11 swatch samples. $65.00

PATMORE, Coventry. *Florilegium Ammantis.* 1849 London. 1st ed. scarce. VG $22.00

PATON, Alan. *Ah, But Your Land Is Beautiful.* 1982 NY. 1st ed. dj. M $11.00

PATON, Alan. *Sponono.* 1965 NY. 1st ed. dj. EX $14.00

PATON, Alan. *Tales From a Troubled Land.* 1961 NY. 1st ed. dj. EX $14.00

PATON, Alan. *Too Late the Phalarope.* 1953 Cape Town. 1st ed. sgn. VG $175.00

PATON, William Agnew. *Down the Islands: Voyage to Caribbees.* 1887 NY. Scribner. Ills 1st ed. 301 p. $50.00

PATRICK, V. *Pope of Greenwich Village.* 1979 NY. 1st ed. dj. EX $10.00

PATRIDGE, William. *Practical Treatise on Dying of Wool, Cotton, & Skein Silk.* 1823 NY. 1st ed. 12mo. 288 p. calf. G $150.00

PATTEN, Marguerite. *International Cookery in Color.* 1972 London. dj. EX $15.00

PRAGER, Arthur. *Rascals at Large; or, Clue in Old Nostalgia.* 1971 NY. 1st ed. dj. EX $35.00

PRANDTL, Ludwig. *Essentials of Fluid Dynamics & Applications to Hydraulics.* no date. (1952) NY. Hafner. 452 p. rebound. $35.00

PRASAD, Rama. *Nature's Finer Forces.* 1894 251 p. VG $65.00

PRATHER, Richard S. *Kill the Clown.* 1973 Gold Lion. 1st ed. dj. VG $15.00

PRATHER, Richard S. *Kubla Khan Caper.* 1966 Trident Pr. 1st ed. dj. xl. $7.50

PRATT, Charles Stuart. *By-O-Baby Ballads.* 1886 Boston. Ills F Childe Hassam. $250.00

PRATT, Fletcher. *Alien Planet.* 1962 Avalon. dj. EX $5.00

PRATT, Fletcher. *Civil War in Pictures.* 1955 Garden City. dj. VG $20.00

PRATT, Fletcher. *Double in Space.* 1951 Doubleday. 1st ed. VG $15.00

PRATT, Fletcher. *Double Jeopardy.* 1952 Doubleday. dj. xl. $10.00

PRATT, Fletcher. *Heroic Years: 14 Years of the Republic 1801-1915.* 1934 Smith Haas. Ills. 352 p. dj. EX $8.00

PRATT, Fletcher. *Secret & Urgent Codes & Ciphers.* 1939 NY. 1st ed. VG $20.00

PRATT, Fletcher. *Stanton: Lincoln's Secretary of War.* 1953 Norton. 1st ed. 520 p. maps. dj. EX $12.00

PRATT, Fletcher. *Undying Fire.* 1953 Ballantine. 1st ed. dj. EX $45.00

PRATT, Fletcher. *Witches 3.* 1952 Twayne. 1st ed. dj. VG $35.00

PRATT, Fletcher. *World of Wonder.* 1951 Twayne. 1st ed. dj. VG $20.00

PRATT, James Bissett. *Religious Consciousness.* 1927 NY. 488 p. VG $25.00

PRATT, James Bissett. *What Is Pragmatism?* 1909 NY. 256 p. index. EX $25.00

PRATT, Joseph H. *Year with Sir William Osler.* 1949 Hopkins Pr. 1st ed. dj. EX $32.50

PRATT, Joseph. *Proceedings of Annual Convention of NC Good Roads Assn.* 1913 Raleigh. 8vo. 127 p. wraps. xl. VG $7.50

PRATT, R. *Picture Garden Book & Gardener's Assistant.* 1944 NY. Ills. $25.00

PRATT, Theodore. *Murder Goes to the World's Fair.* no date. Eldon. VG $25.00

PREAUD, Tanara. *Sevres Porcelain.* 1980 WA. Smithsonian. 4to. wraps. $15.00

PREBLE, George H. *History of Origin & Development of Steam Navigation.* 1883 Phil. 1st ed. 8vo. EX $85.00

PREBLE, R. *Pneumonia & Pneumococcus Infections.* 1905 Chicago. Head. EX $17.00

PREISS, Bryon. *Dragon World.* 1979 Bantam. 1st ed. sgn. no dj issued. $35.00

PRENTICE, George D. *Biography of Henry Clay.* 1831 Hartford. 1st ed. full tree calf. EX $150.00

PRENTICE, T.M. *Weeds & Wild Flowers.* 1973 Salem. dj. EX $40.00

PRENTIS, Noble. *History of KS.* 1899 Winfield. Ills. 379 p. $12.00

PRESBREY, Frank. *History & Development of Advertising with Illustrations.* 1929 NY. 1st ed. 8vo. 642 p. VG $45.00

PRESCOTT, George B. *Electric Telephone.* 1890 NY. Revised 2nd ed. 795 p. VG $50.00

PRESCOTT, George B. *Electricity & the Electric Telegraph.* 1877 NY. Appleton. Ills. 978 p. xl. $50.00

PRESCOTT, Kenneth W. *Complete Graphic Works of Ben Shahn.* 1973 Quadrangle. Ills. oblong 4to. 272 p. dj. $85.00

PRESCOTT, L.F. *Great Campaign of 1896.* c 1896. Ills. 12mo. 536 p. blue cloth. $9.00

PRESCOTT, William H. *Conquest of Peru.* no date. NY. 2 vol set. EX $125.00

PRESLEY, Dee. *Elvis, We Love You Tender.* 1980 NY. 1st ed. dj. VG $27.50

PRESSER, J. *Destruction of Dutch Jews.* 1969 NY. Ills. dj. VG $35.00

PRESTAGE. *Chivalry: Historical Significance & Civilizing Influence.* 1928 London. Ills 1st ed. 231 p. VG $27.50

PRESTON, A. *Dreadnought to Nuclear Submarine.* 1980 London. Ills. EX $8.00

PRESTON, A. *Warships of the World.* 1980 London. Ills. dj. EX $20.00

PRESTON, Margaret J. *Handful of Monographs: Continental & English.* 1886 NY. Randolph. 1st ed. 13 albumen prints. EX $95.00

PRESTON, William. *Illustrations of Masonry.* 1821 London. Whittaker. 13th ed. 8vo. VG $25.00

PRETORIUS, P.J. *Jungle Man.* 1948 Dutton. Ills. 256 p. dj. VG $11.50

PREVOST, A. *Manon Lescaut.* 1888 Phil. Ills M Leloir. EX $50.00

PRICE, Anthony. *Col. Butler's Wolf.* 1973 Crime Club. 1st ed. dj. xl. $6.00

PRICE, Anthony. *October Men.* 1974 Crime Club. 1st ed. dj. xl. $5.00

PRICE, Anthony. *Private Contentment.* 1984 Atheneum. 1st ed. dj. EX $15.00

PRICE, Bruce. *Into the Unknown.* 1968 Platt Munk. 306 p. dj. EX $8.00

PRICE, E. Hoffman. *Far Lands, Other Days.* 1975 Chapel Hill. 1st ed. dj. EX $40.00

PRICE, Eugenia. *Beloved Invader.* 1965 Phil. 1st ed. sgn. dj. EX $32.50

PRICE, G.F. *Across the Continent with the 5th Cavalry.* 1959 Antiquarian Pr. reprint of 1883. 706 p. EX $120.00

PRICE, L.W. *Mountains & Man: Study of Processes & Enviroment.* 1981 CA U Pr. Ills 1st ed. 506 p. dj. EX $18.00

PRICE, M.E. *Child's Book of Myths.* 1924 2nd ed. 6 plts. VG $20.00

PRICE, Mary & Vincent. *Treasury of Great Recipes.* 1974 NY. Grosset Dunlap. Ills Kredel. $40.00

PRICE, Reynolds. *Annual Heron.* 1980 Albondocani. Ltd ed. 1/300. sgn. wraps. EX $40.00

PRICE, Reynolds. *Finding Themselves: Essays & Scenes.* 1972 NY. Atheneum. 1st ed. sgn. dj. EX $50.00

PRICE, Reynolds. *Generous Man.* 1966 NY. Atheneum. 1st ed. sgn. dj. EX $30.00

PRICE, Reynolds. *Long & Happy Life.* 1962 Atheneum. 1st ed. dj. EX $85.00

PRICE, Reynolds. *Permanent Errors.* 1970 NY. Atheneum. 1st ed. 8vo. dj. EX $60.00

PRICE, Reynolds. *Things Themselves.* 1972 NY. 1st ed. dj. EX $25.00

PRICE, Richard. *Blood Brothers.* 1976 Boston. Houghton Mifflin. 1st ed. dj. $12.00

PRICE, Richard. *Breaks.* 1983 Simon Schuster. 1st ed. dj. EX $20.00

PRICE, Richard. *Ladies' Man.* 1978 Houghton. 1st ed. dj. EX $20.00

PRICE, Richard. *Wanderers.* 1974 Houghton. 1st ed. dj. EX $35.00

PRICE, Ross Lambart. *2 Americas: Account of Sport & Travel.* 1877 London. Sampson Low. 1st ed. 368 p. $75.00

PRICHARD, H.H. *Hunting Camps in Wood & Wilderness.* 1910 London. Ills 1st ed. 4to. $50.00

PRICHARD, H.H. *Through Heart of Patagonia with Illustrations.* 1902 NY. Appleton. 1st Am ed. photos. 346 p. $125.00

PRICHARD, H.H. *Through Trackless Labrador.* 1911 London. cloth. dj. VG $40.00

PRICHARD, H.H. *Where Black Rules White: Journey Across & About Haiti.* 1900 Westminster. Constable. 1st ed. photos. VG $75.00

PRICKETT, R.J. *African Ark.* 1974 NY. dj. EX $15.00

PRIDEAUX, H. *Old & New Testament Connected in History of the Jews.* 1720 London. 8vo. leather. G $85.00

PRIEST, Christopher. *Anticipations.* London. 1st ed. EX $15.00

PRIEST, Christopher. *Darkening Island.* 1972 Harper Row. 1st ed. dj. VG $9.00

PRIEST, Christopher. *Fugue for Darkening Island.* London. 1st ed. EX $45.00

PRIEST, Christopher. *Glamour.* London. 1st ed. sgn. EX $20.00

PRIEST, Christopher. *Infinite Summer.* 1979 Scribner. 1st ed. dj. EX $11.50

PRIEST, Christopher. *Perfect Lover.* 1977 Scribner. 1st ed. dj. VG $12.50

PRIEST, Christopher. *Space Machine.* 1976 Harper Row. 1st ed. dj. EX $12.50

PRIESTLEY, J.B. *Blackout in Gretley.* 1943 Clipper. dj. EX $30.00

PRIESTLEY, J.B. *Bright Day.* 1946 Heinemann. 2nd ed. $15.00

PRIESTLEY, J.B. *Daylight on Saturday.* 1943 Harper. 1st ed. dj. xl. $10.00

PRIESTLEY, J.B. *Delight: Reflections by Priestley.* 1949 NY. 1st ed. dj. EX $20.00

PRIESTLEY, J.B. *Edwardians.* 1970 NY. 1st ed. 4to. dj. VG $18.00

PRIESTLEY, J.B. *English Journey.* 1934 NY. 2nd print. VG $12.00

PRIESTLEY, J.B. *English.* 1973 London. 1st ed. 4to. dj. VG $18.00

PRIESTLEY, J.B. *Festival at Farbridge.* 1951 Heinemann. 1st ed. VG $30.00

PRIESTLEY, J.B. *Found, Lost, Found.* 1977 Stein Day. 2nd ed. dj. xl. $5.00

PRIESTLEY, J.B. *Good Companions.* 1930 Musson. VG $25.00

PRIESTLEY, J.B. *Good Companions.* 1929 Harper. 1st Am ed. dj. EX $65.00

PRIESTLEY, J.B. *Salt Is Leaving.* 1975 Harper Row. dj. VG $10.00

PRIESTLEY, J.B. *Salt Is Leaving: Novel of Suspense.* 1966 1st Am ed. dj. VG $15.00

PRIESTLEY, J.B. *Saturn Over the Water.* 1961 Heinemann. 1st ed. dj. VG $25.00

PRIESTLEY, J.B. *Shapes of Sleep.* 1962 Heinemann. 1st ed. dj. VG $25.00

PRIESTLEY, J.B. *Sir Michael & Sir George.* no date. Little Brown. 2nd ed. dj. VG $7.50

PRIGOGNE, I. *Introduction to Thermodynamics of Irreversible Processes.* 1961 NY. Interscience. 2nd ed. 119 p. $10.00

PRIME, William C. *Pottery & Porcelain of All Time & Nations.* 1878 NY. Harper. Ills. 8vo. 531 p. EX $125.00

PRIMEAU, Ronald. *Beyond Spoon River: Legacy of Edgar Lee Masters.* 1981 TX U Pr. 1st ed. 217 p. dj. VG $12.00

PRINCE, J.H. *How Animals Hunt.* 1980 Elsevier Nelson. Ills 1st ed. $8.00

PRINCE, L.B. *Spanish Mission Churches of NM.* 1977 Rio Grande Pr. reprint of 1915. 4to. VG $25.00

PRINCE, Thomas. *Bibliotheca Curiosa: Chronicle of New England.* 1887 Edinburgh. 1/250. 5 vol set. wraps. $85.00

PRINCE, Thomas. *Natural & Moral Government & Agency of God.* 1749 Boston. ¾-morocco. scarce. $200.00

PRINCE, Walter F. *Enchanted Boundary.* 1930 Boston. Society for Psychic Research. $22.00

PRINCE, Walter F. *Noted Witnesses for Psychic Occurences.* 1963 NY U Books. 336 p. dj. EX $22.00

PRITCHARD, J. *Sir George Cayley: Inventor of the Aeroplane.* 1962 NY. 1st Am ed. dj. $22.50

PRITCHARD, P.C.H. *Living Turtles of the World.* 1967 PCH. Ills. 288 p. VG $18.00

PRITCHARD, W. *Angler's Guide to Rivers & Lakes of North Wales.* c 1860s. Wrexham. maps. VG $60.00

PRITCHARD & TREBBAU. *Turtles of Venezuela.* 1984 Ills Voltolina. Special Patron ed. sgns. EX $250.00

PRITCHETT, V.S. *Books in General.* no date. NY. dj. VG $7.50

PRITCHETT, V.S. *On Edge of the Cliff.* 1979 NY. 1st ed. dj. M $12.00

PROCTER, Maurice. *Body To Spare.* no date. Book Club ed. dj. VG $4.00

PROCTER, Maurice. *Hideaway.* 1968 Harper Row. 1st ed. dj. xl. $5.00

PROCTER, Maurice. *His Weight in Gold.* no date. Book Club ed. dj. VG $4.00

PROCTER, Maurice. *Homicide Blonde.* 1965 Harper Row. 1st ed. dj. VG $10.00

PROCTER, Maurice. *Rogue Running.* no date. Book Club ed. dj. VG $4.00

PROCTER, Maurice. *2 Men in 20.* no date. Book Club ed. xl. $3.00

PROCTER. *Victoria Regina.* 1861 London. 1st ed. 1st print. G $30.00

PROCTOR, Alexander P. *Sculptor in Buckskin: Autobiography.* 1971 OK U Pr. 1st ed. slipcase. EX $30.00

PRODAN, Mario. *Art of the T'ang Potter.* 1961 NY. Viking. Studio Book. 186 p. dj. $85.00

PROKOSCH, Frederic. *America, My Wilderness.* 1972 NY. 1st ed. dj. EX $8.00

PROKOSCH, Frederic. *Ballad of Love.* 1960 Farrar. 1st ed. dj. EX $15.00

PROKOSCH, Frederic. *Voices.* 1983 Farrar. Uncorrected proof. EX $30.00

PRONZINI, Bill. *Arbor House Treasury of Horror.* 1981 Arbor House. dj. EX $30.00

PRONZINI, Bill. *Blowback.* no date. Book Club ed. VG $3.00

PRONZINI, Bill. *Cambodia File.* 1981 Doubleday. 1st ed. $10.00

PRONZINI, Bill. *Cat's Paw.* 1983 Richmond. 1st ed. 1/50. sgn. red cloth. $75.00

PRONZINI, Bill. *Eye.* 1984 St. Martin. 1st ed. dj. VG $14.00

PRONZINI, Bill. *Great Tales of Horror & Supernatural.* 1985 Castle. VG $10.00

PRONZINI, Bill. *Killing in Xanadu.* 1980 Richmond. 1st ed. sgn. issued unbound. $45.00

PRONZINI, Bill. *Nightshades.* no date. Book Club ed. dj. VG $4.00

PRONZINI, Bill. *Snatch.* 1971 Random House. 1st ed. dj. xl. VG $4.00

PRONZINI, Bill. *Stalker.* Random House. 2nd ed. dj. G $7.50

PRONZINI, Bill. *Stalker.* 1971 NY. 1st ed. $40.00

PROSKAUER, J.J. *Spook Crooks!* 1932 Chicago. 1st ed. VG $18.00

PROSKE, B.G. *Brookgreen Gardens Sculpture.* 1968 private print. Ills. 374 p. M $25.00

PROUDFIT, A. *Practical Godliness.* 1813 Salem. 12mo. 399 p. leather. G $26.00

PROUST, Marcel. *Past Recaptured.* 1959 Modern Lib. dj. G $12.50

PROVENSEN, Alice & Martin. *Leonardo Da Vinci Pop-Up Book.* 1985 NY. Viking. Ills 2nd print. M $12.50

PROVENSEN, Alice & Martin. *1st Noel.* 1959 NY. Golden Pr. Ills. 8vo. EX $12.00

PROZINI & MALZBERG. *Night Screams.* 1979 Chicago. 1st ed. dj. EX $20.00

PRUCHA, F.P. *Churches & the Indian Schools 1888-1912.* 1979 NE U Pr. Ills. 178 p. dj. VG $9.00

PRUSSING. *Estate of George Washington, Deceased.* 1927 Boston. 1st ed. dj. VG $42.50

PRY & WHITE. *Big Trees.* 1930 Stanford U Pr. G $12.00

PRYOR, Mary. *American Annual Monitor for 1860.* 1860 NY. G $12.00

PRYOR, Mary. *Life Story of 100 Years Ago.* 1888 Phil. 2nd ed. G $12.00

PUCKETT, Newbell. *Folk Beliefs of the Southern Negro.* 1926 Chapel Hill. 1st ed. 644 p. VG $75.00

PUCKLE, Bertram. *Funerals & Customs: Their Origins & Development.* 1926 London. Ills 1st ed. VG $15.00

PUCKLE, James. *Club; or, Gray Cap for Green Head.* 1834 London. Ills. green cloth. VG $17.00

PUFFENDORF, Samuel. *Introduction to History of Kingdoms & States of Europe.* 1697 London. 8vo. full calf. $65.00

PUGIN, A.C. & A.W. *Gothic Architecture.* 1927 Cleveland. Jansen. 5 vols in 2. EX $50.00

PULLEN, J.J. *20th ME Volunteer Regiment in Civil War.* 1957 Lippincott. Ills 1st ed. 338 p. dj. VG $27.50

PULLITZER, Ralph. *Over the Front in an Aeroplane.* 1915 Burt. Ills. 159 p. dj. VG $28.00

PULVER, Jeffrey. *Biographical Dictionary of Old English Music.* 1927 London. Kegan Paul. VG $30.00

PULVER, Jeffrey. *Dictionary of Old English Music & Musical Instruments.* 1923 London. Kegan Paul. VG $30.00

PUNSHON, E.R. *Conqueror Inn.* 1944 Macmillan. 1st ed. xl. G $6.00

PUPPI, Lionello. *Complete Paintings of Caneletto.* 1968 NY. 1st ed. dj. VG $25.00

PURCHA, Francis Paul. *American Indian Policy in Crisis.* 1976 Norman. 1st ed. dj. VG $18.00

PURCHAS, T.A.R. *Spiritual Adventures of a Business Man.* 1929 London. Psychic Pr. 239 p. G $11.00

PURDY, James. *Children Is All.* 1963 Secker Warburg. 1st English ed. dj. EX $25.00

PURDY, James. *Eustace Chisholm & Works.* 1967 Farrar. 1st ed. dj. EX $25.00

PURDY, James. *In a Shallow Grave.* 1975 Arbor House. 1st ed. dj. EX $20.00

PURDY, James. *Jeremy's Version.* 1970 Doubleday. 1st ed. dj. EX $25.00

PURDY, James. *On the Rebound.* 1970 Black Sparrow. 1st ed. 1/300. sgn. EX $90.00

PURDY, James. *Proud Flesh.* 1980 Northridge. 1st ed. 1/250. sgn. cloth. dj. $40.00

PURDY, James. *Scrap of Paper & the Berry Picker.* 1981 Los Angeles. Ltd ed. 1/330. sgn. cloth. EX $75.00

PURDY, James. *63: Dream Place.* 1957 Gollancz. 1st English ed. dj. VG $25.00

PURNELL, Idella. *Wishing Owl.* 1931 NY. Macmillan. Ills Dehlsen. 1st ed. EX $20.00

PURSELL, Carroll W. *Early Stationary Steam Engines in America.* 1969 Smithsonian. Ills 1st ed. 152 p. VG $15.00

PURSER, Philip. *4 Days to the Fireworks.* 1965 Walker. 1st Am ed. dj. VG $7.50

PURSH, Frederick. *Journal of a Botanical Excursion in Northeastern PA & NY.* 1869 Phil. $75.00

PURTELL, Joseph. *Tiffany Touch.* 1971 Random House. Ills 1st ed. dj. $25.00

PUTNAM, E. *Old Salem.* 1886 Boston. Houghton Mifflin. 120 p. $12.50

PUTNAM, Eban. *Holden Genealogy.* 1923 & 1926. Boston. 2 vol set. $75.00

PUTNAM, G. *Political Debates Between A. Lincoln & S.A. Douglas.* 1926 3rd ed. 8vo. 661 p. G $35.00

PUTNAM, G.P. *Last Flight of Amelia Earhart.* 1937 NY. Ills 1st ed. 226 p. xl. G $5.00

PUTNAM. *Lady.* 1911 Sturgis & Walton. 12mo. 323 p. $7.50

PUZO, Mario. *Fools Die.* 1978 NY. 1st ed. dj. M $10.00

PUZO, Mario. *Sicilian.* 1984 NY. 1st ed. sgn. dj. M $35.00

PUZO, Mario. *Sicilian.* 1984 Simon Schuster. 1st ed. dj. M $12.00

PYLE, Howard. *Howard Pyle's Book of Pirates.* 1921 NY. 1st ed. 4to. VG $85.00

PYLE, Howard. *Howard Pyle's Book of the American Spirit.* 1923 NY/London. Harper. 1st ed. 1st issue. EX $100.00

PYLE, Howard. *Jack Ballister's Fortunes.* 1895 NY. 1st ed. VG $65.00

PYLE, Howard. *Merry Adventures of Robin Hood.* 1933 NY. Scribner. Brandywine ed. rare. EX $150.00

PYLE, Howard. *Merry Adventures of Robin Hood.* 1921 NY. Scribner. Ills Pyle. VG $20.00

PYLE, Howard. *Otto of the Silver Hand.* 1888 Scribner. Ills 1st ed. 179 p. VG $65.00

PYLE, Howard. *Otto of the Silver Hand.* 1927 Scribner. Ills. 172 p. green cloth. VG $25.00

PYLE, Howard. *Pepper & Salt.* no date. NY. Harper. not 1st ed. VG $22.00

PYLE, Howard. *Price of Blood.* 1899 Boston. Ills 1st issue. VG $75.00

PYLE, Howard. *Robin Hood.* 1946 Scribner. New ed. dj. EX $10.00

PYLE, Howard. *Ruby of Kishmoor.* 1908 Harper. Ills Pyle. 1st ed. gray cloth. $20.00

PYLE, Howard. *Story of the Grail & Passing of Arthur.* 1910 NY. Ills 1st ed. tan cloth. VG $80.00

PYLE, Katharine. *Tales of Folk & Fairies.* 1919 Little Brown. Ills 1st ed. 8vo. VG $40.00

PYLE, Katherine. *Giant's Ruby & Other Fairy Tales.* 1903 Little Brown. Ills. 8vo. 292 p. VG $25.00

PYNCHON, Thomas. *Crying of Lot 49.* 1966 NY. 1st ed. dj. VG $40.00

PYNCHON, Thomas. *Crying of Lot 49.* 1966 NY. 1st ed. inscr. dj. EX $125.00

PYNCHON, Thomas. *Journey into the Mind of Watts.* 1983 Westminster. 1st ed. red wraps. $10.00

PYNCHON, Thomas. *Low-Lands.* 1978 London. Ltd 1st ed. 1/1,500. wraps. $20.00

PYNCHON, Thomas. *Secret Integration.* 1980 London. 1st ed. wraps. EX $10.00

PYNCHON, Thomas. *Slow Learner: Early Stories.* 1985 London. 1st ed. dj. EX $22.00

PYNCHON, Thomas. *Small Rain.* no date. London. 1st ed. wraps. EX $15.00

PYNE, S.J. *Biography of Grove Karl Gilbert.* 1980 TX U Pr. Ills. 306 p. dj. EX $20.00

PYNE, W.H. *World in Miniature: England, Scotland, & Ireland.* 1827 Ills. 4 vols in 2. ¾-calf. $475.00

Q

QUACKENBOS, John D. *Body & Spirit*. 1916 NY. 1st ed. 282 p. EX $35.00

QUAIFE, Milo. *Chicago & the Old Northwest: 1673*. 1913 Chicago U Pr. EX $125.00

QUAIFE, Milo. *Chicago Highways: Old & New*. 1923 Keller. Ills 1st ed. EX $35.00

QUAIFE, Milo. *John Askin Papers*. 1928 Detroit. Ltd ed. 1/1,000. sgn. 2 vols. $200.00

QUAIFE, Milo. *Siege of Detroit in 1763*. 1958 Chicago. EX $50.00

QUAIN, Richard. *Dictionary of Medicine*. 1884 NY. 8th ed. 1,816 p. ½-leather. $35.00

QUANTRILL, Malcolm. *Reimi Pietella: Architecture*. Rizzoli. 4to. wraps. $10.00

QUARLES, E.A. *American Pheasant Breeding & Shooting*. 1916 Wilmington. Ills. wraps. fair. $17.00

QUAYLE, Eric. *Collector's Book of Books*. 1971 London. Ills. dj. $20.00

QUAYLE, Eric. *Collector's Book of Books*. 1971 NY. dj. VG $35.00

QUAYLE, William A. *Beside Lake Beautiful*. 1922 Ills 3rd ed. inscr. EX $25.00

QUAYLE, William A. *Prairie & Sea*. 1905 Cincinnati/NY. Ills. fair. $18.00

QUEEN, Ellery. *Brown Fox Mystery*. 1955 Little Brown. 4th ed. dj. VG $15.00

QUEEN, Ellery. *Calamity Town*. no date. Grosset Dunlap. dj. G $6.00

QUEEN, Ellery. *Calamity Town*. 1942 Little Brown. 1st ed. xl. fair. $5.00

QUEEN, Ellery. *Challenge to the Reader*. 1938 Stokes. VG $30.00

QUEEN, Ellery. *Chinese Orange Mystery*. 1934 Stokes. 1st ed. xl. $12.50

QUEEN, Ellery. *Devil To Pay*. 1946 Tower. VG $5.50

QUEEN, Ellery. *Devil To Pay*. 1942 Triangle. 5th ed. $5.00

QUEEN, Ellery. *Double Double*. no date. Book Club ed. VG $3.00

QUEEN, Ellery. *Ellery Queen Omnibus*. no date. Grosset Dunlap. G $5.00

QUEEN, Ellery. *Ellery Queen's Faces of Mystery*. 1977 Dial Pr. 1st ed. dj. VG $10.00

QUEEN, Ellery. *Ellery Queen's Veils of Mystery*. 1980 Dial Pr. 1st ed. dj. VG $12.50

QUEEN, Ellery. *Ellery Queen's 20th Anniversary Annual*. 1965 Random House. 1st ed. dj. VG $14.00

QUEEN, Ellery. *Finishing Stroke*. 1958 NY. 1st ed. dj. EX $20.00

QUEEN, Ellery. *Masterpieces of Mystery*. 1979 Davis. 20 vol set. no djs issued. EX $300.00

QUEEN, Ellery. *New Adventures of Ellery Queen*. no date. Triangle. dj. VG $7.00

QUEEN, Ellery. *NY Murders*. no date. Book Club ed. dj. VG $6.00

QUEEN, Ellery. *Perfect Crime*. 1942 Grosset Dunlap. VG $8.50

QUEEN, Ellery. *Queen's Awards 1949*. 1950 Little Brown. 3rd ed. VG $15.00

QUEEN, Ellery. *Red Chipmunk Mystery*. 1946 Lippincott. 1st ed. dj. VG $45.00

QUEEN, Ellery. *Rogues' Gallery*. 1945 Little Brown. 1st ed. 8vo. dj. EX $45.00

QUEEN, Ellery. *Rogues' Gallery*. 1945 Little Brown. 3rd ed. VG $15.00

QUEEN, Ellery. *Roman Hat Mystery*. 1948 Tower. $10.00

QUEEN, Ellery. *Siamese Twin Mystery*. 1942 Triangle. dj. VG $7.00

QUEEN, Ellery. *Sporting Detective Stories*. 1946 Faber. VG $20.00

QUEEN, Ellery. *There Was an Old Woman*. 1943 Little Brown. 1st ed. VG $30.00

QUEEN, Ellery. *To the Queen's Taste*. 1946 Little Brown. 1st ed. VG $30.00

QUEEN, Ellery. *Tradedy of X*. 1978 CA U Pr. VG $10.00

QUEEN, Ellery. *10 Days' Wonder*. 1948 Little Brown. VG $7.00

QUEEN, Ellery. *4 of Hearts*. 1946 Tower. 1st ed. VG $6.50

QUEEN, Ellery. *4 of Hearts*. 1941 Triangle. 3rd ed. VG $5.50

QUEENY, E.M. *Cheechako*. 1941 Scribner. 1st ed. rare. VG $75.00

QUEENY, E.M. *Prairie Wings: Pen & Camera Flight Studies*. 1946 Phil. 1st ed. G $200.00

QUEENY, E.M. *Prairie Wings: Pen & Camera Flight Studies*. 1947 Phil. 1st trade ed. $115.00

QUEENY, E.M. *Prairie Wings: Pen & Camera Flight Studies*. 1979 Schiffer. Ills. 4to. 256 p. EX $40.00

QUENNELL, Peter. *Masques & Poems*. 1922 Golden Cockerell. 1/375. sgn. $75.00

QUENTIN, Patrick. *Black Widow*. no date. Book Club ed. $3.50

QUENTIN, Patrick. *Darker Grows the Valley*. 1935 Cassell. 1st ed. xl. G $20.00

QUENTIN, Patrick. *Follower*. no date. Book Club ed. dj. VG $4.00

QUENTIN, Patrick. *Follower*. 1950 Simon Schuster. 1st ed. dj. VG $15.00

QUENTIN, Patrick. *Green-Eyed Monster*. 1960 Gollancz. 1st ed. dj. VG $20.00

QUENTIN, Patrick. *Man with 2 Wives*. no date. Book Club ed. VG $3.00

QUENTIN, Patrick. *Ordeal of Mrs. Snow & Other Stories*. 1962 NY. 1st print. dj. VG $10.00

QUENTIN, Patrick. *Puzzle for Players*. no date. Simon Schuster. xl. $5.00

QUENTIN, Patrick. *Run to Death*. no date. Book Club ed. dj. G $3.00

QUENTIN, Patrick. *Run to Death*. 1948 Simon Schuster. VG $7.00

QUENTIN, Patrick. *Shadow of Guilt*. no date. Book Club ed. dj. VG $4.00

QUICK, Clifford. *Why Endure Rheumatism & Arthritis?* no date. Allen Unwin. VG $10.00

QUICK, Jim. *Trout Fishing & Trout Flies*. 1957 Countryman Pr. Ills. 252 p. dj. VG $10.00

QUICK, Michael. *American Portraiture in Grand Manner 1720-1920*. 1981 Los Angeles. Ills. 4to. 228 p. wraps. $30.00

QUIGLEY, Carroll. *Tragedy & Hope*. 1966 NY. 1st ed. dj. EX $50.00

QUILLER-COUCH, Arthur. *Brother Copas*. 1911 NY. 1st ed. EX $12.00

QUILLER-COUCH, Arthur. *Castle Door*. no date. Book Club ed. dj. EX $3.50

QUILLER-COUCH, Arthur. *Oxford Books of Ballads*. 1955 cloth. $20.00

QUILLER-COUCH, Arthur. *Shorter Stories*. 1944 Dent. 1st ed. dj. VG $16.00

QUILLER-COUCH, Arthur. *12 Dancing Princesses & Other Fairy Tales*. Doran. Ills K Neilsen. 244 p. $225.00

QUINCEY, J. Wong. *Chinese Hunter*. no date. (1940) Ills. 382 p. dj. VG $60.00

QUINN, A.H. *Edgar Allan Poe: Letters & Documents in E. Pratt Free Lib*. 1941 NY. Scolars Facsimiles. 1/500. VG $35.00

QUINN, Edward. *Max Ernst.* 1984 Barcelona. Poligrafa. Ills. folio. dj. $150.00

QUINN, P.T. *Pear Culture for Profit.* 1869 NY. Ills 1st ed. 12mo. 136 p. $25.00

QUINN, Seabury. *Alien Flesh.* 1977 Oswald Train. 1st ed. dj. EX $9.00

QUINN, Seabury. *Phantom Fighter.* 1966 Sauk City. 1st ed. dj. EX $30.00

QUINN, Sister Bernetta. *Ezra Pound.* 1972 Columbia. 1st ed. dj. EX $20.00

QUINTERO. *If You Don't Dance They Beat You.* 1974 Little Brown. 1st ed. dj. M $15.00

QUINTON, Robert. *Strange Adventures of Captain Quinton.* 1912 Christian Herald. 486 p. VG $18.00

R

RABACK, Dr. C.W. *Mysteries of Astrology & the Wonders of Magic.* 1854 Boston. 238 p. VG $135.00

RABAN, Jonathan. *Old Glory: American Voyage.* 1981 NY. 1st ed. dj. EX $25.00

RABB, K.M. *J. Parson's Tour Through IN in 1840.* 1920 NY. 1st ed. 391 p. dj. VG $27.50

RABELAIS. *Works of Rabelais.* 1927 Bodley Head. Ills Pape. Ltd ed. 2 vol set. $95.00

RABINOWITZ, A. *Jaguar: Struggle & Triumph in the Jungles of Belize.* 1986 Arbor House. Ills 1st ed. 368 p. dj. EX $18.00

RACKHAM, Arthur. *Allie's Fairy Book.* 1915 London. 12 plts. fair. $17.00

RACKHAM, Arthur. *Arthur Rackham's Book of Pictures.* 1913 London. 1st trade ed. rebound. EX $225.00

RACKHAM, Arthur. *Arthur Rackham's Book of Pictures.* 1979 Avenel. dj. EX $9.00

RACKHAM, Arthur. *Arthur Rackham's Book of Pictures.* 1927 Heinemann. EX $195.00

RACKHAM, Arthur. *Cinderella.* 1919 Heinemann. Ills Ltd Deluxe ed. 1/300. VG $850.00

RACKHAM, Arthur. *Cinderella.* 1919 London. Evans. Deluxe ed. 1/300. sgn. EX $895.00

RACKHAM, Arthur. *Compleat Angler.* 1931 London. VG $52.00

RACKHAM, Arthur. *Gulliver's Travels.* 1909 Dent Dutton. 1st ed. 4to. 291 p. cloth. EX $95.00

RACKHAM, Arthur. *Night Before Christmas.* no date. Oxford U Pr. dj. G $15.00

RACKHAM, Arthur. *Peer Gynt.* no date. Phil. 1st Am ed. dj. $115.00

RACKHAM, Arthur. *Peter Pan in Kensington Gardens.* 1919 Scribner. 16 color plts. VG $65.00

RACKHAM, Arthur. *Peter Pan in Kensington Gardens.* 1907 London. 50 plts. gilt calf. fair. $32.00

RACKHAM, Arthur. *Puck of Pook's Hill.* 1906 Doubleday Page. 4 plts. xl. G $22.00

RACKHAM, Arthur. *Ring of the Niblung.* 1939 Garden City. 48 color plts. dj. $135.00

RACKHAM, Arthur. *Romance of King Arthur.* 1917 NY. Macmillan. 1st ed. gilt green cloth. $145.00

RACKHAM, Arthur. *Siegfried & the Twilight of the Gods.* 1911 NY. 1st trade ed. G $40.00

RACKHAM, Arthur. *Sleeping Beauty.* no date. Evans. Deluxe ed. 1/625. sgn. 110 p. $795.00

RACKHAM, Arthur. *Some British Ballads.* no date. London. 1/575. VG $8.50

RACKHAM, Arthur. *Tales From Shakespeare.* 1939 Temple Pr. 12 plts. $25.00

RACKHAM, Arthur. *Undine.* 1909 London. Ltd ed. 1/250. 4to. sgn. EX $450.00

RACKHAM, Arthur. *Where the Blue Begins.* 1922 Lippincott. Ills. 4to. blue cloth. VG $45.00

RACKHAM, Arthur. *Wind in the Willows.* 1940 Heritage. Ills 1st ed. slipcase. VG $45.00

RACKHAM, Arthur. *Wind in the Willows.* 1954 NY. 12 color plts. dj. VG $25.00

RACKHAM, Bernard. *Early Staffordshire Pottery.* 1951 London. Faber. Ills. 8vo. 62 p. dj. $45.00

RADCLIFFE, Ann. *Mysteries of Udolpho.* 1803 London. 5th ed. 4 vol set. VG $50.00

RADCLIFFE, Garnett. *Flower Gang.* 1930 Boston. Houghton Mifflin. 1st ed. dj. $10.00

RADCLIFFE, William. *Fishing From Earliest Times.* 1926 Murray. Revised ed. 494 p. scarce. EX $65.00

RADCLIFFE, William. *Fishing From Earliest Times.* 1921 Dutton. 1st ed. VG $45.00

RADCLIFFE-BROWN, A.B. *Adaman Islanders.* 1948 Free Pr. Ills 1st Am ed. 510 p. VG $18.00

RADER, Dotson. *Blood Dues.* 1973 Knopf. 1st ed. dj. EX $15.00

RADFORD, R.L. *Sylvia Sanders & the Tangled Web.* 1946 Whitman. dj. VG $7.00

RADFORD, William. *Steel Square & Its Uses.* 1907 Chicago. Ills. 2 vol set. VG $30.00

RADIGUET, Raymond. *Devil in the Flesh.* 1948 Black Sun. VG $45.00

RADIN, Paul. *Road of Life & Death: Ritual Drama of American Indians.* 1945 NY. Pantheon. 1st ed. VG $20.00

RADKE, E.F. *New Angles on Bass Fishing.* 1955 Greenburg. Ills. 188 p. VG $7.50

RADLEY, Shelia. *Who Saw Him Die?* 1987 Scribner. 1st ed. dj. VG $15.00

RADUE, W.F. *Diseases of Children.* 1908 Chicago. Clinic Pub. 176 p. $20.00

RAE, John B. *American Automobile: Brief History.* 1934 Chicago Ills 1st ed. 265 p. dj. VG $10.00

RAE, John B. *American Automobile: Brief History.* 1965 Chicago. G $10.00

RAE, John. *Grasshopper Green & the Meadow Mice.* 1922 Volland. Ills 1st ed. 12mo. VG $18.00

RAE, John. *Lucy Locket, Doll with the Pocket!* 1928 Volland. Ills 6th print. $40.00

RAE, John. *New Adventures of Alice.* 1917 Volland. Ills. 4to. G $30.00

RAE, William E. *Treasure of Outdoor Life.* 1975 NY. dj. VG $14.00

RAEBURN, Harold. *Mountaineering Art.* 1920 NY. Ills 1st ed. EX $35.00

RAEMAEKERS, Louis. *Raemaekers' Cartoons.* 1916 NY. 1st ed. G $45.00

RAFFALOVICH, G. *Benito Mussolini.* 1923 Owl. wraps. G $50.00

RAFFERTY, Kathleen. *Dell Crossword Dictionary.* 1964 Delacorte. 1st ed. dj. VG $7.00

RAFINESQUE. *Western Minerva; or, American Annals.* 1949 Peter Smith. reprint. EX $40.00

RAGG, Lonsdale. *Some of My Tree Friends.* c 1932. De La More Pr. 8vo. 31 p. VG $50.00

RAHT, Carlysle. *Romance of Davis Mountain & Big Bend Country.* 1919 Rathbooks. Ills. presentation. 381 p. $30.00

RAILE, Vilate. *So There!* 1942 Bookmark Pr. Ills Dickman. 1st ed. VG $10.00

RAIMON, De Loi. *Trails of the Troubadors.* 1926 London/NY. 1st ed. VG $17.50

RAINES, W.M. *Border Breed.* 1944 Triangle. 4th ed. $6.00

RAINES, W.M. *Daughter of the Dons.* 1914 Ills Hutchinson. 320 p. $5.00

RAINES, W.M. *Famous Sheriffs & Outlaws.* no date. Perma. G $5.00

RAINES, W.M. *Famous Sheriffs & Western Outlaws.* 1944 New Home Library. 294 p. EX $15.00

RAINES, W.M. *Tangled Trails.* 1921 1st ed. dj. VG $25.00

RAINES, W.M. *To Ride the River With.* 1936 Houghton Mifflin. VG $12.50

RAINES, W.M. *TX Man.* 1928 Doubleday Doran. VG $12.00

RAINES, W.M. *Yukon Trail.* 1942 Triangle. 7th ed. dj. VG $9.00

RAINEY, G. *When, How, & Why of OK.* 1939 private print. 61 p. VG $10.00

RAINEY, Mrs. George. *In Memory.* 1949 Enid, OK. private print. Ills. pb. EX $20.00

RAINS, Marie Custis. *Lazy Liza's Tricks.* 1953 Phil. Ills Neville. 1st ed. dj. VG $22.50

RAINSFORD, Marcus. *Historical Account of Black Empire of Haiti.* 1805 London. Albion. Ills 1st ed. 4to. maps. 467 p. $300.00

RAINWATER & FELGER. *Collector's Guide to Spoons Around the World.* 1976 NY. Ills 1st ed. 406 p. dj. EX $35.00

RAIT, R.S. *Royal Palaces of England.* 1911 NY. Ills. 377 p. $25.00

RALBOTT & HOBART. *Biographical Directory of Railway Officials of America.* 1885 Chicago. 1st ed. EX $40.00

RALFS, J. *British Desmidieae.* 1848 London. Ills 1st ed. $125.00

RALPH, Julian. *On Canada's Frontier.* 1892 NY. Ills Remington. 1st ed. EX $75.00

RALPH, Julian. *Our Great West.* 1893 NY. Ills 1st ed. VG $25.00

RAMAZZINI, Bernardini. *Diseases of Workers.* 1940 Chicago U Pr. Trans W Wright. 1st ed. $45.00

RAMBOSSEON, J. *Les Pierres Precieuses.* 1870 Paris. Ills. 8vo. 298 p. ½-morocco. $45.00

RAMIE, G. *Picasso's Ceramics.* 1976 NY. 1st ed. dj. EX $45.00

RAMP, L.C. & D.L. *Civil War in the Indian Territory.* 1975 Presidential Pr. Ills. dj. EX $35.00

RAMPA, T. Lobsang. *3rd Eye.* 1958 Doubleday. Ills 1st Am ed. dj. VG $10.00

RAMPA, T. Lobsang. *3rd Eye.* 1956 London. 1st ed. dj. scarce. EX $85.00

RAMSAY, David. *History of American Revolution.* 1893 Dublin. 2 vols in 1. brown leather. VG $45.00

RAMSAY, John. *American Potters & Pottery.* 1939 Clinton, MA. Ills 1st ed. biblio. 304 p. $55.00

RAMSAY, William. *Argon: New Constituent of the Atmosphere.* 1896 WA. 4to. wraps. VG $75.00

RAMSAY, William. *Essays Biographical & Chemical.* 1908 London. Constable. 1st ed. sgn. 247 p. $95.00

RAMSDEN, Charles. *French Bookbinders 1789-1848.* 1950 London. Ills 1st ed. 4to. 228 p. EX $185.00

RAMSEY, Carolyn. *Cajuns on the Bayous.* 1957 Hastings House. Ills. 300 p. dj. VG $15.00

RAMSEY & LAWRENCE. *Outdoor Living Room.* 1932 Macmillan. 126 p. blue cloth. VG $20.00

RAND, A. *Fountainhead.* 1943 IN. 1st ed. G $15.00

RAND, Austin L. *American Water & Game Birds.* 1956 Dutton. Ills 1st ed. 4to. 239 p. EX $15.00

RAND, Ayn. *Atlas Shrugged.* 1957 NY. 1st print. xl. $25.00

RAND, C. *Nostalgia for Camels.* 1957 Little Brown. 1st ed. dj. EX $12.00

RAND, E.S. *Treatise on Hardy & Tender Bulbs & Tubers.* 1866 Boston. 1st ed. 12mo. 306 p. G $25.00

RAND, Edward K. *Quest of Virgil's Birthplace.* 1930 Cambridge. Harvard. 1st ed. VG $15.00

RAND, James. *Run for the Trees.* 1966 NY City. 1st Am ed. dj. VG $35.00

RAND, Paul. *Thoughts on Design.* 1947 1st ed. dj. VG $50.00

RANDALL, Bob. *Calling.* 1981 Simon Schuster. Advance copy. dj. EX $15.00

RANDALL, J.H. *Landscape & Looking Glass: Willa Cather's Search for Value.* 1960 Riverside Pr. 1st ed. 423 p. dj. $20.00

RANDALL, J.H. *New Light on Immortality; or, Significance of Research.* 1921 NY. 1st ed. 174 p. EX $15.00

RANDALL, Jane. *When Toys Could Talk.* 1939 Saalfield. Ills Peat. 4to. 22 p. VG $25.00

RANDALL, Randolph C. *James Hall: Spokesman for the New West.* 1964 OH U Pr. VG $12.00

RANDELL, Brian. *Origins of Digital Computers.* 1982 Berlin. Verlag. 3rd ed. 580 p. EX $30.00

RANDHAWA & GALBRAITH. *Scenes, Themes, & Legends of Indian Painting.* 1968 Boston. Houghton Mifflin. $25.00

RANDI. *Houdini: His Life & Art.* 1977 Ills 1st ed. dj. EX $15.00

RANDISI, Robert J. *Eyes Have It: 1st Private Eye Writers of America Anthology.* 1984 NY. Ltd 1st ed. 1/250. sgns. slipcase. EX $55.00

RANDLE, Gen. E.H. *Safi Adventure.* 1965 Clearwater. presentation. $35.00

RANDOLPH, Edmund. *Hell Among the Yearlings.* 1955 Norton. Ills 1st Am ed. 308 p. dj. EX $25.00

RANDOLPH, Edmund. *Hell Among the Yearlings.* 1978 Chicago. Lakeside Classic. EX $10.00

RANDOLPH, Isham. *Gleanings From a Harvest of Memories.* 1937 Columbia. inscr. VG $40.00

RANDOLPH, John W. *World of Wood, Field, & Stream: Outdoorsman's Collection.* no date. Holt. Ills John Groth. dj. VG $4.00

RANDOLPH, John. *Marsmen in Burma.* 1946 TX. Ltd 1st ed. sgn. VG $87.50

RANDOLPH, John. *TX Brags.* 1952 Tomball, TX. private print. Ills. pb. EX $3.00

RANDOLPH, Mary. *VA Housewife.* 1836 Baltimore. $125.00

RANDOLPH, Paschal Beverly. *After Death: Disembodiment of Man.* 1866 Revised 4th ed. 260 p. VG $55.00

RANDOLPH, Paschal Beverly. *Eulis: History of Love.* 1906 4th ed. 221 p. G $65.00

RANDOLPH, Vance. *From an Ozark Holler.* 1933 NY. 1st ed. dj. VG $25.00

RANDOLPH, Vance. *Funny Stories About Hillbillies.* 1944 Haldeman Julius. 24 p. pb. EX $5.00

RANDOLPH, Vance. *Funny Stories From AR.* 1943 Haldeman Julius. 24 p. pb. EX $5.00

RANDOLPH, Vance. *Ozark Mountain Folks.* 1932 Vanguard. Ltd ed. 1/250. sgn. dj. $25.00

RANDOLPH, W. Eliot. *Wilmer Opthalmological Institute 1925-1975.* 1976 Baltimore. Williams Wilkins. VG $15.00

RANHOFFER, Charles. *Epicurean.* 1920 Chicago. G $95.00

RANKINE, John. *Never the Same Door.* 1967 Dobson. 1st ed. dj. EX $14.00

RANKINE, John. *Ring of Garamas.* 1971 Dobson. 1st ed. $15.00

RANSLEBEN, Guido E. *100 Years of Comfort in TX: Centennial History.* 1974 Naylor. Revised Enlarged ed. sgn. dj. $25.00

RANSOM, J.C. *Kenyon Critics.* 1951 World. 1st ed. dj. VG $30.00

RANSOME, Arthur. *Oscar Wilde: A Critical Study.* 1913 NY. VG $25.00

RANSOME, Arthur. *Russian Fairy Tales.* no date. NY. Peter Pauper. 122 p. slipcase. $40.00

RANSOME, Stephen. *Frazer Acquittal.* 1955 Crime Club. 1st ed. dj. VG $10.00

RANSOME, Stephen. *Sin File.* 1965 Dodd Mead. dj. VG $10.00

RANSOME-WALLIS, P. *Royal Navy.* 1962 London. Ills 3rd ed. 64 p. wraps. G $5.00

RAO, Raja. *Serpent & the Rope.* 1960 London. Murray. 1st ed. VG $35.00

RAPHAEL, Frederic. *Somerset Maugham & His World.* 1976 NY. 1st ed. dj. M $10.00

RAPPAPORT, A. *Love Affairs of Vatican.* c 1912. London. Ills. VG $15.00

RASCOE, B. *Theodore Dreiser Monograph.* 1925 NY. 1st ed. dj. EX $12.00

RASCOE, Burton. *American Reader.* 1938 Chicago. dj. VG $20.00

RASCOE, Burton. *Belle Starr: Bandit Queen.* 1941 NY. Ills 1st ed. dj. VG $15.00

RASHLEIGH, Ralph. *Adventures of Ralph Rashleigh: Penal Exile in Australia.* 1929 London. Ills. 349 p. VG $22.50

RASKIN, Saul. *Hagadah for Passover.* 1941 NY. Ills. VG $40.00

RASKY, Frank. *Polar Voyagers.* 1976 McGraw Hill. cloth. VG $10.00

RASTELL, John. *Pastime of People; or, Chronicles of Divers Realms.* 1811 London. Ills. 4to. 299 p. VG $150.00

RATAJ, K.; & ZUKAL, R. *Aquarium Fishes & Plants.* 1971 Spring. Ills. 132 p. VG $5.00

RATCHFORD, J.W. *Some Reminiscences of Persons & Incidents of the Civil War.* 1971 Shoal Creek. facsimile of 1909. EX $30.00

RATCLIFF, A.J.J. *History of Dreams.* 1923 Boston. VG $20.00

RATH, E.J. *6th Speed.* 1908 NY. Moffat. 1st ed. VG $10.00

RATH, Ida. *Boy Planet Seeker.* 1963 Dodge City. inscr. VG $35.00

RATH, Ida. *Star That Did Not Twinkle.* 1963 Antonio. Naylor. G $20.00

RATH, Ida. *Year of Charles.* 1955 Antonio. Naylor. 1st ed. G $15.00

RATHBONE, Basil. *In & Out of Character.* 1962 Doubleday. 1st ed. dj. VG $32.50

RATHBONE, Julian. *Diamonds Bid.* 1967 Walker. 1st ed. dj. EX $10.00

RATHBONE, Julian. *Euro-Killers.* 1979 Pantheon. 1st ed. dj. VG $12.50

RATHBONE, Julian. *Watching the Detectives.* 1983 Pantheon. 1st ed. dj. VG $14.00

RATHBONE, Perry T. *Westward the Way: Character & Development of LA Territory.* 1954 St. Louis. dj. EX $35.00

RATHBONE & TARPLEY. *Fabrics & Dress.* 1931 Houghton Mifflin. 430 p. $5.00

RATHBUN, M.J. *Grapsoid Crabs of America.* 1918 USNM. Ills. 461 p. cloth. EX $60.00

RATHBUN, M.J. *Oxystomatous & Allied Crabs of America.* 1937 Smithsonian. Ills. 278 p. wraps. VG $30.00

RATHBUN, M.J. *Spider Crabs of America.* 1925 USNM. Ills. 613 p. cloth. EX $60.00

RATIGAN, William. *Great Lakes Shipwrecks & Survivals.* 1960 Galahad. Revised ed. 333 p. dj. VG $11.00

RAU, Santha Rama. *East of Home.* 1950 NY. dj. VG $10.00

RAVEN, R. *Golden Dreams & Leaden Realities.* 1853 NY. 12mo. cloth. G $45.00

RAVEN, Simon. *Boys Will Be Boys.* 1963 London. 1st ed. dj. VG $20.00

RAVEN, Simon. *Brother Cain.* 1959 London. 1st ed. dj. VG $27.00

RAVEN, Simon. *Close of Play.* 1962 London. 1st ed. dj. EX $40.00

RAVEN & ROBERTS. *Class Destroyers of WWII.* 1979 London. Ills. 56 p. wraps. EX $10.00

RAVENEL. *Charleston: Place & People.* 1906 NY. 1st ed. VG $30.00

RAVENSCROFT. *Spear of Destiny.* 1973 NY. $35.00

RAVITCH, Michael L. *Romance of Russian Medicine.* 1937 NY. Liveright. 1st ed. VG $20.00

RAVITZ, Abe. *Clarence Darrow & the American Literary Tradition.* 1962 Western Reserve U Pr. 1st ed. $10.00

RAWLINGS, A.L. *Theory of Gyroscopic Compass & Its Deviations.* 1944 NY. Macmillan. Ills 2nd ed. 182 p. dj. VG $12.00

RAWLINGS, Marjorie K. *Cross Creek Cookery.* 1942 Scribner. 1st ed. dj. VG $15.00

RAWLINGS, Marjorie K. *Cross Creek.* 1942 NY. 1st ed. dj. VG $25.00

RAWLINGS, Marjorie K. *Cross Creek.* 1942 Scribner. 1st ed. dj. EX $50.00

RAWLINGS, Marjorie K. *Marjorie Kinnan Rawlings' Cookbook.* 1960 London. 1st ed. dj. VG $28.00

RAWLINGS, Marjorie K. *Yearling.* 1938 NY. Scribner. Ills Shenton. 1st ed. dj. VG $35.00

RAWLINGS, Marjorie K. *Yearling.* 1939 NY. Ills Wyeth. 1st ed. VG $50.00

RAWLS, Wilson. *Where the Red Fern Grows.* 1961 Doubleday. sgn. $20.00

RAWMAEKERS, Louis. *Kultur in Cartoons.* 1917 NY. 1st ed. EX $35.00

RAWSON, Marion N. *Candle Days: Story of Early American Arts & Implements.* 1927 NY/London. 1st ed. dj. VG $35.00

RAWSON, Marion N. *Candle-Day Art.* 1938 Dutton. 1st ed. dj. $12.50

RAWSON, P. *Art of Drawing.* 1984 NY. Ills. 106 p. $30.00

RAWSON, P.S. *Indian Sword.* 1969 Arco. Ills. 108 p. dj. EX $10.00

RAY, C.; & CIAMPI, E. *Underwater Guide to Marine Life.* 1956 Barnes. Ills. 338 p. dj. EX $10.00

RAY, Dorothy. *Artists of the Tundra & the Sea.* 1961 WA U Pr. dj. $17.50

RAY, Dorothy. *Eskimo Art: Tradition & Innovation in North AK.* 1977 WA U Pr. $12.00

RAY, Ginger. *Bending Cross.* 1949 Rutgers. VG $10.00

RAY, Gordon N. *Letters of William Makepiece Thackeray.* 1945 Harvard U Pr. 4 vol set. xl. G $35.00

RAY, Joseph M. *President: Rex, Princeps, Imperator?* 1969 TX Western Pr. 1st ed. 101 p. cloth. M $12.00

RAY, Joseph M. *Thomason: Autobiography of a Federal Judge.* 1971 TX Western Pr. 1st ed. 131 p. cloth. dj. $12.00

RAY, Man. *Man Ray: Self-Portrait.* 1963 Boston. Little Brown. 1st ed. dj. $50.00

RAY, Michele. *2 Shores of Hell.* 1968 NY. Ills. 217 p. dj. VG $15.00

RAYBURN, O.E. *Eureka Springs Story.* 1954 Times Echo. Ills. 80 p. pb. EX $5.00

RAYER, F.G. *Tomorrow Sometimes Comes.* 1951 Home/Van Thal. 1st ed. VG $15.00

RAYMOND, Alex. *Flash Gordon in the Caverns of Mongo.* 1936 NY. Grosset Dunlap. 1st ed. dj. $125.00

RAYMOND, Alex. *Flash Gordon: Into the Water World of Mongo.* 1971 NY. Nostalgia. 8vo. cloth. VG $22.50

RAYMOND, Henry. *Life, Public Services, & State Papers of Abraham Lincoln.* 1865 NY. G $30.00

RAYMOND, James F. *Lost Colony.* 1891 Phil. Petersen. 1st ed. VG $40.00

RAYMOND, Litzka. *How To Read Palms.* 1950 Perma. $5.00

RAYMOND, Louise. *Child's Story of the Nativity.* 1943 Random House. Ills Masha. 4to. dj. EX $15.00

RAYMOND, M. *God Goes to Murderer's Row.* 1951 Bruce. dj. VG $9.00

RAYMOND, Margaret. *Linnet on the Threshold.* 1930 NY. Jr Literary Guild. Ills. G $7.00

RAYMOND, P.E. *Prehistoric Life.* 1939 Harvard U Pr. Ills. 324 p. VG $17.50

RAYMOND, Steve. *Year of the Angler.* 1973 Winchester. Ills 1st ed. 205 p. dj. EX $12.50

RAYNAL, Maurice. *History of Modern Painting.* 1905 Skira. 3 vol set. $125.00

RAYNE, Mrs. M.L. *What Can a Woman Do?; or, Her Position in Business World.* 1884 Detroit. cloth. VG $20.00

RAYTER, Joe. *Stab in the Dark.* 1955 Mill Morrow. 1st ed. dj. G $15.00

RAYZER, G. *Flowering Cacti.* 1984 Hippocrene. Ills. 181 p. EX $12.00

READ, George H. *Last Cruise of the Saginaw.* 1912 Boston. Ltd ed. 1/150. VG $30.00

READ, Grantly Dick. *Childbirth Without Fear.* 1957 British Book Service. dj. VG $6.00

READ, Herbert. *Art Now.* 1936 London. Revised ed. EX $12.50

READ, Herbert. *Innocent Eye.* 1933 London. 1st ed. dj. EX $20.00

READ, Herbert. *Staffordshire Pottery Figures.* 1929 London. Duckworth. Ills. 4to. cloth. $75.00

READ, John. *Alchemist in Life, Literature, & Art.* 1947 London. Nelson. 1st ed. sgn. 100 p. $30.00

READ, John. *Henry Moore: Portrait of an Artist.* 1979 London. 1st ed. dj. VG $15.00

READ, K. *High Valley.* 1965 Scribner. Ills. 266 p. dj. EX $12.00

READ, M.C. *Archeology of OH.* c 1888. Cleveland. Ills. 117 p. fair. $65.00

READ, Miss. *No Holly for Miss Quinn.* 1976 Boston. Houghton Mifflin. 1st ed. dj. $15.00

READ, Miss. *Over the Gate.* 1965 Boston. 1st ed. dj. M $18.00

READ, Opie. *Bolanyo.* 1897 Chicago. Ills Parrish. 1st ed. G $22.00

READ, Opie. *Starbucks.* 1902 Chicago. VG $25.00

READ, Susannah. *Needleworker's Constant Companion.* 1978 NY. Ills. VG $30.00

READ, Thomas B. *Female Poets of America.* 1866 Phil. Ills. 478 p. full leather. EX $48.00

READ. *Astronomical Dictionary.* 1817 New Haven. Woodward. 16mo. 207 p. $7.50

READ. *Village Affairs.* 1st Am ed. dj. EX $23.50

READE, Charles. *Cloister & the Hearth.* 1861 NY. 1st Am ed. $60.00

READE, Charles. *Cloister & the Hearth.* 1926 London. Harrap. Ills E Paul. 706 p. $5.00

READE, Charles. *Cloister & the Hearth.* 1893 Ills Johnson Harper. 2 vols. $12.50

READE, Hamish. *Comeback for Stark.* 1968 Putnam. dj. VG $10.00

READER'S DIGEST. *Book of British Birds.* 1969 1st ed. dj. EX $25.00

READER'S DIGEST. *Great World Atlas.* 1963 1st ed. folio. 232 p. VG $7.00

READER'S DIGEST. *Marvels & Mysteries of Our Animal World.* 1964 Ills. 4to. 320 p. dj. EX $10.00

READER'S DIGEST. *Natural Wonders of the World.* 1980 Ills. 4to. 463 p. maps. EX $10.00

READING. *Arrows Over TX.* 1960 Naylor. 1st ed. dj. EX $60.00

REAGAN, John H. *Memoirs of John H. Reagan.* 1906 Neale Pub. 8vo. cloth. xl. VG $95.00

REAGAN, Ronald. *Where's the Rest of Me.* 1965 NY. 1st ed. dj. VG $17.50

REAGE, Pauline. *Return to the Chateau.* 1971 Grove Pr. 1st ed. 100 p. dj. $50.00

REATH, Nancy Andrews. *Weaves of Hand-Loom Fabrics.* 1927 Phil. Ills. 8vo. VG $45.00

RECHY, John. *Sexual Outlaw.* 1977 Grove Pr. 1st ed. dj. VG $15.00

RECHY. *Numbers.* 1967 NY. 1st ed. dj. G $12.00

RECINOS & GOETZ. *Annals of Cakchiquels & Title of the Lords of Totonicapan.* 1953 OK U Pr. 1st ed. dj. VG $12.00

REDDING, J. Saunders. *No Day of Triumph.* 1942 NY. Harper. 716 p. $4.50

REDDISH, Claude. *Chronicle of Memories.* 1950 Miami. 1st ed. presentation. EX $50.00

REDFIELD, Edith S. *Seattle Memories.* 1930 Boston. Ills 1st ed. VG $35.00

REDFORD, Robert. *Outlaw Trail.* 1978 London. 1st ed. dj. VG $12.00

REDGATE, John. *Killing Season.* no date. Book Club ed. VG $3.00

REDGROVE, H. Stanley. *Alchemy: Ancient & Modern.* 1922 London. Rider. Ills 2nd ed. 144 p. VG $20.00

REDMAN, L.A. *Einstein Delusion & Other Essays.* 1926 San Francisco. Robertson. 1st ed. 217 p. VG $20.00

REDNER, Morton. *Getting Out.* 1971 NY. Walker. 1st ed. dj. M $15.00

REDPATH, James. *Guide to Haiti.* 1861 Boston. 1st ed. fld map. 180 p. VG $75.00

REDPATH, James. *Public Life of Capt. John Brown.* 1860 Boston. Ills 1st ed. 12mo. 407 p. $32.00

REDWAY, L.D. *History of Medical Society of Westchester Co. 1797-1947.* EX $25.00

REECE, Maynard. *Waterfowl: Art of Maynard Reece.* 1985 Abrams. Ills. 4to. 179 p. dj. EX $45.00

REED, Alma. *Mexican Muralists.* 1960 Crown. 1st ed. dj. $20.00

REED, Andrew. *Rolls Plumbe: Authentic Memoir of a Child.* c 1857. Am Tract Soc. VG $10.00

REED, C.A. *American Game Birds.* 1912 private print. Ills. 64 p. VG $10.00

REED, C.A. *American Game Birds.* 1912 Reed. Ills 1st ed. 64 p. VG $14.00

REED, C.A. *Guide to Taxidermy.* 1908 Reed. Ills. 304 p. G $14.00

REED, C.A. *North American Birds' Eggs.* 1904 NY. fair. VG $20.00

REED, Douglas. *Next Horizon.* 1946 Cape. 4th ed. VG $5.00

REED, Earl H. *Silver Arrow & Other Romances of Dune Country.* 1926 Chicago. 1st ed. sgn. VG $25.00

REED, Earl H. *Sketches in Jacobia.* 1919 private print. G $40.00

REED, Ishmael. *Flight to Canada.* 1976 Random House. 1st ed. dj. EX $30.00

REED, Ishmael. *Last of LA Red.* 1974 Random House. 1st ed. dj. EX $30.00

REED, J. Eugene. *Masterpieces of German Art.* c 1880s. Phil. folio. 2 vol set. ¾@-morocco. $125.00

REED, John. *Apology for the Rite of Infant Baptism.* 1806 Providence. 16mo. mottled calf. VG $40.00

REED, Kit. *Fort Privilege.* 1985 Doubleday. 1st ed. $15.00

REED, Kit. *Killer Mice.* 1976 Gollancz. 1st ed. dj. EX $14.00

REED, Kit. *Magic Time.* 1980 Putnam. 1st ed. dj. xl. $5.00

REED, Kit. *Revenge of the Senior Citizens Pluss.* 1986 Doubleday. 1st ed. dj. VG $15.00

REED, Louis. *Burning Springs.* 1985 Huntington, WV. Ills. 275 p. wraps. EX $10.00

REED, Myrtle. *Book of Clever Beasts.* 1904 NY. Ills Newell. G $22.00

REED, Myrtle. *Flowers of the Dusk.* 1910 Putnam. 341 p. $27.00

REED, Stanley. *All Color Book of Oriental Carpets & Rugs.* 1972 Crescent Crown. Ills. 72 p. dj. $22.50

REED, Stanley. *Oriental Rugs & Carpets.* 1972 London. Octopus. Ills. 96 p. dj. $18.50

REED, Walt. *Great American Illustrators.* 1979 NY. Ills. 159 p. EX $17.50

REED, Walt. *Harold Von Schmidt Draws & Paints the Old West.* 1972 Northland. 1st ed. dj. EX $40.00

REED, Walt. *Illustrator in America.* 1966 NY. 1st ed. dj. VG $40.00

REED, William. *Olaf Wieghorst.* 1976 Northland. $15.00

REED & BEAMONT. *Typhoon & Tempset at War.* 1974 London. Allan. 1st ed. EX $15.00

REELING, Viola C. *Evanston: Its Land & Its People.* 1928 IL. Ills. 468 p. VG $40.00

REEP, Diana. *Rescue & Romance.* 1982 Popular Pr. VG $15.00

REES, J.R. *Brotherhood of Letters.* 1889 NY. 1st Am ed. 271 p. $10.00

REESE, David M. *Phrenology.* 1836 NY. 1st ed. 195 p. VG $45.00

REEVE, Arthur B. *Craig Kennedy Listens In.* no date. Mckinlay Stone Mackenzie. VG $10.00

REEVE, Arthur B. *Craig Kennedy on the Farm.* no date. Mckinlay Stone Mackenzie. $12.50

REEVE, Arthur B. *Ear in the Wall.* no date. Hodder Stoughton. VG $9.00

REEVE, Arthur B. *Gold of Gods.* 1915 McClelland. 1st Canadian print. $12.00

REEVE, Arthur B. *War Terror.* 1915 Harper. VG $15.00

REEVE, J. Stanley. *Fox Hunting Formalities.* 1958 reprint. 8vo. 15p. wraps. EX $5.00

REEVE, J. Stanley. *Fox Hunting Formalities.* 1930 Derrydale. Ills. 54 p. VG $75.00

REEVES, Col. Ira L. *Ol' Rum River.* 1931 Chicago. presentation. G $40.00

REEVES, John. *Murder Before Matins.* 1984 Doubleday. 1st ed. dj. EX $13.00

REGARDIE, Israel. *Art & Meaning of Magic.* 1971 100 p. dj. EX $23.00

REGARDIE, Israel. *Garden of Pomegranates.* 1970 St. Paul. Revised 2nd ed. dj. VG $20.00

REGARDIE, Israel. *Golden Dawn.* 1971 MN. 2 vol set. $75.00

REGARDIE, Israel. *Romance of Metaphysics.* 1946 Chicago. Aries Pr. 1st ed. VG $45.00

REGARDIE, Israel. *12 Steps to Spiritual Enlightenment.* 1969 Sangreal. 96 p. VG $16.00

REICHE, Charles. *15 Discourses on Marvellous Works of Nature.* 1781 Phil. 180 p. juvenile. scarce. VG $125.00

REID, A. *Oddments, Inklings, Omens, Moments, & Poems.* 1959 Boston. 1st ed. dj. EX $12.00

REID, A.J. *Letters of Long Ago.* 1936 Caxton. 2nd ed. sgn. 138 p. dj. $15.00

REID, B.L. *Man From NY: John Quinn & His Friends.* 1968 NY. Oxford. Ills. 4to. 708 p. cloth. dj. $35.00

REID, C. *Figure Painting in Watercolor.* 1976 NY. Ills. 160 p. $25.00

REID, C. *Flower Painting in Oil.* 1976 NY. Ills. 168 p. $25.00

REID, D. *Mushrooms & Toadstools.* 1980 Kingfisher. Ills. 1st ed. 124 p. EX $10.00

REID, Edith G. *Great Physician: Short Life of Sir William Osler.* 1942 London. Oxford U Pr. dj. VG $15.00

REID, Edward. *Grim Reapers: Anatomy of Organized Crime in America.* 1969 Chicago. 1st ed. 344 p. dj. scarce. EX $35.00

REID, G.K. *Ecology of Inland Waters & Estuaries.* 1965 Reinhold. Ills. 375 p. xl. G $10.00

REID, J. *Life of Christ in Woodcuts.* 1930 NY. Ills 1st ed. slipcase. EX $25.00

REID, James D. *Telegraph in America & the Morse Memorial.* 1866 NY. plts. rebound. $60.00

REID, James. *Song of Songs.* 1931 Farrar Rinehart. 1st ed. dj. $35.00

REID, Mayne. *Cliff Climbers; or, Lone Home in the Himalayas.* 1882 NY. VG $20.00

REID, Mayne. *Rifle Rangers; or, Adventures in Southern Mexico.* c 1870s. NY. Dewitt. Ills. green cloth. VG $35.00

REID, T.W. *Land of Bey: Being Impressions of Tunis Under the French.* 1892 London. 1st ed. VG $35.00

REID, T.W. *Traits & Stories of Ye Olde Cheshire Cheese.* 1882 London. VG $40.00

REID, V.S. *New Day: Novel of Jamaica.* 1949 Knopf. 1st ed. dj. EX $25.00

REID, W.M. *Mohawk Valley: Legends & History.* 1901 NY. Putnam. Ills. rebound. $55.00

REIGER, George. *Fishing with McClane.* 1975 Prentice Hall. 1st ed. dj. VG $20.00

REIGER. *Zane Grey Cookbook.* 1961 1st ed. dj. EX $20.00

REIK, Theodore. *Psychology of Sex Relations.* 1945 Farrar Rinehart. dj. G $10.00

REILLY, C.W. *English Poetry of WWI.* 1978 London. 402 p. $17.50

REILLY, Helen. *Day She Died.* 1962 Random House. 1st ed. dj. xl. $6.00

REILLY, Helen. *Ding-Dong Bell.* 1958 Random House. 1st ed. dj. xl. $7.50

REILLY, Helen. *Follow Me.* 1960 Random House. 1st ed. dj. VG $14.00

REILLY, Helen. *Mr. Smith's Hat.* 1936 Crime Club. 1st ed. xl. G $15.00

REILLY, Helen. *Murder at Angler's Island.* 1945 Random House. dj. G $25.00

REILLY, Helen. *Murder at Arroways.* 1950 Random House. 1st ed. dj. xl. $7.50

REILLY, Helen. *Not Me, Inspector.* 1959 Random House. dj. xl. $6.00

REILLY, Helen. *Velvet Hand.* 1953 Random House. 1st ed. dj. VG $35.00

REILLY, J.C. *Navy Destroyers of WWII.* 1983 Poole. Ills. 160 p. dj. EX $18.00

REILLY, Paul. *Introduction to Regency Architecture.* 1948 London. Art Technics. G $20.00

REILLY, Robin. *Rest to Fortune: Life of Maj. Gen. James Wolfe.* 1960 London. Ills. 367 p. $35.00

REILLY, Robin. *Wedgwood.* 1972 NY. World. Ills. 8vo. 80 p. dj. $10.00

REILLY, Robin. *Wedgwood-Jasper Collector Guide.* 1972 NY. World. Ills. cloth. dj. $15.00

REILLY, Sidney. *Britain's Master Spy: Adventures of Sidney Reilly.* 1932 NY. 1st ed. VG $50.00

REILLY & RAE. *Physico-Chemical Methods.* 1953 5th ed. 2 vol set. $45.00

REINER, Laurence E. *Buy or Build?* 1973 Prentice Hall. VG $3.00

REINFELD, F. *Story of Civil War Money.* 1959 Sterlings. Ills. 93 p. VG $20.00

REINHARDT, Hans. *Holbein.* 1938 Paris. Hyperion Pr. Ills. dj. EX $45.00

REINHARDT, Richard. *Out West on the Overland Train.* 1967 Palo Alto. 1st ed. dj. VG $20.00

REIS, J.S. *Battle with the Slum.* 1902 NY. Macmillan. 465 p. VG $15.00

REISLER, Oliver. *Philosophy & Concepts of Modern Science.* 1935 Macmillan. 1st ed. 323 p. dj. VG $15.00

REISLER, Oliver. *Promise of Scientific Humanism.* 1940 NY. 1st ed. dj. G $35.00

REISMAN, David. *Thomas Sydenham, Clinician.* 1926 NY. Hoeber. 1st ed. VG $15.00

REISMAN, Marty. *Money Player.* 1974 Morrow. 1st ed. dj. EX $5.00

REITELL, Charles. *Let's Go Fishing.* 1931 Whittlesey House. 1st ed. G $10.00

REITER, J.S. *Women.* 1979 Time Life. Revised ed. 240 p. leather. EX $15.00

REITMAN, Dr. Ben L. *Sister of the Road: Autobiography of Boxcar Bertha.* c 1937. Gold Label. $25.00

REITSCH, Hanna. *Flying Is My Life.* 1954 NY. Ills 1st ed. 246 p. G $35.00

REMARQUE, E.M. *Arch of Triumph.* 1945 NY. 1st ed. dj. EX $17.00

REMARQUE, E.M. *Heaven Has No Favorites.* 1961 NY. 1st ed. dj. M $20.00

REMARQUE, E.M. *Night in Lisbon.* 1964 NY. 1st ed. dj. EX $12.00

REMENHAM, John. *Lurking Shadow.* no date. MacDonald. dj. xl. $5.00

REMENHAM, John. *Peacemaker.* 1947 MacDonald. 1st ed. dj. VG $7.00

REMER, Theodore G. *Serendipity & the 3 Princes.* 1965 OK U Pr. 1st ed. inscr. dj. EX $8.50

REMINGTON, Frederic. *Crooked Trails.* 1898 Harper. 1st ed. tan/green cloth. G $85.00

REMINGTON, Frederic. *Daughter of the Sioux.* 1903 NY. 1st ed. VG $25.00

REMINGTON, Frederic. *Done in the Open.* 1902 NY. Ills 1st ed. 2nd issue. $75.00

REMINGTON, Frederic. *Done in the Open.* 1903 NY. Ills. VG $50.00

REMINGTON, Frederic. *Done in the Open.* 1902 NY. Russell. Ltd 1st ed. 1/250. sgn. suede. $650.00

REMINGTON, Frederic. *Frederic Remington Book.* 1966 NY. Ltd ed. 1/500. sgn. slipcase. $350.00

REMINGTON, Frederic. *Frederic Remington's Own West.* 1960 NY. Dial. Ills 1st ed. VG $17.50

REMINGTON, Frederic. *John Erskine of Yellowstone.* 1902 NY. Ills 1st ed. VG $35.00

REMINGTON, Frederic. *Men with the Bark On.* 1900 NY. Harper. Ills 1st ed. 208 p. $100.00

REMINGTON, Frederic. *Men with the Bark On.* 1890 NY. VG $60.00

REMINGTON, Frederic. *Pony Tracks.* 1895 NY. Ills 1st ed. $200.00

REMINGTON, Frederic. *Pony Tracks.* 1982 Am Legacy. Ills. 221 p. dj. EX $15.00

REMINGTON, Frederic. *Remington's Frontier Sketches.* 1969 Franklin. Ills. oblong 4to. EX $12.00

REMINGTON, Frederic. *Remington's Frontier Sketches.* 1898 Chicago. Werner. 1st ed. slipcase. $600.00

REMISE, J.; & FONDIN, Jean. *Golden Age of Toys.* 1967 Edita Lausanne. Ills. folio. 254 p. dj. $85.00

RENARD, Jules. *Bucoliques.* 1898 Paris. inscr. VG $37.50

RENARD, Jules. *Natural Histories: Bestiary.* 1966 Braziller. Ills Toulouse-Lautrec. 1st ed. $25.00

RENAULT, Mary. *Fire From Heaven.* 1969 NY. 1st ed. dj. VG $10.00

RENAULT, Mary. *Mask of Apollo.* 1966 NY. Pantheon. 1st ed. dj. VG $35.00

RENAULT, Mary. *Praise Singer.* 1978 NY. Pantheon. 1st ed. dj. EX $25.00

RENDALL, F. Geoffrey. *Clarinet.* 1957 London. Revised 2nd ed. dj. VG $30.00

RENDELL, Ruth. *Best Man To Die.* 1970 Doubleday. 1st ed. dj. EX $17.50

RENDELL, Ruth. *Death Notes.* no date. Book Club ed. dj. VG $3.00

RENDELL, Ruth. *Fever Tree.* 1982 Pantheon. 1st Am ed. dj. EX $12.00

RENDELL, Ruth. *From Doon with Death.* 1964 Doubleday. 1st ed. dj. xl. $5.00

RENDELL, Ruth. *Judgement in Stone.* 1978 Doubleday. dj. VG $7.50

RENDELL, Ruth. *Killing Doll.* 1984 Pantheon. 1st Am ed. dj. EX $13.00

RENDELL, Ruth. *Life Flesh.* no date. London. 1st ed. sgn. $28.00

RENDELL, Ruth. *New Girl Friend.* no date. BOMC. EX $5.00

RENDELL, Ruth. *Speaker of Mandarin.* 1938 NY. Pantheon. 1st Am ed. dj. VG $12.50

RENDELL, Ruth. *Talking to Strange Men.* 1987 London. Uncorrected proof. VG $30.00

RENDELL, Ruth. *Unkindness of Ravens.* 1985 Pantheon. 1st ed. dj. VG $15.00

RENEAU, Jack & Susan. *CO Biggest Bucks & Bulls.* 1980 CO Springs. 1st ed. sgn. M $18.00

RENNELL, James. *Geographical System of Herodotus.* 1800 London. maps. calf. $475.00

RENNER, F.G. *Charles M. Russell Art in Amon Carter Collection.* 1966 Austin. Ills 1st ed. 148 p. dj. EX $35.00

RENO, Marie R. *Final Proof.* 1976 Harper Row. 1st ed. dj. xl. $5.00

RENO, Marie R. *Final Proof.* no date. Book Club ed. dj. VG $3.00

RENOIR, Jean. *Renoir, My Father.* 1962 Boston. Little Brown. photos. EX $6.00

REPPLIER, Agnes. *Essays in Miniature.* 1892 NY. Webster. 1st ed. EX $20.00

RESNICK, Mike. *Eros Ascending.* 1984 Phantasia. Ltd 1st ed. sgn. dj. slipcase. $40.00

RESNICK, Mike. *Eros at Zenith.* 1984 Phantasia. Ltd 1st ed. sgn. dj. slipcase. $40.00

RESSE, John. *Looters.* 1968 Random House. 1st ed. dj. EX $12.50

RESSLER, T.W. *Treasury of American Indian Tales.* 1957 Bonanza. reprint. 310 p. dj. EX $6.00

RESTOUT, D.; & HAWKINS, R. *Landowska on Music.* 1965 London. Ills 1st English ed. dj. VG $22.00

RETI, Richard. *Masters of Chessboard.* 1932 NY. 5th ed. G $26.00

REUSSWIG, William. *Picture Report of the Custer Fight.* 1967 Hastings House. Ills. 184 p. dj. EX $30.00

REVEL, J.F. *On Proust.* 1972 London. 1st ed. 4to. dj. EX $11.00

REVI, Albert C. *American Cut & Engraved Glass.* 1965 London. Nelson. folio. white linen. dj. EX $45.00

REVI, Albert C. *Collectible Iron, Tin, & Copper.* 1974 Castle. dj. VG $7.00

REVI, Albert C. *19th Century Glass: Its Genesis & Development.* 1967 NY. Galahad. Revised ed. 301 p. dj. $65.00

REVI, Albert C. *19th Century Glass: Its Genesis & Development.* 1959 NY. Nelson. Ills. 4to 288 p. dj. $20.00

REVIERS-HOPKINS, A.E. *Sheraton Period.* 1927 London. Heinemann. Ills. 12mo. VG $55.00

REWALD, John. *History of Impressionism.* 1973 Boston. Ills Revised 4th ed. 4to. dj. $40.00

REWALD, John. *Les Fauves.* 1953 MOMA. Ills. 4to. 49 p. wraps. $30.00

REWALD, John. *Post-Impressionism From Van Gogh to Gauguin.* 1978 MOMA. Ills. 4to. 592 p. cloth. dj. $60.00

REWALD, John. *Woodcuts of Aristide Maillol.* 1951 NY. Pantheon. Ills. 4to. dj. VG $30.00

REXROTH, Kenneth. *In What Hour?* 1940 1st ed. dj. EX $125.00

REXROTH, Kenneth. *New British Poets.* no date. New Directions. inscr. EX $150.00

REXROTH, Kenneth. *100 Poems From the Chinese.* New Directions. 1st ed. EX $25.00

REY, Guido. *Peaks & Precipices: Scrambles in Dolomites & Savoy.* 1914 NY. Dodd Mead. Ills 1st Am ed. rebound. EX $75.00

REY, H.A. *Find the Constellations.* 1954 Boston. Houghton Mifflin. Ills. index. $22.50

REY, J.D. *Guillermo Roux.* Rizzoli. 4to. dj. $18.00

REYNOLDS, Andrea. *Palladio & the Winged Device.* 1948 NY. Ills. $30.00

REYNOLDS, Francis J. *Master Tales of Mystery.* 1915 Collier. G $5.00

REYNOLDS, Helen W. *Dutch Houses in the Hudson Valley Before 1776.* 1929 NY. Holland Society/Payson Clark. $225.00

REYNOLDS, Hughes. *Coosa River Valley.* 1944 Hobson Pr. VG $45.00

REYNOLDS, J. *Andrae Palladio.* 1948 NY. 8vo. cloth. dj. EX $30.00

REYNOLDS, J.A. *Heraldry & You.* 1961 Nelson. Ills. 176 p. dj. VG $9.00

REYNOLDS, James. *Panorama of Austria.* 1956 NY. Ills 1st ed. dj. VG $15.00

REYNOLDS, Jan. *William Callow, R.W.S.* 1980 London. Batsford. tall 4to. dj. $50.00

REYNOLDS, John. *Windmills & Watermills.* 1975 NY. Praeger. Ills 2nd print. 196 p. dj. VG $15.00

REYNOLDS, Lloyd J. *Professor of Art.* 1957 Portland. Revised ed. wraps. VG $10.00

REYNOLDS, Quentin. *Curtain Rises.* 1944 NY. 1st ed. inscr. VG $25.00

REYNOLDS, Quentin. *Dress Rehearsal.* 1943 Blue Ribbon. Ills. dj. $10.00

REYNOLDS, Quentin. *Fiction Factory.* 1955 NY. 1st ed. dj. EX $20.00

REYNOLDS, Quentin. *Minister of Death.* 1960 Viking. 1st ed. photos. dj. EX $20.00

REYNOLDS, V. *Tibet: Lost World.* 1978 1st trade ed. pb. VG $25.00

REZNIKOFF, C. *Testimony: US 1885-1890.* 1965 San Francisco. 1st ed. dj. EX $12.00

REZNIKOFF, Charles. *Manner Music.* 1977 Black Sparrow. Ltd 1st ed. 1/200. 8vo. dj. EX $30.00

REZNIKOFF. *By the Waters of Manhattan.* 1930 Boni. Paper Books. 1st ed. G $15.00

RHEAD, Louis. *American Trout Stream Insects.* 1916 NY. 1st ed. VG $40.00

RHEAD, Louis. *Book of Fish & Fishing.* 1908 NY. 1st ed. VG $20.00

RHEIMS, Maurice. *Flowering of Art Nouveau.* 1966 NY. Abrams. Ills. 450 p. cloth. $85.00

RHINE, J.B. *New Frontiers of Mind.* 1937 NY. 1st ed. dj. VG $15.00

RHOADS, Dorothy. *Bright Feather & Other Maya Tales.* 1932 Garden City. Doubleday Doran. 1st ed. EX $20.00

RHODE, E.S. *Story of the Garden.* 1922 Boston. xl. VG $15.00

RHODE, John. *Death at the Dance.* 1952 London. 1st ed. dj. VG $35.00

RHODE, John. *Death of an Author.* 1947 London. 1st ed. dj. VG $40.00

RHODE, John. *Murder at Derivale.* 1958 London. 1st ed. dj. VG $35.00

RHODE, John. *Peril at Cranbury Hill.* 1930 London. 1st ed. dj. $35.00

RHODE, John. *Poison for 1.* 1934 Dodd Mead. 1st ed. G $20.00

RHODE, John. *Shadow of an Alibi.* no date. Dodd Mead. VG $12.50

RHODE, John. *Vanishing Diary.* 1961 Dodd Mead. dj. xl. $5.00

RHODE, John. *Venner Crime.* 1933 London. Odhams. 1st ed. VG $30.00

RHODE, Robert H. *Sucker Money.* 1927 Chelsea House. VG $10.00

RHODES, Frederick Leland. *Beginnings of Telephony.* 1929 Harper Row. Ills 1st ed. 261 p. VG $20.00

RHODES, R. *Ozarks.* 1974 Time Life. Ills. 184 p. EX $10.00

RHODES, R. Crompton. *Shakespeare's 1st Folio.* 1923 Appleton. 1st ed. 147 p. VG $17.50

RHYNER, P.; & MANNIX, D.P. *Wildewt Game.* 1958 Lippincott. Ills. 320 p. VG $10.00

RHYS, Ernest. *English Fairy Book.* no date. Stokes. G $27.50

RHYS, Ernest. *English Fairy Tales.* no date. (1906) NY/London. Ills Cole. EX $65.00

RHYS, Ernest. *Everyman Remembers.* 1932 NY. Cosmo. 1st ed. plts. cloth. VG $10.00

RHYS, Grace. *History of Ali Baba & the 40 Thieves.* 1895 Dent. Ills HG Fell. 16mo. 63 p. VG $25.00

RHYS, Jean. *Sleep It Off Lady.* 1976 NY. 1st ed. dj. EX $10.00

RHYS, Jean. *Tigers Are Better Looking.* 1947 NY. 1st ed. dj. EX $12.50

RHYS, John Llewelyn. *England Is My Village.* 1941 NY. 1st Am ed. 198 p. dj. VG $20.00

RIBAUT, Jean. *Whole & True Discovery of Terra, FL.* 1927 facsimile of 1563 London ed. $80.00

RICCI, Franco Maria. *Tamara de Lempicka with Journal of d'Annunzio's Housekeeper.* 1977 Rizzoli. Ltd ed. 1/3,000. slipcase. EX $95.00

RICCIARDI, M. *Vanishing Africa.* 1971 NY. Morrow. 1st ed. dj. VG $50.00

RICCIUTI, E.R. *Killers of the Sea.* 1973 Walker. Ills 1st ed. 308 p. dj. EX $12.00

RICCIUTI, E.R. *Wildlife of the Mountains.* 1979 Abrams. Ills. 232 p. VG $16.00

RICCIUTI, I. *New Orleans Domestic Architecture.* 1938 Helburn. 4to. EX $75.00

RICE, Alice Hegan. *Captain June.* 1907 NY. Century. Ills Weldon. 1st ed. 8vo. VG $15.00

RICE, Anne. *Belinda.* 1986 Arbor House. 1st ed. dj. EX $20.00

RICE, Anne. *Belinda.* 1986 Arbor House. Review copy. dj. EX $25.00

RICE, Anne. *Cry to Heaven.* 1982 Knopf. 1st ed. dj. VG $15.00

RICE, Anne. *Exit to Eden.* 1985 Arbor House. 1st ed. dj. EX $25.00

RICE, Anne. *Feast of All Saints.* 1979 NY. 1st ed. dj. EX $12.00

RICE, Anne. *Interview with the Vampire.* no date. Book Club ed. dj. VG $4.00

RICE, Anne. *Interview with the Vampire.* 1976 NY. 1st ed. dj. EX $37.50

RICE, Craig. *April Robin Murders.* no date. Book Club ed. dj. VG $4.00

RICE, Craig. *Having Wonderful Crime.* 1944 Tower. VG $15.00

RICE, Craig. *Having Wonderful Crime.* 1944 Nicholson Watson. G $12.50

RICE, Craig. *Having Wonderful Crime.* 1944 Simon Schuster. 2nd ed. VG $15.00

RICE, Craig. *Home Sweet Homicide.* 1946 Tower. dj. VG $20.00

RICE, Craig. *Knocked for a Loop.* no date. Book Club ed. dj. VG $4.00

RICE, Craig. *My Kingdom for a Hearse.* 1957 1st ed. dj. VG $7.00

RICE, Craig. *Right Murder.* 1943 Tower. 2nd ed. $10.00

RICE, Dennis G. *Derby Porcelain: Golden Years 1750-1770.* 1983 London. David & Charles. Ills. 4to. $60.00

RICE, Elmer. *Living Theatre.* 1959 NY. Harper. 1st ed. 306 p. $4.00

RICE, Elmer. *Show Must Go On.* 1949 Viking. dj. VG $7.00

RICE, F.P. *America's Favorite Fishing: Guide to Angling for Panfish.* 1964 Outdoor Life. Ills 1st ed. 285 p. VG $5.00

RICE, J. *Relativity: Systematic Treatment of Einstein's Theory.* 1923 London. Longman. 1st ed. 397 p. VG $12.00

RICE, Robert. *Business of Crime.* 1956 Farrar Straus. 1st ed. dj. VG $9.00

RICE, Tamara. *Russian Icons.* no date. NY. 48 color plts. VG $22.50

RICE & GAVSHON. *Sinking of the Belgrano.* 1984 London. Ills. 218 p. maps. dj. EX $18.00

RICE & STOUDT. *Shenandoah Pottery.* 1929 Strasburg. Ills 1st ed. cloth. $60.00

RICH, Daniel Catton. *Henri Rousseau.* 1942 MOMA. Art Institute Chicago. 1st ed. $15.00

RICH, L.D. *Mindy.* 1959 Lippincott. 1st ed. dj. $4.00

RICH, L.D. *Natural World of Louise Dickinson Rich.* 1962 Dodd Mead. Ills. 195 p. dj. EX $8.00

RICH, L.D. *We Took to the Woods.* 1942 Lippincott. Ills. 322 p. G $7.00

RICHARD, John. *Story of the English People.* no date. Donohue. 4 vol set. dj. G $12.50

RICHARD, Timothy. *New Testament of Higher Buddhism.* 1910 China. 269 p. VG $65.00

RICHARDS, Allen. *Market to Market.* 1961 Macmillan. 1st ed. dj. VG $7.00

RICHARDS, Bob. *Heart of a Champion.* 1959 sgn. 159 p. dj. VG $18.00

RICHARDS, Clay. *Death of an Angel.* 1963 Bobbs Merrill. 1st ed. dj. VG $14.00

RICHARDS, Clay. *Gentle Assassin.* 1964 Bobbs Merrill. dj. G $12.50

RICHARDS, Clay. *Who Steals My Name.* 1964 Bobbs Merrill. 1st ed. dj. xl. $5.00

RICHARDS, Colin. *Bowler Hats & Stetsons.* no date. Bonanza. dj. VG $5.00

RICHARDS, Eva. *Arctic Mood.* 1949 Caxton. Ills. 282 p. dj. VG $7.00

RICHARDS, Grant. *Author Hunting by an Old Literary Sportsman.* 1934 NY. Ills 1st ed. VG $25.00

RICHARDS, I.D. *Story of a River Town: Little Rock in the 19th Century.* 1969 private print. 144 p. maps. dj. EX $12.00

RICHARDS, Laura E. *Little Master.* 1913 Boston. Estes. 1st ed. EX $125.00

RICHARDS, Laura E. *Please!* 1936 ME. 1st ed. inscr. wraps. EX $15.00

RICHARDS, Milton. *Tom Blake's Mysterious Adventure.* 1929 Saalfield. G $5.00

RICHARDS, T. Addison. *Tallulah & Jocassee; or, Romances of Southern Landscape.* 1852 Charleston, SC. 1st ed. VG $80.00

RICHARDSON, Albert D. *Beyond the MS.* 1867 Hartford. Ills. 8vo. brown cloth. G $30.00

RICHARDSON, Albert D. *Beyond the MS.* 1867 Hartford. Ills. full leather. EX $40.00

RICHARDSON, Albert D. *Beyond the MS.* 1869 Hartford. Ills New ed. EX $17.50

RICHARDSON, Albert D. *Personal History of Ulysses S. Grant.* 1868 Hartford. Ills. 8vo. 560 p. maps. xl. VG $28.00

RICHARDSON, Albert D. *Personal History of Ulysses S. Grant.* 1868 NY. Ills. full leather. G $30.00

RICHARDSON, Albert D. *Secret Service, the Field, the Dungeon, & the Escape.* 1865 Hartford. Ills. 8vo. 512 p. xl. VG $25.00

RICHARDSON, Albert D. *Secret Service, the Field, the Dungeon, & the Escape.* 1865 Hartford. Ills 1st ed. 8vo. 512 p. VG $45.00

RICHARDSON, Albert D. *Secret Service.* 1866 Hartford. VG $75.00

RICHARDSON, B. *Strangers Devour the Land.* 1976 Knopf. Ills. 342 p. VG $4.00

RICHARDSON, Guy. *My Abraham Lincoln Radio & Other Addresses.* 1937 Boston. Baker Taylor. Ills. scarce. $45.00

RICHARDSON, Henry Handel. *Maurice Guest.* 1908 London. 1st ed. VG $50.00

RICHARDSON, John. *Arctic Expedition in Search of Sir John Franklin.* 1852 NY. Ills. VG $75.00

RICHARDSON, John. *Arctic Searching Expedition of Sir John Franklin.* 1969 NY. 2 vol set. $22.50

RICHARDSON, John. *Georges Braque.* 1962 Paris. La Bibliotheque des Arts. $50.00

RICHARDSON, John. *Wonders of Yellowstone Region: Explored in 1870-1871.* 1876 Blackie & Son. Ills. maps. $65.00

RICHARDSON, M. *Fascination of Reptiles.* 1972 Hill Wang. Ills. 240 p. dj. VG $18.00

RICHARDSON, Mrs. A. *Lover of Queen Elizabeth.* no date. London. 8vo cloth. VG $10.00

RICHARDSON, O.W. *Thermionic Vacuum Tubes.* 1933 London. Methuen. 2nd ed. dj. VG $30.00

RICHARDSON, W. *House on Nauset Marsh.* 1955 Norton. Ills. 221 p. dj. VG $10.00

RICHARDSON, William H. *Washington & the Enterprise Against Powles Hook.* 1938 Jersey City. Ills. maps. VG $35.00

RICHERAND, A. *Elements of Physiology.* 1818 Phil. 8vo. 621 p. full leather. G $45.00

RICHERAND, A. *Elements of Physiology.* 1821 Hardy. calf. VG $50.00

RICHEY, David. *How To Catch Trophy Fresh-Water Game Fish.* 1979 Outdoor Life. Ills. 394 p. dj. EX $12.00

RICHEY, David. *Steelheading for Everybody.* 1976 Stackpole. Ills. 224 p. dj. EX $10.00

RICHLER, Mordecai. *Shovelling Trouble.* 1973 London. 1st ed. dj. VG $20.00

RICHMAN, Philip. *Bird Painter's Sketchbook.* 1931 London. Ills. 4to. $35.00

RICHMOND, M.E. *Long View.* 1930 Russel Sage Foundation. dj. VG $10.00

RICHMOND, R. *Woman in TX: Mrs. Percy V. Pennybacker.* 1941 San Antonio. Naylor. 7 plts. 367 p. $10.00

RICHMOND, Rev. Leigh. *Annals of the Poor.* no date. Philadelphia. $15.00

RICHTER, Conrad. *Aristocrat.* 1968 Knopf. 1st ed. dj. VG $15.00

RICHTER, Conrad. *Brothers of No Kin.* 1924 NY. 1st ed. sgn. VG $45.00

RICHTER, Conrad. *Lady.* 1957 Knopf. 1st ed. dj. VG $15.00

RICHTER, Conrad. *Sea of Grass.* 1937 Knopf. 1st ed. dj. EX $35.00

RICHTER, Conrad. *Town.* 1950 NY. 1st ed. 433 p. cloth. G $15.00

RICHTER, Conrad. *Trees.* 1940 NY. Ltd 1st ed. 1/250. slipcase. $60.00

RICHTER, E.H. *Prints: Their Technique & History.* 1914 Boston. 137 p. cloth. VG $25.00

RICHTER, Gisela. *Handbook of Greek Art.* 1960 NY. Revised 2nd ed. 421 p. VG $25.00

RICHTER, Gisela. *Sculpture & Sculptors of Greeks.* 1930 New Haven. Ills. 8vo. 613 p. $50.00

RICHTER, Louis M. *Chantilly in History & Art.* 1914 Scribner. 305 p. $30.00

RICKENBACKER, Edward V. *Edward V. Rickenbacker: Autobiography.* 1967 Englewood Cliffs. 5th print. $15.00

RICKENBACKER, Edward V. *Fighting the Flying Circus.* 1919 NY. Ills 1st ed. inscr. 371 p. $95.00

RICKENBACKER, Edward V. *Fighting the Flying Circus.* 1965 NY. Doubleday. 296 p. dj. $6.00

RICKENBACKER, Edward V. *7 Came Through.* 1943 NY. Doubleday. 118 p. dj. $5.00

RICKER, E.M. *Togo's Fireside Reflections.* 1928 ME. Ills. G $12.00

RICKS, Melvin. *AK Bibliography.* 1977 Binford Mort. 1st ed. cloth. M $28.00

RIDDEL, John. *In the Worst Possible Taste.* 1932 Scribner. Ills Covarrubias. 1st ed. dj. $47.50

RIDE, W.D.L. *Guide to the Native Mammals of Australia.* 1970 Oxford U Pr. Ills. 264 p. dj. EX $48.00

RIDEING, W.H. *Boys in the Mountains & on the Plains.* 1882 Appleton. Ills. VG $27.50

RIDEING, W.H. *Overland Express.* 1970 private print. Ills Ltd ed. 1/650. VG $35.00

RIDGE, W.P. *London Types.* 1926 London. 1st ed. 8vo. EX $50.00

RIDING, Laura. *Lara & Francisca.* 1931 Seizin Pr. Ltd ed. 1/200. sgn. $300.00

RIDING, Laura. *Love As Love, Death As Death.* 1928 London. Seizin Pr. Ltd ed. 1/175. sgn. $275.00

RIDPATH, J.C. *Story of South Africa.* 1902 Guelph, Ontario. Ills. cloth. $25.00

RIDPATH, John. *Life & Times of Gladstone.* 1898 Chicago. 1st ed. gilt cloth. VG $15.00

RIDSON, P.J. *Wireless.* c 1924. London. Ills. G $250.00

RIEFENSTAHL, L. *Coral Gardens.* 1978 Harper Row. Ills 1st Am ed. 4to. dj. EX $25.00

RIEMAN, Terry. *Vamp Till Ready.* 1954 Harper. 1st ed. dj. VG $9.00

RIES, Karl. *Dora-Kurfurst und Rote 13.* 1964 Ills 1st ed. German/English text. dj. VG $65.00

RIESENBERG, Felix. *Cape Horn.* 1939 Dodd Mead. charts William Briesemeister. $30.00

RIESENBERG, Lt. H.E. *I Dive for Treasure.* 1942 NY. 1st ed. 331 p. black cloth. $55.00

RIESENBERG, Lt. H.E. *Treasure Hunter.* 1945 NY. Ills 1st ed. 260 p. M $55.00

RIGGS, S.R. *Psalm Wowapi: Book of Psalms in Dakota Language.* 1887 NY. 1st ed. 133 p. VG $50.00

RIJNHART, Susie. *With the Tibetans in Tent & Temple.* 1902 Revell. VG $25.00

RILEY, James Whitcomb. *Afterwhiles.* 1891 Bowen Merrill. inscr. $40.00

RILEY, James Whitcomb. *Book of Joyous Children.* 1902 NY. Ills Vawter. 1st ed. VG $40.00

RILEY, James Whitcomb. *Boys of Old Glee Club.* 1907 Indianapolis. Ills Vawter/Booth. 1st ed. G $20.00

RILEY, James Whitcomb. *Child Rhymes with Hoosier Pictures.* 1905 Indianapolis. 1st ed. EX $17.00

RILEY, James Whitcomb. *Defective Santa Claus.* 1904 Bobbs Merrill. Ills Relyea/Vawter. dj. VG $12.50

RILEY, James Whitcomb. *Flying Islands of the Night.* 1913 Indianapolis. Ills Franklin Booth. EX $75.00

RILEY, James Whitcomb. *Flying Islands of the Night.* 1892 Indianapolis. 1st ed. dj. white wraps. VG $75.00

RILEY, James Whitcomb. *Hoosier Romance.* 1868 Century. Ills J Woolcott. 8vo. cloth. $15.00

RILEY, James Whitcomb. *Love Lyrics.* 1888 Bobbs Merrill. Ills Dyer. VG $15.00

RILEY, James Whitcomb. *Old Sweetheart of Mine.* 1902 Indianapolis. Ills Christy/Keep. 1st ed. $40.00

RILEY, James Whitcomb. *Old Swimmin' Hole & 'Leven More Poems.* 1920 Chicago. 1st ed. 12mo. dj. wraps. $45.00

RILEY, James Whitcomb. *Out to Old Aunt Mary's.* 1904 Indianapolis. Ills Christy. 1st ed. G $15.00

RILEY, James Whitcomb. *Poems Here at Home.* 1893 NY. 1st ed. rebound. EX $95.00

RILEY, James Whitcomb. *Raggedy Man.* 1919 Bobbs Merrill. Ills EF Betts. 1st ed. VG $75.00

RILEY, James Whitcomb. *Rubaiyat of Doc Sifers.* 1897 NY. Century. Ills Relyea. 1st ed. $12.50

RILEY, James Whitcomb. *Selected Poems.* 1931 Bobbs Merrill. 1st ed. VG $10.00

RILEY, James Whitcomb. *Songs of Summer.* 1909 Indianapolis. Bobbs Merrill. EX $20.00

RILEY, James Whitcomb. *While the Heart Beats Young.* 1906 Indianapolis. Ills EF Betts. 4to. cloth. EX $105.00

RILEY, James Whitcomb. *Works of James Whitcomb Riley.* 1913 Indianapolis. Ills. 6 vol set. xl. VG $95.00

RILEY, James Whitcomb. *Works of James Whitcomb Riley.* 1898 NY. Homestead ed. 10 vol set. $85.00

RILEY, Robert. *Fashion Makers: Photographic Record.* 1968 NY. Crown. Ills. dj. G $10.50

RILEY, Woodbridge. *American Thought From Puritanism to Pragmatism.* 1915 NY. 373 p. EX $35.00

RILKE, Rainer Maria. *Later Poems.* no date. Hogarth. Ltd 1st English ed. $22.50

RILKE, Rainer Maria. *Letters to a Young Poet.* 1934 Norton. 1st Am ed. dj. VG $30.00

RILLA, Wolf. *A Through Z of Movie Making.* 1970 Viking. VG $9.00

RIMMEL, Eugene. *Book of Perfumes.* 1865 London. Ills. presentation. VG $90.00

RIMMER, C.H. *Figure Drawing for Children.* 1893 Boston. Lathrop. Ills. 8vo. cloth. VG $15.00

RIMSKY-KORSAKOFF, N.A. *My Musical Life.* 1923 NY. EX $25.00

RINARD, J. *Creatures of the Night.* 1977 Nat'l Geog Soc. Ills. 32 p. EX $8.00

RINEHART, Mary Roberts. *After House.* no date. Burt. G $5.00

RINEHART, Mary Roberts. *After House.* 1914 Boston. 1st ed. dj. VG $15.00

RINEHART, Mary Roberts. *Album.* 1943 Triangle. 3rd ed. dj. VG $10.00

RINEHART, Mary Roberts. *Bat.* 1928 Cassell. 2nd ed. VG $12.50

RINEHART, Mary Roberts. *Breaking Point.* no date. Burt. VG $7.50

RINEHART, Mary Roberts. *Circular Staircase.* 1943 Triangle. 6th ed. dj. VG $7.00

RINEHART, Mary Roberts. *Circular Staircase.* 1908 Indianapolis. Ills L Ralph. 1st ed. EX $75.00

RINEHART, Mary Roberts. *Fightened Wife.* no date. Black. dj. VG $4.00

RINEHART, Mary Roberts. *Great Mistake.* 1946 Triangle. dj. VG $15.00

RINEHART, Mary Roberts. *K.* no date. Grosset Dunlap. dj. G $15.00

RINEHART, Mary Roberts. *Long Live the King.* no date. Burt. G $5.00

RINEHART, Mary Roberts. *Lost Ecstasy.* no date. Grosset Dunlap. Photoplay ed. $20.00

RINEHART, Mary Roberts. *Lost Ecstasy.* 1944 Tower. 2nd ed. dj. VG $10.00

RINEHART, Mary Roberts. *Lost Ecstasy.* 1927 Doran. 1st ed. dj. VG $14.00

RINEHART, Mary Roberts. *Man in Lower 10.* no date. Grosset Dunlap. VG $20.00

RINEHART, Mary Roberts. *Red Lamp.* 1925 Doubleday Doran. 1st ed. G $20.00

RINEHART, Mary Roberts. *Swimming Pool.* 1952 Rinehart. 1st ed. dj. VG $16.00

RINEHART, Mary Roberts. *Tish.* no date. Burt. VG $7.50

RINEHART, Mary Roberts. *Tish.* 1916 Boston. 1st ed. VG $20.00

RINEHART, Mary Roberts. *When a Man Marries.* 1909 Bobbs Merrill. Ills H Fisher. 1st ed. VG $12.50

RINEHART, Mary Roberts. *Yellow Room.* 1945 Farrar Rinehart. 1st ed. VG $15.00

RING, Adam. *Killers Play Rough.* 1946 Crown. 1st ed. dj. G $9.00

RINGEL, F.J. *America As Americans See It.* 1932 Literary Guild. Ills 1st ed. 8vo. 365 p. VG $20.00

RIPLEY, E. *Leonardo da Vinci.* 1952 Oxford U Pr. Ills. VG $8.50

RIPLEY, Henry & Martha. *Hand-Clasp of the East & West: Story of Pioneer Life.* 1914 Denver, CO. 1st ed. 8vo. VG $25.00

RIPLEY, Mary. *Chinese Rug Book.* 1927 Stokes. 1st ed. $15.00

RIPLEY, Ozark. *Sport in Field & Forest.* 1926 Appleton. Ills 1st ed. 180 p. VG $12.00

RIPLEY, Roswell S. *War with Mexico.* 1970 NY. reprint. 2 vol set. $35.00

RIPLEY, S.D. *Synopsis of the Birds of India & Pakistan.* 1961 Bombay. Nat Hist Soc. 1st ed. 702 p. $35.00

RIPLEY, Sherman. *Raggedy Animal Book.* 1928 Rand McNally. Ills Cady. 96 p. green cloth. $20.00

RIPLEY, Thomas. *They Died with Their Boots On.* 1937 NY. Sun Dial. VG $25.00

RIPLEY, Warren. *Artillery & Ammunition of the Civil War.* 1970 Promontory. Ills. 4to. 384 p. dj. EX $25.00

RIPLEY, Warren. *Artillery & Ammunition of the Civil War.* 1970 Van Nostrand. Ills 1st ed. 4to. 374 p. EX $55.00

RIPPEY, S. *Sunny-Sulky Book.* 1935 Rand McNally. 60 p. VG $10.00

RIPPINGALE. *Queensland & Great Barrier Reef Shells.* 1961 Brisbane. Ills 1st ed. 1/200. sgn. VG $85.00

RIPPY & NELSON. *Crusaders of the Jungle.* 1936 Chapel Hill. 1st ed. 401 p. xl. VG $12.00

RISER, N.W.; & MORSE, M.P. *Biology of the Turbellaria.* 1974 McGraw Hill. Ills 1st ed. 530 p. dj. EX $25.00

RISTER, C.C. *Command on the Frontier: Gen. Phil Sheridan in the West.* 1944 OK U Pr. Ills 1st ed. 244 p. dj. EX $60.00

RISTER, C.C. *Fort Griffen on the TX Frontier.* 1956 OK U Pr. 2nd print. dj. EX $18.00

RISTER, C.C. *Fort Griffen on the TX Frontier.* 1956 OK U Pr. Ills 1st ed. 216 p. VG $14.00

RISTER, C.C. *Southwestern Frontier 1865-1881.* 1928 Cleveland. Clark. 1st ed. scarce. EX $135.00

RITCHIE, Andrew Carnduff. *Abstract Painting & Sculpture in America.* 1951 NY. MOMA. Ills. 4to. 159 p. dj. $30.00

RITCHIE, Andrew Carnduff. *Charles Demuth.* 1950 MOMA. Ills. 4to. 96 p. dj. $25.00

RITCHIE, Andrew Carnduff. *Masters of British Painting 1800-1950.* 1956 MOMA. Ills. 4to. 160 p. dj. $20.00

RITCHIE, Andrew Carnduff. *Sculpture of the 20th Century.* 1952 MOMA. Ills. 4to. 238 p. $30.00

RITCHIE, Carson A. *Art of the Eskimo.* 1979 NY. Barnes. Ills. 4to. 175 p. dj. $20.00

RITCHIE, Carson A. *Modern Ivory Carving.* 1972 NY. Barnes. 1st ed. dj. EX $20.00

RITCHIE, Carson A. *Shell Carving History & Technique.* 1974 NY. Barnes. Ills. 4to. 208 p. dj. $25.00

RITSON, Joseph. *Essay on Abstinence of Animal Food As a Moral Duty.* 1802 London. 1st ed. 8vo. 236 p. VG $90.00

RITTEL, Rudolf. *Great Men & Movements in Israel.* 1929 NY. dj. G $20.00

RITTENHOUSE, J.D. *Maverick Tales: True Stories of Early TX.* 1971 Winchester. 248 p. pb. VG $15.00

RITTENHOUSE, J.D. *Santa Fe Trail: Historical Bibliography.* 1986 private print. Ltd ed. 1/500. sgn. pb. EX $35.00

RITTER, Elizabeth. *Parasols Is for Ladies.* 1941 Winston. 1st ed. Negro juvenile. VG $40.00

RITTER, Richard H. *Arts of the Church.* 1947 Boston. 1st ed. dj. VG $15.00

RITTER & GADBOIS. *You've Had It: Story of Basic Training.* 1950 NY. cartoons. 28 p. wraps. VG $12.50

RITTLINGER, H. *Photography & Nude.* 1961 London. dj. EX $17.50

RITZ, David. *Man Who Brought the Dodgers Back to Brooklyn.* 1981 Simon Schuster. 1st ed. dj. EX $25.00

RIVERA, Geraldo. *Special King of Courage.* 1976 NY. 1st ed. sgn. dj. EX $25.00

RIVERA & WOLFE. *Portrait of Mexico.* 1937 NY. Ills 1st ed. photos. plts. $37.50

RIVERAIN, J. *Concise Encyclopedia of Explorations.* 1969 Collins Follett. Ills. dj. VG $14.00

RIVERO, Mariano Edward. *Peruvian Antiquities.* 1853 NY. Putnam. Ills 1st ed. 306 p. cloth. $100.00

RIVES, R.W. *Coaching Club.* 1935 NY. Derrydale. 1/300. EX $200.00

RIVIERE, Bill. *L.L. Bean Guide to Outdoors.* 1981 NY. dj. EX $15.00

RIVIERE, Robert & Sons. *Smaller Classical Dictionary.* no date. London. ½-calf. G $15.00

RIVOLIER, J. *Emperor Penguins.* 1958 Speller. Ills 1st ed. 131 p. dj. EX $12.50

RIZAL. *Rizal's Poems.* 1962 Manila. Centennial ed. 4to. 182 p. $18.00

ROARK, Garland. *Should the Wind Be Fair.* 1960 Garden City. Doubleday. 1st ed. dj. VG $25.00

ROBACKER, E.F. *Arts of the PA Dutch.* 1975 NY. Ills. 240 p. $16.50

ROBACKER, E.F. *PA Dutch Stuff: Guide to Country Antiques.* 1946 Phil. PA U Pr. 163 p. $25.00

ROBBINS, Chandler. *Sermon Preached Before John Hancock & Samuel Adams.* 1791 Boston. 1st ed. 51 p. wraps. G $45.00

ROBBINS, Charles Henry. *Gam: Group of Whaling Stories.* 1899 New Bedford. Ills 1st ed. 203 p. G $15.00

ROBBINS, Harold. *Betsy.* 1971 NY. 1st ed. dj. EX $11.00

ROBBINS, Harold. *Dreams Die 1st.* 1977 Simon Schuster. 1st ed. dj. VG $10.00

ROBBINS, Harold. *Good-Bye Janette.* 1981 Simon Schuster. 1st ed. dj. VG $12.50

ROBBINS, Harold. *79 Park Avenue.* 1955 NY. 1st ed. dj. $16.00

ROBBINS, M. *Refrain of Roses.* 1965 Denver. Swallow. incr. dj. $15.00

ROBBINS, R. *Outlines of Ancient & Modern History.* 1843 Hartford. Ills. 12mo. 2 vols in 1. $15.00

ROBBINS, R.W. *Discovery at Walden Pond.* 1947 8vo. sgn. dj. VG $20.00

ROBBINS, Todd. *Who Wants a Green Bottle? & Other Uncanny Tales.* 1926 Philip Allan. 1st ed. VG $60.00

ROBBINS, Tom. *Even Cowgirls Get the Blues.* 1976 Boston. Houghton Mifflin. 1st ed. dj. $65.00

ROBBINS, Tom. *Jitterbug Perfume.* 1984 Bantam. Review copy. $18.00

ROBBINS, Tom. *Jitterbug Perfume.* 1984 Bantam. Advance copy. wraps. EX $25.00

ROBBINS, Tom. *Jitterbug Perfume.* 1984 Bantam. 1st ed. dj. EX $15.00

ROBBINS, Tom. *Still Life with Woodpecker.* 1980 Bantam. 1st ed. dj. M $20.00

ROBERGE. *Timber Country.* 1973 Caxton. 1st ed. photos. dj. EX $50.00

ROBERSON, Charles L. *Historical Rooms From Manor Houses of England.* 1921 London. EX $24.00

ROBERTS, Bruce. *Faces of SC.* 1976 Garden City. 1st ed. dj. VG $10.00

ROBERTS, Bruce. *Springs From the Parched Ground.* 1950 private print. sgn. dj. EX $30.00

ROBERTS, Cecil. *Man Arose.* 1941 NY. Macmillan. Intro Willkie. sgn. EX $30.00

ROBERTS, Cecil. *8 for Eternity.* 1947 Hodder Stoughton. 1st ed. G $3.50

ROBERTS, Charles. *Kings in Exile.* 1910 NY. Macmillan. Ills 1st ed. 8vo. 298 p. $25.00

ROBERTS, E. *NY.* 1887 1st ed. American Commonwealth Series. $40.00

ROBERTS, Edwards. *Shoshone & Other Western Wonders.* 1888 Harper. Ills. 275 p. fair. $4.00

ROBERTS, Edwards. *Shoshone & Other Western Wonders.* 1888 NY. Ills 1st ed. VG $35.00

ROBERTS, Eizabeth. *Black Is My True Love's Hair.* 1938 NY. Ltd 1st ed. 1/175. slipcase. $40.00

ROBERTS, F. *River Basin Surveys.* 1960 Smithsonian. Ills. 337 p. maps. EX $20.00

ROBERTS, G. *English Origins of New England Families.* 1985 Geneal Pub. 3 vol set. djs. EX $45.00

ROBERTS, Henry W. *Aviation Radio.* 1945 NY. Morrow. Ills. inscr. 637 p. dj. $35.00

ROBERTS, Howard. *Big 9.* 1948 NY. dj. G $15.00

ROBERTS, J. *My Congo Adventure.* 1963 London. Jarrolds. Ills 1st ed. dj. VG $20.00

ROBERTS, James Hall. *Q Document.* no date. Book Club ed. dj. VG $3.00

ROBERTS, Job. *PA Farmer.* 1804 Phil. Bertram. 224 p. $100.00

ROBERTS, K. *Battle of Cowpens.* 1958 Ills 1st ed. 8vo. 111 p. dj. VG $25.00

ROBERTS, Keith. *Chalk Giants.* 1975 Berkley Putnam. 1st ed. dj. EX $25.00

ROBERTS, Keith. *Chalk Giants.* 1974 Hutchinson. 1st ed. dj. xl. $7.50

ROBERTS, Kenneth. *Antiqueamania.* 1928 NY. 1st ed. dj. EX $50.00

ROBERTS, Kenneth. *Biographical Sketch.* 1936 Doubleday Doran. 1st ed. VG $30.00

ROBERTS, Kenneth. *Boon Island.* 1956 Garden City. 1st ed. dj. EX $20.00

ROBERTS, Kenneth. *Boon Island.* 1956 Doubleday. 1st ed. dj. VG $15.00

ROBERTS, Kenneth. *Captain Caution.* 1949 London. 1st English ed. dj. VG $15.00

ROBERTS, Kenneth. *Captain Caution.* 1966 Doubleday. 310 p. dj. EX $6.00

ROBERTS, Kenneth. *FL.* 1926 Harper. Ills 1st ed. VG $25.00

ROBERTS, Kenneth. *Henry Gross & His Dowsing Rod.* 1951 Garden City. 1st ed. dj. VG $17.50

ROBERTS, Kenneth. *Henry Gross & His Dowsing Rod.* 1951 NY. 1st ed. presentation. sgn. dj. EX $75.00

ROBERTS, Kenneth. *I Wanted To Write.* 1949 Doubleday. 1st ed. dj. EX $25.00

ROBERTS, Kenneth. *Lydia Bailey.* 1947 NY. Ltd 1st ed. 1/1,050. sgn. $125.00

ROBERTS, Kenneth. *Northwest Passage.* 1937 NY. 1st ed. sgn. dj. VG $40.00

ROBERTS, Kenneth. *Northwest Passage.* 1938 Doubleday Doran. 709 p. dj. EX $6.00

ROBERTS, Kenneth. *Oliver Wiswell.* 1940 NY. Doubleday Doran. 1st trade ed. $20.00

ROBERTS, Kenneth. *Oliver Wiswell.* 1940 Doubleday. Ltd ed. sgn. $100.00

ROBERTS, Kenneth. *Trending into ME.* 1938 Boston. Arundel ed. 1/727. slipcase. $325.00

ROBERTS, Kenneth. *Trending into ME.* 1985 reprint of Arundel ed. dj. EX $35.00

ROBERTS, Kenneth. *Trending into ME.* 1938 Boston. Ills Wyeth. Ltd 1st ed. sgns. $275.00

ROBERTS, Kenneth. *Trending into ME.* 1938 Little Brown. Ills NC Wyeth. 1st ed. EX $35.00

ROBERTS, Kenneth. *Water Unlimited.* 1957 Doubleday. 1st ed. dj. $17.50

ROBERTS, Leslie. *There Shall Be Wings.* 1960 London. Ills 1st ed. 290 p. dj. $27.50

ROBERTS, M.F. *Turtles.* 1980 Ills. 93 p. wraps. $5.00

ROBERTS, Patricia. *Table Settings, Entertaining, & Etiquette: History & Guide.* 1967 NY. 1st ed. EX $20.00

ROBERTS, Peter. *Victoria de Los Angeles.* 1982 London. Ills. dj. VG $25.00

ROBERTS, T. *Accurate Home Estimating.* 1947 Milwaukee. Ills. 285 p. $15.00

ROBERTS, Ursula. *Health, Healing, & You.* 1965 124 p. dj. EX $15.00

ROBERTS, W.A. *Lake Pontchartrain.* 1946 Bobbs Merrill. Ills. 376 p. maps. dj. VG $10.00

ROBERTSON, A.J. *ABC of Golf.* 1923 London. 12mo. 110 p. $35.00

ROBERTSON, D. *Sea Survival: A Manual.* 1975 NY. 1st ed. dj. VG $27.50

ROBERTSON, Florence H. *Shadow Land: Stories of the South.* 1906 Boston. Ills 1st ed. 12mo. 91 p. VG $30.00

ROBERTSON, G. *Account of Discovery of Tahiti.* 1955 London. Folio Soc. Ills. 127 p. VG $17.50

ROBERTSON, J.K. *Book of Lettering.* 1926 London. Black. Ills. 8vo. 48 p. VG $20.00

ROBERTSON, J.M. *Pagan Christs.* 1966 NY. 171 p. dj. M $18.00

ROBERTSON, J.P. *Letters on Paraguay Comprising Account of 4 Year Residence.* 1838 London. Murray. 1st ed. 2 vol set. VG $150.00

ROBERTSON, J.W. *Land of the Evergreens: Pictorial Review of Delmarva.* 1963 Eastern Shore News. dj. VG $18.50

ROBERTSON, J.W. *Study of Edgar Allan Poe.* 1921 San Francisco. 1st ed. 424 p. EX $45.00

ROBERTSON, Manning. *Everyday Architecture.* c 1923. NY. McDevitt Wilson. G $22.00

ROBERTSON, R.B. *Of Whales & Men.* 1954 Knopf. Ills. 300 p. VG $8.00

ROBERTSON, Stephen L. *Shropshire Racket.* 1937 London. Ills Derrick. 1st ed. dj. VG $30.00

ROBERTSON, Terence. *Shame & Glory.* 1962 Canada. Ills 1st ed. 432 p. dj. VG $22.50

ROBERTSON, William. *Historical Disquisition of India.* 1799 London. 3rd ed. VG $95.00

ROBERTSON, William. *History of America.* 1912 Phil. 2 vol set. leather. G $35.00

ROBERTSON, William. *History of America.* 1818 London. 24mo. 400 p. ½–leather. G $12.00

ROBERTSON, William. *History of America.* 1803 London. 8vo. 4 vol set. leather. $10.00

ROBERTSON, William. *History of Scotland.* 1759 London. 2 vol set. xl. $125.00

ROBERTSON, William. *Life of Miranda.* 1929 Chapel Hill. Ills 1st ed. 2 vol set. EX $75.00

ROBERTSON & HARRIS. *Soapy Smith: King of the Frontier Con Men.* 1961 NY. Ills 1st ed. 244 p. dj. VG $22.50

ROBERTSON-MILLER, E. *Butterfly & Moth Book.* 1920 Scribner. Ills. 249 p. G $5.00

ROBESON, Paul. *Here I Stand.* 1958 NY. sgn. dj. $35.00

ROBINS, Edward. *Romances of Early America.* 1902 Phil. Ills 1st ed. 268 p. $25.00

ROBINSON, A. Mary. *Emily Bronte.* 1893 Oston. 1st ed. EX $15.00

ROBINSON, B.W. *Shotgun & Rifle in North American Game Fields.* 1925 Appleton. Ills 1st ed. 387 p. VG $20.00

ROBINSON, Bill. *Berth to Bermuda.* 1961 Princeton. Ills. dj. VG $8.00

ROBINSON, C. *Discoveries in West Until 1519.* 1848 Richmond. 1st ed. rebound. G $70.00

ROBINSON, C. *Rook.* no date. c 1920. London. 4to. G $25.00

ROBINSON, Charles. *Old Naval Prints: Their Artists & Engravers.* 1924 London. Ltd ed. 1/1,500. 4to. blue cloth. $175.00

ROBINSON, Charles. *Our Sentimental Garden.* 1914 Lippincott. gilt green cloth. VG $45.00

ROBINSON, Charles. *4 Gardens.* 1912 Lippincott. 1st ed. 161 p. purple cloth. $40.00

ROBINSON, D.H. *Dangerous Sky.* 1973 London. Ills. dj. EX $20.00

ROBINSON, D.M. *Ancient Sinope: Historical Account.* 1906 Baltimore. John Hopkins. VG $12.00

ROBINSON, E.A. *Amaranth.* 1934 NY. 1st ed. dj. EX $20.00

ROBINSON, E.A. *Cavender's House.* 1929 NY. 1st ed. dj. EX $20.00

ROBINSON, E.A. *Children of the Night.* 1897 Boston. Badger. 1st ed. 1/500. VG $100.00

ROBINSON, E.A. *Matthias at the Door.* 1931 NY. 1st ed. dj. EX $15.00

ROBINSON, E.A. *Sonnets 1889-1927.* 1928 NY. Rudge. 1/561. sgn. EX $40.00

ROBINSON, E.A. *Sonnets.* 1927 NY. Crosby Gaige. Ltd ed. sgn. VG $30.00

ROBINSON, E.A. *Talifer.* 1933 NY. Ltd ed. 1/273. sgn. slipcase. VG $75.00

ROBINSON, E.A. *Talifer.* 1933 NY. Macmillan. 1st trade ed. sgn. dj. $25.00

ROBINSON, Eric. *Partners in Science: James Watt & Joseph Black.* 1970 Harvard U Pr. Ills. 502 p. dj. EX $15.00

ROBINSON, F.C. *Bluebird.* 1920 Dodd Mead. Ills. VG $35.00

ROBINSON, Fayette. *Mexico & Her Military Chieftains.* 1848 Hartford. 1st ed. cloth. $80.00

ROBINSON, G. *Old Wagon Show Days.* 1925 Cincinnati. Ills 1st ed. 250 p. VG $22.50

ROBINSON, George. *Bait Casting.* 1941 Barnes. Ills. 66 p. VG $5.00

ROBINSON, George. *Fly Casting.* 1942 Barnes. Ills. 66 p. dj. G $5.00

ROBINSON, H.P. *Letters on Landscape Photography.* 1888 NY. Ills. 8vo. VG $85.00

ROBINSON, H.P. *Pictorial Effect in Photography.* 1881 Phil. 1st ed. 8vo. VG $115.00

ROBINSON, J.B. *Pictures of Slavery & Anti-Slavery.* 1863 fair. $30.00

ROBINSON, J.H. *Dr. Silver-Knife; or, Hunters of the Rocky Mountains.* 1850 Boston. 1st ed. wraps. EX $125.00

ROBINSON, Kim Stanley. *Icehenge.* London. 1st ed. sgn. EX $45.00

ROBINSON, Kim Stanley. *Wild Shore.* London. 1st ed. sgn. EX $50.00

ROBINSON, L. *Further Letters of John Butler Yeats.* 1920 Dundrum. Cuala Pr. Ltd ed. 81 p. $65.00

ROBINSON, M.L. *Runner of the Mountain Tops: Life of Louis Agassiz.* 1939 Random House. Ills. 264 p. dj. VG $10.00

ROBINSON, Mabel L. *Robin & Tito.* 1930 NY. Macmillan. Ills Burns. $15.00

ROBINSON, Marilynne. *Housekeeping.* 1980 Farrar. 1st ed. dj. VG $20.00

ROBINSON, Mary. *Amateur's Guide to the Night.* 1983 Knopf. 1st ed. dj. EX $12.00

ROBINSON, Mary. *Day.* 1979 Random House. Uncorrected proof. $35.00

ROBINSON, Rollo S. *Shots at Mule Deer.* 1972 NY. sgn. dj. EX $25.00

ROBINSON, Rowland E. *Hunting Without a Gun & Other Papers.* 1905 NY. 1st ed. 2nd state. 391 p. $25.00

ROBINSON, S. *Antimony.* 1980 Dell. 1st ed. wraps. VG $50.00

ROBINSON, S. *Fact for Farmers.* 1868 NY. Ills. gilt leather. VG $35.00

ROBINSON, Selma. *City Child.* 1931 Farrar. Ills Kent. 1st ed. 8vo. 64 p. $35.00

ROBINSON, Victor. *Pathfinders in Medicine.* 1929 NY. Medical Life Pr. 2nd ed. VG $25.00

ROBINSON, Victor. *Story of Medicine.* 1936 NY. Tudor. 2nd print. VG $25.00

ROBINSON, W. *Mushroom Culture: Its Extension & Improvement.* 1870 London. 1st ed. 172 p. xl. $25.00

ROBINSON, W.A. *10,000 Leagues Over the Sea.* 1932 NY. Putnam. Ills 1st ed. 8vo. dj. G $35.00

ROBINSON, W.H. *Bill the Minder.* 1912 Holt. 1st Am ed. gilt olive cloth. $325.00

ROBINSON, W.H. *Bill the Minder.* 1912 London. Ills Robinson. 1/380. 4to. $275.00

ROBINSON, W.H. *Rabelais, Gargantua, & Pantagruel.* 1904 London. Ills. 2 vol set. VG $85.00

ROBINSON, W.H. *Witchery of Rita & Waiting for Tonti.* 1919 Phoenix. 1st ed. scarce. VG $75.00

ROBINSON, W.H. *Works of Rabelais.* no date. London. private print. $30.00

ROBISON, Andrew. *Piranesi: Early Architectural Fantasies.* 1986 Chicago U Pr. Ills. oblong folio. 241 p. dj. $55.00

ROBISON, James. *Rumor & Other Stories.* 1985 Summit. 1st ed. dj. VG $15.00

ROBISON, Mary. *Days.* 1979 NY. Knopf. Uncorrected proof. VG $50.00

ROBISON, Mary. *Days.* 1979 NY. Knopf. Review copy. EX $35.00

ROBOTTI, F.D. *Chronicles of Old Salem.* 1948 Salem. 1st ed. dj. $8.50

ROBOTTI, F.D. *Key to NY.* 1964 NY. Tricentennial ed. 1st print. $20.00

ROBOTTI, F.D. *Whaling & Old Salem.* 1962 Bonanza. reprint. 292 p. dj. VG $10.00

ROBOTTI, F.D. *Whaling & Old Salem.* 1950 Newcomb/Gauss. 1st ed. dj. VG $27.50

ROCA, P.M. *Paths of the Padres Through Sonora.* 1967 Tucson. 1st ed. dj. EX $60.00

ROCA, P.M. *Spanish Jesuit Churches in Mexico's Tarahumara.* 1979 Tucson. 1st ed. 369 p. dj. VG $20.00

ROCH, Carl. *Zeichnungen Altdeutscher Meister zur Zeit Dures.* 1922 Dresden. cloth. VG $95.00

ROCH, Philip. *Circles of Time.* 1981 Seaview. Advance copy. dj. EX $12.00

ROCHESTER, E.F. *Rochester Family in America 1640-1934.* 1934 NY. 4to. 77 p. $40.00

ROCK, B. *Storms.* 1947 private print. inscr. G $10.00

ROCKOW, H.K. *Creative Home Decorating.* 1946 NY. Ills. 323 p. $12.50

ROCKWELL, Carey. *Danger in Deep Space.* no date. Grosset Dunlap. dj. EX $20.00

ROCKWELL, Carey. *Sabotage in Space.* no date. Grosset Dunlap. $15.00

ROCKWELL, Norman. *Golden Anniversary Book of Scouting.* 1959 NY. 2nd ed. dj. VG $40.00

ROCKWELL, Norman. *My Adventures As an Illustrator.* 1960 NY. dj. VG $15.00

ROCKWELL, Norman. *Scrapbook for a Young Boy.* 1979 NY. Abbeville. poem by Mendoza. VG $25.00

ROCKWELL, Norman. *Willie Was Different: Tale of Ugly Thrushing.* 1969 Funk Wagnall. 1st ed. beige cloth. dj. VG $35.00

ROCKWELL, Norman. *Willie Was Different: Tale of Ugly Thrushing.* 1969 Funk Wagnall. octavo. white linen. dj. EX $35.00

ROCKWELL, R.H. *My Way of Becoming a Hunter.* 1955 Norton. Ills 1st ed. 285 p. dj. VG $15.00

ROCKWELL, Wilson. *Memoirs of a Lawman.* 1962 Denver. dj. VG $15.00

ROCKWOOD, Roy. *Bomba & the Hostile Chieftain.* no date. Cupples Leon. $10.00

ROCKWOOD, Roy. *Bomba at the Giant Cataract.* no date. Cupples Leon. VG $7.50

ROCKWOOD, Roy. *Bomba at the Moving Mountain.* no date. Cupples Leon. dj. VG $12.00

ROCKWOOD, Roy. *Bomba in the Land of Burning Lava.* no date. Cupples Leon. dj. VG $10.00

ROCKWOOD, Roy. *Bomba in the Steaming Grotto.* no date. Cupples Leon. dj. VG $10.00

ROCKWOOD, Roy. *Lost on the Moon.* no date. Whitman. VG $15.00

ROCKWOOD, Roy. *Through the Air to the North Pole.* no date. Cupples Leon. G $15.00

ROCKWOOD, Roy. *Wizard of the Sea.* 1900 NY. Burt. dj. EX $20.00

RODALE, J.I. *Encyclopedia of Common Diseases.* 1971 Rodale. 8th ed. VG $15.00

RODALE, J.I. *Encyclopedia of Organic Gardening.* 1972 Rodale. 19th ed. dj. VG $12.50

RODALE, J.I. *Stone Mulching in the Garden.* 1949 Rodale. 164 p. dj. G $10.00

RODALE, Robert. *Sane Living in a Mad World.* 1972 Rodale Pr. 1st ed. dj. $4.00

RODD, Ralph. *Midnight Murder.* 1931 Crime Club. 1st ed. VG $20.00

RODEN, H.W. *You Only Hang Once.* 1945 Triangle. 4th ed. dj. VG $7.00

RODEN, Robert. *Famous Presses: Cambridge Press 1683-1692.* 1905 NY. 1st ed. 1/750. VG $85.00

RODGERS, D. *House in My Head.* 1967 NY. Ills. 254 p. $18.00

RODGERS, Dorothy. *Personal Book.* 1977 NY. Harper Row. Ills. dj. EX $20.00

RODIER, Paul. *Romance of French Weaving.* 1936 NY. Tudor. $27.50

RODIER, Paul. *Romance of French Weaving.* 1931 NY. Stokes. xl. fair. $25.00

RODIER, Paul. *Romance of French Weaving.* 1931 NY. dj. slipcase. EX $45.00

RODIN, Auguste. *Cathedrals of France.* 1965 Boston. Beacon. Intro Herbert Read. $25.00

RODMAN, O.H.P. *Handbook of Salt-Water Fishing.* 1940 Lippincott. Ills. 269 p. dj. VG $7.50

RODMAN, Selden. *Airmen: Poem in 4 Parts.* 1941 NY. 1st ed. dj. G $20.00

RODMAN, Selden. *Insiders.* 1960 LA U Pr. 1st ed. dj. $15.00

RODMAN, Selden. *Portrait of the Artist As an American: Ben Shahn.* 1951 Harper. Ills. 4to. 180 p. dj. $40.00

RODMAN, Seldon. *Mortal Triumph & Other Poems.* 1932 NY. 1st ed. dj. VG $17.50

RODMAN, Seldon. *Revolutionists: Tragedy in 3 Acts.* 1942 NY. Ills 1st ed. 193 p. $7.50

RODWELL, Anne. *Child's 1st Step to English History.* 1844 Ills. cloth. VG $45.00

RODZINSKI, Halina. *Our 2 Lives.* 1976 Scribner. $10.00

ROE, Edward P. *Success with Small Fruits.* 1880 NY. Ills Winslow Homer. 1st ed. G $30.00

ROE, F.G. *Indian & the Horses.* 1974 OK U Pr. Ills 1st ed. 433 p. VG $30.00

ROE, F.G. *Sporting Prints of the 18th & Early 19th Centuries.* 1927 NY. Payson Clarke. 1st Am ed. 4to. $70.00

ROE, Fred. *Old Oak Furniture.* 1908 Chicago. Ills. 339 p. G $35.00

ROE, Ivan. *Salamander Touch.* 1972 Hutchinson. 1st ed. VG $5.50

ROE, Joseph E. *English & American Tool Builders.* 1916 New Haven. 8vo. 315 p. VG $100.00

ROEDER. *Juarez & His Mexico.* 1947 NY. 1st ed. 2vol set. slipcase. EX $60.00

ROEHM, Marjorie Catlin. *Letters of George Catlin & His Family.* 1966 Berkely. dj. VG $18.00

ROEINE, M. *Henry E. Sigerist on Sociology of Medicine.* 1937 MD. VG $15.00

ROESSEL, R. *Pictorial History of Navajo 1860-1910.* 1980 Rough Rock. 1st ed. 240 p. VG $25.00

ROESSLE, Theodore. *How To Cultivate & Preserve Celery.* 1860 Albany. 1st ed. plts. EX $60.00

ROESSLER, Arthur. *John Constable.* 1911 Berlin. VG $25.00

ROESSLER, Arthur. *Josef Danhauser.* 1946 Wien. 60 plts. $8.00

ROESSLER, Arthur. *Kritische Fragmente.* 1918 Wien. 1/70. 101 p. ½-leather. $75.00

ROETHKE, Theodore. *Lost Son.* 1949 London. 1st ed. dj. EX $60.00

ROETHKE, Theodore. *Lost Son.* 1948 Garden City. 1st ed. sgn. VG $50.00

ROETHKE, Theodore. *Open House.* 1941 NY. Ltd 1st ed. dj. VG $350.00

ROETHKE, Theodore. *Words for the Wind.* 1958 Garden City. 1st ed. dj. EX $375.00

ROFFMAN, Jan. *Walk in the Dark.* 1970 Crime Club. 1st ed. dj. VG $10.00

ROGERS, Agnes. *Women Are Here To Stay.* 1949 NY. Ills. dj. $7.50

ROGERS, B. *Books.* 1945 private print. inscr. VG $60.00

ROGERS, B. *Essays of Montaigne.* 1902-1904. Boston. 1/265. 3 vol set. VG $600.00

ROGERS, B. *New Year's Eve.* 1923 NY. Lamb. VG $25.00

ROGERS, B. *Will Rogers: Story of His Life.* 1941 Garden City. photos. 312 p. $4.00

ROGERS, Bruce. *Paragraphs on Printing.* 1943 NY. Rudge. Ills. 147 p. cloth. M $125.00

ROGERS, Bruce. *Unholy Bible Story by Bruce Rogers.* 1936 NY. Maverick. 1st ed. 1/40. dj. EX $100.00

ROGERS, D.B. *Prehistoric Man of Santa Barbara Coast.* 1929 Santa Barbara. Ills 1st ed. 452 p. maps. VG $47.50

ROGERS, Dale Evans. *Grandparents Can.* 1983 Old Tappan, NJ. 128 p. dj. EX $4.00

ROGERS, Dale Evans. *My Spiritual Diary.* 1955 Old Tappan, NJ. 144 p. dj. EX $4.00

ROGERS, Dorothy. *House in My Head.* 1967 NY. 1st ed. dj. VG $15.00

ROGERS, Dorothy. *My Favorite Things.* 1964 NY. Ills 1st ed. 282 p. dj. VG $12.00

ROGERS, Fairman. *Manual of Coaching.* 1900 Phil/London. Lippincott. Ills Ltd 1st ed. $400.00

ROGERS, Garet. *Brother Surgeons.* 1957 London. 1st ed. dj. M $22.00

ROGERS, Glendon J. *Stories Along the Kern.* 1958 San Francisco. Ills. sgn. 103 p. $12.50

ROGERS, H.C.B. *History of Artillery.* 1975 Citadel. 1st ed. 230 p. dj. VG $30.00

ROGERS, J. *Old Public Schools of England.* 1938 London. 1st ed. VG $10.00

ROGERS, James H. *America Weighs Her Gold.* 1931 Yale. dj. $20.00

ROGERS, Joel Townsley. *Stopped Clock.* 1958 Simon Schuster. 1st ed. dj. VG $25.00

ROGERS, John William. *Finding Literature on the TX Plains.* 1931 Dallas. Southwest Pr. 57 p. EX $75.00

ROGERS, John William. *Lusty Texans of Dallas.* 1951 Dutton. 1st ed. 384 p. dj. EX $20.00

ROGERS, John. *Sport in Vancouver & Newfoundland.* 1912 NY. 1st Am ed. VG $60.00

ROGERS, Julia Ellen. *Trees.* 1926 NY. 291 p. dj. $5.00

ROGERS, L. *Leprosy.* 1925 London. Ills. 301 p. G $18.00

ROGERS, L.W. *Ghosts in Shakespeare.* 1955 Theosophical Pr. 3rd print. VG $16.00

ROGERS, Lebbeaus Harding. *Kite Trust.* 1900 NY. Kite Trust Pub. 1st ed. VG $25.00

ROGERS, Lela E. *Ginger Rogers & Riddle of Scarlet Cloak.* 1942 Whitman. dj. VG $7.50

ROGERS, Robert. *Journals of Major Robert Rogers.* 1966 Readex. facsimile of 1765. 236 p. EX $8.00

ROGERS, Samuel. *Human Life.* 1819 London. Ills. G $10.00

ROGERS, Samuel. *Italy: A Poem.* 1830 London. Cabell Moxon. Ills 1st ed. VG $100.00

ROGERS, Samuel. *Poems.* 1843 London. fore-edge of Winchester. $375.00

ROGERS, Samuel. *Poems.* 1834 London. Ills Stothard. EX $75.00

ROGERS, Samuel. *Poems.* 1912 London. VG $180.00

ROGERS, W. *Cruising Voyage Around the World.* 1928 Ills. VG $10.00

ROGERS, W.G. *Wise Men Fish Here: Frances Steloff & Gotham Book Mart.* 1965 Harcourt. 1st ed. dj. $12.50

ROGERS, Will. *Ether & Me; or, Just Relax.* 1929 Putnam. 1st ed. VG $35.00

ROGERS, Will. *How We Elect Our Presidents.* 1952 Boston. 1st ed. 175 p. $50.00

ROGERS & BEARD. *5,000 Years of Glass.* 1937 NY. Stokes. Ills 2nd print. 303 p. VG $10.00

ROGET, Peter M. *Thesaurus of English Words.* 1854 Boston. 1st Am ed. VG $85.00

ROHAN, Jack. *Yankee Arms Maker: Incredible Career of Samuel Colt.* 1935 NY. Ills Revised ed. 378 p. dj. $17.50

ROHAN, Michael. *Anvil of Ice.* London. 1st ed. sgn. EX $36.00

ROHMER, Sax. *Bat Wing.* 1925 Cassell. 3rd ed. VG $25.00

ROHMER, Sax. *Brood of the Witch Queen.* 1924 Doubleday Page. 1st ed. G $45.00

ROHMER, Sax. *Brood of the Witch Queen.* 1927 Pearson. 5th ed. G $20.00

ROHMER, Sax. *Daughter of Fu Manchu.* 1931 Doubleday Doran. 1st ed. G $15.00

ROHMER, Sax. *Day the World Ended.* 1930 Crime Club. 1st ed. G $25.00

ROHMER, Sax. *Devil Doctor.* 1973 Tom Stacey. dj. EX $15.00

ROHMER, Sax. *Drums of Fu Manchu.* 1939 Crime Club. 1st ed. $45.00

ROHMER, Sax. *Emperor of America.* 1929 Crime Club. 1st ed. xl. rebound. $10.00

ROHMER, Sax. *Fire Tongue.* 1922 NY. Ills 1st ed. EX $20.00

ROHMER, Sax. *Green Eyes of Bast.* 1920 McBride. 1st ed. VG $25.00

ROHMER, Sax. *Mask of Fu Manchu.* 1955 Cassell. VG $15.00

ROHMER, Sax. *Moon of Madness.* 1933 Cassell. VG $40.00

ROHMER, Sax. *Mystery of Dr. Fu Manchu.* no date. Methuen. 2nd ed. fair. $20.00

ROHMER, Sax. *Quest of the Sacred Slipper.* 1939 Caxton. G $25.00

ROHMER, Sax. *Return of Dr. Fu Manchu.* 1916 NY. 1st ed. VG $60.00

ROHMER, Sax. *Return of Sumuru.* Gold Medal. pb. VG $15.00

ROHMER, Sax. *Romance of Sorcery.* 1914 London. Ills 1st ed. presentation. $80.00

ROHMER, Sax. *Sins of Sumuru.* 1950 London. 1st ed. dj. VG $55.00

ROHMER, Sax. *Trail of Fu Manchu.* 1936 London. 2nd ed. dj. G $18.00

ROHMER, Sax. *White Velvet.* 1936 Doubleday Doran. 1st ed. VG $75.00

ROJO, Richard. *My Friend Che.* 1968 Dial. 1st ed. dj. $10.00

ROLAND, E.P. *Eroberer der Lufte.* no date. (1908) Stuttgart. Ills 160 p. VG $55.00

ROLFE, R.T. & F.W. *Romance of the Fungus World.* 1974 Dover. reprint of 1925. 308 p. wraps. $8.00

ROLLIN, Charles. *Ancient History of Egyptians, Carthaginians, Assyrians, Etc.* 1846 NY. Harper. 1st Complete Am ed. 2 vol set. $120.00

ROLLINS, A.W. *Story of a Ranch.* 1885 NY. Ills. 16mo. $35.00

ROLLINS, Philip. *Cowboy.* 1922 NY. 1st ed. EX $35.00

ROLLINS, Philip. *Gone Haywire: Tenderfoot on MT Range in 1886.* 1939 NY. Ills 1st ed. dj. EX $30.00

ROLLINSON, J.K. *Pony Trails in WY.* 1941 Caxton. Ills 1st ed. VG $25.00

ROLLINSON, J.K. *WY Cattle Trails.* 1948 Caxton. Ltd 1st ed. sgn. dj. EX $75.00

ROLLO, W.K. *Fly Fishing: Practical Hints on the Sport.* 1947 Witherby. Ills. 143 p. dj. G $13.50

ROLVAG, O.E. *Giants in the Earth: Saga of the Prairie.* 1927 Harper. 1st ed. VG $18.00

ROMAINS, J. *Verdun.* 1939 NY. Knopf. 500 p. $4.00

ROMANES, G. *Mental Evolution in Man.* 1888 London. 1st ed. G $50.00

ROMBAUER, Irma. *Cookbook for Girls & Boys.* 1946 Indianapolis. Ills 1st ed. 243 p. VG $32.50

ROMBAUER. *Joy of Cooking.* 1936 Bobbs Merrill. 2nd ed. dj. VG $50.00

ROME, C. *Owl Who Came To Stay.* 1980 Crown. Ills. 144 p. dj. EX $10.00

ROMER, A.S. *Osteology of Reptiles.* 1968 Chicago U Pr. Ills. 772 p. EX $30.00

ROMERO, George A. *Dawn of the Dead.* 1978 St. Martin. 1st ed. dj. EX $45.00

ROMERO, Pablo Bush. *Mexico & Africa From the Sights of My Rifle.* c 1950. Mexico. 1st ed. 1/1,000. sgn. dj. EX $200.00

ROMERO, Pablo Bush. *My Adventures with Tigers & Lions.* no date. c 1950. Ills. 1/1,000. sgn. EX $200.00

RONALD, James. *This Way Out.* 1939 Lippincott. 1st ed. dj. xl. $10.00

RONBLOM, H.K. *Spy Without a Country.* 1965 NY. 1st ed. dj. VG $10.00

RONDA, J.P. *Lewis & Clark Among the Indians.* 1986 NE U Pr. Ills. 310 p. dj. M $25.00

RONNS, Edward. *Terror in the Town.* 1947 McKay. VG $10.00

ROOD, R. *Elephant Bones & Lonely Hearts.* 1977 Greene. 163 p. dj. VG $5.00

ROOKE, Leon. *Shakespeare's Dog.* 1983 Knopf. 1st Am ed. dj. EX $15.00

ROONEY, Andy; & HUTTON, B. *Story of Stars & Stripes.* 1970 Farrar. dj. G $15.00

ROOS, Kelley. *Bad Trip.* 1971 Dodd Mead. 1st ed. dj. xl. $5.00

ROOS, Kelley. *Triple Threat.* 1949 AA Wyn. 1st ed. dj. G $20.00

ROOSEVELT, Eleanor. *Christmas 1940.* 1986 St. Martin. 1st Am ed. 8vo. 61 p. dj. EX $7.50

ROOSEVELT, Eleanor. *India & the Awakening East.* 1953 NY. dj. VG $18.00

ROOSEVELT, Eleanor. *Indian & the Awakening East.* 1953 NY. Ills 1st ed. inscr. dj. $150.00

ROOSEVELT, Eleanor. *It's Up To the Women.* 1933 1st ed. 8vo. 263 p. G $15.00

ROOSEVELT, Eleanor. *On My Own.* 1958 NY. Ills. inscr. cloth. VG $75.00

ROOSEVELT, Eleanor. *This I Remember.* 1949 NY. Ills 1st ed. sgn. cloth. $60.00

ROOSEVELT, Eleanor. *This I Remember.* 1949 NY. Ltd 1st ed. sgn. slipcase. EX $95.00

ROOSEVELT, Eleanor. *This I Remember.* 1949 NY. Ltd ed. 1/1,000. 8vo. sgn. blue cloth. $100.00

ROOSEVELT, Elliott. *Murder & the 1st Lady.* no date. Book Club ed. dj. VG $4.00

ROOSEVELT, Franklin D. *Public Papers & Addresses of Franklin D. Roosevelt.* 1938 Random House. 5 vol set. djs. slipcase. EX $75.00

ROOSEVELT, Kermit. *Long Trail.* 1921 NY. sgn. EX $20.00

ROOSEVELT, Kermit. *Sentimental Safari.* 1963 Knopf. Ills 1st ed. 286 p. dj. EX $12.50

ROOSEVELT, T. & K. *East of the Sun & West of the Moon.* no date. Scribner. Ills. 284 p. VG $10.00

ROOSEVELT, T. & K. *East of the Sun & West of the Moon.* 1926 Scribner. $30.00

ROOSEVELT, Theodore. *African Game Trails.* 1926 Scribner. 4 vol set. EX $7.00

ROOSEVELT, Theodore. *African Game Trails.* 1910 Syndicate. dj. G $30.00

ROOSEVELT, Theodore. *African Game Trails.* 1910 NY. Scribner. 1st ed. VG $40.00

ROOSEVELT, Theodore. *Average Americans.* 1919 NY. Ills 1st ed. 12mo. 252 p. G $27.00

ROOSEVELT, Theodore. *Book Lover's Holidays in the Open.* 1916 NY. 1st ed. VG $35.00

ROOSEVELT, Theodore. *Book Lover's Holidays in the Open.* 1925 Scribner. Ills. 373 p. VG $6.50

ROOSEVELT, Theodore. *Deer Family.* 1902 NY. Ills Carl Rungus. 1st ed. EX $45.00

ROOSEVELT, Theodore. *Fear God & Take Your Own Part.* 1914 NY. Doran. VG $40.00

ROOSEVELT, Theodore. *Good Hunting: Pursuit of Big Game in the West.* 1907 Harper. Ills 1st ed. 12mo. 107 p. $20.00

ROOSEVELT, Theodore. *Hunting Adventures in West.* 1927 Putnam. Ills Remington. 1st ed. 366 p. $40.00

ROOSEVELT, Theodore. *Outdoor Pastimes.* 1925 Scribner. Ills. 409 p. VG $8.00

ROOSEVELT, Theodore. *Outdoor Pastimes.* 1905 Scribner. Ills 1st ed. 369 p. VG $45.00

ROOSEVELT, Theodore. *Ranch Life & Hunting Trail.* 1981 Time Life. reprint of 1888. 186 p. M $25.00

ROOSEVELT, Theodore. *Ranch Life & Hunting Trail.* 1969 Winchester. Ills. 4to. 186 p. dj. EX $20.00

ROOSEVELT, Theodore. *Ranch Life & Hunting Trail.* 1888 NY. Ills Remington. 1st ed. VG $285.00

ROOSEVELT, Theodore. *Rough Riders.* 1900 NY. Putnam. leather. EX $35.00

ROOSEVELT, Theodore. *Rough Riders.* 1899 NY. 1st ed. dj. VG $75.00

ROOSEVELT, Theodore. *Strenuous Life.* 1900 NY. 1st ed. G $25.00

ROOSEVELT, Theodore. *Theodore Roosevelt: Autobiography.* 1923 Scribner. Ills. 597 p. G $19.00

ROOSEVELT, Theodore. *Theodore Roosevelt: Autobiography.* 1913 NY. Ills 1st ed. 647 p. cloth. EX $15.00

ROOSEVELT, Theodore. *Through the Brazilian Wilderness.* 1925 Scribner. Ills. 410 p. maps. VG $14.00

ROOSEVELT, Theodore. *Trailing the Giant Panda.* 1929 NY/London. Ills. fair. $35.00

ROOSEVELT, Theodore. *Trailing the Great Panda.* 1929 NY. Scribner. dj. $65.00

ROOSEVELT, Theodore. *Wilderness Hunter.* 1900 NY. ¾-leather. EX $45.00

ROOSEVELT, Theodore. *Winning of the West.* 1900 Putnam. Alleghany ed. 4 vol set. VG $50.00

ROOSEVELT, Theodore. *Works of Theodore Roosevelt.* NY. Putnam. 12mo. ¾-calf. 15 vol set. $225.00

ROOSEVELT, Theodore. *Works of Theodore Roosevelt.* 1923-1925. NY. Memorial ed. 24 vol set. EX $300.00

ROOT, A.I. & E.R. *ABC & XYZ of Bee Culture.* 1929 Root. Ills. 815 p. VG $13.00

ROOT, Elihu. *Military & Colonial Policy of US* Cambridge. 1916 Cambridge U Pr. cloth. VG $30.00

ROOT, R.R. *Landscape Garden Series.* c 1920s. Garden Pr. boxed. VG $35.00

ROPER, Daniel. *50 Years of Public Life.* 1941 Duke U Pr. Ills. cloth. VG $20.00

ROPER, Freeman C.S. *Catalogue of Works on the Microscope.* no date. Bronxville. Smith. M $15.00

ROPER, R. *Royo Country.* 1973 NY. 1st ed. dj. EX $12.00

ROPER, W.F. *Experiments of a Handgunner.* 1949 Stackpole Heck. Ills 1st ed. 202 p. dj. EX $28.00

RORER, Mrs. S.T. *Good Ways in Cooking.* 1889 Hart. wraps. $30.00

ROREX, Robert A.; & FONG, W. *18 Songs of a Nomad Flute: 14th Handscroll in MOMA.* 1974 NY. slipcase. EX $25.00

RORICK, Isabel Scott. *Mr. & Mrs. Cugat.* 1946 Tower. dj. VG $10.00

ROSA, J.G. *Gunfighter: Man or Myth.* 1969 OK U Pr. Ills. 229 p. dj. EX $20.00

ROSA, J.G. *Guns of the American West.* 1985 Crown. Ills 1st ed. 192 p. dj. EX $45.00

ROSA, Joseph. *They Called Him Wild Bill.* 1964 Norman. 1st ed. dj. EX $50.00

ROSA, Juimaraes. *Devil To Pay in the Back Lanes.* 1963 Knopf. 1st ed. dj. VG $22.50

ROSCOE, J. *25 Years in East Africa.* 1969 Negro U Pr. reprint of 1921. 288 p. EX $15.00

ROSCOE, Thomas. *History of Painting in Italy.* 1826 London. 6 vols in 5. $200.00

ROSCOE, Thomas. *Works of Jonathan Swift.* 1880 with clippings/letters. $75.00

ROSE, Augustus F. *Jewelry Making & Design.* 1949 Worcester, MA. Ills. gilt tan linen. $27.50

ROSE, Barbara. *American Art Since 1900.* 1967 NY. Praeger. World of Art Series. 320 p. $12.50

ROSE, Bernice. *Drawings of Roy Lichtenstein.* 1987 MOMA. Ills. square 4to. cloth. dj. $37.50

ROSE, Bernice. *Jackson Pollock: Drawing into Painting.* 1980 MOMA. Ills. oblong 4to. 96 p. wraps. $10.00

ROSE, Billy. *Wine, Women, & Words.* 1948 Simon Schuster. Ills 1st ed. 1st print. VG $20.00

ROSE, E.W. *Cathedrals & Cloisters of Midland France.* 1907 NY. Ills. 766 p. 2 vol set. M $75.00

ROSE, H.W. *Colonial House of Worship in America.* 1963 NY. Ills. 574 p. $38.00

ROSE, R. *Living Magic.* 1956 Rand McNally. Ills 1st ed. 240 p. VG $10.00

ROSEAMAN, I.P. *Leatherwork.* 1954 London. Ills. 75 p. $8.50

ROSEBUSH, W.E. *Frontier Steel: Men & Their Weapons.* 1958 Nelson. Ills 1st ed. 355 p. dj. EX $22.50

ROSEN, S.R. *Judge Judges Mushrooms.* 1982 Highlander. Ills. 92 p. wraps. EX $5.00

ROSENBACH, A.S.W. *Book Hunter's Holiday.* 1936 NY. 1st ed. VG $45.00

ROSENBACH, A.S.W. *Book Hunter's Holiday.* 1936 Boston. Ltd ed. 1/760. sgn. slipcase. $110.00

ROSENBACH, A.S.W. *Books & Bidders.* 1927 Boston. 1st ed. sgn. $65.00

ROSENBACH, A.S.W. *Unpublishable Memoirs.* 1924 London. 1st ed. VG $30.00

ROSENBERG, C.G. *Jenny Lind: Her Life, Struggles, & Triumphs.* 1850 NY. String Townsend. Ills. 82 p. $95.00

ROSENBERG, D. *Chosen Days: Celebrating Jewish Festivals in Poetry & Art.* 1980 London. 1st ed. 231 p. $12.00

ROSENBERG, Harold. *Artworks & Packages.* 1969 NY. Horizon. Ills. 4to. 232 p. dj. $40.00

ROSENBERG, M.M. *IA on the Eve of Civil War: Decade of Frontier Politics.* 1972 OK U Pr. 1st ed. 262 p. map. dj. EX $32.00

ROSENBERG, Samuel. *Naked Is the Best Disguise.* 1974 Bobbs Merrill. 1st ed. dj. VG $15.00

ROSENFELD, Paul. *Men Seen.* 1925 NY. 380 p. dj. VG $10.00

ROSENTHAL, M.L. *Randall Jarrell.* 1972 MN U Pr. 1st ed. 8vo. wraps. EX $12.50

ROSENTHAL & GELB. *1 More Victim.* 1967 NY. 1st ed. dj. EX $20.00

ROSKE, R.J. *Everyman's Eden: History of CA.* 1968 Macmillan. Ills 1st print. 624 p. VG $20.00

ROSMAN, Alice Grant. *Jock the Scot.* 1930 Minton Balch. Ills. 4to. 204 p. dj. VG $35.00

ROSNER, Charles. *Printer's Progress: Comparative Survey 1851-1951.* 1951 Harvard Pr. Ills 1st ed. 4to. VG $20.00

ROSS, A. *Fur Hunters of the Far West.* 1967 OK U Pr. Ills. 304 p. dj. VG $30.00

ROSS, A.M. *Birds of Canada.* 1872 Toronto. Ills 2nd ed. 152 p. VG $27.50

ROSS, Alexander. *Adventures of the 1st Settlers on the OR or Columbian River.* 1969 Citadel. 388 p. map. dj. EX $7.50

ROSS, Barnaby. *Tragedy of X.* 1932 NY. VG $10.00

ROSS, E.S. *Insects Close Up: Pictorial Guide for the Photographer.* 1953 CA U Pr. Ills. 81 p. VG $10.00

ROSS, E.S. *Spirited Life: Bertha M. Miller & Children's Books.* 1973 Boston. 1st ed. dj. EX $20.00

ROSS, I. *1st Lady of the South: Life of Mrs. Jefferson Davis.* 1958 NY. Harper. 1st ed. presentation. dj. EX $27.50

ROSS, M.D. *West of Alfred J. Miller.* 1951 OK U Pr. dj. VG $35.00

ROSS, Nancy Wilson. *Waves: Story of Girls in Blue.* 1943 NY. Ills 1st ed. inscr. 214 p. dj. $35.00

ROSS, Sam. *Empty Sleeve: Biography of Luicus Fairchild.* 1964 WI Hist Soc. sgn. dj. $15.00

ROSS & EMERSON. *Wonders of Barnacles.* 1974 Dodd Mead. Ills. 78 p. dj. EX $5.00

ROSSBACH, Ed. *Baskets As Textile Art.* 1973 Van Nostrand. Ills. 199 p. dj. $45.00

ROSSELL, H.E. *Principles of Naval Architecture.* 1939 NY. Society of Naval Architects. $17.50

ROSSELL, J.E. *History of MD Hunt Club 1894-1954.* 1954 Baltimore. Waverly. 1/1,000. sgn. 174 p. $95.00

ROSSER, NEWTON, & GROSS. *Mathematical Theory of Rocket Flight.* 1947 McGraw Hill. Ills 1st ed. 2nd imp. 276 p. $10.00

ROSSETTI, Christina. *Speaking Likenesses.* 1874 London. 1st ed. 8vo. G $65.00

ROSSETTI, Dante Gabriel. *Ballads & Sonnets.* 1903 Portland. Ltd ed. 1/450. 334 p. $35.00

ROSSETTI, Dante Gabriel. *3 Rossettis.* 1937 Harvard U Pr. 1st ed. 4to. dj. EX $100.00

ROSSETTI, William Michael. *Life of John Keats.* 1887 London. 1st ed. G $45.00

ROSSI, Paul A.; & HUNT, David. *Art of the Old West.* 1971 Knopf. Deluxe ed. slipcase. boxed. EX $350.00

ROSSI, Paul A.; & HUNT, David. *Art of the Old West.* 1985 Castle. reprint. dj. EX $35.00

ROSSITER, Oscar. *Tetrasomy 2.* 1974 Doubleday. 1st ed. dj. EX $8.00

ROSSMAN, L.A. *Christianizing the Chippewas.* 1949 Grand Rapids. 9 p. blue wraps. VG $8.00

ROSSNER, Judith. *Looking for Mr. Goodbar.* 1975 NY. 1st ed. dj. EX $12.00

ROSTAND, Edmond. *Cyrano de Bergerac.* 1936 Ltd Ed Club. Ills Sauvage. 199 p. M $85.00

ROSTAND, Edmond. *Cyrano de Bergerac.* 1901 Paris. EX $50.00

ROSTAND, Robert. *D'Artagnan Signature.* 1976 Putnam. 1st ed. dj. VG $7.00

ROSTANY, Pierre. *Yves Klein.* 1982 Abrams. 4to. dj. $35.00

ROSTEN, Norman. *4th Decade.* 1945 NY. 2nd print. inscr. VG $25.00

ROSTOV, Charles I. *Chinese Carpets.* 1983 NY. Abrams. Ills. 224 p. dj. $60.00

ROSTRON, Sir Arthur. *Home From the Sea.* 1931 Macmillan. 1st ed. $25.00

ROSZAK, Theodore. *Dreamwatcher.* 1985 Doubleday. 1st ed. dj. EX $15.00

ROTCH, A. Lawrence. *Conquest of Air; or, Advent of Aerial Navigation.* 1907 NY. Moffat Yard. Ills. 192 p. $25.00

ROTH, Charles B. *Key to Your Personality.* 1949 Perma. VG $5.00

ROTH, Holly. *Sleeper.* 1955 Simon Schuster. 1st ed. dj. VG $10.00

ROTH, L. *Package Design.* 1981 NY. Ills. 212 p. $32.50

ROTH, Philip. *Anatomy Lesson.* 1983 NY. 1st ed. dj. M $10.00

ROTH, Philip. *Anatomy Lesson.* 1983 Farrar. Ltd 1st ed. 1/300. sgn. EX $75.00

ROTH, Philip. *Anatomy Lesson.* 1984 Cape. Uncorrected proof. EX $30.00

ROTH, Philip. *Anatomy Lesson.* 1983 Farrar. 1st trade ed. dj. EX $20.00

ROTH, Philip. *Breast.* 1972 Holt. 1st ed. dj. EX $20.00

ROTH, Philip. *Ghost Writer.* Franklin. 1st ed. full leather. M $36.00

ROTH, Philip. *Ghost Writer.* 1979 Cape. 1st English ed. dj. EX $20.00

ROTH, Philip. *Good-Bye, Columbus.* Modern Lib. 1st ed. dj. M $32.00

ROTH, Philip. *Good-Bye, Columbus.* 1959 Boston. Houghton Mifflin. 1st ed. dj. $75.00

ROTH, Philip. *Great American Novel.* 1973 NY. Holt. 1st ed. dj. VG $30.00

ROTH, Philip. *Letting Go.* 1962 Random House. 1st ed. dj. EX $60.00

ROTH, Philip. *My Life As a Man.* 1974 Holt. 1st ed. dj. VG $15.00

ROTH, Philip. *Our Gang.* 1971 NY. 1st ed. dj. $12.00

ROTH, Philip. *Portnoy's Complaint.* 1969 NY. Stated 1st ed. dj. EX $10.00

ROTH, Philip. *Professor of Desire.* 1978 Cape. 1st English ed. dj. EX $20.00

ROTH, Philip. *Professor of Desire.* 1977 NY. 1st ed. dj. EX $20.00

ROTH, Philip. *Quand Elle Etait Gentille.* 1971 Paris. 1st French ed. 8vo. wraps. M $200.00

ROTH, Philip. *When She Was Good.* 1967 Random House. 1st ed. dj. EX $35.00

ROTH, Philip. *Zuckerman Unbound.* 1981 Farrar. 1st ed. 1/350. sgn. slipcase. $75.00

ROTH, Robert. *Sand in the Wind.* 1973 Boston. 1st ed. dj. M $12.00

ROTHE, Hans. *Daumier und das Theater.* 1925 Leipzig. Ills. wraps. VG $45.00

ROTHENSTEIN, John. *Augustus John.* 1944 London. Phaidon. Ills. 4to. dj. VG $30.00

ROTHERT, Otto. *Outlaws of Cave-In-Rock.* 1924 Cleveland. VG $125.00

ROTHSCHILD, M.; & CLAY, T. *Fleas, Flukes, & Cockoos: Study of Bird Parasites.* 1957 Macmillan. Ills. 305 p. dj. EX $12.00

ROTTENSTEINER, Franz. *Science Fiction Book.* 1975 Seabury. dj. EX $15.00

ROUECHE, Berton. *Curiosities of Medicine.* 1963 Boston. 1st ed. 338 p. dj. EX $25.00

ROUECHE, Berton. *Greener Grass & Some People Who Found It.* 1948 NY. Harper. 1st ed. dj. EX $30.00

ROUECHE, Berton. *11 Blue Men & Other Narratives of Medical Detection.* 1953 Boston. Little Brown. 1st ed. 215 p. $10.00

ROUGHHEAD, W. *Malice Domestic.* 1928 Edinburgh. Ills 1st ed. inscr. VG $45.00

ROULE, L. *Fishes: Their Journeys & Imigrations.* 1933 Norton. Ills 1st Am ed. 270 p. G $10.00

ROUNDTREE, Henry. *Enchanted Wood.* no date. Estes. Ills. 12mo. 101 p. VG $18.00

ROURKE, C. *Audubon.* 1936 Harcourt Brace. Ills. 342 p. VG $10.00

ROUSCH, L.L. *History of Rousch Family in America.* 1928 Strasburg, VA. 747 p. VG $50.00

ROUSE, B. *Letters of Ellen Glasgow.* 1958 NY. 1st ed. dj. VG $20.00

ROUSE, Parke. *Great Wagon Road From Philadelphia to the South.* 1973 NY. 1st ed. Am Trails Series. dj. $12.50

ROUSSEAU, J.J. *Confessions of Jean-Jacques Rousseau.* 1904 Phil. Gebbie. Ills. 4 vol set. VG $275.00

ROUSSEAU, J.J. *Confessions of Jean-Jacques Rousseau.* Nonesuch. 1/800. 2 vol set. slipcase. VG $225.00

ROUSSEAU, J.J. *Melanges.* 1781 Geneve. 4 vol set. G $75.00

ROUSSET, D. *No Other Kingdom.* 1947 Reynal Hitchcock. 1st ed. VG $25.00

ROUTH, Francis. *Early English Organ Music From Middle Ages to 1837.* 1973 NY. dj. VG $25.00

ROWAN, Carl. *Pitiful & Proud.* 1956 NY. Review copy. dj. G $10.00

ROWAN, Ruth Dinkins. *Helping Children with Learning Disabilities.* 1977 Abingdon. dj. VG $5.00

ROWANS, V. *Loving Couple.* 1956 NY. Crowell. 1st ed. dj. VG $10.00

ROWE, Ann Pollard. *Century of Change in Guatemalan Textiles.* 1981 NY. Relations. Ills. 151 p. xl. $15.00

ROWE, J.G. *Lightship Pirates.* 1928 Cupples Leon. VG $7.50

ROWE, Percy. *Great Atlantic Air Race.* 1977 Ontario. dj. G $20.00

ROWELL, Margit. *Joan Miro.* 1970 NY. Abrams. Ills. 4to. slipcase. $90.00

ROWES, Barbara. *Grace Slick.* 1980 Garden City. Ills 1st ed. dj. VG $10.00

ROWLAND, Amy Z. *Handcrafted Doors & Windows.* 1982 Emmaus. Rodale. Ills. index. $12.50

ROWLAND, D. *Courts, Judges, & Lawyers of MS 1798-1935.* 1935 Jackson. $10.00

ROWLAND, Henry A. *Physical Papers of Henry August Rowland.* 1902 Baltimore. Johns Hopkins. 4to. 704 p. $125.00

ROWLANDS, J.J. *Cache Lake Country.* 1959 Norton. Ills 272 p. dj. VG $6.00

ROWLANDS, J.J. *Cache Lake Country.* 1947 NY. Ills. G $15.00

ROWLANDSON, Mary. *Narrative of Captivity & Restoration of Mary Rowlandson.* 1930 Boston. Ltd ed. 1/1,500. dj. EX $45.00

ROWLEY, G. *Flowering Succulents.* 1959 England. Morris. Ills. dj. VG $11.00

ROWNTREE, Harry. *Stories From Grimm.* c 1900. London/NY. 16mo. 116 p. $20.00

ROWSE, A.L. *Shakespeare the Man.* 1973 NY. 1st ed. dj. M $11.00

ROWSE, A.L. *What Shakespeare Read & Thought.* 1981 NY. 1st ed. dj. M $11.00

ROWSE, A.L. *William Shakespeare.* 1963 Harper Row. 1st ed. $15.00

ROY, Claude. *Hans Erni.* 1955 Geneve. Cailler. Ills. 8vo. wraps. $30.00

ROY, Lillian Elizabeth. *Polly in NY.* 1922 Grosset Dunlap. Ills. $4.00

ROYCE, S. *Deterioration & Race Education.* 1878 Boston. 12mo. 585 p. brown cloth. G $17.00

ROYKO, M. *Up Against It.* 1967 Chicago. 1st ed. dj. VG $22.50

ROYLE, J. Forbes. *On Culture & Commerce of Cotton in India & Elsewhere.* 1851 London. 1st ed. 8vo. 607 p. $75.00

RUARK, R.C. *Grenadine Etching.* 1947 Doubleday. 1st ed. sgn. 270 p. dj. VG $35.00

RUARK, R.C. *Grenadine's Spawn.* 1952 Doubleday. 1st ed. 253 p. dj. VG $12.50

RUARK, R.C. *Honey Badger.* 1965 McGraw Hill. 534 p. VG $8.00

RUARK, R.C. *Honey Badger.* 1965 NY. 1st Am ed. dj. EX $30.00

RUARK, R.C. *Horn of the Hunter.* 1953 Doubleday. Ills. 315 p. VG $15.00

RUARK, R.C. *Horn of the Hunter.* 1953 Garden City. Doubleday. 1st ed. EX $50.00

RUARK, R.C. *I Didn't Know It Was Loaded.* 1948 Doubleday. 1st ed. EX $30.00

RUARK, R.C. *Old Man & the Boy.* c 1957. NY. 18th print. dj. VG $35.00

RUARK, R.C. *Old Man & the Boy.* 1957 Holt. Ills 1st ed. 303 p. dj. EX $45.00

RUARK, R.C. *Old Man & the Boy.* 1958 2nd ed. dj. EX $37.50

RUARK, R.C. *Old Man's Boy Grows Older.* 1961 NY. Holt. 1st ed. dj. VG $45.00

RUARK, R.C. *Old Man's Boy Grows Up.* 1961 NY. 1st ed. dj. EX $40.00

RUARK, R.C. *Poor No More.* 1959 Holt. 1st ed. 706 p. VG $12.50

RUARK, R.C. *Something of Value.* 1955 NY. 1st ed. dj. VG $12.50

RUARK, R.C. *Use Enough Gun.* 1966 NY. 1st ed. dj. VG $35.00

RUARK, R.C. *Use Enough Gun.* 1966 New Am Lib. dj. EX $20.00

RUARK, R.C. *Women.* 1967 NY. 1st ed. $35.00

RUARK, Robert. *Uhuru (Africa Today).* 1962 NY. 1st ed. 555 p. VG $12.00

RUBENS, Alfred. *History of Jewish Costume.* 1967 Funk. 1st ed. dj. $15.00

RUBENSTEIN, A. *My Young Years.* 1973 NY. Knopf. 1st ed. dj. VG $10.00

RUBIN, Jerry. *Do It!* 1970 NY. 3rd print. HrdCvr. EX $15.00

RUBIN, Jerry. *Growing at 37.* 1976 Evans. 1st ed. dj. EX $15.00

RUBIN, Jerry. *We Are Everywhere.* 1971 NY. 1st ed. dj. EX $22.00

RUBIN, Reuven. *My Life, My Art: Autobiography & Selected Paintings.* 1974 NY. 4to. dj. VG $22.50

RUBIN, Theodore. *Through My Own Eyes.* 1982 Macmillan. dj. $4.00

RUBIN, William. *Andre Masson.* 1976 MOMA. Ills. 4to. 323 p. wraps. $9.00

RUBIN, William. *Anthony Caro.* 1974 MOMA. Ills. 4to. 196 p. wraps. $8.00

RUBIN, William. *Cezanne.* 1977 MOMA. Ills. 4to. 416 p. cloth. dj. $45.00

RUBIN, William. *De Chirico.* 1982 MOMA. Ills. 4to. 208 p. cloth. dj. $35.00

RUBIN, William. *Frank Stella Monograph.* 1970 MOMA. Ills. 4to. 176 p. dj. $25.00

RUBIN, William. *Frank Stella 1970-1987.* 1987 MOMA. Ills. 4to. 208 p. dj. $45.00

RUBIN, William. *Pablo Picasso.* 1980 MOMA. Ills 1st ed. 4to. wraps. $25.00

RUBIN, William. *Paintings of Gerald Murphy.* 1974 MOMA. Ills. 4to. 48 p. wraps. $20.00

RUBIN, William. *Primitivism in 20th Century Art.* 1985 MOMA. 4to. 720 p. dj. boxed. 2 vols. $100.00

RUBIN, William. *Surrealism & Their Heritage.* 1968 MOMA. Ills. oblong 4to. 252 p. dj. $12.50

RUBINOWICZ, D. *Das Tagebuch des Dawid Rubinowicz.* 1985 East Berlin. Ills. German text. G $10.00

RUBY, Robert; & BROWN, John A. *Spokane Indians.* 1970 Norman. dj. VG $25.00

RUCHAMES, L. *John Brown Reader.* 1959 NY/London. Schuman. 431 p. $17.50

RUD, Anthony. *Devil's Heirloom.* 1924 NY. 1st ed. wraps. $15.00

RUDAUX, Lucien. *Larousse Encyclopedia of Astronomy.* 1967 Prometheus. dj. xl. $15.00

RUDDER, Robert. *Literature of Spain in English Translation: A Bibliography.* 1975 NY. dj. VG $12.00

RUDIGER, M. *Waldtraut According to Chronicle of Pastor of Hinrichshagen.* 1898 Chicago. 8vo. 279 p. VG $25.00

RUDKIN, Margaret. *Pepperidge Farm Cookbook.* 1976 NY. dj. EX $10.00

RUDKIN, Margaret. *Pepperidge Farm Cookbook.* 1963 Ills Blegvad. 1st ed. 440 p. dj. VG $12.00

RUDLOE, J. *Sea Brings Forth.* 1968 Knopf. Ills 1st ed. 261 p. dj. EX $6.00

RUDLOE, J. *Time of the Turtle.* 1980 Penguin. Ills. 273 p. wraps. EX $5.00

RUDOFSKY, B. *Now I Lay Me Down To Eat.* 1980 Garden City. 1st ed. dj. VG $27.50

RUDOLPH, Wolf & Evelyne. *Ancient Jewelry From Collection of Burton Y. Berry.* 1973 IN U Art Mus. Ills. 4to. 275 p. wraps. $35.00

RUE, L.L. *Deer of North America.* 1981 Outdoor Life. Ills. 463 p. dj. EX $14.00

SCHERF, Margaret. *Judicial Body.* 1957 Crime Club. 1st ed. dj. VG $20.00

SCHERMAN, Katharine. *Spring on an Artic Island.* 1956 Little Brown. Ills. 331 p. maps. dj. VG $8.00

SCHERTZ, H.P. *Legends of LA.* 1922 New Orleans. New Orleans Journal. 83 p. $10.00

SCHIDER, F. *Plastich Anatomischer Handatloas.* 1922 Leipzig. Ills Stuck. VG $100.00

SCHIFF, Bessie. *Travelling Gallery.* 1936 Chicago. Ills Emma Brock. 1st ed. $15.00

SCHIFF, Stuart. *Mad Scientists.* 1980 Garden City. 1st ed. dj. M $15.00

SCHIFF, Stuart. *Whispers IV.* 1983 1st Am ed. dj. EX $15.00

SCHIFF & LIEBER. *World Fantasy Awards Vol. II.* 1980 Doubleday. 1st ed. dj. EX $12.50

SCHIFF & YA'ARI. *Israel's Lebanon War.* 1985 London. maps. dj. EX $18.00

SCHIFFER, Margaret B. *Historical Needlework of PA.* 1968 NY. Scribner. Ills. 4to. dj. $20.00

SCHIFFER, Margaret B. *History of Needlework of PA.* 1968 Scribner. 1st ed. folio. linen. dj. EX $25.00

SCHIMMEL, Julie. *Art & Life of W. Herbert Dunton 1878-1936.* 1984 TX U Pr. Ills 1st ed. 4to. dj. EX $25.00

SCHINDLER, Valentine. *Institutionum Hebraicarum Libri Sex in Hebrew & Latin.* 1612 Wittebergae. Henckelii. 8vo. calf. $500.00

SCHISGALL, Oscar. *Devil's Daughter.* 1932 Fiction League. 1st ed. VG $25.00

SCHIWETZ, E.M. *Buck Schiwetz' TX.* 1960 UT. Ills 1st ed. 4to. 134 p. dj. $10.00

SCHLEE, Ann. *Rhine Journey.* 1981 Holt. 1st Am ed. dj. EX $16.00

SCHLEE, S. *Edge of an Unfamiliar World: History of Oceanography.* 1973 Dutton. Ills 1st ed. 398 p. dj. EX $15.00

SCHLEGEL, Frederick. *Lectures on History of Literature: Ancient & Modern.* 1844 NY. New ed. cloth. VG $20.00

SCHLESINGER, Arthur M. *Colonial Merchants & American Revolution.* 1966 NY. dj. VG $10.00

SCHLESINGER, Arthur M. *Politics of Upheaval.* 1960 Houghton Mifflin. 1st print. $10.00

SCHLESINGER, Arthur M. *1,000 Days.* 1965 Boston. 1,087 p. dj. EX $7.00

SCHLESINGER & FOX. *History of American Life.* 1929 Macmillan. 12 vol set. EX $50.00

SCHLEY, W.S.; & SOLEY, J.R. *Rescue of Greely.* 1885 Scribner. Ills. 277 p. fld maps. EX $45.00

SCHLIEMANN, Dr. Henry. *Tiryns: Prehistoric Palace of King of Tiryns.* no date. NY. Ills 1st ed. 4to. EX $275.00

SCHLIEMANN. *Narrative of Researches & Discoveries at Mycenae.* 1878 NY. Ills. VG $100.00

SCHLOSSER, Ignace. *Book of Rugs: Oriental & European.* 1963 NY. Crown. Ills. 318 p. G $40.00

SCHMALENBACH, Werner. *Kurt Schwitters.* 1967 NY. Abrams. Ills. 4to. dj. $125.00

SCHMEDDING. *Cowboy & Indian Trader.* 1951 Caxton. dj. $45.00

SCHMIDLY, D. *TX Mammals East of the Balcones Fault Zone.* 1983 TX A&M U Pr. Ills 1st ed. 400 p. wraps. EX $14.00

SCHMIDT, G.P. *Princeton & Rutgers: 2 Colonial Colleges of NJ.* 1964 dj. VG $12.00

SCHMIDT, Karl Patterson. *Homes & Habits of Wild Animals.* 1934 Chicago. Donohue. Ills Weber. sgn. EX $35.00

SCHMIDT, Max. *Primitive Races of Mankind: Study of Ethnology.* 1926 Boston. Ills. 360 p. $20.00

SCHMIDT, Oscar C. *Practical Railroading.* 1913 Phil. 5 vol set. EX $300.00

SCHMIDT, Oscar C. *Practical Treatise on Automobiles.* 1911 Am Textbook Co. Ills. 2 vol set. ¾-leather. $50.00

SCHMIDT, Stanley. *From Mind to Mind.* 1984 Doubleday. 1st ed. $15.00

SCHMIDT, Stanley. *War & Peace: Possible Futures From Analog.* 1983 NY. 1st ed. dj. VG $8.00

SCHMIDT. *Doberman Pinscher.* 1935 Judy Pub. 3rd ed. $15.00

SCHMUTZLER, Robert. *Art Nouveau.* 1962 NY. Abrams. Ills. 322 p. cloth. dj. $125.00

SCHNABEL, A. *Reflections on Music.* 1924 NY. VG $15.00

SCHNEIDER, Bill. *Where the Grizzly Walks.* 1977 Mountain Pr. Ills. 191 p. maps. dj. EX $10.00

SCHNEIDER, H.W. *Puritan Mind.* 1930 NY. 1st ed. VG $10.00

SCHNEIDER, Isadore. *Comrade Mister.* 1934 NY. Equinox Co-Op Pr. Ltd ed. VG $35.00

SCHNITZLER, Arthur. *Casanova's Homecoming.* Ills Kent. Ltd ed. 1/1,499. 153 p. EX $55.00

SCHOBEL, Johannes. *Fine Arms & Armor: Treasures in the Dresden Collection.* 1975 NY. Putnam. $22.50

SCHOENBERGER, Dale. *Gunfighters.* 1971 Caxton. Ills. 4to. 207 p. dj. EX $27.00

SCHOENBERGER. *Drawings of Mathis Gothart Nithart.* 1948 Bittner. Ills. 4to. dj. EX $35.00

SCHOENER. *American Jewish Album.* 1983 Rizzoli. folio. wraps. $9.00

SCHOENRICH, O. *Legacy of Christopher Columbus.* 1949 Glendale. 2 vol set. $45.00

SCHOETTLE, Edwin J. *Sailing Craft.* 1937 Macmillan. Ills Parker. G $36.00

SCHOFF, Wilfred H. *Periplus of Erythraean Sea.* 1912 London. $50.00

SCHOFIELD, M. *Decorative Art & Modern Interiors.* 1974 NY. Ills. 176 p. $32.50

SCHOFIELD, R.E. *Scientific Autobiography of Joseph Priestley.* 1966 Cambridge. MIT Pr. 1st ed. xl. VG $15.00

SCHOFIELD, William H. *English Literature From Norman Conquest to Chaucer.* 1925 London. G $9.00

SCHOFIELD. *46 Years in the Army.* 1897 NY. Ills. inscr. cloth. VG $110.00

SCHOLEM, Gershom G. *On the Kabbalah & Its Symbolism.* 1960 NY. Schocken. 1st ed. 216 p. $22.50

SCHOMBURG, Robert H. *Description of British Guiana: Geographical & Statistical.* 1840 London. Simpkin Marshall. 1st ed. $250.00

SCHON, M.A. *Muscular System of the Red Howling Monkey.* 1968 Ills. 183 p. wraps. EX $10.00

SCHONBACH, Morris. *Radicals & Visionaries: History of Dissent in NJ. Vol. XII.* 1964 dj. VG $12.00

SCHONBERG, Harold. *Great Conductors.* 1967 Simon Schuster. 384 p. dj. $6.50

SCHONBERGER, Arno. *Rococo Age: Art & Civilization of the 18th Century.* 1960 NY. Ills 1st Am ed. VG $85.00

SCHOOLCRAFT, Henry R. *Notes on the Iroquois.* 1847 Albany. 1st ed. EX $275.00

SCHOOLCRAFT, Henry R. *Personal Memoirs of a Residence of 30 Years with Indians.* 1851 Lippincott Grambo. 1st ed. EX $175.00

SCHOONMAKER, W.J. *World of the Woodchuck.* 1966 Lippincott. Ill 1st ed. 4to. 146 p. dj. EX $8.50

SCHOONMAKER & MARVEL. *American Wines.* 1941 NY. Duell Sloan Pearce. 1st ed. $15.00

SCHOONMAKER & MARVEL. *Complete Wine Book.* 1935 Simon Schuster. Revised 2nd ed. maps. G $10.00

SCHORR, Daniel. *Clearing the Air.* 1977 Houghton Mifflin. dj. VG $10.00

SCHOTTMULLER, F. *Furniture & Interior Decoration of Italian Renaissance.* 1921 NY. Brentano. Ills. 4to. cloth. dj. VG $110.00

SCHRADE, Hubert. *Bauten des Dritten Reiches.* 1937 Leipzig. dj. G $20.00

SCHRADER, F.F. *Germans in the Making of America.* 1972 NY. 1st ed. $35.00

SCHREINER, Olive. *Stories, Dreams, Allegories.* 1923 NY. 1st ed. VG $12.50

SCHREINER, Olive. *Trooper Peter Halket of Mashonaland.* 1897 Boston. 1st ed. VG $17.50

SCHREINER. *Pictorial History of TX Rangers.* 1969 1st ed. dj. VG $35.00

SCHRENKEISEN, Ray. *Fishing for Bass, Muskalonge, Pike, & Panfishes.* 1937 Doubleday Doran. Ills 1st ed. $6.50

SCHRENKEISEN, Ray. *Fishing for Salmon & Trout.* 1937 Doubleday Doran. 1st ed. dj. G $7.50

SCHROEDER, Doris. *Annie Oakley in Danger at Diablo.* 1955 Whitman. G $5.00

SCHROEDER, Francis. *Anatomy for Interior Designers.* 1954 NY. Whitney. 2nd ed. 2nd print. $18.00

SCHROEDINGER, Erwin. *What Is Life?* 1947 NY. Macmillan. later ed. 91 p. VG $15.00

SCHRUMACHER, Emile C. *Nothing's Sacred on Sunday.* 1951 Crowell. dj. VG $20.00

SCHUBERT, Paul. *Electric Word: Rise of Radio.* 1928 NY. Macmillan. 1st ed. 8vo. 311 p. dj. VG $20.00

SCHUBERT, Walter C. *Die Deutsche Werbe Graphik.* 1927 Francken Land. Ills. folio. 252 p. EX $400.00

SCHULBERG, Budd. *Disenchanted.* 1950 Random House. 1st ed. dj. VG $20.00

SCHULBERG, Budd. *Harder They Fall.* 1947 NY. 1st ed. dj. EX $15.00

SCHULBERG, Budd. *Sanctuary V.* 1969 World. 1st ed. dj. EX $20.00

SCHULBERG, Budd. *Water Front.* 1955 Random House. 1st ed. 1st print. VG $16.00

SCHULBERG, Budd. *What Makes Sammy Run?* 1941 Random House. dj. EX $20.00

SCHULER, Elizabeth. *Gardens Around the World.* 1964 Abrams. dj. VG $22.00

SCHULER, Montgomery. *Westward the Course of the Empire.* 1906 NY. EX $35.00

SCHULTHESS, Emil. *Antarctica.* 1960 NY. 1st ed. dj. VG $25.00

SCHULTZ, B. *Colonial Hempstead.* 1937 1st ed. 8vo. 392 p. G $35.00

SCHULTZ, J.W. *Many Strange Characters: MT Frontier Tales.* 1982 OK U Pr. 1st ed. 143 p. dj. EX $15.00

SCHULTZ, J.W. *Quest of the Fish-Dog Skin.* 1913 Boston. Ills 1st ed. VG $35.00

SCHULTZ, J.W. *White Beaver.* 1930 Boston. 1st ed. dj. VG $25.00

SCHULTZ, L.P. *Ways of Fishes.* 1948 Van Nostrand. Ills. 264 p. dj. VG $10.00

SCHULZ, Charles M. *Charlie Brown Christmas.* 1977 NY. Scholastic Books. Ills. EX $8.00

SCHULZ, Charles M. *Snoopy Come Home Movie Book.* 1972 NY. Holt. Ills 1st ed. 8vo. 126 p. dj. $12.50

SCHULZ, E.D. *TX Wild Flowers.* 1928 Laidlaw. Ills. 505 p. VG $18.00

SCHUMACHER, G. *Deepest Valley: Guide to Owens Valley.* 1963 Sierra Club. 2nd print. $10.00

SCHUMAKER, E. *Last Paradises.* 1967 Doubleday. Ills. 4to. dj. EX $18.00

SCHURE, Edouard. *Krishna & Orpheus: Great Initiates of East & West.* 1919 London. Rider. 154 p. VG $25.00

SCHUSSLER, Hermann. *Locality of the Broderick-Terry Duel on September 13, 1859.* 1916 San Francisco. VG $80.00

SCHUSTER & EGAN. *Printed Kate Greenaway: Catalogue Raisonne.* 1986 London. Schuster. Ills. 304 p. dj. M $100.00

SCHUTZ, Benjamin M. *All the Old Bargains.* 1985 Blue Jay. 1st ed. sgn. dj. EX $25.00

SCHUTZ. *When Mammoths Roamed the Frozen Earth.* 1929 NY. Cape Smith. 1st ed. 197 p. VG $22.50

SCHUYLER, Eugene. *Turkistan: Notes of Journey in Russian Turkistan. Vol. I.* 1877 NY. fld maps. xl. $15.00

SCHUYLER, James. *What's for Dinner?* 1978 Black Sparrow. Ltd 1st ed. sgn. dj. EX $35.00

SCHWARTZ, C.W.; & E.R. *Wild Animals of MO.* 1964 MO U Pr. Ills. 4to. 341 p. EX $25.00

SCHWARTZ, Lynn. *Balancing Acts.* 1981 Harper. 1st ed. sgn. dj. EX $30.00

SCHWARTZ, Marvin D. *American Furniture of the Colonial Period.* 1976 NY. MOMA. 8vo. dj. $15.00

SCHWARZ, Ted. *Hillside Strangler.* 1981 Doubleday. 1st ed. dj. EX $10.00

SCHWATKA, F. *Along AK's Great River.* 1983 AK Northwest. Ills. 95 p. pb. EX $8.00

SCHWATKA, F. *Along AK's Great River.* 1898 Chicago. fld map. EX $50.00

SCHWATKA, F. *Along AK's Great River.* 1885 NY. G $70.00

SCHWATKA, F. *In the Land of Cave & Cliff Dwellers.* 1893 NY. $10.00

SCHWATKA, F. *Summer in AK.* 1891 Phil. Ills. G $30.00

SCHWEITZER, Albert. *Aus Meinem Leben un Denken.* 1932 Leipzig. Ills 1st ed. 211 p. EX $75.00

SCHWEITZER, Albert. *J.S. Bach.* 1947 NY. Macmillan. VG $30.00

SCHWIEBERT, E. *Nymphs.* 1973 Winchester Pr. 4to. cloth. dj. EX $25.00

SCHWIEBERT, E. *Rememberances of Rivers Past.* 1972 Macmillan. Ills 1st ed. 287 p. dj. EX $13.50

SCHWINN. *50 Years of Schwinn Built Bicycles.* 1945 Chicago. Ills 1st ed. 92 p. VG $60.00

SCIASCIA, Leonardo. *1 Way or Another.* 1977 Harper Row. 1st ed. dj. VG $5.00

SCIDMORE, Eliza. *Jinrikisha Days in Japan.* 1891 Harper. Ills. 8vo. 386 p. VG $30.00

SCOBEE, Barry. *Old Fort Davis.* 1947 San Antonio. 1st ed. sgn. dj. VG $25.00

SCOBEY & MC GRATH. *Celebrity Needlepoint.* 1972 Dial. 1st ed. folio. 166 p. $25.00

SCOPPETTONE, Sandra. *Suzuki Beane.* 1961 Doubleday. Ills Fitzhugh. 1st ed. dj. M $25.00

SCORESBY, Rev. W. *Journal of a Voyage to Australia.* 1859 London. 1st ed. 8 vol set. navy cloth. $250.00

SCORTIA, Thomas N. *Best of Thomas N. Scortia.* 1981 Garden City. Review copy. dj. EX $10.00

SCORTIA, Thomas N. *Caution! Inflammable!* 1975 Doubleday. 1st ed. dj. xl. $5.00

SCORTIA, Thomas N. *Nightmare Factor.* 1978 Doubleday. 1st ed. dj. VG $10.00

SCORTIA, Thomas N. *Strange Bedfellows.* 1972 Random House. 1st ed. dj. EX $15.00

SCOTT, A.C. *Kabuki Theatre of Japan.* 1955 London. 1st ed. VG $15.00

SCOTT, Alma. *Wanda Gag: Story of an Artist.* 1949 MN U Pr. Ills. 8vo. 325 p. wraps. M $40.00

SCOTT, Alma. *Wanda Gag: Story of an Artist.* 1949 MN U Pr. Ills. 8vo. cloth. xl. VG $18.00

SCOTT, Eleanor. *1st 20 Years of the Santa Fe Opera.* 1976 Santa Fe. Ills. oblong 4to. dj. VG $25.00

SCOTT, Eugene. *Tennis Experience.* 1979 Larrouse. Ills. dj. EX $17.50

SCOTT, G.C. *Fishing in American Waters.* 1869 Harper. Ills 1st ed. 484 p. VG $45.00

SCOTT, George R. *Phallic Worship.* 1952 NY. Ills 1st ed. dj. EX $15.00

SCOTT, J. *Story of the 32nd IA Infantry Volunteers.* 1896 NV. 1st ed. VG $85.00

SCOTT, J.D. *Discovering the American Stork.* 1976 Harcourt Brace. Ills 1st ed. 64 p. dj. VG $8.00

SCOTT, J.D. *Forests of the Night.* 1959 Rinehart. Ills. 216 p. dj. EX $20.00

SCOTT, J.D.; & SWEET, O. *Moose.* 1981 Putnam. Ills. 4to. dj. EX $8.00

SCOTT, Janet Laura. *Children Across the Sea.* 1931 Saalfield. Ills 1st ed. VG $20.00

SCOTT, Janet Laura. *Shoes, Ships, & Sealing Wax.* 1920 Volland. Ills 1st ed. dj. VG $25.00

SCOTT, Jeremy. *Mandrake Root.* 1946 Jarrolds. VG $30.00

SCOTT, Job. *Journal of Life, Travels, & Gospel Labors of Job Scott.* no date. NY. 1st ed. VG $45.00

SCOTT, John Reed. *Princess Dehra.* 1908 Lippincott. 2nd ed. VG $12.50

SCOTT, John. *Behind the Urals.* 1942 Cambridge. 279 p. $5.00

SCOTT, John. *Story of Sigma Nu.* 1927 Indianapolis. Ills. 556 p. VG $25.00

SCOTT, M. Gladys. *Analysis of Human Motion: Textbook in Kinesiology.* 1946 NY. Ills 3rd ed. 388 p. VG $10.00

SCOTT, Michael. *Tom Cringle's Log.* 1927 NY. Ills 1st ed. $45.00

SCOTT, Paul. *On Writing & the Novel.* 1987 NY. Morrow. proof. wraps. $35.00

SCOTT, Peter. *Observations of Wildlife.* 1980 Cornell U Pr. Ills 1st ed. 4to. dj. EX $15.00

SCOTT, Peter. *Wild Chorus.* 1938 London. Country Life Ltd. 1/250. VG $375.00

SCOTT, Peter. *Wild Chorus.* 1942 London. Ills. G $11.00

SCOTT, Peter. *World Atlas of Birds.* 1974 Crescent. Ills. 4to. 272 p. dj. EX $22.00

SCOTT, R.L. *Between the Elephants Eyes.* 1954 Dodd Mead. 243 p. map. dj. EX $12.50

SCOTT, R.L. *Damned to Glory.* 1944 NY. $15.00

SCOTT, Sir Walter. *Border Antiquities of England & Scotland.* 1814 London. Longman. 4vo. 2 vol set. G $190.00

SCOTT, Sir Walter. *Fortunes of Nigel.* no date. Edinburgh. 12mo. 2 vol set. VG $200.00

SCOTT, Sir Walter. *Ivanhoe.* no date. McKay. Ills Greiffenhagen. 8vo. EX $25.00

SCOTT, Sir Walter. *Journals of Sir Walter Scott From Original Manuscript.* 1891 NY. 2 vol set. EX $20.00

SCOTT, Sir Walter. *Lady of the Lake.* no date. Lauriat. Ills Estes. dj. VG $30.00

SCOTT, Sir Walter. *Lady of the Lake.* 1863 London. Bennett. Ills T Ogle. VG $110.00

SCOTT, Sir Walter. *Lady of the Lake.* 1870 Edinburgh. 11 tipped-in photos. morocco. $175.00

SCOTT, Sir Walter. *Letters on Demonology & Witchcraft.* 1831 NY. 1st Am ed. 16mo. $45.00

SCOTT, Sir Walter. *Marmion: Tale of Flodden Field.* 1810 2 vols. full leather. $75.00

SCOTT, Sir Walter. *St. Bonan's Well.* 1824 Phil. 2 vol set. $60.00

SCOTT, Sir Walter. *Waverley Novels.* c 1850. Rossyln ed. 23 vol set. G $150.00

SCOTT, Sir Walter. *Works of Johathan Swift.* 1883 Boston. Ltd ed. 1/250. 19 vol set. EX $175.00

SCOTT, W. *Giant Judge; or, Story of Sampson, Hebrew Hercules.* 1858 San Francisco. Whitton Towne. 1st ed. 324 p. $75.00

SCOTT, W.T. *New & Selected Poems.* 1967 Garden City. 1st ed. dj. EX $10.00

SCOTT. *Office at Home.* 1985 NY. Scribner. dj. EX $5.00

SCOTT-ELLIOT, W. *Man's Place in the Universe.* 1902 London. Theosophical Pub. 132 p. VG $45.00

SCOTT-ELLIOT, W. *Story of Atlantis.* 1896 London. Theosophical Pub. 1st ed. EX $65.00

SCOTTO, Renata; & ROCA, O. *More Than a Diva.* 1984 NY. 1st ed. dj. VG $15.00

SCOURSE, N. *Victorians & Their Flowers.* 1983 Timber. 195 p. EX $25.00

SCRIBNER, F. *Fungus Diseases of the Grape & Other Plants.* 1890 NJ. Lovett. 136 p. green cloth. G $15.00

SCROPE, G.P. *Geology & Extinct Volcanos of Central France.* 1858 Lodnon. 2nd ed. 258 p. VG $45.00

SCROPE, G.P. *Ueber Volkane.* 1872 Berlin. German Trans of 1862. $35.00

SCROPE, G.P. *Volcanos: Character of Their Phenomena.* 1862 London. 2nd ed. 490 p. VG $48.00

SCRUGGS, William L. *Columbian & Venezuelian Republics.* 1900 Little Brown. Ills 1st ed. 350 p. VG $75.00

SCUDDER, H. *American Commonwealths: OH.* 1888 12mo. 427 p. brown cloth. G $10.00

SCULLY, Vincent. *Earth, Temple, & Gods.* 1969 NY. Revised ed. dj. $25.00

SCULLY, Vincent. *Frank Lloyd Wright.* 1960 NY. Braziller. G $20.00

SCULLY, William C. *White Hecatomb.* 1897 NY. Holt. 1st ed. VG $10.00

SCULLY, William. *Brazil: Provinces & Chief Cities; Manners & Customs.* 1866 London. Murray. Ills 1st ed. 398 p. $100.00

SEABROOK, William. *Adventures In Arabia.* 1927 NY. Ills. 346 p. dj. $15.00

SEABROOK, William. *Jungle Ways.* 1931 Blue Ribbon. Ills. 308 p. G $8.00

SEABROOK, William. *Magic Island.* 1929 Harcourt. Ills 1st ed. 336 p. VG $10.00

SEABROOK, William. *No Hiding Place.* 1942 Phil. 1st ed. dj. VG $10.00

SEABROOK, William. *Witchcraft: Its Power in the World Today.* 1940 NY. 1st ed. dj. VG $20.00

SEABURY, Stowe Joseph. *Reflections of a Moose Hunter.* 1921 Boston. private print. VG $15.00

SEALE, W. *Biography of Margaret Lea Houston.* 1970 OK U Pr. Ills 1st ed. 287 p. dj. EX $35.00

SEAMAN, N.G. *Relics of the Pacific Northwest.* 1946 Binfords Mort. Ills. 157 p. dj. EX $27.00

SEARLS, Hank. *Lost Prince.* 1969 World. 1st ed. dj. VG $10.00

SEARS, C. *Gleanings From Old Shaker Journals.* 1916 Boston. Houghton Mifflin. Ills 1st ed. $48.00

SEARS, F. *Fruit Growing Projects.* 1928 Macmillan. 383 p. VG $10.00

SEARS, Hugh. *What's New in the Air Corps.* 1941 NY. Grosset Dunlap. dj. VG $8.00

SEARS, John van der Zee. *My Friends at Brook Farm.* 1912 NY. 1st ed. 12mo. 172 p. VG $20.00

SEARS, Mary H. *Hudson Crossroads.* 1954 NY. Exposition. 1st ed. dj. EX $15.00

SEARS, P.B. *Deserts on the March.* 1935 OK U Pr. 231 p. VG $8.00

SEARS, P.B. *Lands Beyond the Forest.* 1969 Prentice Hall. Ills. 206 p. dj. EX $8.00

SEARS, Robert. *Pictorial Description of the US.* 1853 NY. Ills. 8vo. 648 p. $45.00

SEARS, Stephen W. *Automobile in America.* 1977 NY. Am Heritage. Ills. 352 p. dj. $30.00

SEATTLE, M.L. *All the Brave Promises.* 1966 Delacorte. 1st ed. dj. EX $30.00

SEATTLE, M.L. *Fight Night on Sweet Saturday.* 1964 Viking. 1st ed. dj. EX $35.00

SEDGWICK, Henry D. *Pro Vita Monastica.* 1923 Boston. 1st ed. EX $45.00

SEDGWICK, N.M. *Young Shot.* 1940 London. Ills. VG $25.00

SEE, Carolyn. *Rest Is Done with Mirrors.* 1970 Boston Little Brown. 1st ed. $30.00

SEEGER, Alan. *Letters & Diary.* 1917 NY. 4th print. 12mo. 218 p. VG $17.50

SEEGER, Alan. *Poems.* December 1916. NY. 1st ed. dj. EX $45.00

SEEGER, Eugene. *Chicago the Wonder City.* 1893 Chicago. VG $75.00

SEELEY, Mable. *Beckoning Door.* 1950 Crime Club. 1st ed. dj. VG $20.00

SEELEY, Mable. *Chuckling Fingers.* 1941 Book League of Am. VG $12.50

SEELEY, Mable. *Crying Sisters.* 1944 Triangle. dj. G $15.00

SEEMAN. *River of Life: Story of Man's Blood From Magic to Science.* Norton. Ills 1st ed. 256 p. dj. VG $7.00

SEFERIS, George. *On the Greek Style.* 1966 NY. dj. VG $35.00

SEFI, A.J. *Introduction to Advanced Philately.* 1932 London. dj. G $50.00

SEGAL, Erich. *Fairy Tale.* 1973 NY. 1st ed. dj. M $10.00

SEGAL, Erich. *Love Story.* 1970 NY. 1st ed. dj. EX $12.00

SEGAL, Lore. *Lucinella.* 1976 NY. Farrar. 1st ed. dj. EX $20.00

SEGUIN, E. *Family Thermometry.* 1873 NY. xl. VG $150.00

SEGUIN, E. *Myelitis of the Anterior Horns.* 1877 NY. $150.00

SEGUR, A. *Country of 36,000 Wishes.* 1930 London. Heinemann. Ills 1st ed. G $35.00

SEGUR, A. *Snow Queen & Other Tales.* 1962 Golden Pr. Ills Deluxe 2nd ed. 4to. VG $20.00

SEGUR, Madame. *Wise Little Donkey.* 1931 Whitman. Ills Brock. 1st ed. cloth. $30.00

SEIB, C.B. *1 Man's Escape to the Woods.* 1971 Doubleday. Ills. 108 p. dj. EX $6.00

SEIDEN, O.J. *Survivor of Babi-Yar.* 1980 Boulder. dj. G $10.00

SEIDMAN, L.I. *Once in the Saddle: Cowboys Frontier 1866-1896.* 1973 Knopf. Ills. 199 p. dj. EX $11.00

SEIFERT, Elizabeth. *Hospital Zone.* 1948 NY. 361 p. dj. $4.00

SEIGMEISTER, E. *Music Lover's Handbook.* 1943 Morrow. dj. VG $15.00

SEIICHIRO, Takahashi. *Kaigetsudo.* 1959 Rutland. 1st Am ed. wraps. $20.00

SEITZ, William C. *Art Israel: 26 Painters & Sculptors.* 1964 MOMA. Ills. 4to. 88 p. cloth. dj. $20.00

SEITZ, William C. *Art of Assemblage.* 1961 MOMA. Ills. 8vo. 176 p. cloth. $15.00

SEITZ, William C. *Hans Hofmann Monograph.* 1963 MOMA. Ills 1st ed. 4to. 64 p. wraps. $30.00

SEITZ, William C. *Hans Hofmann Monograph.* 1972 Arno Pr. reprint. cloth. xl. $15.00

SEITZ, William C. *Mark Tobey Monograph.* 1962 MOMA. Ills. 4to. 112 p. wraps. $10.00

SEITZ, William C. *Paintings, Drawings, & Studies of Arshile Gorky.* 1962 MOMA. Ills. 8vo. 56 p. wraps. $15.00

SEITZ, William C. *Responsive Eye.* 1965 MOMA. Ills. 4to. 56 p. wraps. $15.00

SEITZ, William C. *Seasons & Moments of Claude Monet.* 1960 MOMA. Ills. 8vo. 64 p. wraps. $20.00

SEJOURNE, L. *Un Palacio en la Ciudad de los Dioses: Teotihuacan.* 1959 Mexico. Ills. 4to. 215 p. dj. VG $50.00

SEKIDA, Katsuki. *Zen Training Methods & Philosophy.* 1975 NY. Weatherhill. $25.00

SELDES, G. *7 Lively Arts.* 1924 Ills 1st ed. 398 p. G $40.00

SELDES, George. *Catholic Crisis.* 1939 Messner. inscr. VG $20.00

SELDES, Gilbert. *Movies Came From America.* 1937 London/NY. Ills. 120 p. dj. VG $17.50

SELDIS, Henry J. *Henry Moore in America.* 1973 Praeger. Ills. 4to. 238 p. cloth. $60.00

SELIGMAN, A. *Voyage of the Cap Pilar.* 1941 London. Ills. maps. G $10.00

SELINKO, Annemarie. *Desiree.* 1953 NY. 1st ed. dj. EX $16.00

SELL, F.E. *American Deer Hunter.* 1950 Stackpole Heck. Ills. 174 p. dj. VG $15.00

SELL, F.E. *Deer Hunter's Guide.* 1964 Stackpole. Ills. 192 p. dj. VG $10.00

SELL, H.B.; & WEYBRIGHT, V. *Buffalo Bill & the Wild West.* 1955 Oxford U Pr. Ills. 278 p. dj. EX $18.00

SELLE, Carol O. *Larry Rivers Drawings 1949-1969.* no date. Ills. folio. spiral bdg. $50.00

SELLECK, Charles M. *Norwalk After 250 Years.* 1901 South Norwalk. Ills. 387 p. $35.00

SELLIN, Thorsen. *Pioneering in Penology.* 1949 Phil. PA U Pr. VG $12.00

SELLING, Lowell S. *Men Against Madness.* 1940 Greenberg, NY. VG $14.00

SELLINGS, Arthur. *Power of X.* 1968 Dobson. 1st ed. dj. EX $12.00

SELLINGS, Arthur. *Quy Effect.* 1966 Dobson. 1st ed. dj. VG $12.00

SELLNER, E. *History of Costume Design.* 1928 Ills. portfolio. dj. VG $38.00

SELOU, Salomon de la. *Poema de los Siete Tratados.* 1952 Mexico. Ills Familia. 1/1,000. sgn. M $150.00

SELOUS, F.C. *African Nature Notes & Reminiscences.* 1908 London. 1st ed. 1st issue. VG $110.00

SELOUS, F.C. *Hunter's Wanderings in Africa.* 1976 Rhodesia. facsimile of 1881. dj. EX $40.00

SELOUS, F.C. *Hunter's Wanderings in Africa.* 1981 Zimabbwe. dj. VG $45.00

SELOUS, F.C. *Sunshine & Storm in Rhodesia.* 1968 Rhodesia. facsimile of 1896. dj. EX $30.00

SELOUS, F.C. *Travel & Adventure in Southeast Africa.* 1972 Rhodesia. Ills. 503 p. fld map. dj. EX $60.00

SELOUS, F.C. *Travel & Adventure in Southeast Africa.* 1893 Rowland Ward. 1st ed. VG $75.00

SELOUS, Percy. *Travel & Big Game.* 1897 NY. Ills. 195 p. VG $40.00

SELWYN-BROWN, A. *Physician Throughout the Ages.* 1928 Capehart Brown. 1st ed. 2 vol set. G $50.00

SELZ, Peter. *Alberto Giacometti.* 1965 Doubleday. Ills. 4to. 119 p. cloth. dj. $30.00

SELZ, Peter. *Mark Rothko Monograph.* 1961 MOMA. Ills. 4to. 44 p. wraps. $10.00

SELZ, Peter. *New Images of Man.* 1959 MOMA. Intro P Tillich. 4to. dj. $35.00

SELZ & CONSTANTINE. *Art Nouveau.* 1959 MOMA. Ills. dj. VG $25.00

SEMMENS, Raphael. *Rebel Raider: Account of R. Semmes Cruise in C.S.S. Sumter.* 1948 Chapel Hill. Ills. green cloth. VG $20.00

SEMMES, R. *Service Afloat & Ashore During the Mexican War.* 1851 Cincinnati. Ills. fld map. cloth. $65.00

SENART, Emile. *Caste in India: Facts & the System.* 1930 London. Methuen. 1st ed. VG $15.00

SENDAK, Maurice. *Hector Protector & As I Went Over the Water.* 1965 Harper Row. 4to. dj. EX $25.00

SENDAK, Maurice. *In the Night Kitchen.* 1st ed. EX $30.00

SENDAK, Maurice. *Juniper Tree & Other Tales From Grimm.* 1973 Farrar Straus. 1st ed. 2nd print. 2 vol set. $30.00

SENDAK, Maurice. *King Grisly Beard.* 1973 NY. 8vo. EX $10.00

SENDAK, Maurice. *Where the Wild Things Are.* 1963 NY. Harper Row. Ills. dj. EX $12.50

SENDAK & MARGOLIS. *Some Swell Pup.* 1976 NY. 1st ed. dj. EX $12.50

SENDREY, Alfred. *Music in Ancient Israel.* 1969 NY. Ills. dj. VG $37.00

SENNETT, Ted. *Hollywood Musicals.* 1981 NY. Abrams. folio. cloth. dj. EX $45.00

SEPHARIAL. *Book of Charms & Talismans.* no date. Phil. dj. VG $15.00

SER, Giovanni. *Pecorone.* 1898 London. Soc of Bibliophiles. 3 vols. $150.00

SERANNE, Ann. *Epicures' Companion.* 1962 NY. EX $10.00

SEREDY, Kate. *Chestry Oak.* 1948 NY. Viking. Ills 1st ed. 8vo. dj. EX $25.00

SEREDY, Kate. *Good Master.* 1947 NY. juvenile. dj. VG $22.50

SEREDY, Kate. *Good Master.* 1938 NY. Viking. Ills 5th print. 8vo. 210 p. VG $15.00

SEREDY, Kate. *Lazy Tinka.* 1962 NY. Viking. Ills 1st ed. 4to. 56 p. dj. VG $30.00

SEREDY, Kate. *Listening.* 1936 NY. Viking. Ills 1st ed. $30.00

SEREDY, Kate. *Open Gate.* 1943 NY. Viking. Ills 1st ed. blue cloth. M $20.00

SEREDY, Kate. *Open Gate.* 1943 NY. Viking. 1st ed. 4to. dj. VG $10.00

SEREDY, Kate. *Singing Tree.* 1946 NY. Viking. Ills. dj. $10.00

SEREDY, Kate. *Tree for Peter.* 1941 NY. 1st ed. dj. VG $27.50

SEREDY, Kate. *White Stag.* 1937 NY. Viking. 1st ed. sgn. dj. EX $30.00

SERGEL, S.L. *Language of Show Biz: Dictionary.* 1973 Chicago. Dramatic Pub. dj. VG $18.50

SERLING. *Left Seat.* 1966 Doubleday. 1st ed. dj. VG $22.50

SERRA, Pere A. *Miro & Mallorca.* 1986 NY. Rizzoli. Ills. 4to. 293 p. dj. $50.00

SERRES, Raoul. *Voltaire: Candide et Autres Contes.* 1947 Petit Angers. Ltd ed. 4to. 278 p. wraps. $40.00

SERVEN, James E. *Colt Firearms From 1836.* 1979 Stackpole. Revised ed. 4to. dj. EX $25.00

SERVEN, James E. *Colt Firearms 1836-1954.* 1954 Santa Ana, CA. private print. inscr. EX $95.00

SERVENTY, V. *Singing Land.* 1972 Scribner. Ills 1st ed. 96 p. dj. EX $12.00

SERVICE, E.R. *Profile of Primitive Culture.* 1958 Harper. Ills. 474 p. G $10.00

SERVICE, R.W. *Complete Poems of Robert Service.* 1943 Dodd Mead. 180 p. dj. VG $14.00

SERVICE, R.W. *Rhymes of a Red Cross Man.* 1916 NY. 1st ed. VG $30.00

SERVICE, R.W. *Rhymes of a Rolling Stone.* 1915 Dodd Mead. 172 p. G $8.00

SERVICE, R.W. *Songs of a Sourdough.* 1908 Briggs. 106 p. VG $12.00

SERVICE, R.W. *Why Not Grow Young?* 1928 NY. VG $20.00

SERVICE, Robert. *Ballads of a Bohemian.* 1921 Barse Hopkins. 220 p. VG $7.50

SERVICE, Robert. *Harper of Heaven.* 1948 Dodd Mead. 1st ed. VG $22.50

SERVIEN, Pius. *Probabilities et Quanta.* 1948 Paris. Hermann. 1st ed. 69 p. wraps. $20.00

SERVISS, Garrett P. *Pleasures of the Telescope.* 1906 NY. Appleton. Ills. 200 p. VG $18.00

SETON, Anya. *Hearth & Eagle.* 1948 Houghton Mifflin. dj. VG $10.00

SETON, Anya. *Winthrop Woman.* 1958 Boston. Houghton Mifflin. 586 p. G $5.00

SETON, Cynthia. *Private Life.* 1982 Norton. proof. wraps. VG $10.00

SETON, E.T. *Animal Heroes.* 1905 Scribner. 1st ed. $50.00

SETON, E.T. *Arctic Prairies: Journey in Search of the Caribou.* 1911 Scribner. Ills 1st ed. 415 p. maps. VG $55.00

SETON, E.T. *Arctic Prairies: Journey in Search of the Caribou.* 1911 Scribner. Ills 1st ed. wraps. EX $85.00

SETON, E.T. *Book of Woodcraft & Indian Lore.* 1923 Doubleday Page. Ills. G $13.00

SETON, E.T. *Book of Woodcraft.* 1921 Garden City. Ills. 590 p. G $7.00

SETON, E.T. *Boy Scouts of America.* 1910 NY. 1st ed. wraps. G $225.00

SETON, E.T. *Gospel of the Red Man.* 1936 NY. 1st ed. 121 p. dj. VG $18.00

SETON, E.T. *Johnny Bear, Lobo, & Other Stories.* 1935 Scribner. Ills 1st ed. 162 p. G $13.00

SETON, E.T. *Lives of the Hunted.* 1901 NY. Ills 1st ed. VG $45.00

SETON, E.T. *Lives of the Hunted.* 1919 Scribner. Ills. 360 p. G $7.00

SETON, E.T. *Lives of the Hunted.* 1936 Scribner. VG $22.00

SETON, E.T. *Lives of the Hunted.* 1967 Schocken. Ills. 350 p. dj. EX $10.00

SETON, E.T. *Monarch the Big Bear.* 1904 NY. 1st ed. G $25.00

SETON, E.T. *Preacher of Cedar Mountain.* 1917 Doubleday Page. VG $16.50

SETON, E.T. *Rolf in the Woods.* 1911 Garden City. 1st ed. EX $55.00

SETON, E.T. *Story of a Gray Squirrel.* 1922 Scribner. Ills 1st ed. scarce. VG $25.00

SETON, E.T. *Studies in Art Anatomy of Animals.* 1896 London. 1st ed. 96 p. green cloth. VG $300.00

SETON, E.T. *Trail of the Sandhill Stag.* 1900 NY. Ills 2nd imp. G $25.00

SETON, E.T. *Trail of the Sandhill Stag.* 1910 NY. 8th imp. square 8vo. VG $15.00

SETON, E.T. *Trail of the Sandhill Stag.* 1917 Scribner. Ills. 93 p. VG $7.00

SETON, E.T. *Trail of the Sandhill Stag.* 1899 NY. Scribner. 1st ed. beige cloth. $25.00

SETON, E.T. *Trail of the Sandhill Stag.* 1899 NY. Ltd 1st ed. 1/250. leather. VG $65.00

SETON, E.T. *Wild Animals at Home.* c 1913. Grosset Dunlap. Ills. G $7.50

SETON, E.T. *Wild Animals I Have Known.* 1926 Scribner. Ills. 298 p. dj. EX $10.00

SETON, E.T. *Wild Animals I Have Known.* 1900 NY. Scribner. Ills. fair. $75.00

SETON, E.T. *Wood Myth & Fable.* 1905 NY. Ills 1st ed. VG $27.50

SETON, E.T. *World of Ernest Thompson Seton.* 1976 NY. Ills 1st ed. dj. EX $35.00

SETON, E.T. *2 Little Savages.* 1903 Doubleday. Ills 1st ed. VG $27.50

SETTLE, Mary Lee. *Blood Tie.* 1977 Houghton Mifflin. 1st ed. dj. $25.00

SETTLE, Mary Lee. *Empire on Wheels.* 1949 Stanford. dj. VG $35.00

SETTLE, Mary Lee. *Killing Ground.* 1982 Farrar. Ltd 1st ed. sgn. slipcase. EX $60.00

SETTLE, Mary Lee. *Killing Ground.* 1982 NY. Farrar. 1st ed. dj. VG $25.00

SETTLE, Mary Lee. *Prisons.* 1973 NY. Putnam. 1st ed. dj. EX $25.00

SETTLE, Mary Lee. *Scapegoat.* 1980 Random House. 1st ed. dj. VG $30.00

SETTLE, Mary Lund & Raymond W. *Saddles & Spurs.* 1955 NY. reprint. dj. VG $15.00

SEUSS. *Cat in the Hat Comes Back!* 1958 1st ed. 8vo. 63 p. dj. VG $45.00

SEVERIN, M.F. *Making a Bookplate.* 1949 London. Ills. 88 p. $16.50

SEVERIN, T. *Explorers of the MS.* 1968 Knopf. Ills 1st Am ed. 294 p. dj. VG $5.00

SEVERSON, John. *Modern Surfing Around the World.* 1964 NY. Doubleday. 1st ed. xl. G $16.00

SEVILLIAS, E. *Athens to Auschwitz.* 1983 Athens. Lycabettus. Ills. dj. G $20.00

SEWALL, Marcia. *Little Wee Tyke.* 1979 NY. Atheneum. Ills Sewall. 1st ed. dj. EX $7.50

SEWALL, Richard B. *Life of Emily Dickinson.* 1975 Farrar Straus. 2nd print. 2 vol set. boxed. M $32.50

SEWARD, A.F. *Star Gazers of Egypt.* 1919 Chicago. 265 p. EX $33.00

SEWARD, Anna. *Memoirs of Dr. Darwin 1731-1802.* 1804 London. VG $20.00

SEWARD, George F. *Chinese Immigration: Social & Ecomomical Aspects.* 1881 NY. Scribner. 1st ed. 8vo. VG $65.00

SEWEL, William. *History of People Called Quakers.* 1722 London. folio. full leather. VG $45.00

SEWELL, Anna. *Black Beauty.* no date. London. Ills. green cloth. $95.00

SEWELL, Anna. *Black Beauty.* c 1920s. London. Jarrolds. 291 p. VG $95.00

SEWELL, Anna. *Black Beauty.* 1970 Clasic Pub. Ills M Rois. 1st ed. cloth. EX $15.00

SEWELL, Anna. *Great Chicago Fire.* 1871 private print. 1st ed. fld map. VG $50.00

SEXTON, Anne. *Book of Folly.* 1972 Boston. 1st ed. dj. EX $20.00

SEXTON, Anne. *To Bedlam & Part Way Back.* 1960 Houghton. 1st ed. dj. EX $100.00

SEXTON, Anne. *To Bedlam & Part Way Back.* 1960 Boston. 1st ed. 1st print. $25.00

SEXTON, Anne. *Transformations.* 1971 Boston. Ills B Swan. 1st ed. dj. EX $30.00

SEXTON, Anne. *Words for Dr. Y.* 1978 Boston. 1st ed. dj. M $17.00

SEYMOUR, Charles. *Intimate Papers of Colonel House.* 1926 Riverside Pr. 4 vol set. EX $130.00

SEYMOUR, Charles. *Intimate Papers of Colonel House.* 1926 Houghton Mifflin. 2 vol set. $25.00

SEYMOUR, F.W. *Story of the Red Man.* 1934 Tudor. Ills. 421 p. maps. VG $17.00

SEYMOUR. *Baseball: Early Years' Golden Age.* 1960 NY. 1st ed. 2 vol set. boxed. VG $27.50

SEYMOUR-JONES, A. *Sheep & Its Skin.* 1913 London. Ills. VG $15.00

SEYMOUR-SMITH. *Robert Graves.* 1956 London. 1st ed. wraps. VG $15.00

SEZNAC, Jean. *Survival of the Pagan Gods.* 1953 NY. Bollingen Foundation. 1st ed. $30.00

SHACKELTON, R. *Book of Chicago.* 1920 Phil. Ills 1st ed. 354 p. VG $45.00

SHACKLEFORD, W.Y. *Gun Fighters of the Old West.* 1943 Haldeman Julius. 24 p. pb. VG $10.00

SHACKLETON, Elizabeth. *Touring Through France.* 1925 Phil. Ills. 4to. 407 p. VG $20.00

SHADBOLT, M.; & RUHEN, O. *Isles of the South Pacific.* 1971 Nat'l Geog Soc. Ills. 211 p. fld map. dj. VG $10.00

SHAFFNER. *Secession War in America.* 1862 London. map. G $60.00

SHAH, Sayed Idries. *Oriental Magic.* 1957 NY. 206 p. dj. VG $22.50

SHAH, Sayed Idries. *Secret Lore of Magic: Book of the Sorcerers.* 1957 London. Muller. 314 p. dj. VG $22.50

SHAH, Sayed Idries. *Secret Lore of Magic: Book of the Sorcerers.* 1958 NY. dj. VG $8.50

SHAHN, Ben. *Ecclesiastes.* 1971 NY. Grosman. dj. VG $18.50

SHAHN, Ben. *Haggadah for Passover.* 1965 Boston. Trans Cecil Roth. VG $15.00

SHAHN, Ben. *Hamlet.* 1959 NY. Ills. VG $25.00

SHAKESPEARE, William. *As You Like It.* London. Hodder Stroughton. Ills. 8vo. $25.00

SHAKESPEARE, William. *Dramatic Works.* no date. Gall Ingis. Ills. $4.00

SHAKESPEARE, William. *Dramatische Werke.* 1905 Berlin. 4th ed. blue cloth. 8 vol set. $75.00

SHAKESPEARE, William. *Hamlet: CBS Television Script.* 1959 CBS. Ills. wraps. dj. VG $25.00

SHAKESPEARE, William. *King Henry the 5th.* 1951 Heritage. Ills Kredel. folio. slipcase. $17.50

SHAKESPEARE, William. *Merchant of Venice.* 1935 London. Ills Eric Gill. full leather. $25.00

SHAKESPEARE, William. *Midsummer Night's Dream.* Ills Morse. scissor-cut silhouettes. 88 p. $80.00

SHAKESPEARE, William. *Midsummer Night's Dream.* 1955 Grabhorn. Ills M Grabhorn. 1/180. 4to. $195.00

SHAKESPEARE, William. *National Shakespeare.* no date. London. Mackenzie. 3 vol set. $400.00

SHAKESPEARE, William. *Poems of William Shakespeare.* 1967 Cambridge. Ltd Ed Club. slipcase. EX $60.00

SHAKESPEARE, William. *Poems of William Shakespeare.* 1830 London. Dove. 8vo. 152 p. ½-red leather. $50.00

SHAKESPEARE, William. *Tempest.* no date. London/NY. Ills Rackham. VG $50.00

SHAKESPEARE, William. *Tragedy of Anthony & Cleopatra.* 1960 Grabhorn. Ills M Grabhorn. 1/185. EX $200.00

SHAKESPEARE, William. *Works of William Shakespeare in 15 Vols.* 1881 London. Ills Gilbert. 4to. morocco. $500.00

SHAKESPEARE, William. *Works of William Shakespeare.* 1901-1904. London. 1/1,000. 10 vols in 5. $250.00

SHAKESPEARE, William. *Works of William Shakespeare.* 1929 NY. Nonesuch. Ltd ed. 1/1,600. 7 vol set. $550.00

SHAKESPEARE, William. *Works of William Shakespeare.* 1888 NY. Ltd ed. 1/500. 3 vol set. VG $550.00

SHAKESPEARE, William. *19 Sonnets.* 1946 NY. Golden Eagle. Ltd ed. 8vo. dj. $65.00

SHAMBAUGH, Bertha. *Amana That Was & Amana That Is.* 1932 IA State Hist Soc. 1st ed. EX $65.00

SHANGE, Ntozake. *Daugther's Geography.* 1983 St. Martin. Ltd 1st ed. 1/250. slipcase. $40.00

SHANGE, Ntozake. *3 Pieces.* 1981 St. Martin. 1st ed. dj. EX $13.00

SHANKAR, Ravi. *My Music, My Life.* 1968 Delhi. Ills. 4to. G $25.00

SHANKLE, G. *American Nicknames: Their Origin & Significance.* 1955 NY. 3rd ed. $22.50

SHANKS, B. *Wilderness Survival.* 1980 Universe. Ills. 208 p. dj. EX $10.00

SHANNON, Dell. *Appearances of Death.* 1977 Morrow. 1st ed. dj. EX $13.00

SHANNON, Dell. *Coffin Corner.* 1966 Morrow. dj. xl. $7.50

SHANNON, Dell. *Crime File.* 1974 Morrow. 1st ed. dj. xl. $6.00

SHANNON, Dell. *Crime File.* 1974 Morrow. 1st ed. dj. EX $20.00

SHANNON, Dell. *Death by Inches.* 1967 London. Gollancz. 1st ed. dj. VG $15.00

SHANNON, Dell. *Death of a Busybody.* 1963 Morrow. 1st ed. xl. $5.00

SHANNON, Dell. *Destiny of Death.* 1984 Morrow. 1st ed. dj. VG $15.00

SHANNON, Dell. *Felony at Random.* 1979 Morrow. 1st ed. dj. VG $12.50

SHANNON, Dell. *Whim To Kill.* 1971 Morrow. 1st ed. dj. xl. $7.50

SHANNON, Monica. *Eyes for the Dark.* 1928 Garden City. Ills Millard. 1st ed. EX $40.00

SHANNON, Monica. *Tawnymore.* 1931 Garden City. Ills Jean Charlot. 1st ed. VG $25.00

SHAPIRO, Irwin. *Golden Book of America.* 1957 Simon Schuster. 1st ed. VG $7.50

SHAPIRO, Irwin. *Story of Yankee Whaling.* 1959 Am Heritage. Ills. 153 p. maps. VG $7.00

SHAPIRO, Irwin. *Walt Disney's Old Yeller.* 1957 Simon Schuster. Ills Schmidt/Dreany. 1st ed. $7.50

SHAPIRO, Irwin. *Yankee Thunder: Legendary Life of Davy Crockett.* 1945 NY. Ills Daugherty. juvenile. dj. $20.00

SHAPIRO, Karl. *Adult Bookstore.* 1976 Random House. 1st ed. dj. VG $15.00

SHAPIRO, Karl. *Beyond Criticism.* 1953 NE U Pr. 1st ed. EX $15.00

SHAPIRO, Karl. *Burgeois Poet.* c 1964. NY. 1st ed. blue cloth. dj. VG $17.50

SHAPIRO, Karl. *Edsel.* 1971 Bernard Geis. 1st ed. dj. EX $25.00

SHAPIRO, Karl. *Essay on Rhyme.* 1945 Reynal Hitchcock. 1st ed. dj. $35.00

SHAPIRO, Karl. *In Defense of Ignorance.* 1960 Random House. 1st ed. dj. EX $25.00

SHAPIRO, Karl. *Poems of a Jew.* 1968 Random House. 1st ed. dj. EX $25.00

SHAPIRO, Karl. *Randall Jarrell.* 1967 Washington. Lib of Congress. 8vo. wraps. $20.00

SHAPIRO, Karl. *To Abolish Children.* 1968 Quadrangle. 1st ed. sgn. dj. EX $60.00

SHAPIRO, Karl. *To Abolish Children.* 1968 Quadrangle. 1st ed. dj. VG $20.00

SHAPIRO, Karl. *Trial of a Poet.* 1947 Reynal Hitchcock. 1st ed. dj. $20.00

SHAPIRO, Karl. *White-Haired Lover.* 1968 Random House. 1st ed. dj. EX $20.00

SHAPIRO, Michael Edward. *Sculpture & Drawings of Jim Dine.* 1984 NY. Ills. 4to. 40 p. wraps. $20.00

SHARAFF, Irene. *Broadway & Hollywood: Costumes Designed by Irene Sharaff.* 1976 Van Nostrand. 1st ed. dj. EX $8.00

SHARKEY, Jack. *Murder Maestro Please.* 1960 Schuman. 1st ed. xl. fair. $5.00

SHARP, Abbie. *History of the Spirit Lake Massacre.* 1923 Des Moines. Ills 9th ed. 386 p. VG $27.50

SHARP, Abbie. *History of the Spirit Lake Massacre.* 1895 Des Moines. Ills. VG $52.50

SHARP, Ann Pearsall. *Little Garden People & What They Do.* 1938 Akron. Ills Marion Bryson. $16.00

SHARP, Dallas Lore. *Watcher in the Woods.* 1915 NY. Century. 127 p. VG $4.00

SHARP, Dallas Lore. *Where Rolls the OR.* 1914 Boston. 12mo. 251 p. $50.00

SHARP, Margery. *Bernard into Battle.* 1978 Little Brown. Ills Morrill. 1st Am ed. dj. $20.00

SHARP, Margery. *Bernard the Brave.* 1977 Little Brown. Ills Morrill. 1st ed. dj. EX $20.00

SHARP, Margery. *Martha, Eric, & George.* 1964 Boston. Little Brown. 1st ed. $10.00

SHARP, Margery. *Miss Bianca & the Bridesmaid.* 1972 Little Brown. Ills Blegvad. 1st ed. dj. EX $25.00

SHARP, Thomas. *Dissertation on Pageants or Dramatic Mysteries.* 1825 Coventry, England. 4to. VG $75.00

SHARP, William. *Poems: Selected & Arranged by Mrs. William Sharp.* 1912 London. 1st ed. inscr. G $45.00

SHARP. *Country Dance Book. Part II.* 1913 London. Novello. Revised 2nd ed. $15.00

SHARPE, L.W. *How To Draw Merchant Ships.* 1945 London. Ills. dj. G $6.50

SHARPE, P.B. *Rifle in America.* 1938 Morrow. 1st ed. inscr. dj. VG $55.00

SHARPE, Ruth. *Tristram of Lyonesse.* 1949 NY. Greenburg. Ills Richard Sharpe. 1st ed. $30.00

SHARPE, Tom. *Great Pursuit.* 1977 London. dj. EX $45.00

SHARPE, Tom. *Vintage Stuff.* 1982 London. 1st ed. dj. VG $20.00

SHARPE, Tom. *Wilt On High.* 1984 London. 1st ed. sgn. dj. EX $30.00

SHATTUCK, George Burbank. *Bahama Islands.* 1905 NY. Macmillan. Ills 1st ed. 630 p. VG $100.00

SHATTUCK, H.R. *Woman's Manual of Parliamentary Law.* 1896 Lee Shepherd. Revised 6th ed. VG $10.00

SHATTUCK, William. *Secret of Black Butte; or, Mysterious Mine.* 1897 Boston. Ills 1st ed. VG $35.00

SHATTUCK. *Proust's Binoculars.* 1963 NY. 1st ed. dj. EX $11.00

SHAW, Arnold. *World of Soul: Black America's Contribution to Pop Music.* 1970 NY. Cowles. 1st ed. VG $18.00

SHAW, Bernard. *Intelligent Woman's Guide to Socialism & Capitalism.* 1928 NY. Brentano. 1st Am ed. EX $18.00

SHAW, Bob. *Cosmic Kaleidoscope.* 1976 Gollancz. 1st ed. dj. EX $25.00

SHAW, Bob. *Cosmic Kaleidoscope.* 1977 Doubleday. $10.00

SHAW, Edward. *Civil Architecture; or, Complete System of Building.* 1832 Boston. 2nd ed. 4to. 97 plts. calf. EX $325.00

SHAW, Elton. *Body Taboo.* 1937 1st ed. VG $20.00

SHAW, F.G. *Science of Fly Fishing for Trout.* 1925 Scribner. Ills. 341 p. dj. G $12.50

SHAW, G.B. *Adventures of the Black Girl in Her Search for God.* 1932 London. 1st ed. VG $25.00

SHAW, G.B. *Apple Cart.* 1930 London. EX $16.00

SHAW, G.B. *Back to Methuselah.* 1939 Ltd Ed Club. sgn J Farleigh. cloth. dj. EX $55.00

SHAW, G.B. *Collected Works.* 1930 NY. Ltd ed. 1/1,790. 30 vol set. $145.00

SHAW, G.B. *Complete Plays with Prefaces.* 1963 Dodd Mead. 6 vol set. djs. VG $50.00

SHAW, G.B. *How To Settle the Irish Question.* 1917 Dublin. 1st ed. 32 p. blue wraps. $30.00

SHAW, G.B. *Lady, Wilt Thou Love Me?* 1980 NY. 1st ed. dj. M $17.00

SHAW, G.B. *Man & Superman.* 1905 NY. Brentano. G $15.00

SHAW, G.B. *Plays: Pleasant & Unpleasant.* 1898 London. 1st ed. 2 vol set. EX $650.00

SHAW, G.B. *Pygmalion & Candida.* 1974 Ltd Ed Club. Ills/sgn C Hutton. 1/2,000. VG $30.00

SHAW, G.B. *Saint Joan: Chronicle Play in 6 Scenes & Epilogue.* 1924 Brentano. VG $17.50

SHAW, G.B. *Widowers' Houses.* 1893 London. 1st ed. VG $100.00

SHAW, G.B. *Wreath of Stars.* 1977 Doubleday. 1st ed. dj. VG $15.00

SHAW, G.B. *9 Plays.* 1935 Dodd Mead. VG $12.00

SHAW, G.E. *Malayan Agriculture.* 1924 Singapore. 305 p. wraps. VG $10.00

SHAW, Henry. *Alphabets, Numerals, & Devices of the Middle Ages.* 1845 London. 48 plts. VG $325.00

SHAW, Henry. *Art of Illumination.* 1870 London. Ills 2nd ed. 4to. 66 p. VG $150.00

SHAW, Henry. *Dresses & Decorations of the Middle Ages.* 1858 London. Bohn. Ills. 4to. VG $450.00

SHAW, Hubert K. *Families of the Pilgrims.* 1956 Boston. Mayflower Descendants. VG $45.00

SHAW, Irwin. *Acceptable Losses.* 1982 NY. 1st ed. dj. M $12.00

SHAW, Irwin. *Beggar Man, Thief.* 1977 NY. 1st ed. dj. M $12.00

SHAW, Irwin. *Beggar Man, Thief.* 1977 Franklin Lib. 1st ed. full leather. EX $35.00

SHAW, Irwin. *God Was Here But He Left Early.* 1973 NY. 1st ed. dj. EX $14.00

SHAW, Irwin. *Love on a Dark Street.* 1965 NY. 1st ed. dj. EX $15.00

SHAW, Irwin. *Mixed Company.* 1950 Random House. 1st ed. dj. EX $50.00

SHAW, Irwin. *Nightwork.* 1980 Delacorte. 1st ed. dj. VG $15.00

SHAW, Irwin. *Short Stories: 5 Decades.* 1978 NY. 1st ed. sgn. dj. M $25.00

SHAW, Irwin. *Top of the Hill.* 1979 Delacorte. 1st ed. dj. VG $15.00

SHAW, Irwin. *2 Weeks in Another Town.* 1960 Cape. 1st English ed. dj. EX $20.00

SHAW, J. *Hard-Boiled Omnibus.* 1946 NY. Simon Schuster. 367 p. $52.50

SHAW, L.M. *Current Issues.* 1908 NY. Ills. cloth. VG $20.00

SHAW, Lloyd. *Cowboy Dances.* 1939 Caldwell. Ills 1st ed. sgn. dj. EX $40.00

SHAW, Lloyd. *Cowboy Dances.* 1952 Caxton. 13th print. VG $10.00

SHAW, Lloyd. *True History of Some of the Pioneers of CO.* 1909 Denver. Ills 1st ed. 268 p. scarce. $40.00

SHAW, Peter. *Character of John Adams.* 1976 Chapel Hill. dj. VG $10.00

SHAW, R.C. *Across the Plains in 49.* 1948 Lakeside Pr. Ills. 16mo. 170 p. EX $18.50

SHAW, Rev. S.B. *Great Revival in Wales.* c 1905. Chicago. $30.00

SHAW, Samuel. *Narrative of Travels of James Bruce to Abyssinia.* 1790 London. 1st ed. rebound. G $65.00

SHAW, Simeon. *Nature Displayed: Part I, Astronomy & Physics.* 1823 London. fld map. G $50.00

SHAW, W.T. *China or Denny Pheasant in OR.* 1908 Phil. G $20.00

SHAW-SPARROW, Walter. *John Lavery & His Work.* no date. Boston. Estes. 4to. 243 p. $50.00

SHAWN, Ted. *1,001 Night Stands.* 1960 Garden City. 1st ed. inscr. dj. VG $45.00

SHAY, Edith & Frank. *Sand in Their Shoes.* 1951 Boston. 1st ed. VG $12.50

SHAY, Felix. *Elbert Hubbard of East Aurora.* 1926 NY. Ills 1st ed. dj. EX $25.00

SHAY, Frank. *Deep Sea Chanties.* 1925 London. Ills EA Wilson. 4to. $85.00

SHAYLOR, Joseph. *Fascination of Books.* 1912 London. 1st ed. VG $40.00

SHEA, John G. *PA Dutch & Their Furniture.* 1980 NY. Nostrand. Ills. dj. VG $10.00

SHEA, Michael. *Fat Face.* 1987 Seattle. Intro Wagner. 1/300. sgns. dj. $45.00

SHEA, Michael. *Fat Face.* 1987 Seattle. 1st trade ed. SftCvr. M $15.00

SHEA, Michael. *Fat Face.* Axolotl. Ltd 1st ed. sgn. dj. M $40.00

SHEAHAN, James W. *Great Conflagration. Chicago: Its Past, Present, & Future.* 1871 Ills. fld map. ½-leather. EX $95.00

SHEARER. *Robert Potter: Remarkable North Carolinian & TX.* 1951 Houston. 1st ed. VG $25.00

SHEARMAN, Montague. *Athletics & Football.* 1887 Boston/London. Ills. 410 p. $25.00

SHECKLEY, Robert. *Crompton Divided.* 1978 NY. 1st Am ed. dj. M $25.00

SHECKLEY, Robert. *Game of X.* 1965 Delacorte. 1st ed. dj. VG $50.00

SHEEAN, Vincent. *Between the Thunder & the Sun.* 1943 Random House. inscr. G $10.00

SHEEAN, Vincent. *11th Hour.* 1939 London. Hamilton. 1st ed. inscr. dj. G $20.00

SHEEHAN, Donald. *This Was Publishing: Chronicle of Book Trade in Gilded Age.* 1952 IN U Pr. 1st ed. dj. VG $20.00

SHEEHAN, Murray. *Eden.* 1928 Dutton. 3rd ed. G $6.00

SHEEHAN, N. *Arnheiter Affair.* 1971 NY. 1st ed. sgn. dj. VG $25.00

SHEERAN, James. *Confederate Chaplain in a War Journal.* 1960 Bruce. 1st ed. dj. $7.50

SHEIL, M.P. *Prince Saleski & Cummings King Monk.* 1977 Sauk City. 1st ed. 220 p. dj. EX $12.50

SHELDON, Charles. *Wilderness of Danali.* 1960 NY. New ed. 412 p. dj. EX $12.50

SHELDON, Charles. *Wilderness of North Pacific Coast Islands.* 1912 Scribner. Ills 1st ed. 246 p. VG $17.50

SHELDON, Charles. *Wilderness of the Upper Yukon.* 1919 Scribner. Ills 2nd ed. G $225.00

SHELDON, G.W. *American Painters.* 1879 NY. 83 plts. $150.00

SHELDON, George. *History of Deerfield, MA.* 1895 Deerfield. 1st ed. 2 vol set. VG $125.00

SHELDON, Harold P. *Tranquility Revisited.* 1940 NY. Derrydale. Ills Ltd ed. 1/485. 4to. $175.00

SHELDON, Richard. *Poor Prisoner's Defense.* 1949 Simon Schuster. VG $10.00

SHELDON, W.G. *Book of American Woodcock.* 1971 MA U Pr. Ills 2nd ed. 4to. dj. EX $10.00

SHELDRICK, D. *Orphans of Tsavo.* 1967 McKay. Ills 1st Am ed. 159 p. dj. EX $18.00

SHELFORD, R.W. *Naturalist in Borneo.* 1917 NY. Ills 1st ed. 331 p. G $75.00

SHELFORD, V.E. *Ecology of North America.* 1964 IL U Pr. Ills. 610 p. maps. dj. EX $30.00

SHELLER, R. *Name Was Olney.* 1980 Franklin. Ills. 171 p. dj. EX $14.00

SHELLEY, Mary W. *Frankenstein; or, Modern Prometheus.* 1984 Berkeley. CA U Pr. Ills Moser. $30.00

SHELLEY, Mary W. *Letters of Mary Shelley.* 1918 Harper. Ltd ed. 1/448. VG $17.50

SHELLEY, Percy Bysshe. *Complete Poetical Works.* 1921 London. gilt leather. VG $20.00

SHELLEY, Percy Bysshe. *Poetical Works.* 1892 London. Chiswick. 5 vol set. VG $65.00

SHELLEY, Percy Bysshe. *Sensitive Plant.* no date. London. Ills Robinson. VG $60.00

SHELLEY, Percy Bysshe. *Shelley's Prose of the Trumpet of a Prophecy.* 1954 Albuquerque. NM U Pr. 1st ed. VG $22.50

SHELLEY, Percy Bysshe. *Zastrozzi.* 1955 London. Ltd ed. 1/200. dj. boxed. VG $85.00

SHELLEY, Percy Bysshe. *6 Hymns of Homer.* 1929 Halcon Pr. Ltd ed. 1/450. VG $40.00

SHELTON, Jason S. *Strike at Shane's.* 1893 Boston. Am Humane Ed Soc. 1st ed. VG $250.00

SHELTON, L. *Charles M. Russell: Cowboy, Artist, & Friend.* 1962 NY. 1st ed. dj. EX $13.00

SHEM, Samuel. *Fine.* 1984 St. Martin. Advance copy. wraps. EX $20.00

SHENBERG, Yitzhak. *Under the Fig Tree.* 1948 Schocken. 1st Am ed. dj. VG $20.00

SHENSTONE, W.A. *Methods of Glass Blowing & Working Silica in Oxy-Gas Flame.* 1907 London. Longman Green. 6th print. VG $12.00

SHENSTONE, W.A. *Methods of Glass Blowing & Working Silica in Oxy-Gas Flame.* 1918 London. 10th imp. 12mo. 95 p. $15.00

SHEPARD, Ernest H. *Holly Tree & Other Christmas Stories.* no date. NY. Scribner. 4to. 192 p. VG $35.00

SHEPARD, Lucius. *Jaguar Hunter.* 1987 Sauk City. 1st ed. dj. M $22.00

SHEPHERD, A. *Flight of the Unicorns.* 1965 London. Elek. Ills 1st ed. dj. VG $15.00

SHEPHERD, Grant. *Silver Magnet: 50 Years in a Mexican Silver Mine.* 1938 1st ed. xl. VG $10.00

SHEPHERD, Jack. *Adams Chronicles.* 1976 Boston. dj. VG $25.00

SHEPHERD, Jean. *Wanda Hickey's Night of Golden Memories.* 1971 Doubleday. 1st ed. inscr. dj. EX $25.00

SHEPHERD, Michael. *Road to Gandolfo.* 1975 NY. 1st ed. dj. $20.00

SHEPPARD, A.T. *Art & Practice of Historical Fiction.* 1930 London. EX $25.00

SHEPPARD, Thomas F. *Lourmarin in the 18th Century: Study of a French Village.* 1971 Baltimore. 262 p. $20.00

SHEPPERD, Tad. *Pack & Paddock.* 1938 Derrydale. Ills Paul Brown. 1/950. EX $70.00

SHERBOURNE, James. *Death's Gray Angel.* 1981 Houghton. Advance copy. dj. EX $10.00

SHERIDAN, P.H. *Personal Memoirs.* 1888 NY. 1st ed. 2 vol set. EX $55.00

SHERIDAN, R.B. *Jaunts & Jollities of Renowned Sporting Citizen J. Jorrocks.* 1932 Ltd Ed Club. sgn G Ross. brown cloth. VG $25.00

SHERIDAN, R.B. *School for Scandal & Rivals.* 1934 Oxford. Ills Rene Sussan. 4to. VG $50.00

SHERIDAN, R.B. *School for Scandal & Rivals.* 1930 London. full leather. VG $20.00

SHERIDAN, R.B. *Sheridiana; or, Anecdotes of R.B. Sheridan.* 1826 London. ½-calf. VG $70.00

SHERIDAN, R.B. *Trip of Scarborough: A Comedy.* 1781 London. 1/4 calf. VG $125.00

SHERMAN, Allan. *I Can't Dance.* 1964 Harper. Ills Hoff. 1st ed. dj. $10.00

HERMAN, Harold M. *Tahara in the Land of Yucatan.* 1933 Goldsmith. dj. VG $20.00

SHERMAN, Harold M. *Tahara: Boy Mystic of India.* 1933 Goldsmith. dj. VG $20.00

SHERMAN, Jane. *Drama of Denishawn Dance.* 1979 Middletown. Ills 1st ed. dj. VG $25.00

SHERMAN, John. *Sherman's Recollections of 40 Years in House & Senate.* 1896 Chicago. VG $35.00

SHERMAN, John. *Trenton Falls Illustrated.* 1868 NY. Orr. Ills. VG $35.00

SHERMAN, Loren A. *Science of the Soul.* 1895 1st ed. 414 p. VG $35.00

SHERMAN, William T. *Personal Memoirs.* 1891 NY. Webster. 2 vols in 1. VG $37.50

SHERRILL, C.H. *Stained Glass Tours in France.* 1908 NY. Lane. 1st ed. VG $25.00

SHERROD, Robert. *History of Marine Corps Aviation in WWII.* 1952 WA. 1st ed. $25.00

SHERROD, Robert. *Tarawa: Story of a Battle.* 1944 Duell Sloan. 1st ed. 183 p. dj. VG $15.00

SHERRY, Edna. *Survival of the Fittest.* 1960 Dodd Mead. 1st ed. dj. VG $12.50

SHERWOOD, E.W. *Rainbow Hoosier.* no date. Indianapolis. VG $25.00

SHERWOOD, Mary. *Wishing Cap.* 1833 NY. Day. $35.00

SHERWOOD, R. *Idiot's Delight.* 1936 NY. inscr. dj. EX $85.00

SHERWOOD, Robert. *Petrified Forest.* 1935 NY. Scribner. Review copy. dj. EX $75.00

SHERWOOD, Robert. *There Shall Be No Night.* 1940 NY. 1st ed. dj. VG $15.00

SHICK, Alice. *Serengeti Cats.* 1977 Lippincott. Ills Joel Shick. dj. VG $15.00

SHIEL, M.P. *Children of the Wind.* 1923 Knopf. 1st ed. VG $30.00

SHIEL, M.P. *How the Old Woman Got Home.* 1928 NY. Macy. 1st ed. EX $17.50

SHIEL, M.P. *Lord of the Sea.* 1901 NY. Stokes. 1st ed. 1st issue. G $20.00

SHIEL, M.P. *Prince Zaleski & Cummings King Monk.* 1977 Mycroft Moran. 1st ed. dj. EX $15.00

SHIEL, M.P. *Purple Cloud.* 1963 Gollancz. dj. VG $25.00

SHIEL, M.P. *Purple Cloud.* 1946 World. dj. VG $30.00

SHIEL, M.P. *Shapes in the Fire*. 1896 London. G $50.00

SHIEL, M.P. *Xelucha*. 1975 Arkham House. 1st ed. dj. VG $15.00

SHIEL, M.P. *Yellow Danger*. 1899 NY. Fenno. 1st ed. VG $20.00

SHIEL, M.P. *Young Men Are Coming*. 1937 NY. Vanguard. 1st ed. dj. VG $25.00

SHIELDS, Cornelius. *Racing with Cornelius Shields & the Masters*. 1974 NY. Prentice Hall. dj. EX $66.00

SHIELDS, G.O. *Big Game of North America*. 1890 Chicago. 1st ed. VG $17.00

SHIELDS, G.O. *Cruisings In Cascades*. 1889 NY/Chicago. $38.00

SHIELDS, G.O. *Hunting in the Great West*. no date. Belford Clarke. Ills. rebound. $28.00

SHILLITOE, Alan. *2nd Chance*. 1981 London. 1st ed. sgn. dj. EX $22.00

SHIMER, J.A. *This Sculptured Earth: Landscape of America*. 1959 Columbia U Pr. Ills. 255 p. map. VG $10.00

SHINE, Deborah. *Thrilling Detective Stories*. 1980 Octopus. VG $6.00

SHINGLETON, R.G. *John Taylor Wood: Sea Ghost of the Confederacy*. 1982 GA U Pr. Ills. 242 p. maps. dj. EX $19.00

SHINN, C.H. *Mining Camps: Study in American Frontier Government*. 1965 Harper. Torch Book. 1st ed. pb. VG $7.50

SHINN, E. *Christ Story*. 1943 Phil/Toronto. 1st ed. dj. EX $20.00

SHINNO, Tat. *Flower Arrangements To Copy*. 1966 Doubleday. Ills 1st ed. 246 p. dj. $25.00

SHIPLEY, Joseph T. *Art of Eugene O'Neill*. 1928 WA U Pr. 1st ed. wraps. $30.00

SHIPMAN, Louis Evan. *D'Arcy of the Guards; or, Fortunes of War*. 1899 Chicago. Stone. 1st ed. 12mo. 238 p. VG $65.00

SHIPPEY, Lee. *Los Angeles Book*. 1950 Boston. Houghton Mifflin. 1st ed. 8vo. $40.00

SHIRAS, G. *Hunting Wildlife with Camera & Flashlight*. 1936 WA. 2 vol set. VG $27.50

SHIRAS, Wilmar H. *Children of the Atom*. 1978 Pennyfarthing. dj. EX $15.00

SHIRCLIFF, S.N. *Jungle Islands*. 1930 Putnam. Ills 1st ed. VG $22.50

SHIRER, William L. *Berlin Diary*. 1941 Knopf. 1st ed. VG $20.00

SHIRER, William L. *Consul's Wife*. 1956 Little Brown. 1st ed. dj. VG $20.00

SHORE, Wendy. *Ukiyo-e*. 1980 Woodbine Books. 30 p. EX $12.00

SHORES, Christopher F. *Fighter Aces*. 1975 London. Hamlyn. 1st ed. EX $20.00

SHORT, John T. *North Americans of Antiquity*. 1880 NY. Harper. Ills. 8vo. brown cloth. VG $150.00

SHORT, Luke. *Coroner Creek*. 1946 Macmillan. 1st ed. dj. xl. $6.00

SHORT, Luke. *Sunset Graze*. 1942 Doubleday Doran. 1st ed. xl. $5.00

SHORT, Michael. *Gustav Holst 1874-1934: Centenary Documentation*. 1974 London. dj. VG $30.00

SHORT, W. *Cheechakos*. 1964 Random House. Ills 1st ed. 244 p. dj. EX $10.00

SHORTER, Clement. *Complete Poems of Charlotte Bronte*. 1923 NY. 1st ed. VG $22.50

SHORTT, Adam; & DOUGHTY, A.E. *Canada & Its Provinces*. 1914-1917. England. 1/875. 23 vol set. $1100.00

SHOWELL, Romola. *Learning About Insects & Small Animals*. 1972 Ladybird. VG $4.00

SHRIDHARANI, Krishnalal. *Mahatma & the World*. 1946 Duell Sloan. dj. G $12.00

SHRUBSOLE, E.S. *Fisherman's Handbook*. 1904 Bodley Head. Ills. 189 p. G $10.00

SHUFFREY, L.A. *English Fireplace & Its Accessories*. 1912 London. Ills WG Davie. cloth. VG $95.00

SHULL, A.F. *Principles of Animal Biology*. no date. McGraw Hill. Ills. 425 p. VG $8.00

SHULLMAN, Irving. *Valentino*. 1967 NY. Ills 2nd ed. 499 p. $12.50

SHULMAN, Alix Kates. *On the Stroll*. 1981 Knopf. 1st ed. dj. VG $10.00

SHULMAN, Irving. *Square Trap*. 1953 Little Brown. 1st ed. dj. EX $15.00

SHULMAN, Max. *Tender Trap*. 1955 NY. 1st ed. dj. EX $15.00

SHULMAN, Max. *Zebra Derby*. 1946 NY. Doubleday. Ills 1st ed. dj. $15.00

SHUMWAY, DURRELL, & FREY. *Conestoga Wagon: 1750-1850*. 1964 private print. Ills. inscr Durrell. 4to. dj. $50.00

SHURE, David. *Hester Bateman: Queen of English Silversmiths*. 1959 NY. dj. VG $25.00

SHUTE, Henry. *Real Boys*. 1905 NY. Dillingham. Ills 1st ed. VG $18.00

SHUTE, Nevil. *Checquer Board*. 1947 Heinemann. dj. VG $30.00

SHUTE, Nevil. *Far Country*. 1952 Heinemann. 1st English ed. dj. VG $35.00

SHUTE, Nevil. *In the Wet*. 1953 Heinemann. 1st English ed. dj. VG $32.00

SHUTE, Nevil. *Legacy*. 1950 Morrow. 1st Am ed. dj. VG $20.00

SHUTE, Nevil. *No Highway*. 1951 Heinemann. 7th ed. VG $10.00

SHUTE, Nevil. *On the Beach*. 1957 Heinemann. 1st ed. inscr. dj. VG $90.00

SHUTE, Nevil. *On the Beach*. 1957 Morrow. 1st Am ed. 8vo. 320 p. dj. EX $65.00

SHUTE, Nevil. *Ordeal*. 1939 NY. Morrow. 1st ed. dj. VG $15.00

SHUTE, Nevil. *Pastoral*. 1944 Morrow. 1st Am ed. dj. VG $20.00

SHUTE, Nevil. *Rainbow & the Rose*. 1958 London. 1st ed. 306 p. dj. VG $25.00

SHUTE, Nevil. *Requiem for a Wren*. 1955 London. 1st ed. dj. VG $30.00

SHUTE, Nevil. *Round the Bend*. 1951 NY. 341 p. dj. $8.00

SHUTE, Nevil. *Stephen Morris*. 1961 London. 1st ed. dj. VG $20.00

SHUTE, Nevil. *Town Like Alice*. 1950 London. 1st ed. dj. VG $25.00

SHUTE, Nevil. *Vinland the Good*. 1946 Heinemann. 1st English ed. dj. VG $50.00

SHUTE, Nevil. *What Happened to the Corbetts?* 1939 London. 1st ed. VG $15.00

SHUTE, Nevil. *What Happened to the Corbetts?* 1953 London. dj. EX $18.00

SIANG, Song. *100 Years History of Chinese in Singapore*. 1967 Malaya U Pr. 1st ed. dj. $20.00

SIBLEY, Celestine. *Christmas in GA*. 1964 NY. Doubleday. sgn. dj. EX $10.00

SIBLEY, Celestine. *Malignant Heart*. 1958 Crime Club. 1st ed. dj. VG $12.50

SIBLEY, H.H. *Iron Face: Adventures of Jack Frazer*. 1950 Caxton. Ltd ed. 1/500. EX $45.00

SIBLEY, William G. *French 500 & Other Papers*. 1933 Lakeside Pr. 1st ed. 1/600. sgn. 108 p. $45.00

SIBLEY, William G. *French 500 & Other Papers*. 1901 Gallipolis, OH. 1st ed. 303 p. fair. $65.00

SIBSON, Francis H. *Unthinkable.* 1933 NY. Harrison Smith. 1st ed. VG $45.00

SICHEL, Pierre. *Jersey Lily.* 1958 Prentice Hall. Ills 1st ed. 456 p. dj. VG $15.00

SICK, Helmut. *Ornitologia Brasileira.* 1984 Brasil. Portuguese text. 2 vol set. M $45.00

SIDEMAN & FRIEDMAN. *Europe Looks at the Civil War.* 1960 NY. Orion. dj. VG $20.00

SIDGWICK, N.V. *Some Physical Properties of the Covalent Link in Chemistry.* 1922 Ithica. Cornell U Pr. 1st ed. xl. VG $20.00

SIDNEY, Margaret. *Golden West.* 1886 Boston. Ills. square 8vo. 388 p. VG $12.50

SIDNEY, Margaret. *Stories Polly Pepper Told.* 1899 Boston. Ills Etheldred Barry. VG $10.00

SIDNEY, Margaret. *5 Little Peppers & How They Grew.* 1881 Boston. Ills. gilt cloth. G $35.00

SIDNEY, Margaret. *5 Little Peppers & How They Grew.* 1948 Grosset Dunlap. Ills. VG $6.00

SIDNEY, Sylvia. *Sylvia Sidney Needlepoint Book.* 1968 Van Nostrand. Ills. 120 p. pb. $12.50

SIDNEY, Sylvia. *Sylvia Sidney Needlepoint Book.* 1968 Van Nostrand. Ills. 120 p. dj. $25.00

SIEBER, Roy. *African Textiles & Decorative Arts.* 1972 NY. MOMA. Ills. 4to. 240 p. wraps. VG $40.00

SIEDENTOPF, A.R. *Last Stronghold of Big Game.* 1946 McBride. Ills 1st ed. 202 p. dj. VG $18.00

SIEGLER, H.R. *NH Nature Notes.* 1962 Equity. Ills. 317 p. dj. VG $22.00

SIEMEL, Sasha. *Tigrero!* 1953 Prentice Hall. Ills. 266 p. dj. VG $10.00

SIENKIEWICZ, Henryk. *Pan Michael.* 1898 NY. Federal Book Co. 1st ed. VG $10.00

SIENKIEWICZ, Henryk. *Whirlpools.* 1910 Boston. 1st ed. EX $12.00

SIERRA CLUB. *Last Redwoods & the Parkland of Redwood Creek.* 1969 Ills. 160 p. VG $9.00

SIGERIST, Henry E. *American Medicine.* 1934 NY. Norton. 1st ed. VG $25.00

SIGERIST, Henry E. *Great Doctors: Biographical History of Medicine.* 1933 London. Ills 1st ed. VG $40.00

SIGERIST, Henry E. *Medicine & Human Welfare.* 1947 Yale U Pr. dj. VG $12.50

SIGERIST, Henry E. *Socialized Medicine in Soviet Union.* 1937 Norton. VG $12.50

SIGERSON. *Dull Day in London.* 1920 London. Intro Thomas Hardy. 1st ed. VG $22.50

SIGOURNEY, Mrs. L.H. *Man of Uz & Other Poems.* 1862 Hartford. 1st ed. A bdg. wraps. $60.00

SIGOURNEY, Mrs. L.H. *Poems.* 1841 Leavitt Allen. Ills. VG $15.00

SIKES, S.K. *Natural History of the African Elephant.* 1971 Am Elsevier. Ills. 397 p. dj. EX $20.00

SILBERSTANG, Edwin. *Playboy's Book of Games.* Playboy. 5th ed. dj. EX $10.00

SILL, E.R. *Around the Horn: Journal* Dec. 10, 1861 to March 25, 1862. 1944 New Haven. Ills 2nd ed. dj. VG $15.00

SILL, William. *Underground Railroad.* 1872 Phil. Porter Coates. G $55.00

SILLER, Van. *Paul's Apartment.* 1948 Crime Club. 1st ed. xl. G $5.00

SILLIMAN, Benjamin. *Tour to Quebec in the Autumn of 1819.* 1822 London. 1st English ed. 8 vol set. $65.00

SILLITOE, Alan. *Death of William Posters.* 1965 Knopf. 1st Am ed. dj. VG $25.00

SILLITOE, Alan. *Key to the Door.* 1962 NY. 1st ed. dj. EX $15.00

SILLITOE, Alan. *Ragman's Daughter.* 1964 NY. 1st Am ed. dj. EX $15.00

SILLITOE, Alan. *Road to Volvograd.* 1964 Knopf. 1st Am ed. cloth. VG $10.00

SILLITOE, Alan. *Start in Life.* 1970 London. 1st ed. dj. EX $15.00

SILLITOE, Alan. *Storyteller.* 1979 NY. Simon Schuster. 1st ed. dj. $25.00

SILLITOE, Alan. *Tree on Fire.* 1968 Doubleday. 1st Am ed. dj. VG $20.00

SILONE, Ignazio. *And He Hid Himself.* 1946 NY. 1st ed. dj. EX $15.00

SILONE, Ignazio. *Bread & Wine.* 1937 Harper. 1st Am ed. dj. VG $20.00

SILONE, Ignazio. *Fontamara: Novel of Modern Italy.* 1934 NY. Harrison Smith. Advance copy. $12.50

SILONE, Ignazio. *Handful of Blackberries.* 1953 Harper. 1st Am ed. dj. VG $15.00

SILSBEE, Mrs. *Willie Winkie's Nursery Songs.* 1859 Boston. $18.00

SILTZER, Frank. *Newmarket.* 1923 London. cloth. VG $50.00

SILVAIN, Gerard. *Images et Traditions Juives.* 1950 Paris. folio. dj. EX $100.00

SILVERBERG, Robert. *Book of Skulls.* 1972 Scribner. 1st ed. dj. EX $27.50

SILVERBERG, Robert. *Chains Of Sea.* 1973 Nelson. 1st ed. dj. EX $10.00

SILVERBERG, Robert. *Dying Inside.* 1972 Scribner. 1st ed. dj. EX $25.00

SILVERBERG, Robert. *Gilgamesh the King.* 1985 Gollancz. dj. EX $22.50

SILVERBERG, Robert. *Homefaring.* 1983 Phantasia. Ltd 1st ed. sgn. dj. slipcase. $17.50

SILVERBERG, Robert. *Infinite Jests.* 1974 Chilton. 1st ed. dj. EX $17.50

SILVERBERG, Robert. *Lord of Darkness.* 1983 Arbor House. 1st ed. dj. EX $17.50

SILVERBERG, Robert. *Lord Valentine's Castle.* 1980 NY. 1st ed. dj. VG $10.00

SILVERBERG, Robert. *Lord Valentine's Castle.* 1980 NY. Ltd ed. 1/250. sgn. slipcase. $60.00

SILVERBERG, Robert. *Lost Cities & Vanished Civilizations.* 1962 NY. 177 p. dj. EX $4.00

SILVERBERG, Robert. *Project Pendulum.* 1987 Walker. Ltd 1st ed. 1/350. slipcase. $55.00

SILVERBERG, Robert. *Revolt on Alpha C.* 1955 Crowell. 1st ed. rebound. xl. $7.50

SILVERBERG, Robert. *Sunrise on Mercury.* 1975 Nashville. 1st ed. dj. M $15.00

SILVERBERG, Robert. *Tomorrow's World.* 1969 Meredith. 1st ed. dj. VG $25.00

SILVERBERG, Robert. *Unfamiliar Territory.* 1973 NY. 1st ed. dj. EX $12.50

SILVERBERG, Robert. *Vanentine Pontifex.* 1983 Arbor House. 1st ed. dj. VG $25.00

SILVERBERG, Robert. *World Inside.* 1976 Millington. dj. EX $15.00

SILVERBERG, Robert. *World Inside.* 1971 Doubleday. 1st ed. dj. EX $20.00

SILVERBERG, Robert. *World of the Ocean Depths.* 1968 Meredith. 1st ed. dj. xl. $20.00

SILVERBERG, Robert. *World's Fair, 1992.* 1970 Follett. 1st ed. dj. xl. $10.00

SILVERS, Phil. *This Laugh Is on Me.* 1973 Prentice Hall. 1st ed. dj. VG $15.00

SILVERSTEIN, Sheldon T. *Giving Tree.* 1964 Harper Row. Ills 1st trade ed. dj. EX $15.00

SILVERSTEIN, Sheldon T. *Lafcadio: Lion Who Shot Back.* 1963 1st ed. review slip laid in. dj. M $16.00

SIMAK, Clifford D. *Choice of Gods.* 1972 NY. 1st ed. dj. VG $15.00

SIMAK, Clifford D. *City.* 1954 Weidenfeld Nicolson. VG $30.00

SIMAK, Clifford D. *Fellowship of the Talisman.* 1978 Del Rey. 1st ed. dj. EX $10.00

SIMAK, Clifford D. *Special Deliverance.* 1982 Del Rey. 1st ed. dj. EX $20.00

SIMAK, Clifford D. *Strangers in the Universe.* 1952 NY. 1st ed. VG $17.50

SIMAK, Clifford D. *Time & Again.* 1951 Simon Schuster. 1st ed. dj. VG $100.00

SIMAK, Clifford D. *Visitors.* 1980 Del Rey. 1st ed. dj. EX $20.00

SIMAK, Clifford D. *Where the Evil Dwells.* 1982 Del Rey. 1st ed. dj. EX $20.00

SIMENON, George. *Aunt Jeanne.* 1983 Harcourt. 1st Am ed. dj. EX $14.00

SIMENON, George. *Disappearance of Odile.* no date. Harcourt Brace. 2nd ed. dj. VG $10.00

SIMENON, George. *Hatter's Phantoms.* 1976 Harcourt Brace. dj. EX $10.00

SIMENON, George. *Inspector Maigret & the Strangled Stripper.* 1954 Crime Club. 1st ed. dj. G $15.00

SIMENON, George. *Lodger.* 1983 Harcourt. 1st Am ed. dj. EX $13.00

SIMENON, George. *Long Exile.* 1983 Harcourt. 1st Am ed. dj. EX $16.00

SIMENON, George. *Maigret & the Apparition.* no date. Hall. Large Print ed. dj. VG $10.00

SIMENON, George. *Maigret & the Man on the Bench.* 1975 NY. 1st Am ed. dj. EX $8.00

SIMENON, George. *Maigret & the Toy Village.* 1979 NY. dj. M $15.00

SIMENON, George. *Maigret Afraid.* 1983 Harcourt. 1st Am ed. dj. EX $15.00

SIMENON, George. *Maigret Bides His Time.* 1985 Harcourt Brace. 1st ed. dj. EX $13.00

SIMENON, George. *Maigret Has Doubts.* 1982 Harcourt. 1st ed. dj. EX $14.00

SIMENON, George. *Maigret in Court.* 1983 Harcourt. 1st Am ed. dj. EX $12.00

SIMENON, George. *Maigret to the Rescue.* 1946 Routledge. dj. G $7.50

SIMENON, George. *Maigret's Boyhood Friend.* 1970 NY. 1st Am ed. dj. VG $8.00

SIMENON, George. *Night Club.* 1979 NY. 1st Am ed. dj. EX $5.00

SIMENON, George. *November.* 1970 Harcourt. 1st Am ed. dj. EX $15.00

SIMENON, George. *Sunday & Little Man From Archangel.* 1966 Harcourt. 1st Am ed. dj. EX $20.00

SIMENON, George. *Tidal Wave.* 1954 Garden City. 1st Am ed. VG $8.00

SIMENON. *Striptease.* 1958 Paris. 1st trade ed. 12mo. 242 p. G $85.00

SIMIN, Howard. *500 Years of Art & Illustration of Albrecht Durer.* 1947 Cleveland/NY. World. Ills. 4to. 476 p. G $32.00

SIMMEL. *It Can't Always Be Caviar.* 1965 Blond. dj. VG $8.00

SIMMONITE, W.S; & CULPEPER, N. *Simmonite-Culpeper Herbal Remedies.* 1957 London. 123 p. index. EX $18.00

SIMMONS, Albert D. *Flight: Selection of 12 Sporting Photographs.* no date. EX $75.00

SIMMONS, Albert Dixon. *Wing Shots: Series of Camera Studies of American Game Birds.* 1936 NY. Derrydale. Ltd ed. 1/950. gilt cloth. EX $100.00

SIMMONS, Dan. *Song of Kali.* 1985 Bluejay. Uncorrected proof. wraps. EX $50.00

SIMMONS, Dan. *Song of Kali.* 1985 NY. 1st ed. sgn. dj. M $30.00

SIMMONS, J.R. *Historic Trees of MA.* 1919 Boston. photos. G $30.00

SIMMONS, Jack. *St. Pancras Station.* 1969 London. Allen Unwin. Ills. dj. VG $18.00

SIMMONS, Marc. *On the Santa Fe Trail.* 1986 KS U Pr. Ills 1st ed. 149 p. EX $24.00

SIMON, Andre. *Bibliotheca Bacchica.* 1972 Holland Pr. 2 vols in 1. VG $65.00

SIMON, Andre. *Concise Encyclopedia of Gastronomy.* 1952 NY. 1st ed. dj. VG $20.00

SIMON, Andre. *Dictionary of Gastronomy.* 1949 NY. Farrar Straus. 264 p. dj. VG $18.50

SIMON, Andre. *In the Twilight.* 1969 London. dj. EX $15.00

SIMON, Andre. *Wines of World.* 1968 McGraw Hill. Ills. 700 p. $18.00

SIMON, Bill. *Effective Card Magic.* 1952 NY. VG $10.00

SIMON, Claude. *Wind.* 1959 NY. Braziller. 254 p. $5.00

SIMON, H. *Chameleons & Other Quick-Change Artists.* 1973 Dodd Mead. Ills. 157 p. dj. EX $14.00

SIMON, H. *Date Palm: Bread of the Desert.* 1978 Dodd Mead. Ills 1st ed. 158 p. dj. EX $20.00

SIMON, Oliver. *Printer & Playground: Autobiography.* 1956 London. Ills 1st ed. 8vo. dj. VG $18.00

SIMON, Paul. *1-Trick Pony.* 1980 NY. 1st ed. dj. M $12.00

SIMONDS, Frank H. *History of World War.* 1917 Doubleday Page. Review ed. 5 vol set. G $40.00

SIMONOV, Konstantine. *Days & Nights.* 1945 Simon Schuster. G $12.50

SIMONS, Lt. Col. David G. *Man High.* 1960 NY. 1st ed. dj. VG $15.00

SIMONSON, Lee. *Part of a Lifetime.* 1949 NY. Ills 1st ed. dj. VG $55.00

SIMPSON, Bruce L. *Development of Metal Castings Industry.* 1948 Chicago. Ills. 4to. 246 p. dj. VG $20.00

SIMPSON, Charles T. *FL Wildlife.* 1932 NY. sgn. $15.00

SIMPSON, Claude M. *British Broadside Ballad & Its Music.* 1966 New Brunswick. dj. VG $35.00

SIMPSON, Colin. *Lusitania.* 1972 Little Brown. 1st ed. dj. EX $20.00

SIMPSON, Colin. *Plumes & Arrows.* no date. Sydney. Halstead Pr. 415 p. $17.50

SIMPSON, Dorothy. *Last Seen Alive.* 1985 Scribner. 1st ed. dj. EX $14.00

SIMPSON, G.G. *Discoveries of the Lost World.* 1984 Yale U Pr. Ills 1st ed. 222 p. dj. EX $22.00

SIMPSON, G.G. *Geography of Evolution: Collected Essays.* 1965 Chilton. Ills 1st ed. 249 p. dj. VG $16.00

SIMPSON, G.G. *Life of the Past: Introduction to Paleontology.* 1954 Yale U Pr. Ills. 198 p. dj. VG $12.00

SIMPSON, G.G. *Penguins: Past & Present, Here & There.* 1976 Yale. Ills. 150 p. dj. EX $6.00

SIMPSON, George. *Fur Trade & Empire.* 1931 Harvard. 1st ed. $50.00

SIMPSON, Harriette. *Mountain Path.* 1926 Covici Friede. 1st ed. G $70.00

SIMPSON, James Young. *Physicians & Physic.* 1856 Edinburgh. $100.00

SIMPSON, James Young. *Selected Obstetrical & Gynecological Works.* 1871 NY. Wood. 800 p. $125.00

SIMPSON, Jean. *Frozen Food Cookbook.* 1962 CT. EX $10.00

SIMPSON, Jeffrey. *Way Life Was: Photographic Treasury From American Past.* 1974 NY. 1st ed. dj. EX $25.00

SIMPSON, Louis. *Best Hour of the Night.* 1983 Ticknor. Advance copy. dj. EX $14.00

SIMPSON, Stephen. *Lives of George Washington & Thomas Jefferson.* 1833 Phil. 1st ed. 389 p. $65.00

SIMPSON, William. *Buddhist Praying Wheel.* 1970 University Books. Ills. dj. VG $15.00

SIMPSON. *Blue Grass Houses & Their Traditions.* 1932 Lexington. 2nd ed. 4to. 408 p. VG $25.00

SIMS, A.E. *Witching Weed.* no date. London. Harrap. 207 p. dj. $25.00

SIMS, George. *Coat of Arms.* 1984 London. Macmillan. 1st ed. dj. EX $15.00

SIMS, George. *Last Best Friend.* 1968 NY. Stein Day. dj. VG $10.00

SIMS, J.P. *Philadelphia Assemblies 1748-1948.* 1948 Phil. Ltd ed. 1/2,400. 51 p. VG $10.00

SIMS, Orland L. *Cowpokes, Nesters, & So Forth.* 1969 Austin. Ltd ed. 1/250. sgn. boxed. $65.00

SIMS, Orland L. *Cowpokes, Nesters, & So Forth.* 1970 Austin. Encino. 1st ed. dj. EX $35.00

SIMS, Patterson. *Concentration of Works of Charles Burchfield.* 1980 Whitney Mus. Ills. 8vo. 32 p. wraps. $3.00

SIMS, Patterson. *Concentration of Works of Charles Sheeler.* 1980 NY. Ills. 8vo. 32 p. wraps. $3.00

SIMS, Patterson. *Concentration of Works of Gaston Lachaise.* 1980 Whitney Mus. Ills. 8vo. 32 p. wraps. $3.00

SIMS, Patterson. *Concentration of Works of John Sloan.* 1980 NY. Ills. 8vo. 32 p. wraps. $3.00

SIMS, Patterson. *Concentration of Works of Maurice B. Prendergast.* 1980 NY. Whitney. Ills. 32 p. $3.00

SIMS, Patterson. *Works of Stuart Davis From a Permanent Collection.* 1980 NY. Ills. 8vo. 32 p. wraps. $3.00

SIMSON, Alfred. *Travels in Wilds of Ecuador & Exploration of Putumayo River.* c 1886. London. Ills. possible 1st ed. 270 p. $50.00

SINCLAIR, Andrew. *Project.* 1960 Simon Schuster. 1st ed. dj. EX $10.00

SINCLAIR, May. *Mary Olivier.* 1919 NY. 1st Am ed. dj. EX $8.00

SINCLAIR, May. *Mr. Waddington of Wyck.* 1921 NY. VG $5.00

SINCLAIR, May. *Rector of Wyck.* 1925 NY. VG $5.00

SINCLAIR, Upton. *Another Pamela.* 1950 Viking. 1st ed. dj. VG $10.00

SINCLAIR, Upton. *Between 2 Worlds.* 1941 NY/Pasadena. author pub. 1st ed. dj. VG $40.00

SINCLAIR, Upton. *Cry for Justice.* 1915 Winston. VG $45.00

SINCLAIR, Upton. *Damaged Goods.* 1913 Phil. VG $15.00

SINCLAIR, Upton. *Dragon Harvest.* 1945 NY. 1st ed. dj. VG $12.00

SINCLAIR, Upton. *Jungle.* 1906 Doubleday Page. 1st ed. 1st state. $100.00

SINCLAIR, Upton. *Limbo on the Loose.* 1948 Girard. wraps. EX $55.00

SINCLAIR, Upton. *Mammonart.* 1925 Pasadena. 1st ed. wraps. VG $35.00

SINCLAIR, Upton. *Mannassas.* 1904 NY. Macmillan. 1st ed. VG $25.00

SINCLAIR, Upton. *Metropolis.* 1908 NY. Moffat. 1st ed. VG $20.00

SINCLAIR, Upton. *Money Writes.* 1927 NY. Boni. 1st ed. 227 p. G $10.00

SINCLAIR, Upton. *O Shepard Speak!* 1949 Viking. 1st ed. dj. VG $20.00

SINCLAIR, Upton. *Profits of Religion.* 1918 Pasadena. Sinclair. 1st ed. VG $15.00

SINCLAIR, Upton. *Return of Lanny Budd.* 1953 NY. 1st ed. dj. VG $40.00

SINCLAIR, Upton. *Samuel the Seeker.* 1923 Pasadena. Sinclair. 2nd ed. dj. $15.00

SINCLAIR, Upton. *They Call Me Carpenter.* 1922 Pasadena. 1st ed. 12mo. 225 p. wraps. VG $35.00

SINCLAIR, Upton. *Wide Is the Gate.* 1943 NY. Viking. 1st ed. dj. VG $20.00

SINCLAIR, Upton. *World To Win.* 1946 Viking. 1st ed. dj. EX $12.00

SINGER, Bant. *Don't Slip Delaney.* 1954 Collins. 1st ed. dj. VG $15.00

SINGER, Charles. *Short History of Medicine.* 1928 NY. 368 p. dj. $15.00

SINGER, D.J. *Big Game Fields of America, North & South.* 1914 Doran. Ills Bull. 368 p. G $22.50

SINGER, Hans W. *Die Modern Graphik.* 1914 Leipzig. Seemann. 547 p. $150.00

SINGER, Isaac Bashevis. *Alone in the Wild Forest.* 1971 Farrar. Ills 1st ed. dj. EX $30.00

SINGER, Isaac Bashevis. *Collected Stories.* 1982 NY. Ltd 1st ed. 1/450. sgn. boxed. $75.00

SINGER, Isaac Bashevis. *Crown of Feathers.* 1973 Farrar. 1st ed. dj. EX $25.00

SINGER, Isaac Bashevis. *Day of Pleasure.* 1969 Farrar. 1st ed. dj. VG $25.00

SINGER, Isaac Bashevis. *Death of Methuselah.* 1988 Cape. Uncorrected proof. EX $55.00

SINGER, Isaac Bashevis. *East of Eden.* 1939 NY. 1st ed. dj. EX $10.00

SINGER, Isaac Bashevis. *Estate.* 1969 NY. Farrar. 1st ed. dj. VG $40.00

SINGER, Isaac Bashevis. *Family Moskat.* 1950 NY. Knopf. 1st ed. dj. VG $35.00

SINGER, Isaac Bashevis. *Fearsome Inn.* 1967 NY. Scribner. 1st trade ed. dj. VG $30.00

SINGER, Isaac Bashevis. *Golem.* 1982 NY. Farrar. Ltd 1st ed. sgn. slipcase. EX $65.00

SINGER, Isaac Bashevis. *Image & Other Stories.* 1985 Farrar. Ltd 1st ed. sgn. slipcase. EX $90.00

SINGER, Isaac Bashevis. *Love & Exile.* 1985 Cape. 1st English ed. dj. EX $20.00

SINGER, Isaac Bashevis. *Old Love.* 1980 London. 1st ed. dj. M $12.00

SINGER, Isaac Bashevis. *Old Love.* 1979 Farrar. proof. wraps. $85.00

SINGER, Isaac Bashevis. *Old Love.* 1979 NY. 1st ed. dj. M $15.00

SINGER, Isaac Bashevis. *Passions & Other Stories.* 1976 London. 1st ed. dj. M $12.00

SINGER, Isaac Bashevis. *Penitent.* 1983 Farrar. Advance copy. dj. EX $20.00

SINGER, Isaac Bashevis. *Reaches of Heaven.* 1980 NY. Farrar. 1st trade ed. $15.00

SINGER, Isaac Bashevis. *Reaches of Heaven.* 1980 NY. Farrar. 1st ed. dj. EX $25.00

SINGER, Isaac Bashevis. *Short Friday.* 1964 Farrar. 1st ed. dj. EX $35.00

SINGER, Isaac Bashevis. *Short Friday.* 1964 Phil. 1st ed. dj. $20.00

SINGER, Isaac Bashevis. *Shosha.* 1978 NY. 1st ed. dj. M $12.00

SINGER, Isaac Bashevis. *Slave.* 1962 NY. Farrar. 1st ed. dj. VG $40.00

SINGER, Isaac Bashevis. *Steel & Iron.* 1969 NY. 1st ed. dj. EX $10.00

SINGER, Isaac Bashevis. *Stories of Children.* 1984 Farrar. Ltd 1st ed. sgn. slipcase. EX $50.00

SINGER, Isaac Bashevis. *When Shlemiel Went to Warsaw & Other Stories.* 1968 Farrar Straus. Ills Zemach. 1st print. dj. EX $25.00

SINGER, Isaac Bashevis. *Yentl: Yeshiva Boy.* 1983 NY. Ills Fasconi. 1/450. sgns. M $75.00

SINGER, Isaac Bashevis. *Young Man in Search of Love.* 1978 NY. Ltd 1st ed. sgn. slipcase. EX $100.00

SINGER, Paul. *Early Chinese Gold & Silver.* 1972 China House Gallery. 72 p. $18.50

SINGER. *Power of Light.* 1983 Robson. 1st English ed. dj. EX $15.00

SINGEWALD, Joseph T. *Report on the Iron Ores of MD.* 1911 Baltimore. Johns Hopkins. 337 p. VG $20.00

SINGH, Arjan. *Tiger Haven.* 1973 Harper Row. Ills 1st Am ed. 237 p. dj. EX $18.00

SINGH, Arjan. *Tiger Haven.* 1973 Harper Row. Ills 1st Am ed. 232 p. dj. VG $8.50

SINGH, Arjan. *Tiger Heaven.* 1973 London. Macmillan. Ills 1st ed. dj. $25.00

SINGH, Kesri. *Tiger of Rajasthan.* 1959 Hale. Ills. 191 p. dj. EX $22.00

SINISTRARI, Ludo Vinco Maria. *Demonality.* 1927 London. Fortune Pr. Ltd ed. 127 p. $125.00

SINNETT, A.P. *Collected Fruits of Occult Teachings.* 1919 London. 307 p. VG $26.00

SINNETT, A.P. *Incidents in the Life of Madame Blavatsky.* 1886 London. Redway. 1st ed. 324 p. VG $65.00

SIODMAK, Curt. *City in the Sky.* 1975 Barrie Jenkins. 1st ed. dj. EX $10.00

SIODMAK, Curt. *3rd Ear.* 1971 Putnam. 1st ed. dj. VG $10.00

SIPLEY, L.W. *Half Century of Color.* 1951 NY. Ills. EX $17.50

SIREN, Osvald. *Early Chinese Paintings from A.W. Bahr Collection.* 1938 London. Chiswick. 1/750. EX $250.00

SIREN, Oswald. *Historie de la Peinture Chinoise. Vol. II.* 1930 Paris. G $50.00

SIREN, Oswald. *Chinese Painting.* 1973 Hacker. Ills. 4to. 7 vol set. $125.00

SIRINGO, Charles A. *Lone Star Cowboy.* 1919 Santa Fe. 1st ed. $85.00

SIRINGO, Charles A. *TX Cowboy; or, 15 Years on Hurricane Deck of Spanish Pony.* 1950 Sloane. 1st ed. dj. xl. VG $17.50

SIRINGO, Charles A. *TX Cowboy; or, 15 Years on Hurricane Deck of Spanish Pony.* 1886 Chicago. 2nd ed. 347 p. G $45.00

SIRKIS, Nancy. *Newport Pleasures & Palaces.* 1963 NY. Viking. 1st ed. dj. EX $30.00

SISLEY, Nick. *Deer Hunting Across North America.* 1975 NY. dj. EX $17.00

SITWELL, Edith. *Alexander Pope.* 1930 London. Ills Whistler. 1st ed. sgn. $35.00

SITWELL, Edith. *Atlantic Book of British & American Poetry.* 1958 Boston. 1st ed. sgn. dj. VG $32.50

SITWELL, Edith. *Book of the Winter.* 1950 London. sgn Davenport. 86 p. VG $18.00

SITWELL, Edith. *Collected Poems of Edith Sitwell.* 1930 London. Duckworth. 1st ed. dj. EX $75.00

SITWELL, Edith. *English Eccentrics.* 1957 NY. 1st Am ed. dj. EX $35.00

SITWELL, Edith. *Fanfare for Elizabeth.* 1946 London. 1st ed. dj. EX $20.00

SITWELL, Edith. *Gardeners & Astronomers.* 1953 NY. 1st ed. dj. VG $60.00

SITWELL, Edith. *Green Song.* 1944 Macmillan. 1st ed. dj. EX $40.00

SITWELL, Edith. *Song of the Cold.* 1948 Vanguard. 1st Am ed. dj. VG $15.00

SITWELL, Osbert. *Argonaut & Juggernaut.* 1919 London. 1st ed. dj. VG $22.50

SITWELL, Osbert. *Death of a God.* 1949 Macmillan. 1st ed. dj. VG $35.00

SITWELL, Osbert. *Demos the Emperor.* 1949 London. Ltd 1st ed. 1/500. wraps. EX $38.00

SITWELL, Osbert. *Discursions.* 1925 London. Ills 1st ed. VG $25.00

SITWELL, Osbert. *Queen Mary & Others.* 1975 Day. 1st Am ed. photos. 171 p. tan linen. VG $7.00

SITWELL, Osbert. *Selected Poems.* 1943 London. 1st ed. dj. EX $20.00

SITWELL, Sacheverall. *All Summer in a Day.* 1926 Doran. 1st ed. dj. EX $35.00

SITWELL, Sacheverall. *Portugal & Madeira.* 1954 London. 1st ed. dj. EX $15.00

SITWELL, Sacheverell. *Baroque & Rococo.* 1967 NY. 1st Am ed. dj. $35.00

SITWELL, Sacheverell. *British Architects & Craftsmen.* 1945 London. Pan. Ills Revised ed. 320 p. $18.50

SITWELL, Sacheverell. *German Baroque Art.* 1927 London. Ills 1st ed. VG $30.00

SITWELL, Sacheverell. *Hunters & Hunted.* 1948 NY. 1st ed. dj. $18.00

SITWELL, Sacheverell. *Tropical Birds From Plates by John Gould.* 1948 London. Batsford Color Books. 1st ed. $10.00

SITWELL, Sacheverell. *2 Poems, 10 Songs.* 1929 London. Ltd 1st ed. 1/275. sgn. EX $85.00

SITWELL, Sachverell. *Gothic North.* 1929 Boston. VG $20.00

SITWELL & BLUNT. *Great Flower Books 1700-1900.* 1956 London. Biblio ed. 1/295. slipcase. EX $875.00

SIZER, Nelson. *Heads & Faces.* 1892 NY. leather. VG $15.00

SIZER, Nelson. *40 Years in Phrenology.* 1882 NY. Fowler & Wells. 1st ed. VG $35.00

SIZER, Theodore. *Recollections of John Ferguson Weir 1969-1913.* 1957 NY. EX $25.00

SJOMAN. *I Was Curious: Diary for Making of Film.* 1968 Grove. 1st ed. dj. M $15.00

SJOWALL & WAHLOO. *Locked Room.* 1973 NY. Pantheon. 1st ed. VG $12.50

SJOWALL & WAHLOO. *Terrorists.* 1977 London. 1st ed. dj. EX $18.00

SJOWALL & WAHLOO. *Terrorists.* 1976 NY. 1st ed. dj. VG $10.00

SKADOPLOS, C.D. *People's Guide.* 1920 St. Louis. VG $20.00

SKEETERS, Paul. *Maxfield Parrish: Early Years.* no date. Chartwell. VG $35.00

SKELTON, C. *Engravings of Eric Gill.* 1983 Wellingborough. 1st ed. boxed. VG $250.00

SKELTON, R.A. *Decorative Printed Maps of 15th & 18th Centuries.* 1952 London. Ills 1st ed. dj. VG $85.00

SKELTON, R.A. *Vinland Map & Tartar Relation.* 1965 New Haven. 3rd print. 4to. dj. EX $20.00

SKELTON, R.A. *Vinland Map & Tartar Relation.* 1965 Yale. 3rd print. dj. VG $18.00

SKEYHILL, Tom. *Sergeant York: Last of the Long Hunters.* 1930 Phil. Ills. presentation. sgn. $175.00

SKIDMORE, Hubert. *Hawk's Nest.* 1941 Doubleday. 1st ed. dj. VG $27.50

SKIDMORE, Hubert. *I Will Lift Up My Eyes.* 1936 Doubleday. 1st ed. dj. VG $35.00

SKINNER, C.E. *Molds, Yeasts, & Actino-mycetes.* 1947 NY. 2nd ed. 409 p. VG $10.00

SKINNER, Cornelia Otis. *Madame Sarah.* 1966 Boston. Houghton Mifflin. 356 p. $6.00

SKINNER, Cornelia Otis. *Soap Behind the Ears.* 1941 NY. 1st ed. sgn. VG $20.00

SKINNER, H. *Jiu-Jitsu.* 1904 NY. Ills. VG $12.00

SKINNER, M.P. *Guide to the Winter Birds of NC Sandhills.* 1928 Albany. Ills. fair. $20.00

SKIRKA & SWANK. *Africa Antelope.* 1971 NY. Winchester. $95.00

SKOLSKY, Syd. *Evenings with Music.* 1944 Dutton. 1st ed. inscr. G $10.00

SKURKA, Norma. *NY Times Book of Interior Design.* 1976 NY. 1st ed. EX $25.00

SKUTCH, A. *Bird Watcher's Adventures in Tropical America.* 1977 TX U Pr. Ills Gardner. 327 p. dj. EX $20.00

SKUTCH, A. *Birds of Tropical America.* 1983 TX U Pr. Ills 1st ed. 305 p. dj. EX $30.00

SKVORECKY, Joseph. *Bass Saxophone.* 1979 NY. 1st ed. dj. EX $10.00

SKVORECKY, Joseph. *Miss Silver's Past.* 1974 NY. 1st ed. dj. EX $25.00

SLADEK, J. *Red Noise.* 1982 Cheap Street. Ills Bash. 1/26. sgns. wraps. $250.00

SLADEK, J. *Tik-Tok.* 1983 Gollancz. 1st ed. dj. EX $45.00

SLAGG, Winifred N. *Riley County, KS.* 1968 private print. dj. G $16.00

SLATER, Francis Carey. *Selected Poems.* 1947 London. Oxford. 1st ed. dj. VG $12.50

SLATER, J.H. *Book Collecting: Guide for Amateurs.* 1892 London. $45.00

SLATER, J.H. *How To Collect Books.* 1905 London. Chiswick Pr. 1st ed. VG $35.00

SLATER, Michael. *Catalogue of the Suzannet Charles Dickens Collection.* 1975 London. dj. EX $55.00

SLATON, Vivian. *Tiny Town.* 1929 NY. Row Peterson. $7.00

SLAUGHT, H.E. *Elementary Algebra.* 1915 Allyn Bacon. fair. $2.50

SLAUGHTER, Frank G. *In a Dark Garden.* 1946 Doubleday. 435 p. $5.00

SLAVITT, D.R. *Dozens.* 1981 LSU Pr. 1st ed. dj. EX $12.00

SLAYTON, Robert. *Back of the Yards.* 1986 Chicago. 1st ed. dj. EX $22.50

SLESINGER, Tess. *Time: The Present.* 1935 Simon Schuster. 1st ed. $20.00

SLESSER, M. *Red Peak.* 1964 NY. 1st Am ed. dj. VG $10.00

SLESSOR, John. *Central Blue.* 1956 London. Ills 1st ed. 709 p. G $25.00

SLEZAK, Leo. *Song of Motley.* 1938 London. Ills. G $55.00

SLICER, Thomas R. *From Poet to Premier.* 1909 NY. Ltd ed. 1/1,250. G $25.00

SLINEY, Eleanor Mathews. *Forward Ho!* 1960 NY/WA. Ills 1st ed. 332 p. dj. $6.00

SLOAN, Donald. *Shadow Catcher.* 1940 NY. 1st ed. dj. VG $15.00

SLOAN, Howard N. & Lucille L. *Pictorial History of American Mining.* 1970 NY. Crown. Ills 1st ed. 4to. 342 p. dj. $15.00

SLOANE, Eric. *Eric Sloane's Weather Book.* 1952 NY. dj. EX $25.00

SLOANE, Eric. *Museum of Early American Tools.* c 1964. NY. dj. VG $20.00

SLOANE, H.N. & L.L. *Pictorial History of American Mining.* 1970 Crown. 4to. 342 p. dj. EX $10.00

SLOANE, William. *Edge of Running Water.* 1939 Farrar Rinehart. 1st ed. VG $12.50

SLOANE, William. *To Walk the Night.* 1946 Tower. dj. VG $25.00

SLOBODKIN, Louis. *Clear the Track for Michael's Magic Train.* 1945 NY. Macmillan. Ills 1st ed. 4to. 46 p. dj. G $25.00

SLOCOMBE, George. *White-Plumed Henry, King of France.* 1931 NY. 1st ed. G $12.50

SLOCUM, Joshua. *Around the World in the Sloop Spray.* 1905 NY. VG $20.00

SLOCUM, Joshua. *Sailing Alone Around the World.* 1900 Century. 1st ed. VG $35.00

SLOSSON, Annie T. *Fishin' Jimmy.* 1898 NY. cloth. EX $40.00

SLOTER, J. *Eloy.* no date/place. 1st ed. 64 p. VG $30.00

SLOURNOY, Theodore. *Spiritism & Psychology.* 1911 NY. 1st ed. 354 p. EX $26.00

SMALL, A. *Birds of CA.* 1974 Winchester. Ills. 310 p. maps. dj. EX $18.00

SMALL, Austin J. *Avenging Ray.* 1930 Crime Club. VG $15.00

SMALL, Austin J. *Vantine Diamonds.* 1930 Crime Club. 1st ed. G $20.00

SMALL, G.L. *Blue Whale.* 1971 Columbia U Pr. Ills. 248 p. dj. EX $18.00

SMALLEY. *Animals Came In.* 1930 Morrow. EX $15.00

SMART, Alastair. *Assisi Problem & the Art of Giotto.* 1971 Oxford. Clarendon. Ills. 4to. 330 p. $75.00

SMART, P. *International Butterfly Book.* 1975 Crowell. Ills. 4to. 275 p. dj. EX $30.00

SMEDLEY, Agnes. *Battle Hymn of China.* 1943 NY. Book Find Club. dj. VG $10.00

SMEDLEY, Agnes. *China Fights Back.* 1938 London. Gollancz. Book Club ed. VG $20.00

SMEDLEY, Agnes. *Daughter of Earth.* 1929 NY. Coward. 1st ed. VG $25.00

SMEDLEY, Alfred. *Some Reminiscences.* 1900 London. 143 p. G $20.00

SMELLIE, William. *Anatomical Tables with Explanations.* 1787 Edinburgh. Ills. folio. VG $625.00

SMILES, Samuel. *George & Robert Stephenson: Lives of Engineers.* 1879 London. Ills. 388 p. VG $25.00

SMILES, Samuel. *Life of a Scotch Naturalist: Thomas Edward.* 1877 NY. Ills George Reid. $30.00

SMILEY, Jane. *At Paradise's Gate.* 1981 Simon Schuster. proof. $10.00

SMILEY, Jane. *Duplicate Keys.* 1984 Knopf. Advance copy. wraps. EX $30.00

SMILIES, S. *Publisher & Friends: Memoir & Correspondence of J. Murray.* 1891 London. Ills. 2 vol set. $100.00

SMITH, A.E. *Up to Now: An Autobiography.* 1929 NY. Ltd ed. sgn Mary Breckinridge. $60.00

SMITH, A.H. *Field Guide to Western Mushrooms.* 1975 MI U Pr. Ills. 280 p. VG $15.00

SMITH, A.H. *How To Know the Gilled Mushrooms.* 1979 Brown. Ills. 334 p. EX $15.00

SMITH, A.H. *Mushroom Hunter's Field Guide.* 1969 MI U Pr. Revised ed. 264 p. EX $12.00

SMITH, A.H.; & WEBER, N.S. *Mushroom Hunter's Field Guide.* 1980 MI U Pr. Ills. sgn. 316 p. EX $13.00

SMITH, A.M. *Sport & Adventure in Indian Jungle.* 1904 London. Ills 1st ed. 307 p. G $50.00

SMITH, A.M. *US Mint with US & Colonial Coins.* 1881 Phil. Ills. 120 p. wraps. VG $25.00

SMITH, Aaron. *Atrocities of Pirates; or, Faithful Narrative of Sufferings.* 1824 NY. Lowry. 1st Am ed. 158 p. $200.00

SMITH, Adam. *Enquiry into Nature & Causes of Wealth of Nations.* 1863 Edinburgh. 8vo. ½ -morocco. VG $125.00

SMITH, Adam. *Enquiry into Nature & Causes of Wealth of Nations.* 1880 Oxford. 2 vol set. red cloth. VG $75.00

SMITH, Alexander. *Dream Thorp: 8 Essays by Alexander Smith.* no date. NY. Peter Pauper. 8vo. 138 p. VG $25.00

SMITH, Alson J. *Men Against the Mountains.* 1965 NY. Ills 1st ed. maps. 320 p. dj. $12.50

SMITH, Andre. *Art & the Subconscious: Drawings by Andre Smith.* 1937 Maitland, FL. Ills Ltd ed. 1/500. sgn. VG $45.00

SMITH, Anita. *As True As the Barnacle Tree.* 1939 Woodstock, NY. 1/1,000. 8vo. wraps. EX $25.00

SMITH, Anthony. *Jambo: African Balloon Safari.* 1963 Dutton. Ills 1st ed. 272 p. dj. EX $15.00

SMITH, B.F. *Road to Nuremberg.* 1981 NY. dj. G $15.00

SMITH, Barbara C. *After the Revolution: Smithsonian History of Everyday Life.* 1985 Random House. 1st ed. dj. EX $10.00

SMITH, Bertha. *Yosemite Legends.* 1904 San Francisco. Elder. Ills Lundborg. VG $28.00

SMITH, Betty. *Joy in the Morning.* 1963 Harper. 1st ed. sgn. dj. VG $25.00

SMITH, Bill. *Vaudevillians.* 1976 NY. Ills 1st ed. dj. VG $10.00

SMITH, Bradley. *Mexico: History in Art.* 1968 Garden City. Ills. $45.00

SMITH, Bradley. *USA: History in Art.* 1982 NY. Revised ed. 268 plts. 296 p. dj. $35.00

SMITH, C. Alphonso. *O Henry Biography.* 1916 Garden City. 1st ed. VG $37.50

SMITH, C.W. *Lone Wolf & the Hidden Empire.* 1947 Whitman. dj. VG $12.50

SMITH, C.W. *TX.* 1946 Haldeman Julius. 26 p. pb. EX $5.00

SMITH, Calvin J. *Handbook for Travellers Through the US.* 1849 NY. Ills. 233 p. $165.00

SMITH, Chard P. *Housatonic River.* 1946 NY. 1st ed. VG $15.00

SMITH, Charles F. *Games & Recreational Methods.* 1947 NY. 704 p. $5.00

SMITH, Charles W. *Pacific Northwest Americana: Checklist.* 2nd ed. enlarged. VG $50.00

SMITH, Charles. *Ancient & Present State of County & City of Waterford.* 1747 Dublin. 1st ed. 8vo. 380 p. boxed. $375.00

SMITH, Charles. *Marines in the Revolution.* 1975 WA. EX $65.00

SMITH, Clark Ashton. *Abominations of Yondo.* 1960 Arkham House. dj. VG $85.00

SMITH, Clark Ashton. *Abominations of Yondo.* 1972 Neville Spearman. dj. EX $25.00

SMITH, Clark Ashton. *Genius Loci.* 1972 Neville Spearman. dj. VG $25.00

SMITH, Clark Ashton. *Lost Worlds.* 1944 Arkham House. 1st ed. dj. $50.00

SMITH, Clark Ashton. *Lost Worlds.* 1971 London. 1st English ed. dj. EX $25.00

SMITH, Clark Ashton. *Other Dimensions.* 1970 Sauk City. 1st ed. dj. EX $30.00

SMITH, Clark Ashton. *Poems in Prose.* 1964 Sauk City. 1st ed. dj. EX $125.00

SMITH, Clark Ashton. *Spells & Philtres.* 1958 Arkham House. 1st ed. inscr. dj. VG $300.00

SMITH, Clark Ashton. *Tales of Science & Sorcery.* 1964 Arkham House. 1st ed. dj. EX $75.00

SMITH, Cyril Stanley. *From Art to Science.* 1980 Cambridge. MIT Pr. Ills. 118 p. $20.00

SMITH, Cyril Stanley. *Sources for the History of Science of Steel 1532-1786.* 1968 Cambridge. MIT Pr. Ills 1st ed. 357 p. EX $12.00

SMITH, Daniel. *Stedman's Wanderings in Interior of South Africa.* 1856 NY. VG $20.00

SMITH, Darrell H. *Panama Canal.* 1927 Johns Hopkins. 413 p. VG $42.50

SMITH, Dave. *Onliness.* 1984 Baton Rouge. proof. wraps. EX $20.00

SMITH, Dave. *Southern Delights.* 1984 Croissant. Ltd ed. 1/100. sgn. dj. VG $30.00

SMITH, David R. *Conrad's Manifesto: Preface to a Career.* Gehenna Pr. Ltd ed. 1/1,100. boxed. VG $65.00

SMITH, Dodie. *I Capture the Castle.* 1948 Boston. 1st ed. dj. VG $8.50

SMITH, E. Boyd. *Farm Book.* 1982 Boston. Houghton Mifflin. 1st ed. dj. $12.00

SMITH, E. Boyd. *Fun in the Radio World.* 1923 NY. Ills 1st ed. $42.50

SMITH, E. Boyd. *Seashore Book.* 1912 1st ed. oblong 4to. VG $36.00

SMITH, E. Boyd. *So Long Ago.* 1944 Jr Lit Guild. Ills Smith. 4to. 36 p. cloth. $25.00

SMITH, E. Boyd. *Story of Noah's Ark.* 1905 Boston. 1st ed. EX $35.00

SMITH, E.E. *Children of the Lens.* 1954 Fantasy. 1st ed. dj. VG $40.00

SMITH, E.E. *Children of the Lens.* 1954 Reading. Fantasy. 1st trade ed. dj. VG $25.00

SMITH, E.E. *Galactic Patrol.* 1950 Fantasy. 1st ed. dj. VG $40.00

SMITH, E.E. *Gray Lensman.* no date. Gnome Pr. 1st ed. dj. VG $20.00

SMITH, E.E. *Lost in Space.* 1959 NY. Avalon. 1st ed. dj. EX $15.00

SMITH, E.E. *Nomad.* 1950 Phil. Prime Pr. 1st ed. dj. EX $15.00

SMITH, E.E. *Skylark of Space.* 1946 Providence. Hadley. 1st ed. dj. $100.00

SMITH, E.E. *Skylark of Space.* 1947 Providence. Hadley. 2nd ed. inscr/sgn. VG $35.00

SMITH, E.E. *Skylark of Valeron.* 1949 Fantasy. 1st ed. dj. VG $45.00

SMITH, E.E. *Skylark of Valeron.* 1949 Fantasy. 1st trade ed. sgn. VG $50.00

SMITH, E.E. *Skylark 3.* 1948 Fantasy. 1st trade ed. sgn. VG $50.00

SMITH, E.E. *Triplanetary.* 1950 Fantasy. 1st trade ed. dj. $20.00

SMITH, E.E. *Troubled Star.* 1975 NY. Avalon. 1st ed. dj. EX $15.00

SMITH, E.E. *Venus Equilateral.* 1949 Phil. Prime Pr. 1st ed. 2nd print. dj. $10.00

SMITH, E.E. *Vortex Plaster.* 1960 Hickville. 1st ed. dj. VG $35.00

SMITH, E.E. *1st Lensman.* 1948 Fantasy. 1st ed. VG $25.00

SMITH, E.E. *2nd Stage Lensmen.* 1953 Fantasy. 1st ed. dj. VG $40.00

SMITH, E.F. *James Cutbush: American Chemist 1788-1823.* 1980 NY. Arno Pr. reprint of 1919. 94 p. M $10.00

SMITH, E.F. *Joseph Priestly in America 1794-1804.* 1920 Phil. 8vo. 172 p. blue cloth. xl. EX $45.00

SMITH, E.L. *Early Home Remedies.* 1968 Applied Arts. Ills. 4to. 42 p. pb. VG $8.00

SMITH, E.L.; SLATER, V.W. *Field of Occult Chemistry.* 1954 London. Theosophical Pub. 2nd ed. VG $13.00

SMITH, E.W. *Treasury of the ME Woods.* 1958 Fell. Ills. 295 p. dj. EX $18.50

SMITH, Edmond Reuel. *Araucanians; or, Notes of Tour Among Indian Tribes of Chili.* 1855 NY. Harper. Ills 1st ed. 335 p. cloth. $50.00

SMITH, Edmond Reuel. *Araucanians; or, Notes of Tour Among Indian Tribes of Chili.* 1855 NY. 1st ed. xl. scarce. $30.00

SMITH, Edward. *Account of a Journey Through North Eastern TX in 1849.* 1849 London. maps. $2500.00

SMITH, Edward. *Frogs Who Wanted a King.* 1977 NY. Ills Margot Zemach. $20.00

SMITH, Elbert H. *Ma-Ka-Tai-Me-She-Kia-Kiak; or, Black Hawk & Scenes in West.* 1848 NY. 1st ed. 299 p. green cloth. G $45.00

SMITH, Elias. *Sermons.* 1808 Exeter, NH. 1st ed. black calf. rebound. $80.00

SMITH, Eliza. *Compleat Housewife.* 1741 London. Ills. 8vo. $150.00

SMITH, Ellen Calusha. *How To Shade Emboidered Flowers & Leaves.* 1889 Chicago. 127 p. 4to. $50.00

SMITH, Ethan. *View of the Hebrews; or, Tribes of Israel in America.* 1825 Poultney. 2nd ed. calf. $225.00

SMITH, Eva Munson. *Woman in Sacred Song.* 1888 Standard. 883 p. G $25.00

SMITH, F. *Father Kino in AZ.* 1966 Phoenix. 1st ed. 142 p. VG $25.00

SMITH, F. Hopkinson. *Charcoals of New & Old NY.* 1912 Garden City. Ills 1st ed. 4to. 142 p. $40.00

SMITH, F. Hopkinson. *Colonel Carter of Cartersville.* 1891 Boston. Ills Kemble. 2nd state. EX $24.00

SMITH, F. Hopkinson. *Colonel Carter's Christmas.* 1903 NY. Ills Yohn. 1st ed. EX $18.00

SMITH, F. Hopkinson. *In Dicken's London.* 1914 Scribner. Ills 2nd ed. 127 p. VG $20.00

SMITH, F. Hopkinson. *Venice of Today.* 1896 NY. Ills. 1/540. folio. sgn. morocco. VG $275.00

SMITH, Francis. *Vox Populi; or, People's Claim to Their Parliaments.* 1681 London. 16 p. wraps. soiled. $125.00

SMITH, Frank A. *Corpse in Handcuffs.* 1969 Macmillan. 1st ed. dj. EX $8.00

SMITH, Fredrika Shumway. *Magic City.* 1949 Boston. dj. EX $10.00

SMITH, G. Berkeley. *Real Latin Quarter.* 1901 NY. 1st ed. VG $35.00

SMITH, G.M. *Fresh-Water Algae of the US.* 1950 McGraw Hill. Ills. 719 p. VG $25.00

SMITH, G.M. *Windsinger.* 1976 Sierra Club. Ills. 175 p. EX $8.00

SMITH, G.T. *Birds of the Southwestern Desert.* 1965 Doubleshoe. Ills. 68 p. EX $11.00

SMITH, George Adam. *Historical Geography of the Holy Land.* 1895 NY. 692 p. 6 fld maps. VG $95.00

SMITH, George E. *Prisoner of War: 2 years with Vietcong.* 1971 Berkeley. Ramposts Pr. 1st ed. dj. EX $25.00

SMITH, George O. *Hellflower.* 1953 Abelard. 1st ed. dj. VG $20.00

SMITH, George O. *Troubled Star.* no date. Avalon. dj. VG $15.00

SMITH, George O. *Venus Equilateral.* 1949 Prime Pr. 2nd ed. VG $15.00

SMITH, George. *Narrative of Visit to Consular Cities of China & Hong Kong.* 1847 NY. Ills. 8vo. 467 p. ¾-calf. EX $200.00

SMITH, Grant H. *History of the Comstock Lode 1850-1920.* 1943 Reno. EX $30.00

SMITH, H. *Stina: Story of a Cook.* 1947 7th ed. dj. EX $10.00

SMITH, H. Allen. *Desert Island Decameron.* 1945 Doubleday. dj. EX $15.00

SMITH, H. Allen. *Larks in the Popcorn.* 1948 Doubleday. 1st ed. VG $15.00

SMITH, H. Allen. *Life & Legend of Gene Fowler.* 1977 NY. 1st ed. dj. VG $10.00

SMITH, H. Allen. *Lost in the Horse Latitudes.* 1945 Doubleday. VG $7.00

SMITH, H. Allen. *Low Man on a Totem Pole.* 1945 Blakiston. dj. VG $12.50

SMITH, H. Allen. *Pig in the Barber Shop.* 1958 Little Brown. 1st ed. dj. VG $15.00

SMITH, H. Allen. *Return of the Virginian.* 1974 Doubleday. 1st ed. dj. VG $10.00

SMITH, H. Allen. *3 Smiths in the Wind.* 1946 Doubleday. 1st ed. dj. VG $20.00

SMITH, H. Clifford. *Sulgrave Manor & the Washingtons.* 1933 NY. VG $50.00

SMITH, H. Maynard. *Inspector Frost in the City.* 1930 Doubleday. 1st ed. VG $17.50

SMITH, H. Maynard. *Inspector Frost in Crevenna Cove.* 1933 Minton Balch. 1st Am ed. xl. $10.00

SMITH, H.H. *Brazil, Amazons, & the Coast.* 1879 London. Sampson Low. 8vo. fld map. VG $75.00

SMITH, H.H. *War on Powder River.* 1966 McGraw Hill. 1st ed. 320 p. dj. VG $27.50

SMITH, H.L. *Pollyanna of the Orange Blossoms.* 1924 Boston. Ills 1st ed. 313 p. VG $8.00

SMITH, H.L. *Pollyanna's Debt of Honor.* no date. Grosset. VG $7.50

SMITH, H.V. & A.H. *How To Know the Non-Gilled Fleshy Fungi.* 1973 Brown. Ills. 402 p. EX $14.00

SMITH, Harry W. *Life & Sports in Aiken & Those Who Made It.* 1935 NY. Ills Ltd ed. 1/950. 237 p. $60.00

SMITH, Harvey. *Gang's All Here.* 1941 Princeton. 325 p. G $50.00

SMITH, Henry Justin. *Chicago: A Portrait.* 1931 NY. Century. Ills. EX $35.00

SMITH, Homer. *Kamongo.* 1932 Viking. VG $5.00

SMITH, Homer. *Man & His Gods.* 1952 Boston. 1st ed. dj. EX $10.00

SMITH, Hugh. *Fresh-Water Fishes of Siam or Thailand.* 1946 Smith Inst. Ills. 620 p. VG $35.00

SMITH, J. *Irish Diamonds.* 1847 London. Chapman Hall. Ills Phiz. VG $128.00

SMITH, J. Frazer. *White Pillars: Architecture of the South.* 1941 NY. Bramhall. dj. EX $25.00

SMITH, J. Russell. *North America.* 1925 Harcourt Brace. fld map. VG $10.00

SMITH, J.B. *Economic Entomology.* 1906 Lippincott. Revised ed. 475 p. cloth. VG $12.00

SMITH, J.H. *Famous Old Recipes.* 1908 Phil. VG $20.00

SMITH, J.L. *Treatise of Diseases of Infancy & Childhood.* 1879 4th ed. leather. VG $25.00

SMITH, J.L.B. *Search Beneath the Sea.* 1956 Holt. Ills. 260 p. dj. VG $15.00

SMITH, Jerome V.C. *Trout & Angling.* 1929 NY. Derrydale. Ills Ltd ed. 1/325. 8vo. $850.00

SMITH, Jessie Wilcox. *At the Back of the North Wind.* 1919 McKay. 8 plts. VG $65.00

SMITH, Jessie Wilcox. *Boys & Girls of Book Land.* 1923 Phil. McKay. 1st ed. dj. VG $95.00

SMITH, Jessie Wilcox. *Child's Book of Country Stories.* 1925 NY. Duffield. 1st ed. 4to. G $25.00

SMITH, Jessie Wilcox. *Child's Garden of Verses.* 1905 Scribner. 1st ed. 12 color plts. VG $65.00

SMITH, Jessie Wilcox. *Child's Garden of Verses.* 1905 NY. Scribner. 1st ed. 12 plts. EX $125.00

SMITH, Jessie Wilcox. *Children of Dickens.* 1947 Scribner. 4to. 259 p. $40.00

SMITH, Jessie Wilcox. *Dicken's Children.* 1912 NY. Ills 1st ed. EX $45.00

SMITH, Jessie Wilcox. *Dicken's Children.* 1912 NY. Scribner. Ills 1st ed. VG $30.00

SMITH, Jessie Wilcox. *In the Closed Room.* 1904 NY. Ills 1st ed. $25.00

SMITH, Jessie Wilcox. *Jessie Wilcox Smith's Mother Goose.* 1914 Dodd Mead. 1st ed. oblong 4to. G $65.00

SMITH, Jessie Wilcox. *Little Child's Book of Stories.* 1935 NY. VG $50.00

SMITH, Jessie Wilcox. *Little Goose.* 1918 NY. Dodd Mead. Ills 1st ed. 8vo. 176 p. $150.00

SMITH, Jessie Wilcox. *Mother Goose.* 1986 Derrydale. Ills. folio. 173 p. EX $30.00

SMITH, Jessie Wilcox. *Twas the Night Before Christmas.* 1912 Houghton. Ills. small 4to. VG $55.00

SMITH, Jessie Wilcox. *Water Babies.* 1937 NY. 4 plts. VG $25.00

SMITH, Jim. *Nimbus & Crown Jewels.* 1981 Ills 1st Am ed. VG $7.50

SMITH, L. Walden. *Saddles Up.* 1937 San Antonio. Ills 1st ed. dj. VG $20.00

SMITH, L.B. *American Game Preserve Shooting.* 1937 Garden City. Deluxe ed. 175 p. VG $10.00

SMITH, L.B. *Fur or Feather: Days with Dog & Gun.* 1946 Scribner. 1st ed. 144 p. G $10.00

SMITH, L.B. *Sunlight Kid & Other Western Verses.* 1935 Dutton. 1st ed. photos. VG $17.50

SMITH, L.L.; & DOUGHTY, R.W. *Amazing Armadillo: Geography of a Folk Critter.* 1984 TX U Pr. Ills 1st ed. 134 p. dj. EX $13.00

SMITH, Laurence Dwight. *Reunion.* 1946 Samuel Curl. 1st ed. VG $10.00

SMITH, Lee. *Black Mountain Breakdown.* 1980 NY. Putnam. 1st ed. dj. EX $10.00

SMITH, Lee. *Cakewalk.* 1981 NY. Putnam. 1st ed. dj. M $15.00

SMITH, Lee. *Oral History.* 1983 Putnam. 1st ed. dj. EX $15.00

SMITH, Lillian. *Journey.* 1954 World. 1st ed. dj. EX $20.00

SMITH, Lillian. *Killers of the Dream.* 1949 Norton. 1st ed. inscr. dj. VG $20.00

SMITH, Lillian. *Memory of a Large Christmas.* 1962 Norton. Ills C McMillan. 1st ed. dj. $15.00

SMITH, Lillian. *1 Hour.* 1959 Harcourt. 1st ed. dj. VG $20.00

SMITH, Lloyd. *Hangin' Around the OH Bar.* 1983 NY. 1st ed. dj. M $12.00

SMITH, Logan Pearsall. *Afterthoughts.* 1932 London. Ltd ed. 1/100. VG $15.00

SMITH, Logan Pearsall. *Philadelphia Quaker: Letters of Hannah Whitall Smith.* 1950 1st Am ed. 234 p. dj. VG $20.00

SMITH, M. *Middleman.* 1967 Boston. 1st ed. dj. EX $20.00

SMITH, M. *Moon Lamp.* 1976 NY. 1st ed. dj. EX $12.00

SMITH, M.R. *Harpers Ferry Armory & the New Technology.* 1977 Cornell U Pr. Ills 1st ed. 363 p. dj. VG $35.00

SMITH, Mark. *Death of the Detective.* 1974 Knopf. 1st ed. dj. EX $20.00

SMITH, Mark. *Doctor Blues.* 1983 Morrow. 1st ed. dj. VG $15.00

SMITH, Martin Cruz. *Gorky Park.* 1981 NY. 1st ed. dj. EX $18.00

SMITH, Martin Cruz. *Gypsy in Amber.* 1971 Putnam. 1st ed. dj. VG $30.00

SMITH, Martin Cruz. *Nightwing.* 1977 Norton. 1st ed. dj. M $22.50

SMITH, Martin Cruz. *Nightwing.* no date. Norton. 3rd ed. dj. VG $10.00

SMITH, N. *Golden Doorway to Tibet.* 1949 Bobbs Merrill. dj. EX $15.00

SMITH, N.A. *Boys & Girls in Book Land.* 1923 Phil. McKay. Ills JW Smith. 4to. 100 p. dj. $30.00

SMITH, Norman. *History of Dams.* 1972 Secaucus. Citadel Pr. 1st Am ed. dj. EX $10.00

SMITH, O.W. *Gold on the Desert.* 1956 Albuquerque. 1st ed. 249 p. dj. VG $20.00

SMITH, O.W. *Trout Lore.* 1917 Stokes. Ills 1st ed. 203 p. EX $15.00

SMITH, P. *Daughters of the Promised Land.* 1970 Little Brown. 1st ed. VG $8.50

SMITH, P.C.F. *Journals of Ashley Bowen.* 1973 Salem. 2 vol set. boxed. EX $45.00

SMITH, P.W. *Fishes of IL.* 1979 IL U Pr. Ills. 4to. maps. dj. EX $22.50

SMITH, Page. *John Adams.* 1962 Doubleday. 1st ed. 2 vol set. dj. EX $20.00

SMITH, Patricia. *Modern Collector's Dolls.* 1973 Ills. 310 p. dj. EX $12.00

SMITH, Patti. *7th Heaven.* 1972 Telegraph Books. 1/50. wraps. $50.00

SMITH, Paul C. *Personal File.* 1964 Appleton Century. 1st ed. VG $6.00

SMITH, Paul Jordan. *Key to Ulysses.* 1927 Pascal Covici. 1st ed. dj. VG $40.00

SMITH, Philip C. *Frigate Essex Papers.* 1974 Salem. 1st ed. 1/1,100. EX $35.00

SMITH, R. *Tree Crops.* 1953 NY. 408 p. VG $8.00

SMITH, R.L. *Ecology & Field Biology.* 1966 Harper Row. Ills. 686 p. maps. G $8.00

SMITH, R.L. *Venomous Animals of AZ.* 1982 AZ U Pr. Ills. 4to. 134 p. wraps. EX $14.00

SMITH, R.M. *Story of Pope's Barrels.* 1960 Stackpole. Ills. 4to. 203 p. dj. EX $60.00

SMITH, R.P. *So It Doesn't Whistle.* 1951 NY. 1st ed. dj. VG $15.00

SMITH, Red. *On Fishing Around the World.* 1963 NY. Ills 1st ed. dj. EX $30.00

SMITH, Red. *Out of the Red.* 1950 Knopf. Ills Mullin. 1st ed. 294 p. $25.00

SMITH, Rex Alan. *Moon of Popping Tree.* 1975 NY. 1st ed. dj. VG $10.00

SMITH, Robert. *Air & Rain: Beginnings of Chemical Climatology.* 1872 London. Ills. VG $150.00

SMITH, Robert. *Modern Writing.* 1955 NY. Arrowhead. 275 p. $4.00

SMITH, S. Compton. *Chili Con Carne.* 1857 NY. G $8.00

SMITH, S.B. *TN History.* 1974 Knoxville. 1st ed. 8vo. 498 p. dj. EX $40.00

SMITH, S.E. *US Marine Corps in WWI.* 1969 NY. dj. VG $20.00

SMITH, Seba. *Western Captive; or, Times of Tecumseh.* 1842 NY. 48 p. wraps. $100.00

SMITH, T. *Richard Snowden Andrews.* 1910 Baltimore. 1st ed. scarce. VG $85.00

SMITH, T.M. *Nature of the Beast.* 1963 Coward McCann. Ills 1st Am ed. 206 p. dj. VG $10.00

SMITH, Tevis Clyde. *Cardboard God.* 1970 private print. inscr. VG $20.00

SMITH, Thorne. *Bishop's Jaegars.* 1933 Doubleday Doran. VG $12.00

SMITH, Thorne. *Did She Fall?* 1937 Sun Dial. VG $7.50

SMITH, Thorne. *Passionate Witch.* 1941 Doubleday Doran. 1st ed. dj. G $30.00

SMITH, Thorne. *Passionate Witch.* 1942 Dial. dj. VG $10.00

SMITH, Thorne. *Rain in the Doorway.* 1933 Doubleday Doran. 1st ed. VG $20.00

SMITH, Thorne. *Stray Lamb.* 1941 Triangle. 6th ed. VG $6.00

SMITH, Thorne. *Topper Takes a Trip.* no date. Sun Dial. red cloth. dj. G $8.00

SMITH, Thorne. *Turnabout.* 1931 Doubleday Doran. 1st ed. VG $17.50

SMITH, W. Anderson. *Temperate Chile: Progressive Spain.* 1899 London. Black. 1st ed. fld map. 399 p. VG $75.00

SMITH, W.B. *Moscow Mission 1946-1949.* 1950 London. Heinemann. G $15.00

SMITH, W.H.B. *Book of Rifles.* 1963 Harrisburg. VG $12.00

SMITH, W.H.B. *Mauser Rifles & Pistols.* 1954 Harrisburg. Stackpole. 4th print. 236 p. $15.00

SMITH, W.H.B. *Small Arms of the World.* 1962 Harrisburg. VG $16.00

SMITH, Wilbur. *Angels Weep.* 1982 Heinemann. dj. VG $17.50

SMITH, Wilbur. *Before I Forget.* 1971 Chicago. Moody Pr. dj. $5.00

SMITH, Wilbur. *Cry Wolf.* 1977 Doubleday. 1st Am ed. dj. VG $20.00

SMITH, Wilbur. *When the Lions Fade.* 1964 NY. 1st ed. dj. VG $35.00

SMITH, William. *Dictionary of Greek & Roman Biography & Mythology Vol II.* 1880 London. Murray. VG $30.00

SMITH, William. *Hawley & Family of Peoria.* 1902 Chicago. 1st trade ed. presentation. $35.00

SMITH, William. *History of Province of NY From 1st Discovery to 1732.* 1792 Phil. 2nd Am ed. full calf. VG $95.00

SMITH, William. *Traveller's Tree.* 1980 Persea. Ills Hinzdovsky. 1st trade ed. $15.00

SMITH, Woodham. *Great Hunger.* 1962 Harper. 1st ed. dj. VG $15.00

SMITH, Worth. *Miracle of the Ages.* 1934 MA. dj. VG $35.00

SMITH & JUDAH. *Chronicles of Gringos: US Army in Mexican War 1846-1848.* 1969 Albuquerque. 1st ed. dj. EX $30.00

SMITH. *And Miles To Go.* 1967 Little Brown. 1st ed. dj. VG $22.50

SMOLEN & COHEN. *Day in Life of Canada.* 1984 Collins. 1st ed. folio. dj. M $20.00

SMOLLETT, T. *Adventures of Gil Blas of Santillane.* c 1820. London. Cook ed. 3 vol set. VG $40.00

SMOLLETT, Tobias. *Adventures of Roderick Random.* 1815 London. Walker. 568 p. $40.00

SMYTH, C. Piazzi. *Our Inheritance in the Great Pyramid.* 1880 London. 4th ed. 677 p. maps. VG $125.00

SMYTH, J.D. *Physiology of Cestodes.* 1969 Oliver Boyd. Ills 1st ed. 279 p. dj. EX $15.00

SMYTH, William Henry. *Sketch of Present State of Island of Sardinia.* 1828 London. Murray. Ills. map. 351 p. EX $35.00

SMYTHE, Henry. *Atomic Energy for Military Purposes.* 1945 Princeton. dj. EX $255.00

SNAITH, J.C. *Araminta.* 1923 McLeod. 1st ed. VG $8.00

SNAITH, J.C. *Cousin Beryl.* 1929 Appleton. VG $10.00

SNEAD, Sam. *Education of a Golfer.* 1962 NY. 1st ed. dj. VG $20.00

SNEAD, Sam. *Quick Way To Better Golf.* 1938 Photo Sales Co. Ills. folio. EX $75.00

SNELL, Carroll. *Alice in Orchestralia.* 1946 NY. Doubleday. Ills. dj. VG $7.00

SNELL, Edmund. *Z Ray.* 1932 Phil. 1st ed. dj. VG $25.00

SNELL, Roy J. *Secret Mark.* 1923 Reilly Lee. sgn. VG $5.00

SNELLER, A.G. *Vanished World.* 1964 Syracuse U Pr. Ills. 365 p. dj. EX $12.00

SNELLING, H. *History & Practice of Art of Photography.* 1970 reprint of 1849. 12mo. cloth. $20.00

SNELLING, O.F. *Rare Books & Rarer People.* 1982 London. 1st ed. dj. EX $20.00

SNELLING, W.J. *Tales of the Northwest.* 1971 Haines. reprint. dj. EX $10.00

SNIVELY, W.D. *Satan's Ferryman.* 1968 Unger. Ills. 244 p. dj. VG $25.00

SNODGRASS, R.E. *Crustacean Metamorphosis.* 1956 Smithsonian. Ills. 78 p. wraps. $6.00

SNODGRASS, R.E. *Evolution of the Annelida: Onychophora & Arthropoda.* 1938 Smithsonian. Ills. 159 p. VG $14.00

SNODGRASS, R.E. *Insect Metamorthosis.* 1954 Smithsonian. Ills. 124 p. wraps. $8.00

SNODGRASS, W.D. *In Radical Pursuit.* 1975 NY. 1st ed. dj. $18.00

SNOW, C.P. *Corridors of Power.* 1964 London. 1st ed. dj. EX $16.00

SNOW, C.P. *Sleep of Reason.* 1968 NY. 1st ed. dj. VG $10.00

SNOW, C.P. *Strangers & Brothers.* 1972 Scribner. Omnibus ed. 11 vols in 3. VG $35.00

SNOW, Edgar. *Stalin Must Have Peace.* 1947 NY. 1st print. dj. $50.00

SNOW, Edward Rowe. *Famous Lighthouses of New England.* 1945 no place. 1st ed. xl. G $15.00

SNOW, Edward Rowe. *Ghosts, Gales, & Gold.* 1972 Dodd Mead. 2nd ed. dj. EX $17.50

SNOW, Edward Rowe. *Great Atlantic Adventures.* 1970 272 p. dj. VG $9.00

SNOW, Edward Rowe. *Mutiny & Murder.* 1959 306 p. dj. VG $9.00

SNOW, Edward Rowe. *Pilgrim Returns to Cape Cod.* 1946 Ills 1st ed. fld map. dj. EX $20.00

SNOW, Edward Rowe. *Pirates & Buccaneers of Atlantic Coast.* 1944 MA. Ills 1st ed. dj. EX $18.00

SNOW, Edward Rowe. *Romance of Boston Bay.* 1944 Boston. Ills 1st ed. 319 p. $15.00

SNOW, Edward Rowe. *Romance of Casco Bay.* 1975 Dodd Mead. inscr. dj. VG $20.00

SNOW, Edward Rowe. *Secrets of the North Atlantic Islands.* 1950 Dodd Mead. inscr. dj. VG $12.50

SNOW, Edward Rowe. *Storms & Shipwrecks of New England.* 1944 no place. 2nd ed. xl. G $15.00

SNOW, Edward Rowe. *Story of Minot's Light.* 1955 West Hanover. Ills 2nd ed. $25.00

SNOW, Edward Rowe. *True Tales of Buried Treasure.* 1955 Dodd Mead. 7th ed. inscr. dj. VG $22.00

SNOW, Jack. *Dark Music & Other Spectral Tales.* 1947 Herald. 1st ed. dj. VG $45.00

SNOW, Jack. *Magical Mimics in Oz.* 1946 Reilly Lee. 1st ed. dj. VG $150.00

SNOW, Jack. *Shaggy Man of Oz.* 1949 Chicago. Reilly Lee. Ills Kramer. $130.00

SNOW, William P. *Lee & His Generals.* 1867 NY. Ills. 4to. 500 p. G $40.00

SNOWMAN, A. Kenneth. *Art of Carl Faberge.* 1955 London. Faber. Ills 2nd imp. 4to. dj. $65.00

SNOWMAN, A. Kenneth. *Art of Carl Faberge.* 1964 Boston. Revised Enlarged 2nd ed. dj. $150.00

SNOWMAN, A. Kenneth. *Carl Faberge: Goldsmith to the Imperial Court of Russia.* 1979 NY. Greenwich/Crown. Ills. dj. $35.00

SNOWMAN, A. Kenneth. *18th Century Gold Boxes of Europe.* 1966 Boston Book & Art Shop. dj. $250.00

SNYDER, Earl. *General Leemy's Circus.* 1953 NY. 1st ed. 175 p. dj. VG $27.50

SNYDER, Fairmont. *Rhymes for Kindly Children.* 1916 Volland. Ills Gruelle. 11th ed. VG $25.00

SNYDER, Gerald. *In the Footsteps of Lewis & Clark.* 1970 Nat'l Geog Soc. Ills. 215 p. maps. dj. VG $13.00

SNYDER, H.M. *Snyder's Book of Big Game Hunting.* 1950 Greenburg. Ills. 302 p. dj. VG $32.50

SNYDER, John J. *Philadelphia Furniture & Its Makers.* 1975 Main Street. Ills. 4to. 158 p. wraps. $25.00

SOAL, S.G.; & BATEMAN, F. *Modern Experiments in Telepathy.* 1954 NY. Yale U Pr. 425 p. VG $18.00

SOBOTTA, Dr. Johannes. *Atlas of Human Anatomy.* 1930 NY. Revised ed. 4to. 3 vol set. $45.00

SOBOTTA, Dr. Johannes. *Textbook of Histology & Microscopic Anatomy.* 1930 NY. 4to. TB. 2 vol set. $45.00

SOBY, James Thrall. *After Picasso.* 1935 Hartford. 4to. 60 plts. $75.00

SOBY, James Thrall. *Georges Rouault.* 1945 MOMA. Ills. 4to. 132 p. cloth. dj. $20.00

SOBY, James Thrall. *Graphic Art of Ben Shahn.* 1957 Braziller. Ills. 4to. 139 p. cloth. dj. $35.00

SOBY, James Thrall. *Juan Gris.* 1958 MOMA. Ills. 4to. 128 p. cloth. xl. $30.00

SOBY, James Thrall. *Rene Magritte.* 1965 MOMA. Ills. 4to. 80 p. wraps. $20.00

SOBY, James Thrall. *Yves Tanguy.* 1955 MOMA. Ills. 4to. 72 p. wraps. $20.00

SOBY, James Thrall. *20th Century Italian Art.* 1949 MOMA. Ills. 4to. 144 p. dj. $27.50

SODDY, Frederick. *Chemistry of Radioelements.* 1911 London. Longman. 1st ed. $40.00

SODDY, Frederick. *Story of Atomic Energy.* 1949 London. Nova Atlantis. 1st ed. 136 p. $85.00

SOFFAN, Linda Usra. *Women of United Arab Emirates.* 1980 London. Croom Helm Ltd. 1st ed. dj. EX $30.00

SOFTLY, Barbara. *Magic People Around the World.* 1970 NY. Ills Vera Bock. 1st ed. EX $7.50

SOHL, Jerry. *Altered Ego.* 1954 Rinehart. 1st ed. $12.50

SOKAL, R.R.; & ROHLF, F.J. *Biometry: Principles & Practice in Biological Research.* 1969 Freeman. 776 p. VG $18.00

SOKOLOFF, Dr. Boris. *Napolean: Doctor's Biography.* 1937 NY. 1st ed. EX $45.00

SOLEY, James Russell. *Boys of 1812 & Other Naval Heroes.* 1888 Boston. Ills. 338 p. VG $17.50

SOLEY, James Russell. *Sailor Boys of '61.* 1888 Boston. Ills. VG $20.00

SOLEY, James Russell. *Sailor Boys of '61.* 1887 Boston. Ills. 381 p. juvenile. G $25.00

SOLMS-LAUBACH, E. *Die Schonsten Jagdbilder ans Europaischen Sammlungen.* 1961 Verlag. Ills. square 4to. dj. EX $55.00

SOLOMON, Brad. *Open Shadow.* 1978 Summit. 1st ed. dj. EX $15.00

SOLOMON, D. *Marijuana Papers.* 1966 Bobbs Merrill. VG $12.50

SOLON, L.M. *Art of the Old English Potter.* 1906 NY. 8vo. gilt cloth. VG $20.00

SOLONOMSKY, Nicolas. *Music of Latin America.* 1945 NY. VG $18.00

SOLZHENITSYN, Aleksandr. *August 1944.* 1972 Farrar. 1st Am ed. dj. VG $25.00

SOLZHENITSYN, Aleksandr. *Cancer Ward.* 1968 Bodley Head. 1st English ed. dj. VG $40.00

SOLZHENITSYN, Aleksandr. *Gulag Archipelago.* 1973 Harper. 1st Am ed. dj. EX $12.00

SOLZHENITSYN, Aleksandr. *Lenin in Zurich.* 1976 London. 1st English ed. dj. VG $22.00

SOLZHENITSYN, Aleksandr. *Lenin in Zurich.* 1976 Farrar. 1st Am ed. dj. EX $20.00

SOLZHENITSYN, Aleksandr. *Oak & the Calf.* 1980 Harper. 1st trade ed. dj. VG $15.00

SOLZHENITSYN, Aleksandr. *Prussian Nights.* 1977 NY. 1st ed. dj. M $12.00

SOLZHENITSYN, Aleksandr. *Stories & Prose Poems.* 1971 Farrar Straus. 1st Am ed. dj. EX $15.00

SOLZHENITSYN, Aleksandr. *1 Day in the Life of Ivan Denisovich.* 1963 Dutton. 1st ed. 8vo. dj. EX $16.00

SOLZHENITSYN, Aleksandr. *1 Day in the Life of Ivan Denisovich.* 1963 Praeger. 1st ed. dj. G $15.00

SOLZHENITSYN, Aleksandr. *1st Circle.* 1968 Collins. 1st English ed. dj. EX $40.00

SOLZHENITSYN, Aleksandr. *1st Circle.* 1968 Harper. 1st Am ed. dj. EX $12.00

SOMERS, John. *Brethern of the Axe.* 1927 NY. Dutton. 1st ed. VG $10.00

SOMERVELL, D.C. *Reign of King George.* 1935 NY. $8.00

SOMERVILLE, H. *Sceptre: 17th Challenger.* 1959 NY. 1st Am ed. dj. VG $25.00

SOMERVILLE, William. *Chace.* 1929 NY. Ills Bewick. Ltd ed. 1/375. VG $35.00

SOMMER, E. *Contemporary Costume Jewelry.* 1974 NY. Ills. 224 p. $20.00

SOMMER, Francois. *Man & Beast in Africa.* 1954 NY. Citadel. 1st ed. dj. VG $45.00

SOMMER, Scott. *Lifetime.* 1981 Random House. 1st ed. dj. EX $15.00

SOMMER, Scott. *Nearing's Grace.* 1979 Taplinger. 1st ed. dj. EX $20.00

SOMMERFELD, Arnold. *Atombau und Spektrallinien.* 1919 Braunschweig. 1st ed. 550 p. VG $95.00

SOMMERFELD, Arnold. *3 Lectures on Atomic Physics.* no date. NY. Dutton. 1st ed. 70 p. dj. G $20.00

SONDERN, Frederic. *Brotherhood of Evil.* 1959 Farrar Straus. dj. VG $7.50

SONDERSON, Ivan. *Follow the Whale.* 1956 Bramhall House. 1st ed. dj. VG $45.00

SONNICHSEN, C.L. *Billy King's Tombstone.* 1951 Caxton. Ills. dj. VG $15.00

SONNICHSEN, C.L. *Cowboys & Cattle Kings.* 1950 Norman. 1st ed. VG $25.00

SONNICHSEN, C.L. *Mescalero Apaches.* 1970 OK U Pr. Ills. 204 p. maps. dj. EX $18.00

SONNICHSEN, C.L. *Roy Bean: Law West of the Pecos.* 1958 Devin Adair. Ills. 207 p. dj. VG $10.00

SONNISCHSEN & MORRISON. *Alias Billy the Kid.* 1955 NM U Pr. Ills 1st ed. dj. VG $30.00

SONTAG, Susan. *Benefactor.* 1963 Farrar. 1st ed. dj. VG $35.00

SONTAG, Susan. *Brother Carl.* 1974 Farrar. 1st ed. dj. EX $20.00

SONTAG, Susan. *Death Kit.* 1976 Farrar. 1st ed. dj. VG $15.00

SONTAG, Susan. *Etcetera.* 1978 Farrar. 1st ed. dj. EX $12.00

SONTAG, Susan. *Illness As Metaphor.* 1978 Farrar. 1st ed. dj. EX $15.00

SONTAG, Susan. *On Photography.* 1977 NY. 1st ed. dj. VG $30.00

SONTAG, Susan. *Styles of Radical Will.* 1969 Farrar. 1st ed. dj. VG $30.00

SONTAG, Susan. *Susan Sontag Reader.* 1982 Farrar. 1st trade ed. dj. VG $17.50

SONTAG, Susan. *Under the Sign of Saturn.* 1980 Farrar. 1st ed. sgn. dj. EX $30.00

SOPHOCLES. *Antigone.* 1975 Ltd Ed Club. Ills/sgn Bennett. 4to. 127 p. $30.00

SORENSEN, Theodore. *Kennedy.* 1965 NY. Harper Row. 783 p. dj. VG $7.50

SORENSON, H.D. *Decoy Collector's Guide.* 1968 private print. Ills. 128 p. wraps. VG $18.00

SORLIER, Charles. *Chagall's Posters: Catalogue Raisonne.* 1975 NY. Crown. Ills. folio. 159 p. dj. $100.00

SOROKIN, Pitrim A. *Social & Cultural Dynamics.* 1972 NY. Bedminster Pr. 4 vol set. $75.00

SORRENTINO, Gilbert. *Blue Pastoral.* 1983 North Point. 1st ed. dj. EX $18.00

SORRENTINO, Gilbert. *Imaginative Qualities of Actual Things.* 1971 Pantheon. 1st ed. dj. EX $30.00

SORRENTINO, Gilbert. *Mulligan Stew.* 1980 Marion Boyars. 1st English ed. dj. EX $20.00

SORRENTINO, Gilbert. *Perfect Fiction.* 1968 Norton. 1st ed. dj. EX $40.00

SORRENTINO, Gilbert. *Sky Changes.* 1966 NY. Hill Wang. 1st ed. dj. EX $35.00

SORRENTINO, Gilbert. *Splendide Hotel.* 1973 New Directions. Ltd ed. sgn. dj. EX $35.00

SORRENTINO, Gilbert. *Steel Work.* 1970 Pantheon. 1st ed. dj. EX $35.00

SOSIN, Mark. *Angler's Bible.* 1975 Stoeger. Ills 1st ed. wraps. VG $20.00

SOSIN, Mark; & DANCE, Bill. *Practical Black Bass Fishing.* 1975 Crown. Ills. 216 p. wraps. G $7.50

SOTOMAYOR, Antonio. *Balloons: 1st 100 Years.* 1972 NY. 1st ed. 4to. 41 p. dj. VG $50.00

SOULAVIE, John Lewis. *Historical & Political Memoirs of Reign of Louis XVI.* 1802 London. 6 vol set. xl. VG $245.00

SOULE, F. *Annals of San Francisco & History of CA.* 1966 Osborne. reprint. $25.00

SOULE, F. *Annals of San Francisco & History of CA.* 1855 NY. 1st ed. EX $150.00

SOULE, G. *Mystery Monsters of the Deep.* 1981 Watts. Ills. 134 p. dj. EX $10.00

SOUTHERN, R. *Stage Setting for Amateurs & Professionals.* 1946 London. Faber. 1st ed. 2nd print. dj. VG $20.00

SOUTHERN, Terry. *Blue Movie.* 1970 World. 1st ed. 1st print. dj. VG $20.00

SOUTHERN, Terry. *Candy.* no date. Putnam. 4th ed. $10.00

SOUTHEY, R. *All for Love & the Pilgrim to Compostella.* 1829 London. 1st ed. 1/4 leather. G $50.00

SOUTHEY, R. *Tour in the Netherlands.* 1902 Boston. Riverside. Ltd ed. 1/519. VG $25.00

SOUTHEY, R. *Vision of Judgement.* 1821 London. 1st ed. VG $60.00

SOUTHEY, Thomas. *Chronological History of West Indies.* 1827 London. Longman. 1st ed. 3 vol set. $300.00

SOUTHWARD, E.C. *Pogonophora of the Northwest Atlantic: Nova Scotia to FL.* 1971 Smithsonian. Ills. 12 p. wraps. $6.00

SOWERBY, G. *Conchological Manual.* 1852 London. Ills 4th ed. $45.00

SOWERBY, John E. *British Wild Flowers.* 1914 1780 Ills. cloth with gilt edges. $200.00

SOWERBY, John E. *British Wild Flowers.* 1882 180 plts. ¾-leather. $250.00

SOWLS, L.K. *Peccaries.* 1984 AZ U Pr. Ills. 251 p. maps. dj. EX $25.00

SOYINKO, Wole. *Madmen & Specialists.* 1971 NY. Hill Wang. dj. EX $30.00

SPACKMAN, W.M. *Heyday.* 1953 NY. Ballantine. 1st ed. dj. EX $75.00

SPACKMAN, W.M. *Heyday.* 1963 NY. Baltimore. 1st ed. scarce. VG $65.00

SPACKMAN, W.M. *Little Decorum for Once.* 1985 Knopf. 1st ed. dj. EX $13.00

SPALDING, Baird T. *Life & Teachings of Masters of the Far East.* 1927 Los Angeles. De Vorss. Sun Series. 3 vols. $25.00

SPARANO, V.T. *Complete Outdoors Encyclopedia.* 1977 Outdoor Life. Ills. 4to. 622 p. dj. VG $8.00

SPARANO, V.T. *Complete Outdoors Encyclopedia.* 1977 Outdoor Life. Ills. 4to. 622 p. dj. EX $14.00

SPARK, Muriel. *Abyss of Crewe.* 1974 Viking. 1st Am ed. dj. VG $15.00

SPARK, Muriel. *Collected Poems I.* 1967 Macmillan. 1st ed. inscr. dj. EX $40.00

SPARK, Muriel. *Driver's Seat.* 1970 Knopf. 1st ed. dj. VG $15.00

SPARK, Muriel. *Fanfarlo & Other Verse.* 1952 Kent. Hand Flower Pr. 1st ed. EX $65.00

SPARK, Muriel. *Girls of Slender Means.* 1963 NY. 1st ed. dj. M $12.00

SPARK, Muriel. *Hothouse by the East River.* 1973 Macmillan. 1st ed. dj. VG $20.00

SPARK, Muriel. *Loitering with Intent.* 1981 Coward McCann. 1st Am ed. dj. VG $12.50

SPARK, Muriel. *Mandelbaum Gate.* 1965 NY. 1st ed. dj. VG $12.50

SPARK, Muriel. *Memento Mori.* 1959 Lippincott. 1st Am ed. dj. EX $30.00

SPARK, Muriel. *Only Problem.* 1984 Putnam. Advance copy. dj. EX $20.00

SPARK, Muriel. *Prime of Miss Jean Brodie.* 1961 NY. 1st ed. dj. EX $30.00

SPARK, Muriel. *Prime of Miss Jean Brodie.* 1961 London. 1st ed. dj. EX $35.00

SPARK, Muriel. *Public Image.* 1968 Knopf. 1st Am ed. dj. VG $20.00

SPARK, Muriel. *Stories of Muriel Spark.* 1985 Dutton. 1st Am ed. dj. EX $20.00

SPARK, Muriel. *Stories of Muriel Spark.* 1985 Dutton. Uncorrected proof. EX $35.00

SPARK, Muriel. *Takeover.* 1976 NY. Viking. 1st ed. dj. VG $15.00

SPARK & STANFORD. *My Best Mary: Letters of Mary Wollstonecraft Shelley.* 1973 London. Wingate. 240 p. red cloth. VG $10.00

SPARKES & MOORE. *Hetty Green: Witch of Wall Street.* 1935 NY. EX $25.00

SPARKES & MOORE. *Hetty Green: Witch of Wall Street.* 1935 NY. dj. G $15.00

SPARKS, J. *Discovery of Animal Behavior.* 1982 Little Brown. Ills 1st Am ed. 288 p. dj. EX $22.00

SPARKS, J.; & SOPER, T. *Owls: Their Natural & Unnatural History.* 1979 Taplinger. Ills. 206 p. dj. EX $12.50

SPARKS, Jared. *Life of Benjamin Franklin*. 1856 Boston. Ills. 8vo. 612 p. brown cloth. $20.00

SPARKS, Jared. *Life of George Washington*. 1842 Boston. 12mo. 330 p. 2 vol set. xl. G $12.00

SPARKS, Jared. *Life of George Washington*. 1852 Boston. Ills 8vo. 562 p. VG $24.00

SPARKS, Jared. *Life of George Washington*. 1854 no place. Ills. 12mo. 344 p. xl. $20.00

SPARROW, Gerald. *Vintage Victorian Murder*. c 1971. London. 1st ed. presentation. dj. VG $18.00

SPARROW, W.S. *Angling in British Art*. 1923 London. EX $195.00

SPARROW, W.S. *British Sporting Arts From Barlow to Herring*. 1922 Scribner. $175.00

SPARROW, W.S. *Women Painters of the World*. 1905 NY. Ills 1st Am ed. 4to. cloth. VG $65.00

SPAYTH, Henry. *Draughts or Checkers for Beginners*. 1866 NY. Ills. 12mo. cloth. $25.00

SPEARMAN, F.H. *Nan of Music Mountain*. 1916 NY. Ills Wyeth. $20.00

SPEARMAN, F.H. *Whispering Smith*. no date. Hodder Stoughton. VG $7.50

SPEARMAN, F.H. *Whispering Smith*. 1906 Scribner. Ills Wyeth. G $10.00

SPEARS, J.R. *Gold Diggings of Cape Horn: Study of Life Tierra del Fuego*. 1895 NY. Putnam. Ills 1st ed. 319 p. VG $75.00

SPEARS, J.R. *History of MS Valley*. 1903 NY. G $35.00

SPEARS, J.R. *History of Our Navy 1775-1898*. 1899 NY. 5 vol set. VG $85.00

SPEARS, J.R. *History of Our Navy*. 1897 NY. Ills. cloth. VG $50.00

SPEARS, J.R. *History of the MI Valley*. 1903 NY. VG $55.00

SPEATH, Sigmund. *Read 'Em & Weep*. 1926 NY. Ills 1st ed. $15.00

SPECHT, Richard. *Johannes Brahms*. 1930 NY. Trans Eric Blom. VG $20.00

SPECK, F.G. *Naskapi Savage Hunters of Labrador Peninsula*. 1935 Norman, OK. Ills 1st ed. 248 p. VG $47.50

SPECK, Gordon. *Samuel Hearne & the Northwest Passage*. 1963 Caxton. Ills. 337 p. dj. EX $6.50

SPECTOR, Benjamin. *History of Tufts College Medical School*. 1943 Tufts Medical Alumni Soc. VG $12.50

SPEED, Harold. *Practice & Science of Drawing*. 1920 London. Ills. $40.00

SPEED, Joshua F. *Reminiscences of Abraham Lincoln & Notes of Visit to CA*. 1896 Louisville. Bradley Gilbert. 67 p. wraps. $95.00

SPEER, Albert. *Inside the 3rd Reich*. 1970 Macmillan. 1st ed. dj. G $10.00

SPEIDEL, Hans. *Invasion 1944*. 1950 Chicago. Ills 1st ed. 176 p. dj. VG $45.00

SPEISER, Werner. *Art of China*. 1961 NY. 1st Am ed. dj. $20.00

SPEKE, J. *Journal of the Discovery of the Source of the Nile*. 1864 NY. 1st Am ed. G $60.00

SPELL, L. & H. *Forgotten Men of Cripple Creek*. 1959 Denver. Ills 1st ed. sgn. dj. VG $20.00

SPELL, Lota M. *Pioneer Printer Samuel Banks in Mexico & TX*. 1963 TX U Pr. 8vo. 230 p. dj. M $22.00

SPELLMAN, F. *Prayers & Poems*. 1946 NY. Scribner. VG $25.00

SPELTZ, Alexander. *Styles of Ornament*. c 1910. Grosset Dunlap. fair. $30.00

SPELTZ, Alexander. *Styles of Ornament*. 1923 Chicago. Regan. Ills. 8vo. 647 p. $20.00

SPEMANN, Wilhelm. *Das Museum eine Anleitung zum Genuss Werke Bildender Kunst*. c 1910s. Stuttgart. 160 plts. 107 p. $125.00

SPENCE, B. *Harpooned: Story of Whaling*. 1980 Greenwhich. Ills. dj. EX $17.50

SPENCE, Clark C. *Territorial Politics & Government in MT*. 1975 Urbana. 1st ed. dj. VG $12.00

SPENCE, E.F. *Pike Fisher*. 1928 Black. London. Ills. 264 p. G $15.00

SPENCE, Joseph. *Polymetis*. 1755 London. folio. 361 p. full calf. EX $100.00

SPENCE, Lewis. *Myths of the North American Indians*. 1904 London. 8vo. 393 p. VG $85.00

SPENCER, Bella Z. *Tried & True; or, Love & Loyalty*. 1868 Springfield. 8vo. 394 p. brown cloth. $14.00

SPENCER, Bernard. *Aegean Islands & Other Poems*. 1948 Doubleday. 1st ed. dj. EX $25.00

SPENCER, D.A. *Color Photography in Practice*. 1952 NY. 3rd ed. VG $12.50

SPENCER, D.A. *Color Photography in Practice*. 1938 NY. Pitman. cloth. dj. VG $20.00

SPENCER, D.A. *Photography Today*. 1936 Oxford U Pr. $15.00

SPENCER, Elizabeth. *Knights & Dragons*. 1965 McGraw Hill. 1st ed. sgn. dj. EX $85.00

SPENCER, Elizabeth. *Knights & Dragons*. 1965 NY. 1st ed. dj. EX $20.00

SPENCER, Elizabeth. *Light in Piazza*. 1960 McGraw Hill. 1st ed. dj. EX $35.00

SPENCER, Elizabeth. *Marilee*. 1981 Jackson, MS. 1st trade ed. sgn. wraps. $10.00

SPENCER, Elizabeth. *Marilee*. 1981 MS U Pr. 1st ed. 1/300. sgn. dj. EX $35.00

SPENCER, Elizabeth. *Mules*. 1982 Palaemon. Ltd 1st ed. 1/150. sgn. EX $30.00

SPENCER, Elizabeth. *No Place for an Angel*. 1967 McGraw Hill. 1st ed. dj. EX $30.00

SPENCER, Elizabeth. *No Place for an Angel*. 1967 McGraw Hill. 1st ed. sgn. dj. EX $45.00

SPENCER, Elizabeth. *Salt Line*. 1985 Penguin. 1st ed. sgn. EX $20.00

SPENCER, Elizabeth. *Salt Line*. 1984 NY. Doubleday. 1st ed. sgn. dj. EX $40.00

SPENCER, Elizabeth. *Ship Island & Other Stories*. 1968 McGraw Hill. Ltd ed. 1/150. sgn. dj. EX $75.00

SPENCER, Elizabeth. *This Crooked Way*. 1952 Dodd Mead. 1st ed. dj. scarce. EX $75.00

SPENCER, Elizabeth. *Voice at the Back Door*. 1956 McGraw Hill. 1st ed. dj. EX $65.00

SPENCER, H. *Spencerian Key to Practical Penmanship*. 1867 NY. 8vo. 176 p. VG $75.00

SPENCER, J.A. *History of the US*. no date. NY. Johnson Fry. wraps. VG $150.00

SPENCER, J.W. *Confederate Guns of Navarro County*. 1986 TX U Pr. Ills Ltd ed. 1/500. dj. EX $30.00

SPENCER, Richard H. *Genealogical & Memorial Encyclopedia of State of MD*. 1919 NY. Ills 1st ed. 4to. EX $55.00

SPENCER, S. *World Within World*. 1951 NY. 1st ed. dj. EX $12.00

SPENCER, Scott. *Last Night at the Brain Thieves' Ball*. 1973 Boston. Houghton Mifflin. 1st ed. dj. $20.00

SPENDER, J.A. *Public Life*. 1925 London. 1st ed. 2 vol set. EX $45.00

SPENDER, Stephen. *Burning Cactus*. 1936 London. 1st ed. dj. EX $65.00

SPENDER, Stephen. *European Witness*. 1946 NY. Reynal Hitchcock. 1st ed. 8vo. $35.00

SPENDER, Stephen. *Forward From Liberalism*. 1937 NY. 1st Am ed. sgn. VG $37.50

SPENDER, Stephen. *Generous Days.* 1971 NY. 1st ed. dj. EX $12.00

SPENDER, Stephen. *Journals 1939-1983.* 1985 Franklin Lib. 1st ed. sgn. full leather. dj. $45.00

SPENDER, Stephen. *Letters to Christopher.* 1980 Santa Barbara. Ltd 1st ed. 1/250. sgn. dj. EX $35.00

SPENDER, Stephen. *Poems.* 1933 Faber. 1st ed. VG $50.00

SPENDER, Stephen. *Ruins & Visions.* 1942 Random House. 1st Am ed. dj. VG $35.00

SPENDER, Stephen. *Trial of a Judge.* 1938 Random House. 1st Am ed. sgn. dj. VG $35.00

SPENDER, Stephen. *W.H. Auden: A Tribute.* 1975 NY. 1st ed. dj. M $17.00

SPENDER & HOCKNEY. *China Diary.* 1982 Abrams. dj. VG $25.00

SPENDER. *2 Winters in Norway.* 1902 London. VG $25.00

SPENSER, E. *Prothalamion & Epithalamion.* 1902 Boston. Riverside. Ltd ed. 1/419. VG $55.00

SPENSER, Edmund. *Shepherds's Calender.* 1930 London. Cresset. Ills Nash. 1/350. VG $95.00

SPERLICH, E.K. *Guatemalan Back-Strap Weaving.* 1980 OK. Ills. 176 p. $30.00

SPERRY, Armstrong. *Wagons Westward.* 1936 Winston. 1st ed. VG $20.00

SPEWACK, Bella & Samuel S. *Clear All Wires.* 1932 London. 1st ed. inscr. VG $20.00

SPEWACK, Samuel. *Skyscraper Murder.* 1928 Macaulay. 2nd ed. VG $15.00

SPICER-SIMSON & SHERMAN. *Men of Letters of the British Isles.* 1924 NY. Rudge. Ills Ltd ed. 1/530. VG $45.00

SPIEGELBERG, Herbert. *Phenomenological Movement.* 1960 Hague. inscr. 2 vol set. VG $35.00

SPIELMANN & LAYARD. *Kate Greenaway.* 1905 NY. Putnam. 1st Am ed. 2nd print. VG $70.00

SPIER, Peter. *Christmas!* 1983 Doubleday. Ills 1st ed. 4to. 32 p. dj. VG $15.00

SPIES, Werner. *Victor Vasarely.* 1971 NY. Abrams. Ills. 4to. 206 p. dj. $65.00

SPILLANE, Mickey. *By-Pass Control.* 1966 Dutton. 1st ed. xl. $10.00

SPILLANE, Mickey. *Day of Guns.* 1964 Dutton. 1st ed. dj. VG $20.00

SPILLANE, Mickey. *Deep.* 1961 NY. Dutton. 1st ed. 8vo. dj. VG $15.00

SPILLANE, Mickey. *Deep.* 1961 London. 1st ed. dj. $12.50

SPILLANE, Mickey. *My Gun Is Quick.* 1950 Dutton. 1st ed. dj. VG $48.00

SPILLANE, Mickey. *Tomorrow I Die.* 1984 Mysterious Pr. 1st ed. dj. EX $20.00

SPILLANE, Mickey. *Twisted Thing.* 1966 Dutton. 1st ed. dj. xl. $10.00

SPILLER, Burton L. *Firelight.* 1937 Derrydale. Ills LB Hunt. 1/950. EX $180.00

SPILLER, Burton L. *Grouse Feathers.* 1972 NY. Ills Hunt. dj. VG $10.00

SPILLER, Burton L. *More Grouse Feathers.* 1972 Crown. Ills Hunt. 4to. 238 p. dj. EX $20.00

SPINAGE, C.A. *Book of the Giraffe.* 1968 London. Collins. Ills. 191 p. dj. EX $22.50

SPINDEN, H. *Ancient Civilizations of Mexico & Central America.* 1948 Ills. 270 p. fld map. VG $20.00

SPINRAD, Norman. *Songs From the Stars.* 1980 Simon Schuster. 1st ed. dj. EX $12.00

SPLAN, John. *Life with the Trotters.* 1889 White. 450 p. inscr. VG $30.00

SPOCK, L.E. *Guide to the Study of Rocks.* 1962 Harper. Ills. 298 p. dj. VG $6.00

SPOFFORD, Harriet Prescott. *Titian's Garden & Other Poems.* 1897 Boston. Copeland Day. 1st ed. 1/500. $55.00

SPOFFORD, J. *Gazetteer of MA.* 1828 Newburyport. 1st ed. map. calf. $30.00

SPORE, Dr. William D. *Peripatetic M.D.* 1899 Mexico. 162 p. green cloth. VG $125.00

SPORTS AFIELD. *Treasury of Waterfowl.* 1957 Prentice Hall. Ills. 4to. 143 p. VG $20.00

SPRACKLAND, R.G. *All About Lizards.* 1977 Ills. 127 p. wraps. $5.00

SPRAGUE, Kurth. *Promise Kept.* 1975 Austin. Ills Groth. Ltd ed. sgns. EX $65.00

SPRAGUE, Marshall. *Gallery of Dudes.* 1967 Boston. 1st ed. dj. VG $10.00

SPRAGUE, Marshall. *Massacre: Tragedy at White River.* 1957 Boston. 1st ed. dj. VG $20.00

SPRAGUE, Marshall. *Money Mountain.* 1953 Boston. 1st ed. dj. VG $17.50

SPRING, Agnes Wright. *Caspar Collins: Life Exploits of Indian Fighter.* 1927 Columbia U Pr. EX $35.00

SPRING, Agnes Wright. *Cheyenne & Black Hills Stage.* 1949 Glendale. 1st ed. VG $85.00

SPRING, James W. *Boston & the Parker House.* 1927 Boston. private print. Ills. VG $25.00

SPRING, Norma. *Roaming Russia, Siberia, & Middle Asia.* 1973 Seattle. Ills 1st ed. 191 p. VG $12.50

SPRINGS, Elliot White. *Clothes Make the Man.* 1949 446 p. G $15.00

SPROAT, I. *Wodehouse at War.* 1981 Ticknor Fields. 1st ed. dj. VG $20.00

SPRUILL, Steven G. *Keepers of the Gate.* 1977 Doubleday. 1st ed. dj. xl. $5.00

SPRUNT, A. *North American Birds of Prey.* 1955 Harper. Ills 1st ed. 227 p. VG $40.00

SPRY, Constance. *Favorite Flowers.* 1959 London. Dent. 1st ed. gilt cream cloth. VG $8.00

SPURR, George G. *Fight with a Grizzly Bear: Story of Thrilling Interest.* 1886 Boston. Spurr. 1st ed. 8vo. brown wraps. $175.00

SPURRIER, S. *Illustration: Its Practice in Wash & Line.* 1933 London. Ills. 128 p. VG $18.00

SPURZHEIM, G. *Anatomy of the Brain with View of Nervous System.* 1926 London. Ills 1st English ed. VG $250.00

SPYRI, Johanna. *Grotli's Children: Story of Switzerland.* 1924 NY. Blue Ribbon. 265 p. $4.00

SPYRI, Johanna. *Heidi.* 1921 Rand McNally. Windermere Series. VG $30.00

SPYRI, Johanna. *Heidi.* 1922 McKay. Ills JW Smith. 1st ed. VG $16.00

SPYRI, Johanna. *Heidi.* 1945 NY. Grosset Dunlap. Ills Sharp. $4.00

SPYRI, Johanna. *Mazli: Story of the Swiss Valleys.* 1921 NY. Blue Ribbon. 265 p. $4.00

SPYRI, Johnson. *Cornelli.* 1920 NY. Burt. 275 p. $5.00

SQUIER, E. George. *Peru: Incidents of Travel & Exploration in Land of Incas.* 1877 NY. Harper. Ills 1st ed. 599 p. $150.00

SQUIRE, John. *Cheddar Gorge: Book of English Cheeses.* 1938 NY. Macmillan. Ills Shepard. 1st Am ed. EX $40.00

SQUIRE, John. *Cheddar Gorge: Book of English Cheeses.* 1938 NY. Ills EH Shepard. 1st Am ed. G $25.00

SQUIRE, Lorene. *Wildfowling with a Camera.* 1938 Lippincott. Ills. 4to. 217 p. $20.00

SRONKOVA, Olga. *Gothic Woman's Fashion.* 1954 Prague. Trans Hort. 1st ed. 265 p. dj. $85.00

ST. GEORGE, Eleanor. *Old Dolls.* 1950 NY. dj. VG $14.00

ST. JOHN, Elizabeth. *Sammy the White House Mouse.* 1976 Handel Pub. Ills Quiram. 1st ed. VG $12.50

ST. JOHN, Philip. *Rocket Jockey.* 1952 Phil. Winston. 1st ed. dj. VG $20.00

ST. JOHN, Robert. *From the Land of Silent People.* 1942 NY. 352 p. dj. G $5.00

ST. JOHNS, Adela. *Field of Honor.* 1938 Dutton. 1st ed. dj. $8.50

ST. MARTIN & NELSON. *Boy: Photographic Essay.* 1964 NY. Book Horizons. 1st ed. VG $25.00

STABLEFORD, Brian M. *Paradise Game.* 1976 Dent. 1st ed. sgn. dj. VG $25.00

STACEY, T. *Hostile Sun.* 1954 London. 2nd print. dj. VG $6.00

STACKPOLE, E.J. *Fredericksburg Campaign.* 1957 Bonanza. reprint. 297 p. maps. dj. EX $16.00

STAEBLER, E. *Food That Really Schmecks.* 1968 Toronto. 1st ed. sgn. dj. VG $25.00

STAENDER, V. *Adventures with Arctic Wildlife.* 1970 Caxton. Ills. 260 p. VG $8.00

STAFFORD, E.N. *Laban Stafford: His Ancestors & Descendants.* 1962 no place. 4to. 286 p. VG $25.00

STAFFORD, E.P. *Big E (Carrier Enterprise).* 1962 Random House. 1st ed. dj. VG $25.00

STAFFORD, Jean. *Boston Adventure.* 1944 NY. Harcourt. 1st ed. dj. EX $25.00

STAFFORD, Jean. *Children Are Bored on Sunday.* 1953 NY. Harcourt. 1st ed. dj. VG $30.00

STAFFORD, Jean. *Mountain Lion.* 1947 Harcourt. 1st ed. dj. VG $20.00

STAFFORD, W. *Travelling Through the Dark.* 1962 NY. Harper. 1st ed. dj. EX $10.00

STAFFORD, William. *Quiet of the Land.* 1979 NY. Nadja. Ltd ed. 1/200. sgn. dj. EX $85.00

STAFFORD, William. *Stories That Could Be True: New & Collected Poems.* 1977 NY. 1st ed. sgn. dj. VG $45.00

STAFFORD, William. *Things That Happen.* 1980 BOMC. 1/10 Roman # copies. sgn. $125.00

STAFFORD, William. *Tuned in Late 1 Night.* 1978 Old Deerfield/Dublin. 1st ed. $50.00

STAFFORD, William; & BELL, M. *Correspondence in Poetry.* 1983 Boston. Godine. 1/150. sgns. slipcase. $60.00

STAGG, Albert. *Almadas & Alamos.* 1978 Tucson. 1st ed. dj. VG $7.50

STAGGE, Jonathan. *Death of My Darling Daughters.* 1945 Crime Club. 1st ed. VG $15.00

STAHL, P.J. *Letters of a French Cat.* 1954 Rodale Miniature Books. dj. EX $10.00

STANDARD, M.N. *Colonial VA: Its People & Customs.* 1917 Phil. Ltd 1st ed. 8vo. 376 p. G $75.00

STANDING BEAR, Chief Luther. *Land of the Spotted Eagle.* 1933 Riverside. Ills 1st ed. 259 p. dj. VG $65.00

STANDING BEAR, Chief Luther. *My People, the Sioux.* 1928 Houghton Mifflin. 1st ed. dj. $95.00

STANFORD, Alfred. *Men, Fish, & Boats.* 1934 Morrow. 1st ed. VG $30.00

STANISLAVSKY, Konstantin. *Stanislavsky on the Art of the Stage.* 1961 NY. Hill Wang. 1st Am ed. VG $8.00

STANLEY, A. Caroline. *Order No. 11: Tale of the Border.* 1904 Century. Ills Harry Edwards. $12.50

STANLEY, A.P. *Historical Memorials of Westminster Abbey.* 1882 NY. Ills. 2 vol set. 422 p. $38.00

STANLEY, A.P. *Memorials of Westminster Abbey.* 1876 London. Murray. Ills 4th ed. G $60.00

STANLEY, F. *Yankee Story.* 1964 private print. Ltd ed. 1/40. sgn. pb. EX $5.00

STANLEY, Henry M. *In Darkest Africa.* 1890 NY. Ills 1st ed. 2 vol set. G $35.00

STANLEY, Henry M. *In Darkest Africa.* 1890 NY. 1st ed. 2 vol set. VG $75.00

STANLEY, Henry M. *In Darkest Africa.* 1890 NY. Scribner. 1st ed. ¾-leather. rebound. $125.00

STANLEY, Henry M. *In Darkest Africa.* 1891 NY. Ills 2nd Am ed. 2 vol set. $35.00

STANLEY, Henry M. *In Darkest Africa. Vol. I.* 1890 NY. Scribner. Ills. rebound. VG $25.00

STANLEY, Henry M. *Slavery & the Slave Trade in Africa.* 1893 NY. Ills 1st ed. 12mo. cloth. $125.00

STANLEY, Henry M. *Through Dark Continent; or, Sources of the Nile.* 1878 NY. 1st ed. 2 vol set. EX $80.00

STANLEY, Henry M. *Through South Africa.* 1898 London. 1st ed. sgn. VG $200.00

STANLEY, Henry. *India in the War.* 1915 London. 16 plts. VG $25.00

STANLEY, Johnson. *Stamp Collector: Guide to World's Postage Stamps.* 1929 London. Revised ed. VG $15.00

STANLEY, Leo. *Men at Their Worst.* 1940 NY. Appleton. EX $11.50

STANLEY, Louis. *How To Be a Better Woman Golfer.* 1952 NY. Ills. 127 p. dj. $5.00

STANSBURY, H. *Exploration & Survey of Valley of Great Lake of UT.* 1853 WA. Ills. 8vo. 495 p. scarce. $70.00

STANSBURY, H. *Lake of the Great Dismal.* 1925 Boni. Intro Don Marquis. map. VG $20.00

STANSBURY, H. *Valley of the Great Salt Lake: New Route Through Mounts.* 1852 Phil. Ills. fld plts. VG $95.00

STANTLEY, Charles. *Student & Singer.* 1893 London. 2nd ed. VG $35.00

STANTON, Daniel. *Journal of Life, Travels, & Labors of Minister of Jesus.* 1772 Phil. 1st ed. $80.00

STANTON, Edward. *Dreams of the Dead.* 1892 Boston. Lee Shepard. 1st ed. VG $40.00

STANTON, Henry T. *Poems of the Confederacy.* 1900 Louisville. VG $17.50

STANTON, Shelby L. *Rise & Fall of an American Army.* 1985 Novato, CA. 411 p. dj. EX $22.50

STANTON, Shelby L. *Vietnam Order of Battle.* 1986 NY. Ills. 396 p. dj. VG $42.50

STANTON, William. *Great US Exploring Expedition of 1838-1842.* 1975 CA U Pr. Ills. 433 p. dj. EX $20.00

STANWOOD, Brooks. *7th Child.* 1981 Londen Pr. dj. EX $10.00

STANWOOD, D.A. *Memory of Eva Ryker.* 1978 NY. 1st ed. dj. M $11.00

STANWOOD. *Direct Ancestry of Jacob Wendell of Portsmouth, NH.* 1882 Ltd ed. 49 P. $45.00

STAPLEDON, Olaf. *Far Future Calling.* 1979 Oswald Train. 1st ed. dj. EX $12.00

STAPLEDON, Olaf. *Star Maker.* 1937 Methuen. 1st ed. VG $35.00

STAPLETON, Ruth Carter. *Brother Billy.* 1978 Harper Row. 1st ed. dj. EX $8.00

STARBUCK, Alexander. *History of the American Whale Fishery to Year 1876.* 1964 NY. Argosy Antiquarian. 2 vol set. $27.50

STARBUCK, George. *Space-Saver Sonnets.* 1986 Bits Pr. 1st ed. 1/255. wraps. EX $10.00

STARK, J.H. *Loyalists of MA.* 1910 Boston. Ills. fld maps. plts. 509 p. $25.00

STARK, Richard. *Deadly Edge.* 1971 Random House. 1st ed. dj. xl. $10.00

STARKEY, Marion. *Devil in MA.* 1950 NY. VG $25.00

STARNES, Richard. *Another Mug for the Bier.* 1950 Lippincott. 1st ed. VG $8.00

STAROKADOMISKIY, L.M. *Charting the Russian Northern Sea Route.* 1976 Montreal. 322 p. dj. EX $20.00

STARR, George Ross. *How To Make Working Decoys.* 1978 Winchester. Ills. 4to. 164 p. dj. EX $25.00

STARR, J.W. *Lincoln & the Railroads.* 1927 NY. 1st ed. 325 p. $35.00

STARR, M. Allen. *Atlas of Nerve Cells.* 1896 NY. Ills. xl. G $295.00

STARR, M. Allen. *Familiar Forms of Nervous Disease.* 1890 NY. 330 p. cloth. xl. $95.00

STARR, R.F.S. *Indus Valley Painted Pottery.* 1941 Princeton U Pr. Ills. VG $20.00

STARRETT, Vincent. *Bookman's Holiday.* 1942 NY. 1st print. VG $25.00

STARRETT, Vincent. *End of Mr. Garment.* 1932 Toronto. Doubleday. 1st ed. dj. VG $27.50

STARRETT, Vincent. *Quick & the Dead.* 1965 Sauk City. 1st ed. dj. EX $40.00

STARRETT, Vincent. *Seaports in the Moon.* 1928 Doubleday Doran. 1st ed. dj. $50.00

STARRETT, Vincent. *Studies in Sherlock Holmes.* 1944 NY. 1st ed. dj. VG $100.00

STATHAM, P.; & ERICKSON, R. *Dictionary of Western Australians 1829-1914.* 1979 Australia U Pr. 3 vol set. M $45.00

STATLER, Oliver. *Black Ship Scroll.* 1964 Tuttle. 2nd Am ed. dj. EX $30.00

STATLER, Oliver. *Japanese Inn.* 1961 Random House. Ills 1st print. 365 p. VG $15.00

STAUFFER, Donald A. *Saint & Hunchback.* 1946 Simon Schuster. dj. xl. $5.00

STAVELEY, Gaylord. *Broken Waters Sing.* 1971 Little Brown. Ills. 283 p. VG $10.00

STAZZI, F. *Italian Porcelain.* 1967 NY. Ills. 128 p. $15.00

STEAD, C. *Beauties & Furies.* 1936 NY. 1st ed. dj. EX $20.00

STEAD, Christina. *Dark Places of the Heart.* 1966 NY. 1st ed. dj. EX $15.00

STEAD, Christina. *Puzzleheaded Girl.* 1967 Holt. 1st ed. dj. VG $20.00

STEAD, William T. *If Christ Came to Chicago.* reprint. red cloth. xl. EX $45.00

STEARNS, Marshall. *Along the Trail.* 1936 private print. VG $90.00

STEARNS, R.P. *Science in the British Colonies of America.* 1970 IL U Pr. facsimile. 760 p. dj. EX $30.00

STEBBING, E.P. *Diary of a Sportsman Naturalist in India.* 1920 John Lane. Ills. 298 p. VG $38.50

STEBBING, H. *Christian in Palestine.* c 1870. London. Ills Bartlett. 4to. G $20.00

STEBBING, T.R.R. *History of Crustacea.* 1893 Appleton. Ills. 466 p. VG $18.00

STEBBINS, Henry M. *Rifles: A Modern Encyclopedia.* 1958 Harrisburg. Stackpole. Ills. 376 p. $17.50

STEBBINS, Lucy & Richard. *Enchanted Wanderer: Life of Carl Maria von Weber.* 1940 NY. presentation. dj. G $18.00

STEBBINS, N.L. *Yacht Portraits of Leading American Yachts.* no date. NY. Brentano. Ills. 4to. VG $300.00

STED, Richard. *They All Bleed Red.* 1954 Simon Schuster. 1st ed. dj. VG $8.00

STEDMAN, Capt. J.G. *Narrative of a 5 Years' Expedition Against Revolted Negroes.* 1971 Imprint Soc. Ills Ltd ed. slipcase. EX $125.00

STEDMAN, E.C. *American Anthology.* 1906 Boston. inscr. VG $150.00

STEDMAN, E.C. *Blameless Prince.* 1869 Fields Osgood. 1st ed. 12mo. $15.00

STEEL, F.R. *Fishing Tackle Digest.* 1946 Paul Richmond. Ill 1st ed. 138 p. wraps. VG $25.00

STEEL, Johannes. *Future of Europe.* 1945 Holt. 1st ed. inscr. dj. VG $20.00

STEEL, Kurt. *Ambush House.* 1943 Harcourt Brace. 1st ed. VG $10.00

STEEL, Kurt. *Murder in G-Sharp.* 1938 Triangle. VG $10.00

STEEL, R. *Sharks of the World.* 1986 Facts on File. Ills. 192 p. dj. EX $24.00

STEELE, Chester K. *Golf Course Mystery.* 1919 NY. 1st ed. 8vo. 303 p. $40.00

STEELE, F. *House Beautiful Gardening Manual.* 1926 Boston. 152 p. cloth. VG $20.00

STEELE, Richard. *Plays.* 1712 London. Collected 1st ed. scarce. VG $110.00

STEELE, Richard. *Tatter & Guardian.* c 1830. 1 vol ed. $50.00

STEELMAN, R. *Call of the Arctic.* 1960 Coward McCann. 316 p. maps. VG $10.00

STEEMAN, Andre. *6 Dead Men.* 1932 Farrar Rinehart. 1st ed. G $17.50

STEEVES, Harrison R. *Good Night Sheriff.* 1941 NY. 1st ed. presentation. $75.00

STEFANSSON, Evelyn. *Here Is AK.* 1956 Scribner. Revised ed. 178 p. dj. VG $10.00

STEFANSSON, V. *Adventure of Wrangel Island.* 1925 Macmillan. Ills 1st ed. 424 p. VG $35.00

STEFANSSON, V. *Fat of the Land.* 1956 NY. Macmillan. 1st ed. sgn. 339 p. VG $30.00

STEFANSSON, V. *Friendly Artic: Story of 5 Years in Polar Regions.* 1922 Macmillan. Ills. 784 p. fld map. VG $55.00

STEFANSSON, V. *Great Adventures & Explorations.* 1947 Dial. 788 p. maps. dj. VG $12.00

STEFANSSON, V. *Great Adventures & Explorations.* 1952 NY. Revised ed. 788 p. dj. $12.50

STEFANSSON, V. *Greenland.* 1942 NY. 1st ed. EX $45.00

STEFANSSON, V. *Greenland.* 1944 Doubleday Doran. Ills. dj. VG $14.00

STEFANSSON, V. *Hunters of the Great North.* 1922 Harcourt Brace. Ills. 301 p. G $8.00

STEFANSSON, V. *Hunters of the Great North.* 1922 Harcourt Brace. Ills. 301 p. VG $12.50

STEFANSSON, V. *My Life with Eskimos.* 1927 Macmillan. Ills. maps. EX $20.00

STEFANSSON, V. *My Life with Eskimos.* 1919 NY. Macmillan. 2nd ed. sgn. VG $30.00

STEFANSSON, V. *Ultima Thule.* 1940 NY. 1st print. cloth. G $25.00

STEFFEN, R. *US Military Saddles 1812-1943.* 1976 OK U Pr. Ills. 158 p. dj. EX $20.00

STEFFENS, Josephine B. *Letitia Berkeley.* 1899 AM Stokers. inscr. G $15.00

STEGNER, Wallace. *Angle of Repose.* 1971 London. Heinemann. 1st ed. dj. VG $20.00

STEGNER, Wallace. *Angle of Repose.* 1971 Doubleday. 1st ed. 8vo. 569 p. dj. EX $25.00

STEGNER, Wallace. *Beyond 100th Meridian.* 1954 Boston. 1st ed. dj. VG $30.00

SWISHER, J.A. *IA Department of the Grand Old Army of the Republic.* 1936 IA Hist Soc. Ills. 194 p. EX $20.00

SWITZER, Lois E. *Over the Counter & Under the Shelf.* 1982 OH. Ills 1st ed. 148 p. dj. M $12.50

SYDEHAM, Thomas. *Treatise of Gout & Dropsy.* 1971 reprint of 1788. VG $15.00

SYKES, P. *History of Exploration.* 1934 London. VG $22.50

SYKES, P. *Westerly Trend.* 1944 Tucson. 1st ed. EX $55.00

SYKOROVA, Dr. Libuse. *Gauguin Woodcuts.* 1963 London. 1st ed. dj. EX $37.50

SYLVESTER, C.H. *Journeys Through Bookland.* 1922 Chicago. 10 vol set. EX $60.00

SYLVESTER, C.H. *Journeys Through Bookland.* 1909 Bellows Reeve. 10 vol set. G $40.00

SYMONDS, R.W. *English Furniture From Charles II to George II.* 1929 NY. International Studio. 1/500. $250.00

SYMONS, A.J.A. *Quest for Corvo.* 1934 NY. 1st ed. dj. VG $22.50

SYMONS, Arthur. *Notes on Joseph Conrad with Some Unpublished Letters.* 1926 London. Ltd 1st ed. 8vo. sgn. VG $27.00

SYMONS, Arthur. *Parisian Nights: Book of Essays.* 1926 Beaumont Pr. Ltd ed. 1/310. EX $75.00

SYMONS, Julian. *Bland Beginning.* 1949 London. 1st ed. dj. VG $50.00

SYMONS, Julian. *Charles Dickens.* 1951 London. 1st ed. dj. EX $35.00

SYMONS, Julian. *Detective Story in Britain.* 1962 London. 1st ed. wraps. VG $25.00

SYMONS, Julian. *End of Solomon Grundy.* 1964 London. 1st ed. dj. VG $22.00

SYMONS, Julian. *Murder! Murder!* 1961 London. 1st book ed. wraps. VG $18.00

SYMONS, Julian. *3 Pipe Problem.* 1975 NY. 1st Am ed. dj. VG $7.00

SYMONS, Julian. *31st of February.* 1950 London. Gollancz. 1st ed. dj. VG $27.00

SYNGE, J.M. *Autobiography of J.M. Synge.* 1965 Dublin. Dolmen. 1st ed. 8vo. cloth. EX $100.00

SYNGE, J.M. *Interviews & Recollections.* 1977 NY. 1st ed. dj. M $12.00

SYNGE, J.M. *Riders to the Sea.* 1911 Boston. 1st Am ed. VG $30.00

SZARKOWSKI, John. *Looking at Photographs: 100 Pictures of Collection of MOMA.* 1973 NY. 1st ed. dj. EX $35.00

SZARKOWSKI, John. *Mirrors & Windows: American Photography Since 1960.* 1978 MOMA. Ills. oblong 4to. 152 p. $12.50

SZARKOWSKI, John. *Walker Evans.* 1971 NY. dj. EX $35.00

SZARKOWSKI, John; & YAMAGUSHI. *New Japanese Photography.* 1974 MOMA. Ills. bilingual. 4to. 111 p. $10.00

SZE, Mai-Ma. *Tao of Painting.* 1956 NY. Pantheon. Ills 2nd ed. 4to. cloth. dj. $200.00

SZENT-GYORGYI, A. *Nature of Life.* 1948 Academy Pr. 1st ed. inscr. dj. $12.50

SZONYI, D.M. *Holocaust: Annotated Bibliography Resource Guide.* 1985 Ktav. G $15.00

SZONYI, D.M. *Holocaust: Annotated Bibliography Resource Guide.* 1985 NY. G $22.00

SZOSTAK & LEIGHTON. *In the Footsteps of John Paul II.* 1980 1st ed. 2nd print. $10.00

SZYK, Arthur. *Anderson's Fairy Tales Illustrated by Szyk.* no date. NY. Grosset Dunlap. VG $10.00

SZYK, Arthur. *Book of Ruth.* 1947 NY. Ills Szyk. $35.00

TABER, Edward M. *Stowe Notes, Letters, & Verses.* 1913 Boston. Ills. $15.00

TABER, Gladys. *Another Path.* 1963 Phil. 2nd ed. dj. VG $15.00

TABER, Gladys. *Another Path.* 1963 Lippincott. 1st ed. dj. VG $18.00

TABER, Gladys. *Book of Stillmeadow.* Large Print ed. 4to. 414 p. dj. EX $30.00

TABER, Gladys. *Country Chronicle.* 1974 Phil. Lippincott. Ills. 220 p. $18.50

TABER, Gladys. *Country Chronicle.* no date. Family Bookshelf. 2nd ed. dj. $15.00

TABER, Gladys. *Especially Dogs.* 1968 Phil. Lippincott. 1st ed. dj. VG $25.00

TABER, Gladys. *Especially Spaniels.* 1945 Phil. Macrae Smith. 253 p. $17.50

TABER, Gladys. *My Own Cape Cod.* 1970 Phil. 2nd ed. dj. EX $12.50

TABER, Gladys. *My Own Cookbook.* 1972 NY. 1st ed. dj. VG $50.00

TABER, Gladys. *Nurse in Blue.* 1944 Phil. Blakiston. $20.00

TABER, Gladys. *Still Cove Journal.* 1981 NY. Harper. 1st ed. dj. EX $22.50

TABER, Gladys. *Stillmeadow & Sugarbridge.* 1953 1st ed. dj. VG $25.00

TABER, Gladys. *Stillmeadow Album.* 1969 NY. Ills Shepard. 2nd ed. dj. EX $10.00

TABER, Gladys. *Stillmeadow Cookbook.* 1965 Lippincott. dj. VG $37.50

TABER, Gladys. *Stillmeadow Kitchen.* 1947 Phil. 1st ed. dj. VG $47.50

TABER, Gladys. *Stillmeadow Road.* 1984 NY. dj. EX $6.50

TABER, Gladys. *Stillmeadow Sampler.* 1959 Phil. Ills Shenton. 282 p. dj. EX $15.00

TABER, William. *DE Trees.* 1937 Dover. 250 p. VG $15.00

TAFFRAIL. *Sea Ventures of Britain.* 1925 London. Ills. 5 fld maps. VG $22.00

TAFT, J. *Practical Treatise on Operative Denistry.* 1968 Phil. Ills 2nd ed. 8vo. rebound. VG $80.00

TAFT, Robert. *Artist & Illustrators of the Old West.* 1953 Scribner. Ills. 400 p. dj. EX $30.00

TAFT, Robert. *Photography & the American Scene.* 1942 NY. 4to. cloth. EX $45.00

TAGGARD, G. *Calling Western Union.* 1936 NY. 1st ed. dj. EX $17.00

TAGORE, A.N. *Rook.* 1925 Phil. Ills. G $20.00

TAGORE, Rabindranath. *Gitanjali.* 1913 London. Intro Yeats. 12th ed. EX $35.00

TAINE, Hippolyte. *History of English Literature.* no date. NY. Nottingham Soc. Ltd Deluxe ed. $125.00

TAINE, John. *Iron Star.* 1930 NY. 1st ed. VG $25.00

TAINE, John. *Quayle's Invention.* 1927 NY. 1st ed. VG $20.00

TAKAHASHI, Masayoshi. *Color Atlas of Cancer Cytology.* 1981 Tokyo/NY. 2nd ed. dj. boxed. EX $65.00

TAKAHASHI, Seichiro. *Traditional Woodblock Prints of Japan.* 1973 Weatherhill. Ills. 175 p. dj. EX $45.00

TAKEUCHI, Tom. *Minidoka Interlude.* 1943 Hunt, ID. 1st ed. bilingual. 2 vol set. $450.00

TALBERT, Bill. *Tennis Observed.* 1967 Barre, MA. folio. dj. VG $25.00

TALBOT, Frederik A. *Moving Pictures: How They Are Made & Worked.* 1912 Phil. 340 p. VG $100.00

TALLANT, R. *Romantic New Orleanians.* 1950 Dutton. 384 p. G $5.00

TALLANT, R. *Voodoo in New Orleans.* 1946 NY. 1st ed. G $15.00

TALLANT, R. *Voodoo in New Orleans.* 1946 NY. 1st ed. dj. VG $22.50

TALLEUR, R.W. *Fly Fishing for Trout: Guide for Adult Beginners.* 1974 Winchester. Ills. 260 p. dj. EX $10.00

TALLEY, T. *Negro Folk Rhymes.* 1922 NY. Special Autograph 1st ed. G $85.00

TALLY, Joseph M. *Child's Guide to Jesus.* 1902 Switzerland. Ills. miniature book. VG $25.00

TALMAGE, John. *Cora Harris: Lady of Purpose.* 1968 GA U Pr. Ills 1st ed. 179 p. dj. VG $20.00

TALMAGE, T.D. *Social Dynamite; or, Wickedness of Modern Society.* 1889 Chicago. Ills. 8vo. 574 p. red cloth. G $16.00

TAMPION, J. *Dangerous Plants.* 1982 Universe. Ills. 176 p. dj. EX $12.00

TANAVOLI, Parviz. *Shahsavan: Iranian Rugs & Textiles.* 1985 NY. Rizzoli. Ills. oblong 4to. 435 p. dj. $90.00

TANIZAKI, J. *Makioka Sisters.* 1957 NY. 1st ed. dj. EX $20.00

TANKA, Sen'o. *Tea Ceremony.* 1973 Tokyo/NY. Kodanscha. Ills 1st ed. 214 p. $45.00

TANNENBAUM, Samuel A. *Handwriting of the Renaissance.* 1930 Columbia U Pr. 210 p. G $20.00

TANNER, Clara Lee. *Southwest Indian Painting: Changing Art.* 1973 AZ U Pr. 2nd ed. VG $35.00

TANNER, Fred W. *Practical Bacteriology.* 1933 NY. TB. 235 p. $4.00

TANNER, H. *Guns of the World.* 1977 NY. Ills. $15.00

TANNER, J.R. *Tudor Constitutional Documents 1485-1603.* 1951 2nd ed. $35.00

TANNER, Ogden. *Ranchers.* 1977 Time Life. Ills 1st ed. 4to. leather. EX $14.00

TARBELL, F.B. *History of Greek Art.* 1923 NY. Ills. 295 p. $12.50

TARBELL, Ida M. *He Knew Lincoln.* 1909 NY. Ills. 12mo. 40 p. VG $18.00

TARBELL, Ida M. *Life of Abraham Lincoln.* 1924 NY. Sangamon ed. 4 vol set. $65.00

TARBELL, Ida M. *Life of Abraham Lincoln.* 1902 NY. McClure. 2 vol set. $45.00

TARBOX, Increase N. *Sir Walter Raleigh & His Colony in America.* 1884 Boston. Ltd 1st ed. 1/250. sgn. EX $95.00

TARDIEU, Jean. *Bazaine, Aquarelles et Dessins.* 1968 Paris. Derriere Le Miroir. 1/150. $100.00

TARG, William. *American Books & Their Prices.* 1941 Chicago. Black Archer. Ltd ed. 1/500. $22.50

TARG, William. *American West.* 1946 Cleveland. 1st ed. 595 p. gray cloth. VG $14.00

TARG, William. *Bibliophile in the Nursery.* 1957 Cleveland. 1st ed. 8vo. dj. VG $50.00

TARG, William. *Bouillabaisee for Bibliophiles: Treasurey of Booklist Lore.* no date/place. Ills 1st ed. 8vo. cloth. VG $28.00

TARG, William. *Making of the Bruce Rogers' World Bible.* 1949 Cleveland. Ltd ed. 1/1,875. slipcase. $50.00

TARKINGTON, Booth. *Beasley's Christmas Party.* 1909 Harper. Ills. VG $20.00

TARKINGTON, Booth. *Beasley's Christmas Party.* 1911 Harper. Ills RS Clements. $8.50

TARKINGTON, Booth. *Beauty & the Jocobin.* 1912 NY. 1st ed. dj. EX $15.00

TARKINGTON, Booth. *Cherry.* 1903 Harper. VG $12.00

TARKINGTON, Booth. *His Own People.* 1907 NY. 1st ed. dj. VG $15.00

TARKINGTON, Booth. *In the Arena.* 1905 McClure. 1st ed. $12.50

TARKINGTON, Booth. *Looking Forward & Others.* 1926 Doubleday. $14.00

TARKINGTON, Booth. *Penrod.* 1912 NY. 1st ed. 1st issue. EX $150.00

TARKINGTON, Booth. *Presenting Lily Mars.* 1933 Garden City. 1st ed. dj. EX $20.00

TARKINGTON, Booth. *Rumbin Galleries.* 1937 Doubleday. 1st ed. 8vo. inscr. dj. EX $125.00

TARKINGTON, Booth. *Some Old Portraits.* 1939 NY. 1st trade ed. 8vo. VG $45.00

TARKINGTON, Booth. *Works of Booth Tarkington.* 1918 Garden City. Ltd ed. 1/565. sgn. VG $125.00

TARN, W.W. *Treasure of the Isle of Mist.* 1934 Putnam. Ills Robert Lawson. 184 p. VG $15.00

TARNACRE, Robert. *Beyond the Swamps.* 1929 London. Lane. 1st ed. VG $35.00

TARRANT, M. *Christmas Garland.* 1942 Boston. 1st ed. EX $25.00

TARTAR, V. *Biology of Stentor.* 1961 Pergamon. Ills. 413 p. dj. VG $15.00

TASSI, Dan. *Mind & Time & Space.* 1962 Phil. 1st print. dj. VG $25.00

TASTU, Madame Amable. *Education Maternelle.* 1852 Paris. Ills. 4to. ½ leather. dj. VG $50.00

TATE, Alfred O. *Edison's Open Door: Life of Thomas Alva Edison.* 1938 NY. 1st ed. sgn. dj. G $45.00

TATE, Allen. *Collected Poems 1922-1947.* 1948 NY. 1st ed. inscr. dj. M $145.00

TATE, Allen. *Constant Defender.* 1983 Ecco. 1st ed. dj. EX $14.00

TATE, Allen. *Forlorn Demon.* 1953 Chicago. 1st ed. dj. EX $25.00

TATE, Allen. *Memoirs & Opinions 1926-1974.* 1975 Chicago. 1st ed. inscr. dj. EX $60.00

TATE, Allen. *Memories & Essays: Old & New.* 1976 Carcanet. 1st English ed. VG $30.00

TATE, Allen. *On the Limits of Poetry.* 1948 Denver. Swallow. 1st ed. dj. VG $80.00

TATE, Allen. *Reason in Madness.* 1941 Putnam. 1st ed. dj. EX $95.00

TATE, Allen. *Selected Poems.* 1937 NY. Scribner. 1st ed. dj. scarce. EX $125.00

TATE, Allen. *Southern Vanguard.* 1947 NY. 1st ed. dj. EX $50.00

TATE, Allen. *Translation of Poetry.* 1972 GPO. 1st ed. EX $25.00

TATE, G.H.H. *Mammals of Eastern Asia.* 1947 Macmillan. Ills 1st ed. 366 p. G $18.00

TATE, James. *Destination.* 1967 Randall. Ltd 1st ed. 1/126. sgn. EX $45.00

TATE, James. *Hottentrot Ossuary.* 1974 Cambridge. Ltd 1st ed. 1/50. sgn. dj. EX $65.00

TATHAM, David. *Winslow Homer in 1880's: Watercolors, Drawings, & Etchings.* 1984 Syracuse. Ills. oblong 8vo. 32 p. wraps. $10.00

TAUBENHAUS, J.J. *Diseases of Greenhouse Crops.* 1920 NY. 429 p. G $25.00

TAUBERT, Sigfred. *Pictures & Texts About Book Trade.* 1966 NY. Bowker. Ills. 2 vol set. slipcase. EX $100.00

TAUBES, F. *Better Frames for Your Pictures.* 1953 NY. Ills. 144 p. $8.50

TAVERNER, Eric. *Trout Fishing From All Angles.* 1933 Seely Service. Ills. 444 p. dj. EX $27.50

TAWES, W.I. *Creative Bird Carving.* 1969 Tidewater. Ills. 207 p. dj. EX $15.00

TAYLERSON, A.W.F. *Revolver 1889-1914.* 1971 Crown. Ills. 324 p. dj. EX $20.00

TAYLOR, A.D. *Forest Hill Park.* 1938 Ills. 4to. fld map. VG $25.00

TAYLOR, A.N. *Coming Empire; or, 2,000 Miles in TX on Horseback.* 1936 Dallas. Turner. Revised ed. VG $12.50

TAYLOR, A.S. *Poisons in the Relation to Medical Jurisprudence & Medicine.* 1875 Lea. Ills 3rd ed. 788 p. EX $60.00

TAYLOR, Ann. *Reciprocal Duties of Parents & Children.* 1825 Boston. 1st Am ed. $45.00

TAYLOR, Bayard. *Boys of Other Countries.* 1876 NY. 1st ed. VG $65.00

TAYLOR, Bayard. *Eldorado.* 1850 London. 2nd ed. 2 vols in 1. $60.00

TAYLOR, Bayard. *Picturesque Europe.* 1878 NY. Ills. 3 vol set. EX $250.00

TAYLOR, Bayard. *Picturesque Europe.* 1875 NY. 1st ed. 3 vol set. leather. VG $175.00

TAYLOR, Benjamin. *World on Wheels & Other Sketches.* 1874 Chicago. SC Griggs. $65.00

TAYLOR, Benjamin. *World on Wheels.* 1874 Lakeside Pr. G $27.50

TAYLOR, C. *Yankee Doodle.* 1945 NY. Intro CW Williams. 1st ed. VG $25.00

TAYLOR, C. Clarke. *John Updike: A Bibliography.* 1968 Kent State. 1st ed. 8vo. black cloth. VG $10.00

TAYLOR, C.B. *Montague; or, Is This Religion?* 1833 London. Smith Elder. New ed. 12mo. VG $20.00

TAYLOR, Charles Fayette. *On the Mechanical Treatment of Diseases of Hip Joint.* 1873 NY. Ills. scarce. VG $325.00

TAYLOR, D. *Treasury of Stephen Foster.* 1946 NY. 1st print. 224 p. VG $10.00

TAYLOR, D.C. *John L. Stoddard.* 1935 NY. 1st ed. VG $20.00

TAYLOR, Deems. *Pictorial History of the Movies.* 1950 NY. Revised 1st ed. VG $10.00

TAYLOR, E. *Wedding Group.* 1968 Viking. dj. VG $15.00

TAYLOR, Elizabeth. *Mrs. Palfrey at the Claremont.* 1971 Chatto Windus. 1st ed. dj. VG $15.00

TAYLOR, Emily. *Dear Charlotte's Boys & Other Stories.* no date. London. Ills Whimper. VG $20.00

TAYLOR, F. Sherwood. *Alchemists: Founders of Modern Chemistry.* 1949 NY. Ills. 246 p. EX $35.00

TAYLOR, Francis Henry. *50 Centuries of Art.* 1954 NY. dj. $25.00

TAYLOR, Griffith. *Antarctic Adventure & Research.* 1930 NY. Ills 1st ed. G $20.00

TAYLOR, Harold. *Art & Intellect, Moral Values, & Experience of Art.* 1960 MOMA. Ills. 8vo. 62 p. wraps. $5.00

TAYLOR, Henry H. *Knowing, Collecting, & Restoring Early American Furniture.* 1930 Lippincott. Ills. 156 p. $25.00

TAYLOR, J.G. *Great Western Short Stories.* 1967 Am West Pub. slipcase. $15.00

TAYLOR, J.H. *Beavers: Their Ways.* 1904 Washburn, ND. 1st ed. VG $90.00

TAYLOR, J.W. *African Zoo in the Family.* 1965 Emerson. Ills. 185 p. dj. EX $14.00

TAYLOR, John Russell. *Art Nouveau Book in Britain.* 1966 London. Ills. EX $40.00

TAYLOR, John. *African Rifles & Cartridges.* 1977 Gun Room Pr. Ills. 431 p. dj. EX $17.50

TAYLOR, John. *African Rifles & Cartridges.* 1948 Georgetown, SC. Small Arms Pub. 1st ed. EX $150.00

TAYLOR, John. *Pondoro: Last of the Ivory Hunters.* 1955 Simon Schuster. Ills 1st ed. 354 p. dj. VG $25.00

TAYLOR, John. *Witchcraft Delusion in Colonial CT.* 1908 NY. Grafton. 172 p. $17.50

TAYLOR, Joshua C. *Futurism.* 1961 Garden City. Ills. 4to. 154 p. cloth. dj. $35.00

TAYLOR, Joshua C. *William Page: American Titian.* 1957 Chicago U Pr. G $20.00

TAYLOR, Louise. *Horse America Made.* 1944 Louisville. 1st ed. VG $10.00

TAYLOR, Malcolm. *Knight of the Air.* 1938 Boston. Christopher Pub. 1st ed. dj. $12.50

TAYLOR, Marie. *Mysterious 5.* 1930 Boston. Christopher Pub. 1st ed. dj. $12.50

TAYLOR, Mrs. H.J. *Last Survivor.* 1932 San Francisco. Ills. 22 p. $15.00

TAYLOR, P. *Woman of Means.* 1950 NY. 1st ed. dj. VG $75.00

TAYLOR, P.G. *Pacific Flight: Story of Lady Southern Cross.* no date. London. VG $25.00

TAYLOR, Peter. *Early Guest.* 1982 Palaemon Pr. Ltd ed. 1/140. sgn. wraps. $50.00

TAYLOR, Peter. *Long 4th & Other Stories.* 1948 NY. Harcourt. 1st ed. dj. EX $100.00

TAYLOR, Peter. *Old Forest & Other Stories.* 1985 NY. Dial. Uncorrected proof. EX $50.00

TAYLOR, Peter. *Old Forest & Other Stories.* 1985 Garden City. 1st ed. dj. M $12.00

TAYLOR, Peter. *Summons to Memphis.* 1986 NY. Knopf. Uncorrected proof. EX $50.00

TAYLOR, Peter. *Summons to Memphis.* 1986 NY. 1st ed. sgn. dj. M $60.00

TAYLOR, Peter. *Summons to Memphis.* 1987 London. Chatto Windus. 1st ed. dj. EX $30.00

TAYLOR, Peter. *Summons to Memphis.* 1986 NY. Knopf. 1st ed. dj. EX $35.00

TAYLOR, Phoebe Atwood. *Crimson Patch.* 1936 NY. Norton. 1st ed. EX $20.00

TAYLOR, Phoebe Atwood. *Deadly Sunshade.* 1940 NY. Norton. reprint. 1st issue. $45.00

TAYLOR, Phoebe Atwood. *Proof of the Pudding.* 1945 London. Collins. 1st ed. dj. VG $25.00

TAYLOR, Phoebe Atwood. *Spring Harrowing.* 1939 NY. Review copy. dj. EX $65.00

TAYLOR, R. *Ridin' the Rainbow: Father's Life in Tucson.* 1944 NY. Ills. sgn. dj. VG $8.00

TAYLOR, R.A. *Leonardo the Florentine.* 1929 NY. Ills. 580 p. VG $25.00

TAYLOR, Ransom. *Die Malerin Tini Rupprecht.* 1968 Muchen. Ills 1st ed. dj. EX $25.00

TAYLOR, Robert Lewis. *Adrift in a Boneyard.* 1947 NY. Doubleday. 1st ed. dj. VG $25.00

TAYLOR, Robert Lewis. *2 Roads to Guadalupe.* 1955 London. 1st English ed. dj. EX $18.00

TAYLOR, Robert. *W.C. Fields: His Follies & Fortunes.* 1949 Garden City. Doubleday. Ills 1st ed. $17.50

TAYLOR, Samuel. *Sabrina Fair.* 1954 NY. 1st ed. dj. EX $17.00

TAYLOR, T. *Sword & Swastika.* 1952 Simon Schuster. rebound. xl. G $15.00

TAYLOR, T.U. *Austin Dam.* 1910 Austin. Ills. 85 p. wraps. $30.00

TAYLOR, Walter. *4 Years with General Lee.* 1878 Appleton. $25.00

TAYLOR, William. *CA Life.* 1858 NY. Carlton Porter. fair. $20.00

TAZEWELL, Charles. *Littlest Angel.* 1946 Chicago. later print. 8vo. dj. VG $10.00

TEAGUE, C.C. *50 Years a Ranger.* 1944 no place. Ills 2nd ed. 199 p. $10.00

TEAGUE, W.D. *Design This Day: Technique of Order in Machine Age.* 1940 NY. Ills 1st ed. VG $65.00

TEALE, E.W. *Adventures in Nature.* 1959 Dodd Mead. Ills. 304 p. dj. EX $8.00

TEALE, E.W. *Autumn Across America.* 1956 Dodd Mead. Ills. 386 p. VG $8.00

TEALE, E.W. *Golden Throng: Book About Bees.* 1945 Dodd Mead. Ills. 208 p. VG $8.00

TEALE, E.W. *Naturalist Buys an Old Farm.* 1974 Dodd Mead. Ills. 306 p. dj. EX $10.00

TEALE, E.W. *North with the Spring.* 1953 Dodd Mead. Ills. 358 p. dj. VG $8.00

TEALE, E.W. *Walden: An Interpretation.* 1946 NY. Ills 1st ed. dj. VG $25.00

TEALE, E.W. *Wandering Through Winter.* 1965 Dodd Mead. Ills. 370 p. dj. VG $6.00

TEBBEL, John. *American Indian Wars.* c 1960. NY. Ills 1st ed. EX $8.50

TEFFT, B.F. *Life of Daniel Webster.* 1854 Porter Coates. tan bdg. $14.50

TEGETMEIR, W.B. *Pheasants: Natural History & Practical Management.* 1897 London. 3rd ed. 237 p. $50.00

TEGETMEIR, W.B. *Pheasants: Natural History & Practical Management.* 1904 London. Ills. VG $50.00

TEGNER, Henry. *Game for the Sporting Rifle.* 1963 London. dj. EX $18.00

TEICHERT, Minerva K. *Drowned Memories.* 1925 no place. sgn. 37 p. wraps. VG $25.00

TELEKI, Gloria Roth. *Baskets of Rural America.* 1975 NY. Dutton. Ills. 202 p. dj. $25.00

TEMPLE, A.G. *Art of Painting in the Queen's Reign.* 1897 London. Chapman Hall. 4to. 77 plts. $60.00

TEMPLE, Augusta A. *Flowers & Trees of Palestine.* 1929 London. 1st ed. dj. VG $35.00

TEMPLE, Nigel. *Seen & Not Heard: Garland of Fancies for Victorian Children.* 1970 NY. 1st Am ed. dj. VG $10.00

TEMPLE, Shirley. *Fairyland.* 1985 Random House. 5th print. dj. VG $12.00

TEMPLE, William. *Space Travel.* 1954 Prentice Hall. Ills Henry Billings. dj. VG $8.00

TENGGREN, Gustaf. *Good Dog Book.* 1924 Boston. Houghton Mifflin. Ills. VG $20.00

TENGGREN, Gustaf. *5 Bedtime Stories.* no date. Golden Pr. Big Golden Book. $10.00

TENNANT, Emma. *Wild Nights.* 1980 NY. Harcourt. 1st ed. dj. VG $20.00

TENNISON, E.M. *Elizabethan England 1553-1625.* 1933-1961. 4to. 13 vol set. $850.00

TENNYSON, Alfred Lord. *Ballads & Other Poems.* 1880 London. 1st ed. G $25.00

TENNYSON, Alfred Lord. *Ballads & Other Poems.* 1906 London. full leather. VG $20.00

TENNYSON, Alfred Lord. *Death of Oenone, Akber's Dream, & Other Poems.* 1892 London. G $30.00

TENNYSON, Alfred Lord. *Demeter & Other Poems.* 1889 London. EX $17.00

TENNYSON, Alfred Lord. *Devil & Lady.* 1930 NY. Ltd ed. 1/500. dj. VG $20.00

TENNYSON, Alfred Lord. *Fairy Lillian & Other Poems.* 1888 Boston. Estes Lauriat. Ills Humphrey. $45.00

TENNYSON, Alfred Lord. *Gareth & Lynette.* 1872 London. 1st ed. G $20.00

TENNYSON, Alfred Lord. *Idylls of the King.* 1869 London. Enlarged 1st ed. blue calf. $50.00

TENNYSON, Alfred Lord. *In Memoriam.* 1933 London. Nonesuch. VG $24.00

TENNYSON, Alfred Lord. *Last Tournament.* 1872 Boston. Osgood. EX $30.00

TENNYSON, Alfred Lord. *Locksley Hall: 60 Years After.* 1886 London. 1st ed. EX $25.00

TENNYSON, Alfred Lord. *Morte d'Arthur.* 1912 Chatto Windus. Ills Sangorski. 4to. dj. EX $50.00

TENNYSON, Alfred Lord. *Poetic & Dramatic Works of Alfred Lord Tennyson.* 1929 NY. Ltd ed. 1/500. 7 vol set. $80.00

TENNYSON, Alfred Lord. *Unpublished Early Poems.* 1931 London. Ltd 1st ed. 1/1,500. VG $45.00

TENNYSON, Alfred Lord. *Works of Alfred Lord Tennyson.* 1904 Boston. Riverside. 4 vol set. xl. $165.00

TERENCE. *Andria.* 1971 Verona. Ills Kredel. 1/160. slipcase. $400.00

TERKEL, Studs. *Division Street: America.* 1967 Pantheon. 1st ed. dj. EX $35.00

TERKEL, Studs. *Working.* 1974 Pantheon. 1st ed. dj. EX $20.00

TERRELL, J. *Bunkhouse Papers.* 1971 NY. Ills Bjorklund. dj. VG $12.00

TERRELL, J. *Indian Women of the Western Morning.* 1974 NY. 1st ed. 214 p. dj. EX $10.00

TERRES, J.K. *Audubon Book of True Nature Stories.* 1958 NY. dj. EX $12.00

TERRES, J.K. *Flashing Wings: Drama of Bird Flight.* 1968 Doubleday. Ills 1st ed. 177 p. dj. EX $12.50

TERRY. *Rawhide Tree: Story of Florence Reynolds in Rodeo.* 1957 Clarendon Pr. Ills HB Bugbee. 1st ed. $55.00

TESSIER, T. *Phantom.* 1982 Atheneum. 1st ed. dj. EX $60.00

TEY, Josephine. *Franchise Affair.* 1948 London. 1st ed. dj. $45.00

THACKER, James. *American New Dispensatory.* 1813 Boston. 2nd ed. rebound. G $75.00

THACKERAY, William M. *Collection of Letters of Thackeray.* 1887 NY. 1st ed. G $20.00

THACKERAY, William M. *Denis Duval.* 1867 London. 1st English ed. G $30.00

THACKERAY, William M. *Fitz-Boodle Papers.* 1857 London. full leather. $90.00

THACKERAY, William M. *History of Pendennis.* 1850 London. 2 vol set. rebound cloth. VG $145.00

THACKERAY, William M. *Interesting Event.* 1904 Gadshill. Ltd ed. 1/250. 32 p. G $45.00

THACKERAY, William M. *Reading a Poem.* 1911 Grolier Club. slipcase. EX $70.00

THACKERAY, William M. *Rebecca & Rowena.* 1850 London. Ills Doyle. 1st ed. 4to. $100.00

THACKERAY, William M. *Rose & Ring; or, History of Prince Giglio & Prince Bulbo.* 1898 London. Smith Elder. Ills. 8vo. 128 p. $16.00

THACKERAY, William M. *Sketches After English Landscape Painters.* no date. London. Ills. xl. VG $75.00

THACKERAY, William M. *Thackerayana: Notes & Anecdotes.* 1875 London. Chatto & Windus. 1st ed. VG $135.00

THACKERAY, William M. *Vanity Fair.* 1910 London. full leather. VG $25.00

THACKERAY, William M. *Virginians.* 1859 NY. American Books. 1st ed. VG $30.00

THACKERAY, William M. *Virginians.* 1858 London. 1st book ed. 2 vol set. EX $150.00

THACKERAY, William M. *Works of William M. Thackeray.* 1874 London. 8vo. 3/4 calf. 12 vol set. $100.00

THACKERY, William S. *Henry Esmond.* 1956 Heritage. Ills Ardizzone. 1st ed. wraps. $20.00

THANE, E. *Majestic Land.* 1950 Bobbs Merrill. Ills 1st ed. $8.50

THANET, Octave. *Book of True Lovers.* 1899 NY. sgn. $45.00

THARP, Louise Hall. *Peabody Sisters of Salem.* 1950 Boston. Ills 1st ed. inscr. dj. $20.00

THATCHER, James. *American Medical Biography of 1828.* Milford. reprint of 1828. VG $20.00

THAUSING, Julius. *Malzbereitung und Bierfabrication.* 1898 Leipzig. Ills. 4to. 1,080 p. G $25.00

THAYER, Alexander Wheelock. *Life of Ludwig van Beethoven.* 1921 NY. 3 vol set. EX $120.00

THAYER, Bert Clark. *August in Saratoga.* 1937 Sagamore Pr. 109 photos. 4to. VG $25.00

THAYER, G. *Concealing Coloration in Animal Kingdom.* 1909 Ills 1st ed. 4to. EX $100.00

THAYER, William Roscoe. *Letters of John Holmes to James Russell Lowell & Others.* 1917 Boston. VG $9.50

THAYER, William Roscoe. *Life & Letters of John Hay.* 1915 Boston. 2 vol set. VG $30.00

THEAL, G.M. *South Africa.* 1897 London. Ills. 12mo. 442 p. cloth. xl. $11.00

THEN, John N. *Christmas Comes Again.* 1939 Bruce Pub. Ills. 8vo. 135 p. dj. VG $10.00

THEOBALD, J. *Wells Fargo in AZ Territory.* 1978 Tempe. 1st ed. 210 p. dj. VG $25.00

THEROUX, Paul. *Black House.* 1974 1st English ed. dj. EX $35.00

THEROUX, Paul. *Consul's File.* 1977 Boston. 1st ed. dj. $12.00

THEROUX, Paul. *Fong & the Indians.* 1963 Boston. Houghton Mifflin. 1st ed. dj. $35.00

THEROUX, Paul. *Girls at Play.* 1969 Boston. Houghton Mifflin. 1st ed. dj. $35.00

THEROUX, Paul. *Jungle Lovers.* 1971 Boston. Houghton Mifflin. 1st ed. dj. $35.00

THEROUX, Paul. *London Embassy.* 1983 Houghton. 1st ed. dj. EX $15.00

THEROUX, Paul. *London Snow.* 1980 Ills Ltd ed. 1/300. sgn. EX $60.00

THEROUX, Paul. *Mosquito Coast.* 1982 Houghton. Ltd ed. 1/350. sgn. slipcase. $75.00

THEROUX, Paul. *Mosquito Coast.* 1982 NY. 1st trade ed. sgn. dj. EX $20.00

THEROUX, Paul. *O-Zone.* 1986 Hamilton. 1st ed. dj. EX $25.00

THEROUX, Paul. *Old Patagonian Express.* 1979 Boston. 1st ed. sgn. dj. EX $50.00

THEROUX, Paul. *Picture Palace.* 1978 Boston. 1st ed. dj. M $12.00

THEROUX, Paul. *Sailing Through China.* 1983 Russell. 1st trade ed. dj. EX $15.00

THEROUX, Paul. *Sinning with Annie.* 1972 Boston. Houghton Mifflin. 1st ed. dj. $35.00

THEROUX, Paul. *Waldo.* 1968 London. 1st English ed. dj. EX $90.00

THETFORD, Owen. *British Naval Aircraft 1912-1958.* 1958 London. Ills 1st ed. 426 p. EX $30.00

THIEL, Y.G. *Artists & People.* 1959 NY. Ills. 327 p. VG $15.00

THIMM, Franz. *Bibliotheca Shakespeareana.* 1872 London. 118 p. gilt navy cloth. G $25.00

THIRKELL, Angela. *High Rising & Wild Strawberries.* 1951 NY. Knopf. 1st Borzoi ed. 2 vol set. djs. $37.50

THIRKELL, Angela. *High Rising & Wild Strawberries.* 1951 NY. Knopf. 1st ed. 2 vol set. boxed. VG $30.00

THIRKELL, Angela. *Love at All Ages.* 1959 London. 1st ed. dj. VG $18.00

THIRKELL, Angela. *Love at All Ages.* 1959 NY. Knopf. 1st Am ed. $20.00

THIRKELL, Angela. *Northbridge Rectory.* 1942 NY. Knopf. 1st Am ed. dj. EX $22.50

THIRKELL, Angela. *Peace Breaks Out.* 1946 London. 1st ed. dj. VG $22.00

THIRKELL, Angela. *Pomfret Towers.* 1928 London. Hamish Hamilton. 1st ed. sgn. $95.00

THIRY, Paul & Mary. *Eskimo Artifacts Designed for Use.* 1977 Seattle. Superior Pub. dj. slipcase. M $35.00

THOBALD. *Moholy-Nagy: Vision in Motion.* 1947 Chicago. folio. 371 p. linen. dj. EX $60.00

THOM & FISK. *Book of Cheese.* 1821 NY. Rural TB Series. VG $20.00

THOMAS, A. *Gardening in Hot Countries.* 1965 Faber. 207 p. dj. VG $10.00

THOMAS, Alfred Barnaby. *Teodoro de Croix & Northern Frontier of New Spain 1776-83.* 1941 OK U Pr. dj. EX $35.00

THOMAS, B. Stanton. *Life & Times of Lincoln's Secretary of War.* 1962 1st ed. 8vo. 656 p. VG $25.00

THOMAS, B.F. *Goodwin's Town Officer.* 1837 Worcester, MA. 12mo. 365 p. leather. G $18.00

THOMAS, Bertram. *Arabs.* 1927 London. Butterworth. 1st print. G $35.00

THOMAS, C. *Frontier Schoolmaster.* 1880 Montreal. 1st ed. VG $35.00

THOMAS, D.G. *US Silencer Patents 1888-1972.* 1973 Paladin. Ills. 4to. 2 vol set. EX $25.00

THOMAS, D.M. *Ararat.* 1983 Viking. Advance copy. dj. EX $50.00

THOMAS, D.M. *Ararat.* 1983 Dennys. 1st Canadian ed. dj. EX $15.00

THOMAS, D.M. *Ararat.* 1983 NY. 1st ed. sgn. dj. M $15.00

THOMAS, D.M. *Boris Godunov.* 1985 6th Chamber Pr. 1st ed. 1/30. slipcase. EX $225.00

THOMAS, D.M. *Flute Player.* 1979 London. Gollancz. 1st ed. dj. EX $40.00

THOMAS, D.M. *Flute Player.* 1979 NY. 1st ed. sgn. dj. M $22.00

THOMAS, Denis. *Picasso & His Art.* 1975 NY. folio. 128 p. dj. $40.00

THOMAS, Dylan. *Adventures in the Skin Trade.* 1955 London. 1st English ed. dj. EX $120.00

THOMAS, Dylan. *Adventures in the Skin Trade.* 1955 London. 1st Separate ed. 1st issue. VG $85.00

THOMAS, Dylan. *Beach of Falesa.* 1963 NY. 1st ed. dj. M $24.00

THOMAS, Dylan. *Beach of Falesa.* 1954 London. 1st ed. dj. EX $45.00

THOMAS, Dylan. *Child's Christmas in Wales.* no date. (1969) Ills Eichenberg. 1st ed. dj. $35.00

THOMAS, Dylan. *Child's Christmas in Wales.* 1954 New Directions. 1st Am ed. dj. EX $40.00

THOMAS, Dylan. *Collected Letters.* 1985 Toronto. 982 p. dj. EX $28.00

THOMAS, Dylan. *Collected Poems.* 1953 New Directions. VG $25.00

THOMAS, Dylan. *Death of the King's Canary.* 1977 NY. 1st ed. dj. M $12.00

THOMAS, Dylan. *Map of Love.* 1939 London. 1st ed. VG $75.00

THOMAS, Dylan. *Outing.* 1971 London. 1st ed. wraps. EX $18.00

THOMAS, Dylan. *Portrait of the Artist As a Young Dog.* 1945 London. 1st ed. wraps. VG $20.00

THOMAS, Dylan. *Prospect of the Sea.* 1955 London. 1st ed. dj. VG $55.00

THOMAS, Dylan. *Quite Early 1 Morning.* 1954 New Directions. 1st Am ed. dj. EX $50.00

THOMAS, Dylan. *Quite Early 1 Morning.* 1954 New Directions. 1st ed. G $20.00

THOMAS, Dylan. *Quite Early 1 Morning.* 1954 London. 1st ed. 1st issue. dj. VG $75.00

THOMAS, Dylan. *Under Milk Wood.* 1957 London. dj. VG $10.00

THOMAS, Dylan. *Under Milk Wood.* 1954 New Directions. VG $25.00

THOMAS, Dylan. *Under Milk Wood.* 1969 Guernsey. Ltd 1st ed. 1/250. wraps. EX $27.00

THOMAS, Dylan. *20 Years A'Growing.* 1964 London. 1st ed. dj. VG $30.00

THOMAS, E.M. *Confederate Nation 1861-1865.* 1979 Harper Row. Ills 1st ed. 384 p. dj. EX $18.00

THOMAS, E.M. *Harmless People.* 1959 Knopf. Ills. 266 p. EX $13.00

THOMAS, E.M. *Mary at the Farm & Book of Recipes.* 1915 Norristown, PA. VG $25.00

THOMAS, Earl of Dundonald. *Narrative of Services: Liberation of Chili, Peru, & Brazil.* 1859 London. Ridgway. 1st ed. 2 vol set. G $125.00

THOMAS, Gordon; & WITTS, M.M. *San Francisco Earthquake.* 1971 NY. Book Club ed. dj. VG $12.00

THOMAS, Isaiah. *History of Printing in America.* 1874 Albany. Munsell. 2nd ed. 2 vol set. $120.00

THOMAS, Isaiah. *History of Printing in America.* 1970 NY. reprint of 1874. 650 p. dj. EX $15.00

THOMAS, J.J. *Rural Affairs.* Vols. II-VI. 1873 Albany. $65.00

THOMAS, James A. *Pioneer Tobacco Merchant in the Orient.* 1928 Durham. xl. $60.00

THOMAS, Jean. *Ballad Makin' in the Mountians of KY.* 1939 NY. VG $25.00

THOMAS, Jean. *Devil's Ditties.* 1931 Chicago. $20.00

THOMAS, Joseph. *Observations of Borzoi.* 1912 Boston/NY. 1st ed. VG $170.00

THOMAS, Joseph. *Universal Pronouncing Dictionary of Biography & Mythology.* 1870 Lippincott. 4to. 2 vol set. 1/2 morocco. G $100.00

THOMAS, L. *Medusa & the Snail.* 1979 Viking. 175 p. dj. VG $6.00

THOMAS, Lowell. *Count Luckner: Sea Devil.* 1927 NY. Garden City. dj. VG $50.00

THOMAS, Lowell. *So Long Until Tomorrow.* 1977 NY. 1st ed. dj. VG $15.00

THOMAS, Lowell. *With Lawrence in Arabia.* 1924 NY. reprint. VG $10.00

THOMAS, Norman. *America's Way Out.* 1931 NY. inscr. cloth. VG $25.00

THOMAS, Norman. *Appeal to the Nations.* 1947 NY. 1st ed. dj. EX $12.00

THOMAS, R. *Glory of America.* 1850 Hartford. Ills. 12mo. 574 p. leather. G $40.00

THOMAS, Rolla L. *Eclectic Practice of Medicine.* 1922 John Scudder. Ills 4th ed. EX $22.50

THOMAS, Rowan T. *Born in Battle.* 1944 Phil. Ills 1st ed. 367 p. dj. G $32.50

THOMAS. *Disney Animation.* 1981 NY. Abbeville. 1st ed. 2nd print. $55.00

THOMASON, John W. *Gone to TX.* 1937 NY. 1st ed. VG $45.00

THOMPKINS, Peter. *Magic of Obelisks.* 1981 NY. Harper Row. Ills 1st ed. 470 p. dj. EX $20.00

THOMPSON, Blanche Jennings. *All the Silver Pennies.* 1967 NY. Macmillan. Ills Arndt. 1st print. dj. EX $15.00

THOMPSON, C.J.S. *Mysteries & Secrets of Magic.* no date. NY. 320 p. dj. M $24.00

THOMPSON, C.J.S. *Mystery & Lore of Apparitions with Accounts of Ghosts.* 1930 London. 1st ed. 331 p. EX $31.00

THOMPSON, C.J.S. *Mystery & Romance of Astrology.* 1969 Detroit. reprint of 1929. 296 p. EX $26.00

THOMPSON, Clara M. *Interpersonal Psychoanalysis.* 1964 Basic. dj. EX $16.50

THOMPSON, D. *ME Forms of Architecture.* 1976 Camden. 1st ed. dj. EX $20.00

THOMPSON, Francis. *Shelley: An Essay.* 1909 Mosher Pr. 1st ed. 1/900. dj. $15.00

THOMPSON, Francis. *Sister Songs.* 1895 London. 1st ed. G $50.00

THOMPSON, G.M. *Search for the Northwest Passage.* 1975 Macmillan. Ills 1st Am ed. 288 p. EX $20.00

THOMPSON, George. *View of the Holy Land.* 1850 Wheeling. 1st ed. 8vo. 496 p. VG $50.00

THOMPSON, Hunter S. *Fear & Loathing in Las Vegas.* 1971 NY. dj. VG $48.00

THOMPSON, Hunter S. *Generation of Swine.* no date. Uncorrected proof. wraps. $75.00

THOMPSON, Hunter S. *Hell's Angels.* 1967 NY. 1st ed. dj. VG $60.00

THOMPSON, Jim. *After Dark, My Sweet.* 1955 NY. Popular Lib. 1st ed. scarce. $50.00

THOMPSON, Jim. *Hell of a Woman.* 1954 NY. Lion. 1st ed. scarce. EX $65.00

THOMPSON, Jim. *Kill-Off.* 1957 NY. Lion. 1st ed. EX $45.00

THOMPSON, Jim. *TX by the Tail.* 1965 Greenwich. Fawcett. 1st ed. pb. EX $10.00

THOMPSON, John S. *Mechanism of the Linotype.* 1908 Chicago. Inland Printer. disbound. $25.00

THOMPSON, Kay. *Eloise in Moscow.* 1959 Simon Schuster. Ill Knight. 1st print. dj. EX $50.00

THOMPSON, Kay. *Eloise in Paris.* 1957 NY. Ills 1st ed. dj. VG $35.00

THOMPSON, Kay. *Eloise.* 1957 London. Ills Knight. 1st ed. dj. G $50.00

THOMPSON, Kay. *Eloise.* 1955 Simon Schuster. Ills Knight. 2nd print. dj. $32.00

THOMPSON, Kay. *Eloise.* 1955 NY. 3rd ed. EX $20.00

THOMPSON, Kay. *Eloise.* 1955 Simon Schuster. 1st ed. dj. VG $65.00

THOMPSON, L. *Melville's Quarrel with God.* 1952 Princeton. 1st ed. VG $30.00

THOMPSON, Lawrence. *Robert Frost: Years of Triumph.* 1970 NY. Holt. 1st ed. dj. EX $20.00

THOMPSON, M. *Birds From North Borneo.* 1966 KS U Pr. wraps. EX $4.00

THOMPSON, Maurice. *Boys' Book of Sports & Outdoor Life.* 1886 NY. Ills 1st ed. 352 p. $35.00

THOMPSON, Merwin Stone. *Ancient Mariner Recollects.* c 1966. Oxford, OH. Ills 1/1,500. $25.00

THOMPSON, Morton. *Not As a Stranger.* 1955 NY. 1st ed. dj. EX $12.00

THOMPSON, R.T. *Col. James Neilson: Business Man of Early Machine Age.* 1940 New Brunswick. Rutgers. 359 p. dj. VG $12.50

THOMPSON, R.W. *At Whatever Cost: Story of the Dieppe Raid.* 1957 NY. 1st Am ed. 215 p. dj. VG $12.50

THOMPSON, Robert F. *Black Gods & Kings: Yoruba Art at UCLA.* 1976 IN U Pr. Ills. 4to. dj. VG $50.00

THOMPSON, Ruth Plumley. *Pirates of Oz.* 1931 Chicago. Reilly Lee. dj. VG $50.00

THOMPSON, Ruth Plumly. *Ojo in Oz.* 1933 Reilly Lee. dj. VG $85.00

THOMPSON, Ruth Plumly. *Princess of Cozytown.* 1922 Chicago. Ills JL Scott. 1st ed. EX $45.00

THOMPSON, Silvanus P. *Elementary Lessons in Electricity & Magnetism.* 1884 London. Ills 1st ed. 456 p. cloth. VG $35.00

THOMPSON, Toby. *Positively Main Street: Unorthodox View of Bob Dylan.* 1971 NY. G $12.00

THOMPSON. *Scotland: Her Songs & Scenery As Sung by Her Bards.* 1868 London. Ills. 8vo. gilt cloth. G $110.00

THOMSON, Belinda. *Post-Impressionists.* 1983 Secaucus, NJ. Ills 1st ed. 198 p. dj. EX $35.00

THOMSON, George. *Foreseeable Future.* 1955 Cambridge. 1st ed. 166 p. dj. VG $10.00

THOMSON, J.A. *Biology of Birds.* 1923 Macmillan. Ills. 436 p. VG $8.00

THOMSON, James. *Biographical & Critical Studies.* 1896 London. EX $20.00

THOMSON, Jeff. *Deer Hunter.* 1974 Auckland. wraps. VG $8.00

THOMSON, Joseph John. *Conduction of Electricity Through Gases.* 1903 Cambridge. 1st ed. 544 p. xl. G $40.00

THOMSON, Joseph John. *Electron in Chemisty.* 1923 Phil. Franklin Institute. 1st ed. VG $50.00

THOMSON, Joseph John. *Treatise on the Motion of Vortex Rings.* 1883 London. Macmillan. 1st ed. 8vo. $300.00

THOMSON, Richard. *Faithful Account of Processions & Ceremonies.* 1820 London. 8vo. 99 p. VG $50.00

THOMSON, Samuel. *Guide to Health; or, Botanic Family Physican.* 1835 Boston. 1st ed. 12mo. 166 p. G $35.00

THOMSON, W.M. *Land & the Bible.* 1874 London. Ills T Nelson. VG $25.00

THOMSON. *Seasons.* 1927 London. Nonesuch. 4to. cloth. EX $75.00

THONE, F.E. *Trees & Flowers of Yellowstone National Park.* 1923 Haynes. Ills. 70 p. EX $5.00

THORBURN, Grant. *40 Years Residence in America: Life of a Seedsman.* 1834 Boston. 1st ed. cloth. EX $60.00

THOREAU, H.D. *Annotated Walden.* 1970 NY. 1st ed. dj. VG $37.50

THOREAU, H.D. *Canoeing in Wilderness.* 1916 Boston/NY. Ills Will Hammell. VG $60.00

THOREAU, H.D. *Cape Cod.* 1865 Boston. 1st ed. 1/2,000. green cloth. $325.00

THOREAU, H.D. *Cape Cod.* 1968 Ltd Ed Club. Ills RJ Holden. 1/1,500. M $110.00

THOREAU, H.D. *Cape Cod.* 1914 Boston. Ills Charles Olcott. G $22.00

THOREAU, H.D. *Cape Cod.* 1896 Boston. Ills Amelia Watson. 2 vol set. $210.00

THOREAU, H.D. *Civil Disobedience.* 1969 Boston. Godine. Ltd ed. 1/650. boxed. $40.00

THOREAU, H.D. *Collected Poems of Henry David Thoreau.* 1943 Chicago. 1st trade ed. EX $70.00

THOREAU, H.D. *Complete Works of Thoreau.* 1906 Boston/NY. Walden 1st ed. 20 vol set. EX $625.00

THOREAU, H.D. *Complete Works of Thoreau.* 1949 Walden ed. 14 vol set. green cloth. VG $250.00

THOREAU, H.D. *Early Spring in MA.* 1881 Boston. 1st ed. G $40.00

THOREAU, H.D. *Essays & Other Writings of Henry David Thoreau.* 1891 London. 1st ed. EX $100.00

THOREAU, H.D. *Excursions.* 1863 Boston. 1st ed. 1/1,558. green cloth. $425.00

THOREAU, H.D. *Journal of Thoreau.* 1984 Salt Lake City. 14 vol set. M $200.00

THOREAU, H.D. *Letters to Various Persons.* 1865 Boston. 1st ed. 1/2,100. black cloth. $195.00

THOREAU, H.D. *Living Thoughts of Thoreau.* 1939 NY. VG $20.00

THOREAU, H.D. *ME Woods.* 1864 Boston. 1st ed. 1/1,450. purple cloth. $400.00

THOREAU, H.D. *ME Woods.* 1915 Boston. Riverside Pocket ed. VG $25.00

THOREAU, H.D. *Men of Concord.* 1936 Boston. Ills Wyeth. 1st ed. cloth. EX $65.00

THOREAU, H.D. *Plea for Capt. John Brown.* 1969 Boston. Ltd ed. 1/750. dj. boxed. EX $55.00

THOREAU, H.D. *Service.* 1902 1st/only print. 1/500. VG $80.00

THOREAU, H.D. *Sir Walter Raleigh.* Bibliophile Soc. Ltd ed. G $50.00

THOREAU, H.D. *Thoreau's Thoughts.* 1890 Boston/NY. Intro Blake. VG $55.00

THOREAU, H.D. *Thoreau's Writings.* 1899 Boston. Riverside ed. 11 vol set. EX $750.00

THOREAU, H.D. *Transmigration of 7 Brahmans.* 1932 NY. Rudge. Ltd ed. 1/1,200. VG $75.00

THOREAU, H.D. *Transmigration of 7 Brahmans.* 1932 NY. 1st ed. 2nd print. dj. EX $85.00

THOREAU, H.D. *Walden.* 1897 Boston. Holiday ed. 2 vol set. EX $150.00

THOREAU, H.D. *Walden.* 1854 Boston. 1st ed. EX $1450.00

THOREAU, H.D. *Walden.* 1915 Boston. Riverside Pocket ed. VG $25.00

THOREAU, H.D. *Walden.* 1946 NY. Ills Charles Locke. VG $30.00

THOREAU, H.D. *Walden.* 1909 Boston. Bibliophile Soc. 1/483. 4to. $500.00

THOREAU, H.D. *Week on Concord & Merrimack.* 1966 WV Pulp Paper. EX $30.00

THOREAU, H.D. *Week on Concord & Merrimack.* 1868 Boston. 2nd ed. 1st print. 1/2 calf. $325.00

THOREAU, H.D. *Week on Concord & Merrimack.* 1975 Ltd Ed Club. slipcase. M $100.00

THOREAU, H.D. *Writings of Henry David Thoreau.* 1894 Boston. Riverside ed. 11 vol set. EX $300.00

THOREAU, H.D. *Yankee in Canada.* 1881 Boston. Later ed. xl. EX $15.00

THORNBOROUGH, L. *Great Smoky Mountains.* 1937 Crowell. Ills. 147 p. EX $20.00

THORNDIKE, Lynn. *Sphere of Sacrobosco & Its Commentators.* 1949 Chicago. 8vo. 496 p. dj. $35.00

THORNDIKE, Rachel Sherman. *Sherman Letters.* 1894 NY. Ills 1st ed. blue cloth. G $20.00

THORNDYKE, Helen Louise. *Honey Bunch: Her 1st Summer on an Island.* 1929 Grosset Dunlap. Ills Rogers. 1st ed. EX $12.00

THORNDYKE, Helen Louise. *Honey Bunch: Her 1st Visit to the City.* 1923 NY. 1st ed. EX $15.00

THORNDYKE, L. *History of Magic & Experimental Science During 1st 13th C.* 1923 London. 2 vol set. G $65.00

THORNE, Diane. *How To Draw the Dog.* 1950 Watson Guptill. 1st ed. dj. VG $17.50

THORNE, Mrs. James Ward. *American Rooms in Miniature.* 1982 Chicago. 9th ed. wraps. $5.00

THORNE, Mrs. James Ward. *Miniature Rooms: Architectural Models.* 1940 World's Fair. Official Catalog. VG $20.00

THORNLEY, I. *England Under the Yorkists 1460-1485.* 1920 London. VG $20.00

THORNTON, I. *Darwin's Islands: Natural History of the Galapagos.* 1971 Ills. 322 p. dj. EX $14.00

THORON, Ward. *Letters of Mrs. Henry Adams.* 1936 Boston. 1st ed. dj. VG $20.00

THORP, R.W. *Doc W.F. Carver: Spirit Gun of the West.* 1957 Clarke. Ills 1st ed. 266 p. dj. VG $42.50

THORP, Roderick. *Detective.* 1966 NY. 1st ed. dj. EX $16.00

THORWALD, Jurgen. *Dismissal: Last Days of Ferdinand Sauerbruch.* 1962 NY. Pantheon. 1st ed. dj. VG $12.00

THORWALD, Jurgen. *Illusion: Soviet Soldiers in Hitler's Armies.* 1975 NY. Harcourt. 1st Am ed. 342 p. dj. VG $10.00

THRALL, R.T. *Digestion & Dyspepsia.* 1873 NY. Wells. 1st ed. cloth. VG $20.00

THRAPP, Dan. *Victorio & Mimbres Apaches.* no date. OK U Pr. 1st ed. dj. EX $23.00

THRASHER, Halsey. *Hunter & the Trapper.* 1868 NY. Judd. 1st ed. 12mo. 91 p. $50.00

THRASHER, Halsey. *Hunter & the Trapper.* 1911 NY. 12mo. cloth. $30.00

THROCKMORTON, C.W. *Genealogical & Historic Account of Throckmorton Family.* 1930 Ills. 503 p. 1/2 leather. EX $65.00

THRUDEAU, Edward Livingston. *Autobiography of Edward Livingston Thrudeau.* 1916 NY. Lea Febiger. Ills. VG $20.00

THRUM, Thomas G. *Hawaiian Folk Tales.* 1907 Chicago. Ills 1st ed. $20.00

THUILLIER, Jacques. *Rubins' Life of Marie de Medici.* 1967 NY. Abrams. Ills. folio. dj. slipcase. $175.00

THURBER, James. *Alarms & Diversions.* 1957 NY. 1st ed. dj. EX $15.00

THURBER, James. *Beast in Me & Other Animals.* 1949 London. 1st ed. dj. VG $25.00

THURBER, James. *Credos & Crimes.* 1962 London. 1st ed. dj. VG $35.00

THURBER, James. *Credos & Curios.* 1962 NY. 1st ed. dj. EX $17.00

THURBER, James. *Fables for Our Time.* 1940 NY. 1st ed. dj. VG $37.50

THURBER, James. *Further Fables for Our Time.* 1956 NY. 1st ed. dj. EX $12.00

THURBER, James. *Further Fables for Our Time.* 1956 London. 1st ed. dj. EX $25.00

THURBER, James. *Men, Women, & Dogs.* 1943 NY. 1st ed. VG $15.00

THURBER, James. *Seal in the Bedroom.* 1932 1st ed. 4to. EX $45.00

THURBER, James. *White Deer.* 1945 NY. 1st ed. dj. VG $22.50

THURBER, James. *Wonderful O.* 1957 Ills Simont. 2nd print. 8vo. dj. VG $22.50

THURBER, James. *Years with Ross.* 1959 London. 1st ed. dj. VG $30.00

THURBER, James. *13 Clocks & the Wonderful O.* 1974 London. dj. VG $10.00

THURBER, James. *13 Clocks.* 1950 Simon Schuster. Ills Marc Simont. VG $22.50

THURSTON, Carl. *Wild Flowers of Southern CA.* 1936 Pasadena. 412 p. EX $20.00

THURSTON, Lucy. *Life & Times of Lucy Thurston.* 1934 Ann Arbor. Ills 3rd ed. VG $35.00

THWAITE, Ann. *Waiting for the Party: Life of Frances Hodgson Burnett.* 1974 NY. 1st ed. dj. EX $20.00

THWAITES, R.G. *Father Marquette.* 1911 Appleton. Ills. 244 p. fld maps. EX $13.00

THWAITES, R.G. *How George Rogers Clark Won the Northwest & Other Essays.* 1903 Chicago. 1st ed. EX $65.00

TIBBLES, T.H. *Buckskin & Blanket Days: Memoirs of a Friend of the Indians.* 1957 Doubleday. 1st ed. 336 p. G $5.00

TICE, Clara. *Tales & Novels of J. De La Fontaine.* 1929 Holland. private print. Ills Ltd ed. $140.00

TICE, George. *Urban Romantic: Photographs of George Tice.* 1982 Boston. Special Ltd 1st ed. 1/100. dj. $325.00

TIDY, Rev. Gordon. *Surtees on Fishing.* 1931 NY. Ills Ltd ed. 1/500. dj. EX $100.00

TIEDJENS, V. *More Food From Soil Science.* 1965 NY. 300 p. dj. VG $5.00

TIFFANY, F. *Dorothea Lynde Dix.* 1890 Houghton Mifflin. VG $18.50

TIGGS, Oscar Lovell. *Chapters in History of Arts & Crafts Movement.* 1902 Chicago. Bohemia Guild. 198 p. $115.00

TIGHE, Richard. *Short Account of Life & Writings of Late Rev. William Law.* 1813 London. full leather. VG $135.00

TILGHMAN, Zoe. *Marshal of the Last Frontier.* 1964 2nd print. EX $75.00

TILGHMAN, Zoe. *Outlaw Days: True History of Early Day OK Characters.* 1926 Harlow. Ills. 138 p. pb. EX $20.00

TILKE, Max. *Costumes of Eastern Europe.* 1926 London. Ills. folio. 32 p. VG $250.00

TILLE, Alex. *Yule & Christmas: Their Place in the Germanic Year.* 1899 London. Ltd ed. 8vo. 218 p. VG $60.00

TILLETSON. *Grand Canyon Country.* 1929 Stanford U Pr. 1st ed. VG $25.00

TILLMAN, H.W. *When Men & Mountains Meet.* 1946 Cambridge. EX $25.00

TILLOTSON, Geoffrey. *Pope & Human Nature.* 1958 cloth. dj. xl. VG $20.00

TILTON, J.F. *Capt. George Fred.* 1928 Garden City. Ills 1st ed. 295 p. VG $25.00

TIMBS, J. *Clubs & Club Life in London.* 1967 Detroit. $20.00

TIME LIFE. *Time Life Picture Cookbook.* 1959 Ills 2nd print. folio. photos. 292 p. G $11.00

TIMMERMAN, J. *John Steinbeck's Fiction.* 1986 Norman. 1st ed. 8vo. M $22.50

TIMMERMAN, J. *Longest War.* 1982 Knopf. Advance copy. dj. EX $15.00

TIMMONS, Wilbert H. *Morelos of Mexico: Priest, Soldier, Statesman.* 1963 El Paso. TX Western Pr. Ltd ed. dj. EX $75.00

TINDALE, Thomas K. & Harriet. *Handmade Papers of Japan.* 1952 Rutland/Tokyo. 1st ed. 4 vols. wraps. $2800.00

TINDALL, W. *James Joyce: His Way of Interpreting the Modern World.* 1950 NY. 134 p. VG $12.00

TINKER, B. *Mexican Wilderness & Wildlife.* 1978 TX U Pr. Ills. 131 p. dj. EX $10.00

TINKER, E.L. *Horsemen of the Americas & the Literature They Inspired.* 1967 TX U Pr. Revised 2nd ed. 4to. dj. EX $30.00

TINKER, Frances & Edward. *Old New Orleans Strife: The '70s.* 1931 NY. green cloth. dj. M $55.00

TINKER, Jack. *Barefoot & the Open Road.* 1938 NY. Viking. Ills 1st ed. EX $10.00

TINKLE, Lon. *American Original: Life of J. Frank Dobie.* 1978 Little Brown. Ills 1st ed. 264 p. dj. VG $17.00

TINTEROW, Gary. *Master Drawings by Picasso.* 1981 NY/Braziller. Fogg Art Museum. Ills. 4to. $45.00

TIPPING, H. Avray. *Grinling Gibbons & Woodwork of His Age.* 1914 London. folio. 259 p. cloth. VG $150.00

TITCHENELL, Elsa-Brita. *Once Round the Sun.* 1950 Pasadena. Ills Gruelle. 1st ed. $25.00

TITMARSH, M.A. *Irish Sketchbook.* 1845 London. Chapman Hall. 2nd ed. VG $180.00

TITMARSH, M.A. *Mrs. Perkins' Ball.* no date. Chapman Hall. Ills. 46 p. G $40.00

TITTERTON, George F. *Aircraft Materials & Processes.* 1941 NY. Pitman. Revised ed. dj. G $20.00

TOBE, J. *Proven Herbal Remedies.* 1969 Canada. 304 p. dj. VG $10.00

TOBER, Barbara. *Bride.* 1984 Abrams. 4to. $7.50

TOBIN. *Letters of George Ade.* 1973 Purdue. 1st ed. dj. VG $10.00

TOBY, M. *Courtship of Eddie's Father.* 1961 NY. 1st ed. dj. EX $10.00

TOD, James. *Travels in Western India.* 1839 London. 4to. 9 plts. 1/2 calf. G $175.00

TODD, Rev. John. *Early Settlement & Growth of Western IA.* 1906 Des Moines. 12mo. cloth. xl. VG $25.00

TODKILL, Anas. *My Lady Pocahontas.* 1885 Houghton Mifflin. G $35.00

TOFFLER, Alvin. *Future Shock.* 1970 NY. 1st ed. dj. EX $12.00

TOFFLER, Alvin. *3rd Wave.* 1980 NY. 1st ed. dj. M $12.00

TOKLAS, Alice B. *Aromas & Flavors of Past & Present.* 1959 London. 1st ed. dj. VG $40.00

TOLAND, John. *Last 100 Days.* 1966 NY. 1st print. dj. EX $20.00

TOLKIEN, J.R.R. *Farmer Giles & Of Ham.* 1966 London. Allen Unwin. Ills 5th imp. dj. $15.00

TOLKIEN, J.R.R. *Father Christmas Letters.* 1976 Houghton. Ills. folio. white cloth. dj. $30.00

TOLKIEN, J.R.R. *Father Christmas.* 1976 Houghton. 1st Am ed. dj. EX $25.00

TOLKIEN, J.R.R. *Hobbit.* 1938 Boston. 1st Am ed. VG $150.00

TOLKIEN, J.R.R. *Lord of Rings.* no date. HrdCvr pirated ed. 3 vol set. $125.00

TOLKIEN, J.R.R. *Mr. Bliss.* 1983 Houghton. 1st Am ed. dj. EX $25.00

TOLKIEN, J.R.R. *Return of the King.* 1956 Houghton. 1st ed. dj. EX $150.00

TOLKIEN, J.R.R. *Road Goes Ever On.* 1978 Houghton. Revised 2nd ed. dj. VG $15.00

TOLKIEN, J.R.R. *Road Goes Ever On.* 1967 Boston. Houghton Mifflin. 1st ed. dj. $60.00

TOLKIEN, J.R.R. *Silmarillion.* 1977 London. 1st ed. dj. M $26.00

TOLKIEN, J.R.R. *Silmarillion.* 1977 Boston. 1st ed. dj. M $17.00

TOLKIEN, J.R.R. *Smith of Wootton Major.* 1968 London. Allen Unwin. 3rd imp. VG $10.00

TOLKIEN, J.R.R. *Smith of Wootton Major.* 1967 Boston. 1st ed. dj. EX $12.00

TOLKIEN, J.R.R. *Unfinished Tales.* 1980 Boston. 1st ed. dj. M $15.00

TOLKIEN, J.R.R. *2 Towers.* 1966 Boston. Houghton Mifflin. 2nd ed. xl. $10.00

TOLKIEN, J.R.R. *2 Towers.* 1955 Houghton. 1st Am ed. dj. EX $50.00

TOLLER, Ernest. *Look Through the Bars.* 1937 Farrar. Ills. inscr. G $12.50

TOLLER, Jane. *Turned Woodware for Collectors.* 1976 Cranbury, NJ. Ills. 8vo. 176 p. dj. $20.00

TOLSON, Francis. *Hermathenae; or, Moral Emblems & Ethnic Tales. Vol. I.* c 1740. London. xl. EX $800.00

TOLSTOY, Alexandra. *Tolstoy: Life of My Father.* 1953 NY. Ills 1st ed. inscr. cloth. dj. $40.00

TOLSTOY, Leo. *Anna Karenina.* 1939 Random House. Ills P Reisman. slipcase. $30.00

TOLSTOY, Leo. *Anna Karenina.* 1886 NY. Crowell. 1st ed. VG $150.00

TOLSTOY, Leo. *Invaders.* 1887 NY. 1st Am ed. EX $35.00

TOLSTOY, Leo. *Ivan Styitch.* 1887 NY. 1st Am ed. VG $75.00

TOLSTOY, Leo. *War & Peace.* 1938 Ills/sgn Freedman. 6 vol set. $60.00

TOLSTOY, Leo. *War & Peace.* 1949 Garden City. Ills. 741 p. $12.50

TOLSTOY, Leo. *War & Peace.* c 1965. Geneva. 3 vol set. VG $25.00

TOLSTOY, Leo. *What To Do?* 1887 NY. 1st ed. EX $17.00

TOLSTOY, Leo. *Works of Leo Tolstoy in 13 Vols.* 1885-1888. NY. Crowell. 8vo. blue cloth. $150.00

TOMES, Robert. *Battles of America.* 1861 NY. 3 vol set. VG $150.00

TOMKINS, Calvin. *Lewis & Clark Trail.* 1965 Harper Row. Ills 1st ed. inscr/sgn. dj. EX $14.00

TOMKINS, Calvin. *Living Well Is the Best Revenge.* 1971 NY. Viking. dj. VG $25.00

TOMKINSON, Constance. *Les Girls.* 1956 Boston. Ills 1st ed. dj. EX $15.00

TOMLIN, Maurice. *Catalogue of Adam Period Furniture.* 1972 Victoria/Albert Mus. 4to. $30.00

TOMLINSON, H.M. *All Our Yesterdays.* 1930 NY. 1st ed. dj. EX $15.00

TOMLINSON, H.M. *Mingles Yarn.* 1958 Indianapolis. 1st ed. dj. EX $15.00

TOMLINSON, H.M. *Sea & Jungle.* 1912 London. Duckworth. VG $65.00

TOMORY, Peter. *Life & Art of Henry Fuseli.* 1972 NY. Praeger. Ills. 4to. 254 p. dj. $60.00

TOMPKINS & BIRD. *Secret Life of Plants: Relations Between Plants & Men.* 1973 Harper. 1st ed. EX $8.50

TONEYAMA, Kojin. *Popular Arts in Mexico.* 1974 Weatherhill. 1st English ed. 226 p. $50.00

TONKIN, D. *My Partner, the River.* 1958 Pittsburgh, PA. Ills 1st ed. 276 p. dj. VG $27.50

TOOLE, K.R. *20th Century MT: State of Extremes.* 1972 OK U Pr. Ills. dj. EX $15.00

TOOLEY, R.V. *Maps & Map Makers.* 1961 Bonanza. Ills. 140 p. dj. EX $17.00

TOOLEY & BRICKER. *Landmarks of Map Making.* 1972 NY. Crowell. $70.00

TOOR, Frances. *Mexican Popular Arts.* 1939 Mexico. Frances Toor Studios. 107 p. $45.00

TOPOLSKI, Felix. *Portrait of George Bernard Shaw.* 1947 NY. Oxford. Ltd Am ed. 1/1,000. VG $30.00

TOPOLSKI, Felix. *88 Pictures by Topolski.* 1951 London. 4to. $30.00

TOPPING, E.S. *Chronicles of the Yellowstone.* 1968 Ross Haines. reprint of 1883. 279 p. dj. EX $22.00

TOPPING, E.S. *Chronicles of the Yellowstone.* 1968 Minneapolis. 1st ed. dj. VG $20.00

TOROSIAN, Michael. *Aurora.* 1987 Toronto. Lumiere Pr. 1st ed. 1/50. sgn. $135.00

TORRANCE, Arthur. *Tracking Down the Enemies of Man.* 1938 Sears. Intro Fishbein. VG $10.00

TORRENS, R.G. *Secret Rituals of the Golden Dawn.* 1973 London. 304 p. VG $35.00

TOUDOUZE, Gustave. *Le Roy Soleil.* 1904 Ills M Leloir. French text. cloth. $250.00

TOURGEE, Albion. *Fool's Errand & the Invisible Empire.* 1880 NY. Ills. 8vo. 2 vols in 1. fair. $20.00

TOURGEE, Albion. *Fool's Errand & the Invisible Empire.* 1880 NY. brown cloth. EX $30.00

TOURNEUR, Cyril. *Works of Cyril Tourneur.* 1929 London. Fanfrolico. Ltd ed. 1/750. VG $50.00

TOURTELLOT, A.B. *Charles River.* 1941 NY. 1st ed. G $12.00

TOUSEY, Frank. *How To Hunt & Fish.* 1889 NY. 60 p. wraps. VG $25.00

TOUSLEY, A.S. *Where Goes the River: Canoe Trip on MS.* c 1928. IA City. 296 p. dj. VG $15.00

TOUSSAINT, Franz. *Lost Flute & Other Chinese Lyrics.* 1929 NY. Elf. Ltd ed. 1/1,950. slipcase. EX $20.00

TOUSSAINT, Pierre. *Memoir of Pierre Toussaint.* 1854 Boston. 3rd ed. 124 p. xl. VG $25.00

TOWBRIDGE, W.R.H. *Cagliostro: Splendour & Misery of a Master of Magic.* 1910 NY. 1st Am ed. 8vo. 312 p. $35.00

TOWLE, Virginia Rowe. *Vigilante Woman.* 1966 South Brunswick. 182 p. dj. $30.00

TOWN, Salem. *Town's New Speller & Definer.* 1874 NY. Ills. 12mo. 168 p. G $12.00

TOWNE, C.W. *Her Majesty MT.* 1914 Butte. 1st ed. presentation. wraps. $10.00

TOWNE, C.W.; & WENTWORTH, E. *Cattle & Men.* 1955 OK U Pr. 1st ed. dj. EX $40.00

TOWNE, M. *Treasures in Truck & Trash.* 1949 NY. 205 p. VG $8.50

TOWNER, Wesley. *Elegant Auctioneers.* 1970 Hill Wang. Ills 1st ed. 632 p. dj. EX $15.00

TOWNLEY, Edward. *Practical Treatise on Humanity to Honey Bees.* 1843 NY. 1st ed. 12mo. 162 p. VG $100.00

TOWNSEND, C.W. *Sand Dunes & Salt Marshes.* 1913 Boston. Ills 1st ed. inscr. G $45.00

TOWNSEND, Charles. *Records of Changes in Color Among Fishes.* 1929 NY. Ills 1st ed. $75.00

TOWNSEND, George Alfred. *Life, Crime, & Capture of John Wilkes Booth.* NY. facsimile of 1865. 1/1,000. M $10.00

TOWNSEND, John S.E. *Motion of Electrons in Gases.* 1924 Oxford. Clarendon Pr. 1st ed. 35 p. $15.00

TOWNSEND, L.T. *Mosaic Record & Modern Science.* 1881 Boston. 1st ed. 86 p. EX $45.00

TOWNSEND, Virginia. *Dorothy Draycott's Tomorrows.* 1897 Boston. 1st ed. dj. VG $125.00

TOWNSEND, W.G. Paulson. *Modern Decorative Art in England. Vol. I.* 1922 NY/London. Batsford. Ills. 149 p. $145.00

TOWNSEND, Whelan. *Wilderness Hunting & Wildcraft.* 1927 Marshalltown. Ills 1st ed. 338 p. VG $42.50

TOWNSHEND, R.B. *Tenderfoot in CO.* 1968 Norman. 1st ed. 1st print. dj. VG $18.00

TOYLAND, John. *Ships in the Sky.* 1957 NY. xl. VG $18.00

TOYNBEE, A. *German Terror in France.* 1917 London. Hodder Stoughton. 1st ed. $65.00

TOYNBEE, A. *Greek Historical Thought.* 1924 London. 1st ed. EX $20.00

TOYNBEE, A. *Progress & Poverty: Criticism of Mr. Henry George.* 1883 London. 1st ed. wraps. G $30.00

TOYNBEE, A. *Study of History Vol. XII.* 1961 NY. Oxford U Pr. 2nd ed. dj. VG $27.50

TOYNBEE, A. *Study of History.* 1954 London. Oxford. 10 vol set. VG $150.00

TOZZER, A.M. *Excavation of Santiago, Mexico.* 1921 GPO. G $20.00

TRACHTENBERG, Joshua. *Devil & the Jews.* 1943 New Haven. Ills. dj. EX $45.00

TRACHTMAN, Paul. *Gunfighters.* 1974 Time Life. Ills. 238 p. EX $15.00

TRACY, M.C.; & HAVELOCK-BAILE. *Colonizer: Saga of Stephen F. Austin.* 1940 El Paso. 1st ed. dj. EX $10.00

TRAHERNE, Michael. *Be Quiet & Go Angling.* 1949 Butterworth. Ills 1st ed. 200 p. G $8.50

TRAILL, Mrs. C.P. *In the Forest; or, Pictures of Life & Scenery in Canada.* 1890 London. Nelson. Ills. 12mo. EX $45.00

TRAILL, Mrs. C.P. *Studies of Plant Life in Canada.* 1885 Ottawa. Woodberry. Ills Chamberlain. $250.00

TRAITSER, John E. *Basic Gunsmithing.* 1979 Tab Books. Ills. 288 p. EX $12.50

TRAPP, Frank A. *Attainment of Delacroix.* 1970 John Hopkins. Ills. 4to. 393 p. dj. $95.00

TRASK, Spencer. *Bowling Green.* 1898 NY. Putnam. Ills 1st ed. VG $20.00

TRAUBEL, Horace. *Camden's Compliment to Walt Whitman.* 1889 Phil. 1st ed. EX $55.00

TRAUTMAN, M.B. *Fishes of OH.* 1957 OH U Pr. Ills. 4to. 683 p. dj. VG $25.00

TRAVEN, B. *March to the Monteria.* 1971 Hill Wang. 1st ed. dj. EX $11.00

TRAVEN, B. *Rebelion de Los Colgados.* 1986 Sayrols. Spanish text. pb. EX $7.50

TRAVER, R. *Danny & the Boys.* 1951 NY/Cleveland. World. 1st ed. dj. VG $50.00

TRAVER, R. *Trouble Shooter.* 1943 NY. 1st ed. dj. EX $85.00

TRAVERS, Morris W. *Experimental Study of Gases.* 1901 London. Macmillan. Ills. 323 p. xl. VG $70.00

TRAVERS, P.L. *Mary Poppins & Mary Poppins Comes Back.* 1937 Reynal Hitchcock. VG $10.00

TREADWELL, E.G. *Cattle King: Dramatized Biography of Henry Miller of CA.* 1931 Macmillan. Ills 1st ed. $45.00

TREDGOLD, Thomas. *Tracts on Hydraulics.* 1836 London. Taylor. 2nd ed. xl. $95.00

TREDWELL. *Monograph on Privately Printed Books.* 1881 Brooklyn. 1st ed. 4to. 161 p. wraps. $30.00

TREECE, Henry. *Collected Poems by Henry Treece.* 1946 NY. 1st Am ed. dj. G $30.00

TREFETHEN, J.B. *American Crusade for Wildlife.* 1975 Winchester. Ills. 409 p. dj. EX $14.00

TREGASKIS, Richard. *Guadalcanal Diary.* 1943 NY. 1st ed. dj. VG $12.00

TREMAIN, Rose. *Swimming Pool Season.* 1985 Summit. 1st Am ed. dj. EX $17.00

TREMBLY, R. *Trails of an Alaskan Game Warden.* 1985 AK Northwest. Ills. 176 p. wraps. EX $10.00

TRENCH, B. Le Poer. *Men Among Mankind.* 1963 Ills. 207 p. dj. VG $24.00

TRENHOLM, Virginia. *WY Pageant.* 1946 Casper. sgn. dj. G $20.00

TRESIDER & HOSS. *Trees of Yosemite.* 1932 Stanford. 1st ed. dj. EX $32.00

TREVELYAN, G. Otto. *Life & Letters of Lord Macaulay.* 1876 NY. 2 vols set. VG $65.00

TREVELYN, Marie. *Land of Arthur: Its Heroes & Heroines.* 1895 London. 1st ed. VG $40.00

TREVES, F. *Country of Ring & Book.* 1913 London. Cassell. Ills. maps. VG $20.00

TREVOR, William. *Angels at the Ritz.* 1975 London. Bodley. Uncorrected proof. $65.00

TREVOR, William. *Beyond the Pale.* 1981 London. 1st ed. dj. EX $30.00

TREVOR, William. *Day We Got Drunk on Cake.* 1968 NY. Viking. Advance copy. VG $35.00

TREVOR, William. *Fools of Fortune.* 1983 London. 1st ed. dj. EX $25.00

TREVOR, William. *Love Department.* 1966 NY. Viking. 1st ed. dj. EX $30.00

TREVOR, William. *Other People's Worlds.* 1980 London. 1st ed. dj. EX $40.00

TRIGG, Elwood. *Demons & Divinities.* 1973 NJ. 238 p. dj. M $18.00

TRIGG, Roberta. *Haworth Idyll.* 1946 Richmond, VA. sgn. EX $30.00

TRILLING, Lionel. *Gathering of Fugitives.* 1957 London. 1st ed. dj. EX $12.00

TRILLING, Lionel. *Opposing Self.* 1955 NY. 1st ed. dj. EX $17.00

TRILLING, Lionel. *Sincerity & Authenticity.* 1972 Harvard U Pr. 1st ed. dj. EX $15.00

TRIMBLE, Lawrence. *Strongheart: Story of a Wonder Dog.* 1926 Whitman. Ills. 8vo. 20 p. $12.00

TRIMPEY, Alice. *Story of My Dolls.* 1935 Racine. dj. EX $24.00

TRINE, Grace H. *Dreams & Voices.* 1920 Womans Pr. NY. 1st ed. G $30.00

TRIPLETT, F. *Life, Times, & Treacherous Death of Jesse James.* 1970 Promontory. Ills. 344 p. dj. EX $5.00

TRIPP, A. *Crests From the Ocean World.* 1855 Boston. 12mo. 408 p. gilt blue cloth. $20.00

TROLLOPE, Anthony. *Last Chronicle of Barset.* 1867 London. 1st ed. 2 vol set. fair. $35.00

TROLLOPE, Anthony. *West Indies & the Spanish Main.* 1860 NY. 1st Am ed. 385 p. G $35.00

TROLLOPE, Francis. *Life & Adventures of Jonathan Jefferson Whitlaw.* 1836 London. 2nd ed. 3 vol set. EX $200.00

TROLLOPE, Mrs. *Domestic Manners of the Americans.* 1832 4th ed. G $50.00

TROSTEL, Scott D. *Bradford, the Railroad Town.* 1987 Fletcher, OH. 2nd print. 4to. maps. 152 p. M $25.00

TROW, W.S. *City in the Mist.* 1984 Boston. Review ed. dj. EX $10.00

TROY, J. Ben. *Adventures of a Hunting Retriever.* 1984 Oshkosh. Ills 1st ed. 4to. EX $14.00

TRUDEAU, Gary. *Doonesbury Chronicles.* c 1975. Holt. 1st ed. dj. VG $25.00

TRUDEL, Jean. *Silver in New France.* 1974 Ottawa. Nat'l Gallery of Canada. $45.00

TRUE, Dan. *Family of Eagles.* 1980 Everest House. Ills 1st ed. 159 p. dj. VG $14.00

TRUEBLOOD, Sarah E. *Cats by the Way.* 1904 Lippincott. Ills 1st ed. 115 p. cloth. VG $20.00

TRUEBLOOD, Ted. *Angler's Handbook.* 1949 Crowell. Ills 1st ed. 434 p. VG $15.00

TRUEBLOOD, Ted. *Ted Trueblood Hunting Treasury.* 1978 McKay. Ills. 348 p. dj. EX $10.00

TRUMAN, N.E. *Oedipus: King; by Sophocles.* 1946 Hopbon. inscr. dj. VG $40.00

TRUMAN, Nevil. *Historic Costuming.* 1937 London. Ills 3rd imp. 152 p. G $10.00

TRUMBALL, Charles G. *Pilgrimage to Jerusalem.* 1905 Phil. Ltd 1st ed. 1/735. sgn. VG $45.00

TRUMBO, Dalton. *Night of the Aurochs.* 1979 Viking. 1st ed. dj. EX $15.00

TRUMBULL, John. *M'Fingal.* 1881 NY. 1st ed. EX $16.00

TRYCKARE, T. *Whale.* 1968 Simon Schuster. Ills 1st ed. 287 p. dj. VG $26.00

TRYCKARE, T.; & CAGNER, E. *Lore of Sport Fishing.* 1976 Crown. Ills 1st ed. 4to. dj. EX $30.00

TSCHICHOLD, J. *Designing Books.* no date. NY. 1st Am ed. 4to. EX $50.00

TSCHUDI. *Travels in Peru.* 1847 London. 1st English ed. rebound. $40.00

TSE-TUNG, Mao. *Selected Military Writings.* 1963 China. 1st ed. dj. slipcase. EX $30.00

TSUJII, K. *Mastery of Japanese Flower Arrangement.* 1940 Kyoto. Ills 1st ed. $35.00

TUCHOLSKY, Kurt. *Deutschland.* 1972 MA U Pr. 4to. dj. VG $20.00

TUCKER, G. *Dawn Like Thunder.* 1963 Indianapolis. 1st ed. 487 p. maps. dj. VG $15.00

TUCKER, G. *Hancock the Superb.* 1960 Indianapolis. 1st ed. dj. VG $32.50

TUCKER, G. *Poltroons & Patriots.* 1954 Indianapolis. 1st ed. 2 vol set. djs. boxed. $40.00

TUCKER, John R. *Constitution of the US.* 1899 2 vol set. sgn John Dos Passos. $40.00

TUCKER, Sophie. *Some of These Days.* 1945 NY. 1st ed. sgn. VG $45.00

TUCKER, William J. *Man & His Destiny.* 1967 London. Pythagorean Pub. 187 p. VG $25.00

TUCKER, Wilson. *Year of the Quiet Sun.* 1975 Gregg. 1st HrdCvr ed. M $25.00

TUCKERMAN, H.T. *America & Her Commentators.* 1864 1st ed. 460 p. fair. $55.00

TUCKETT, Ivor. *Evidence for the Supernatural.* 1932 London. 16mo. 146 p. $20.00

TUDOR, Tasha. *Amy's Goose.* 1977 NY. Crowell. Ills 1st ed. 4to. 32 p. dj. VG $40.00

TUDOR, Tasha. *Around the Year.* 1957 no place. 1st Walck ed. oblong 12mo. dj. $25.00

TUDOR, Tasha. *Dolls' Christmas.* 1950 Oxford. Ills 1st ed. dj. EX $20.00

TUDOR, Tasha. *Take Joy.* 1966 1st ed. dj. EX $50.00

TUDOR, Tasha. *Tasha Tudor's Favorite Stories.* 1965 Lippincott. Ills 2nd print. 8vo. 131 p. $20.00

TUDOR, Tasha. *1st Poems of Childhood.* 1967 Platt Munk. Ills Tudor. 8vo. 45 p. dj. $18.00

TUER, Andrew W. *Forgotten Children's Books.* 1898 London. Ills 1st ed. G $50.00

TUER, Andrew W. *History of the Horn Book.* 1979 NY. reprint. EX $20.00

TUER, Andrew W. *Of London Street Cries & Cries of Today.* 1885 NY. Ills 1st ed. 16mo. G $25.00

TUFTS, Eleanor. *American Women Artists 1830-1930.* 1987 WA. Nat'l Museum of Women in Arts. $35.00

TUFTS, R. *Principles Behind Rules of Golf.* 1961 Pinehurst. dj. EX $6.50

TULLY, Jim. *Circus Parade.* 1927 NY. Ills Gropper. 3rd ed. 8vo. VG $35.00

TUME, Lynelle. *Latin American Cookbook.* 1979 NJ. EX $10.00

TUMULTY, Joseph P. *Woodrow Wilson As I Know Him.* 1921 Doubleday. 1st ed. 8vo. inscr. VG $25.00

TUNNARD, Christopher. *City of Man.* 1953 NY. Ills 1st ed. dj. EX $20.00

TUNNARD, Christopher. *Man-Made America: Chaos or Control?* 1967 New Haven. Yale U Pr. G $35.00

TURGENEV, Ivan. *Torrents of Spring.* 1976 Westport. Ltd Ed Club. Ills/sgn L Salay. $50.00

TURGENIEFF, Ivan. *Novels & Stories.* 1903 NY. Scribner. 16 vol set. $225.00

TURKLE, Brinton. *Moonlion Castle.* 1970 NY. 1st Am ed. dj. VG $7.50

TURKUS. *Murder Inc.* 1951 NY. 1st ed. dj. VG $22.50

TURNBULL, C.M. *Mountain People.* 1972 Simon Schuster. Ills. 309 p. map. dj. EX $14.00

TURNER, A. Logan. *Joseph Baron Lister 1827-1927.* 1927 Edinburgh/London. Oliver Boyd. $35.00

TURNER, H.A.B. *Collector's Guide to Staffordshire Pottery Figures.* 1971 London. Ills. 294 p. $28.00

TURNER, H.H. *Architectural Practice & Procedure.* 1925 London. 339 p. VG $15.00

TURNER, H.H. *Astronomical Discovery.* 1904 London. Arnold. 225 p. xl. VG $12.00

TURNER, J.E. *History of 1st Inebriate Asylum in the World.* 1888 NY. Ills 1st ed. 8vo. 503 p. xl. G $25.00

TURNER, John Frayn. *V.C.'s of the Air.* 1960 London. Ills 1st ed. 187 p. dj. VG $27.50

TURNER, Noel. *American Silver Flatware 1837-1910.* 1972 Ills. dj. VG $16.00

TURNER, Sharon. *History of the Anglo-Saxons.* 1823 3 vol set. 3/4 leather. $75.00

TURNER, Wallace B. *CO Woman's College.* 1962 Boulder. 1st ed. dj. VG $25.00

TUSA, Ann & John. *Nuremberg Trial.* 1984 Atheneum. 1st ed. dj. EX $20.00

TUSKA, Jon. *Billy the Kid.* 1983 Westport. Ills 1st ed. 236 p. cloth. EX $20.00

TUTHERLY, H. *Military Science & Art of War.* 1898 Burlington, VT. Ills. 8vo. 338 p. G $30.00

TUTTLE, Hudson. *Religion of Man & Ethics of Science.* 1906 Chicago. Progressive Thinker Pub. EX $22.00

TUWIM, Julian. *Wiersze de la Dzieci.* 1954 Warsaw. Ills O Siemaszko. $15.00

TWAIN, Mark. *Adventures of Huckleberry Finn.* 1885 NY. 1st Am ed. VG $180.00

TWAIN, Mark. *Adventures of Tom Sawyer.* 1937 Heritage. Ills Rockwell. VG $25.00

TWAIN, Mark. *American Claimant.* 1892 NY. Webster. Ills Dan Beard. 1st ed. EX $80.00

TWAIN, Mark. *Autobiography & 1st Romance of Mark Twain.* 1871 NY. Ills 1st ed. 1st state. 471 p. $150.00

TWAIN, Mark. *Christian Science.* 1907 NY/London. Harper. 1st ed. VG $55.00

TWAIN, Mark. *Clemens of the Call: Mark Twain in San Francisco.* 1969 Berkeley. CA U Pr. dj. EX $50.00

TWAIN, Mark. *CT Yankee in King Arthur's Court.* 1889 NY. 1st ed. 1st state. $125.00

TWAIN, Mark. *CT Yankee in King Arthur's Court.* 1917 NY. Harper. G $20.00

TWAIN, Mark. *Double-Barrelled Detective Story.* 1902 London/NY. 1st ed. EX $75.00

TWAIN, Mark. *Fireside Conversation in 1601 at Ye Time of Queen Elizabeth.* 1925 private print. Airdale Series. 1/500. wraps. $27.50

TWAIN, Mark. *Fireside Conversation in 1601.* 1955 Earth Pub. Ills R Roth. 8vo. wraps. VG $17.50

TWAIN, Mark. *Following the Equator.* 1897 Hartford. 1st ed. 1st issue. 8vo. cloth. $70.00

TWAIN, Mark. *Letters From the Earth.* 1959 Harper. 1st ed. dj. VG $22.50

TWAIN, Mark. *Prince & the Pauper.* 1882 Boston. 1st ed. 1st issue. $125.00

TWAIN, Mark. *Pudd'nhead Wilson & Those Extraordinary Twins.* 1894 Hartford. 1st Am ed. VG $100.00

TWAIN, Mark. *Pudd'nhead Wilson.* 1974 Ltd Ed Club. Ills/sgn J Groth. 1/2,000. VG $35.00

TWAIN, Mark. *Roughing It.* 1982 Time Life. reprint of 1872. 591 p. EX $18.00

TWAIN, Mark. *Sketches.* 1880 Toronto. Complete 1st ed. VG $45.00

TWAIN, Mark. *Speeches.* 1910 NY. VG $45.00

TWAIN, Mark. *Stolen White Elephant.* 1882 1st ed. VG $55.00

TWAIN, Mark. *Tale of Rats.* 1878 San Francisco. 1st ed. gilt cloth. EX $225.00

TWAIN, Mark. *Tom Sawyer Abroad.* 1894 NY. Ills Dan Beard. G $150.00

TWAIN, Mark. *Tramp Abroad.* 1880 Toronto. Belford. 1st Canadian ed. G $95.00

TWATA, Seido. *Japanese Flower Arrangement.* no date. NY. Studio. EX $35.00

TWEEDALE, Violet. *Ghosts I Have Seen & Other Psychic Experiences.* 1919 London. 312 p. fair. $22.00

TWEEDY, M. *Color Treasury of Sea Shells.* 1971 NY. Ills. 64 p. $10.00

TWIGLEY, Katherine. *Gods Await.* 1926 Point Loma. VG $20.00

TWISS, R. *Tour in Ireland in 1775.* 1777 Dublin. 3rd ed. G $50.00

TWISS, Travers. *OR Territory: Its History & Discovery.* 1846 NY. 1st Am ed. VG $60.00

TWOMBLY. *Frank Lloyd Wright.* 1973 Harper. 1st ed. dj. VG $22.50

TYLER, Anne. *Accidental Tourist.* 1986 NY. Knopf. Ltd 1st ed. sgn. M $75.00

TYLER, Anne. *Accidental Tourist.* 1985 NY. Knopf. 1st ed. sgn. dj. EX $50.00

TYLER, Anne. *Celestial Navigation.* 1974 NY. 1st ed. dj. EX $35.00

TYLER, Anne. *Dinner at the Homesick Restaurant.* 1982 NY. Knopf. Uncorrected proof. VG $90.00

TYLER, Anne. *Dinner at the Homesick Restaurant.* 1982 NY. Knopf. 1st ed. dj. EX $20.00

TYLER, Anne. *Morgan's Passing.* 1980 Knopf. 1st ed. dj. EX $50.00

TYLER, D. *Stream Conquers the Atlantic.* 1939 Appleton. Ills 1st ed. 425 p. dj. VG $30.00

TYLER, Moses Coit. *History of American Literature 1607-1783.* 1967 Chicago. dj. EX $6.00

TYLER, Ron. *Visions of America: Pioneer Artists in a New Land.* 1983 NY. Thames Hudson. 4to. 208 p. dj. $35.00

TYMMS, W.R. *Art of Illuminating As Practiced in Europe.* 1860 99 full-page plts. EX $450.00

TYNAN, Katharine. *Flower of Peace.* 1914 London. Review ed. $45.00

TYNAU, Kenneth. *Show People: Profiles in Entertainments.* 1979 NY. 317 p. dj. EX $18.00

TYNDALE, Walter. *Below the Cataracts.* 1907 60 plts. VG $28.50

TYNDALL, John. *Forms of Water in Clouds & Rivers, Ice & Glaciers.* 1876 London. King. 6th ed. 192 p. $25.00

TYNDALL, John. *Fragments of Science for Unscientific People.* 1871 London. 1st ed. G $30.00

TYNDALL, John. *Fragments of Science for Unscientific People.* 1871 NY. Appleton. 1st Am ed. 422 p. VG $35.00

TYNDALL, John. *Lectures on Light Delivered in US in 1872-1873.* 1873 NY. Appleton. 1st ed. 194 p. VG $35.00

TYNDALL, John. *Lessons in Electricity at the Royal Institution 1875-1876.* 1877 NY. Appleton. 113 p. $20.00

TYNDALL, John. *New Fragments.* 1892 NY. Appleton. 500 p. VG $20.00

TYNDALL, John. *Notes on Electrical Phenomena & Theories.* 1870 London. Longman. 1st ed. 40 p. VG $30.00

TYNDALL, John. *Sound.* 1880 NY. Appleton. 3rd ed. 448 p. $12.00

TYREE, M.C. *Housekeeping in Old VA.* 1965 Louisville. reprint of 1879. EX $25.00

TYRELL, G.N.M. *Grades of Significance.* 1947 London. Rider. 221 p. G $13.00

TYRRELL, R. & E. *Hummingbirds: Their Life & Behavior.* 1985 Crown. Ills. 256 p. dj. EX $30.00

TYSON, George. *Arctic Experiences: History of the Polaris Expedition.* 1874 NY. Harper. 1st ed. VG $110.00

TYSON, Job. *Discourse on Colonial History of Eastern & Southern States.* 1842 Phil. 1st ed. 64 p. wraps. VG $75.00

U

UBBELOHDE, Carl. *CO Reader.* 1973 Pruett. 342 p. EX $13.00

UDELSON, Joseph H. *Great Television Race.* 1982 AL U Pr. sgn. dj. EX $10.00

UDRY, Janice May. *Moon Jumpers.* 1959 Harper Row. Ills Sendak. 1st ed. 4to. G $45.00

UHDE-BERNAYS, Hermann. *Feuerbach des Meisters Gemalde.* 1913 Stuttgart. 196 p. $65.00

ULLMAN, J.R. *Kingdom of Adventure: Everest.* 1947 Sloane. Ills. 411 p. maps. dj. VG $10.00

ULLMAN, J.R. *Tiger of the Snows.* 1955 NY. 2nd print. dj. VG $6.50

ULLMAN, S. *Valentino As I Knew Him.* 1926 NY. Ills 1st ed. 8vo. VG $25.00

ULRICH, Heinz. *How the Experts Catch Trophy Fish.* 1969 Barnes. Ills 1st ed. 194 p. dj. EX $10.00

UNDERDOWN, Emily. *Gateway to Chaucer.* no date. Nelson. Ills Anderson. 4to. VG $50.00

UNDERHILL, Reuben L. *From Cowhides to Golden Fleece: Narrative of CA. 1832-1858.* Stanford U Pr. 1st ed. VG $35.00

UNDERWOOD, G. *Our Falkland's War.* 1983 Liskeard. Ills. 144 p. EX $12.50

UNDERWOOD, Michael. *Goddess of Death.* 1982 St. Martin. 1st ed. dj. EX $10.00

UNDERWOOD & MILLER. *Kingdom of Fear.* Ltd ed. 1/500. sgns. dj. slipcase. EX $100.00

UNGER, Frederick William. *Roosevelt's African Trip.* 1909 Scull. G $20.00

UNGERER, Tomi. *Beast of Monsieur.* 1971 Racine. 1st ed. dj. VG $15.00

UNITARIAN WOMEN OF GARDNER. *Ye Loaves & Fishes.* 1939 Gardner, MA. VG $48.00

UNNA, Warren. *Coppa Murals.* 1952 San Francisco. Ltd ed. 1/350. VG $85.00

UNTERMEYER, Louis. *Britannica Library of Great American Writing.* 1960 Phil. Lippincott. 2 vol set. $40.00

UNTERMEYER, Louis. *From Another World.* 1939 Harcourt. 1st ed. inscr. VG $45.00

UNTERMEYER, Louis. *Letters of Robert Frost.* 1963 NY. Holt. 1st ed. dj. EX $20.00

UNTERMEYER, Louis. *Poems of Edgar Allan Poe.* 1943 NY. Ltd Ed Club. 1/1,100. boxed. $65.00

UNTERMEYER, Louis. *Treasury of Laughter.* 1956 Simon Schuster. Ills Corcos. 712 p. VG $12.00

UNTERMEYER, Louis. *Treasury of Ribaldry.* 1956 Hanover. 675 p. VG $9.00

UPDIKE, John. *Assorted Prose.* 1965 NY. Knopf. 1st ed. 8vo. yellow cloth. dj. $50.00

UPDIKE, John. *Bech Is Back.* 1982 NY. Knopf. 1st ed. dj. EX $12.00

UPDIKE, John. *Bech: A Book.* 1970 NY. Ltd 1st ed. sgn. slipcase. $50.00

UPDIKE, John. *Bech: A Book.* 1970 Knopf. 1st trade ed. dj. EX $30.00

UPDIKE, John. *Bottom's Dream.* 1969 NY. 1st ed. $25.00

UPDIKE, John. *Buchanan Dying.* 1974 NY. Knopf. 1st ed. EX $20.00

UPDIKE, John. *Carpentered Hen.* 1958 Harper. 1st ed. rare. VG $50.00

UPDIKE, John. *Carpentered Hen.* 1982 Knopf. 1st ed. dj. EX $12.00

UPDIKE, John. *Centaur.* 1963 NY. Knopf. 1st ed. dj. VG $30.00

UPDIKE, John. *Centaur.* 1963 Cape. 1st English ed. dj. EX $45.00

UPDIKE, John. *Coup.* 1979 London. 1st ed. dj. M $15.00

UPDIKE, John. *Coup.* 1978 Knopf. 1st ed. dj. EX $20.00

UPDIKE, John. *Couples.* 1968 London. Deutsch. 1st ed. dj. VG $25.00

UPDIKE, John. *Couples.* 1968 Knopf. 1st ed. dj. VG $30.00

UPDIKE, John. *Emersonianism.* 1985 Ewert. 1st ed. 1/203. sgn. VG $75.00

UPDIKE, John. *Facing Nature.* 1985 Knopf. 1st ed. sgn. dj. M $45.00

UPDIKE, John. *Hawthorne's Creed.* 1981 Targ. Ltd ed. 1/250. sgn. EX $60.00

UPDIKE, John. *Hugging the Shore.* 1986 Knopf. Review ed. dj. EX $35.00

UPDIKE, John. *Jester's Dozen.* 1984 Lord John. Ills Ltd ed. 1/150. sgn. EX $75.00

UPDIKE, John. *Marry Me.* 1976 Knopf. Review copy. $25.00

UPDIKE, John. *Marry Me.* 1976 Knopf. 1st trade ed. dj. EX $20.00

UPDIKE, John. *Marry Me.* 1976 NY. 1st ed. dj. M $30.00

UPDIKE, John. *Midpoint & Other Poems.* 1969 NY. Ltd ed. 1/350. sgn. boxed. $110.00

UPDIKE, John. *Midpoint & Other Poems.* 1969 Knopf. 1st trade ed. dj. EX $35.00

UPDIKE, John. *Midpoint & Other Poems.* 1969 Deutsch. 1st English ed. dj. VG $30.00

UPDIKE, John. *Month of Sundays.* 1975 NY. 1st ed. dj. M $15.00

UPDIKE, John. *Month of Sundays.* 1975 Knopf. 1st trade ed. dj. EX $15.00

UPDIKE, John. *More Stately Mansions.* 1986 Nouveau. Ltd ed. 1/300. sgn. VG $65.00

UPDIKE, John. *Museums & Women & Other Stories.* 1972 Knopf. 1st ed. dj. EX $45.00

UPDIKE, John. *Museums & Women.* 1972 Knopf. 1st trade ed. dj. EX $25.00

UPDIKE, John. *Music School.* 1966 NY. Knopf. 1st ed. 1st issue. dj. M $95.00

UPDIKE, John. *Music School.* 1966 NY. 1st ed. 2nd state. dj. EX $35.00

UPDIKE, John. *Of the Farm.* 1965 Knopf. 1st ed. dj. EX $45.00

UPDIKE, John. *People One Knows.* 1980 Lord John. 1st ed. 1/100. slipcase. $110.00

UPDIKE, John. *Picked Up Pieces.* 1975 NY. Knopf. 1st ed. EX $20.00

UPDIKE, John. *Picked Up Pieces.* 1975 Knopf. 1st ed. dj. M $35.00

UPDIKE, John. *Pigeon Feathers.* 1962 NY. 1st ed. dj. EX $55.00

UPDIKE, John. *Problems & Other Stories.* 1979 NY. Knopf. 1st ed. dj. EX $25.00

UPDIKE, John. *Rabbit Redux.* 1971 NY. Knopf. 1st ed. dj. EX $30.00

UPDIKE, John. *Rabbit Redux.* 1971 Knopf. 1st trade ed. dj. EX $20.00

UPDIKE, John. *Rabbit Run.* 1960 NY. Knopf. 1st ed. 8vo. dj. VG $65.00

UPDIKE, John. *Roger's Version.* 1986 NY. Knopf. Ltd 1st ed. 1/350. boxed. M $125.00

UPDIKE, John. *Roger's Version.* 1986 Franklin Soc. 1st ed. sgn. full leather. EX $45.00

UPDIKE, John. *Same Door.* 1959 NY. dj. EX $65.00

UPDIKE, John. *Selected Stories.* 1985 Random House. Audiobooks 1st ed. M $15.00

UPDIKE, John. *Some Unrecorded Letters of Caroline Norton.* 1934 Merrymount Pr. private print. 1/75. inscr. EX $275.00

UPDIKE, John. *Talk From the '50s.* 1979 Northridge. 1st ed. 1/300. EX $70.00

UPDIKE, John. *Telephone Poles.* 1963 NY. Knopf. 1st ed. dj. EX $25.00

UPDIKE, John. *Trust Me.* 1987 NY. Knopf. Uncorrected proof. VG $65.00

UPDIKE, John. *Trust Me.* 1987 Random House. Audiobooks 1st ed. M $15.00

UPDIKE, John. *Witches of Eastwick.* 1984 London. 1st ed. dj. M $12.00

UPDIKE, John. *Witches of Eastwick.* Franklin Lib. 1st ed. sgn. VG $75.00

UPDIKE, John; & LEVINE, David. *Pens & Needles: Caricatures.* 1969 Boston. Ltd ed. 1/300. sgns. dj. $65.00

UPHAM, Caroline E. *Salem Witchcraft in Outline.* 1891 MA. Ills. 161 p. EX $30.00

UPHAM, Elizabeth. *Little Brown Monkey.* 1949 Platt Munk. Ills Hartwell. 4to. VG $15.00

UPTON, E. *Military Policy of US.* 1912 GPO. 3rd ed. 495 p. VG $20.00

UPTON, George P. *Letters of Peregrine Pickle.* 1869 Chicago. EX $150.00

UPTON, Harriet Taylor. *Our Early Presidents: Their Wives & Children.* 1890 Boston. Ills. 395 p. cloth. G $20.00

URESOVA, L. *Bohemian Glass.* 1965 Victoria/Albert Mus. 4to. $10.00

URIS, Leon. *Angry Hills.* 1955 Random House. 1st ed. dj. VG $25.00

URIS, Leon. *Exodus.* 1958 Garden City. 1st ed. dj. VG $32.00

URIS, Leon. *Topaz.* 1967 NY. 1st ed. dj. EX $15.00

URSIN, M.J. *Guide to Fishes of the Temperate Atlantic Coast.* 1977 Dutton. Ills. 262 p. dj. EX $10.00

URWIN, Gregory J.W. *Custer Victorious.* 1983 East Brunswick. 1st ed. dj. VG $25.00

US CARTRIDGE CO. *Where To Hunt American Game.* 1898 Lowell. VG $25.00

US DEPARTMENT INTERIOR. *Waterfowl Tomorrow.* 1964 GPO. Ills 1st ed. 4to. 770 p. VG $20.00

US NAVY DEPARTMENT. *Civil War Naval Chronology.* 1971 GPO. Ills. 4to. 1,090 p. EX $95.00

USSHER, A. *Face & Mind of Ireland.* 1950 NY. Intro Gogarty. 191 p. dj. VG $18.00

UTLEY, Robert M. *Reno Court of Inquiry.* 1983 Fort Collins. 2nd ed. sgn. EX $65.00

UTLEY. *4 Fighters of Lincoln County.* 1986 Ltd 1st ed. 1/150. EX $75.00

UTTERLIN. *Neither Fear Nor Hope.* 1964 NY. 1st ed. dj. EX $22.50

UTTLEY, Allison. *Great Adventure of Hare.* 1952 London. Heinemann. Ills. dj. G $7.00

UTTLEY, Allison. *Wise Owl's Story.* 1969 London. Collins. Ills Tempest. 64 p. $7.50

V

VACHSS, Andrew. *Flood.* 1985 Fine. 1st ed. dj. EX $18.00

VAIHINGER, H. *Kommentar zu Kant's Kritik der Reinen Vernunft.* 1922 Stuttgart. 2nd ed. 4to. 2 vol set. $30.00

VAIL, R.W.G. *Voice of the Old Frontier.* 1970 reprint of 1949. VG $50.00

VALE, C. *Spirit of St. Louis.* no date. Doran. 1st ed. dj. VG $15.00

VALE, R.B. *How To Hunt American Game.* 1950 Stackpole. 3rd print. dj. G $20.00

VALE, R.B. *How To Hunt American Game.* 1946 Military Service. Ills. dj. EX $10.00

VALENTINE, David. *Manual of the Corporation of NY.* 1860-1861. NY. Ills. maps. charts. rebound. $125.00

VALENTINE, G. *Chromosone Disorders: Introduction for Clinicians.* 1979 Phil. Lippincott. 2nd ed. VG $20.00

VALENTINER, W.R. *Hals: des Meisters Gemalde in 318 Abbildungen.* 1921 Stuttgart. Ills. 4to. German text. VG $30.00

VALENTINO, Rudolph. *Day Dreams.* 1923 NY. 1st ed. 8vo. VG $25.00

VALENZUELA, Luisa. *Clara.* 1976 Harcourt. 1st Am ed. dj. EX $20.00

VALERIE, C. *Caulle, Tiberlli et Prospertie.* 1772 Birmingham. Baskerville. 12mo. rebound. VG $250.00

VALERY, Paul. *Introduction to the Method of Leonardo da Vinci.* 1929 London. Curwen. Ltd ed. 1/875. 4to. $50.00

VALIN, Jonathan. *Days of Wrath.* 1982 Congdon. 1st ed. dj. EX $13.00

VALIN, Jonathan. *Dead Letter.* 1981 Dodd Mead. 1st ed. dj. EX $15.00

VALIN, Jonathan. *Life's Work.* 1986 Delacorte. Advance copy. wraps. EX $25.00

VALIN, Jonathan. *Natural Causes.* 1983 Congdon. 1st ed. dj. EX $14.00

VALJEAN, Nelson. *John Steinbeck: Errant Knight.* 1975 San Francisco. dj. EX $8.50

VALLENTIN, Antonina. *Leonardo da Vinci.* 1938 NY. 1st Am ed. $20.00

VALLERY-RADOT, Rene. *Life of Pasteur.* 1919 London. reprint. 484 p. rebound. $15.00

VAMBERY, Arminus. *Travels in Central Asia in Year 1863.* 1865 NY. Ills. pocket map. ¾-calf. VG $135.00

VAN AMEE, Lida Ostram. *Adirondack Idyl.* 1893 Dillingham. 1st ed. VG $20.00

VAN BENEDEN, P.J. *Animal Parasites & Messmates.* 1889 Appleton. Ills. 274 p. G $10.00

VAN BUREN. *Abraham Lincoln's Pen & Voice: Letters of Lincoln.* 1890 Cincinnati. Clarke. 1st ed. VG $60.00

VAN CAMPEN, H. *Our American Game Birds.* 1941 Ills Lynn Bogue Hunt. VG $32.50

VAN DE WATER, F.F. *Glory Hunter: Life of General Custer.* Bobbs Merrill. Burt ed. 2nd state. VG $35.00

VAN DE WATER, F.F. *In Defense of Worms & Other Angling Heresies.* 1970 Freshet. 182 p. slipcase. EX $8.50

VAN DE WATER, F.F. *Lake Champlain & Lake George.* 1946 Bobbs Merrill. Ills 1st ed. 381 p. maps. VG $14.00

VAN DE WATER, F.F. *Real McCoy.* 1931 Doubleday. Ills 1st ed. 305 p. dj. VG $15.00

VAN DER MARCK. *Arman.* 1984 Abbeville. 4to. dj. $15.00

VAN DER POST, Laurens. *Face Beside the Fire.* 1953 London. Hogarth. 1st ed. VG $35.00

VAN DER WAALS, J.D. *Die Continuitat des Gasformigen und Flussigen Zustandes.* 1899 Leipzig. 182 p. xl. $25.00

VAN DEVENTER, H.R. *Telephonology.* 1910 NY. Ills. 590 p. rebound. $30.00

VAN DOREN, Carl. *Secret History of the American Revolution.* 1941 NY. 1st ed. sgn. dj. $40.00

VAN DOREN, Mark. *Travels of William Bartram.* no date. Dover. Ills. 414 p. pb. EX $12.00

VAN DYKE, Henry. *Creelful of Fishing Stories.* 1932 Scribner. 1st ed. 420 p. VG $15.00

VAN DYKE, Henry. *Fisherman's Luck & Other Uncertain Things.* 1905 Scribner. Ills. 285 p. G $7.50

VAN DYKE, Henry. *Spirit of Christmas.* 1905 NY. 1st ed. dj. EX $20.00

VAN DYKE, Henry. *Spirit of Christmas.* 1933 Scribner. Ills Chagall. 12mo. dj. EX $15.00

VAN DYKE, Henry. *Story of the Other Wise Man.* 1920 NY. Ills Flanagan. 1st ed. EX $30.00

VAN DYKE, J.C. *Desert.* 1903 NY. G $12.00

VAN DYKE, T.S. *Southern CA.* 1886 NY. VG $35.00

VAN DYKE, Theodore. *Game Birds at Home.* 1895 NY. 1st ed. 219 p. $25.00

VAN DYNE, Edith. *Aunt Jane's Nieces Abroad.* 1906 Chicago. Ills. juvenile. G $22.50

VAN DYNE, Edith. *Aunt Jane's Nieces on Vacation.* Reilly Britton. 1st ed. VG $22.00

VAN DYNE, Edith. *Mary Louise in the County.* 1916 Chicago. Reilly Lee. dj. VG $35.00

VAN GOGH, Vincent. *Letters to Emile Bernard.* 1938 NY. 1st ed. dj. VG $52.00

VAN GULIK, Robert. *Judge Dee at Work.* 1967 London. 1st English ed. dj. EX $15.00

VAN GYTENBEEK, R.P. *Way of a Trout.* 1972 Lippincott. Ills 1st ed. 146 p. dj. EX $11.50

VAN HEUVEL, J.A. *El Dorado: Narrative of Circumstances.* 1844 NY. Winchester. 1st ed. 165 p. VG $150.00

VAN HISE, C.R. *Conservation of Natural Resources in the US.* 1910 Macmillan. Ills 1st ed. 8vo. VG $10.00

VAN HOOK, Weller. *Future Way.* 1928 Chicago. Rajput Pr. 220 p. VG $15.00

VAN LEER CARRICK, Alice. *Next-to-Nothing House.* 1922 Boston. Atlantic Monthly Pr. G $25.00

VAN LINSCHATEN, Jan. *Dutch Marco Polo.* 1964 NY. Ills. 8vo. cloth. dj. G $15.00

VAN LOHUIZEN-DE LEEUW, J.E. *Indo-Japanese Metalwork.* 1984 Stuttgart. Linden Mus. Ills. 218 p. $30.00

VAN LOON, H.W. *Arts.* 1939 NY. Ills. 677 p. $18.50

VAN LOON, H.W. *Arts.* 1937 NY. 677 p. dj. $25.00

VAN LOON, H.W. *How To Look at Pictures.* 1938 NY. Ills. 77 p. VG $8.50

VAN LOON, H.W. *Tolerance.* 1925 Boni Liveright. G $20.00

VAN MELLE, P. *Shrubs & Trees for the Small Place.* 1953 NY. 298 p. dj. G $8.00

VAN MELSEN, Andrew G. *From Atomos to Atom.* 1952 Pittsburgh. Duquesne U Pr. 1st ed. dj. VG $16.00

VAN MELVIN. *Big Heart.* 1957 San Francisco. Fearon. 4to. cloth. VG $45.00

VAN ORMAN, Richard A. *Room for the Night: Hotels of the Old West.* c 1966. NY. Bonanza. dj. VG $20.00

VAN RENSSELAER, Mrs. John K. *Devil's Picture-Books: History of Playing Cards.* 1893 NY. Ills 2nd ed. 4to. 207 p. VG $75.00

VAN RENSSELAER, Mrs. John K. *Goede Vrouw of Mana-Ha-Ta: At Home & in Society 1609-1760.* 1898 Scribner. 418 p. orange cloth. $35.00

VAN RENSSELAER, Stephen. *American Firearms.* 1948 Watkins Glen. Ltd 1st ed. sgn. VG $60.00

VAN RENSSELAER, Stephen. *Points on Buying a Horse.* 1904 no place. 60 p. $25.00

VAN SINDEREN, Adrian. *As We Go Galloping Along.* 1939 NY. private print. slipcase. $25.00

VAN STOCKUM, Hilda. *Kersti & St. Nicholas.* 1940 Viking. Ills 1st ed. 4to. 71 p. $18.00

VAN TASSEL, S. *19th Hole: Tales of the Fair Green.* 1901 NY. Ills 1st ed. EX $35.00

VAN THIENEN, Frithjof. *Great Age of Holland.* 1951 London. Harrap. Ills. dj. $20.00

VAN VECHTEN, C. *Music After the Great War.* 1915 Schirmer. 1st ed. VG $55.00

VAN VECHTEN, C. *Nigger Heaven.* 1951 Avon. EX $40.00

VANN & DIXON. *Brumback-Hotsinpiller Genealogy.* 1961 Englewood. 1st ed. 323 p. EX $45.00

VANN FOWLER, Albert. *Cranberry Lake 1845-1959.* 1959 Adirondack Mus. Ltd ed. 1/500. 160 p. $15.00

VANN. *TX Institute of Letters 1936-1966.* 1967 Encino. Ltd ed. sgn. EX $35.00

VAQUEZ & BORDET. *Le Coeur et l'Aorte: Etudes de Radiologie Clinique.* 1918 Paris. Bailliere. 2nd ed. G $8.00

VARADARAJAN, Lotika. *Ajrakh & Related Techniques.* 1983 Ahmedabad. New Order Book. Ills 71 p. VG $98.00

VARE, Robert. *Buckeye: Study of Coach Woody Hayes.* 1974 1st ed. 240 p. VG $9.50

VARGAS LLOSA, Mario. *Capt. Pantoja & the Special Service.* 1978 Harper. 1st Am ed. dj. VG $17.00

VARGAS LLOSA, Mario. *Green House.* 1968 Harper. 1st Am ed. dj. VG $17.00

VARGAS LLOSA, Mario. *Time of the Hero.* 1966 NY. Grove. 1st ed. dj. EX $25.00

VARLEY, John. *Ophiuchi Hotline.* 1977 NY. 1st ed. sgn. dj. EX $40.00

VARLEY, John. *Titan.* 1979 Berkeley/Putnam. sgn. dj. VG $65.00

VARLEY, John. *Wizard.* 1980 NY. Putnam. 1st ed. dj. EX $50.00

VARNEDOE, Kirk. *Vienna 1900: Art, Architecture, & Design.* 1986 NY. Ills. 4to. 320 p. cloth. dj. $50.00

VARNER, J. & J.J. *Dogs of the Conquest.* 1983 OK U Pr. Ills 1st ed. 238 p. dj. EX $20.00

VARNEY, G.J. *Gazetteer of the State of ME.* 1882 Boston. VG $40.00

VARNEY, G.L. *Reminiscences of Henry Clay Barnabee.* 1913 Boston. Chapple. 1st ed. sgn. $50.00

VASSILYEV, A.T. *Ochrana.* 1930 Phil. 1st ed. 305 p. EX $35.00

VASSOS, John. *Ballad of Reading Gaol.* 1928 Dutton. dj. VG $50.00

VASSOS, John. *Kubla Khan.* 1933 Dutton. 1st ed. VG $45.00

VASSOS, John. *Salome.* 1927 Dutton. Ills Wilde. dj. VG $50.00

VASTA, Edward. *Middle English Survey.* 1968 Notre Dame Pr. 2nd print. dj. VG $12.50

VAUGHAN, A.J. *Personal Record of 13th Regiment, TN Infantry.* 1975 Brentwood, TN. Ltd ed. 1/500. green cloth. EX $15.00

VAUGHAN, George Tully. *Papers on Surgery & Other Subjects.* 1932 WA. Roberts. Ills 1st ed. 408 p. VG $15.00

VAUGHAN, V.C. *Infection & Immunity.* 1915 Chicago. 1st ed. 238 p. VG $110.00

VAVRA, Jaroslav R. *Das Glas & die Jahrtausende.* 1955 Prague. Artia. Ills. 199 p. cloth. $175.00

VEATCH, A.C. *Quito to Gogota.* 1917 NY. VG $20.00

VEBLEN, Thorstein. *Theory of Business Enterprise.* 1904 NY. 1st ed. VG $45.00

VECSEY, George. *Getting Off the Ground: Pioneers of Aviation Speak.* 1979 NY. Dutton. Ills. 304 p. dj. xl. $10.00

VEDDER, E.B. *Beriberi.* 1913 NY. Ills 1st ed. 427 p. VG $120.00

VEDDER, Elihu. *Rubaiyat of Omar Kayyam.* 1894 Boston. Houghton. VG $60.00

VEDDER. *Rook.* 1886 Boston. Houghton Mifflin. 4to. VG $75.00

VEGETIUS. *De le Militari.* 1553 Paris. Ills. full calf. G $575.00

VEHSLAGE & HALLETT. *Diseases of Nose, Throat, & Ear.* 1900 NY. Boericke Runyon. 1st ed. VG $25.00

VELARDE, Pablita. *Old Father, the Storyteller.* 1960 Globe. sgn. EX $20.00

VELIKOVKSY. *Peoples of the Sea.* 1977 Doubleday. 1st ed. gilt blue cloth. dj. $15.00

VELIKOVSKY. *Worlds in Collision.* 1950 Doubleday. 6th print. 401 p. dj. VG $5.00

VENABLES, Bernard. *Gentle Art of Angling.* 1955 Reinhardt. Ills 1st ed. 186 p. G $7.50

VENABLES, Robert. *Experienced Angler.* 1827 London. 12mo. ½-leather. $150.00

VENEGAS, Miguel. *Natural & Civil History of CA.* 1759 London. 1st ed. 2 vol set. full calf. $1000.00

VENEZI, J. *Hungarian Cuisine.* 1958 Budapest. VG $15.00

VENTER, Al J. *Terror Fighters.* 1969 Capetown. Ills. 152 p. dj. VG $12.50

VENTURI, Lionello. *Cezanne.* 1978 NY. Skira/Rizzoli. Ills. 176 p. $35.00

VENTURI, Lionello. *Italian Painting: Creators of the Renaissance.* 1950 London. folio. 2 vol set. $135.00

VENTURI, Lionello. *Italian Painting: Creators of the Renaissance.* 1950 Skira. dj. VG $35.00

VERKADE, D.W. *Yesterday of an Artist Monk.* 1930 NY. 304 p. VG $12.50

VERLAINE. *Jadis et Naguere.* 1936 Paris. Ills Bernard Naudin. leather. $60.00

VERLET, Pierre. *Book of Tapestry History & Technique.* 1978 NY. 1st Am ed. dj. $95.00

VERLET, Pierre. *French Royal Furniture.* 1963 London. Barrie Rockliff. 201 p. dj. $75.00

VERNE, Jules. *Michael Strogoff.* 1955 NY. Scribner. Ills Wyeth. dj. xl. VG $15.00

VERNE, Jules. *Steam House. Part I. Demon of Cawnpore.* 1881 NY. 12mo. 262 p. $15.00

VERNE, Jules. *20,000 Leagues Under the Sea.* 1936 Rand McNally. Windermere Series. VG $15.00

VERNER, Elizabeth O'Neil. *Mellowed by Time.* 1947 2nd ed. sgn. dj. EX $20.00

VERNON, Edward. *Account of Expedition to Carthegena with Notes.* 1743 London. Cooper. 3rd ed. ¾-calf. $100.00

VERNON, Edward. *Original Papers Relating to Expedition to Carthegena.* 1744 London. Cooper. 1st ed. 154 p. $250.00

VERRAL, Charles S. *Zorro & the Secret Plan.* 1958 Simon Schuster. Ills H Greene. 1st ed. VG $7.50

VERRILL, A.H. *Strange Birds & Their Stories.* 1938 Page. Ills. 203 p. dj. VG $8.00

VERTREES. *Pearls & Pearling.* 1913 NY. Ills. VG $25.00

VERVLIET, H.D. *Book Through 5,000 Years.* 1972 London. Ills. boxed. EX $95.00

VERZONE, Paolo. *Art of Europe.* 1968 NY. 1st Am ed. dj. $25.00

VESEY-FITZGERALD, Brian. *British Game.* 1946 London. Ills. VG $12.00

VESTAL, Stanley. *Jim Bridger: Mountain Man.* 1946 Morrow. Ills. 333 p. maps. dj. VG $20.00

VESTAL, Stanley. *Queen of the Cow Towns: Dodge City.* 1952 NY. 1st ed. dj. VG $22.50

VESTAL, Stanley. *Short Grass Country.* 1941 NY. 1st ed. dj. VG $22.50

VESTAL, Stanley. *Sitting Bull: Champion of the Sioux.* 1965 OK U Pr. 346 p. EX $18.00

VIARDOT, Louis. *Masterpieces of French Art.* 1883 Phil. folio. 2 vol set. xl. VG $1150.00

VIAUX, Jacqueline. *French Furniture.* 1964 London. Benn. Ills. 200 p. dj. $40.00

VIAUX, Jacqueline. *French Furniture.* 1964 NY. Putman. Ills. 8vo. 200 p. dj. $20.00

VICTOR, Frances Fuller. *Atlantis Arisen; or, Talks About OR.* 1891 Phil. 1st ed. 8vo. 412 p. G $40.00

VICTOR, Frances Fuller. *River of the West.* 1974 Oakland. 1st ed. dj. VG $32.50

VICTOR, O.J. *History of American Conspiracies: Record of Treason.* 1863 1st ed. 579 p. full leather. $55.00

VICTOR, O.J. *History of Southern Rebellion.* c 1861. NY. Ills. brown cloth. G $22.00

VICTORIN, Capt. Herald. *Eaglet.* 1933 Macmillan. 1st ed. blue cloth. G $8.00

VIDAL, Gore. *City & the Pillar.* 1948 Dutton. 1st ed. dj. VG $25.00

VIDAL, Gore. *Creation.* 1981 Random House. 1st ed. dj. VG $15.00

VIDAL, Gore. *Duluth.* 1983 Random House. 1st ed. dj. EX $14.00

VIDAL, Gore. *Evening with Richard Nixon.* 1972 NY. 1st ed. dj. EX $15.00

VIDAL, Gore. *Judgement of Paris.* 1952 NY. 1st ed. dj. EX $45.00

VIDAL, Gore. *Lincoln: A Novel.* 1984 Frankin Lib. 1st ed. full leather. M $45.00

VIDAL, Gore. *Myra Breckinridge.* 1968 Little Brown. 1st ed. dj. EX $30.00

VIDAL, Gore. *Reflections on a Sinking Ship.* 1969 Boston. 1st ed. dj. EX $10.00

VIDAL, Gore. *1876.* 1976 Random House. 1st ed. dj. EX $20.00

VIDAL, Gore. *2nd American Revolution & Other Essays.* 1982 Random House. Advance copy. dj. EX $18.00

VIERECK & LITTLE. *AK Trees & Shrubs.* 1972 GPO. 265 p. VG $15.00

VIGNON, Paul. *Shroud of Christ.* c 1902. Dutton. Ills. 4to. 170 p. VG $50.00

VILAS, C.N. & N.R. *FL Marine Shells.* 1945 Aberdeen. Ills. 150 p. dj. G $8.00

VILLAR, Captain R. *Robbery & Violence at Sea Since 1980.* 1985 Greenwich. maps. dj. EX $22.50

VILLARD, O.G. *John Brown 1800-1859: Biography 50 Years After.* 1910 Boston. Ills. VG $35.00

VILLEE, C.A.; & DETHIER, V.G. *Biological Principals & Processes.* 1971 Saunders. Ills. 1,009 p. EX $18.00

VILLIARD, P. *Raising Small Animals for Fun & Profit.* 1973 Winchester. Ills. 160 p. dj. EX $11.00

VILLIERS, Alan. *Cruise of the Conrad.* 1937 NY. Ills 1st ed. dj. VG $35.00

VILLIERS, Alan. *Men, Ships, & the Sea.* 1962 Nat'l Geo Soc. Ills 1st ed. 436 p. dj. EX $18.00

VILLIERS, Alan. *Wild Ocean: Story of North Atlantic & Men Who Sailed It.* 1957 326 p. VG $9.00

VILLIERS, George. *Poems 1919-1929.* 1947 London. 1st ed. dj. EX $12.00

VILLIGER, Dr. *Brain & Spinal Cord.* 1912 Phil. EX $18.00

VILLON, Francois. *Lyrical Poems of Francois Villon.* 1979 NY. Ltd Ed Club. 1st ed. 8vo. VG $40.00

VINCENT, Frank. *Around & About South America: 20 Months Quest & Query.* 1890 NY. Appleton. Ills 1st ed. 473 p. VG $100.00

VINCENT, Frank. *Land of the White Elephant.* 1884 NY. Harper. Ills. 8vo. inscr. 383 p. $40.00

VINCENT, Harry. *Sea Fish of Trinidad.* 1910 private print. Ills 1st ed. 97 p. maps. EX $27.50

VINCENT, Howard. *Daumier & His World.* 1968 Evanston. Northwestern U Pr. 269 p. $35.00

VINCENT, Howard. *Trying Out of Moby Dick.* 1949 Boston. EX $20.00

VINCENZ, S. *On the High Uplands: Sagas, Songs, Tales, & Legends.* 1955 NY. 8vo. dj. VG $10.00

VINE, Barbara. *Dark-Adapted Eye.* 1986 Bantam. Advance copy. wraps. EX $35.00

VINGE, V. *Marooned in Realtime.* 1986 Bluejay. 1st ed. sgn. dj. EX $27.50

VINGE, V. *Peace War.* 1984 Bluejay. 1st ed. sgn. dj. EX $30.00

VINING, E. *Biography of Rufus M. Jones.* 1958 Ills 1st ed. 347 p. dj. VG $25.00

VIORST, Judith. *Alexander & the Terrible, Horrible, No Good, Very Bad Day.* 1977 Atheneum. Ills Ray Cruz. 14th ed. dj. M $12.00

VIRCHOW, Rudolph. *Cellular Pathology.* c 1867. NY. Revised 2nd ed. 554 p. EX $350.00

VIROUBOVA, Anna. *Memories of the Russian Court.* 1923 NY. wraps. EX $45.00

VISSCHER, William L. *Thrilling & Truthful History of Pony Express.* 1946 Powner. reprint. dj. EX $20.00

VISSCHER, William L. *Thrilling & Truthful History of Pony Express.* 1908 Chicago. Ills. 98 p. $32.50

VITELES, M. *Industrial Psychology.* 1932 NY. 1st ed. 8vo. cloth. 652 p. VG $15.00

VIVEKANADA, Swami. *Karma Yoka: 8 Lectures.* 1896 NY. 34 p. G $22.00

VIVEKANADA, Swami. *Lectures on Raja Yoga.* 1897 London. 234 p. G $26.00

VIZINCZEY, Stephen. *Rules of Chaos.* 1969 NY. 1st ed. dj. VG $12.50

VLACH, John M. *Afro-American Tradition in Decorative Arts.* 1978 Cleveland. Ills. 175 p. xl. $18.50

VLACH, John M. *Charleston Blacksmith: Work of Philip Simmons.* 1981 Athens. GA U Pr. Ills. 154 p. $12.50

VLIET, R.G. *Scorpio Rising.* 1985 NY. Uncorrected proof. wraps. EX $35.00

VOGT, H. *Burden of Guilt.* 1964 Oxford U Pr. Ills. SftCvr. $15.00

VOGT, H. *Burden of Guilt.* 1968 NY. 2nd ed. dj. VG $15.00

VOGT, Paul. *Best of Christian Rohlfs.* 1964 NY. Atlantis. Ills. 4to. 89 p. dj. $35.00

VOLBACH, W. Fritz. *Early Decorative Textiles.* 1969 London. Ills. 157 p. dj. $12.50

VOLKOV, Solomon. *Testimony: Memoirs of Dmitri Shostakovich.* 1979 Harper. 1st ed. dj. VG $8.50

VOLLARD, A. *Degas: Intimate Portrait.* 1927 NY. Ills 1st ed. dj. VG $30.00

VOLTAIRE. *Candide.* 1929 NY. Ills R Kent. dj. VG $45.00

VOLTAIRE. *Candide.* 1949 Ills S Adler. Intro C Van Doran. Ltd 1st ed. $55.00

VOLTAIRE. *Candide.* 1927 NY. Bennett Lib. reprint. $25.00

VOLTAIRE. *Candide.* 1930 3 Sirens Pr. Ills M Blaine. VG $8.00

VOLTAIRE. *Le Brutus avec un Discours sur la Tragedie.* 1731 Paris. EX $325.00

VOLTAIRE. *Princess of Babylon.* 1927 London. 1/1,500. 8vo. VG $28.00

VON ARCHENHOLTZ, Johann W. *History of Pirates, Free-Booters, or Buccaneers of America.* 1807 London. 1st ed. 12mo. ½-calf. $125.00

VON BOEHN, Max. *Dolls & Puppets.* 1932 London. VG $65.00

VON BOEHN, Max. *Fashions From the Middle Ages Through the 19th Century.* 1923-1937. Munchen. 8 vol set. VG $225.00

VON BOEHN, Max. *Vom Kaiserreich zur Republik.* 1917 Berlin. Ills. 507 p. ¾-leather. VG $55.00

VON BONIN, Gerhardt. *Essay on Cerebral Cortex.* 1950 Thomas. 1st ed. 150 p. VG $55.00

VON CHAMISSO, A. *Sojourn at San Francisco Bay 1816.* 1936 Grabhorn. Ills Louis Choris. Ltd ed. EX $150.00

VON ECKARDT, Wolf. *Mid-Century Architecture in America.* c 1961. Baltimore. VG $30.00

VON ELTERLEIN, Ernst. *Beethoven's Pianoforte Sonatas.* no date. London. Reeves. VG $8.00

VON ERFFA & STALEY. *Paintings of Benjamin West.* 1986 New Haven. Ills. folio. cloth. dj. $75.00

VON FALKE, Otto. *Majolica.* 1907 Berlin. Verlag. G $25.00

VON FLAKE, Jacob. *Art in the House.* 1879 Boston. Ills 1st Am ed. 4to. 356 p. $65.00

VON FRIEDEN, L. *Mushrooms of the World.* 1969 Bobbs Merrill. Ills. 439 p. dj. EX $20.00

VON HAGEN, V.W. *Frederick Catherwood.* 1950 NY. Oxford U Pr. dj. EX $18.00

VON HAMMER, Joseph. *Ancient Alphabets & Hieroglyphic Characters Explained.* 1806 1st ed. 8vo. G $200.00

VON HARBOR, Thea. *Rocket to the Moon.* 1977 Boston. 1st HrdCvr ed. EX $20.00

VON HOFFMAN, Nicholas. *2, 3, Many More.* 1969 Chicago. 1st ed. dj. VG $12.50

VON HUMBOLDT, Alexander. *Cosmo: Sketch & Physical Description of the Universe.* no date. NY. 5 vols in 2. VG $35.00

VON KARMAN, Theodore. *Daniel Guggenheim Airship Institute Publication No. 1.* 1933 Akron. 68 p. wraps. VG $15.00

VON KARMAN, Theodore. *Wind & Beyond: Theodore Von Karman, Pioneer in Aviation.* 1967 Boston. Ills 1st ed. 376 p. $17.50

VON KARMAN, Theodore. *Wind & Beyond: Theodore Von Karman, Pioneer in Aviation.* 1967 Little Brown. Ills 2nd ed. 376 p. dj. EX $15.00

VON KLENNER, Katharine. *Greater Revelation.* 1925 NY. 259 p. VG $22.00

VON KULTERMAN, U. *Kenzo Tange 1946-1969.* 1970 Zurich. Artemis. Ills. trilingual. VG $85.00

VON LANG, J. *Martin Bormann: Man Who Manipulated Hitler.* 1979 Random House. Ills. VG $12.50

VON MANSTEIN, E. *Lost Victories.* 1958 Chicago. 1st ed. dj. EX $35.00

VON MELLENTHIN, F.W. *Panzer Battles.* 1956 Norman, OK. Ills 1st ed. maps. dj. EX $45.00

VON MELLENTHIN, F.W. *Panzer Battles.* 1964 Norman, OK. dj. EX $15.00

VON MOLO, Walter. *Fugen des Seins.* 1924 Leipzig. Ills Jaechet. 1/550. sgns. $475.00

VON PERCKHAMMER, H. *China & the Chinese.* c1940. London. Routledge. Ills. 12mo. $20.00

VON SALDERN, Axel. *Brooklyn: Triumph of Realism.* 1967 Greenwich. Ills. 4to. 187 p. cloth. dj. $25.00

VON SCHALBRENDORFF, F. *Secret War Against Hitler.* 1965 NY. Ills. dj. G $20.00

VON WAGNER, Dr. Wilhelm. *Hellas: Das Land und Volk der Alten Griechen.* 1911 Leipzig. Spamer. Ills. 675 p. cloth. VG $37.50

VON WINNING, H. *Pre-Columbian Art of Mexico & Central America.* NY. Abrams. Ills. folio. cloth. dj. VG $150.00

VON WUTHENAU, Alexander. *Art of Terra Cotta Pottery in Pre-Columbian Central America.* 1965 NY. Greystone. Ills. 203 p. dj. $20.00

VONNEGUT, Kurt. *Bluebeard.* 1987 NY. 1st ed. dj. M $15.00

VONNEGUT, Kurt. *Bluebeard.* 1987 NY. Ltd ed. 1/500. sgn. slipcase. $60.00

VONNEGUT, Kurt. *Breakfast of Champions.* 1973 Delacorte. 1st ed. dj. EX $20.00

VONNEGUT, Kurt. *Cat's Cradle.* 1963 NY. 1st ed. sgn. dj. VG $125.00

VONNEGUT, Kurt. *Dead-Eye Dick.* 1982 NY. 1st ed. sgn. dj. M $20.00

VONNEGUT, Kurt. *Dead-Eye Dick.* 1982 Delacorte. 1st trade ed. dj. EX $15.00

VONNEGUT, Kurt. *Galapagos.* 1985 Delacorte. 1st ed. dj. EX $7.00

VONNEGUT, Kurt. *Galapagos.* 1985 Sgn Ltd Eds. 1st ed. full leather. M $80.00

VONNEGUT, Kurt. *Galapagos.* 1985 Delacorte. Advance copy. EX $50.00

VONNEGUT, Kurt. *Jailbird.* 1979 Delacorte. 1st trade ed. dj. EX $20.00

VONNEGUT, Kurt. *Mother Night.* 1966 NY. Harper. Review copy. 1st HrdCvr ed. M $125.00

VONNEGUT, Kurt. *Mother Night.* 1966 NY. 1st HrdCvr ed. dj. EX $80.00

VONNEGUT, Kurt. *Mother Night.* 1966 Greenwich. Fawcett. 1st ed. pb. $25.00

VONNEGUT, Kurt. *Nothing Is Lost Save Honor.* 1985 Nouveau Pr. 1st ed. 1/300. sgn. EX $65.00

VONNEGUT, Kurt. *Palm Sunday.* 1981 London. 1st English ed. dj. EX $20.00

VONNEGUT, Kurt. *Palm Sunday.* 1981 Delacorte. Ltd 1st ed. sgn. slipcase. M $60.00

VONNEGUT, Kurt. *Palm Sunday.* 1981 Delacorte. 1st trade ed. dj. EX $20.00

VONNEGUT, Kurt. *Player Piano.* 1952 NY. 1st ed. dj. VG $160.00

VONNEGUT, Kurt. *Sirens of Titan.* 1959 Dell. 1st ed. pb. EX $15.00

VONNEGUT, Kurt. *Slapstick.* 1976 Delacorte. 1st trade ed. dj. EX $15.00

VONNEGUT, Kurt. *Slapstick.* 1976 Franklin Lib. Ills Robert A Parker. Ltd ed. $35.00

VONNEGUT, Kurt. *Sun, Moon, Star.* 1980 Harper. 1st ed. folio. dj. VG $12.00

VONNEGUT, Kurt. *Welcome to the Monkey House.* 1968 NY. Delacorte. 1st ed. dj. VG $35.00

VORONOFF, Serge. *Sources of Life.* 1943 Boston. Humphries. 1st Am ed. dj. VG $20.00

VOSBURGH, W.S. *Cherry & Black: Career of Mr. Pierre Lorillard on Turf.* 1916 private print. 1st ed. 158 p. EX $45.00

VOSE, Ruth Hurst. *Glass: Connoisseur's Illustrated Guide.* 1975 London. 1st ed. dj. EX $25.00

VOSS, G.L. *Cephalopods of the Philippine Islands.* 1963 Ills. 180 p. wraps. $18.00

VOYCE, Arthur. *Russian Architecture: Trends in Nationalism & Modernism.* 1948 NY. Philosophical. Ills. 296 p. $25.00

VREELAND, F. *Dishonored.* 1931 Grosset Dunlap. dj. EX $8.00

VROOMAN, J. *Clarisa Putman of Tribes Hill.* 1950 NY. 1st ed. VG $22.50

VUKELICH, George. *Fisherman's Beach.* 1962 NY. 1st ed. dj. EX $10.00

WA-SHA-QUON-ASIN (GRAY OWL). *Tales of an Empty Cabin.* 1936 NY. photos. G $15.00

WADDELL, L. Austine. *Buddhism of Tibet; or, Lamaism.* 1935 2nd ed. 598 p. dj. G $60.00

WADE, Allan. *Bibliography of Writings of William Butler Yeats.* 1951 London. 1st ed. dj. VG $95.00

WADLEY, N. *Cubism.* 1970 London. Ills. 189 p. $18.00

WADSWORTH, Wallace. *Paul Bunyan & His Great Blue Ox.* 1951 Doubleday. Ills Will Crawford. G $7.00

WAGENKNECHT. *Fireside Book of Christmas Stories.* 1945 Bobbs Merrill. Ills. 8vo. gilt cloth. VG $7.00

WAGENKNECHT. *Marilyn Monroe: Composite View.* 1969 1st ed. dj. EX $45.00

WAGNER, A. *Campaign of Koniggratz.* 1889 Leavenworth. Ills. 8vo. 121 p. gray cloth. $28.00

WAGNER, A.R. *Heralds & Heraldry in Middle Ages.* 1956 London. 2nd ed. dj. EX $20.00

WAGNER, Ernest F. *Foundation to Flute Playing.* 1918 NY. Fischer. pb. VG $12.00

WAGNER, Henry R. *60 Years of Book Collecting.* 1952 Roxburge Club. 1st ed. 8vo. rare. VG $60.00

WAGNER, Richard. *Ring of Niblung.* 1910 London. Ills Rackham. gilt cloth. VG $55.00

WAGNER, Richard. *Ring of Niblung.* 1911 NY. Ills Rackham. G $38.00

WAGNER & CAMP. *Plains & the Rockies: Critical Bibliography 1800-1865.* Ills 4th ed. 8vo. 745 p. EX $120.00

WAGONER, J.J. *History of Cattle Industry in Southern AZ 1540-1940.* 1952 Tucson. 1st ed. 132 p. wraps. VG $15.00

WAHL, Jan. *Teeny, Tiny Witches.* 1979 Putnam. Ills Margot Tomes. 4to. 48 p. $7.50

WAHL, P.; & TOPPEL, D.R. *Gatling Gun.* 1966 Jenkins. Ills 1st ed. 4to. dj. EX $30.00

WAHL, Ralph. *Come Wade the River.* 1971 Superior. Ills 1st ed. 128 p. dj. EX $18.50

WAINWRIGHT. *History of Philadelphia Electric Co.: 1881-1961.* 1961 Phil. 1st ed. 8vo. 416 p. dj. VG $15.00

WAITE, Arthur E. *Book of Ceremonial Magic.* 1911 London. Rider. Ills. VG $110.00

WAITE, Arthur E. *Complete Manual of Occult Divination.* 1972 NY U Books. djs. 2 vol set. EX $45.00

WAITE, Arthur E. *Hermetic & Alchemical Writings of Paracelsus the Great.* 1967 NY. Universe Books. 1/500. 2 vols. $250.00

WAITE, Arthur E. *Hidden Church of the Holy Grail.* 1909 London. 1st ed. 714 p. rebound. VG $75.00

WAITE, Arthur E. *Holy Kabbalah.* 1929 Macmillan. Ills. 4to. 636 p. VG $65.00

WAITE, Arthur E. *Lives of Alchemystical Philosophers.* 1888 London. Redway. 1st ed. 315 p. EX $145.00

WAITE, Arthur E. *Mysteries of Magic.* 1897 London. 2nd ed. sgn. VG $196.00

WAITE, Arthur E. *Mysteries of Magic.* 1974 NJ. Universe Books. 523 p. dj. VG $35.00

WAITE, Arthur E. *Real History of the Rosicrucians.* 1887 London. Redway. 1st ed. 446 p. EX $135.00

WAITE, Arthur E. *Secret Doctrine in Israel.* no date. (1950) NY. Ills. 330 p. EX $45.00

WAITE, Arthur E. *Shadows of Life & Thought.* 1938 London. Ills. 388 p. rebound. VG $85.00

WAITE, Arthur E. *Strange Houses of Sleep.* 1906 London. Ltd 1st ed. 1/250. sgn. EX $235.00

WAKEFIELD, Dan. *Selling Out.* 1985 Little Brown. 1st ed. dj. EX $17.00

WAKEFIELD, Dan. *Under the Apple Tree.* 1982 Delacorte. 1st ed. dj. EX $15.00

WAKEFIELD, H.R. *Ghost Stories.* 1934 Cape. VG $30.00

WAKEFIELD, H.R. *Imagine a Man in a Box.* 1931 Appleton. 1st ed. VG $45.00

WAKEFIELD, H.R. *Strayers From Sheol.* 1961 Arkham House. 1st ed. dj. EX $20.00

WAKEFIELD, Priscilla. *Brief Memoir of Life of William Penn.* 1833 NY. 2nd ed. VG $25.00

WAKEFIELD, Tom. *Love Siege.* 1979 London. 1st ed. dj. M $10.00

WAKEMAN, I. *Sins of Philip Fleming.* 1959 NY. 1st ed. dj. EX $20.00

WAKOSKI, Diane. *Looking for the King of Spain.* 1974 Black Sparrow. 1st ed. wraps. EX $22.00

WAKOSKI, Diane. *Saturn's Ring.* 1982 Targ. Ltd ed. 1/250. sgn. EX $45.00

WAKOSKI, Diane. *Variations on a Theme.* 1976 Black Sparrow. 1st ed. EX $12.00

WAKSMAN, Selman A. *Humus: Origins, Chemical Composition, & Importance.* 1936 Williams Wilkins. VG $37.50

WALCHA, Otto. *Meissen Porcelain.* 1981 NY. Putnam. Ills Frewel/Beyer. 516 p. dj. $60.00

WALDECK, T.J. *On Safari.* 1946 Harrap. London. Ills 1st ed. 160 p. G $15.00

WALDEN, H.T. *Familiar Fresh-Water Fishes of America.* 1964 Harper Row. Ills 1st ed. 324 p. dj. VG $12.00

WALDEN, H.T. *Last Pool.* 1972 Crown. reprint. dj. EX $7.50

WALDEN, H.T. *Upstream & Down.* 1938 Macmillan. Ills 1st ed. 367 p. VG $12.50

WALDENBERG, Patrick. *Alain le Yaounac.* 1969 Paris. Derriere Le Miror. wraps. $40.00

WALDMAN, Max. *On Theater.* 1971 Doubleday. Ills. dj. VG $15.00

WALDROP, Howard. *All About Strange Monsters of Recent Past.* 1987 KS City. Ills 1st ed. 1/600. slipcase. $35.00

WALDSEEMULLER, M. *Cosmographie Introductio.* 1907 NY. facsimile. fld maps. EX $65.00

WALETT, Francis G. *Boston Gazette 1774.* 1972 Imprint Soc. 1/1,950. folio. G $15.00

WALEY, Arthur. *Translations From the Chinese.* 1941 NY. Knopf. Ills Baldridge. slipcase. EX $15.00

WALGAMOTT, Charles. *6 Decades Back: Early Days in ID.* 1936 Caxton. VG $65.00

WALKER, Alexander. *Columbia: Geographical, Statistical, Agricultural, Etc.* 1822 London. Baldwin. Ills 1st ed. $100.00

WALKER, Alexander. *General Andrew Jackson.* 1890 Phil. G $17.50

WALKER, Alexander. *Intermarriage.* 1839 NY. Ills 1st Am ed. VG $18.00

WALKER, Alice. *Horses Make a Landscape Look More Beautiful.* 1984 Harcourt. 1st ed. dj. EX $15.00

WALKER, B.S. *Great Divide.* 1973 Time Life. Ills. 184 p. EX $8.00

WALKER, E.S. *Treetops Hotel.* 1962 Hale. London. Ills. sgn. 190 p. dj. EX $16.00

WALKER, Ernest. *History of Music in England.* 1924 Oxford. 2nd ed. VG $20.00

WALKER, F. *San Francisco's Literary Frontier.* 1939 NY. Knopf. Ills. 400 p. dj. VG $20.00

WALKER, F.A. *General Hancock.* 1894 NY. Ills 1st ed. 12mo. 332 p. G $12.00

WALKER, Frederick. *Practical Kites & Aeroplanes: How To Make & Work Them.* 1909 London. Ills. 80 p. G $22.50

WALKER, George. *View of North America in Its Former & Present State.* 1781 Glasgow. Root. ¾-green leather. $1000.00

WALKER, H. *Walker Expedition to Quebec in 1711.* 1953 Navy Records Soc. 1st ed. $65.00

WALKER, Jeanie Mort. *Life of Captain Joseph Fry.* 1875 Hartford. 1st ed. 589 p. G $65.00

WALKER, John. *National Gallery of Art in Washington, D.C.* 1963 NY. 339 p. wraps. $20.00

WALKER, Joseph Cooper. *Historical Memoir on Italian Tragedy.* 1799 London. 14 plts. cloth. rebound. EX $55.00

WALKER, Kenneth. *Mystic Mind.* 1965 Emerson Books. dj. VG $12.00

WALKER, L.C. *Ecology & Our Forests.* 1972 Barnes. Ills. 175 p. dj. EX $5.00

WALKER, Margaret Coulson. *Our Birds & Their Nestlings.* 1904 NY. Am Book Co. 8vo. photos. gray cloth. EX $10.00

WALKER, Marie. *Freeing Our Mental Forces.* 1925 MA. 188 p. VG $18.00

WALKER, Marie. *Make of Yourself What You Will.* 1920 200 p. VG $12.00

WALKER, Stella A. *Sporting Art of England 1700-1900.* 1972 NY. dj. $45.00

WALKER, Sydney. *Aviation Principles: Both Present & Future.* c 1913. London. People's Book Series. $25.00

WALKER, T. *Red Salmon, Brown Bear: Story of an Alaskan Lake.* 1971 World. Ills 1st ed. 226 p. dj. EX $10.00

WALKER, Thomas. *Journal of Exploration in Spring of Year 1750.* 1888 Boston. 1st ed. 69 p. VG $95.00

WALKOWITZ, A. *Isadora Duncan in Her Dances.* 1945 Girand, KS. 1st ed. 4to. sgn. $100.00

WALKUP, Fairfax Proudfit. *Dressing the Part.* 1950 Appleton. 4to. 423 p. VG $35.00

WALL, John. *Briding Thoroughbreds.* 1946 NY. Ills 1st ed. dj. VG $20.00

WALL, John. *Horseman's Handbook on Practical Breeding.* 1939 Myrtle Beach. Ills 1st ed. 308 p. $25.00

WALL & WILLIAMS. *Following General Sam Houston From 1793 to 1863.* 1935 Austin. 1st ed. dj. EX $40.00

WALLACE, A.R. *Man's Place in the Universe.* 1903 NY. 1st ed. 326 p. $25.00

WALLACE, A.R. *World of Life.* 1911 NY. Ills 1st ed. 441 p. $30.00

WALLACE, Brenton G. *Patton & His 3rd Army.* 1946 Harrisburg. Ills 1st ed. 231 p. cloth. VG $35.00

WALLACE, D.M. *Russia.* 1877 Holt. 1st ed. maps. VG $40.00

WALLACE, D.R. *Dark Range: Naturalists Night Notebook.* 1978 Sierra Club. Ills 1st ed. 131 p. dj. EX $15.00

WALLACE, D.R. *Idle Weeds: Life of a Sandstone Ridge.* 1980 Sierra Club. Ills. 1st ed. 183 p. dj. EX $12.00

WALLACE, Dillon. *Long Labrador Trail.* 1911 McClurg. Ills. 316 p. G $10.00

WALLACE, Dillon. *Lure of the Labrador Wild.* 1905 Revell. 6th ed. green cloth. VG $25.00

WALLACE, Dillon. *Lure of the Labrador Wild.* c 1905. NY. 10th ed. VG $20.00

WALLACE, Dillon. *Packing & Portaging.* 1916 Outing. Ills. 133 p. dj. VG $14.00

WALLACE, E.; & HOEBEL, E.A. *Comanches: Lords of the Southern Plains.* 1969 OK U Pr. Ills. 381 p. dj. VG $20.00

WALLACE, E.S. *28th Division in World War.* 1923 Pittsburgh. 1st ed. 5 vol set. EX $275.00

WALLACE, Edgar. *Day of Unity.* 1930 NY. 1st Am ed. dj. VG $20.00

WALLACE, Edgar. *Devil Man.* 1931 NY. VG $10.00

WALLACE, Edgar. *On the Spot.* 1931 NY. 1st ed. G $8.00

WALLACE, Edgar. *Ringer Returns.* 1931 NY. 1st ed. dj. VG $12.00

WALLACE, Edgar. *Terror Keep.* 1927 NY. 1st ed. dj. VG $15.00

WALLACE, Edgar. *Terror.* 1932 London. Collins. VG $15.00

WALLACE, Edgar. *Writing in Barracks.* 1900 London. 1st ed. scarce. $75.00

WALLACE, Elizabeth. *Mark Twain & Happy Island.* 1913 Chicago. McClurg. 1st ed. 140 p. VG $55.00

WALLACE, Grange Byron. *Way to Game Abundance: Explanation of Game Cycles.* 1949 Scribner. 1st ed. dj. VG $14.50

WALLACE, I. *Chapman Report.* 1960 NY. 1st ed. dj. EX $10.00

WALLACE, I. *3 Sirens.* 1963 NY. 1st ed. dj. EX $10.00

WALLACE, Irving. *27th Wife.* 1961 Simon Schuster. 1st ed. dj. VG $17.50

WALLACE, Ivy L. *Pookie & the Gypsies.* 1957 Collins. 10th print. 4to. $15.00

WALLACE, Ivy L. *Pookie in Search of a Home.* 1957 Collins. Ills 5th print. 4to. $15.00

WALLACE, Lew. *Ben Hur.* 1901 NY. Players ed. 12mo. 552 p. G $40.00

WALLACE, Lew. *Ben Hur.* 1960 Ltd Ed Club. sgn Mugnaini. slipcase. EX $40.00

WALLACE, Lew. *Fair God.* 1899 Boston. Ills E Pape. 1st ed. 2 vols. $60.00

WALLACE, P. *Conrad Weiser: Friend of Colonist & Mohawk.* 1945 Phil. Ills 1st ed. dj. VG $30.00

WALLACE, R. *Grand Canyon.* 1972 Time Life. Ills. 184 p. EX $8.00

WALLACE, R. *HI.* 1973 Time Life. Ills. 184 p. maps. EX $8.00

WALLACE, Susan E. *Ginevra; or, Old Oak Chest.* 1887 NY. Worthington. Ills Lew Wallace. $20.00

WALLACE, Susan E. *Land of Pueblos.* 1888 NM. Ills 1st ed. 285 p. VG $30.00

WALLACE, Susan E. *Land of Pueblos.* 1888 NY. 1st ed. VG $17.50

WALLACE, W.M. *Traitorous Hero: Life of Benedict Arnold.* 1954 NY. Ills 1st ed. dj. VG $15.00

WALLACE & BENEKE. *Managing Tenant-Operated Farm.* 1956 Ames. 264 p. VG $5.00

WALLACK, L.R. *Anatomy of Firearms.* 1965 Simon Schuster. Ills 1st ed. inscr/sgn. dj. EX $20.00

WALLACK, L.R. *Modern Accuracy in Bench Rest Shooting.* 1951 Greenburg. Ills. 4to. 151 p. dj. EX $18.50

WALLER, John L. *Colossal Hamilton: Biography of Andrew Jackson Hamilton.* 1969 TX Western Pr. 1st ed. 152 p. cloth. dj. M $12.00

WALLER, Mary E. *Daughter of the Rich.* 1927 Boston. Ills. juvenile. VG $25.00

WALLIHAN, A.G. *Camera Shots at Big Game.* c 1895. Ills. 4to. $75.00

WALLING, H.F.; & GRAY, O.W. *New Topographical Atlas of State of P.A.* 1872 Phil. Ills. folio. maps. cloth. VG $200.00

WALLIS, G.A. *Cattle Kings of the Staked Plains.* 1964 Sage. Ills. 164 p. dj. EX $5.00

WALPOLE, Horace. *Apple Trees.* 1932 Golden Cockerell. Ills Lamb. $50.00

WALPOLE, Horace. *Castle of Otranto.* 1975 Westerham. 1/2,000. 4to. slipcase. EX $50.00

WALPOLE, Horace. *Letter to Editor of Miscellanies of Thomas Chatterton.* 1779 Strawberry Hill. Kirgate. 8vo. $225.00

WALPOLE, Horace. *Letters of Horace Walpole to Horace Mann.* 1833 London. Bentley. 2nd ed. 3 vol set. $125.00

WALPOLE, Hugh. *Above the Dark Circus.* 1931 London. Ltd ed. 1/200. sgn. VG $35.00

WALPOLE, Hugh. *Cathedral.* 1931 NY. Ltd ed. 1/500. dj. slipcase. $35.00

WALPOLE, Hugh. *Hans Frost.* 1929 Garden City. 1st ed. dj. EX $12.00

WALPOLE, Hugh. *Jeremy.* 1919 NY. Doran. Ills Shepard. 1st Am ed. dj. $30.00

WALPOLE, Hugh. *Judieth Paris.* 1931 London. Ltd ed. 1/350. sgn. $35.00

WALPOLE, Hugh. *Portrait of a Man with Red Hair.* 1925 NY. Doran. Large Paper ed. 1/250. sgn. EX $60.00

WALSER, M. *Marriage in Philippsburg.* 1961 Norfolk. 1st ed. dj. EX $18.00

WALSER, R. *Thomas Wolfe: Undergraduate.* 1977 Durham, NC. Duke U Pr. Ills. dj. VG $7.50

WALSH, J.J. *Catholic Churchmen in Science.* 1906 Phil. EX $12.00

WALSH, Justin. *To Print the News & Raise Hell.* 1969 Chapel Hill. 1st ed. dj. VG $18.00

WALSH, Rev. Robert. *Notices of Brazil in 1828 & 1829.* 1831 Boston. Richard. 1st Am ed. 2 vol set. $125.00

WALSH, S. *Anglo-American General Encyclopedia 1702-1967.* 1968 NY. EX $35.00

WALSH, Thomas. *Prison Ship & Other Poems.* 1909 Boston. 1st ed. presentation. G $30.00

WALTARI, Mika. *Egyptian.* 1949 NY. 1st ed. dj. EX $17.00

WALTER, John. *Sword & Bayonet Makers of Imperial Germany.* 1973 Lyon Pr. Ills 1st ed. dj. EX $7.00

WALTER, Nehemiah. *Faithfulness in the Ministry Derived From Christ.* 1723 Boston. 1st ed. disbound. $80.00

WALTON, Evangeline. *Witch House.* 1945 Arkham House. 1st ed. inscr. dj. EX $55.00

WALTON, George. *Sentinel of the Plains.* 1973 Prentice Hall. 1st ed. fld map. G $9.00

WALTON, Izaak. *Compleat Angler.* c 1924. London. Hodder Stoughton. 1st trade. $100.00

WALTON, Izaak. *Compleat Angler.* 1936 Heritage Pr. Ills. 241 p. slipcase. EX $25.00

WALTON, Izaak. *Compleat Angler.* 1953 Stackpole. Revised ed. 192 p. EX $20.00

WALTON, Thomas. *Steel Ships: Their Construction & Maintenance.* 1901 London/Phil. Ills. gilt cloth. EX $85.00

WALTON. *Whale Fishery of New England.* 1915 Boston. VG $35.00

WAMBAUGH, Joseph. *Black Marble.* 1978 Delacorte. 1st ed. dj. EX $12.00

WANDREI, Donald. *Eye & the Finger.* 1944 Arkham House. 1st ed. dj. VG $125.00

WANDREI, Donald. *Poems for Midnight.* 1964 Sauk City. 1st ed. sgn. dj. EX $120.00

WANDREI, Donald. *Strange Harvest.* 1965 Arkham House. Ltd ed. 1/2,000. dj. EX $65.00

WANDREI, Donald. *Web of Easter Island.* 1948 Arkham House. Ltd ed. 1/3,000. dj. VG $55.00

WARBURG, Fred. *Occupation for Gentlemen.* 1960 Boston. 1st ed. dj. EX $12.00

WARBURTON, S. *Silent Watcher; or, York As Seen From Agamenticus.* 1897 Boston. Heintzemann. Ills. 70 p. $12.50

WARD, A. Dorrance. *3 Ozark Streams, Log of Moccasin, & Wilma.* 1937 Richmond, MO. sgn. tree bark bdg. VG $20.00

WARD, Barbara. *Only 1 Earth.* 1972 NY. 1st ed. dj. M $10.00

WARD, Clarence. *Medieval Church Vaulting.* 1915 Princeton U Pr. G $22.00

WARD, D. *Bits of Silver: Vignettes of the Old West.* 1961 Hastings House. 306 p. dj. EX $18.00

WARD, F.K *Burma's Icy Mountains.* 1949 London. 1st ed. dj. EX $25.00

WARD, Harry P. *Some American College Bookplates.* 1915 Columbus, OH. Ltd ed. 1/500. sgn. EX $50.00

WARD, J.C. *Geology of Northern Part of English Lake District.* 1876 London. Ills. 132 p. VG $60.00

WARD, John. *Young Mathematician's Guide.* 1719 London. 3rd ed. 8vo. full leather. G $65.00

WARD, L. *Vertigo.* 1937 Random House. Ills 1st ed. VG $40.00

WARD, L.; & HICKS, G. *Story of John Reed.* 1935 Equinox. dj. G $50.00

WARD, L.F. *Guide to the Flora of WA & Vicinity.* 1881 WA. 1st ed. VG $25.00

WARD, Lynd. *God's Man.* 1933 NY. VG $25.00

WARD, Lynd. *God's Man.* 1929 NY. Ills 1st ed. VG $95.00

WARD, Lynd. *Nic of the Woods.* 1965 Boston. Houghton Mifflin. 1st print. $40.00

WARD, Lynd. *Wild Pilgrimage.* 1932 NY. Harrison Smith/Robert Haas. G $40.00

WARD, Rowland. *Records of Big Game.* 1962 Africa. 11th ed. buckskin. rebound. $85.00

WARDLE, Patricia. *Victorian Silver & Silverplate.* 1963 NY. Nelson. Ills. tall 8vo. 238 p. dj. $30.00

WARHOL, Andy. *'a.'* 1968 NY. Grove Pr. 1st ed. sgn. wraps. VG $35.00

WARHOL, Andy. *Philosophy of Andy Warhol.* 1975 NY. 1st ed. initialed AW. dj. EX $75.00

WARING, George. *Elements of Agriculture.* 1870 NY. Tribune. Revised ed. 254 p. G $10.00

WARING, George. *Sanitary Drainage of Houses & Towns.* 1881 Boston. Ills 2nd ed. 366 p. VG $25.00

WARING, Janet. *Early American Stencils on Walls & Furniture.* 1968 NY. Dover. Ills. 4to. 158 p. wraps. $15.00

WARLOCK, Peter. *English Ayre.* 1926 Oxford U Pr. EX $15.00

WARNER, C.D. *On Horseback: Tour in VA, NC, & TN; Notes of Mexico & CA.* 1888 Boston/ NY. 1st ed. 8vo. 331 p. cloth. $27.50

WARNER, C.D. *Roundabout Journey.* 1884 Boston. 12mo. 360 p. gilt blue cloth. $20.00

WARNER, C.D. *Studies in the South & West.* c 1889. NY. 12mo. 484 p. $10.00

WARNER, Deborah Jean. *Alvin Clark & Sons: Artists in Optics.* 1968 Smithsonian. Ills. 120 p. EX $18.00

WARNER, Langdon. *Craft of Japanese Sculptor.* 1936 NY. Japan Soc/Morrill Pr. 1st ed. $75.00

WARNER, Sylvia Townsend. *Cat's Cradle Book.* 1960 London. 1st ed. dj. VG $27.00

WARNER, Sylvia Townsend. *Flint Anchor.* 1954 London. Chatto Windus. 1st ed. VG $35.00

WARNER, Sylvia Townsend. *Lolly Willowes & Mr. Fortunes Maggot.* 1966 NY. Ltd ed. 1/600. EX $25.00

WARNER, Sylvia Townsend. *Mr. Fortunes Maggot.* 1927 London. 1st ed. dj. VG $55.00

WARNER, Sylvia Townsend. *Teacher.* 1963 NY. 1st ed. VG $15.00

WARNER. *Glen Loates: Brush with Life.* 1984 Scarborough. 1st ed. sgn. dj. EX $42.00

WARREN, Arthur. *George Westinghouse 1846-1914: A Tribute.* Ills. 12mo. 32 p. $17.00

WARREN, D.M. *System of Physical Geography: Phenomena of Atmosphere.* 1856 Phil. Ills 1st ed. 4to. 1/2 calf. $60.00

WARREN, E.R. *Mammals of CO.* 1910 Putnam. Ills 1st ed. 300 p. EX $20.00

WARREN, Earl. *Republic If You Can Keep It.* 1972 NY. cloth. VG $80.00

WARREN, J. Mason. *Surgical Observations with Cases & Operations.* 1867 Boston. Ills Bufford. cloth. VG $300.00

WARREN, Robert Penn. *All the King's Men.* 1946 Harcourt Brace. 1st ed. 1st imp. 8vo. dj. $45.00

WARREN, Robert Penn. *All the King's Men.* 1953 Modern Library. 1st ed. dj. VG $15.00

WARREN, Robert Penn. *All the King's Men.* 1948 London. 1st ed. dj. VG $75.00

WARREN, Robert Penn. *Audubon.* 1969 Random House. 1st ed. dj. VG $35.00

WARREN, Robert Penn. *Band of Angels.* 1955 Random House. 1st ed. inscr. dj. VG $75.00

WARREN, Robert Penn. *Being Here: Poetry 1977-1980.* 1980 Random House. 1st ed. sgn. dj. EX $40.00

WARREN, Robert Penn. *Brother to Dragons.* 1953 Random House. 1st ed. sgn. dj. EX $70.00

WARREN, Robert Penn. *Cave.* 1959 Random House. 1st ed. sgn. dj. VG $55.00

WARREN, Robert Penn. *Chief Joseph of the Nez Perce.* 1986 Random House. 1st ed. sgn. dj. EX $35.00

WARREN, Robert Penn. *Chief Joseph of the Nez Perce.* 1983 Random House. Ltd ed. 1/250. slipcase. EX $100.00

WARREN, Robert Penn. *Chief Joseph of the Nez Perce.* 1983 NY. 1st ed. dj. VG $25.00

WARREN, Robert Penn. *Democracy & Poetry.* 1975 Harvard U Pr. 1st ed. dj. EX $35.00

WARREN, Robert Penn. *Flood.* 1964 Random House. 1st trade ed. dj. M $25.00

WARREN, Robert Penn. *Homage to Theodore Dreiser.* 1971 Random House. 1st ed. sgn. dj. EX $45.00

WARREN, Robert Penn. *John Greenleaf Whittier's Poetry.* 1971 MNU Pr. 1st ed. sgn. dj. EX $40.00

WARREN, Robert Penn. *Meet Me in the Green Glen.* 1971 Random House. 1st ed. dj. EX $35.00

WARREN, Robert Penn. *Place To Come To.* 1977 Random House. 1st ed. sgn. dj. EX $35.00

WARREN, Robert Penn. *Place To Come To.* 1977 Random House. Ltd 1st ed. 1/350. 401 p. VG $75.00

WARREN, Robert Penn. *Promises: Poems 1954-1956.* 1957 Random House. 1st ed. sgn. dj. EX $75.00

WARREN, Robert Penn. *Who Speaks for the Negro?* 1965 Random House. 1st ed. sgn. dj. EX $55.00

WARREN, Robert Penn. *Wilderness.* 1961 Random House. 1st ed. sgn. dj. EX $60.00

WARREN, Robert Penn. *Wilderness.* 1961 Random House. 1st ed. dj. EX $50.00

WARREN, Robert Penn. *World Enough & Time.* 1950 Random House. Special KY ed. 1/1,000. dj. EX $250.00

WARREN, Robert Penn. *World Enough & Time.* 1950 Random House. 1st ed. dj. VG $50.00

WARREN, S. *Farthest Frontier: Pacific Northwest.* 1949 NY. 1st print. dj. VG $8.00

WARREN, Samuel. *Now & Then: Through a Glass Darkly.* 1854 London. Blackwood. sgn. VG $25.00

WARREN, T.R. *Shooting, Boating, & Fishing.* 1871 Scribner. Ills. 165 p. VG $25.00

WARREN, William; & BRAKE, B. *House of Klong: Bangkok Home & Collection of James Thompson.* 1968 NY. Ills. dj. VG $25.00

WARRICK, F.W. *Experiments in Psychics.* 1939 London. Ills. 339 p. xl. VG $60.00

WARTENBERG, R. *Diagnostic Tests in Neurology.* 1953 Phil. Ills 1st ed. 228 p. VG $85.00

WASHBURN, C. *Come into My Parlor.* 1936 Nat'l Lib Pr. 1st ed. 255 p. dj. VG $20.00

WASHBURN, Charles A. *History of Paraguay with Notes of Personal Observations.* 1871 Boston. Lee Shepard. 1st ed. 627 p. $150.00

WASHBURNE, E.B. *Edwards Papers.* 1884 Chicago. Chicago Hist Soc. VG $35.00

WASHBURNE, Heluiz. *Little Elephant Catches Cold.* c 1937. Chicago. 1st ed. 8vo. VG $15.00

WASHBURNE. *Land of the Good Shadows: Life Story of Anauta.* 1940 NY. 1st ed. inscr. VG $25.00

WASHER, R. *Sheffield Bowie & Pocket Knife Makers, 1825-1925.* 1974 Vinall. Ills. 144 p. dj. EX $13.50

WASHINGTON, Booker T. *Up From Slavery.* 1901 NY. 1st ed. EX $55.00

WASHINGTON, George. *Correspondence with the Continental Congress.* 1906 Library of Congress. EX $65.00

WASHINGTON, George. *Writings of George Washington From Original Manuscript.* c 1940s. WA. 39 vol set. $850.00

WASHINGTON, H.A. *Writings of Thomas Jefferson.* 1857 NY. 10 vol set. $950.00

WASSERMANN, J. *Bula Matari.* 1933 Liverwright. 1st Am ed. EX $10.00

WASSERMANN, J. *Wedlock.* 1926 NY. 1st ed. dj. EX $15.00

WASSING, Rene. *African Art.* 1968 Abrams. Ills 1st ed. dj. EX $50.00

WASSON, R. Gordon. *Soma: Divine Mushroom of Immortality.* 1968 Ltd ed. slipcase. EX $60.00

WATERBURY, J.B. *Voyage of Life Suggested by Cole's Allegorical Paintings.* 1852 Boston. MA Sabbath School Soc. 180 p. $20.00

WATERER, John W. *Leather & Craftsmanship.* 1950 London. Faber. Ills. 4to. cloth. dj. $45.00

WATERFIELD, Hermione. *Faberge: Imperial Eggs & Other Fantasies.* 1980 NY. Bramhall House. Ills. 4to. dj. $30.00

WATERFIELD, M. *Flower Groupings in English, Scotch, & Irish Gardens.* 1907 London. Ills. $27.50

WATERHOUSE, Benjamin. *Botanist: Botanical Part of a Course of Lectures.* 1811 Boston. 1st ed. calf. $185.00

WATERHOUSE. *Harunobo & His Age.* 1964 London. Ills 1st ed. spiral bdg. VG $45.00

WATERMAN, C.F. *Hunter's World.* 1976 NY. 1st ed. dj. EX $20.00

WATERMAN, C.F. *Hunting in America.* 1973 Ridge Pr. Ills. 4to. 250 p. dj. EX $15.00

WATERMAN, C.F. *Hunting Upland Birds.* 1972 Winchester. Ills. 311 p. dj. EX $10.00

WATERS, Bernard. *Modern Training, Handling, & Kennel Management.* 1889 private print. Ills 1st ed. 373 p. VG $28.50

WATERS, Frank. *Midas of the Rockies.* 1949 Sage. Ills. 347 p. VG $18.00

WATERS, Frank. *Midas of the Rockies.* 1937 NY. 1st ed. dj. VG $32.50

WATERS, W.G. *Novellino of Masuccio.* 1895 London. Ills ER Hughes. 2 vol set. $50.00

WATERTON, C. *Essays on Natural History, Chiefly Ornothology.* 1851 & 1858. 2nd & 3rd series. 2 vols in 1. $22.50

WATKIN, William Ward. *Church of Tomorrow.* 1936 NY. Harper. fair. $12.00

WATKINS, Leslie. *Unexploded Man.* 1968 Morrow. 1st Am ed. dj. VG $12.00

WATKINS, Lura Woodside. *Early New England Potters & Their Wares.* 1950 Cambridge. Harvard U Pr. Ills. 291 p. $25.00

WATKINS, Lura Woodside. *Early New England Potters & Their Wares.* 1968 Hamden. Archon Books. reprint of 1950. $55.00

WATKINS, T. *Gold & Silver in the West.* 1971 Palo Alto. dj. $20.00

WATKINS, Vernon. *Breaking of the Wave.* 1979 Suffolk. Ipswich. 1st ed. dj. wraps. EX $15.00

WATKINS. *Grand CO.* 1969 CA. 1st ed. 4to. dj. VG $20.00

WATKINS-PITCHFORD, Denys. *Little Gray Men.* 1951 NY. Ills. juvenile. VG $25.00

WATKINSON, Ray. *William Morris As Designer.* 1967 NY. Reinhold. Ills. 84 p. $30.00

WATROUS, George R. *History of Winchester Firearms 1866-1966.* 1966 no place. 1st ed. boxed. VG $32.50

WATSON, Alfred E.T. *Sporting & Dramatic Career.* 1918 London. 1st ed. G $30.00

WATSON, E.W. *Composition in Landscape & Still Life.* 1959 NY. Ills. 208 p. $18.50

WATSON, E.W. *40 Illustrators & How They Work.* 1947 NY. Ills 2nd ed. cloth. VG $25.00

WATSON, E.W. *40 Illustrators & How They Work.* 1947 Watson Guptill. 1st ed. 318 p. $40.00

WATSON, E.W. *40 Illustrators & How They Work.* 1946 NY. 1st ed. dj. EX $45.00

WATSON, Elizabeth C. *Metropolitan Mother Goose.* c 1927. NY. Ills Emma Clark. wraps. G $5.00

WATSON, F.E.; & LUTZ, F.E. *Our Common Butterflies.* 1926 Ills. 21 p. wraps. VG $13.00

WATSON, F.J.B. *Furniture.* 1956 London. Clowes. Ills. 360 p. $75.00

WATSON, Forbes. *John Quinn 1870-1925.* 1926 Pigeon Hill. Ills. 4to. 200 p. wraps. $50.00

WATSON, Frederick. *Hunting Pie.* 1931 Derrydale. Ills Paul Brown. 1/750. dj. EX $160.00

WATSON, Idelle. *True Story of a Real Garden.* 1922 NY. 183 p. VG $10.00

WATSON, J. Madison. *Manual of Calisthenics.* 1889 NY. 8vo. 144 p. cloth. VG $30.00

WATSON, James D. *Molecular Biology of the Gene.* 1965 NY. Benjamin. Ills 1st ed. 494. dj. xl. $18.00

WATSON, P. *Sea Shepherd: My Fight for Whales & Seas.* 1982 Norton. Ills 1st ed. 258 p. dj. EX $8.00

WATSON, P.F. *Artificial Breeding of Non-Domestic Animals.* 1978 Academic Pr. Ills. 376 p. dj. EX $20.00

WATSON, Richard. *Life of Rev. John Wesley.* 1831 Emory Waugh. 1st Am ed. leather. G $95.00

WATSON, Thomas E. *Life & Times of Thomas Jefferson.* 1903 NY. Ills 1st ed. 534 p. cloth. EX $35.00

WATSON, Virginia. *Princess Pocahontas.* 1916 PA. Ills GE Wharton. G $35.00

WATSON, Virginia. *With Cortez the Conquerer.* 1917 Phil. Ills Schoonover. 1st ed. 4to. $40.00

WATSON, Virginia. *With Cortez the Conqueror.* 1917 NY. Ills. $15.00

WATSON, W. *Art of Dynastic China.* 1981 Abrams. 4to. dj. $65.00

WATSON, Wendy M. *Italian Renaissance Majolica From W.A. Clark Collection.* 1986 London. Ills. 192 p. wraps. $20.00

WATSON, William. *Style in Arts of China.* 1974 London. Ills. wraps. $10.00

WATSON. *Savage Club.* 1907 London. G $25.00

WATT, Roberta. *4 Wagons West: Story of Seattle.* 1931 Binfords Mort. Ills. 390 p. VG $11.00

WATT, Roberta. *4 Wagons West: Story of Seattle.* c 1931. Portland. dj. M $30.00

WATTS, Alan W. *Way of Zen.* 1959 dj. VG $13.00

WATTS, Isaac. *Divine & Moral Songs for Children.* 1866 NY. Ills. 12mo. 116 p. leather. G $12.00

WATTS, Isaac. *Improvement of Mind; or, Supplement to Art of Logic.* 1798 London. ½-calf. VG $95.00

WATTS, Isaac. *Improvement of Mind; or, Supplement to Art of Logic.* 1813 WA. leather. G $25.00

WATTS, Isaac. *Improvement of Mind; or, Supplement to Art of Logic.* 1819 NY. 16mo. 327 p. leather. G $15.00

WATTS, Isaac. *Improvement of Mind; or, Supplement to Art of Logic.* 1741 London. 1st ed. calf. $175.00

WATTS, Isaac. *Logic; or, Right Use of Reason in Enquiry After Truth.* 1924 London. 8vo. full calf. VG $45.00

WATTS. *Dictionary of the Old West.* 1977 Knopf. 1st ed. dj. VG $12.00

WATTY, Piper. *Mother Goose Rhymes & Animal Stories.* 1929 Platt Munk. Ills Eulalie/Burd/Gurney. EX $25.00

WAUER, R.H. *Birds of Big Bend National Park.* 1973 TX U Pr. Ills. 223 p. wraps. EX $10.00

WAUGH, Alec. *Hot Countries.* 1930 Farrar Rhinehart. Ills Ward. $15.00

WAUGH, Alec. *Island in the Sun.* 1955 Farrar Straus. yellow cloth bdg. $11.00

WAUGH, Alec. *My Place in the Bazaar.* 1961 Farrar. 1st Am ed. dj. EX $14.00

WAUGH, Auberon. *Consider the Lilies.* 1968 Little Brown. 1st Am ed. dj. EX $25.00

WAUGH, Auberon. *Path of Daliance.* 1964 Simon Schuster. 1st Am ed. dj. EX $35.00

WAUGH, Auberon. *Who Are the Violets Now?* 1965 Simon Schuster. 1st Am ed. dj. EX $30.00

WAUGH, Evelyn. *Diaries of Evelyn Waugh.* 1976 Boston. 1st ed. dj. M $18.00

WAUGH, Evelyn. *Helena.* 1950 Chapman Hall. 1st English ed. dj. VG $45.00

WAUGH, Evelyn. *Little Learning: 1st Volume of an Autobiography.* 1964 London. 1st ed. dj. EX $40.00

WAUGH, Evelyn. *Loved Ones.* 1948 Boston. 1st Am ed. sgn. dj. EX $25.00

WAUGH, Evelyn. *Scott-King's Modern Europe.* 1949 Little Brown. 1st Am ed. dj. EX $40.00

WAUGH, Evelyn. *Tourist in Africa.* c 1960. Boston. Little Brown. 1st ed. dj. EX $50.00

WAUGH, F.A. *Dwarf Fruit Trees.* 1916 NY. Ills. G $10.00

WAUGH, Norah. *Corsets & Crinolines.* 1954 4to. 176. dj. VG $45.00

WAUGH, Norah. *Cut of Women's Clothes 1600-1930.* 1969 NY. Theatre Arts Books. dj. $65.00

WAUGH, W.T. *James Wolfe: Man & Solider.* 1928 Montreal/NY. Louis Carrier. red bdg. dj. VG $20.00

WAYBRENN, Ned. *Art of Stage Dancing.* 1925 NY. 1st ed. 8vo. 382 p. scarce. VG $75.00

WAYLAND, Francis. *Memoir of Life & Labors of Francis Wayland.* 1867 2 vol set. VG $15.00

WAYLAND, John W. *Fairfax Line: Thomas Lewis' Journal of 1746.* 1925 VA. Henkle Pr. 8vo. red cloth. VG $85.00

WAYMAN, Norbury L. *Life on the River.* 1971 NY. Bonanza. 1st ed. 4to. 338 p. dj. VG $10.00

WEARIN, Otha D. *Clarence Ellsworth: Artist of the Old West.* 1967 Shennandoah. Ltd ed. 1/750. dj. VG $40.00

WEARIN, Otha D. *Statues That Pour: Story of Character Bottles.* 1965 Denver. Sage. Ills. 8vo. cloth. dj. $15.00

WEATHERBY, W.J. *Conversations with Marilyn.* 1976 2nd ed. dj. EX $27.50

WEATHERLY, F.E. *Maids of Lee.* Caldecott. Color Picture Book. $25.00

WEATHERS, W.W. *Birds of Southern CA Deep Canyons.* 1983 CA U Pr. Ills 1st ed. 266 p. dj. EX $27.00

WEAVER, Gordon. *Give Him a Stone.* 1975 Crown. 1st ed. dj. EX $15.00

WEAVER, John. *VA in American Poems.* 1921 Knopf. 2nd imp. inscr. fair. $10.00

WEAVER, Sir Lawrence. *Lutyens Houses & Gardens.* 1921 London. 1st ed. 203 p. EX $75.00

WEBB, Charles. *Love, Roger.* 1969 Boston. Houghton Mifflin. dj. EX $15.00

WEBB, James. *Adventures in Santa Fe Trade 1844-1847.* 1931 Glendale. Clark. 1st ed. EX $75.00

WEBB, Sydney & Beatrice. *History of Trade Unionism.* 1894 London/NY. Longman. 8vo. cloth. VG $40.00

WEBB, W. *Tables of Products.* 1775 London. leather. VG $22.00

WEBB, W.P. *Great Frontier.* 1979 TX U Pr. 434 p. dj. EX $17.00

WEBB, W.P. *Great Plains.* 1936 NY. 8vo. 525 p. dj. VG $37.50

WEBB, W.P. *History As High Adventure.* 1969 Pemberton. Ltd ed. 1/350. slipcase. $40.00

WEBB, W.P. *TX Rangers.* 1935 Boston/NY. Ills. 8vo. red cloth. VG $45.00

WEBBER, Andrew Lloyd. *Joseph & the Amazing Technicolor Dream Coat.* 1982 NY. 1st ed. dj. M $12.00

WEBBER, C.W. *Romance of Natural History.* 1853 London. Ills. 447 p. VG $200.00

WEBBER, Georgiana. *Anyone for Orchids?* 1978 Schiffer Ltd. dj. EX $10.00

WEBER, Bruce. *Fine Line: Drawing with Silver in America.* 1985 Palm Beach. Ills. 4to. 103 p. wraps. $22.50

WEBER, Carl J. *Thomas Hardy in ME.* 1942 Portland, ME. Ltd ed. 1/425. VG $30.00

WEBER, Carl Otto. *Chemistry of India Rubber Including Theory of Vulcanization.* 1909 London. Ills. xl. G $75.00

WEBER, D. *Taos Trappers: Fur Trade in Far Southwest 1540-1846.* 1971 OK U Pr. 1st ed. dj. $22.50

WEBER, Edward Joseph. *Catholic Church Buildings: Their Planning & Furnishing.* 1927 NY. Wagner. Ills 1st ed. inscr. VG $45.00

WEBLY. *Life, Death, & Futurity.* 1863 NY. VG $25.00

WEBSTER, D. *Myth & Maneater: Story of the Shark.* 1963 Norton. Ills 1st Am ed. 223 p. VG $11.00

WEBSTER, F. *Private Correspondence of Daniel Webster.* 1857 Boston. 2 vol set. VG $150.00

WEBSTER, G.C.; & HALL, L. *Journal of a Trip Around the Horn.* 1970 private print. Ills Ltd ed. 1/650. VG $40.00

WEBSTER, H.T. *Who Dealt This Mess?* 1948 Doubleday. 1st ed. dj. VG $17.50

WEBSTER, H.T.; & ZERN, E. *To Hell with Fishing.* 1945 Appleton Century. Ills. dj. EX $9.00

WEBSTER, J. *Duchess of Malfi.* 1930 London. Bodley Head. Ills Keen. boxed. $17.00

WEBSTER, J.W. *Parkman Murder: Trial of Prof. John W. Webster.* no date. (1850) Boston. 1st ed. self wraps. VG $95.00

WEBSTER, J.W. *2 True CA Stories.* 1893 San Franicsco. 1st ed. $60.00

WEBSTER, Jean. *Daddy Long Legs.* Motion Picture ed. cloth. EX $15.00

WEBSTER, Leslie T. *Rabies in Animals & Men.* 1942 NY. Macmillan. 1st ed. 168 p. cloth. xl. VG $25.00

WEBSTER, Noah. *American Selection of Lessons in Reading & Speaking.* 1805 Hudson Goodwin. 16th ed. 536 p. brown leather. $55.00

WEBSTER, Noah. *American Selection of Lessons in Reading & Speaking.* 1793 Boston. Thomas Andrews. 4th ed. 239 p. $65.00

WEBSTER, Noah. *American Spelling Book.* 1804 Boston. 1st ed. 8vo. G $45.00

WEBSTER, Noah. *American Spelling Book.* 1944 Portland. Sanborn Carter. VG $40.00

WEBSTER, Noah. *American Spelling Book.* 1819 Hudson Hartford. G $40.00

WEBSTER, Noah. *American Spelling Book.* 1848 Cooledge, NY. 7 Ills. cloth. rare. VG $65.00

WEBSTER, Noah. *American Spelling Book.* 1805 Albany. Revised 1st imp. VG $50.00

WEBSTER, Noah. *American Spelling Book.* 1843 Wells River. 8 Ills. VG $40.00

WEBSTER, Noah. *Compendious Dictionary of the English Language.* 1806 Hartford/New Haven. 12mo. $350.00

WEBSTER, Noah. *Dictionary of English Language.* 1832 NY. White. 16mo. 536 p. brown leather. $100.00

WEBSTER, Noah. *Grammatical Institute of the English Language. Part II.* 1784 Hartford. 1st ed. $160.00

WEBSTER, Noah. *Letter to Governors, Instructors, & Trustees.* 1798 NY. 1st ed. wraps. $280.00

WEBSTER, Noah. *Webster's New International Dictionary.* 1943 2nd ed. VG $60.00

WECHSBERG, J. *Blue Trout & Black Truffles.* 1966 NY. EX $10.00

WECHSBERG, J. *Glory of the Violin.* 1973 Viking. 1st ed. dj. VG $25.00

WECHSLER, H. *Great Prints & Printmakers.* 1967 Abrams. EX $28.00

WECTER, D. *Mark Twain in 3 Moods.* 1948 Friends of Hunt Lib. 1/1,200. $75.00

WECTER, Dixon. *Saga of American Society 1607-1937.* 1937 Scribner. $17.50

WEECH. *Pioneer Town: Pima Centennial History.* 1979 Eastern AZ Mus. 1st ed. M $45.00

WEEDEN, Howard. *Bandana Ballads.* 1899 Doubleday McClure. 1st ed. VG $25.00

WEEGEE. *Weegee's People.* 1946 NY. 1st ed. 4to. VG $25.00

WEEKS, J.E. *Diseases of the Eye.* 1910 NY. Ills 1st ed. 944 p. VG $85.00

WEEKS, Jeanne G. *Rugs & Carpets of Europe & the Western World.* 1969 Phil. Chilton. Ills. 252 p. dj. $25.00

WEEKS, John. *Easy Method of Managing Bees.* 1839 Brandon, VT. 4th ed. 16mo. 96 p. $50.00

WEGELIN, Oscar. *Early American Fiction 1774-1830.* 1913 NY. Revised Ltd ed. 1/102. $45.00

WEGELIN, Oscar. *Early American Plays 1714-1830.* 1905 NY. Revised 2nd ed. 1/200. $45.00

WEGELIN, Oscar. *Early American Poetry 1650-1799.* 1903 NY. Ills Ltd ed. 1/150. VG $45.00

WEGELIN, Oscar. *Early American Poetry 1800-1820.* 1907 NY. Ltd ed. 1/150. 81 p. $45.00

WEHLE, H.B. *American Miniatures 1730-1850.* 1937 NY. 48 plts. 127 p. $30.00

WEHLE, R.G. *Wing & Shot: Gun Dog Training.* 1971 Country Pr. Ills. 4to. dj. EX $22.50

WEICK, F. *Aircraft Propeller Design.* 1930 McGraw Hill. 1st ed. 8th imp. 294 p. VG $18.00

WEICK, F. *Birds of Prey of the World.* 1980 Hamburg/Berlin. Ills 1st ed. 4to. 159 p. EX $85.00

WEIDMAN, J. *Death of Dickie Draper.* 1965 NY. 1st ed. dj. EX $10.00

WEIDMAN, J. *Letter of Credit.* 1940 NY. 1st ed. dj. EX $20.00

WEIDMAN, J. *Traveller's Cheque.* 1954 Garden City. 1st ed. dj. EX $15.00

WEIDMAN, J. *4th Street East.* 1970 NY. Ltd 1st ed. 1/350. sgn. boxed. $30.00

WEIGLEY, R.F. *Eisenhower's Lieutenants.* 1981 Bloomington. 1st ed. dj. VG $25.00

WEILL, Alan. *Poster: World-Wide Survey & History.* 1985 Boston. dj. EX $35.00

WEINBAUM, Stanley. *Red Peri.* 1952 Reading. 1st ed. dj. EX $35.00

WEINER, Joel. *Great Britain: Foreign Policy & Span of Empire.* 1972 NY. Chelsea House. 3 vol set. $45.00

WEINSTEIN, E.A. *Woodrow Wilson: Medical & Psychological Biography.* 1981 Princeton. 1st ed. dj. EX $20.00

WEINTRAUB, Stanley. *Beardsley.* 1967 Braziller. 1st print. yellow cloth. dj. $10.00

WEINTRAUB. *Wit & Wisdom of Mae West.* 1967 Putnam. Ills. dj. VG $26.00

WEIR, Capt. Robert. *Riding & Polo.* 1891 London. Ills 2nd ed. 8vo. 423 p. $35.00

WEISE, A.J. *Discoveries of America to the Year 1525.* 1884 NY. 1st ed. 12 maps. EX $35.00

WEISE, A.J. *History of the City of Troy.* 1876 Troy, NY. 8vo. 400 p. green cloth. $26.00

WEISENBERGER, F.P. *Idol of the West: Fabulous Career of Rollin Mallory Daggett.* 1965 Syracuse U Pr. Ills 1st ed. dj. VG $10.00

WEISGARD, Leonard. *Who Dreams of Cheese.* 1950 Scribner. Ills. 4to. dj. $18.00

WEISS, P. *Trotsky in Textile.* 1972 NY. 1st ed. dj. EX $10.00

WEISS, W. *Der Kreig im Westen.* 1941 Munchen. dj. $20.00

WEISS & ENGLISH. *Psychosomatic Medicine.* 1943 Phil. Saunders. 1st ed. 2nd print. VG $25.00

WEISSE, John A. *Obelisk & Freemasonry.* 1880 NY. 1st ed. 178 p. VG $145.00

WEISSMANN, Elizabeth. *Mexico in Sculpture 1521-1821.* 1959 Cambridge. 1st ed. 8vo. 224 p. VG $25.00

WELCH, James. *Death of Jim Loney.* 1979 NY. 1st ed. dj. EX $15.00

WELCH, James. *Riding the Earth Boy 40.* 1976 NY. Harper. 1st ed. dj. EX $20.00

WELCH, William H. *Relation of Yale to Medicine.* 1901 Yale. xl. G $15.00

WELCOME, Henry S. *Story of Metlakahtla.* 1887 Saxon. Ills 2nd ed. 483 p. EX $75.00

WELD, E.F. *Ransomed Bride: A Tale.* 1946 NY. 1st ed. $50.00

WELD, H. Hastings. *Benjamin Franklin: His Autobiography.* 1859 NY. Ills. 8vo. 549 p. ½-leather. $25.00

WELDON, Fay. *Female Friends.* 1974 St. Martin. 1st Am ed. dj. EX $20.00

WELDON, Fay. *Life & Loves of a She-Devil.* 1983 Pantheon. Advance copy. dj. EX $15.00

WELDON, Fay. *Words of Advice.* 1977 Random House. 1st Am ed. dj. EX $15.00

WELLARD, J. *George Patton: Man Under Mars.* 1946 NY. 1st ed. dj. VG $22.50

WELLARD, J. *Great Sahara.* 1965 Dutton. Ills 1st ed. 350 p. dj. VG $10.00

WELLARD, J. *Man in a Helmet.* 1947 London. Ills 1st ed. dj. VG $25.00

WELLER, C.E. *History of the Typewriter.* 1918 La Porte, IN. 1st ed. 12mo. inscr. 87 p. VG $35.00

WELLES, Orson. *Invasion From Mars: Interplanetary Stories.* 1949 NY. Dell. 1st ed. M $20.00

WELLES, P. *Baby Hip.* 1967 NY. 1st ed. dj. EX $10.00

WELLES, R.E. & F.B. *Bighorn of Death Valley.* 1961 GPO. Ills. 195 p. wraps. EX $8.00

WELLMAN, M.W. *Dead & Gone: Crimes of NC.* 1954 Chapel Hill. dj. VG $35.00

WELLMAN, M.W. *Fastest of the River.* 1957 1st ed. cloth. G $20.00

WELLMAN, M.W. *Rebel Boast: 1st at Bethel, Last at Appomattox.* 1956 Holt. Ills 1st ed. 317 p. maps. VG $25.00

WELLMAN, P.I. *Comancheros.* 1952 Doubleday. 1st ed. VG $20.00

WELLMAN, P.I. *Dynasty of Western Outlaws.* 1961 1st ed. dj. EX $35.00

WELLMAN, P.I. *Glory, God, & Gold: Narrative Work of Pioneer West.* 1959 London. 1st English ed. dj. VG $18.00

WELLMAN, P.I. *Indian Wars of the West.* 1956 Doubleday. Ills. 484 p. maps. dj. EX $20.00

WELLMAN, P.I. *Iron Mistress.* 1951 Garden City. Book Club ed. dj. VG $10.00

WELLMAN, P.I. *Spawn of Evil.* 1964 NY. 1st ed. dj. VG $22.50

WELLMAN, P.I. *Trampling Herd.* 1939 Carrick Evans. 1st ed. 433 p. VG $30.00

WELLS, A. Wade. *Hail to the Jeep.* 1946 Harper. Ills. 120 p. dj. VG $32.50

WELLS, A.M. *Miss Marks & Miss Wolley.* 1978 Houghton Mifflin. dj. VG $8.50

WELLS, B.W. *Natural Gardens of NC.* 1932 Chapel Hill. Ltd 1st ed. 1/500. sgn. 458 p. $25.00

WELLS, C. *Idle Idylls.* 1900 NY. Ills 1st ed. EX $20.00

WELLS, C. *Short Stories & Poems.* 1928 Doubleday. Ills 1st ed. VG $12.50

WELLS, Carolyn. *Book of Humorous Verse.* 1941 Garden City. Revised ed. 1,011 p. VG $10.00

WELLS, Carolyn. *Merry-Go-Round.* 1901 Russell. Ills Newell. 1st ed. 152 p. VG $40.00

WELLS, Carveth. *6 Years in the Malay Jungle.* 1925 Garden City. Ills. 261 p. VG $10.00

WELLS, Edmund. *Argonaut Tales.* 1927 NY. 1st ed. EX $60.00

WELLS, H.G. *Adventures of Tommy.* 1935 Poughkeepsie. Artist/Writer Guild. 4to. $25.00

WELLS, H.G. *Christina Alberta's Father.* 1925 London. Cape. 1st ed. sgn. gilt cloth. EX $90.00

WELLS, H.G. *Croquet Player.* 1937 NY. Viking. 1st Am ed. dj. VG $35.00

WELLS, H.G. *Crux Ansata: Indictment of the Roman Catholic Church.* 1944 Agora, NY. 2nd print. 116 p. cloth. VG $37.00

WELLS, H.G. *Experiment in Autobiography.* 1934 1st ed. 718 p. VG $18.00

WELLS, H.G. *Joan & Peter.* 1918 London. 1st ed. G $25.00

WELLS, H.G. *Time Machine.* 1931 Random House. Ills Dwiggins. 1st ed. EX $20.00

WELLS, H.G. *World of William Clissold.* 1926 London. inscr/sgn. 3 vol set. $70.00

WELLS, Henry P. *American Salmon Fisherman.* 1886 Harper. Ills 1st ed. 166 p. EX $30.00

WELLS, Henry W. *Merrill Moore: Poet & Psychiatrist.* 1955 NY. Twayne. 1st ed. dj. EX $25.00

WELLS, Henry W. *Poet & Psychiatrist: Merrill Moore.* 1955 Dublin. Dolmen Pr. 1/700. 8vo. wraps. $20.00

WELLS, James W. *Exploring & Travelling 3,000 Miles Through Brazil.* 1886 London. Sampson Low. 1st ed. 2 vols. $125.00

WELLS, John. *Wells' Illustrated National Handbook of Documents.* 1857 Cincinnati. VG $45.00

WELLS, R. *Covered Bridges in America.* 1931 NY. Ills 1st ed. 135 p. $37.50

WELLS, S. *New Physiognomy; or, Signs of Character.* 1866 NY. 1st ed. VG $30.00

WELLS, William V. *Life & Public Services of Samuel Adams.* 1865 Boston. 3 vol set. VG $85.00

WELLS & HOOPER. *Modern Cabinet Work: Furniture & Fitments.* 1918 Phil/London. Revised 2nd ed. 50 plts. VG $65.00

WELLS-GOSLING, N. *Flying Squirrels: Gliders in the Dark.* 1985 Smithsonian. Ills. 128 p. maps. EX $24.00

WELO, Samuel. *Trade Mark & Monogram Suggestions.* 1937 NY. VG $18.00

WELTY, Earl M.; & TAYLOR, F.J. *76 Bonanza.* 1966 CA. Union Oil Co. 4to. dj. VG $22.50

WELTY, Eudora. *Acrobats in the Park.* 1980 Lord John. Ltd ed. 1/300. sgn. EX $90.00

WELTY, Eudora. *Bride of the Innisfallen.* 1955 Harcourt. 1st ed. inscr. dj. VG $30.00

WELTY, Eudora. *Collected Stories of Eudora Welty.* 1980 Harcourt. 1st ed. sgn. dj. EX $50.00

WELTY, Eudora. *Collected Stories of Eudora Welty.* 1980 NY. Harcourt. 1st trade ed. dj. EX $35.00

WELTY, Eudora. *Eye of the Story.* 1979 Vintage. 1st ed. wraps. EX $15.00

WELTY, Eudora. *Images of South: Visits with Eudora Welty & Walker Evans.* 1977 South Folklore. 1st ed. sgn. wraps. M $35.00

WELTY, Eudora. *Lives of MS Authors 1817-1967.* 1981 MS U Pr. 1st ed. dj. EX $35.00

WELTY, Eudora. *Losing Battles.* 1970 NY. 1st ed. inscr. dj. EX $55.00

WELTY, Eudora. *Losing Battles.* 1982 London. 1st ed. dj. EX $45.00

WELTY, Eudora. *Mothers & Daughters.* 1987 Aperture. 1st ed. dj. EX $25.00

WELTY, Eudora. *Optimist's Daughter.* 1973 Deutsch. dj. EX $35.00

WELTY, Eudora. *Optimist's Daughter.* 1973 Fawcett. 1st ed. pb. wraps. EX $20.00

WELTY, Eudora. *Optimist's Daughter.* 1972 NY. 1st ed. dj. EX $20.00

WELTY, Eudora. *Ponder Heart.* 1954 London. 1st English ed. dj. VG $85.00

WELTY, Eudora. *Robber Bridegroom.* 1978 Harvest. 1st ed. sgn. wraps. EX $25.00

WELTY, Eudora. *Robber Bridegroom.* 1942 Doubleday. 1st ed. EX $25.00

WELTY, Eudora. *Robber Bridegroom.* 1987 Harcourt. Ills/sgn Barry Moser. 1st ed. $30.00

WELTY, Eudora. *Short Stories.* 1950 NY. Ltd 1st ed. 1/1,500. wraps. $75.00

WELTY, Eudora. *Wide Net.* 1945 Bodley Head. 1st ed. scarce. VG $75.00

WELTY, Eudora. *1 Writer's Beginnings.* 1984 Harvard U Pr. Ltd 1st ed. 1/350. boxed. M $125.00

WELTY, Eudora. *1 Writer's Beginnings.* 1984 Cambridge. 1st ed. inscr. dj. VG $30.00

WELTY, Eudora. *3 Papers on Fiction.* 1962 Smith College. 1st ed. wraps. M $75.00

WELTY, J.C. *Life of Birds.* 1963 Knopf. Ills 1st ed. 546 p. dj. VG $10.00

WELZL, Jan. *30 Years in the Golden North.* 1932 Macmillan. 336 p. fld map. G $10.00

WENDELL, Barrett. *Rankell's Remains.* 1887 Boston. scarce. EX $15.00

WENDELL, G. *Bird Carving: Guide to a Fascinating Hobby.* 1961 Bonanza. Ills. 115 p. dj. EX $15.00

WENDT, H. *Sex Life of Animals.* 1965 Simon Schuster. Ills. 383 p. EX $6.00

WENDT, Lloyd; & KOGAN, Herman. *Lords of the Levee: Story of Bathouse John & Hinky-Dink.* 1943 1st ed. VG $35.00

WENDT & KOGAN. *Bet a Million.* 1948 Bobbs Merrill. Ills 1st ed. 357 p. dj. VG $17.50

WENDT. *Give the Lady What She Wants.* 1952 Chicago. 1st ed. sgn. VG $20.00

WENHAM, Edward. *Practical Book of American Silver.* 1949 Phil. 1st ed. VG $30.00

WENIGER, D. *Cacti of TX & Neighboring States.* 1984 TX U Pr. Ills 1st ed. 356 p. dj. EX $25.00

WENTWORTH, E. *America's Sheep Trails.* 1948 IA State Pr. 1st ed. dj. $30.00

WENTWORTH, Patricia. *Gazebo.* 1958 London. 1st English ed. inscr. dj. EX $100.00

WENTWORTH. *Forges in Strong Fires.* 1948 Caxton. Ltd ed. 1/1,000. sgn. dj. EX $37.50

WENTZ, Roby. *Grabhorn Press: A Biography.* 1981 San Francisco. 1st ed. 4to. dj. VG $115.00

WENTZEL, H. *Die Luneberger Ratsstube von A von Soest.* 1947 Hamburg. Ills. dj. wraps. $15.00

WENZEL, Marian. *House Decoration in Nubia.* 1972 Toronto. Ills. 4to. 238 p. dj. $20.00

WERNER, A. *Butterflies & Moths.* 1956 Random House. Ills. 4to. 175 p. dj. EX $30.00

WERNER, Alfred. *Modigliani the Sculptor.* 1962 NY. Golden Griffin/Arts Inc. 4to. $60.00

WERNER, Carl Avery. *Tobacco Land.* no date. NY. 1st ed. VG $17.00

WERNER, Herbert A. *Iron Coffins: Personal Account of German U-Boat Battle.* 1969 NY. Ills 1st ed. 364 p. dj. EX $25.00

WERNER, Jane. *Child's Book of Bible Stories.* 1944 Random House. Ills Masha. 4to. 54 p. dj. VG $12.50

WERNER, M.R. *Brigham Young.* 1925 London. Ills 1st ed. VG $15.00

WERNER, M.R. *Tammany Hall.* 1928 Garden City. Ills 1st ed. 586 p. $12.00

WERPER, B. *Tarzan & the Abominable Snowmen. Series #4.* 1965 Golds. 1st ed. wraps. EX $35.00

WERPER, B. *Tarzan & the Snake People. Series #3.* 1964 Golds. 1st ed. wraps. EX $35.00

WERSTEIN, I. *Marshal Without a Gun: Tom Smith.* 1959 Messner. 192 p. dj. EX $5.00

WERTHAM, Frederick. *Seduction of the Innocent.* 1954 Rinehart. 2nd ed. dj. G $40.00

WERTHAM, Frederick. *World Within.* 1947 Wertham. inscr. G $10.00

WESCOTT, Glenway. *Good-Bye WI.* 1928 Ltd 1st ed. 1/250. inscr. boxed. VG $65.00

WESLEY, Charles. *Negro Labor in the US 1850-1925.* 1927 Vanguard. 2nd ed. presentation. $30.00

WEST, Charles C. *Aroostock Woods.* 1892 Houlton, ME. wraps. scarce. VG $65.00

WEST, Dorothy H.; & SHOR, R. *Children's Catalogue.* 1961 NY. Wilson. 10th ed. VG $20.00

WEST, Jessamyn. *Cress Delahanty.* 1953 NY. 1st ed. dj. EX $15.00

WEST, Jessamyn. *Leafy Rivers.* 1967 NY. 1st ed. dj. EX $15.00

WEST, L. *Making an Etching.* 1932 London. Ills. xl. VG $35.00

WEST, Mae. *Diamond Lil.* 1949 NY. dj. VG $17.50

WEST, Morris L. *Tower of Babel.* 1968 NY. 1st ed. dj. M $10.00

WEST, Nathaniel. *Day of the Locust.* 1951 London. 1st ed. dj. VG $40.00

WEST, Paul. *Alley Jaggers.* 1966 NY. Harper. 1st ed. VG $15.00

WEST, Paul. *Caliban's Filibuster.* 1971 NY. 1st ed. dj. EX $15.00

WEST, Paul. *Quality of Mercy.* 1961 London. Chatto Windus. 1st ed. EX $25.00

WEST, R. *New Meaning of Treasons.* 1964 NY. dj. G $12.50

WEST, Rebecca. *Black Lamb & Gray Falcon.* 1944 London. 2 vol set. VG $25.00

WEST, Rebecca. *Black Lamb & Gray Falcon.* 1941 Viking. 2 vol set. djs. EX $35.00

WEST, Rebecca. *Black Lamb & Gray Falcon. Vol. II.* 1941 NY. 1st ed. dj. EX $15.00

WEST, Richard. *Lincoln's Navy Department.* 1943 Bobbs Merrill. Ills 1st ed. 279 p. dj. VG $25.00

WEST, Roy B. *Rocky Mountain Cities.* 1949 NY. 1st ed. dj. VG $25.00

WEST, T.W. *History of Architecture in England.* 1966 NY. McKay. 2nd ed. dj. VG $20.00

WESTCOTT, A. *Mahan on Naval Warfare.* 1919 Boston. Ills. 12mo. 372 p. blue cloth. $16.00

WESTCOTT, G. *Images of Truth.* 1963 London. 1st English ed. dj. VG $15.00

WESTCOTT, Glenway. *Grandmothers.* 1927 Harper. G $12.50

WESTCOTT, W. Wynn. *Introduction to Study of Kabalah.* 1926 London. Watkins. 2nd ed. 72 p. VG $35.00

WESTCOTT, W. Wynn. *Numbers: Their Occult Power & Mystic Virtues.* 1911 NY. Allied Pub. 3rd ed. 127 p. VG $22.00

WESTCOTT, W. Wynn. *Pymander of Hermes. Collectanea Hermetica Vol. II.* 1926 London. Watkins. 2nd ed. 72 p. VG $35.00

WESTCOTT, W. Wynn. *Pymander of Hermes. Collectanea Hermetica Vol. II.* 1894 London. 1st ed. 117 p. VG $95.00

WESTERDIJK, Peter. *African Metal Implements, Weapons, Tools, & Regalia.* 1984 Greenvale, NY. Ills. 48 p. $18.50

WESTERGAARD, Waldemar. *Danish West Indies Under Company Rule.* 1917 NY. Macmillan. Ills 1st ed. VG $50.00

WESTERMEIER, Clifford P. *Trailing the Cowboy: His Life & Lore.* 1955 Caxton. 1st ed. sgn. dj. EX $55.00

WESTING, Fred. *Locomotives That Baldwin Built.* 1966 192 p. dj. VG $9.50

WESTLAKE, Donald E. *Levine.* 1984 Mysterious Pr. 1st ed. dj. EX $15.00

WESTLAKE, Donald E. *Up Your Banners.* 1969 Macmillan. 1st ed. sgn. dj. EX $35.00

WESTLAKE, Donald E. *Why Me?* 1983 Viking. 1st ed. dj. EX $25.00

WESTLAKE & GARFIELD. *Gangway!* 1973 Barker. 1st English ed. dj. EX $15.00

WESTMAN, James. *Why Fish Bite & Why They Don't.* 1961 Prentice Hall. Ills. 211 p. dj. VG $10.00

WESTMORE, H.C. *Last of the Great Scouts.* 1899 Chicago. 1st ed. 2nd issue. G $20.00

WESTON, Brett. *Voyage of the Eye.* 1975 Millerton. Aperture. 1st ed. cloth. dj. $40.00

WESTON, C. & E. *CA & the West.* 1940 Duell Sloan. 1st ed. 4to. cloth. VG $70.00

WESTON, Christine. *Dark Wood.* 1946 NY. 1st ed. dj. EX $12.00

WESTON, Edward. *Cats of Wildcat Hill.* 1947 Duell Sloan. 1st ed. 4to. cloth. EX $185.00

WESTON, Edward. *Daybooks of Edward Weston. Vol. I: Mexico.* 1961 Eastman House. 1st ed. cloth. dj. EX $45.00

WESTON, Edward. *Leaves of Grass.* 1942 Ltd Ed Club. 1/1,500. sgn. 2 vol set. VG $425.00

WESTON, Edward. *Life & Photos.* 1979 Aperture. Revised ed. dj. EX $75.00

WESTON, Edward. *My Camera on Point Lobos.* 1950 Boston. 1st ed. spiral bdg. dj. EX $145.00

WETHERED, Newton. *Medieval Craftsmanship & the Modern Amateur.* 1923 London. Ills 1st ed. G $25.00

WETJEN, Albert R. *Fiddlers' Green.* 1931 Little Brown. Ills Horvath. 1st ed. VG $10.00

WETMORE, Helen Cody. *Last of the Great Scouts: Life Story of W.F. Cody.* 1889 Duluth. 1st ed. 267 p. VG $40.00

WETZEL, C.M. *Trout Flies: Natural & Imitation.* 1979 Stackpole. Ltd Facsimile ed. 4to. dj. EX $12.00

WEYER, E.M. *Strangest Creatures on Earth.* 1953 Sheridan. 255 p. VG $5.00

WEYMAN, Stanley. *Castle Inn.* 1898 NY. 1st ed. VG $35.00

WEYMAN, Stanley. *Count Hannibal.* 1901 NY. G $20.00

WHARTON, Don. *Roosevelt Omnibus.* 1934 Knopf. 1st ed. VG $20.00

WHARTON, Edith. *Book of the Homeless.* 1916 NY. Scribner. VG $25.00

WHARTON, Edith. *Children.* 1928 Appleton. 1st ed. VG $10.00

WHARTON, Edith. *Crucial Instances.* 1901 Scribner. 1st ed. VG $22.50

WHARTON, Edith. *Ethan Frome.* 1911 NY. 1st ed. 1st issue. VG $135.00

WHARTON, Edith. *Fruit of the Tree.* 1907 NY. Ills 1st ed. M $25.00

WHARTON, Edith. *Gods Arrive.* 1932 NY. 1st ed. dj. EX $30.00

WHARTON, Edith. *Hermit & Wild Woman.* 1908 NY. 1st ed. dj. EX $50.00

WHARTON, Edith. *House of Mirth.* 1905 NY. 1st ed. EX $65.00

WHARTON, Edith. *House of Mirth.* 1975 Ltd Ed Club. Ills/sgn Quackenbush. 230 p. $50.00

WHARTON, Edith. *Hudson River Bracketed.* 1929 NY. Appleton. wraps. VG $75.00

WHARTON, Edith. *Italian Backgrounds.* 1905 NY. 1st ed. EX $75.00

WHARTON, Edith. *Italian Villas & Their Gardens.* 1904 Century. Ills Parrish. 1st ed. VG $95.00

WHARTON, Edith. *Madame de Treymes.* 1907 NY. Ills 1st ed. VG $20.00

WHARTON, Edith. *Reef.* 1912 NY. VG $10.00

WHARTON, Edith. *Summer.* 1917 NY. 1st ed. G $5.00

WHARTON, Edith. *Touchstone.* 1900 NY. 1st ed. $30.00

WHARTON, Edith. *Twilight Sleep.* 1927 NY. 2nd print. VG $7.00

WHARTON, George. *Works of the Late Most Excellent Philosopher & Astronomer.* 1683 London. Collected 1st ed. leather. VG $500.00

WHARTON, John F. *Theory & Practice of Earning a Living.* 1945 Simon Schuster. 236 p. dj. G $15.00

WHARTON, William. *Birdy.* 1979 NY. 1st ed. dj. EX $25.00

WHARTON, William. *Dad.* 1981 Knopf. 1st ed. dj. EX $20.00

WHARTON, William. *Midnight Clear.* 1982 Cape. 1st English ed. dj. EX $15.00

WHEAT, Carl I. *Book of CA Gold Rush.* 1949 Grabhorn. Ltd ed. 1/500. $110.00

WHEAT, Carl I. *Pioneer Press of CA.* 1948 Oakland. Grabhorn. Ltd ed. 1/450. dj. $150.00

WHEAT, E.H. *Jacob Lawrence: American Painter.* 1986 Seattle. Ills. 272 p. $50.00

WHEAT, Peter. *Fishing As We Find It.* no date. Warne. Ills. 154 p. VG $8.50

WHEAT & BRUN. *Maps & Charts Published in America Before 1800.* 1969 Yale. 1st ed. $45.00

WHEATLEY, Dennis. *Total War.* 1942 London. 1st ed. presentation. wraps. $30.00

WHEELER, Burton. *Yankee From the West.* 1962 NY. EX $20.00

WHEELER, C.B. & R.W. *With Scissors & Pen: Silhouettes & Verse.* c 1932. NY. 8vo. 111 p. dj. VG $25.00

WHEELER, E.S. *Scheyichbi & Strand; or, Early Days Along the DE.* 1876 Lippincott. 116 p. VG $42.00

WHEELER, G.C. & J.N. *Ants of ND.* 1963 ND U Pr. Ills. 326 p. wraps. EX $18.00

WHEELER, George. *History of Brunswick, Topsham, & Harpswell, ME.* 1878 Boston. map. G $45.00

WHEELER, Homer W. *Buffalo Days: 40 Years in Old West.* 1925 Indianapolis. Ills 2nd ed. 16 plts. 369 p. G $65.00

WHEELER, K. *Railroaders.* 1973 Time Life. Ills. 240 p. leather. EX $15.00

WHEELER, Monroe. *Last Works of Henri Matisse.* 1961 MOMA. Ills. 4to. 46 p. wraps. $18.00

WHEELER, Monroe. *Modern Painters & Sculptors As Illustrators.* 1936 MOMA/Rudge. Ills Ltd 1st ed. 1/2,500. 4to. $45.00

WHEELER, Monroe. *Soutine.* 1950 MOMA. Cleveland Mus of Art. 4to. dj. $30.00

WHEELER, Monroe; & REWALD, J. *Modern Drawings.* 1944 MOMA. Ills. 4to. 104 p. cloth. dj. $20.00

WHEELER, Opal. *Sing for America.* 1944 Dutton. Ills G Tenggren. 1st ed. 4to. $25.00

WHEELER, Opal. *Sing for Christmas.* 1943 Dutton. Ills G Tenggren. 1st ed. $20.00

WHEELER, Opal. *Sing in Praise.* 1946 NY. Ills M Torrey. 1st ed. dj. EX $17.50

WHEELER, Opal. *Stars Over Bethlehem.* 1952 NY. Ills C Price. 1st ed. sgn. EX $14.00

WHEELER, W.M. *Ants.* 1926 NY. Ills. 663 p. dj. EX $35.00

WHEELER, W.M. *Mosiacs & Other Anomalies Among Ants.* 1937 Harvard U Pr. Ills. 95 p. EX $16.00

WHEELER & DEUCHER. *Edward MacDowell & His Cabin in the Pines.* 1968 NY. Ills Greenwalt. 16th print. G $12.50

WHEELER. *Sessions S. Paiute.* 1965 Caxton. 1st ed. map. dj. EX $10.00

WHEELER-BENNET, John W. *Nemesis of Power: German Army in Politics 1918-1945.* 1954 NY. Ills. 829 p. G $22.50

WHEELOCK, Julia S. *Boys in White: Experience of Hospital Agent in WA.* 1870 NY. 1st ed. 12mo. 274 p. G $38.00

WHEELWRIGHT, Edmund March. *School Architecture.* 1901 Rogers Manson. Ills. photos. plans. $40.00

WHEELWRIGHT, John T. *New Chance Acquaintance: Trifle Served Up on 12 Plates.* 1880 Boston. Williams. Ills 1st ed. 8vo. $45.00

WHEILDON, William W. *New History of Battle of Bunker Hill.* 1875 Boston. Ills. 8vo. fld map. 55 p. VG $65.00

WHELEN, J. *Why Not Load Your Own?* 1951 Revised 2nd ed. dj. VG $22.50

WHELEN, Townsend. *Hunting Rifle.* 1940 Harrisburg, PA. 1st ed. VG $25.00

WHELEN, Townsend. *Telescopic Rifle Sights.* 1944 Plantersville. Ills 2nd ed. G $15.00

WHELPLEY, G.F. *Practical Instruction in Art of Letter Engraving.* 1984 NY. 2nd ed. VG $15.00

WHERRY, E.T. *Wild Flower Guide.* 1948 Doubleday. 202 p. cloth. VG $12.00

WHEWELL, W. *History of Inductive Sciences From Earliest to Present Time.* 1847 London. Expanded 2nd ed. gilt leather. $100.00

WHICHER, George. *This Was a Poet.* 1938 Scribner. 1st ed. 8vo. 336 p. VG $20.00

WHIDDEN, Capt. John. *Old Sailing Ship Days.* 1925 Boston. Ills 1st ed. dj. EX $35.00

WHIFFEN, E.T. *Outing Lore: Guide for the Modern Angler.* 1928 Neale. 185 p. dj. G $13.50

WHIGHAM, H.J. *How To Play Golf. New Edition.* 1898 Chicago. Stone. Ills. photos. 8vo. 335 p. $150.00

WHISTLER, Eden V. *Baronet & Butterfly.* 1899 NY. Russell. 8vo. red morocco. rebound. EX $300.00

WHISTLER, J.M. *Eden Versus Whistler.* 1899 Paris. 4to. cloth. $225.00

WHISTLER, J.M. *Gentle Art of Making Enemies.* c 1890s. London. 1st trade ed. cloth. $85.00

WHISTLER, Rex. *Designs for the Theatre. Parts I & II.* 1947 London. 1st ed. plts. wraps. VG $40.00

WHISTON, William. *Memoirs of the Life & Writings of Mr. William Whiston.* 1749 London. 1st ed. 8vo. 2 vol set. VG $200.00

WHITAKER, Evelyn. *Laddie.* c 1900. NY. Caldwell. Ills. 12mo. G $8.00

WHITAKER, R. *Common Indian Snakes: Field Guide.* 1978 Macmillan. Ills. 154 p. wraps. EX $12.00

WHITE, Alma. *Titanic Tragedy: God Speaking to the Nations.* 1913 Bound Brook. Ills 1st ed. 211 p. scarce. EX $75.00

WHITE, Charles L. *Drums Through the Ages.* 1960 Los Angeles. Ills 1st ed. dj. VG $30.00

WHITE, E. *Caracole.* 1985 NY. Review ed. dj. EX $10.00

WHITE, E.B. *Charlotte's Web.* 1952 Harper Row. Ills G Williams. dj. M $22.00

WHITE, E.B. *Ho Hum.* 1931 NY. 4th ed. dj. VG $20.00

WHITE, E.B. *Stuart Little.* 1945 NY/London. Ills Williams. 1st ed. dj. EX $50.00

WHITE, E.B. *1 Man's Meat.* 1942 NY. Harper. 1st ed. dj. EX $35.00

WHITE, E.B. *2nd Tree From the Corner.* 1954 Harper. 1st ed. dj. VG $40.00

WHITE, Ernest William. *Cameos From Silver Land; or, Experiences of Naturalist.* 1881-1882. London. John van Voorst. set. $100.00

WHITE, Gilbert. *Natural History of Selborne.* 1911 London. Macmillan. Ills G Collins. $15.00

WHITE, Gilbert. *Natural History of Selborne.* 1854 London. full leather. G $25.00

WHITE, Gilbert. *Natural History of Selbourne.* 1960 Cresset. Ills. 296 p. dj. EX $20.00

WHITE, Gilbert. *White's Selborne for Boys & Girls.* no date. Blackwell. Ills 1st ed. VG $15.00

WHITE, Gleeson. *English Illustration of the '60s.* 1906 London. Corrected 3rd ed. VG $60.00

WHITE, Gleeson. *Practical Designing: Handbook of Preparation of Drawings.* 1893 London. George Bell. xl. VG $40.00

WHITE, Gwen. *Book of Dolls.* 1956 NY. dj. EX $20.00

WHITE, J. *National Gallery of Ireland.* 1969 NY. Ills. 224 p. $45.00

WHITE, James P. *Birdsong.* 1977 Providence. Copper Beech. presentation. $20.00

WHITE, John H. *American Railroad Passenger Car.* 1978 John Hopkins. dj. VG $20.00

WHITE, John H. *Great Yellow Fleet.* 1986 186 p. dj. EX $20.00

WHITE, John. *Journal of a Voyage to New South Wales.* 1790 London. 65 plts. ½-leather. $3000.00

WHITE, John. *Troubles of Jerusalem's Restoration.* 1646 London. cloth. rebound. VG $60.00

WHITE, Leslie T. *Harness Bull.* 1937 Harcourt. 1st ed. inscr. G $17.50

WHITE, Leslie T. *Me Detective.* 1936 Harcourt. 1st ed. inscr. G $17.50

WHITE, Margaret. *Boys & Girls at Work & Play.* c 1930. NY. Am Book Co. Ills. VG $12.50

WHITE, Minor. *Mirrors, Messages, & Manifestations.* 1969 NY. Aperture. 1st ed. 4to. cloth. EX $115.00

WHITE, Palmer. *Poiret.* 1973 NY. Potter. Ills. 4to. 192 p. dj. $45.00

WHITE, Paul Dudley. *Heart Disease.* 1938 NY. Macmillan. 2nd ed. 745 p. VG $20.00

WHITE, Paul Dudley. *Heart Disease.* 1931 NY. Macmillan. 1st ed. G $35.00

WHITE, S. *History of American Troops During War Under Fenton.* 1896 Rochester, NY. Ltd ed. 1/300. EX $25.00

WHITE, S.E. *African Campfires.* 1913 NY. 1st ed. VG $25.00

WHITE, S.E. *Forest.* 1905 McClure Phillips. Ills. cloth. $14.50

WHITE, S.E. *Forest.* 1903 NY. Outlook Co. Ills Fogarty. 1st ed. 8vo. $25.00

WHITE, S.E. *Gold.* 1913 Doubleday Page. Ills 1st ed. $15.00

WHITE, S.E. *Land of Footprints.* 1912 NY. 1st ed. VG $25.00

WHITE, S.E. *Lions in the Path.* 1926 NY. 1st ed. VG $35.00

WHITE, S.E. *Mountians.* 1904 NY. 1st ed. $35.00

WHITE, S.E. *Shipper & Newfounder.* 1931 NY. Ills Webster. 1st ed. VG $25.00

WHITE, S.E. *Silent Places.* 1904 NY. 6th print. EX $20.00

WHITE, S.E. *Unobstructed Universe.* 1940 Dutton. 1st ed. 12mo. 320 p. dj. VG $18.00

WHITE, S.E. *Wild Geese Calling.* 1940 Literary Guild. blue cloth. VG $10.00

WHITE, T. *Our War with Spain for Cuba's Freedom.* c 1898. no place. Ills. 8vo. 416 p. G $15.00

WHITE, T.H. *Book of Merlyn.* 1982 Austin. 1st ed. dj. EX $25.00

WHITE, T.H. *Goshawk.* 1951 London. 1st ed. dj. EX $45.00

WHITE, T.H. *Goshawk.* 1960 London. dj. VG $18.00

WHITE, Thomas. *Beauties of Occult Science Investigated.* 1810 London. 8vo. 436 p. $135.00

WHITE, William A. *Autobiography of William A. White.* 1946 Macmillan. dj. G $8.00

WHITE, William A. *Martial Adventures of Henry & Me.* 1918 NY. 1st ed. sgn. EX $17.00

WHITE, William Charles. *Album of Chinese Bamboos.* 1939 Toronto. 1st ed. 4to. EX $50.00

WHITE & JACOBY. *Thunder Out of China.* 1946 NY. G $10.00

WHITEHEAD, J.H.C. *Mathematical Works of J.H. Whitehead.* 1963 Macmillan. 4th ed. dj. EX $60.00

WHITEHILL, Walter M. *Analecta Biographica.* 1969 New England Portraits. dj. EX $12.00

WHITELEY, Opal. *Story of Opal.* 1920 Boston. Ltd ed. 1/650. 8 plts. VG $48.00

WHITING, Edward E. *Calvin Coolidge: His Ideals of Citizenship.* 1924 Boston. Wilde. dj. VG $20.00

WHITLEY, Edna T. *KY Ante-Bellum Portraiture.* 1956 Colonial Dames. Ills Ltd ed. 1/1,000. 4to. $85.00

WHITMAN, Walt. *American Bard.* 1982 NY. 1st trade ed. square 8vo. dj. $35.00

WHITMAN, Walt. *Drum Taps.* 1865 NY. 1st ed. 2nd issue. 12mo. G $105.00

WHITMAN, Walt. *Leaves of Grass.* 1951 Peter Pauper. Ills Boyd Hanna. 1/1,100. VG $140.00

WHITMAN, Walt. *Leaves of Grass.* no date. Peter Pauper. Ills Curry. VG $15.00

WHITMAN, Walt. *Leaves of Grass.* 1942 Ltd Ed Club. sgn. 2 vol set. slipcase. VG $300.00

WHITMAN, Walt. *Leaves of Grass.* 1940 Doubleday. Ills Daniel. boxed. VG $15.00

WHITMAN, Walt. *Leaves of Grass.* 1892 Phil. McKay. VG $135.00

WHITMAN, Walt. *Leaves of Grass.* 1976 Paddington Pr. 4to. cloth. dj. EX $55.00

WHITMAN, Walt. *Letters of Anne Gilchrist & Walt Whitman.* 1919 Garden City. VG $16.00

WHITMAN, Walt. *November Boughs.* 1888 Phil. 1st ed. $90.00

WHITMAN, Walt. *NY Dissected.* 1936 NY. VG $25.00

WHITMAN, Walt. *Selected Poems of Walt Whitman.* 1892 NY. 1st ed. cloth. EX $135.00

WHITMAN, Walt. *Specimen Days & Collections.* 1883 Phil. 1st ed. 2nd issue. EX $125.00

WHITMAN, Walt. *Specimen Days in America.* 1887 London. Scott. 1st ed. VG $65.00

WHITMAN, Walt. *There Was a Child Went Forth.* 1968 Northampton. Gehenna Pr. Ills/sgn Taylor. $140.00

WHITMAN, Walt. *Walt Whitman in Camden.* 1938 Camden. Ltd 1st ed. 1/1,100. $60.00

WHITMAN, Wanda Wilson. *Songs That Changed the World.* 1969 NY. Crown. dj. VG $15.00

WHITMONT, Edward. *Symbolic Quest: Basic Concepts of Analytical Psychology.* 1969 Jung Foundation. 1st ed. dj. $20.00

WHITNEY, Albert W. *Man & the Motor Car.* 1938 Detroit. later print. 12mo. 264 p. G $10.00

WHITNEY, Caspar. *Flowing Road.* 1913 Lippincott. photos. 319 p. VG $40.00

WHITNEY, Caspar. *Jungle Trails & Jungle People.* 1905 NY. 1st ed. VG $23.50

WHITNEY, Caspar. *On Snowshoes to the Barren Ground.* 1896 NY. Ills Remington. 1st ed. 8vo. $50.00

WHITNEY, E.A. *Complete Guide to Watercolor Painting.* 1966 NY. Ills. 176 p. $22.50

WHITNEY, J. Parker. *Reminiscences of a Sportsman.* 1906 NY. 1st ed. inscr. EX $35.00

WHITNEY, Thomas R. *Defense of the American Policy.* c 1856. NY. 12mo. 369 p. red cloth. G $40.00

WHITNEY. *Hawaiian America.* 1902 Harper. VG $30.00

WHITTEMORE. *George Washington in Sculpture.* 1933 Boston. 1st ed. sgn. 203 p. G $35.00

WHITTEN, Les. *Alchemist.* 1973 NY. 1st ed. presentation. dj. EX $45.00

WHITTEN, T. *Gibbons of Siberut.* 1982 Dent. London. Ills 1st ed. 207 p. dj. EX $17.00

WHITTIER, John Greenleaf. *Among the Hills & Other Poems.* 1869 Boston. Ills 1st ed. green cloth. VG $40.00

WHITTIER, John Greenleaf. *Miriam & Other Poems.* 1871 Boston. 1st ed. G $25.00

WHITTIER, John Greenleaf. *PA Pilgrim.* 1872 Boston. 1st ed. EX $30.00

WHITTIER, John Greenleaf. *Panorama.* 1856 Boston. 1st ed. VG $25.00

WHITTIER, John Greenleaf. *Poems.* 1939 Phil. 1st ed. 12mo. cloth. $60.00

WHITTIER, John Greenleaf. *Snow-Bound.* 1939 Windham. Hawthorne House. 1st ed. $20.00

WHITTIER, John Greenleaf. *Snow-Bound.* 1866 Boston. 1st ed. 2nd state. VG $35.00

WHITTIER, John Greenleaf. *Snow-Bound.* 1930 NY. Ltd Ed Club. boxed. $38.00

WHITTIER, John Greenleaf. *Tent on the Beach & Other Poems.* 1867 Boston. 1st ed. $25.00

WHITTIER, John Greenleaf. *To the Lighthouse.* 1981 Harcourt Brace. 1st ed. 8vo. slipcase. EX $20.00

WHITTLE, Sir Frank. *Story of a Pioneer.* 1953 London. Muller. Ills 1st ed. 320 p. VG $25.00

WHITTLE, T. *Some Ancient Gentlemen.* 1966 Taplinger. 244 p. dj. VG $12.00

WHITTMANN, Otto. *New England Glass Company 1818-1888.* 1963 Toledo. Toledo Mus Art. 80 p. wraps. $15.00

WHITTON, Blair. *American Clockwork Toys 1862-1900.* 1981 Exton, PA. Schiffer. Ills. 4to. 224 p. $25.00

WHYTE, Alexander. *Characters & Characteristics of William Law.* 1893 London. 328 p. VG $75.00

WIBBERLEY, Leonard. *Last Stand of Father Felix.* 1974 Morrow. 1st ed. dj. EX $8.00

WIBBERLEY, Leonard. *Time of the Lamb: Christmas Story.* 1961 NY. Ives Washburn. Ills Kredel. VG $8.50

WIBERG, H. *Christmas at Tomtens Farm.* 1968 NY. dj. EX $20.00

WICKENDEN, J. *Claim in the Hills.* 1957 Rinehart. 275 p. dj. VG $10.00

WICKENDEN, L. *Make Friends with Your Land.* 1949 NY. 132 p. dj. G $4.00

WICKERSHAM, James. *Bibliography of AK Literature.* 1927 Cordova, AK. 1st ed. presentation. EX $165.00

WICKERSHAM, James. *Old Yukon.* 1938 WA. Ills. 8vo. maps. blue cloth. $25.00

WICKES, G. *Americans in Paris.* 1969 NY. Doubleday. 1st ed. cloth. dj. VG $15.00

WICKEY, H. *Thus Far: Growth of an American Artist.* 1941 NY. Ills. 3,030 p. $25.00

WICKSTEED, Joseph H. *Blake's Innocence & Experience.* 1928 London. dj. VG $65.00

WICKWIRE, Franklin P. *British Subministers & Colonial America 1763-1783.* 1966 Princeton. 216 p. $18.00

WIDTSOE, A. John. *Discourses of Bringham Young.* 1925 Deseret Book Co. $32.50

WIEDERSEIM, Grace. *Molly & the Unwiseman Abroad.* 1910 Lippincott. Ills 2nd print. 8vo. 252 p. $40.00

WIEGAND. *Chester A. Arthur Conspiracy.* 1983 1st ed. dj. VG $7.00

WIENER, Leo. *Anthology of Russian Literature.* 1902 NY. 1st ed. 8vo. 2 vol set. $30.00

WIENER, Norbert. *Cybernetics: Control & Communication in Animal & Machine.* 1950 NY. Wiley. 8th print. 194 p. dj. VG $12.00

WIENER, Norbert. *Ex-Prodigy: My Childhood & Youth.* 1953 Simon Schuster. Ills 2nd print. 309 p. dj. VG $12.00

WIER, Allen. *Things About To Disappear.* 1978 Baton Rouge. LA U Pr. 1st ed. wraps. $20.00

WIER, Dara. *All You Have in Common.* 1984 Pittsburgh. Carnegie Mellon. 1st ed. pb. $15.00

WIER, Dara. *Blood Hook & Eye.* 1977 Austin. TX U Pr. 1st ed. dj. EX $75.00

WIESE, Kurt. *Return of Silver Chief.* 1943 Winston. Ills 1st ed. 211 p. dj. VG $22.00

WIESEL, Elie. *Beggar in Jerusalem.* 1970 NY. Special 1st ed. sgn. EX $25.00

WIESEL, Elie. *Beggar in Jerusalem.* 1970 Ltd ed. 1/250. sgn. glassine wraps. boxed. EX $50.00

WIESEL, Elie. *Golem.* 1983 Summit. Ills 1st ed. dj. EX $15.00

WIESEL, Elie. *Jews of Silence.* 1966 Holt. 1st ed. dj. EX $30.00

WIESEL, Elie. *Legends of Our Time.* 1968 Holt. 1st ed. dj. EX $25.00

WIESEL, Elie. *Messengers of God.* 1976 Random House. 1st ed. dj. EX $20.00

WIESEL, Elie. *Oath.* 1973 Random House. 1st ed. dj. EX $20.00

WIESEL, Elie. *Souls On Fire.* 1972 Random House. 1st Am ed. dj. EX $20.00

WIESEL, Elie. *Testament.* 1981 Summit. 1st ed. dj. EX $15.00

WIESEL, Elie. *Zalman; or, Madness of God.* 1974 Random House. 1st ed. dj. EX $18.00

WIESEL, Elie. *5th Son: A Novel.* 1985 Franklin Lib. 1st ed. sgn. full leather. M $40.00

WIGGIN, Kate Douglas. *Old Peabody Pew.* 1907 Boston. Houghton Mifflin. Ills 1st ed. $15.00

WIGGIN, Kate Douglas. *Timothy's Quest.* 1890 Boston. Houghton Mifflin. gilt cloth. $15.00

WIGGIN, Kate Douglas. *Arabian Nights.* 1924 NY. Scribner. Ills Parrish. 339 p. VG $35.00

WIGGIN, Kate Douglas. *Arabian Nights.* 1919 NY. Scribner. Ills Parrish. 339 p. M $100.00

WIGGIN, Kate Douglas. *Bird's Christmas Carol.* 1941 Boston. Ills J Gillespie. dj. EX $12.50

WIGGIN, Kate Douglas. *Bird's Christmas Carol.* 1912 NY. Ills Wireman. VG $15.00

WIGGIN, Kate Douglas. *Bird's Christmas Carol.* 1894 Boston. Houghton Mifflin. VG $9.50

WIGGIN, Kate Douglas. *Froebel's Occupations.* 1897 Boston. VG $30.00

WIGGIN, Kate Douglas. *Homespun Tales.* 1907 Boston. Ills. G $15.00

WIGGIN, Kate Douglas. *Penelope's Irish Experiences.* 1901 Boston. 1st ed. VG $18.00

WIGGIN, Kate Douglas. *Penelope's Postscripts.* 1915 Boston. 1st ed. VG $15.00

WIGGIN, Kate Douglas. *Rebecca of Sunnybrook Farm.* 1903 Boston. 1st ed. 1st issue. EX $50.00

WIGGIN, Kate Douglas. *Romance of a Christmas Card.* 1916 Houghton Mifflin. Ills Hunt. G $15.00

WIGGIN, Kate Douglas. *Story of Waitsill Baxter.* 1913 Boston. 1st ed. VG $15.00

WIGGIN, Kate Douglas. *Summer in Canon.* 1894 Boston. Houghton Mifflin. VG $10.00

WIGGIN, Kate Douglas. *Susanna & Sue.* 1909 Boston. 1st ed. EX $28.00

WIGGIN, Kate Douglas. *Timothy's Quest.* 1898 Boston. VG $12.50

WIGGLESWORTH, V.B. *Physiology of Insect Metamorphosis.* 1954 Cambridge U Pr. Ills. 152 p. dj. EX $13.00

WIGHT, F.S. *Arthur G. Dove.* 1958 CA U Pr. Ills. 4to. dj. $50.00

WIGHT, F.S. *Milestones of American Painting in Our Century.* 1949 NY. Ills. 134 p. $15.00

WIKAN, Unni. *Behind the Veil in Arabia: Women in Oman.* 1982 Baltimore. John Hopkins. 1st ed. dj. EX $30.00

WILBERT, Johannes. *Warao Basketry: Form & Function.* 1975 UCLA. Ills. 86 p. $15.00

WILBOUR, C.E. *Travels in Egypt.* 1936 Brooklyn. 1/1,000. 8vo. 22 plts. 614 p. $125.00

WILBUR, K.M.; & YONGE, C.M. *Physiology of Mollusca.* 1964 Academic Pr. Ills. 681 p. dj. EX $55.00

WILBUR, Marguerite Eyer. *John Sutter: Rascal & Adventurer.* 1949 NY. Liveright. Ills 1st ed. 371 p. $10.00

WILBUR, Richard. *Ceremony & Other Poems.* 1950 NY. 1st ed. dj. EX $35.00

WILBUR, Richard. *Elizabeth Bishop: Memorial Tribute.* 1982 Albondocani. 1st ed. 1/174. sgn. wraps. M $35.00

WILBUR, Richard. *Mind Reader.* 1976 NY. 1st ed. dj. EX $35.00

WILBUR, Richard. *Opposites.* 1973 Harcourt. 1st ed. dj. EX $15.00

WILBUR, Richard. *Things of This World.* 1956 NY. 1st ed. dj. EX $35.00

WILBUR, Richard. *Whale & Other Uncollected Translations.* 1982 NY. Ltd 1st ed. 1/10. M $250.00

WILBUR, S. *Life of Mary Baker Eddy.* 1923 Boston. Christian Science Pub. 406 p. $10.00

WILCOCKE, Samuel Hull. *History & Description of Republic of Buenos Ayres.* 1820 London. Sherwood. 2nd ed. 576 p. $75.00

WILCOCKS, Alexander. *Tides: Theory of 2 Forces.* 1855 Phil. Ills 1st ed. 12mo. EX $125.00

WILCOX, Carrie. *American Legion in TX 1919-1949.* 1951 Dallas. Ills 1st ed. 520 p. dj. VG $25.00

WILCOX, Ella Wheeler. *Custer & Other Poems.* 1896 WB Conkey. VG $20.00

WILCOX, Ella Wheeler. *Maurine & Other Poems.* 1888 Chicago. G $7.00

WILCOX, James. *North Gladiola.* 1985 Harper. 1st ed. dj. EX $16.00

WILCOX, R. Turner. *Mode in Footwear From Antiquity to Present Day.* 1948 NY. Ills 1st ed. 4to. 190 p. dj. $40.00

WILCOX, R. Turner. *Mode in Furs.* 1951 NY. 4to. 257 p. dj. VG $37.50

WILCOX, R. Turner. *Mode in Hats & Headdress.* 1946 NY. Ills. 332 p. dj. VG $45.00

WILCOX, R. Turner. *Mode in Hats & Headdress.* 1959 NY. dj. EX $12.00

WILDE, Lady. *Social Studies.* 1893 London. 1st ed. VG $30.00

WILDE, Oscar. *Ballad of Reading Gaol.* 1924 London. Ills Masereel. ½-calf. $250.00

WILDE, Oscar. *Ballad of Reading Gaol.* 1902 Boston. Ltd ed. 1/550. 12mo. dj. VG $65.00

WILDE, Oscar. *Ballad of Reading Gaol.* 1937 Ltd Ed Club. sgn Zhenya Gay. sheepskin. VG $50.00

WILDE, Oscar. *Complete Works of Oscar Wilde.* 1927 Connoisseur ed. 12 vol set. G $45.00

WILDE, Oscar. *Happy Prince.* Putnam. reprint of 1908. G $8.00

WILDE, Oscar. *Happy Prince.* 1918 London. Duckworth. 1st ed. 4to. dj. VG $95.00

WILDE, Oscar. *Intentions.* 1891 London. 1st ed. VG $45.00

WILDE, Oscar. *Picture of Dorian Gray.* 1925 NY. Ills Keen. gilt cloth. VG $25.00

WILDE, Oscar. *Picture of Dorian Gray.* 1930 Liveright. Ills Majeska. Ltd 1st ed. EX $75.00

WILDE, Oscar. *Picture of Dorian Gray.* 1957 NY. Ltd Ed Club. 1/1,500. boxed. M $50.00

WILDE, Oscar. *Poems in Prose & Private Letters.* 1919 8vo. orange wraps. scarce. $65.00

WILDE, Oscar. *Poems.* 1881 Boston. 1st Am ed. G $100.00

WILDE, Oscar. *Poems.* 1927 NY. Boni. Ills De Bosschere. 1/2,000. VG $22.00

WILDE, Oscar. *Salome.* 1927 NY. Ills Vassos. dj. $50.00

WILDE, Oscar. *Salome.* 1930 Dutton. Ills/inscr John Vassos. dj. EX $75.00

WILDE, Oscar. *Salome.* 1920 London. Ills Beardsley. 1st ed. 4to. $85.00

WILDE, Oscar. *Soul of Man Under Socialism.* 1910 Boston. 1st Am ed. G $37.50

WILDENSTEIN, George. *Chardin.* 1969 Greenwhich, CT. Ills Revised/Enlarged ed. dj. $150.00

WILDER, Alexander. *History of Medicine.* 1901 New England Electic Pub. EX $37.50

WILDER, F.L. *Sporting Prints.* 1974 Viking. Ills. 4to. 224 p. EX $25.00

WILDER, Laura Ingalls. *Little Town on the Prairie.* 1953 Ills Williams. Uniform ed. 8vo. dj. VG $15.00

WILDER, Laura Ingalls. *Long Winter.* 1940 NY. Harper. Ills Sewell/Boyle. reprint. $30.00

WILDER, Laura Ingalls. *These Happy Golden Years.* 1943 Harper. Ills Sewell/Boyle. 1st ed. dj. $15.00

WILDER, Laura Ingalls. *West From Home: Letters of Laura Ingalls Wilder.* 1915 San Francisco. Ills 1st ed. dj. EX $17.50

WILDER, Louise Beebe. *Color in My Garden.* 1918 NY. Ltd ed. G $45.00

WILDER, Robert. *Sea & Stars.* 1967 NY. Putnam. $10.00

WILDER, Robert. *Wind From the Carolinas.* 1964 NY/London. Putnam. $10.00

WILDER, Thornton. *Bridge of San Luis Rey.* 1929 NY. Boni. pb. $7.50

WILDER, Thornton. *Bridge of San Luis Rey.* 1929 NY. Ills C Leighton. 1st ed. dj. $32.50

WILDER, Thornton. *Ides of March.* 1948 Harper. 1st ed. dj. EX $35.00

WILDER, Thornton. *Long Christmas Dinner.* 1931 NY. 1st ed. dj. EX $17.00

WILDER, Thornton. *Our Century.* 1947 NY. Ltd 1st ed. 1/1,000. EX $15.00

WILDER, Thornton. *Theophilus North.* 1973 NY. Harper Row. 1st ed. inscr/sgn. dj. EX $47.00

WILDER, Thornton. *Theophilus North.* 1973 NY. 1st ed. dj. EX $15.00

WILDER, Thornton. *Woman of Andros.* 1930 London/NY. Ltd 1st ed. 1/260. sgn. EX $40.00

WILDER, Thornton. *8th Day.* 1967 NY. 1st ed. dj. EX $17.00

WILDSMITH, B. *Bible Stories.* 1969 NY. 1st ed. dj. EX $25.00

WILDSMITH, B. *12 Days of Christmas.* Revised ed of 1972. dj. EX $25.00

WILEY, B.I. *Road to Appomattox.* 1956 Memphis. 1st ed. dj. EX $15.00

WILEY, Frank W. *MT & the Sky.* c 1966. 1st ed. M $45.00

WILEY, Richard T. *Sim Greene & Tom the Tinker's Men.* 1907 Phil. Ills. 380 p. VG $9.50

WILHELM, Kate. *Listen, Listen.* 1981 Boston. Houghton Mifflin. 1st ed. VG $10.00

WILHELM, Richard. *Secret of the Golden Flower: Chinese Book of Life.* 1962 Harcourt Brace. Intro Jung. Ills. dj. VG $22.00

WILHELM, Walt. *Last Rig to Battle Mountain.* 1970 Morrow. Ills 1st ed. 308 p. dj. VG $25.00

WILIAMS, H.L. *America's Small Houses: Personal Homes of Designers.* 1964 NY/London. Ills. 4to. dj. EX $50.00

WILK, Christopher. *Furniture & Interiors.* 1981 MOMA. Ills. 4to. 224 p. wraps. $12.50

WILKES, C. *Life in OR Before the Emigration.* 1974 & 1975. OR Book Soc. 2 vol set. VG $70.00

WILKIN, Esther. *So Big.* 1968 NY. Golden Pr. Ills 1st print. G $7.50

WILKIN, Karen. *Works of Helen Frankenthaler on Paper 1949-1984.* 1984 Internat'l Exhibitions. 4to. $35.00

WILKINS, Eithne. *Rose-Garden Game: Tradition of Beads & Flowers.* 1969 London. 1st ed. dj. VG $35.00

WILKINS, George H. *Flying the Arctic.* 1929 Grosset Dunlap. Ills. 336 p. G $18.00

WILKINS, Hubert. *Thoughts Through Space.* 1951 Hollywood. 1st ed. dj. VG $42.50

WILKINS, John. *Mathematical Magic; or, Wonders That May Be Performed.* 1680 London. 2nd ed. 8vo. 295 p. $300.00

WILKINSON, A.E. *Modern Strawberry Growing.* 1913 Doubleday. 210 p. VG $5.00

WILKINSON, C. *William Dampier.* 1929 London. 1st ed. dj. EX $20.00

WILKINSON, Charles K. *Iranian Ceramics.* 1963 NY. Asia House/Abrams. Ills. 4to. $40.00

WILKINSON, D. *Land of the Long Day.* 1956 London. Ills. 261 p. maps. dj. $15.00

WILKINSON, F. *Small Arms.* 1966 Hawthorne. Ills 1st Am ed. 256 p. dj. EX $12.00

WILKINSON, J. Gardner. *Popular Account of Ancient Egyptians.* 1854 London. Revised ed. 2 vol set. VG $75.00

WILKINSON, Margaret. *Autobiography of Emma Harding Britten.* 1900 London. 273 p. G $33.00

WILKINSON, O.N. *Old Glass.* 1968 NY. Philosophical Lib. 200 p. dj. $15.00

WILLAN, Robert; & BATEMAN, T. *Delineations of Cutaneous Diseases.* 1849 London. Ills. 4to. G $275.00

WILLARD, Emma. *History of USA; or, Republic of America.* 1831 NY. 8vo. 424 p. $50.00

WILLARD, J.A. *History of Simon Willard: Inventor & Clockmaker.* 1911 private print. Ltd 1st ed. 1/500. 133 p. xl. $125.00

WILLCOX, D. *Wood Design.* 1968 NY. Ills. 144 p. $20.00

WILLEFORD, Charles. *Miami Blues.* 1984 NY. St. Martin. 1st ed. dj. VG $25.00

WILLETT, Prof. J.E. *Wonders of Insect Life.* 1871 Phil. Ills. 12mo. $40.00

WILLEY, B. *Darwin & Butler: 2 Versions of Evolution.* 1960 Chatto Windus. 113 p. dj. EX $10.00

WILLIAM, H. Noel. *Last Loves of Henri of Navarre.* 1925 NY. Dingwall Rock Ltd. 8vo. $24.00

WILLIAM, N.L. *Sir Walter Raleigh.* 1962 London. Ills 1st ed. dj. VG $12.00

WILLIAM, Robert. *Dictionary of Ancient Celtic Language of Cornwall.* 1845 London. Trubner. 4to. G $100.00

WILLIAMS, A.B. *Shrimps, Lobsters, & Crabs of the Atlantic Coast.* 1984 Smithsonian. Ills. 568 p. EX $45.00

WILLIAMS, A.C. *Angling Diversions.* no date. Jenkins. Ills. 266 p. G $8.50

WILLIAMS, A.C. *Dictionary of Trout Flies & Flies for Sea Trout & Grayling.* 1949 London. Ills 1st ed. dj. VG $50.00

WILLIAMS, Albert. *Pioneer Pastorate & Times.* 1879 San Francisco. VG $45.00

WILLIAMS, Archibald. *Conquering the Air.* 1930 NY. Ills 1st ed. 366 p. VG $15.00

WILLIAMS, B. *Happy End.* 1939 Derrydale. Ltd ed. 1/1,250. VG $35.00

WILLIAMS, Ben Ames. *House Divided.* 1947 Boston. 1st ed. sgn. 2 vol set. djs. $65.00

WILLIAMS, Ben Ames. *Time of Peace.* 1942 Houghton. 1st ed. dj. EX $20.00

WILLIAMS, Benjamin S. *Select Ferns & Lycopods: British & Exotic.* 1873 London. Ills 2nd ed. 12mo. 353 p. $50.00

WILLIAMS, Beryl. *Young Faces in Fashion.* 1956 Phil. Lippincott. 1st ed. 176 p. $20.00

WILLIAMS, C. Wye. *On Heat in Its Relation to Water & Steam.* 1861 London. Longman. Ills Revised 2nd ed. $40.00

WILLIAMS, C.P. *Lone Elk: Life Story of Bill Williams.* 1935 Denver. John Van Male. Ltd 1st ed. EX $185.00

WILLIAMS, Catherine R. *Biography of Revolutionary Heroes: W. Barton & S. Olney.* 1839 Providence. private print. 312 p. $25.00

WILLIAMS, Charlean M. *Old Town Speaks: Recollections of WA, Hempstead Co., AR.* 1951 Houston. Anson Jones. Ills 1st ed. VG $50.00

WILLIAMS, E. *Headlong: A Novel.* 1981 NY. 1st Am ed. sgn. dj. EX $35.00

WILLIAMS, E. Noel. *Queen Margot.* 1907 NY/London. Harper. VG $40.00

WILLIAMS, F.B. *On Many Seas: Life & Exploits of Yankee Sailor.* 1897 NY. cloth. fair. $75.00

WILLIAMS, G.M. *Passionate Pilgrim.* 1931 NY. G $20.00

WILLIAMS, G.M. *Priestess of the Occult.* 1946 NY. 1st ed. G $12.00

WILLIAMS, Garth. *Baby Animals.* 1952 Simon Schuster. Ills. VG $10.00

WILLIAMS, George F. *Bullet & Shell.* 1883 NY. Ills Forbes. 8vo. 454 p. G $32.00

WILLIAMS, Harold. *Whaling Family.* no date. Houghton Mifflin. Ills. dj. VG $18.00

WILLIAMS, Harry. *Lincoln & His Generals.* 1952 NY. Knopf. 1st ed. 363 p. VG $15.00

WILLIAMS, Henry L. *Great Houses of America.* 1969 NY. Ills 2nd print. VG $50.00

WILLIAMS, Henry L. *Old American Houses & How To Restore Them.* 1946 NY. Doubleday. G $15.00

WILLIAMS, Henry T. *Pacific Tourist Illustrated Transcontinental Travel Guide.* 1878 NY. 1st ed. 1st issue. scarce. $125.00

WILLIAMS, Howard. *Ethics of Diet.* 1883 London. 1st ed. 336 p. gilt cloth. EX $45.00

WILLIAMS, Iolo A. *Early English Watercolors & Some Cognate Drawings.* 1952 London. Connoisseur. 1st ed. 266 p. VG $125.00

WILLIAMS, Iolo A. *18th Century Bibliographies.* 1924 London. 1st ed. $65.00

WILLIAMS, J. *Personal Eye.* 1973 Millerton. Ills. 4to. EX $20.00

WILLIAMS, J.A. *Man Who Cried I Am.* 1967 Little Brown. 1st ed. dj. EX $25.00

WILLIAMS, J.D. *America Illustrated.* c 1883. Boston. Ills. 4to. 121 p. G $15.00

WILLIAMS, J.D. *America.* 1879 NY. Ills. 121 p. G $35.00

WILLIAMS, J.H. *Bandoola.* 1954 Doubleday. Ills. 256 p. dj. G $5.00

WILLIAMS, J.H. *Elephant Bill.* 1950 Doubleday. Ills 1st ed. 250 p. dj. VG $10.00

WILLIAMS, J.L. *Not Wanted.* 1923 NY. 1st ed. inscr. 83 p. VG $15.00

WILLIAMS, J.L. *They Still Fall in Love.* 1929 Scribner. inscr. VG $15.00

WILLIAMS, J.P. *Alaskan Adventure.* 1952 Stackpole. Ills. 299 p. G $10.00

WILLIAMS, J.R. *Out Our Way.* 1943 NY. Scribner. 1st ed. VG $45.00

WILLIAMS, J.S. *History of the Invasion & Capture of WA.* 1857 NY. $35.00

WILLIAMS, J.W. *Big Ranch Country.* 1954 Terry Bros. Ills 1st ed. 307 p. dj. VG $40.00

WILLIAMS, Joan. *Conversations with Tennessee Williams.* 1986 MS U Pr. 1st ed. dj. EX $25.00

WILLIAMS, Joan. *County Woman.* 1982 Little Brown. 1st ed. sgn. dj. EX $30.00

WILLIAMS, Joan. *Knightly Quest.* 1966 New Directions. 1st ed. dj. EX $75.00

WILLIAMS, Joan. *Morning & Evening.* 1961 Atheneum. 1st ed. sgn. dj. EX $60.00

WILLIAMS, John. *Broken Landscape.* 1949 Swallow. 1st ed. inscr. dj. VG $75.00

WILLIAMS, John. *Captain Blackman.* 1972 Doubleday. 1st ed. dj. M $20.00

WILLIAMS, John. *Nightsong.* 1961 NY. 1st ed. dj. VG $17.50

WILLIAMS, John. *Nothing But the Night.* 1948 Swallow. 1st ed. inscr. dj. VG $85.00

WILLIAMS, John. *Pariah.* 1983 Little Brown. 1st ed. sgn. dj. EX $35.00

WILLIAMS, John. *Redeemed Captive Returning to Zion.* 1774 Boston. 5th ed. wraps. $100.00

WILLIAMS, Jonathan. *Blues & Roots, Rue & Bluets: Garland for Appalachians.* 1971 NY. Ills Nicholas Dean. G $30.00

WILLIAMS, Joy. *State of Grace.* 1973 Garden City. Doubleday. 1st ed. EX $25.00

WILLIAMS, L. *Samba & the Monkey Mind.* 1965 Norton. Ills 1st ed. 146 p. dj. EX $8.00

WILLIAMS, Mary Floyd. *History of San Francisco Committee of Vigilance.* 1921 CA U Pr. wraps. VG $90.00

WILLIAMS, Mrs. H.D. *Year in China.* 1864 NY. Intro WC Bryant. 1st ed. VG $60.00

WILLIAMS, Owen Glen. *Owen Glen.* 1950 Houghton. 1st ed. dj. EX $20.00

WILLIAMS, Paul R. *New Homes for Today.* 1946 Hollywood. Murray Gee. fair. $20.00

WILLIAMS, R. *Toward Conquest of Beriberi.* 1961 Harvard U Pr. inscr. VG $12.50

WILLIAMS, R.H. *With the Border Ruffians: Memories of Far West 1852-1868.* 1907 London. Ills 1st ed. xl. VG $30.00

WILLIAMS, S.C. *History of American Indians.* 1973 Promontory. 508 p. dj. EX $8.50

WILLIAMS, S.C. *History of American Indians.* 1930 TN. G $40.00

WILLIAMS, S.C. *History of the Lost State of Franklin.* 1933 Blue & Gray Pr. facsimile. 378 p. EX $15.00

WILLIAMS, S.C. *Report on the Helicopter & Its Role As a Transport Vehicle.* 1955 NY. 1st ed. blue cloth. VG $40.00

WILLIAMS, S.C. *TN During the Revolutionary War.* 1944 Nashville. 1st ed. VG $25.00

WILLIAMS, Samuel B. *Digital Computing Systems.* 1959 McGraw Hill. Ills 1st ed. 229 p. xl. $10.00

WILLIAMS, Stanley T. *Life of Washington Irving.* 1935 Oxford U Pr. 2 vol set. $40.00

WILLIAMS, Stephen W. *American Medical Biography.* 1845 Greenfield, MA. VG $125.00

WILLIAMS, Susan. *Footprints of Elephant Bill.* 1963 McKay. Ills 1st Am ed. 224 p. dj. EX $18.00

WILLIAMS, T.H. *Life History of the US.* 1975 NY. Ills. 4to. 160 p. 5 vol set. VG $10.00

WILLIAMS, Tennessee. *Androgyne, Mon Amour.* 1977 New Directions. 1st ed. dj. EX $25.00

WILLIAMS, Tennessee. *Baby Doll.* 1956 NY. 1st ed. dj. VG $50.00

WILLIAMS, Tennessee. *Camino Real.* 1953 Norfolk. 1st ed. dj. EX $25.00

WILLIAMS, Tennessee. *Cat on Hot Tin Roof.* 1956 Secker. dj. EX $42.00

WILLIAMS, Tennessee. *Collected Stories.* 1985 New Directions. Intro G Vidal. 1st ed. dj. EX $20.00

WILLIAMS, Tennessee. *Eccentricities of Nightingale with Summer & Smoke: 2 Plays.* 1964 NY. 1st ed. Advance copy. VG $45.00

WILLIAMS, Tennessee. *Glass Menagerie.* 1948 Lehmann. dj. scarce. VG $65.00

WILLIAMS, Tennessee. *Milk Train Doesn't Stop Here Anymore.* 1964 London. 1st ed. dj. EX $22.00

WILLIAMS, Tennessee. *Moise & the World of Reason.* 1975 NY. 1st ed. inscr. dj. EX $75.00

WILLIAMS, Tennessee. *Moise & the World of Reason.* 1976 Allen. 1st English ed. dj. EX $30.00

WILLIAMS, Tennessee. *Period of Adjustment.* 1961 Secker Warburg. 1st English ed. dj. EX $60.00

WILLIAMS, Tennessee. *Roman Spring of Mrs. Stone.* 1950 NY. 1st ed. dj. EX $45.00

WILLIAMS, Tennessee. *Rose Tattoo.* 1951 New Directions. 1st ed. dj. VG $30.00

WILLIAMS, Tennessee. *Small Craft Warnings.* 1973 Secker Warburg. 1st English ed. dj. EX $35.00

WILLIAMS, Tennessee. *Summer & Smoke.* 1948 NY. 1st ed. dj. EX $45.00

WILLIAMS, Tennessee. *Summer & Smoke.* 1952 Lehmann. dj. VG $40.00

WILLIAMS, Tennessee. *Sweet Bird of Youth.* 1959 NY. 1st ed. dj. scarce. VG $60.00

WILLIAMS, Tennessee. *Sweet Bird of Youth.* 1961 Secker Warburg. 1st English ed. dj. EX $50.00

WILLIAMS, Tennessee. *Wagon Full of Cotton.* 1949 Lehmann. dj. VG $40.00

WILLIAMS, William Carlos. *Forward for Yankee Doodle: A Drama.* 1945 NY. 1st ed. $15.00

WILLIAMS, William Carlos. *In the American Grain.* 1925 Norfolk. G $20.00

WILLIAMS, William Carlos. *Make Light of It.* 1950 NY. 1st ed. dj. EX $35.00

WILLIAMS & FISHER. *Elements of Theory & Practice of Cookery.* 1912 NY. Macmillan. 1st ed. G $20.00

WILLIAMS & PARRY. *Riddle of the Reich.* 1941 NY. 351 p. $25.00

WILLIAMSON, H.F. *Winchester: Gun That Won the West.* 1963 Barnes. Ills. 4to. 494 p. dj. EX $18.50

WILLIAMSON, Henry. *Phasian Bird.* 1950 Little Brown. Ills 1st ed. 276 p. EX $10.00

WILLIAMSON, Jack. *Humanoids.* 1949 NY. Simon Schuster. 1st ed. dj. $12.50

WILLIAMSON, Jack. *Legion of Time.* 1952 Fantasy. 1st ed. dj. VG $20.00

WILLIAMSON, Jack. *Legion of Time.* 1952 Reading. 1st ed. dj. EX $25.00

WILLIS, Helen. *Tennis.* 1928 Scribner. 1st ed. EX $25.00

WILLIS, J.C. *Handbook for Resident & Traveller.* 1907 Peradeniya. Ills 1st ed. 8vo. cloth. EX $50.00

WILLIS, N.P. *American Scenery with Plates by W.H. Bartlett.* 1852 London. 2 vol set. ¾-morocco. $300.00

WILLIS, N.P. *American Scenery.* 1971 Barre, MA. Imprint Soc. Ills 4to. 362 p. $50.00

WILLIS. *Thesaurus Rerum Ecclesiasticarum.* 1763 London. calf. $65.00

WILLISON, G.F. *Here They Dug for Gold.* 1931 Brentanos. Ills 1st ed. 299 p. VG $20.00

WILLISON, John. *Sacramental Meditations & Advices.* 1794 Phil. 287 p. full leather. G $35.00

WILLISTON, S.W. *Water Reptiles of Past & Present.* 1914 Chicago. Ills 1st ed. 251 p. G $30.00

WILLOUGHBY, M. *US Coast Guard in WWII.* 1957 Naval Insitute. 4to. 348 p. cloth. dj. VG $20.00

WILLS, Geoffrey. *English Furniture 1550-1760.* 1971 NY. Doubleday. Ills 4to. 261 p. dj. $25.00

WILLS, Geoffrey. *English Looking Glasses.* 1965 NY. Barnes. Ills 4to. cloth. dj. $45.00

WILLS, George. *Candlesticks.* 1974 Potter Crown. Ills 120 p. $25.00

WILLS, H. *15-30: Story of a Tennis Player.* 1937 Scribner. Ills. VG $7.50

WILLS, M.M.; & IRWIN, H.S. *Roadside Flowers of TX.* 1961 TX U Pr. Ills. 295 p. dj. EX $15.00

WILLS, Royal B. *Business of Architecture.* 1941 NY. Ills. 210 p. $15.00

WILLSBERGER, Johann. *Zauberhafte Gehause der Zeit.* 1974 Dusseldorf. 4to. 112 plts. EX $40.00

WILMERDING, John. *American Art.* 1976 Middlesex. Penguin. 1st ed. 4to. 322 p. $85.00

WILMERDING, John. *Robert Salmon: Painter of Ship & Shore.* Salem, MA. Peabody Mus. Ills. 4to. VG $100.00

WILMERDING, John. *Winslow Homer.* 1972 NY. Praeger. Ills. 4to. dj. $60.00

WILSON, A.N. *Wise Virgin.* 1982 London. Secker Warburg. 1st ed. VG $20.00

WILSON, Adrian. *My 1st Publication.* 1961 Book Club CA. Ltd ed. 1/475. VG $40.00

WILSON, Alexander. *American Ornithology.* 1829 Phil. 1st ed. folio. 76 color plts. $1600.00

WILSON, Angus. *Anglo-Saxon Attitudes.* 1956 London. 1st ed. dj. EX $20.00

WILSON, Angus. *Bit Off the Map.* 1957 NY. 1st ed. dj. EX $12.00

WILSON, C.A. *Legends & Mysteries of the Maori.* 1932 London. 1st ed. presentation. dj. VG $35.00

WILSON, Carol. *Green Chinatown Quest.* 1931 Stanford U Pr. inscr. $25.00

WILSON, Carrie. *Fashions Since Their Debut.* 1939 Scranton. Ills. 4to. VG $10.00

WILSON, Colin. *Adrift in Soho.* 1961 Houghton. 1st Am ed. dj. EX $35.00

WILSON, Colin. *Janus Murder Case.* 1984 Granada. 1st ed. dj. EX $25.00

WILSON, Colin. *Necessary Doubt.* 1964 Trident. 1st Am ed. dj. VG $25.00

WILSON, Colin. *Outsider.* 1956 Houghton. 1st Am ed. dj. EX $40.00

WILSON, Colin. *Religion & the Rebel.* 1957 Gollancz. 1st ed. dj. EX $50.00

WILSON, Colin. *Ritual in the Dark.* 1960 London. 1st ed. dj. VG $55.00

WILSON, Colin. *Space Vampires.* 1976 Random House. 1st ed. dj. EX $30.00

WILSON, Colin. *Spider World.* 1987 London. Tower. 1st ed. sgn. dj. M $35.00

WILSON, Colin. *Strindberg.* 1972 Random House. 1st Am ed. dj. EX $20.00

WILSON, Colin. *Violent World of Hugh Greene.* 1963 Houghton. 1st Am ed. dj. EX $30.00

WILSON, E. *Axel's Castle.* 1931 NY. 1st ed. VG $20.00

WILSON, E. *Devils & Canon Barham.* 1973 NY. 1st ed. EX $20.00

WILSON, E. *System of Human Anatomy: General & Special.* 1847 Phil. Lea Blanchard. 3rd Am ed. $40.00

WILSON, E.B. *Development of Renilla.* 1883 Royal Soc. Ills. 4to. EX $15.00

WILSON, E.B. *Early America at Work.* c 1963. NY. 8vo. 188 p. dj. VG $11.00

WILSON, E.B. *Early Southern Towns.* 1967 South Brunswick. dj. VG $30.00

WILSON, E.B. *Vanishing America.* c 1961. NY. Ills. 8vo. red cloth. VG $10.00

WILSON, E.G. *Famous Old Euclid Avenue, Cleveland, OH.* 1932 Cleveland. Ills 1st ed. sgn. 325 p. dj. $60.00

WILSON, E.H. *America's Greatest Garden.* 1925 Boston. Ills 2nd ed. 123 p. VG $30.00

WILSON, E.H. *More Aristocrats of the Garden.* 1928 Boston. Ills. $17.50

WILSON, E.H. *Romance of Our Trees.* 1920 NY. Ltd ed. photos. fair. $11.00

WILSON, E.L. *Wilson's Quarter Century in Photography.* 1899 NY. Ills. 8vo. dj. EX $45.00

WILSON, Earl. *I Am Gazing into My Eightball.* 1945 Garden City. 1st ed. dj. EX $20.00

WILSON, Earl. *Pike's Peak or Bust.* 1946 Garden City. Ills John Groth. 1st ed. dj. $12.00

WILSON, Edith. *My Memoir.* 1939 Bobbs Merrill. Ills 1st ed. VG $10.00

WILSON, Edith. *My Memoir.* 1939 Indianapolis. Ills Ltd ed. cloth. $90.00

WILSON, Edmund. *Apologies to the Iroquois.* 1960 NY. 1st book ed. dj. VG $36.00

WILSON, Edmund. *Twenties.* 1975 NY. 1st ed. dj. M $11.00

WILSON, Edmund. *Window on Russia.* 1972 NY. 1st ed. dj. M $15.00

WILSON, Erica. *Needle Play.* 1975 NY. Scribner. Ills. 189 p. dj. $12.50

WILSON, Erica. *Quilts of America.* 1979 Birmingham. Oxmor. 218 p. gold linen. EX $25.00

WILSON, Ethel. *Swamp Angel.* 1954 Toronto. Macmillan. 1st ed. VG $35.00

WILSON, Eunice. *History of Shoe Fashions.* 1970 London. Pitman. reprint. Ills. 4to. 350 p. dj. $40.00

WILSON, F.A. *Some Annals of Nahant, MA.* 1928 Boston. Ills. 412 p. VG $27.50

WILSON, F.E. *Advancing the OH Frontier: Saga of the Old Northwest.* 1953 Long. reprint of 1937. 126 p. dj. EX $18.00

WILSON, F.P. *Keep.* 1981 NY. 1st ed. dj. EX $20.00

WILSON, Francis. *Eugene Field I Knew.* 1898 NY. Scribner. Ills Ltd ed. 1/216. VG $35.00

WILSON, George. *Yesterday's Philadelphia.* 1975 Miami. Ills. sgn. 152 p. dj. VG $25.00

WILSON, Guy. *Geometry for Architects.* 1975 Champaign, IL. Stipes Pub. G $15.00

WILSON, H.V.P. *Geraniums Pelargoniums.* 1946 NY. 1st ed. 248 p. dj. $12.00

WILSON, H.V.P. *Joy of Geraniums.* 1965 NY. 364 p. dj. VG $12.00

WILSON, Helen. *African Violets.* 1966 Van Nostrand. VG $12.50

WILSON, Herbert E. *Lore & Lure of Yosemite.* 1923 San Francisco. VG $15.00

WILSON, J.C. *3-Wheeling Through Africa.* 1936 Bobbs Merrill. Ills. 351 p. G $5.00

WILSON, James. *Complete Dictionary of Astrology.* 1885 Boston. 406 p. VG $35.00

WILSON, Jimmie E. *Big Red 1.* 1967 Tokyo. Ills. 4to. 272 p. VG $75.00

WILSON, Meredith. *There I Stood with My Piccolo.* 1948 Garden City. 1st ed. dj. VG $12.00

WILSON, Meredith. *Who Did What to Fedalia?* 1952 NY. 1st ed. dj. EX $25.00

WILSON, Neill C. *Treasure Express.* 1936 NY. G $12.00

WILSON, Peter M. *Southern Exposure.* 1927 Chapel Hill. VG $15.00

WILSON, R. *Beloved Physician.* 1928 NY. Macmillan. VG $35.00

WILSON, R. *Benjamin K. Green: Bibliography.* 1977 Flagstaff. 1st ed. 158 p. dj. VG $20.00

WILSON, R.A. *Modern Book Collecting.* 1980 NY. Knopf. 1st ed. inscr. dj. EX $15.00

WILSON, R.L. *Rampant Colt: Story of a Trademark.* 1969 Haas. Ills. 107 p. dj. EX $17.50

WILSON, R.L. *Theodore Roosevelt: Outdoorsman.* 1971 Winchester. Ills 1st ed. 278 p. dj. EX $25.00

WILSON, Richard. *Those Idiots From Space.* 1957 NY. 1st ed. 8vo. wraps. $50.00

WILSON, Sandy. *This Is Sylvia.* 1955 Ills 1st ed. dj. VG $15.00

WILSON, Sloan. *Summer Place.* 1958 NY. 1st ed. dj. EX $10.00

WILSON, Theodora. *Through the Bible.* no date. Collins. reprint of 1938. VG $20.00

WILSON, Thomas. *Swastika: Its History & Migration.* 1896 Smithsonian. 200 plts. 250 p. VG $145.00

WILSON, Thomas. *Transatlantic Sketches; or, Travelling West Indies & US.* 1860 Montreal. Lovell. 1st ed. inscr. M $75.00

WILSON, William. *LBJ Brigade.* 1966 London. MacGibbon. 1st ed. scarce. VG $40.00

WILSON, Woodrow. *George Washington.* 1896 NY. Harper. Ills 1st ed. VG $20.00

WILSON. *Anti-Slavery Measures in Congress.* 1864 Boston. inscr. cloth. $60.00

WILSTACH, Paul. *Hudson River Landings.* 1933 Indianapolis. 1st ed. VG $25.00

WILSTACH, Paul. *Mount Vernon: Washington's Home & Nation's Shrine.* 1916 NY. Ills Ltd ed. sgn. VG $35.00

WILTSEE, E. *Pioneer Mines & Pack Mule Express.* 1931 San Francisco. Ills. fld map. 112 p. scarce. $150.00

WINANT, Lewis. *Firearms Curiosa.* 1961 St. Martin. Ills. 281 p. dj. EX $15.00

WINCHELL, C.M. *Guide to Reference Books.* 1951 Chicago. 4to. 645 p. green cloth. G $8.00

WINCHELL. *Aborigines of MN.* 1911 St. Paul. MN Hist Soc. Ills. G $15.00

WINCHESTER, Alice. *American Antiques in Words & Pictures.* 1944 NY. Ills. 95 p. $7.50

WINCHESTER. *Winchester Ammunition Handbook.* 1965 NY. dj. VG $10.00

WIND, Herbert W. *World of P.G. Wodehouse.* 1971 104 p. dj. VG $9.00

WINDHAM, Donald. *Tanaquil.* 1977 Holt. 1st ed. dj. EX $20.00

WINDHAM, Donald. *2 People.* 1965 Coward McCann. 1st ed. dj. EX $20.00

WINDLE, John T.; TAYLOR, R.M. *Early Architecture of Madison, IN.* 1986 Madison, IN. Ills. 4to. 246 p. $30.00

WINDSOR, Duke of. *Crown & the People.* 1954 NY. dj. EX $22.00

WINDY, Bill. *Poor American in Ireland & Scotland.* 1913 San Francisco. Ben Goodkind. VG $15.00

WINGERT, Paul. *Sculpture of William Zorach.* 1938 NY. 1st ed. 4to. VG $20.00

WINGFIELD, Sheila. *Collected Poems 1938-1981.* 1982 Hill. Advance copy. wraps. M $25.00

WINIFIELD, G.F. *China: Land & People.* 1948 NY. dj. VG $12.00

WINKLER, E.W. *Secret Journals of the Senate: Republic of TX 1836-1845.* 1911 Austin. 337 p. wraps. $55.00

WINKLER, F.A. *Railroad Conductor.* 1948 Spokane. Pacific Book Co. 1st print. VG $12.00

WINKLER, J. *Incredible Carnegie.* 1931 Vanguard. Ills 1st ed. 307 p. dj. VG $18.00

WINN, Matthew J. *Down the Stretch.* 1945 NY. photos. dj. G $20.00

WINSHIP. *Woofus, the Woolly Dog.* c 1944. Whitman. VG $15.00

WINSLOW, Carleton M. *Architecture & Gardens of San Diego Exposition.* 1926 San Francisco. Elder. Ills. 8vo. cloth. $40.00

WINSLOW, D.G. *Essentials of Design.* 1924 NY. Ills. 255 p. $10.00

WINSLOW, Ola E. *American Broadside Verse From Imprints of 17th & 18th C.* 1930 New Haven. Ltd 1st ed. 1/500. sgn. 224 p. $85.00

WINSOR, Frederick. *Space Child's Mother Goose.* 1958 Simon Schuster. Ills Parry. 1st ed. dj. VG $30.00

WINSOR, Justin. *Memorial History of Boston.* 1880 Ticknor. 4 vol set. VG $140.00

WINSOR, Justin. *MS Basin.* 1895 NY. VG $25.00

WINSOR, Justin. *Narrative & Critical History of America.* 1889 Boston. 8 vol set. xl. G $85.00

WINSOR, Justin. *Reader's Handbook of the American Revolution 1761-1783.* 1880 8vo. 328 p. G $25.00

WINSOR, Kathleen. *Lovers.* 1952 London. 1st ed. dj. EX $15.00

WINSTEDT, R. *Indian Art.* 1947 London. Ills. 200 p. $10.00

WINSTON, Alexander. *No Man Knows My Grave: Privateers & Pirates 1665-1715.* 1969 1st print. 265 p. dj. VG $9.00

WINSTON, R.W. *Andrew Johnson: Plebian & Patriot.* 1928 NY. 1st ed. EX $12.00

WINSTON, R.W. *Andrew Johnson: Plebian & Patriot.* 1932 NY. sgn. EX $35.00

WINTER, Douglas. *Stephen King: Art of Darkness.* 1984 NY. 1st trade ed. dj. EX $35.00

WINTER, Ella. *I Saw the Russian People.* 1946 Boston. 5th print. sgn. dj. VG $10.00

WINTER, Ella. *Red Virtue.* 1933 Harcourt. 1st ed. inscr. dj. G $15.00

WINTER, Nevin O. *FL: Land of Enchantment.* 1918 Boston. Page. Ills. 8vo. map. cloth. G $45.00

WINTER, Nevin O. *TX the Marvellous: State of 6 Flags.* 1936 Garden City. Revised ed. 337 p. VG $13.00

WINTER, Nevin O. *TX the Marvellous: State of 6 Flags.* 1916 Boston. Page. 1st ed. VG $35.00

WINTER, Nevin O. *TX the Marvellous: State of 6 Flags.* 1936 Garden City. Revised Centennial ed. EX $35.00

WINTERICH, John T. *Collector's Choice.* 1928 NY. 1st ed. blue cloth. VG $20.00

WINTERS, Lea Lowell. *True Hard Scrabble.* 1974 Phil. sgn. cloth. dj. $15.00

WINTERS, Yvor. *Primitivism & Decadence.* 1937 Arrow Eds. 1st ed. $25.00

WINTERS, Yvor. *Uncollected Essays & Reviews.* 1974 Allen Lane. 1st English ed. dj. EX $20.00

WINTHROP, Robert. *Life & Letters of John Winthrop, Governor of MA Bay.* 1864 Boston. 1st ed. EX $45.00

WINWAR, Frances. *Puritan City: Story of Salem.* 1938 NY. 1st ed. VG $30.00

WIRT, William. *Sketches of the Life & Character of Patrick Henry.* 1852 Hartford. 8vo. 468 p. G $24.00

WISE, Jennings C. *Red Man in the New World Drama: Political-Legal Study.* 1931 WA. Ills 1st ed. 4to. VG $60.00

WISE. *Inside View of Mexico & CA.* 1849 NY. 1st ed. EX $50.00

WISEMAN, R.F. *Complete Horseshoeing Guide.* 1968 OK U Pr. Ills 1st ed. 238 p. dj. VG $13.00

WISLON, Ernest H. *Aristocrats of Trees.* 1930 Boston. Stratford. 1st ed. 279 p. VG $80.00

WISLON, Joseph. *Naval Hygiene.* 1879 Phil. Ills Sinclair. 2nd ed. VG $175.00

WISNER, B. *How To Catch Salt-Water Fish.* 1955 Essy. Ills. 247 p. dj. VG $7.50

WISTAR, Isaac Jones. *Autobiography of 1827-1905.* 1937 Phil. 1st trade ed. fld map. 528 p. $35.00

WISTER, John C. *Peonies.* 1962 WA. EX $35.00

WISTER, Owen. *Journey in Search of Christmas.* 1904 NY. Ills Remington. VG $35.00

WISTER, Owen. *Journey in Search of Christmas.* 1905 NY. Harper. Ills. 93 p. $25.00

WISTER, Owen. *Journey in Search of Christmas.* 1904 Harper. Ills Remington. 1st ed. M $75.00

WISTER, Owen. *Lady Baltimore.* 1906 Bailey Macmillan. VG $12.50

WISTER, Owen. *Members of the Family.* 1911 Macmillan. Ills HT Dunn. $22.50

WISTER, Owen. *Mother.* 1907 NY. Dodd. Ills J Rae. 1st ed. VG $15.00

WISTER, Owen. *Virginian.* Grosset Dunlap. reprint. EX $7.50

WISTRICH, R. *Who's Who in Nazi Germany.* 1982 NY. Bonanza. dj. EX $15.00

WITHERS, Alexander Scott. *Chronicles of Border Warfare.* 1961 Parsons, WV. reprint. 447 p. VG $35.00

WITHERS, Alexander Scott. *Chronicles of Border Warfare.* 1915 Cincinnati. New ed. 447 p. red cloth. EX $50.00

WITHERS, Hartly. *Money Changing.* 1913 London. 1st ed. 8vo. cloth. dj. VG $16.00

WITHINGTON, A. *Hawaiian Tapestry.* 1937 Harper. Ills D Staten. VG $20.00

WITHINGTON, Sidney. *2 Dramatic Episodes of New England Whaling.* 1929 Marine Hist Assn. wraps. VG $10.00

WITKEN, Lee. *10 Year Salute: Withen Gallery 1969-1979.* 1979 Danbury, NH. Ltd 1st ed. 1/100. sgn. EX $225.00

WITKIN, L.; & LONDON, B. *Photographic Collectors' Guide.* 1979 NY Graphic Soc. 1st ed. 4to. cloth. dj. EX $55.00

WITTER, Dean. *Meanderings of a Fisherman.* no date. private print. Ills. 4to. EX $20.00

WITTER, Dean. *Shikar.* 1961 private print. Ills. 4to. 65 p. $15.00

WITTER, Dean. *Shikar.* 1961 San Francisco. Ills. sgn. 65 p. EX $40.00

WITTER, Dean. *Solo Safari.* no date/place. Ills. sgn. 52 p. VG $40.00

WITTKOWER, Rudolf. *Art & Architecture in Italy 1600-1750.* 1958 NY. Penguin. xl. G $30.00

WODEHOUSE, P.G. *Aunts Aren't Gentlemen.* 1975 Barrie Jenkins. 2nd ed. dj. EX $22.50

WODEHOUSE, P.G. *Aunts Aren't Gentlemen.* 1974 London. 1st ed. dj. VG $35.00

WODEHOUSE, P.G. *Author! Author!* 1962 NY. 1st Am ed. dj. VG $40.00

WODEHOUSE, P.G. *Bachelors Anonymous.* 1974 Simon Schuster. 1st ed. dj. EX $20.00

WODEHOUSE, P.G. *Bachelors Anonymous.* 1973 Barrie Jenkins. 1st ed. dj. EX $25.00

WODEHOUSE, P.G. *Barmy in Wonderland.* 1978 London. dj. EX $27.00

WODEHOUSE, P.G. *Big Money.* no date. Jenkins. 4th ed. dj. VG $65.00

WODEHOUSE, P.G. *Bill the Conqueror.* no date. Goodchild. 1st Canadian ed. $35.00

WODEHOUSE, P.G. *Brinkley Manor.* 1939 Triangle. 5th ed. dj. VG $35.00

WODEHOUSE, P.G. *Butler Did It.* 1957 Simon Schuster. 1st ed. dj. xl. $12.50

WODEHOUSE, P.G. *Cocktail Time.* 1958 London. 1st ed. 2nd issue. dj. EX $28.00

WODEHOUSE, P.G. *Code of the Woosters.* 1938 Doubleday Doran. 1st ed. VG $12.00

WODEHOUSE, P.G. *Company for Henry.* 1967 London. 1st ed. dj. VG $35.00

WODEHOUSE, P.G. *Crime Wave at Blandings.* Sun Dial Pr. G $8.00

WODEHOUSE, P.G. *Damsel in Distress.* 1975 Barrie Jenkins. dj. VG $20.00

WODEHOUSE, P.G. *Do Butlers Burgle Banks?* 1968 Simon Schuster. 1st Am ed. dj. EX $25.00

WODEHOUSE, P.G. *Do Butlers Burgle Banks?* 1968 NY. 1st ed. dj. xl. G $10.00

WODEHOUSE, P.G. *Do Butlers Burgle Banks?* 1968 Jenkins. 1st ed. dj. EX $15.00

WODEHOUSE, P.G. *Eggs, Beans, & Crumpets.* 1940 NY. 1st ed. dj. VG $40.00

WODEHOUSE, P.G. *Few Quick Ones.* London. 1st English ed. VG $18.00

WODEHOUSE, P.G. *Fish Preferred.* 1929 Doubleday Doran. 1st ed. G $55.00

WODEHOUSE, P.G. *Frozen Assets.* 1964 Jenkins. 1st ed. dj. xl. $20.00

WODEHOUSE, P.G. *Full Moon.* 1947 Garden City. 1st Am ed. dj. VG $75.00

WODEHOUSE, P.G. *Full Moon.* 1947 Jenkins. 1st ed. $60.00

WODEHOUSE, P.G. *Galahad at Blandings.* 1965 London. 1st English ed. dj. VG $70.00

WODEHOUSE, P.G. *Galahad at Blandings.* 1965 Jenkins. 1st ed. dj. xl. $20.00

WODEHOUSE, P.G. *Girl in Blue.* 1971 Simon Schuster. 1st ed. dj. EX $35.00

WODEHOUSE, P.G. *Gold Bat.* 1974 Souvenir Pr. dj. EX $15.00

WODEHOUSE, P.G. *Gold Bat.* 1923 London. 3rd issue. VG $50.00

WODEHOUSE, P.G. *Gold Omnibus.* 1973 London. 1st ed. dj. VG $60.00

WODEHOUSE, P.G. *Gold Without Tears.* 1924 NY. 1st ed. VG $75.00

WODEHOUSE, P.G. *Head of Kay's.* 1924 London. 3rd print. VG $40.00

WODEHOUSE, P.G. *Heavy Weather*. no date. Jenkins. 5th print. G $25.00

WODEHOUSE, P.G. *Heavy Weather*. 1933 McClelland Stewart. 1st ed. VG $60.00

WODEHOUSE, P.G. *Hot Water*. no date. Jenkins. 2nd ed. dj. VG $40.00

WODEHOUSE, P.G. *Hot Water*. 1932 McClelland Stewart. 1st ed. VG $50.00

WODEHOUSE, P.G. *Ice in the Bedroom*. 1961 Jenkins. 1st ed. dj. VG $35.00

WODEHOUSE, P.G. *In Legion*. 1929 NY. Stated 1st ed. G $20.00

WODEHOUSE, P.G. *Indiscretions of Archie*. 1921 Doubleday Doran. VG $35.00

WODEHOUSE, P.G. *Jeeves & the Tie That Binds*. 1971 NY. 1st ed. dj. VG $8.50

WODEHOUSE, P.G. *Jeeves & the Tie That Binds*. 1971 Simon Schuster. 1st ed. dj. EX $25.00

WODEHOUSE, P.G. *Jeeves in the Offing*. 1960 Jenkins. 1st ed. dj. EX $60.00

WODEHOUSE, P.G. *Jill the Reckless*. 1922 London. 2nd ed. cloth. VG $45.00

WODEHOUSE, P.G. *Joy in the Morning*. 1946 NY. 1st ed. dj. VG $25.00

WODEHOUSE, P.G. *Joy in the Morning*. 1947 Zephyr. pb. dj. $45.00

WODEHOUSE, P.G. *Laughing Gas*. 1936 McClelland Stewart. 1st ed. VG $50.00

WODEHOUSE, P.G. *Lord Emsworth & Others*. 1956 Jenkins. VG $20.00

WODEHOUSE, P.G. *Luck of the Bodkins*. 1935 McClelland Stewart. 1st ed. VG $75.00

WODEHOUSE, P.G. *Luck of the Bodkins*. 1975 Barrie Jenkins. dj. EX $25.00

WODEHOUSE, P.G. *Meet Mr. Mulliner*. no date. Burt. dj. VG $30.00

WODEHOUSE, P.G. *Mike at Wrykyn*. 1953 Meredith Pr. 1st ed. dj. VG $60.00

WODEHOUSE, P.G. *Money for Nothing*. no date. Jenkins. 2nd ed. $35.00

WODEHOUSE, P.G. *Money in the Bank*. 1942 Clipper Books. dj. VG $60.00

WODEHOUSE, P.G. *Most of P.G. Wodehouse*. 1960 Simon Schuster. 1st ed. dj. VG $30.00

WODEHOUSE, P.G. *Mr. Mulliner Speaking*. 1930 Garden City. 1st ed. $15.00

WODEHOUSE, P.G. *Much Obliged Jeeves*. 1971 Barrie Jenkins. 2nd ed. dj. EX $25.00

WODEHOUSE, P.G. *Mulliner Omnibus*. 1935 London. 1st ed. VG $38.00

WODEHOUSE, P.G. *No Nudes Is Good Nudes*. 1970 Simon Schuster. 1st ed. dj. G $8.00

WODEHOUSE, P.G. *No Nudes Is Good Nudes*. 1970 NY. 1st ed. dj. EX $30.00

WODEHOUSE, P.G. *Not George Washington*. 1980 Continuum. dj. EX $12.50

WODEHOUSE, P.G. *Nothing But Wodehouse*. 1946 Doubleday. dj. VG $35.00

WODEHOUSE, P.G. *Nothing Serious*. 1951 Doubleday. 1st ed. dj. VG $35.00

WODEHOUSE, P.G. *Nothing Serious*. 1951 Doubleday. 1st ed. xl. $25.00

WODEHOUSE, P.G. *Pearls, Girls, & Monty Bodkin*. 1972 Barrie Jenkins. 1st ed. dj. EX $30.00

WODEHOUSE, P.G. *Pelican at Blandings*. 1969 Jenkins. 1st ed. $35.00

WODEHOUSE, P.G. *Perfect's Uncle*. 1972 Souvenir Pr. dj. EX $15.00

WODEHOUSE, P.G. *Performing Flea*. 1953 London. 1st ed. EX $50.00

WODEHOUSE, P.G. *Piccadilly Jim*. no date. Jenkins. Popular ed. dj. VG $40.00

WODEHOUSE, P.G. *Pothunters*. 1972 Souvenir Pr. dj. EX $12.50

WODEHOUSE, P.G. *Pothunters*. 1925 London. 2nd print. VG $50.00

WODEHOUSE, P.G. *Prince & Betty*. 1912 WJ Watts. Popular ed. VG $250.00

WODEHOUSE, P.G. *Quick Service*. 1941 Longman Green. 1st Canadian ed. VG $40.00

WODEHOUSE, P.G. *Right Ho, Jeeves*. 1934 McClelland Stewart. 1st ed. VG $60.00

WODEHOUSE, P.G. *Sam the Sudden*. 1925 Methuen. 1st ed. VG $75.00

WODEHOUSE, P.G. *Service with a Smile*. 1961 London. 1st ed. dj. VG $35.00

WODEHOUSE, P.G. *Something New*. 1977 Ballantine. 2nd ed. pb. VG $4.50

WODEHOUSE, P.G. *Sunset at Blandings*. 1977 Chatto Windus. 1st ed. dj. EX $25.00

WODEHOUSE, P.G. *Ukridge*. 1924 Jenkins. 1st ed. VG $50.00

WODEHOUSE, P.G. *Uncle Dynamite*. 1948 Jenkins. 1st ed. xl. VG $30.00

WODEHOUSE, P.G. *Uncle Fred in the Springtime*. 1939 McClelland Stewart. 1st ed. $75.00

WODEHOUSE, P.G. *Uncollected Wodehouse*. 1976 Seabury. 1st ed. dj. EX $35.00

WODEHOUSE, P.G. *Very Good Jeeves*. 1930 Doubleday Doran. 1st ed. VG $12.00

WODEHOUSE, P.G. *Very Good Jeeves*. 1930 McClelland Stewart. 1st ed. VG $60.00

WODEHOUSE, P.G. *White Feather*. 1972 Souvenir Pr. dj. EX $12.50

WODEHOUSE, P.G. *William Tell Told Again*. 1904 AC Black. 1st ed. G $200.00

WODEHOUSE, P.G. *Wodehouse Nuggets*. 1983 Hutchinson. 1st ed. dj. EX $17.50

WODEHOUSE, P.G. *Wodehouse on Crime*. 1981 E Queen Mystery Club. 1st ed. $20.00

WODEHOUSE, P.G. *Wodehouse on Golf*. 1940 Doubleday Doran. 1st ed. xl. $35.00

WODEHOUSE, P.G. *Wodehouse on Wodehouse*. 1983 Penguin. 2nd ed. EX $10.00

WODEHOUSE, P.G. *World of Blandings*. 1976 Barrie Jenkins. dj. EX $25.00

WODEHOUSE, P.G. *World of Mr. Mulliner*. 1972 Barrie Jenkins. 1st ed. dj. VG $25.00

WODEHOUSE, P.G. *Young Men in Spats*. 1936 McClelland Stewart. 1st ed. VG $50.00

WODEHOUSE, P.G. *Young Men in Spats*. 1984 Penguin. 4th print. pb. EX $5.00

WODEHOUSE, P.G. *Young Men in Spats*. 1936 Jenkins. 1st ed. xl. VG $40.00

WODEHOUSE, P.G. *5 Complete Novels*. 1983 Avenel. 1st ed. dj. EX $15.00

WODEHOUSE & BOLTON. *Bring on the Girls*. 1953 NY. 1st ed. dj. VG $35.00

WODEHOUSE & BOLTON. *Bring on the Girls*. 1954 London. 1st English ed. dj. VG $80.00

WOIWODE, Larry. *Beyond the Bedroom Wall*. 1975 NY. 1st ed. dj. EX $15.00

WOIWODE, Larry. *Poppa John*. 1981 NY. 1st ed. dj. EX $10.00

WOIWODE, Larry. *What I'm Going To Do, I Think*. 1969 NY. 1st ed. dj. EX $10.00

WOLCOTT, Imogene. *New England Yankee Cookbook*. 1939 NY. reprint. EX $10.00

WOLDERING. *Art of Egypt*. 1963 Greystone. Ills 1st ed. 256 p. dj. VG $15.00

WOLF, A. *Higher Education in Nazi Germany for World Conquest*. 1944 London. 1st ed. dj. VG $25.00

WOLF, Abraham. *Science, Technology, & Philosophy in 16th & 17th Centuries.* 1939 NY. Macmillan. 1st ed. 8vo. VG $95.00

WOLF, B. *Morton Livingston Schamberg.* 1963 Phil. Ills. folio. 125 p. cloth. dj. $85.00

WOLF, B. *Reveries of an Outdoor Man: Tales of Field & Stream.* 1946 Putnam. Ills. 181 p. dj. VG $8.00

WOLF, E.R. *Sons of the Shaking Earth.* 1959 Chicago U Pr. Ills. 303 p. maps. dj. EX $15.00

WOLF, Gary K. *Generation Removed.* 1977 Doubleday. 1st ed. dj. EX $10.00

WOLF, Lucien. *Sir Moses Montefiore: Centennial Biography.* 1885 NY. Harper. blue cloth. VG $45.00

WOLF, Simon. *American Jew As Patriot, Soldier, & Citizen.* 1895 Phil. 1st ed. sgn. VG $125.00

WOLF & FLEMING. *Rosenbach: Biography.* 1960 London. 1st ed. dj. VG $55.00

WOLF & FLEMING. *Rosenbach: Biography.* 1960 Cleveland. xl. VG $20.00

WOLF & FLEMING. *Rosenbach: Biography.* 1960 Cleveland. 1st ed. dj. EX $60.00

WOLF & RUBBER. *Story of Glory & Greed.* 1936 NY. 1st ed. 8vo. 533 p. VG $15.00

WOLFE, B. *Portrait of Mexico.* 1937 NY. Ills Diego Rivera. 1st ed. dj. $42.50

WOLFE, Bernard. *Magic of Their Singing.* 1961 Scribner. 1st ed. dj. VG $25.00

WOLFE, Gene. *Urth of the New Sun.* 1987 Ultramarine. Ltd ed. 1/150. sgn. dj. M $150.00

WOLFE, Gene. *Wolfe Archipelago.* 1983 Ziesing Bros. Ills Ltd ed. 1/200. sgns. $125.00

WOLFE, Humbert. *Cursory Rhymes.* 1927 London. Ills A Rutherston. 1/500. sgn. $35.00

WOLFE, Humbert. *Uncelestial City.* 1930 NY. 1st ed. dj. EX $15.00

WOLFE, T. *Western Journal: Daily Log of Great Parks Trip, June 1938.* 1951 Pittsburgh. 1st ed. dj. VG $35.00

WOLFE, Thomas. *From Bauhaus to Our House.* 1981 NY. Farrar. 1st ed. dj. M $15.00

WOLFE, Thomas. *From Death to Morning.* 1935 Scribner. 1st ed. VG $60.00

WOLFE, Thomas. *Hills Beyond.* 1941 Harper. 1st ed. dj. EX $75.00

WOLFE, Thomas. *Mannerhouse.* 1948 NY. Ltd 1st ed. 1/500. dj. boxed. $115.00

WOLFE, Thomas. *Of Time & River.* 1935 NY. Scribner. 1st Am ed. dj. EX $60.00

WOLFE, Thomas. *Portable Thomas Wolfe.* 1946 NY. Viking. 1st ed. dj. EX $10.00

WOLFE, Thomas. *Purple Decades.* 1982 Farrar. 1st ed. dj. EX $18.00

WOLFE, Thomas. *Purple Decades.* 1982 NY. Ltd ed. 1/450. sgn. boxed. M $50.00

WOLFE, Thomas. *Radical Chic & Mau-Mauing the Flak Catchers.* 1970 Farrar. 1st ed. dj. EX $15.00

WOLFE, Thomas. *Radical Chic & Mau-Mauing the Flak Catchers.* 1970 NY. 1st ed. sgn. dj. EX $35.00

WOLFE, Thomas. *Story of a Novel.* 1936 Scribner. 1st ed. dj. EX $125.00

WOLFE, Thomas. *Story of a Novel.* 1936 NY. 1st ed. 93 p. dj. VG $65.00

WOLFE, Thomas. *Web & the Rock.* 1939 NY/London. Harper. 8vo. blue cloth. dj. $70.00

WOLFE, Thomas. *Web & the Rock.* 1947 London. 1st English ed. dj. $50.00

WOLFE, Thomas. *You Can't Go Home Again.* 1940 NY. 1st ed. blue cloth. VG $40.00

WOLFE, Tom. *Bonfires of Vanities.* 1987 Farrar. 1st ed. 1/250. sgn. slipcase. $100.00

WOLFE, Tom. *Right Stuff.* 1979 NY. 1st ed. presentation. dj. EX $65.00

WOLFE, Tom. *Right Stuff.* 1979 NY. 1st ed. dj. M $15.00

WOLFERT, Ira. *Act of Love.* 1948 Simon Schuster. inscr. dj. fair. $7.50

WOLFF, Dr. Paul. *My First 10 Years with Leica.* no date. NY. 4to. plts. white cloth. VG $150.00

WOLFF, Geoffrey. *Black Sun.* 1976 NY. 1st ed. $16.00

WOLFF, Paul. *Meine Erfahrungen Mit der Leica.* 1934 Frankfurt. Ills 1st ed. 4to. cloth. $80.00

WOLFF, Tobias. *Back in the World.* 1985 Houghton. 1st ed. dj. EX $20.00

WOLFF, Tobias. *Back in the World.* 1985 Boston. 1st ed. sgn. EX $30.00

WOLFF, Tobias. *Barracks Thief.* 1984 NY. Ecco. 1st ed. sgn. dj. EX $35.00

WOLFF, Tobias. *Barracks.* 1984 NY. Ecco. 1st ed. dj. EX $20.00

WOLFF, Tobias. *Hunters in the Snow.* 1982 Cape. 1st English ed. dj. EX $30.00

WOLFF, Tobias. *Hunters in the Snow.* 1982 Cape. Uncorrected proof. EX $40.00

WOLFF, Tobias. *In the Garden of the North American Martyrs.* 1981 NY. Ecco. 1st ed. dj. VG $45.00

WOLFF, W. *Island of Death.* 1948 NY. Augustin. 1st ed. 4to. cloth. dj. EX $35.00

WOLFF, W. *Island of Death.* 1973 Hacker. Ills. 228 p. EX $15.00

WOLFLEY, L. *Report of Governor of AZ 1889.* 1889 WA. 1st ed. 24 p. wraps. VG $30.00

WOLITZER, Hilma. *In the Flesh.* 1977 Morrow. 1st ed. dj. EX $20.00

WOLLE, F. *Desmids of US.* 1884 Bethlehem. Ills. VG $50.00

WOLLE, Muriel Sibell. *Bonanza Trail.* 1955 Bloomington. Crown. Ills. 8vo. EX $22.50

WOLLE, Muriel Sibell. *Bonanza Trail.* 1952 NY. 1st ed. dj. VG $22.50

WOLLE, Muriel Sibell. *Stampede to Timberline.* 1949 Boulder. 2nd ed. dj. VG $20.00

WOLLEBIO, Johanne. *Compendium Theologiae Christinsnae.* 1760 London. 16mo. 266 p. leather. VG $20.00

WOLLHEIM, Donald. *Mike Mars Astronaut.* 1961 Doubleday. Ills Orbaan. 1st ed. dj. VG $16.00

WOLTERS, R.A. *Gun Dog: Revolutionary Rapid Training Method.* 1973 Dutton. Ills. 150 p. G $5.00

WOLTERS, R.A. *Gun Dog: Revolutionary Rapid Training Method.* 1961 Dutton. VG $8.00

WOMAN'S DAY. *Woman's Day Encyclopedia of Cookery.* 1966 Fawcett. 3rd ed. 12 vol set. G $40.00

WONS, Anthony. *Tony's Scrapbook.* 1930 Reilly Lee. Ills. 12mo. red cloth. $8.00

WOOD, Barry. *What Price Football.* 1932 Boston/NY. Houghton Mifflin. 1st ed. $30.00

WOOD, D. *Narrow Margin: Battle of Britain 1930-1940.* 1961 McGraw Hill. 1st ed. dj. EX $20.00

WOOD, E.M. *Reef Corals of the World.* 1983 Ills. 4to. 256 p. maps. EX $25.00

WOOD, Edward J. *Wedding Day in All Ages & Countries.* 1869 NY. 297 p. VG $30.00

WOOD, Ernest. *Great Systems of Yoga.* 1954 NY. 168 p. dj. EX $14.00

WOOD, Ernest. *Vedanta Dictionary.* 1964 Philosophical Lib. dj. VG $6.00

WOOD, George B. *Address on Centennial of Founding of PA Hospital.* 1851 Phil. Ills. VG $85.00

WOOD, George L. *7th Regiment.* 1865 NY. 1st ed. 304 p. VG $95.00

WOOD, Grant. *Farm on the Hill.* 1936 NY. Scribner. Ills 1st ed. 4to. 78 p. $35.00

WOOD, J.G. *Athletic Sports & Recreations for Boys.* 1861 London. Ills. 12mo. 144 p. $25.00

WOOD, J.G. *Our Living World.* 1885 Hess. 30 Prang plts. 2 vol set. $115.00

WOOD, John. *Suppressed History of Administration of John Adams.* 1846 Phil. ¾-leather. VG $75.00

WOOD, M. *History of General Federation of Women's Clubs.* 1912 NY. VG $25.00

WOOD, Ruth Kedzie. *Tourist's CA.* 1914 NY. Dodd Mead. 1st ed. map. EX $30.00

WOOD, Stanley. *Over Range to Golden Gate.* 1903 San Francisco. EX $20.00

WOOD, T. Martin. *George du Maurier: Satirist of the Victorians.* 1913 London. 4to. $75.00

WOOD, W. *Reminiscences of Big I.* 1956 Jackson. EX $15.00

WOOD. *Natural History of Man: Africa.* 1868 London. Ills. ½-leather. $25.00

WOODALL, Ronald. *Magnificent Derelicts.* 1977 WA U Pr. 1st ed. dj. EX $25.00

WOODBERRY, G. *100 Books in English Literature.* 1967 NY. Grolier. Kraus reprint. 8vo. VG $25.00

WOODBURY. *Battlefronts of Industry: Westinghouse in WWII.* 1948 Chapel Hill. 1st ed. dj. VG $15.00

WOODFORD, M.H. *Manual of Falconry.* 1977 Black. London. Ills. 194 p. dj. EX $10.00

WOODFORDE, Christopher. *Norwich School of Glass Painting in the 15th Century.* 1950 London/NY. Cumberlege/Oxford. 233 p. dj. $50.00

WOODGATE, W.B. *Boating.* 1888 Boston/London. Ills Ltd ed. dj. M $200.00

WOODHOUSE, B. *Talking to Animals.* 1974 Stein Day. Ill. 208 p. G $5.00

WOODIN, A. *Home Is the Desert.* 1965 Macmillan. Ills. 247 p. VG $10.00

WOODROFFE, J.F. *Upper Reaches of Amazon.* 1914 NY. Macmillan. 1st ed. 304 p. VG $35.00

WOODRUFF, Hiram. *Trotting Horse of America.* 1868 NY. 1st ed. VG $35.00

WOODS, Frederick. *Bibliography of Works of Sir Winston Churchill.* 1963 London. 1st ed. 8vo. 340 p. dj. EX $50.00

WOODS, K.P. *From Dusk to Dawn.* 1892 NY. scarce. EX $14.00

WOODS, Ralph L. *Treasury of the Familiar.* 1945 7th print. 751 p. dj. VG $10.00

WOODS, Ralph L. *World of Dreams.* 1947 Random House. dj. VG $12.00

WOODS, Sara. *Call Back Yesterday.* 1983 NY. 1st Am ed. dj. VG $7.00

WOODS, Stuart. *Chiefs.* 1981 Norton. 1st ed. dj. EX $18.00

WOODVILLE, William. *Medical Botany.* 1810 London. 271 plts. ½-morocco. $900.00

WOODWARD, Arthur. *Indian Trade Goods.* 1967 Binfords Mort. Ills. 4to. 38 p. wraps. EX $4.00

WOODWARD, Asbel. *Life of General Nathaniel Lyon.* 1862 Hartford. map. 360 p. VG $25.00

WOODWARD, G.S. *Cherokees.* 1965 OK U Pr. Ills. 355 p. maps. VG $18.00

WOODWARD, George E. *Woodward's Ornamental & Fancy Alphabets, Monograms, Titles.* no date. no place. folio. 80 p. G $195.00

WOODWARD, W.E. *Meet General Grant.* 1928 Literary Guild. Ills. 512 p. VG $10.00

WOODWARD, W.E. *Meet General Grant.* 1946 Liveright. Ills. 524 p. EX $15.00

WOODWARD, W.E. *Meet General Grant.* 1928 NY. 1st ed. gilt leather. rebound. $35.00

WOODWARD, William. *French Quarter Etchings of Old New Orleans.* 1938 New Orleans. 1st ed. 4to. dj. VG $25.00

WOOLCOTT, A. *2 Gentlemen & a Lady.* 1928 Ills Edwina. 1st ed. 8vo. 121 p. VG $50.00

WOOLF, D. *Wall to Wall.* 1962 NY. 1st ed. dj. EX $10.00

WOOLF, S.J. *Here Am I.* 1941 NY. Ills 1st print. 369 p. dj. $25.00

WOOLF, Virginia. *Between the Acts.* 1941 1st Am ed. dj. VG $40.00

WOOLF, Virginia. *Books & Portraits.* 1978 NY. 1st ed. dj. M $15.00

WOOLF, Virginia. *Common Reader.* 1925 Hogarth. 1st ed. 8vo. G $75.00

WOOLF, Virginia. *Flush.* 1933 NY. 1st ed. 12mo. red cloth. EX $15.00

WOOLF, Virginia. *Fresh-Water.* 1976 NY. 1st ed. dj. M $10.00

WOOLF, Virginia. *Room of One's Own.* 1929 NY/London. 1/492. sgn. 159 p. M $65.00

WOOLF, Virginia. *Street Haunting.* 1930 Westgate Pr. 1/500. sgn. EX $45.00

WOOLF, Virginia. *Writer's Diary.* 1954 NY. 1st ed. dj. EX $35.00

WOOLLCOTT, Alexander. *Letters of Alexander Woollcott.* 1944 NY. Viking. 1/262. 2 vol set. slipcase. $65.00

WOOLLEY, Sir Leonard. *Abraham: Recent Discoveries & Hebrew Origins.* 1936 NY. 1st ed. EX $25.00

WOOLNER, F. *Grouse & Grouse Hunting.* 1974 Crown. Ills. 4to. 192 p. dj. EX $6.50

WOOLNER, F. *Timberdoodle: Practical Guide to the American Woodcock.* 1974 Crown. Ills. 4to. 168 p. dj. EX $10.00

WOOLNOTH, William. *Ancient Castles of England & Wales.* 1825 London. Large Paper 1st ed. 4to. EX $85.00

WOOLRICH, Cornell. *Nightwebs.* 1971 Harper. 1st ed. sgn. dj. EX $25.00

WORCESTER. *Philippines: Past & Present.* 1930 Macmillan. dj. VG $25.00

WORCHESTER, Thomas K. *Portrait of CO.* 1976 Portland. 1st ed. dj. VG $15.00

WORDSWORTH, Christopher. *Greece: Pictorial, Descriptive, & Historical.* 1853 London. New ed. full calf. $135.00

WORDSWORTH, William. *Our English Lakes, Mountains, & Waterfalls.* 1870 London. Provost. Ills T Ogle. 8vo. VG $125.00

WORDSWORTH, William. *Poems.* 1973 Cambridge. Ills/sgn O'Connor. slipcase. $65.00

WORDSWORTH, William. *Poetical Works of William Wordsworth.* 1897 London. 7 vol set. VG $100.00

WORK, M. *Whist of Today.* 1897 Phil. 16mo. 201 p. G $7.00

WORKMAN, W.D. *Bishop From Barnwell: Political Life & Times of E. Brown.* 1963 Columbia, SC. 1st ed. sgn Brown. dj. VG $35.00

WORMALD, F. *Benedictional of St. Ethelwold.* 1959 NY. 8 plts. dj. EX $25.00

WORMINGTON, H.M. *Prehistoric Indians of the Southwest.* 1968 Denver Mus. Ills. 191 p. EX $22.00

WORSELY & GRIFFITH. *Romance of Lloyds.* 1934 NY. 1st ed. cloth. dj. VG $13.00

WORSHAM, J.H. *Jackson's Foot Cavalry.* 1964 Jackson, TN. reprint. dj. VG $25.00

WORTH, C.B. *Mosquito Safari: Naturalist in Southern Africa.* 1971 Simon Schuster. Ills 1st ed. 316 p. dj. EX $15.00

WORTH, C.B. *Naturalist in Trinidad.* 1967 Lippincott. Ills 1st ed. dj. EX $20.00

WORTHEN, Helen Harlow. *Perimeters.* 1980 NY. Uncorrected proof. M $12.00

WORTMAN, Elmo. *Almost Too Late.* 1981 Random House. 1st ed. 211 p. maps. dj. EX $12.00

WOUK, Herman. *Aurora Dawn.* 1947 Simon Schuster. dj. VG $10.00

WOUK, Herman. *Inside, Outside.* 1985 Little Brown. 1st ed. dj. EX $20.00

WOUK, Herman. *Youngblood Hawke.* 1962 NY. 1st ed. dj. VG $12.00

WPA WRITER'S PROGRAM. *Almanac for Bostonians.* 1939 1st ed. EX $45.00

WPA WRITER'S PROGRAM. *Birds of the World.* 1938 Chicago. Ills 1st ed. 205 p. map. VG $32.50

WPA WRITER'S PROGRAM. *Guide to Death Valley.* 1939 Boston. 1st ed. map. dj. VG $32.50

WPA WRITER'S PROGRAM. *Guide to Evergreen State.* 1941 Portland. Binford Mort. map. dj. EX $30.00

WPA WRITER'S PROGRAM. *Guide to New Orleans.* 1938 Boston. 1st ed. dj. VG $32.50

WPA WRITER'S PROGRAM. *Maritime History.* 1941 NY. Garden City. 1st ed. dj. VG $32.50

WPA WRITER'S PROGRAM. *MT: Profile in Pictures.* 1941 NY. 1st ed. dj. VG $45.00

WPA WRITER'S PROGRAM. *New England Hurricane.* 1938 Boston. EX $45.00

WPA WRITER'S PROGRAM. *OK: Guide to the Sooner State.* 1941 OK U Pr. Ills. 445 p. EX $15.00

WPA WRITER'S PROGRAM. *San Francisco.* 1973 reprint of 1940. dj. EX $20.00

WPA WRITER'S PROGRAM. *TN State Guide.* 1939 Viking. 1st ed. pocket map. dj. VG $55.00

WPA WRITER'S PROGRAM. *WA: City & Capital.* 1937 Ills. 1,141 p. maps. VG $20.00

WPA WRITER'S PROGRAM. *Washington D.C. City Guide.* 1937 WA. 1st ed. pocket map. $47.50

WREN, R. *New Encyclopedia of Botanical Drugs.* 1970 England. 400 p. dj. VG $20.00

WREN & MC KAY. *3rd Baffle Book.* 1930 NY. 1st ed. VG $9.00

WRENSCH, Frank A. *Horses in Sport.* 1937 NY. Ltd 1st ed. 1/250. slipcase. $30.00

WRIGHT, Blanche Fisher. *Favorite Rhymes for Little Tots.* 1921 Rand McNally. Ills. EX $35.00

WRIGHT, Blanche Fisher. *Real Mother Goose.* 1926 Rand McNally. Ills. 300 rhymes. 4to. $25.00

WRIGHT, Bruce S. *Black Duck Spring.* 1966 Dutton. Ills 1st ed. 191 p. dj. VG $12.50

WRIGHT, Charles. *Absolutely Nothing To Get Alarmed About.* 1973 Farrar. 1st ed. dj. EX $25.00

WRIGHT, Charles. *Wig.* 1966 Farrar. 1st ed. dj. EX $25.00

WRIGHT, Chauncey. *Letters of Chauncey Wright.* 1878 Cambridge. private print. 2nd issue. VG $40.00

WRIGHT, Christopher. *French Painters of the 17th Century.* 1985 Boston. Little Brown. 4to. 288 p. dj. $30.00

WRIGHT, Dare. *Lonely Doll.* 1957 Doubleday. VG $25.00

WRIGHT, Dare. *Look at a Colt.* 1969 NY. dj. VG $25.00

WRIGHT, Doreen. *Bobbin Lace Making.* 1971 London. Ills. 4to. blue linen. dj. EX $25.00

WRIGHT, Doreen. *Complete Guide to Basket Weaving.* 1972 NY. Ills. 144 p. $15.00

WRIGHT, Frank Lloyd. *Autobiography of Frank Lloyd Wright.* 1932 NY. 1st ed. sgn. VG $45.00

WRIGHT, Frank Lloyd. *Drawings of a Living Architecture.* 1959 NY. 1st ed. xl. $40.00

WRIGHT, Frank Lloyd. *Future of Architecture.* 1953 1st ed. dj. EX $75.00

WRIGHT, Frank Lloyd. *Future of Architecture.* 1965 Horizon. 1st ed. dj. VG $45.00

WRIGHT, Frank Lloyd. *Genius & the Mobocracy.* 1949 Duell Sloan. 1st ed. dj. VG $60.00

WRIGHT, Frank Lloyd. *Japanese Print.* 1967 NY. sgn. slipcase. EX $90.00

WRIGHT, Frank Lloyd. *Man in Possession of His Earth.* 1962 Doubleday. 1st ed. dj. VG $95.00

WRIGHT, Frank Lloyd. *Natural House.* 1954 Horizon. 1st ed. dj. VG $55.00

WRIGHT, Frank Lloyd. *Natural House.* 1954 NY. Ills. tall 8vo. 223 p. dj. EX $35.00

WRIGHT, Frank Lloyd. *Testament.* 1957 NY. 1st ed. VG $35.00

WRIGHT, G. *Art of Caricature.* 1904 NY. Baker Taylor. 1st ed. 8vo. VG $22.50

WRIGHT, G.F. *Asiatic Russia.* 1902 NY. McClure. Ills 1st ed. 2 vol set. VG $50.00

WRIGHT, G.N. *Rhine, Italy, & Greece.* c 1850. London. Ills Fisher. leather. $15.00

WRIGHT, George. *Complete Bird Fancier.* 1785 Dublin. 16mo. 62 p. $75.00

WRIGHT, Harold Bell. *Ma Cinderella.* 1932 NY. 1st ed. VG $100.00

WRIGHT, Harold Bell. *Their Yesterdays.* 1912 Chicago. 1st ed. dj. EX $35.00

WRIGHT, Harold Bell. *Uncrowned King.* 1910 Chicago. Ills Neill. 1st ed. G $17.50

WRIGHT, J. *My Father Who Is on Earth.* 1946 NY. Ills 1st ed. dj. VG $35.00

WRIGHT, J.W. *Long Ago.* 1925 Pr in Forest. inscr. 61 p. VG $20.00

WRIGHT, James. *Reply to Matthew Arnold.* 1981 Logbridge. Ltd ed. 1/500. EX $15.00

WRIGHT, James. *Temple in Nimes.* 1982 Metacom. 1st ed. 1/150. wraps. EX $35.00

WRIGHT, James. *To a Blossoming Pear Tree.* 1977 NY. 1st ed. dj. M $15.00

WRIGHT, L.B. *Arts in America: Colonial Period.* 1966 NY. Ills. 4to. dj. EX $27.50

WRIGHT, L.B. *1st Gentleman of VA: Qualities of Colonial Ruling Class.* 1940 San Marino. dj. G $35.00

WRIGHT, M.O. *Citizen Bird.* 1897 NY. Ills Fuertes. 1st ed. 430 p. $90.00

WRIGHT, M.O. *Wabeno the Magician.* 1899 NY. Ills Gleeson. 1st ed. 346 p. $40.00

WRIGHT, M.W.E. *Memoirs of Marshal Count de Rochambeau.* 1838 Paris. 1st ed. 12mo. ¾-leather. VG $265.00

WRIGHT, Morris. *God's Country & My People.* 1968 NY. 1st ed. dj. VG $22.50

WRIGHT, Morris. *Inhabitants.* 1946 NY. 1st ed. dj. VG $75.00

WRIGHT, Mr. Julia McNair. *Complete Home Encyclopedia of Domestic Life & Affairs.* 1883 Phil. Ills. VG $20.00

WRIGHT, Olgivanna Lloyd. *Our House.* 1959 Horizon. 1st ed. dj. VG $30.00

WRIGHT, Richard. *American Hunger.* 1977 NY. 1st ed. dj. M $15.00

WRIGHT, Richard. *Black Boy.* 1945 Harper. 1st ed. dj. G $15.00

WRIGHT, Richard. *In the Middle of a Life.* 1973 Farrar. 1st ed. dj. EX $20.00

WRIGHT, Richard. *Long Dream.* 1958 NY. 1st ed. dj. VG $25.00

WRIGHT, Richard. *Native Son.* 1940 NY. 1st ed. dj. EX $45.00

WRIGHT, Richard. *Native Son.* 1940 Harper. 5th ed. inscr. G $15.00

WRIGHT, Richard. *Revels in Jamaica 1682-1838.* 1937 NY. Dodd Mead. Ills. 387 p. VG $12.50

WRIGHT, Richard. *12 Million Black Voices: Folk History of Negro in US.* 1941 NY. Ills 1st ed. 4to. xl. VG $55.00

WRIGHT, Richardson. *Hawkers & Walkers in Early America.* 1927 Lippincott. 1st ed. VG $15.00

WRIGHT, Robert W. *Vision of Judgement.* 1867 NY. 12mo. $30.00

WRIGHT, Stephen. *Meditations in Green.* 1983 NY. Scribner. 1st ed. dj. EX $20.00

WRIGHT, Thomas. *History of Scotland.* c 1890. Edinburgh. 4to. 6 vol set. $125.00

WRIGHT, W.H. *Black Bear.* 1910 NY. Ills. $25.00

WRIGHT, W.J. *Greenhouses: Their Construction & Equipment.* 1946 NY. Ills. 269 p. $12.50

WRIGHT, William. *Heiress of Rich Life: Marjorie Meriweather Post.* 1978 New Republic. 1st ed. sgn. dj. VG $35.00

WRIGHT & FAYLE. *History of Lloyd's: From Founding to Present.* 1928 London. Macmillan. 1st ed. 475 p. VG $50.00

WRIGHT & LE BAR. *Devil's Highway.* 1932 NY. Appleton. 3rd print. red cloth. VG $20.00

WRIGHT & UPHAM. *Greenland Ice Fields & Life in North Atlantic.* 1896 NY. Appleton. 1st ed. xl. $20.00

WROLIDGE, Thomas. *Select Collection of Drawings From Curious Antique Gem.* 1768 London. 4to. 2 vol set. EX $180.00

WROTH, L.C. *Voyages of G. da Verrazzano 1524-1528.* 1970 Yale U Pr. Review ed. dj. EX $50.00

WROTH, Lawrence. *Abel Buell of CT.* 1958 Wesleyan U Pr. Revised 2nd ed. 1st print. dj. $15.00

WROTH, Lawrence. *Colonial Printer.* 1938 Portland. 1/1,500. boxed. EX $125.00

WROTH, Lawrence. *History of Printed Book.* 1938 Ltd Ed Club. 1/1,800. VG $120.00

WULFF, Lee. *Let's Go Fishing: Boy's Book on Fresh-Water Fishing.* 1939 Lippincott. Ills. 101 p. VG $7.50

WULFF, Lee. *Sportsman's Companion.* 1968 Harper Row. Ills 1st ed. 4to. dj. EX $10.00

WULFFEN, Dr. Erich. *Woman as a Sexual Criminal.* 1934 NY. Am Ethnological Pr. 1st Am ed. $60.00

WYATT, Colin. *Call of the Mountains.* 1963 NY. Beechurst. Ills 1st Am ed. blue cloth. VG $16.00

WYATT, H. *William Harvey.* 1924 Boston. Small Maynard. 214 p. xl. $8.00

WYATT, Isabel. *King Beattle Tamer & Other Lighthearted Wonder Tales.* 1963 NY. McKay. Ills Jauss. 1st ed. dj. EX $10.00

WYETH, Andrew. *Merryman.* 1978 Houghton Mifflin. 1st print. $175.00

WYETH, Betsy James. *Stray.* 1979 NY. Ills Jamie Wyeth. 1st ed. dj. $10.00

WYETH, Betsy. *Letters of N.C. Wyeth 1901-1945.* 1971 Boston. 1st ed. plts. dj. EX $35.00

WYETH, N.C. *Robin Hood.* 1917 McKay. green cloth. VG $20.00

WYLDE, James. *Circle of Sciences.* c 1870. London. Ills. 4to. 4 vol set. $150.00

WYLIE, I.A.R. *Rambles in Black Forest.* 1911 Boston. Ills Liegich/English. 325 p. $30.00

WYLIE, Philip. *Denizens of the Deep.* 1953 NY. 1st ed. dj. VG $25.00

WYLIE, Philip. *Innocent Ambassadors.* 1957 NY. 1st ed. sgn. dj. VG $30.00

WYLIE, Philip. *Tomorrow.* 1954 Rinehart. 1st ed. dj. EX $30.00

WYLIE, T.A. *IN University 1820-1887.* 1890 Indianapolis. Burford. Ills. 472 p. VG $25.00

WYLIE & BALMER. *When Worlds Collide.* 1932 Phil/NY. Lippincott. dj. VG $20.00

WYLLIE, I. *Cuckoo.* 1981 Universe. Ills. 176 p. $14.00

WYMAN. *Trees for American Gardens.* 1955 Macmillan. Ills. photos. maps. index. VG $9.50

WYNDHAM, John; & PARKER, L. *Outward Urge.* 1959 London. 1st English ed. dj. VG $30.00

WYNNE, John H. *Fables of Flowers for the Female Sex.* 1773 London. Ills 1st ed. 173 p. $100.00

WYSONG, T.T. *Rocks of Deer Creek, Harford County, MD.* 1880 Baltimore. 123 p. EX $45.00

WYSS, Johann. *Swiss Family Robinson.* 1916 Rand McNally. Ills Winter. Windemere ed. VG $20.00

WYSUPH, C.L. *Psychoanalytic Drawings of Jackson Pollock.* 1970 NY. Horizon. Ills. 4to. 123 p. wraps. $30.00

Y

YABUTA, Shinji. *Nurimono.* no date. Tokyo. Chap Book. EX $20.00

YALE. *Story Pictures of Clothing, Shelter, & Tools.* 1939 photos. TB. VG $12.50

YAMANAKA, K. *Jiu-Jitsu.* 1920 NJ. Ills. VG $25.00

YAMAWAKI, Haruki. *Japan in the Beginning of the 20th Century.* 1903 Tokyo. Ills. map. 800 p. xl. G $12.00

YAMAZAKI, Akira. *Japanese Art of Kusaki-Zome Nippon Colors.* 1958 Kamakura. Getumei-Kai. 1/200. boxed. M $350.00

YANEZ, Agustin. *Edge of the Storm.* 1963 UT Pr. 1st ed. dj. EX $25.00

YANG, Martin C. *Chinese Village: Taitou in Shantung Province.* 1945 Columbia U Pr. dj. VG $15.00

YARKER, John Jr. *Notes on Scientific & Religious Mysteries of Antiquity.* 1872 London. 158 p. rebound. VG $85.00

YARMOLINSKY, Av. *Turgenev: The Man, The Art, & His Age.* 1926 NY. Century. $22.50

YARWOOD, Doreen. *English Costume From 2nd Century BC to 1972.* 1972 London. Ills. 4to. 302 p. dj. EX $55.00

YARWOOD, Doreen. *English Home: 1,000 Years of Furniture & Decoration.* 1956 NY. Ills. 4to. dj. VG $22.50

YATES, H. *70 Miles From a Lemon.* 1947 Boston. Ills 1st ed. dj. VG $25.00

YATES, R. *Lower CO River: Bibliography.* 1974 Yuma. 1st ed. 153 p. VG $25.00

YATES, Richard. *Good School.* 1978 Delacorte. 1st ed. dj. EX $15.00

YATES, Richard. *Liars in Love.* 1981 Delacorte. 1st ed. dj. EX $15.00

YATES, Richard. *Young Hearts Crying.* 1984 Delacorte. 1st ed. dj. EX $17.00

YATES, Richard. *11 Kinds of Loneliness.* 1962 Boston. Little Brown. 1st ed. dj. VG $50.00

YAZZIE, A.W. *Navajo Police.* 1980 Rough Rock. 1st ed. 144 p. wraps. VG $10.00

YEAGER, B. *100 Girls: New Concepts in Glamour Photography.* 1965 NY/London. 4to. photos. dj. VG $40.00

YEATS, E.L.; & SHELTON, H. *History of Nolan County, TX.* 1975 Sweetwater. Shelton. dj. sgn. EX $30.00

YEATS, Jack B. *Treasure of the Garden.* London. Elkin Mathews. 1st ed. 4to. $160.00

YEATS, Jack Butler. *Essays: Irish & American.* 1918 Dublin/London. 1st ed. 12mo. cloth. VG $35.00

YEATS, William Butler. *Ballylee.* 1983 Lewisburg. Ltd ed. 1/150. green leather. $40.00

YEATS, William Butler. *Bounty of Sweden.* 1925 Dublin. Caula Pr. Ltd ed. 1/400. $150.00

YEATS, William Butler. *Collected Poems.* 1933 London. 1st ed. VG $16.00

YEATS, William Butler. *Discoveries: Volume of Essays.* 1907 Dundrum. Dun Emer Pr. 1st ed. 1/200. $275.00

YEATS, William Butler. *Dramatis Personae.* 1936 NY. 1st ed. VG $35.00

YEATS, William Butler. *Early Poems & Stories.* 1925 Macmillan. 1st Am ed. 8vo. cloth. dj. EX $90.00

YEATS, William Butler. *Full Moon in March.* 1935 London. 1st ed. dj. VG $110.00

YEATS, William Butler. *Hour Glass, Cathleen Ni Houlihanm, Pot of Broth.* 1904 London. Chiswick. 1st ed. dj. VG $95.00

YEATS, William Butler. *King of the Great Clock Tower.* 1934 Dublin. Cuala Pr. Ltd ed. 1/400. $150.00

YEATS, William Butler. *King's Threshold.* 1911 Shakespeare Head Pr. wraps. $40.00

YEATS, William Butler. *Passages From Letters of Dundrum, Ireland.* Cuala Pr. 1/400. $175.00

YEATS, William Butler. *Reveries Over Childhood & Youth with Trembling of the Veil.* 1927 NY. Macmillan. 1st Am ed. 1/250. 8vo. sgn. EX $300.00

YEATS, William Butler. *Vision.* 1893 NY. 1st Am ed. VG $100.00

YEATS, William Butler. *Wind Among the Reads.* 1899 NY/London. Land. 1st print. VG $65.00

YEATS, William Butler. *Winding Stair.* 1929 NY. 1st ed. sgn. VG $200.00

YEE, Chiang. *Silent Traveller in San Francisco.* 1964 NY. Norton. 1st ed. dj. VG $12.00

YELLEN, S. *Passionate Shepherd.* 1957 NY. 1st ed. dj. EX $12.00

YEOMAN, R.S. *Guide Book of US Coins.* 1948 Whitman. 1st ed. EX $12.00

YEOMAN, R.S. *Yeoman Red Book of US Coins.* 1954 Racine. 8th ed. VG $25.00

YEPSOEN, R.B. *Organic Plant Protection.* 1977 Rodale. Ills. 688 p. VG $10.00

YERBY, Frank. *Old Gods Laugh.* 1964 NY. 1st ed. dj. $15.00

YERBY, Frank. *Sarcen Blade.* 1952 NY. dj. EX $8.00

YERKOW, C. *Modern Judo.* 1942-1958. Ills. 3 vol set. VG $25.00

YESUDIAN, Selvarajan. *Yoga & Health.* 1953 Harper. dj. G $10.00

YEVTUSHENKO, Yevgeny. *Dove in Santiago.* 1982 Viking. 1st Am ed. dj. EX $15.00

YEVTUSHENKO, Yevgeny. *From Desire to Desire.* 1976 Doubleday. 1st Am ed. dj. EX $15.00

YEVTUSHENKO, Yevgeny. *Selected Poems.* 1962 Dutton. 1st Am ed. dj. EX $30.00

YIVO. *Life Struggle & Uprising in Warsaw Ghetto.* 1963 NY. Ills. English/Yiddish text. $35.00

YLLA. *Dogs.* 1945 NY. 1st ed. dj. EX $20.00

YOKOYAMA, S.; & OSHIMA, E. *Judo.* 1915 Tokyo. Nishodo. Ills 1st ed. $35.00

YONGE, Charlotte M. *Dove in the Eagle's Nest.* 1924 NY. Duffield. Ills Stevens. 1st ed. VG $20.00

YONGE, Charlotte M. *Young Folk's History of Rome.* 1879 Lathrop. Ills 1st ed. 12mo. EX $15.00

YORKE, F.R.S. *Modern House.* 1935 London. 4to. gray cloth. VG $25.00

YOSHIDA, Toshi. *Varieties of the Japanese Print.* 1967 Tokyo. Ills. sgn. oblong 4to. $60.00

YOSHIKAWA, E. *Heike Story.* 1956 NY. 1st ed. dj. EX $12.00

YOST, Karl. *Bibliography of the Published Works of C.M. Russell.* 1971 Lincoln. Ills. 4to. dj. EX $42.50

YOST, Nellie. *Call of the Range, NE: History of Its Cattle Industry.* 1966 Denver. 1st ed. dj. EX $35.00

YOST, Nellie. *Medicine Lodge: Story of a KS Frontier Town.* 1970 Sage. Ills 1st ed. 237 p. dj. EX $20.00

YOST. *Frank & Lillian Gilbreth: Partners for Life.* 1949 Rutgers. 1st ed. VG $12.00

YOUMANS, Edward Livingston. *Culture Demanded by Modern Life.* 1867 NY. G $50.00

YOUMANS, Eliza A. *Lessons in Cookery.* 1878 NY. 1st Am ed. VG $55.00

YOUNG, Al. *Ask Me Now.* 1980 McGraw Hill. 1st ed. dj. EX $15.00

YOUNG, Alex. *History of the Netherlands.* 1884 Boston. 1st ed. EX $35.00

YOUNG, B. *Confederate Wizards of the Saddle.* 1958 KY. VG $25.00

YOUNG, C.E. *Dangers of the Trail in 1865: Narrative of Actual Events.* 1912 Geneva, NY. Ills. sgn. $35.00

YOUNG, Charles Van Patten. *Courteney & Cornell Rowing.* 1923 Cornell Pub. Ills. 107 p. $25.00

YOUNG, Desmond. *Rommel.* 1950 London. Later ed. dj. EX $15.00

YOUNG, E.R. *Stories From Indian Wigwams & Northern Campfires.* 1915 Abingdon Pr. G $20.00

YOUNG, E.R. *Stories From Indian Wigwams & Northern Campfires.* 1893 NY. 293 p. $22.00

YOUNG, Edward. *Complaint; or, Night Thoughts on Life, Death, & Immortality.* 1772 Edinburgh. 12mo. 360 p. leather. G $75.00

YOUNG, Edward. *Poetical Works of Edward Young.* 1852 London. Pickering. leather. EX $195.00

YOUNG, Francis Brett. *Black Roses.* 1929 London. 1st ed. dj. EX $15.00

YOUNG, Francis Brett. *Jim Redlake.* 1930 London. 1st ed. dj. EX $15.00

YOUNG, Frank. *Advertising Layout.* 1928 NY. Ills. 4to. EX $17.50

YOUNG, G.F. *Medici.* no date. London. 2 vol set. VG $22.00

YOUNG, G.O. *AK-Yukon Trophies Won & Lost.* 1947 WV. Standard Pub. Ills 1st ed. dj. $225.00

YOUNG, Hugh. *Genital Abnormalities, Hermaphroditism, & Related Diseases.* 1837 Baltimore. Williams Wood. VG $47.50

YOUNG, Hugh. *Surgeon's Autobiography.* 1940 NY. Harcourt Brace. 1st ed. EX $16.50

YOUNG, L. *Science of Hypnotism.* 1931 Chicago. VG $8.00

YOUNG, L.E. *Chief Episodes in the History of UT.* 1912 Lakeside Pr. 1st ed. 51 p. cloth. $85.00

YOUNG, L.S. *Life & Heroic Deeds of Dewey & Battles in Philippines.* c 1899. Phil. Ills. 8vo. 504 p. VG $17.00

YOUNG, Marguerite. *Angel in the Forest.* 1945 NY. 1st ed. 313 p. dj. VG $18.00

YOUNG, Mary Elizabeth. *Redskins, Ruffleshirts, & Redskins.* 1961 Norman. 1st ed. dj. VG $45.00

YOUNG, Roland. *Thorne Smith: His Life & Times.* 1934 Doubleday. 1st ed. wraps. scarce. EX $65.00

YOUNG, S.H. *AK Days with John Muir.* 1915 Revell. Ills. 226 p. VG $25.00

YOUNG, S.P. *Last of the Loners.* 1970 Macmillan. Ills 1st ed. 316 p. dj. VG $14.00

YOUNG, S.P. *Puma: Mysterious Cat.* 1946 Am Wildlife Inst. G $30.00

YOUNG, Stark. *Pavilion.* 1951 NY. Scribner. 1st ed. dj. EX $20.00

YOUNG, Stark. *Queen of Sheba.* 1922 NY. Theatre Arts. 1st ed. wraps. $95.00

YOUNG, Stark. *Torches Flare.* 1928 NY. Scribner. 1st ed. presentation. dj. EX $75.00

YOUNG, Stark. *3 1-Act Plays.* 1921 Cincinnati. Stewart Kidd. 1st ed. EX $45.00

YOUNG & GOLDMAN. *Puma: Mysterious American Cat.* 1946 WA. 1st ed. 8vo. puma skin bdg. EX $250.00

YOUNG & HOWELL. *Minor Tactics of Chess.* 1896 Boston. 2nd ed. 12mo. 221 p. G $20.00

YOUNG & WIDSTOE. *Life Story of Brigham Young.* 1930 NY. Ills 1st ed. 388 p. dj. VG $45.00

YOUNG. *Real HI.* 1899 NY. Ills. VG $45.00

YOUNT, John. *Hardcastle.* 1980 NY. Marek. 1st ed. sgn. M $25.00

YOUNT, John. *Trapper's Last Shot.* 1973 Random House. 1st ed. dj. EX $30.00

YOUNT, John. *Wolf at the Door.* 1967 Random House. Advance copy. dj. VG $45.00

YOUNT, John. *Wolf at the Door.* 1967 Random House. 1st ed. VG $30.00

YOUSSOUPOFF, Prince Felix. *Rasputin.* 1927 NY. 246 p. VG $45.00

YUNG, K.K. *National Portrait Gallery.* 1981 NY. 4to. $45.00

YUTANG, Lin. *Between the Tears & Laughter.* 1943 John Day. dj. G $15.00

Z

ZABRISKIE, George A. *Ships' Figureheads in & About NY.* 1946 Ormond Beach. Ills. 21 p. dj. VG $22.50

ZAHARIAS, Babe Didrikson. *This Life I've Led.* 1955 Barnes. 1st ed. dj. VG $17.50

ZAHL, P.A. *Flamingo Hunt.* 1952 Bobbs Merrill. Ills 1st ed. 270 p. VG $10.00

ZAHM, Albert F. *Aerial Navigation.* 1911 NY. Appleton. Ills 1st ed. 496 p. VG $45.00

ZAHN, Leopold. *Mortiz Von Schwind.* 1922 Munchen. Recht. cloth. $75.00

ZAMMATTIO, Carlo. *Leonardo the Scientist.* 1980 Ills. 192 p. dj. EX $9.00

ZAMPETTI, Pietro. *Complete Paintings of Giorgione.* 1968 NY. 1st Am ed. dj. $25.00

ZANGWILL, Israel. *Italian Fantasies.* no date. London. 8vo. 369 p. VG $45.00

ZANGWILL, Israel. *Mantle of Elijah.* 1900 London. 1st ed. dj. VG $63.00

ZAPF, Hermann. *Hunt Roman: Birth of a Type.* 1965 Pittsburgh. 1st ed. 1/750. sgn. dj. VG $50.00

ZAPF, Hermann. *Pen & Graver: Alphabets & Pages of Calligraphy.* 1952 NY. oblong folio. VG $150.00

ZASSENHAUS, H. *Walls Resisting the 3rd Reich.* 1974 Boston. $17.50

ZAVIN, Theodora. *Everybody Bring a Dish Cookbook.* 1974 NY. EX $10.00

ZEBROSKI, George. *Sun Spacer.* 1984 NY. Uncorrected proof. wraps. EX $15.00

ZECHLIN, R. *Complete Book of Handicrafts.* 1967 MA. Ills. 347 p. $22.50

ZEILLER, Martin. *Itinearium Hispaniae & Lustaniae.* 1656 Amsterdam. 19 fld plts. EX $575.00

ZEILLER, W. *Tropical Marine Fishes of Southern FL & the Bahama Islands.* 1975 Barnes. Ills. dj. EX $17.50

ZEIS, Paul. *American Merchant Marine Policy Since the Civil War.* 1936 Princeton. private print. 446 p. leather. $100.00

ZEISBERGER, David. *David Zeisberger's History of the North American Indians.* 1910 Columbus. 189 p. maroon cloth. VG $75.00

ZEISBERGER, David. *Diary of David Zeisberger: Moravian Missionary.* 1885 Cincinnati. 8vo. 2 vol set. xl. $55.00

ZEITLIN, Ida. *Skazki: Tales & Legends of Old Russia.* 1926 Doran. Ills. 4to. black cloth. $60.00

ZEITLIN, Jacob. *Types of Poetry.* 1926 NY. 1st ed. xl. G $30.00

ZEITLIN, Jake. *Book Stalking at Home & Abroad.* 1987 Dallas. 1st ed. wraps. $15.00

ZEITLIN, Jake. *Whispers & Chants.* 1927 San Francisco. 1st ed. sgn. VG $75.00

ZELAZNY, Roger. *Unicorn Variations.* 1983 Timescape. 1st print. dj. EX $30.00

ZEMACH, Margot. *Frogs Who Wanted a King.* 1977 NY. 4 Winds Pr. Ills 1st ed. 4to. 58 p. dj. VG $12.50

ZENZINOV, V.; & LEVINE, I.D. *Road to Oblivion.* 1931 McBride. Ills 1st ed. 250 p. G $5.00

ZERBE. *Automobiles: Every Boy's Mechanical Library.* 1915 Cupples. Ills 1st print. $28.00

ZERN, Ed. *How To Tell Fish From Fishermen.* 1947 Appleton Century. Ills. G $5.50

ZETLIN, Mikhail. *Five.* 1959 NY. Ills. dj. VG $25.00

ZEVI, B. *Architecture As Space.* 1957 NY. Ills. dj. EX $30.00

ZIEGLER & BARNELL. *Zen of Base & Ball.* 1964 Simon Schuster. Ills 1st print. dj. VG $16.00

ZIEL, Ron. *Twilight of Steam Locomotives.* 1963 Grosset Dunlap. Ills. 4to. 208 p. VG $10.00

ZIERBOGEL, S. *Dissertatio Anatomico Physiologica.* 1760 Upsala U. Latin text. 56 p. VG $35.00

ZIEROLD, Norman. *Little Charley Ross: America's 1st Kidnapping for Ransom.* 1967 Little Brown. Ills. 301 p. dj. EX $10.00

ZIGROSSER, Carl. *Childe Hassam.* 1916 NY. Ills. 32mo. 62 p. wraps. $25.00

ZIGROSSER, Carl. *Prints & Their Creators.* 1974 NY. Crown. Ills 2nd Revised ed. 136 p. $45.00

ZIGROSSER, Carl. *Rockwellkentiana.* 1933 NY. Harcourt. Ills Rockwell Kent. $37.00

ZIMELLI & VERGERIO. *Decorative Ironwork.* 1969 London. Hamlyn. Ills. 159 p. dj. $12.50

ZIMEN, E. *Wolf: His Place in the Natural World.* 1981 Souvenir. Ills. 373 p. dj. EX $22.00

ZIMMER, H. *Myth & Symbols in Indian Art & Civilization.* 1946 Pantheon. Ills. 248 p. dj. EX $10.00

ZIMMERMAN, A.F. *Francisco de Toledo: 5th Vicroy of Peru 1569-1581.* 1938 Caldwell. Caxton. 1st ed. 307 p. xl. VG $15.00

ZIMMERMAN, Paul. *Los Angeles Dodgers.* 1960 NY. Coward McCann. 1st ed. dj. VG $12.00

ZIMMERMAN, W.F.A. *Kalifornein och Guldfebern.* 1862 Stockholm. Ills. ½-leather. $95.00

ZIMMERMANN, E. *Grasesse Fuhrer fur Sammler.* 1922 Berlin. Ills. 8vo. brown cloth. $95.00

ZINSSER, Hans. *Rats, Lice, & History.* 1935 Boston. Little Brown. 3rd ed. leather. $25.00

ZISTEL, Era. *Hi Fella.* 1977 Phil. Ills Oughton. 1st ed. dj. M $12.00

ZITTLE, John H. *Correct History of John Brown's Invasion at Harper's Ferry.* 1905 Hagerstown, MD. 1st ed. 259 p. G $50.00

ZIV, Frederic. *Valiant Muse: Anthology of Poems by Poets Killed in War.* 1936 NY. sgn. VG $25.00

ZOLA, Emile. *Germinal.* 1942 Nonesuch. 1st ed. dj. slipcase. EX $28.00

ZORN, Friedrich Albert. *Grammar of the Art of Dancing.* 1905 Boston. Ills. 4to. 302 p. VG $45.00

ZOUCH, Thomas. *Life of Izaak Walton.* 1826 London. Ills. 8vo. ½-calf. VG $95.00

ZUBAKOV, Vasily. *Heroic Leningrad.* 1974 Moscow. Novosti. wraps. VG $15.00

ZUKOFSKY, L. *A-24.* 1972 NY. 1st ed. dj. EX $15.00

ZUKOFSKY, L. *Found Objects.* 1964 Georgetown. 1st ed. wraps. VG $20.00

ZUTZ, Don. *Double Shotgun.* 1978 Winchester. Ills. 266 p. dj. EX $12.50

ZVORYKIN, B. *Firebird & Other Russian Fairy Tales.* 1978 NY. Viking. 1st Am ed. dj. VG $35.00

ZWEIG, A. *Axe of Wandsbek.* 1947 NY. 1st ed. dj. EX $10.00

ZWEIG, A. *Education Before Verdun.* 1936 NY. 1st ed. dj. VG $15.00

ZWEIG, Von Friderike M. *Stefan Sweig.* 1961 Germany. Kindlers Klassiche. photos. $15.00

ZWINGER, A. *Beyond the Aspen Grove.* 1970 Random House. Ills 1st ed. 368 p. dj. VG $18.00

ZWORYKIN, V.K. *Photoelectricity & Its Applications.* 1949 NY. Wiley. Rewritten ed. 494 p. xl. $15.00

Bookbuyers

In this section of the book we have listed buyers of books and related material. When you correspond with these dealers, be sure to enclose a self-addressed stamped envelope if you want a reply. Do not send lists of books for appraisal. If you wish to sell your books, quote the price you want or send a list and ask if there are any on the list they might be interested in and the price they would be willing to pay. If you want the list back, be sure to send a S.A.S.E. large enough for the listing to be returned. When you list your books, do so by author, full title, publisher and place, date, edition, and condition, noting any defects on cover or contents.

Remember, when contacting a book dealer, either quote a price or ask if there is any material on the list that he would be interested in and how much he would be willing to pay. Remember, too, a self-addressed stamped envelope is important.

Edward Abbey
Authors of the West
191 Dogwood Dr.
Dundee, OR 97115

Alcoholics Anonymous
1939-1954.
Paul Melzer Fine Books
P.O. Box 1143
Redlands, CA 92373; 714-792-7299

Robert Richshafer
1214 SE 11th Ave.
Deerfield Beach, FL 33441; 305-429-1559 or
1800 Vine St.
Cincinnati, OH 45210

Louisa May Alcott
The Barrow Bookstore
79 Main St.
Concord, MA 01742

All Authors, All Subjects
Charles Apfelbaum Books
39 Flower Rd.
Valley Stream, NY 11581

American Indians
Old Erie Street Bookstore
2128 E 9th St.
Cleveland, OH 44115

Literature
Modern First Editions
Ken Lopez, Bookseller
51 Huntington Rd.
Hadley, MA 01035

Americana
Also military history.
Art Carduner
6228 Greene St.
Philadelphia, PA 19144

Donald Magee
Newport Book Store
109 Bellevue Ave.
Newport, RI 02840

19th Century Shop
1047 Hollins St.
Baltimore, MD 21223

The Bookseller Inc.
521 W Exchange St.
Akron, OH 44302; 216-762-3101

John L. Heflin Jr.
5708 Brentwood Trace
Brentwood, TN 37027; 615-373-2917

Gordon Totty
Scarce Paper Americana
347 Shady Lake Parkway
Baton Rouge, LA 70810; 504-766-8625

Also ephemera, autographs, maps, broadsides, historical newspapers, photographica, directories, etc.
Robert Richshafer
1214 SE 11th Ave.
Deerfield Beach, FL 33441; 305-429-1559
or
1800 Vine St.
Cincinnati, OH 45210

Old Books
811 Royal St.
New Orleans, LA 70116

R.M. Weatherford Books
P.O. Box 5
Southworth, WA 98386; 206-871-3617

Western, general, early guides, maps, atlases.
Trotting Hill Park Books
P.O. Box 1324
Springfield, MA 01101; 413-567-6466

Anthropology
R.M. Weatherford Books
P.O. Box 5
Southworth, WA 98386; 206-871-3617

Antiques
Heritage Books
410-C W Felicita Ave.
Escondido, CA 92025; 619-746-6601

Archaeology
Robin Bledsoe, Bookseller
(formerly Blue Rider Books)
1640 Massachusetts Ave.
Cambridge, MA 02138; 617-576-3634

Also ancient Egypt, Near East, pictograph and petrograph rock art, etc.
Hyman & Sons Rare Books
2341 Westwood Blvd., #2-3
Los Angeles, CA 90064

Architecture
Academy Book Store
10 W 18th St.
New York, NY 10011

V.L. Green Booksellers
19 E 76th St.
New York, NY 10021; 212-439-9194

Arthur H. Minters Inc.
39 W 14th St., Room 401
New York, NY 10011; 212-989-0593

Also gardens.
C. Richard Becker, Bookseller
238 W 14th St.
New York, NY 10011-7217; 212-243-3789

Archery
Melvin Marcher, Bookseller
6204 N Vermont
Oklahoma City, OK 73112

Art
Decorative from 1928 to 1970, industrial and furniture design, design periodicals from 1928 to 1960, Arts & Craft Movement, etc.
American Decorative Arts
9 Market St.
Northampton, MA 01060

B.R. Artcraft Co.
Baldwin, MD 21013

Decorative.
Arch Books
5916 Drew Ave., S
Minneapolis, MN 55410

20th C and modern illustrated.
Arthur H. Minters Inc.
39 W 14th St., Room 401
New York, NY 10011; 212-989-0593

Fine and applied.
David Holloway, Bookseller
6760 SW 76th Terrace
S Miami, FL 33143; 305-665-5567

All aspects.
Davis & Schorr Art Books
P.O. Box 56054
Sherman Oaks, CA 91413-1054; 818-787-1322

British and American from 1850 to 1950.
Pharos Books
P.O. Box 17
Fair Haven Station
New Haven, CT 06513; 203-562-0085

Decorative and applied.
Rick Barandes
61 4th Ave.
New York, NY 10003

Especially history.
Robin Bledsoe, Bookseller
(formerly Blue Rider Books)
1640 Massachusetts Ave.
Cambridge, MA 02138; 617-576-3534

C. Richard Becker, Bookseller
238 W 14th St.
New York, NY 10011-7217; 212-243-3789

William & Victoria Dailey Ltd.
8216 Melrose Ave.
P.O. Box 69160
Los Angeles, CA 90069; 213-658-8515

American.
Nancy Scheck
Art Reference Books
164 Boulevard
Scarsdale, NY 10583; 914-723-6974

Astrology
Middle Earth Book Shop
Paul B. Hudson
2791 E 14 Mile
Sterling Heights, MI 48310; 313-979-7340

Todd Pratum
Out-of-Print & Rare Books
843 37th Ave.
San Francisco, CA 94121

Atlases
Pre-1870.
Gordon Totty
Scarce Paper Americana
347 Shady Lake Parkway
Baton Rouge, LA 70810; 504-766-8625

The Philadelphia Print Shop Ltd.
8441 Germantown Ave.
Chestnut Hill
Philadelphia, PA 19118; 215-242-4750

Autographs
Also manuscripts and documents.
19th Century Shop
1047 Hollins St.
Baltimore, MD 21223

Letters, manuscripts, documents.
Paul Melzer Fine Books
P.O. Box 1143
Redlands, CA 92373; 714-792-7299

Aviation

Antheil Booksellers
2177 Isabelle Ct.
N Bellmore, NY 11710

Caravan Book Store
550 S Grand Ave.
Los Angeles, CA 90071

Baseball

Butternut & Blue
3411 Northwind Rd.
Baltimore, MD 21234

Pre-1960.
John Kashmanian
38 Forest View Dr.
N Providence, RI 02904

Bibles

Early.
The Family Album
International Library Agents
R.D. 1, Box 42
Glen Rock, PA 17327; 717-235-2134

Holy Land Treasures
1200 Edgehill Dr.
Burlingame, CA 94010

Bibliographies

About Books
P.O. Box 5717
Parsippany, NJ 07054

Biographies

Bookphil Book Search Service
P.O. Box 706
Hilliard, OH 43026; 614-876-0442

Black History and Literature

Beasley Books
1533 W Oakdale
Chicago, IL 60657

Fran's Bookhouse
69 W Schoolhouse Lane
Philadelphia, PA 19144

Books About Books

About Books
P.O. Box 5717
Parsippany, NJ 07054

Book Buyers Shop
1305 S Shepherd
Houston, TX 77019

Also printing.
Key Books
Raymond D. Cooper
2 W Montgomery St.
Baltimore, MD 21230; 301-539-5020

Especially children's books, authors, and illustrators; by mail or phone only.
Arch Books
5916 Drew Ave., S
Minneapolis, MN 55410; 612-927-0298

Books by Conservative Authors

Sumac Books
R.D. #1, Box 197
Troy, NY 12180

Book Trade Periodicals

About Books
P.O. Box 5717
Parsippany, NJ 07054

Boxing

John Kashmanian
38 Forest View Dr.
North Providence, RI 02904

Boy Scout

Richard Shields
The Carolina Trader
P.O. Box 769
Monroe, NC 28110; 704-289-1604

California

Old, unusual.
Paul Melzer Fine Books
P.O. Box 1143
Redlands, CA 92373; 714-702-7299

American Bookstore
608 E Olive
Fresno, CA 93728

Cape Cod

Cape Cod Books
C. Mildred Chamberlin
P.O. Box 794
E Orleans, MA 02643

Cats

The Literary Cat
4932 Oakwood Ave.
La Canada, CA 91011

Ceramics and Pottery

Also other decorative arts, catalogue resumes of artists, and painted finishes.
V.L. Green Booksellers
18 E 76th St.
New York, NY 10021; 212-439-9194

Exhibitions.
American Decorative Arts
9 Market St.
Northampton, MA 01060

Marc Chagall

Fine illustrated.
Paul Melzer Fine Books
P.O. Box 1143
Redlands, CA 92373; 714-792-7299

Chicago

Phyllis Tholin Books
824 Ridge Terrace
Evanston, IL 60201; 312-475-1174

By Chicago authors.
Chicago Historical Bookworks
831 Main St.
Evanston, IL 60202; 312-869-6410

Children's Books

Noreen Abbot Books
2666 44th Ave.
San Francisco, CA 94116; 415-664-9464

Fran's Bookhouse
69 W Schoolhouse Lane
Philadelphia, PA 19144

The Literary Cat
4932 Oakwood Ave.
La Canada, CA 91011

Cinema

Also television, photography, filming technology, and history.
Hampton Books
Rte. 1, Box 202
Newberry, SC 29108

Jose Cisneros

HI Books
6509 N Mesa
El Paso, TX 79912

Civil War

Also judicial and political history, Lincolniana, militaria, etc.
Daniel Weinberg
Abraham Lincoln Book Shop
18 E Chestnut St.
Chicago, IL 60610

Butternut & Blue
3411 Northwind Rd.
Baltimore, MD 21234

Richard Shields
The Carolina Trader
P.O. Box 769
Monroe, NC 28110; 704-289-1604

Books, documents, letters, photos, envelopes, North and South, Confederate money, slavery items, etc.
John L. Heflin Jr.
5708 Brentwood Trace
Brentwood, TN 37027

Related ephemera including newspapers, magazines, documents, letters, stereoviews, photographs, strategy books, etc.
Gordon Totty
Scarce Paper Americana
347 Shady Lake Parkway
Baton Rouge, LA 70810; 504-766-8625

Sandlin's Books & Bindery
70 W Lincolnway
Valparaiso, IN 46383; 219-462-9922

Coats of Arms

Tuttle Antiquarian Books Inc.
P.O. Box 541
28 S Main St.
Rutland, VT 05710-0541

Cookbooks and Culinary Arts

Caravan Book Store
550 S Grand Ave.
Los Angeles, CA 90071

Art Carduner
6228 Greene St.
Philadelphia, PA 19144

Heritage Books
410-C W Felicita Ave.
Escondido, CA 92025; 619-746-6601

Communism

Sumac Books
R.D. #1, Box 197
Troy, NY 12180

County Histories

Tuttle Antiquarian Books Inc.
P.O. Box 541
28 S Main St.
Rutland, VT 05710-0541

Cryptography

Elm
P.O. Box 28255
Washington, DC 20038

Charles Darwin

Amaranth Books
P.O. Box 527
Iowa City, IA 52240

Derrydale Press

Gary L. Estabrook Books
P.O. Box 61453
Vancouver, WA 98666

Detective Fiction

Beasley Books
1533 W Oakdale
Chicago, IL 60657

The Book Baron
1236 S Magnolia Ave.
Anaheim, CA 92804; 714-527-7022

Dolls

And anything related.
Doll Works
1400 St. Andrews Place B
Santa Ana, CA 92705

Drawing and Drawings

Nancy Scheck
Art Reference Books
164 Boulevard
Scarsdale, NY 10583; 914-723-6974

Early American and European Imprints

The Family Album
International Library Agents
R.D. 1, Box 42
Glen Rock, PA 17327; 717-235-2134

Economics
Jeremy Norman & Co. Inc.
442 Post St.
San Francisco, CA 94102-1579

Espionage
Also terrorism.
Elm
P.O. Box 28255
Washington, DC 20038

Also crime.
Bookphil Book Search Service
P.O. Box 706
Hilliard, OH 43026; 614-876-0442

Ethnic Studies
Alcuin Books
2120 E Apollo Ave.
Tempe, AZ 85283

Exploration and Voyages
Older material.
Paul Melzer Fine Books
P.O. Box 1143
Redlands, CA 92373; 714-792-7299

Expositions
Especially sports related.
Harvey Abrams Books
P.O. Box 732
State College, PA 16804

Far East
Alcuin Books
2120 E Apollo Ave.
Tempe, AZ 85283

Firearms and Edged Weapons
Melvin Marcher, Bookseller
6204 N Vermont
Oklahoma City, OK 73112

First Editions
Academy Book Store
10 W 18th St.
New York, NY 10011

The Aleph
831 Main St.
Evanston, IL 60202; 312-869-6410

Authors of the West
191 Dogwood Dr.
Dundee, OR 97115

Karl M. Armens Books
740 Juniper Dr.
Iowa City, IA 52245

20th century.
Nouveau Rare Books
5005 Meadow Oaks Park Dr.
P.O. Box 12471
Jackson, MS 39236

Pride & Prejudice Books
Diane & Merrill Whitburn
11 N Hill Rd.
Ballston Lake, NY 12019

Football
John Kashmanian
38 Forest View Dr.
N Providence, RI 02904

Gambling and Gaming
Phone or mail only.
Bob Rosenberger Rare Books
6592 Madeira Hills Dr.
Cincinnati, OH 45243; 513-271-8477

Gardening and Horticulture
Also agriculture and landscape architecture.
The American Botanist Booksellers
D. Keith Crotz
1103 W Truitt Ave.
Chillicothe, IL 61523; 309-274-5254

Out of print only.
V.L. Green Booksellers
19 E 76th St.
New York, NY 10021; 212-439-9194

Patricia Ledlie, Bookseller
P.O. Box 90, Bean Rd.
Buckfield, ME 04220; 207-336-2969

Genealogies
Tuttle Antiquarian Books Inc.
P.O. Box 541
28 S Main St.
Rutland, VT 05710-0541

Geology and Mineralogy
Andy's Book Shop Inc.
78 Main St.
Littleton, NH 03561

Albert G. Clegg
P.O. Box 306
Eaton Rapids, MI 48827

Great Lakes
Chicago Historical Bookworks
831 Main St.
Evanston, IL 60202; 312-869-6410

Zane Grey
Gary L. Estabrook Books
P.O. Box 61453
Vancouver, WA 98666

Authors of the West
191 Dogwood Dr.
Dundee, OR 97115

Haggadot
Holy Land Treasures
1200 Edgehill Dr.
Burlingame, CA 94010

Nathaniel Hawthorne
The Barrow Bookstore
79 Main St.
Concord, MA 01742

Herbals
The American Botanist Booksellers
D. Keith Crotz
1103 W Truitt Ave.
Chillicothe, IL 61523; 309-274-5254

Carl Hertzog
HI Books
6509 N Mesa
El Paso, TX 79912

Historical Newspapers
Robert Richshafer
1214 SE 11th Ave.
Deerfield Beach, FL 33441; 305-429-1559 or
1800 Vine St.
Cincinnati, OH 45210

History
American Bookstore
608 E Olive
Fresno, CA 93728

All aspects.
Alcuin Books
2120 E Apollo Ave.
Tempe, AZ 85253

American.
Austin Book Shop
Bernard Titowsky, Bibliographer
P.O. Box 36
Kew Gardens, NY 11415; 718-441-1199

Signed American and European.
Robert F. Batchelder
1 W Butler Ave.
Ambler, PA 19002; 215-643-1430

Bookphil Book Search Service
P.O. Box 706
Hillard, OH 43026; 614-876-0442

Religious.
The Grands
P.O. Box 783
8 Woodland Rd.
Valley Stream, NY 11582

Sandlin's Books & Bindery
70 W Lincolnway
Valparaiso, IN 46383; 219-462-9922

William & Victoria Dailey Ltd.
8216 Melrose Ave.
P.O. Box 69160
Los Angeles, CA 90069; 213-658-8515

Holocaust
Also American Judaica, Zionism, Hebraica, Holy Land, antique ritual silver, Bibles, etc.
Holy Land Treasures
1200 Edgehill Dr.
Burlingame, CA 94010

The Grands
P.O. Box 783
8 Woodland Rd.
Valley Stream, NY 11582

Herbals
Horror
Pandora's Books Ltd.
P.O. Box 54
Neche, ND 58265

The Aleph
831 Main St.
Evanston, IL 60202; 312-869-6410

Horses and Equestrian Sports
Including horse racing, polo, sidesaddle riding, carriages, driving, etc.
Robin Bledsoe, Bookseller
(formerly Blue Rider Books)
1640 Massachusetts Ave.
Cambridge, MA 02138; 617-576-3634

Especially carriages and driving, and books authored or illustrated by Paul Brown or George Ford Morris.
October Farm Horse Books
Barbara Cole
Rte. 2, Box 183-C
Raleigh, NC 27610

Humor
The Book Chest
125 E 87th St.
New York, NY 10228

Hunting and Fishing
Melvin Marcher, Bookseller
6204 N Vermont
Oklahoma City, OK 73112

Also related subjects.
Gary L. Estabrook Books
P.O. Box 61453
Vancouver, WA 98666

Hydrology
Albert G. Clegg
P.O. Box 306
Eaton Rapids, MI 48827

Illustrated Books
Noreen Abbot Books
2666 44th Ave.
San Francisco, CA 94116; 415-664-9464

Indiana
Sandlin's Books & Bindery
70 W Lincolnway
Valparaiso, IN 46383; 219-462-9922

Jazz and Blues
Beasley Books
1533 W Oakdale
Chicago, IL 60657

Jewelry and Gems
The Gemmary
P.O. Box 816
Redondo Beach, CA 90277

James Joyce

Pre-1940.
Paul Melzer Fine Books
P.O. Box 1143
Redlands, CA 92373; 714-792-7299

Judaica

American.
Holy Land Treasures
1200 Edgehill Dr.
Burlingame, CA 94010

Hyman & Sons Rare Books
234 Westwood Blvd., #2-3
Los Angeles, CA 90064

All forms.
The Grands
P.O. Box 783
8 Woodland Rd.
Valley Stream, NY 11582

King Arthur

Also anything related.
Charles E. Wyatt Inc.
P.O. Box 2883
Vista, CA 92083

Ku Klux Klan

Bookworm & Silverfish
P.O. Box 639
Wytheville, VA 24382; 703-686-5813

Lakeside Classics

Chicago Historical Bookworks
831 Main St.
Evanston, IL 60202; 312-869-6410

Laos

Fiction and non-fiction.
Dalley Book Service
90 Kimball Lane
Christiansburg, VA 24073

Latin America

Alcuin Books
2120 E Apollo Ave.
Tempe, AZ 85283

Law

Austin Book Shop
Bernard Titowsky, Bibliographer
P.O. Box 36
Kew Gardens, NY 11415; 718-441-1199

Library Consultants and Appraisers

The Family Album
International Library Agents
R.D. 1, Box 42
Glen Rock, PA 17327; 717-235-2134

Lincolniana

Daniel Weinberg
Abrahm Lincoln Book Shop
18 E Chestnut St.
Chicago, IL 60610

Literature

Alcuin Books
2120 E Apollo Ave.
Tempe, AZ 85283
American Bookstore
608 E Olive
Fresno, CA 93728

Black Oak Books
1491 Shattuck Ave.
Berkeley, CA 94709

English first editions; business by appointment.
T.S. Vandoros Rare Books
5827 Highland Terrace
Middleton, WI 53562; 608-836-8254

Book Buyers Shop
1305 S Shepherd
Houston, TX 77019

David Holloway, Bookseller
6760 SW 76th Terrace
S Miami, FL 33143; 305-665-5567

Heritage Books
410-C W Felicita Ave.
Escondido, CA 92025; 619-746-6601

Old Erie Street Bookstore
2128 E 9th St.
Cleveland, OH 44115

American and British from 1850 to 1950.
Pharos Books
P.O. Box 17
Fair Haven Station
New Haven, CT 06513; 203-562-0085

William & Victoria Dailey Ltd.
8216 Melrose Ave.
P.O. Box 69160
Los Angeles, CA 90069; 213-658-8515

Magazines and Periodicals

Watchtower, Scientific American, and Overland Monthly.
AAAA Books
P.O. Box 2817
Providence, RI 02907

Design from 1928 to 1960.
American Decorative Arts
9 Market St.
Northampton, MA 01060

Rick Barandes
61 4th Ave.
New York, NY 10003

Manuscripts

Charles Apfelbaum Books
39 Flower Rd.
Valley Stream, NY 11581

Maritime

Antheil Booksellers
2177 Isabelle Ct.
N Bellmore, NY 11710

Steamship.
Thomas & Susan Bjorkman
128 Lake Dr. E
Wayne, NJ 07470

Martha's Vineyard

Cape Cod Books
C. Mildred Chamberlin
P.O. Box 794
E Orleans, MA 02643

Masonic Books

Bookworm & Silverfish
P.O. Box 639
Wytheville, VA 24382; 703-686-5813

Larry McMurtry

Fiction first editions.
Geographic Enterprises
P.O. Box 246
Mesquite, TX 75149; 214-289-7107

Medicine

Jeremy Norman & Co. Inc.
442 Post St.
San Francisco, CA 94102-1579

Key Books
Raymond D. Cooper
2 W Montgomery St.
Baltimore, MD 21230; 301-539-5020

Metaphysics

Middle Earth Book Shop
Paul B. Hudson
2791 E 14 Mile
Sterling Heights, MI 48310; 313-979-7340

Militaria

Antheil Booksellers
2177 Isabelle Ct.
N Bellmore, NY 11710

Sea and air.
Bookphil Book Search Service
P.O. Box 706
Hilliard, OH 43026; 614-876-0442

All out of print, all wars, all services.
Carl Sciortino-Militaria
P.O. Box 6424
Scottsdale, AZ 85261

Mining

Also mineralogy.
The Gemmary
P.O. Box 816
Redondo Beach, CA 90277

John Muir

First editions.
Geographic Enterprises
P.O. Box 246
Mesquite, TX 75149; 214-289-7107

Amaranth Books
P.O. Box 527
Iowa City, IA 52240

Museum of Modern Art

Catalogs.
Nancy Scheck
Art Reference Books
164 Boulevard
Scarsdale, NY 10583; 914-723-6974

Music

Jazz, rock, musicals, big band, etc.
Austin Book Shop
Bernard Titowsky, Bibliographer
P.O. Box 36
Kew Gardens, NY 11415; 718-441-1199

Black Oak Books
1491 Shattuck Ave.
Berkeley, CA 94709

Theory, history, compositions, classical vocal sheet music, biographies, etc.
Books & Music Ltd.
801 E Salem Ave.
Indianola, IA 50125-2733

Mysticism

Mythistory
Douglas Gunn Books
819 Quinby Ave.
Wooster, OH 44691

Mythology

Todd Pratum
Out-of-Print & Rare Books
843 37th Ave.
San Francisco, CA 94121

Mysteries

Also detective.
Karl M. Armens Books
740 Juniper Dr.
Iowa City, IA 52245

First editions.
David Holloway, Bookseller
6760 SW 76th Terrace
S Miami, FL 33143; 305-665-5567

Pandora's Books Ltd.
P.O. Box 54
Neche, ND 58265

Nantucket

Cape Cod Books
C. Mildred Chamberlin
P.O. Box 794
E Orleans, MA 02643

National Geographic

Geographic Enterprises
P.O. Box 246
Mesquite, TX 75149; 214-289-7107

Natural History

All aspects.
Melvin Marcher, Bookseller
6204 N Vermont
Oklahoma City, OK 73112

Patricia Ledlie, Bookseller
P.O. Box 90, Bean Rd.
Buckfield, ME 04220; 207-336-2969

The Philadelphia Print Shop Ltd.
8441 Germantown Ave.
Chestnut Hill
Philadelphia, PA 19118; 215-242-4750

Naval
Antheil Booksellers
2177 Isabelle Ct.
N Bellmore, NY 11710

New England States
New Hampshire, Vermont, and Maine.
Andy's Book Shop Inc.
78 Main St.
Littleton, NH 03561

New Orleans
Old Books
811 Royal St.
New Orleans, LA 70116

New Mexico
HI Books
6509 N Mesa
El Paso, TX 79912

Nursing
History, Florence Nightingale, medicine, alternative healing, related ephemera.
Trotting Hill Park Books
P.O. Box 1324
Springfield, MA 01101; 413-567-6566

Occult
Hyman & Sons Rare Books
2341 Westwood Blvd., #2-3
Los Angeles, CA 90064

Ohio
The Bookseller Inc.
521 W Exchange St.
Akron, OH 44302; 216-762-3101

Olympic Games
Harvey Abrams Books
P.O. Box 732
State College, PA 16804

Opera
Books & Music Ltd.
801 E Salem Ave.
Indianola, IA 50125-2733

Orange Judd Co.
The American Botanist Booksellers
D. Keith Crotz
1103 W Truitt Ave.
Chillicothe, IL 61523; 309-274-5254

Original Comic Art
The Book Chest
125 E 87th St.
New York, NY 10028

Pacific Islands
The Cellar Book Shop
18090 Wyoming
Detroit, MI 48221

Paleontology
Albert G. Clegg
P.O. Box 306
Eaton Rapids, MI 48827

Pennsylvania Americana
The Family Album
International Library Agents
R.D. 1, Box 42
Glen Rock, PA 17327; 717-235-2134

Performing Arts
Art Carduner
6228 Greene St.
Philadelphia, PA 19144

Philosophy
Academy Book Store
10 W 18th St.
New York, NY 10011

Middle Earth Book Shop
Paul B. Hudson
2791 E 14 Mile
Sterling Heights, MI 48310; 313-979-7340

Photography
Karl M. Armens Books
740 Juniper Dr.
Iowa City, IA 52245

Charles Apfelbaum Books
39 Flower Rd.
Valley Stream, NY 11581

Black Oak Books
1491 Shattuck Ave.
Berkeley, CA 94709

The Broken Diamond
19 N Broadway
Billings, MT 59101

Arnold Sadow
All Photography Books
40 Reservoir St., 510
Brockton, MA 02401; 508-587-6074

Plants
Exotic; mail order only.
Myron Kimnach
5508 N Astell Ave.
Azusa, CA 91702

Playing Cards
Business by phone or mail only.
Bob Rosenberger Rare Books
6592 Madeira Hills Dr.
Cincinnati, OH 45243

Poetry
American and British from 1850 to 1950.
Pharos Books
P.O. Box 17
Fair Haven Station
New Haven, CT 06513; 203-562-0085

POW
Elm
P.O. Box 28255
Washington, DC 20038

Press Books
Book Buyers Shop
1305 S Shepherd
Houston, TX 77019

Mail order only.
Myron Kimnach
5508 N Astell Ave.
Azusa, CA 91702

Business by appointment.
T.S. Vandoros Rare Books
5827 Highland Terrace
Middleton, WI 53562; 608-836-8254

Prints and Cartoons
The Book Chest
125 E 87th St.
New York, NY 10028

Prints and Printmakers
Nancy Scheck
Art Reference Books
164 Boulevard
Sarsdale, NY 10583; 914-723-6974

Proofs and Galleys
Modern First Editions
Ken Lopez, Bookseller
51 Huntington Rd.
Hadley, MA 01035

Pulps
Pandora's Books Ltd.
P.O. Box 54
Neche, ND 58265

The Aleph
831 Main St.
Evanston, IL 60202; 312-869-6410

Railroads and Railroadiana
Frederick N. Arone
377 Ashforde Ave.
Dobbs Ferry, NY 10522

Thomas & Susan Bjorkam
128 Lake Dr. E
Wayne, NJ 07470

Rare Books and Fine Bindings
Fran's Bookhouse
69 W Schoolhouse Lane
Philadelphia, Pa 19144

Mail order only.
Myron Kimnach
5508 N Astell Ave.
Azusa, CA 91702

Paul Melzer Fine Books
P.O. Box 1143
Redlands, CA 92373; 714-792-7299

Also unusual medicine, nursing, conservation, ecology, polution control, etc.
Trotting Hill Park Books
P.O. Box 1324
Springfield, MA 01101; 413-567-6466

Old Erie Street Bookstore
2128 E 9th St.
Cleveland, OH 44115

Sandlin's Books & Bindery
70 W Lincolnway
Valparaiso, IN 46383; 219-462-9922

Business by appointment.
T.S. Vandoros Rare Books
5827 Highland Terrace
Middleton, WI 53562; 608-836-8254

Vieux Livres D'Europe Inc.
14 E 73rd St., Suite 4-B
New York, NY 10021; 212-861-5694

Amistad Enterprises
71 Nordica Drive
Croton, NY 10520; 914-271-5368

Reference
Antiques and collecting.
C. Richard Becker, Bookseller
238 W 14th St.
New York, NY 10011-7217; 212-243-3789

Religion
American Bookstore
608 E Olive
Fresno, CA 93728

Rhode Island
Donald Magee
Newport Book Store
109 Bellevue Ave.
Newport, RI 02840

Russia
Especially Russian royalty, communism, pre-1940 China, Tibet, Eastern Europe, etc.
Sumac Books
R.D. #1, Box 197
Troy, NY 12180

By appointment only.
The Literary Cat
4932 Oakwood Ave.
La Canada, CA 91011

Scholarly Books
Theory, Greek and Roman oratory, rhetoric, etc.
Pride & Prejudice Books
Diane & Merril Whitburn
11 N Hill Rd.
Ballston Lake, NY 12019

Science and Technology
Key Books
Raymond D. Cooper
2 W Montgomery St.
Baltimore, MD 21230; 301-539-5020